Campaigning for President in America, 1788–2016

Campaigning for President in America, 1788–2016

Scott John Hammond, Robert North Roberts, and Valerie A. Sulfaro

 GREENWOOD™

An Imprint of ABC-CLIO, LLC

Santa Barbara, California • Denver, Colorado

Library of Congress Cataloging-in-Publication Data

Names: Hammond, Scott J. | Roberts, Robert North | Sulfaro, Valerie A.

Title: Campaigning for president in America, 1788-2016 / Scott John Hammond, Robert North Roberts, Valerie A. Sulfaro.

Description: Santa Barbara, California : Greenwood, 2016. | Includes bibliographical references.

Identifiers: LCCN 2015046107 | ISBN 9781440848902 (hardback) | ISBN 9781440848889 (paperback) | ISBN 9781440850790 (ebook)

Subjects: LCSH: Presidents—United States—Election—History—Encyclopedias. | Political campaigns—United States—History—Encyclopedias. | Presidential candidates—United States—History—Encyclopedias. | Political parties—United States—Platforms—Encyclopedias.

Classification: LCC JK524.R57 2016 | DDC 324.70973—dc 3 LC record available at http://lccn.loc.gov/2015046107

ISBN: 978-1-4408-4890-2 (hardcover)
ISBN: 978-1-4408-4888-9 (paperback)
EISBN: 978-1-4408-5079-0

20 19 18 17 16   1 2 3 4 5

This book is also available as an eBook.

Greenwood
An Imprint of ABC-CLIO, LLC

ABC-CLIO, LLC
130 Cremona Drive, P.O. Box 1911
Santa Barbara, California 93116-1911
www.abc-clio.com

This book is printed on acid-free paper ∞

Manufactured in the United States of America

To Deborah, Caitlin, and William Roberts;
Chereé, Adriana, and Neil Hammond;
and Jack McCaslin,
for their unconditional love and support.

Contents

Note to Our Readers

The manuscript for the current volume was prepared and finished during the early stages of the 2015/2016 presidential campaign season, and our final draft was delivered to our publisher the day following the South Carolina Democratic primary. Thus our discussion of that campaign is already incomplete. Since then, we now know that Sec. Clinton has improved her position by managing to win primaries and caucuses in seven more states, raising her delegate total to 577 as of this writing. Sen. Sanders managed to win four states during Super Tuesday, and at this point can claim 386 delegates. While Sen. Sanders remains a viable candidate, these results reinforce our position that Hillary Clinton, given events through March 1, should win the nomination of her party and is the likeliest candidate to be elected to the presidency. On the Republican side, Donald Trump still holds the lead in delegates after Super Tuesday, but Sen. Cruz remains within striking distance, and Sen. Rubio, with a win in Minnesota, cannot be ruled out at this point. Sen. Rubio must now rely on his home state of Florida to sustain his campaign. Auspiciously, that primary is to be held on the Ides of March. Currently, as this book goes to press, Sen. Rubio is a distant second in the polls to Mr. Trump, and it is unclear whether or not he has enough time to gain the momentum necessary to score a needed win in the Sunshine State. Should Sen. Rubio lose Florida, the nomination for the Grand Old Party is most likely to become a two-way contest from this point forward to the California primary.

Having said all of this, it is our hope that the necessarily incomplete discussion of the 2016 campaign within this volume proves to be helpful in at least a small way. Finally, we hope that this book provides a solid introduction to both the history of presidential campaigns as well as the various qualities and elements that continue to remain meaningful. Democracy depends on rational, civil discourse, and civil discourse in turn relies on informed participants interacting as fellow citizens within the public arena. When civil discourse is abandoned, and rational dialogue gives way to reactive and unreflective emotion, democracy becomes vulnerable to the designs of demagogues and enthralled by the force of personality. This is not to say that there is no place for emotion in politics; many of the greatest moments in political campaigns stir the human heart. Rather, this is simply to remind us that only those emotions that elevate us—those emotions that are supported by careful reason and shared through the civil debate over which means is best to achieve our shared ends as Americans—work to the benefit and improvement of our institutions and the realization our national purpose. It is our hope that the outcome of the campaign that is now unfolding before us will uplift our democracy and enable us to share together all that is true and good within the American spirit.

Scott John Hammond
Robert North Roberts
Valerie A. Sulfaro
March 2, 2016

Preface

Four years have passed since the release of the second edition of this work, a three-volume set that was produced to serve primarily as a library collections reference source and as an introductory tool for serious students of politics interested in both the history of presidential campaigning and in the various features and dynamics that currently define presidential politics. This three-volume edition was itself an expansion of a single-volume work that had been published several years before, composed with the same basic intention. Both the single-volume first edition and the three-volume second edition featured, in addition to the elements mentioned above, several entries describing campaign slogans as well as entries focused on specific issues written independently of the longer campaign narratives. So as to produce a more streamlined edition more amenable and accessible to a wider readership, all of the stand-alone entries on campaign slogans and most of the more dated campaign issues have been removed for this new volume, maintaining the inclusion of those campaign issues that are still current as well as retaining the campaign narrative chronicle that accounted for a large portion of both the first and second editions. Additionally the number of separate entries explaining major campaign events has also been reduced, those being primarily retained within the narratives themselves. There are a few exceptions to this editorial decision, but generally the narratives cover events that in previous editions would have merited an independent entry. In sum, this third edition is an attempt at combining elements of the first two: the inclusion of a considerable number of topic-specific entries as in the first and second volumes combined with the longer narratives as they were expanded in the three-volume set (the second volume). This volume also possesses qualities of its own, as a few new topic-specific entries have been added, while older entries have been updated and strengthened. All of these modifications are designed to assist readers in their efforts to further understand presidential campaign politics, to answer some questions about presidential campaigning, and to stimulate the more committed students toward further research.

Presidential politics is a rich, complex, and vitally important facet of American democracy. But knowledge of political history seems to be on the wane as increasingly fewer students appear on college campuses with a reasonable grasp of the fundamental events, actors, institutions, issues, episodes, controversies, themes, principles, and ideas pertaining to the development of American political culture and the story of American democracy. Admittedly, while a new encyclopedia by itself cannot serve as the sufficient corrective for the current state of political education, it can supply a mine of information that will stimulate the thinking student onward toward richer, deeper veins. This work is designed with that very purpose in mind. This volume, it must be remembered, will only support the initial stages of a student's inquiry and help to foster in a modest way the continued legacy of a particularly fascinating and relevant aspect of the American political past—presidential politics and its colorful, and at times indecipherable, multifaceted history of idealism, cynicism, high aspiration, overweening ambition, persuasion, enthusiasms, honesty, deception, bombast, inspiration, human nobility and folly, embittered rivalry, inventive strategy, sincere promise, masked intentions, scandalmongering, grace, inconsolable disappointment, unrestrained elation, the admirable and the contemptible, the moments of personal heroism, the revelation of flawed character, unrestrained elation, and devastating heartbreak.

Political rhetoric is as old as politics itself, dating at least to the establishment of democracy in ancient Athens and long preceding the high oratory of Greek leaders such as Pericles and Demosthenes, and Romans statesmen such as Cato the Elder and Cicero. American presidential campaigning, by comparison, is still a new phenomenon within the long arc of the political history of the world, and in many ways it continues to show the signs of growing pains that usually accompany the early stages of development. And yet, from the perspective of Americans, this history is built on tried and true traditions, exhibits its own legacy, and follows its own comfortable (or perhaps for some, uncomfortable), predictable patterns and sturdy continuities. In an attempt to understand the history and nature of presidential campaigning more thoroughly, this work discusses an aspect of politics—presidential politics—that can at times still exhibit the unpredictable vigor characteristic of the new, and in so doing is itself influenced by the youthful energy of American democracy; and as such, this work is directed at an audience of readers who approach new fields of the intellect with the openness and enthusiasm of the young everywhere. Perhaps more importantly, this volume aims at drawing the attention of students to the deep connections between our current political culture and the political history that has shaped it. In reading through the campaign histories, careful students will recognize themes, connections, constants, and variables when they direct their attention to those facets of presidential politics that are more current, more evidently pertinent to what is important now. It is in this spirit that our readers are exhorted to continue their quest beyond the front and back covers here, and to truly chart the often turbulent and yet always alluring seas of the American political drama.

Acknowledgments

We extend abundant gratitude to many who have either directly or indirectly contributed to this project. Specifically, we thank John Wagner, Vince Burns, Michelle Scott, Pete Feely, and all their associates at ABC-CLIO/Greenwood for applying their energy and skill to marshaling our work into print. A debt of gratitude is owed to John Wagner in particular, without whom we would not have joined this effort, and whose patience and flexibility enabled us to bring the manuscript to its conclusion. Doubtless we also owe a portion of our gratitude to our students, for whether they are aware of it or not, necessity required their having to share our attention with this project—which was under hard deadline from the beginning—at least for a short time in the fall of 2015. More important, in working with our students and discussing American politics over the years, we have gained the experience and insight requisite to this project, thus in a real way our students have made this volume possible.

Among those who indirectly assisted our efforts, we acknowledge an intellectual, academic debt to John Sides (at George Washington University) and Lynn Vavrek (at UCLA), who through their work in *The Gamble* and unbeknownst to them provided us with a valuable resource in more deeply and thoroughly understanding the 2012 campaign, which was the central component of this edition's revision. At several points in this volume we cite or quote Sides and Vavrek when attempting to more adequately explain the events and dynamics of the 2012 contest. More broadly, we also drew on many other scholars in the process of our research, too many to enumerate, at least without the risk of unduly leaving someone out. That said, there are a few who are noticeably influential in the development of this book. In writing the campaign narratives, the exhaustive work of Arthur M. Schlesinger, Fred Israel, and William P. Hansen was especially valuable. Additionally, a good deal of insight was borrowed from the recent work of our colleague here at James Madison University, Marty Cohen, and his collaborators David Karol, Hans Noel, and John Zaller. There are many others as well, but those identified here were exceedingly important as reliable resources for us, serving as gateways to other scholarship throughout the field, and we encourage our readers to follow these scholars through those gateways.

Finally and above all we also thank our families, to whom this volume is dedicated, for their patient understanding throughout the all-too-brief but exceedingly hectic duration of this project. Any further remarks in this regard would fall short of the extent of our gratitude for them and our debt to them.

Introduction

Presidential campaigning as a manifestation of both the principles and the dynamics of American political culture has been marked by noteworthy changes throughout its historical progression, but in significant ways identifiable aspects of this particular political phenomenon have endured substantively unchanged. Today politicians with presidential ambitions behave in ways not unlike their forerunners, and while under the comforting influence of sentimental remembrance we are tempted to regard the politics, and the politicians, of the past as loftier than what is presently familiar, or as somehow more genuine in the comparison to what we now experience, a more careful and fair appraisal of our own times in contrast to what has proceeded us may likely disclose a closer resemblance than our nostalgic yearnings will allow. Candidates still court party insiders, depend on the largesse of donors, rely on the steady commitment of party activists and the seasoned expertise of advisers, grapple with a vigilant media, joust against the competition at all stages, consult with image-weavers and hoopla spinners, even curry the favor of popular comedians and other celebrities in vogue, and all this while exposing themselves to the irregular, distracted gaze of the voting public through the effervescent spectacle that is the modern campaign trail. These features are what we have come to expect from any modern presidential campaign, and we expect them because they are not in essence by any means new; quite to the contrary, in some variation they are nearly as old as American political campaigning itself. Changes in delivery and the nature of timing throughout the flow of a campaign season certainly set contemporary campaigning apart from the past—technology by itself, as with so many things, is a major factor in transforming the dynamics of current political campaigning—and the techniques of showmanship, the rapidity and brevity of communication, the threshold of correct form and good taste, and the texture of political language, among other things, are indeed distinct from what was normal in the experience of previous generations; tweets, sound bites, memes, viral videos, the rise and expansion of public informality, the intensified and ubiquitous spotlight glare cast on personal lives and private issues—all characterize the political terrain of the latter twentieth and early twenty-first century in ways that would all appear decidedly foreign, and likely disconcerting, to those generations of voters in our past—and all of these features and more do in fact lend a singular quality to the nature of the current political basic situation. Nevertheless, there remain strong resemblances between the style, and even the substance, of the all-too-garish campaigns today and what we now tend to look back upon with a sense of loss, for how often do we speak of bygone eras as something better, cleaner, sounder? Without question, changes have occurred and differences are real, and yet there is much that demonstrates the continuity of essential things.

What are those "essential things" from which we are able to derive, and sustain, this continuity? Foremost among any itemized account of these durable aspects of presidential politics stands the basic fact that those politicians whose ambitions are resolved toward gaining the White House must win the confidence and support of the electorate, the people themselves. Granted, as we all well know, it is a matter of fact that the Electoral College, the management of which is directed by the legislatures of the several states, technically still elects the president as authorized by Article II of the federal Constitution. But the history of campaigning is not the history of winning over appointed electors; the history of campaigns is a long, often repetitive, at times dramatic, and at its edges somewhat curious chronicle of the competition for the people's favor, a spectacularly theatrical but ultimately serious popularity contest with the highest possible stakes. Electors still cast the formal, certified ballots that determine who will serve as president, but they in turn, while remaining faceless to most Americans—even the nominated candidates who have earned their votes—are on Election Day elected by the citizens of the various states who are assured of the elector's pledged commitment to the voter's choice. Officially, citizens choose between those electors committed to the candidate that they support for the presidency, and while they may not vote for these electors by name, it is they, not the candidate, for whom they officially cast their ballot. That these names remain mostly anonymous—anonymous but not secret—reveals the dynamic at work, for while the votes are directly for the unknown electors, they are in fact cast for the actual candidate, however indirectly. Who among us enters the voting booth with the intent to vote for electors? Rather, uppermost in the voter's mind are thoughts about and commitments to the candidates themselves. And as indirect as this may be under the language of the Constitution, the candidates well know whose support they must gain, and who they must persuade in the process, and thus the necessity and inevitability of presidential campaigning, of taking one's case before the people themselves. This is the way it has been throughout most of the republic's political history, or at least that history as developed since the popular vote was first tallied and recorded on a national scale in 1824, even during those times in which the right of suffrage was not universally protected, in which the nation's democracy was still striving to spring forth in its fullness, even under circumstances and prejudices resistant to it.

While it is commonplace to observe, and even complain of, the discrepancies between the Electoral College and the popular vote, and not without good reason, by and large the outcome of the popular vote has been consonant with the Electoral College, even though the respective percentages are typically different. With the important exceptions of three elections (1876, 1888, and 2000), the Electoral College has followed the popular will; in two of those elections (1876 and 2000), the final outcome was contingent on a decision by the Supreme Court. An additional case, the 1824 election—a four-candidate race that did not produce a majority in either the Electoral College or among the tallied popular vote—was decided in the House of Representatives according to procedure as established under the Constitution, the second and last time in American history in which the House determined the election of the president (the first being the election of 1800 wherein the House selected Thomas Jefferson after a tie with Aaron Burr in the Electoral College tally, an election that occurred before the practice of recording the popular vote for the president). In the 1824 election, candidate Andrew Jackson actually received the higher number of popular votes as well as more votes in the Electoral College among the four competitors; however, in both cases he won only a plurality, not the mandatory Electoral College majority, and thus the decision fell to the House, resulting in the selection of John Quincy Adams. Along with the 1824 outcome, those three exceptions in 1876, 1888, and 2000 in which the Electoral College overrode the recorded popular vote may easily be perceived as failures of democracy—the silencing of the people's voice—and thus evidence that the Electoral College is both dated and undemocratic. Moreover, simple electoral math guarantees a discrepancy between the popular tally and the electoral tally in each election. An election can be as close as imaginable in the popular vote, and yet the winner can still come away with a more convincing Electoral College victory. For example, in the famously tight election of 1960, won by Senator John F. Kennedy by just slightly under 113,000 votes—49.7 percent of the popular vote cast for Senator Kennedy and 49.6 percent cast for his rival, Vice President Richard Nixon—a more persuasive victory of 56 percent of the Electoral College votes was enjoyed by the senator (an Electoral College count of 303 to 219, or 56% to 40%). For good reasons, this election has become familiar to students of political history as one of the closest in American political history because of the small margin among the popular voters, for we know that this is what really matters to Americans, and not the larger margin in the Electoral College. Moreover, it is even possible, although only slightly so, to win each state's popular vote by one vote while sweeping all fifty states in the Electoral College, but the odds of this happening are decidedly long. Nonetheless, it is a fact that in most cases a candidate's victory is amplified by the Electoral College, but it is mathematically conceivable, although improbable, that a wide margin of victory in the popular vote would be matched by a narrower percentage in the Electoral College under certain circumstances. The point of this is simply to illustrate the odd relationship between the popular vote for the president—or more accurately the popular vote for those electors pledged to in turn cast their votes for that designated candidate—and the Electoral College. This eccentricity has at various times perplexed and even frustrated Americans, and yet, even after the exceedingly controversial and frustrating election of 2000, a veritable comedy of errors, no serious effort to work for the amendment of the Constitution to abolish or even modify the Electoral College has occurred. Prior to that election, one might have predicted that the Electoral College would remain untouched until a case arose wherein the electors neutralized the popular will, as in the case of the 2000 general election. And yet, fifteen years later, the system remains in place, no effort to amend it having been mounted. For all our perplexity and episodic disgruntlement with regard to the Electoral College, it is still the constitutional procedure under which the president of the United States is chosen. Few Americans would openly admit to approving of the Electoral College's continued existence—it is more common to dismiss it, even contemptuously deride it as antiquated and pointless in a modern, more enlightened democracy—and yet, even after the fractured and embarrassingly inept election of 2000, no groundswell to abolish it has surfaced.

What might explain and clarify this dissonance merits further study, but the reasons behind the establishment of the Electoral College are clear and familiar. The American Founders sought a compromise between the direct election of the president by the people on the one hand and the appointment of the president by Congress on the other, the latter undesirable on grounds that it would transgress the margins set for the separation of power, the former intolerable for dread of the unreliability of the popular judgment and the serious risk of demagoguery. Additionally, the Founders anticipated that the Electoral College would be better equipped to foster the kind of expertise requisite to an intelligent, mature choice with regard to the selection of a chief executive; left to the people alone—who are not of necessity the most dependable judges of political ability and moral character—politicians capable of winning elections through their charms but less qualified to govern effectively might gain the presidency. "The process of election [via the Electoral College] affords a moral certainty," Alexander Hamilton explained in *Federalist 69*,

> that the office of the President will seldom fall to the lot of any man who is not in an eminent degree endowed with the requisite qualifications. Talents for low intrigue, and the little arts of popularity, may alone suffice to elevate

a man to the first honors in a single State; but it will require other talents, and a different kind of merit, to establish him in the esteem and confidence of the whole Union, or to make him a successful candidate for the distinguished office of the President of the United States. It will not be too strong to say that there will be a constant probability of seeing the station filled by characters pre-eminent for ability and virtue.

Now, this is not to argue that the Electoral College in practice guarantees or even encourages the most talented and virtuous to seek or win the White House, but it does explain the intent, at least in part, of those Founders who considered this institution to be the best compromise between direct election by the people (with its attendant foibles, caprice, and vulnerability to pandering demagogues) and selection by individuals from or by another branch of the government, which could itself blur the designed boundaries between the branches of government and slant toward oligarchy, or worse, toward despotism. More than democracy, the Framers sought the balanced dispersal of power, for concentration of power in either the people or among their talented elites were regarded as both equally distasteful prospects. Discernment of ability, detachment from popular passion (and naïveté), and protection from the ambitions and anxieties of particular interests, the venality of the self-serving, and the intrigues of "cabals"—in a word, the prevention of "tumult and disorder" and the evils of its consequences were all, in the judgment of Hamilton and those of like mind, sufficient reasons to institute a separate, dispassionate body for the selection of this eminent, momentous, and yet at the time still largely undefined office. Perhaps a vague, subconscious resonance with these reasons abides within the American citizenry to this day; thus, even though there is an enduring impression among the politically informed that the Electoral College is a musty relic of the past, there may yet be a residual, albeit still more enduring intuition, sympathetic to the rationale behind maintaining the institution, modified by and within the practices of the democratic processes of party politics. Ultimately, with the four exceptions noted above, the ongoing maintenance of this method of selecting the president has, in its own idiosyncratic way, aligned with the more democratically established popular will detected within limitations; and while incongruity has occurred in the past and the popular vote on a handful of occasions has been overridden—a scenario that remains a possibility for any future election—for the most part the Electoral College simply and typically confirms the popular vote while lending it greater weight as a function of the disparate proportions, and thus candidates earnestly petition their many and varied appeals to people.

Campaigning to earn the people's confidence and endorsement from the voting booth has been elemental to presidential elections since the mid-1820s, that aspect of presidential politics being the most constant of all. Equally persistent through-out the history of presidential politics is the nature of partisan commitment. While few political scientists and presidential observers would deny the importance of campaigning, it remains a long-established fact that most voters are set in their allegiances and have determined how they will vote well before the general election, perhaps well before the earliest signs that the campaign season is under way. As with anything, there are exceptions; there are indeed voters within the general public who from the start of the campaign season remain uncommitted, waiting for something to be said or done that will persuade them toward one direction or the other; but those exceptions aside, most likely voters are guided by their own partisan tendencies, loyalties to specific politicians, and behavioral proclivities. Many other variables must be factored in, such as the state of the economy (perhaps the most important factor in determining an election's outcome) during the election year, or the presence of a crisis abroad, and yes, the level of a candidate's personal appeal across a broad and diverse population; all of these and more do have some influence in helping to determine the outcome in November, but the fact holds that a large segment of the likely voting population know how they will cast their ballot, campaign efforts notwithstanding. Most of us follow our tendencies, the patterns that we have adopted in the past; even if we are politically inactive, we nonetheless lean one direction and follow that direction on Election Day even if the candidate holding the standard of our party of preference is not for us an inspiring choice. It has often been observed that American political parties lack the discipline of their counterparts in Europe, a comparison that in many tangible ways still obtains. Nevertheless, absent the more deeply set fidelities of European parties, American voters still persist in their own engrained habits; they still abide by their own partisan commitments and prefer to follow those ideological markers that lead them in support of those they deem to be the right candidates. There is more ideological fixity in American political culture than most of us may realize, and while our expressed desire to keep an open mind, to wait for candidates to make their case, and to form a decision only after all the evidence is laid out before us, is no doubt sincere for many among us, it is unlikely that campaigning, for all the expense and spectacle attendant to it, will move those who are predisposed to vote for x to abandon their affinities and commit their vote to y. And while campaigning is an expected and requisite component of the democratic process, only a small fraction of votes are influenced by it. In the closest elections, an artfully crafted campaign does make a difference, along with other factors of various and often unexpected kinds, but in general much of what occurs on Election Day is not necessarily the result of persuasive campaigning, but more realistically the expression of that portion of the electorate that has managed to organize and motivate its perennial adherents, to muster out their loyal rank and file. Even the more objective among us often find the certainties that we're already looking for, and while this is not meant to assert that there is little hope of objectivity with regard to truth—quite the contrary, for truth is inherently objective—it is nonetheless an admission that those certainties that we do adopt throughout our lives, and especially with regard to decisions committed in response to political questions and even larger social issues, are to an extent refracted by our perceptions, fitted to our expectations, bent by our inclinations, hewn to our hopes, and molded by our existential background. Even for those of us who might have committed a dramatic shift in ideological propensities—and such shifts do happen for some people during the course of their lives—we move from one pattern and reliance on its markers to another pattern defined by new markers and signposts. Human freedom generates possibility, and for this reason no election is a foregone conclusion; but human habit often forecloses electoral possibilities a priori.

Perhaps these tendencies help explain why political parties are inevitable within any polity shaped by democratic processes. While the Framers designed a process for presidential selection that they deemed compatible with republican principles, inserted within the Constitution itself the expectation of at least some democratic processes such as the election of representatives, guaranteed for the states republican government and those dimensions of democracy expected thereby, and defined da capo the very act of establishing the Constitution as legitimized by the people as a whole, they made no mention of party politics, if not perhaps hoping to discourage partisanship from the beginning, at least hoping to diminish its role in designing the future of the American polity. And yet parties materialized, and relatively quickly, a natural outgrowth of a pluralistic political culture characterized by debate and division. Equally compelling, the party system that grew out of this institutional architecture, and the cultural foundations upon which it is anchored, coalesced around bipartisan allegiances, and while additional parties have come and gone, for the most part politics in America has been propelled forward on the energy of two major parties, and for the last 160 years the same two parties: Democrats and Republicans in all their at times inexplicable permutations. Moreover, these parties have, historically and with comparison to other party systems, gravitated toward the center, and while at various times throughout American history we can accurately speak of the electorate being pulled toward the right or left, in the long view American political parties, while certainly containing noticeable elements that lean hard to one extreme or the other, have been moored to the center. This is not always the case. In recent years, for example, we can speak of the ideological base of the Republican Party as having adopted, for the past two to three decades, attitudes and policies aligned more closely to the right, and it remains to be seen whether or not those dynamics that have fashioned moderate parties in America will self-correct. Political volatility, by its very nature, is a short-term phenomenon; when we assess the long term, the measure of stability is brought into focus. In any event, should a shift in one direction or the other eventually prove to be long-term, the bipartisan structure is likely to remain in place, even if the focus has itself fixed on a new point.

A third constant that can be observed over the course of American political history involves the potent influence of media. Within any political regime, the tools used for communication and the dissemination of information help to frame our perspective and thereby direct our discourse. What events are covered in the media, which elements are stressed, how the information about these elements is conveyed, and the manner in which subsequent conversations about a given event are directed, all contribute to the packaging of our experiences and inadvertently limit the scope of what we can know. So much of what we know about the world beyond our immediate experiences is dependent upon a communication network that processes and compartmentalizes information for us. This is not a deliberate act of controlling knowledge, as the conspiracy-anxious among us might conclude, but rather simply a facet of the structure of the communicative environment. Certainly, some journalists working within the media can and do shape the information that they share, and perhaps for their own purposes, but even when members of the media earnestly seek to adhere to a standard of neutrality, a perspective still sets constraints on which information we are given, how it is dispensed, and what is therein emphasized. In a presidential campaign, which is a complex national event with the capacity to overwhelm our senses and thus one that actually requires that the ordinary mind of the voter undertake a considerable degree of filtering to reasonably process the unfolding spectacle, the media provides a necessary, even critical service for the voting public. We live in an information-fixated age, and the manner in which that information is delivered is vital to the democratic process. With or without intent, the media is responsible for its share in shaping a presidential campaign, in the selection of which politicians to follow and how what they say and do are reported, as well as which issues blinker a candidate's campaign agenda and rhetoric. Democratic government is deeply dependent on communication, and for this reason, media is an elemental constant in presidential campaign history.

Conceding this, even an exceedingly influential media cannot always anticipate what will happen or channel the news according to some set of hidden, subconscious patterns; the more effective candidates assert themselves into the process in ways that cannot be ignored. For this reason we cannot always anticipate which candidate will arise as the sustained front-runner, nor can we confidently predict, beyond reasoned conjecture, what even comfortable front-runners may do to strengthen or weaken their own efforts. Front-runners can be overtaken by events, dark horses propelled by unexpected opportunities, media favorites self-destruct, once seemingly invulnerable incumbents succumb to circumstances, and ostensible pacesetters collapse under pressure. In a real sense, presidential campaigning is as much about survival as it is about qualification, the need to survive often controlling the convictions shared and the competencies revealed.

There are many aspects about presidential campaigning that have endured over the generations, and many that have undergone flux and uncertainty. Through all this, the presidency captivates the American public like no other elective office across the republic's political landscape. At the risk of leaning on a cliché, the White House is the Mt. Everest of American democracy, even if its occupant is not solely determined by what we would hope to be purely democratic procedures. Democracy is nonetheless insistent that a free citizenry will always be the one constant that grounds any political process, as well as the principal agent of change in the structure and dynamics of a political community. The promise of the presidency is ineradicably a democratic promise, and every credible person who has sought or held the office has understood this, even as their actions have not always reflected this inner awareness. Presidents carry the appellation "Leader of the Free World" for a reason; those who select them for office are therefore charged with the sober duty of raising up a personage equal to that immense responsibility. We rest our hopes on the president; more deeply, the promise of the presidency rests on our own capacity for self-government and the expression of a reasoned freedom; and the virtues of our candidates, those who succeed in their efforts and those who fail, are in the end only as sound as the virtues we have cultivated within ourselves.

Guide to Related Topics

Campaign Strategies

Astro-Turfers
Dark Money
Frontloading
Going Rogue
Ground War/Ground Game
Internet Campaigning
Invisible Primary

Maverick
Money Ball
Negative Campaigning
Poll-Driven Campaign
Silent Majority
Wedge Issue

Campaign Tactics

Astroturfers
Campaign Ads/Political Ads
Microtargeting
Paid Media
Retail Politics

Sound Bite
Symbolic Racism
Talking Points
Wedge Issue

Campaign Tools

Big Data
Campaign Ads
Cattle Call
Dark Money
Internet Campaigning
Media Event
Paid Media

Photo Opportunity
Presidential Debates
Retail Politics
Social Media
Talking Points
Tracking Poll

Defeat of Incumbent President

Campaign of 1800
Campaign of 1828
Campaign of 1840

Campaign of 1888
Campaign of 1892
Campaign of 1912

Campaign of 1932   Campaign of 1980
Campaign of 1976   Campaign of 1992

Disputed Presidential Elections

Campaign of 1800   Campaign of 1876
Campaign of 1824   Campaign of 2000

Economic Issues and Presidential Campaigns

Americans for Prosperity (AFP)   Immigration Issue
Americans for Tax Reform   Independent Advocacy Groups
Bread-and-Butter Issues   Keynesian Economics
Corporations and Personhood   Pocketbook Issue
Dark MoneyEarmark   Prosperity Issue
Economic Inequality Issue   Right to Work
Education Reform Issue   Social Security Issue
Energy Issue   Tea Party Movement
Environmental Issue   Trade Issues
Health Care Issue   Troubled Asset Relief Program (TARP)

Efforts at and Issues Involving Electoral Reform

Butterfly Ballot   National Voter Registration Act
Campaign Finance Reform   of 1993
Civil Rights Reforms   Provisional Ballot
Early Voting   Voting Reform Issue
Frontloading   Voting Rights Act of 1965
Get-Out-the-Vote (GOTV) Programs   Women's Equality Issue

Elections Decided by Electoral College Contrary to Popular Vote*

Campaign of 1876   Campaign of 2000
Campaign of 1888

Elections Decided in the House of Representatives

Campaign of 1800   Campaign of 1824

Elections Involving a Supreme Court Decision or Participation of Supreme Court Justices

Campaign of 1876 (involved Supreme   Campaign of 2000 (*Bush v. Gore)*
  Court justices participating in an
  Electoral Commission)

*All elections are and always have been technically decided by the Electoral College.

Elections of Notable Political, Social, and Cultural Import

1789: The first presidential election under the recently ratified Constitution.

1800: The first transition of the presidency between rival parties.

1824: The first election in which the popular vote for the presidency was recorded and published at the national level.

1860: The first and only election that precipitated secession and, ultimately, civil war.

1868: Freed slaves participate in their first presidential election.

1876–1877: The end of Reconstruction weakens the brief influence—and in some parts of the country, entirely eliminates the exercise—of the African American vote.

1912: The only election in which a candidate nominated by one of the two major parties received fewer votes than a third-party candidate.

1920: The first election in which women could vote at the national level (in previous elections, women were able to vote at the state level in some states).

1928: Includes the first Roman Catholic to be nominated for the presidency by a major party.

1940: First and only election in which an incumbent president ran for and was elected to a third term (followed by election to a fourth term in 1944).

1960: Includes the first Roman Catholic to be elected president.

1964: Includes the first Roman Catholic to be nominated for the vice presidency.

1968: The first presidential election to be held after the passage of the 1965 Voting Rights Act helping to reestablish the influence of the African American vote that had been severely diminished throughout much of the Union with the end of Reconstruction in 1877.

1976: The first election in which all adult citizens over the age of eighteen were allowed to vote.

1984: Includes the first woman to be nominated for the vice presidency.

2000: Includes the first Jewish candidate to be nominated for the vice presidency.

2008: Includes the first person of African American descent to be elected president of the United States, the first Catholic to be elected to the vice presidency, and the second woman to be nominated for vice president by a major party.

2012: Includes reelection of the first and only African American president as well as the first Mormon to be nominated for president by a major party.

Emotion and Presidential Campaigns

Anti-Catholicism
Birther
Bread-and-Butter Issues
Checkers Speech
Culture War
"Daisy Girl" Campaign Ad
Going Rogue
Gun Control Issue
Immigration Issue
Nativism
Negative Campaigning

Pocketbook Issue
Presidential Coattails
Race Relations Issue
Rally Around the Flag Effect
Red Meat Issue
Silent Majority
Sister Souljah Moment
Sound Bite
Symbolic Racism
Talk Radio
Wedge Issue

Events

Cattle Call
Caucus
CPAC
Media Event

Netroots Nation/YearlyKos
    Convention
Photo Opportunity
Presidential Debates
Super Tuesday

Ideological Affiliations, Contexts, and Propensities

Blue and Red States
Compassionate Conservatism
Goldwater Conservative
Libertarianism
Neoconservatives
Partisan Sorting

Populists
Progressivism
RINO
Tea Party Movement
Values Voters
Women's Equality Issue

Important Legislation Affecting Presidential Campaigns and Elections

Civil Rights Reforms
Jim Crow Laws
National Voter Registration Act

Voting Reform Issue
Voting Rights Act of 1965
Women's Equality Issue

International Affairs, Foreign Policy, and War and Peace

American Exceptionalism
Anti-Catholicism
"Daisy Girl" Campaign Ad
Environmental Issue
Goldwater Conservative

Immigration Issue
Isolationism
Manifest Destiny
Nativism Issue
War and Peace Issue

Landslide Presidential Elections, Popular Vote (Winner Received More Than 54 Percent of *Popular* Vote), Listed Chronologically, Not by Rank

Campaign of 1828 (Andrew Jackson over John Quincy Adams)

Campaign of 1832 (Andrew Jackson over Henry Clay)

Campaign of 1864 (Abraham Lincoln over George B. McClellan)

Campaign of 1872 (Ulysses S. Grant over Horace Greeley)

Campaign of 1904 (Theodore Roosevelt over Alton Parker)

Campaign of 1920 (Warren G. Harding over James Cox)

Campaign of 1924 (Calvin Coolidge over John W. Davis)

Campaign of 1928 (Herbert Hoover over Al Smith)

Campaign of 1932 (Franklin D. Roosevelt over Herbert Hoover)

Campaign of 1936 (Franklin D. Roosevelt over Alfred Landon)

Campaign of 1940 (Franklin D. Roosevelt over Wendell Willkie)

Campaign of 1952 (Dwight D. Eisenhower over Adlai Stevenson)

Campaign of 1956 (Dwight D. Eisenhower over Adlai Stevenson)

Campaign of 1964 (Lyndon Johnson over Barry Goldwater)

Campaign of 1972 (Richard Nixon over George McGovern)

Campaign of 1984 (Ronald Reagan over Walter Mondale)

Media Coverage of Presidential Campaigns

Cable News Network (CNN)

C-SPAN

Exit Polling

Free Media

Horse-Race Campaign Coverage

Larry King Live

Netroots Nation

New Media

Paid Media

Photo Opportunity

Political Cartoons

Poll-Driven Campaign

Presidential Debates

Soft News

Sound Bite

Spin Doctor

Swift Boating

Talk Radio

Tracking Poll

Twenty-Four-Hour News Cycle

Money and Presidential Campaigns

Americans for Prosperity (AFP)

Americans for Tax Reform

Buckley v. Valeo (1976)

Campaign Ads

Campaign Finance Reform

Corporations and Personhood

Dark Money

Earned Media

501c Group

527 Group

Independent Advocacy Groups

Internet Campaigning

Paid Media

Political Ads

Retail Politics
Social Media

Super PAC
Women's Equality Issue

Polling and the Use of Statistical Data

Big Data
Moneyball
Poll-Driven Campaign

Poll of Polls
Tracking Poll

Realigning Presidential Elections

Campaigns of 1828 and 1832
Campaigns of 1856 and 1860
Campaign of 1896

Campaigns of 1932 and 1936
  (prefigured by 1928)
Campaign of 1980

Social Issues and Presidential Campaigns

Abortion Controversy
Affirmative Action
Anti-Catholicism
Birther
Civil Rights Reform
Civil Service Reform
Compassionate Conservatism
Culture War
Education Reform Issue
Gender Gap
Gun Control Issue
Health Care Issue
Immigration Issue
Jim Crow Laws
LGBTQ Issues
Libertarianism
Moral Majority

MoveOn
Nativism Issue
Neoconservatives
Populists
Poverty Issue
Prosperity Issue
Race Relations Issue
Right to Work
Silent Majority
Sister Souljah Moment
Social Security Issue
Symbolic Racism
Tea Party Movement
Values Voters
Wedge Issue
Women's Equality Issue

Television and Presidential Campaigns

Campaign Ads
Checkers Speech
"Daisy Girl" Campaign Ad
Dark Money
Earned Media
501c Group

527 Group
Going Viral
Media Event
Negative Campaigning
Paid Media
Photo Opportunity

Political Ads
Presidential Debates
Social Media

Soft News
Sound Bite
Twenty-Four-Hour News Cycle

Voter Behavior, Trends, and Patterns

Battleground State
Big Data
Campaign Ads
Culture War
Early Voting
Frontloading
Focus Group
Gender Gap
Get-Out-the-Vote (GOTV) Programs
Likely Voter
Marriage Gap
Median Voter Theory

Microtargeting
Moneyball
Pocketbook Issue
Presidential Coattails
Sociotropic Voting
Superdelegate
Surge and Decline Theory
Tracking Poll
Undecideds
Valence Issue
Values Voters

Issues, Strategies, Practices, and Events

Abortion Controversy

During the **Campaign of 1972**, abortion emerged as an important campaign issue as several notable cases wound their way through the court system. A spring 1972 report by the President's Commission on Population Growth and the American Future urged the liberalization of abortion laws and making contraceptives available for teenagers to limit unwanted pregnancies. Nevertheless, Republican president Richard Nixon, running for a second term, expressed strong opposition to these recommendations. Despite strong pressure from women in the Democratic Party, presidential nominee and South Dakota senator George McGovern tried to avoid taking a firm stand on the issue by arguing that abortion laws should be left to the states. An August 1972 Gallup poll found that 64 percent of the American public believed that a decision to have an abortion should be left solely to the woman and her doctor.

The 1973 landmark Supreme Court decision in *Roe v. Wade,* sharply limiting the ability of states to prohibit abortions, turned abortion into a hot-button issue for subsequent presidential campaigns. Relying upon the privacy rationale in the 1965 Supreme Court decision in *Griswold v. Connecticut* that struck down a Connecticut ban on the sale of contraceptives to married women, the high court extended the right to privacy, established in the *Griswold* ruling, to adult women choosing abortion in the first trimester of a pregnancy, while also allowing for abortion in the second trimester in cases when maternal health is at risk. Although many women's groups applauded the Court's decision, many social conservatives regarded the decision as an assault on the sanctity of life, and as another example of the Supreme Court making law rather than strictly interpreting the Constitution.

In the **Campaign of 1976,** legal abortion and the *Roe v. Wade* decision became major campaign issues. Now a major force in the Republican Party, social conservatives managed to push through a strong anti-abortion plank to the party's platform. During his primary challenge to President Gerald Ford, former California governor Ronald Reagan openly advocated a constitutional amendment banning abortion in all fifty states. During the primary battle and general election campaign, President Ford only supported a constitutional amendment that returned to the States the authority to regulate abortions. Interestingly, the Democratic presidential nominee, former Georgia governor Jimmy Carter, expressed his opposition to abortion while simultaneously opposing a proposed constitutional amendment banning abortions or returning to the states regulatory responsibility regarding any restrictions that might be imposed on the controversial procedure.

The **Campaign of 1980** signaled a major split between the Republican and Democratic parties on the abortion issue. Beginning with the 1980 Republican National Convention and continuing through all subsequent GOP conventions, Republican platforms have included a call for a constitutional amendment banning abortion. Every Democratic convention since 1980 has reaffirmed support for the *Roe v. Wade* decision. As social conservatives grew in importance within the Republican Party, Republican presidential candidates found themselves subject to a "right to life" litmus test. The growing importance of women voters to the Democratic Party, on the other hand, placed great pressure on Democratic presidential candidates to hold a "pro-choice" position.

Despite the divergent positions of the Democratic and Republican parties on the abortion issue, little evidence exists that the abortion issue had much effect on swing voters from the **Campaign of 1980** through the **Campaign of 2008**. However, considerable evidence exists that abortion has played a major role in mobilizing activists and core voters by both the Republican and Democratic parties. For instance, during the **Campaign of 1992** and **Campaign of 1996,** Bill Clinton and the Democratic Party used the pro-choice issue to mobilize women by emphatically warning that a Republican president would have the power to nominate Supreme Court justices who would overturn the *Roe* decision. In the **Campaign of 2000,** the Democratic Party and their nominee, Vice President Al Gore, devoted time and resources to highlight his strong pro-choice position. Whether or not this effort influenced the outcome of the election is unclear. Republican nominee George W. Bush, during this campaign, avoided most discussions of abortion, noting that *Roe v. Wade* was "settled law." Similarly, in the **Campaign of 2004,** the Republican Party devoted large sums to target social conservatives in Ohio and other **battleground states**, emphasizing Bush's traditional values, including his more outspoken role as a critic of legal abortion. The success of the Bush reelection campaign in targeting pro-life social conservatives proved crucial in Bush's narrow electoral vote victory.

By the **Campaign of 2008**, the abortion controversy became overshadowed by the specter of failing financial institutions, sizable increases in the ranks of the unemployed, and an upsurge in home foreclosures. However, new attempts by states to tightly regulate abortion in the wake of the 2010 Republican victories at the state (and federal) level, combined with a conservative Supreme Court willing to restrict abortions, has consequently reignited this debate. In the **Campaign of 2012**, Democrats claimed that the GOP was waging a "war on women," and in an attempt to distance himself from his party's hardline position, GOP nominee Mitt Romney broke ranks with his party's platform and suggested that he would not support a personhood amendment to the U.S. Constitution that did not permit exceptions for rape and incest. Both political parties have vowed to make abortion a theme in the **Campaign of 2016**, although as of this writing the abortion issue has been largely ignored owing to the strange tenor of the preprimary polemics focusing on controversies involving immigration, terrorism, gun control, and religious freedom. That said, Democrats continue to advocate the pro-choice position and to advance the "war on women" narrative. The entirety of the GOP field remains committed to the pro-life position, with almost all of the candidates supporting a federal ban on all abortions after twenty weeks.

See also Campaign of 1980; Campaign of 1992; Campaign of 1996; Campaign of 2000; Gender Gap; Moral Majority; Red Meat Issue; Wedge Issue

Additional Resources

Alvarez, R. Michael, and John Brehm. *Hard Choices, Easy Answers: Values, Information, and American Public Opinion.* Princeton, NJ: Princeton University Press, 2002.
Fiorina, Morris P. *Culture War? The Myth of a Polarized America.* New York: Pearson Longman, 2005.
Hillygus, D. Sunshine, and Todd G. Shields. *The Persuadable Voter: Wedge Issues in Presidential Campaigns.* Princeton, NJ: Princeton University Press, 2008.
Wald, Kenneth D. *Religion and Politics in the United States.* Washington, DC: Congressional Quarterly Press, 1997.

Affirmative Action

The Title VII provision of the 1964 Civil Rights Act prohibits private employers from discriminating against either employees or job applicants on the basis of race, religion, gender, and country of national origin. However, Title VII does not place an affirmative obligation on employers to increase the diversity of their organizations. In September 1965, President Lyndon Johnson issued Executive Order 11246, which prohibited federal contractors from discriminating against both employees and applicants for positions on the basis of race, creed, color, or national origin. Two years later, the Johnson administration amended the language of the executive order prohibiting federal contractors from discriminating on the basis of gender as well, and directed federal contractors to take affirmative steps to increase the diversity of their organizations in the areas of race, gender, and national origin.

Throughout the 1970s, Republican and Democratic presidential administrations strongly supported affirmative action programs. Both Republican president Richard Nixon (1969–1974) and Democratic president Jimmy Carter (1977–1981) continued the federal government's commitment to increasing the diversity of government agencies. In October 1978, for example, President Carter signed into law the Civil Service Reform Act, which required all federal agencies to take affirmative steps to increase the number of members of underrepresented groups in their organizations.

Despite strong presidential and congressional support for affirmative action programs, the late 1970s saw a grassroots backlash against programs designed to give underrepresented minorities a preference in hiring for government jobs. Critics of affirmative action argued that such programs violated the Civil Rights Act of 1964 and the Equal Protection Clause of the Fourteenth Amendment, an argument supported by the Supreme Court in *University of California v. Bakke* (1978). The court ruled that the admission policy of the university's law school, which gave African American applicants preference in admissions, violated Section VI of the 1964 Civil Rights Act. The decision signaled the beginning of strict scrutiny of government-mandated affirmative action programs by the Supreme Court.

The public backlash against affirmative action coincided with bad economic times; the energy crisis of the late 1970s contributed to a sluggish economy and job losses, particularly in the manufacturing sector. Large numbers of blue-collar workers lost their jobs to lower-priced foreign competition, most notably in the automotive industry. The **Campaign of 1980** marked the end of the consensus between the Republican and Democratic parties on affirmative action. The 1980 Republican Party platform included a plank that opposed any government-mandated hiring quotas for minorities. In contrast, the 1980 Democratic Party platform included a plank reaffirming affirmative action programs as necessary remedies correcting the historical injustice of discriminatory hiring practices. Not surprisingly, the Democratic platform in the **Campaign of 1984** continued to promote affirmative action as a means to "repair the legacy of discrimination in American society," whereas the Republican platform sharply criticized the use of "quotas" as inherently unfair.

These partisan differences reflected sharply different beliefs about the role of government in society, as well as differences in the core elements of each party's political coalition. While Americans are generally supportive of the notion of societal equality, how this is to be accomplished is an enduring source of conflict. Conservatives, in large measure, support "equality of opportunity" policies, in which the government attempts to level the playing field but does not act in a way that influences societal outcomes. Liberals are more concerned with "equality of outcomes," or the distribution of opportunities and rewards in society, predominantly supporting government remedies addressing inequalities. In addition to these philosophical differences, the Republican Party during this era relied heavily on white voters (particularly white males), whereas racial minorities represent an increasingly larger segment of the Democratic Party.

In the **Campaigns of 1984** and **1988**, President Reagan and Vice President Bush, respectively, used affirmative action as part of a broader strategy designed to depict the Democratic Party and their nominees, Walter Mondale and Michael Dukakis, respectively, as too liberal. As a result, many blue-collar and working-class partisans who had voted Democratic from the New Deal through the 1970s found their party loyalties challenged. Some of these voters defected to the Republican Party during this era, while others may have avoided the polls entirely. While the Republican Party was able to successfully characterize the Democrats as out of touch with (white) Middle America, this strategy was also effective because whites still constituted 86 percent of the electorate when President Reagan was reelected in 1984. Republican candidates after the Reagan-Bush era faced a very different, more racially diverse pool of voters.

From the **Campaign of 1992** onward, affirmative action did not play a direct role in either Democratic or Republican campaigns. A series of Supreme Court decisions starting in the late 1980s and continuing through the present day has sharply limited the government's ability to give preference to members of underrepresented groups in hiring, admissions to colleges and universities, and awarding of government contracts. In 1997, California voters approved a constitutional amendment banning all forms of affirmative action in public employment, higher education, and public contracting. In 2008, voters in Nebraska approved a similar ban on affirmative action, while Colorado voters refused to impose a ban. The Supreme Court upheld Michigan's 2006 ban in 2012, in *Schuette v. Coalition to Defend Affirmative Action*. In *Schuette*, the Court affirmed the right of Michigan voters to ban affirmative action via referendum.

While no longer debated overtly as a policy, concerns about affirmative action simmer beneath the surface of American politics. Paradoxically, while whites still constitute a majority of the electorate (74% in 2008 and 72% in 2012), many whites are concerned about their loss of political and economic power at the same time that members of ethnic minority groups and women find themselves facing less discrimination. A 2014 survey conducted by the Public Religion Research Institute found that 52 percent of white Americans believed that discrimination against whites constituted a social problem as serious as discrimination against minorities. This view was more likely to be expressed by conservatives, with 76 percent of Tea Party identifiers and 61 percent of Republicans believing that anti-white discrimination was a serious problem, up from a similar survey four years previously. White Independents (53%) and white Democrats (37%) were far less likely to subscribe to this belief. White men were more likely to see discrimination against whites than were white women; this view also tended to increase with age and decreased as a function of education. Among religious groups, white evangelical Protestants were more likely to claim that discrimination against whites was a problem than other denominations.

At the same time, many whites appear to be indifferent to the enduring problems of racism in American society. A 2013 study by the Pew Research Center evaluated perceptions of discrimination against African Americans by the police, in housing, in employment, in the criminal justice system, in public schools, in voting, in obtaining health care, and in receiving service in restaurants and stores. The study found that 49 percent of all whites believed that African Americans experienced no discrimination in any of these areas (whereas only 13% of blacks and 24% of Latinos shared this perception). Whites were less likely to perceive discrimination against African Americans if they were male, lived in a rural location, and self-identified as ideologically conservative. Sixty percent of white Republicans claim that African Americans experience no racial discrimination whatsoever, approximately twice the rate of white Democrats (and similar to the findings of the Public Religion Research Institute Survey). Thus, it appears that conservative and Republican voters are less cognizant of, or less concerned about, discrimination against non-whites, and substantially more likely to view whites, who remain numerically and culturally dominant, as being marginalized.

These differing perceptions of power and threat underlie the parties' policy differences on immigration and on civil rights, and their preference for nostalgia for a past era as opposed to one that embraces sociodemographic change.

See also Campaign of 1996; Campaign of 2000; Immigration Issue; Race Relations Issue; Tea Party Movement; Wedge Issue

Additional Resources

Gilens, Martin. *Why Americans Hate Welfare: Race, Media, and the Politics of Anti-Poverty Policy.* Chicago: University of Chicago Press, 2000.

Jones, Robert B., and Daniel Cox. "Old Alignments, Emerging Fault Lines: Religion in the 2010 Election and Beyond: Findings from the 2010 Post-Election American Values Survey." Public Religion Research Institute, November 2010.

Keen, Judy. "Affirmative Action Takes New Turn for '96." *USA Today,* June 13, 1995, p. 5A.

McClosky, Herbert, and John Zaller. *The American Ethos: Public Attitudes toward Capitalism and Democracy.* Cambridge, MA: Harvard University Press, 1987.

Parker, Christopher S., and Matt A. Barreto. *Change They Can't Believe In: The Tea Party and Reactionary Politics in America.* Princeton, NJ: Princeton University Press, 2013.

Teixiera, Ruy, and Alan Abramowitz. "The Decline of the White Working Class and the Rise of a Mass Upper Middle Class." Brookings Working Paper, April 2008.

American Exceptionalism

The use of the term "exceptional" to describe American culture originated with Alexis de Tocqueville, who noted that Americans were in an exceptional position as English-speaking people exploring "the wilds of the new world." In Tocqueville's usage, the term "exceptional" indicated uniqueness but not moral superiority (indeed, Tocqueville also commented on rampant, grasping consumerism as an undesirable trait shared by Americans). Citizens of the United States at that time enjoyed political rights not found elsewhere in the world, and high rates of immigration contributed to a society in which many—but by no means all—ethnic and religious cultures could live peacefully together when compared to contemporary European societies (although this social stability was short-lived, preceding the eruption of a historic civil war a few decades later). Thus, for Tocqueville, the United States constituted a grand and unique social and political experiment.

Even earlier than Tocqueville, Massachusetts Bay Colony governor John Winthrop declared in 1630 that settlers in the American territory had been chosen by God to create a Christian society and that the economic prosperity of this settlement would be an indication of God's favor. The United States was, in this view, a shining "city upon a hill" setting an example for peoples around the world. Elements of Tocqueville's admiration of the American political system, combined with Winthrop's belief in Divine Providence, fostered a worldview that accorded the United States a special role among the community of nations. According to this worldview, now known as American exceptionalism, the structural traits of the United States as a nation, particularly its democratic political institutions, civic-spiritedness, frontier sensibilities, celebration of individual liberty comingled with egalitarian aspirations, and enduring capitalist economic institutions and attitudes, represent an ideal system, a uniquely blessed society. Moreover, the powerful position that the United States has achieved and sustained in global politics is deemed a sign of divine favor.

As a consequence, so the thinking goes, exporting these political and economic institutions to other nations is both desirable and generous. Beliefs about the superiority of American institutions are accompanied by beliefs about the superiority of American judgment and actions. Americans pride themselves on their enlightened, tolerant attitudes toward diversity, and for their independent-minded thinking. As historian James Q. Wilson notes, Americans are, in fact, unique when compared with European democracies, exhibiting higher levels of expressed patriotism, attributing economic status to individual efforts that are within their range of control, and stressing abiding belief in God.

Advocates of territorial expansion and the extension of American political and economic influence abroad have claimed American exceptionalism as a moral justification. Some argue that this exceptionalism has encouraged commitment of the military abroad absent congressional declarations of war. Additionally, principal leadership in the United Nations, as well as the adoption of the Marshall Plan and the institution of the Peace Corps by President Kennedy have been viewed by some as efforts motivated by American exceptionalism. American reliance on military intervention abroad has most recently occurred through President George W. Bush's efforts to liberate Iraqis from Saddam Hussein and the Afghanis from the Taliban, and by President Barack Obama's efforts to aid militants in toppling the Qaddafi regime in Libya as well as his use of force against extremists in Afghanistan (i.e., the Surge in Afghanistan), drone strikes against terrorists, and most recently his resolve to support opposition to ISIL/ISIS in Syrian and Iraq.

In contemporary politics, American exceptionalism is most strongly associated with President Ronald Reagan. He explicitly mentioned Winthrop's "shining city on the hill" during his nomination acceptance speech in the **Campaign of 1984**, proclaiming that, "We said we would once again be respected throughout the world, and we are." Reagan also reaffirmed the belief that the United States was a special nation, entitled to interact with other nations from a position of power: "We came together in a national crusade to make America great again, and to make a new beginning. Well, now it's all coming together. With our beloved nation at peace, we're in the midst of a springtime of hope for America. Greatness lies ahead of us." Reagan used similar language in other speeches, including his 1989 farewell address. As early as 1952 Reagan identified the source of this national greatness during a commencement address proclaiming that he "always thought of America as a place in the divine scheme of things that was set aside as a promised land."

A majority of Americans still adhere to the philosophy that the United States is a divinely favored nation possessing exceptional qualities. A poll conducted by the Public Religion Research Institute (PRRI) in late 2010 found that 58 percent of Americans surveyed believe that "God has granted America a special role in human history." Moreover, there were clear partisan differences in beliefs about American exceptionalism. Overwhelming majorities of Republicans (75%) and Tea Party identifiers (76%) affirmed this belief, compared to only 43 percent of Independents and only 30 percent of Democrats. More darkly, researchers also noted that those who subscribe to the notion of American exceptionalism are also more inclined to believe that there is a justifiable use for torture, and that military strength is more important than diplomacy as a tool for ensuring world peace.

Given these partisan differences in the general public, it was not surprising that candidates in the **Campaign of 2012** incorporated American exceptionalism into their campaigns. Democrat Barack Obama addressed the topic of American exceptionalism on numerous occasions, earliest among them his speech at the 2004 Democratic convention. When asked during a press conference whether he subscribed to the view that the United States was "uniquely qualified to lead the world," Obama responded, "I believe in American exceptionalism, just as I suspect that the Brits believe in British exceptionalism and the Greeks believe in Greek exceptionalism." Obama further noted that "we have a core set of values that are enshrined in our Constitution, in our body of law, in our democratic practices, in our belief in free speech and equality that, although imperfect, are exceptional."

Obama's Republican critics blasted his response, complaining that he is too ready to apologize to the world for America's good fortune. Former Alaska governor Sarah Palin criticized Obama for his perceived failure to acknowledge that the United States is different from other countries, noting in her 2010 book that "when President Obama insists that all countries are exceptional, he's saying that none is, least of all the country he leads." Former Pennsylvania senator Rick Santorum echoed this sentiment, telling a group of college Republicans, "Don't kid yourself with the lie. America is exceptional." GOP hopefuls Newt Gingrich, Mitt Romney, Mike Pence, and Mike Huckabee made similar claims in their writings and public appearances, offering a stridently nationalistic interpretation of American exceptionalism that has come to be a hallmark of Republican campaign rhetoric in contemporary elections.

Some of the President's defenders suspect insidious motivations of a personal nature influenced by hidden attitudes of racism underlying these criticisms. The implication here is that the President, a person of color and therefore someone who, as the argument goes, has not shared the "mainstream" American experience and is consequently in some inexplicable way incapable of fully appreciating the values that Americans honor. This type of critique is typified by former New York City mayor Rudy Giuliani, who declaimed that, "I know this is a horrible thing to say, but I do not believe the president loves America. He wasn't brought up the way you were brought up and I was brought up, through love of this country."

Obama did not dispense with American exceptionalism in its entirety, however; he has repeatedly referred to the United States as an "indispensable nation," suggesting that it should continue to play an important role in world affairs. President Obama's rhetoric throughout his administration suggests that he believes the United States to be special; however, his interpretation of exceptionalism has tended to focus on the domestic aspects of American policy rather than its role in global affairs. In his speech commemorating the fiftieth anniversary of the march on Selma, Alabama, the president suggested that the struggle for civil rights was one of the things that made America exceptional—in particular, the hard-fought battle by those long oppressed to compel the country to honor its commitment to equality. As President Obama explained that day on the Edmund Pettus bridge:

> What Selma does perhaps better than any other moment in our history is to vindicate the faith of our founders; to vindicate the idea that ordinary folks—not of high station, not born to wealth or privilege or to certain religious belief—are able to shape the destiny of their nation. You can't get more American than that. This is the most American of ideas. The most American of moments.

Obama's Selma speech also served as a rebuttal of Giuliani and, in some respects, set the stage for the campaign to come. He emphasized the changes in American society as something to be welcomed, and the future as something to be anticipated: "That's what America is. Not stock photos or airbrushed history, or feeble attempts to define some of us as more American than others. We respect the past but we don't pine for the past. We don't fear the future; we grab for it. America is not some fragile thing."

The Republican hopefuls in the **Campaign of 2016** have tapped into American exceptionalism in many ways, often in the context of demographic changes throughout the nation. Senator Ted Cruz defended the view of America as "a shining city on a hill," a vision that he claimed was slipping away under Obama and claiming the erosion of U.S. power in the community of nations. Similarly, Donald Trump has played to these concerns, dramatically donning a "Make America Great Again" baseball cap throughout his campaign. In 2012, Trump had argued with comedian Bill Maher about the relevance of American exceptionalism, maintaining that the United States could be restored to global dominance if only the GOP could regain the White House. Jeb Bush spoke admiringly of the Marshall Plan, suggesting that only a great country such as the United States could have executed such a feat. Former secretary of state Hillary Clinton, the Democratic front-runner, differs from her predecessor in that she has endorsed American exceptionalism by name, and implied that she would be more willing to use military force overseas to defend U.S. interests, and in so doing promote the story and purpose of the United States as a leader among the nations of the world.

See also Isolationism

Additional Resources

Bacevich, Andrew. *The Limits of Power: The End of American Exceptionalism*. New York: Metropolitan Books, 2008.

The Brookings Institution. *Democracy in America: Reexamining American Exceptionalism.* Panel on Alexis de Tocqueville hosted by the Brookings Institution, Washington, DC, April 23, 2008. http://www.brookings.edu/events/2008/0423_america.aspx. Accessed September 10, 2015.

Brooks, Stephen. *American Exceptionalism in the Age of Obama.* New York: Routledge, 2013.

"A History of Exceptionalism." Post Politics, *Washington Post*, November 24, 2010.

Jaffe, Greg. "Obama's New Patriotism." *Washington Post*, June 3, 2015.

Jones, Robert B., and Daniel Cox. "Old Alignments, Emerging Fault Lines: Religion in the 2010 Election and Beyond: Findings from the 2010 Post-Election American Values Survey." Public Religion Research Institute, November 2010.

Lipset, Seymour Martin. *American Exceptionalism: A Double-Edged Sword.* New York: W. W. Norton and Co., 1997.

McClosky, Herbert, and John Zaller. *The American Ethos.* Cambridge, MA: Harvard University Press, 1987.

Palin, Sarah. *American by Heart: Reflections on Family, Faith, and Flag.* New York: HarperCollins, 2010.

Pease, Donald A. *The New American Exceptionalism.* Minneapolis: University of Minnesota Press, 2009.

Reagan, Ronald. "Remarks Accepting the Presidential Nomination at the Republican National Convention in Dallas, Texas," August 23, 1984. http://www.reagan.utexas.edu/archives/speeches/1984/82384f.htm. Accessed September 10, 2015.

Romney, Mitt. *No Apology: The Case for American Greatness.* New York: St. Martin's Press, 2010.

Schuck, Peter H., and James Q. Wilson, eds. *Understanding America: The Anatomy of an Exceptional Nation.* Washington, DC: Public Affairs, 2008.

Tumulty, Karen. "American Exceptionalism: An Old Idea and a New Political Battle." *Washington Post*, November 29, 2010.

Vowell, Sarah. *The Wordy Shipmates.* New York: Riverhead Books, 2009.

Americans for Prosperity (AFP)

Americans for Prosperity Foundation (AFP) is an anti-taxation advocacy group founded and financed by David and Charles Koch, the billionaire brothers who own Koch Industries of Wichita, Kansas, in 2004. The Kochs also founded (and funded) AFP's predecessor, Americans for a Sound Economy, as well as the Cato Institute and the National Center for Policy Analysis, and numerous other free-enterprise, libertarian-oriented think tanks. AFP is a **501(c) group**, which means that they do not disclose their donor list. The group's stated policy goals include "removing unnecessary barriers to entrepreneurship and opportunity" and "restoring fairness to our judicial system by stemming the tide toward 'overcriminalization' of economic activity spurred by over-active attorneys general," as well as "pointing out evidence of waste, fraud, and abuse," tax reduction, and halting "the encroachment of government in the economic lives of citizens."

AFP boasts of having over one hundred field organizers, thirty fully staffed state affiliates, and 1.6 million members, although the latter figure cannot be verified. AFP provides a forum for conservative candidates running for office, by hosting political dinners and policy summits. In the summer of 2009, AFP created Patients United Now to organize hundreds of rallies against President Obama's proposed health care reforms. The group also promotes **Tea Party movement** candidates, offering training sessions in grassroots political activities and, according to journalist Jane Mayer, providing lists of candidates for the Tea Party to target and **talking points** for members to utilize (leading critics to characterize the movement as **astroturfers**). Beginning in 2008, the group has also hosted the yearly RightOnline conference. RightOnline was intended to create a forum for conservative bloggers and activists that was similar to the liberal **Netroots** conference. The Kochs also underwrite Generation Opportunity, a 501(c)(4) group focused on conservative youth mobilization, although this is done through their TC4 Trust and Freedom Partners. Generation Opportunity ran ads encouraging young people to "opt out of Obamacare" and financed ads against endangered Democratic incumbent senators in the 2014 midterm elections.

Americans for Prosperity has funded state legislative and gubernatorial candidates who were committed to limiting the role of public-sector unions, opposing reforms in minimum wage laws, opposing new health care regulations, reducing taxes, and limiting regulations on businesses more generally. In particular, the organization contributed to the 2010 gubernatorial campaign of Scott Walker in Wisconsin, as well as numerous other state legislative candidates. Shortly after the newly elected Republicans were sworn into office in January 2011, Walker and the Republican legislature attempted to ban collective bargaining for public-sector unions (with the exception of firefighters and police officers). Large protests followed, and the Koch brothers' role in funding federal elections became a topic of media scrutiny. AFP began to run ads in Wisconsin and other Midwestern states that portrayed public-sector union members as enjoying unfair privileges that other workers don't get, and of failing to do their fair share to reduce state deficits. During the midterm elections of 2010, AFP spent over $40 million, a record sum for the group, on a combination of campaign donations, rallies, door-to-door voter canvassing, and attack ads, the vast bulk of which benefited Republican candidates.

In the **Campaign of 2012**, AFP spent an estimated $122 million according to Michael Beckel of *Primary Source*, albeit with somewhat less success, prompting an internal audit of their electoral targeting and spending practices after Obama was reelected. In particular, the group and its benefactors are concerned about environmental regulations on industry, particularly those aimed at global climate change (most notably, cap-and-trade). They also seek to reduce corporate and individual tax rates and to expand oil exploration and production in the United States. They have also actively campaigned against minimum wage legislation. In many ways, AFP has come to perform many of the functions that the GOP has traditionally performed, and it can be viewed as a rival to the GOP for conservative influence and agenda setting. They are on track to play an influential role in the **Campaign of 2016**, with the expectation that they will spend $125 million in 2015 in preparation for the election, and many times this amount the following year to promote the GOP candidate.

Additional Resources

Americans for Prosperity. http://www.americansforprosperity.org. Accessed September 5, 2015.

Americans for Prosperity State Chapters. http://www.americansforprosperity.org/state -chapters. Accessed September 5, 2015.

Beckel, Michael. "Koch-Backed Nonprofit Spent Record Cash in 2012." *Primary Source*, November 14, 2013.

Gold, Matea. "Koch-Backed Network Aims to Spend Nearly $1 Billion in Run-Up to 2016." *Washington Post*, January 26, 2015.

Hamburger, Tom, Kathleen Hennesset, and Neela Banerjee. "Koch Brothers Now at Heart of GOP Power." *Los Angeles Times*, February 6, 2011.

Harris, Paul. "The Koch Brothers: All the Influence Money Can Buy." *The Guardian*, April 8, 2011.

Lawler, Joseph. "Jane Mayer's Violent Assault on the Koch Brothers." *American Spectator*, August 23, 2010.

Lipton, Eric. "Billionaire Brothers' Money Plays Role in Wisconsin Dispute." *New York Times*, February 21, 2011.

Mayer, Jane. "Covert Operations: The Billionaire Brothers Who Are Waging a War Against Obama." *New Yorker*, August 30, 2010.

RightOnline Conference. http://www.rightonline.com. Accessed September 5, 2015.

Vogel, Kenneth P. "Secret Koch Memo Outlines Plans for 2016." *Politico*, April 22, 2015. http://www.politico.com/story/2015/04/koch-brothers-2016-election-memo-117238 .html. Accessed September 5, 2015.

Americans for Tax Reform

Founded by anti-tax crusader Grover Norquist in 1986, this anti-taxation advocacy group is best known for the Taxpayer Protection Pledge in which political officials and candidates for political office vow to "oppose any and all tax increases." According to the organization, signing the pledge is a necessity for any Republican candidate, as well as any Democratic candidate running in a Republican-leaning district. The organization holds itself as the sole arbiter in determining whether a candidate or officeholder has honored the pledge. Breaking the pledge carries the implicit risk of a primary election challenge, with Norquist and ATR helping to fund a more suitably anti-taxation challenger. Every GOP presidential candidate since 1986, with the exception of Bob Dole in 1996, has signed on to the Taxpayer Protection Pledge.

Since 1993, Norquist has also held a weekly "Wednesday Meeting" for conservative activists, officeholders, and lobbyists. Drake Bennett, writing for *Business Week*, characterizes Norquist as "a single unelected actor with a single issue, he holds immense power over the Republican Party's fiscal platform, and through it, the national policy debate."

While most of the GOP field in the **Campaign of 2016** is committed, at least in principle, to the Norquist pledge, not all of the candidates have officially signed on, Jeb Bush being among those more notably absent.

Additional Resources

Americans for Tax Reform. "What Is the Taxpayer Protection Pledge?" http://www.atr .org/taxpayer-protection-pledge. Accessed September 5, 2015.

Bennett, Drake. "Grover Norquist, the Enforcer." *Business Week*, May 26, 2011.

Berg, Rebecca. "Jeb Still Won't Sign Grover's Anti-Tax Pledge." *Real Clear Politics*, May 2, 2015. http://www.realclearpolitics.com/articles/2015/05/02/jeb_still_wont_sign_grovers _anti-tax_pledge_126469.html. Accessed September 5, 2015.

Franklin, Daniel, and A.G. Newmyer III. "Is Grover Over? Norquist's Anti-Tax Jihad Stumbles in the States." *Washington Monthly*, March 2005.

Anti-Catholicism

From the nineteenth century through the 1960 presidential election, anti-Catholicism played a major role in American presidential politics. Historians trace anti-Catholicism in the presidential campaigns to the Protestant Reformation in sixteenth-century Europe. The Reformation spawned a number of Protestant denominations and churches that rejected papal authority and opposed the major beliefs, teachings, and liturgical practices of the Catholic Church. The split between Protestant denominations and the Catholic Church touched off a religious war between European Protestants and Catholics. Sadly, these animosities spread to the colonies.

The vast majority of early settlers to the colonies belonged to Anglican, Calvinist, Baptist, Lutheran, Methodist, Congregationalist, Unitarian, and other

Protestant sects. Even though large numbers of Catholics settled in Maryland, relatively few Catholics lived in the colonies during the eighteenth century. From the Revolutionary War through the early decades of the nineteenth century, anti-Catholicism was not a visible factor in national politics. However, the First Great Awakening (1730s–1770s) and the Second Great Awakening (1800s–1850s) led to a significant increase in the role of religion in American society. Equally important, the number of Catholic immigrants also surged in the 1840s. The largest group of Catholic immigrants came from Ireland as the result of the potato famine and settled in the eastern portion of the United States. By the 1840s, Democratic urban political machines, such as New York City's Tammany Hall, became heavily dependent on these immigrant voters to maintain their political power.

During the late 1840s and early 1850s, growing anti-immigrant and anti-Catholic sentiment led to the establishment in New York of a secret society dedicated to denying immigrants political power. Members of the society came to be known as Know-Nothings because of their refusal to admit belonging to the secret society. The members of this society established the American Party as their political arm in 1854. The success of the American Party in winning state and local elections led the party to run its own presidential candidate, former president Millard Fillmore, in 1856. Although Fillmore won 21 percent of the popular vote, he managed to win only the electoral votes of Maryland. Support for the American Party in the North collapsed after the 1856 election, largely due to the party's support for pro-slavery policies.

In the aftermath of the Civil War, the decline of the Democratic Party reduced the political power of Catholic voters, leading to a decline in anti-Catholic sentiment. By the 1880s, the era of Reconstruction was over and the Democratic Party reemerged as a national political force, reigniting anti-Catholic sentiment as Democratic candidates in northern states once again relied heavily on the Catholic immigrant vote to win elections.

In particular, anti-Catholic sentiment played a major role in the final hours of the **Campaign of 1884** between Democrat Grover Cleveland and Republican nominee James G. Blaine. Both Blaine and Cleveland needed New York's electoral votes to win the presidential election, and Cleveland needed New York City's Tammany Hall organization to get out the Catholic immigrant vote. On October 29, 1884, Blaine attended a meeting of pro-Blaine Protestant clergy in New York City. During his introduction of Blaine, Reverend Samuel D. Burchard commented that "we are Republicans, and don't propose to leave our party and identify ourselves with the party whose antecedents have been 'Rum, Romanism, and Rebellion.' " With only days remaining before the election, the well-publicized remarks mobilized New York Catholics to turn out to vote for Cleveland, enabling him to take New York's electoral votes and defeat Blaine.

Beginning in the 1890s, and continuing through the beginning of World War I in 1917, the United States experienced new waves of immigration, largely from southern European countries. Many of these immigrants were Catholic as well. This rise in immigration in the early decades of the twentieth century coincided with the reemergence of the Ku Klux Klan (KKK), which expanded its attacks beyond African Americans to include immigrants, Catholics, and Jews. This public backlash against immigrants precipitated numerous immigration reforms, including the 1924 Immigration Act, which imposed strict quotas on the number of individuals other countries could send to the United States.

Against this backdrop, New York governor Al Smith became the first Roman Catholic to win a presidential nomination when he was tapped by Democrats during the **Campaign of 1928**. Even though the Republican presidential nominee, Quaker Herbert Hoover, did not attack Smith's religion, many Republican partisans trotted out the old canard that, if elected president, Smith would obey the Pope's bidding on political issues rather than serve the needs of the American people. Smith's defeat made both the Democratic and Republican parties more nervous about nominating a Catholic for the presidency.

From 1928 to 1960, no Catholic candidate received the presidential nomination of either political party. Then, in 1960, Massachusetts senator John F. Kennedy won the Democratic nomination after a series of competitive primary victories. Throughout the campaign, Kennedy faced questions regarding the role his religion might play in his decisions as president. On September 12, 1960, Kennedy dealt directly with the issue in speech before the Greater Houston Ministerial Association in Texas. In an effort to end the controversy, Kennedy stated, "I believe in an America where the separation of church and state is absolute, where no Catholic prelate would tell the president (should he be Catholic) how to act, and no Protestant minister would tell his parishioners for whom to vote; where no church or church school is granted any public funds or political preference; and where no man is denied public office merely because his religion differs from the president who might appoint him or the people who might elect him." Presidential election experts generally agree that Kennedy's speech played a major role in defusing the Catholic issue, contributing to Kennedy's narrow victory over the Republican nominee, Richard Nixon.

By the 2000 presidential election, evangelical Christians emerged as a major influence on the Republican Party. Early in the 2000 Republican primary season, Texas governor George W. Bush and Arizona senator John McCain fought for crucial Republican votes. During the South Carolina Republican primary, Bush made a visit to Bob Jones University, located in Greenville, South Carolina. Bob Jones, the founder of the college, had a reputation for making anti-Catholic statements, and the college had a previous history of whites-only admissions and had banned interracial dating (both of which have since been eliminated). While Bush's visit to the Bob Jones campus undoubtedly aided him in winning over the heavily white, evangelical Protestant voters in the South Carolina primary, the event created unpleasant fallout for the candidate in other parts of the country, particularly among African American and Catholic voters. In a February 27, 2000, letter to Cardinal John O'Connor, the Roman Catholic archbishop of New York, Bush expressed regret for failing to disassociate himself from the anti-Catholic statements associated with Bob Jones. The apology did not end the controversy. Bush sharply criticized McCain for allegedly tacitly supporting push polls by his supporters that implied that Bush was anti-Catholic.

In the **Campaign of 2004**, the Democratic Party nominated Catholic Massachusetts senator John Kerry as its presidential nominee. During the campaign, Archbishop Raymond Burke of St. Louis forbade Kerry from receiving communion in his diocese because of Kerry's pro-choice position on the abortion issue. During the campaign, a number of Catholic bishops openly criticized Kerry on this topic, leading to controversies among Catholic voters about whether it was appropriate for the Church to make recommendations about their decisions at the ballot box.

Religion once again emerged as a controversy in the **Campaign of 2008** when Democratic nominee Barack Obama was forced to defend his religious affiliation and distance himself from incendiary statements made by the pastor of his Protestant Chicago church, Rev. Jeremiah Wright. Nevertheless, his choice of Catholic running mate Joe Biden stirred no reaction. Furthermore, Obama was able to win 52 percent of the Catholic vote seven percentage points higher than Kerry's Catholic tally in 2004. Obama's Catholic support was earned against heavy criticism from a number of Catholic bishops, including then-archbishop Raymond Burke of St. Louis, who referred to the Democrats as "the party of death," and the suggestion by Bishop Joseph Martino of Scranton that abortion should be the primary issue guiding the votes of Catholics.

More recently, anti-Muslim remarks shared by two Republicans campaigning for the 2016 nomination have exposed prejudices remarkably similar to those directed against Catholics just a few decades earlier. Donald Trump proposed a ban against all Muslims entering the country, reminiscent of the anti-Catholic nativism of the nineteenth century and its loud twentieth-century echoes; and, it should be noted, a suggestion roundly rejected within Mr. Trump's own party. Prior to Trump's posturing, Dr. Ben Carson bluntly claimed that the idea of a Muslim president runs contrary to the principles of the Constitution—ignoring the Constitution's prohibition against religious tests—a comment that, *mutatis mutandis,* would have been targeted against Catholics even as late as the mid-twentieth century. Attitudes such as these are what prompted Catholic Senator John Kennedy's eloquent and insightful September 12, 1960, address in Houston two months before his election to the presidency. Residues, at times strong, of anti-Catholicism remain in American culture, but in mainstream politics Catholics no longer confront the same bigotry that hobbled Al Smith and that was so deftly deflected by John Kennedy. Given recent comments during the 2016 campaign, it is evident that anti-religious prejudices are, at least for the moment, focused elsewhere to the detriment of the American pursuit of a free and just society.

See also Abortion Controversy; Campaign of 1960

Additional Resources

Dulce, Benton, and Edward J. Richter. *Religion and the Presidency: A Recurring American Problem.* New York: MacMillan, 1962.
Hunter, James Davison. *Culture Wars: The Struggle to Define America.* New York: Basic Books, 1992.

Astroturfers

"Astroturfer" is a pejorative term used to describe a faux grassroots movement. "Grasstops" is a somewhat friendlier euphemism to describe the small core of political elites who often direct the activities of so-called grassroots movements, and Washington, DC, lobbying firms often describe their ability to provide "grassroots and grasstops support." True grassroots movements generally do not rely on Washington PR firms but are organized instead from the bottom up. Astroturfers, or grasstops, on the other hand, represent their activities as bottom-up; but in reality, they have a top-down structure through which political or community leaders rally local citizens to support elite-driven causes.

In contemporary politics, the term "astroturfer" is often used by liberals to disparage the **Tea Party movement**. While much of the Tea Party movement is locally organized and there is no central leadership structure, many notable Tea Party-affiliated organizations are run by well-connected individuals with deep ties to the Republican Party establishment, such as Freedom Works and Americans for Prosperity.

Additional Resources

Beder, Sharon. "Public Relations' Role in Manufacturing Artificial Grass Roots Coalitions." *Public Relations Quarterly* 43, no. 2 (Summer 1998): 21–23.
Smith, Ben. "The Summer of Astroturf." Politico, August 21, 2009.

Battleground State

The outcome of American presidential elections is determined not by the popular vote, but by the number of states a candidate can win. The worth of each state is, in effect, that state's number of Electoral College votes. On first blush, it may appear that candidates would concentrate their resources on the states with the most electoral votes, since winning these states results in the largest payoff. However, another important factor to consider is that candidates have limited sums of both time and money available to them. These limitations force candidates to act strategically. Candidates would prefer not to invest resources in states where the outcome is near certain, preferring instead to put their dollars and time to work in those states where they will be most useful—namely, where the election is expected to be close. These are the states most commonly referred to as "battleground states" (or "swing states").

Voters in battleground states are barraged with televised ads throughout the campaign season and are favored with candidate visits. They are also targets for mobilization efforts by candidates' campaigns, political parties, and other activist groups. And they turn out to vote in higher numbers than do citizens who live in less competitive states. Political scientists believe this is because these voters have lower information costs, more effort is spent in mobilizing them, and they are also more likely to believe their vote will count.

Throughout much of American electoral history, political parties have had geographic bases of strength. And in many political eras, a single party has been dominant. Thus, the number of states where the political parties have been competitive has waxed and waned over time. For example, after the Civil War, the Republican Party entered a political era in which they were dominant, which meant that Republican presidential candidates had many states in which they faced little electoral competition. After Reconstruction ended, the Democratic Party once again dominated the South, a position of power that strengthened as southern states moved to strip African American voting rights through the imposition of **Jim Crow laws**. "The Solid South" refers to the era, roughly from the post-Reconstruction era to the early to mid-1960s, when the Democratic Party was the only viable political actor in this region.

From the mid-1960s through the 1980s, the electoral competitiveness of many states increased as the Democratic stranglehold on the South loosened, **Rockefeller Republicans** competed with liberal Democrats in the Northeast, and the Midwest continued to provide opportunities to both major parties. By the 1990s, political analysts observed that many states had become fairly predictable in their voting behavior. New England states, with the exception of New Hampshire, opted for Democrats in most presidential elections. Southern states, with the exceptions of Florida, Louisiana, and Arkansas, were generally voting Republican. States in the Midwest, such as Kansas, Missouri, and Nebraska, routinely voted Republican as well. Not only were many states becoming predictable, but the number of states where one party won by a landslide were becoming more common. In half of all states, the winning presidential candidate's margin of victory usually exceeded 10 percent.

By the **Campaign of 2000**, only a handful of states were deemed by the press to be battleground states. Most political analysts designated fourteen to twenty states as swing or battleground states, although that list narrowed considerably in the months leading up to the election. For both the **Campaign of 2000** and the **Campaign of 2004**, the states labeled as battleground states prior to Election Day were virtually identical. After all of the votes were in, only a few states in 2004 were truly competitive. The winning candidate's margin of victory was less than 8 percent in only thirteen states (Colorado, Florida, Iowa, Michigan, Minnesota, Nevada, New Hampshire, New Jersey, New Mexico, Ohio, Oregon, Pennsylvania, and Wisconsin). In 2000, New Mexico selected Al Gore by a very narrow margin; John Kerry fared better in that state in 2004.

In the **Campaign of 2008**, the picture changed as the resources of the candidates changed. Specifically, Democratic nominee Barack Obama opted to forgo public funding in both the primary season and the general election. While donations to the Obama campaign were still subject to federal donation limits, Obama was free to raise as much money as he could within these constraints, and to spend as much as he raised. In 2008, it is estimated that Obama's campaign spent $740.6 million.

John McCain, on the other hand, opted out of public funding for the primary season but accepted public funding for the general election, a decision he soon came to regret. Because candidates who accept public funding are subject to spending ceilings, McCain found himself with far fewer resources in the fall of 2008; his campaign spent only $227.7 million. He was forced to abandon his campaign in states like Michigan, which was considered a battleground state, to shore up support in states like Indiana, Virginia, North Carolina, and Georgia—places that had been considered safe Republican states, but where Obama had been spending a lot of time and money, and where polls were showing him closing in on McCain.

In June 2008 *The Washington Post* listed sixteen states as battleground states: Colorado, Florida, Iowa, Michigan, Minnesota, Missouri, Nevada, New Hampshire, New Jersey, New Mexico, North Carolina, Ohio, Oregon, Pennsylvania, Virginia, and Wisconsin. In eight of those states, all of the four preceding presidential elections were won by the same political party. Only three states could claim an evenly divided history of presidential voting over the four previous elections. And all but three states were on the list of states that had competitive outcomes in 2004.

Of the battleground states listed by the *Washington Post* that June, Obama won all but Missouri in November. Additionally, Obama picked up Indiana, which had been considered safe for Republicans, and one electoral vote from Nebraska (one of only two states that does not allocate all of its electoral votes to the popular vote winner in the state).

In the **Campaign of 2012**, the candidates of both major political parties opted out of the public funding system. Barack Obama, the Democratic nominee, raised slightly more money in direct campaign donations ($715,150,163 to Romney's $443,363,696), whereas Mitt Romney, the GOP nominee, relied more on his **super PAC** and other outside groups to raise and spend money on his behalf ($804,815,645 to Obama's $423,568,154). Both candidates had similar resources, and the battleground contracted significantly relative to 2008. Only five states were decided by less than 5 percent of the vote: Ohio, Virginia, Florida, Colorado, and North Carolina. Those states received more than three-quarters of all of the advertising spent by candidates and outside groups during the general election campaign, and almost all of the candidate visits during this time period, according to an analysis by the *Washington Post*. Indeed, half of all ad dollars were spent in Florida, Ohio, and Virginia alone.

Experts anticipate a similar set of battleground states in the upcoming campaign of 2016. Florida, Virginia, Ohio, Iowa, New Hampshire, and Colorado are expected to continue to be competitive, and Nevada may be as well. Changes in voting laws may influence the competitiveness of North Carolina in the short term—although states such as North Carolina, Georgia, Texas, and Arizona may become more competitive in 2020 or 2024 as a result of ongoing demographic changes that are more likely to reduce the dominance of the Republican Party in those states. Conversely, demographic shifts in states such as Michigan and Wisconsin may work to the GOP's advantage during this same time period.

See also Blue and Red States; Campaign Finance Reform

Additional Resources

Balz, Dan. "Each Party Is Set to Hunt the Other's Usual Ground." *Washington Post*, June 8, 2008.

"Battleground States." *Washington Post*, June 8, 2008. http://www.washingtonpost.com/wp-dyn/content/graphic/2008/06/08/GR2008060800566.html. Accessed September 5, 2015.

Center for Responsive Politics. "2012 Presidential Race." http://www.opensecrets.org/pres12/. Accessed September 5, 2015.

McKee, Seth. "Was Turnout Significantly Higher in Battleground States in the 2000 Presidential Election?" Paper presented at the annual meeting of the American Political Science Association, August 28, 2002.

Palmer, Brian. "When Did We Start Talking about Landslide Elections?" Slate, November 3, 2010.

Panagopoulos, Costas. "Campaign Dynamics in Battleground and Nonbattleground States." *Public Opinion Quarterly* 73, no. 1 (Spring 2009): 119–29.

Salant, Jonathan D. "Spending Doubled as Obama Led First Billion-Dollar Race in 2008." *Bloomberg News*, December 26, 2008. http://www.bloomberg.com/apps/news?pid=newsarchive&sid=aerix76GvmRM. Accessed September 5, 2015.

Travers, Karen, and Kate Barrett. "Breaking Down the Battleground States." *ABC News*, October 24, 2008. http://abcnews.go.com/Politics/story?id=6096271&page=1. Accessed September 5, 2015.

Washington Post. "Mad Money: TV Ads in the 2012 Presidential Campaign." http://www.washingtonpost.com/wp-srv/special/politics/track-presidential-campaign-ads-2012/. Accessed September 5, 2015.

Wolak, Jennifer. "The Consequences of Presidential Battleground Strategies for Citizen Engagement." *Political Research Quarterly* 59 (September 2006): 353–61.

Zimmer, Ben. "Mailbag Friday: Landslide." Visual Thesaurus, November 7, 2008. http://www.visualthesaurus.com/cm/wordroutes/1600/. Accessed September 5, 2015.

Big Data

In the twenty-first century, political strategists have sought ways to harness the increasingly sophisticated advances in data mining with the vast arrays of information available about modern consumers. Rather than rely on church membership lists or magazine and newspaper subscription databases, as campaigns throughout the twentieth century have done, modern-day strategists engage in more targeted predictions based on a larger array of data, including online purchasing and social network relationships, and other detailed sociodemographic and lifestyle information.

The goal of using such a vast array of data is to pinpoint precisely the type of voter that is amenable to the candidate's message, and to avoid wasting time and scarce resources on voters who are either already firmly on the candidate's side (and thus don't require further persuasion) or firmly in the opponent's camp (and thus aren't likely to be receptive to persuasion). The more adept a campaign is at figuring out where its candidate's support is, and who the most flexible voters are likely to be, the better it will be at tailoring the candidate's message to attract those voters, and at not wasting resources in the pursuit of votes.

On the political left, the Analyst Institute, founded shortly before the **Campaign of 2008**, performs data analytic services for a range of Democratic Party clients. On the right, there has been little coordinated effort to engage in any party-wide, systematic data analytic effort. Rather, candidates have relied on a series of party-approved vendors who have operated quasi-independently of each other. However, this may be changing, as the Republican National Committee has contracted with an outside vendor to build an in-house data analytic arm aptly named Para Bellum Labs, whose task is the coordination of existing party voter databases with GOP vendors and candidates to provide the type of ongoing analysis that the Obama campaign was able to build for the **Campaigns of 2008** and **2012**. Other companies, often founded by individuals with a social science or other behavioral research background, now compete with traditional political consultants to provide services to political campaigns. During the 2016 contest for the Republican presidential nomination, Texas senator Ted Cruz's campaign credited psychological data and analytics for his ascent in the polls.

See also Get-Out-the-Vote (GOTV) Programs; Microtargeting; Moneyball

Additional Resources

Gallagher, Sean. "Built to Win: Deep Inside Obama's Campaign Tech." Ars Technica, November 14, 2012. http://arstechnica.com/information-technology/2012/11/built-to-win-deep-inside-obamas-campaign-tech/.

Gallagher, Sean. "The GOP Arms Itself for the Next 'War' in the Analytics Arms Race." Ars Technica, February 27, 2014. http://arstechnica.com/information-technology/2014/02/the-gop-arms-itself-for-the-next-war-in-the-analytics-arms-race/.

Hamburger, Tom. "Cruz Campaign Credits Psychological Data and Analytics for Its Rising Success." *The Washington Post*, December 13, 2015.

Issenberg, Sasha. *The Victory Lab.* New York: Crown, 2012.

Birther

"Birther" is a pejorative term used to refer to individuals who believe that Barack Obama was not born in the United States and is therefore constitutionally ineligible to serve as president. Official records in Hawaii indicate that Obama was born in Hawaii to an American mother and a Kenyan father. Birthers believe Obama's actual place of birth to be in Kenya.

In an April 2010 *New York Times*/CBS poll, 58 percent of Americans indicated that they believed Obama was born in the United States, while 20 percent believed he was born in another country and another 23 percent were not sure. A year later, a YouGov poll conducted by Adam Berinsky of MIT in April 2011 produced similar results: 55 percent believed Obama was born in the United States, 15 percent claimed he was not, and 30 percent were not sure.

In May 2011, responding to a series of groundless remarks about his place of birth (including accusations from billionaire celebrity Donald Trump), President

Obama publicly released his official birth certificate. In a *Washington Post*/ABC poll conducted soon afterward, 70 percent of Americans now believed that Obama was born in Hawaii, and 86 percent said that their best guess was that Obama was born in the United States. Of the 10 percent who still believed Obama was born abroad, most only indicated a suspicion of this, while 1 percent claimed that they had seen "solid evidence" of an overseas birth. Only 7 percent of Democrats in the *Washington Post* poll thought that Obama might have been born overseas (compared to 15% a year before). Republicans were more likely to be skeptical of Obama's birthplace (14%), but this number, too, was down substantially from a year before (when it was 31%).

Berinsky, too, found a brief surge in the number of Americans who believed Obama was born in the United States after the release of the long form of the birth certificate—67 percent of Americans in his poll now felt that the president was a natural-born citizen (with Republicans reporting lower levels of persuasion relative to Democrats). However, the effects of this new information were short-lived. By January of 2012, only 59 percent of Americans he polled believed the president was born in the United States, and by July 2012, the number was back to 55 percent.

In the **Campaign of 2012**, 51 percent of GOP primary voters believed that Obama was not born in the United States, according to a poll conducted by Public Policy Polling (whereas 28% were sure that he was). Sarah Palin's and Mike Huckabee's supporters exhibited the highest rates of birthers.

Suspicions about the country of Obama's birth are more common among those who seek out conservative media sources. A recent Fairleigh Dickinson poll found that while 19 percent of Americans believe that President Obama is probably not or definitely not an American citizen, 30 percent of *Fox News* viewers exhibit this belief. Other polls have found birtherism more common among self-identified members of the **Tea Party movement**, among Southerners, among rural residents, and among less-educated citizens. Emory researcher Alan Abramowitz found that birtherism was more common among whites than it was among nonwhites, and that predictors of birtherism include ideology and partisanship as well as racial resentment. Similarly, University of Delaware researcher Eric Hehman found that whites with higher rates of racial prejudice tended to rate Obama's job performance more poorly and to evaluate him as less American than other respondents. Perceptions of Obama as Muslim, or as somehow not being a valid American citizen, appear to be driven, in part, by an element of racial animosity.

Birtherism may resurface in the **Campaign of 2016** for several reasons. First, birther Donald Trump is now a highly visible candidate in the GOP primaries. Second, another GOP candidate, Texas senator Ted Cruz, finds himself in precisely the situation that birthers suggested Barack Obama faced: Ted Cruz had a Cuban-born father and a U.S.-born mother, and he himself was born in Canada.

He is claiming birthright citizenship on the basis of his mother's American citizenship (presumably, the same basis Obama could have used for claiming American citizenship even if he had, in fact, been born in Kenya, which he was not). In May 2015, GOP candidate Rand Paul ran an ad questioning Cruz's eligibility for the presidency based on his Canadian citizenship.

Birtherism is also surfacing in state laws regarding ballot access. In May 2011, Republican Arizona governor Jan Brewer vetoed a bill that would have required any candidate running for public office in Arizona to produce their birth certificate. However, numerous other states are entertaining similar measures.

See also Campaign of 2008; Symbolic Racism

Additional Resources

Abramowitz, Alan I. "The Race Factor: White Racial Attitudes and Opinions of Obama." Sabato's Crystal Ball, May 12, 2011. http://www.centerforpolitics.org/crystalball/articles/aia2011051201. Accessed September 5, 2015.

Berinsky, Adam. "The Birthers Are (Still) Back." July 11, 2012. YouGov US. https://today.yougov.com/news/2012/07/11/birthers-are-still-back/. Accessed September 5, 2015.

Cassino, Dan. "Ignorance, Partisanship Drive False Beliefs About Obama, Iraq." Fairleigh Dickinson University's Public Mind Poll, January 7, 2015. http://publicmind.fdu.edu/2015/false/. Accessed September 5, 2015.

Cohen, Jon. "Poll: Number of 'Birthers' Plummets." *Washington Post*, May 5, 2011.

Hehman, Eric, Samuel L. Gaertner, and David F. Dovidio. "Evaluations of Presidential Performance: Race, Prejudice, and Perceptions of Americanism." *Journal of Experimental Social Psychology* 47, no. 2 (March 2011): 430–35.

Jensen, Tom. "Huckabee Tops GOP Field; 51% Are Birthers and Love Palin." Public Policy Polling, February 15, 2011. http://www.publicpolicypolling.com/pdf/PPP_Release_US_0215.pdf. Accessed September 5, 2015.

New York Times/CBS News Poll: National Survey of Tea Party Supporters, April 5–12, 2010. http://documents.nytimes.com/new-york-timescbs-news-poll-national-survey-of-tea-party-supporters. Accessed September 5, 2015.

Blue and Red States

In common parlance, the term "blue state" refers to a state that consistently votes for a Democratic candidate in presidential elections. This term first became popular in the aftermath of the **Campaign of 2000**. Prior to this time, many Republican presidential candidates (such as Ronald Reagan and Bob Dole) used the color blue in their campaign graphics, and electoral voting maps displayed by television broadcasters often represented the states differently than they do now, with states won by Republicans cast in blue. Since coverage of the Campaign of 2000, however, blue has come to be associated with the Democrats, red with the Republicans. A close examination of voting results at the county level reveals a tendency toward "red" rural and interior regions, and "blue" urban and coastal regions—depicted on this level, a map of the United States would be mostly red, with pockets of blue along the coast and corresponding to metropolitan areas. It is not unusual to observe a "blue" city surrounded by "red" counties.

The term "blue state" connotes an element of electoral stability for Democrats in presidential politics. Most of the states that were blue in 2000 stayed blue in 2004, 2008, and 2012. These include California, Connecticut, Delaware, the District of Columbia, Hawaii, Illinois, Maine, Maryland, Massachusetts, Michigan, Minnesota, New York, Oregon, Pennsylvania, Rhode Island, Vermont, Washington, and Wisconsin.

Conversely, the term "red state" has become shorthand for referring to a state that usually favors Republican candidates in presidential elections. Red states are found primarily in the South, portions of the Midwest, and in the Rocky Mountain West. Twenty-one states voted Republican in 2000, 2004, 2008, and 2012. These are Alabama, Alaska, Arkansas, Arizona, Georgia, Idaho, Kansas, Kentucky, Louisiana, Mississippi, Missouri, Montana, North Dakota, Oklahoma, South Carolina, South Dakota, Tennessee, Texas, Utah, West Virginia, and Wyoming. Nebraska is often counted as a red state as well, but in the **Campaign of 2008**, it cast one of its electoral votes for Democratic nominee Barack Obama.

"Purple states" are states that are neither red nor blue; that is, they are states whose electoral votes did not consistently favor one political party over the course of the **Campaign of 2000**, the **Campaign of 2004**, the **Campaign of 2008**, and the **Campaign of 2012**. Currently, these states include Colorado, Florida, New Hampshire, New Mexico, North Carolina, Iowa, Indiana, Nevada, Ohio, and Virginia. Because purple states have exhibited more electoral volatility than other states, it may be tempting to view "purple state" as synonymous with labels such as "swing state" or "battleground state." However, doing so would underestimate the amount of electoral competition that has occurred in many states in recent presidential campaigns. For example, states such as Michigan and Pennsylvania have proven to be quite competitive, and while the Democrats have managed to capture these states in all four elections, the margins of victory have been slim. On the other hand, in purple states such as New Hampshire and Virginia, winning candidates have often had far more comfortable margins of victory.

Labels such as "blue state" and "red state" are often used to generalize a state's overall political disposition; voters in states that are consistently red in a presidential election are assumed to behave conservatively in elections for other offices as well, with voters in blue states presumed to be more generally liberal. Such assumptions are often misleading, however. For example, voters in West Virginia tend to favor Republican candidates in presidential elections, but they often vote for Democratic candidates for Congress, for governor, and in other state and local elections. Unlike other GOP-leaning states, West Virginians exhibit strong support for labor unions, due, in a large part, to the state's role as a coal mining state. Most red states have cities and counties where Democrats are more likely to win elections than are Republicans, and most blue states have areas of the state that are more conservative and favor GOP candidates.

See also Battleground State

Additional Resources

Bishop, Bill. *The Big Sort: Why Clustering of Like-Minded Americans Is Tearing Us Apart.* New York: Houghton Mifflin Harcourt, 2008.
Chinni, Dante, and James Gimpel. *Our Patchwork Nation.* New York: Gotham, 2010.
Gelman, Andrew, et al. *Red State, Blue State, Rich State, Poor State.* Expanded ed. Princeton, NJ: Princeton University Press, 2009.
Zeller, Tom. "Ideas and Trends: One State, Two State, Red State, Blue State." *New York Times*, February 8, 2004.

Blue State. *See* Blue and Red States

Bread-and-Butter Issues

The media and political experts frequently make use of the phrase "bread-and-butter issue" to describe issues that directly affect the financial security of Americans, where "bread" and "butter" are metaphors for Americans' ability to put food on the dinner table. Such issues include unemployment, the cost of living, health care, aid to the poor, and entitlements (Social Security and Medicare). Bread-and-butter issues are often thought to be particularly useful for mobilizing the party faithful and attracting undecided voters who might be willing to select the candidate who best appeals to their pocketbook.

The **Campaign of 1932** was a watershed in American policy, with Franklin Delano Roosevelt (FDR) ushering in a new era in which the federal government assumed direct responsibility for the economic prosperity of the nation as well as the personal financial well-being of American families. Roosevelt's policies focused on keeping unemployment and prices low through government intervention. In particular, FDR was an advocate of **Keynesian economics** as a means for blunting the effects of economic downturns. According to this philosophy, the government should tax in times of economic prosperity to generate sufficient revenue to spend its way out of future recessions. Specifically, the Roosevelt administration embraced the creation of a social safety net that included Social Security, government jobs programs, and the expanded use of government grants to state and local governments to stimulate economic growth. In the post-FDR era, the basic guiding philosophy underlying the New Deal was tacitly accepted by political elites in both parties, with the two Republican presidents who served after presidents Roosevelt and Truman had already established and sustained their New Deal and Fair Deal policies actually adhering to the basic structure instituted by their Democratic predecessors. Republican President Eisenhower made no effort to dismantle the New Deal and embarked on a major public works project of his own, creating a national interstate highway system. Republican President Nixon, who followed presidents Kennedy and Johnson, later implemented wage and price controls to strengthen a troubled economy, and he proposed a guaranteed minimum income, declaring at one point, "We are all Keynesians now."

By the late 1970s, Republicans began to rethink Keynesianism. The **Campaign of 1980** was notable in that the Republican Party primaries illustrated the fundamental disagreements within the party on the best approach to the economy. Ronald Reagan's rejection of Keynes and his advocacy of Milton Friedman's supply-side economics philosophy were a clear break from past party policies. Reagan argued that dramatic decreases in government spending, coupled with large tax decreases, would stimulate the economy and thus generating more tax revenue while also saving the government money over the long run. Republican primary opponent George H. W. Bush, an economics major while at Yale, derided Reagan's policies as "voodoo economics." Over time, presidential candidates on both sides of the political aisle advocated tax cuts of some sort, with the primary emphasis on the middle class (with Mondale's **Campaign of 1984** serving as a notable exception).

During the **Campaign of 2000**, Republican presidential nominee George W. Bush made middle-class tax cuts a centerpiece of his campaign, and Democratic nominee Al Gore followed suit. Once elected, Bush significantly pared down the federal income tax rate, with the largest gains being recognized by the most affluent. Bush argued, in the spirit of Reagan, that such tax breaks would serve as an economic stimulus, with the wealthy using their windfall to make purchases that would create jobs for all Americans. The Bush tax cuts changed the parties' approaches to the tax issue for later elections. From the **Campaign of 2004** onward, Democrats promised to repeal the Bush tax cuts for the wealthiest Americans. Republicans, on the other hand, have argued that eliminating the Bush tax cuts (or other tax subsidies, both corporate and individual) would constitute a tax increase, which they strenuously opposed. The **Campaign of 2012** was a continuation of this debate. Democratic incumbent Barack Obama argued that the rising federal debt necessitated frugality, suggesting that the country could ill afford to offer tax breaks to those who could most afford to pay. The Republican Party, on the other hand, united around a federal debt reduction proposal by Wisconsin representative Paul Ryan that, among other things, offered the wealthy additional tax reductions on the premise that this would spur investment and economic growth. When Mitt Romney became the GOP nominee, he selected Ryan as his running mate, and he defended the Bush tax cuts for wealthier Americans on the grounds that these individuals were "job creators."

Also notable during the **Campaign of 2000** was a proposal by Bush to partially privatize Social Security. Gore defended the existing system, arguing that he would put Social Security in a "lock box" to protect it for future generations. Bush's privatization proposal failed to garner public support, and he quickly abandoned it. The conventional political wisdom has been that Americans, while concerned about the long-term viability of Social Security, are generally supportive of the system. Social Security is often termed the "third rail" of American politics, which implies that attempts to reform the system are politically risky. Yet in the **Campaign of 2012**, both parties were forced by circumstances produced by the economic turmoil that began in 2008 to navigate the third rail. Ryan had proposed reforms in both Social Security and Medicare, with the latter being replaced by a system of fixed-rate vouchers. Democrats resisted attempts to reform both programs, despite growing questions about their continued viability, particularly with the retirement of the baby boomers, which was predicted to severely tax the resources of both programs. Romney and Ryan backed off of the voucher system, suggesting that it would be phased in and would apply to younger Americans but not those set to receive benefits in the near future. The GOP candidates also expressed a commitment to repealing the Affordable Care Act (also known as "Obamacare"), passed during Obama's first term, while the Democrats expressed continued support for Obamacare.

What is now called the Great Recession effectively dominated the last act of the Campaign of 2008, reverberating throughout the Campaign of 2012. However, by the **Campaign of 2016** economic indicators were encouraging. As a result, tax cuts have not played a central role in the campaign, nor has the repeal of the Affordable Care Act, although Republican candidates still advocate its abolition. Even Social Security reform has lost its sense of urgency, as candidates discussed less-radical reforms to keep the system intact for future generations. Democrats support increasing the minimum wage and are likely to continue to do so in future campaigns.

Bread-and-butter issues have been particularly visible in presidential elections that have occurred during periods of economic downturn or eras of high inflation.

The **Campaigns of 1896, 1932, 1976, 1980, 1992,** and **2008** are all examples of elections where bread-and-butter issues dominated political discourse.

See also Red Meat Issue

Additional Resources

Eulau, Heinz, and Michael Lewis-Beck, eds. *Economic Conditions and Electoral Outcomes: The United States and Western Europe.* New York: Algora Publishing, 1985.

Hillygus, D. Sunshine, and Todd G. Shields. *The Persuadable Voter: Wedge Issues in Presidential Campaigns.* Princeton, NJ: Princeton University Press. 2008.

Kiewiet, D. Roderick. *Microeconomics and Micropolitics: Electoral Effects of Economic Issues.* Chicago: University of Chicago Press, 1983.

Mackuen, Michael B., Rober S. Erikson, and James A. Stimson. *The Macro Polity.* New York: Cambridge University Press, 2002.

Norpoth, Helmut, Jean-Dominique Lafay, and Michael S. Lewis-Beck, eds. *Economics and Politics: The Calculus of Support.* Ann Arbor: University of Michigan Press, 1991.

Tufte, Edward R. *Political Control of the Economy.* Princeton, NJ: Princeton University Press, 1980.

Buckley v. Valeo (1976)

In the 1976 U.S. Supreme Court decision *Buckley v. Valeo*, the court ruled on the constitutionality of key provisions of the Federal Election Campaign Act of 1974 (FECA). The high court upheld the constitutionality of the limits on individual contributions to federal campaigns and candidates. The high court also upheld the requirement that candidates disclose the amount of campaign contributions and the names of contributors. The high court, however, found that the First Amendment prohibited Congress from limiting the size of independent political expenditures and also precluded limits on personal spending by candidates in general elections (except in presidential elections when candidates agree to accept public funding).

The decision had significant impact on political campaigns because it permitted interest groups to run their own independent campaign ads in opposition to presidential candidates, leading to the formation and multiplication of political action committees (PACs) and other political groups that acted independently (though often with the silent approval) of the actual political candidates. During the **Campaign of 1988**, for example, an independent group, the National Security Political Action Committee, produced and funded the airing of the instantly controversial and now infamous Willie Horton ad. During the **Campaign of 2004**, an independent group called the Swift Boat Veterans for Truth produced and paid to air the Swift Boat ads that criticized Democratic nominee John Kerry's service record in the Vietnam War; the ad campaign became known as **swift boating**. Similarly, the independent group MoveOn funded numerous television and print ads attacking President George W. Bush during this campaign. In the **Campaign of 2008**, the American Issues Project spent over $2 million to produce and broadcast the Bill Ayers ads, alleging that Democratic presidential nominee Barack Obama had a close relationship with a former radical associated with the Weather Underground, a violent antiwar group that had bombed government buildings in protest of the Vietnam War. Decades later, in *Citizens United v. Federal Election Commission (2010)*, the U.S. Supreme Court held that the First Amendment prohibited Congress from limiting involvement of a nonprofit corporation in a political campaign. The decision meant that independent groups now could raise unlimited funds and could use those funds to directly advocate for or against the election of a candidate for federal office. During the 2012 presidential campaign, the most active and well-funded independent **super PACs** were Restore Our Future and American Crossroads, in support of Republican nominee Mitt Romney, and Priorities USA Action, supporting President Obama's reelection efforts. These and other groups were not officially linked to either candidate's campaign, but they did fund activities and advertisements in pursuit of their respective election. In the early phase of the campaign for 2016, the number of super PACs has continued to proliferate, often beginning their fund-raising and expenditure efforts well in advance of a candidate's official announcement. While these events have happened long after the *Buckley* decision and in part as a consequence of later cases and developments, many constitutional scholars credit *Buckley v. Valeo* for laying the foundation for the Citizens United decision.

See also Campaign Finance Reform

Additional Resources

Banks, Christopher P., and John Clifford Green. *Superintending Democracy: The Courts and the Political Process.* Akron, OH: University of Akron Press, 2001.

"Congressional Campaign Finance: History, Facts, and Controversy." Washington, DC: Congressional Quarterly, 1992.

MoveOn.Org. 2004 MoveOn PAC Action Archive. http://pol.moveon.org/archive. Accessed September 22, 2015.

Butterfly Ballot

The butterfly ballot was designed by the Palm Beach County, Florida, election board prior to the **Campaign of 2000** for use in a punch card voting machine. The butterfly ballot format has a vertical array of holes in the center of the ballot where the voter must punch out their candidate preference with a stylus. The candidates' names are arranged in columns to both the left and the right of this vertical line of holes (presumably, resembling the wings of a butterfly, whereas the holes to be punched resemble the body of a butterfly).

While the butterfly design had been used in numerous elections prior to the **Campaign of 2000**, the consequences of its use in Palm Beach in 2000 were monumental. The ballot design, in which the presidential candidate was listed on one line, with the running mate listed below, was confusing for some voters. Some voters misread the line associated with the hole to be punched and selected Reform Party candidate Pat Buchanan, when they intended to vote for Democrat Al Gore. Political scientists estimate that this cost Gore approximately two thousand misdirected votes in Palm Beach County. Other voters were under the impression that two holes needed to be punched, one for the presidential nominee and the other for the running mate. Thus, 6,607 of Gore's votes were discarded because the voter had also punched out the hole for the adjacent candidate (in this case, Buchanan). According to the *Palm Beach Post*, the discarded votes for Gore totaled more than ten times the margin by which George W. Bush won the state (and its twenty-five electoral votes).

In response to the disputed election of 2000, critics widely argued that states needed to reform their voting methods, equipment, and procedures. Many states have since moved to electronic, computer-scanned voting machines and increased early voting to reduce the length of voting lines.

Additional Resources

CNN. "Newspaper: Butterfly Ballot Cost Gore White House." CNN Politics, March 11, 2001. http://articles.cnn.com/2001-03-11/politics/palmbeach.recount_1_gore -buchanan-gore -and-reform-party-butterfly-ballot?_s=PM:ALLPOLITICS. Accessed September 22, 2015.

Correspondents of the *New York Times*. *Thirty-Six Days: The Complete Chronicle of the 2000 Presidential Election Crisis*. New York: Times Books, 2001.

"Florida 2000." Vote: The Machinery of Democracy (online exhibit), Smithsonian Institution, National Museum of American History, Behring Center. http://americanhistory .si.edu/vote/florida.html. Accessed September 22, 2015.

Toobin, Jeffrey. *Too Close to Call: The Thirty-Six-Day Battle to Decide the 2000 Election*. New York: Random House, 2002.

2000 Florida Ballots Project. http://electionstudies.org/florida2000. Accessed September 22, 2015.

Wand, Jonathan N., Kenneth W. Shotts, Jasjeet S. Sekhon, Walter R. Mebane Jr., Michael C. Herron, and Henry E. Brady. "The Butterfly Did It: The Aberrant Vote for Buchanan in Palm Beach County, Florida." *American Political Science Review* 95, no. 4 (December 2001): 793–810.

Campaign Ads

The **Campaign of 1952** marked the beginning of the use of television to broadcast presidential campaign ads. From the **Campaign of 1924** through the **Campaign of 1948**, presidential campaigns made extensive use of print media and radio to deliver campaign messages to millions of voters in their own homes. Radio ads typically consisted of half-hour talks by candidates, paid for by political campaigns. Following this practice, the majority of television ads broadcast in 1952 were half-hour speeches as well. It did not take long for campaign strategists to realize that this tactic bored viewers and also failed to capitalize on the persuasive potential of visual imagery. Campaign managers sought out advice from Madison Avenue and began to create thirty-second television spot ads for political candidates that employed the same basic principles that were also being used to sell consumers laundry soap and other household products.

The Republican ads in support of their nominee, General Dwight Eisenhower, proved particularly effective. Themes such as "I Like Ike" and "Eisenhower Answers America" were catchy and helped to humanize Eisenhower in the minds of the voters. In the years that followed, spot ads became an integral part of the presidential campaign process. Campaigns produced biographical ads to introduce candidates to prospective voters and to highlight a candidate's qualifications for holding higher office. Issue ads were produced to familiarize voters with a candidate's positions on important public policy matters, and they also helped campaigns point out flaws in their opponents' proposals. Campaigns also created testimonial ads in which well-known public officials and entertainment celebrities endorsed a candidate. Campaigns continued to broadcast important campaign speeches by their candidate as well, although over time, these have been reduced to short clips and sound bites. While the early years of spot ads tended to be primarily positive in nature, over time, spot ads became increasingly centered on criticism of opponents. Contemporary ads that are primarily positive in nature tend to be funded by the campaigns of political candidates. Ads that are more negative in tone are more likely to emanate from political parties or **independent advocacy groups**.

One of the most notorious negative ads was also one of the earliest. Incumbent president Lyndon Johnson's campaign sought to portray Republican nominee Barry Goldwater as an extremist in the **Campaign of 1964**. It crafted the **"Daisy Girl" campaign ad** to suggest to voters that Goldwater might have an itchy nuclear trigger finger and could not be trusted to keep the peace between the United States and the Soviet Union. While the "Daisy Girl" ad was broadcast only once, on September 7, 1964, it received extensive news coverage, and to this day, most Americans have had an opportunity to view this ad. In modern parlance, the "Daisy Girl" ad "went viral," which is undoubtedly one of the reasons why provocative and controversial negative ads continue to be a feature of modern political campaigns. President Johnson's campaign also broadcast another television ad cynically alleging a link between Sen. Goldwater and the Ku Klux Klan, even though the Arizona senator had no relationship with that organization, nor did he agree with its positions or attitudes. The television ad in question projected images of cross-burning, hooded Klansmen accompanied by voice-over narration quoting an Alabama Klan leader itemizing the Klan's hatred of equality for African Americans, "Catholicism and Judaism, and all the other isms," followed by his enthusiastic approval of the senator: "I like Barry Goldwater, he needs our help!" Both the "Daisy Girl" ad and the "KKK" spot illustrate the extent to which even candidates in a comfortable position, such as President Johnson in 1964, will go to discredit their opposition.

Negative ads often accuse candidates of changing their position, or "flip-flopping," on an issue, implying that the candidate cannot be trusted to keep his or her campaign promises once elected. Alternatively, an ad may attempt to link a candidate with an unpopular political figure, producing a guilt-by-association effect. Negative ads often attempt to induce a sense of fear in the viewer, not only by implying catastrophic outcomes if a candidate were to be elected, but also by enhancing the message with black-and-white imagery and ominous music. Candidates with previous electoral experience can expect to find themselves criticized for policy failures (and candidates who lack previous experience in office can expect to find themselves criticized for their inexperience). Ads that compare a candidate with the opponent on a series of policy issues are common; such ads generally attempt to highlight favorable elements of one candidate's experience while at the same time attacking the record of the opponent.

The trend over time has been toward an increased use of negative ads of all types. The Wesleyan Median Project conducted a series of studies on the **Campaign of 2012**. In their examination of the first three weeks of October, for example, they found that 73.3 percent of Obama's ads were negative (they contained only a critique of Romney), and another 20.3 percent were contrast ads (where Obama was contrasted with Romney). Only 6.3 percent of Obama's ads during this period were positive. Romney had more positive ads during this time—11.9 percent of his ads only mentioned his candidacy. 51.1 percent of Romney's ads contrasted his candidacy with Obama's, and 36 percent were purely negative. Of groups promoting the Democratic candidate, 88.7 percent of ads were purely negative, and of groups promoting the Republican candidate, 95.2 percent were purely negative, suggesting that spending by outside groups is focused on attack ads rather than on the promotion of a candidate.

During this same three-week period in the **Campaign of 2008**, Obama's campaign was far more positive, running 37 percent of ads that were solely positive, and far less negative, running 43.2 percent of ads that were purely negative.

Compared to Mitt Romney four years later, John McCain ran a similar amount of purely negative ads in 2008 (49.2%) and more positive ads than Romney (24%). In the **Campaign of 2004**, however, the picture was a bit different, most notably because of striking asymmetries in how the candidates chose their strategies. In the first three weeks of October, 55.4 percent of George W. Bush's ads were strictly negative, while only 2.7 percent of John Kerry's were. A surprising 55.8 percent of Kerry's ads were wholly positive, while only 27.4 percent of Bush's were.

The Wesleyan Media Project also noted that as presidential campaign ads have become more negative, so too have the negative emotions associated with these ads. During a three-week period in October in the **Campaign of 2012**, they noted that 86.1 percent of pro-Romney ads and 70 percent of pro-Obama ads relied on anger (a number that went up for the pro-Romney ads as the campaign progressed). The second most common emotion elicited in a pro-Romney ad was fear, which they noted in 36 percent of ads. In the case of Obama, the second most common emotion was sadness, present in 47.3 percent of ads. Emotions like enthusiasm were evident in approximately a quarter of ads favoring each candidate, while other positive emotions such as pride were even more rare.

Critics of negative campaigning argue that the increased use of negative ads has produced a general public disaffection with politics and politicians. On the other hand, defenders of negative campaigning argue that there is nothing inappropriate about a political campaign revealing the questionable record of an opponent or the inconsistent positions taken by a candidate. According to this line of reasoning, negative campaigning provides voters with essential information about a candidate's shortcomings.

In the aftermath of the *Citizens United* decision, the number of actors involved in the funding and broadcasting of political ads has proliferated, and so too have the places and manner of dissemination of these ads. Radio, broadcast television, billboards, and print media (newspapers and magazines) remain staples in the world of campaign advertising, but they have been joined by cable television, Internet ads, YouTube videos, and even video game billboards as candidates and advocacy groups seek out more avenues for disseminating their messages.

See also MoveOn; Negative Campaigning; Paid Media; Swift Boating

Additional Resources

Ansolabehere, Stephen, and Shanto Iyenger. *Going Negative: How Attack Ads Shrink and Polarize the Electorate.* New York: Free Press, 1995.

Buell, Emmett H., and Lee Sigelman. *Attack Politics: Negativity in Presidential Campaigns since 1960.* Lawrence: University of Kansas Press, 2008.

David, Mark. *Going Dirty: The Art of Negative Campaigning.* Lanham, MD: Rowman & Littlefield, 2009.

Geer, John G. *In Defense of Negativity: Attack Ads in Presidential Campaigns.* Chicago: University of Chicago Press, 2006.

Jamieson, Kathleen Hall. *Packaging the Presidency: A History and Criticism of Presidential Campaign Advertising.* New York: Oxford University Press, 1996.

The Living Room Candidate: Presidential Campaign Commercials 1952–2008. http://www.livingroomcandidate.org/. Accessed September 24, 2015.

Patterson, Thomas E. *Out of Order.* New York: Knopf, 1993.

Wesleyan Media Project. "2012 Shatters 2004 and 2008 Records for Total Ads Aired." 2012. http://mediaproject.wesleyan.edu/releases/2012-shatters-2004-and-2008-records-for-total-ads-aired/. Accessed September 24, 2015.

West, Darrell W. *Air Wars: Television Advertising in Election Campaigns, 1952–2000.* Washington, DC: Congressional Quarterly, 2001.

Campaign Finance Reform

From the ratification of the Constitution through the early twentieth century, there were few efforts by Congress to regulate political parties and how they conducted presidential campaigns. By the 1820s, a national political party system was in place, and parties attracted volunteers by rewarding them with government jobs after the election (a practice known as patronage, or more colorfully, the "spoils system"). Parties also financed campaigns by collecting donations from party members who had been placed in government jobs (10% of their salary was not uncommon). In the aftermath of the Civil War, advocates of **civil service reform** lobbied Congress for federal protections for government employees that would preclude them from being compelled to engage in politicking to keep their jobs. In 1883, in the aftermath of the assassination of President James A. Garfield by the infamous "disappointed office seeker," Congress passed the Civil Service Reform Act (Pendleton Act), which included a provision prohibiting federal employees from asking their colleagues to make political contributions. This was the first major effort to limit the campaign donations to political parties. This legislation, however, did little to stop political parties from exploiting other sources of campaign revenue.

In the **Campaign of 1896**, Mark Hanna, who directed Republican nominee William McKinley's campaign, raised millions of dollars in corporate campaign contributions. This enabled McKinley to mount a successful nationwide campaign against the populist Democratic nominee, William Jennings Bryan. The Republican Party continued to rely on corporate funding in the **Campaign of 1900** and the **Campaign of 1904**. Embarrassed by public disclosures of these practices, in 1905 President Theodore Roosevelt proposed banning corporate contributions to presidential campaigns. Subsequently Congress passed the Tillman Act of 1907 prohibiting corporations from financing federal election campaigns. In the aftermath of the Teapot Dome scandal, the Federal Corrupt Practices Act of 1925 was enacted to eliminate the loopholes in the Tillman Act. It required limited disclosure of political party contributions and placed spending limits on federal campaigns. The Taft-Hartley Act of 1947 expanded restrictions on political contributions by corporations, unions, and federally chartered banks to candidates for federal office. Most political observers agreed that, while helpful, these attempts to limit corporate influence on federal elections were ineffective. Corporations continued to seek out exceptions and loopholes for each new law that was enacted.

In 1971, Congress passed the Federal Election Campaign Act (FECA), which placed strict disclosure requirements on campaign contributions to candidates in federal elections. The disclosure limits applied to donations to campaigns and to contributions to political action committees (PACs). FECA also limited the amount campaigns could spend on political advertising. The original act, however, did not place limits on how much an individual could contribute to a candidate's campaign, or what corporations and unions could contribute to PACs. In an effort to reduce reliance on special interest contributions, the Revenue Act of 1971 allowed individual $1.00 donations to the presidential campaign fund through an option provided on their federal tax returns, with the money committed to a public financing system funding presidential candidates (to begin with the **Campaign of 1976**). Among other things, the Watergate scandal revealed that several corporations had made sizable donations to President Richard Nixon's reelection campaign in exchange for political favors. In 1974, Congress amended the FECA, limiting individual contributions to federal campaigns to $1,000 and requiring that all corporate and union contributions to campaigns be made through PACs. The law placed a spending cap on candidates' campaign expenditures and limited how much candidates could donate to their own campaigns. The FECA amendments also established the Federal Election Commission (FEC) to enforce these regulations.

Critics on both sides of the aisle argued that the 1974 FECA law went too far in limiting how much candidates could spend at election time. The Supreme Court agreed. In *Buckley v. Valeo* (1976) the court found unconstitutional limits on total campaign expenditures. The court also struck down limits on independent expenditures by individuals. However, the court upheld the disclosure requirements and the donation limits for both campaigns and PACs, arguing that these served to reduce the appearance of corruption in federal elections. Candidates who voluntarily accepted public financing of their presidential campaigns were still subject to spending limits. The FEC later ruled that political parties could accept unlimited donations (referred to as "soft money") for the sole purpose of what were termed "party-building activities." These activities included voter registration and get-out-the-vote efforts, fund-raising activities, and other "voter education" activities.

Political parties took advantage of the soft money exception as a means to evade some contributor limits under FECA. Subsequently both the Democratic and the Republican parties raised tens of millions of dollars in large contributions from wealthy individuals. By the 1990s, these extensive soft money donations funded issue ads, which had every appearance of being an electioneering activity in that they promoted or attacked a political candidate. The parties believed that as long as these ads did not contain the phrases "vote for" or "vote against," they could be classified as voter education (for which purpose the parties could accept unlimited donations), rather than electioneering (in which case, donations were subject to strict limits). The FEC accepted this interpretation by declining to prosecute the parties for violations.

Alarm over the growing influence of soft money on presidential campaigns eventually led Congress to pass the Bipartisan Campaign Finance Reform Act of 2002 (BCRA). The Abramoff influence-peddling scandal that became public around this time pressured many reluctant legislators to support the bill. This law prohibited national political parties from raising any soft money, and raised the maximum amount of individual contributions from $1,000 to $2,000, with later contributions indexed to inflation (which was not a provision in the original legislation). The BCRA also prevented **independent advocacy groups** from running campaign ads in close proximity to a primary election (not within thirty days) or a federal general election (not within sixty days). In December 2003, the Supreme Court ruled in *McConnell v. FEC* that the BCRA's ban on soft money contributions was constitutional. However, in January 2010, the court, in *Citizens United v. FEC*, found unconstitutional restrictions on independent expenditures. The decision permitted independent groups to raise and spend unlimited funds from donors. While the court again upheld disclosure requirements, independent groups have found creative ways to evade these, most recently, by forming **501(c) groups**. Candidates' campaigns have also found ways to benefit from independent expenditures, relying on **super PACs** to help promote their political campaigns. In April 2014, the Supreme Court further modified its position on campaign finance reform in *McCutcheon vs. FEC*, striking down the cap on the total contributions an individual can make during the course of a campaign, while leaving in place the cap on individual donations for candidates and political parties.

The **Campaign of 2016** posed a unique challenge to existing campaign finance laws. While almost all candidates have relied on support from independent groups, the candidacy of Republican Jeb Bush, in particular, appears to have violated the spirit, if not the letter, of laws enacted limiting candidates' coordination with outside groups. Bush specifically held off officially declaring his candidacy, even as he made campaign appearances, raised funds, and suggested publicly (on numerous occasions) that he was a candidate for president. He argued that this enabled him to coordinate with the super PAC that was raising money on his behalf (and, because it was considered an outside advocacy group, unlike his official campaign organization, it could accept donations of unlimited size), directly soliciting funds for the super PAC from donors and helping to plan the activities of the super PAC. Bush's plan was to raise $100 million through the super PAC and to assist in planning its strategy, prior to his official announcement of his candidacy, when he would be barred from engaging in such activities and could only raise funds through his campaign (which would be subject to strict donor limits). What was controversial about Bush's behavior was that while he postponed his official declaration of his candidacy, he was clearly behaving as a candidate during this time. Bush told audiences he was a candidate for president, and he made campaign speeches—behaviors that appeared to preclude his involvement with the super PAC. However, a deeply divided FEC made it clear that they were unwilling and unable to prosecute any candidate for campaign violations, seemingly leaving the door open to candidates' attempts to challenge the rules. Bush was not the only candidate to coordinate with an outside group during a time period when he or she was already a declared candidate for office, or clearly behaving as such. Rather, Bush's flouting of the rules illustrated how toothless the current regime was, and the necessity of adopting enforcement practices that reflect the contemporary campaign environment.

See also 527 Group

Additional Resources

"Major Provisions of the Bipartisan Campaign Reform Act of 2002." Campaign Finance Law Quick Reference for Reporters. Federal Elections Commission. http://www.fec .gov/press/bkgnd/bcra_overview.shtml. Accessed September 18, 2015.

Mann, Thomas E. "Bipartisan Campaign Reform Act: Success or Failure?" The Campaign Legal Center. Brookings Institute. April 10, 2007. http://www.brookings.edu /opinions/2007/0410uspolitics_mann.aspx. Accessed September 18, 2015.

Mutch, Robert E. *Buying the Vote: A History of Campaign Finance Reform*. New York: Oxford University Press, 2014.

Post, Robert C. *Citizens Divided: Campaign Finance Reform and the Constitution*. Cambridge, MA: Harvard University Press, 2014.

Smith, Melissa M., Glenda C. Williams, Larry Powell, and Gary A. Copeland. *Campaign Finance Reform: The Political Shell Game*. New York: Lexington Books, 2010.

Cattle Call

This term is generally used to refer to a sponsored campaign event where multiple contests for the same (or similar) political offices put in an appearance to demonstrate their viability. For GOP candidates, such events are often sponsored by state or local GOP groups (and include Lincoln-Reagan dinners, or events named for these icons individually), by independent advocacy groups such as the National Rifle Association or **Americans for Prosperity**, by conservative media organizations such as RedState, or by conservative umbrella groups, such as the Values Voters Summit and CPAC. For Democratic candidates, state party organizations have historically used Jefferson-Jackson dinners as political events, although there has been some movement recently to jettison the names of these former slave-owning presidents and rebrand these events.

See also Netroots Nation

Additional Resource

Berman, Russell. "Is the Democratic Party Abandoning Jefferson and Jackson?" *The Atlantic,* July 28 2015. http://www.theatlantic.com/politics/archive/2015/07/will-the -democratic-party-abandon-thomas-jefferson-andrew-jackson/399722/. Accessed September 5, 2015.

Caucus

In the late eighteenth and early nineteenth centuries, political parties made use of congressional caucuses (termed "king caucuses" due to Congress's role as king-maker) to select their respective presidential candidates. The first use of the congressional caucus followed President George Washington's decision not to seek a third term as president, when Congress found itself in need of a means to nominate his successor. In the **Campaign of 1796**, the Federalist faction in Congress nominated John Adams as its presidential nominee and Charles Cotesworth Pinckney as its vice presidential nominee, although candidates at that time did not run on a joint ticket. The Anti-Federalist faction in Congress selected Thomas Jefferson as its presidential nominee and Aaron Burr as its vice presidential nominee. Because the president and vice president were not elected on a joint ticket, Adams, who won the most votes, was selected president, and his adversary, Jefferson, became vice president by virtue of coming in second in the race. In the **Campaign of 1800**, the efforts of the Anti-Federalists to avoid a repeat of the 1796 election led to an outcome where no candidate received a majority of the Electoral College vote, sending the election to the House of Representatives.

The Twelfth Amendment to the Constitution permitted candidates to run on a joint ticket, and this, along with the demise of the Federalist faction as a national force, created pressure for reform in the presidential nomination process. By the **Campaign of 1824**, criticism of the king caucus led to a revolt by a number of Democratic-Republican (formerly Anti-Federalist) candidates who refused to seek the endorsement of the congressional caucus, with Andrew Jackson of Tennessee among the most vocal. When no candidate received a majority of votes in the Electoral College, the presidential contest was again decided by the House of Representatives. This ultimately led to the demise of the king caucus as a means of nominating presidential candidates.

The end of the king caucus did not mean the end of the use of the caucus system in presidential elections, however. By the 1840s, fissures in the old Democratic-Republican Party once again led to distinct factions, which then nominated their own candidates for office under their own party labels. These newly emerging political parties used party caucuses to select delegates to national political conventions. The party caucus system typically involves supporters of a party attending meetings organized on the city or county level and sending delegates pledged to support their candidate to a state party convention, proportional to their degree of support at the local caucus. The state convention delegates then vote to determine which candidate their state will support at the party's national nominating convention (although rules on how delegates are allocated vary by state).

Caucuses remained the standard means for selecting presidential candidates throughout much of the twentieth century, and they are still the method used by most third parties for candidate nomination. While some states did hold primaries prior to the **McGovern-Fraser reforms**, these were not always binding, and as late as the **Campaign of 1968**, Democratic presidential candidate Hubert Humphrey was able to win his party's nomination without winning a single primary. This changed during the 1970s, as states increasingly opted to let voters select delegates to the national convention during primaries, rather than leaving the decision to the small group of party activists that attended caucuses. The earliest caucus in the political campaign season still occurs in Iowa, the most famous among the remaining caucuses. The campaign scheduling process for the **Campaigns of 2008, 2012,** and **2016** have also elevated the role of the Nevada caucus.

Additional Resource

Berg-Andersson, Richard E. "How Did We Get Here, Anyway? An Historical Analysis of the Presidential Nominating Process." The Green Papers. http://www.thegreenpapers .com/Hx/NomProcess.html. Accessed September 5, 2015.

Character Issue

Throughout electoral history, alleged acts of personal impropriety have plagued presidential campaigns. During the **Campaign of 1800,** political opponents attacked Thomas Jefferson with accusations of atheism, and they circulated rumors that he shared intimacies with one of his female slaves (a rumor only recently determined to be likely true). Despite the rumor, Jefferson went on to defeat President John Adams for the presidency. During the **Campaign of 1828,** supporters of incumbent president John Quincy Adams spread vicious rumors about Democratic presidential candidate Andrew Jackson. One such widely circulated rumor alleged that Jackson's wife, Rachel, had married him before she had obtained a legal divorce from her first husband. Jackson's opponents also published the so-called coffin handbill, which alleged that Jackson had ordered the execution of a number of his soldiers without just cause.

Similarly, supporters of Andrew Jackson circulated their own rumors about John Quincy Adams. One rumor alleged that Adams had procured the sexual services of an American girl on behalf of the Russian czar while serving as ambassador to Russia. Jackson's supporters also attacked Adams for having a billiard table in the White House, claiming that it was purchased with public funds. (Adams did have a billiard table, but he paid for it with personal funds.) Of greater importance to the ultimate outcome of the election, supporters of Jackson accused Adams of a "corrupt bargain" with Henry Clay that permitted Adams to win the presidency in 1824, when neither Jackson nor Adams had won enough electoral votes to win the election outright. By throwing his support to Adams, Clay guaranteed Adams victory when the House of Representatives made the final determination of the election outcome. After his election, Adams then appointed Clay as secretary of state in what Jackson supporters characterized as a quid pro quo, implying that Adams had bribed Clay.

During the **Campaign of 1844,** supporters of Democratic presidential candidate James K. Polk spread rumors that Whig Party candidate Henry Clay frequented brothels in Washington, DC, and engaged in heavy gambling and blasphemy. Supporters of Clay retaliated, alleging that Polk had sold many of his slaves to slave traders. In later elections, attacks focused more on personality than on misdeeds. During the **Campaign of 1860,** Northern Democratic candidate Stephen Douglas criticized Lincoln as a "horrid-looking wretch, sooty and scoundrelly in aspect, a cross between the nutmeg dealer, the horse-swapper and the nightman." Supporters of Lincoln frequently referred to Stephen Douglas as the "Little Giant" in an effort to point out that Douglas was a diminutive five foot four, implying that as a short individual, Douglas could not command respect. In the **Campaign of 1872,** Liberal Republicans attempted to weaken support for President Ulysses S. Grant by depicting Grant as a drunkard who was unaware of the massive corruption within his own administration.

Presidential campaign historians regard the **Campaign of 1884** as one of the nastiest in American history. New York governor Grover Cleveland received the nomination of the Democratic Party, and long-time Republican leader James G.

Blaine received the Republican presidential nomination. With few major issues dividing the Democratic and Republican parties, both sides looked for other ways to discredit the other's nominee. Cleveland supporters pounded Blaine for a 1870s influence-peddling scandal in which Blaine took payments from a railroad in exchange for helping it win federal land grants. The so-called Mulligan Letters scandal had already cost Blaine the 1876 Republican presidential nomination, and critics believed that reviving it would have a similar negative outcome in 1884. To counter these attacks, Blaine's Republican supporters made the most of a July 1884 story in the Buffalo *Evening Telegraph* alleging that Cleveland had fathered an illegitimate child. Instead of denying the allegation, Cleveland admitted to having an affair with the woman in 1874, and he explained that he had taken financial responsibility for the child. By getting out in front of the issue, Cleveland successfully defused the controversy. The race between Blaine and Cleveland remained close until the final weeks of the campaign. In the end, Cleveland pulled out a narrow election victory, largely due to the fact that New York State's powerful Irish Catholic vote perceived Blaine to be anti-Catholic.

Throughout much of the twentieth century, major print and broadcast media outlets abided by an unwritten rule that the private lives of presidential candidates were generally off limits. Warren Harding was elected to the presidency in 1920, but his marital infidelity did not become known until after his untimely death in 1923. Franklin Delano Roosevelt's long-term affair with Lucy Mercer, and his death while on vacation with her in Warm Springs, went unmentioned in the press. Similarly, no mention was made during the **Campaign of 1952** of rumors of General Dwight Eisenhower's close personal relationship with his driver, Army captain Kay Summersby, while serving together during World War II. While the press corps was aware of rumors of John F. Kennedy's womanizing well before he ran for president in the **Campaign of 1960**, no mention was made of them until after his death.

During the 1970s, however, media coverage of the private and public lives of political candidates began to change. During the **Campaign of 1972**, Democratic presidential nominee George McGovern made the decision to replace his chosen running mate, Missouri senator Thomas Eagleton, after media reports that Eagleton had received electroshock therapy treatments for depression. In the **Campaign of 1976**, Democratic presidential candidate Jimmy Carter drew sharp criticism for giving an interview to *Playboy* in which he admitted to having lust in his heart. Many political experts would point to the *Playboy* controversy as contributing to Carter's decline in presidential preference polls.

A turning point in media coverage of presidential candidates' personal lives occurred during the Democratic primary season in the **Campaign of 1988**. The leading candidate, former Colorado senator Gary Hart, faced rumors of marital infidelity. In an effort to quell these rumors, Hart challenged reporters to "follow him around," guaranteeing a boring time for all. Soon after, a reporter saw a young woman enter Hart's Washington, DC, townhouse, fueling suspicion in the press corps that Hart had something to hide. Unbeknownst to him, Hart was being followed, and in early May 1987, the *Miami Herald* published a story (with photos) about Hart partying with model Donna Rice on a yacht aptly named *Monkey Business*. The media feeding frenzy that ensued led Hart to drop out of the race for the Democratic nomination. Even though Hart subsequently reentered the contest, he was unable to establish himself as a serious contender for the nomination, and he soon disappeared from the political scene.

During the Democratic primary **Campaign of 1992**, Arkansas governor Bill Clinton found himself forced to deal with a tabloid story about a long-term affair with Gennifer Flowers. There were also allegations that Clinton used improper influence in seeking a military deferment to avoid the draft during the Vietnam War. To the surprise of many political experts, these character issues did not derail Clinton's campaign. As the Clinton campaign had hoped, voters were more concerned about their economic well-being than about Clinton's personal life, and Clinton went on to win the election. Despite efforts by Republican presidential nominee Bob Dole to turn the **Campaign of 1996** into a referendum on the Whitewater scandal and other Clinton administration ethics controversies, Clinton went on to easily win the reelection in 1996 as well, buoyed by the economic recovery.

In the **Campaign of 2000,** Republican presidential nominee George W. Bush was forced to confront rumors of heavy drinking and drug use during in his youth. Bush reassured voters that these were youthful indiscretions, that his marriage to Laura had transformed him, and that he no longer had any substance abuse problems. Late in the campaign, a Maine Democratic operative contacted several media sources with evidence that Bush had been cited for driving under the influence in 1976 while visiting his parents' home in Maine, some time after he claimed to have stopped drinking. Bush confirmed the reports, although he maintained that he was currently a sober and responsible family man. These revelations had little effect on Bush's standing in the polls.

Military service (or the lack thereof) became an issue again in the **Campaign of 2004,** as Bush sought reelection. His competitor, Democratic nominee John Kerry, had served on a United States Navy swift boat during the Vietnam War, while Bush had served in the Texas National Guard (viewed during that era as a means of avoiding dangerous combat). Democrats alleged that Bush's father, former president George H. W. Bush, had pulled strings to get his son into the Guard at a time when the waiting list was long and student deferments were no longer available. (Bush's running mate, Dick Cheney, had received five deferments and never served, declaring, "I had other priorities in the 1960s than military service").

Similar charges had been leveled against Dan Quayle, George H. W. Bush's vice president, in the **Campaign of 1988**. In response, Bush's supporters argued that Kerry's actions in Vietnam were anything but heroic, suggesting that he endangered the troops under his command and that he was inappropriately awarded a Purple Heart.

In the **Campaign of 2008**, former POW and Arizona senator John McCain was the Republican nominee, and the Democrats nominated Illinois senator Barack Obama, who was too young to have served in Vietnam. The candidates had other liabilities, however. McCain had been married once before, and Democrats alleged that he began dating his current wife, Cindy, while he was still married to his first wife. McCain's first wife came to his defense. Obama was criticized for the inflammatory comments made by his long-time minister, the Reverend Jeremiah Wright. Republicans also attempted to link Obama to former Weather Underground member and domestic terrorist Bill Ayers. The poor state of the economy in 2008, and Obama's attempts to link McCain's policies to those of his unpopular predecessor George W. Bush, helped to mitigate the effects of character issues during the campaign.

The **Campaign of 2012** contained remarkably few character attacks. GOP voters were already fairly united in their hatred of incumbent president Barack Obama, primarily as a function of his policies and his perceived lack of patriotism (the latter more likely a function of his party, and potentially his ethnicity, than his character). GOP nominee Mitt Romney was subjected to some early attacks by his opponent for his business activities with Bain Capital—in particular, those instances where Bain purchased businesses that eventually laid off American employees. Romney was also accused of concealing taxable earnings in the Cayman Islands as a means of tax evasion.

It is far more likely that character will be an issue in the **Campaign of 2016**. Democratic front-runner Hillary Clinton has faced scrutiny for her actions as secretary of state during the terrorist attack on the U.S. consulate in Benghazi in 2012 in which four people, including U.S. ambassador Christopher Stevens, were killed. GOP critics also suggest that the Clinton Foundation received improper political donations. Clinton has also failed to release most of her e-mail messages from her time as secretary of state, when she used a private e-mail address and server that she retained after leaving office. Most of her GOP opponents face similar scrutiny for their public and private behaviors, ranging from improper business dealings with corrupt individuals (Jeb Bush), to improper political pressure for personal ends (Chris Christie), to improper coordination of fund-raising in previous campaigns (Scott Walker), to being financially supported by an affluent donor in exchange for political favors (Marco Rubio), to failure to support the Civil Rights Act (Rand Paul), for example. Other candidates (e.g., Donald Trump, Ted Cruz,

Ben Carson, Carly Fiorina) have engaged in conduct or made remarks that may be offensive to some portion of the electorate and that may be perceived as a character liability by their party leadership. Just recently Mr. Trump signaled his intention to target the campaign of Democratic frontrunner and former secretary of state Hillary Clinton by dredging up a past pocked by unseemly marital infidelities committed by her husband, former president Bill Clinton, a personal history that Mr. Trump has curiously deemed an indictment of Secretary Clinton's own character.

See also Campaign of 1824; Swift Boating

Additional Resources

Bailey, Thomas. *Presidential Saints and Sinners.* New York: Free Press, 1981.

Nicholas, Peter, and Byron Tau. "Emails Show Clinton Was Warned Over Security in Benghazi Ahead of Attack." *Wall Street Journal*, May 22, 2015. http://www.wsj.com/articles/hillary-clintons-benghazi-emails-to-be-released-by-state-department-1432309888. Accessed September 5, 2015.

Roberts, Robert North. *Ethics in Government: An Encyclopedia of Investigations, Scandals, Reforms, and Legislation.* Westport, CT: Greenwood Press, 2001.

Checkers Speech

In early July 1952, the Republican National Convention nominated thirty-nine-year-old senator Richard M. Nixon as General Dwight D. Eisenhower's vice presidential running mate. Prior to receiving the nomination, Nixon had established a reputation as a strong anti-communist and an expert on foreign affairs. On September 18, 1952, the *New York Post* published a story with the headline, "Secret Rich Men's Trust Fund Keeps Nixon in Style beyond His Salary." The story alleged that a group of seventy-six California businessmen had provided Nixon with a secret personal slush fund in excess of $18,000. The story proved extremely embarrassing for the Republican Party, and Eisenhower was under enormous pressure to drop Nixon from the ticket. Only a few years before, a number of alleged influence-peddling controversies had tarnished the reputation of the Truman administration, and the Republican Party had used these controversies as part of its campaign strategy to win back the White House for the first time since 1932. It was therefore inconceivable that Republicans would risk charges of hypocrisy in coming to Nixon's defense.

Realizing that he faced almost certain removal from the ticket, Nixon decided to take his case directly to the people rather than addressing the scandal in a press conference. On September 23, 1952, in a nationally televised address to the American people, Nixon defended himself against the allegations and denied breaking any laws or regulations. After defending his honesty and integrity, Nixon emphasized his modest upbringing and lifestyle, noting that his wife, Pat, did not own a mink but, rather, sported a "respectable Republican cloth coat." Even more effective in building sympathy for his plight was Nixon's sentimental story about Checkers, the dog given to him and his family by a campaign supporter. Nixon characterized Checkers as an example of a campaign gift in an attempt to minimize the seriousness of the accusations against him:

> A man down in Texas heard Pat on the radio mention the fact that our two youngsters would like to have a dog. And believe it or not, the day before we left on this campaign trip we got a message from Union Station in Baltimore, saying they had a package for us. We went down to get it. You know what it was? It was a little cocker spaniel dog in a crate that he'd sent all the way from Texas, black and white, spotted. And our little girl Tricia, the six year old, named it "Checkers." And you know, the kids, like all kids, love the dog, and I just want to say this, right now, that regardless of what they say about it, we're gonna keep it.

The speech was given on a Hollywood set designed to look like a room in an average American home. Nixon's gamble worked. The speech attracted fifty-five million viewers, a record that remained unbroken for eight years (edged out by the Nixon-Kennedy televised debate in 1960). The Eisenhower campaign received thousands of telegrams supporting Nixon's place on the ticket, and on Election Day, the Eisenhower-Nixon ticket won a landslide victory. Nixon's Checkers speech foreshadowed the growing importance of television in presidential campaigns as a tool that enables candidates to transmit their message directly to the voters, unfiltered by print and broadcast journalists. Ironically, many political historians attribute Nixon's loss to John F. Kennedy in the 1960 presidential election to Nixon's poor performance in the first of four televised **presidential debates**.

See also Campaign of 1952; Campaign of 1960

Additional Resources

Lagesse, David. "The 1952 Checkers Speech: The Dog Carries the Day for Richard Nixon." *U.S. News and World Report*, January 17, 2008.

Nixon, Richard M. "Checkers." The History Place: Great Speeches Collection. http://www.historyplace.com/speeches/nixon-checkers.htm. Accessed October 12, 2015.

"Richard M. Nixon 'Checkers' Speech." PBS: *The American Experience.* http://www.pbs.org/wgbh/amex/presidents/37_nixon/psources/ps_checkers.html. Accessed October 12, 2015.

Super, John C., ed. *The Fifties in America.* Ipswich, MA: Salem Press, 2005.

Wells, William T. "A Fantasy Theme Analysis of Nixon's 'Checkers' Speech." *Electronic Journal of Communication* 6, no. 1 (1996).

Civil Rights Issue

The concept of civil rights is broad and encompasses the protection from political and economic discrimination based on race, ethnicity, country of origin, religion, gender, social class, and, in contemporary politics, sexual orientation. Numerous groups throughout American history have endured deprivations of basic rights, and the manner in which politicians and political parties have responded to this discrimination has varied, both a function of the era and the type of group being targeted. While discrimination against African Americans is often viewed as the primary interpretation of civil rights, blacks in American are but one of many groups who have faced discriminatory treatment in the United States. It has been argued that what is particularly noticeable about the situation of African Americans is that the scope of the discrimination they endured has been particularly intense. Native Americans also suffered deeply unjust and culturally destructive discrimination throughout American history with fatal consequences. Discrimination against women has been equally egregious. Unlike other groups victimized by discrimination, most African Americans are descendants of slaves who were treated as property and frequently regarded as subhuman.

President Lincoln's Emancipation Proclamation, issued on January 1, 1863, freed all slaves living in states not already under Union control, and it was the first presidential directive dealing with the issue of civil rights in American history. In the aftermath of the Civil War, Radical Republicans in Congress passed the Thirteenth Amendment, which abolished slavery everywhere in the United States; the Fourteenth Amendment, guaranteeing all citizens equal protection and due process; and the Fifteenth Amendment, prohibiting the federal government and the states from denying any male his right to vote on account of his race or condition of former servitude. These amendments were soon ratified by the states. To enforce these newly created constitutional rights, Congress passed a series of civil rights laws in 1866, 1870, 1871, and 1875. During the Reconstruction era, this legislation gave the federal government the legal tools to combat the growing influence of the Ku Klux Klan in the South, and it protected the voting rights of newly enfranchised African American men. As a result of these efforts, newly enfranchised African American voters in the former Confederacy were devoutly loyal to the Republican Party, which then became known as the party of civil rights.

The disputed presidential **Campaign of 1876** effectively brought Reconstruction to an end and also ended the aggressive federal enforcement of civil rights laws aimed at protecting African Americans from discrimination. Within a decade, the Democratic Party regained effective political control of all of the former Confederate states, almost exclusively through the support of white voters. And with this newfound political control, Democratic parties in almost every southern state quickly pushed for the enactment of **Jim Crow laws** aimed at denying African Americans the extensive rights they were guaranteed under the Constitution and supporting legislation just after the Civil War, including the right to vote

Around this same time, states began enacting legislation to limit the voting and citizenship rights of immigrant Americans, particularly those of Asian descent. Congress, controlled by Republicans, passed the Chinese Exclusion Act of 1882, which prevented Chinese persons from immigrating to the United States and banned them from ever becoming citizens. By the end of the 1880s, laws were enacted permitting the expulsion of immigrants and imposing bans against the importation of skilled labor. In 1891, Congress established the Bureau of Immigration to maintain stricter limits on immigrants from southern and eastern Europe, and Ellis Island became an immigrant screening station a year later.

During this period, the roles of the political parties in support of civil rights for minority groups changed. While the Democratic Party sought to subjugate African Americans in the South, it early sought out the votes of new immigrants in the urban North and Midwest. And, by absorbing elements of the **Populist** movement near the end of the nineteenth century, the party also became more closely associated with the economic rights of the disadvantaged. The complementary progressive movement, particularly the administrations of Republican president Theodore Roosevelt and Democratic president Woodrow Wilson, sought reforms in workplace safety, child labor, workplace hours and rules, wages, and public health. Progressives saw government as uniquely positioned to solve many of society's ills, and as progressivism crossed party lines, it was able to claim many accomplishments during the early part of the twentieth century.

Through the Progressive Era, the Republican Party remained the party of civil rights, with party platforms consistently endorsing the theme of universal rights for all Americans. However, the party also became strongly associated with economic prosperity and the rights of corporations, with a strong commitment to capitalism and the protection of business interests, including government investment in infrastructure and enacting sizable tariffs on imported goods (the progressives were only a wing of the larger party). The split was one of occupation and region rather than one of class; northern industrialized states backed the Republicans, worker and owner alike, whereas more agricultural areas (primarily in the South and the West) looked to the Democratic Party for support. These geographical divisions over occupation, overlaid by preexisting divisions based on race, kept the existing political coalitions stable during this time period.

Hostility toward immigrants continued into the twentieth century. During World War I, the administration of Democrat Woodrow Wilson (as well as many state governments of all political stripes) prosecuted Americans, particularly those of German descent, for criticism of the war and other "subversive activities." When the war was over, Wilson refused to issue amnesty to these individuals, leaving his Republican successor, Herbert Hoover, to pardon these individuals who were guilty, in many cases, of little more than exercising their right to free speech. In 1917, Congress passed the Immigration Act, which required English literacy tests of all adolescent immigrants (over age sixteen) and banned immigration from Asia in its entirety. In 1921 Congress established quotas on immigration from perceived undesirable regions, such as southern and eastern Europe. This was followed by the Immigration Act of 1924 imposing bans on Asian immigrants, tight restrictions on southern and eastern Europeans, and based on prior legislation reinforcing naturalization eligibility only to whites and Africans.

Native Americans ironically found themselves in a similar position to those who were born overseas—until 1924, they were not considered U.S. citizens, and states with sizable Native American populations generally had constitutional provisions barring them from participating in elections (which continued in many areas until 1948).

During World War II, discrimination against immigrants worsened as Americans of both political parties were gripped by xenophobia fueled by the impending war and the poor domestic economy. New immigrants were fingerprinted when entering the United States, and American citizens of Japanese descent were forcibly removed from their homes and interned in camps in the western part of the United States, a policy that was upheld by the Supreme Court in *Korematsu v. U.S.* (1944). Latin American immigrants were permitted to enter the United States for work purposes with the advent of the bracero program during the war, but they were expected to leave once their contract was fulfilled, and they were not eligible to apply for citizenship. Despite American opposition to Hitler's policies in Europe, in 1939, the United States turned away the MS *St. Louis*, a vessel carrying over nine hundred refugees from Germany, most of them Jewish. While the Roosevelt administration initially appeared amenable to admitting the refugees, U.S. law would not permit it, and Roosevelt's cabinet unsuccessfully attempted to persuade Cuba and Canada to accept the passengers. The ship returned to Europe, where perhaps one-third of its passengers eventually died in Hitler's concentration camps.

It was not until 1944 that President Roosevelt, under pressure from party activists and Jewish Americans already in the United States, took action to relocate Jewish refugees from Europe displaced by the war. He established a War Refugee Board and created an open port of entry for Jewish refugees (although access was limited to those fleeing Allied-controlled areas, which offered little protection for Jews facing the greatest dangers to their survival). While the Displaced Persons Act of 1948 permitted a larger number of war refugees (including Jewish refugees) to resettle in the United States, much of the quota was reserved for Northern Europeans. And while Asian immigrants were once again permitted to enter the United States, their quotas were set extremely low. By the 1950s, race was eliminated as a consideration for citizenship, although quotas for Asian Americans continued to be low. The era of McCarthyism was fueled, in part, by lingering suspicions of outsiders and the potentially dangerous political ideologies that they espoused. It was not until 1965 that national origin immigration quotas were officially abolished.

Discrimination against African Americans followed a somewhat different path. Like other groups, they continued to be disenfranchised in much of the United States throughout the twentieth century despite being officially classified as citizens. Neither political party seemed inclined to address this problem. While African Americans continued to identify with the party of Lincoln, it produced very little in the way of political payoff. While a majority of African Americans supported Democrat Franklin Delano Roosevelt in the **Campaign of 1932**, a majority of most other groups did so as well. Like the rest of America, blacks had been hit hard by the Depression and stood to gain from Roosevelt's New Deal. By the **Campaign of 1936**, their support for Roosevelt increased substantially, and their commitment to the Democratic Party endured through the elections that followed.

The coalition built by Roosevelt in the Campaign of 1932 was unique in terms of the extent to which it reached—no other electoral coalition before or since has been able to cross lines of race, religion, region, gender, and social class. Roosevelt had strong support from most sociodemographic groups, and once in office, the New Deal programs he implemented had far-reaching effects, alleviating some of the misery of poverty, providing for employment for those out of work, and creating federal protections for organized labor. Nonetheless, discrimination did occur against African Americans during the implementation at the local level of many New Deal programs. President Roosevelt's wife, Eleanor, was a strong supporter of civil rights, and she pressured her husband to work harder to promote equality in America. Eleanor earned accolades and criticism when she was photographed at Howard University being escorted by two male African American students, and again in 1939 when she resigned her membership in the Daughters of the American Revolution over their refusal to allow African American singer Marion Anderson to perform in their auditorium.

Between 1932 through 1944, pressure increased on the Democratic Party to embrace civil rights by including pro-civil right planks in its party platforms. However, accommodating the demands of the pro-civil rights camp risked the Democratic Party's base of white voters in the South. African Americans served their country loyally in World War II, but they remained in segregated units. Philip A. Randolph threatened to march on Washington to protest discriminatory treatment in wartime industry employment, and to head off the potential controversy,

Roosevelt issued an executive order prohibiting such discrimination. However, ending hiring discrimination (on paper, at least) was not the same as ending segregated work environments.

In the summer of 1947, Eleanor Roosevelt and Harry Truman spoke to delegates from the National Association for the Advancement of Colored People from the steps of the Lincoln Memorial, where they articulated their beliefs about equality for African Americans. Soon thereafter, in 1948, a fight erupted at the Democratic National Convention over the inclusion of a pro-civil rights plank in the party platform, which had been endorsed by northern delegates but was heatedly opposed by the South. Delegates from southern states threatened to walk out of the convention if the plank was adopted. Nevertheless, in response to the efforts of a young senator from Minnesota, Hubert Humphrey, the convention voted to adopt the plank.

A number of southern delegates angrily stormed out of the convention, and some formed the pro-segregation Dixiecrat Party, which fielded South Carolina governor Strom Thurmond as its presidential nominee. This same summer, President Harry Truman desegregated the U.S. military via executive order, thus firmly establishing the Democratic Party's commitment (outside of the South) to racial equality. Many political observers predicted that the loss of the South would cost Truman dearly, and they argued that he would be unable to win the election without the support of this traditionally Democratic region. While Thurmond and the Dixiecrats were able to win a total of thirty-nine electoral votes (all from southern states), Truman managed to pull off an upset victory in the 1948 election over Republican nominee Thomas Dewey.

Throughout the 1950s and early 1960s, both the Democratic and Republican parties included civil rights planks in their party platforms, but progress on ending institutional racism was slow. Civil rights leaders turned to the Supreme Court as an effective strategy in combatting state-mandated segregation. In the landmark case of *Brown v. Board of Education* (1954), the Supreme Court held that the Equal Protection Clause of the Fourteenth Amendment prohibited states from operating segregated public school systems. In the aftermath of the *Brown* decision, Republican president Dwight Eisenhower used federal troops to enforce court-ordered desegregation in the South, assuring that civil rights would be a major issue in subsequent presidential campaigns.

Research by political scientists Edward Carmines and James Stimson shows that well into the early 1960s, congressional support for civil rights was largely a bipartisan affair. However, the passage of the Civil Rights Act of 1964 and the Voting Rights Act of 1965 caused many southern whites to abandon the Democratic Party. The loss of the once stalwart and formidably unified bloc of southern Democrats in Congress and the demise of the liberal/moderate wing of the

Republican Party in the Northeast helped to exacerbate existing fissures already opened around the issue of civil rights.

By the **Campaign of 1964,** the Republican Party was deeply divided. A new generation of conservative Republicans, led by Arizona senator Barry Goldwater, took up the historically Democratic cause of states' rights, with the purpose of using the doctrine to limit federal interference with segregation in the South. Goldwater notably argued that states should be left to decide on their own if they wished to end segregation, a position that appealed to disgruntled white Democrats in the South who felt abandoned by their party (although it remains unclear whether Goldwater personally supported segregation during this time). Despite the passage of the Civil Rights Act, Johnson was able to win a sizable victory in the 1964 election. In part, this may have been due to his successful efforts to portray his opponent as an unstable extremist, but it probably also mattered that the Voting Rights Act (and the white backlash that followed) had not yet occurred. By the **Campaign of 1968**, however, Democrats could no longer expect to win the white vote in the South.

After Democratic front-runner Robert Kennedy was assassinated on the eve of the California primary in 1968, a violent and protest-laced Democratic convention named Hubert Humphrey as its nominee. Humphrey had a long history of support for civil rights, and as a consequence, he earned the support of many newly enfranchised black voters. Humphrey's opponent, Richard Nixon, also expressed support for the Civil Rights Act, although his campaign conducted a "southern strategy" designed to appeal to white Southerners through the use of **symbolic racism** themes. Some voters were dissatisfied with options presented to them by the two major parties and threw their support behind former Alabama governor (and former Democrat) George Wallace, who ran as the nominee of the pro-segregation American Independence Party. Wallace campaigned against the forced racial integration of public schools and attacked opponents of the Vietnam War as unpatriotic. He managed to win nearly ten million votes and carried five states, earning forty-six electoral votes (and, as was the case with the Dixiecrats before him, all were in the South). Wallace's candidacy created serious problems (by design) for Humphrey, who, as a champion of civil rights throughout his political career, was unwilling to cozy up to segregationists in order to win back white southern Democrats who were now siding with Wallace and his third party.

The Republican Party continued to express strong support for the principles of civil rights, although Nixon continued his southern strategy in the **Campaign of 1972** and took a strong position in opposition to mandatory school busing programs as a means to integrate public schools. Nominee George McGovern and the Democratic Party expressed support for civil rights and advocated both school busing and the goal of school integration more generally. McGovern lost in a landslide, in part because his views on economic and social reform were considered too extreme for many voters.

Four years later, the Democratic Party nominated Jimmy Carter, another ardent advocate of civil rights. Carter also advocated the Equal Rights Amendment as a means of protecting women from discrimination in employment. Carter's opponent in the **Campaign of 1976** was Gerald Ford, who had been a little-known Republican congressman from Grand Rapids, Michigan, before Vice President Spiro Agnew's abrupt resignation (on tax evasion charges). Not long after Nixon made Ford his new vice president, Nixon himself was forced to resign (to avoid being impeached during the Watergate scandal), catapulting Ford into the White House. Ford had a long history as a political moderate, and, like Carter, he was a supporter of civil rights and equal rights for women. Ford's wife, Betty, was a passionate spokeswoman for the ERA, and the Fords' centrist views made them unpopular with their party's growing base of social conservatives, many of whom voted for his opponent, Ronald Reagan, in the Republican primary. Ford's pardon of his disgraced predecessor, combined with a weak economy, undoubtedly harmed him far more than any positions that he took on civil rights or women's rights. Carter, a Georgia native, carried every southern state, with the exception of Virginia, in one of the very few post-civil rights era elections where a Democrat was able to win over white voters in the South.

By the **Campaign of 1980**, the political climate had changed, particularly for the Republican Party, which now had a strong Christian conservative element as part of its base. The 1980 Republican Party platform notably lacked its previous commitment to the ERA and, for the first time, contained language advocating the restriction of **abortion** rights. Reagan also campaigned against affirmative action, and his subsequent defense of Bob Jones University's racially discriminatory admissions policy created a lasting rift between the Republican Party and black voters. However, these positions proved to be popular with southern white voters, who were among Reagan's strongest supporters.

Reagan's opposition to affirmative action continued in the **Campaign of 1984**, and his vice president, George H. W. Bush, incorporated it into his successful bid for the White House in the **Campaign of 1988**. Both Reagan and Bush continued to draw votes from southern whites, while at the same time losing African American voters, a disparity that appeared to grow larger with each new election year. The Republican Party's use of convicted felon Willie Horton (who was African American) to attack Democratic nominee Michael Dukakis only served to exacerbate this trend.

Also notable, civil rights activist Jesse Jackson ran for the Democratic Party's nomination in both 1984 and 1988, the first African American since Shirley Chisholm to do so. Jackson's presence in the campaign kept the Democratic Party focused on issues relating to civil rights and poverty, and African American voter registration and turnout rose in these years as a response to his candidacy.

In the **Campaign of 1992**, Democratic nominee Bill Clinton, an Arkansas native, was able to use Bush's refusal to expand federal civil rights protections as a means to mobilize large numbers of African American voters. Bush's campaign, weighed down by a faltering economy and a third-party challenge from Texas business mogul H. Ross Perot, was unable to overcome the numerous obstacles that lay in its path. A notable Bush achievement in the area of civil rights was the passage of the Americans with Disabilities Act in 1990. The act imposed federal access guidelines on businesses and public agencies throughout the nation, granting disabled Americans unprecedented legal protections in seeking and retaining employment, educational support, and access to public agencies and accommodations. The act was a source of controversy among some conservatives, who viewed it as an unfunded federal mandate on state and local governments and an unfair restriction on the business community.

While generally hewing to the Republican Party's now traditional position on affirmative action and the expansion of civil rights legislation, Republican nominee Bob Dole sought to improve his party's standing among African Americans in the **Campaign of 1996**. In an attempt to reach out to the African American community, Dole selected former New York representative Jack Kemp, who had served as secretary of housing and urban development under President George H. W. Bush, as his running mate. At the time, Kemp was one of the few Republican Party notables who were viewed favorably by African American voters. Despite this effort, Dole fared poorly among black voters.

Eight years later, Republican incumbent George W. Bush suggested that the Democratic Party was taking black voters for granted in the **Campaign of 2004**. Bush criticized the Democrats for failing to produce improvements in the lives of African Americans, and for engaging in primarily symbolic shows of support for the black community. Ironically, Bush's refusal to speak to the NAACP during the campaign (and in the preceding 2000 campaign as well) conveyed its own kind of symbolism. While Bush pushed his proposed school vouchers program as a sort of civil rights package to attract black voters, he generally did not book campaign events for African American audiences (the major exceptions were the few occasions where he spoke at predominantly African American private schools). Like Reagan, Bush had also campaigned at Bob Jones University (which still banned interracial dating at the time) in his first presidential campaign, and while he later apologized for offending Catholics, he pointedly omitted an apology to African American voters. These factors contributed to the even lower rates of African American support for the Republican Party in the early 2000s.

In the **Campaign of 2008,** Democrat Barack Obama became the first African American to receive the nomination of a major political party. While Obama attempted to downplay his multiracial background during the campaign, instead emphasizing his all-American upbringing at the hands of his Kansas grandparents, concerns about his race lurked beneath the surface. His wife, Michelle Obama, was criticized for expressing the sentiment that her husband's electoral viability finally made her proud to be an American. The Obama's family minister, the Rev. Jeremiah Wright, came under fire for sermons where he criticized the progress of racial equality in America, causing Obama to publicly distance himself from his friend. Perhaps most nefarious element of the campaign was the recurring accusation that Obama had not really been born in the United States and was therefore not eligible to hold the office of president, regardless of his popularity among voters. A corollary to this birtherism conspiracy painted Obama as a closeted Muslim (he is a Christian), with the implication that he was somehow foreign, not like other Americans, and had loyalties that resided elsewhere. By 2008, it was no longer socially acceptable to openly oppose a candidate on the basis of his race; however, in the wake of September 11, 2001, it had become acceptable to criticize a candidate on the basis of religion, if that religion happened to be Islam. Both forms of criticism serve the same purpose, namely, to suggest that the candidate is not a regular American like everyone else, and doesn't share mainstream American values. It labels the candidate an outsider, and even inherently un-American. Political scientists view it as a coded form of racism.

Besides race, gender equality was a topic of controversy in the 2008 election. Obama took Republican nominee John McCain to task for voting against the Lilly Ledbetter Act, which protected women's ability to sue for violations of existing equal pay laws. The candidates also differed on gay rights. While Obama, like John Kerry before him, was not willing to advocate gay marriage (although he did express support for civil unions), he did promise to eliminate the military's "don't ask, don't tell" (DADT) policy for gay service members if elected. DADT was signed into law by Bill Clinton, who'd accepted it as a compromise when his promise to rescind the existing ban on gay service members met with political opposition. McCain took a more guarded approach to same-sex marriage. Like many Republicans, he needed to balance the demands of social conservatives within his party to support a constitutional amendment to ban same-sex marriage (a position McCain did not support) and the increasingly liberal social environment on gay rights. McCain implied that he did not mind states permitting civil unions, and he suggested that the military make the decision about whether to retain DADT. (Two years later, when a survey of military personnel suggested that a majority supported eliminating the policy, McCain lobbied hard to keep it in place, openly parting ways with his wife, Cindy, and daughter, Meghan, who appeared in ads promoting the policy's repeal.) Both candidates also took a moderate approach to immigrant rights, each allowing some scenario where undocumented residents might apply for citizenship. The one aspect of civil rights that was never directly addressed in the campaign was the civil rights of African Americans. Obama was reluctant to draw any attention to his own ethnic background, and McCain was concerned about being viewed as a racist.

The **Campaign of 2012** was a continuation of the events of 2008, with scant mention of civil rights except for continued GOP opposition to same-sex marriage and continued GOP opposition to offering any legal protections for those who were residing in the country without the legal authorization to do so. Republican nominee Mitt Romney affirmed his support for women's rights in the workplace but declined to support equal pay legislation on the grounds that existing protections were sufficient. Romney became the first Republican candidate in decades to speak before the NAACP; however, he gave his standard campaign speech promising to repeal the Affordable Care Act, and he was booed by some of the audience members. At his next campaign event, he criticized the NAACP audience, claiming that their primary interests were in receiving more "free stuff" from government, and that he was not interested in providing handouts to the undeserving. On the Democratic side, Barack Obama touted his passage of the Ledbetter Act, which was the first piece of legislation that he had authorized upon being elected president. He also touted his success in persuading Congress to repeal DADT, and he was overseeing the transition for openly gay service members, as well as promoting military reforms that would permit women service members to serve in combat roles. By the 2012 election, Obama had changed his beliefs on same-sex marriage and now supported extending marriage rights to gay couples. In a further modification of a previous position, Obama also opposed letting states decide whether or not to permit same-sex marriage, arguing that it should be a federally protected right in every state. Like McCain before him, Romney received almost all of his support from white voters, losing African Americans, Latinos, and Asian Americans by sizable margins.

In the **Campaign of 2016**, similar dynamics were at play. In the run-up to the primaries, GOP hopeful Jeb Bush, like Romney before him, suggested that African American voters were primarily interested in "free stuff"; while the remark demonstrated insensitivity to the concerns of nonwhites about civil rights, it was particularly tone-deaf in the aftermath of events in Ferguson, Missouri, and the continued instances of police brutality against African American citizens that characterized the political climate at the time. Numerous public opinion polls suggested that white Americans were more likely than they had previously been to believe that African Americans and other people of color were subjected to unequal treatment by the justice system, and in employment and housing. Other

GOP candidates such as Rand Paul exhibited concern about racial disparities in how the legal system treated citizens, and the Black Lives Matter movement had even put Democratic candidates on the defensive, interrupting campaign speaking events and challenging them to propose real-world solutions to these racial disparities instead of simply criticizing the system. Conservatives, in particular, tended to respond to the Black Lives Matter movement with the suggestion that #AllLivesMatter; indeed, this debate surfaced in numerous political speeches, during candidate debates, and in political discourse throughout the campaign.

Late in June 2015 the Supreme Court in *Obergefell v. Hodges* held that states must permit marriage between same-sex couples. In response, the Democratic Party strongly supported the decision. By contrast, responses within the Republican leadership and among GOP presidential aspirants varied. Some elements of the Republican Party felt that the resolution of the issue by the Supreme Court provided a final answer to the question about who was legally permitted to marry; these individuals expressed differing personal beliefs about the morality of homosexuality and the social desirability of same-sex marriage but maintained that the ruling, once issued, must be respected. Others challenged the legitimacy of the ruling and the Court's right to issue it, advocating for a constitutional amendment to compel states to recognize only those marriages between one man and one woman. Conservatives also argued that both private individuals and businesses should be able, with legal protection, to consciously object to the ruling and refuse to abide by it, as an expression of religious principles. Many GOP candidates rallied behind a local Kentucky elected official who refused to issue marriage licenses, despite federal court rulings ordering her to do so, on the grounds that she had religious objections to issuing licenses to same-sex couples. She was eventually jailed for contempt of court by a conservative federal judge (the son of a former GOP senator from Kentucky), and a handful of GOP presidential candidates traveled to Kentucky to attend a rally on her behalf. Other Republicans sought to put the issue to rest by arguing that the rule of law must be respected.

Recent public opinion polls show that there are major generational shifts taking place in public attitudes on civil rights. Younger voters are far more likely than their older counterparts to endorse interracial dating and marriage, and to oppose discrimination on the basis of race, gender, religion, and sexual orientation. Changes are also occurring in public attitudes on affirmative action. White voters, long opposed to affirmative action, have become slightly more supportive, whereas African American voters, long supportive of affirmative action, have become slightly less supportive. It seems that both groups are moving slowly toward a consensus on the issue, with the consensus area being more centrist. It may also be that these changes reflect the advantages some whites (particularly males) now derive from affirmative action. Some of the lawsuits now working their way through the courts come from Asian Americans, who are challenging affirmative action on the grounds that it tends to artificially limit the number of Asians at an institution, which helps whites and other minorities at the expense of higher-performing Asian American students who should be evaluated on their merit. Despite these changes, racial differences in partisanship still persist, with the vast majority of African American (and Latino) voters still supporting the Democratic Party, and a majority of white voters supporting the Republican Party.

One of the newest fronts in the struggle for civil rights in America involves Muslim Americans and Arab Americans, who face increasing levels of social hostility in the aftermath of the September 11, 2001, attacks against the United States. Members of these groups (or individuals presumed to be members of these groups) have faced intimidation and violence, and occasionally even death, and a generally hostile public climate. Americans in cities and states throughout the nation have attempted to prevent Muslims from building mosques in their towns (most significantly, the so-called Ground Zero mosque that was to be built several blocks from the site of the World Trade Center), and states like Oklahoma have passed legislation ostensibly to outlaw sharia law, but which also has the clearly intended effect of limiting the religious freedoms of Muslim Americans. More chillingly, in two Republican primary debates in the spring of 2011, most of the participants (save Ron Paul and Mitt Romney) stated that they would be unwilling to hire a Muslim if they were elected, on the grounds that the individual might be a terrorist, and they expressed concern about sharia law. (Jon Huntsman and Rick Perry were not yet in the race.) In the **Campaign of 2016**, Republican hopeful Ben Carson argued that a Muslim should not be permitted to become president of the United States, because Islam is antithetical to the Constitution. Republican aspirant Donald Trump went further still by advocating a temporary moratorium on the immigration of Muslims to the United States and proposing the establishment of a database tracking Syrian—presumably Muslim Syrian—refugees with the ambiguous suggestion that such a database could possibly be expanded to Muslims without qualification, but his actual position has seemed vague and inconsistent. As quoted by PolitiFact's Lauren Carroll, Mr. Trump has explained that "[T]he suggestion was made and (it's) certainly something we should start thinking about . . . what I want is a watch list. I want surveillance programs. Obviously, there are a lot of problems. . . . But, certainly, I would want to have a database for the refugees, for the Syrian refugees that are coming in because nobody knows where they're coming from."

After years of partisan debate, the Matthew Shepard and James Byrd, Jr., Hate Crimes Act was passed in 2009. The act was named for Matthew Shepard, a college student who had been tortured and murdered in 1998 for his sexual orientation, and James Byrd Jr., an African American man who was tortured and murdered by white supremacists in that same year. In the aftermath of these brutal killings, Democrats lobbied for a federal hate crimes law to give prosecutors more ammunition in cases where individuals are victimized because of some aspect of their group identity. This was viewed as particularly important for the LGBTQ community, because minority sexual orientation has generally not been considered a protected group that is covered by the tenets of the Civil Rights Act (although the EEOC argued differently in 2015). Republicans have generally opposed hate crimes laws on the grounds that they are superfluous. They note that both Shepard's and Byrd's murderers were convicted without such laws, and they oppose additional penalties being imposed on criminals as a function of the traits of the victim. While hate crimes now carry federal penalties, gays and lesbians still lack federal protection from employment and housing discrimination, along with the other legal protections that most Americans take for granted. While the Supreme Court ruled in *Romer v. Evans* (1996) that states could single out gays and lesbians for legal discrimination, minority sexual orientation is still not a federally protected class in the area of civil rights.

Some states and localities have attempted to pass legislation to protect children from bullying in public schools and other public facilities. As is the case with hate crime legislation, the intent is protect children who are gay or who are non-gender conforming from harassment in school, as well as children who suffer from a disability, but it could also be used to protect members of other minority groups (i.e., group identification associated with gender, ethnicity, or religion). This, too, has become a partisan issue. Many conservative parents object to anti-bullying laws on the grounds that they interfere with parental rights, and in particular, parents' decisions about how to teach their children about morality. They argue that schools should not be teaching their children to tolerate lifestyles and behaviors that their families' religious beliefs may not tolerate. Liberals are more likely to support anti-bullying legislation, claiming that whatever a person's beliefs about another's lifestyle, values, ethnicity, or religion, those views should not permit them to subject another to harassment. Their emphasis tends to be on the rights of the individuals who are being singled out for treatment that may be harmful, and the notion that it impedes a productive learning environment for that child. Conservatives are more concerned about the prospect that students may be punished for things that they say to others, and that this constitutes an infringement on their speech and religious rights.

See also Affirmative Action; Birther; Education Reform Issue; Immigration Issue; Jim Crow Laws; LGBTQ Issues; Nativism Issue; Race Relations Issue; Symbolic Racism; Voting Reform Issue; Voting Rights Act of 1965; Women's Equality Issue

Additional Resources

Carroll, Lauren. "In Context: Donald Trump's Comments on a Database of American Muslims." PolitiFact, November 24, 2015.

DuBois, W. E. B. *Black Reconstruction in America, 1860–1880*. n.p.: S. A. Russell Co., 1956.

Mayer, Jeremy D. *Running on Race: Racial Politics in Presidential Campaigns, 1960–2000*. New York: Random House, 2002.

Rosen, Robert N. *Saving the Jews: Franklin D. Roosevelt and the Holocaust*. New York: Basic Books, 2007.

Valentino, Nicholas A., and David O. Sears. "Old Times There Are Not Forgotten: Race and Partisan Realignment in the Contemporary South." *American Journal of Political Science* 49, no. 3 (July 2005): 672–688.

Woodward, C. Vann. *Origins of the New South, 1877–1913*. Baton Rouge: Louisiana State University Press, 1971.

Woodward, C. Vann. *The Strange Career of Jim Crow*. Revised ed. New York: Oxford University Press, 1971.

Civil Service Reform

In the eighteenth and nineteenth centuries, government positions were staffed by the family and friends of influential political officials, and government contracts were awarded to those with a personal relationship to government administrators, rather than on the basis of an open, competitive bidding process. These practices are collectively referred to as the "spoils system," because they are rooted in the notion that to the victor (of the election) go the spoils (well-paying public jobs, government contracts). Between 1828 and 1880, the spoils system (also known as political patronage) grew rapidly as the size of the country expanded and state and local governments embarked on more ambitious infrastructure projects. By the 1870s, many Americans were concerned that the spoils system was creating dangerously high levels of political disruption and leading to dysfunctional government. In response to such concerns, there emerged a good-government coalition of political reformers who lobbied to establish a professional civil service system as a means to restore integrity to government. Not surprisingly, neither the Republican nor the Democratic parties warmly embraced these proposed reforms. Both parties had relied heavily upon patronage to reward loyal party workers who drummed up the voters they needed to win elections, and those who were awarded government jobs usually paid back a portion of their salary to the political party that gave them the job (often 10%). It was therefore in the financial and electoral interest of political parties to keep the spoils system in place.

Early in 1872, the controversy over civil service reform led to a major split within the Republican Party. Establishment leaders wanted nothing to do with civil service reform. In sharp contrast, a reform wing of the party pressed for civil service reforms and other good-government measures. This reform wing was highly critical of the administration of President Grant due to the widespread corruption within his administration. When Republican Party leaders refused to adopt the reform agenda, the liberal Republican wing left the party in protest. Liberal Republicans then held a convention of their own and nominated New York publisher Horace Greeley as their presidential candidate. Lacking an alternative candidate, the Democratic Party endorsed Greeley as well. During the **Campaign of 1872**, Grant gave the appearance of embracing civil service reform in an attempt to downplay the problems in his own administration. Greeley lost to President Grant in a landslide. Grant and the Republican Party promptly abandoned their support for civil service reform and returned to politics as usual.

In the **Campaign of 1880**, the Republican Party nominated James Garfield for president and Chester A. Arthur for vice president. Both Garfield and Arthur had a long record of supporting political patronage. These nominations dismayed reformers within the Republican Party who had believed that the party was moving away from patronage when it nominated Rutherford B. Hayes four years earlier. Despite internal dissent over the Garfield/Arthur ticket, the Republican nominees went on to narrowly win the election. Charles J. Guiteau, forever known as the "disappointed office-seeker," shot President Garfield in July 1881, which thrust Chester Arthur into the presidency. To the surprise and anger of many Republican supporters of the patronage system, President Arthur threw his support behind the enactment of civil service reform legislation. Congress passed and Arthur signed into law the Civil Service Reform Act of 1883, more commonly known as the Pendleton Act. The law established an independent Civil Service Commission to conduct competitive examinations to fill a relatively small number of positions. The legislation also prohibited political assessments of civil service employees.

The Hatch Act, passed in 1939 and modified in 1993, further limited political activities in public employment at the federal, state, and local levels (although political appointees are subject to much looser restrictions). Specifically, the Hatch Act forbids public employees from engaging in political activities while on duty (including wearing or displaying items that express support for a party or candidate), engaging in or hosting political fund-raisers even when off duty, working for a partisan voter registration drive, holding office in a political club or party, or using any federal property (including Internet access or e-mail accounts) for campaign-related or partisan purposes. Employees may not be questioned about their political affiliation during the hiring process, and supervisors may not attempt to influence their vote in any way.

The passage of the Pendleton Act effectively ended civil service reform as a national political issue. Gradually, a series of presidential administrations would extend merit system protection to a majority of federal employees.

Recent events at the state level, though, have suggested that changes in the rights of federal employees may be on the horizon, and that such changes may become campaign issues sooner rather than later. In the **Campaign of 2016**, GOP candidates Scott Walker, John Kasich, and Chris Christie have all presided over the curtailment of collective bargaining rights of public sector employees in their states (although in some instances, police officers and firefighters were exempted, and in the case of Ohio, voters repealed those limitations via referendum a short time later). All have promised to bring such changes to the federal workforce as well. Walker, in particular, claims that even after stripping public-sector employees of their collective bargaining rights in Wisconsin, those workers still have better protections than most federal workers. The Government Executive Web site disagrees, suggesting that federal employees already are not free to bargain over wages, because those are set by Congress. They are also not free to strike. Employees in Wisconsin could bargain over wages. Government Executive also points out that despite this, federal employees can and do retain the ability to bargain over working conditions, something that Wisconsin employees are no longer free to do.

At the state level, GOP governors have passed reforms prohibiting unions from automatically collecting dues from employees, which is a blow to the political power of those unions because a portion of those dues goes to political lobbying efforts. At the federal level, employees already are not required to join a union or pay its dues. Thus, civil service reform is likely to focus on reducing civil service job protections, reducing health care costs by increasing employee contributions, and reducing pension benefits. Downsizing the federal workforce and privatizing more of its functions is another dimension of modern-day civil service reform.

See also Campaign of 1876; Right-to-Work Issue

Additional Resources

Katz, Eric. "How Scott Walker Could Bust Federal Employee Unions and Cut Fed's Pay." Government Executive, July 13, 2015. http://www.govexec.com/pay-benefits/2015/07/how-scott-walker-could-bust-federal-employee-unions-and-cut-feds-pay/117643/. Accessed September 5, 2015.

Mosher, Frederick C. *Democracy and the Public Service.* New York: Oxford University Press, 1982.

Common Core. *See* Education Reform Issue

Compassionate Conservatism

During the **Campaign of 2000**, Republican presidential nominee George W. Bush attempted to appeal to independent voters and women by framing himself as a "compassionate conservative." The Bush campaign understood that President George H. W. Bush in 1992 and Senator Bob Dole in 1996 had lost their presidential election bids largely due to the fact that independent voters, particularly independent women, voted for Clinton. In the 1996 election, Jack Kemp, the Republican nominee for vice president, angered Republican conservatives by arguing that the Republican Party needed to moderate its positions on a number of important social issues related to poverty and equality if it wished to recapture the White House by closing the **gender gap**. George W. Bush chose to heed Kemp's advice.

Reflecting the compassionate conservatism theme, the Bush campaign made a calculated decision to make education reform a top priority, despite the fact that the federal government had a relatively minor role to play in the funding or management of K–12 public schools in the United States. The Republican Party had historically opposed federal funding of public education in recent elections (with Ronald Reagan famously expressing his desire to eliminate the Department of Education entirely), so Bush's decision to promote reforming the system, complete with expanded federal funding, was a major policy shift. Somewhat surprisingly, the Bush campaign proposed the establishment of national performance standards for K–12 public schools across the country, and tied performance improvements to federal funds. The Bush campaign and the Republican Party placed much of the blame for failing schools on public employee teachers' unions, and they also emphasized school choice, in which parents would be permitted to remove their child from a public school that received a failing performance score to a better-performing school (with federal funding for that child transferring to the new school). Also reflecting the compassionate conservatism theme, the Bush campaign proposed to make much heavier use of nonprofit organizations along with faith-based organizations to help less fortunate members of society.

In an attempt to counter the Bush campaign's effort to appeal to moderate women, Democratic nominee Al Gore's campaign argued that compassionate conservatism did not include protecting the right of women to terminate an unwanted pregnancy. Rather, Gore argued that compassionate conservatism constituted a cynical effort to repackage Republican policies that would force the less fortunate members of society to fend for themselves. To drive home this point, the Gore campaign stressed that Bush refused to support the expansion of the Medicare program to include prescription drug coverage for the elderly (a policy Bush later endorsed), or any other programs directed at increasing health care coverage for those without insurance.

In the end, the compassionate conservatism theme failed to close the gender gap in key **battleground states**. Gore won more popular votes, although Bush won the presidency by winning a narrow victory in Florida (after the Supreme Court halted the vote recount in *Bush v. Gore*), giving Bush barely enough electoral votes to gain a majority.

Additional Resources

Nagourney, Adam. "Ideas and Trends; Republicans Stalk a Slogan, Hunting for Themselves." *New York Times*, June 20, 1999, section 4, p. 1.

Neal, Terry M. "Bush Outlines Charity-Based Social Policies." *Washington Post*, July 23, 1999, p. A02.

Conservation Issue. *See* Environment Issue

Conservative Political Action Conference. *See* CPAC (Conservative Political Action Conference)

Corporations and Personhood

Corporate personhood is a legal fiction recognizing the autonomy of private, incorporated bodies and establishing specific legal rights comparable to but not identical with the legal, political, constitutional, and moral rights of natural persons or private citizens. A private corporation is thereby regarded as an artificial person, a separate entity "personified" by the law and treated as a person in a limited way. According to *Black's Legal Dictionary*, a legal or "juridical person" is an "entity, as a firm, that is not a single natural person, as a human being, authorized by law with duties and rights, recognized as a legal authority having a distinct identity, a legal personality." A "corporation" or "corporate person" is viewed, according to *Black's*, as "having a personality and existence distinct from that of its several members, and which is, by the same authority, vested with the capacity of continuous succession, irrespective of changes in its membership, either in perpetuity or for a limited term of years, and of acting as a unit or single individual in matters relating to the common purpose of the association." Since *Dartmouth College v. Woodward*, the 1819 landmark Supreme Court case under Chief Justice John

Marshal, American law has recognized corporations as "persons" in a limited, abstract, and legal sense, and thus enjoying rights under the law in a way similar to the rights of persons. Or, as Marshal himself wrote in his 1819 opinion, a private corporation is "an artificial being, invisible, intangible, and existing only in contemplation of law." Corporations, according to this concept, therefore only possess some rights enjoyed by individuals, such as the right to contract and engage in free trade, and the right to bring suit at civil law, but this does not mean that a corporation is morally or even politically identical to a natural person and thereby bears all the rights natural to a human being. More accurately, a legal corporate person possesses limited rights when compared to the full scope of civil rights inherent within individual citizens. Corporations, by this understanding, resemble persons in that they possess some rights, but they are not identical to human beings. Nevertheless, some confusion has occurred in recent years regarding the status of corporate persons, owing to the 2010 Supreme Court case *Citizens United v. Federal Election Commission*. Without grasping what is meant by the concept of a legal person abstractly construed, many in the public have been led to believe that corporations have the identical rights as a flesh-and-blood person—that they are in fact like people in what they can and cannot do, both legally and politically. While these perceptions are grounded in a general misunderstanding of the concept of a legal person in contrast to a natural person—a human being and an autonomous citizen—there are good reasons for citizens to be alarmed at the potential for abuse in the construction and application of legal personhood under *Citizens United*.

In *Citizens United v. Federal Election Commission* (2010), by a vote of five to four, the U.S. Supreme Court held that nonprofit corporations, like individuals, had a First Amendment right to engage in political speech. Despite the fact that the decision dealt with the political activities of a nonprofit corporation, the decision applies to any type of for-profit or nonprofit corporation. This holding effectively reversed more than a century of U.S. Supreme Court decisions granting Congress and state legislatures the authority to limit the use of corporate funds to influence the outcome of local, state, and federal elections, and it opened the door for individuals and for-profit and nonprofit corporations to increase their role in influencing the outcome of elections at the local, state, and federal levels. *Citizens United* permits individuals and any for-profit corporation to make unlimited anonymous contributions to "nondisclosing" nonprofit groups established under 501(c)(4) and 501(c)(6) of the federal tax code. *Citizens United*, however, did not end the ban on coordinated campaigning between independent advocacy groups and candidates for federal office, including those running for president of the United States.

Campaign finance scholars trace the effort to control corporate influence on elections to the **Campaign of 1896** in which Ohio governor and Republican nominee William McKinley, whose campaign was directed by influential industrialist

Mark Hanna, raised millions of dollars from corporations to fund a nationwide campaign against populist Democratic nominee William Jennings Bryan. In the **Campaign of 1900**, the Republican Party made effective use of large corporate campaign contributions to support McKinley's reelection. In the Campaign **of 1904**, the Republican Party relied heavily on corporate contributions to help incumbent president Theodore Roosevelt, who had recently ascended to the presidency on the assassination of President McKinley, win election to a second, full term.

After Roosevelt's landslide victory, reports surfaced of the large contributions by corporations to his reelection campaign. In sharp contrast to McKinley, Roosevelt had established a record of opposing the political influence of large corporations. Deeply embarrassed, Roosevelt moved quickly to defuse the growing controversy by proposing legislation banning corporations from directly contributing to federal election campaigns. In 1907, Congress passed the Tillman Act, which prohibited corporations and national banks from making direct campaign contributions to candidates for federal office. Despite the passage of the Tillman Act and other campaign finance laws, corporate contributions continued to find their way into campaigns for federal office through the 1960s. In 1971, Congress passed the Federal Election Campaign Act (FECA). The law put in place strict disclosure requirements for campaign contributions and expenditures. To deal with the lack of transparency in indirect corporate and union contributions to campaigns for federal office, the FECA authorized corporations and unions to establish PACs (political action committees) to make contributions to candidates for federal office and to political parties.

From the mid-1970s forward, both Congress and the Supreme Court addressed the ongoing problem of private corporate influence in political elections, Congress establishing the Federal Election Commission in 1974 and the Supreme Court further defining the law by upholding mandatory disclosure and contribution limits imposed on corporations while also ruling that expenditure limits on individuals and independent advocacy groups were unconstitutional (*Buckley v. Valeo*, 1976). These actions did not alter the long-standing interpretation of the Constitution regarding corporations as not possessing the same First Amendment right to freely engage in political speech, a right guaranteed for all individual citizens; that is, natural persons. In fact, restrictions on corporations, as well as on other organizations such as labor unions, only became tighter in the wake of *Buckley*. Organizations could work around these restrictions (e.g., through the use of "soft money"), but by and large, the concept that corporate persons were different from real persons with respect to free speech and political action remained clear legally and morally. Those tactics that allowed wealthy donors and groups to get around campaign finance constraints were addressed by Congress in 2002 under the Bipartisan Campaign Finance Reform Act (BCRA), which banned soft money contributions to political parties but then raised individual contribution limits. Critics of these restrictions argued that limiting the political speech of independent advocacy groups would have a chilling impact on political discourse. In 2003, the U.S. Supreme Court ruled in *McConnell v. FEC* that the soft money ban did not violate the Constitution.

Then, in 2010, the U.S. Supreme Court in *Citizens United v. FEC* held that nonprofit corporations primarily engaged in political activity had the same rights as individuals to participate in political discourse. In the aftermath of *Citizens United*, a small number of rich individual and corporate donors have become the principal source of a large percentage of campaign contributions funneled through independent advocacy groups, which are now free to accept unlimited contributions in support of a candidate or to oppose the election of a candidate for federal office. This development opened a new discourse about the meaning of corporate personhood and any resemblance between this legal concept and the personhood of autonomous individuals. It was within this context that a Republican nominee for president during the 2012 campaign, Mitt Romney, responding to an angry heckler at a campaign event who loudly challenged Romney's position against raising corporate taxes, stated, "Corporations are people, my friend. . . . Everything corporations earn ultimately goes to people. Where do you think it goes?" Gov. Romney's response in the heat of the moment indicates that he misconstrued what is meant by corporate personhood, for again, the law does not in fact equate corporations with individual persons or view them as "people" in general; but rather, the law only views corporations as legal persons for the sake of the protection of certain rights—primarily property rights— that allow them to operate more freely.

Quite recently the discussion over the nature and extent of corporate personhood has involved issues distinct from political campaign contributions and the "free political speech" of corporations. In *Burwell v. Hobby Lobby* (2014), the Supreme Court affirmed a decision that recognized the religious right of what is defined as a "closely held corporation"; that is, a corporation in which at least half of its shares are owned by four persons or less—one likely to be family-owned. Specifically, the Court held that a closely held company, Hobby Lobby, could claim an exemption from a law to which its owners objected on religious grounds—in this case, provisions in the Patient Affordable Care Act that allowed for female employees to fund contraception under their insurance coverage—provided that there is a "less restrictive means" to allow the relevant services under the ACA to be delivered to the insured. This case dealt directly with the Religious Freedom Restoration Act (1993), an uncontroversial law passed with bipartisan support during the Clinton administration, now interpreted by the Roberts Court to allow owners of a closely held company to object to the provision of contraceptives for their female employees in violation of their private religious values. This is not to say that the corporation itself has a right to freedom of religion in the same way as a natural person—Hobby Lobby does not go to church—but only that a corporation owned by individuals holding specific religious beliefs in conflict with the federal law in question does not have to comply to a mandate against their religious values. In other words, the Hobby Lobby ruling does not assert that a corporate person is equal to a natural person. As the Court explained, "[The text of the Religious Freedom Restoration Act] shows that Congress designed the statute to provide very broad protection for religious liberty and did not intend to put merchants to such a choice. It employed the familiar legal fiction of including corporations within RFRA's definition of 'persons,' but the purpose of extending rights to corporations is to protect the rights of people associated with the corporation, including shareholders, officers, and employees. Protecting the free-exercise rights of closely held corporations thus protects the religious liberty of the humans who own and control them."

Even so, some argue that the Court has established a precedent allowing for broader latitude, and potential abuse, with regard to a corporation's obligations under the law vis-à-vis religious freedom. Sensing this, in her dissent, Associate Justice Ruth Bader Ginsburg wrote, "Suppose an employer's sincerely held religious belief is offended by health coverage of vaccines, or paying the minimum wage or according women equal pay for substantially similar work?" Justice Ginsburg elaborated further, "Would the exemption the Court holds RFRA demands for employers with religiously grounded objections to the use of certain contraceptives extend to employers with religiously grounded objections to blood transfusions (Jehovah's Witnesses); antidepressants (Scientologists); medications derived from pigs, including anesthesia, intravenous fluids, and pills coated with gelatin (certain Muslims, Jews, and Hindus); and vaccinations (Christian Scientists, among others)? According to counsel for Hobby Lobby, 'each one of these cases . . . would have to be evaluated on its own.'"

At the time the ruling was announced, prospective Republican presidential candidates Ted Cruz, Rand Paul, and Bobby Jindal all expressed their support of Hobby Lobby, while Democratic candidate Hillary Clinton voiced her disappointment. Democratic presidential candidate Bernie Sanders is on record as opposing corporate personhood, having proposed in 2011 a constitutional amendment that would prohibit the extension of "the rights of natural persons" to "for-profit corporations, limited liability companies, or other private entities established for business purposes."

Prior to the Hobby Lobby case, the Court ruled that a federal program requiring raisin growers to reserve a portion of their crop for federally managed redistribution is unconstitutional under the Fifth Amendment (*Horne v. Dept. of Agriculture,* 2013), in effect extending rights held by natural persons to artificial persons; furthermore, since the Hobby Lobby case, the Court has more recently ruled that the Fourth Amendment's protections against illegal searches extends to hoteliers, thereby ruling invalid a local ordinance that allowed the police to examine guest registries without a warrant (*Los Angeles v. Patel*, 2015). These cases do not redefine corporations as "people," nor do they establish a principle equating artificial persons with natural persons. However, in terms of corporate personhood, the question remains: To what extent is a fictional person *similar* to a natural person? Fictional, corporate persons certainly must rely on protection under the law and thus possess specific legal rights, such as the right to contract, but how far is this to be extended in comparison to the rights held by individual citizens? To what extent these and similar, related questions will be raised in 2016 remains to be seen, but if 2012 is any indication, the comparison of the legal fiction of a corporate person to a natural person is likely to resurface at some point. We know Sen. Sanders's official position; beyond that, only time will reveal whether or not the issue is still important enough to the candidates to raise, and where they will stand should the discussion be renewed.

Additional Resources

Black's Law Dictionary. Second ed. http://thelawdictionary.org/.

Confessore, Nicholas, Sarah Cohen, and Karen Yourish. "Small Pool of Rich Donors Dominates Election Giving." *New York Times*, August 1, 2015. http://www.nytimes.com/2015/08/02/us/small-pool-of-rich-donors-dominates-election-giving.html. Accessed September 5, 2015.

Epstein, Richard A. "Citizens United v. FEC: The Constitutional Right That Big Corporations Should Have But Do Not Want." *Harvard Journal of Law & Public Policy* 34, no. 2 (2011): 639–61.

Federal Election Commission. "Appendix 4: The Federal Election Campaign Laws: A Short History." http://www.fec.gov/info/appfour.htm. Accessed September 5, 2015.

Liptak, Adam. "Justices, 5-4, Reject Corporate Spending Limit." *New York Times*, January 21, 2010. http://www.nytimes.com/2010/01/22/us/politics/22scotus.html. Accessed September 5, 2015.

McGrath, Leah Goodman. "Dark Money." *Newsweek Global* 63, no. 14 (October 10, 2014): 12–16.

Sprague, Robert, and Mary Ellen Wells. "The Supreme Court as Prometheus: Breathing Life into the Corporate Supercitizen." *American Business Law Journal* 49, no. 3 (2012): 507–56. http://www.law.virginia.edu/html/alumni/uvalawyer/f11/personhood.htm. Accessed September 5, 2015.

CPAC (Conservative Political Action Conference)

The Conservative Political Action Conference, hosted yearly by the American Conservative Union, attracts policy makers, political pundits, political activists, and potential political candidates to the nation's capital for a discussion of the conservative issues of the day. Outside of the Republican National Convention, it is the largest Republican political event in the nation, with attendance at times exceeding ten thousand persons.

Speakers at CPAC often include presidential hopefuls, current and retired Republican officeholders at the state and federal levels, and political pundits such as Rush Limbaugh, Ann Coulter, David Horowitz, and the late Andrew Breitbart. The event also includes a straw poll of presidential hopefuls. Like most straw polls, CPAC isn't terribly predictive; in 2010, only 2,400 attendees cast ballots, and of those, Ron Paul won a plurality (due in large part to the large number of college students in attendance, a group that has tended to give Paul very high levels of support). In 2015, Rand Paul won the straw poll (Jeb Bush came in a distant fifth, behind Scott Walker, Ted Cruz, and Ben Carson). While the straw poll isn't particularly predictive, the event is an important outreach opportunity, and most political analysts believe that Republican candidates who are serious about a presidential run will court their conservative base by attending CPAC.

See also Cattle Call

Additional Resource

American Conservative Union, CPAC Web site. http://www.conservative.org/cpac/. Accessed September 5, 2015.

Culture War

The term "culture war" loosely refers to a clash of worldviews that is often rooted in nonpolitical principles but later spills over into the political arena. The concept of a struggle between conflicting cultures within a single social matrix, or two competing subcultures within a larger, more loosely defined culture, is not a new one. Nor is it one that is exclusively American. Over the last two decades, this notion has increasingly become a topic of public debate.

Historically, one can identify antagonistic value sets throughout American history. In the nineteenth century, for example, there existed a deep conflict between Protestant and Catholic worldviews that manifested in political ways. Additionally, a geographically fixed culture conflict existed between northern and southern states during the decades prior to the Civil War, a conflict that was rooted in the morality and the economic necessity of slavery.

In the latter part of the nineteenth century and into the twentieth century, there were several axes of polarization in American politics. Differences emerged between conservative and progressive worldviews (evident in both major political parties), and there were also deep disagreements on the nature of American society as a whole and the moral values upon which it rested. The temperance movement, for example, gained enough momentum to obtain an amendment to the Constitution prohibiting the production and consumption of alcohol. Even though the Prohibition Party never made any significant electoral gains, in the end, the prohibition movement achieved its goal (at least for a time). Prohibition was often used as a measure of a candidate's moral values, bringing private morality into the political arena.

By the 1920s, American society developed fissures over more weighty measures than personal habits. In particular, the tensions between science and faith (epitomized in the notorious Scopes "Monkey Trial"), new public attitudes toward the role of women in society that clashed with long-standing traditions, new discussions regarding race, and the continuation of the Protestant-Catholic divide (albeit in a more subdued manner than the virulent anti-Catholicism of the Know-Nothing movement) all became sources of social and political controversy. Some would argue that the Red Scares of the early 1920s and the 1950s were by-products of deeper divisions in American society, in particular concerns about immigrants and suspicions about intellectuals. Finally, the cultural clash that led to the social unrest of the 1960s and early 1970s may represent the kind of cultural struggle meant by the term "culture war." Many of the social tensions that influenced the second half of the twentieth century emanated from the 1960s, particularly the conflict between traditional values, which emphasized community and responsibility, and the 1960s counterculture movement, which emphasized individuality and freedom (itself the heir to the beat culture of the 1950s).

In contemporary politics, the notion of a culture war is most closely associated with events of the early 1990s and the rise of the **Moral Majority** in the 1970s and 1980s. The modern culture war involves a politically active community of religious fundamentalism and its connections to conservative political leaders and policies. This discussion is framed in terms of a clash between Judeo-Christian values and "secular humanism." At the Republican convention in the **Campaign of 1984**, Jeanne Kirkpatrick claimed that American liberals were more inclined to attack their own country and its policies than they were to criticize problems in other countries. Kirkpatrick observed, "When Marxist dictators shoot their way into power in Central America, the San Francisco Democrats don't blame the guerrillas and their Soviet allies. They blame United States policies of 100 years ago. But then they always blame America first." Kirkpatrick's accusation draws attention to the deep ideological antagonisms that stem from these disparate worldviews.

In 1998, Allan Bloom's *Closing of the American Mind* sounded the alarm about the United States' degenerating culture and the deeply flawed, self-absorbed, amoral, and overly cynical system of higher education accelerating this social decay. University of Virginia sociologist James Davison Hunter published his now-famous exposition, *Culture Wars*, in 1992. Hunter traced the historical antecedents of the current cultural conflict and identified the issues that have contributed to these divisions, such as disagreements about the morality and necessity of abortion, the influence of feminism in contemporary culture, gay rights (specifically the debate over gay marriage), the value of patriotism, universal health care, entitlement programs, school prayer, evolution (and how evolution is taught in public schools), environmentalism (particularly debates over global warming), gun rights, the culture of "academia," "political correctness," and the merits of "multiculturalism."

In presidential politics, the phrase "culture war" is derived from a speech delivered at the GOP convention during the **Campaign of 1992**. There, presidential candidate and conservative pundit Patrick Buchanan intoned, "There is a religious war going on in our country for the soul of America. It is a cultural war, as critical to the kind of nation we will one day be as was the Cold War itself. And in that struggle for the soul of America, Clinton and Clinton are on the other side, and George Bush is on our side. And so, we have to come home, and stand beside him." Even though Buchanan's campaign to dislodge President Bush, a political moderate, was not successful, his *Kulturkampf* jeremiad seeped into the GOP platform:

> The culture of our Nation has traditionally supported those pillars on which civilized society is built: personal responsibility, morality, and the family. Today, however, these pillars are under assault. Elements within the media, the entertainment industry, academia, and the Democrat Party are waging a guerrilla war against American values. They deny personal responsibility, disparage traditional morality, denigrate religion, and promote hostility toward the family's way of life. Children, the members of our society most vulnerable to cultural influences, are barraged with violence and promiscuity, encouraging reckless and irresponsible behavior. This undermines the authority of parents, the ones most responsible for passing on to their offspring a sense of right and wrong. The lesson our Party draws is important—that all of us, individuals and corporations alike, have a responsibility to reflect the values we expect our fellow citizens to exhibit. And if children grow to adulthood reflecting not the values of their parents but the amorality with which they are bombarded, those who send such messages cannot duck culpability.

Buchanan's declaration and the related platform plank, in hindsight, appear to be the culmination of cultural tensions that had been brewing for at least a generation, but at the time they were viewed by conservative Republicans as a new and forceful voice against the decadence of the counterculture. Democrats, on the other hand, viewed this declaration of war as nothing less than a call for a new kind of social repression. Much of political dialogue since Buchanan's definitive moment has been framed in terms of a culture clash. Democrats and Republicans not only represent different ideological positions, but now, rightly or wrongly, they are seen as the political extensions of conflicting cultural values.

While the **Campaign of 2000** was less influenced by the "culture war" mood, the **Campaign of 2004** and especially the **Campaign of 2008** were infused with culture-clash symbolism and rhetoric, a trend that intensified in the Campaign of 2012. In addition to Bill and Hillary Clinton, President Obama in particular has been singled out by his more strident critics as harboring un-American and, in some cases, anti-American values. During the **Campaign of 2008**, Republicans criticized Obama's association with figures on the radical left, and some of his more vocal critics argued that his overall agenda is to reshape the United States on the model of "European-style socialism." (Similar criticisms were made by opponents of George W. Bush, as it has become common in American politics to depict one's enemy as Hitler, or to claim a similarity to the Nazis or totalitarians generally.)

Undercurrents of these tensions stewed beneath the campaign rhetoric and tactics of the 2012 presidential campaign, occasionally rising to the surface. Some of President Obama's critics sustained their indictment of his credentials as an American, not only the birther crackpots but also those critics who continued their condemnation of the president's approach to economic issues, deeming them contrary to the free-market principles of American society and suggesting that the president's vision of American culture and society were somehow corrupted by ideas alien to the principles and values upon which the country was established. In a word, according to some voters on the oppositional right, the president was the standard-bearer of a weird hybrid of European socialism, anti-colonialist self-loathing, and globalist design. From the other direction, the Republican nominee, former Massachusetts governor Mitt Romney, was persistently depicted as an aloof plutocrat, too patrician to connect to the common man, too patriarchal to recognize marginalized voices, and too comfortably ensconced in his privilege to appreciate the egalitarian aspirations of the American promise. Surprisingly, the governor's Mormon faith, which many expected could have become an issue for certain elements in the electorate (e.g., evangelical Protestants), proved to be of little concern. With former speaker of the house Newt Gingrich in the race for the GOP nomination, many anticipated that he would forge ahead as a spokesman for one side of the culture war, given his overall track record in that regard. It was Mr. Gingrich, after all, who was noted for provocative statements redolent with "culture war" polemic, statements such as a 2008 remark that the country was threatened by "a gay and secular fascism" seeking "to impose its will on the rest of us," or a 2010 indictment of President Obama for using racially charged tactics to lure Republican Hispanic Americans to the Democratic Party, or saying that poor children do not possess a work ethic and that President Obama is an effective "food stamp president." However, at least for a short time during the first quarter of 2012, the most prominent "culture warrior" among the field of candidates was Pennsylvania senator Rick Santorum, a vocal opponent of same-sex marriage and publicly funded contraception. During the early phase of his campaign for the nomination, Sen. Santorum, remarking on the "dangers of contraception in this country," explained his position that artificial birth control permitted "license to do things in a sexual realm that are counter to how things are supposed to be." For the senator, sexuality is grounded in marriage, and marriage is about procreation and the responsible rearing of children. Abortion, for any reason, the senator affirmed, is an assault on the sanctity of life. Culture warriors on the other side of these controversies were keen to exploit the ammunition handed to them by the senator; not only was he charged with the promotion of excessive public control over personal affairs, but he was also accused of intolerance and even bigotry, and his family was mocked for the manner in which they had grieved for the death of a newborn child.

Inflammatory statements in the 2015–2016 campaign season continue to reveal cultural divisions: Donald Trump's blunt, irresponsible generalizations about the character of undocumented immigrants, his immature attitudes toward women, his position regarding possible restrictions unqualifiedly imposed against Syrian refugees, his public, stereotyped suspicion of Muslims, and his outrageous mockery of the disabled; Bernie Sanders's simplistic diatribes against the rich; Carly Fiorina's strident charges against Planned Parenthood; Ben Carson's random and unsubstantiated claim that a Muslim presidency would conflict with the principles of the U.S. Constitution; and Jeb Bush's confusing declaration against "a multicultural society" all indicate that the "culture war" divisions are still tangible fissures within the topography of the nation's social landscape, continuing to influence the track of American political development.

Activists on both sides of the cultural divide trot out their particular varieties of history to vindicate their ideological positions, and not surprisingly, each side finds a version of history suited to its beliefs. This is perhaps the true battleground for the culture warrior, if indeed the culture war exists. (Many political scientists argue that it does not.) While the use of history for ideological purposes is not new in American politics, the current conflict is notable for its intensity, its scope, and its sense of urgency. The parties and their supporters are more polarized than they have been for generations. Throughout much of American political history, an underlying sense of a commonly understood narrative abided and was endorsed (to some degree) by the mainstream parties. But in recent decades, the meaning of American history itself seems to have become a topic of debate, with a substantial gulf erupting between these competing ideological camps. Historically, once elections were over, the more aggressive and divisive rhetoric that had emerged during the campaign would usually recede, and political leaders could negotiate compromise solutions to the problems of the day. In recent years, that rhetorical storm does not appear to be calmed after Election Day. And compromise between the parties seems to be increasingly, and to the frustration of the American public, a thing of the past.

See also Campaign of 2012; Values Voters

Additional Resources

Bloom, Allan. *The Closing of the American Mind.* New York: Simon & Schuster, 1988.

Fiorina, Morris P., Samuel J. Abrams, and Jeremy C. Pope. *Culture War? The Myth of a Polarized America.* New York: Longman, 2005.

Hartman, Andrew. *A War for the Soul of America: A History of the Culture Wars.* Chicago: University of Chicago Press, 2015.

Hunter, James Davison. *Culture Wars: The Struggle to Control the Family, Art, Education, Law and Politics in America.* New York: Basic Books, 1992.

Kreeft, Peter. *How to Win the Culture War: A Christian Battle Plan for Society.* Madison, WI: IVP Press.

Levine, Lawrence W. *The Opening of the American Mind.* Boston: Beacon Press, 1997.

Nash, Gary B., Charlotte Antoinette Crabtree, and Ross E. Dunn. *History on Trial: Culture Wars and the Teaching of the Past.* New York: Vintage Books, 2000.

"Daisy Girl" Campaign Ad (1964)

Though Democratic and Republican presidential candidates first began using television as a medium for broadcasting campaign ads in the **Campaign of 1952**, such ads remained relatively tame (although not always positively themed). This situation changed with the **Campaign of 1964.** That year, the Democratic Party nominated President Lyndon Johnson, who had assumed the presidency after the assassination of President John Kennedy. Somewhat surprisingly, conservative Arizona senator Barry Goldwater captured the Republican Party nomination. Prior to becoming the nominee, Goldwater had made a number of controversial statements regarding civil rights and the use of military force overseas. Despite the fact that few political observers believed that Goldwater had a realistic chance of defeating the popular Johnson, the Johnson campaign took the Goldwater challenge quite seriously.

Instead of focusing on the accomplishments of the Johnson administration, such as the passage of the Civil Rights Act of 1964 and the "war on poverty," the Johnson campaign decided to launch an unprecedented negative assault against Goldwater, depicting him as dangerous and volatile. The Johnson campaign broadcast numerous radio and television ads painting Goldwater as an extremist who was willing to engage in atomic brinkmanship. With the October 1962 Cuban Missile Crisis still fresh in the minds of tens of millions of Americans, the Johnson campaign's attack reached its highest pitch with the television broadcast of the "Daisy Girl" ad, viewed by many as the first modern political attack advertisement.

The ad begins with a small girl at play in a field of flowers, plucking petals from daisies and innocently counting aloud as they fall. Her voice fades, and a disembodied voice rises with the ominous cadence of a rocket launch countdown. Suddenly, the screen fills with the nightmarish mushroom cloud of an exploding atomic bomb, obliterating the little girl and her surroundings. As the atomic death cloud billows, the grave voice of Lyndon Johnson darkly warns, "These are the stakes: to make a world in which all of God's children can live or to go into the dark. We must love each other or we must die." Concluding the ad, the announcer urges the audience to "vote for President Johnson on November 3. *The Stakes Are Too High for You to Stay Home.*" Goldwater's name is never mentioned, and his image is never shown. Nevertheless, the ad outraged the Goldwater campaign and received harsh criticism from editorial writers. As a result, the Johnson campaign broadcast the ad only once, during an episode of NBC's *Monday Night at the Movies* when the film *David and Bathsheba* was being broadcast. The original viewing audience was approximately fifty million, for which the Johnson campaign paid $25,000.

While the audience for the original airing was sizable, the single showing would have otherwise limited its reach. However, the extensive media coverage of the ad controversy played into the hands of the Johnson campaign by drawing the ad to the attention of voters who had not seen it when it originally aired. And the subsequent media analysis of the ad drew attention to Goldwater's more bellicose posture regarding the permissible use of nuclear weapons, which included Goldwater's refusal to rule out the use of tactical nuclear weapons in Vietnam. The ad remains one of the most widely viewed campaign ads in American history, with each new generation of voters experiencing it anew at some point in their lifetime. It has also been copied (in varying degrees) by numerous candidates over the years; the most recent is Republican contender Mike Huckabee, who shows his own little girl plucking petals from a flower as he attempts to portray the threat posed by the nuclear deal that the Obama administration is negotiating with Iran.

See also Negative Campaigning

Additional Resources

Faber, Harold. *The Road to the White House: The Story of the 1964 Election.* New York: McGraw Hill, 1965.

Geer, John. *In Defense of Negativity: Attack Ads in Presidential Campaigns.* Chicago: University of Chicago Press, 2008.

Jamieson, Kathleen Hall. *Packaging the Presidency: A History and Criticism of Presidential Campaign Advertising*. New York: Oxford University Press, 1984.

Killough, Ashley. "Lyndon Johnson's 'Daisy' Ad, Which Changed the World of Politics, Turns 50." *CNN*, September 8, 2014. http://www.cnn.com/2014/09/07/politics/daisy-ad-turns-50/. Accessed September 5, 2015.

Mann, Robert. *Daisy Petals and Mushroom Clouds: LBJ, Barry Goldwater, and the Ad That Changed American Politics*. Baton Rouge: Louisiana State University Press, 2011.

Ross, Janell. "LBJ's 'Daisy': An Ad So Effective It Just Had to Be Copied—A Lot." *Washington Post*, July 12, 2015. http://www.washingtonpost.com/news/the-fix/wp/2015/07/12/lbjs-daisy-and-ad-so-effective-it-just-had-to-be-copied-a-lot-video/. Accessed September 5, 2015.

White, Theodore. *The Making of the President, 1964*. New York: Atheneum Publishers, 1965.

Dark Money

This term is used to refer to spending by **independent advocacy groups** on federal (and, increasingly, state and local) elections. In particular, the term references money that is contributed to those groups by anonymous sources—which occurs when those groups claim nonprofit status as social welfare groups instead of political organizations—501(c)(4) groups—or when some other aspect of the contribution process enables donors to mask their identity (such as contributing under the guise of a limited liability corporation or other shell corporation, or as another nonprofit whose members are not disclosed).

According to Trevor Potter (former chair of the Federal Election Commission) and Bryson Morgan, in the **Campaign of 2004**, after the passage of the Bipartisan Campaign Act of 2002 (McCain-Feingold), 96.5 percent of funding sources were fully disclosed. In the subsequent midterm, that number had only budged by a couple of percentage points. By the **Campaign of 2012**, $1.03 billion (approximately) was spent by outside groups on campaign-related activities. Of that, it has been estimated that more than 40 percent of those funds involved undisclosed sources. The amount of undisclosed spending in the **Campaign in 2016** is expected to climb even higher for a variety of reasons, including early attempts by candidates (Jeb Bush in particular) to raise funds outside of traditional candidate committees in order to facilitate unlimited (and perhaps undisclosed) donations, and the lack of FEC and IRS enforcement of existing campaign finance regulations and tax laws that would otherwise serve to limit such contributions.

While critics of *Citizens United* have argued that the Supreme Court's decision to permit independent advocacy groups to engage in unlimited spending (as long as it is not coordinated with a political party or candidate), the Court has, in fact, always upheld the principle of disclosure. In *Citizens United*, Justice Kennedy even argued that rational, informed citizens could decide for themselves how to evaluate the speech of outside groups—a presumption based on the notion that citizens would know the identities of the groups engaging in the outside spending and who their donors were. Kennedy's assumptions were quickly upended as independent advocacy groups sought out loopholes in the tax code that permitted them to keep their funding sources secret from the public.

The portions of the tax code being used to conceal donors' identities were designed by Congress for social welfare and educational groups, and the IRS prohibits their use by entities whose primary activity is electioneering. (The language of the original 1954 tax code says that the organizations must operate exclusively for social welfare purposes. A 1959 IRS regulation interpreting this law suggests that organizations need only operate primarily for social welfare purposes. This later interpretation has created the loophole.) However, this restriction is rarely enforced. Beginning in 2012, under pressure to do something to stem the tide of dark money in American politics, the IRS began to more carefully scrutinize groups claiming 501(c)(4) status—a process that conservatives, and Tea Party groups in particular, claim targeted them unfairly. In fact, the overwhelming majority of political groups claiming to be social welfare nonprofits have, in fact, been conservative groups, and during this time, many of the newly formed Tea Party organizations were organizing themselves in this fashion as well. However, there is evidence that the IRS conducted searches for Tea Party groups in particular, as part of an investigation of possible abuses of the tax code, fueling concerns that the organization had underlying partisan motives. The IRS actions provoked a backlash, particularly among Republicans, who held congressional hearings in 2013 to determine whether the IRS was engaging in partisan politics. Under pressure to limit their scrutiny of 501(c)(4) groups, the IRS opted for a new tactic: to attempt to protect the integrity of the tax code by educating groups about its meaning, and to signal its intent to uniformly enforce the code at some future date.

In the spring of 2014, the IRS announced new rules governing the conduct of 501(c)(4) groups in order to provide clearer guidelines for what types of political activities such groups could engage in without losing their tax exempt (and nondisclosure) status, including prohibitions on direct and indirect participation or intervention in political campaigns on behalf of or in opposition to a candidate for public office and direct or indirect candidate activity. The new rules were opposed by a variety of conservative and liberal advocacy groups, as well as the American Civil Liberties Union. Under political pressure to leave the current regime intact, the IRS declared in May 2015 that it was suspending the rules for the **Campaign of 2016** and would be considering additional revisions after further public input.

The Campaign of 2016 is marked by an explosion of dark money contributions and election-related spending by dark money groups.

See also Campaign Finance Reform; 501(c) Group; 527 Group

Additional Resources

Potter, Trevor, and Bryson B. Morgan. "The History of Undisclosed Spending in U.S. Elections and How 2012 Became the Dark Money Election." *Notre Dame Journal of Law, Ethics, and Public Policy* 27, no. 2 (2013): 383–479.

Smith, Melissa M., and Larry Powell. *Dark Money, Super PACs, and the 2012 Election.* New York: Lexington Books, 2014.

"Democrat in Name Only" (DINO). *See* RINO

DINO. *See* RINO

Dirty Tricks. *See* Negative Campaigning

Drill, Baby, Drill! *See* Energy Issue

Early Voting

Early voting, also called in-person absentee voting, occurs when a state law permits citizens to vote prior to Election Day. In some cases, ballots are cast at satellite polling locations during the week, and in many instances, locations are open on Saturdays as well. While all states offer some form of absentee voting, only thirty-three states permit early voting. The start time for the early voting process varies across states as well. In some states, early voting begins the weekend prior to the election, and in others, it may begin forty-five days prior to the election. States vary in how many days they make available for early voting, how many hours they make available for the process, and whether they permit early voting on evenings or weekends.

As is the case with absentee voting, some states offer no-excuse early voting, where registered voters may cast a ballot early for any reason, while other states limit those who are eligible to vote early. In the **Campaign of 2008**, half a dozen states permitted citizens to cast their ballots prior to the first presidential debate. In other states, early voting took place fifteen to twenty-six days prior to Election Day. The practice of casting a ballot prior to Election Day, which was quite rare prior to the **Campaign of 2000**, has been on the rise. In the **Campaign of 2004**, just under 20 percent of all ballots were cast prior to Election Day. George Mason University voting specialist Michael McDonald calculated that 25.7 percent of all ballots cast in the 2008 presidential election were early, either in person or by absentee ballot. Others claim that this figure is even higher. Early and absentee voting changes election dynamics, placing greater emphasis on earlier events and limiting the effects of events that happen closer to Election Day. This also serves to shorten the length of the campaign season itself, giving candidates less time to communicate their message to voters.

In the **Campaign of 2012**, for the first time in decades, the trend in early voting has been in the direction of reversal. According to the Brennan Center for Justice at New York University, five states scaled back the ability to vote prior to Election Day, most notably in the area of early voting. In the **Campaign of 2016**, voters in additional states will find that their opportunity to cast a ballot prior to Election Day is more limited. North Carolina, for example, reduced seventeen days of early voting to ten. In the aftermath of the 2012 election, Ohio cut their Sunday early voting, which was widely used by African American churches for voter mobilization efforts referred to as "Souls to the Polls" drives. Ohio also eliminated its "Golden Week," a period where registration and early voting overlapped, enabling citizens to register and vote simultaneously prior to Election Day. Voting after 5:00 PM on weekdays was eliminated as well. The American Civil Liberties Union sued, and Ohio reached a settlement with the ACLU to restore evening voting hours and Sunday voting; Golden Week, however, was not restored. Georgia appears poised to follow suit; in 2008, it had offered forty-five days of early voting, but by 2011, it had pared this down to twenty-one. The legislature is considering further reducing the number of early voting days to twelve. These examples illustrate the overall pattern of change at the state level between 2008 and 2012; states continued to offer early voting, but the availability of this option was often dramatically limited after the 2008 election.

See also Voting Reform Issue

Additional Resources

Diemer, Tom. "Election Day Has Already Come in Some Early-Voting States." *Politics Daily*, posted September 22, 2010.

Early Voting Information Center, Reed College. http://www.earlyvoting.net/blog. Accessed October 13, 2015.

McDonald, Michael. "2008 Early Voting Statistics." United States Elections Project, George Mason University. http://elections.gmu.edu/early_vote_2008.html. Accessed October 13, 2015.

National Conference of State Legislatures. "Absentee and Early Voting." February 11, 2015. http://www.ncsl.org/research/elections-and-campaigns/absentee-and-early-voting .aspx#early. Accessed October 13, 2015.

Phillips, Michael M. "Parties Seek Edge from Early Voters." *Wall Street Journal*, September 22, 2010, online edition.

Sullivan, Amy. "Virginia Sounds the Starting Gun for Early Voting." *Time*, September 19, 2008.

Weiser, Wendy R., and Lawrence Norden. "Voting Law Changes in 2012." Brennan Center for Justice, NYU School of Law. October 3, 2011. http://www.brennancenter.org/content /resource/voting_law_changes_in_2012/. Accessed October 13, 2015.

Earmark

"Earmark" is another term for pork-barrel project. The term refers to funds in the federal budget allocated for projects in a legislator's home district, presumably for the primary purpose of advantaging the legislator's constituency, and thus the legislator's own reelection chances. Senator John McCain campaigned against the practice of earmarking during his run for the White House in the **Campaign of 2008**; however, his running mate Sarah Palin's efforts to secure federal funds for the notorious "Bridge to Nowhere" damaged his credibility on this front.

Some members of Congress, such as Senator Robert Byrd of West Virginia and Senator Alphonse D'Amato (nicknamed "Senator Pothole") of New York, were infamous for their ability to direct federal monies to their districts, and they trumpeted such projects in their reelection bids.

Public opinion data suggests that voters are not particularly troubled by earmarks, as long as those earmarks go to benefit their own districts. According to a Pew Research/National Journal poll conducted during the 2010 midterms, 53 percent of citizens overall (and 47% of Republicans and 66% of Democrats) said that they would be more likely to vote for legislators who have a record of directing federal funds to their home districts. Only 12 percent of respondents (17% of Republicans and 6% of Democrats) said that they were less likely to vote for a candidate who had used earmarks to benefit their district. The remaining citizens were indifferent.

Additional Resources

"Earmarks Could Help Candidates in Midterms; Palin and Tea Party Connections Could Hurt." Pew Center for People and the Press, August 2, 2010. http://people-press.org /report/642/. Accessed September 29, 2015.

Frisch, Scott A. *The Politics of Pork: A Study of Congressional Appropriations Earmarks (Financial Sector of the American Economy)*. Lanham, MD: Routledge Press, 1998.

Frisch, Scott A., and Sean Q. Kelly. *Cheese Factories on the Moon: Why Earmarks Are Good for American Democracy*. St. Paul, MN: Paradigm Publishers, 2011.

Earned Media

The terms "earned media" and "free media" refer to the ability of a political campaign to generate media coverage of its candidate or campaign issues without having to pay for it. Over time, the rising cost of television advertising and the **frontloading** of the presidential campaign season have forced political campaigns to devote large percentages of their campaign budgets to the purchase of airtime. This has made it important for campaigns to structure events that elicit favorable press coverage without the need to purchase airtime.

The **retail politics** practiced during the early days of the primary season affords candidates countless opportunities to be seen interacting directly with regular people, which is undoubtedly why this campaign style has not totally died out over time. Candidates also schedule press conferences, release provocative **talking points** or tweets, hold town hall meeting events, go on whistle-stop campaign tours by train or bus, and participate in rallies and other constructed events to draw media coverage. Campaign events are often scheduled at schools, factories, military bases, or retirement centers to generate photo opportunities that will portray candidates in a favorable light. The rise of the **twenty-four-hour news cycle** has virtually guaranteed candidates some amount of coverage for any event that their campaigns stage. And the advent of newer technology such as the Internet has greatly expanded opportunities for campaigns to generate coverage for their candidates.

In the **Campaign of 2016**, GOP hopeful Donald Trump became notorious for his ability to generate earned media coverage, making a seemingly endless series of controversial statements, calling out his political opponents for perceived inadequacies, and accusing the press of incompetence and bias in their coverage of him, often in late-night tweets to his many followers. These manufactured controversies served the purpose of keeping him continuously in the media limelight during the **invisible primary**, without Trump having to spend campaign funds or his personal wealth in exchange for the coverage. As a consequence, Trump performed well in the polls, as he literally crowded the other candidates off of the front page and out of the airwaves.

See also Soft News

Additional Resources

Patlak, Dan. "How to Get on the Radio: A Big Earned Media Campaign Opportunity." *Campaign and Elections*, June 2001, p. 62.

Zavattro, Staci M. "Brand Obama: The Implications of the Branded President." *Administrative Theory and Praxis* 32, no. 1 (2010): 123–129.

Economic Inequality Issue

Major parties in the United States have always claimed that their political agenda was the surest remedy for redressing income imbalances. This abiding confidence has historically been fueled by numerous factors, most notably the United States' seemingly inexhaustible abundance of natural resources, unflappable Yankee ingenuity, unique good fortune, promotion of entrepreneurial sensibilities, and an ingrained "Protestant work ethic." American culture has always held fast, even in the bleakest of times, to the notion that anyone can secure an easy and affluent life by working hard enough or by having the right kind of luck.

As the United States entered the world stage as an industrial giant in the latter nineteenth and early twentieth centuries, politicians and public officials became increasingly concerned with addressing the increasing economic disparities between the spectacularly wealthy and the miserably impoverished. These disparities, in the midst of a burgeoning economy and incalculable abundance, inspired the progressive movement. During this time period, both the Democratic and Republican parties possessed progressive wings, and these groups, along with the populist third parties of the era, pushed for major economic reforms such as safer working conditions in factories, the creation of public hospitals, wage reform, limits on child labor, an eight-hour workday, and a progressive federal income tax. With the economic boom of the 1920s, the possibility of eliminating poverty seemed well within reach.

However, the global depression in the 1930s shattered these illusions—that is, until advocates for the poor and vulnerable found their voice in the presidency of Democrat Franklin Delano Roosevelt. Numbering among his famous "four freedoms" the freedom from want, Roosevelt affirmed the basic American principle that poverty could and should, by right, be eradicated from society. Roosevelt developed an "economic bill of rights" that endorsed a right to prosperity, and in so doing, he advanced the idea that every citizen was entitled to live a life free from the miseries of poverty. FDR's New Deal policies shaped the manner in which the federal government addressed poverty for generations to come. By instituting a range of entitlement programs and social safety nets—most notably the Social Security program—the Roosevelt administration transformed the role of the federal government in the economic sphere and changed attitudes, in both parties, about the government's responsibility for dealing with the indigent and the economically disadvantaged. These attitudes pervaded the administrations of Harry Truman, Dwight Eisenhower (although a Republican, he embraced the tenets of the New Deal, much to the chagrin of his more conservative colleagues), John Kennedy, and particularly Lyndon Johnson.

By the advent of the **Campaign of 1964**, urban and rural poverty had become major political issues. "White flight" from major urban centers had left inner cities with extremely high levels of poverty, rising crime rates, substandard housing, hunger, and a host of other social problems. Rural areas were facing similar crises. Democratic incumbent Lyndon Johnson defeated Republican nominee Barry Goldwater in a landslide, giving Johnson the votes he need to push his Great Society program through Congress. Johnson's efforts involved an unprecedented expansion of antipoverty programs, including Medicaid, food stamps, the National School Lunch Act, the Child Nutrition Act, and the Housing and Urban Development Act—in all, the largest package of antipoverty reforms since Roosevelt's New Deal three decades earlier. Congress also indexed the Social Security program to inflation and appropriated funds to aid local school systems with high numbers of students from poor families. While the Johnson administration found it difficult to deliver both the guns it needed for the war in Vietnam and the butter to supply the needy, LBJ's "war on poverty" defined his domestic agenda and continued to influence American public policy well into the 1970s. Republican president Richard Nixon famously flirted with a negative income tax as a means of reducing poverty during this era, and his administration embarked on a revenue-sharing program to provide federal funds for improvements in living standards in the nation's inner cities.

However, the economically depressed latter years of the 1970s and into the early 1980s contributed to growing discontent with social welfare programs. Sharp lines formed separating the major political parties regarding problems associated with poverty and income inequality across the United States. The Reagan administration promoted an essentially laissez-faire economic policy in which the benefits given to corporations and investors would "trickle down" to middle- and working-class Americans, ultimately raising living standards for all. Reagan portrayed recipients of government aid as "welfare queens" who would rather live off of the public dole than find a paying job. Reagan's critics attacked what they derisively termed "trickle-down economics" as the former failed policies of the Gilded Age with a new label. Reagan's opponents also expressed concerns about the lack of compassion in leaving the fate of the poor to the caprices of the market. Nonetheless, even though "Reaganomics" never achieved complete implementation (Reagan himself was less ideological on these positions than both his supporters and critics had anticipated), the electoral success of Reagan and his successor, George H. W. Bush (who had previously criticized trickle-down theories as "voodoo economics"), forced Democrats to modify their approach to meliorist programs.

President Clinton typified the New Democrat through his attempt to develop a "third way" that attempted to incorporate, with mixed results, a greater sensitivity to unfettered, dynamic markets without completely abandoning social programs supportive of the poor. Clinton's failed health care reforms and alterations in the welfare system are representative of this shift in attitudes among Democrats, a shift that to many analysts occurred in response to the Reagan Revolution, ostensibly "pulling the country to the right" and reopening questions about entitlement programs that had previously been regarded as closed. Clinton's dismantling of Aid to Families with Dependent Children typified the new approach to social programs, and one that previous Democrats, from FDR through Carter, would have found unacceptable. But the Clinton administration enjoyed an economic boom; the 1990s was probably the most prosperous decade since the 1950s and one of the more prosperous decades in history. Poverty was certainly not overcome, but the spirit of the nineties was one of considerable optimism regarding the future of the American economy.

Thus, the **Campaign of 2000** was not shaped by the kind of concerns that existed in the **Campaign of 1992** when Bill Clinton, reminding his fellow candidates that "It's the Economy, Stupid," defeated an incumbent president during an economic downturn. Democratic nominee Al Gore and Republican nominee George W. Bush were not as focused on the issue of poverty and economic uncertainty that fixed the attention of the candidates in 1992. The closest either candidate came to discussing issues of income inequality was in their competing plans to remedy the Social Security program, and in their competition to offer prescription drug benefits to elderly Medicare recipients (neither of which was a means-tested program). Bush, in fact, sought to distance himself from the harsher rhetoric associated with the Reagan years by using a new slogan, "compassionate conservatism."

The **Campaign of 2004** occurred at the height of the housing bubble and in the midst of two wars. The country had been enjoying a jobless recovery; while many Americans were not personally better off (and too many were deeply in debt), most were unconcerned about the lurking problems underlying the economy and focused more on the threat of terrorism. The foreclosure crisis, the stock market crash, a spate of bank failures, and the advent of the Great Recession during the **Campaign of 2008** were stark reminders to many voters that bankruptcy and poverty, and all of the miseries that attend them (such as the loss of housing and medical care), remained tangible possibilities. When more Americans feared becoming members of the lower class, the concerns of the lower class suddenly became more salient and pressing. Americans voted en masse to remove the incumbent Republican Party from power.

However, by the **Campaign of 2012**, while the economy had undergone some improvement, however gradual, for many Americans things remained very much as they were in 2008. Many Americans were jobless, even while many corporations enjoyed profitability. Many still struggled to pay their bills, while the media broadcast news stories about corporations that paid no federal taxes and even collected millions, or billions, of dollars in government subsidies. Banks and investment firms received federal bailout funds, while small business owners and homeowners found themselves filing for bankruptcy and many were still in danger of losing their homes. The poor remained poor, and for the first time in a very long time, the middle class worried about joining their ranks. The 2010 census estimated that one in seven Americans was at or below the poverty line, with Latinos and African Americans disproportionately represented in the ranks of the underprivileged. Incumbent president Barack Obama's approach to reelection was to focus on those who were struggling to get by, and to convince them that if reelected, he'd use the resources and institutions of government to help them, including mortgage reform, extension of unemployment benefits and programs for the poor, expansion of college assistance for the poor and middle class, programs for veterans, expansion of health care benefits, and job creation (through the stimulus bill and government assistance for the private sector). Republicans countered that such programs were too costly, particularly given the burgeoning federal debt. Presidential candidate Mitt Romney famously explained in a CNN interview in the early days of the primary season that he was not concerned about the very poor, because they had a social safety net to protect them (he also noted that he was not concerned about the very rich). Newt Gingrich called Obama "the food stamp president" and suggested that federal labor laws be revised so that children of poor families could be put to work in their neighborhood schools as janitors so they could learn an appropriate work ethic. As the rhetoric indicates, presidential candidates are not very accustomed to seeking the votes of the poor, and often they lack basic information about the lifestyles of the poor in America.

This rhetoric changed in the **Campaign of 2016**. The Republican Party placed newfound emphasis on income inequality, with candidates sounding sympathetic to working-class voters. Even so, Republican aspirants persistently and uniformly embraced a flat income tax, a position incompatible with those working-class sympathies. Democratic candidates crusaded against the excesses of big business and an unfair tax code that enables hedge fund managers to pay a fraction of the rate that most workers were required to pay, despite earning millions. They have also renewed their commitment to raising the minimum wage.

Yet many party activists, particularly among the ranks of the Republicans, are demanding major cuts in domestic programs, including those that benefit the poor and people who are about to slip through the cracks. States, strapped for cash, have moved to limit unemployment benefits and Medicaid eligibility, despite the rising numbers of citizens in their states who rely on these programs as their economic circumstances become more precarious. Voters will be required to assess how much they value government assistance for the needy, and the extent to which they are willing to pay for it (in terms of higher taxes for the wealthy, higher taxes for corporations, higher deficits, or some combination of the above).

And as the poor remain, the American promise remains, a promise that indeed sustains the hope that a better life awaits for all, and that, as the political theorist John Rawls once conjectured, those who are the least advantaged will nonetheless still benefit from the just, fair society that beckons us onward.

See also Keynesian Economics; Prosperity Issue

Additional Resources

Blau, Joel, with Mimi Abramovitz. *The Dynamics of Social Welfare Policy.* New York: Oxford University Press, 2000.

Burton, C. Emory. *The Poverty Debate: Politics and the Poor in America.* Westport, CT: Greenwood Press, 1992.

Freedland, Tom, and John Bridgeland. "A New Study on the Political Media: Poverty Is Getting More Coverage." Spotlight on Poverty, 2008. http://spotlightonpoverty.org /spotlight-exclusives/a-new-study-on-the-political-media-by-tom-freedman-and-john -bridgeland/.

Greenwald, Glenn. "Barack Obama Is Gutting the Core Principles of the Democratic Party." *Guardian*, July 27, 2011.

Harrington, Michael. *The Other America: Poverty in the United States.* New York: Macmillan, 1963.

Hofstadter, Richard. *Social Darwinism in American Thought.* Boston: Beacon Press, 1992.

MacAskill, Ewen. "Four Million Additional Americans Fall into Poverty in One Year." *Guardian*, September 16, 2010.

Patterson, James T. *America's Struggle Against Poverty in the Twentieth Century.* Cambridge, MA: Harvard University Press, 2000.

Phillips, Kevin. *The Politics of Rich and Poor: Wealth and the American Electorate in the Reagan Aftermath.* New York: Random House, 1990.

Piven, Frances Fox, and Richard A. Cloward. *Poor People's Movements: Why They Succeed, How They Fail.* New York: Vintage, 1978.

Education Reform Issue

Although the federal Department of Education was established in 1867 to aid public schools in developing effective instruction, primary and secondary education remained the sole purview of state and local governments well into the twentieth century. The earliest federal involvement in education occurred in the realm of postsecondary education. In 1862, Congress passed the Morrill Act, which granted states large parcels of land (based on the size of their congressional delegation) to be sold for the purpose of creating colleges for the study of agriculture, military science, and engineering. Congress initially limited the act to those states that had remained in the Union during the Civil War. The second Morrill Act, passed in 1890, expanded the land grant program to southern states and gave the federal Office of Education (later the Department of Education) the responsibility for administering the program.

In 1917, the federal government expanded its interest in vocational training to the high school level through the passage of the Smith-Hughes Act. The legislation provided federal funding for the establishment of vocational education programs in the nation's high schools, and it mandated that states submit reports on their progress in training teachers, developing curricula, and attracting students. The George-Reed Act of 1929 extended the Smith-Hughes program to encompass home-economics instruction. The George-Barden Act of 1946 substantially increased federal contributions to vocational programs, with agricultural programs receiving the largest share of funds.

The advent of World War II led to an increased federal role in primary and secondary education. Under the Lanham Act of 1941, the federal government provided funds for the construction, maintenance, and operation of nearly a thousand public schools across the nation. This assistance was viewed as an essential part of the nation's overall war effort; as families migrated to towns with military bases while relatives trained for service overseas (or were deployed), local governments were poorly equipped to deal with the influx of children in the schools. Congress viewed federal funds as a crucial means of supporting the educational needs of military families and for the towns that housed military installations. When the war ended, extensions to the act provided for local governments to be given surplus military buildings to use for schools.

On the postsecondary education front, President Franklin Delano Roosevelt signed the Servicemen's Readjustment Act of 1944, also known as the GI Bill, helping soldiers, sailors, and marines reenter the civilian workforce. In addition to bonuses, low-interest loans, and unemployment pay, the GI Bill provided for vocational training and postsecondary education for millions of Americans. Tuition and fees were paid directly to colleges and universities under the GI Bill, allowing for nearly half of the sixteen million World War II veterans to complete some form of educational training while also underwriting a financial boon for colleges and universities. According to the American Council on Education, by 1947, 49 percent of all students admitted to college were veterans.

Less than a decade later, these benefits were drastically reduced by the Veterans Adjustment Act of 1952, which gave veterans a flat fee that could be used toward college. By the time of the Vietnam War, benefits had been reduced again, leaving veterans with few career options after leaving the service. Just as important, this legislation reduced the diversity of students at the nation's colleges and provided far fewer opportunities for working-class Americans to gain the skills they needed to reach the middle class.

For prospective college students who lacked military service, financial assistance was limited to private scholarships and grants. This effectively limited higher educational opportunities to the more affluent members of society and made it difficult for the children of working-class families to get ahead. It took an arms race with the Soviet Union to bring about reforms in higher education that would make a college degree more accessible to a greater proportion of American society. In 1957, the Soviets launched Sputnik, cementing fears that the United States was falling far behind the Soviets in mathematics and science education.

To ensure the nation's competitiveness in the space race, Congress enacted the National Defense Education Act of 1958, which funded improvements in primary and secondary science education, made funds available for college loans and graduate fellowships in science-related fields of study, and provided funds for the study of foreign languages. The college loan program was eventually expanded to cover all academic disciplines, and it became known as the Perkins loan program.

Other measures to improve the affordability of higher education came in the 1960s. As part of his "war on poverty," President Lyndon Johnson signed the Equal Opportunity Act of 1964. This legislation created the federally funded college work-study program, which provided colleges with funds to employ lower-income students on campus, giving students the opportunity to work their way through college. The 1965 Higher Education Act created the Guaranteed Student Loan program, which enabled needy students to borrow funds at low rates of interest, with repayment guaranteed by the federal government in the event of default. The Higher Education Act amendments of 1972 created the Basic Opportunity Grants Program, now known as the Pell Grant program. Pell Grants are available for students from lower- and middle-income families to fund undergraduate education, and, unlike student loans, they do not need to be repaid. The 1976 reauthorization of the act instituted the requirement that a student make satisfactory academic progress to be eligible for federal financial assistance. In 1978, the Middle Income Student Assistance Act made all students, regardless of family income, eligible for federally guaranteed student loans.

The election of President Reagan in the **Campaign of 1980** signaled big changes in federal funding for education. The 1981 Omnibus Budget Reconciliation Act once again limited student loan eligibility to low-income families. In 1982, Congress passed legislation requiring that all males under the age of twenty-six be registered for Selective Service to be eligible for any federal financial assistance. Later legislation restricted the total number of years of eligibility for Pell Grants. Over time, Pell Grants failed to keep up with college tuition costs, which were rising faster than the rate of inflation. Democratic nominee Barack Obama's mobilization efforts were focused heavily on younger voters in the **Campaign of 2008**, and he vowed to increase federal aid to lower-income students. Obama also criticized his opponent, John McCain, for McCain's recent vote against an expansion of the GI Bill. McCain defended his vote, arguing that it was simply not financially feasible to increase government spending in a time of crushing budget deficits. In 2010, Congress passed the Student Aid and Fiscal Responsibility Act on a party-line vote. Republicans objected to the price tag; Democrats argued that the expanded eligibility and increased payments for Pell Grants were necessary to make college affordable for middle-class families.

A current controversy in federal funding of higher education revolves around for-profit institutions of higher learning. In recent years, such institutions have mushroomed, and the primary sources of their operating budgets (as well as their profits) are Pell Grants and federally guaranteed student loan funds. The Department of Education under Obama sought to limit federal funds for any institution where student loan default rates were excessive, where job placement rates were excessively low, or where false information was provided during the recruitment of students. Congressional Republicans have been opposed to these limitations, arguing that they unfairly regulate business. Over time, one of the major changes in higher education has been the reduction of need-based financial aid and the expansion of merit-based financial aid. The result of this change has been a gradual decrease in the number of students from low-income families attending college.

Other changes in higher education have centered on combating racial and gender discrimination in enrollments, instruction, and access to educational facilities. The Civil Rights Act of 1964 prevented any federally funded institution from engaging in discrimination based on race or national origin. The act proved critical in compelling public schools and universities to desegregate. According to education researcher Gary Orfield, only 1.2 percent of African Americans in the South were attending integrated schools in 1964; by 1968, 32 percent of black students were in integrated schools.

In 1970, Congress passed legislation requiring that colleges and universities have non-racially discriminatory admissions policies in order to be eligible for tax-exempt status. Title VI of the Civil Rights Act already prohibited students from receiving federal financial assistance to attend institutions that did not meet this requirement. Bob Jones University in South Carolina quickly found itself in violation of the new law. A religious institution with a strict, conservative Christian interpretation of the bible, Bob Jones did not begin admitting African American students until 1971, and even then, admission was permitted only to blacks who were married (an interracial dating ban continued into the twenty-first century). A Supreme Court decision in 1976 upheld the 1970 antidiscrimination law, and the IRS quickly moved to charge the institution with a tax code violation. The case wound its way to the Supreme Court and was on the docket for the early spring of 1982. This put President Ronald Reagan in a bit of a quandary; he had attempted (but failed) to convince Congress to eliminate the 1970 law a year earlier, and he had unsuccessfully sought an exemption for the institution. Initially, the Reagan Adminisration attempted to drop the prosecution of the case, although a public backlash forced him to back off from these efforts. This funding dispute did not prevent Republican candidates from making public appearances at Bob Jones. During the 2000 Campaign Republican nominee George W. Bush stirred controversy by speaking on the Bob Jones campus, and the backlash following that event caused future candidates to steer clear of any association with the institution. Fifteen years would pass before a visit from another credible Republican presidential aspirant occurred, with both Senator Ted Cruz and Dr. Ben Carson speaking there during the 2015 pre-primary season.

Reagan was also notable for his vocal opposition to affirmative action in higher education (and elsewhere); both Jimmy Carter and Walter Mondale continued to support affirmative action, as has every Democratic presidential candidate since this time. A series of Supreme Court decisions that have effectively ended race-based admissions criteria have ultimately rendered this issue less relevant in contemporary presidential campaigns.

In primary and secondary education, antidiscrimination measures have been more limited, with an emphasis on school integration (and, to a lesser extent, equality in funding). In the wake of *Brown v. Board of Education* (1954), many school systems were slow to desegregate, engaging in lengthy legal battles that occasionally closed down the public school system in many towns in the South for a number of years. School funding formulas have historically been the domain of the state, and while *Brown* required schools to integrate with all due haste, it did not mandate equality in school funding, either as a function of ethnic composition or of social class. In the **Campaign of 1964**, Democrat Lyndon Johnson's "war on poverty" platform included federal assistance programs for low-income and minority students, while opponent Barry Goldwater campaigned on a states' rights platform. It was Goldwater's belief that the role of the federal government in education (and many other areas) should be limited, and that states should be free to make their own choices about school desegregation and school funding. Johnson used his electoral victory to provide federal funds to improve inner-city and rural schools, to assist low-income and minority children to prepare for entering school through the Head Start program, and to provide free school lunches for the needy.

By the **Campaign of 1968**, both the Democratic and Republican party platforms endorsed public school desegregation. American Independent Party candidate George Wallace, on the other hand, ran on a platform almost entirely devoted to protecting racial segregation. Where the Democrats and Republicans differed was on school busing. Busing was viewed by many liberals as a necessary means of remedying de facto segregation (that is, school segregation that does not result from discriminatory laws but instead from segregated neighborhoods, a process that had been exacerbated by the urban unrest and "white flight" of the era). As long as informal social practices confined minorities to ethnic enclaves where few funds were allocated for school improvements, busing supporters believed that minority children would continue to be disadvantaged. Conservatives objected to taxpayers' funds being used for schools that would not benefit their own children, and to the burdens imposed on children by compelling them to be transported great distances to attend school. The busing controversy expanded beyond the South and into the Northeast and Midwest, as cities like Boston and Detroit found themselves under court orders to bus children to remedy problems of de facto segregation. In the early 1970s, the Supreme Court limited busing across county lines but otherwise permitted the practice to continue. Busing continued to be a controversy that not only divided the political parties, but also served as a **wedge issue** for some Democrats who were not opposed to school integration in principle but had qualms about the toll that busing would take on their own children. This wedge caused some Democrats to support candidates such as Richard Nixon, Ronald Reagan, and George H. W. Bush for their adamant opposition to busing. The school busing controversy eventually came to an end when the nation's final forced busing program in the Charlotte-Mecklenburg (North Carolina) schools was halted in 2001.

Other forms of discrimination in education have also been the topic of educational reform. Title IX of the Education Amendments of 1972 prohibited discrimination on the basis of sex at institutions receiving federal funding. This rule became controversial on many college campuses in the early years of the twenty-first century, as gender imbalances at many public institutions required colleges and universities to either expand the number of school-financed sports for women (which most claimed that they could not afford) or reduce the number of school-financed sports for men. In 1990, President George H. W. Bush signed the Americans with Disabilities Act (ADA), which required government agencies, localities, and public accommodations to provide access (and employment protections) for the disabled. Many Republicans initially criticized the legislation, arguing that it was an unfunded government mandate that placed a heavy burden on businesses and local governments. However, over time, opposition to the law has abated. Nevertheless, many universities have failed to fully conform to the requirements of the ADA, and as more disabled persons join the ranks of college students, this controversy may be rekindled.

In addition to issues of financial assistance and discrimination, the level of federal involvement in education spending and oversight remains a source of campaign controversy. During the **Campaign of 1976**, Jimmy Carter and his Republican opponent Gerald Ford argued over the creation of a cabinet department for education. Ford argued that establishing a cabinet-level department would give the federal government too much control over primary and secondary education. Carter strongly endorsed more federal involvement, including federal funding, in K–12 education. Once elected, Carter set about lobbying Congress for his cabinet post, and the Department of Education was created in 1980. Ronald Reagan notoriously advocated the elimination of the department in the **Campaign of 1980**. Reagan won the election, but the department stayed. Unlike Carter, who saw the federal government as the solution to the nation's education problems, Reagan looked to the private sector for solutions. He advocated providing taxpayers with vouchers that could be used for either public or private schools as an alternative to federal funding of public education. The issue of school vouchers was promoted by Republican candidates throughout the 1980s and 1990s, whereas Democratic candidates were vociferously opposed to any diversion of public funds for private schools. The parties have also differed on the desirability of ESL (English as a second language) programs. Several Republican Party platforms have advocated making English the official language of the United States, which would preclude ESL instruction in public schools. Democrats have traditionally defended ESL programs.

In the **Campaign of 2000**, Republican George W. Bush offered a new twist on the voucher system. He proposed to create federal standards for public school quality. Parents of children who attended schools deemed to be "failing" would have the option of diverting the federal funds allotted for their child to another public school in their area, or even a private institution if they desired. Democratic nominee Al Gore stressed the need for federal funds for increased teacher pay and the construction and renovation of public-school buildings to reduce class sizes. In return, Gore received strong support from public-employee teachers' unions. School assessment and vouchers were surprisingly popular reforms with African American voters, whose children were most likely to be attending low-quality public schools. In the aftermath of the election, Bush worked closely with Democratic senator Ted Kennedy to pass No Child Left Behind, a program that established mandatory federal testing standards for schools, grades school performance, and ties federal aid to improvements in school performance. Despite its bipartisan origins, No Child Left Behind has become controversial, and in unexpected places. Teachers' unions dislike devoting instructional time to assessment, and school administrators fret over the report cards they receive. Non-native speakers and special-education students are tested at grade level under No Child Left Behind, which schools complain artificially depresses scores in regions with high percentages of immigrant families. An assortment of states (both liberal and conservative) already had assessment tests in place before No Child Left Behind, and they have resented federal efforts to control their assessment process. However, in the **Campaign of 2004**, Democratic nominee John Kerry did not campaign against No

Child Left Behind; rather, he argued that some aspects of the legislation needed to be fixed.

Similarly, in the **Campaign of 2008**, Obama did not reject No Child Left Behind in its entirety. Rather, he advocated charter schools as an alternative to failing public schools, a move that angered many public-school teachers. John McCain defended No Child Left Behind and argued that parents should be allowed to divert their tax dollars to private schools if suitable public schools did not exist in their area. After being elected, Obama appointed Arne Duncan as his education secretary. Duncan's association with the school accountability movement furthered the skepticism over Obama among public teacher unions.

Teachers' unions continued to back Obama in the **Campaign of 2012** despite their distaste for many elements of his education agenda. This has had less to do with their enthusiasm for Obama than it has for their dislike of the policies being advocated by his Republican opponents. In numerous states with Republican governors or Republican-dominated legislators, there has been a concerted effort to lower public teacher pay and to limit health care and retirement benefits in the aftermath of the 2010 midterms. These moves were endorsed by Republican presidential candidates, and they were decried by opponents and public-employee unions as an attack on teachers.

Also at issue is Obama's Race to the Top program, which offered states an opportunity to compete for federal funds to implement innovative reforms. Republican presidential candidates criticized the program as an unwarranted intrusion on states' rights and a waste of taxpayer dollars. Yet, despite all of the controversy over federal tax dollars being used for public education, less than ten cents of every dollar spent on primary and secondary education comes from the federal government.

Public-sector employee pay and benefits, and teacher accountability, continue to be mainstays of the GOP agenda on education in the **Campaign of 2016**. All of the GOP hopefuls express skepticism about public-sector unions, and several (Christie, Walker, Kasich) have actively attempted to limit teachers' collective bargaining rights in their states. Those who have served as governors also tout their support for charter schools and other alternatives to public schools (particularly Jeb Bush, Jindal, and Huckabee) and their opposition to the Common Core standards adopted in many states to provide a new set of teaching and learning standards in the twenty-first century for students across the nation (here, Jeb Bush is a notable exception). While Common Core standards were developed as a cooperative effort among the states, the GOP has come to view them as a federal program that is foisting national standards on local schools. The Democratic Party is more divided on the topic of education. Some Democrats support the standardized testing and teacher accountability model represented by No Child Left Behind; others are increasingly hostile to this model and encourage parents and children to decline to participate in standardized tests altogether. Some Democrats would prefer a return to traditional public schools where teachers have more flexibility and testing plays a less central role. Others would prefer an emphasis on more teacher training, a more effective testing model, retention of only the most talented and qualified teachers, and the development of charter schools. None of the Democratic candidates, including Hillary Clinton, have made it clear how they will manage the divide between the traditional pro-teachers' union constituency in their party and the educational reformers. For the Democrats, more than for the Republicans, education appears to be a **wedge issue**.

See also Affirmative Action; Civil Rights Issue

Additional Resources

Besze, Susan. "Learning Division: Bush, Gore Offer Different Ideas on Reform for Nation's Schools." *Denver Post*, October 22, 2000, p. A1.

Chait, Jonathan. "Will Hillary Clinton Continue Education Reform?" *New York Magazine*, July 13, 2015. http://nymag.com/daily/intelligencer/2015/07/will-hillary-clinton-continue-education-reform.html. Accessed September 5, 2015.

"Civil Rights 101," Leadership Conference on Civil and Human Rights. http://www.civilrights.org/resources/civilrights101/desegregation.html. Accessed September 5, 2015.

Epstein, Reid J. "GOP Candidates Return to Bob Jones University, as Party Shifts Right." *The Wall Street Journal,* November 13, 2015.

FoxNews.Com. "Inside the GOP, the Question Is, Where Do You Stand on Common Core?" June 20, 2014. http://www.foxnews.com/politics/2014/06/20/inside-gop-question-is-where-do-stand-on-common-core/. Accessed September 5, 2015.

Haberman, Aaron. "Into the Wilderness: Ronald Reagan, Bob Jones University, and the Political Education of the Christian Right." *Historian* 67, no. 2 (Spring 2005): 234–53.

Henig, Jeffrey R. *The End of Exceptionalism in American Education: The Changing Politics of School Reform.* Cambridge, MA: Harvard University Press, 2013.

Hochcschild, Jennifer, and Nathan Scovronick. *The American Dream and the Public Schools.* New York: Oxford University Press, 2004.

Marshall, M. J., and R. J. McKee. "From Campaign Promises to Presidential Policy: Education Reform in the 2000 Election." *Educational Policy* 16 (March 2002): 96–118.

Miller, Jake. "Could Common Core Cause a Republican Civil War in 2016?" *CBS News*, February 20, 2015. http://www.cbsnews.com/news/will-common-core-cause-a-republican-civil-war-in-2016/. Accessed September 5, 2015.

National Public Radio. "The Legacy of School Busing." *Morning Edition*, April 28, 2004.

Toppo, Greg. "Where They Stand: McCain, Obama Split on Education." *USA Today*, October 14, 2008.

U.S. Department of Education. "The Federal Role in Education." http://www2.ed.gov/about/overview/fed/role.html. Accessed September 5, 2015.

U.S. Department of Justice. "Title IX of the Educational Amendments of 1972." http://www.justice.gov/crt/about/cor/coord/titleix.php. Accessed September 5, 2015.

Williams, Conor P. "In 2016, Democrats Have a Good Reason to Run Against Obama's Education Record." *New Republic*, June 3, 2014. http://www.newrepublic.com/article/117989/hillary-clintons-education-policy-other-implications-2016. Accessed September 5, 2015.

Energy Issue

Through the nineteenth century, few Americans gave a second thought to the possibility of energy shortages. Vast deposits of coal powered the Industrial Revolution, and it was not until the early twentieth century that oil became a national concern. To assure a reliable supply of oil for the U.S. Navy, Congress set aside a number of petroleum reserves located on federal lands in Elk Hills, California, and Teapot Dome, Wyoming. Concerns about securing a sufficient oil supply ended in the 1920s with the discovery of vast new western oil fields in Texas and Oklahoma. At that time it appeared that the United States had an unlimited supply of oil.

However, the outbreak of World War II placed a heavy demand on the U.S. domestic supply of oil; these supplies were even more heavily taxed when the war ended and American demand for automobiles skyrocketed. Changes in the transportation industry shifted much of the freight traffic from trains to trucks, and the postwar economic boom furthered the demand for oil. By the 1950s, the United States could no longer rely solely on domestic sources to meet its growing need for petroleum. Furthermore, incidents of accidental oil spills began to raise concerns about the environmental consequences of domestic oil extraction. A large spill—at the time the largest in American history—that occurred off the coast of Santa Barbara, California, in 1969 was particularly alarming, contributing to suspicions revolving around the oil industry in general. By 1970, the United States produced only 69 percent of the oil it consumed, with the bulk of the imports coming from the Middle East. The Yom Kippur War of 1973 created upheaval in the world's oil market. The Organization of the Petroleum Exporting Countries (OPEC) exploited American and European dependence on imported oil by dramatically limiting the supply as a means to drive up the price. During the 1970s, the price of gasoline and home heating fuel skyrocketed, and the limited supply led to long lines at gas stations throughout the United States. Several frigid winters in the late 1970s merely worsened the economic plight of American consumers, who were already facing high unemployment and rising prices.

The postwar demand for oil paralleled similar changes in the demand for electricity. As the economy boomed and the rural electrification projects of the New Deal expanded the use of electricity in American homes, the country continued to be heavily dependent on the coal industry to power homes, businesses, and factories. Yet coal extraction continued to be a dangerous and dirty industry, with miners risking illnesses such as black lung disease and injury due to cave-ins and collapses. Additionally, coal-fired power plants were a major source of air pollution for neighboring regions. The search for a cleaner-burning source of electricity that was less reliant on nonrenewable resources helped to facilitate the development of the nuclear power industry, although its appeal was short-lived. In 1978, the Three Mile Island nuclear plant near Harrisburg, Pennsylvania, suffered a partial meltdown in one of its two reactors, resulting in the release of radioactive gases into the environment around the facility. Although no immediate deaths were associated with the Three Mile Island accident and the effect on public health in the vicinity was less than initially feared, it was nevertheless a widely publicized event producing a high level of anxiety, and as a consequence the general public quickly cooled to the idea of nuclear power. No new nuclear power facility has been built in the United States since this accident.

During the **Campaign of 1980**, the Democratic and Republican parties adopted very different tactics for dealing with the energy crisis. Democratic incumbent Jimmy Carter stressed the need for conservation of both fuel and electricity (including lowering the speed limit to 55 miles per hour) and advocated higher fuel economy rates for automobiles (such as the 1978 Energy Tax Act that levied a special tax on gas guzzlers), more energy-efficient mass transit, and the use of alternative energy sources. Republican nominee Ronald Reagan advocated the increased domestic production of oil, coal, natural gas, and other traditional sources of energy. While the energy crisis alone did not sink the Carter campaign, his inability to resolve these problems undoubtedly damaged his candidacy.

By the 1980s, other sources of oil were being developed, and energy prices fell as production gradually increased. However, the process was slow. The American automobile industry suffered in the early 1980s as its domestic customers turned to the less expensive, more fuel-efficient cars that were being imported from Japan. By the **Campaign of 1984**, the domestic economy (including the automobile industry) began to rebound, and Reagan was easily reelected. Opposition to extraction of oil, particularly in the Alaskan wilderness, did for a time increase in the wake of the 1989 *Exxon Valdez* spill in Alaska's Prince William Sound, but for the most part, the petroleum industry weathered the disaster, and with continued low prices for gasoline and other petroleum products, incentives for the consumption of oil strengthened. Americans once again returned to their love of large automobiles, and Congress aided and abetted this trend by weakening CAFE (Corporate Average Fuel Economy) regulations and permitting automakers to classify more vehicles as light trucks to further skirt fuel-efficiency requirements. While gasoline prices were mentioned briefly in the **Campaign of 2000**, when Republican nominee George W. Bush claimed that his relationship with the Saudis put him in a better position to bargain over gas prices, it was not until the **Campaign of 2008** that oil imports became a serious topic of debate. During this election, rising oil prices forced both candidates to propose strategies to deal with the problem. Democratic nominee Barack Obama emphasized investing more resources in alternative sources of energy, as well as improving fuel efficiency of American vehicles. Republican nominee John McCain argued that greater domestic production of energy would lower prices. He advocated drilling in the Arctic National Wildlife Refuge in Alaska, as well as in the Gulf of Mexico and the Chesapeake Bay. McCain running mate Sarah Palin's slogan became "Drill, baby, drill!"

The explosion of the Deepwater Horizon rig in the Gulf of Mexico in the spring of 2010, and the resulting leak of approximately five million gallons of oil into the Gulf over a three-month period, led to environmental damage in coastal areas and a somewhat lessened level of enthusiasm for offshore drilling in environmentally sensitive areas. It also refueled Democratic Party opposition to offshore energy exploration. Ironically, just prior to the Deepwater accident, Obama had reversed course and stated that he would permit new offshore-drilling permits to be issued. In the **Campaign of 2012**, Obama, under pressure from activists within his own party, again preached caution on offshore drilling, as well as on the construction of the proposed Keystone oil pipeline to transport tar sands oil from northwest Canada to the Gulf. The Republican Party made the exploitation of domestic sources of energy—including the Keystone pipeline, offshore oil exploration, fracking for natural gas, and "clean" coal technology—a cornerstone of its campaign.

Nuclear energy, as an alternative to coal and natural gas, has generally remained off the political agenda in the United States. The close call at Three Mile Island, followed a few years later by the disastrous core meltdown of the Chernobyl nuclear plant in Ukraine (in the former Soviet Union) in 1986 merely served to increase Americans' worries about the safety of nuclear power and the safe disposal of spent nuclear fuel for decades thereafter. The storage of depleted fuel at Yucca Mountain in Nevada (a measure strongly opposed by the local population) remains controversial. The topic of nuclear power made a brief resurgence in the **Campaign of 2004**, when incumbent president George W. Bush campaigned on expanding the domestic nuclear power industry as a cleaner alternative to coal. This was not a focus of the **Campaign of 2008**, and after the core meltdown at the Fukashima Daiichi reactor in Japan on the heels of an earthquake (and subsequent tsunami) in March 2011, it is unlikely to be an issue in future campaigns. Rather, citizens in countries throughout Europe and Asia have pressured their governments to discontinue their reliance on the use of nuclear power altogether.

Unlike nuclear power, coal-fired power plants have remained a topic of controversy at election time. One area of controversy deals with the mining practices in the coal industry. While the Carter administration attempted to create federal regulations for the burgeoning surface mining (also known as strip mining) industry, President Reagan's secretary of the interior, James Watt, preferred to streamline these regulations, leaving much of the oversight up to the states (although Congress thwarted many of his plans). It was also during the Reagan era that coal-fired power plants of the Midwest first came under criticism for contributing to the problem of acid rain in the Northeast and Canada, leading to renewed concerns about coal as an energy source. Democratic nominee Michael Dukakis unsuccessfully attempted to take the Reagan administration to task in the **Campaign of 1988**, although he was not able to make this a major campaign issue.

It was not until the **Campaign of 2000** that attention was once again placed on the mining and burning of coal for electricity. Democratic nominee Al Gore, by then an avowed environmentalist, criticized the coal industry for air pollution and for contributing to the greenhouse gases that were causing global climate change. Gore won the popular vote but lost the Electoral College vote, in part due to his loss of the traditionally Democratic state of West Virginia, a major coal producer. Four years later, the country was at war in two nations in the Middle East, and scant attention was paid to energy or the environment.

By the **Campaign of 2008**, the Iraq war had ceased to dominate the campaign, and Americans once again turned their attention to problems on the home front. In addition to alternative energy sources (solar, wind, wave), Obama advocated limiting greenhouse gases with a cap-and-trade system in which companies essentially bid on vouchers to pollute. The rationale of this system is that profit-seeking companies will economize to sell their vouchers (rather than use them), creating a market-based incentive to limit pollutants. McCain acknowledged during the campaign that global warming was a problem, but he argued that there were more effective means to address it. By the **Campaign of 2012**, the political climate had changed somewhat. The GOP still opposed cap-and-trade on the grounds that it was an unfair infringement on American businesses and would render them unprofitable. But most GOP hopefuls (with the exception of Mitt Romney, the eventual nominee, and Jon Huntsman) denied that global climate change was even occurring, or that humans had the ability to influence the temperature of the Earth. The science of climate change remains a topic of partisan debate, with Democrats more sympathetic to arguments about both the existence of climate change and the need for the federal government to act, and Republicans more skeptical on both counts.

Partisan differences over the extraction of domestic sources of energy persist. Republicans appear to favor nonrenewable sources such as oil, coal, and natural gas and thus the GOP is sensitive to environmental regulations that place limitations on energy-related industries and their methods, even when controversial (e.g., hydraulic fracturing, or fracking). Democrats tend to focus on renewable sources of energy such as solar, wind, biodiesel, and other alternative fuel sources, but they are not uniformly averse to the continued extraction and processing of petroleum resources. That said, Democrats remain more inclined to favor increased government investment in new energy technologies designed to wean the economy from fossil fuels, hoping to generate less expensive consumer versions of these energies for everyday use.

See also Environment Issue

Additional Resources

Dao, James. "The 2000 Campaign: The Vice President: Gore to Unveil a Plan to Foster Change Energy." *New York Times*, June 26, 2000.

Daynes, Byron W., and Glen Sussman. *White House Politics and the Environment: Franklin D. Roosevelt to George W. Bush.* College Station: Texas A&M Press, 2010.

Jackson, David. "McCain Calls to Lift U.S. Oil Drilling Ban." *USA Today*, June 17, 2008.

Rutledge, Ian. *Addicted to Oil: America's Relentless Drive for Energy Security.* London: I. B. Tauris, 2006.

Uslaner, Eric. *Shale Barrel Politics: Energy and Legislative Leadership.* Palo Alto, CA: Stanford University Press, 1989.

Environment Issue

No president played a more seminal role in lending credibility and momentum to the conservation movement than Theodore Roosevelt. His administration made unprecedented efforts to establish a national policy to conserve the nation's abundant natural resources during a time when the Industrial Revolution threatened to deplete the vast wilderness in the West. As the nineteenth century drew to a close, the needs of the burgeoning industrial sector led to major improvements in transportation and infrastructure, and it fueled demands for cheap energy. Massive coal-mining operations sprung up in a number of eastern states such as Pennsylvania, West Virginia, Virginia, and Kentucky. Congress, eager to aid in the process of industrialization, granted private individuals and corporations the right to extract natural resources from federal lands in exchange for a fee. As the demand for coal, timber, and other natural resources increased, a fledgling conservation movement sounded an alarm that unregulated extraction of resources threatened the future of the country. The late nineteenth-century conservation movement sought to preserve the natural condition of federal land and place pressure on the Interior Department to protect the environment instead of focusing solely on the development of federal lands. The conservation movement faced intense opposition from political and corporate interests who adamantly opposed any effort to limit their access to natural resources.

One of the earliest political conflicts between these two forces occurred in the battle over Yellowstone National Park. Despite being designated a national park, there were no laws protecting the wildlife or other natural resources within its boundaries. By the end of the nineteenth century, mining and railroad interests threatened to permanently disrupt the habitat of the park. Extensive lobbying by the wilderness group Boone and Crockett persuaded President Grover Cleveland to sign legislation protecting Yellowstone's natural resources in 1894.

The cause of conservation found a friend in Theodore Roosevelt. Roosevelt had a lifelong fascination with nature and was an ardent admirer of famed environmentalist and author John Muir. In 1903, President Roosevelt went camping in the Yosemite Valley with Muir. The trip persuaded Roosevelt to expand the boundaries of Yosemite National Park to include Yosemite Valley and other adjacent areas. Similarly, a visit to Pelican Island in Florida in 1903 convinced Roosevelt that the majestic birds needed to be protected from the threats posed by the millinery industry, and he created the Pelican Island Bird Reservation, one of more than fifty such wildlife refuges that he would establish during his time in office.

In the **Campaign of 1904**, Roosevelt, who had become president upon the assassination of President William McKinley in September 1901, easily won election to a full four-year term. Roosevelt ran on a platform that included support for new conservation programs, rooted in the principles of scientific management of natural resources that he had developed decades earlier as a founding member of the Boone and Crockett Club. For the first time, the conservation movement had a strong ally in the White House. Roosevelt created the Bureau of Forestry in the Department of the Interior and appointed well-known conservationist Gifford Pinchot as the bureau's "chief forester." With the support of Roosevelt, Pinchot instituted a number of reforms to conserve the nation's resources. Roosevelt created eighteen national monuments during his time in office, including the Grand Canyon National Monument in Arizona.

Roosevelt declined to run for another term, and in 1908, the Republican Party nominated William Howard Taft in his stead. Taft went on to easily win the **Campaign of 1908** on a Republican platform that promised, in part, to continue Roosevelt's conservation policies. Shortly after assuming the presidency, however, Taft angered the conservation movement by nominating Richard A. Ballinger, a friend of western business interests, as secretary of the interior. When Ballinger announced his support for opening large tracts of Alaskan land for the extraction of natural resources, the conservation movement criticized him for favoring the interests of his pro-development friends. In 1910, Ballinger dismissed Louis Glavis, an Interior Department employee responsible for overseeing federal lands in Alaska, for opposing his development decision. Chief forester Pinchot then released an open letter sharply criticizing Ballinger for the firing and for the decision to open Alaskan lands to development. President Taft responded by dismissing Pinchot for insubordination.

The Pinchot-Ballinger controversy had a major effect on the relationship between former president Theodore Roosevelt and President Taft. Many progressive Republicans attacked Taft for abandoning Roosevelt's progressive agenda. In the **Campaign of 1912**, Roosevelt launched an unsuccessful effort to win the Republican nomination for president. When the Republican convention renominated Taft for a second term, Roosevelt launched a third-party campaign under the auspices of the Bull Moose Party, which was composed of progressive Republicans. Woodrow Wilson, the nominee of the Democratic Party, went on to win the 1912 presidential election, largely because Roosevelt and Taft split the Republican vote.

Elected to office in the **Campaign of 1928**, Republican Herbert Hoover shared some of the sensible-use ethic that underscored the progressives' approach to conservation (although he openly feuded with Gifford Pinchot). As historian Kendrick Clements notes, by the 1920s, many federal agencies had bureaus devoted specifically to conservation or environmental concerns, and both chambers of Congress had formed powerful committees to deal with these issues. Hoover was an engineer by trade, and this influenced his approach to conservation. He was also suspicious of public-sector solutions to problems, believing that voluntary, private-sector initiatives were more effective. Hoover's goal was the efficient, centralized organization of the federal government's various environmental entities, reduction of industrial waste, efficient production of energy, and the conservation of natural resources so that they could be utilized by future generations. As secretary of commerce, Hoover played a major role in negotiating the Colorado River Compact, which allocated water use among the various states along its boundaries. He also negotiated the compact that created the Hoover Dam, which then began construction under his presidency. Hoover's creation of a Timber Conservation Board in 1930 was primarily to limit overproduction of timber and to eliminate waste in timber harvesting. He was not interested in protecting forests from development; rather, he was interested in sustainable use. Similarly, the limits Hoover placed on oil permits on federal land were not to protect the land itself, but instead to limit overproduction (which he viewed as inefficient) in the oil industry. Ultimately, Hoover's interests lay in promoting practices that made businesses more profitable and produced jobs for workers.

Elected to the presidency in the **Campaign of 1932**, Franklin Roosevelt threw his full support behind various conservation programs as part of his New Deal. Roosevelt's Civilian Conservation Corps (CCC) helped to rebuild the national park system. Workers in the CCC worked on fire prevention in national forests, planted billions of trees, constructed hundreds of parks, cleaned up rural streams and stocked them with fish, controlled erosion, implemented flood-control projects, and created park trails and picnic areas. The Works Progress Administration (WPA) not only repaired and built transportation infrastructure, but also cleared slums and reforested blighted areas. The Tennessee Valley Authority (TVA) is best known for its electrification of rural America, but the program also replanted logged-out forests, restored soil that had been eroded due to overfarming, developed sustainable agriculture practices, and restored the natural habitats of fish and other wildlife. While Franklin Roosevelt's primary goal was the useful employment of millions of out-of-work Americans, he chose to focus much of that effort on environmental conservation and on making America's green spaces more accessible to its citizens.

During the 1950s, decades of air and water pollution began to threaten the health and safety of millions of Americans, as thick coats of smog blanketed the nation's cities and waterways became contaminated by refuse and industrial waste. The publication of books such as Rachel Carson's *Silent Spring* in 1962, which demonstrated the harm to human and animal life from the use of the pesticide DDT, helped to usher in a new era of environmentalism, and activists set goals far beyond conserving the nation's natural resources. The new emphasis was on restoring the health of an environment severely damaged by the Industrial Revolution, along with large amounts of pollution caused by reliance on the automobile for transportation, the burning of coal to generate electric power, and the use of pesticides in agriculture.

Support for environmental regulations was more bipartisan during this time period than it had been in previous eras. President Lyndon Johnson's wife, Lady Byrd, promoted a program to "Keep America Beautiful," which involved limits on the use of public billboards along highways, limiting the size and location of waste facilities, and using public funds to beautify the nation's highways and byways. By the 1970s, several states began deposit programs for beverage containers to encourage recycling. Most notably during this time period, two major pieces of legislation were enacted. The Clean Air Act of 1970 gave the federal government the power to develop standards for measuring and limiting industrial air pollutants. The Environmental Protection Agency (EPA) was established in 1971 to implement the Clean Air Act. The Clean Air Act was further amended in 1977 and 1990, giving the federal government new enforcement powers when air quality did not meet federal standards, and expanding goals to limiting acid rain and damage to the ozone layer. The Federal Water Pollution Control Act of 1948 was amended substantially in 1972 and again in 1977, giving the federal government the authority to regulate the discharge of pollutants and wastewater, and to set federal guidelines for contaminants in all bodies of water. The legislation also created grants for building wastewater treatment facilities.

The bipartisan coalition to improve air and water quality began to unravel with the **Campaign of 1980**. Republican nominee Ronald Reagan argued that excessive federal environmental regulations were risking American jobs and constraining general economic prosperity. Throughout the 1980s, Reagan battled Democrats in Congress over drilling for oil in the Arctic National Wildlife Refuge. A mere ten days after a Senate committee finally agreed in 1989 to allow limited drilling, the *Exxon Valdez* ran aground in Prince William Sound, spilling eleven million gallons of oil. With this environmental devastation on the nightly news for months, the issue of drilling for oil in Alaska quietly slid off of the political agenda. From 1980 to the present time, Democratic presidential candidates have generally shown strong support for the federal government's role in protecting the environment. The Republican position has generally reflected the sentiment expressed by Reagan—namely, that federal regulations are not the best means to solve the problem.

Democrat Bill Clinton used his time in office to create nineteen national monuments (via the existing 1906 Antiquities Act) and to establish the Joshua Tree National Park. In his last days in office, his administration issued rules to limit commercial and recreational use of national parks and monuments, including a controversial ban on snowmobiles in the Yellowstone and Grand Teton national parks after an EPA study that blamed snowmobiles, powerboats, and off-road vehicles for their substantial contribution to the nation's air pollution (because they have long been exempted from pollution regulations on other vehicles). The snowmobile ban was promptly overturned by Clinton's successor, George W. Bush.

During the **Campaign of 2000**, Vice President Al Gore, author of *Earth in the Balance*, argued that the state of the environment was precarious and that Americans' use of fossil fuels was contributing to a catastrophic change in the global climate. Gore supported the ratification of the Kyoto Protocol, an international pact to limit greenhouse gases. His opponent, Republican nominee George W. Bush, argued that the effect of human action on the planet was not a point on which all scholars agreed and suggested that drastic action would be premature. Bush opposed the Kyoto Protocol, arguing that it put American businesses at a competitive disadvantage relative to other countries. Gore's plan to limit fossil fuel consumption was not popular in West Virginia, a state that had historically voted for Democrats but was also heavily reliant on the coal industry. Gore lost West Virginia; had he managed to win the state, the Florida recount would not have been a factor in determining the outcome of the presidential race, and Gore would have easily earned the necessary electoral votes to win the election.

In the **Campaign of 2008**, the environmental debate shifted to offshore oil drilling. While Republican governors such as Jeb Bush (Florida) and Arnold

Schwarzenegger (California) had opposed offshore drilling during their tenure in office, arguing that it risked the environment and their states' tourism industries, the Republican Party in general took a different tack. Republican voters chanted "Drill, baby, drill" at their campaign events (reminiscent of the "Burn, baby, burn" slogan chanted by participants in the Los Angeles riots in the 1960s), while Democratic candidates assured their voters that they would never permit an expansion of offshore drilling (although Obama changed his mind after being elected).

The **Campaign of 2012** continued the 2008 debate over offshore drilling. In the interim, the country had experienced a disastrous spill at the BP Deepwater Horizon offshore drill site in the Gulf of Mexico in the summer of 2010, and Obama's plans to allow limited offshore drilling were put on hold. Democrats used the BP spill as evidence that offshore drilling was a dangerous and risky process, and they suggested that allowing the Keystone oil pipeline plan to proceed over land would potentially involve similar leaks and spills. The GOP defended Keystone, arguing that it would create jobs, although support for offshore drilling became less of a campaign centerpiece. Instead, the GOP began to promote "clean coal" and fracking for natural gas as viable domestic energy sources—while Obama and the Democrats focused on the environmental costs of pursuing these energy policies.

Another emerging environmental issue involves the use of dams and levees to control flooding and to generate hydroelectricity. During the late 1950s and the early 1960s, the Glen River Canyon (north of the Grand Canyon) was dammed to regulate the distribution of water from the Colorado River. While environmentalists had agreed to the project to spare the Dinosaur National Monument, they soon had regrets. A last-minute trip down the canyon by the director of the Sierra Club revealed breathtaking natural formations and numerous Native American artifacts, but soon this was all submerged under Lake Powell. Edward Abbey's influential novel *The Monkey Wrench Gang* is a fantasy about sabotaging this dam. A number of the Colorado River diversion projects are being reevaluated, as are many of the numerous levees along the Mississippi River, as scientists try to determine whether these levees contributed to the damage from Hurricane Katrina by limiting the Mississippi Delta's ability to absorb the overflow. The stormy spring of 2011 led the U.S. Army Corps of Engineers to breach some of the levees on the Mississippi, flooding some areas, to protect major cities from rising waters. Letting some U.S. waterways and shorelines have more natural boundaries is a current topic of debate.

In the 2012 and 2016 presidential campaigns, the debate over the nature and causes of climate change has emerged as a major issue, with conservatives more inclined toward skepticism of the evidence supporting recent conclusions about the Earth's climate and the patterns of change now observed, and liberals typically trusting the objectivity of the science behind it.

Additional Resources

Carson, Rachel. *Silent Spring.* Boston: Houghton Mifflin Harcourt, 2002.

Clements, Kendrick A. "Herbert Hoover and Conservation, 1921–1933." *American Historical Review* 89, no. 1 (February 1984): 67–88.

Gore, Al. *Earth in the Balance.* Boston: Houghton Mifflin, 1992.

Kamieniecki, Sheldon, and Michael Kraft, *The Oxford Handbook of U.S Environmental Policy.* New York: Oxford University Press, 2013.

Killingsworth, M. Jimmie, and Jacqueline S. Palmer. *Ecospeak: Rhetoric and Environmental Politics in America.* Carbondale: Southern Illinois University Press, 1992.

Roosevelt, Theodore. "John Muir: An Appreciation.' *Outlook* (January 16, 1915): 27–28. http://www.sierraclub.org/john_muir_exhibit/life/appreciation_by_Roosevelt.aspx. Accessed September 5, 2015.

Shogren, Elizabeth. "For 30 Years, a Political Battle Over Oil and ANWR." NPR, November 10, 2005.

Stewart, Doug, Lisa Drew, and Mark Wexler. "How Conservation Grew from a Whisper to a Roar." *National Wildlife* (December–January 1999): 22.

"TR's Legacy—The Environment." PBS, *The American Experience.* http://www.pbs.org/wgbh/amex/tr/envir.html. Accessed September 5, 2015.

U.S. Environmental Protection Agency. "Clean Air Act." http://www.epa.gov/air/caa. Accessed September 5, 2015.

U.S. Environmental Protection Agency. "National Pollutant Discharge Elimination System, Clean Water Act." http://cfpub.epa.gov/npdes/cwa.cfm?program_id=45. Accessed September 5, 2015.

Faithless Elector

Members of the Electoral College are chosen by state legislatures, according to the U.S. Constitution. Since 1836 (with the exception of South Carolina), voters, rather than state legislatures, have selected party-designated slates of electors who are pledged to support their party's nominee to represent the plurality of voters in the state. In all states but two (Maine and Nebraska), the party of the plurality vote-winner gains 100 percent of the electors voting for the state. In Maine and Nebraska, electors are assigned on the basis of the plurality of votes for each House district, with the additional two electors being assigned on the basis of the statewide popular vote.

In some instances, electors have cast a ballot for someone other than the candidate to whom they were pledged when the Electoral College convened in December. A faithless elector is an elector who fails to support the party's candidate when the Electoral College meets. While faithless electors are rare, political observers are concerned about them nonetheless. After all, presidential elections are already an indirect process. Citizens (often unwittingly) cast their votes for a slate of unnamed electors who merely promise to reflect their wishes during the real election, a month later. If electors vote according to their own personal whims, voter decisions on Election Day are essentially meaningless.

While it is theoretically possible for a faithless elector to alter the outcome of a presidential election, this has never happened. In large part, this is because electors are selected by state political parties, and so they have a strong incentive to support their party's ticket. When electors are faithless, it is often to support a rival candidate from their own political party, although there are also notable instances of defections in support of a specific political policy (for example, in three twentieth-century cases, electors defected to support a pro-segregation candidate).

Recent documented instances of faithless electors include the following:

- 2004 (an unknown Minnesota elector for John Kerry voted instead for his running mate, John Edwards)
- 2000 (a DC elector for Al Gore cast a blank ballot)
- 1988 (a West Virginia elector for Michael Dukakis voted instead for his running mate, Lloyd Bentsen)
- 1976 (a Washington elector for Gerald Ford voted instead for Ronald Reagan, who had lost to Ford in the Republican primary)
- 1972 (a Virginia elector for Nixon voted instead for a Libertarian)
- 1968 (a North Carolina elector for Nixon voted instead for George Wallace, the pro-segregation candidate from the American Independent Party)
- 1960 (an Oklahoma elector for Nixon voted instead for Harry Byrd Sr., a pro-segregation senator from Virginia)
- 1956 (an Alabama elector for Adlai Stevenson voted instead for an Alabama judge)
- 1948 (a Tennessee elector for Truman voted instead for Strom Thurmond, who had defected from the Democratic Party to run on the States' Rights ticket on a pro-segregation platform)

Currently, twenty-six states (as well as the District of Columbia) require that electors vote for the candidate to whom they pledged their support (although some exceptions are made when that candidate is deceased by the time the electoral vote is to be cast). However, twenty-four states have no such requirement. Even when electors are required to vote for the candidate to whom they have pledged, few states have penalties for ignoring the requirement: three states (North Carolina, Oklahoma, and Washington) impose a monetary fine; two (New Mexico and South

Carolina) subject faithless electors to criminal prosecution; and Utah automatically removes and replaces electors who fail to uphold their pledge.

Additional Resources

The Green Papers. "2000 Electors for President and Vice President of the United States." July 6, 2004 http://www.thegreenpapers.com/G00/Electors.html. Accessed October 15, 2015.

Federal Employees. *See* Civil Service Reform

501(c) Group

After the passage of the Bipartisan Campaign Reform Act of 2002, which banned soft-money contributions to political parties and retained limits on PAC and individual contributions, many political analysts predicted that unions, corporations, and other organized interests would use **527 groups** to advance their political agendas. As long as 527 groups were engaging in independent issue advocacy (rather than promoting a specific candidate), contributions to such groups were not subject to any limits, and there were no limits on their election spending. However, they must disclose their contributors. Many political analysts believed that large donors would still want to influence election outcomes, and if they could not contribute large sums directly to political parties anymore, they would contribute to other groups that would engage in the same types of activities.

While 527-group donations and expenditures did surge after 2002, hitting a high mark of $424 million in the **Campaign of 2004**, they quickly abated as large donors sought to conceal their identities. Such donors seeking greater anonymity have turned in recent years to section 501(c) of the federal tax code. The 501(c) designation—in particular, the 501(c)(4) designation—is reserved for charitable and social welfare organizations, and such are not permitted to have electioneering as a primary purpose. These 501(c) organizations are beyond the regulatory scope of the Federal Elections Commission (because they are not deemed campaign organizations), and the IRS does not require that they disclose the identity of their donors.

In 2004, 501(c) groups spent approximately $60 million on federal elections, according to the Campaign Finance Institute (CFI). CFI estimates that in the **Campaign of 2008**, overall 501(c) spending tripled as donors increasingly sought to conceal their identities. They found that many industries and interest groups that had previously utilized 527 groups were redirecting their resources toward 501(c) groups, particularly those groups associated with conservative causes. Republican-leaning 501(c) groups spent twice as much as Democratic-leaning 501(c) groups in 2008. However, Democratic-leaning 527 groups outspent Republican-leaning 527 groups at a similar rate, suggesting that many liberal-leaning groups had yet to make the transition to 501(c) groups. This asymmetry continued into the **Campaign of 2012**. The Center for Responsive Politics estimated that in the 2012 election, liberal-leaning non-disclosing groups (their term for 501(c) groups) spent approximately $33.6 million, while conservative-leaning groups spent approximately $265.5 million. While the IRS had initially indicated that it would be enforcing the rules on groups claiming to be 501(c)(4)s more strictly in future elections, in the spring of 2015, it backed off of proposed new regulations, delaying any discussion of reform until well after the **Campaign of 2016**.

See also Campaign Finance Reform; Independent Advocacy Groups; Super PAC

Additional Resources

Center for Responsive Politics. "Types of Advocacy Groups." http://www.opensecrets.org /527s/types.php. Accessed September 29, 2015.

Weissman, Steve, and Suraj Sazawal. "501(c) Groups Emerge as Big Players Alongside 527s." Campaign Finance Institute, October 31, 2008. http://www.cfinst.org/press /PReleases/08-10-31/Outside_Soft_Money_Groups_in_2008_Election.aspx. Accessed September 29, 2015.

Weissman, Steve, and Suraj Sazawal. "Soft Money Political Spending by 501(c) Nonprofits Tripled in 2008 Election." Campaign Finance Institute, February 25, 2009. http:// www.cfinst.org/press/releases_tags/09-02-25/Soft_Money_Political_Spending_by _Nonprofits_Tripled_in_2008.aspx. Accessed September 29, 2015.

527 Group

Section 527 of the Internal Revenue Service tax code refers to a political organization that engages in issue advocacy at the local, state, or federal level. 527 groups are nonprofit and tax-exempt. However, contributions are not tax-deductible to the person making them. For the purpose of taxation, the IRS considers political party organizations, campaign organizations associated with candidates for office, political action committees (PACs), and other organized political entities as falling within the scope of section 527 (this would include super PACs). All 527 groups are required to file disclosure forms detailing their income sources and their expenses with the IRS on a routine basis. The Federal Elections Commission (FEC), however, only requires that political parties, candidates' campaign organizations, and PACs disclose this information on a specified schedule; all other 527s are exempt from the strict schedule of FEC disclosure. This means that exempt 527 groups can operate with more secrecy than other 527 groups, at least in the short term.

While exempt 527 groups engage in electioneering activities similar to those of traditional PACs, they are subject to less regulation by the FEC. While PACs must have a minimum number of donors, and there are limits to how much an individual can contribute to a PAC, there are no such limits on exempt 527 groups. Thus, they have become attractive means for corporations, unions, other organized interests, and even individuals to spend large amounts of money on federal elections with much less scrutiny of their activities.

After the Bipartisan Campaign Reform Act of 2002 prohibited outside groups from making unlimited contributions to political parties for voter education and **get-out-the-vote (GOTV) programs**, 527 group activity surged. Stephen Weissman and Ruth Hassan estimate that federally focused 527 spending leaped from $151 million in 2002 to $424 million in the **Campaign of 2004**. In subsequent elections, 527 spending declined, totaling about $200 million in the **Campaign of 2008**. Nevertheless, 527 spending still accounted for half of all outside spending in the 2008 election, according to the Campaign Finance Institute. One of the primary reasons for the decline in 527 spending is that donors have been moving toward **501(c) groups**, which are subject to far fewer regulations. This trend continued into the **Campaign of 2012**, when the Center for Responsive Politics estimates that federally focused 527 groups spent approximately $153 million on the election.

Some of the most notorious examples of 527 spending can be found in the **Campaign of 2004**, where Swift Boat Veterans for Truth and **MoveOn** were responsible for financing some of the most controversial ads in the election. In the **Campaign of 2008**, Democrats were the primary beneficiaries of 527 spending, and Republicans were the primary beneficiaries of 501(c) spending.

See also Campaign Finance Reform; Independent Advocacy Groups; Super PAC; Swift Boating

Additional Resources

Center for Responsive Politics. "527s: Advocacy Group Spending." https://www.open secrets.org/527s/index.php?filter=F#split. Accessed September 29, 2015.

Center for Responsive Politics. "Types of Advocacy Groups." http://www.opensecrets .org/527s/types.php. Accessed September 29, 2015.

Internal Revenue Service. "Tax Information for Political Organizations." April 8, 2010. http://www.irs.gov/charities/political/index.html. Accessed September 29, 2015.

Malbin, Michael J. *The Election after Reform: Money, Politics, and the Bipartisan Campaign Reform Act.* Lanham, MD: Rowman & Littlefield, 2006.

Weissman, Steve, and Ruth Hassan. "BCRA and the 527 Groups." In Michael J. Malbin, ed. *The Election after Reform: Money, Politics, and the Bipartisan Campaign Reform Act*. Lanham, MD: Rowman & Littlefield, 2006.

Weissman, Steve, and Suraj Sazawal. "Soft Money Political Spending by 501(c) Nonprofits Tripled in 2008 Election." Campaign Finance Institute, February 25, 2009. http://www.cfinst.org/press/releases_tags/09-02-25/Soft_Money_Political_Spending_by_Nonprofits_Tripled_in_2008.aspx. Accessed September 29, 2015.

Focus Groups

Presidential campaigns and the news operations covering them routinely make use of focus groups to gather insights regarding campaign issues from small groups of potential voters. The 1988 presidential campaign of George Bush, for example, used a focus group to evaluate the effectiveness of using the Massachusetts furlough program as an issue against Democratic nominee Michael Dukakis, the state's governor. On furlough from a Massachusetts prison, Willie Horton raped a woman and attacked her fiancé. Bush focus groups indicated that the furlough issue would play very well with a wide cross-section of voters. Subsequently, the Bush campaign made extremely effective use of the furlough issue to depict Dukakis as soft on crime.

Electronic news operations made use of focus groups to evaluate the effectiveness of candidates during and after presidential debates of the **Campaign of 2000**. Some news operations made use of dial group technology that permitted focus group participants to indicate their moment-to-moment reactions throughout the debate.

By the late 1990s, critics alleged that presidential campaigns had grown overly dependent on focus groups for developing campaign strategy, and news operations received criticism for relying too much on polls and focus groups to measure public reaction to presidential debates and other events.

Additional Resource

Hunter, Pamela. "Using Focus Groups in Campaigns: A Caution." *Campaign and Elections*, August 2000, p. 38.

Free Media. *See* Earned Media

Frontloading

"Frontloading" is a term that describes the late-twentieth- and early-twenty-first-century trend of states moving their presidential primaries to earlier and earlier times on the electoral calendar. Through the 1970s and 1980s, the presidential primary season ran from late January/February through June. State primaries and caucuses were distributed throughout these months, giving presidential candidates opportunities to visit and campaign in most states. Moreover, this type of scheduling permitted candidates to raise money throughout the primary season, and the slow accrual of delegates made it possible for a candidate to gain momentum for an unexpected, come-from-behind victory.

By the **Campaign of 2000**, most states began to schedule their primaries and caucuses as early as possible, hoping to benefit from the media coverage and tourism benefits enjoyed by traditionally early states such as Iowa and New Hampshire. The end result was that by March 14, 2000, Democrat Al Gore and Republican George W. Bush had both garnered enough delegate support that each was guaranteed his party's eventual nomination. This effectively eliminated the role of later primaries and caucuses from the selection process; voters residing in those states had no meaningful say over their party's nominee, as that decision had already been made before they even had a chance to go to the polls. Candidates like Republican hopeful John McCain, who lacked the name recognition of George W. Bush, found themselves denied of the opportunity to mount an effective campaign. McCain's victory in the Michigan primary came far too late in the primary season (February 22) to enable him to earn any momentum—too many delegates had already been awarded to Bush.

States adapted quickly to this turn of events, and more states scheduled their primaries at earlier dates in the **Campaign of 2004**. In that election, Republican incumbent George W. Bush and Democrat John Kerry had earned their parties' nominations by March 9, 2004—again, despite the nominating conventions being months away. After the 2004 elections were over, both the Democratic and Republican national parties attempted to limit frontloading for the first time. Both parties adopted rules that would penalize states that held elections prior to February 5 in the upcoming **Campaign of 2008**. The Democratic Party, in an attempt to be sensitive to legitimate concerns from states that claimed that the needs of their region were being ignored, let states apply for exemptions to the rules; this process led to the creation of new, early slots for the South Carolina primary and the Nevada caucus. The Republican Party offered no such exemptions; however, its rules penalized only early primaries, not early caucuses. Despite warnings from both political parties, two states plunged ahead and scheduled primaries prior to February 5. Michigan held its primary on January 15, 2008, and Florida held its primary on January 29, 2008. The Democratic Party required that all of its candidates remove their names from the Michigan and Florida ballots, and that no candidate actively campaign in either state. Michigan and Florida lost all of their voting delegates to the Democratic National Convention (although an agreement was eventually reached on a restoration formula, but this occurred months later).

Hillary Clinton alone remained on the Democratic ballot in Michigan, which she claimed was an oversight (although she later attempted to claim those delegates). The Republican Party reduced the convention delegations of Florida, Michigan, and South Carolina by 50 percent.

The scheduling of early primary dates by Michigan and Florida in the Campaign of 2008 did not occur in isolation. As a consequence, New Hampshire was compelled to reschedule its primary to an even earlier date, and Iowa was compelled to schedule its caucus to a date prior to the New Hampshire primary. Until 1976, the New Hampshire primary had been held in mid-March. In the 1980s, it crept up to the end of February. In 2000, it was moved to February 1, almost three weeks earlier than it was four years before. By 2004, it had slipped into January, and by the Campaign of 2008, it had been pushed up to January 8.

After the Campaign of 2008, both political parties once again resolved to deal with the problem of frontloading. While the Republican Party had initially been pleased that its nominee, John McCain, had sewn up the nomination early in the campaign season, thus avoiding the potential for fracturing party unity, the neck-and-neck race between Democrats Hillary Clinton and Barack Obama garnered constant media attention throughout the spring. As the Democratic candidates battled each other through June, the Republican nominee was sidelined by the media, and Republican voter enthusiasm waned as their party's race wound down. Rather than generate ill will and long-term grudges, the protracted Democratic contest seemed to generate voter enthusiasm and interest among Democratic voters.

Both parties sought to generate this same kind of enthusiasm for the **Campaign of 2012**. Working together, they negotiated an agreement that banned January primaries and permitted only four states (Iowa, New Hampshire, Nevada, and South Carolina) to hold campaign events prior to March 1. Moreover, the Republican Party also barred states that held primaries in February or March from using a winner-take-all delegate allocation. (The Democrats already allocated delegates proportionally, regardless of when a primary was held.) Florida, Michigan, and Arizona all held primaries prior to March 1, and all ran afoul of the rules (and incurred the delegate reduction penalty). Missouri's primary was held on February 7, but because it was not used for the purpose of delegate allocation (rather, it was a "beauty contest" primary), the state was not penalized. Colorado and Minnesota held their caucuses in February; however, only the first phase of the caucuses were held in that month, and delegates were awarded at a later phase, thus no party rules were violated. It appeared quite evident that the penalties imposed in the 2008 and 2012 elections were not sufficient to deter many states from violating political party rules on primary election scheduling.

The **Campaign of 2016** marked a departure from these recent trends. No primaries or caucuses were scheduled for January for the first time in two decades. The Iowa caucus was slated for February 1, and the New Hampshire primary was scheduled the following week, on February 9. The next campaign event did not occur until the South Carolina primary on February 20 (the Republicans) and 27 (the Democrats), followed by the Nevada caucuses (February 20 for the Democrats and February 23 for the GOP). Other states' primaries and caucuses were held on March 1 or thereafter, ending with a series of state primaries on June 7 (including CA, MT, NJ, NM, and SD), the District of Columbia primary on June 14, and the culmination of a series of state caucuses in mid-June. This created a more compressed schedule but also provided for smaller allotments of delegates throughout the campaign season, rather than a few large allocations early on. Because GOP events held prior to mid-March also entail a proportional instead of a winner-take-all allocation of delegates (similar to the Democrats, who use proportionality for all events), such a system seems designed to make the playing field more competitive in scenarios where there is no clear nationwide front-runner. When there is a consensus on a front-runner, and when that front-runner enjoys national rather than regional support, most systems do not impair such candidates from handily winning their party's nomination. However, frontloaded schedules clearly advantage those who are well positioned to quickly consolidate electoral gains; systems that are not frontloaded make it easier for candidates who are competitive, but who are not overwhelming favorites, to stay in the race; they also tend to placate elements of the party rank and file who may otherwise believe that their concerns are not being heard. And, as the Democratic primary season of 2008 demonstrated, systems that provide a more level playing field may lengthen the duration of the primary season when there is more than one competitive candidate (or, potentially, when the candidate field is one that is overwhelmingly weak and without a clear favorite).

See also Super Tuesday

Additional Resources

Busch, Andrew E. *The Front-Loading Problem in Presidential Nominations.* Washington, DC: Brookings, 2003.

Frontloading HQ. http://frontloading.blogspot.com/. Accessed October 13, 2015.

The Green Papers. "2016 Presidential Primaries, Caucuses, and Conventions Chronologically." http://www.thegreenpapers.com/P16/events.phtml?s=c. Accessed October 13, 2015.

"Thrusters v. Laggards: The High Tide of Frontloading Has Passed and Now Seems to be Ebbing." *Economist*, April 20, 2011.

Gay Rights Issue. *See* LGBTQ Issues

Gender Gap

The concept of the gender gap relies on the assumption that men and women have differing political interests, and that these interests can be discerned through their choices at the ballot box. In the earliest eras of American democracy, women's opportunities for political influence were severely limited. Denied the right to vote or even to own property, women were forced to depend on their fathers or their husbands to represent their political interests. In some localities during this time period, widows were permitted to vote in local school elections; however, there was little pressure to expand the franchise prior to the 1848 Seneca Falls Convention, where founders of the fledgling women's rights movement first gathered to express their support for both the abolition of slavery and the expansion of the franchise to women, the poor, and to African Americans.

In 1869 the Wyoming Territory guaranteed women full suffrage, which remained law when Wyoming became a state in 1890. In 1893 the state of Colorado followed suit, joined three years later by Utah and Idaho. From 1910, beginning with Oregon, through 1918, eleven more states, most of them west of the Mississippi (with the exception of Michigan and New York) guaranteed full suffrage for women, bringing the total to fifteen states, with several more allowing limited suffrage (e.g., allowing participation in primary elections—which at that time were not nearly as significant as they are today—and participation in specified municipal elections). By 1919, only seven states denied suffrage altogether, and ten more restricted suffrage to the most local matters (e.g., school bond and taxation proposals). Most, but by no means all, of these states were in the South. In 1920, the United States Constitution was amended—the Nineteenth Amendment—guaranteeing all women the right to vote at all levels: federal, state, and local. In the decades that followed, women's voting patterns did not differ substantially from those of men. That is to say, women voted according to their social class, their religion, their geography, and even their ethnicity. It was not until the emergence of the women's rights movement that men and women first saw their political interests diverge. By the late 1970s, the Republican Party and the Democratic Party offered very different positions on the ratification of the Equal Rights Amendment, equal pay, and abortion rights. And gender differences in vote choice began to emerge.

By the **Campaign of 1988**, pollsters and political scientists found evidence of a growing gender gap between Republican Party and Democratic Party supporters. Specifically, Democratic candidates at all levels received a higher percentage of votes from women than did Republican candidates. Republican candidates, on the other hand, received a higher percentage of white male voters. Moreover, there also appeared to be a **marriage gap** among women voters: exit polls indicated that Democratic candidates performed very well with unmarried, college-educated women, whereas the Republican Party fared better with middle-class, married women.

The gender gap has become a major feature of the political landscape of the United States, appearing in all subsequent presidential elections (with the arguable exception of the **Campaign of 2008**, in which Democratic nominee Barack Obama fared well with both men and women). In their study of the gender gap in the **Campaign of 2012**, Maxwell, Ford-Dowe, Jimeno, and Shields found that much of the gender gap occurred outside of the South, where 60 percent of women supported Obama, compared to only 45 percent of men. In the South, they found very little evidence of a gender gap: 49.6 percent of Southern women voted for Obama, as did 48.3 percent of Southern men. This pattern is evident among white voters as well as Latino voters (but not African American voters, who overwhelmingly supported Obama regardless of gender or geography). 53.8 percent of white women residing outside of the South supported Obama, but 52 percent of white men outside of the South supported Romney. However, among Southern whites, 66.6 percent of women supported Romney, as did 65 percent of men. Similar to the rise in support for Romney among white women in the South, the researchers found that Latino women in the South tended to support Romney at higher rates than Latino women outside of the South. Their data show that 73 percent of non-Southern Latino women voted for Obama, whereas his support dropped in the South to only 55 percent of Latino women. This research suggests that the gender gap is influenced by race, ethnicity, and geography.

Preliminary research by Maxwell et al. found that although Hillary Clinton was preferred by three out of five voters, women were twice as likely to express support for her than were men. Men expressed a preference for Jeb Bush, Marco Rubio, or Chris Christie over Clinton when offered the option, suggesting the continuation of the gender gap in the **Campaign of 2016**. While most voters preferred a candidate of their own party to any alternative, Republican women were more likely than GOP men to express a preference for Clinton over the three GOP candidates offered, suggesting that women voters in the GOP may be dissatisfied with their party's large field of almost exclusively male candidates (Carly Fiorina being the only exception) and the lack of progress on the cultivation of a more diverse group of potential nominees.

While political candidates often refer to health care, education, and reproductive rights as "women's issues," these issues are not the underlying source of the gender gap. Rather, public opinion data continue to show that women and men differ most on issues related to the death penalty, gun rights, and military involvement in other nations. Specifically, women are less likely than men to support the death penalty, more likely to favor gun control, and less likely to favor the use of force abroad.

See also Campaign of 1992; Campaign of 1996; Campaign of 2000; Campaign of 2004; Women's Equality Issue

Additional Resources

Carroll, Susan J., and Richard Logan Fox. *Gender and Elections*: *Shaping the Future of American Politics*. New York: Cambridge University Press, 2010.

Maxwell, Angie, Pearl Ford-Dowe, Rafael Jimeno, and Todd Shields. "Is There a War on Women? Attitudes about Women in the Workplace." Report from the 2012 Blair Center-Clinton School Poll (2012), Diane D. Blair Center of Southern Politics and Society, University of Arkansas. http://blaircenterclintonschoolpoll.uark.edu/6759.php. Accessed September 5, 2015.

Get-Out-the-Vote (GOTV) Programs

Historically, the task of mobilizing voters was the responsibility of political parties, and the organized interests that supported a party contributed manpower and other expertise in marshaling the voters needed to secure an electoral victory. Changes in the financial landscape, wrought by campaign finance reform in the 1970s and afterward, and Supreme Court decisions about spending by outside independent advocacy groups, in addition to changes in the technological landscape (such as the advent of television advertising and the rise of computer-driven market research), have altered the traditional role of political parties in getting out the vote for their candidates. Political parties, buffeted by campaign finance loopholes in the 1980s and 1990s but seduced by the lure of television advertising, focused their resources on advertising as a means to attract voters, abandoning traditional door-to-door, face-to-face modes of contact. At the same time, elections overall became more candidate-centered and less party-centered, reducing partisan ties that tend to keep voters showing up to the polls from one election to the next. As court decisions permitted outside groups to rival, or even exceed, party spending at election time, new sources of influence came to rival those of political parties.

Yet some surprising changes have taken place in voter mobilization behaviors. For the first time since the mid-1960s, voter turnout has been on the rise. The **Campaigns of 2004**, **2008**, and **2012** were all marked by substantially higher turnout than the norm, and they constituted a clear departure from the decades-long trend of declining voter turnout. The increase in voter turnout was no fluke; rather, it occurred as a result of deliberate, systematic efforts by political parties and their candidates to generate voter mobilization. With each subsequent election, parties and candidates have sought novel means for reaching out to voters, yet they have also reemphasized some of the more time-honored get-out-the-vote-techniques used by parties of earlier generations.

Particularly on the left, collaboration between academic researchers and political activists has led to the use of field experiments to study the effectiveness of various GOTV strategies, and the results of these experiments have often been used to craft subsequent campaign strategies. Among the most influential research has been that conducted by Donald Green and Alan Gerber, then political scientists at Yale, who conducted a series of controlled experiments in the 1990s on the effects of campaign contact and voting. Green and Gerber found that phone contact was no more effective than receiving no contact whatsoever, with mailers generating only a slight bump in turnout. Their major finding was that in-person contact yielded a sizable increase in an individual's likelihood of turning out to vote. Green and Gerber and their students attracted the attention of candidates from both parties, as well as outside groups such as the AFL-CIO, and with the cooperation of various campaigns, candidates over the years experimented in altering the content of mailers, homing in on important media markets, changing the content of television ads to adapt to crucial audiences, using paid and volunteer callers for phone banks, and using various forms of personal contact. These experiments were an important factor in creating a more scientific approach to political campaigns. And, just as importantly, they led to the appearance of political and behavioral scientists in campaign management.

For example, the Analyst Institute, formed just prior to the 2008 election, conducts behavioral science experiments on elections around the country in order to generate strategies for Democratic campaigns. Its staff are involved in the planning of the Democratic Party's national campaign efforts, as well as its House and Senate strategies. In the Campaigns of 2008 and 2012, Democrat Barack Obama's campaign organization had a reputation for its devotion to a scientific, data-oriented approach to campaigning, and it developed a formidable in-house, data-oriented voter identification and mobilization effort. While the scope of Obama's campaigns differed across the two elections (in 2008, he targeted a larger group of states and voters, including those who did not usually vote Democratic, but by 2012, his focus was on his Democratic base), in both instances, his campaign relied on getting voter turnout rates up in his must-win states. To accomplish this, the Obama campaign used a number of novel tactics, among them, asking people to make a plan about how they were going to vote on Election Day (with the campaign sending reminders about the date, polling hours in their state, and their polling location), and a subtle form of social pressure in which potential voters were provided with the names of their neighbors who had recently voted as part of a vote reminder (with the implication that their neighbors would also know whether they had voted).

The campaign of Republican John McCain was underfunded in the Campaign of 2008, having agreed to take public funds for the general election. It did not have the luxury of waging a battle in every state in which it was competitive, pulling out of states such as Michigan well before Election Day, and thus lacked the resources to invest in analytics. Republican Mitt Romney was far better financed in the Campaign of 2012, although much of his resources were controlled by **super PACs** and other outside groups, rather than by his campaign organization. This limited the campaign's ability to directly engage in a sophisticated GOTV effort. Romney did not prioritize the ground game in the campaign, maintaining a fraction of the field offices that the Obama campaign had. Additionally, some GOP-controlled legislatures in states such as Florida had passed limitations on nonpartisan voter registration drives. This negatively affected the Romney campaign, which lacked the field presence in Florida that the Obama campaign had, forcing the GOP to spend valuable funds late in the race on a last-ditch effort to register potential supporters that the League of Women Voters used to register for free. However, the Romney campaign did attempt to emulate some of the Obama campaign's tactics, crafting a strategy it termed "Orca" in order to combat "Narwhal," Obama's vaunted in-house GOTV operation. Orca was supposed to enable GOP volunteers manning the polls on Election Day to quickly input data on which voters had already showed up, letting Romney campaign staff at the Boston headquarters send out phone reminders to prospective Romney voters before the polls closed. But poor planning and an under-resourced system led Orca to malfunction, leaving volunteers frustrated and the Romney campaign adrift. It is unclear whether Romney's inability to connect with voters on Election Day cost him the election; however, it was viewed as a symptom of other problems with the management of the campaign.

In the Campaign of 2015/2016, to this point, Republican candidate Senator Ted Cruz in particular has devoted considerable resources to the use of psychological data and analytics to stimulate support among likely voters.

See also Battleground State; Big Data; Early Voting; Ground War; Microtargeting; Voter Eligible Population (VEP) Turnout; Voting Reform Issue

Additional Resources

Allen, Cathy. "Get Out Your Vote." *Campaigns and Elections* 21, October 2000, p. 20.

CIRCLE: The Center for Research on Civic Learning and Engagement, Tufts University. http://www.civicyouth.org. Accessed September 29, 2015.

Green, Donald P., and Alan S. Gerber. *Get Out the Vote: How to Increase Voter Turnout.* 2nd ed. Washington, DC: Brookings Institute, 2008.

Hamburger, Tom. "Cruz Campaign Credits Psychological Data and Analytics for Rising Success." *The Washington Post*, December 12, 2015.

Issenberg, Sasha. *The Victory Lab*. New York: Crown, 2012.

National Conference of State Legislatures. "Absentee and Early Voting." http://www.ncsl
.org/default.aspx?tabid=16604. Accessed September 29, 2015.

Rosenstone, Steven J., and John Mark Hansen. *Mobilization, Participation, and Democracy in America*. New York: Longman, 2002.

Going Rogue

The term "going rogue" was originally used by the campaign staff of Republican presidential candidate John McCain to describe instances in which McCain's running mate, Alaska governor Sarah Palin, strayed from the campaign's message (and the advice of her handlers) during the **Campaign of 2008**. Palin took pride in advertising her independence, and she later used the phrase as a title for her autobiography. The term quickly evolved, and it is now used to refer to any instance of a candidate going off-message or departing from the party line on a political issue. Perhaps the blunt and unrestrained rhetorical style of GOP candidate Donald Trump adds another connotation to the phrase "going rogue," but that remains a question of future usage and the manner in which atypical, even controversial behavior of serious candidates is rewarded.

Additional Resources

Bash, Dana, Peter Hamby, and John King. "Palin's 'Going Rogue,' McCain Aide Says." *CNN Politics*, October 25, 2008. http://articles.cnn.com/2008-10-25/politics/palin.tension
_1_sarah-palin-nicolle-wallace-tracey-schmitt?_s=PM:POLITICS. Accessed September 22, 2015.

Dickerson, John. "Palin's Campaign vs. McCain's." *Slate*, October 20, 2008. http://www
.slate.com/id/2202658/. Accessed September 22, 2015.

Smith, Ben. "Palin Allies Report Rising Camp Tension." Politico, October 25, 2008. http://
www.politico.com/news/stories/1008/14929.html. Accessed September 22, 2015.

Snow, Kate. "Game On: Palin Book Blitz Begins: Former McCain Aides Rebut Claims in 'Going Rogue.'" *ABC News*, November 16, 2009. http://abcnews.go.com/GMA/sarah
-palin-angers-mccain-aides-rogue/story?id=9090753. Accessed September 22, 2015.

Going Viral

"Going viral" denotes that phenomenon which occurs through social media as disseminated through the Internet and that is often, but not necessarily, in the form of a video through which news of an event, or simply the event itself, is received by an exceedingly large and exponentially growing number of people within a short duration of time. To "go viral," as the name implies, is to spread through cyberspace with the rapidity of a virus replicating itself throughout a population. An event or story is recorded—again, often as a video, but it could just as easily be an audio clip or some brief text containing a remark, quote, or gaffe—posted on a popular Web site or social medium such as YouTube or Twitter, and saturates the entire Internet within a matter of hours. Given that laptop computers, electronic tablets, and smartphones enable consumers to instantaneously gain access to Internet news with an expanded degree of mobility, flexibility, and speed, it is now possible for an event to go viral in a matter of minutes. The source of a viral story or video could be anywhere; it could initially be posted by a candidate, a campaign operative, a member of the press, or any private citizen with the access and skill to use the Internet accordingly. Once an event goes viral on the Internet, it is often repeatedly reported in the broadcast media, as more television news outlets are drawing stories from the latest viral videos and tweets circulating through social media. Once the incident is circulating through both the Internet and the twenty-four-hour news cycle, it quickly becomes nearly universally known to the general public. One can easily surmise what this means for presidential campaigns.

Arguably one of the more famous examples of a political episode going viral would be Howard Dean's "screaming" incident in the aftermath of the 2004 Iowa Caucus. After having lost in Iowa, Dean, who had been considered the front-runner up to that point, in an attempt to bolster confidence among his supporters, at one point cut loose with an ear-splitting scream that went viral on the Internet and was replayed numerous times in the twenty-four-hour television news loop. In the 2006 Virginia senatorial campaign, former governor and incumbent senator George Allen, the Republican nominee for the open Senate seat, publicly and deliberately referred to S. R. Sidarth, a young Democratic campaign tracker who was shadowing Allen's events, as "macaca," which was immediately recognized as a racial slur, although Allen denied that this was his meaning or his intent. This story and image went viral and proved damaging to Allen's campaign—he lost his seat to challenger Jim Webb in a tight election—and to his long-term career, which for many of his supporters within the party included the possibility of a run for the White House. During the 2008 New Hampshire primary campaign, a short video of Sen. Hillary Clinton showing vulnerability went viral on YouTube after first being broadcast on television. In the **Campaign of 2012**, numerous gaffes went viral, among them Gov. Rick Perry's "oops" moment and Gov. Romney's "47 percent" remark. But it's not simply gaffes that go viral: The president's "horses and bayonets" jibe during the third debate spread rapidly through the Internet. Less flattering to the president was viral video capturing a comment made while mistakenly assuming that he was off-mic, in which he assured the president of Russia that he would enjoy "more flexibility" to act after his reelection. In the early stages of the 2015–2016 campaign season, celebrity billionaire and GOP candidate

Donald Trump's observations and remarks had inundated both the Internet and the cable news cycle. His imprudent remarks about immigrants, his proclivities for blunt language and dramatic statements, his taunting of other candidates, and his rude posture toward television anchorwoman and debate moderator Megyn Kelly, as well as his perplexing treatment during a press conference of another broadcast journalist, Jorge Ramos, have dominated social media over the Internet as well as both broadcast and print media.

Since the advent of television coverage, presidential campaign moments have been spread across the media with greater rapidity and to a larger extent, which could offer the temptation to present retrospectives of famous campaign moments that might be exhibited as precursors to "going viral," episodes such as Sen. Edmund Muskie "crying" at a press conference during the 1972 New Hampshire primary, and breaking news about Sen. Thomas Eagleton, the 1972 Democratic nominee for vice president, having received in the previous decade electroshock therapy as a psychiatric treatment for depression and debilitating stress. In the case of the former, Sen. Muskie, during an outdoor press conference conducted during a light snow, displayed emotion when answering unkind allegations about his wife that were in fact disseminated by dirty tricksters working for incumbent president Nixon's campaign, and he appeared to choke up and blink back tears, a moment that was seized upon by his opponents to impugn Sen. Muskie's character: A man who would so easily come to tears is not the man for the White House. Interestingly, when President Reagan cried at the funeral for the lost astronauts of the *Challenger* disaster, it was also a moment that "went viral" but an example of tears shed to the opposite effect, in this case conveying the president's sincerity and sensitivity.

Other examples of "viral moments" that circulated prior to the Internet might include Vice President Mondale riffing off of a popular hamburger commercial as a pointed criticism of a rival candidate; or an annoyed Ronald Reagan, then a candidate for president, refusing to yield the microphone at a primary debate in 1980; or sadly comical images of a helmeted Gov. Michael Dukakis riding atop an army tank. As viral moments they might seem anachronistic *prima facie,* as they preceded both widespread use of the Internet and the twenty-four-hour news cycle, but they did quickly reach a wide audience and were familiar to the general public, elements of what it means to go viral. If a comment or incident is widely disseminated, like a rapidly spread rumor, then it qualifies as having gone viral. Probably the most famous example of a forerunner of a viral image or message is the familiar **"Daisy Girl"** television ad produced by President Lyndon Johnson's 1964 election campaign. The ad was so inflammatory that it was shelved after just one broadcast, but that one broadcast nearly instantaneously stirred a national discussion, and it succeeded in influencing the manner in which many voters reacted to the president's Republican challenger, Arizona senator Barry Goldwater. Some researchers have suggested that the "Daisy Girl" ad was one of the first instances of something going viral—in this case, due to media coverage of the ad and the controversies and discussions that ensued. Moments such as these do illustrate that modern media, at least with the ascent of television followed by the popularity of the Internet as a source of instant information, has been colored by the manner in which information about a candidate's statements and conduct, both good and bad, reach a wide population among consumers of the news and users of social media. In a real sense, even before television, the old-fashioned rumor mill could influence how a public official was perceived. President Warren Harding earned a reputation as a womanizer (and father of a child out of wedlock), with the consequence that both he and his presidency were dismissed as shallow, ineffective, and—owing to the Teapot Dome scandal (unrelated to his personal foibles)—corrupt. But historians have more recently rehabilitated the reputation of the Harding presidency, the president's own personal issues notwithstanding. While President Harding's reputation did not spread virally, the dissemination of stories about his personal conduct might qualify as an example of a "viral" story that preceded even television. Interestingly, President Kennedy's infidelities were well-protected secrets during his short lifetime, an example of journalists deliberately withholding information about a public official, and yet those who knew the president were aware of his proclivities and habits.

"Going viral" can work to a candidate's advantage or disadvantage. In the examples above, Gov. Reagan's refusal to yield the mic benefited his image as a strong, determined, indomitable leader, while Gov. Dukakis's effort to visually convey that same kind of toughness while riding in a tank was risible. In some cases an incident gone viral, while stirring considerable coverage and exercised conversation, has little to no effect in the final analysis. For example, Gov. Romney's "47 percent" remark, while infuriating to his critics, in the end was inconsequential to his campaign. In other cases, going viral has a double effect, both good and bad. In the current case of Donald Trump, many of his untoward comments have gone viral, causing considerable furor with regard to his image and conduct while at the same time perplexingly drawing new supporters. Trump is adept at turning negative press to his advantage like no other presidential candidate before him, surviving controversial remarks that would have destroyed the campaigns of most candidates. This ability to turn bad press to good is again reminiscent of that most famous forerunner of the viral video, the "Daisy Girl" ad, for much of the agitation about that television spot was critical of the Johnson campaign for using Cold War terror tactics to slur the opposition, but even though Johnson received criticism, it forced a reexamination of Sen. Goldwater's stance with regard to how the military should be used, and to what extent the United States should go to win conflicts abroad, especially the war in Vietnam.

As YouTube and other social media outlets are used more deliberately by campaigns at all levels, viral videos, rapidly breaking news stories, remarks from candidates (including announcements, controversial claims, and occasional gaffes), and political messages will continue to gain the attention of Internet consumers. With the creation of YouTube's Election Hub, for example, political campaigning appears to be entering a new phase in the dissemination of information. Now that the Internet has become a popular disseminator of information, the management of the media is no longer the province of experts, no longer directed by professional journalists or serving professional campaign operatives alone. The Internet enables anyone to post news of an event in their own way, and anyone's video or tweet can spread with rapidity and ubiquity in ways that have no real precedent. In the age of the Internet, "going viral" illustrates what happens when "the press" becomes anyone with a camera, and it is but one more result of the introduction and continuing growth of online political communication, and it will no doubt remain a fixture of presidential campaigning into the foreseeable future.

Additional Resources

Hendricks, John Allen, and Schill, Dan. *Presidential Campaigning and Social Media.* Oxford: Oxford University Press, 2015.

McNair, Brian. *An Introduction to Political Communication.* Fifth ed. Lanham, MD: Routledge Press, 2011.

Vernallis, Carol. "Audiovisual Change: Viral Web Media and the Obama Campaign." *Cinema Journal* 50, no. 4 (Summer 2011): 73–97.

Goldwater Conservative

While the term "Goldwater conservative" originally described supporters of 1964 Republican presidential candidate and states' rights advocate Senator Barry Goldwater of Arizona, it has increasingly come to define one specific ideological approach to the relationship between the power of the federal government and the rights of citizens. Specifically, Goldwater conservatives believe in limited government involvement in the economy, but they also believe in limiting government involvement in the personal lives of individuals, separating the Goldwater species of conservatism from the social conservative movement that emerged in the latter decades of the twentieth century, long after Goldwater's failed 1964 campaign. In contrast to the social conservatives in the GOP, Goldwater was an early supporter of abortion rights (at the state level), and his support for abortion rights expanded over the course of his career. In the early 1990s, he also became an advocate for gay men and women, arguing that they should be able to serve openly in the military, observing, "You don't have to be straight to be in the military; you just have to be able to shoot straight." A strong believer in the separation of church and state, Goldwater was skeptical about the influence of the religious right on the Republican Party and bluntly critical of Rev. Jerry Falwell's Moral Majority and the political ambitions of televangelist Pat Robertson.

Some political commentators may characterize Goldwater conservatives as libertarians; however, Goldwater himself cannot be so characterized. Unlike contemporary libertarians, who tend to espouse isolationism, Goldwater supported a strong military and an activist U.S. foreign policy as a means to thwart the spread of Soviet influence, and he was often viewed as an extremist for his willingness to use military force whenever it was expedient to do so. Moreover, during the 1980s, he began to accept a more moderate attitude toward the scope of the federal government; still, Senator Goldwater continued to identify himself with the principles of smaller, less intrusive government, and he generally supported the policies of President Ronald Reagan. Save for the Iran-Contra blunder, for the most part, Goldwater admired the Reagan presidency. That said, Sen. Goldwater found himself increasingly estranged from his party's social conservatism and its reliance on the support of religious fundamentalism. He fervently disassociated himself from those elements within the Republican Party who presumed to be his heirs, referring to the GOP in 1989 as being led by "a bunch of kooks." In 1996 he observed that he and Republican presidential nominee Sen. Bob Dole were, compared to contemporary GOP conservatives, the "new liberals" in the party.

In retrospect, Sen. Goldwater appears to be a different breed of cat compared to nearly every variety of conservatism in American politics today. Some might claim Kentucky senator Rand Paul as the true heir to the Goldwater legacy, and Sen. Paul does share the Goldwater faith in limited government and expansive individual freedom, but Paul's isolationism couldn't be farther from Goldwater's commitment to national defense. Barry Goldwater's impact on American politics doubtless continues to reverberate throughout the American ideological topography, and his quixotic 1964 presidential campaign remains a potent ideological touchstone, but the species "Goldwater conservative" might today be as rare as vacuum tubes.

See also Campaign of 1964; Rockefeller Republican

Additional Resources

Buckley, William F., Jr. *Flying High: Remembering Barry Goldwater.* New York: Basic Books, 2008.

Bush, Andrew, John W. Dean, and Barry M. Goldwater Jr. *Pure Goldwater.* New York: Palgrave Macmillan, 2008.

Goldwater, Barry M. *The Conscience of a Conservative.* Princeton, NJ: Princeton University Press, 2007.

Perlstein, Rick. *Before the Storm: Barry Goldwater and the Unmaking of the American Consensus.* Second ed. New York: Nation Books, 2009.

Sherman, Elizabeth Tanner, ed. *Barry Goldwater and the Remaking of the American Political Landscape.* Tucson: University of Arizona Press, 2013.

Ground War

This is the portion of the presidential campaign that tends to focus on the **get-out-the-vote (GOTV)** effort at the grassroots, or on the ground, in contrast with the "air war" that candidates wage on the airwaves. It is sometimes referred to as the "ground game" portion of a political campaign, in reference to its strategic element.

Get-out-the-vote activities were largely neglected by presidential candidates from the early 1960s through the 1990s. During this era, many campaign managers felt that television ads were a more effective means of generating voter turnout than more labor-intensive, traditional GOTV strategies. While political parties and interest groups still engaged in GOTV activities, these efforts too waned over time as Americans grew less inclined to engage in volunteerism more generally, and labor unions lost their pool of members on which the Democratic Party had long relied for such efforts.

Voter turnout stagnated and declined during this era, but political campaigns continued to view GOTV activities as too expensive and therefore not cost-effective in the long run. Instead, they sought out market research strategies that would enable them to more effectively target their potential supporters in the electorate as a means of generating turnout. In the aftermath of the hotly contested **Campaign of 2000**, political candidates and political parties came to realize that with an almost evenly divided electorate, every vote counted, and the candidate who could mobilize the most supporters would have an edge on Election Day. Republican incumbent George W. Bush's campaign focused its efforts on mobilizing its evangelical Christian base in the **Campaign of 2004**, and in the end, Bush achieved a very narrow victory over Democratic nominee John Kerry.

The **Campaign of 2008** marked a new era in GOTV activities. Democratic nominee Barack Obama amassed a substantial campaign war chest after forgoing the public financing system that would have limited his expenditures. Obama used these funds to campaign in states such as Virginia, Georgia, Indiana, and North Carolina, where Democratic candidates had not performed well for decades. His campaign also invested in GOTV activities that targeted younger voters and ethnic minorities, all of whom had historically low voter turnout rates. Republican nominee John McCain lacked the resources to engage in similar activities. Many political analysts believe that these differences helped Obama defeat his opponent, becoming the first African American president in U.S. history.

However, in the **Campaign of 2012**, Democratic incumbent Obama faced a challenger with more comparable financial resources. Sides and Vavreck argue that while Romney may have had strong fund-raising skills, he made very different choices about how to use those funds than Obama did, and those differences were most evident in the ground game. Nationwide, they counted 786 field offices associated with Obama's campaign and only 284 associated with Romney's campaign. While Romney invested some resources in states where Obama had few offices (Utah, Missouri), on balance, it was more often the case that the Obama campaign invested in field offices in states that the Romney campaign ignored (i.e., Washington, Oregon, Idaho, Montana, California, Arizona, Texas, Oklahoma, Arkansas, Mississippi, Alabama, Georgia, South Carolina, and Connecticut). Sides and Vavreck tallied up candidate advantage by county and found 187 counties in the United States where there was an Obama field office but not a Romney field office.

How Romney and Obama used their field offices tended to differ as well. Sides and Vavreck noted that Obama's field offices tended to be located in counties that leaned Democratic, such that they would help to benefit Obama's reelection chances. Moreover, this appeared to be the primary or sole objective of those field offices. Romney's field offices, on the other hand, were situated such that they benefited local candidates, and their operations seemed to be centered on that task. Sides and Vavreck conducted a statistical analysis that showed that having one field office (or more) tended to improve Obama's vote share (controlling for other factors such as ads) but that having one Romney field office (or more) had no discernible effect on Romney's vote share. However, they also note that even if Obama had had fewer field offices, he likely still would have won the election, albeit by a slightly smaller margin.

These studies suggest that in the **Campaign of 2016**, fund-raising alone won't be the primary determinant of a candidate's electoral success. Rather, how the candidates, their parties, and their outside supporters use their resources at the local level to mobilize voters will play a large role in determining who wins in November. At present the Trump campaign may prove to be an outlier.

Additional Resources

Bailey, Eric. "Campaign 2000: Foot Soldiers Fight to Boost Turnout." *Los Angeles Times*, October 29, 2000, p. A1.

Ball, Molly. "Obama's Edge: The Ground Game That Could Put Him Over the Top." *The Atlantic*, October 12, 2012.

Bergen, Daniel E., Alan S. Gerber, Donald P. Green, and Costas Panagopoulos. "Grassroots Mobilization and Voter Turnout in 2004." *Public Opinion Quarterly* 69, no. 5 (2005): 760–77.

Darr, Joshua P., and Matthew S. Levendusky. "Relying on the Ground Game: The Placement and Effect of Campaign Field Offices." *American Politics Research* 42 (May 2014): 529-48.

Sides, John, and Lynn Vavreck. *The Gamble: Choice and Chance in the 2012 Presidential Election.* Princeton, NJ: Princeton University Press, 2013.

Gun Control Issue

Handgun control became a major **wedge issue** beginning with the **Campaign of 1976** and continuing through the **Campaign of 2008**. Throughout the period, the Democratic Party and its nominees generally supported restricting access to handguns in an effort to reduce gun violence. In contrast, the Republican Party and its candidates have resisted additional restrictions on handguns on the grounds that the Second Amendment protects the right of citizens to bear arms. Throughout this era, the Republican Party made use of the gun control issue to characterize the Democratic Party as soft on crime, suggesting that gun rights were necessary to protect honest citizens from well-armed criminals.

During the 1920s and early 1930s, an intense wave of gun violence swept the nation as Prohibition led to widespread bootlegging and associated criminal activities. This violence raised a national outcry for the federal government to regulate guns, and in response to this pressure, Congress passed the National Firearms Act of 1934. This act limited the general public's access to machine guns and short-barreled (or sawed-off) shotguns and rifles. In 1938, Congress passed the Federal Firearms Act, which required all gun dealers to obtain a federal firearms license. Equally important, the law required gun dealers to record the names and addresses of individuals who purchased firearms.

During the 1960s, the United States experienced an unprecedented increase in crime, particularly in major metropolitan areas, and by the end of the decade, many of the nation's largest cities had experienced race riots as well. Some experts blamed the increase in crime on easy access to guns. Sociologists and criminologists saw other factors at work as well, including rising rates of urban poverty as whites took flight to the suburbs, leaving eroding tax bases and deteriorating neighborhoods in their wake. Exacerbating this new wave of violence were the assassinations of high-profile public figures, most of whom had strong associations with the civil rights movement, including President John F. Kennedy in 1963, civil rights activist Malcolm X in 1965, civil rights activist Martin Luther King in 1968, and Democratic presidential candidate Robert Kennedy in 1968. During the **Campaign of 1972**, Alabama governor and pro-segregation presidential candidate George Wallace was shot while attending a campaign event, and he was permanently paralyzed as a result of his wounds. These shocking acts of gun violence once again put pressure on Congress to make American streets safer.

In the **Campaign of 1968**, Republican nominee Richard Nixon made restoring law and order the centerpiece of his domestic agenda. The Republican Party platform blamed the increase in crime on failed Democratic policies but at the same time acquiesced to public pressure to deal with the gun issue. Specifically, the platform adopted by Republicans in 1968 supported the "enactment of legislation to control indiscriminate availability of firearms," while protecting the Second Amendment rights of citizens "to collect, own and use firearms for legitimate purposes." Significantly, by the Campaign of 1972, President Nixon and the Republican Party called for "laws to control the improper use of handguns." Similarly, the 1972 Democratic Party platform encouraged a crackdown on illegal "Saturday night specials." Even though both the 1968 and 1972 Republican Party platforms included planks pledging to protect gun ownership, gun rights were not a major campaign issue in either the Campaign of 1968 or the Campaign of 1972, primarily because both political parties sought to place some limits on handgun ownership.

The Campaign of 1976 marked a major shift in the gun rights position of the Republican Party. Between 1972 and 1976, conservatives assumed a more prominent role in the Republican Party. Backed by the National Rifle Association (NRA), these conservative Republicans expressed their strong opposition to federal handgun registration laws. Despite two failed assassination attempts against President Gerald Ford, the Republican Party platform sought to use gun control as a wedge issue to attract independents and conservative Democratic voters, particularly in the South. The Democratic Party and its nominee Jimmy Carter called for handgun registration and a federal ban on the sale of cheap handguns ("Saturday night specials"), which had previously been subject only to import bans and state-level bans.

During the **Campaigns of 1980**, **1984**, and **1988**, major differences continued to emerge between the Democratic and Republican parties on the gun control issue. Shortly after Reagan's 1981 presidential inauguration, John Hinckley Jr. shot President Reagan; a Secret Service agent; a Washington, DC, police officer; and Reagan's press secretary, James Brady, in a foiled assassination attempt on the president. All four were seriously wounded; Reagan recovered, but Brady was paralyzed and confined to a wheelchair. Forced to retire, Brady turned his energies to new cause: handgun control. Reagan supported Brady's efforts, but Congress, under strong pressure from the National Rifle Association, failed to deliver any significant legislation during this time. Instead, the Armed Criminal Act of 1986 increased federal penalties for those already prohibited from owning a firearm, and that same year, Congress banned the sale of "cop killer" bullets.

Brady and his wife, Sarah, formed Handgun Control Inc. to lobby Congress for additional reforms. The Brady Bill, which included a federal background check on gun purchases and imposed a seven-day waiting period (eventually decreased to five days in the final passage), was winding its way through the legislature in the spring of 1991. President George H. W. Bush was reluctant to sign, and Republicans in the House were attempting to block the bill. In an op-ed column in the *New York Times*, Ronald Reagan openly advocated the provisions of the Brady Bill, noting that he had supported a far lengthier waiting period while governor of California. Reagan also privately encouraged Bush to sign the bill. The legislation eventually passed and was signed by President Clinton in late 1993 (and later expired under a Republican Congress in 2004).

During the **Campaign of 1992**, Democratic nominee Bill Clinton successfully downplayed support for new gun control measures, which temporarily defused the issue. Yet Clinton proved successful in pushing through Congress the 1994 Violent Crime Control and Law Enforcement Act, which included a ten-year ban on the manufacture and sale of automatic weapons to civilians (also known as the assault weapons ban). This legislation was a response to the 1989 school shooting in Stockton, California, in which thirty-four students and a teacher were shot and five children died, and a subsequent California shooting that killed eight. In both instances, semi-automatic weapons were used. Interestingly, Clinton did not pay a heavy political price for his support for the Brady Bill or the assault weapons ban, and he was easily reelected in the **Campaign of 1996**. Clinton's good fortune was most likely due, in part, to the NRA's tin ear. After the Oklahoma City bombing in the spring of 1995, an NRA spokesperson distributed fund-raising literature that was highly critical of the federal Bureau of Alcohol, Tobacco, and Firearms, calling agents "jack-booted thugs" and accusing the agency of Nazi tactics and "murdering law-abiding citizens." Former president George H. W. Bush publicly resigned his NRA membership in disgust.

In both the **Campaign of 2000** and the **Campaign of 2004**, the Republican Party used the gun control issue to appeal to voters who had previously voted for Clinton in conservative states such as West Virginia, Tennessee, and Missouri. Republican nominee George W. Bush warned voters that Democratic nominees Al Gore and John Kerry would impose serious limitations on their gun rights, and the NRA ran numerous issue ads in these states as well. Gore and Kerry both reaffirmed their commitment to gun rights, and each went on a high-profile hunting trip during his campaign. This was a fairly pointless endeavor; by this time, white male voters, particularly those who were rural or who lived in the South, had long abandoned the Democratic Party and were unlikely to be reassured by these attempts to placate them on gun rights. The assault rifle ban expired during the administration of George W. Bush. Supporters of the ban took out a full-page ad in the *New York Times* with Osama bin Laden's photo and text that suggested that Bin Laden and his supporters were excited about the impending expiration of the ban.

Gun control remained an issue in the **Campaign of 2008**, even though neither candidate discussed the issue a great deal. Republican vice presidential nominee Sarah Palin openly touted her experiences in hunting wolves from helicopters in Alaska, sending cues to Republican voters about her candidate's position on gun rights. Democratic nominee Barack Obama, on the other hand, made no attempt to go on a hunting trip during the campaign. Obama appeared most comfortable in suits and ties and was at ease with his image as an urbanite. Voters drew their own conclusions, and many Republicans became convinced that Obama would engage in a major push to take their guns away if he was elected. These fears were fanned by the NRA; in a direct mail campaign to its members, the group claimed that Obama would introduce sweeping changes to current gun control laws if elected (although PolitiFact debunked most of the items on the NRA's ten-point list). Shortly after Obama took office, several individuals engaged in shooting sprees that appeared to be related to fears that Obama was coming for their guns.

In 2009, the Supreme Court struck down the District of Columbia's handgun restrictions, at the time among the strictest in the nation. While the court argued that a total ban on handgun ownership was unconstitutional, Justice Scalia suggested that some regulations would be considered permissible, including registration laws, laws meant to keep guns out of the hands of mentally unstable persons or criminals, and laws meant to limit guns in sensitive areas such as schools or government buildings. The NRA went on to challenge gun control laws on the books in numerous other states and municipalities in the wake of this ruling, ushering in a new era of controversy over gun rights that was centered on the states (and to a lesser extent, local governments), rather than on reforms at the federal level.

Unlike the violence of previous decades, mass shootings in more recent years have not led to a social or political consensus about the role of guns in American society. Indeed, the massacre of students at Virginia Tech in April 2007 did not substantially change the dialogue of the 2008 presidential campaign. It was framed as more of a mental health issue than a gun violence issue and attributed to the depravity of a single individual rather than to a systemic failure of government or society, and thus it was not viewed as a problem in need of a solution. It did appear that most Americans shared concerned about guns getting into the hands of the wrong people, a topic about which they were reminded in January 2011 when GOP representative Gabrielle Giffords and eighteen others were gunned down during a campaign event, but opinions have remained divided on how best to accomplish this. Gun rights supporters believe that the solution is to expand legal gun ownership, in part by making it easier to carry a concealed weapon and by allowing guns in more places such as airports, churches, government buildings, and college campuses. Gun control advocates argue that gun show loopholes on criminal background checks need to be closed, that default purchases after incomplete background checks need to be ended, that large ammunition clips should be limited, and that there should be better safeguards to prevent mentally unstable persons from purchasing firearms. In a polarized partisan political environment, it is perhaps unsurprising that Americans' views about the remedies for gun violence are similarly polarized: either we need easier access to a wider range of firearms or we need less access to a more restricted range of firearms.

Americans' beliefs about the remedies to gun violence have been challenged in recent years by a rising tide of mass shootings. *Mother Jones* documented seventy-one mass shootings from 1982 to 2012 and found that most of the shooters obtained their guns legally. In the **Campaign of 2012**, candidates had to contend with several grisly events. On July 20, 2012, James Holmes shot seventy people at a movie theater in Aurora, Colorado; on August 5, Wade Michael Page, an Army veteran, shot ten people at a Sikh temple in Wisconsin; there were four other incidents where five or more people were shot. Perhaps the most distressing incident of 2012 occurred after the conclusion of the 2012 campaign, on December 14, when Adam Lanza shot his mother as well as twenty children and six adults at the Sandy Hook Elementary School in Newtown, Connecticut. Lanza's targeting of the schoolchildren was deliberate, in emulation of a 2011 massacre in Norway of seventy-seven people, most of them juveniles, by Anders Breivik.

Facing pressure from President Obama, the public, and the families of the victims of these incidents, the Senate held a series of votes on gun-related measures in April 2014. Each of the proposals needed sixty votes to be taken up by the House. A bipartisan proposal by GOP senator Pat Toomey (PA) and Democratic senator Joe Manchin (WV) to expand federal background checks to include purchases made at gun shows and over the Internet received only fifty-four votes. Republicans Charles Grassley (NE) and Ted Cruz (TX) proposed to remove individuals who have been involuntarily committed to a mental health facility from the criminal background check database immediately upon their release; this received fifty-two votes in support. A proposal to reinstate the ban on assault rifles received forty, and a ban on large magazine clips received only forty-six votes. A proposed federal ban on straw purchases received fifty-eight votes, as did a proposal to increase the federal penalties for gun traffickers (the latter of which was backed by the NRA). Some of the votes would have loosened restrictions on firearm ownership; most of these failed as well. The Senate rejected a proposal that would have compelled any state with a concealed-carry law, regardless of how strict its requirements were, to accept a concealed-carry permit from any other state; it received fifty-seven votes. A measure to leave the determination of whether a mentally ill veteran should be permitted to own a firearm to a judge (and only a judge) received only fifty-six votes. However, the Senate did vote to pass, by a vote of sixty-seven to thirty, penalties on states for releasing gun data. Voting was partisan across all of the proposals, with Democrats favoring gun control and Republicans favoring gun rights.

Sadly, the mass shootings continue parallel to the 2015/2016 presidential campaign season. Deadly shootings in Emanuel African Methodist Episcopal Church in Charleston, South Carolina; Northern Arizona University in Flagstaff; Oregon's Umpqua Community College; and the terrorist shooting in San Bernardino, California, among many others, are tragically symptomatic of the crisis of mindless violence in American society. Consequently, the regulation of firearms has again become a topic of debate in the **Campaign of 2016**, if for no other reason than that Democrats are now predominantly in favor of more regulation of guns (with the curious exception of candidate Bernie Sanders) and Republicans are predominantly opposed to such policies. While not running (or eligible) for reelection, incumbent president Obama has sternly commented with increasing anger and frustration about the routinization of these incessant eruptions of violence. Republican candidates, to a person, have dug in on the protection of Second Amendment, at least as it is construed by those who view any regulation of guns as a threat to liberty. Among the more controversial comments was a remark uttered by GOP candidate Dr. Ben Carson, arguing that imposing restrictions on gun ownership is more tragic than a bullet-ridden body, a comment that he has recently defended. While comments such as these are received with a degree of incredulity to many Americans, there is little risk that assuming such a position will move many likely voters. One's position on firearms regulations has become a cultural and partisan divide that makes for a safe campaign topic for a party's base of supporters.

The divide in congressional voting closely resembles the divide in public opinion. According to the Pew Center for People and the Press, in the winter of 2015, for the first time, the survey found support for gun rights as a priority edging support for gun control (52% to 46%). Expanded background checks are favored by 85 percent of the public, and preventing mentally ill persons from purchasing firearms is almost as popular. Fully 67 percent of the public would support a federal database to track firearm purchases. But in other areas, such as an assault rifle ban, the public reflects divisions similar to those in the Senate. Most of the change in public opinion over time has come from changes in Republicans, who have become dramatically more supportive of gun rights and more opposed to gun control than they were in earlier eras. The attitudes of Democrats have been more stable. The outcome is a stark partisan divide, which is also reflected in patterns of gun ownership.

Federal inaction on gun violence has led to pressure for policy reform at the state level. The Law Center to Prevent Gun Violence notes that in the two years after Sandy Hook, while seventy state laws were passed that weaken gun regulation and sixty-four laws were passed that strengthen it, the net effect has been that eight states substantially strengthened their regulation of firearms and four states substantially weakened it. After Sandy Hook, Alabama, Louisiana, and Missouri sought to protect gun rights in their state constitutions with a strict scrutiny clause, setting a very high bar for any municipality that would attempt to regulate firearms within state boundaries. This creates challenges for the states themselves as they seek to maintain existing bans on the possession of firearms by felons, and by people with domestic protection orders against them; such laws may not meet the requirements of strict scrutiny. Connecticut, however, chose to strengthen its background checks to include all gun and ammunition purchases, along with a ban on large-capacity magazines and some kinds of automatic and semi-automatic rifles.

Pennsylvania became a testing ground for a new strategy in pursuing gun rights in the courts. Forty-six states, Pennsylvania among them, bar local governments from passing gun control measures that are stricter than those at the state level. When local governments found the state unresponsive to their requests for new laws to prevent individuals with domestic protection orders from possessing firearms, they enacted policies on their own, knowing that local residents would be unlikely to mount a legal challenge. In response, the state government enacted new legislation in 2014 that permitted any state resident or organization to which they belong, whether they could demonstrate that they had been harmed by the policy or not, to challenge municipal regulations on firearms (for example, local bans on carrying firearms in parks, or requiring that a lost or stolen gun be reported). Successful plaintiffs would receive reimbursement for all of their court costs plus punitive damages, all at taxpayer expense. The NRA (based in Virginia) began to sue cities throughout Pennsylvania (as did Texas-based U.S. Law Shield and Pennsylvania-based Firearms Owners Against Crime), most of whom could not afford to defend their gun ordinances in court. Pittsburgh and Philadelphia could, however, and in June 2015, the NRA lost its suit on the grounds that the law itself was invalid (because it was tacked onto a scrap metal bill, in violation of a single-subject rule). Pennsylvania may yet pass a clean version of this law, and other states may follow its lead. This would shift the political debate about gun rights to the local level, and it would pit wealthy advocacy groups against municipalities that are often strapped for cash.

The rise in gun violence has also influenced political advocacy, with new groups entering the public debate over the role of guns in American society. In 2006, then New York City mayor Michael Bloomberg and then Boston mayor Thomas Menino formed Mayors Against Illegal Guns, a group that advocates for regulations on firearms. The group launched an effort entitled "Everytown for Gun Safety" in the 2014 midterm elections, spending $50 million on ads targeting lawmakers who opposed measures such as nationwide background checks on gun purchases. Moms Against Guns in America, founded by Shannon Watts in 2012 after Sandy Hook, is a grassroots network of gun control activists with a presence in all fifty states. It merged with Mayors Against Illegal Guns in December 2013. At present, these groups constitute the most visible elements of the gun control movement in the United States. Their adversaries are the NRA (which remains the best-funded, most cohesive voice for gun rights) and a plethora of other national and grassroots-level advocacy groups.

At the grassroots level, gun rights advocacy is exemplified by the open-carry movement. In the summer of 2014, Open Carry Texas (OCT), a gun rights group, engaged in armed demonstrations throughout the state in an attempt to normalize the appearance of guns in public places and to protest Texas's ban on the open carrying of handguns. Members, armed with long guns and assault rifles, marched on towns and neighborhoods and gathered at restaurants and stores as part of their public relations strategy. The gun control advocacy group Moms Demand Action for Gun Sense in America publicized photos of the heavily armed members of OCT in restaurants and stores in an attempt to pressure those businesses to ban firearms from their establishments, and to portray the public display of firearms as scary and threatening. They achieved a measure of success: Target, Starbucks, Wendy's, Chili's, Applebee's, Jack in the Box, Sonic, and Chipotle all banned firearms from their stores after photos of armed customers circulated online. The NRA, in an open letter on its Web site, suggested that such demonstrations were "downright scary" and might damage the gun rights cause.

Similar demonstrations by open-carry groups in other states followed, as the open display of firearms became a form of political speech and appeared to extend to causes beyond the Texas open-carry handgun ban. Heavily armed protesters staged two separate demonstrations at a Muslim community center in Phoenix in May 2015. And during the August 2014 violence in Ferguson, Missouri, OCT (whose members are almost all white, and mostly male) announced plans to march through the Fifth Ward, a predominantly black neighborhood, in Houston. The pro-gun group was met by the equally armed New Black Panther Party, which questioned OCT's motives and suggested that its members were insurgents in the Fifth Ward. Also in Texas, the Huey P. Newton Gun Club, formed by African American gun rights activists to protest recent shootings of unarmed people of color by law enforcement, marched on Dallas and started the #BlackOpenCarry movement. The Oath Keepers, a predominantly white gun rights group, demonstrated in Ferguson in the summer of 2015 and at the one-year anniversary protests as well, and it reached out to the #BlackOpenCarry movement to coordinate a protest with black gun rights groups. The Huey P. Newton Gun Club noted, however, that the two groups have very different objectives—the Oath Keepers and other mostly white gun rights groups were concerned about civil liberties, whereas the

#BlackOpenCarry movement was primarily concerned about human rights. This distinction reveals the role that race has played in shaping American politics; a history of segregation, Jim Crow, and other forms of discrimination (legal and not) continues to shape the lens through which citizens view the world, and to affect the way citizens are treated by others, thus influencing political priorities. More recently the connection between gun violence and terrorism has significantly complicated the gun control debate.

See also Race Relations Issue; Red Meat Issue

Additional Resources

Associated Press. "2008 Candidates on Spot Over Gun Control: Va. Tech Rampage Certain to Set Off Debate among Presidential Contenders." MSNBC, April 18, 2007. http://www.msnbc.msn.com/id/18170829/. Accessed October 13, 2015.

Doherty, Carroll. "A Public Opinion Trend That Matters: Priorities for Gun Policy." Pew Research Center, Fact Tank, January 9, 2015. http://www.pewresearch.org/fact-tank/2015/01/09/a-public-opinion-trend-that-matters-priorities-for-gun-policy/.

Edsall, Thomas B. "Gore, Democrats Face Challenge in Wooing South." *Washington Post*, September 28, 2000, p. A4.

Holmes, Steven A. "Gun Control Bill Backed by Reagan in Appeal to Bush." *New York Times*, March 29, 1992.

Reagan, Ronald. "Why I'm For the Brady Bill." *New York Times*, March 29, 1992.

Smith, Ben. "Obama Most Anti-Gun Candidate Ever, Will Ban Guns." Politico, August 6, 2008.

Spitzer, Robert J. *The Politics of Gun Control.* Sixth ed. New York: Paradigm, 2014.

Wildermuth, John. "Bush, Gore Trade Fire over Gun Control." *San Francisco Chronicle*, October 10, 2000, p. A1.

Winkler, Adam. *Gunfight: The Battle over the Right to Bear Arms in America.* New York: W. W. Norton and Co., 2013.

"Yes, and Outlaw Apple Pie as Well." PolitiFact, September 23, 2008. http://www.politifact.com/truth-o-meter/statements/2008/sep/23/national-rifle-association/yes-and-outlaw-apple-pie-as-well. Accessed October 13, 2015.

Health Care Issue

Health care policy has been a perennial political issue in the United States in one form or another. Its scope is broad, including disease detection and prevention, federally funded medical research, food and drug safety, and health insurance. While health care has been a public policy concern since the inception of the nation, the role of the federal government in this area is somewhat newer. Historically, public health has been viewed as the domain of state and local governments. As

Americans migrated from rural to urban areas during the Industrial Revolution, city planners focused on improvements in sanitation and water quality to combat the spread of infectious disease. According to the Centers for Disease Control and Prevention (CDC), by the turn of the twentieth century, forty of the forty-five states had public health departments, and cities and counties began establishing local health departments in 1908. State and local governments dealt with issues of sewage and solid waste disposal, water treatment (including fluoridation), food and drug safety, animal control, insect eradication, and personal hygiene. State and local governments began providing diphtheria and tetanus vaccines in 1949, and the federal government provided funding for the poliovirus vaccine in 1955.

The role of the federal government in medical research can be traced back to the earliest agencies of disease prevention. In 1798, the U.S. Marine Hospital Service (MHS), a precursor to the U.S. Public Health Service, was established to provide medical care for sailors. Each month, twenty cents was deducted from the paycheck of each sailor to fund this service. By the 1880s, Congress had tasked the MHS with inspecting passengers on ships to prevent the spread of disease, and the MHS also issued quarantines to prevent the spread of disease. In 1887, the MHS established a medical research laboratory, which evolved into the National Institutes of Health (NIH) in 1930. The National Cancer Institute was created in 1937 and was folded into the NIH in 1944. These actions established the federal government as a key actor in the funding and conducting of medical research to both fight disease and promote preventative care.

In 1908, the Democratic Party became the first national political party to devote an entire plank of its party platform to urging greater government involvement in protecting the safety of the nation's food supply and in other public health issues, including safety and hygiene issues related to high-density urban tenements. The progressive movement, counting among its supporters legislators from both sides of the political aisle, was perhaps the strongest voice for the development of public and charitable hospitals, along with better sanitation and health care for the nation's poor.

Germany had adopted a system of universal health care in the late nineteenth century. While progressive reformers saw the German model as a potential solution to U.S. health care problems, by World War I, the virulent anti-German sentiment that pervaded the nation had tainted the national health care debate. Candidates and elected officials of both major political parties denounced anything resembling the German-style system. After the years that followed, opponents of government-run health care programs recycled the rhetoric from the Red Scare of the early 1920s. The American ethos of rugged individualism contributed to the strong opposition to "European" and "collectivist" notions of state-provided or state-regulated health care, a sentiment that still exists today. Strong public and political opposition to a government-run health care system forced President Franklin Roosevelt to abandon proposals to include health insurance as part of the legislation creating the Social Security system in 1935. It would take three decades for the government to provide health insurance, and even then, the program benefited only the elderly (and was not means-tested).

During World War II, the United States experienced the largest expansion of private health insurance in its history. Due to federally mandated controls on wages, employers were limited in the types of benefits they could offer to attract and retain employees. High salaries were out of the question, but the wage controls did not preclude employers providing low-cost health insurance as a benefit. Many employers, particularly in the manufacturing sector, jumped on health insurance as a means to attract quality labor. After the war, Blue Cross and Blue Shield associations proliferated, due in no small measure to the desire of both doctors and hospitals to have a system of assured payments from their patients. These indemnity plans worked much like other insurance products and were purchased by employers as well as by individuals and families.

During the latter half of the 1940s and into the early 1950s, President Harry Truman became the first president to openly endorse compulsory national health insurance. Critics termed the proposal "socialized medicine," the American Medical Association lobbied hard against the program, and Republicans in Congress decried the proposal as a communist plot, successfully blocking the proposed legislation. Yet by the early 1960s, it had become increasingly apparent that health insurance plans provided by employers or purchased by individuals were out of the reach of those who most needed it. Elderly Americans, no longer in the workforce and living on fixed incomes, had no access to employer-provided plans and lacked the means to purchase individual plans. Even if they were able to qualify, the premiums were sky-high. A serious illness, and the medical bills that followed, could easily bankrupt elderly Americans. (Indeed, even now, major medical problems continue to be the primary cause of bankruptcies in the United States, even for those with health insurance.) With strong support from President Lyndon Johnson and congressional Democrats, in 1965, Congress established the Medicare program to provide health insurance for Americans over the age of sixty-five and the Medicaid program to provide health insurance for poor Americans. The Medicare program was funded with a new payroll tax, and those eligible for coverage paid a small premium. The cost of the Medicaid program was to be split between the federal government and the states.

By the 1970s, rising health care costs continued to limit the affordability of health care for many Americans. In the aftermath of the **Campaign of 1972**, Republican incumbent Richard Nixon took up the cause of health care reform, seeking a way to provide for Americans not old enough to be eligible for Medicare and not poor enough to be eligible for Medicaid. In a spring 1972 speech to Congress on the topic, Nixon endorsed the use of federal funds for an assortment of publicly financed health care programs. In his 1974 State of the Union address, Nixon proposed a Comprehensive Health Insurance Act that would have guaranteed health care to all uninsured Americans, charging citizens based on the amount they could afford to pay. Democratic senator Ted Kennedy offered his own health care reform bill, and Congress sought to structure a compromise, which was ultimately derailed by the Watergate scandal. After Nixon's resignation, his successor, President Gerald Ford, endorsed the cause of health care reform but saw his primary responsibility as dealing with the now-ailing economy.

Attempts to expand health care coverage were quickly overshadowed by more pressing concerns. The country had entered a serious economic recession, marked by both high rates of inflation and high unemployment. In the **Campaign of 1976**, Democrat Jimmy Carter campaigned on controlling health care costs, not expanding health care access. Kennedy continued to push Congress to enact more substantive reforms, and Carter created a plan that was implemented beginning in 1983. When Carter attempted to expand Medicaid coverage for children, Congress did not vote on his proposal. In 1980, Carter achieved his long-held goal of creating a stand-alone Department of Education. The former Department of Health, Education, and Welfare (HEW) became the Department of Health and Human Services (HHS), with a specific focus on health care issues.

The poor state of the economy, and later the spiraling budget deficit, kept health care out of the presidential campaigns of the 1980s. Ronald Reagan had little interest in expanding health care coverage and focused more on paring down domestic spending. The advent of the human immunodeficiency virus (HIV) and AIDS during this era also distracted Americans from the broader question of health care. Democrats criticized Reagan for his slow response to the AIDS crisis and his reluctance to increase federal funding for AIDS research, and the topic of expanded health care coverage soon fell off of the political agenda.

It was not until the **Campaign of 1992** that health care reform once again became a major campaign issue. Democratic nominee Bill Clinton promised a major overhaul of the nation's health care system, and early public opinion polls showed that voters were supportive. Indeed, pollsters had been asking about federally subsidized health care since the 1970s, and throughout, it had remained a popular political reform among citizens. After the election, Clinton appointed his wife, Hillary Rodham Clinton, to chair a health care insurance reform working group. Clinton and representatives from key federal agencies fashioned an extensive series of changes to the nation's health insurance system, and Clinton's health security plan was introduced in Congress in September 1993.

The health insurance industry quickly embarked on an aggressive effort to defeat Clinton's proposed reforms, running a series of fourteen television ads featuring "Harry and Louise." In the ads, Harry and Louise represent a white, middle-class couple who voice their concern (and even panic) that health care reform will be costly, will ration their access to treatment, and will force them to abandon their trusted family doctor in favor of one selected for them by the government. The ads ran for a year and are viewed by many political analysts as one the key factors in undermining Clinton's attempts to enact health care reforms. Clinton and the Democrats abandoned the reforms in the fall of 1994.

While Clinton's promised health care overhaul never came to fruition, in 1996, Congress passed the Health Insurance Portability and Accountability Act (HIPAA), which restricted (but did not eliminate) the use of preexisting condition rules to deny insurance coverage for medical conditions, set federal privacy standards for medical records, and established tax incentives for the purchase of long-term care insurance. In 1997, the State Children's Health Insurance Program (SCHIP) was created to provide insurance for low-income children whose parents earn too much to be eligible for Medicaid, but for whom private insurance is too costly. In the years that followed, Democrats continued to advocate changes in the health care system, while Republicans praised the quality of medical care in the United States as the best in the world and cautioned against attempts to change the existing system.

In the **Campaign of 2000**, despite the existence of a budget surplus, the debate over health care reform revolved around a single group of individuals—the elderly. Republican George W. Bush and Democrat Al Gore both offered plans to add government-funded prescription drug coverage to the existing slate of Medicare benefits. There was little discussion of the medical needs of those under sixty-five, and both candidates' plans were to offer federal subsidies for prescriptions regardless of the affluence of the individual.

It was not until the Democratic primaries in the **Campaign of 2004** that a more extensive vision of health care reform became part of the political debate. Democratic hopeful Howard Dean, a medical doctor, was the first (and only) major party candidate in decades to call for a federally regulated, single-payer, universal health care system in the months leading up to the Democratic primaries. While Dean failed to win his party's nomination, he set the stage for the **Campaign of 2008**, where most Democratic candidates offered proposals to extend health insurance to most Americans.

Also at issue in the Campaign of 2004 was federal funding for stem cell research. Republican incumbent George W. Bush opposed the use of embryonic stem cells for medical research and sought to limit most stem cell research in the United States. Bush's conservative Christian base argued that the use of stem cells, particularly embryonic stem cells, for medical research was immoral. Bush's opponent, John Kerry, advocated stem cell research, arguing that it had the best prospect for combating many of the diseases that continued to defy the search for a cure. Medical research was, at best, a minor issue in the election, and neither Bush nor Kerry advocated any reform of the health insurance industry.

In the Campaign of 2008, Democratic hopefuls Hillary Clinton and Barack Obama battled over whose health care reform proposal covered the most Americans, and for the most affordable price. Also at issue was SCHIP, passed back in 1997. The program had since proved to be a political hot potato, and in 2007 the bipartisan bill to reauthorize the program was vetoed by then president George W. Bush, who objected to both the $60 billion price tag and the Democrats' attempts to expand the number of individuals eligible for the program. The SCHIP debate spilled over into the Campaign of 2008, where Democrats attempted to portray their opponents as callous and anti-child. Republican nominee John McCain, under pressure to respond to the Democrats' health care agenda, offered a private-sector alternative, which Republicans touted as the most cost-effective (and least socialist) means to address the widely acknowledged problems with medical care in the United States. By the end of the campaign, the country had slid into a recession, and other issues captured the political spotlight.

Three months after being elected, President Barack Obama signed a bill to reauthorize SCHIP after the measure had passed through Congress on a party-line vote. Democrats characterized the bill's passage as a "lifeline" for struggling American families, whereas Republicans argued that it was "a foundation stone for socialized medicine in the United States." In the spring of 2009, Obama also introduced a plan to provide universal health insurance, which was widely decried by angry conservatives at town hall meetings throughout the summer. Members of the fledgling Tea Party movement took up the cause of opposition to health care reform, holding protests in Washington, disrupting legislators' town hall meetings with constituents, and holding rallies around the nation. Obama wrangled with both Democrats and Republicans over various versions of the bill, and in the fall of 2010, Congress passed the Patient Protection and Affordable Care Act, often referred to as "Obamacare" by its detractors. The act eliminated preexisting conditions as an exclusion criterion for health insurance companies and set up a federally subsidized high-risk insurance pool for Americans with serious health issues who were unable to obtain insurance on the private market. States would either have to participate in the federal pool or set up their own high-risk pools that complied with federal guidelines. Families that had health insurance would be able to offer coverage to children through the age of twenty-six, whether they were dependents or not. And, over time, all Americans would be compelled to purchase some form of private health insurance. The federal government would subsidize the cost of policies for those with low incomes.

Compulsory insurance has proved to be politically controversial (although Republicans have offered variants on this theme in the past as alternatives to a government-financed single-payer system). Democrats and an unlikely ally, health insurance companies, argued that to balance out the costs from requiring that insurers offer reasonably priced policies to the sickest Americans, they also needed to be able to write policies for the least sick Americans (who are most likely to be young and to have jobs that lack health insurance). Several states sued the federal government in an attempt to strike down the law in its entirety, or at least the mandatory-coverage portion of the law. In July of 2012, the Supreme Court upheld the constitutionality of the mandate portion of the Affordable Care Act, arguing that the requirement that Americans purchase health care or pay a fine was similar to a tax. The Court struck down the compulsory Medicaid expansion portion of the ACA, however; as a consequence, not all states have expanded their Medicaid programs to cover those too poor to receive coverage under the ACA but who earn too much to be covered under their existing Medicaid guidelines. A further challenge to the ACA rested on whether the act authorized the federal government to create a health care exchange (and to provide subsidies) for states that refused to create their own; in June 2015, the Supreme Court ruled that the language of the Act did not appear to preclude the federal government from creating exchanges on behalf of states or from providing subsidies for the purchase of insurance through such exchanges. A more recent constitutional challenge has been brought by Republicans in the House of Representatives, questioning the manner in which the executive is using appropriated funds.

In the spring of 2011, President Obama added a rule to federal health care guidelines that required health insurance companies to provide contraception to women free of charge, on the grounds that it was a form of preventative care. Medicaid was also required to offer contraception to its clients free of charge. In February 2012, Republican presidential hopefuls took up the issue of the contraception mandate, arguing that it unfairly forced Catholic hospitals and universities (and other religious employers) to provide coverage that violated their faith, and painting Obama and the Democrats as hostile to Christian values.

More generally, Republican presidential candidates in the **Campaign of 2012** were, without exception, opposed to "Obamacare." Ironically, much of the plan was modeled on an earlier policy created by Republican nominee Mitt Romney when he was governor of Massachusetts. Romney was placed in the uncomfortable position of having to criticize a policy that he had helped to create. Obama continued to defend his health care reforms, and public opinion polls showed that while Americans had concerns about the concept of the program, they favored most of the individual elements. It is notable that the legislation was crafted so that the most popular elements of the proposal (elimination of preexisting condition limits, extension of health care benefits to children through age twenty-six) were already in place prior to the election, while the most controversial elements (e.g., the mandated purchase of insurance) were not scheduled to be implemented until after the election was over. This put Republican candidates in the awkward position of attacking a policy that was already providing some popular benefits to voters. Repealing the policy, as the Republican Party advocated, meant eliminating some of the coverage that voters currently had for preexisting conditions, and withdrawing coverage for their adult children. Moreover, the costs of this coverage were being borne by insurance companies, not the government, so repealing these benefits, in the short run, would do little to reduce the federal deficit. This was the argument being made by Obama and the Democrats, who suggested that problems with the legislation be fixed, rather than repealing the legislation in its entirety.

In June 2014, the Supreme Court issued a ruling in a challenge to the contraception mandate portion of the Affordable Care Act. While the ACA already contained exemptions for religious institutions, it did not exempt nonreligious employers from providing contraceptive coverage. In the *Hobby Lobby* decision, the Court ruled that closely held private corporations whose owners had firmly held religious beliefs could not be compelled to pay for their employees to receive coverage for contraception. The ruling expanded the rights of corporations in important ways. The earlier *Citizens United* ruling had suggested that corporations had free-speech rights in elections, rights equivalent to those of individual citizens. *Hobby Lobby* appeared to suggest that corporations also had religious beliefs that they could claim protection for, even when the entities were not themselves religious. Moreover, the decision weighed the religious rights of a corporation against a woman's access to health care, and determined that burdening the corporation's religious expression was the more serious concern. Most certainly, it suggested that contraception was something other than a health issue; it was a moral issue and should be debated in the public sphere as such.

The religious exception, or moral objection argument, has been used in other areas as well, most notably, in challenges to the implementation of the Supreme Court's ruling on same-sex marriage. The extent to which the Court will be willing to limit the rights of same-sex couples in the face of sincere objections by those whose religious beliefs condemn homosexuality is yet to be determined.

The passage of time has made the ACA a far less vitriolic political issue. Republicans in the **Campaign of 2016** still proposed repealing the legislation, but no coherent alternative has been offered, suggesting less focus within the GOP than one would expect from appearances. Most of the GOP hopefuls were adamant about defunding Planned Parenthood; the focus on contraception and women's health (in addition to abortion, which has been a conservative staple since the **Campaign of 1980**) suggests that these have become cultural as well as health topics for Republicans. The Democratic candidates were equally committed to

Planned Parenthood, the availability of contraception, and the preservation of the ACA.

One of the newer areas of public debate in 2016 was mandatory vaccination. In the spring of 2015, California experienced an outbreak of measles primarily due to a significant number of unvaccinated children. More generally, some childhood illnesses have become more common as parents have opted not to vaccinate their children, aided by lax laws in some states that permit parents to cite religious or personal reasons for avoiding vaccines. There is no partisan or geographic correlation with patterns of personal and religious exemptions from childhood vaccination schedules required by states. Nor is there a partisan pattern to those who oppose mandatory vaccinations on principle (although Pew finds that in recent months, there is a slight tendency for Republicans to be more likely to oppose mandatory vaccinations; however, this sentiment is uncommon, overall). Such individuals can be found on both the conservative and the liberal ends of the ideological spectrum, driven by extreme levels of distrust in government and in the pharmaceutical industry, respectively. Numerous presidential candidates weighed in on the role of government in compelling the vaccination of its citizens. GOP candidates Chris Christie (although he has since revised his opinion), Rand Paul, Scott Walker, and Carly Fiorina have defended parents' right to choose not to vaccinate their children. GOP candidates Jeb Bush, Ted Cruz, Bobby Jindal, Ben Carson, Mike Huckabee, Rick Santorum, George Pataki, and Marco Rubio have expressed support for mandatory vaccinations. Democrat Hillary Clinton also expressed support for mandatory vaccinations (although she had previously spoken up for parental rights).

See also Culture War; LGBTQ Issues; Women's Equality Issue

Additional Resources

Boychuk, Gerard William. *National Health Insurance in the United States and Canada: Race, Territory, and the Roots of Difference.* Washington, DC: Georgetown University Press, 2008.

Hacker, Jacob S. *The Road to Nowhere: The Genesis of President Clinton's Plan for Health Security.* Princeton, NJ: Princeton University Press, 1997.

Hoffman, B. "Health Care Reform and Social Movements in the United States." *American Journal of Public Health* 93, no. 1 (January 2003): 75–85.

Kaiser Family Foundation. "Timeline: History of Health Reform Efforts in the U.S." http://kff.org/health-reform/timeline/history-of-health-reform-efforts-in-the-united -states/. Accessed November 28, 2015.

"President Nixon's Special Message to Congress Proposing a Comprehensive Health Insurance Plan, February 6, 1974." http://www.kaiserhealthnews.org/Stories/2009 /September/03/nixon-proposal.aspx.

"Richard Nixon's Special Message to Congress on Health Care, March 2, 1972." http:// www.presidency.ucsb.edu/ws/index.php?pid=3757#axzz1XllmiRej.

Skocpol, Theda. *Boomerang: Health Care Reform and the Turn against Government.* New York: W. W. Norton and Co., 1997.

Stout, David. "Bush Vetoes Children's Health Bill." *New York Times*, October 3, 2007.

Washington Post Staff. *Landmark: The Inside Story of America's New Health Care Law and What It Means for Us All.* New York: PublicAffairs Books, 2010.

Horse-Race Campaign Coverage

The term "horse-race campaign coverage" refers to the news media's tendency to use a game framework for reporting about political events. The candidates and political parties represent dueling sides in a pitched battle to win the vote on Election Day. Public opinion **tracking polls** are used as a scorecard to illustrate who is leading the pack and who is behind. The candidates' issue positions become part of the game, viewed through the lens of strategic maneuvering to capture the support of a particular sociodemographic group. Political analysts are interviewed for their expert opinions on which candidate has the lead and what it will take for a particular candidate to win the race.

Studies of media coverage of political campaigns over time have clearly demonstrated that horse-race coverage has become the dominant theme in election news.

According to the Project for Excellence in Journalism (PEJ), 52 percent of total media coverage (print, broadcast, cable, online) of the **Campaign of 2008** was devoted to the horse race. These stories accounted for 53 percent of all print media stories about the campaign and 54.3 percent of the election coverage on the five most popular political news Web sites (AOL, Yahoo, Google News, CNN.com, and MSNBC.com).

By the **Campaign of 2012**, horse-race coverage declined slightly, constituting 38 percent of the coverage of the final two months of the campaign, and also playing a less prominent role during the primary season, according to PEJ. However, PEJ noted that during the three-week period surrounding the presidential debates, horse-race coverage spiked to 47 percent of all stories—the highest for any point of the campaign, and also constituting the most dominant narrative of the debates themselves.

Political scientists are concerned about horse-race coverage because it often comes at the expense of in-depth analysis of complex issues, leaving voters with little quality information on which to base their vote. Moreover, while such coverage does create a sense of excitement among individuals who are highly engaged in politics, for many other citizens, particularly those without strong partisan attachments, it may lead to more cynicism about political candidates and a feeling of detachment from the electoral process.

Additional Resources

Kurtz, Howard. "On TV, Covering 'the Issues' from A to Zzzzzz." *Washington Post*, July 3, 2000, p. C1.

Patterson, Thomas E. *Out of Order*. New York: Knopf, 1993.

Pew Research Center and Project for Excellence in Journalism. "The Final Days of the Media Campaign 2012." Project for Excellence in Journalism, November 19, 2012. http://www .journalism.org/2012/11/19/final-days-media-campaign-2012/. Accessed September 5, 2015.

Project for Excellence in Journalism. "The Color of News." Journalism.org, October 29, 2008. http://www.journalism.org/2008/10/29/the-color-of-news/.

Rosenstiel, Thomas B. "Fascination with Tactics Dominates Political Coverage." *Los Angeles Times*, November 4, 1988, Part I, p. 12.

Rosenstiel, Tom, Mark Jurkowitz, and Tricia Sartor. "How the Media Covered the 2012 Primary Campaign." Project for Excellence in Journalism, April 23, 2012. http://www .journalism.org/2012/04/23/romney-report/. Accessed September 5, 2015.

Immigration Issue

Through the late nineteenth century, the United States encouraged immigration and maintained an open-door policy. From the early seventeenth century through the mid-nineteenth century, Protestants made up a large percentage of new immigrants to North America, although a number of Jewish and Catholic immigrants arrived in the American colonies well before the American Revolution. The colony of Maryland began as a haven for Catholics in the seventeenth century, and Catholics from Spain settled in Florida and the American Southwest as early as the sixteenth century, well before Jamestown. By and large, though, the vast majority of the earliest settlers were Protestant.

By the early nineteenth century, increasing numbers of Catholic immigrants from Italy, Ireland, and Poland began arriving in the United States, and many went to work building the canals and railroads of the Eastern Seaboard, later becoming an integral part of the labor force in the nation's coal mines and textile mills. By the mid-1850s, the growing number of Irish-Catholic immigrants provoked an increasingly virulent nativism among xenophobic and anti-Catholic Americans, leading to the establishment of the American Party, more commonly known as the Know-Nothings. The Know-Nothings proposed tighter restrictions on European immigration and sought to discourage Catholics from holding political office or gaining any influence in American public life (laws that remain on the books in some states, although they are no longer enforced). Following the Civil War, repressed anti-immigrant sentiments reemerged, and a number of states passed new laws restricting immigration and making it difficult for new immigrants to participate in the electoral process. In 1875, the Supreme Court found state limitations on immigration unconstitutional on the grounds that only the federal government had the authority to regulate immigration. By the early 1880s, growing concern with Chinese immigration in the West led to increased pressure on Congress to enact additional laws restricting immigration. In 1880, the national conventions of the Republican, Democratic, and Greenback parties all endorsed restrictions on Chinese immigration, which was considered to be a matter of "grave concern." In response, Congress passed the Chinese Exclusion Act of 1882. In 1884, the Republican and Democratic national conventions called for full enforcement of the Chinese Exclusion Act. Between 1885 and 1887, Congress enacted a series of laws further prohibiting certain laborers from immigrating to the United States, many of which targeted immigrants from Asia.

In 1891, Congress established an Immigration Service within the Treasury Department to screen immigrants. Despite these new, restrictive immigration laws, immigration to the United States accelerated during the period from 1880 through the early days of World War I, and a large percentage of these immigrants were from southern European countries such as Italy and Greece. Initially, immigrants from these countries drew little attention, but as their numbers swelled, alarms were raised. In response to the even higher volume of immigration after World War I, Congress passed the Immigration Acts of 1921 and 1924, which created a quota system that severely limited immigration from Asia and established a preference system for immigrants that favored residents of northern European countries. It was not until the Magnuson Act of 1943 that Chinese persons were eligible to become citizens of the United States, and it would take another twenty years for the Immigration Act of 1965 to eliminate ethnic quotas.

Immigrants often found themselves the targets of political discrimination, as was the case with many German immigrants, who were prosecuted for sedition during World War I, and many American-born citizens of Japanese descent, who were forcibly sent to internment camps in the western United States during World War II. Concerns about American communist sympathizers in the 1950s led far right-wing political groups such as the John Birch Society to crusade for draconian limits on immigration (a position that the group continues to endorse).

During the 1940s, the Roosevelt administration and the Mexican government undertook a cooperative venture called the "bracero program," which involved a series of laws and executive agreements designed to encourage the temporary migration of Mexican workers to the United States to be hired for contract work, which helped to addressed the labor shortages in the United States during World War II. Half a million Mexican laborers had been deported from the United States during the Great Depression; thus the bracero program not only supplied needed labor for American employers, but it also promised to serve as a fresh start for U.S.-Mexican relations with regard to the treatment of migrant workers. The bracero program ended for most employers after the war, but it continued in the agricultural sector until its expiration in 1964.

The bracero program officially ended during the Johnson administration, but migrant workers continued to flow northward to work the fields of California, Arizona, Colorado, New Mexico, and Texas, eventually spreading eastward and northward. The ensuing migrations swelled the population of immigrant workers from south of the border, many of whom were working in the country without permission from (or under the protection of) American law. Federal law did permit certain illegal aliens to obtain legal residence status, but these provisions applied to few migrant workers.

The bracero program was opposed by the charismatic Latino activist Cesar Chavez and his National Farm Workers Association (which eventually became the United Farm Workers [UFW] union) on the grounds that it failed to protect the rights of migrant workers, who lacked the right to unionize, and thus they were easily fired if they refused to work for the low wages and in the poor working conditions offered by their employers. In 1965, Chavez's group, in conjunction with several other migrant workers' organizations, initiated a nonviolent boycott against the growers of table grapes in Delano, California. Chavez enlisted the support of student groups and church groups and ultimately took his case to the American consumer, persuading more than ten million Americans to forgo buying table grapes over the course of the boycott. In the **Campaign of 1968**, Democratic hopeful Robert Kennedy joined Chavez to celebrate the end of a fast that Chavez had embarked on, and in return, Chavez and the UFW endorsed Kennedy's candidacy (the support of Chavez and the UFW had played an important role in his short-lived electoral success; tragically Kennedy was later assassinated on the night of his victory in the California primary). The UFW ultimately signed a labor contract with the Delano growers in 1969 that provided for fairer hiring and working conditions for migrant labor in the industry. When the contract expired four years later, the UFW joined up with the Teamsters (and, ultimately, the AFL-CIO) to strike for a new contract. The strike turned violent, and the UFW called it off, instead lobbying California governor Jerry Brown for greater legal protection. Their initial success proved to be short-lived, as later administrations provided more leeway for growers and fewer rights for migrant workers.

Despite their precarious legal position, migrant workers continued to stream into the United States, both legally and illegally. By the 1980s, tensions over immigration policy resurfaced, spurred by this growth in immigration, mostly from Latin America. In the fall of 1980 alone, approximately 124,000 Cubans arrived in the United States as part of the Mariel boatlift (most of whom were permitted to stay in the United States under the unique "wet-feet, dry-feet" policy governing Cuban immigrants, who are not deported if their feet come into contact with

American soil before they are detained by law enforcement officials). In 1986, President Ronald Reagan signed into law the Immigration and Reform Control Act, which tightened border security and increased penalties for employers who knowingly hired illegal immigrants, but which also offered amnesty to any immigrant who had entered the country illegally prior to 1982. At the time, the legislation was part of a bipartisan compromise between the Democratic-controlled Congress and the Republican president. For the most part, immigration policy was not a source of controversy in presidential campaigns during much of the twentieth century, despite being a source of controversy in society more generally. In part, this was due to a shared view on immigration by both major parties. For example, despite recent legislative efforts to stem the tide of illegal immigration, the Republican Party platform in the **Campaign of 1988** still recognized the valuable contributions made by immigrants to the United States, while also reaffirming the right of the country to control its borders.

However, in the **Campaign of 1992**, this situation changed. The Republican Party platform called for strengthening border patrol activities to prevent further growth in illegal immigration, and it advocated rolling back the number of migrant laborers working outside of the purview of the law. In contrast, the Democratic platform emphasized the contributions made by immigrants to American society and did not call for further limits on immigration or tougher measures to identify and deport illegal immigrants. Republican incumbent George H. W. Bush defended his decision to repatriate Haitian refugees who were fleeing political violence and poverty in their home country, while Democratic nominee Bill Clinton criticized the repatriation as lacking in compassion (although after he was elected, Clinton too found himself repatriating Haitians, and he later sent U.S. troops to Haiti to restore the deposed Aristide, presumably hoping that the presence of a democratically elected leader would stem the flow of Haitian refugees).

The nation's overall mood began to turn sharply against illegal immigrants during the Clinton years. In 1994, the state of California passed Proposition 187, a voter-initiated referendum known as the Save Our State (or SOS) Initiative, which was designed to prevent illegal residents and their children from receiving public benefits such as emergency health care and public education (although it contained no provisions to deport these individuals, who were crucial to the state's agriculture industry). The courts eventually struck down the law, but the measure had long-lasting consequences for politics in California and the nation as a whole. Support for Proposition 187 broke down largely along party lines, with most support coming from Republican voters. The measure was endorsed by then Republican governor Pete Wilson (who had presidential aspirations at the time). Democrats sharply opposed the measure. Latino voters in California also opposed the measure, although they did not vote in large numbers, presumably believing that the measure would never pass. Ironically, one consequence of Proposition 187 was that its passage served to mobilize the Latino community in California and elsewhere and made it more difficult for Republican candidates to do well in future statewide elections in California.

In the **Campaign of 1996**, the Republican National Convention approved a platform plank stating that illegal aliens should not receive public benefits other than emergency aid. The Democratic Party platform criticized Republicans for attempting to deprive immigrant children of their access to education. Instead, Democrats supported increasing civil and criminal sanctions against employers who hired illegal immigrants.

In the **Campaign of 2000**, the Republican National Convention nominated Texas governor George W. Bush, who (like his brother, Florida governor Jeb Bush) was known for his moderate views on immigration. In a critical change in the GOP platform, Republicans again applauded the role of immigrants in building the United States and abandoned their earlier proposals for new legislation that would have deprived illegal immigrants of social services. This change helped Bush tailor his message to the growing number of Hispanic voters, many of whom supported his candidacy. In the **Campaign of 2004**, incumbent president Bush proposed a new guest worker program that would permit some seven million non-residents to work in the United States for a limited amount of time. His challenger, Democrat John Kerry, criticized the guest worker program as too narrow and instead suggested legislation that would benefit undocumented residents who were already working in the United States. Kerry proposed legislation that would put millions of undocumented aliens on the road to citizenship. Both the Bush and Kerry campaigns competed vigorously for the votes of millions of Hispanic voters. Latino voters turned out in record numbers, with over seven million Latino voters casting ballots on Election Day, an increase of well over a million from the previous election.

Bush's efforts to court the Latino vote in 2004 paid off. The Hispanic vote had historically been more favorable toward the Democratic Party (although Reagan made some inroads in the **Campaign of 1980**). In 2004, Bush received somewhere between 30 percent and 40 percent of the Latino vote (depending on the survey used), which is at or near a record level for a Republican presidential candidate (and an improvement on his own performance in 2000). After winning the 2004 election, President Bush proposed comprehensive immigration reform legislation, including a path to citizenship for undocumented residents, but he was unable to convince a Republican-dominated Congress to enact his reforms.

Most of the current efforts to ease restrictions on immigration in the United States center on the children and families of illegal immigrants. In 2001, Congress (with the support of President Bush) proposed the Development, Relief, and

Education for Alien Minors Act (DREAM), which would have granted permanent residency (under certain conditions) to children of undocumented residents. The legislation enjoyed bipartisan support; Republican senators John McCain and Orrin Hatch signed on as cosponsors. This bill has been reintroduced in various forms over the years but has failed to pass in the Senate. Additionally, some Republicans who initially supported the legislation have shifted their position. Democrats have generally endorsed the passage of the newest incarnation of the DREAM Act. Obama lobbied hard for passage of the act, although he was also criticized by immigrants' rights groups for achieving record levels of deportations during his first term.

The Republican candidates for president were, on the whole, far more critical of attempts to ease up on immigration restrictions in the **Campaign of 2012** compared to McCain only four years earlier. During the primary season, GOP hopefuls all supported building a fence of some sort along the U.S. border with Mexico (varying in size and features, including whether it was electrified), a position Republican nominee John McCain also endorsed in the **Campaign of 2008** (although McCain also endorsed a path to citizenship at some indeterminate point after the border had been secured). Mitt Romney expressed strong opposition to the DREAM Act and suggested that by creating a hostile environment for illegal immigrants in the United States, they would self-deport.

After the 2012 election, Congress failed to make any progress on immigration reform in spite of the efforts of future 2016 presidential aspirants Senators Ted Cruz and Marco Rubio, who participated in passing a reform proposal in the Senate in July 2013, only to see the bill defeated in the House. After the 2014 midterm, Obama addressed the nation in a televised evening appearance to announce that he was using his power to issue an executive order to offer temporary protection to individuals who had been brought to the United States illegally as children (the targets of the DREAM Act). They would be permitted to work legally, subject to a fee and a background check. His action was not a path to citizenship, and because it was an executive action, it could be reversed by a later president. Obama's pitch came with an appeal to American values: "What makes us Americans is our shared commitment to an ideal—that all of us are created equal, and all of us have a chance to make of our lives what we will." Republicans in Congress suggested that Obama's move would preclude any immigration reform being passed, which most political scientists viewed as an empty threat (in that this appeared unlikely regardless).

Because Congress remains divided on immigration, it remains an issue in the **Campaign of 2016**. In the first GOP debate, the candidates, including those viewed as moderates on the topic such as Jeb Bush and Marco Rubio, were endorsing the creation of a two-thousand-mile wall with an interior electronic tracking system, similar to what they advocated in the 2012 campaign. But the party has not settled on all facets of this complex issue. Donald Trump, for example, has consistently hewed to a hard line with regard to immigration, while Marco Rubio has been subjected to increasing and intensifying criticism for his support of the failed 2013 Senate immigration reform bill. Most candidates, including Bush, were critical of sanctuary cities (those cities that refuse to act as agents for Immigration Control and Enforcement by querying the immigration status of anyone they encounter in their duties, and deporting those who cannot prove that they are in the United States legally) and suggested that they would withhold federal funds from those cities. The law enforcement community remains divided about questioning crime victims, bystanders, and witnesses about their immigration status; many fear it will hamper their efforts to investigate crime and may result in crime victims being reluctant to contact law enforcement. Ironically, those who support cooperation with the federal government on this issue tend not to be those who have favorable attitudes toward the federal government more generally.

Most notoriously, this attitude is demonstrated in the voice of GOP hopeful Donald Trump, who has alleged that the vast majority of those who cross the borders illegally, Mexicans in particular, are murderers, rapists, and drug dealers. Trump further accuses the Mexican government of deliberately sending criminal elements to the United States. "Our leaders are stupid," Trump declaims, "our politicians are stupid, and the Mexican government is much smarter, much sharper, much more cunning, and they send the bad ones over because they don't want to pay for them, they don't want to take care of them. Why should they, when the stupid leaders of the United States will do it for them? And that's what's happening, whether you like it or not."

Trump's recommendations regarding immigration have dominated a good portion of his campaign, and he has received both an unexpected amount of support and considerable criticism for his assertions about immigrants. Wanting to erect a wall on the southern border, Trump has persistently dug in on his claims that immigrants are a disruptive and dangerous element. In a recent and disturbing turn of events, two thugs beat and urinated on a homeless Latino man in Boston, an event that spurred the outrage of Boston's mayor but was met with a different reaction from Mr. Trump, who explained that he "hadn't hear about" the event, and then, while admitting that "it would be a shame" that such a thing would happen, he seized the opportunity to reflect upon the character and desires of his followers, who "are very passionate. They love this country and they want this country to be great again. I will say that, and everybody here has reported it." Trump's comments have been viewed as chillingly demagogic by some, and yet in the days following both the incident and Trump's reaction, his standing in the recent polls remains strong.

Because the federal government has been viewed as reluctant to take up the task of comprehensive immigration reform, much of the current political debate over immigration policy is being driven by actions taken at the state and local levels. For example, several states have recently passed legislation that tasks local law enforcement officials with enforcing a strict immigration policy, including requiring residents to carry proof of citizenship papers at all times (Arizona) and restricting where those who cannot prove legal residence may live and work (Alabama). The Obama administration challenged these laws, maintaining that border and immigration policy is solely within the scope of the federal government. Arizona is also among the states that seek to challenge the notion that children born in the United States to parents who are here illegally are automatically citizens. While the Fourteenth Amendment guarantees "birthright citizenship," these states are seeking to institute a separate status of state citizenship, wherein the U.S. citizenship status of the parents determines the state citizenship status of the child. Arizona and Kansas currently require proof of U.S. citizenship in order to cast a ballot in an election. In the Campaign of 2016, several GOP hopefuls have indicated that they would like to end birthright citizenship. Donald Trump, Ben Carson, Lindsey Graham, Ted Cruz, Bobby Jindal, Scott Walker, Rick Santorum, and Mike Huckabee have all suggested that children born in the United States to parents who are not legal residents should not be considered citizens (despite the language of the Fourteenth Amendment that guarantees otherwise, as currently interpreted by the Supreme Court), and that birthright citizenship as a legal practice should be abolished. To that end Sen. Graham has cosponsored proposed legislation that would change the construction of the Fourteenth Amendment in a way that would no longer support birthright citizenship for children of undocumented aliens. This harkens back to the rhetoric of the late nineteenth century, when opponents of Asian immigration to the United States denounced birthright citizenship.

While some candidates, such as John Kasich and Chris Christie, are less clear on the issue, there are a few who oppose denying birthright citizenship. Jeb Bush, Carly Fiorina, Marco Rubio, and George Pataki have all rejected proposals to amend the Constitution to abolish birthright citizenship. Responding to the question, Gov. Jeb Bush impatiently remarked, "I think that people born in this country ought to be American citizens. Okay, now we got that over with," a comment that was welcomed by many who are concerned about the potentially xenophobic tone sounded by candidates such as Trump and Graham; nevertheless, Gov. Bush received considerable criticism for having unapologetically and repeatedly used the term "anchor baby" in alleging that some undocumented immigrants deliberately enter the United States to give birth to their children while guaranteeing for them American citizenship. While refusing to apologize for using the term, the governor did try to explain himself further by awkwardly claiming that the designation "anchor baby" is "frankly, more related to Asian people." While Mr. Trump's comments regarding undocumented immigrants are the more volatile, it would appear that Gov. Bush is encountering an equal or greater amount of criticism for his use of the term "anchor baby," even though he does not oppose birthright citizenship.

Since the September 11, 2001, terrorist attacks on the World Trade Center and the Pentagon, national concerns about immigration have expanded to encompass an additional focus—the infiltration of America's borders by potential terrorists. The September 11 attacks were accompanied by a new strain of nativism that percolated up through the general population from more ideologically charged fringe groups. Whereas in the past, Catholics of all stripes (especially Irish, Italian, and Polish Catholics), Jews, East Asians (especially Chinese and Japanese immigrants), and Hispanics became targets of anti-immigrant bigotry, after the terrorist bombings on 9/11, Muslims and anyone of Arab or Middle Eastern descent were singled out as *personae non gratae*. In some places Sikhs, ignorantly mistaken for Muslims because of their tradition of wearing turbans, were victimized in the aftermath of the terrorist attacks. Cities have attempted to ban the construction of mosques, and states such as Oklahoma have banned the practice of sharia law, all motivated by the perception that Islam is a religion that is inherently antidemocratic and that those who practice the religion all harbor nefarious intentions toward the United States. In the 2012 GOP primary debates, candidates were asked if they would be willing to hire a Muslim as a cabinet member. Only Mitt Romney, a Mormon, said yes. This posture evokes memories of the Know-Nothing anti-Catholicism and anti-Semitism of the past; and while the majority of Americans recognize the distinction between Islam as a religion and the beliefs of a smaller number of religious extremists, the volume of anti-Muslim attitudes from various quarters cannot go unnoticed. The terrorist attack in Paris in November 2015, which cost 130 lives, followed by the San Bernardino, California, terrorist shooting in December has directed even more intensified attention to immigration policy and raised the level of anxiety over immigration on the campaign trail, especially among GOP candidates. Donald Trump, most notably and not without controversy, had initially proposed imposing a temporary prohibition against Muslim Syrian refugees seeking entrance into the United States, a proposal accompanied by perceived implications that Mr. Trump holds as untrustworthy Muslims in general. Directly following the San Bernardino tragedy, Mr. Trump called for a temporary but "total and complete shutdown of all Muslims entering the United States," a proposal that has been soundly rejected throughout the GOP, stridently condemned by Republican speaker of the house Paul Ryan and especially criticized among presidential candidates.

Governor Bush defined Mr. Trump's reaction as "unhinged," Senator Rubio noted the unconstitutionality of the proposal, and even Senator Cruz, who has consistently appeared more concerned about alienating the Trump faction and somewhat sympathetic with the attitudes underlying Trump's comments, cautiously distanced himself from Trump's xenophobic generalizations regarding Muslim immigrants.

See also Anti-Catholicism; Nativism Issue; Voting Reform Issue

Additional Resources

Barabak, Mark Z. "Campaign 2000; Bush Softens Sharp Edges of Republican Platform." *Los Angeles Times*, July 28, 2000, p. A1.

Daniels, Roger, and Otis L. Graham Jr. *Debating American Immigration: 1882–Present.* Lanham, MD: Rowman & Littlefield, 2001.

Downes, Lawrence. "A Republican Broadside on Immigrants." Taking Note, *New York Times*, August 7, 2015. http://takingnote.blogs.nytimes.com/2015/08/07/a-republican -broadside-on-immigrants/. Accessed September 5, 2015.

Graham, Otis L., Jr. *Immigration Reform and America's Unchosen Future.* Bloomington, IN: Author House, 2008.

LeMay, Michael C., and Elliot Robert Barkan. *U.S. Immigration and Naturalization Laws and Issues.* Westport, CT: Greenwood Press, 1999.

Peralta, Eyder. "Obama Goes It Alone, Shielding Up to 5 Million Immigrants from Deportation. National Public Radio, November 20, 2014. http://www.npr.org/sections /thetwo-way/2014/11/20/365519963/obama-will-announce-relief-for-up-to-5-million -immigrants. Accessed September 5, 2015.

Swain, Carol M. *Debating Immigration.* Cambridge: Cambridge University Press, 2007.

"Will Rick Perry Throw the Tea Party Under the Bus?" *Mother Jones*, August 25, 2011.

Independent Advocacy Groups

Independent advocacy groups began to appear in presidential elections after the Federal Election Campaign Act of 1971 (and subsequent amendments in 1974 and 1976) placed limits on the amount of money that individuals and groups could donate directly to political candidates and political parties. The FECA formally recognized political action committees (PACs) and permitted them to raise hard money contributions for the express purpose of advocating the election or defeat of candidates for federal office (subject to regulations on the group's size and the amount of money it could accept). The FECA also permitted PACs to contribute directly to the campaigns of candidates for federal office (with limits on both the amount of these contributions and the maximum number of candidates to receive funding). The majority of these traditional PACs represented businesses, labor organizations, or single-issue interest groups such as the National Rifle Association (NRA) or the Sierra Club. The FECA required PACs to register with the Federal Election Commission (FEC) and to comply with strict hard money contribution limits as well as disclosure requirements for their donors.

In the landmark case of ***Buckley v. Valeo*** (1976), the Supreme Court upheld the constitutionality of campaign contribution limits on individuals and PAC donations to candidates and parties. However, the high court held that Congress lacked the authority to limit or prohibit independent political expenditures by private individuals or interest groups, clearing the way for interest groups to increase their independent political expenditures. Many of these organizations would later go on to form **527 groups** and **501(c) groups** to further evade the few remaining regulations on independent groups. The Bipartisan Campaign Reform Act of 2002 (BCRA) placed additional limits on the types of donations that could be made to political parties, which furthered the growth of independent advocacy groups.

Independent advocacy groups have been responsible for many of the most controversial (and negative) campaign ads in recent history, including the infamous Willie Horton ad in the **Campaign of 1988** and the Swift Boat ads in the **Campaign of 2004**. Negative ads run by independent groups can be safely disavowed by political candidates even as they reap the benefits from these attacks on their opponents.

While the BCRA prohibited independent groups from financing campaign ads thirty days before a primary election and sixty days before a general election, the *Citizens United v. Federal Election Commission* decision in early 2010 effectively eliminated these restrictions. Moreover, *Citizens United* overturned a century-old ban that had prohibited corporations and unions from directly paying for ads supporting or opposing candidates for federal office, on the grounds that corporations were entitled to the same free-speech rights as individuals. The subsequent 2010 midterms witnessed a rise in 527 and 501(c) group spending by a host of corporations, unions, and murky independent political groups whose membership remained concealed (despite disclosure requirements being upheld by the Supreme Court). In the **Campaign of 2012**, independent spending moved from corporations and unions to **super PACs** that were far more closely connected to candidates' political campaigns, a practice that threatens to undermine the existing regime of campaign finance regulations.

See also Campaign Finance Reform; Swift Boating

Additional Resource

Center for Responsive Politics. "Types of Advocacy Groups." http://www.opensecrets.org /527s/types.php. Accessed September 29, 2015.

Internet Campaigning

By the late 1990s, it was expected that a presidential candidate would have some sort of campaign Web site. Candidates used their Web sites to publicize their issue positions and to present their image to the American public. In short, candidate Web sites were little more than glorified versions of the traditional campaign brochure. The advantage to having a Web site was that it made the dissemination of campaign materials much less expensive than traditional printing. Plus, candidates could also solicit funds and announce campaign events, and Web sites could quickly be updated as the need arose, so they were multifunctional. In the primary season of the **Campaign of 2000**, Republican hopeful John McCain was notable for raising $3.7 million in campaign funds online, although in the end, he failed to earn his party's nomination. One of the drawbacks to relying too much on an Internet-based strategy during this era was that most voters did not seek out campaign information online. The Internet was still primarily the domain of young persons, and this age group has historically been among those least interested in political campaigns and voting.

In the **Campaign of 2004**, Democratic hopeful Howard Dean tried to change the way candidates used the Internet. Dean was the first candidate to appear in a chat room, where he interacted directly with prospective voters—many of them younger people who wouldn't normally be interested in politics. His campaign also used Web sites such as Meetup.com for grassroots organizing (eventually creating their own automated system) and raised a record amount (at the time) of funds online, mostly in small donations. Dean's supporters wrote handwritten letters to registered voters in Iowa and compiled their own database of volunteers to further assist in their outreach efforts. And Dean closely followed the blogs of his supporters to determine what issues were important to them and adjusted his campaign accordingly. While Dean ultimately lost his party's nomination to John Kerry, his campaign provided a blueprint for future candidates who sought to use the Internet in ways that were less traditional, and it also provided useful examples for more decentralized ways to organize grassroots support.

By the time the **Campaign of 2008** rolled around, many candidates had recognized the potential that Dean saw in the Internet four years earlier. In particular, Republican hopeful Ron Paul and Democratic hopefuls John Edwards and Barack Obama developed sophisticated, interactive Web sites and integrated these with overarching campaign strategies designed to encourage supporters to mobilize on their behalf at the grassroots level. The Obama campaign employed Facebook cofounder Chris Hughes as a campaign strategist and quickly established an online presence using a variety of sites, including Facebook, MySpace, LinkedIn, Twitter, YouTube, Flickr, Digg, BlackPlanet, AsianAve, MiGente, and Glee. By the general election, Obama had over two million Facebook supporters, while his opponent, John McCain, barely reached six hundred thousand. Even in the primary season, hopeful Hillary Clinton was handily outnumbered on Facebook by Obama supporters, an early indication of his campaign's advantage in the digital realm. Political analysts believe that Obama's online presence was more than a virtual phenomenon—Obama was consistently able to perform well in caucuses, in large part because his campaign was able to organize and mobilize large numbers of young voters to show up for these events.

By Election Day, Obama had over 112,000 people regularly following him on Twitter, whereas McCain had only 4,600 (after a belated effort to set up a Twitter account in the waning days of the campaign). The Obama campaign used Twitter to collect more detailed sociodemographic information from its followers, enabling it to tailor its campaign communications so that supporters would be notified of events, via e-mail and text messages, in their geographical area. And Obama's supporters retweeted his messages to their friends. The BarackObama.com channel on YouTube contained over eighteen hundred video files and attracted more than eighteen million visits (and ninety-seven million views), whereas the JohnMcCain.com channel contained only three hundred and thirty videos and attracted only two million visits (and twenty-five million views). Obama's campaign even developed an iPhone app for its supporters.

Similarly, Republican hopeful Ron Paul was a notable presence in the campaign, primarily because of his ability to reach out to his supporters online. Like Obama, Paul was especially popular among voters, and like Obama, Paul invested considerable time in his online presence. Most notably, Paul raised a record $4.2 million in twenty-four hours online during November 2007. The Paul campaign generated attention by tying the fund-raising drive to Guy Fawkes Day, and even created video mash-ups of the Fawkes character in *V for Vendetta* and posted them on YouTube as part of the event. Paul was able to raise funds from over thirty-seven thousand donors during this drive, which put him ahead of all other GOP candidates in funds raised in the last quarter of 2007.

In addition to the candidates devoting more resources to online activities in 2008, so too did the media. The Democratic and Republican conventions provided press credentials to bloggers, who provided real-time coverage of events to their readers online. Facebook and ABC shared news content and cohosted online forums about the campaign. And YouTube and CNN paired up to cohost presidential debates, which were made available for viewing on television and online (making it more likely that voters would have an opportunity to view them).

By the **Campaign of 2012**, Twitter, the microblogging Web site, had expanded in importance, with the number of active users increasing by a factor of ten since the 2008 election. Democrat Barack Obama had 20.42 million followers on Twitter during the campaign, while Republican Mitt Romney had 1.225 million followers, one indication that the Obama campaign was, once again, dominant when it came to campaigning online and through social media. Obama's content was retweeted by followers approximately twenty times more than Romney's content was retweeted. Both Obama and Romney had Facebook profiles as well, and like with Twitter, they used the site to post updates about daily events, photos of their travels, and comments about events going on in the world. Obama's content received more than twenty-nine million likes over the course of the campaign, compared to the just under eight million likes received by Romney's content, again suggesting something about the reach of the content being disseminated by the campaigns—more people were sharing Obama's content on both Twitter and Facebook, broadcasting it far beyond those viewers who originally chose to follow him or access his profile. Obama had a similar advantage on his Pinterest account (four times as many followers as Romney), his Instagram account (1.4 million followers compared to Romney's 38,000), and Spotify (where 14,600 people subscribed to his playlist, compared to the 400 people who subscribed to Romney's). A systematic ability to maintain this many online accounts requires a great deal of campaign organization, and a recognition that the candidate's public image is no longer defined by interactions with broadcast and print media alone.

A candidate's Internet presence is a means for the candidate to create a public image that is sympathetic and friendly, and it even permits candidates to exhibit their sense of humor—something that isn't as easy to do in the formal confines of presidential debates, or in the impersonal setting of a mass rally. Candidates may also choose to use their Internet presence, as Howard Dean did, to create new opportunities for voter interaction. For example, on August 29, 2012, Democratic incumbent Barack Obama answered questions on a Reddit thread entitled "Ask Me Anything." Reddit users asked Obama about items both serious (specifics about his tax policy, his commitment to NASA) and lighthearted (his favorite basketball player, the recipe for the microbrew served at the White House).

Although online contributions were nothing new by 2012, in this election, for the first time, the Federal Elections Commission permitted campaign contributions to be made in the form of a text message. While texting donations to organizations like the Red Cross during times of disaster have long been used for fund-raising drives for other nonprofits, FEC rules had prevented candidates from easily raising funds from donors via mobile phones. Rather, online donors have had to use a computer in order to enter the needed information to document their contribution. Changing the device that can be used to make a donation, and the type of application in which a supporter can make a donation, makes it easier and more cost-effective for candidates to raise donations online—both in terms of the number of donors reached (it broadens the potential scope) and the size of the donations (it makes it easier to reach small-dollar donors). Direct mail and phone banking are far more costly, reach a smaller potential base of supporters, and tend to have a far lower rate of return for dollars spent. Based on surveys conducted in late September, the Pew Research Center found that 13 percent of Americans had contributed to a political campaign in 2012. Yet Pew found that texting remained the least common avenue for political donations up to that time, being utilized by only 10 percent of those who had given money to a candidate. Significantly, 67 percent of donors had given money in person, sent a donation through the mail, or given a donation over the phone—decidedly traditional forms of fund-raising. Half of those polled had also made a contribution online or through e-mail, suggesting that using the Internet for fund-raising, overall, has become a common form of fund-raising for those who contribute to political candidates. (Pew found that one in ten Americans had made a charitable donation of any kind using a text via cell phone, compared to one in one hundred Americans who had made such a donation to a political candidate in 2012.) Democrats were twice as likely to contribute online or via text, whereas Republican voters were more likely to contribute funds in more traditional ways. There were no partisan differences in overall likelihood of contributions, however, suggesting that it is the candidates and their fund-raising strategies that are the main sources of difference in type of donation.

In the **Campaign of 2016**, CNN broke records for debate viewership when it live-streamed its coverage of the second GOP debate, enabling online viewers to watch the event as it unfolded. *Fox News*, which had hosted the first GOP debate, did not stream the event, restricting viewership to those with cable access. As Americans, particularly millennials, have abandoned expensive satellite and cable subscriptions, the *Fox News* format left sizable segments of the viewing public in the dark. The CNN debate was more widely viewed and more widely covered by the press (and was even live-tweeted by Democratic hopeful Bernie Sanders), which established a model for the coverage of future campaign events: In order to generate visibility, and to maximize viewership, the transmission of such events cannot be limited to traditional broadcast sources.

Online fund-raising had broken new records in 2016 as well. By the end of September 2015, Democratic hopeful Bernie Sanders had raised $1 million online, far earlier than any other candidate had managed to accomplish such a feat. By mid-September of 2015, Twitter announced a partnership with Square that permitted candidates who subscribed to the Square payment system to embed a donation button in their Twitter feed, enabling interested donors to click on the button, input a donation amount, and also enter their name, address, and other information required by the FEC (all without leaving the app or the feed).

Throughout 2015 Donald Trump used Twitter and other social media platforms to great effect, mastering the craft of repeatedly stirring controversy to his political advantage. Nowadays, all candidates are expected to have Web sites, to tweet the daily events of their campaign, to be part of an online community on Facebook and elsewhere, and to routinely post campaign materials on YouTube. More effective campaigns use their online interactions with supporters as a means to disseminate information, but also to interact with and organize supporters, and to harvest data about the electorate for later use in data analytic models. Public opinion polls suggest that older voters are an expanding presence online, and particularly in the use of **social media** sites. As more voters rely on these technologies, candidates will be compelled to adapt their campaign strategies to this changing world of social mass media or risk finding their campaigns widely ignored.

See also Big Data; Twenty-Four-Hour News Cycle

Additional Resources

Bimber, Bruce, and Richard Davis. *Campaigning Online: The Internet in U.S. Elections.* New York: Oxford University Press, 2003.

Fraser, Matthew, and Soumitra Dutta. "Obama's Win Means Future Elections Must Be Fought Online." *Guardian*, November 7, 2008.

Lapowsky, Issie. "Campaign Donation Buttons Come to Twitter, Thanks to Square." *Wired*, September 15, 2015.

Obama, Barack. "I Am Barack Obama, President of the United States." Reddit thread, August 29, 2012. https://www.reddit.com/comments/z1c9z/i_am_barack_obama_president_of _the_united_states/. Accessed October 6, 2015.

Smith, Aaron, and Maeve Duggan. "Presidential Campaign Donations in the Digital Age." Pew Research Center for Internet, Science, and Technology, October 25, 2012. http:// www.pewinternet.org/2012/10/25/presidential-campaign-donations-in-the-digital-age/.

Walensky, Robyn, and the Associated Press. "Ron Paul Sets Online Fundraising Record with $4.2 Million in One Day." FoxNews.com, November 6, 2007.

Wolf, Gary. "How the Internet Invented Howard Dean." *Wired*, December 1, 2004.

Wortham, Jenna. "The Presidential Campaign on Social Media." *New York Times* interactive, October 8, 2012. http://www.nytimes.com/interactive/2012/10/08/technology /campaign-social-media.html. Accessed October 6, 2015.

Invisible Primary

Coined by journalist Arthur Hadley in 1976 to describe a "pre-primary" process, beginning as early as the outcome of the previous general election, in which candidates promote their prospects as future nominees to party leaders and fund-raisers, the "invisible primary," according to political scientists Cohen, Karol, Noel, and Zaller, is in general terms an unobserved interval of time prior to the opening of the primary/caucus season wherein candidates labor for the requisite support to win their party's nomination. As described by Cohen, Zaller, et al., it is in the invisible primary that candidates "meet, woo and gain the public support of leading members of their party." These "leading members" are further identified as including "office holders, party officials, interest group leaders, citizen-activists, and anyone else who works regularly for the party," such as "fund raisers" and "ideologues," and we hazard to venture that influential media figures are also in the mix. While sounding public opinion remains important, the invisible primary, described by some as "exhibition season," plays a critical role in determining who will succeed in state primaries and caucuses, and by extension, who will ultimately win the party's nomination for president. The invisible primary is, therefore, as Sides and Vavreck observe, a means "to recruit [candidates] or perhaps discourage them," through the deliberate "efforts of party leaders" long before the first caucus or primary occurs.

For Cohen et al., the importance of the unseen endorsement of party leadership cannot be gainsaid; the invisible primary has become the "modern analog to the smoke-filled rooms" that shaped the direction of the national nominating connections before the ascent of the modern primary system following the internal reforms of the nominating process during the late 1960s and early 1970s, especially the reforms instituted in the Democratic Party in 1972 in response to the McGovern-Fraser Commission. Those reforms, which were more or less emulated by the Republican Party, were designed to democratize the presidential nomination process, to grant more "power to the people" by abolishing the party boss and the smoke-filled room. Democratization makes perfect sense in a democratic polity, and yet as the appearance of the invisible primary might demonstrate, some needs find a way to be filled in spite of our best efforts to suppress them.

While direct, authorized presidential primaries had been around as early as 1912, they were merely popularity contests to test the viability of candidates who were already on the inside track; one could gain the party's nomination without winning a single primary. But with the reforms that shaped the political landscape of the 1970s, they assumed new relevance in presidential politics, and the constellation of primaries and caucuses expanded. Consecutive Democratic nominations for president of first Sen. George McGovern in 1972 and then Gov. Jimmy Carter in 1976 were the consequence of this new process, two candidates who likely would have been otherwise marginal in the more traditional national convention system as dominated by bosses, insiders, and elites. The reformed primary system also encouraged Gov. Ronald Reagan's serious challenge against incumbent president Gerald Ford, who won the nomination, in 1976. These examples were enough to illustrate a marked change—a more democratic change, as it were, in which the rank and file played a major role, and this was met with some resistance by insiders and principal activists in both parties. A new and largely unobserved dynamic grew out of the reforms of the 1970s to replace the smoke-filled room, a dynamic that developed its own structure and established its own patterns: the invisible primary.

Popularity among the general public and within the media and the ability to generate abundant funding are important qualities for any candidate, but there is evidence to support the notion that "winning" in the invisible primary is paramount. Without gaining the support of the party leadership itself—of prominent officeholders at national and state levels, of leading activists in the precincts and invested insiders at all levels—no candidate can mount a credible campaign for the nomination. This support is, as suggested above, won quietly from the inside, not necessarily deliberately concealed but nonetheless beyond the public's view. Even before succeeding at the crucial necessity of fund-raising, it can be said that the unofficial, unpublicized support of prominent party leaders is the first and requisite step. Cohen et al. detail the appearance of Texas governor George Bush on the scene during the prelude to the 2000 campaign, the exhibition season that was not exhibited, in which he gathered the support of thirty-one governors, "8 of 9 from the most populous states," and from there managed to launch an irresistible bid for the nomination. Low-profile endorsements from several of these governors were tendered prior to Gov. Bush's announced intention to run, leading to the accumulation of financing that would far exceed that of any other candidate in the race. Gov. Bush was not a secret; he was a well-known public figure, and both his political ambitions as reported by the press and his exposure to potential supporters in private channels were important. In the accounts offered by political scientists like Cohen and Zaller, Sides and Vavreck, or John Aldrich, the invisible primary is not unlike a multilayered conversation, part of which is indeed visible, but a good part of it is obscured from the gaze of the general public. Negotiating throughout this conversation, party insiders and prospective candidates engage in a mutual relationship involving a candidate's skill at self-promotion and the party insider's demonstration of interest and potential commitment, all done without media scrutiny and therefore more candidly. As stated above, this is not meant to conceal an inner cabal of kingmakers, or even to return to older practices (e.g., bosses and machine favorites) that antedate the reforms of the seventies, but rather it is a means to supply what was lost before the primary system; that is, a way to screen candidates without relying on the caprices of public opinion. Public opinion remains potent, and all candidates seek to build a favorable relationship with the electorate; this is natural to democracy. Leadership is also natural to democracy; it is natural to politics, and the invisible primary, if it is indeed an accurate depiction of the reality of campaigns, in its own way is a vehicle for leadership independent of the strains that accompany the quest for popularity. If the analogy holds, the invisible primary is the smoke-filled room unconstrained by walls yet equally mysterious to those uninitiated in the interior processes of democratic politics. Anything is subject to abuse, and the activity that occurs in the invisible primary is no different, but the fact that it is an influence in the nominating process does not mean the destruction of the nominating process.

More narrowly, one might describe the invisible primary as those processes that occur between the emergence of a candidate and the establishment of fundraising—in particular, the appearance of such money generators as super PACs. However, while this is doubtless a part of the invisible primary dynamic, it is about more than the money. Party insiders do recognize the importance of forwarding candidates who can draw funding, but a candidate's campaigning skills, ability to inspire loyalty, and insider appeal are priorities. Even more important than funding is the search for candidates who can unify the party and give it the common cause needed to win the White House. Establishing a candidate who can bring unity to the party is central, as Cohen et al. explain: "An especially important common feature [of the invisible primary] is that individuals of diverse preferences—here ideological preferences—must converge on a choice that might not be many people's ideal choice." The invisible primary will not satisfy those who are ardently committed to a candidate with purist proclivities; rather, it is through this mostly hidden stage of the nominating process that such true believers are screened out, leaving a more pragmatic candidate who can be considered optimal to the highest number of factions. Once a candidate proves to the party loyalists that he or she can provide this kind of unity and leadership, the candidate's status as early frontrunner is more likely. Significantly, the money must be there, patronage must be secured, and rival spending must be matched or exceeded, but money alone does not earn nominations; money without prestige, loyalty, and trust among the party insiders cannot win elections. Money is necessary to a winning campaign, but it is not by itself sufficient.

As mentioned above, the invisible primary both "recruits and discourages" candidates, and while the former is likely to occur long before the primary season, the latter is likely to extend into it. An example shared by Dan Balz and Sides and Vavreck is provided by the 2012 campaign of Newt Gingrich, whose campaign was hobbled by eroded support from party insiders. Some of this could be observed by the public, but much of it stemmed from efforts by many insiders to dissuade Gingrich from continuing his campaign. In Gingrich's case, the opposition to his campaign became increasingly visible the longer he sustained it, but Sides and Vavreck claim that this opposition, once it became more public, "provided a somewhat uncommon glimpse into the conversations ongoing during the invisible primary." More recently, Nate Silver at fivethirtyeight.com, commenting on the fleetingly anticipated entrance of former governor and 2012 Republican nominee Mitt Romney into the race for the 2016 nomination, observed that Romney was engaged in the conversation and negotiations of the "invisible primary . . . [in an attempt to persuade] influential Republicans that Bush is too moderate, that Rubio isn't ready, that Paul is too far afield and so forth." This may serve as a more accurate example of the nature of the invisible primary than the Gingrich case in 2012, and, given the eventual transitory nature of Romney's interest in 2016, one might conclude, although with a dose of conjecture, that this time he failed to stir interest or support among party insiders— that he lost the invisible primary and wisely withdrew. Of that we cannot be sure, but Silver's account of Romney's momentary presence in the conversation may provide another visible glimpse into principally invisible processes.

Given the nature of the invisible primary, if it is as many political scientists and commentators believe it to be, we can only conclude that this unobserved but crucial conversation is under way at present, and we can only speculate on how it will play out as we move further into the 2016 campaign season. As of late December 2015, former Florida Governor Jeb Bush, while failing to gain attention in the polls, nevertheless still led his rivals in the number of insider endorsements. This changed in February 2016 with Sen. Marco Rubio catching, and then eclipsing Gov. Bush in the quantity of endorsements. According to a recent article by Aaron Bycoffe at FiveThirtyEight, in which candidates are assigned an endorsement score based on public support from members of the House of Representatives (one point per endorsement), the Senate (five points per endorsement), and state governors (ten points per endorsement), Sen. Rubio had accumulated 97 endorsement points by Feb. 21, followed by Gov. Bush with 46, Gov. Chris Christie with 36, Gov. Mike Huckabee with 25, Sen. Ted Cruz with 22, and Gov. John Kasich with 22. Having lost significantly in the South Carolina primary, and losing ground to Sen. Rubio in the endorsement race, Gov. Bush, who began his campaign as the likely front runner, withdrew from the campaign. Donald Trump—the frontrunner as measured by the public polls—has yet to receive an endorsement (as of Feb. 21, 2016), with Ben Carson having received just one endorsement point. Whether or not Mr. Trump can continue to dominate the public, visible campaign given his utter inability to gain any insider endorsements remains to be seen, but as of this writing he has managed to win primaries in New Hampshire and South Carolina even though he has no support from party insiders. On the Democratic side, former secretary of state Hillary Clinton has almost universal support within the invisible primary in spite of Vermont senator Bernie Sanders's widely captivating campaign, and she is also now enjoying stronger numbers in the polls in most states, although not across all groups. Should Sec. Clinton and Sen. Rubio gain the nominations of their respective parties, it would thereby seem to lend additional credence to the importance of the invisible primary as concluded by many political scientists and analysts, perhaps confirming the analogy depicting the invisible primary as the re-embodiment of the "smoke-filled room." At present, the campaign of Donald Trump could still throw a spanner in the works.

Additional Resources

Aldrich, John. "The Invisible Primary and Its Effects on Democratic Choice." *PS: Political Science and Politics* 42, no. 1 (January 2009): 33–38.

Balz, Dan. *Collision 2012: Obama vs. Romney and the Future of Elections in America.* New York: Viking, 2013.

Bycoffe, Aaron. "The Endorsement Primary." FiveThirtyEight. December 28, 2015. http://projects.fivethirtyeight.com/2016-endorsement-primary/.

Cohen, Marty, David Karol, Hans Noel, and John Zaller. "The Invisible Primary in Presidential Nominations, 1980–2004." In William G. Mayer, ed. *The Making of Presidential Candidates.* Lanham, MD: Rowman & Littlefield Publishers, Inc., 2008, pp. 1–38.

Cohen, Marty, David Karol, Hans Noel, and John Zaller. *The Party Decides: Presidential Nominations before and after Reform.* Chicago: University of Chicago Press, 2008.

Hadley, Arthur. *The Invisible Primary.* Englewood Cliffs, NJ: Prentice-Hall, 1976.

Sides, John, and Lynn Vavreck. *The Gamble: Choice and Chance in the 2012 Presidential Election.* Princeton, NJ: Princeton University Press, 2013.

Silver, Nate. "Romney and the GOP's Five-Ring Circus." FiveThirtyEight. http://fivethirtyeight.com/datalab/romney-and-the-gops-five-ring-circus/. Accessed August 25, 2015.

Isolationism

From 1895 through 1904, the United States joined a number of European powers in expanding its global sphere of influence. After a victory over Spain in the Spanish-American War, the subsequent acquisition of American colonies in the Caribbean and Pacific established the United States as an international power in its own right. However, by the **Campaign of 1904**, growing concern over the impact of expansionism on American democratic values led the Democratic National Convention to include in its platform a strongly worded plank denouncing imperialism.

Even though William McKinley easily won reelection by defeating William Jennings Bryan, a growing number of national political figures criticized the government's ambitions abroad. Influential progressives argued that the country faced too many problems at home to afford to squander its wealth and the lives of its young men on dreams of empire. Through the 1908 presidential election, Republicans vigorously defended expansionism by arguing that the country needed to protect important new markets for American business and industry. Democrats continued to declaim against these undemocratic and grasping imperial ambitions.

By the opening salvos of World War I in August 1914, the American public had tilted away from expansionism and toward isolationism. During the **Campaign of 1916**, incumbent president Woodrow Wilson ran for reelection as the proven peace candidate. Wilson rode the campaign slogan "He Kept Us Out of War" to victory.

Events subsequently overtook Wilson, and in 1917, the United States joined the war against Germany and its allies.

In the war's aftermath, Wilson lobbied hard for U.S. membership in the new League of Nations. While the 1920 Democratic platform supported membership in the League of Nations, the Republican platform expressed strong opposition to the league on grounds that it threatened American sovereignty. Bitter from the high casualties suffered in a seemingly senseless foreign war, wary of political upheaval in Russia, and suspicious of foreign entanglements, the American public moved further toward isolationism throughout the 1920s and 1930s. World War I had taught Americans the dangers of "entangling alliances"; neutrality and isolation prevailed in both public sentiment and national policy.

Despite growing concern in the mid-1930s over the emergence of fascism in Germany and Japanese aggression in Asia, both major party platforms of 1936 continued to express strong opposition to foreign alliances or commitments. But by the 1940 party conventions, Nazi Germany had conquered most of Western Europe and part of Scandinavia while also seizing most of Northern Africa, leaving Britain to stand alone against Hitler, while Japan continued its war of aggression in China. Germany and Japan had amassed substantial military might and demonstrated a clear willingness to use it. Even though the U.S. Navy possessed a sizable fleet, the United States seemed weak compared with Nazi Germany and Imperial Japan. The Republican platform blamed the New Deal policies of the Roosevelt administration for leaving the nation unprepared to defend itself from new threats abroad. And yet, the Republican platform continued to express strong opposition to American participation in foreign wars.

Interestingly, the Democratic platform included a plank pledging that the Roosevelt administration would not involve the United States in a foreign war. Both Republican and Democratic platforms advocated materiel support to free nations in their efforts to resist aggression. But Republican candidate Wendell Willkie, under pressure from his party's isolationist wing, attacked Roosevelt for his lend-lease arrangement with Britain.

Roosevelt continued to publicly insist on his preference for neutrality while quietly but resolutely working behind the scenes—through the provision of materials as well as the combat deployment of the U.S. Navy in the North Atlantic—to assist Britain in their efforts against the Nazis after the fall of France. Ultimately, this issue was decided for him by the Japanese attack on American naval forces at Pearl Harbor, ending American isolationism.

Isolationism has been remarkably absent from most contemporary presidential campaigns. While candidates have disagreed over the manner in which the United States should pursue its interests in world affairs—most notably in the areas of arms control, the promotion of human rights, and the need for military intervention—no major party candidate has advocated withdrawing from global commitments in the post–World War II era. Democrats have historically been more likely to prioritize human rights (particularly Jimmy Carter in the **Campaign of 1976** and the **Campaign of 1980**) and to advocate arms-control treaties and multilateral actions; however, Democrats have occasionally championed greater levels of military spending as well (most notably, Carter in the Campaign of 1980, but also John Kerry in 2004). Republicans have been more likely to prioritize military spending over domestic programs (particularly Ronald Reagan in the Campaign of 1980 and the **Campaign of 1984**, George W. Bush in the **Campaign of 2004**, and John McCain in the **Campaign of 2008**).

The demise of the Soviet Union during the administration of George H. W. Bush led to widespread support among both political parties for a dramatic reduction in military spending and a reallocation of the "peace dividend" to domestic programs. However, the U.S. commitment to continued involvement in world affairs has never been in question. Military interventions to promote human rights in Somalia and Bosnia occurred during the Clinton administration and had strong bipartisan support, although these actions were later criticized by Clinton's political opponents. Similarly, President George W. Bush's decision to invade Afghanistan, and later Iraq, in the wake of the September 11, 2001, attacks had strong bipartisan support as well. By the Campaign of 2004, much of that support had crumbled, and Democratic nominee John Kerry argued that the war in Iraq was a mistake. Kerry continued to support the war in Afghanistan, however, again demonstrating the bipartisan commitment to internationalism that pervaded this era.

In the Campaign of 2008, Democratic nominee Barack Obama campaigned for a withdrawal of U.S. forces from Iraq and a buildup of forces in Afghanistan. Republican nominee John McCain wanted to maintain U.S. troop levels in both conflicts and suggested a possible invasion of Iran if the United States became convinced that Iraq was nearing development of a nuclear weapon. After being elected, Obama pursued troop reductions in Iraq and dramatically increased U.S. forces in Afghanistan, and he engaged in a multilateral military effort with other NATO countries to protect Libyan civilians from retaliation by the Qaddafi regime.

The most vocal advocates for isolationism in recent decades have been third-party candidates. Specifically, in the **Campaign of 2000**, Pat Buchanan and the Reform Party advocated refocusing U.S. foreign policy on the basis of national defense, rather than pursuing American interests overseas. Similarly, the liberal Green Party and the conservative Constitution Party supported an isolationist foreign policy, an agenda that has consistently also been pursued by the Libertarian Party. The libertarian perspective was best exemplified by Ron Paul, a Republican hopeful in the Campaign of 2008 and the Campaign of 2012. A self-declared libertarian, Paul would withdraw the United States from all military involvement overseas as well as from all multilateral organizations and treaties. Paul would limit military spending to what is needed to secure the nation's boundaries. Paul's viewpoint is unique within the Republican Party. Mitt Romney campaigned on strengthening the role of the U.S. military abroad, including the possible use of military force against Iran. While Obama withdrew U.S. troops from Iraq and pledged a 2013 withdrawal of troops from Afghanistan, he also has enthusiastically supported the use of drones in air strikes, and his administration has been involved in several high-profile assassinations of suspected terrorists overseas. At present, in the 2015–2016 campaign season, Lincoln Chaffee appears to most closely resemble the non-interventionist attitudes of Ron Paul. Cong. Paul's son, Sen. Rand Paul, has adopted a foreign policy stance that can be characterized as more "realist" in its substance than that of his father. The emergence of ISIL/ISIS has sparked an intense debate fueled by questions about the proper American response to militant Islamist movements abroad, with almost all Republican candidates critical of President Obama's policies in this regard. Donald Trump in particular has assumed a tough stance toward ISIL/ISIS, commenting on *60 Minutes* that we should confront "ISIS in Iraq" and saying, "You got to knock them out. You got to knock them out. You got to fight them. You got to fight them." Mr. Trump also has expressed admiration for Russia's apparent willingness to fight the extremists in Syria, observing, "Russia wants to get rid of ISIS. We want to get rid of ISIS. Maybe let Russia do it. Let them get rid of ISIS. What the hell do we care?" Remarks such as these are neither isolationist nor interventionist, but rather at best an unrefined variation of political realism. Given the current mood among almost all the candidates competing for the 2016 major party nominations, it would thus appear that isolationism, given the general mood of the electorate, is less likely to gain support among serious presidential contenders.

See also American Exceptionalism; Neoconservatives; War and Peace Issue

Additional Resources

Cole, Wayne S. *Roosevelt and the Isolationists, 1932–45.* Lincoln: University of Nebraska Press, 1983.

Cooper, John Milton. *The Vanity of Power: American Isolationism and the First World War, 1914–1917.* Westport, CT: Greenwood Press, 1969.

Desvarieux, Jessica, and Imtiyaz Delawala. "John McCain Criticizes 2012 GOP Field for Isolationism." ABCNews.com, June 19, 2011.

Dueck, Colin. "GOP Isolationist? No, Just More Jacksonian." *Real Clear Politics*, June 20, 2011.

Jim Crow Laws

At the resolution of the Civil War, the U.S. Constitution was amended to abolish slavery and protect the inherent rights of the previously enslaved. These "Civil

War Amendments" (the Thirteenth, Fourteenth, and Fifteenth amendments) were designed to remedy the inequities and injustices that African Americans had suffered since the earliest days of colonial America. However, even before these amendments were ratified, southern states enacted what became known as "black codes," which severely restricted the liberties of freed slaves and forced upon them a new system of subjugation that, in many ways, resembled their previous condition of slavery. Congress responded by enacting civil rights legislation to legally preempt the black codes, enforced by the presence of the federal military, throughout the states of the former Confederacy. For a time, these federal efforts worked to improve the condition of freed slaves; but by the late 1870s, the mood in Washington had changed, and the goals of Reconstruction were abandoned. (Some argue that President Rutherford B. Hayes was elected in a compromise that gave him an Electoral College victory in exchange for the withdrawal of federal troops, but a formal "compromise" to "end Reconstruction" is not evident with any confidence.)

As the federal government withdrew its presence from the South, new efforts to constrain the liberties of the freedmen were undertaken through a variety of methods, some legal and institutional, others informal and unwritten, that became known as "Jim Crow" laws. The term "Jim Crow" has its origins in a racial slur that harkens back to the 1830s, when minstrel shows with performers singing and dancing in blackface first appeared. The negative stereotypes associated with the Jim Crow minstrel shows paralleled the stereotypes about free slaves that pervaded white culture in the South during the antebellum period, stereotypes that became further ingrained in American popular culture in the latter half of the nineteenth century and continued into the twentieth century. Jim Crow laws imposed segregation (through laws forcing blacks into separate schools and neighborhoods and restricting their access to public transportation, restaurants, and lodging) and deprived African Americans of basic civil rights, most notably, the right to vote. Informally, Jim Crow also refers to the mentality that was imposed upon black Americans from this socially stifling set of unwritten restrictions and unspoken rules on how they were permitted to interact with whites, forcing them at every turn into a subservient and inherently humiliating position.

The deprivation of voting rights sanctioned by Jim Crow severely hampered the influence of African Americans in the selection and election of presidential candidates. Literacy tests, grandfather clauses, and regressive poll taxes deprived African Americans of their electoral influence at every turn. These practices, combined with the more sinister and deadly methods employed by white militant groups such as the Ku Klux Klan and white citizens' councils, effectively reduced the black vote to a slender, marginalized thread within the electorate. Throughout the nineteenth century and into the first three decades of the twentieth century, African Americans universally affiliated themselves with the Republican Party, which was viewed as the party of Emancipation. In spite of legal and extralegal methods aimed at disfranchising African Americans, they made every effort to become politically involved. Even after Reconstruction, African American delegates participated in Republican nominating conventions, albeit in a limited role. One milestone was achieved when, at the 1884 GOP convention, Mississippi delegate John Roy Lynch, an African American, served as temporary convention chair and delivered the keynote address. For the most part, though, these achievements were unusual; and once Reconstruction was over, African Americans were by and large treated as second-class citizens at all levels of society. Jim Crow laws were the most visible reminder of this status. Where African Americans were permitted to exercise their constitutional rights, they continued to vote Republican, and most remained loyal to the GOP even through the **Campaign of 1932**. While some African Americans had supported Democratic nominee Al Smith as early as the **Campaign of 1928**, their movement toward the Democratic Party was gradual; it was not until the **Campaign of 1936** that African Americans voters fully embraced a Democrat, Franklin Delano Roosevelt. Roosevelt's New Deal programs appealed to black voters, and in 1936, over 71 percent cast their ballots for FDR.

In the South, however, white Democrats at the state and local levels continued to support the policies of Jim Crow, and they were aided and abetted in their efforts by the existence of the all-white primary. It was not until 1944, in *Smith v. Allwright*, that the Supreme Court effectively ended this practice in Texas and throughout the South. NAACP lawyers Thurgood Marshall and William Hastie had brought the suit on behalf of Lonnie Smith, an African American citizen who was refused the opportunity to participate in the Texas Democratic primary in 1940. Texas had argued that primaries were party activities and therefore protected by the first amendment, which guarantees freedom of association. Smith and the NAACP argued that primaries were administered by the state and served the function of electing political leaders, and therefore that Smith's federal voting rights were being violated by the race-based ban on nonwhite primary participation. The ruling in this case reversed an earlier decision, *Grovey v. Townsend* (1935), where the Court had ruled that Grovey's Fourteenth and Fifteenth amendment rights were not violated, because the Texas all-white primary was not sanctioned by the state. By the late 1930s, the composition of the Court had changed, and several new Roosevelt appointees contributed to the eight-to-one decision to overturn the practice.

African American gains during this era came from the courts, rather than from the legislative branch, as restrictive covenants, segregated law schools, and segregated public schools were struck down in turn. It was only through bipartisan efforts at the federal level, including the Civil Rights Acts of 1957 and 1960, and particularly the more substantive and effective Civil Rights Act of 1964, as well as the Voting Rights Act of 1965 and the ratification of the Twenty-Fourth Amendment (ending the poll tax), that the Jim Crow disfranchisement of black voters finally came to an end. While African Americans continue to struggle to overcome the lingering effects of Jim Crow, their ability to participate in the electoral process has improved dramatically since the 1960s. Record numbers of African Americans now serve in the House of Representatives. African American legislators are making gains in both state and local government, and in the **Campaign of 2008**, Americans elected the first African American president. President Obama's reelection in the **Campaign of 2012** was also a milestone.

See also Civil Rights Issue; Race Relations Issue

Additional Resources

Grovey v. Townsend, 295 U.S. 45 (1935).
The History of Jim Crow. http://www.jimcrowhistory.org. Accessed September 5, 2015.
Packard, Jerrold M. *American Nightmare: The History of Jim Crow.* New York: St. Martin's Press, 2002.
Smith v. Allwright, 321 U.S. 649 (1944).
Williams, Juan. *Eyes on the Prize.* New York: Penguin Books, 1987.
Woodward, C. Vann. *The Strange Career of Jim Crow.* Oxford: Oxford University Press, 2002.

Keynesian Economics

Keynesian economics is a school of thought associated with the theories developed by British economist John Maynard Keynes and most associated with the economic policies implemented by President Franklin Delano Roosevelt to address the Great Depression. According to Keynes, government can stimulate a lagging economy by manipulating aggregate demand (thus Keynesian economics is often referred to as "demand-side economics"). There are numerous tools government can use to manipulate aggregate demand, including raising or lowering interest rates (to encourage saving or spending by consumers); changing the marginal tax rate or offering greater tax credits (again, to potentially encourage spending); expanding benefits such as Social Security or veterans' benefits, or indexing those benefits to inflation (again, to encourage spending); or job creation, in which the government has a direct role as an employer (as was the case with Roosevelt, and with later programs such as AmeriCorps), or where the government attempts to indirectly create jobs by allocating funds to state or local governments, or to the private sector, with the expectation that these funds will be used for projects that will create employment.

Applications of Keynes's theory have generally revolved around the notion that in poor economic times, the government should be free to spend money to help the nation recover, primarily through some combination of efforts to stimulate aggregate demand. In times of a robust economy, however, government efforts are less needed, and this is when taxes should be raised to pay down debt accrued during past recessions, or to put aside for future times when government assistance may be needed.

Keynesian principles guided much of American economic policy throughout the twentieth century, beginning with President Roosevelt's first term. (FDR's predecessor, Herbert Hoover, had rejected more than minimal government intervention in the economy during the Depression in the belief that, given enough time, any market economy, however stressed, would correct itself, a position that he held at the cost of reelection.) Following World War II, the Roosevelt New Deal and the principles of Keynesian economic theory emerged as the dominant theoretical perspective guiding national policy. Republican and Democratic presidents alike hewed to Keynesian policies through the 1970s, with Republican Richard Nixon famously claiming, "We are all Keynesians now," as he adopted a series of wage and price controls (to limit aggregate demand and slow the inflation rate) during the 1970s and considered implementing a guaranteed minimum income.

The major challenge to Keynesian policies came during Republican Ronald Reagan's campaigns for the White House. Reagan was unsuccessful in his efforts to win his party's nomination in 1976, but he went on to win the presidential election in the **Campaign of 1980**. Reagan's supply-side approach (originally criticized by rival George H. W. Bush as "voodoo economics") provided Republicans with an alternative approach to economic policy, and it was later embraced by Republican nominee George W. Bush in the **Campaigns of 2000** and **2004** (and, to a somewhat lesser extent, by John McCain during the **Campaign of 2008**). The supply-side approach to economic policy continued to dominate the Republican Party agenda in the **Campaign of 2012**, as the party unified behind the budget proposals of Wisconsin representative Paul Ryan. The Democratic nominee, incumbent president Barack Obama, demonstrated an affinity for the tenets of Keynesian economics, particularly in his stimulus plan that provided federal funds to states to protect the jobs of state employees and to spur hiring on construction projects, the government-backed loans to the failing domestic automobile industry, and his opposition to the George W. Bush–era tax cuts for wealthier Americans (on the grounds that their aggregate demand is unaffected by the cuts, and that their tax dollars are needed to fund aid programs for less affluent Americans). Critics of Keynesian politics argue that such policies have contributed to unsustainable levels of national debt, and that fewer regulations on business are a more efficient means of producing economic growth.

Additional Resources

Keynes, John Maynard. *The Essential Keynes.* Penguin Classics. Edited by Robert Skidelsky. New York: Penguin Books, 2016.

Rauchway, Eric. *The Money Makers: How Roosevelt and Keynes Ended the Depression, Defeated Fascism, and Secured a Prosperous Peace.* New York: Basic Books, 2010.

Skildelksy, Robert. *Keynes: A Very Short Introduction.* New York: Oxford Books, 2010.

LGBTQ Issues

Lesbian, Gay, Bisexual, Transgender, and Queer (or Questioning) (LGBTQ) rights did not become a national political issue until the summer of 1969, when patrons of a gay bar in Greenwich Village responded to a police raid with outrage in a series of incidents that became known as the Stonewall Riots. The following summer, the gay community in New York City held its first gay pride parade to commemorate the Stonewall Riots, an event that has been replicated in other cities around the world since that time. Stonewall is often viewed as the beginning of openness about homosexuality in American society, although violence against the gay community, and the criminalization of homosexual relations, continued for several decades after the event. Still, Stonewall began a debate in American politics about the treatment of gay Americans and the varying forms of workplace and other legal discrimination faced by this community. It is a debate that persists to this day.

In the **Campaign of 1972**, the Democratic National Convention adopted the first gay rights platform plank in American history. A majority of Democratic convention delegates viewed support for gay rights as consistent with the commitment of the modern Democratic Party to civil rights. The Republican Party approached gay rights not from the perspective of civil rights but from the perspective of morality. During the 1970s, the **Moral Majority** came to wield a far greater influence over the Republican Party; most members of this movement viewed homosexuality as inconsistent with biblical teachings, and as their role in the GOP coalition grew, so too did the GOP's unwillingness to guarantee members of the LGBTQ community the same rights as heterosexuals.

During the early 1980s, the AIDS epidemic further complicated the gay rights debate. The fact that AIDS first appeared in the gay community raised public health questions about the gay lifestyle, and religious figures associated with the conservative movement, such as Pat Robertson and Jerry Falwell, were quick to suggest that AIDS might be a divine punishment for homosexuality. Gay rights was not a prominent theme in the **Campaign of 1980**. While Ronald Reagan openly courted the Moral Majority, he focused his efforts on abortion and traditional family values, and the first cases of AIDS were not reported until 1981. When Reagan's close friend, actor Rock Hudson, died from AIDS in 1985, Reagan avoided discussing both the disease that killed Hudson and his friend's closeted homosexuality. It has been noted that Reagan did not say the word "AIDS" until 1987. To the consternation of many conservatives, Reagan's surgeon general, the pro-life physician C. Everett Koop, responded to the AIDS crisis by mailing a flyer to every American household outlining safe-sex practices, including condom usage. The threat of AIDS, the public discrimination that ensued, and the lack of federal funding for AIDS research during this era served to mobilize the gay community. Groups such as ACT-UP aggressively demanded public action by lawmakers. But because the community faced a very real public health crisis, most efforts focused on dealing with the crisis, and not on the expansion of rights more generally.

By the 1990s, the gay rights movement attempted to move beyond issues of AIDS funding; homosexual relations were still illegal in many states, and the Supreme Court had recently upheld the constitutionality of state anti-sodomy laws in *Bowers v. Hardwick* (1986). In the **Campaign of 1992**, Democratic presidential nominee Bill Clinton took up the cause of gay rights, promising that if he were elected, he would repeal the existing ban on gay people serving in the military. While Clinton's pledge did not prevent him from being elected, he quickly ran into opposition from both Congress and the military, and eventually a compromise was struck in the form of "don't ask, don't tell" (DADT). Under DADT, if members of the military revealed that they were gay, they were subject to immediate dismissal. If they concealed their sexual orientation, and they were not "outed" by a colleague, they could keep their position. At the time, public opinion polls showed support for DADT as a compromise between an outright ban on service and a complete repeal of the ban.

By the **Campaign of 1996**, the Republican Party began to openly use gay rights as a **wedge issue** for mobilizing Democrats who were not comfortable with homosexuality (those social conservatives who might still be Democrats). The party platform explicitly opposed expanding civil rights or employment laws to prohibit discrimination on the basis of sexual preference or orientation. The Democratic Party platform, on the other hand, supported treating sexual preference and orientation in the same manner as sex, race, creed, religion, and national origin. In an attempt to defuse the conflict and reassure socially conservative Democrats that civil rights for gay persons did not mean that voters would soon be facing the prospect of same-sex marriages in their states, President Clinton signed the Defense of Marriage Act (DOMA) into law shortly before the election. DOMA provided a federal definition of marriage as a legal union between a man and a woman, precluding federal recognition of any same-sex marriage that might be recognized at a state level. While no state was actively considering marrying same-sex couples at this time, the measure seemed to be designed to thwart some of the fear tactics being used by opponents of civil rights for gays and lesbians—namely, that if these groups were given such protections, marriage demands would surely follow.

The 1998 murder of college student Matthew Shepard, who was kidnapped, robbed, assaulted, and tied to a fencepost on a freezing night in Wyoming, in part because he was gay, shocked the nation's conscience and again raised questions about whether crimes against gay persons should be treated as civil rights violations. Two years earlier, in *Romer v. Evans* (1996), the Supreme Court had rejected an amendment to the Colorado Constitution that specifically prohibited laws to prevent discrimination against gays and lesbians. However, the decision did not serve to guarantee gay Americans explicit political equality. In addition to DADT, employment protection for gay persons was still unclear, many states prohibited gays and lesbians from adopting children, and same-sex marriage was not legal in any state. By the **Campaign of 2000**, though, public opinion had shifted. Discrimination in employment on the basis of sexual orientation was no longer socially acceptable to most Americans, and the debate now revolved around whether to grant gays and lesbians the right to marry or enter into civil unions.

In the Campaign of 2000, the Democratic and Republican parties continued to be sharply divided on gay rights issues. In an attempt to mobilize their conservative Christian base, the Republican Party platform included planks in support of traditional marriage, in support of the Boy Scouts of America's right to exclude gays from its ranks, and opposition to DADT (the party preferred to reestablish the ban on service). Republicans also advocated a constitutional amendment to restrict marriage to heterosexual couples, which would prevent states from taking their own actions in support of gay marriage.

The Democratic Party, and its presidential nominee Al Gore, embraced the expansion of gay rights. Specifically, Gore criticized DADT for its lack of compassion and tolerance. Although neither Gore nor the Democratic Party was willing to go as far as to endorse same-sex marriage, the Democratic Party platform did call for the creation of civil unions for the protection of the legal rights of same-sex couples. Significantly, Gore supported Clinton's decision to sign the DOMA, essentially denying gay couples the right to marry. Republican nominee George W. Bush did not equivocate on the same-sex marriage issue. Like the Republican Party platform, Bush rejected the legitimacy of any legal recognition of same-sex unions. Yet Bush did not make gay rights a central issue of his campaign, instead focusing on education reform as a cornerstone of his domestic agenda.

Things changed in the **Campaign of 2004**, as the Bush campaign pursued a reelection strategy that narrowly focused on a core base of supporters. This time around, Bush took a hard line on gay marriage, supporting a constitutional amendment that would bar gay marriage in any state. Democratic nominee John Kerry opposed a constitutional ban on gay marriage but also refused to support the legality of same-sex marriage, preferring instead to advocate for civil unions. Late in the campaign, Bush also expressed his support for state legislation allowing civil unions, despite the fact that the Republican Party platform specifically opposed both same-sex marriage and civil unions. Much more significant to the ultimate outcome of the election, the Republican Party coordinated with a number of state anti-gay marriage and anti-gay civil union initiatives to place defense-of-marriage constitutional amendments on state ballots during the presidential election in an effort to mobilize anti-gay marriage conservatives to turn out to vote. In the end, Bush easily won the popular vote and narrowly won the majority of electoral votes, which political analysts attributed to his ability to mobilize Christian conservatives in a number of key battleground states. Ironically, Bush's vice president, Dick Cheney, later came out in support of same-sex marriage, as did Bush's wife and the nation's First Lady, Laura Bush, who was joined by their daughters.

The **Campaign of 2008** was a more toned-down version of the previous campaign. While economic issues were at the forefront, the nominees were unable to avoid a discussion of gay rights. The Democratic Party and its nominee, Barack Obama, put in place a national outreach program for gay and lesbian voters, promising to focus on LGBTQ rights issues if elected. However, Obama did not support same-sex marriage. On the other hand, Republican nominee John McCain did not attempt to focus on gay rights. McCain expressed support for the continuation of DADT, despite numerous polls showing a lack of public support for the policy. McCain also opposed both same-sex marriages and civil unions, but he supported allowing gay couples to enter into contracts related to their relationships (although it was unclear what such contracts would be). McCain opposed a constitutional amendment to ban same-sex marriage as long as DOMA remained intact (although after the campaign, McCain's wife, Cindy, and his daughter produced ads in support of gay rights and same-sex marriage). In the end, the economy, not gay rights, provided Obama with the issue that permitted him to define himself as the "change" candidate. However, Obama also received strong support (both financially and in terms of votes) from the LGBTQ community.

Once he was elected, the LGBTQ community expected Obama to move quickly to eliminate DADT, which he was reluctant to do. Instead, Obama commissioned a survey of the military and then pressured Congress to retract the rule, which occurred in the last days of 2010 in a party-line vote. The Obama administration later declined to defend the DOMA against further lawsuits, on the grounds that the law was unconstitutional, a move criticized by Republican lawmakers.

The social and legal environment changed dramatically by the time of the **Campaign of 2012**. Same-sex marriage had become legal in seven states. Polls suggested that for the first time, a majority of Americans supported same-sex marriage. Obama's unwillingness to defend DOMA in court created the very real possibility that states that did not permit same-sex marriage might still be compelled to recognize such marriages if they were performed outside of their boundaries for persons who now resided there. The Republican Party's response to these changes was to keep the proposed constitutional amendment to ban same-sex marriage in the party platform. In the 2012 primaries, Ron Paul was the only GOP candidate to oppose the amendment; the eventual Republican nominee, former Massachusetts governor Mitt Romney, supported the constitutional amendment and also expressed his opposition to civil unions (if they provided rights similar to marriage). While the GOP field was divided about whether to reinstate DADT, Romney opposed reinstatement. Democratic nominee Barack Obama, bolstered by favorable shifts in public opinion, came out in support of same-sex marriage during the campaign. It was a risk-free change in strategy for Obama; while most polls found that a slight majority of the public favored same-sex marriage, the rates were substantially higher among Democrats and independents (including groups viewed as more socially conservative such as African Americans, Latinos, and Catholics). Republican voters, on the other hand, remained overwhelmingly opposed in most polls, making support for same-sex marriage far riskier for GOP candidates. This was perhaps best exemplified by the gay combat veteran who was booed by the crowd at a GOP primary debate when he implied that ending DADT was a sign of progress—suggesting that in 2012, at least, some Republican voters felt little sympathy for the concerns of this community.

While same-sex marriage has historically been used as a **wedge issue** by Republicans in their bid to win over socially conservative Democratic voters, the dynamics of this issue appear to have changed in 2012. Now the Democrats were the party that was united on the issue, and the GOP was the party with more divisions (in particular, generational divisions and divisions between evangelical Protestants and other voters). Some Democratic strategists have suggested that slim Democratic margins in states like Ohio and Florida were bolstered by votes from the LGBTQ community, which heavily favored Obama. Others argue that voters who favor same-sex marriage tend to be quite liberal on a host of other issues as well, and so were likely to already be Obama supporters. There is insufficient evidence to demonstrate the narrow claim that enough of these voters were mobilized (rather than converted) to cast a ballot for Obama in 2012, although such an outcome is certainly theoretically possible.

In the aftermath of the 2012 election, federal courts overturned a series of state bans on same-sex marriage, vastly increasing the number of states where same-sex marriage was permitted. The legality of same-sex marriage in the United States was finally answered by the Supreme Court in *Obergefell v. Hodges*. While the ruling federalized same-sex marriage rights, it did not automatically provide parental rights for non-biological parents in same-sex relationships, nor did it provide non-discrimination protections for the LGBTQ community, more generally.

Conservatives unhappy with the *Obergefell* decision attempted to minimize its effect using a similar strategy to that employed by religious and private-sector employers who opposed the contraception mandate in the Affordable Care Act. That is, they suggested that some individuals might have religious objections to same-sex marriage and thus should not be compelled to issue marriage licenses. Several states passed, or attempted to pass, sweeping legislation that granted religious objection status not only to religious institutions who objected to performing same-sex marriages, but also to any private business that did not want to accommodate same-sex couples (such as wedding photographers and bakeries). The laws are ostensibly modeled on the federal Religious Freedom Restoration Act, which protects individuals from violations of their religious freedoms by the federal government. But the state laws are substantively different. They are more broadly written in order to avoid specifically mentioning the LGBTQ community by name, and they do not protect individuals from religious discrimination by the government. Rather, they permit any religious organization, individual, or private business to claim religious discrimination from any activity arising from a transaction with another individual (rather than excluding those interactions to the government alone). Thus, they enable businesses that serve the public to deny service to any customer whose conduct a proprietor might find objectionable for religious reasons (someone from an opposing religion such as Islam; a woman dressed immodestly without a male escort; a person who is in the company of someone other than his or her spouse). Civil rights watchdogs argue that such laws potentially affect hiring (e.g., permitting an employer to refuse to hire Muslims or divorced persons), housing (e.g., landlords can refuse to rent to Muslims, Jews, or anyone whose behavior offends their religious sensibilities), and adoptions (in that it would permit private adoption agencies to refuse to work with gay couples). The Human Rights Campaign notes that such laws require that state governments have compelling interest before they may substantially burden a person's religious practices. Yet these laws are seemingly in conflict with existing protections afforded citizens under the Civil Rights Act—not to be discriminated against as customers at a business, as renters, and as employees.

In Indiana, GOP governor Mike Pence confidently signed such a "conscience protection" bill (also referred to as a "religious freedom" bill) despite pressure from a variety of sources, including the business community, not to do so. Arizona governor Jan Brewer, also a Republican, had refused to sign a similar bill in February 2014 (under the threat of the loss of the Super Bowl). The ensuing public backlash forced the Indiana legislature to amend the legislation after the fact to ensure that businesses could not refuse customers service based on their sexual orientation. Arkansas's conscience protection bill, following on the heels of Indiana's, fell victim to a similar fate, particularly after pressure from Wal-Mart, the state's highest-profile employer. North Carolina passed a narrow religious exemption bill that permitted public officials to recuse themselves from performing same-sex marriages or registering deeds, but which would then suspend them from performing all marriages for at least six months; it was passed over conservative governor Pat McCrory's veto.

Moreover, the *Hobby Lobby* ruling, in which the Supreme Court was willing to grant a religious exemption to a nonreligious organization, has tended to make LGBTQ groups and their allies skeptical that any religious exemption will be narrowly tailored (even if it is originally written as such). In the summer of 2014, the ACLU and a host of LGBTQ organizations including Lambda Legal, the National Gay and Lesbian Task Force, the Transgender Law Center, and the National Center for Lesbian Rights all ended their support of ENDA, the Employment Non-Discrimination Act, on the basis of the religious exemption in the Senate version of the bill. A more comprehensive bill, the Equality Act, originally introduced in 1974, has now replaced ENDA. The Equality Act's purpose is to add gender orientation and identity protections to existing legislation on civil rights (such as the Fair Housing Act, the Equal Credit Opportunity Act, the Civil Rights Act, and the Jury Selection and Service Act). It does not include religious exemptions that would permit discrimination against the LGBTQ community. The Act has yet to pass, and it has become a cornerstone of the LGBTQ community's legal and political agenda.

In July 2015, the Equal Employment Opportunity Commission made a ruling in which it claimed that Title VII of the Civil Rights Act of 1964 prevented employment discrimination on the basis of sexual orientation. The commission argued that sexual orientation stems from discrimination on the basis of sex, which is in the language of the original law. The three-to-two ruling affects federal employees, and potentially private-sector employees who bring a suit to the EEOC; however, it is not binding on the courts. Currently, only twenty states and the District of Columbia have laws that prohibit employment, housing, and accommodation discrimination based on sexual orientation, and only nineteen have laws that prohibit such discrimination based on gender identity. New York and Delaware have nondiscrimination policies in effect as well, but there issued by executive order, not by statute. In New York and Delaware, the only protection that affects gender identity is public employment; public accommodation and housing protections apply to sexual orientation only. In Massachusetts, state law bars discrimination based on gender identity and sexual orientation in both employment and housing but only protects sexual orientation discrimination in public accommodations.

In the **Campaign of 2016**, all of the Democratic Party candidates expressed support for the same-sex marriage ruling, and for the expansion of rights for same-sex couples, including adoption rights and federal nondiscrimination legislation. The GOP candidates were generally critical of the Supreme Court ruling, although the candidates were divided about whether they were willing to accept the Court's ruling and its consequences (Bush, Kasich, Rubio, Carson, Fiorina, Graham, Christie) or whether they favored attempts to undo the ruling via constitutional amendment (Walker, Huckabee, Santorum, Jindal, Cruz). Huckabee also favored reinstating DADT. Ted Cruz suggested that he would be quick to repeal the executive orders Obama had issued that prohibit discrimination by the federal government and federal contractors on the basis of sexual orientation and sexual identity. Both Jindal and Santorum have suggested that they would use executive orders to provide federal "conscience" protections. Overall, however, LGBTQ rights has appeared to be a topic that GOP candidates seem reluctant to discuss, which is consistent with the theory that such rights are now a **wedge issue** for the Republican party, and thus costlier for the GOP coalition than they are for the Democrats.

As gay and lesbian rights continues to openly move into the social mainstream, rights for other stigmatized groups have begun to make their way onto the political agenda as well. (Undoubtedly, the popularity of Laverne Cox in *Orange is the New Black*, and the transformation of Olympic decathlon champion Bruce Jenner to Caitlin Jenner, has helped to facilitate this dialogue.) In the summer of 2015, Defense Secretary Ashton Carter announced a study period to consider allowing transgender persons to openly serve in the military. Eighteen other nations already permit such troops to serve, among these Canada, which has done so since 1992, and Israel, which has permitted gay, lesbian, and bisexual soldiers to serve openly in its military since 1993 and openly transgendered persons to do so since 2013.

Nevertheless, those in the transgender community in the United States continue to experience discrimination because they lack basic civil rights protections that guarantee employment and fair housing to other groups. They are more likely to be homeless than the rest of the population, including the gay and lesbian community. They are also more likely to suffer from problems of addiction or to have untreated mental health problems such as depression, more likely to commit suicide, more likely to be incarcerated, more likely to be victims of assault, and more likely to be murdered, and they have a shorter life expectancy. The glamour of Caitlin Jenner's affluent celebrity lifestyle more reflects a continuation of the life of white male privilege that she experienced for so many decades than it does the typical transgender experience in the United States, although her visibility has caused Americans to discuss the topic of gender identity in new ways and has helped to give the transgender community a public face. Ironically, Jenner is a conservative Republican; she has expectations of continued acceptance by that community. Whether she is able to soften attitudes of social conservatives toward those with nonconforming sexual identities remains to be seen.

See also Civil Rights Issue; Culture War; Wedge Issue

Additional Resources

American Civil Liberties Union. "Non-Discrimination Laws: State by State Information: Map." https://www.aclu.org/map/non-discrimination-laws-state-state-information-map. Accessed September 5, 2015.

Brownfeld, Peter. "Gay Marriage: A Campaign Wedge Issue." FoxNews.com. http://www.foxnews.com/story/0,2933,134442,00.html. Accessed September 5, 2015.

Bull, Chris, and John Gallagher, *Perfect Enemies: The Christian Right, the Gay Movement, and the Politics of the 1990s.* New York: Crown, 1996.

Camia, Catalina. "Gallup Poll: Majority of Americans Support Gay Marriage." *USA Today*, May 20, 2011.

DiGuglielmo, Joey. "Caitlin Jenner, American Hero or 'Arrogant' Dilettante?" *Washington Blade,* August 9, 2015.

Eaklor, Vicki L. *Queer America: A People's GLBT History of the United States.* New York: New Press, 2011.

Edsall, Thomas B. "Bush Abandons 'Southern Strategy': Campaign Avoids Use of Polarizing Issues Employed by GOP Since Nixon's Time." *Washington Post*, August 6, 2000, p. A19.

Human Rights Campaign. "Discrimination by Another Name" February 6, 2015. http://www.hrc.org/press/discrimination-by-another-name-advocates-sound-alarm-on-wave-of-new-state-b.

Mezey, Susan Gluck. *Queers in Court: Gay Rights Law and Public Policy.* New York: Rowman and Littlefield, 2007.

Mucciaroni, Gary. *Same Sex, Different Politics: Success and Failure in the Struggles over Gay Rights.* Chicago: University of Chicago Press, 2008.

New York Times. "Stonewall Rebellion: Times Topics." http://topics.nytimes.com/topics/reference/timestopics/subjects/s/stonewall_rebellion/index.html. Accessed September 5, 2015.

Riggle, Ellen D. B., and Barry L. Tadlock, eds. *Gays and Lesbians in the Democratic Process.* New York: Columbia University Press, 1999.

Rimmerman, Craig A. *The Lesbian and Gay Movements: Assimilation or Liberation?* Second ed. Boulder, CO: Westview Press, 2014.

Rimmerman, Craig A., Kenneth D. Wald, and Clyde Wilcox, eds. *The Politics of Gay Rights.* Chicago: University of Chicago Press, 2000.

Silver, Nate. "Gay Marriage Opponents Now in Minority." *New York Times*, FiveThirtyEight Blog, April 20, 2011.

Smith, Miriam. *Political Institutions and Gay and Lesbian Rights in the United States and Canada.* New York: Routledge, 2008.

Somashekhar, Sandhya, and Peyton Craighill. "Slim Majority Back Gay Marriage, Post–ABC Poll Says." *Washington Post*, March 18, 2011.

Yoshino, Kenji. *Covering: The Hidden Assault on Our Civil Rights.* New York: Random House, 2006.

Libertarianism

As an ideology, libertarianism rests on the premise that the only credible and just agent of choice and personal direction is the unfettered individual. Thus, any effort by an external agent (such as a government or other political institution) to shape an individual's life beyond the individual's consent not only harms individual liberty, but also deprives the person of opportunities to assume personal responsibility and thereby compromises the person's human potential. Libertarians thus regard the political world as the use of power at the expense of personal liberty, and they seek to significantly limit the scope of government activities.

Within the legitimate realm of government action, libertarianism generally permits (with some variation) the government to engage in the protection of private property, the enforcement of contracts between private persons, the arrest and prosecution of criminal activity (which primarily includes acts of violence against persons and the theft or damage of property), and the defense of national sovereign borders and coastline. Beyond these limited ends, libertarians see little role for the state. Rather, libertarians universally envision a social order that encourages and protects the full exercise of individual liberty, guided primarily by personal conscience.

In general, the libertarian creed can be summed up in the famous affirmation by Henry David Thoreau, "That government is best which governs least, and I should like to see it acted up to more rapidly and systematically. Carried out, it finally amounts to this, which also I believe—That government is best which governs not at all and when men are prepared for it, that will be the kind of government which they will have. Government is at best but an expedient; but most governments are usually, and all governments are sometimes, inexpedient." More recently, political theorist Robert Nozick aptly captured the libertarian sentiment: "The minimal state is the most extensive state than can be justified. Any state more extensive violates people's rights." Similarly, the Libertarian Party platform affirms, "Libertarians support maximum liberty in both personal and economic matters. They advocate a much smaller government; one that is limited to protecting individuals from coercion and violence. Libertarians tend to embrace individual responsibility, oppose government bureaucracy and taxes, promote private charity, tolerate diverse lifestyles, support the free market, and defend civil liberties."

Libertarians generally object to all but the most minimal of taxes, and they are particularly opposed to any form of taxation beyond the local level or any tax that is progressive or graduated, in that these coercively redistribute wealth and thus violate the individual's right to freely manage one's own private property. Libertarians bristle at laws that regulate industry or impede free commerce, and they ardently oppose entitlement programs (e.g., Social Security, Medicare, and Medicaid), welfare assistance, sumptuary laws, mandatory insurance, the use of military intervention overseas, publicly funded education, and other publicly funded programs that require increased tax revenues. Privatization is a basic tenet of the libertarian creed (although, as one would expect, some libertarians dissent on this and other topics). By and large, though, libertarians generally agree that most of the services currently provided by the government are better delivered by the private sector, whether for profit in the free market or communally by individuals who volunteer to help supply a public need.

While it is tempting to conclude that libertarians are motivated egoistically (and some libertarians do, in fact, celebrate the pursuit of unrestrained self-interest and even a kind of "selfishness" as praiseworthy ideals), libertarianism in and of itself is not an intrinsically selfish moral or political position. Rather, it is best understood as one view of the most suitable relationship between the government and the individual, with the latter regarded as the sole legitimate agent of personal choice. Some libertarians do indeed flaunt a seemingly selfish ethic, but to generalize this attitude to include all libertarians is both inaccurate and unrealistic. It is also a mistake to define libertarianism as a solely right-wing ideology. Certainly, many libertarians are politically "to the right," particularly on matters regarding taxation and economic policy. However, many libertarians embrace social and moral perspectives that are more closely aligned with liberals (such as privacy rights, opposition to the death penalty, and drug legalization), making it difficult to pigeonhole this ideology into a single location on the liberal–conservative spectrum—a spectrum that is limited by its own oversimplifications and generalizations. Some political observers split libertarianism into "left" and "right" positions, with the latter arguing, for example, that natural resources can be extracted and consumed without restraint (save the legal ownership of another party), while the former supports the need to obtain the consent of the community to properly use, allocate, conserve, and manage such resources.

Libertarianism in the United States has been historically expressed in three ways: (1) through the laissez-faire wings within the two major parties (most elements of the Democrats in the Age of Jackson through Reconstruction, and a faction of the Republican Party since the end of Reconstruction); (2) through the Libertarian Party since its formation in the early 1970s; and (3) within disparate fringe movements loosely associated with libertarian principles. Libertarian strains within the Republican Party have been pronounced; Arizona senator and Republican nominee for president Barry Goldwater is perhaps the most familiar example of this group. However, during the 1960s and early 1970s, more doctrinaire libertarians, disaffected by the Vietnam War and influenced by the counterculture movements of the time, split from the GOP and offered their own view of the ideal society. By 1971, these GOP outcasts had formed their own political party, and since the **Campaign of 1972**, the Libertarian Party has run candidates for the presidency in every election. While Jon Hospers, their first candidate, won scarcely more than 3,000 total votes, the party demonstrated some growth, its nominee Edward Clark winning just around 921,000 votes in the **Campaign of**

1980; but in the following general election, Libertarian nominee David Bergland barely received a quarter of a million votes, a number that was increased to over 430,000 four years later when Ron Paul of Texas temporarily resigned from the Republican Party to serve as the Libertarian standard-bearer in the general election. From 1984 through 2008, the best showing for a Libertarian candidate for president was Bob Barr's 523,433 votes in the **Campaign of 2008**. In 2012 the Libertarian Party, with Gary Johnson as its nominee, exceeded a million votes for the first time, winning 1,275,923, which amounted to 0.99 percent of the popular vote, and while it was the most total votes enjoyed by the party since its inception, it still fell below the 1.06 percent won by Clark in 1980. The numbers reinforce the reality that the Libertarian Party, while well known throughout the electorate, remains at best a decidedly marginal party with little influence in the outcome of presidential elections. Even so, Libertarians have run for office at the state and local levels, and through the Free State Project, the brain child of Yale graduate student Jason Sorens (now an assistant professor of political science at SUNY-Buffalo) and established in 2001, they have been actively recruiting like-minded individuals to migrate to the state of New Hampshire in, ironically, a collective effort to carve out a libertarian stronghold, to the consternation of some residents of the Granite State.

A current misconception associates the **Tea Party movement** with libertarianism, primarily due to the Tea Party's shared dislike of the federal income tax and its faith in free markets. There are, however, many notable differences. Many Tea Partyers hold views on social policies that would not be entertained by most libertarians. While both groups are suspicious of public education, libertarians do not share the Tea Party's belief that religion should have a more central role in government. As a whole, libertarians tend to be isolationists in the realm of foreign policy, whereas many Tea Partyers support U.S. military intervention overseas. Tea Partyers also hold a view of American political culture that is more traditional, and more homogenous, than most libertarians would permit. Most significantly, the Tea Party movement is animated by a strong pulse of populism, a characteristic to which libertarians across the board would react with discomfort.

Currently there are six announced candidates competing for the Libertarian Party's presidential nomination, with two more possible candidates, including 2012 nominee Gary Johnson, showing some support. Beyond the party some libertarian influence can be detected within the GOP, but the predominance of social conservatism among the current GOP pool dampens the libertarian effect. At times real estate mogul and GOP front-runner Donald Trump sounds libertarian tones, particularly in his celebration of personal initiative and free enterprise, but other aspects of his campaign, especially his nationalist proclivities and willingness to undertake expensive projects to regulate cross-border migration, are noticeably anti-libertarian in both substance and style. Kentucky senator Rand Paul, son of Ron Paul, who shares at least in part some libertarian attitudes with his father, is currently running for the Republican nomination for president, but there are those who argue that the younger Paul's libertarian credentials are somewhat mixed. At this point—that is, as of late summer 2015—Sen. Paul's campaign has yet to show evidence of broad support, and it remains scarcely noticed amid the ongoing Trump phenomenon.

See also Isolationism

Additional Resources

Boaz, David. *Libertarianism: A Primer.* New York: Free Press, 1997.
Hammond, Scott John. *Political Theory: An Encyclopedia of Contemporary and Classic Terms.* Westport, CT: Greenwood Press, 2009.
Huebert, Jacob H. *Libertarianism Today.* Santa Barbara, CA: ABC-CLIO/Praeger, 2010.
"Libertarianism." Stanford Encyclopedia of Philosophy http://plato.stanford.edu/entries /libertarianism. Accessed September 1, 2015.
Murray, Charles. *What It Means to Be a Libertarian.* New York: Broadway Books, 1997.
Nozick, Robert. *Anarchy, State and, Utopia.* New York: Basic Books, 1974.

Likely Voter

Part and parcel of predicting the probable outcome of a presidential (or any other) election is determining who is likely to show up to vote on Election Day. Only a subset of the eligible citizens who reside in a geographic area will actually cast a ballot, and the identity of these individuals is not known in advance. Citizens may be willing to express a preference for a political candidate to a pollster, but ultimately, the utility of that preference is a function of the probability that the citizen will vote.

Pollsters have used a variety of strategies over the years for determining whether an individual is a "likely" voter. In some instances, being registered to vote is presumed to make a person a likely voter. However, a dozen states now permit citizens to register to vote on Election Day itself, and Oregon is now automatically registering all eligible citizens at age eighteen. Thus, not all citizens need to be aware of their registration status in advance of the election in order to cast a ballot. Moreover, many registered voters fail to show up on Election Day; registration is, at best, an imperfect measure, particularly if it is not asked proximate to Election Day.

Often, questions about whether or not a citizen is registered are combined with questions about a person's past voting history and whether they know where to vote. Like voter registration, this information is less likely to be helpful if it is being used at a time not proximate to Election Day, particularly for young or first-time voters, who are less likely to have such information at hand before they need to use it.

A citizen's self-reported level of interest in (or enthusiasm for) the campaign is often used as an indication of his or her likelihood of voting, and this may be used in conjunction with measures of vote intent, vote history, voter registration, or knowledge about voting locations. In this scenario, only a citizen who expresses a very high level of interest in (or enthusiasm for) the campaign is treated as likely to vote. Measures of campaign interest and enthusiasm are quite volatile and may respond to the ebb and flow of campaign events, but they don't exhibit much ability to predict future events. Moreover, some cohorts (e.g., young people) exhibit lower levels of interest in campaigns, generally, but may still turn out to vote. In the **Campaign of 2012**, Republican nominee Mitt Romney's campaign team was convinced that he had won the election, based largely on its internal polls of likely voters in **battleground states**. Romney's team constructed likely voter estimates based on levels of voter enthusiasm and found that when looking only at voters who reported the highest levels of enthusiasm, Romney seemed to be performing better than Obama in several of the battleground states. In fact, Romney lost, and the campaign's internal polls were wildly off the mark in some cases. Aside from other sampling problems, it seems likely that Obama's supporters showed up even if they did not exhibit extremely high levels of enthusiasm for the election (and thus perhaps had different motives for voting), a shortcoming of the Romney model.

See also Poll of Polls

Additional Resources

Burns, Alexander. "The GOP Polling Debacle." Politico, November 11, 2012.

Erikson, Robert S., Costas Panagopoulos, and Christopher Wlezien. "Likely (and Unlikely) Voters and the Assessment of Campaign Dynamics." *Public Opinion Quarterly* 68, no. 4 (Winter 2004): 588–601.

Manifest Destiny

Westward expansion became a major political issue in the United States during the 1840s, primarily owing to the consequences of expanding farther west with regard to the ongoing debate over slavery. In addition to this debate and other questions concerning westward expansion, there was a cultural undercurrent shaping the new nation's perceptions of itself and its purposes, perceptions drawn from an understanding of the American republic as more than a nation-state among all others—as somehow the work of an unseen, irresistible Divine Providence. In the summer of 1845, prior to the election of President James K. Polk the following year and the subsequent war with Mexico, an article appeared in *United States Magazine and Democratic Review*, likely penned by the periodical's editor, John L. O'Sullivan, coined a new phrase in asserting that it was America's "manifest destiny to overspread the continent allotted by Providence for the free development of our multiplying millions." The phrase "manifest destiny" would come to symbolize the belief that America's expansion from the Atlantic to the Pacific was divinely ordained, that American success in winning new territory was a manifestation of this divine destiny, and that the American people are therefore, because of their virtues, the natural leaders of all freedom-loving peoples. Advocates of manifest destiny therefore would argue that it was the rightful fate of the United States to expand the nation's territory to fill the natural boundaries marking the continent. Concomitant with this doctrine, the vast territory acquired as a result of victory in the Mexican-American War helped, along with the purchase of the Louisiana Territory four decades earlier, to transform the United States into a bicoastal power. Naturally, this expansionist pressure greatly exacerbated the slavery issue. New territory meant new states, and new states meant that old compromises between free and slave states were to be reexamined, and reexamined compromises meant renewed, and more intense, debates over slavery itself, debates that would only be solved by civil war.

Manifest destiny, while coined as a term to describe a doctrine in 1845, was already well in play as an attitude a good decade earlier. After Texas broke from Mexico in 1836, it sought annexation to the United States. To the great disappointment of Texas, President Martin Van Buren declined to actively support annexation, fearing that admission of Texas as a slave state would reignite the slavery controversy. In 1844, President John Tyler negotiated an annexation treaty with Texas, sending it to the Senate for ratification, where it met with opposition. The Senate's decision not to ratify the treaty sent the issue to the voters and to the campaign for president in 1844.

As the front-runner for the 1844 Democratic presidential nomination, Van Buren made a strategic decision to oppose the annexation of Texas. The decision turned out to be a major mistake, as Democrats strongly supported the annexation of Texas. When the Democratic National Convention met at Baltimore in May 1844, Van Buren no longer had a lock on the presidential nomination. After the convention deadlocked, the party turned to dark-horse candidate James K. Polk, whose proclivities were toward territorial expansion. Rejecting Van Buren's antiannexation position, the Democratic platform expressed support for the reoccupation of Oregon and the annexation of Texas.

The election of Polk significantly strengthened the hands of the supporters of westward expansion. After Polk's election, supporters of expansion made effective use of the "Fifty-Four Forty or Fight" slogan. The slogan referred to the efforts to set the northwestern border of the United States at the 54th parallel. Subsequent negotiations with Britain concluded with a border drawn between Canada and the Oregon Territory at the 48th parallel. Of much greater importance, between 1846 and 1848, Polk conducted the war with Mexico that resulted in adding the territories of the Mexican Cession: Texas, California, the whole of what would become Arizona (with the Gadsden Purchase added later), New Mexico (part of which was once considered western Texas), Nevada, and Utah, as well as the westernmost portion of Colorado and southwestern Wyoming. Manifest destiny, imagined as Liberty's march across the continent, entered the lexicon of American political culture. But Van Buren's fears were soon realized; slavery's fate again was debated without resolution, with war following.

Manifest destiny is an important doctrinal position within the larger context of American history. And while most Americans would view such a doctrine today primarily as something that shaped the American past (for good or ill), in some ways the rhetoric of an American destiny continues to resonate. American politicians and American voters no longer seek or support territorial expansion, but political rhetoric may often reveal a strong residue of manifest destiny in the notion that America is an "exceptional" nation. This in itself is not a new idea, and in some ways it even precedes manifest destiny, with which it is not to be confused but only compared. No less a personage than the great student of democracy and American political culture Alexis de Tocqueville wrote of the unique qualities of the United States vis-à-vis older, tradition-bound European states. Today political rhetoric in general speaks with pride of American achievement past and present, but less triumphantly when compared to the doctrinal attitudes springing from manifest destiny, and it is not uncommon to hear candidates from both major parties speak with sincerity of the special role that America has played, and continues to play, in the progress of democracy and the advance of human rights. The older image of Lady Liberty leading a westward movement for the advance of democracy across an entire continent is no longer in currency, but it is a recognized part of the American legacy, and in some ways the idea of America as the dynamic engine of progress in the world continues to resonate, albeit in ways decidedly different than what was familiar to men such as John L. O'Sullivan and President Polk.

It is not a stretch to connect the current immigration debate to the related ideas of manifest destiny and **American exceptionalism**. In the case of the latter, the notion that the United States is somehow unique influences immigration policy in two conflicted aspects. In the first place, part of what defines the singular qualities of America is its history as a refuge and a place to start anew—a nation of immigrants and a hybrid culture. However, this exceptionalism also influences a second, conflicting notion that fuels an attitude of exclusion, inhibiting access to the American bounty, especially for groups considered to be racially, ethnically, or religiously foreign to the substance of that exceptionalism. In the case of the legacy of manifest destiny, it must be admitted that the concerns regarding undocumented immigrants from south of the border are in part the long-term and ongoing consequence of the Mexican Cession; that is, land gained by the United States as a result of the Mexican-American War. Prior to that war, what we now call the American Southwest was a part of the nation of Mexico, with a history linking its residents to the older Spanish Empire's presence in North America. What was at one time considered to belong to, at first, the numerous Native American tribes of the region, then the Spanish who genetically mixed with those tribes, and then Mexico, was ceded to the United States as a result of American military victory. Rightly or wrongly, these historical facts provide needed context to the problem of transgressions across the southern border. While the history of the region is not at issue in presidential campaigns, it is important to bear in mind as presidential candidates provide their criticisms and offer their solutions.

See also American Exceptionalism; Campaign of 1844

Additional Resources

Greenberg, Amy. *Manifest Destiny and American Territorial Expansion: A Brief History with Documents.* New York: Bedford/St. Martin's, 2011.

Howe, Daniel Walker. *What Hath God Wrought: The Transformation of America, 1815–1848.* Oxford: Oxford University Press, 2009.

Johannsen, Robert Walter, Sam W. Haynes, and Christopher Morris. *Manifest Destiny and Empire: American Antebellum Expansion.* College Station: Texas A&M University Press, 1997.

Stephanson, Andres. *Manifest Destiny: American Expansionism and the Empire of Right.* New York: Hill and Wang, 1995.

Marriage Gap

Some of the most sizable, yet understudied, differences in voting patterns in the American electorate occur between married and unmarried women, and between married women and married men. For example, in the **Campaign of 2000**, Democratic nominee Al Gore won only 48 percent of married women but earned the votes of 63 percent of unmarried women.

In the **Campaign of 2008**, 47 percent of married women voted for Barack Obama, compared to 42 percent of married men. Among unmarried voters,

Obama's support was substantially higher: 66 percent of unmarried women voted for Obama, and 63 percent of unmarried men did as well. The pattern was similar in the **Campaign of 2012**: 66 percent of married women voted for Obama, in contrast to 46 percent of married men. Moreover, 56 percent of single women voted for Obama, whereas only 38 percent of married men did.

Numerous theories have been offered by political scientists to explain these differences. It may be that people who marry are influenced by the political views of their partners, and men, who tend to be more conservative to begin with, are more likely to influence their wives' views than women are to influence their husbands. However, this theory is challenged by the findings of Democratic pollster Celinda Lake, who noted that her studies of the marriage gap found that while 73 percent of married men claimed that their spouses voted for the same candidate that they did, only 49 percent of married women claimed to have voted for the same candidate as their spouses. Or it could be that marriage simply creates more conservative attitudes among voters. Or causality may be reversed: Those who are more conservative to begin with are more likely to get married, and to marry earlier, than those who are more liberal.

See also Gender Gap

Additional Resources

CNN Politics, America's Choice 2012 Election Center. "President: Full Results." http://www.cnn.com/election/2012/results/race/president/. Accessed October 14, 2015.

The Economist. "The Marriage Gap: Think Again, Men." December 15, 2013. http://www.economist.com/blogs/democracyinamerica/2013/12/marriage-gap. Accessed October 14, 2015.

Gallup Organization. "Election Polls: Vote by Groups, 2008." http://www.gallup.com/poll/112132/election-polls-vote-groups-2008.aspx. Accessed October 14, 2015.

Maverick

This label was adopted by Republican candidate John McCain (and subsequently his running mate, Sarah Palin) in the **Campaign of 2008**. Particularly in the general election, McCain argued that he was not a typical Republican candidate. He emphasized occasions in the past where he departed from the majority of his party in Congress, such as his authorship of campaign finance reform legislation, his cosponsorship (with Democratic senator Edward Kennedy of Massachusetts) of a "patient's bill of rights," his support for a legal path to citizenship for illegal immigrants, and his initial opposition to the 2001 tax cuts proposed by President George W. Bush. In a word, Sen. McCain promoted his unconventional sensibilities, claiming that this was the basis for his willingness to strike out on his own without concern for party conformity and in the spirit of a pragmatic approach to politics that is effectively bipartisan or in some sense nonpartisan. As political scientist Stanley Renshon has observed, the senator's "cross party appeal," which is the result of his appearance as a maverick, is "more deeply rooted in his psychology than in his rhetoric or persona," and yet Sen. McCain nonetheless benefits from this image, for according to Prof. Renshon, he "has clearly derived political mileage from his maverick image, and he knows it." In 2008, this strategy enabled him to distance himself from the then unpopular Republican incumbent.

The addition of Alaska governor Sarah Palin to the McCain ticket was used to enhance this imagery. The McCain camp portrayed Palin, then in her first term as governor of Alaska, as a maverick in her own right. They touted her willingness to buck the big oil companies and the leadership of her own party during her tenure in office. These themes were also emphasized in campaign ads such as "Original Mavericks." Gov. Palin's campaign rhetoric drew upon their mutual identification with the maverick label.

Sen. McCain's critics have challenged his purported maverick credentials. For example, as demonstrated by political scientist Benjamin Lauderdale, Sen. McCain's reputation as a maverick is not necessarily consistent with his actual voting record, particularly in the latter years of his political career. According to the conclusions that can be drawn from the data gathered by Lauderdale, Sen. McCain's "maverick score" (or what could awkwardly be identified as "maverickness") peaked in 2001–2002, when he did in fact appear to be more of a maverick when compared to most members of Congress. Since then, his "maverick score" declined steadily, dipping to a point scarcely above the average score for members of Congress in 2007–2008 (as he was running for president in part on the reputation of being a maverick) and in 2011 standing noticeably below the average score. More to the point, Sen. McCain himself repudiates his maverick reputation. In an interview for *Newsweek* in April, 2010, Sen. McCain admitted, "I never considered myself a maverick . . . I consider myself a person who serves the people of Arizona to the best of his abilities." Nevertheless, owing largely in part to his reputation as a maverick (amplified by his brief but memorable alliance with Gov. Palin), Sen. McCain's reputation in the popular imagination remains that of a political maverick.

Additional Resources

Lauderdale, Benjamin E. "Unpredictable Voters in Ideal Point Estimation." *Political Analysis*, 18 (2010): 151–171.

Linkins, John. "John McCain Not a Maverick: Proven with Math!" Huffington Post. May 25, 2011. http://www.huffingtonpost.com/2010/05/06/john-mccain-not-a-maveric _n_566374.html. Accessed October 1, 2015.

Page, Susan. "Which Hopeful Is the New Face of the GOP?" *USA Today*, January 24, 2008.

Renshon, Stanley A. "Psychological Reflections on Barack Obama and John McCain: Assessing the Contours of a New Presidential Administration." *Political Science Quarterly* 123, no. 3 (Fall 2008): 391–433.

McGovern-Fraser Reforms

The Commission on Party Structure and Delegate Selection, first chaired by Senator George McGovern and later chaired by Representative Don Fraser, was tasked with reforming the Democratic nomination process in the aftermath of the violent convention in Chicago in the summer of 1968. The commission ran from 1969 through 1972 and was composed of twenty-eight members.

One of the primary tasks of the commission was to give the average citizen of the Democratic Party a greater role in the party nomination process. Convention delegations could not be composed of state and local party officials. Rather, delegations had to be more broadly representative in terms of race, gender, and age, given the population demographics of the state. And the process for delegate selection had to be open and public, with some element of public participation. The role of party officials was limited to that of **superdelegates**, a small, fixed proportion of delegates who were not committed to candidates as a function of primaries or caucuses in their states. Rather, superdelegates were appointed by the party and were unconstrained in their voting. Most importantly, the national Democratic Party gave itself the power to overrule decisions made by state political parties. This latter power became particularly important in the **Campaign of 2008**, when the Democratic National Committee (DNC) chose not to recognize delegates from the states of Michigan and Florida at their convention, because the parties in those states held primaries on dates forbidden to them by the DNC. (Similarly, the Republican National Committee exacted a penalty on both Florida and South Carolina for deviating from their established primary schedule in 2008.)

Ultimately, many states opted to hold primaries as the simplest means for complying with the new set of rules issued by the commission. Because many state legislatures (even in the South) were controlled by the Democratic Party during this era, the expansion of the primary system tended to affect both political parties. The trend is quite clear. In 1968, only sixteen states held some type of primary, and Hubert Humphrey, the Democratic presidential nominee in the **Campaign of 1968**, did not win a single one of them. By 1972, twenty-two states held presidential primaries, and in 1976, primaries were held in twenty-nine states. Six additional states held primaries in 1980. (Many states skipped Republican primaries in 1984 when Reagan was running unopposed; similarly, many states skipped Democratic primaries in 1996 when Clinton was running unopposed.) By 2008, the number crept up to forty. Just as important, for most sub-presidential nominations, primaries have become the norm.

Political scientists view the reforms recommended by this body as the basis for the modern political primary, with its effects ultimately influencing the nomination process of presidential candidates for Democrats and Republicans alike. Ultimately, the McGovern-Fraser Commission vastly expanded the role of the average citizen in the presidential election process and served to limit the power of political parties over political candidates.

See also Frontloading

Additional Resources

Paulson, Arthur. *Realignment and Party Revival: Understanding American Electoral Politics at the Turn of the Twenty-First Century.* Westport, CT: Praeger, 2000.

Polsby, Nelson W. "The Reform of Presidential Selection and Democratic Theory." *PS: Political Science and Politics* 16, no. 4 (Autumn 1983): 695–698.

Steller, Chris. "40 Years Ago, McGovern-Fraser Commission Paved Way for Challengers Like Obama." *Minnesota Independent*, May 30, 2008.

Stricherz, Mark. "Primary Colors: How a Little-Known Task Force Helped Create Red State/Blue State America." *Boston Globe*, November 23, 2003.

Sundquist, James L. *Dynamics of the Party System: Alignment and Realignment of Political Parties in the United States.* Washington, DC: Brookings, 1983.

Media Event

The modern presidential campaign makes major use of media events to build support for candidates and to obtain free (earned) coverage. During the 1960s, the advent of network nightly news broadcasts permitted campaigns to reach tens of millions of voters without having to buy expensive campaign ads. By the early 1970s, the vast majority of local television stations produced their own evening news shows as well, expanding the scope of coverage even further. By the 1980s, network news operations had expanded to encompass morning news shows such as the *Today* show (NBC) and *Good Morning America* (ABC). Local television outlets followed suit by creating their own morning news shows. During the 1990s, the proliferation of twenty-four-hour news operations provided campaigns with even more opportunities to obtain free coverage of campaign events.

In the **Campaign of 1968**, Republican nominee Richard Nixon's campaign took full advantage of the growing availability of these opportunities for free media coverage. The Nixon campaign carefully staged hundreds of events to maximize national news coverage. In the decades that followed, candidates adapted to the changing media environment in planning their campaign appearances, timing events and strategically locating them such that they would be convenient for the media to cover. The proliferation of local news resources and, later, cable news networks eventually made it feasible for campaigns to stage multiple events on the same day and receive extensive coverage from the vast array of network, cable, and local news operations.

Presidential campaigns have historically used a wide variety of events to obtain **earned media** coverage and to mobilize their supporters. These include activities such as making stump speeches to potential supporters, holding rallies, attending public events (such as state fairs and parades), showing up on daytime and late-night television shows, participating in debates, and attending fund-raising events (although nowadays these tend to be closed to the press). In recent years, candidates have often garnered earned media coverage as a result of content they've posted on social media. In the **Campaign of 2012**, GOP hopeful Donald Trump notoriously took to Twitter to complain about debate moderators, fellow candidates, and members of the press corps; his intemperate tweets were themselves fodder for media coverage.

In the **Campaign of 1992**, presidential candidates borrowed a page from history and turned to several time-honored strategies for creating media events. Democratic nominee Bill Clinton embarked on a bus tour of towns across the United States in which both the visits and the bus itself became topics of media coverage. Candidates also began to make greater use of town meeting events where the candidates take questions from small groups of supporters or average citizens. Much like the traditional stump speech, candidates typically respond with carefully crafted answers. Since the Campaign of 1992, the town-hall-style event has become a fixture of the modern presidential campaign; however, these have increasingly become closed events, as campaigns carefully screen attendees and handpick the audiences.

Presidential campaigns also make heavy use of media events that allow candidates to demonstrate their concern over a particular issue or topic. During the **Campaign of 2000**, for instance, Republican nominee George W. Bush made education reform the top priority of his domestic agenda. As a result, candidate Bush made numerous visits to schools throughout the campaign. In the **Campaign of 2004**, incumbent president Bush visited the troops often in order to remind voters that the country was at war and that he best understood the security threat faced by the nation.

The traditional campaign rally still provides candidates with some of the best photo opportunities of any media event. Rallies generally involve thousands of voters, which enables candidates to be portrayed as having a large public following. During the **Campaign of 2008**, for instance, Democratic nominee Barack Obama's campaign made frequent use of mass rallies. Like most candidates, Obama visited colleges and universities to attract support from young voters and local community members. Obama's St. Louis rally attracted one hundred thousand participants, which produced some visually stunning images of the candidate surrounded by a sea of supporters (an image George W. Bush attempted to evoke in the Campaign of 2004 by visiting the troops in Iraq). Obama attended a similarly large rally at the Brandenburg Gate in Berlin, the same location where President John F. Kennedy once proclaimed, "*Ich bin ein Berliner*" ("I am a Berliner!") and where President Reagan demanded, "President Gorbachev, tear down this wall!" These visual parallels, and Obama's popularity abroad during the campaign, may have lessened some voters' concerns about Obama's lack of foreign policy experience.

In the 2015 lead-in to the Campaign of 2016, Donald Trump effectively used media events to maximize free or unearned media coverage. By the end of 2015, Mr. Trump spent scarcely any money on his campaign while simultaneously receiving intense and persistent coverage throughout the media.

See also Cattle Call; Earned Media

Additional Resources

McCubbins, Matthew D. *Under the Watchful Eye: Managing Presidential Campaigns in the Television Era.* Washington, DC: CQ Press, 1992.

Shaw, Daron R. "The Impact of News Media Favorability and Candidate Events in Presidential Campaigns." *Political Communication* 16, no. 2 (1999): 183–202.

Taibbi, Matt. *Spanking the Donkey.* New York: Broadway Books, 2006.

Median Voter Theory

In 1957, economist Anthony Downs published his classic work, *An Economic Theory of Democracy.* This theoretical work described how, in a two-party system, savvy candidates would attempt to strategically position themselves close to the center of public opinion, which generally meant that they would avoid portraying themselves as extremely liberal or extremely conservative. According to Downs, this strategic positioning would invariably mean that candidates from both political parties would take similar positions on many issues to maximize their potential appeal. "Median voter theory" has come to describe any campaign strategy in which the party or candidate attempts to target the median voter, or the voter in the center of public opinion. This often goes hand in hand with candidates' strategies to target the middle class, or to target potential swing voters.

In the **Campaign of 2004**, incumbent president George W. Bush, with campaign director Karl Rove, employed a risky reelection strategy that disregarded the median voter. Rather than attempt to portray Bush as a moderate Republican, as they had done in the **Campaign of 2000** (by calling him "a uniter not a divider," among other things), they ran on the candidate's conservative record in office instead. Unlike Governor Bush, who had had to contend with a Democratic legislature, President Bush had a Republican legislature and had little need to compromise with his political opponents. Moreover, the country was engaged in controversial wars in both Iraq and Afghanistan. Bush and Rove saw little advantage in attempting to appeal to moderates; rather, they engaged in an extensive effort to mobilize the Republican base, particularly the evangelical Christian component of the base. They relied on grassroots organizations for support and requested church directories to engage in better microtargeting. The strategy worked—Bush squeaked out a close victory over Democratic nominee John Kerry in 2004.

By the **Campaign of 2008**, the nominees of both political parties were once again attempting to appeal to a range of potential voters near the political center. Republican nominee John McCain and his running mate, Sarah Palin, aimed squarely at "Joe Six-Pack," enlisting the efforts of Joe the Plumber in their attempt to target the average American worker. Democratic nominee Barack Obama focused on the middle class as well, promising better jobs, better health care, and an end to the now-unpopular war in Iraq. In the 2012 presidential campaign, Republican challenger Mitt Romney frequently stressed the difficulties confronting the middle class throughout his campaign, and to great effect in his first debate against incumbent President Obama. However, it was not so much Gov. Romney's position on the health of the middle class as his attention to voter attitudes that evinces, in his case, the importance of the median voter. A passing remark by a senior campaign adviser in the Romney camp, Eric Fehrnstrom, aptly matches the concept behind median voter theory. "I think you hit a reset button for the fall campaign," Fehrnstrom observed in commenting about the need to modify strategies and campaign progress. "Everything changes. It's almost like an Etch-A-Sketch. You can kind of shake it up, and we start all over again." The Etch-A-Sketch remark boomeranged on the Romney campaign, as it inadvertently reinforced the popular and ongoing criticism of Romney as an insubstantial flip-flopper, and it offered grist for criticism from other candidates, including Sen. Rick Santorum, a rival for the GOP nomination, and incumbent president Obama. The Etch-a-Sketch comment made by one of his closest advisers was, inadvertently, a much more explicit acknowledgement of median voter theory. It seemed to suggest that Gov. Romney was saying and doing things to position himself strategically with voters rather than from principle or adherence to central values, and that these positions would be altered at will as the electoral need arose.

President Obama, throughout his administration, has attempted to convey his desire to avoid political extremism and attachment to fixed ideological positions, with mixed results, as his critics on the right remain skeptical, and those on the left respond with disappointment. Gov. Romney was in a similar situation during his run for the GOP nomination in 2012, caught between the influential right wing of the party and those seeking a return to a more moderate tone.

Additional Resources

Jacobson, Gary C. *A Divider, Not a Uniter: George W. Bush and the American People.* New York: Longman, 2010.

Shear, Michael D. "For Romney's Trusted Adviser, 'Etch A Sketch' Comment Is a Rare Misstep." *New York Times,* March 21, 2012. nytimes.com/2012/03/22/.

Microtargeting

Microtargeting is a process in which political parties or political campaigns use nontraditional information, often gleaned from marketing research, to more narrowly focus their **get-out-the-vote** efforts. While it is relatively easy for a campaign to ascertain the likelihood of registered voters supporting its candidate based on their zip code or neighborhood, knowing the kind of vehicle they drive, whether they have a hunting license, the types of magazines they subscribe to, and even where they attended college, may enable more precise calculations. Campaigns are now using this nontraditional information to learn more about voters' lifestyles so that they can more effectively target their potential bases of support.

Karl Rove is often credited with some of the first modern uses of microtargeting in a presidential election for his reelection campaign of Republican president George W. Bush in the **Campaign of 2004**. Rove created a database using magazine subscriptions and church directories to pinpoint likely Republican voters, resulting in a narrow Bush victory (owing to a slim majority in the Electoral College, having won fewer popular votes than his Democratic rival, Vice President Gore) and an unusual departure from the traditional median voter strategy. However, magazine subscriptions and church memberships are fairly traditional forms of information that are often used by political campaigns, and while Rove's campaign did eke out a victory in 2004, presuming that it did so on the basis of this, rather than the fact that he was conducting a campaign for an incumbent president who was involved in what was still a fairly popular war, is perhaps overlooking the obvious. What was novel about the Bush team's 2004 strategy was its approach to ad purchases. Rather than rely primarily on prime time ads on major networks, the Bush team focused on channels like the Outdoor Network and other niche programming on specialty cable networks—such ads not only were less expensive to purchase, but more importantly, they also enabled the campaign to reach a more specific audience (e.g., people who enjoyed hunting, people who watched more conservative and family-oriented programming, and people who watched religious television). Thus, the campaign could reach the viewers it felt were more receptive to its message, and not waste funds messaging to voters who were unlikely to cast a ballot for its candidate.

In the **Campaign of 2008**, Democrat Barack Obama's campaign team pioneered the use of more a more personally focused campaign in its bid for the White House. Obama's team often recruited local celebrities to do the voice work for its radio ads or to act as the endorsers for ads run in local media markets. This required having an extensive grassroots network throughout the country and the funds to produce a large number of unique ads. Obama's campaign also purchased embedded ads in eighteen video games on the Xbox Live platform, focusing on ten early-voting states that experts classified as potentially competitive. These included Colorado, Florida, Indiana, Iowa, Montana, Nevada, New Mexico, North Carolina, Ohio, and Wisconsin. The ads began in early October in some states, a bit later in others, and they ran through Election Day. The ads were placed primarily in sports-oriented games, as well as the popular *Guitar Hero*; the intended viewers of these ads were young male gamers, a demographic that has historically been difficult to target. As candidates attempt to broaden the reach of their campaigns using new technology, there will be greater emphasis on nontraditional media in the years to come.

In the **Campaign of 2012**, DSPolitical (a Democratic-affiliated group) and CampaignGrid (a GOP-affiliated group) accumulated numerous pieces of data on Americans' purchasing history, their reading habits, their travel, and other personal habits, and matched this with their voting histories (which are publicly available). The groups acquired information from cookies tracking users' online behavior, as well as from their behavior offline. Online searches and social media behavior are also fodder for such databases. Information is used to create pop-up (including pop-up video) and banner ads online that are tailored to the interests and traits of the individual user.

Incumbent Barack Obama's campaign team created an in-house data analytics section that was quite extensive, code-named Narwhal, which engaged in a variety of field experiments to help the campaign sharpen its ability to target voters. ProPublica studied one Obama fund-raising e-mail message and tracked eleven variations in content, presumably based on the slight differences in demographics of the intended recipients. The Obama campaign also had a Facebook app that would sift through a user's Facebook friends and identify those who matched the traits of a potential Obama supporter; users who downloaded the app would then receive reminders in which they'd be asked to contact those Facebook friends and ask them to vote for the candidate. The Obama campaign's electoral objective was to direct its resources at voters it viewed as "persuadable," rather than those it estimated were already firm supporters, or those who were already deeply committed to Obama's opponent. Thus, the candidate both needed to calculate which voters were already likely to be in his camp and which others might be willing to support him if provided with the proper encouragement. Such calculations required more than the usual amount of information that campaigns rely on to drum up funds from supporters and to try to encourage their base to show up on Election Day, and they emphasize the importance of both data analytics and microtargeting to contemporary campaigns.

The **Campaign of 2016** has revealed further advances in microtargeting. Voters experienced ads on their portable devices, such as phones and tablets, as the focus of microtargeting expanded and campaigns adjusted their strategies to accommodate apps. Campaigns also had to contend with the declining numbers of viewers of broadcast and cable television. Rather than just purchase ad time on television networks, they began turning to satellite and cable companies that supplied DVR boxes to their customers, and they negotiated to download ads directly to customers' DVRs, to be cued up the next time an ad was slated to be run. This enabled political campaigns to have greater control over which customers saw the ads—based on zip codes and other market data they collected about voters, they could determine in advance which households they wanted to have the ads sent to, in effect choosing their potential viewers in advance and not wasting ad revenue on individuals who were unlikely to be receptive to their message.

See also Big Data; Get-Out-the-Vote (GOTV) Programs; Median Voter Theory

Additional Resources

Associated Press. "Video Games Feature Ads for Obama's Campaign." *New York Times*, October 14, 2008.

Hersh, Eitan D. *Hacking the Electorate: How Campaigns Perceive Voters.* New York: Cambridge University Press, 2015.

Issenberg, Sasha. *The Victory Lab: The Secret Science of Winning Campaigns.* New York: Crown, 2012.

Murphy, Tim. "Inside the Obama Campaign's Hard Drive." *Mother Jones*, September/October 2012.

ProPublica. "Message Machine: Reverse Engineering the 2012 Campaign." http://projects .propublica.org/emails/mailings/hey--6. Accessed October 6, 2015.

Wayne, Leslie. "Democrats Take Page from Their Rival's Playbook." *New York Times*, November 1, 2008.

Moneyball

Sports and politics have more in common than many of us would allow, the one consisting of many kinds of games that involve events and decisions that we often take very seriously, the other involving serious decisions and subsequent events that we frequently compare to a game. The practice of "moneyball," which was developed in the sports world by Oakland Athletics baseball executives Billy Beane and Paul DePodesta, illustrates the family resemblance between politics and sports and, more substantively, lends instruction in the potency of understanding factual conditions and the analysis of data. Granted, analyst Nate Sliver, who once worked as a baseball statistician, has observed that sports and politics are not comparable; but one can still be struck by the similarities between data-driven decisions in baseball and more recent presidential campaigning. For both baseball and politics, there is meaning in the numbers; the trick is to know where to find it and how to use it.

Essentially, moneyball is about the concerted application of mathematics: exhaustively mining, interpreting, and intelligently using data in ways that deepen one's knowledge about fundamental realities and consequently suggest more focused team (or campaign) strategies. For the Athletics, Beane and DePodesta, concluding that major league baseball had become "an unfair game" favoring wealthier, large-market teams with deep pockets, adopted the refined statistical methods of sabermetrics, which can be traced back to the statistical modeling developed in the early seventies and employed by baseball guru Bill James, methods that were already emerging among sports statisticians to measure more accurately and with more acutely specified variation the individual situational performance of baseball players. In this model, one looks beyond standard and more generalized measures (such as overall batting average and runs-batted-in) to how a batter/fielder/pitcher performs on the field under a wide variety of specific situations, in order to develop numerous statistical categories that measure numerous performance indicators. In order to assemble the most competitive team for the least amount of money, the Athletics, working with the smallest budget in baseball, consulted complex statistical measures to acquire the most suitable combination of players, most of whom were "undervalued," at the lowest possible cost requisite to producing a winning team. Beane and DePodesta's methods, while utterly counterintuitive to the mentality of baseball executives and on-field managers and coaches at the time, managed to produce three American League pennants and one World Series championship. Rejecting "gut instinct" and intangibles, Beane and DePodesta, influenced by the sabermetrics developed by James and others before him, successfully created a managerial model that relied primarily on research and expert analysis. Numbers have always fascinated baseball fans, and for good reason according to the moneyball mentality, for it is through the numbers that the game can be dissected and understood.

Naturally, these data-soaked methods easily convert to the political arena, wherein decades of quantitative research on voting behavior drawing upon the methods of social and behavioral sciences provide pools of information and databases that enable candidates armed with such knowledge to more intentionally and responsively direct their campaign efforts. Following the lead of baseball's moneyball, political moneyball deemphasizes unquantifiable factors such as "conventional wisdom," "political folklore," "game-changing moments," campaign-spoiling "gaffes," historical analogies, empirically unsubstantiated categories and—as with baseball—gut instinct, and instead emphasizes empirical research along with quantifiable and finely grained analysis of the behavior of those most likely to vote. Through the thorough gathering and critical analysis of measurable facts, the study of election dynamics, and absorbing the results of field experiments, political campaign workers can employ their human and financial resources with greater cost-effectiveness, and are thus able not only to target those voters who hover in the undecided margins and barrage them with persuasive rhetoric and advertisements hoping to sway their decisions, but also to nudge predictably supportive segments of the electorate into actually going to the polls and casting their votes.

Research supports the conclusion that most voters have decided which party to support long before the opening of a campaign season; the key to winning an election is therefore identifying those likely voters who are already inclined to favor a given candidate and then finding and initiating the most reliable stimuli to prompt them to cast their ballots. As with the baseball methods of moneyball, political moneyball is more about knowing what voters will do if stirred into action, rather than trying to win votes through more traditional stumping. This is not to say that campaigning is no longer important; candidates still need to promote themselves before the public. Rather, moneyball is premised on the principle that political behavior is comparatively constant and surprisingly predictable, and that a deep understanding of this enables politicians to campaign more efficiently and effectively, and to subsequently govern more pragmatically.

Political moneyball stresses the importance of localized efforts, such as the reliance on volunteer campaign workers to turn out the vote, rather than imported party activists and prefabricated campaign templates. Local volunteers, embedded in their own communities and neighborhoods, are far more effective in ushering likely voters into action than big-time campaign managers and celebrity cheerleaders. Mobilizing local volunteers is critical to moving the electorate in the right direction, and while a more centralized party organization is still needed, unless the party and political candidates more specifically adapt their strategies to local populations, they will risk losing the attention of those on the margins who, with the proper incentive toward the voting booth, could make the difference between victory or defeat as the votes are tallied. This is particularly the case in close races or in "purple" states and localities, where it is not so much a case of persuading uncommitted voters toward a favorable decision, but rather motivating the likely voters toward their precincts. Nevertheless, with enough data and the development of useful models, some voting behavior can be influenced through specific campaign interventions, so that not only turning out the vote, but also knowing who is really amenable to modifying their political support, can provide political operatives with the tools necessary to win votes precinct by precinct. Far more effective than mass mailings or standardized phone campaigns, personal contact between committed campaign volunteers on the ground and specifically targeted citizens is what is needed to produce votes. Such methods have always been an important part of political campaigning, but now they are being combined with and supported by behavioral research. Without knowing who is voting, why they vote, and how likely they are to participate at the polls on Election Day, slick campaign events, staged rallies, and clever advertisements will be squandered resources. As with baseball, the roots of political moneyball can be traced back to earlier generations, but it is only recently that the data-driven strategies have matured in presidential campaigns.

President Obama's 2012 reelection campaign demonstrates the successful application of some of these data-driven strategies and methods. However, this vote-marshaling approach to presidential campaigning did not suddenly appear in the twenty-first century *ex nihilo*; the tradition of precinct captains charged with riding herd on voters on Election Day and the importance of local political operatives in the old political machine dynamic may serve as rough precedents for the more sophisticated moneyball methods. Even a young Whig politician named Abraham Lincoln, as Sasha Issenberg points out in his book *Victory Lab*, detailed voter-centered political strategies foreshadowing more modern, social science-informed practices. That said, it is during the turn of the last century that we note the full emergence of the science of presidential campaigning. Beginning with the astonishingly close presidential election of 2000—543 Floridian votes making all the difference—the importance of using data to win at the margins has become decidedly more evident to campaign operatives. For example, Matthew Dowd, a notable Republican campaign operative, advocated a more scientific approach to political campaigns prior to the ascent of Barack Obama. Dowd himself was struck by the successful methods of Democratic rivals in turning out the vote during recent campaigns, former First Lady Hillary Clinton's successful campaign for the United States Senate providing one example. By the presidential campaign of 2004, data-driven campaigning was becoming a more visible part of political strategies, and with the efforts of the Obama campaigns of 2008 and 20012, it has become more pronounced.

From what has transpired during the early phase of the Campaign of 2016, moneyball methods and practices continue to be used among serious candidates. Senator Ted Cruz, for example, has invested heavily in accumulating and analyzing psychological data so as to gain an advantage over his competitors. Democratic contender and former secretary of state Hillary Clinton, well-acquainted with the importance of extensive banks of information as a means toward winning a presidential nomination, has implemented a data-driven campaign. While there remains plenty of room for political drama and the allure of larger-than-life personalities, in an increasingly polarized and ideologically fixed electorate, the knowledge gained from empirical research will become even more crucial to the analysis of the nature of electoral politics and the manner in which that knowledge can be converted into electoral success. The ancient Greek philosopher Pythagoras once proclaimed, "All is number," and in a real sense, moneyball politics represents the practical applications of that abstract observation within the amorphous and yet increasingly more predictable world of democratic politics.

Additional Resources

Bluey, Rob. "From 'Moneyball' to Money Bombs: What Sports Analytics Can Teach Political Nerds." *The Atlantic Monthly*, (Online) March 8, 2013.

Green, Donald P., and Alan S. Gerber. *Get Out the Vote: How to Increase Voter Turnout.* Second ed. Washington, DC: The Brookings Institute, 2008.

Isenberg, Sasha. *The Victory Lab: The Secret Science of Winning Campaigns.* New York: Crown Publishers, 2012.

Lewis, Michael. *Moneyball: The Art of Winning an Unfair Game.* New York: W. W. Norton & Company, 2003.

Nickerson, David W., and Todd Rogers. "Political Campaigns and Big Data." *Journal of Economic Perspectives* 28, no. 2 (Spring 2014): 51–74.

Sides, John, and Lynn Vavreck. *The Gamble: Choice and Chance in the 2012 Presidential Election.* Princeton, NJ: Princeton University Press, 2013.

Moral Majority

Breaking from the Baptist practice of maintaining a strict "wall of separation between the garden of the Church and the wilderness of the world," the Reverend Jerry Falwell, a conservative Baptist minister and televangelist, organized a tour of public events promoted as "I Love America" rallies in 1976 in an effort to stimulate a more active political and social conscience among the Evangelical faithful and to draw a tighter connection between religious devotion and patriotic sentiments.

The events raised Falwell's profile within the fundamentalist Protestant community, drawing the attention of other like-minded conservative Christians, such as conservative Catholic activist Paul Weyrich, as well as some leaders within the Jewish community. Through their efforts, the evangelical Falwell and the Catholic Weyrich founded the "Moral Majority," organized primarily to support political candidates and lobby legislatures on issues of particular concern for their faith communities. These issues often involved moral questions such as those raised by the abortion controversy, prayer in school, feminism (specifically, opposition to the Equal Rights Amendment), the state of popular culture, and the rejection of the privacy rights of gay Americans. Headquartered in Lynchburg, Virginia (where Falwell's Thomas Road Baptist Church was located), the Moral Majority at its peak included over four million official members.

The Moral Majority supported the Republican candidate Ronald Reagan in the **Campaign of 1976** and the **Campaign of 1980**, and it quickly become a potent force in electoral politics, especially in the conservative South. Reagan welcomed the group's support and worked closely with Moral Majority activist the Reverend Robert Billings, who would later serve in his administration. Thus, the Moral Majority quickly made political connections with the more conservative elements of the Republican Party, which led to internal party polarization and spurred some moderate and liberal Republicans to change their allegiances. (For example, the independent presidential campaign of moderate Republican John Anderson in the Campaign of 1980 was, in effect, a protest of the Moral Majority's influence on the party.) Within the party, it was clear that moderate Republicans, such as George H. W. Bush, were uncomfortable with the doctrinaire attitude of the Moral Majority wing of the GOP. However, in the **Campaign of 1988**, the Moral Majority endorsed Bush for the presidency, even though televangelist Pat Robertson, who was also a candidate during that election, was far closer to its political and religious positions. While the Moral Majority clearly boosted Reagan's 1980 campaign against the incumbent president, Jimmy Carter, it is less clear that they helped Reagan in his reelection bid during the **Campaign of 1984**. Indeed, an anti-Moral Majority backlash might have helped Walter Mondale counter the group's influence in that election, although this was hardly sufficient to counter Reagan's economic success, and Mondale lost in a landslide. While the Moral Majority has had a strong influence on the composition of the Republican Party coalition, activists later grumbled that Reagan appeared ambivalent about many components of its agenda once he was elected.

By the Campaign of 1988, the Moral Majority began to lose the financial support of many of its core donors and, with this, much of the clout it had earned over the previous decade. Additionally, divisions among the leadership, exposed in part by the Moral Majority's decision to support Bush over Robertson, weakened the organization and diffused its purpose. Finally, other leaders within the evangelical community became disenchanted with the Moral Majority. Notably, Bob Jones, a prominent figure among evangelical Christians in the South, became a vociferous opponent of the Moral Majority; at one point, Jones referred to the Moral Majority as the issue of Satan, primarily because he objected to its ecumenical approach (Jones considered any organization that worked with Catholics, Jews, and Mormons to be no less than an obvious tool of Satan). In 1989, the Moral Majority disbanded as a formal organization.

Falwell attempted to renew the Moral Majority in 2004, but the effort was unsuccessful, and he passed away three years later. While the Moral Majority enjoyed only a few years of real influence during the Reagan era, it remains a significant organization in modern American politics. The political activism of the Christian right initiated by Falwell and Weyrich, despite the brief lifespan of their organization, is largely responsible for sparking the politicization of the evangelical movement and also influencing the political commitment of other faith communities. To a large extent, the association of devout Christians with political conservatism, although inaccurate, is largely the result of the Moral Majority and its leadership.

See also Culture War; Values Voters

Additional Resources

Fowler, Robert Booth, et al. *Religion and Politics in America: Faith, Culture and Strategic Choices*. Fourth ed. Boulder, CO: Westview Press, 2010.

Johnson, Stephen D., and Joseph B. Tamney. "The Christian Right and the 1984 Presidential Election." *Review of Religious Research* 27, no. 2 (1985): 124–33.

Putnam, Robert, and David E. Campbell. *American Grace: How Religion Divides and Unites Us*. New York: Simon & Schuster, 2010.

Wilcox, Clyde, and Carin Robinson. *Onward Christian Soldiers? The Religious Right in American Politics*. Boulder, CO: Westview Press, 2000.

MoveOn

MoveOn is a liberal advocacy group formed in 1998 to oppose the impeachment of then president Bill Clinton. MoveOn was originally founded as a political action committee (PAC), but in the **Campaign of 2004**, it formed a **527 group**, the MoveOn.org Voter Fund, raising millions of dollars to oppose President George W. Bush's reelection. MoveOn set the stage for the formation of other 527 groups such as Swift Boat Veterans for Truth. Because these groups can accept unlimited donations and can engage in unlimited independent campaign spending, they have been criticized as a means for the very wealthy to exert a disproportionate influence on American elections. In June 2008, MoveOn closed shop on its 527 operation but continued to operate as a PAC.

According to the Center for Responsive Politics, in the **Campaign of 2008**, MoveOn spent just under $5 million in independent expenditures in support of Democratic presidential candidate Barack Obama, and just under $1 million in opposition to Republican nominee John McCain. Other major independent expenditures by the group during this period included over $140,000 spent against Republican presidential candidate Rudy Giuliani, just under $250,000 against Republican senator Mitch McConnell (Kentucky), and just under $200,000 in support of other Democratic House and Senate candidates.

While MoveOn supports liberal causes, it has been selective about which liberal candidates it funds. For example, the group spent less than $10,000 in independent expenditures in support of Democrats Hillary Clinton (2008) and John Edwards (2004) in their quest for the party's nomination. Democratic Senate candidate Al Franken of Minnesota received over $10,000 to fund his recount efforts, which ultimately resulted in Franken's victory (many months later) over incumbent Republican senator Norm Coleman.

In the **Campaign of 2012**, MoveOn spent just under $1.2 million in independent expenditures, with approximately $181,000 going to support Democrat Barack Obama's reelection, approximately $863,000 to oppose Republican Mitt Romney's election, and the remainder in opposition to Republican presidential candidate Rick Santorum and in support of Democratic House candidate Brad Schneider of Illinois.

MoveOn's role in the **Campaign of 2016** has been both visible and policy-oriented. The group attempted to fuel Democratic Party support for a "Run, Warren, run" effort in 2014, preferring Senator Elizabeth Warren's (Massachusetts) more progressive views to Hillary Clinton's centrist ones. MoveOn is has recently asked its social media followers to "donate" their social media accounts to it for some specified amount of time as a means of campaign/issue mobilization using a DonateYourAccount tool, similar to what the Obama campaign employed in the Campaign of 2012. And, as Obama's Iranian nuclear deal looked like it might face some Democratic opposition in Congress, MoveOn mobilized its eight million members to express their vocal support for the deal, including the use of field organizers, a six-figure, multiplatform ad buy, and a petition drive against New York Democratic senator Chuck Schumer, who has spoken out in opposition to the deal. MoveOn announced a donors' strike against the Democratic Senatorial Campaign Committee in response to Schumer, hoping to cost Senate Democrats who refuse to support the Iran agreement $10 million in lost campaign contribution pledges during a seventy-two-hour period.

See also Swift Boating

Additional Resources

Berning, Nick. "MoveOn Announces Donor Strike in Response to Schumer's Iran Position." MoveOn.Org, August 6, 2015. http://front.moveon.org/schumer-iran/#.VcfIap1Viko. Accessed September 5, 2015.

Center for Responsive Politics. "MoveOn.Org 2004 Election Cycle." http://www.open secrets.org/527s/527events.php?id=41. Accessed September 5, 2015.

Center for Responsive Politics. "MoveOn.Org Summary, PAC Spending by Cycle—2004." http://www.opensecrets.org/pacs/lookup2.php?strID=C00341396. Accessed September 5, 2015.

Center for Responsive Politics. "Moveon.Org Summary, Independent Expenditures, Communication Costs and Coordinated Expenditures as of April 11, 2013." https://www.opensecrets.org/pacs/indexpend.php?cycle=2012&cmte=C00341396. Accessed September 5, 2015.

Cosgrove-Mather, Bootie. "Attack Ads Skirt Spending Limits." *CBS News*, December 5, 2007.

FactCheck.Org. "MoveOn.Org." August 11, 2010. http://www.factcheck.org/2010/08/moveonorg/. Accessed September 5, 2015.

Johnson, Sasha. "MoveOn.org Shutters Its 527." CNN Political Ticker, June 20, 2008.

Kaye, Kate. "Progressive Political Giant MoveOn Wants Your Twitter Account." AdvertisingAge, July 6, 2015. http://adage.com/article/campaign-trail/progressive-politics-giant-moveon-twitter-account/299352/. Accessed September 5, 2015.

Martin, Jonathan. "MoveOn Looks to Nudge Elizabeth Warren into 2106 Presidential Race." *New York Times*, December 8, 2104. http://www.nytimes.com/2014/12/09/us/politics/looking-to-nudge-senator-elizabeth-warren-into-2016-presidential-race.html. Accessed September 5, 2015.

Weigel, David. "MoveOn Plans 'Mass Mobilization' to Save Iran Deal." *Washington Post*, July 23, 2015. http://www.washingtonpost.com/news/post-politics/wp/2015/07/23/moveon-plans-mass-mobilization-to-save-iran-deal/. Accessed September 5, 2015.

National Voter Registration Act of 1993

Also known as the "Motor Voter" law, this act was signed into law by President Bill Clinton. Its purpose was to make it easier for citizens to vote by requiring states to provide a process for mail-in and in-person registration, and to permit citizens to register to vote when applying for or renewing a driver's license. Other federal agencies that provide services to the public may also be designated as voter registration agencies. The Department of Defense was authorized under the act to develop procedures for voter registration at military recruitment offices. The act also limited states' ability to arbitrarily purge voters from the election rolls (rules that were later modified by the Help America Vote Act [HAVA]).

The U.S. Election Assistance Commission, created in 2002 by HAVA, prepares biannual reports for Congress on the states' implementation of the National Voter Registration Act (NVRA). While there is modest statistical support for the NVRA's effects on increased voter turnout in the United States, there is far more substantial evidence of an increase in voter registration in the period after the legislation was enacted, particularly among voters under the age of thirty. The driver's license renewal component of the law has been far more successful in improving turnout than has mail-in voter registration.

While the NVRA obligates states to register voters at locations where citizens receive public assistance, enforcement of this requirement is notoriously lax. In 2010, the Justice Department notified the states of federal guidelines and warned them about potential legal problems for noncompliance. Thus, many states were required to register poor voters at welfare offices for the first time in the **Campaign of 2012**, as Attorney General Eric Holder engaged in more stringent enforcement of voting rights laws.

Additional Resources

Franklin, Daniel P., and Eric E. Grier. "Effects of Motor Voter Legislation: Voter Turnout, Registration, and Partisan Advantage in the 1992 Presidential Election." *American Politics Research* 25, no. 1 (January 1997): 104–117.

Highton, Benjamin, and Raymond E. Wolfinger. "Estimating the Effects of the National Voter Registration Act of 1993." *Political Behavior* 20, no. 2 (1998): 79–104.

Knack, Stephen. "Does Motor Voter Work? Evidence from State-Level Data." *Journal of Politics* (1995): 796–811.

New York Times. "A Welfare Check and a Voting Card." Editorial, August 9, 2010.

U.S. Election Assistance Commission. "National Voter Registration Act Studies." http://www.eac.gov/research/national_voter_registration_act_studies.aspx. Accessed October 15, 2015.

Nativism Issue

Up through the 1820s, anti-immigration sentiment played a relatively minor role in presidential politics, the anti-Masonry movement of the early 1930s being the first political effort reflecting such sentiment. The anti-Masonry movement grew out of the mysterious disappearance of former Mason William Morgan of New York in 1826. Prior to his disappearance, Morgan had angered Masons by writing a book critical of the fraternal organization. A political movement erupted against "Masonic conspiracies," leading to the formation of the Anti-Masonic Party in 1831. Meeting in Baltimore that year, the Anti-Masonic Party became the first political party in American history to hold a national nominating convention.

Former Mason William Wirt of Maryland was nominated as their candidate for president. The Anti-Masonic Party primarily targeted the Masons but also held anti-immigration positions and xenophobic sentiments.

The "Know-Nothing" movement initiated a second anti-immigration wave during the 1850s. This new wave of xenophobia targeted Catholic immigrants, rather than Masons. When asked about their membership in the movement, many members elusively responded that they "knew nothing" about such a movement.

In February 1856, a group of Know-Nothings formed the American Party, holding their national convention in Philadelphia. The platform supported a preference that all local, state, and federal government positions be filled by native-born citizens. In addition, the platform advocated a requirement that individuals reside in the United States for twenty-one years before being eligible for citizenship. The American Party nominated former president Millard Fillmore for president in the **Campaign of 1856**. It particularly targeted Republican candidate John C. Fremont, accusing him of being a crypto-Catholic in spite of his membership in an Episcopalian congregation. Ironically, Fillmore won the electoral votes of Maryland, a state noted for its strong Catholic heritage.

The Know-Nothings lost steam, attention, and members as the slavery issue further polarized the nation. In the aftermath of the Civil War and Reconstruction, the Ku Klux Klan, which used terror and violence to hatefully repress African Americans while also harboring bitter and bigoted anti-Catholic, anti-Semitic, anti-immigrant, and anti-Northern sentiments, emerged as a particularly militant voice of nativism throughout the South and enjoyed considerable power by the **Campaign of 1880**. Klan repression of the black vote in the South inadvertently contributed to the first election of Grover Cleveland, no friend of the Klan, in the **Campaign of 1884**.

In addition to the rise of the Ku Klux Klan, the post-Civil War era was marred by hostility toward new immigrants from China. Faced with a shortage of laborers during the 1860s, the Central Pacific Railroad brought thousands of Chinese workers to the West to complete the transcontinental railroad. Most of these workers opted to remain in the United States once the project was completed, settling in northern California, particularly in San Francisco; this caused a new wave of xenophobia, now directed against Asians. Both parties included planks in their 1876 platforms calling for restrictions on Chinese immigration. These planks were retained in subsequent platforms, culminating in the passage of the Chinese Exclusion Act of 1882 and the Alien Contract Labor laws of 1885 and 1887.

Between 1890 and the beginning of World War I, millions of new immigrants arrived in the United States from Europe, particularly from the southern and eastern regions of the European continent (where the predominant religious identification was generally Catholic). Following the end of the war, the nation again experienced a surge in immigration, stimulating yet another surge in nativism. Chinese exclusion was again emphasized in the platforms of both parties in the **Campaign of 1920**. Additionally, the Republican platform supported the enactment of immigration quotas. The growing nativism sentiment helped to persuade Congress to pass the immigration acts of 1921 and 1924 that established a quota system for future immigrants.

In the late twentieth century, the rising number of illegal immigrants from Latin America produced renewed insistence on tighter immigration policy and enforcement. Conservative commentator and Republican presidential candidate Pat Buchanan offered provocative (and unflattering) opinions regarding the nature and composition of recent immigration. Buchanan's views reflect one faction of the Republican Party. This faction views immigration as a threat to American jobs, and more broadly, the language and cultural values of immigrants are viewed as a threat to the dominant culture. Most of the Republican candidates for president in the **Campaign of 2012** appeared to endorse this viewpoint, which is not uncommon in an economic downturn. Other Republicans, such as George W. Bush and John McCain, were more tolerant toward illegal immigrants and showed a willingness to negotiate opportunities for them to work legally in the United States or even work toward establishing citizenship. Their faction of the Republican Party tends to view immigration as an asset to the business community.

The presence of wealthy businessman and television celebrity Donald Trump in the **Campaign of 2016** once again raised the specter of nativism. Trump, who had previously been vocally associated with birtherism, centered his campaign for the GOP nomination on the issue of immigration, notoriously claiming that those who entered the United States from Mexico were bringing "drugs, crimes, and rapists" across the border. He contended that everyone illegally residing in the United States needed to be rounded up and deported immediately, and that an enormous wall between the United States and Mexico needed to be constructed that should be paid for, in its entirety, by Mexico. Additionally, Mr. Trump, in recently responding to the Syrian refugee crisis, has publicly speculated, "This could be one of the great military coups of all time if they send them to our country—young, strong people and they turn out to be ISIS . . . Now, probably that won't happen, but some of them definitely in my opinion will be ISIS." Confronting this fear, Mr. Trump has promised to return the refugees to their homeland should he gain the White House, pledging, "If they come in, and if I win, they're going back. They're going back." These attitudes intensified in the aftermath of the December 2015 San Bernardino terrorist shooting, prompting the Trump Campaign to issue the following statement: "Donald J. Trump is calling for a total and complete shutdown of Muslims entering the United States until our country's representatives can figure out what is going on."

While political analysts challenged the validity of Trump's claims about immigration, his rhetoric struck a chord with a sizable number of Republican voters. Pew found that 53 percent of Republicans surveyed believed that immigrants generally made the country worse, and only 31 percent said that they made the country better (whereas majorities of Independents and Democrats felt that immigrants made the country better). Moreover, 71 percent of Republicans held immigrants responsible for worsening crime, and for worsening the economy specifically, concerns not shared by other partisan groups. Sixty-seven percent of Republicans wanted to decrease immigration, and 34 percent wanted to keep it at its current level (only 15 percent wanted to increase immigration). Only 49 percent of Independents, and 33 percent of Democrats, wanted to decrease immigration (as opposed to keeping it the same or increasing it). Trump's GOP challengers scrambled to outdo his rhetoric, with most suggesting that they would be equally hostile toward immigrants; many also took his cue in suggesting that birthright citizenship needed to be ended.

Democratic candidates in recent years have generally been supportive of attempts to expand legal immigration, have been reluctant to deport immigrants who are in the United States illegally if they have committed no other criminal acts, and have been more willing to offer illegal immigrants a path to citizenship. This is probably due, in part, to the ethnic diversity of the Democratic coalition: by the **Campaign of 2012**, most African Americans, Latinos, Asian Americans, and Arab Americans, as well as other minority ethnic groups, were voting for the Democrats, whereas the GOP was attracting almost exclusively white, non-Hispanic voters. Thus, the Democratic Party's rejection of nativism is consistent with the policy interests of its base. As the sociodemographic composition of the nation changes, however, espousing a policy of nativism may make it difficult for GOP candidates to broaden the scope of their party's appeal at a time when the white, non-Hispanic portion of the electorate is shrinking. Among Republican candidates competing for the 2016 nomination, Florida senator Marco Rubio has been targeted by critics within his own party due to the senator's support for moderate immigration reforms submitted to the Senate, and yet defeated in the House, in July 2013.

See also Anti-Catholicism; Birther; Immigration Issue

Additional Resources

Anbinder, Tyler G. *Nativism and Slavery: The Northern Know Nothings and the Politics of the 1850s.* Oxford: Oxford University Press, 1995.

Krogstad, Jens Manuel. "On Views of Immigrants, Americans Largely Split Along Party Lines." Pew Research Center, Fact Tank, September 30, 2015.

Scott, Eugene. "Trump: Bringing Syrian Refugees to U.S. Could Result in Military Coup." *CNN News* online, October 3, 2015. http://www.cnn.com/2015/10/03/politics/donald -trump-syria-refugees-military/index.html. Accessed October 6, 2015.

Negative Campaigning

Throughout the history of American political campaigns, partisans have used a wide variety of methods to criticize their opponents, attacking their positions on issues as well as impugning their personal character. Such accusations have been made verbally by candidates or their surrogates in campaign speeches, they have been whispered by supporters in the form of rumors, they have appeared in print in the form of partisan broadsides and editorials, and they have been broadcast on the airwaves in the form of campaign advertisements.

One time-honored form of negative campaigning has been the use of "dirty tricks," which includes a number of unsavory election practices such as spreading rumors about one's opponent; planting hecklers in the crowd during an opponent's rally; and attempting to suppress, through misinformation or outright intimidation, the voter turnout of groups that are likely to vote for one's challenger. Dirty tricks have a long history in American politics, perhaps because politicians feel that they are effective in providing candidates the edge that they need to win, or perhaps because they are so rarely prosecuted (because they are difficult to substantiate, by their very nature).

Sometimes, the accusations made against candidates are true, but they are manipulated by a campaign to appear damaging. Florida Democrat Claude Pepper's 1950 Senate campaign was once the target of such an attack. His opponent, George Smathers, circulated material charging that Pepper was an "extrovert" who practiced "celibacy" before he was married. While at college, Pepper "matriculated." Moreover, Smathers charged, Pepper's sister was a "thespian" and his brother was a practicing "homo sapien." Voters took the bait, and Pepper lost his reelection bid.

In contemporary politics, the politician most known for employing dirty tricks is Richard Nixon, whose campaign tactics, beginning with his first campaign for Congress and continuing through all three campaigns for the presidency, earned him the nickname "Tricky Dick," although in fairness it must be admitted that his political rival (and erstwhile friend) John F. Kennedy also employed dirty tricks in his various campaigns. That said, few candidates have earned a reputation for dirty tricks matching Mr. Nixon's. In particular, Nixon's Committee to Re-Elect the President (ironically nicknamed CREEP) engaged in a number of illicit activities during the **Campaign of 1972**. Individuals associated with CREEP broke into the office of Daniel Ellsberg's psychiatrist in an effort to find information to discredit Ellsberg, who had leaked the Pentagon Paper\s to the *New York Times*. Nixon campaign workers also forged the "Canuck letter" and the "Muskie sex letter" to discredit Democratic primary challenger Ed Muskie because Nixon preferred to run against another candidate. CREEP also laundered illegal campaign contributions in an attempt to circumvent recently passed campaign finance laws and, most notoriously, broke into and bugged the Democratic National Committee's headquarters at the Watergate Hotel, hoping to find information that would help Nixon win the election as well as prevent feared leaks impugning Nixon's actions with regard to the Vietnam War, including a serious indictment from some quarters claiming that as a candidate in the 1968 campaign, Nixon attempted to illegally interfere with negotiations between belligerents, prolonging the war for his own political advantage. This break-in, and the cover-up that followed, sealed Nixon's fate. By 1974 Nixon was forced to resign to avoid certain impeachment.

The extent of the Nixon campaign's efforts to win the election at any cost has long puzzled political scientists; Nixon was far ahead of McGovern in the polls throughout the campaign, was easily outraising McGovern in campaign funds, and did not at any point appear to be in danger of losing the election. In all likelihood Nixon would have easily won reelection even without resorting to dirty tricks. Much of what seems to have motivated President Nixon, in spite of his comfortable position as the heavy favorite for reelection in 1972, was a fear of leaks that would expose potential tampering with the Vietnam War in 1968 and, perhaps more importantly, his obsession with the political power enjoyed by the Kennedy family, particularly with the prospect of Sen. Edward Kennedy entering the presidential race. President Nixon's complex history with the Kennedys—and his inability to detach his own insecurities from a conflicted mixture of admiration and contempt regarding the Kennedy legacy—explains at least in part much of his willingness to employ the kind of unsavory tactics that have come to characterize, and forever mar, Nixon's political reputation.

In the 2002 midterm campaign, Republican operative Allen Raymond was famously found to have illegally jammed the phone lines of the Democratic Party in New Hampshire to prevent the party from transporting supporters to the polls. Raymond went on to write a book detailing his exploits and explaining how political parties engage in underhanded ploys to gain political advantage. In every presidential election, citizens in some communities receive official-looking mailers telling them that they will be arrested at the polls if they owe back child support or parking tickets (which is false); and fliers are posted in communities listing improper election days, to fool the unwitting into missing their chance to vote. Political scientists remain uncertain of how many voters fail to cast a ballot each year as a result of dirty tricks.

In addition to dirty tricks, opposition research remains a staple of negative campaigning in American elections. This term refers to the long history of political campaigns seeking to discredit their opponents by digging up unflattering personal information about them, unpopular votes they may have cast, and public (or private) statements they have made that might sound unsavory or otherwise troubling to the public at large. Historically, opposition research has been conducted by low-level political operatives. In more recent years, it has become far more professional.

During the **Campaign of 2000**, the BBC trailed opposition researchers for the presidential campaign of Republican nominee George W. Bush. The group, headed by then lawyer and former congressional investigator Barbara Comstock, was staffed primarily with lawyers and congressional investigators for the House committee headed by Representative Dan Burton that had investigated President Bill Clinton during the 1990s. Democratic nominee Al Gore's opposition research team was headed by Chris Lehane, who was responsible for much of the damage control for Bill Clinton during his time in office. "Digging the Dirt" shows how both candidates relied on friendly sources in the news media to disseminate the information they wanted to leak, essentially using the press as a tool to control the narrative of the campaign.

Professional opposition researcher Jason Stanford notes that successful research must be accurate, must strike the right tone, and must address a concern that is viewed by voters as relevant. According to Stanford, rumors of Bill Clinton's infidelities gained little traction in the **Campaign of 1996** or the 1998 midterm elections because voters simply did not care that much about Clinton's personal life.

The advent of the **twenty-four-hour news cycle** has made opposition research far more visible in modern presidential campaigns. Opposition researchers have a wide array of news outlets, both traditional and nontraditional, through which to disseminate information. News organizations, Web sites, and political blogs, eager to feed the public's appetite for new information, have become quicker to embrace the information provided by political campaigns. Democratic candidates Hillary Clinton and Barack Obama had hired opposition research teams at least a year and a half before the election during the **Campaign of 2008**. Similarly, most Republican candidates in the **Campaign of 2012** (except for Michele Bachmann) hired teams of professional opposition researchers a year before the first primary elections took place.

Opposition research may also be disseminated through the unsavory practice of push polling. A push poll involves the use of a telemarketing firm working on behalf of a presidential campaign but concealing that information in its encounters with the people it is "surveying." Rather, push pollsters feign an element of objectivity in the guise of conducting an independent public opinion survey. Recognizing that voters are quite familiar with public opinion polls, campaign managers have reasoned that it might be possible to transform an opinion poll into an instrument of political persuasion. Push polls are designed to convince voters that the survey is legitimate, whereupon voters are provided with damaging information about a candidate and asked whether this information might influence their vote choice. Basically, a push poll is simply a negative campaign ad masquerading as a public opinion poll.

In the **Campaign of 2000**, the Republican primary contest brought considerable media attention to the use of push polls by political campaigns and independent groups. Arizona senator John McCain alleged that the campaign of Texas governor George W. Bush used a push poll to derail the McCain campaign in South Carolina. Specifically, the push poll in question characterized McCain as a cheat and a liar, and it implied that he was the father of an illegitimate African American child, the latter a particularly scurrilous accusation in South Carolina at that time. (The accusation about McCain was not true; the child in question was a Malaysian girl that he and his wife Cindy had adopted; ironically, then South Carolina senator Strom Thurmond actually had fathered an out-of-wedlock African American child, a fact disclosed only after his death.)

Push polls continue to play an important role in both primary and general election campaigns because campaign strategists believe them to be effective in the same way that they believe other negative ads to be effective. The advantage of a push poll is its stealth. Candidates cannot easily determine, much less dispute, the charges being made against them. And because push polls involve telephone conversations, there is little opportunity for the media to broadcast their content, much less analyze the claims being made. Moreover, unlike a negative ad that is broadcast on the airwaves, groups sponsoring push polls are not required to identify themselves to those they call (except in the case of New Hampshire). These factors make it likely that campaigns and other groups will continue to use push polls as a tool to air the most distasteful of accusations about political candidates.

During the 2015/2016 presidential campaign, negative ads again dominated political rhetoric. Main contender Donald Trump relied almost exclusively on negative campaign tactics, particularly targeting Jeb Bush (who he has insulted publicly) and Hillary Clinton (most recently by threatening to remind voters of her husband's history of infidelity), but also poking jabs and jibes at candidates throughout the field. His public aspersions and taunts and mockery of Carly Fiorina, Ben Carson, and Marco Rubio (who he referred to as "a clown") have been especially harsh. Many of Mr. Trump's comments are apparently extemporaneous remarks made during campaign speeches or debate showcases, highlighting Mr. Trump's habit of sharing his unfiltered thoughts on mic and before a crowd.

Political ads continue to be a vehicle for the promotion of negative claims against a political opponent. However, the rise of the Internet and social media has created numerous other outlets for the dissemination of scurrilous accusations against one's political enemies. And technology will undoubtedly provide new opportunities for future candidates to devise dirty tricks that produce misgivings about candidates, and that potentially hinder electoral opportunities for voters.

See also Character Issue; Political Ads

Additional Resources

Ansolabehere, Stephen, and Shanto Iyenger. *Going Negative: How Attack Ads Shrink and Polarize the Electorate.* New York: Free Press, 1995.

Bernstein, Carl, and Bob Woodward. *All the President's Men.* New York: Warner Books, 1976.

Bolger, Glen, and Bill McInturff. "'Push Polling' Stinks." *Campaigns and Elections* 17 (August 1996): 70.

Burns, Eric. "America Enjoys Rich History of Election Hijinks." *Fox News*, January 31, 2004.

"Digging the Dirt." BBC, *Panorama* episode, aired October 22, 2000.

Feld, Karl G. "What Are Push Polls, Anyway?" *Campaigns and Elections* 21 (May 2000): 62.

Geer, John G. *In Defense of Negativity: Attack Ads in Presidential Campaigns.* Chicago: University of Chicago Press, 2006.

Green, Joshua. "Playing Dirty." *Atlantic*, June 2004.

Gumbel, Andrew. *Steal This Vote: Dirty Elections and the Rotten History of Democracy in America.* New York: Nation Books, 2005.

Mark, David. *Going Dirty: The Art of Negative Campaigning.* Lanham, MD: Rowman & Littlefield, 2006.

Matthews, Chris. *Kennedy & Nixon: The Rivalry that Shaped Postwar America.* New York: Touchstone Books, 1996.

Raymond, Allen. *How to Rig an Election: Confessions of a Republican Operative.* New York: Simon & Schuster, 2008.

Schultz, Colin. "Nixon Prolonged Vietnam War for Political Gain." Smithsonian.com, March 18, 2013.

Smith, Ben. "Oppo: From Dark Art to Daily Tool." Politico, August 3, 2011.

Upholdt, Boyce. "Quality Opposition Research." *Campaigns and Elections*, June 12, 2009.

"The Watergate Story." *Washington Post* archive. http://www.washingtonpost.com/wp-srv/politics/special/watergate/index.html. Accessed October 1, 2015.

Neoconservatives

There are numerous schools of thought governing attitudes on foreign policy. Most political scientists believe that there are four primary approaches to the U.S. role in the world: liberal internationalism, realism, neoconservatism, and **isolationism**.

Realism is a school of thought that emphasizes containment and deterrence of the enemy. An overriding concern in realism is long-term political stability and clarity in the understanding and protection of the national interests. This desire for stability has often led foreign policy realists to support unsavory regimes that did not adhere to American political ideals (for example, the shah of Iran, or more recently, deposed Egyptian president Hosni Mubarak and the ruling family of Bahrain), as long as those regimes contributed to regional stability and did not threaten U.S. interests. In short, realists are more concerned with how other nations act on the global stage than they are with how those countries are run internally. During the Cold War, realism guided the arms race with the Soviet Union, which was viewed as a necessary investment to deter an attack on the United States. And realism influenced the decisions to engage in military action in Korea in the 1950s and Vietnam in the 1960s, when it appeared that the Soviets were expanding their sphere of influence in Asia.

Neoconservatives, on the other hand, favor a more activist foreign policy. According to historian Francis Fukuyama, neoconservatives are concerned with democracy, human rights, political institutions, and the belief that U.S. foreign policy should pursue moral ends. In many senses, neoconservatives share the goals of foreign policy liberals. However, there are some key differences. Liberals generally seek nonmilitary means to pursue these goals, and they believe in the ability of international organizations and negotiated, multilateral agreements as the means to create a just and peaceful world. Neoconservatives tend to be more skeptical of organizations like the United Nations and feel that it is unnecessary to rely on alliances with other nations, and they are more willing to commit to unilateral action in addressing crises abroad. They believe that military force can be an effective, decisive means to create a more peaceable world, as long as it is used for moral ends. Neoconservatives seek to undertake regime change, they are not averse to preemptive war, and they believe in **American exceptionalism**, which generally means that they view the United States as having a special role to play in the world (as the sole superpower) and they believe that exporting American democratic principles (and institutions) to other countries is a desirable goal.

While neoconservatism has been influential among both intellectuals and political activists in both political parties, it remained outside of the mainstream for members of the general public until recent years. Among members of the Republican Party, neoconservatives were a decided minority until the **Campaign of 2004**, when many rallied around President George W. Bush and Vice President Dick Cheney's use of military force as a tool for expanding democracy in the Middle East. For many voters, this was the first they had heard of neoconservatism. While Democratic nominee John Kerry was critical of the U.S. decision to go to war in Iraq (once it had been established that Iraq had lacked the weapons of mass destruction that Bush and Cheney used to justify the conflict), he did not claim that he would end military involvement in the region. Nor did Kerry suggest that the United States should withdraw its military forces from Afghanistan. Rather, it appeared that Kerry was tacitly accepting the neoconservative argument that force was sometimes necessary to produce more benevolent and peaceable rulers.

Democratic nominee Senator Barack Obama rejected the basic tenets of neoconservatism in the **Campaign of 2008**, calling for a quick withdrawal of troops from Iraq. However, Obama supported the use of force in Afghanistan because, he argued, the Taliban government had initiated an attack on the United States on September 11, 2001. Obama viewed the war in Afghanistan as primarily defensive in nature. Since that time, Obama sent troops to a third country—Libya—as part of a multilateral force to protect civilians from human rights abuses, and to support the rebels in their attempt to overthrow the existing regime.

The behavior of the Republican presidential candidates in the **Campaign of 2012** ranged from outright isolationist on some occasions to a more traditional neoconservative viewpoint on other occasions. For example, early in the campaign, few candidates were willing to endorse the use of U.S. military forces in Libya, and many pressed for a quicker withdrawal of troops from Afghanistan. Yet most advocated bombing Iran in order to prevent it from developing a nuclear arsenal, and several candidates also suggested that the United States use its military resources in order to depose Fidel Castro. Moreover, all of the candidates (except Ron Paul) professed strong support for the notion of American exceptionalism and endorsed increased spending on defense. Since he was elected president, Barack Obama has altered his approach to foreign policy in ways that reflect more of a realist perspective. He has endorsed a policy of targeted assassination of terrorists abroad (including terrorists who are American citizens), he has stepped up the use of drones in order to pursue military objectives while minimizing the use of American troops, and he has continued many of the foreign policy objectives of his predecessor. At the same time, he has withdrawn American troops from Iraq on schedule and set a quick timetable for the withdrawal of troops from Afghanistan. Thus, while Obama has appeared willing to use military force as an instrument of U.S. foreign policy, he seemed to be more sparing in terms of the number of troops he is willing to use and the duration for which he is willing to use them.

The behavior of the Republican presidential candidates in the **Campaign of 2016** have so far exhibited a seeming resurgence of neoconservative attitudes with regard to the use of military force, particularly in confronting threats from ISIL/ISIS; however, it is always difficult to be sure of the sincerity behind the beating of war drums on the campaign trail. It is one thing to entertain the tactic of "carpet bombing" an enemy abroad as Sen. Cruz has publicly submitted for the public's approval, but quite another thing to issue the command from within the White House.

Additional Resources

Destler, I. M., Celinda Lake, and Frederick T. Steeper. *Misreading the Public: The Myth of a New Isolationism.* Washington, DC: Brookings, 1999.

Ehrman, John. *The Rise of Neoconservatism: Intellectuals and Foreign Affairs, 1945–1994.* New Haven, CT: Yale University Press, 1996.

Friedman, Murray. *The Neoconservative Revolution: Jewish Intellectuals and the Shaping of Public Policy.* New York: Cambridge University Press, 2006.

Fukuyama, Francis. *America at the Crossroads: Democracy, Power, and the Neoconservative Legacy.* New Haven, CT: Yale University Press, 2007.

Halper, Stefan, and Jonathan Clarke. *America Alone: The Neo-Conservatives and the Global Order.* New York: Cambridge University Press, 2004.

Hartz, Louis. *The Liberal Tradition in America.* New York: Harcourt Brace, 1955.

Kristol, Irving. *Neo-Conservatism: The Autobiography of an Idea.* New York: Free Press, 1995.

Lieven, Anatol. *America Right or Wrong: An Anatomy of American Nationalism.* New York: Oxford University Press, 2005.

Nordlinger, Eric. *Isolationism Reconfigured: American Foreign Policy for a New Century.* Princeton, NJ: Princeton University Press, 1995.

Netroots Nation

Netroots Nation is the organization that holds the YearlyKos convention for progressive political bloggers and candidates; it is also currently the name used to refer to the convention itself. Netroots Nation and its predecessor, YearlyKos, are viewed as important forums for liberal activists to shape Democratic Party politics. YearlyKos is widely credited with undermining the candidacy of Democratic senator Joe Lieberman, forcing him to run as an independent (after which he declined to seek reelection). In 2007, all of the Democratic primary candidates for president (with the exception of Joe Biden) attended the YearlyKos convention in Chicago and made their pitches to the new generation of online activists. The 2007 convention's role in Lieberman's candidacy and the 2008 presidential campaign are considered the high-water marks in the political influence of the Netroots Nation community.

In 2011, the convention was held in Minneapolis and was attended by some two thousand bloggers, political activists, and political candidates. That year, RightOnline, bankrolled by the conservative group Americans for Prosperity, also scheduled its conference in Minneapolis, on the same dates and at the same venues. Uncomfortable confrontations between attendees of both conferences occurred, including an uninvited appearance by conservative blogger Andrew Breitbart at Netroots Nation and a flash mob of hijab-wearing women showing up at RightOnline in protest of the activities of some RightOnline attendees. The 2012 Netroots Nation convention was held in Providence, Rhode Island, a smaller, comparatively less accessible city with few major hotels and convention centers, which permitted Netroots to strategically book all of the major venues of any size well in advance and did not give RightOnline the same opportunities to capitalize on **earned media** opportunities that a larger, more centrally located city would have.

Subsequent conferences have exposed ongoing divisions among progressive factions. In 2013 Congresswoman Nancy Pelosi was booed for remarking that NSA whistle-blower Edward Snowden was a lawbreaker, and for supporting President Obama's national security policies. The 2014 convention held in Detroit and attended by Vice President Joseph Biden and Massachusetts senator Elizabeth Warren was mostly calm, but during the 2015 Netroots convention, which was held in Phoenix during summer heat, temperatures rose both inside and out. Attended by only two Democratic candidates for the 2016 presidential nomination, Vermont senator Bernie Sanders and former Maryland governor Martin O'Malley—frontrunner Hillary Clinton selecting not to attend—the convention was marked by protests and frustrated by disorganization and discontent. Gov. O'Malley's speech was interrupted by hecklers and then hijacked by a protester's spokesperson, who, after elements in the audience chanted the slogans "Black lives matter" and "Say her name," was spontaneously invited on stage to speak to the issue of police violence against African Americans, preventing O'Malley from reassuming the podium for a quarter of an hour. When Gov. O'Malley did return to the podium, he voiced his sympathies with the protester's complaint, agreeing that "black lives matter" and then declaring somewhat naïvely that "white lives matter, all lives matter," provoking a cascade of boos and collective groans. When Sen. Sanders took the stage, the heckling continued as the senator, more accustomed to dealing with such tactics, simply ignored the hecklers and used the amplification of his microphone to talk over them. Many in the audience joined the confrontation, shouting over the protesters as well, demanding that they let the senator have his chance to speak to the issues being raised.

The 2016 Netroots Nation convention is currently scheduled to be held in St. Louis in mid-summer and is likely to be influenced by recent memories of the conflict between police and citizens in nearby Ferguson. That painful context, combined with what should be by that time a clear choice in the election of the next president, will likely produce a repetition, and perhaps intensification, of the provocative confrontations that unfolded in the 2011, 2013, and 2015 conventions.

See also Americans for Prosperity

Additional Resources

Cox, Ana Marie. "Why Ambitious Pols Make Their Pilgrimage to Yearly Kos." *Time*, June 9, 2006.

Nagourney, Adam. "Gathering Highlights the Power of the Blog." *New York Times*, June 10, 2006.

Netroots Nation. http:///www.netrootsnation.org. Accessed October 2, 2015.

Rainey, James. "Yearly Kos and Effect: Liberal Activists Celebrate." *Los Angeles Times*, August 4, 2007.

Sherer, Michael. "Cheerful Boos for Hillary." Salon.com, August 6, 2007.

Weigant, Chris. "Where Was Hillary?" Huffington Post, July 20, 2015. http://www.huffington post.com/chris-weigant/where-was-hillary_b_7836984.htmlhuffingtonpost.com. Accessed October 2, 2015.

New Media. *See* Internet Campaigning

Opposition Research. *See* Negative Campaigning

Paid Media

The term "paid media" refers to the expenditure of hard money by presidential campaigns or independent groups to support or oppose the election of a candidate. Nowadays, paid media includes campaign ads broadcast over the radio, broadcast television, cable television, video games, and the Internet. Paid media also includes the purchase of billboard space, Internet banners, Internet billboards, and online pop-up ads.

While the campaign organizations of presidential candidates are the most visible sources of paid media spending, **independent advocacy groups** have become increasingly involved in sponsoring ads as well. The campaign finance reforms of the 1970s limited candidates to spending hard money donations, and, as a consequence, political parties raised soft money to fund ads to promote their nominee (often, these included negative advertising). The Bipartisan Campaign Reform Act of 2002 put an end to the unlimited soft money donations to political parties, leaving parties with only hard money to spend on their electioneering activities. Despite these limits, parties were still able to finance a variety of campaign ads, and they were joined in their efforts by an onslaught of independent advocacy groups, particularly **527 groups**. In 2010, the Supreme Court relaxed the limits on independent spending in federal elections, and **527 groups** and **501(c) groups** grew at an astonishing rate, spending untold sums on the 2010 midterms. In the **Campaign of 2012**, these independent groups narrowed their focus from broad ideological goals to the promotion of specific candidates, essentially becoming an unregulated financing arm of candidates' campaigns. These **super PACs** may soon constitute the bulk of paid media spending in federal elections.

Paid media will likely continue to serve presidential candidates in the years ahead. However, it is possible that other forms of digital media, such as Twitter, or the next unseen innovation on the Internet, could lessen the need for the purchase of expensive time over the airwaves or a share of cyberspace. Given the nature of campaign rhetoric, there will always be a need to use the media to deliver a candidate's message and image, but the importance of hard money paid media has already changed, and it could continue to do so in the near future.

See also Campaign Ads; Negative Campaigning

Additional Resources

Hendricks, John Allen, and Dan Schill. *Presidential Campaigning and Social Media: An Analysis of the 2012 Campaign.* Oxford: Oxford University Press, 2015.

Mentzer, Bruce. "A Political Media Buying Strategy for Using Cable." *Campaigns and Elections* (June 2000): 82–83.

Plouffe, David. *The Audacity to Win.* New York: Viking, 2009.

Partisan Sorting

Historically, Americans' partisanship has been only loosely connected to their liberal-conservative ideology. Political scientists generally found that most Americans lacked the political interest or expertise to make consistent and meaningful connections between political party labels, ideological abstractions such as beliefs about the role of government in society, and their positions on specific policy issues. Identification with a political party label was often based upon long-standing family affinity, and whether a person felt connected to the social groups that they perceived to be part of that party's coalition of support. This lack of ideological rigidity permitted political parties the freedom to adjust their policy positions in response to events (as happened on issues of civil rights and race in the 1960s) and also permitted voters to occasionally select candidates who were personally appealing but did not share their party label (as happened with Eisenhower Democrats in the 1950s and Reagan Democrats in the 1980s, for example).

Beginning in the early 1980s, political scientists noticed that Republican voters were increasingly taking conservative positions on a wide range of issues, and Democratic voters were increasingly taking liberal positions (albeit to a somewhat lesser extent). This trend continued throughout the 1990s and picked up steam in the elections of the twenty-first century. More and more Americans are now willing to commit to a political party label, and political parties themselves are becoming more ideological and more polarized. There are now few conservative Democrats in Congress and even fewer liberal Republicans. The number of party-line votes in Congress has continued to rise, as has the number of filibusters.

The causes of this phenomenon are complex. The rise of party primaries (as a replacement for caucuses) as a means for selecting candidates has served to increase the ideological extremity of the candidates who run for office. The mobilization of the **Moral Majority** in the 1970s and the Christian Right in the 1980s served to politicize many political issues that had not polarized voters in the past. The rise of cable and Internet media has permitted voters to select news sources that match their own ideological leanings (a process known as selective exposure to information). Researchers have also hypothesized that voters' geographic migration and lifestyle choices have further served to isolate citizens into like-minded neighborhoods and communities, which reinforces their preexisting ideological viewpoints and limits their opportunities for interactions with individuals who hold differing opinions.

See also Culture War; Tea Party Movement

Additional Resources

Bishop, Bill. *The Big Sort.* New York: Houghton Mifflin Harcourt, 2008.

Fiorina, Morris P., with Samuel J. Abrams and Jeremy C. Pope. *Culture War? The Myth of a Polarized America.* Third ed. Boston: Longman, 2011.

Levendusky, Matthew. *The Partisan Sort.* Chicago: University of Chicago Press, 2009.

Photo Opportunity

A photo opportunity (or photo op) is essentially a publicity shot, often taken at a campaign event, by a news organization covering that event. While photo ops are part of the normal news-gathering process, political campaigns work hard to craft events that enable their candidates to be portrayed in a favorable way. The retail politicking events early in the campaign season provide numerous opportunities for journalists to photograph candidates interacting one-on-one with ordinary citizens, and such coverage is an important element in a campaign's free media strategy.

Town hall meeting events are another means for generating the all-important photo op, as are whistle-stop campaign events, such as the Clinton-Gore bus tour in the **Campaign of 1992** or the Obama bus tour in the early days of the

Campaign of 2012, or the original "whistle stop" tour of President Harry Truman in his attempt to win election and retain the White House in 1948 after having succeeded President Franklin Roosevelt upon the latter's death. Candidates' speeches can also be shaped to generate a photo op, as well as other appearances such as a visit to a school classroom or attendance at a baseball game, or perhaps meeting a popular celebrity or a visiting dignitary.

Some photo ops simply backfire, such as a photo of a solitary President Nixon walking incongruously on the seashore in dress shoes or 2004 Democratic nominee Sen. John Kerry pheasant hunting in an Iowa field. One of the more notorious photo ops in recent history occurred when then president George W. Bush emerged from a fighter jet on the aircraft carrier USS *Abraham Lincoln* on May 1, 2003, and posed under an enormous "Mission Accomplished" banner to proclaim the cessation of hostilities in Iraq (a strategy that backfired when the war dragged on for the remainder of his presidency).

Democratic nominee Barack Obama exhibited similar showmanship in the **Campaign of 2008**, staging several campaign appearances with an eye toward the photographs they would generate. In St. Louis, Obama spoke to a crowd of one hundred thousand, and the news articles published about the event showed the candidate surrounded by throngs of supporters as far as the eye could see. This reinforced Obama's image as a candidate who was popular with voters, and it also made him appear presidential. A few months earlier, Obama made an appearance at the Brandenburg Gate in Germany, a location normally reserved for heads of state. The photos of Obama surrounded by an enormous crowd of admirers evoked memories of presidents John F. Kennedy and Ronald Reagan, both of whom made major foreign policy statements at the site.

Campaigns micromanage the smallest of details to provide a good photo op. Candidates' ties and suits are selected with an eye toward a favorable contrast with a debate backdrop. Shirtsleeves are rolled up to create an appearance of being hard at work on the campaign trail. Candidates visit schools to be photographed with children, and they visit work sites to be photographed with laborers. Sometimes, even a less-than-flattering image can be exploited to great effect by a campaign, such as in the **Campaign of 1952** when an image of Democrat Adlai Stevenson revealed the hole on the bottom of one of his shoes. The Stevenson campaign early embraced the opportunity to portray its candidate as an average American who wore out the soles of his shoes while he worked tirelessly on the campaign trail.

Every candidate is careful to project the right image, and the photo op is often the cheapest and most effective way of communicating admirable qualities. From photos of a relaxed Kennedy family enjoying each other's company to President Reagan and First Lady Nancy Reagan on horseback, or any given candidate visiting military personnel, volunteering in a soup kitchen, engaging in physical fitness, or simply holding a child, the photographic images can be as effective, perhaps more so, than the most infectious sound bite or appealing catchphrase.

See also Retail Politics

Additional Resource

Hernandez, Debra Gersh. "Improving Election Reporting." *Editor and Publisher* (October 5, 1996): 16–21.

Pocketbook Issue

After World War II, the media began to use the phrase "pocketbook issue" to describe issues that affected the economic well-being of voters. These included unemployment; the cost of food, fuel, and basic necessities; the costs of health care and higher education; and interest rates, which can increase both the cost of living and the cost of doing business (by increasing the price of borrowing). These also include in the postwar years voter concerns over inflation, and subsequently, other issues related to the health of the economy, such as the puzzling stagflation of the 1970s concurrent with the rising cost of energy, and, for example, the housing crisis and debt crises that contributed to the economic stress experienced in 2008–2009. Presidential candidates appreciate these anxieties and are universally inclined to speak to them. Democratic candidate Bill Clinton, campaigning for president in 1992, deftly encapsulated the importance of these kinds of issues to voters with the pithy catch phrase, "It's the economy, stupid."

Doubtless, economic concerns are and always have been important to voters, and both politicians and their consultants as well as journalists and pundits intuitively recognize this and instinctively play to it. However, political scientists are not persuaded that "pocketbook issues," or "pocketbook voting," accurately describes voter behavior when considering economic or financial variables. Generally, political scientists do not include economic issues under a blanket term such as "pocketbook voting"; rather, the term is usually employed as a reference to personal finances. "Sociotropic voting" more aptly encompasses a voter's appreciation of more expansive economic issues and trends, and thus, for political scientists, serves as a more accurate descriptor in allowing for the influence of economic indicators on the voting patterns of individual citizens. When candidate Clinton cheekily observed that "it's the economy, stupid," he was commenting on a sociotropic dynamic, not on a pocketbook anxiety.

Even the dynamics of sociotropic voting are more complex than any summative entry would allow. For example, there are findings suggesting that voters in general, to no fault of their own, aren't really inclined to objectively view the economy or their personal finances, so much of what is described in the media as economic/pocketbook voting is simply routine partisanship and ideologically reflexive behavior. According to political scientist Larry Bartels, people view the economy through a partisan filter—regardless of objective economic conditions. People participating in polls or interviews may tell a pollster or journalist that they're voting for economic reasons, but it is in effect a code for partisan behavior, creating the illusion of pocketbook voting. Those voters who express disappointment with the economy are in reality, according to the findings of Bartels's research, disaffected with a given current administration on partisan, not economic or financial, grounds.

There is more research supportive of findings such as these, findings that reveal an emphasis on "pocketbook" voting to be an exaggeration. In sum, political scientists believe that genuine pocketbook voting is rare. While voters may have intimate knowledge of the decline or expansion of their personal finances, there is little empirical evidence to support the notion that these finances contribute to their choice of a presidential candidate. The available data suggests that voters are far more responsive to national economic conditions than to personal ones. In particular, men are more likely than women to vote on the basis of their personal finances; women are more likely than men to evaluate the condition of the nation as a whole when casting their ballot. Indeed, with a few exceptions, the preponderance of the research suggests that pocketbook voting is not the primary influence in people's decision making. Some studies find that both factors contribute, but pocketbook variables are always far weaker than sociotropic ones. However, some researchers argue that the true effects of pocketbook voting may be underestimated. Nevertheless, the most conclusive and decisive evidence still supports the sociotropic model.

See also Bread-and-Butter Issues; Prosperity Issue

Additional Resources

Bartels, Larry. "Partisanship and Voting Behavior, 1952–1996." *American Journal of Political Science* 44 no. 1 (January 2000): 35–50.

Erikson, Robert S., Michael B. Mackuen, and James A. Stimson. *The Macro Polity.* New York: Cambridge University Press, 2002.

Eulau, Heinz, and Michael Lewis-Beck, eds. *Economic Conditions and Electoral Outcomes: The United States and Western Europe.* New York: Algora Publishing, 1985.

Kiewiet, D. Roderick. *Microeconomics and Micropolitics: Electoral Effects of Economic Issues.* Chicago: University of Chicago Press, 1983.

Norpoth, Helmut, Jean-Dominique Lafay, and Michael S. Lewis-Beck, eds. *Economics and Politics: The Calculus of Support.* Ann Arbor: University of Michigan Press, 1991.

Tufte, Edward R. *Political Control of the Economy.* Princeton, NJ: Princeton University Press, 1980.

Political Ads

The **Campaign of 1952** marked the beginning of the use of television to broadcast presidential campaign ads. From the **Campaign of 1924** through the **Campaign of 1948**, presidential campaigns made extensive use of print media and radio to deliver campaign messages to millions of voters in their own homes. Radio ads typically consisted of half-hour talks by candidates, paid for by political campaigns. Following this practice, the majority of television ads broadcast in 1952 were half-hour speeches as well. It did not take long for campaign strategists to realize that this tactic not only was boring for viewers but also failed to capitalize on the persuasive potential of visual imagery. Campaign managers sought out advice from Madison Avenue and began to create thirty-second television spot ads for political candidates that employed the same basic principles that were also being used to sell consumers laundry soap and other household products.

The Republican ads in support of their nominee, General Dwight Eisenhower, proved particularly effective. Themes such as "I Like Ike" and "Eisenhower Answers America" were catchy and helped to humanize Eisenhower in the minds of the voters. In the years that followed, spot ads became an integral part of the presidential campaign process. Campaigns produced biographical ads to introduce candidates to prospective voters and to highlight a candidate's qualifications for holding higher office. Issue ads were produced to familiarize voters with a candidate's positions on important public policy matters, and they also helped campaigns point out flaws in their opponents' proposals. Campaigns also created testimonial ads in which well-known public officials and entertainment celebrities endorsed candidates. Campaigns continued to broadcast important campaign speeches by their candidates as well, although over time, these have been reduced to short clips and sound bites. While the early years of spot ads tended to be primarily positive in nature, over time, spot ads have become increasingly centered on criticism of opponents. Contemporary ads that are primarily positive in nature tend to be funded by the campaigns of political candidates. Ads that are more negative in tone are more likely to emanate from political parties or **independent advocacy groups**.

One of the most notorious negative ads was also one of the earliest. Incumbent president Lyndon Johnson's campaign sought to portray Republican nominee Barry Goldwater as an extremist in the **Campaign of 1964**. They crafted the **"Daisy Girl" campaign ad** to suggest to voters that Goldwater might have an itchy nuclear trigger finger and could not be trusted to keep the peace between the United States and the Soviet Union. While the "Daisy Girl" ad was broadcast only once, on September 7, 1964, it received extensive news coverage, and to this day, most Americans have had an opportunity to view this ad. In modern terms, the

"Daisy Girl" ad "went viral," which is undoubtedly one of the reasons why provocative and controversial negative ads continue to be a feature of modern political campaigns.

Negative ads often accuse candidates of changing their position on an issue for political gain, playing to the crowd by flip-flopping, and being more concerned with polling figures than with principle or policy, thus implying that the candidate cannot be trusted to keep his or her campaign promises once elected. Alternatively, an ad may attempt to link a candidate with an unpopular political figure, producing an effect of guilt by association. Negative ads often attempt to induce a sense of fear in the viewer, not only by implying catastrophic outcomes if a candidate were to be elected, but also by enhancing the message with black-and-white imagery and ominous music. Candidates with previous electoral experience can expect to find themselves criticized for policy failures (and candidates who lack previous experience in office can expect to find themselves criticized for their inexperience). Ads that compare a candidate with the opponent on a series of policy issues are common; such ads generally attempt to highlight favorable elements of one candidate's experience while at the same time attacking the record of the opponent.

The trend over time has been toward an increased use of negative ads of all types. The Wesleyan Media Project conducted a series of studies on the **Campaign of 2012**. In its examination of the first three weeks of October, for example, it found that 73.3 percent of Obama's ads were negative (they only contained a critique of Romney), and another 20.3 percent were contrast ads (where Obama was contrasted with Romney). Only 6.3 percent of Obama's ads during this period were positive. Romney had more positive ads during this time—11.9 percent of his ads only mentioned his candidacy, 51.1 percent of Romney's ads contrasted his candidacy with Obama's, and 36 percent were purely negative. Of groups promoting the Democratic candidate, 88.7 percent of ads were purely negative, and of groups promoting the Republican candidate, 95.2 percent were purely negative, suggesting that spending by outside groups is focused on attack ads rather than on the promotion of a candidate.

During this same three-week period in the **Campaign of 2008**, Obama's campaign was far more positive, running 37 percent of ads that were solely positive, and far less negative, running 43.2 percent of ads that were purely negative. Compared to Mitt Romney four years later, John McCain ran a similar amount of purely negative ads in 2008 (49.2%) and more positive ads than Romney (24%). In the **Campaign of 2004**, however, the picture was a bit different, most notably because of striking asymmetries in how the candidates chose their strategies. In the first three weeks of October, 55.4 percent of George W. Bush's ads were strictly negative, while only 2.7 percent of John Kerry's were. A surprising 55.8 percent of Kerry's ads were wholly positive, while only 27.4 percent of Bush's were.

The Wesleyan Media Project also noted that as presidential campaign ads have become more negative, so too have the negative emotions associated with these ads. During a three-week October interval in the Campaign of 2012, the project noted that 86.1 percent of pro-Romney ads and 70 percent of pro-Obama ads relied on anger (numbers that went up for the pro-Romney ads as the campaign progressed). The second most common emotion elicited in a pro-Romney ad was fear, which the project noted in 36 percent of ads. In the case of Obama, the second most common emotion was sadness, present in 47.3 percent of ads. Emotions like enthusiasm were evident in approximately a quarter of ads favoring each candidate, while other positive emotions, such as pride, were even more rare.

Critics of negative campaigning argue that the increased use of negative ads has produced a general public disaffection with politics and politicians. On the other hand, defenders of negative campaigning argue that there is nothing inappropriate about a political campaign revealing the questionable record of an opponent or the inconsistent positions taken by a candidate. According to this line of reasoning, negative campaigning provides voters with essential information about a candidate's shortcomings.

In the aftermath of the *Citizens United* decision, the number of actors involved in the funding and broadcasting of political ads has proliferated, and so too have the places and manner of dissemination of these ads. Radio, broadcast television, billboards, and print media (newspapers and magazines) remain staples in the world of campaign advertising, but they have been joined by cable television, Internet ads, YouTube videos, and even video game billboards as candidates and advocacy groups seek out more avenues for disseminating their messages.

See also MoveOn; Negative Campaigning; Paid Media; Swift Boating

Additional Resources

Ansolabehere, Stephen, and Shanto Iyenger. *Going Negative: How Attack Ads Shrink and Polarize the Electorate.* New York: Free Press, 1995.

Buell, Emmett H., and Lee Sigelman. *Attack Politics: Negativity in Presidential Campaigns since 1960.* Lawrence: University of Kansas Press, 2008.

David, Mark. *Going Dirty: The Art of Negative Campaigning.* Lanham, MD: Rowman & Littlefield, 2009.

Geer, John G. *In Defense of Negativity: Attack Ads in Presidential Campaigns.* Chicago: University of Chicago Press, 2006.

Jamieson, Kathleen Hall. *Packaging the Presidency: A History and Criticism of Presidential Campaign Advertising.* New York: Oxford University Press, 1996.

The Living Room Candidate. Presidential Campaign Commercials 1952–2008. http://www.livingroomcandidate.org. Accessed October 15, 2015.

Patterson, Thomas E. *Out of Order.* New York: Knopf, 1993.

Wesleyan Media Project. "2012 Shatters 2004 and 2008 Records for Total Ads Aired." http://mediaproject.wesleyan.edu/releases/2012-shatters-2004-and-2008-records-for -total-ads-aired/. Accessed October 15, 2015.

West, Darrell W. *Air Wars: Television Advertising in Election Campaigns, 1952–2000.* Washington, DC: Congressional Quarterly, 2001.

Poll-Driven Campaign

By the 1970s, advances in polling technology permitted presidential campaigns to gain a better understanding of the impact of specific issues on smaller segments of the electorate, originating with Nixon's in-house team of pollsters hired to gauge the public mood on the issues of the day, directed by Professor David Derge. Not surprisingly, instead of developing a campaign message to appeal to the widest cross-section of the electorate, campaigns developed the ability to develop tailored messages for specific segments of the electorate. By the 1980s, the proliferation of polls, particularly those run by media organizations, placed presidential campaigns in a difficult situation. Moreover, the establishment of the Cable News Network (CNN) gave birth to the **twenty-four-hour news cycle**. The constant reporting of frequently conducted polls that ensued meant that candidates, to maximize their standing in the polls, had to develop strategies to quickly respond to fluctuations in the polls.

During the **Campaign of 1988**, polls showed Republican nominee George H. W. Bush behind Democratic nominee Michael Dukakis by double digits by midsummer. Many political experts believed Dukakis would have little difficulty defeating Bush in November. Yet by early September 1988, Dukakis found himself running neck and neck with Bush, and by early October, Dukakis had fallen behind. Between July and October 1988, the Bush campaign had launched a massive, **wedge issue**-focused media campaign that attacked Dukakis for his support for a prison furlough program, painted Dukakis as unpatriotic for opposing a law requiring public school students to say the Pledge of Allegiance, and characterized him as anti-environment for the pollution in Boston Harbor that persisted while Dukakis was governor of Massachusetts. Even though many political pundits did not regard these issues as particularly important to the future of the country, they proved remarkably effective in influencing public opinion.

During the **Campaign of 2000**, Republican George W. Bush and Democratic nominee Al Gore were running neck and neck in the polls throughout the race. Neither the Bush campaign nor the Gore campaign proved successful in identifying a wedge issue that had the ability to move poll numbers. During the campaign, for example, Bush attempted to attract moderate voters by expressing his strong support for education reform, and by calling himself "a uniter, not a divider." Yet the polls remained unchanged. The 2000 election ended with Gore winning the popular vote but losing the electoral vote to Bush when the U.S. Supreme Court halted the controversial Florida recount, which effectively awarded Florida's electoral votes, and the White House, to Bush.

During the **Campaigns of 2008 and 2012**, the Democratic presidential nominee, Barack Obama, seldom enjoyed more than a slight lead in national polls. Despite this, Obama managed to win both a majority of the popular vote (the first Democrat to win a popular majority since Jimmy Carter in 1976—President Clinton falling just short of a popular majority in his 1996 reelection—and the first presidential candidate to win a majority of the popular vote in two elections since Ronald Reagan) and a comfortable victory in the Electoral College in both general elections. During the campaign of 2012, Republican contenders for their party's nomination held substantial leads in national polls prior to the first caucuses and primaries, dissonant to the final outcome.

While polls continue to command the attention of serious presidential candidates, some campaigns are going still further, supplementing what the polls reveal with other sources of data by harvesting data on other variables within the electorate, such as consumer habits. According to recent reports, the campaign efforts of Republican senator Ted Cruz are attempting to tune into a more varied and expansive pool of data, and it is unlikely that this is a unique example. However, as Eitan Hersh, in a Monkey Cage interview with fellow political scientist John Sides, has explained, reliance on data beyond the actual polling numbers is unwarranted given the complex nature of the data gathered, which may obscure voter motivation as easily as reveal it. Critics of poll-driven campaigns argue that it leads to campaigns focusing on issues able to attract key voting blocs rather than dealing with the most pressing domestic and international problems facing the country. Some political analysts blame the press for creating pressure on political candidates to be responsive to the polls. They point out that instead of focusing on the differences in issue positions between the candidates, media coverage focuses almost exclusively on the standing of presidential campaigns in the polls.

See also Horse-Race Campaign Coverage; Microtargeting

Additional Resources

Getlin, Josh. "Regarding Media: For Whom the Polls Toll—The Candidate Who's Trailing." *Los Angeles Times*, September 18, 2000, p. E1.

Hersh, Eitan. *Hacking the Electorate: How Campaigns Perceive Voters*. Cambridge: Cambridge University Press, 2015.

Patterson, Thomas. *Out of Order*. New York: Knopf, 1993.

Sides, John. "The Real Story about How Data-Driven Campaigns Target Voters." Monkey Cage. http://www.washingtonpost.com/blogs/monkey-cage/wp/2015/07/01/. Accessed September 25, 2015.

Poll of Polls

Beginning in the **Campaign of 2004**, and appearing to an even greater extent in the **Campaign of 2008**, were numerous, almost daily public opinion polls conducted by assorted news organizations, think tanks, and academic institutions. Many news organizations chose to summarize this plethora of polls by simply averaging them (in some cases, regardless of differences in sampling techniques and margins of error). News organizations such as CNN went as far as to claim that their averaging process removed all sampling error (which it did not). All polling contains error; poll results may vary due to systematic sampling bias or random sampling error. In both 2004 and 2008, polling firms varied greatly in how they measured "likely voters," which also led to differences in predictions and created interpretation problems when different strategies were pooled together to calculate an average result.

Aggregation is most helpful when the polling questions are identical or nearly identical (as is the case with a presidential campaign tracking poll) and when the strategy for measuring likely voters is similar. In such cases, aggregation should tend to lower measurement error, because there are now multiple sample means (rather than a single sample mean) being used to calculate the probable location of the true population mean. This is the theory underlying FiveThirtyEight, a prediction-based blog run by Nate Silver, and Pollster, hosted by the Huffington Post. These polls of polls aggregate all available polls taken during a given time period and assign weights based on factors such as sample size and polling technology used (e.g., whether it is a landline-only poll, whether it is automated or has a live interviewer, whether it is conducted online). In the **Campaign of 2012**, Silver's FiveThirtyEight blog predicted Democratic incumbent Barack Obama to win by a small margin over Republican nominee Mitt Romney because this is what the preponderance of the polls (thus adding up to a sufficient number of electoral votes) were predicting. The only poll that predicted otherwise was Gallup, which predicted a win by Romney. This made the Gallup poll an outlier, relative to the other polls. For Gallup to be correct, one would have to make the assumption that Gallup knew something about the electorate that every other poll did not; that is, that every other poll made a fundamental error, and that Gallup had somehow avoided committing this error. In this scenario, it makes more sense to conclude that Gallup is an outlier because Gallup is the poll that is in error. Statistically, it far likelier that one poll is in error than that all polls except one are in error.

See also Poll-Driven Campaign

Additional Resources

FiveThirtyEight. http://fivethirtyeight.com/.
Pollster, Huffington Post. http://elections.huffingtonpost.com/pollster.

Populists

Populism (and by extension, the term "populist") is a loosely conceived concept that refers to popular political movements that intentionally make direct appeals to the will and needs of "the people" and that usually either accompany a grassroots groundswell or are tied to some broadly based organization. Populist candidates and political movements usually offer pledges to improve the condition of the "common man" or "ordinary" person (e.g., "Everyman," "John Q. Citizen," "average working man/woman," "American wage-earner," "tax-paying citizen," "average Joe," or "Joe Six-Pack"). Populist sentiment generally includes the belief that the people as a whole hold the key to commonsense solutions to our nation's problems. Populist rhetoric often exhibits a pronounced concern for the interests of the working and middle classes (often accompanied by strident criticism of the wealthy class and political and business elites), as well as a tendency to celebrate the means of democracy as an end in itself (with suspicion of anything regarded as "undemocratic"). Populist movements throughout American history have also expressed deep dislike of nearly anything associated with the status quo and, in particular, have been notoriously hostile to what they view as "big government" and "big business." Populism encourages political candidates who promote themselves as "outsiders," and it attracts supporters who are somehow disaffected or existentially frustrated by the attitudes, practices, and outcomes of the established political institutions. Populist movements are a democratic phenomenon and are usually democratic in their objectives, but the latter is not always the case, as mass movements, even well-intentioned ones, are not immune to the temptations that are offered in the pandering of demagogues.

Another common thread in American populist movements has been a vigorous sense of patriotism that is, in almost all cases, rooted in a reverence for an idealized version of the past, when society was marked by achievements made possible by virtuous citizens who were guided by wiser and more genuine political leaders. Driven by an egalitarian impulse, populism in its many variants elevates the "common" person and denigrates any leader or policy that might put the interests of the few before the needs of the nation as a whole. Populism often (but not always) generates charismatic leaders and firebrands who come to embody the movement as a whole, and who serve as a rallying symbol for the people's cause.

In American politics, populist tendencies can be traced back to the American Revolution itself, but it was not until the 1820s that populist themes and attitudes began to influence political institutions. The electoral campaigns and presidency of Andrew Jackson were decidedly populist in much of their rhetoric and symbolism, and the **Campaign of 1840** that brought William Henry Harrison to the White House was won through populist imagery and means. By and large, though, the two major parties (at any given point in American history) have been reticent to fan the flames of populism too eagerly. There are important exceptions (such as the **Campaigns of 1828** and 1840), but as a general rule, the larger and more institutionalized the political party, the less likely it is that a candidate with genuine populist credentials and proclivities will receive the support of that party's leadership. However, there have been periods in American history when a major party has sought to embrace a populist movement.

A series of economic crises in the latter half of the nineteenth century sparked a number of radical agrarian groups that sought to limit the powers of big banks and the powerful manufacturing sector of the economy and to redistribute the nation's wealth in a more equitable fashion. As part of this movement, the People's Party (also referred to as the Populists) was formed during the late 1880s/early 1890s to campaign on behalf of the political interests of these groups. In the **Campaign of 1892**, People's Party nominee James Weaver gathered over one million popular votes and twenty-two Electoral College votes (winning Colorado, Idaho, Kansas, Nevada, and North Dakota, and receiving a single electoral vote from Oregon). This was a near-record performance for a third party in a presidential election. While, realistically, the People's Party posed no serious electoral threat to the two major parties, it did help to change the political mood in the country. Both the Democrats and the Republicans included more populist, progressive candidates in their parties, and in the **Campaign of 1896**, a skilled orator and champion of the people, William Jennings Bryan (known as "the Great Commoner"), became the Democratic Party's nominee for the presidency. Bryan eventually lost, but both his nomination and the tenor of his campaign reflected the public's interest in, and desire for, a more populist politics, both in style and substance, thus influencing both major parties.

Populism would flow into the progressivism of the latter part of the nineteenth century and early decades of the twentieth century, continuing to influence wings within both parties. Theodore Roosevelt's Bull Moose candidacy in the **Campaign of 1912**, under the banner of the (soon to be short-lived) Progressive Party, can be considered populist in its approach and demeanor. Populist themes and impulses would be seen in other campaigns in the twentieth century as well, notably in: the **Campaign of 1936**, where Franklin Delano Roosevelt's reaffirmation of his New Deal programs was markedly progressive and laced with a subdued populism; the **Campaign of 1948**, where incumbent president Truman's hard-charging whistle-stop stump speeches and Strom Thurmond's Dixiecrat revolt both exhibited populist strains; the **Campaign of 1968**, where Democratic hopeful Robert Kennedy's doomed campaign and George Wallace's pro-segregation American Party campaign were decidedly populist, with Kennedy's also containing strains of progressivism; the **Campaign of 1972**, where Democratic nominee George McGovern's campaign sought to be the voice of the disenfranchised and the downtrodden; the **Campaign of 1992**, where Republican challenger Pat Buchanan practiced "pitchfork populism" and independent candidate H. Ross Perot campaigned on "common-sense" populism; and the **Campaign of 2004**, where Democratic hopeful Howard Dean introduced an Internet version of populism. Of these, the Campaign of 1992 is of particular interest, in that it nicely illustrates the diversity of populist movements and campaigns. Buchanan's populism was conservative in tone, but it differed from the paleoconservatism that has generally viewed populist appeals as a manipulative and dangerous form of political pandering. Rather, Buchanan's approach to conservatism was infused with a mission to lead the people back to their moral foundations, it contained an emotional appeal rooted in patriotism, and it expressed an abiding discontent with a failed political and economic system that betrayed the purer values of the nation's founding. The Perot campaign, on the other hand, conveyed a pragmatic, "can-do" (and non-ideological) populism, one that scolded the established parties for their selfish incompetence and promised a fresh, third way that would find solutions to the nation's problems outside of the usual "politics-as-usual" lip service. Both Buchanan and Perot portrayed themselves and their causes as coming directly from the people themselves, and both minced no words when it came to biting criticisms of the current political establishment.

More recently, the Tea Party movement seems designed to appeal to populist impulses within the electorate, and both its style and agenda appear to exhibit many populist aspects as well. However, the extent of the Tea Party's core following may not be sufficient to consider it a genuine populist movement. Some would argue that the Tea Party is, in fact, the latest incarnation of American populism, reflected in a tide of grassroots support rising up against the evils of a morally bankrupt and quasi-socialist political establishment. Others argue that while the Tea Party movement may appear to contain some populist traits, upon closer examination, it is a largely media-driven movement with an agenda far too narrow and extreme to appeal to a wider political base. Political scientists Robert Putnam and James E. Campbell find that Tea Party support is most strongly linked with conservatism on social issues, and with a strong desire to see a greater level of religion in government, rather than antigovernment or anti-taxation sentiment. Unlike other populist movements, Tea Party supporters seek to pare down government support for the economically disadvantaged, and their focus is more on individual rights than on political or economic equality. Whether the Tea Party is truly a new form of American populism, or simply an artificial phenomenon sustained by the press, is a question that remains unanswered. There is some evidence that the Tea Party faction has lost some of the momentum it enjoyed in the 2010 midterm elections, but the exact impact that it may have on the 2016 GOP nomination process is as yet unclear. Nevertheless, from a review of recent campaign rhetoric among the current GOP field, Tea Party values and concerns appear to maintain their influence within the party as a whole, even though that influence may be gradually waning when compared to the 2010 and 2012 campaigns.

One might argue that populist impulses explain the current popularity of Donald Trump in his attempt to carry the 2016 Republican standard. Even though Mr. Trump does not meet the typical populist profile owing to his own abundant personal wealth, his message, claims, attitude, and demeanor pluck at those notes resembling populist chords. More substantively, Democratic candidate and Vermont senator Bernie Sanders epitomizes, at least in his rhetoric but also on his record, the anti-establishment, working-class, and grassroots themes that are characteristic of populist movements. As of this writing, both Mr. Trump and Sen. Sanders have attracted a good deal of attention from the media, as well as from a noticeable segment of the voting population; whether or not these candidates can build on this publicity and sustain it among likely voters as the primary and caucus season draws closer remains to be determined, but for the moment, both Mr. Trump and Sen. Sanders evince the ongoing presence of populist qualities and attitudes within the American electorate.

Additional Resources

Kazin, Michael. *The Populist Persuasion: An American History*. Ithaca, NY: Cornell University Press, 1998.

Kuzminksi, Adrian. *Fixing the System: A History of Populism, Ancient and Modern*. New York: Continuum, 2008.

McMath, Robert C., Jr. *American Populism: A Social History, 1877–1898*. New York: Hill & Wang, 1993.

Postel, Charles, *The Populist Vision*. Oxford: Oxford University Press, 2009.

Poverty Issue. *See* Economic Inequality Issue

Presidential Coattails

Presidential elections usually have far broader consequences than simply determining who will serve (or continue to serve) as the nation's chief executive. In many elections, candidates elected to other political offices, such as the House of

Representatives and the Senate, and even positions in state governments, can attribute their victory in part to the outcome of the presidential election. This is referred to as "riding the president's coattails" into office, or the "coattail effect." One of the best examples of the coattail effect appears in the **Campaign of 1964**, when Democratic incumbent Lyndon Johnson's landslide victory was accompanied by a large number of Democrats elected to the 89th Congress. In the **Campaign of 1980**, twelve Senate Democrats lost their seats to Republicans who rode into office on Republican nominee Ronald Reagan's coattails. Reagan's coattails in 1980 were particularly notable because they produced the first Republican majority in the Senate since 1954 (the midterm in President Eisenhower's first term in office).

Democratic nominee Barack Obama's coattails in the **Campaign of 2008** are regarded as the most recent example of this phenomenon, although some pundits view Obama's coattails as due, in part, to the drag of an unpopular Bush presidency rather than an expression of affirmation for the Obama candidacy. Regardless of the reason, the outcome of the 2008 congressional elections provided the new president with a comfortable majority in Congress, at least at the beginning of his term, which enabled Obama to gain the passage of some major congressional legislation, including the stimulus bill, health care reform, and the elimination of the military's "don't ask, don't tell" policy for gay service members.

Indeed, it is this political leverage that makes presidential coattails important. All presidents, as a general pattern, enjoy a "honeymoon" period with Congress (although this period may be dwindling in more recent years), during which congressional leadership is accommodating in passing key elements of the new president's agenda. This honeymoon period will be longer and more fruitful if a new president comes into office with strong support from his or her own party in Congress. If a new president helps to deliver a large congressional majority for his or her party, or dramatically expands the size of an existing majority, Congress is more likely to pursue a legislative agenda that reflects the president's policy goals.

A "negative coattails" effect has also been described; in particular, Jimmy Carter received fewer votes in his quest for the presidency in the **Campaign of 1976** than the total number of votes cast for Democratic candidates in Congress. Thus, it seems likely that Democrats in Congress sustained their majority without any boost from Carter's victory. This may explain, in some part, why Carter was not particularly successful in persuading Democrats in Congress to support his proposed policies. George W. Bush also won the White House absent any presidential coattails in the **Campaign of 2000**; however, this election is unique in that Democratic nominee Al Gore was the winner of the popular vote, and thus it may be more accurately described as Gore's coattails that helped to pull Democrats into Congress that year.

During the 1980s and 1990s, presidential coattails seemed to be dwindling in size. Political scientists have speculated that much of this effect may be due to the rise of split-ticket voting during this era, and to declining levels of political partisanship. In more recent elections, coattails have once again lengthened, coinciding with a decline in split-ticket voting and a resurgence in political partisanship among the electorate. In general, the more Americans are willing to vote a straight party ticket based on the top of the ticket, the more powerful the coattail effect will be. Over time, ballot design and newer voting machine technology have made it increasingly difficult for voters to cast a straight party ticket simply by checking a single box or pulling a single lever. While this may dampen the coattail effect, recent elections appear to indicate that it is nevertheless alive and well.

See also Surge and Decline Theory

Additional Resources

Campbell, James E., and Joe A. Summers. "Presidential Coattails in Senate Elections." *American Political Science Review* 84, no. 2 (June 1990): 513–524.

Cook, Rhodes. "Obama and the Redefinition of Presidential Coattails." Rasmussen Reports, April 17, 2009.

Edwards, George C., III. "The Impact of Presidential Coattails on Outcomes of Congressional Elections." *American Politics Research* 7, no. 1 (January 1979): 94–108.

Presidential Debates

While Americans often associate political debates with the advent of television, what may be the most celebrated of all debates occurred long before this era, and while it was not a debate between presidential candidates, it is now meaningful to us, in part because the two participants would soon become rival candidates in the subsequent presidential campaign, and in a sense, even though they were not running for president at the time they met in debate, it is widely believed that they were even then preparing themselves for that larger stage. It was during the 1858 Senate race in Illinois when Republican Senate nominee Abraham Lincoln engaged in a series of seven debates against Democratic incumbent senator Stephen Douglas—prefiguring their contest for the White House two years later. These debates took place in congressional districts around their home state, and the candidates debated such wide-ranging and substantively critical topics as the abolition of slavery and the Mexican-American War. The format was unusual, involving extended and erudite speeches combined with each candidate posing several questions to the other. While Lincoln lost his race for the Senate to Douglas, the popularity he gained throughout the North during these debates effectively launched his successful run for the presidency two years later, with Douglas this time on the losing end.

Between the election of George Washington in 1788 and the latter half of the twentieth century, no debate was held between presidential candidates from the major parties. Candidates and their surrogates and operatives would rhetorically respond to each other, but from the Washington administration through the Eisenhower administration, there was no event in which the two major candidates joined in formal debate on the same stage or in the same forum. In the modern era, the first presidential debate, which happened to be nationally televised, was held during the **Campaign of 1960**, pitting Massachusetts senator John F. Kennedy against incumbent vice president Richard M. Nixon. On September 26, 1960, Nixon and Kennedy faced each other in the studios of station WBBM in Chicago, Illinois. *CBS News* reporter Howard K. Smith moderated the debate. Sixty-six million viewers tuned in to watch the candidates speak. Democratic nominee Kennedy appeared youthful and healthy, projecting a relaxed demeanor in front of the camera. His manner was confident and knowledgeable, and his personal charm was evident to those who viewed the event on their television screens. Most importantly, Senator Kennedy seemed at ease answering difficult questions regarding foreign and domestic policies. Prior to the debate, political observers had wondered whether the young senator's political inexperience might prove a liability. Equally important, Kennedy used the forum as a means to allay concerns that as a Roman Catholic, he would be obligated to follow the decrees of the pope— effectively, as the suspicion presumed without evidence, giving the Vatican control of the White House.

Exhausted by a long campaign tour and recovering from a recent illness, Vice President Nixon was tired, and he looked it; he was drawn and pale in comparison to Kennedy, with perspiration clearly visible on his forehead throughout the debate, and an unflattering five o'clock shadow and shifting eye movements caused the vice president's aspect to appear vaguely sinister. It did not help that the vice president allowed only minimal application of ineffective makeup to his ashen, whisker-stubbled, and wearied visage prior to the broadcast; that and the heat from glaring studio lights cast a most unflattering image for the Republican hopeful, an image that would be received over millions of televisions nationwide. While both candidates were younger than the typical presidential candidate—at the time Sen. Kennedy was forty-three and Vice President Nixon was forty-seven—the vice president did not exude the same youthful vibrancy exhibited by his Democratic rival. And, while both candidates were well prepared and responded equally with intelligence and confidence, in the end, Senator Kennedy prevailed in the minds of the majority of those who watched the first debate on television, owing to the striking difference in the images they projected. Interestingly, over the years a stubbornly popular folklore has grown around claims that the majority of those who listened to the debate on the radio either considered Nixon's the better performance, or at least concluded that the outcome was even between the two candidates. According to a 1987 study by scholars David Vancell and Sue Pendell, this familiar and universally accepted account is in reality a potent and yet ultimately anecdotal assessment, there being little empirical evidence to support the conclusion that television helped Kennedy while radio either favored Nixon or formed the impression that the two competitors had debated to a draw. There is only one poll conducted after the debate that supports this, a poll in which the television audience did in fact significantly prefer Sen. Kennedy while a radio audience overwhelmingly favored Nixon, but there is little evidence beyond that. Be that as it may, it is a fact that Sen. Kennedy's performance in the debate, any comparison to the vice president aside, did boost his image both in the media and among the electorate, and it's also reasonable to conclude that the debate did not help the vice president. In any event, after the debate the Kennedy campaign was buoyed, and Nixon himself felt disappointed and deflated, at least temporarily. Most importantly, it is this first debate that loomed the largest in importance as the campaign proceeded. Even though three more debates between Kennedy and Nixon followed, and Nixon actually performed better than Kennedy in at least one of those debates and held his own in the others, this first debate contrasting the vigorous Democrat against the haggard Republican—and which enjoyed the highest viewer ratings and stimulated the most conversation and analysis—had the biggest impact and to this day remains one of the more memorable moments in the history of presidential debates. It certainly is the one debate that people still discuss, even though Vice President Nixon managed to win significant debating points in the following debates, especially through his tough response to the serious conflict in East Asia over the disputed islands of Quemoy and Matsu, a response that when contrasted to Senator Kennedy's more hesitant approach to the crisis made the senator, perhaps unfairly, appear green and weak in his attitude toward Cold War enemies such as Mao's China. And yet the first debate is the one that is more consistently remembered as an important Kennedy triumph and, again unfairly, as a setback for Nixon. Kennedy went on to narrowly defeat Nixon in both the popular and Electoral College vote in what remains the closest election in recent history.

Sixteen years would pass before the next presidential candidate debate. In that long interim, President Lyndon Johnson, during the **Campaign of 1964**, had refused to give the Republican nominee, Arizona senator Barry Goldwater, a platform that would guarantee him equal time to explain his conservative positions and ideas. Moreover, President Johnson realized that a debate would more likely hurt than help, as he himself had been impressed by images of the first Kennedy-Nixon debate, and he was not willing to put himself in a position in which the television glare might convey the wrong persona. The president held a solid lead in the polls over his Republican rival, and a debate could risk at least some of that lead.

Still feeling burned by the 1960 debates, Republican nominee and front-runner Richard Nixon refused to debate Democratic nominee and incumbent vice president Hubert Humphrey or the American Independent Party candidate, Alabama governor George Wallace, during the **Campaign of 1968**. Far ahead in the polls, President Richard Nixon saw no strategic or tactical advantage in debating Democratic nominee George McGovern during the **Campaign of 1972**.

Nixon's resignation in 1974 as a result of the Watergate scandal (and the resignation of his initial running mate, Spiro Agnew, after he was indicted on tax charges) catapulted Michigan representative Gerald Ford into the presidency. Two years later, Ford, the only unelected president in the nation's history (he was neither elected as president nor as vice president), was running for election to a full term, and in doing so he gladly agreed to participate in a series of debates against the Democratic nominee and a comparative newcomer to the national political stage, former Georgia governor Jimmy Carter. These debates were sponsored by the nonpartisan League of Women Voters. Both candidates were heavily dependent on public funding for their election bids, and thus they were eager for whatever free media coverage was available. The most memorable moment in the Ford-Carter debates occurred during the second debate on foreign policy issues. *New York Times* reporter Max Frankel asked Ford a question about the Soviet Union's domination of eastern Europe. To the surprise of everyone watching (including Carter), Ford responded, "There is no Soviet domination of eastern Europe." Ford was then given an opportunity to clarify his remarks, yet he still insisted that the Soviet Union did not dominate Poland, Romania, and Yugoslavia. It took more than a week for the Ford campaign to make an effort to explain Ford's comments. Ford's gaffe taught future presidential candidates an important lesson. Candidates needed to prepare for almost every question and stick carefully to a script when answering debate questions. Similar to Sen. Kennedy in 1960, the 1976 debates helped Carter overcome public doubts over his ability to deal with complex foreign policy and domestic issues. Equally important, Carter was able to convince voters that he looked presidential. Carter went on to narrowly defeat Ford on Election Day.

During the **Campaign of 1980**, President Jimmy Carter, adopting a Rose Garden strategy similar to one that was at least temporarily assumed by his predecessor, President Ford, initially refused to debate the Republican nominee, former actor and former California governor Ronald Reagan, much as President Johnson had refused to debate Sen. Goldwater in 1964. The Carter campaign defended its decision by arguing that President Carter needed to remain in the White House to deal with pressing international and domestic problems, including the ongoing Iran hostage crisis. Carter's strategy backfired; the public came to perceive Carter as a hostage in the White House, the Rose Garden strategy giving the appearance that the president was wary of debating his personable Republican challenger. As the polls tightened between Carter and Reagan, the Carter camp decided that the president had no choice but to debate former governor Reagan. Reagan had already debated independent candidate John Anderson (a moderate Republican who had lost his party's nomination to Reagan). Presidential historians credit Reagan's performance in the October 28 debate as crucial to his landslide victory over Carter. Reagan delivered a number of carefully rehearsed sound bites to remind voters of the nation's severe economic problems and the declining standard of living for millions of Americans. Particularly noteworthy was the question Reagan posed to his viewing audience: "Are you better off than you were four years ago?"—a line that instantly defined the governor's challenge to the incumbent president.

Riding high in the polls and having attained a reputation as the "Great Communicator," President Reagan did not shy away from debating the Democratic nominee, former vice president Walter Mondale, in the **Campaign of 1984**. To the surprise of many observers, Reagan uncharacteristically fared rather poorly in the first debate, looking awkward and uncharacteristically bland. Speculation swirled over whether Reagan's age might be slowing him down. Yet, in the October 21 debate, Reagan returned to form, raising the volume on the famous Reagan charm and brushing aside any doubts about his age by quipping that he would not "exploit, for political purposes, my opponent's youth and inexperience," a stylish moment dispelling any doubts that he had lost his touch with the American people. Vice President Mondale would later reveal that he knew he had lost the election at that exact moment. Reagan would go on to defeat Mondale in what has become (at least for the books, as it currently stands) the last landslide in the chronicle of presidential elections.

During the **Campaign of 1988**, Republican nominee Vice President George H. W. Bush was initially reluctant to debate Democratic nominee and Massachusetts governor Michael Dukakis. By the first debate on September 25, Bush had come back from a double-digit deficit in the polls to hold a small lead over his opponent. Neither Bush nor Dukakis committed any major gaffes during the first debate. By the second debate on October 13, Dukakis found himself trailing in the polls by a significant margin. The Bush campaign had successfully defined Dukakis as yet another Northeastern liberal who was soft on crime, eager to raise taxes and impose new and needless federal regulations, and unrealistic about the motivations of rival leaders abroad. In one of the most controversial questions in presidential debate history, the moderator of the debate, Bernard Shaw of the Cable News Network (CNN), asked Dukakis whether he would still oppose the death penalty if his wife "were raped and murdered," an oblique reference to the Bush campaign's Willie Horton ad. Dukakis responded with a tepid, emotionless, and obviously scripted answer that, while meaning to reflect his long opposition to the death penalty, conveyed the appearance of a bloodless bureaucrat. "No, I don't,

Bernard," the governor responded, "and I think you know that I've opposed the death penalty during all of my life. I don't see any evidence that it's a deterrent, and I think there are better and more effective ways to deal with violent crime. We've done so in my own state. And it's one of the reasons why we have had the biggest drop in crime of any industrial state in America; why we have the lowest murder rate of any industrial state in America." Dukakis's lack of emotion when offered such an intimate hypothetical—the rape and murder of his beloved wife—was not well received by political commentators or the public at large, and it represented one of the low points of the Dukakis campaign.

Not only was it a low point for the governor, but it was also a low point in the history of presidential debating. When one objectively examines the substantive quality of the Kennedy-Nixon debates, as well as the Ford-Carter and Carter-Reagan contests, one is struck by the way in which these debates were largely about issues, policies, and ideas. And while the 1984 debate between President Reagan and his challenger, former vice president Mondale, was defined less by substance and more by personality, for the most part the participants were committed to the issues and their ideas about them. In the 1988 debates, a trend away from substance and toward style seemed to become increasingly evident, to the frustration of the voting public. A question such as the hypothetical one involving the governor's wife would not have been tendered even four years earlier, let alone during the more serious debates between Kennedy and Nixon or, for example, Ford and Carter. Owing to this circumstance, the League of Women Voters withdrew its sponsorship of the final debate of the 1988 campaign, declaring that "the demands of the two campaigns would perpetrate a fraud on the American voter." League president Nancy Neuman noted, "It has become clear to us that the candidates' organizations aim to add debates to their list of campaign-trail charades, devoid of substance, spontaneity, and honest answers to tough questions." In particular, the League objected to the sixteen-page negotiated agreement between the candidates demanding control over questioners, the composition of members of the audience, and access for the press, among other things. The candidates refused to debate under any other conditions, and the League backed out of the debate.

In the aftermath of the League's decision, the major political parties established the nonprofit Commission on Presidential Debates (CPD). Because the major parties control the composition of the CPD, it is not a nonpartisan group. The presence of independent candidate Ross Perot in 1992 created problems for the commission. While they would have liked to exclude Perot, he had strong support in public opinion polls and therefore could not reasonably be excluded. The CPD also made a major change in the format of the debates by permitting citizens in the audience to directly ask the candidates questions in a format known as the "town hall meeting."

The first debate using the town hall meeting format took place on October 15 at the University of Richmond in Virginia. President George H. W. Bush received considerable criticism for appearing bored or distracted, even looking at this watch several times during the debate, giving the appearance that he would rather be somewhere else and was not interested in the questions being posed by the audience. In sharp contrast, Bill Clinton welcomed the opportunity to directly interact with members of the audience, and he demonstrated an ability to identify with their concerns. Perot also made a strong impression in the debate, showing a mastery of information about the budget deficit that helped to increase his standing in the polls. Perot's running mate, Admiral James Stockdale, a highly decorated naval officer and former prisoner of war during the Vietnam War, did not fare as well in the vice presidential debate, unfortunately appearing disoriented, confused, and unfocused. The admiral was certainly out of his element, while his competitors, incumbent vice president Dan Quayle and Tennessee senator Al Gore performed comfortably and confidently.

During the **Campaign of 1996**, Democratic incumbent Bill Clinton debated Republican nominee Bob Dole on two occasions, once with a single moderator and once when citizens directly asked questions of the candidates. Ross Perot, again running as a candidate for the newly created Reform Party, was excluded from the debates and unsuccessfully sued to have the CPD eliminated on the grounds that as the sole vehicle for the debates, it was inherently biased against third parties. Both Clinton and Dole were well informed and able to express their ideas and experiences with confidence. The debates had little effect on the larger campaign.

During the **Campaign of 2000**, once again, a popular third-party candidate (Green Party nominee Ralph Nader) was excluded from the debates. By this time, the CPD had formulated specific criteria to limit third-party participation, including requiring that candidates have a reasonable chance at earning the 270 electoral votes needed to win the presidency, and that they demonstrate (through at least five independent national opinion polls) public support of at least 15 percent of the electorate. Democratic nominee and incumbent vice president Al Gore faced the Republican nominee, Texas governor George W. Bush, in three separate debates. Prior to the October 3 debate, Gore held an eight-point lead in the polls. However, during the debate Vice President Gore sighed audibly at several points, sighs that were at times punctuated by the vice president rolling his eyes (which he later claimed was the result of an asthma attack) in response to comments made by his opponent, thus creating a poor impression of a bored, self-satisfied, and conceited know-it-all, shaking his head as his opponent spoke, and at times he appeared to sneer at some of the governor's comments. This in turn helped Gov. Bush, who was able to convince television viewers that he was engaged and enthusiastic about the office of the presidency, someone who was both competent and down-to-earth in his sensibilities. The vice president was certainly capable, but his smug debate performance obscured his genuine abilities, considerable experience, and impressive credentials behind a persona that conveyed a haughty, pretentious posture. Additionally, the vice president at one point actually left his lectern and approached the governor as he was answering a question; Bush, upon noticing the vice president approaching him, nodded reflexively and continued speaking. This was an obvious attempt on the part of the vice president to look assertive, and it may even have been a subconscious effort at intimidation. In the moment it had the effect of making Gore look aggressive and discourteous, and it won some sympathy for Bush, who managed the incident with a noticeable degree of grace. Post-debate polls showed the gap between Gore and Bush narrowing. Viewership for the final two debates dropped sharply, suggesting that voters did not feel that additional useful information would be gleaned from the later debates. The vice presidential debate between Democrat Joe Lieberman and Republican Dick Cheney focused on foreign policy, an area of strength for both candidates, and the collegial atmosphere created by the candidates and their knowledgeable responses were assets for both of their running mates, who were generally perceived to be less experienced in this area. Vice presidential debates are typically, and understandably, less interesting; but in this case both Liebermann and Cheney appeared (at least at this point in time) more appealing than their running mates at the top of the ticket.

During the **Campaign of 2004**, very little of note occurred during the debates of Republican incumbent George W. Bush and Democratic nominee Senator John Kerry. Both candidates were careful not to stray from well-crafted responses, and they broke little new ground. Once again, Mr. Nader, mounting another third-party bid for the White House, was excluded from participating in the debates and was even arrested and removed from the audience, despite possessing a ticket to attend (for which he later sued).

In the **Campaign of 2008**, the presidential debates between Democratic nominee Senator Barack Obama and Republican nominee Senator John McCain probably benefited Obama far more than his opponent, in that they provided the younger Obama with an opportunity to demonstrate his intellect, confidence, and presidential demeanor to the general public. McCain made no substantive gaffes; rather, he simply stood to benefit less, as voters were already familiar with his background from his long time in the Senate and his earlier, unsuccessful run for the Republican nomination for president in 2000. McCain was already a known (and well-respected) quantity. However, at one point McCain inexplicably wandered around the stage, a lapse in form that was noticed and, predictably, lampooned.

The most eventful debate of the Campaign of 2008, and also the most viewed, involved the vice presidential candidates Delaware senator Joe Biden and Alaska governor Sarah Palin. Gov. Palin's political experience prior to the debate consisted of her two years in Alaska's governor's mansion and her previous time spent as mayor of the tiny Alaska town of Wasilla. She was a complete political unknown prior to being tapped by the McCain campaign. Sen. Biden, on the other hand, had a long career in the Senate and had run in the primaries against Sen. Obama and Sen. Hillary Clinton; so, like McCain, he was a known quantity. Biden was placed in a difficult position—should he respond to the barrage of attacks delivered by Palin, or would it look more dignified to ignore them? Palin tended to avoid the questions asked by the moderator, instead giving folksy, scripted replies on themes that she wanted to emphasize. At one point, Palin used a thinly veiled reference to President Ronald Reagan when she responded to a comment by Biden by saying, "There you go again, Joe." On several occasions, Palin winked at the camera. Palin explained her role in the campaign in a pitch to Middle America: "One thing that Americans do at this time, also, though, is let's commit ourselves just every day [to the] American people, Joe Six-Pack, hockey moms across the nation, I think we need to band together and say never again. Never will we be exploited and taken advantage of again by those who are managing our money and loaning us these dollars." The debate appeared to be a draw; pundits were wondering if Palin would commit a major mistake, and she did not, largely because she relied on rehearsed answers to questions that were not necessarily asked of her. Obama went on to easily defeat McCain, in large part because voters blamed the Republicans for the poor state of the economy. Palin's role is more controversial. Some analysts argue that she was critical in mobilizing the evangelical Christian base of the party, who tended to be lukewarm about McCain. Others note that Republican voter turnout overall was down in 2008, potentially because some Republicans found McCain's choice of a running mate too unattractive. Several notable conservatives, including Christopher Buckley, Andrew Sullivan, John Dean, and Colin Powell, expressed support for Obama in 2008, and many of these individuals were critical of the selection of Palin.

Some excitement was generated in the 2012 campaign season debates between incumbent president Obama and the Republican nominee, former Massachusetts governor Mitt Romney. Leading his challenger in the polls going into the first debate in Denver, the president was caught off guard and unprepared as Gov. Romney managed to step up and win the evening. In retrospect, both candidates managed to substantively address issues and policy differences, and compared to some of the presidential debates in the recent past, they were able to sustain their discussion of policy in an intelligent manner. Nevertheless, the president was not himself; in past debates he was fluid and confident, but in this debate he seemed halting and somewhat edgy, even slightly irritable. According to an account detailed by Sides and Vavreck in *The Gamble*, during the post-debate analysis:

A consensus quickly developed in the news media that Romney had not only won the debate but completely dominated. The *National Journal's* Ron

Fournier said that Obama was "peeved and flat" while Romney was "personable and funny, and relentlessly on the attack." *Washington Post* reporters David Nakamura and Philip Rucker perceived Romney's victory in spin-room body language: Republicans like Marco Rubio "paraded triumphantly" while Obama's advisor David Plouffe looked "tired and uncertain" and needed a "handler" to guide him into the room. Andrew Sullivan of the *Daily Beast* [described] Obama's performance [as] "meandering, weak, professorial arguments . . . effete, wonkish lectures." . . . MSNBC's Chris Matthews wailed, "Where was Obama tonight?" And "What was he doing tonight?"

Romney's strong performance, combined with the president's "professorial" and "flat" presentation, seemed to give new life to the Republican effort, and a noticeable blip in the governor's favor did appear in the polls subsequent to the Denver debate, a post-debate bump for Romney that caused alarm for many in the Obama camp. While the polls did indicate that the Romney campaign was injected with new energy, in due course those numbers began to shift downward, the bump receding as the second debate approached, a debate wherein the president reasserted himself. Perhaps drawing upon renewed confidence owing to recent favorable news about the unemployment rate, and perhaps simply determined to answer more forthrightly, the president was more energetic and assertive throughout the town hall forum in the second round. The governor also had his better moments, but for the most part it appeared that the president came away with at best a narrow victory and at worst a draw, thus regaining some ground lost in the first debate. By the third debate, which concentrated on foreign policy, the president was stronger still, with post-debate polls indicating a clear victory for Obama. The vice presidential debate, while lively, had little effect in the polls, but it did restore confidence among Democrats due to Vice President Biden's solid performance against a well-prepared challenger, Congressman Paul Ryan. In the end, the 2012 debates did have more influence on the campaign than the debates in 2008 or 2004, and they may have been the most politically meaningful debates since 1992. These debates by themselves did not change the outcome of the election; however, they did help to sustain the Romney challenge and maybe even allow him a fighting chance, especially after the first debate. As with most presidential debates, the debate of 2012 did change the dynamic of the campaign, but in the end it was not a principal factor in the final result on Election Day. As Sides and Vavreck conclude,

The sum total of the debate season, then, was to create a tighter race but not put Romney in the driver's seat. This was consistent with history and the academic literature: debates have moved the polls but rarely determined the winner of the election.

In additional to the actual debates between presidential nominees, in recent campaign seasons "debate events" involving multiple candidates seeking their party's nomination have drawn considerable attention. Intra-party debates during the primaries are not new, and a few notable moments even have occurred during such affairs, such as Gov. Reagan's refusal to be silenced during a debate among Republican candidates during the 1980 campaign. For the most part, though, the intra-party debates among candidates seeking nomination have been viewed as more preliminary events, not receiving the sort of press coverage that has apparently become the new practice in campaign coverage. In 2012 numerous debates between Republican candidates were held, often contributing to the cycle of surge and decline among various candidates who each in sequence emerged as a temporary (in some cases ephemeral) principal challenger to the party front-runner, who, in the final analysis, was Gov. Romney throughout 2012. In the 2015/2016 campaign season, the Republican Party debates—divided into two tiers, a "first card" set and "second card" set for which candidates would qualify based upon their current position in the national polls (a poorer showing in the polls directs a candidate to the second card event)—have drawn unprecedented interest, due largely to the astonishing ascent of Donald Trump combined with the media's promotion of these pre-primary season exhibitions. Through these debate showcases, Mr. Trump has managed to seize the day by dislodging the presumptive front-runner and scion of the Bush dynasty, Jeb Bush, whose tepid debate performances have opened opportunities for energetic challengers, and by sheer force of will soaked in bravado and bombast, Mr. Trump has grasped that opportunity and dominated the earliest phase of the Republican nominating process. This is not to claim that Mr. Trump has captured the allegiance of the party insiders upon whom the direction of the "invisible primary" depends, but it is nevertheless an observation that through these debate showcases, Mr. Trump has boldly commanded the attention of the media and, consequently, the viewing and voting population. Another candidate and comparative political outsider, Carly Fiorina, has recently succeeded in making her own move toward the upper tier among the candidates, through her skillful performance in the first two debates. During the second debate, Ms. Fiorina appeared to gain the upper hand, outperforming the rest of the field. However, none of the candidates in the second debate fared poorly; mistakes were avoided and gaffes minimized. Mr. Trump held to his previous strategy, and while he did not overwhelm the event as he had in the first round, he emerged from the second debate with his front-runner status intact. Dr. Ben Carson and Sen. Marco Rubio were also well received, and Rubio in particular began to show the stirrings of momentum as a result. Gov. Bush, while not as ineffective as he appeared in the prior event, nonetheless was unable to regain lost ground, still running with the middle of the pack and as yet unable to demonstrate the same conviction and focus as some of his opponents. Both Ms. Fiorina and Gov. Bush were, in the end, unable to use the debates as a means to gain or sustain momentum.

Sen. Rubio continued to make headway during the third debate, primarily at the expense of Gov. Bush, whose lame attempt at criticizing the senator's work ethic backfired, the governor appearing petty, and the senator justly indignant. In a later debate performance, Sen. Rubio performed less effectively as Gov. Chris Cristie mocked as robotic Rubio's tendency to repeat phrases verbatim. Mr. Trump and Dr. Carson did just enough to protect their position in the polls, and Sen. Cruz managed to shift some momentum by scolding the debate moderators for their perceived attempts at provoking personal conflict among the candidates. Cruz built on this momentum in the fourth debate, where both he and Sen. Rubio proved more forceful and focused compared to the rest of the field. Mr. Trump returned to his more aggressive form, and Gov. Bush seemed more animated, while Dr. Carson's overall performance was by far his weakest. The field again targeted Mr. Trump's immigration proposals, with Gov. Bush at one point dismissing Trump's plans as "impossible" and reflecting that any attempts to implement such a radical proposal would damage local communities and compromise American values. Sen. Cruz, while not agreeing with the details of the Trump proposal, did express visible sympathy to the sentiment behind it, while Sen. Rubio remained reticent on the immigration issue. The candidates also shared heated observations about foreign policy, Mr. Trump criticizing the presumption that the United States should serve as the "world's policeman" and Gov. Bush responding that "Donald is wrong on this. He is absolutely wrong on this. We are not going to be the world's policeman, but we sure as hell better be the world's leader." At the end of the fourth debate it was clear that Sen. Cruz had gained considerable momentum, Sen. Rubio had maintained credibility, Mr. Trump had reasserted himself, and Gov. Bush had, at least for the moment, shown at least some signs of life. In the Democrats' first debate, which involved five candidates, the main focus was on former First Lady, senator, and secretary of state Hillary Clinton and Vermont senator Bernie Sanders; additional candidates present were Lincoln Chafee of Rhode Island, Jim Webb of Virginia, and Martin O'Malley of Maryland. Debate analysts generally agree that each of the candidates performed well for the most part, or at least there were no noteworthy mistakes committed. Former secretary of state Clinton exuded the confidence of a front-runner, frequently drawing on her long record of public service while defining herself—perhaps to both make the comparison and mark the contrast with Sen. Sanders—and said that she had long been a "progressive, but a progressive who likes to get things done." Senator Sanders remained true to his form, unabashedly referring to moral principle in his ongoing efforts to overhaul a system rigged to the advantage of wealth.

In large part due to the performances of Mr. Trump and Ms. Fiorina in the early debates and senators Rubio and Cruz in the later debates on the GOP side, as well as skillful efforts from both Sec. Clinton and Sen. Sanders on the Democrats' side, the 2015 debates have drawn significant interest and have proven important—far more important than similar multicandidate, intra-party debates held in previous years—in these early days of the campaign for the 2016 nomination. Four years earlier, the busy and heavily populated debate season did draw some attention, mostly because the candidates were generously supplying plenty of grist for the gaffe mill as well as fueling the surge and decline of the favorite candidate du jour who happened to fill the order "Anyone but Mitt." In the end, very little is remembered about those debates, other than the more comically embarrassing moments, and in retrospect it is clear that Gov. Romney, in spite of the many candidates that emerged to challenge him only to quickly fade, was the front-runner from the beginning. In 2016 the debates have been, at least to this point, far more influential to the direction of the campaign, at least on the Republican side, and while in both substance and style they are not too different from the 2012 events, in outcome the 2016 debates have proved to be far more influential and thus significantly more important.

The ongoing concerns of the League of Women Voters have been borne out by the character of modern debates. With candidates eager to avoid damaging gaffes, presidential and vice presidential debates have become heavily scripted and constricting events, with candidates rarely straying from talking points, even if those talking points are not responsive to the questions that are actually being asked. While debates remain a ritual for all presidential and vice presidential candidates, whether they contribute much useful information to voters is questionable. Polls tend to show that voters feel that their own party's candidate had the strongest performance, regardless of the actual content of the debate.

Additional Resources

Commission on Presidential Debates. "Debate History." http://www.debates.org/index.php?page=debate-history. Accessed October 12, 2015.

Greenberg, David. "Rewinding the Kennedy-Nixon Debates: Did JFK Really Win Because He Looked Better on Television?" Slate, September 24, 2010. http://www.slate.com. Accessed October 12, 2015.

Jamieson, Kathleen Hall, and David S. Birdsell. *Presidential Debates: The Challenge of Creating an Informed Electorate.* New York: Oxford University Press, 1990.

Marietta, Morgan. "The Absolutist Advantage: Sacred Rhetoric in Contemporary Presidential Debate." *Political Communication* 26, no. 4 (2009): 388–411.

Minow, Newton N., and Craig L. LaMay. *Inside the Presidential Debates: Their Improbable Past and Promising Future.* Chicago: University of Chicago Press, 2008.

Northern Illinois University. "The Lincoln-Douglas Debates." http://lincoln.lib.niu.edu/lincolndouglas/index.html. Accessed October 12, 2015.

PBS. "Debating Our Destiny: The 1976 Ford-Carter Debates." http://www.pbs.org/newshour/debating ourdestiny/1976.html. Accessed October 12, 2015.

Schroder, Alan. *Presidential Debates: Fifty Years of High-Risk TV.* New York: Columbia University Press, 2008.

Sides, John, and Lynn Vavreck. *The Gamble: Choice and Chance in the 2012 Presidential Election.* Princeton, NJ: Princeton University Press, 2013.

Stokols, Eli. "Rubio and Cruz Shine at Fourth Debate." Politico, Nov. 10, 2015. http://www.politico.com/story/2015/11/fourth-2016-republican-debate-milwaukee-215694#ixzz3wHtHaf8x.

Vancel, David L., and Sue D. Pendell. "The Myth of Viewer-Listener Disagreement in the First Kennedy-Nixon Debate." *Central States Speech Journal* 38, no. 1 (Spring1987): 16–27.

Prosperity Issue

Alexis de Tocqueville once observed that Americans were keenly focused on securing their material "well-being," acutely perceiving the strong connection drawn between political ideology and economic policy as a typical feature of American political culture. Such concerns were present at the very birth of the republic, generating two disparate alternatives to the pursuit of prosperity: Thomas Jefferson favored an agrarian republic built on the foundations of the self-reliant farmer, and Alexander Hamilton envisioned the creation of an economic colossus driven by commerce and industry. In early presidential politics, the Federalists generally favored Hamilton's policies, whereas the Jeffersonian Republicans generally held the attitudes of their namesake. The Hamiltonians attached their hopes for prosperity on close commercial ties to Britain; whereas the Jeffersonians, influenced by both the French Revolution and the philosophy of the Physiocrats, magnified by a lingering antipathy to Britain, sought closer political and commercial ties to France.

During the Age of Jackson, the Democratic Party was by and large the heir to the Jeffersonian vision, adding the inclination to promote laissez-faire economic attitudes and favoring small business as an important element of an agrarian republic. The Whigs drew upon the doctrine of Hamilton, advocating a close alliance between government and business intended to develop the infrastructure necessary to stimulate manufacturing and trade.

From the late eighteenth century until the Civil War, the tariff issue was an ongoing and divisive debate within presidential politics. By the 1820s, southern states came to regard protective tariffs as a plot by New England and Middle Atlantic states to permanently hobble their economies. High tariffs on British manufactured goods meant reciprocal high tariffs imposed on outgoing southern cash crops. Northeastern manufacturers supported tariffs to protect them from cheaper English and European manufactured goods. Prior to the Civil War, Whigs generally supported high tariffs while Democrats opposed them.

The promise of prosperity became a reliable fixture in the election campaign cycle. However, the issue of which economic course was best for the country, while ever important, became secondary to the more critical moral problems and social concerns confronting the nation over the problem of slavery. But even the debate over slavery, which was principally a moral issue, was on some occasions tied to pecuniary attitudes. In addition to the moral questions, some proponents of slavery claimed its superiority as an economic system, while some opponents of slavery pointed to the economic weaknesses of such an antiquated form of labor. Ultimately the Union victory in the Civil War not only resulted in the abolition of slavery, but it also sealed the economic fate of the republic along Hamiltonian lines: industrial, commercial, urban, and international.

Prosperity issues in the post-Reconstruction period were again polarized, the Republican Party inclining toward high finance and manufacturing, and the Democrats, especially in the South and West, adhering to agrarian and mining interests. The tariff issue was overshadowed by demands for railroad rate regulation and currency reform. The Industrial Revolution made the national economy less dependent upon farm production, but growing farm production and high rail shipping rates made it nearly impossible for farmers to make a profit. Growing discontent among farmers led to the birth of a number of third parties advocating railroad regulation.

Additionally, new labor movements focused on the economic plight of working families, the Industrial Revolution having left millions of Americans at the mercy of powerful corporate trusts. The Greenback Party, Union Labor Party, and Populist Party pressured the other major parties to address farm and labor problems. A peculiar but intensely important debate over the nature of the best monetary system spun out of these differences in the 1890s, Republicans and conservative Democrats hitching prosperity's star to the gold standard, while Democrats advocated the policy of "bimetallism," allowing for the free coinage of silver to augment the circulation of gold. The Republican nominee in 1896, William McKinley, promised voters a "Full Dinner Pail" if they rejected Bryan's "free silver" solution. McKinley and the gold standard prevailed. A mammoth gold strike in Alaska in the late 1890s, accompanied by rising affluence, permanently put the coinage issue to rest.

By 1904, a progressive tide had inundated the country, thereby influencing elements in both major political parties as well as encouraging the appearance of additional minor parties. President Theodore Roosevelt undertook a crusade to break the power of trusts and monopolies once and for all. In spite of an unfortunate split between Roosevelt and his friend and successor, President William Howard Taft, the Taft administration built upon Roosevelt's progressive legacy, although in the latter half of his one-term presidency, Taft reduced the aggressive anti-trust efforts that had previously distinguished his contribution. Following Taft, Democrat Woodrow Wilson pledged to continue progressive policies in his successful 1912 campaign. But in the wake of World War I, disappointed American voters turned their backs on the progressive movement by electing a sequence of pro-business presidents: Warren G. Harding, Calvin Coolidge, and Herbert Hoover.

As the Roaring Twenties yielded to the global Great Depression (which was actually under way in some rural regions in the country prior to the catastrophic stock market crash of October 1929 and the subsequent depression), the best path to prosperity was acutely debated throughout the 1930s, polarized by the New Deal programs of Franklin Roosevelt and framed between the Democratic promotion of state intervention to support and strengthen the economy and Republican faith in the untampered practices of private enterprise protected, but not guided, by the institutions of the state. Thus Republicans became the party of "rugged individualism," insisting that prosperity depended on minimal government activity and individual initiative. These attitudes defined the centers of both parties through the 1960s during the debate over Lyndon Johnson's Great Society and the "war on poverty," and into the early 1970s with the nomination of progressive Democrat George McGovern in 1972.

The severe economic dislocations of the 1970s paved the way for Republican nominee Ronald Reagan's 1980 victory over incumbent president Jimmy Carter. Reagan's presidential debate question that became a de facto campaign slogan, "Are you better off than you were four years ago?" has come to symbolize the **Campaign of 1980** while stimulating a shift in public attitudes regarding government entitlements as guarantors of prosperity. Activist approaches such as the New Deal, Truman's Fair Deal, and the Great Society were widely regarded as having fallen short, and even the Democratic Party moved closer to a less interventionist position, typified by the "third way" economic policies of the Clinton administration in the 1990s.

Bill Clinton purposefully and skillfully emphasized prosperity. His use of the slogan "It's the Economy, Stupid" typifies the successful policy strategy that drove the incumbent president George H. W. Bush from office. Four years later, the booming national economy made it exceptionally difficult for Senator Bob Dole, the Republican nominee, to dislodge Clinton on the **character issue**. Clinton won reelection. Interestingly, Vice President Albert Gore proved unsuccessful in taking credit for eight years of strong economic growth during the **Campaign of 2000**.

While the major parties contain many elements and various opinions regarding the best policies promoting affluence, it is still accurate to say that Democrats are more inclined to "prime the economic pump," Clinton's third way notwithstanding; whereas Republicans remain more firmly devoted to the laissez-faire capitalist vision of Hoover and Reagan.

Shortly after taking office in 2001, President George W. Bush offered Americans a tax rebate, and in 2003, he pushed through Congress one of the largest tax cuts in American history. At the same time, the Bush administration devoted trillions of federal dollars to fighting wars in Afghanistan and Iraq in the aftermath of the September 11, 2001, attacks on the United States. Like Reagan before him, Bush left office with a record federal debt.

The collapse of the housing market bubble in the mid-2000s, combined with a series of shocks to the financial sector from risky investments in mortgage-backed securities (a practice permitted by the gradual easing of regulations on banks and investment firms), led to a catastrophic crisis late in the **Campaign of 2008**. Faced with the impending failure of several large investment firms, President Bush urged Congress to pass his proposed rescue package for the financial sector, known as the **Troubled Asset Relief Program (TARP)**. While Democratic nominee Barack Obama and Republican nominee John McCain both cast votes in favor of TARP in the Senate, House Republicans were initially not convinced that the federal government should be bailing out the private sector. Other businesses around the country were failing, and large numbers of Americans were losing their homes to foreclosure; none of these entities was being offered federal assistance. Bush eventually persuaded a contingent of Republicans that the failure of the big investment firms would have serious repercussions for the rest of the economy, and with mostly Democratic support, TARP was signed into law. Because both major-party candidates had supported the legislation, it was not a topic of controversy in the presidential campaign (although it was controversial). A strong public backlash, particularly among conservative voters, ensured that opposition to TARP would become a hallmark of the Republican campaign in 2012.

In the end, McCain was unable to escape the unpopularity of his predecessor and the public's perception that he was inexperienced in matters of the economy. While Obama promised to get the economy rolling again, it is likely that he received a large portion of his support simply because he presented an alternative to the status quo. Shortly after being elected, Obama got Congress to pass a stimulus bill that pumped federal funds into state and local economies as a means of promoting job growth (or preventing job loss). This, too, proved controversial, as Republicans were overwhelmingly critical of the bill. Several Republican governors, including Bobby Jindal of Louisiana and Rick Perry of Texas, publicly lambasted the bill but accepted the funds anyway.

Two years into the first term of Obama's presidency, economic growth, while evident, was so gradual that the general perception among the American public was one marked by continued anxiety over economic conditions. The economy was recovering, but for many the recovery was imperceptible, and for those who did recognize improvement, it was too little and too slow. Tea Party opponents and critics in the president's own party exhibited emotions running the gamut from fear and outrage (in the case of the Tea Party faction) to deep disillusionment (in the case of the president's more liberal erstwhile allies). Both real and imagined economic problems boosted the Republican Party in the midterm elections and buoyed Republican confidence in the 2012 campaign. There, the economic debate was again marked by distinct attitudes: the president reaffirming the role of activist government and celebrating the more communitarian elements present within American political culture and economic development; his Republican challenger, former Massachusetts governor Mitt Romney, sharply critical of the president's economic vision and ardently celebratory of American free enterprise and personal self-reliance and initiative—themes that resonate throughout the many election cycles running back to the nineteenth century. For Mitt Romney, the wealth of America has been generated by the hard work, independence, and initiative of free individuals in committing to their own choices in free markets, but America under the administration of President Obama, according to Gov. Romney's assessment, was squeezing the middle class, crushing most Americans under the weight of wasteful government programs, intrusive regulation, ineffective tax policies, excessively constrained use of resources, and meddlesome policies that stifle the entrepreneurial spirit. While the president certainly recognized the importance of the entrepreneur, he nevertheless challenged Gov. Romney's understanding of American enterprise with the reminder that America's infrastructure and public works are the inheritance of active government, pointing out that when it came to roads, bridges, canals, and all manner of public infrastructure, the unfettered financier, industrialist, or entrepreneur "did not build that," but rather, the government in behalf of the American public—including the entrepreneur and the financier—did build it. Hence the "rugged individual" versus the "activist community" resurfaced again in the Romney-Obama contest.

The 2016 campaign to date draws this contrast even more pointedly in some ways. This is seen in two candidates in particular: Sen. Bernie Sanders of Vermont, running for the Democratic nomination, and Mr. Donald Trump, a celebrity billionaire who has, at least for the moment, seized Republican front-runner status in the early stages of the campaign for 2016. Sen. Sanders, a self-proclaimed democratic socialist, argues that American prosperity is threatened by the increasingly growing gap in income inequality, a gap that has concentrated the nation's abundant wealth into the hands of the privileged few, while the great majority of Americans are left to struggle and labor in order to meet even their more basic needs. Part of the senator's campaign is based on the advancement of twelve initiatives that include progressivist elements such as "new economic models to increase job creation and productivity"; imposing "a progressive tax system in this country which is based on ability to pay"; the "establishment of worker-owned cooperatives"; increasing the minimum wage; expanding and strengthening the "social safety net" programs such as Social Security, Medicare, Medicaid, and government-sponsored nutrition programs; addressing comparable worth; the development of authentic universal health care coverage; ensuring universally affordable higher education; and reining in the economic, political, and social influence of large corporations, banks, and other financial institutions as embodied on Wall Street. All of these elements, and others not mentioned here, embody the kind of progressivism that has waxed and waned in American political culture since the latter half of the nineteenth century. Former secretary of state Hillary Clinton, still considered the Democratic front-runner in spite of recent inroads carved by the Sanders campaign, has been perceived as another "Wall Street" corporate candidate from the party's left wing, but a closer look at her economic agenda reveals some themes held in common with Sen. Sanders, such as increasing the minimum wage and expanding overtime, strengthening progressive taxation that shifts the revenue burden to the wealthiest citizens, developing profit-sharing between owners and workers, and continuing to address health care costs by fortifying the Affordable Health Care Act, among others. Mr. Trump seeks to lower taxes on corporations, reduce government spending, and impose limits on any future increases in the national debt ceiling, all of which are typical of the economic proposals of Republican candidates. Atypically, Mr. Trump recommends raising personal income tax on the wealthy, a position that at one time was embraced by Republican moderates but is now an unusual recommendation among Republican presidential hopefuls. By and large, the current crop of Republican candidates reiterate much of what has been promoted in recent campaigns, such as Gov. Mitt Romney's 2012 campaign and Sen. John McCain's 2008 campaign, stressing the need to support free markets so as to "grow the economy," meaning primarily the reduction of government regulation of business and industry and rewarding individual initiative and innovation. Again, if one were to compare the substance of the ideas behind the rhetoric, the Democratic Party still more closely resembles the principles of the New Deal, however modified by President Bill Clinton's "third way" during the 1990s, while the Republican Party hews more closely to President Hoover's ideals of less government intervention and the encouragement of a "rugged individualism." As one would expect, both major parties continue to stress the need to strengthen the middle class, and more recently, both parties have expressed concern over the problem of income inequality, although that concern is manifest across a graduated spectrum. American prosperity, in nearly every case, remains a fundamental aspiration in both parties, along with the foundational principles of liberty and equality, however differently construed.

See also Bread-and-Butter Issues; Campaign of 1896; Campaign of 1920; Campaign of 1932; Campaign of 1992; Campaign of 1996; Keynesian Economics; Trade Issue

Additional Resources

Hibbs, Douglas A., Jr. *The American Political Economy: Macroeconomics and Electoral Politics in the United States.* Cambridge, MA: Harvard University Press, 1989.

Indiviglio, Daniel. "The Best and Worst of Mitt Romney's Job Plan." *Atlantic*, September 7, 2011.

Landler, Mark. "Obama Challenges Congress on Jobs Plan." *New York Times*, September 8, 2011.

Stein, Herbert. *Presidential Economics: The Making of Economic Policy from Roosevelt to Reagan and Beyond.* New York: Simon & Schuster, 1984.

Tufte, Edward R. *Political Control of the Economy.* Princeton, NJ: Princeton University Press, 1980.

Provisional Ballot

The **Campaign of 2000** drew public attention to many of the problems that had long plagued American elections, including unreliable voting machines, poor ballot design, and improper election roll purging. While the occasional purging of the rolls is an important antifraud tool for states, which have long used this tactic to remove ineligible voters from voter registration lists (in particular, voters who have moved or who have died), Florida took the practice to new heights. Prior to the 2000 election, the state paid a private firm to create a suspected felon list, and any registered voter with a name resembling (although not necessarily matching) one on this list was dropped from the rolls without notification. The state did not attempt to match age, race, or gender when conducting the purge. As a consequence, thousands of voters showed up on Election Day, only to find that their registration had been improperly canceled by the state. Moreover, the vast majority of the voters affected were African American.

In other states, immigrant groups such as Latinos, Asian Americans, and Middle Eastern Americans had long complained about polling officials improperly demanding birth certificates and proof of citizenship when they showed up to vote, and refusing to provide a ballot if the individual was not carrying this paperwork. College students often reported harassment by local registrars who preferred that they vote elsewhere as well, and there have been examples at the state level, such as modifications made to Florida's election laws, of elected officials altering legal procedures in order to prevent college students from voting in local elections. The closeness of the presidential race in 2000 made clear the electoral consequences of this disenfranchisement, and legislators were concerned that state and local election officials might try to influence future election outcomes by illegally barring some Americans from voting. As it stood at the time, citizens had no legal recourse but to sue after the fact, which was no real remedy for the problem.

Congress passed the Help America Vote Act (HAVA) in 2002. Among other things, HAVA created something called the "provisional ballot." If a voter's name does not appear on the rolls, and the voter believes that he or she registered properly and on time, the voter may receive a provisional ballot. The registrar is then obligated to check the records for potential errors, such as improper data entry or misplaced forms. If the voter did complete the process as required, the ballot will be counted. Provisional ballots are also used for citizens who forget to bring the proper identification with them to the polls, and for citizens whose eligibility to vote is challenged by a poll watcher. While any citizen denied a ballot has the right to demand a provisional ballot, not all citizens are informed of these rights. In some cases, polling staff routinely hand out provisional ballots to voters who appear to be foreign-born, even when those voters are on the rolls, have the proper identification, and are legally entitled to a regular ballot. In the **Campaign of 2004**, the Brennan Center for Justice at the NYU School of Law estimates that only 64.5 percent of provisional ballots were counted. Despite these problems, provisional ballots remain an important safeguard for voters who find themselves improperly purged, or whose paperwork is improperly processed.

Additional Resources

Kingkade, Tyler. "Rep. Dennis Baxley Says He Targeted College Students with Florida Election Reform Law." Huffington Post. http://www.huffingtonpost.com/2012/12/20/dennis-baxley-college-students_n_2340099.html. Accessed October 2, 2015.

Pew Center on the States. "Provisional Ballot Verification." Electionline.Org, January 23, 2008. http://www.pewcenteronthestates.org/uploadedFiles/ballot%20verification.pdf. Accessed October 2, 2015.

Weiser, Wendy R. "Are HAVA's Provisional Ballots Working?" Brennan Center for Justice, New York University School of Law, March 29, 2006. http://www.brennan center.org/page/-/d/download_file_39043.pdf. Accessed October 2, 2015.

Zetter, Kim. "Colorado Agrees to Allow Purged Voters to Vote." Wired.com, October 31, 2008.

Zetter, Kim. "Provisional Ballots Could Decide Election This Year." Wired.com, October 31, 2008.

Zetter, Kim. "Voter Database Glitches Could Disenfranchise Thousands." Wired.com, September 17, 2008.

Purple State. *See* Blue and Red States

Push Polling. *See* Negative Campaigning

Race Relations Issue

Race relations have influenced American politics and society since the founding of the North American colonies in the seventeenth century, and they continue to be a moral and political concern in the dynamics of electoral politics in the twenty-first century. Race has been used as both a carrot and a stick, with most major candidates today eager to promise new forms of equality and harmony beneficial to all races on the one hand (the carrot), and the occasional instance of race bashing and scare tactics (the stick), sometimes overt, other times subtle, employed by more ruthless candidates in elections of the past.

An early example of the latter can be seen in the politics of Reconstruction, with mostly southern Democrats using the race card to evoke fears of a carpet-bag South dominated by greedy Republicans and their new political lackeys, the recently freed slaves. Throughout the nineteenth century and into the early twentieth century, African American voters identified with the GOP, the Party of Lincoln, while Democrats opposed efforts to incorporate the black population fully into the democratic process. This situation remained until the realignment of the 1930s, which produced the Roosevelt Coalition, uniting more black voters with the Democratic Party, although some African Americans remained loyal to the GOP into the early 1960s. In 1932 just over 70 percent of African Americans who could vote supported Democratic candidate Franklin Roosevelt; by 1956 the number of African American voters supporting Democrat Adlai Stevenson dropped to around 60 percent. However, the African American support for Senator John Kennedy in the 1960 general election reached again to approximately 70 percent, after which it rocketed to nearly 95 percent for incumbent president Lyndon Johnson in 1964, due largely to the president's critical role in the passage of the 1964 Civil Rights Act. By the late 1960s and early 1970s, the Democratic Party was firmly established as the principal party of choice for African Americans, while the Republican Party sustains a small, loyal, conservative African American contingent.

Hispanic voters have also historically been associated with the Democratic Party, but not universally. In California and much of the Southwest, as well as the urban Northeast, the Hispanic/Latino vote has been predominantly supportive of Democrats. However, in the Sunbelt states of Florida and Texas, Spanish-speaking voters have inclined toward the GOP in increasing numbers. As the Hispanic population expands, surpassing African Americans as the nation's largest racial minority, the electoral muscle and divided loyalties of the Hispanic vote will become increasingly critical to the outcome of general elections and increasingly desired by major candidates.

Other racial minorities, such as Asian Americans, Arab Americans, and Native Americans, have historically attracted far less electoral attention than the two larger minority groups. During his 1968 campaign for the Democratic nomination, Sen. Robert Kennedy, to the frustration of his campaign handlers, went out of his way to visit Native American reservations as well as spending time with migrant workers, mostly Hispanic, during his fated California primary campaign. Sen. Kennedy's actions, however, were decidedly unusual then, and in many ways they continue to be so. However, as the United States continues to diversify into an increasingly heterogeneous society, these groups should continue to grow in political clout and social influence in the near future.

While race has become less volatile as an issue since the civil rights victories of the 1960s, racial division, suspicion, and bigotry continues to corrupt the undercurrent of political culture. Campaigns in the late twentieth century, in spite of a more general enlightenment regarding race compared to the previous century, could, through implication or inference, cynically play the race card. The "welfare queen" imagery spun by the Reagan campaign led many to draw a racially charged inference singling out impoverished, urban African Americans, and the Willie Horton ad produced by the elder Bush's campaign was perceived as thinly veiled race baiting. Recently, and perhaps as an attempt to correct the impolitic racial tactics of the 1980s, the Republican Party has attempted to overhaul its homogeneous reputation by projecting a more diverse image. The 2000 GOP national convention was noticeably conscious of diversity, with politicians of various races and ethnic backgrounds brought on stage to tout the raised consciousness of the Party of Lincoln.

The **Campaigns of 2000**, **2004**, **2008**, and **2012** followed the trends of the previous decades—in each new election, most minority groups voted in increasing numbers for the Democratic Party. The one anomaly of this trend occurred with Latino voters in 2004. In this election, Republican candidate George W. Bush received approximately 40 percent of the Latino vote, mostly due to his extensive voter-outreach efforts with this community, as well as his more moderate position on immigration issues. His successor in the Campaign of 2008, John McCain, was not able to sustain this level of Latino support, despite McCain's long history of moderation on immigration. A likely factor in McCain's poor showing among Latinos was the anti-immigration rhetoric that marked much of the Republican primary, particularly from the campaign of hopeful Tom Tancredo. McCain's opponents in the primary helped to define the Republican Party label for many Latinos and thwarted his efforts to build upon Bush's success with this community.

McCain's Democratic rival Barack Obama, on the other hand, advocated a path to citizenship for undocumented residents and aired several campaign ads (on television and radio) in which he spoke Spanish to his audience. Democratic primary candidates also competed in a debate on Univision, a Spanish-language channel. Republican candidates declined a similar offer to debate.

The Campaign of 2012 was notable for repeating the pattern of racial polarization that has continued to divide the political parties and their supporters. The Republican nominees battled each other during the primary season in an effort to prove that each supported the most restrictive measures on immigration, with the toughest rhetoric being reserved for undocumented Mexican workers in the

United States. (Texas governor Rick Perry was a notable exception to this pattern.) Republican hopefuls Newt Gingrich and Rick Santorum explicitly linked African Americans with social welfare programs, subtly implying that the primary beneficiaries of government assistance were not white but the primary funders of government assistance were. Efforts by GOP-controlled legislatures to enact voting reforms that restricted early voting (including Florida's efforts to limit "Souls to the Polls," a mobilization drive sponsored by black churches), rollbacks in efforts to re-enfranchise felons, and strict new identification requirements for voters were also viewed as efforts by Republicans to silence the political voices of minority voters. Hispanic voters strongly supported President Obama in the Campaign of 2012 even though Gov. Romney's proposal for "self-deportation" of undocumented residents seemed to many observers as a softer approach to immigration, especially with regard to Hispanic immigrants, than previous positions by GOP candidates.

Yet the racial divisions that have always permeated American society became still more difficult for presidential candidates to ignore in the **Campaign of 2016**. After the shooting of Trayvon Martin, an unarmed African American teen, by George Zimmerman, an armed white member of a neighborhood watch group, and Zimmerman's subsequent exoneration by a Florida jury, black activists sought to publicize the unequal treatment of blacks and whites by the American criminal justice system. They focused their attention on the deaths of people of color at the hands of law enforcement officers, using the moniker Black Lives Matter. Polls at the time had demonstrated that views of the Martin-Zimmerman incident were divided by race, with African Americans more sympathetic to Martin and whites more sympathetic to Zimmerman. But between 2014 and 2015, a series of police shootings of unarmed black men, many of them videotaped, challenged whites' assumptions about how fairly black Americans were being treated at the hands of law enforcement. Their names became familiar to many Americans: Michael Brown (Ferguson), Eric Garner (Staten Island), John Crawford (Dayton), Akai Gurley (Brooklyn), Tamir Rice (Cleveland), Eric Harris (Tulsa), Walter Scott (North Charleston), Freddie Gray (Baltimore), Samuel Dubose (Cincinnati), and other names less familiar (including Sandra Bland in Prairie View, Texas, which was a death in police custody but not a police shooting). Some deaths sparked protests, and even violence. Several viral videos have exposed evident and frequent examples of racism exhibited by white police officers in their encounters with African American citizens. Consequently, Pew finds substantial, stable gaps between blacks and whites regarding confidence in local police and faith in the criminal justice system. Black Lives Matter has been an effective means of publicizing the loss of life and demanding accountability. More broadly, it has become a grassroots movement that has demanded that political candidates respond to questions about how they will solve institutional racism in American society, notoriously disrupting campaign speeches for Democrats Hillary Clinton, Martin O'Malley, and Bernie Sanders. It is also focusing efforts (albeit at a slower pace) on GOP candidates, who have been notably more critical of the movement.

At the same time, the GOP critique of birthright citizenship that emerged in the 2016 campaign has been viewed by Asian Americans and Latinos as a challenge to their legitimate place in American society. Suggesting that more recent immigrant groups should be subject to different standards for what constitutes citizenship than were previous (primarily northern European) groups reveals a more serious, enduring divide about the value that American society places on the rights and cultural inheritance of those who are less familiar with the practices and experiences shared within the dominant culture.

See also Affirmative Action; Civil Rights Issue; Economic Inequality Issue; Immigration Issue; Jim Crow Laws; Symbolic Racism; Voting Reform Issue; Voting Rights Act of 1965

Additional Resources

Biles, Roger. *The South and the New Deal.* Lexington: University Press of Kentucky, 1994.

Craighill, Peyton M. "Martin Luther King's Dream Not Realized, Most Say." *Washington Post*, August 23, 2011.

Drake, Bruce. "Divide between Blacks and Whites on Police Runs Deep." Pew Research Center, April 28, 2015. http://www.pewresearch.org/fact-tank/2015/04/28/blacks-whites -police/. Accessed September 6, 2015.

Frymer, Paul. *Uneasy Alliances: Race and Party Competition in America.* Princeton, NJ: Princeton University Press, 1999.

Mayer, Jeremy D. *Running on Race: Racial Politics in Presidential Campaigns 1960– 2000.* New York: Random House, 2002.

Yoshino, Kenji. *Covering: The Hidden Assault on Our Civil Rights.* New York: Random House, 2007.

Zia, Helen. *Asian American Dreams.* New York: Farrar, Straus and Giroux, 2000.

Rally Around the Flag Effect

Presidential popularity and approval are always boosted during crisis situations, particularly when the crisis is abroad. The outbreak of hostilities with a foreign power, or the threat of an invasion or attack on U.S. interests, will invariably generate a public groundswell of support for the president. Because the president is viewed as the embodiment of the nation as a whole, the public's support of the president in a time of crisis is a means of expressing patriotism and national solidarity.

President William McKinley's popularity was boosted by the outbreak of hostilities with Spain at the onset of the Spanish-American War. Similarly, the Gulf of Tonkin crisis worked to President Johnson's advantage during the Vietnam War (although Johnson soon found, as had many presidents before him, that rallies do not last indefinitely). President Kennedy's approval ratings surged during the Cuban Missile Crisis, and President Carter experienced a rally in public support during his attempt to rescue American hostages in Iran (while the rescue attempt failed, it was the prolonged nature of the crisis itself that ultimately damaged Carter's standing in the polls).

Presidents are also advantaged by being in the White House during wartime. Even when wars are unpopular, the public has generally been reluctant to change leaders in the midst of a conflict. President Franklin Roosevelt would not have been reelected to a third term without the specter of imminent war (and it is unlikely that he would have attempted a third campaign absent the sense of impending conflict). Similarly, President George H. W. Bush saw his lackluster approval ratings skyrocket during Operation Desert Storm in the first Gulf War. Little more than a decade later, President George W. Bush too received a great boost in his approval ratings when the United States was attacked on September 11, 2001, and again when he directed U.S. troops to invade Afghanistan and Iraq. In the **Campaign of 2004**, Bush was able to convince voters to keep him in office despite the increasing unpopularity of the two wars he was conducting overseas. President Obama received a positive bump in the polls upon release of the news of the violent death of Osama bin Laden at the hands of American Navy Seals in May 2011, but by the end of June, his showing in the polls returned to the same level of approval as just prior to the incident.

Rallies, while important to a president's ongoing image before the American public, eventually fade away. As a crisis becomes prolonged, critics of the president's actions begin to emerge, and the public's patriotic devotion to the cause begins to dissipate. Political scientists believe that the White House's ability to control information during a crisis is one of the key factors that initially keep critics at bay. The longer a president is able to monopolize information about the crisis, the longer the rally may last.

Some crises are inherently short-lived. Failed assassination attempts on a president may bring with them a surge of support, but they do not usually involve a sustained sense of crisis, and so generally they will not produce a lengthy rally. Similarly, while President Obama's successful elimination of the architect of the September 11 attacks, Osama bin Laden, earned him accolades in the short run, it did little to stem the criticism of his presidency over the long run.

Additionally, vice presidents who ascend to the White House after the death of a president generally receive a "rally around the flag" bump in their popularity.

Most recently, the deaths of President Franklin Roosevelt and President John Kennedy effectively rallied the public behind their successors, President Harry Truman and President Lyndon Johnson, respectively. Whether or not this rally carries over into the presidential election depends, in part, on timing. Johnson was elected to a full term in less than a year after the death of President Kennedy, benefiting from the public's sympathies for his slain running mate. When Harry Truman ran for a full term in office, a considerable amount of time had passed since the death of his predecessor, and the power of his connection to FDR had faded. Truman found himself in a fight for his political life that he would eventually win (barely), although his victory owed little to his affiliation with Roosevelt, or even to his handling of the culmination of World War II or the outbreak of the Korean War.

Some political analysts regard the "rally around the flag" effect as potentially dangerous, fearing that it could prompt some presidents to irresponsibly provoke crises abroad to divert voters from problems at home. Such actions might endanger the lives of both U.S. forces and innocent civilians on the ground. In such a wag-the-dog scenario, this type of political windfall could even be generated intentionally. While there is no real and direct evidence of such a situation ever happening in presidential elections, the possibility of a president using a crisis situation for personal gain—and even permitting such a situation to arise in the first place, for the sole purpose of strengthening a reelection campaign—cannot be overlooked.

Additional Resources

Brody, Richard A. *Assessing the President.* Palo Alto, CA: Stanford University Press, 1991.

Kernell, Samuel. *Going Public: New Strategies of Presidential Leadership.* Washington, DC: Congressional Quarterly Press, 2006.

Lowi, Theodore J. *The Personal President: Power Invested, Promise Unfulfilled.* Ithaca, NY: Cornell University Press, 1985.

Red Meat Issue

Bread-and-butter issues involve the economy, and **wedge issues** are those that attempt to attract voters across party lines on the basis of some sort of conflict of interest (e.g., racial or religious solidarity, fear of a common enemy). Red meat issues, on the other hand, are not geared toward attracting undecided voters or voters from the opposite party, nor do they tend to deal with economic concerns. Rather, red meat issues are those issues that most appeal to the base of one's own political party, and they usually involve strongly held, core beliefs. Presidential candidates use red meat issues when they are attempting to rally their party's base.

Red meat issues can be ideological. For example, Republicans generally argue that federal government has gotten too big and is trending toward socialism (a common theme over the past hundred years). Democrats, on the other hand, are apt to argue that government is doing too little to help average people, and that government officials are more concerned with the needs of corporate fat cats than they are with regular folks (also a common theme over the past hundred years). Republicans have historically valued candidates who talked tough about communism, wanted a strong national defense, professed strong support for gun rights, opposed government regulations, wanted to lower taxes, opposed affirmative action quotas, and criticized the modern welfare state. Democratic candidates have often focused on strategies for peaceful conflict resolution (including arms control agreements and withdrawing from military conflicts), improving the quality and cost of the education system, supporting civil rights and women's rights, supporting the rights of labor in the marketplace, and providing assistance for the poor.

The **Campaign of 1980** ushered in some new red meat issues—abortion and traditional values. While Republican nominee Ronald Reagan initially used the abortion issue as a wedge (to persuade Catholics, who had long voted Democratic, to cross party lines), party elites and rank-and-file voters have since sorted themselves on this issue, with most pro-life voters now preferring the Republican Party and most pro-choice voters now preferring the Democratic Party. What began as a wedge issue evolved into a red meat issue. Similarly, traditional values have come to be associated with conservative, evangelical Christian voters, who have since 1980 become an integral part of the Republican Party's base of support.

More recent campaigns have produced some new red meat issues. The political parties are strongly divided on the topic of climate change, with the Republican Party challenging the science that purports that climate change is real, while the Democratic Party has embraced climate change as a global problem in need of an immediate solution. Similarly, Republicans want to combat high gas prices by increasing domestic oil production through more offshore drilling as well as drilling in the Arctic National Wildlife Refuge, whereas Democrats believe that such areas are too environmentally sensitive and drilling is too risky. Democrats have agitated for a national health care system for the last several decades, while Republicans are strongly opposed to any attempt to alter the current private sector-based system, and thus they oppose the Affordable Care Act (although it is a private sector-based system in its current inception). The parties also differ on gay rights, with the Republican Party opposing same-sex marriage and gay adoption and (and with some members supporting a reinstatement of the "don't ask, don't tell" policy regarding gays in the military that was first adopted under the Clinton administration). Democrats have generally supported same-sex marriage, gay adoption, and the abandonment of "don't ask, don't tell." They are also more likely to support the expansion of civil rights legislation to LGBTQ groups, more generally.

Republican candidates pawed over the immigration red meat throughout the first few months of the 2015/2016 campaign. Following their failed efforts in the 2012 presidential campaign, some Republicans—most notably Sen. Marco Rubio—threw their support behind comprehensive immigration reform, but by 2016 nearly all GOP hopefuls had abandoned that approach. Donald Trump's provocative comments on the issue of undocumented immigrants, along with controversial statements regarding Muslims, epitomized red meat tactics in an unprecedented manner. Candidates from both parties, for different reasons, are equally inclined to rake over the controversial gun control issue, more red meat to stoke campaign rhetoric.

Additional Resource

Barrett, Grant, ed. *The Oxford Dictionary of American Political Slang.* Oxford: Oxford University Press, 2004.

Red State. *See* Blue and Red States

"Republican in Name Only." *See* RINO

Retail Politics

This is a term used by political analysts to describe a particular type of campaigning tactic, in which candidates engage in personal contact with individual voters in a variety of informal settings such as restaurants, union halls, and even voters' living rooms. For the most part, retail politicking by candidates is part of a bygone era. However, it is still practiced in two states: Iowa and New Hampshire. While, realistically, the types of voters who reside in these states are not representative of most of the nation as a whole, these states hold the earliest presidential caucus and the earliest primary, respectively, and so they serve to introduce the candidates to the nation. Moreover, victories in these early states often set the tone for later campaign events—candidates who are early winners get more campaign contributions, receive more favorable media coverage, and ultimately are viewed as more viable than their competitors.

Because voters in Iowa and New Hampshire have an expectation that they will be able to meet political candidates in person, candidates flock to these states, often making numerous visits years before the presidential election takes place. Some candidates even purchase second homes in one of them with the expectation that their frequent visits will make such homes cost-effective. In the 1970s and 1980s, coverage of events in these two early states constituted a quarter of all election coverage combined. Examples of presidential candidates engaged in retail politicking can be seen in the 1960 cinéma vérité classic *Primary*, directed by Robert Drew, and in the 1993 documentary *The War Room*, directed by Chris Hegedus and D. A. Pennebaker. More recently, what could reasonably called retail politicking influenced the momentum of Sen. Rick Santorum's run in the Iowa caucus, as his informal, personal, and dramatic appearance with his wife in a small-town pizza diner provided his campaign with a pivotal moment. More recently still, what could be called retail politicking seems to be very much alive in Iowa, as recent events such as Donald Trump's helicopter rides seem to indicate. While retail politicking elsewhere in the nation has all but disappeared and other states have begun to rival New Hampshire and Iowa for media attention, the symbolic role of these two early contests remains, and candidates still spend more time in those states, and interact more personally with voters there, than they do in any other state. In the near future, social media may play an increased role in organizing candidate appearances, especially during the heat of a primary or caucus campaign, thus potentially reintroducing reliance on old-style retail politics combined with innovative use of the Internet and related technologies.

Additional Resources

Dimitrova, Daniela V. "The Evolution of Digital Media Use in Election Campaigns: New Functions and Cumulative Impact." In John Allen Hendricks and Dan Schill, eds. *Presidential Campaigning and Social Media*. Oxford: Oxford University Press, 2015.
Polsby, Nelson W., Aaron Wildaskvy, Steven E. Schier, and David A. Hopkins. *Presidential Elections: Strategies and Structures of American Politics*. New York: Rowman & Littlefield, 2011.

Right-to-Work Issue

The term "right-to-work" refers to Section 14(b) of the Taft-Hartley Act of 1947 that amended the National Labor Relations Act of 1935 (NLRA). The NLRA of 1935 granted private-sector employees the right to organize and join unions without fear of retaliation. The NLRA also granted private-sector unions the right to petition the National Labor Relations Board (NLRB) to hold union representation elections, providing employees the opportunity to have a union represent them in negotiations with their employer over wages, hours, and working conditions.

As part of labor negotiations, the NLRA permitted labor and management to agree to a number of different union security provisions, including the closed shop and the union shop. A closed shop provision required management only to hire union members. A union shop provision, in contrast, permitted management to hire individuals who did not belong to the union but required any newly hired employee to join the union or face termination. Organized labor regarded both the closed shops and union shops as essential to the long-term viability of unions, because union members must pay union dues. Shortly after the Republican Party took control of Congress in 1946, Republicans pushed through Congress the Taft-Hartley Act of 1947 that sought to weaken the NLRA. The Taft-Hartley Act banned all closed shops and gave states the right to enact so-called right-to-work laws. A right-to-work law prohibited management and labor from agreeing to include a union shop provision in a collective bargaining agreement. Not surprisingly, unions viewed right-to-work laws as part of efforts to bust organized labor.

From its enactment in 1947 through June 2015, twenty-five states enacted right-to-work laws. Southern states make up the majority of right-to-work states. During the 1970s, large American corporations began to move factories out of largely northern and midwestern states without right-to-work laws to southern right-to-work states. By the 1990s, a number of major foreign automobile and manufacturing companies also began operating plants in southern right-to work states. By the 1980s, the Republican Party emerged as the right-to-work party, as part of its generally hostile attitude toward organized labor. Yet the right-to-work issue did not become a major campaign issue in presidential campaigns, largely because of the need for Republican presidential candidates to compete for blue-collar votes in key Midwestern states such as Michigan, Ohio, and Wisconsin. During the **Campaign of 1980**, for instance, Ronald Reagan, the Republican nominee for president, stressed that he had belonged to a union while he worked as an actor in Hollywood. Reagan served twice as president of the Screen Actors Guild. To have openly advocated the passage of right-to-work laws in these states could have proven politically disastrous. The electoral votes of Wisconsin, Michigan, and Ohio again proved crucial in the presidential elections of 2000 and 2004. Again, right-to-work laws did not become a major campaign issue. In the **Campaign of 2000** and **Campaign of 2004**, Republican presidential nominee George W. Bush did not attempt to make right-to-work a **wedge issue**. Again, in the **Campaign of 2008**, right-to-work did not emerge as a major campaign issue. John McCain, the Republican presidential nominee, had voted for the passage of a national right-to-work law.

The battle over right-to-work laws did not directly impact public-sector union members and collective bargaining. The NLRA only protected the right of private-sector employees to join unions and to have a union represent them in collective bargaining with their employers. Each state has the power to either grant or deny public-sector employees collective bargaining rights. Beginning in the 1960s, states began to grant public employees the right to engage in collective bargaining, much like their private-sector counterparts. In 1959, Wisconsin became the first state to grant public-sector unions the right to negotiate contracts. In *Abood v. Detroit Bd. of Educ.* (1977), the U.S. Supreme Court held that although the First Amendment prohibited union shops in the public sector, the First Amendment's right to freedom of association did not make unconstitutional so-called agency shops that required public employees who did not belong to a union to pay union representation fees. The Court, however, held that public employee unions could not use any of the funds collected from non-union members for political activities.

In 2010, the voters of Wisconsin elected Scott Walker as Wisconsin governor and gave Republicans control of the Wisconsin General Assembly. Elected as part of the anti-Obama 2010 midterm wave, Walker immediately embarked on a campaign to strip most Wisconsin public employees of collective bargaining rights. Early in March 2011, Walker signed into law legislation sharply limiting the collective bargaining rights of Wisconsin state and local government employees, with the exception of police and firefighters. The action, and a subsequently failed effort to recall Walker, turned Walker into a national political figure and helped to move the Republican Party toward taking openly hostile positions on a range of union issues.

In the **Campaign of 2012**, following the lead of Scott Walker, the majority of candidates seeking the Republican presidential nomination expressed open hostility to labor unions and strongly supported the adoption of right-to-work by more states. Of the candidates for the Republican presidential nomination, Mitt Romney cast himself as one of the strongest anti-union candidates since the late nineteenth century. Romney stated that, if elected, he would push a broad anti-union agenda that included supporting the enactment of right-to-work laws by more states. Romney also called for the repeal of a federal law requiring contractors on projects being paid for with federal funds to pay the prevailing local wage, and he supported legislation to prohibit collective bargaining agreements to contain a provision requiring management to withhold union dues from the checks of employees to fund political activities by unions.

The 2012 Republican Party platform adopted one of the most anti-union planks in American history. "The current Administration has chosen a different path with regard to labor, clinging to antiquated notions of confrontation and concentrating power in the Washington offices of union elites. It has strongly supported the anti-business card check legislation to deny workers a secret ballot in union organizing campaigns and, through the use of Project Labor Agreements, barred 80 percent of the construction workforce from competing for jobs in many stimulus projects," stressed the Republican platform. "The current Administration has turned the National Labor Relations Board into a partisan advocate for Big

Labor, using threats and coercion outside the law to attack businesses and, through 'snap elections' and 'micro unions,' limit the rights of workers and employers alike," continued the platform. "We will restore the rule of law to labor law by blocking 'card check,' enacting the Secret Ballot Protection Act, enforcing the Hobbs Act against labor violence, and passing the Raise Act to allow all workers to receive well-earned raises without the approval of their union representative. We demand an end to the Project Labor Agreements; and we call for repeal of the Davis-Bacon Act, which costs the taxpayers billions of dollars annually in artificially high wages on government projects," furthermore stated the plank. And the Republican platform supported the enactment "of a National Right-to-Work law to promote worker freedom and to promote greater economic liberty." Mitt Romney, the Republican presidential nominee, went on to lose the battleground states of Wisconsin, Michigan, and Ohio and the presidency.

Despite the loss of the presidency, Republican state legislators continued to push anti-union measures. In December 2012, the Republican-controlled legislature of Michigan signed a right-to-work law. In March 2015, Wisconsin governor Scott Walker and his state's Republican-controlled legislature passed a right-to-work law, which made Wisconsin the twenty-fifth state with a right-to-work law on the books. In the **Campaign of 2016,** almost all of the candidates seeking the Republican presidential nomination continued with strong anti-union rhetoric. On the other hand, candidates for the Democratic presidential nomination threw their full support behind expanding the rights of unions. The Republican Party had now become the anti-union party, while the Democratic Party continued with the New Deal legacy as the defender of employee workplace rights. By the start of the Campaign of 2016, private-sector union membership had fallen nationwide to 6.6 percent of the workforce, with public-sector union membership holding steady at 35.7 percent of the workforce. By deciding to go after both private-sector and public-sector unions, Republican candidates and the Republican Party made a conscious decision that this part of the electorate would never support Republican candidates. By depicting union members either as privileged or as victims of corrupt union leaders, Republican candidates hope to turn anti-union attacks into an effective wedge issue. On the other side of the political spectrum, the Democratic Party has continued its post-New Deal legacy as the defender of organized labor in both the private sector and the public sector.

Additional Resources

Bureau of Labor Statistics. "Union Members Summary." http://www.bls.gov/news.release/union2.nr0.htm. Accessed October 19, 2015.

Davey, Monica. "Unions Suffer Latest Defeat in Midwest with Signing of Wisconsin Measure." *New York Times*, March 9, 2015. http://www.nytimes.com/2015/03/10/us/gov-scott-walker-of-wisconsin-signs-right-to-work-bill.html. Accessed October 19, 2015.

Greenhouse, Steven. "Wisconsin's Legacy for Unions." *New York Times,* February 22, 2014. http://www.nytimes.com/2014/02/23/business/wisconsins-legacy-for-unions.html. Accessed October 19, 2015.

McClatchy DC. "Romney Targets Labor Unions, Which Could Be Risky Come Fall." February 19, 2012. http://www.mcclatchydc.com/news/politics-government/election /article24724393.html. Accessed October 19, 2015.

Meta, Seema. "Mitt Romney's Anti-Union Tone Could Haunt Him Later." *Los Angeles Times,* February 26, 2012. http://articles.latimes.com/2012/feb/26/nation/la-na-romney -labor-20120226. Accessed October 19, 2015.

National Conference of State Legislatures: Right-to-Work Resources. http://www.ncsl.org /research/labor-and-employment/right-to-work-laws-and-bills.aspx. Accessed October 19, 2015.

Saleh, Ian. "Wisconsin Gov. Scott Walker Signs Collective Bargaining Bill, Bypasses Senate Democrats." *Washington Post*, March 11, 2011. http://www.washingtonpost.com /wp-dyn/content/article/2011/03/11/AR2011031103966.html. Accessed October 19, 2015.

RINO

An acronym for "Republican in name only," RINO is a pejorative term used primarily by Republicans to describe members of their own party that they have deemed to be insufficiently conservative. In the midterm elections of 2010 and in the **Campaign of 2012**, these criticisms came primarily from the **Tea Party movement**. In these elections, Tea Party candidates vigorously challenged those Republicans deemed to be RINOs in Republican primary elections at the state, local, and national levels, with the goal of purging all moderates from the party. During the presidential campaign, Tea Party surrogates offered a host of litmus tests (including a "purity test") for Republican candidates for the White House. Candidates were expected to oppose all forms of tax increases, to be strongly committed to cutting domestic spending (although there was some disagreement about entitlement spending), to oppose same-sex marriage, to oppose legal abortion, to be critical of the Environmental Protection Agency, to oppose cap-and-trade legislation to regulate greenhouse gases, to be critical about theories of global climate change, to support gun rights, to oppose "Obamacare," to oppose the **Troubled Asset Relief Program (TARP)**, to oppose the stimulus bill, and to demonstrate an overall commitment to a smaller federal government. Given the long list of items, it should come as no surprise that Republican candidates were sharply critical of each other's performance on the litmus test.

In the **Campaign of 2016**, the litmus test became much more specific: Would the GOP candidate for president support the eventual party nominee if it did not happen to be him or her? Or, to phrase the question another way, would the candidate promise to refrain from running an independent challenge for the White

House? Only Donald Trump refused to comply with the terms of the litmus test. Trump, previously a supporter of Democratic candidates and long a friend of the Clintons, had long had a reputation as an eccentric and thus showed less of a propensity, overall, to adhere to all of the components of the GOP platform than had the other candidates (supporting, for example, a government-funded health care system, but changing his position on other topics to conform to the party norm). While Trump's refusal to accede to the litmus test certainly left him vulnerable to being tagged a RINO, it is not clear that this in any way hampered his overall popularity with GOP voters.

Democrats have their own version of this term, DINO, to indicate someone who is a "Democrat in name only." This term hasn't played much of a role in presidential elections. It has been more commonly used to describe legislators such as Senator Joe Lieberman, who lost his Democratic primary for the Senate in Connecticut, won reelection as an Independent, caucused with the Democrats, but campaigned with John McCain in the **Campaign of 2008**. Naturally, Democrats questioned Lieberman's loyalty and his Democratic credentials. The Democrats have generally not subjected their members to litmus or purity tests; however, this may be a function of the historic lack of cohesiveness of the Democratic Party.

Additional Resource

Barrett, Grant, ed. *The Oxford Dictionary of American Political Slang.* Oxford: Oxford University Press, 2004.

Rockefeller Republican

Nelson Rockefeller, governor of New York from January 1959 to December 1973 and former vice president of the United States under President Gerald Ford (1974–1977), emerged as the most prominent leader in the moderate to liberal wing of the Republican Party in the late 1950s and throughout the decade of the 1960s. He was particularly visible during the 1964 presidential campaign, representing, along with fellow moderate William Scranton of Pennsylvania, an alternative to conservative Republican Barry Goldwater, a senator from Arizona, who eventually earned the nomination.

Rockefeller Republicans are often characterized as being fiscally conservative and socially liberal; however, such a definition might be oversimplified. Historically, Rockefeller Republicans have been comparatively liberal both on social issues and on economic issues. Indeed, Nelson Rockefeller himself was influenced by the old "Eastern Establishment" of moderate Republicans who were associated with former presidential candidate Thomas Dewey, and what we have called

Rockefeller Republicans have exhibited policy preferences similar to those of President Eisenhower, a political centrist known for his frustration with the party's right. Rockefeller aligned himself as a moderate to liberal on both fiscal and social policy issues, and thus he set himself at odds with limited-government conservatives like Sen. Goldwater, who opposed the expansion of the federal government and bucked against the legacy of the New Deal. Rockefeller, a committed philanthropist who believed in the public value of private charity and the responsible use of one's wealth for social and cultural improvement, nevertheless also viewed active government as a source of positive political and social change. In many ways Nelson Rockefeller epitomized the kind of moderate, pragmatic politics found at the center of both parties in the 1960s and 1970s.

Even though Gov. Rockefeller could not draw the level of support within his party enjoyed by conservatives Barry Goldwater and Ronald Reagan, he nonetheless serves as an archetype for a Republican voice that was particularly influential, at least until the election of Richard Nixon to the White House in 1968. With the Nixon-crafted "southern strategy" that enticed conservative Southern Democrats into the Republican Party, followed by the ascent of the Reagan right in 1976 and its eventual triumph in the election of 1980, the moderate Rockefeller Republican as a political force began to wane. As both major parties continue to become more homogenized and increasingly polarized, the moderating effects of the liberal Republican have been diluted. While the term "Rockefeller Republican" has always been uttered with a degree of derision from the party's right, it is now even more likely to be used as a pejorative in the Republican Party, one aimed at those Republicans who question the more conservative attitudes, policies, and rhetoric that have shaped the party's ideological development since the mid-1970s. From the perspective of the party's right wing, **RINOs**—"Republicans in name only"— are today's Rockefeller Republicans.

Even though the liberal Republican is a rare breed at the national level, there are some who fit that description, at least in part, who are closer to the legacy of Nelson Rockefeller than to today's conservative wing. Christine Todd Whitman (former governor of New Jersey), Olympia Snow (former congresswoman from Maine), and Senator Susan Collins (also of Maine) serve as examples of the more moderate Republican, and prior to his defection to the Democratic Party, Lincoln Chafee, who is currently running for president as a Democrat, could also be described as a Rockefeller moderate, although no longer a Republican one. At one time former Massachusetts governor Mitt Romney, at least prior to his 2012 campaign for president, in which he exhibited a willingness to steer toward the right, would have been included among the more moderate faction, a living model of the Rockefeller Republican, and the same might be said of Sen. John McCain prior to his 2008 campaign for president. Romney's roots go back to the moderate/

liberal Republican of the 1960s, for his father, George Romney, a contemporary of Rockefeller's and governor of Michigan from 1963 to 1969, was known for his liberal positions and policies. During the 2012 campaign, perhaps the best example of a moderate in the race was Utah governor John Huntsman Jr., and in the current campaign for president leading into 2016, New York governor George Pataki's moderate record may best approximate the Rockefeller model.

While it is tempting to declare the moderate Republican extinct, there are those in the party who do not identify with the more stridently conservative ideology and polemics of the right. Upon reflection, this must be the case; even in the current climate that at least rhetorically speaks to ideological purists, the Republican Party has yet to nominate a truly conservative ideologue. While it is true that formerly moderate candidates like McCain and Romney have adjusted their positions in response to the influence of the right, enough of a moderating influence is still present in the party to frustrate the more conservatively pure candidate. Perhaps this is where we find the legacy of Nelson Rockefeller still evident, however faint.

See also Campaign of 1964; Campaign of 1968; Goldwater Conservative

Additional Resources

Gould, Lewis L. *The Republicans: A History of the Grand Old Party.* Oxford: Oxford University Press, 2014.

Kabaservice, Geoffrey. *Rule and Ruin: The Downfall of Moderation and the Destruction of the Republican Party, From Eisenhower to the Tea Party.* Studies in Postwar American Political Development. Oxford: Oxford University Press, 2012.

Richardson, Heather Cox. *To Make Men Free: A History of the Republican Party.* New York: Basic Books, 2014.

Silent Majority

During the volatile, protest-pocked **Campaign of 1968**, the Republican ticket of Richard Nixon and Spiro Agnew called upon the support of the law-abiding "silent majority" in the United States to contribute a sober sensibility to the countercultural politics of the late 1960s. Nixon and Agnew argued that a "silent majority" of Americans supported policies directed at restoring law and order and the continuation of military commitment to South Vietnam. They also made effective use of the "silent majority" to attack the media for alleged liberal bias.

Given the turmoil and social unrest of the 1960s, the "silent majority" theme was well received by Republican partisans, disaffected conservative Democrats, and moderate independents. Critics argued that the Nixon campaign used the slogan to polarize the nation instead of seeking a consensus on how to solve the serious problems facing the nation.

Additional Resource

Levine, Robert A. "The Silent Majority: Neither Simple nor Simple-Minded." *Public Opinion Quarterly* 35 (Winter 1971–1972): 571–577.

Sister Souljah Moment

During a speaking event at Reverend Jesse Jackson's annual Rainbow Coalition Convention in 1992, Democratic presidential candidate and former Arkansas governor Bill Clinton excoriated a fellow convention participant, hip-hop artist and entertainer Sister Souljah (Lisa Williamson), for stridently militant remarks that she had previously voiced during an interview with the *Washington Post* when reacting to the "not guilty" verdict in the infamous Rodney King police brutality trial and subsequent rioting in Los Angeles, remarks in which she had pointedly suggested, "If black people kill black people every day, why not have a week and kill white people? . . . [If] you're a gang member and you would normally be killing somebody, why not kill a white person?" Exercised by her remarks, candidate Clinton upbraided the rapper for engaging in "the kind of hatred we do not honor," further observing that "if you took the words 'white' and 'black,' and you reversed them, you might think David Duke"—a notorious white supremacist and member of the Ku Klux Klan—"was giving that speech." Gov. Clinton's comments in the presence of Rev. Jackson were, significantly, intended as a public rebuke of a combative and extremist position that could be associated with more ideologically polarized but influential elements within his own party and among his supporters, especially within a small segment of the African American community. By doing so, Gov. Clinton vociferously repudiated ongoing sentiments that either were shared by a certain minority contingent within the party, or at were least aligned with the sympathies of some of his potential supporters from the party's left wing. "Sister Souljah moment" has since denoted any example of a politician publically and intentionally denouncing or repudiating an extreme or polarizing and yet influential position within his or her own party, or among his or her supporters more broadly, so as to appear to the wider voting population as even-handed and judicious. More cynically it has also come to connote any statement by a candidate or politician calculated to publically challenge or repudiate a position or attitude held by a comparatively extremist group, or even a special interest, as a way to manipulate potential voters—a staged show of one's political fortitude.

In this specific case, Gov. Clinton's protest raised the ire of Rev. Jackson, who had already previously complained of "a pattern of incidents" that purportedly demonstrated Clinton's deliberate strategy directed at party centrists and independents and designed to illustrate his independence from the "black vote." Controversy stirred by this episode drove a wedge between Clinton and Jackson—who was at the time an important national voice in the African American community and himself a former candidate for president—that remained in place throughout the campaign of 1992. While the Reverend Jesse Jackson was convinced that the content, timing, and venue for Clinton's "Sister Souljah moment" was an unscrupulous "Machiavellian maneuver," one that was not aimed at the party's center but rather, in reality, an act of pandering to "conservative whites," Clinton, in his defense, explained his own version:

> Two of my most important core concerns were combatting youth violence and healing the racial divide. After challenging white voters all across America to abandon racism, if I kept silent on Sister Souljah I might look weak or phony. . . . We have an obligation, all of us, to call attention to prejudice whenever we see it. . . . The political press reported my comments as a calculated attempt to appeal to moderate and conservative swing voters by standing up to a Democratic core constituency. That's how Jesse Jackson saw it, too. He thought I had abused his hospitality to make a demagogic pitch to white voters. . . . I think I was right to speak out against Sister Souljah's apparent advocacy of race-based violence, and I believe most African-Americans agreed with what I said.

Clinton's sincerity notwithstanding, the Sister Souljah moment is, fairly or unfairly, frequently construed as a rhetorical ploy, a calculating device intended to separate a candidate from more controversial attitudes and ideas with which the candidate would otherwise be identified by association. Other examples of Sister Souljah moments in presidential campaigns might include Sen. Bob Dole's comments critical of pro-life Republicans in 1996; comments from both Sen. John McCain and former Gov. Mitt Romney in the 2008 primary campaign season, the former critical of Robert Bork's analysis of the state of American culture ("slouching toward Gomorrah," a popular theme among the GOP's conservative wing), and the latter denouncing divisive positions from the "religious right" (to appease more moderate elements in the party); and perhaps more famously, and more aptly, Senator Obama's repudiation, during the campaign of 2008, of the Rev. Jeremiah Wright's incendiary comments damning America during a sermon delivered at a church that had been attended by the Obama family.

Washington Post columnist Michael Gerson recently suggested that Texas governor Rick Perry, in denouncing Donald Trump's inflammatory rhetoric against immigration issues as they pertain to undocumented immigrants, had a Sister Souljah moment. Mr. Gerson goes further in noting that perhaps the best model for these "small declarations of ideological independence" can be traced back to none other than Abraham Lincoln, "the first great Republican," who rejected influential nativist elements in the early Republican Party by drawing upon the party's own stance against slavery as leverage to lend strength to his own position. Gerson punctuates his point by aptly quoting Lincoln:

> I am not a Know-Nothing . . . That is certain. How could I be? How can anyone who abhors the oppression of Negroes, be in favor of degrading classes of white people? Our progress in degeneracy appears to me to be pretty rapid. As a nation, we begin by declaring that "all men are created equal." We now practically read it "all men are created equal, except Negroes." When the Know-Nothings get control, it will read "all men are created equal, except Negroes, and foreigners, and Catholics." When it comes to this I should prefer emigrating to some country where they make no pretense of loving liberty.

Gerson showcases this quote as perhaps the best example, a century prior, of a candidate denouncing an extreme but potentially prominent minority segment from within his own party—many anti-slavery Know-Nothings shifted their allegiance to the new Republican Party upon the dissolution of the American (or "Know Nothing") Party in the mid-1850s—and risking diminished public support as a consequence. Today Lincoln's comments might be described as something akin to a Sister Souljah moment, but more in the first sense than in the second, more cynical sense. In any event, the legacy of Lisa Williamson and her connection to the ascent of Bill Clinton is refreshed whenever a presidential candidate assumes the role of contrarian against otherwise supportive interests, whether calculated, as some claim, or not, as President Clinton has held in his own account.

See also Campaign of 1992

Additional Resources

Broder, David S. "Clinton's Daring Rebuke to Jackson Sends a Message to White Voters." *Columbus Dispatch*, June 17, 1992.

Clinton, Bill. *My Life*. New York: Alfred A. Knopf, 2004.

Gerson, Michael. "In Opposition to Trumpism, Rick Perry Emerges as a Responsible Voice." *Washington Post*, July 21, 2015.

Piliawsky, Monte. "Racism or Realpolitik? The Clinton Administration and African-Americans." *The Black Scholar* 24, no. 2 (Spring 1994): 2–10.

Social Media

Political candidates have always sought out new ways to appeal to their supporters, and as more Americans have cultivated a social media presence, so too have their political candidates. "Social media" is a catchphrase for media that is interactive and permits some level of networked relationship between individuals or between individuals and groups. So, for example, Facebook and Twitter are commonly used examples of social media, because individuals use these portals to interact with others in ways that are more complex than would be permitted by traditional Web sites, or by the use of blogs or e-mail. Individuals may post political content of their own, or they may view political content posted by others (personal acquaintances, political candidates, or political groups they have joined). Services such as YouTube permit users to post videos, or to view videos posted by others. Videos that elicit a large number of views are said to have "gone viral," as was the case with the "I Got a Crush on Obama" video posted by a fan during the **Campaign of 2008**. According to a 2011 poll by the Pew Internet and American Life Project, 65 percent of all adult users of the Internet use a social networking service. By 2014, 58 percent of all Americans used Facebook alone, according to Pew, with 79 percent of Americans who use only one social networking site claiming fealty to Facebook. Twitter use climbed by 2014 to 19 percent of all Americans, with 21 percent avowing a commitment to Instagram, and similar numbers using LinkedIn and Pinterest.

In the Campaign of 2008, political campaigns as well as their supporters formed groups on Facebook and MySpace to advocate the election of their candidate. Democratic nominee Barack Obama had a much earlier and much more substantial presence on these sites than did Republican nominee John McCain. Obama's popularity on Facebook first began to surge in mid-spring of 2008, and by Election Day, Obama had 2,401,366 Facebook friends, whereas McCain, whose investment in Facebook seemed to have surged only weeks before Election Day, ended up with 623,662 Facebook friends. A similar pattern can be seen on MySpace, where Obama's 840,009 friends on Election Day vastly outnumbered McCain's 218,348. Moreover, the Obama campaign uploaded 1,792 videos on YouTube between November 2006 and Election Day, whereas the McCain campaign uploaded a mere 329 videos.

Similarly, Twitter permits voters to follow politicians they are interested in, and thus it is a form of campaign communication; voters may also have their tweets followed by others, which constitutes a new form of political activism. In the Campaign of 2008, Obama's campaign used Twitter to announce campaign events to supporters, to remind voters to tune in to political debates, and even to declare his nominee for vice president. And, unlike traditional, strictly informative campaign Web sites, Obama's campaign developed a site that was interactive and allowed individuals to tailor its features to suit their personal needs, exploiting elements of social media.

Political campaigns are on a constant quest to find new ways to harness the power of social media to enhance their popularity. Early in the **Campaign of 2012**, Republican hopeful Rick Perry's campaign launched a Twitter account

(@PerryTruthTeam) dedicated to rebutting "unfair" media coverage of the candidate. Followers were invited to e-mail Perry's campaign with examples of biased stories that they would like to see publicized. Perpetual Republican-maybe Sarah Palin has relied heavily on Twitter to inform her followers of her views on political issues, to criticize political leaders and candidates, and to maintain her political image. Mimicking the 2008 Obama campaign, presumptive GOP nominee Mitt Romney tweeted the identity of his running mate to his followers in the 2012 election.

The use of Twitter expanded dramatically in the **Campaign of 2016** as candidates jockeyed for position in the **invisible primary**. Republican hopeful Donald Trump used Twitter to mock his GOP rivals, to blast Democratic candidate Hillary Clinton, and to carry on a petty but vitriolic feud with the news media, and with *Fox News* in particular. Democratic hopeful Bernie Sanders live-tweeted GOP candidate debates, complete with mocking commentary, to the delight of his supporters.

While Twitter offers political candidates the ability to connect instantly to large numbers of supporters, it can also lead to problems for a campaign. John McCain's daughter, political blogger Meghan McCain, points out the potential advantages and pitfalls for politicians who use Twitter to connect with the public. She notes that Twitter is "impulsive" and "unscripted," which can lead to unintended consequences for candidates. The allure of Twitter, McCain points out, is that "at a time when the **twenty-four-hour news cycle** takes away most of the control candidates have over their image, Twitter allows them to be themselves. . . . It is the simplest way to reach the largest audience in the shortest amount of time."

Wikipedia, an online encyclopedia where content is both created and edited by anonymous users, may also be viewed as a form of social media due to its interactive nature. Survey data suggests that as many as half of all college students utilize Wikipedia in their research; the user-driven contributions on the site often form the starting point for research on term papers, and they serve as shortcuts for individuals to learn about political issues. But just as Wikipedia is a tool for users, it is also a tool for the anonymous authors and editors of its ever-changing content, and it may be used as a partisan political tool to discredit a candidate, or to create a sense of legitimacy for a candidate or a policy proposal. In June 2011, potential Republican candidate Sarah Palin visited the Old North Church while on a tour of Boston and described Paul Revere's role in history to a group of reporters in a monologue that was riddled with historical inaccuracies. Palin's supporters then went to great effort to alter the related entries on Wikipedia to reflect Palin's misstatements in an attempt to minimize the damage from her interview. Comedian Stephen Colbert was notable for challenging the viewers of his show, *The Colbert Report,* to tailor Wikipedia entries on a topic to reflect an outlandish claim that he made on his show. Colbert had enough devoted viewers that they were able to effectively preclude their entries from being edited by others, illustrating the dangers inherent in relying on Wikipedia for unsuspecting users.

Social media has become increasingly important to voters, particularly younger voters, as a means of defining their political reality, and its influence appears to be expanding to the broader population According to the Pew Internet and American Life Project, social networking rates among Americans under the age of thirty have remained stable over time, while usage rates among baby boomers have increased dramatically in recent years. Thus, candidate mobilization strategies that rely on social media may be effective in reaching a larger segment of the public in future elections.

See also Internet Campaigning

Additional Resources

Duggan, Maeve, Nicole B. Ellison, Cliff Lampe, Amanda Lenhart, and Mary Madden. "Social Media Update." Pew Research Center: Internet, Science & Tech, January 9, 2015.

Everett, Burgess. "Tweets Highlight Media's Perry, Texas Errors." Politico, August 26, 2011.

Hendricks, John Allen, and Dan Schill. *Presidential Campaigning and Social Media: An Analysis of the 2012 Campaign.* Oxford: Oxford University Press, 2015.

Madden, Mary, and Kathryn Zickuhr. "65% of Online Adults Use Social Networking Sites." *Pew Internet and American Life Project*, August 26, 2011. http://www.pewinternet .org/2011/08/26/65-of-online-adults-use-social-networking-sites/.

McCain, Meghan. "Anthony Weiner Tweeted Me." Daily Beast, June 7, 2011.

TechPresident: Personal Democracy Forum. http://techpresident.com/. Accessed October 2, 2015.

Weiner, Rachel. "Fight Brews Over Sarah Palin on Paul Revere Wikipedia Page." *Washington Post*, The Fix, June 6, 2011.

Social Security Issue

The Social Security program was established under the Social Security Act passed by Congress in 1935 as a prominent part of President Franklin Delano Roosevelt's New Deal, and its purpose was to provide a safety net for elderly Americans to prevent them from falling into poverty. The program is funded by payroll tax contributions from both employers and employees, and these funds are invested in a federally managed trust. The proceeds of this trust are used to pay out benefits to individuals who have already reached retirement age. In its early decades, the Social Security program was not a major source of political controversy. The baby boom that began in the mid-1940s and continued through the 1950s ensured that an influx of new contributors would keep the program afloat for years to come. The first Republican president to succeed Democratic presidents Roosevelt and Harry Truman, Dwight D. Eisenhower, considered Social Security to be a well-established American institution by the time he ascended to the White House in 1953. The program has become more controversial over the past decade because these baby boomers have started to retire and draw benefits, placing a tremendous strain on the program's resources in an era of declining birthrates. While Americans have grown concerned about the long-term viability of the program, Social Security remains a popular entitlement; and historically, few politicians have been willing to propose changing it, leading it to be termed "the third rail" of American politics.

The **Campaign of 1964** demonstrated the clear political risk of proposing major modifications to the Social Security program. Republican nominee Barry Goldwater represented a faction of the Republican Party that sought to sharply reduce the role of the federal government in American society. In particular, Goldwater's supporters wanted to roll back many of the New Deal programs, viewing them as a massive (and expensive) government overreach. In the early days of his campaign, Goldwater discussed the possibility of making Social Security a voluntary system. While Goldwater would later back away from this position, incumbent president Lyndon Johnson accused Goldwater of seeking to destroy Social Security. While national security and civil rights concerns took precedence in this election, criticism of Social Security did little to help Goldwater, who went down in one of the worst defeats in American presidential campaign history. During this era, the only major change to Social Security involved indexing its benefits to inflation, part of President Johnson's Great Society reforms.

However, the specter of the baby boomers' retirement continued to haunt the Social Security program. A series of reports released during the late 1970s indicated that the program needed a major influx of revenue to assure the full benefits of future retirees. In the **Campaign of 1980**, incumbent president Jimmy Carter accused Republican nominee Ronald Reagan of seeking to change the Social Security system. While Reagan had been a vocal opponent of another entitlement program for the elderly in the 1960s (Medicare), he was careful to avoid discussion of Social Security reform in the presidential debates of 1980. After he was elected, Reagan established a bipartisan commission to examine the viability of the Social Security program in 1983. Many of the committee's recommendations were adopted by Congress, including a gradual raising of the retirement age for full benefits to sixty-seven, and requiring self-employed persons to pay the full amount of Social Security payroll tax. In the years that followed, proposals to make major reforms to the Social Security program quickly ran into a political buzz saw.

This changed with the **Campaign of 2000**. George W. Bush, the Republican nominee, proposed a different approach to Social Security reform. Instead of making participation in Social Security voluntary, Bush proposed that individuals be permitted to invest a portion of their Social Security payroll tax in stocks and other investments, with the goal of receiving a higher rate of return. At the time the proposal was made, the economy was booming, as was the stock market. Younger Americans in particular found the proposal to be an attractive alternative to the severely diminished benefits that they otherwise expected to receive from the program upon their retirement. Democratic nominee Al Gore vigorously opposed any changes to the Social Security system, vowing during the presidential debates that he would keep the funds in a lockbox to prevent them from being squandered. In the final weeks of the campaign, Gore ran numerous ads attacking Bush for the proposed reforms, arguing that they would deprive the program of needed operating revenue and ultimately harm its viability. Gore won the popular vote but lost the Electoral College vote after intervention by the Supreme Court ended a controversial Florida recount.

Once again, in the **Campaign of 2004**, Bush proposed to allow individuals to divert part of their Social Security taxes into private individual retirement accounts. And again, the Democratic nominee, this time John Kerry, strongly opposed the proposal on the grounds that allowing individuals to divert funds from the Social Security trust fund would undermine the financial solvency of the trust. The issue was overshadowed by the wars in Iraq and Afghanistan, although public opinion polls showed that Americans retained their suspicions about reforms to this program. After winning the election, Bush pitched his proposed reforms to Congress. However, by this time, the stock market was no longer booming, and Americans were far less confident about risking their retirement funds in the market. The proposal quickly faded away.

Social Security resurfaced once again in the **Campaign of 2008**. The Democratic nominee, Barack Obama, criticized Republican nominee John McCain for his initial support of Bush's proposal for the partial privatization of Social Security. McCain responded by attacking Obama's proposal to raise Social Security payroll taxes on wealthier Americans. The system in place at the time taxed Americans on their earnings up to $102,000 at a rate of 6 percent. Obama proposed to tax those earning between $102,000 and $250,000 at a rate somewhere between 2 and 4 percent on any income earned beyond the threshold of $102,000. The collapse of the stock market between 2006 and 2008 made it difficult for McCain to make a case for market-based Social Security retirement accounts.

Social Security remained a controversial political topic in the **Campaign of 2012**. Most Republican candidates lined up behind Representative Paul Ryan's budget reform proposal, which included a major overhaul of Social Security and

Medicare (essentially privatizing the latter by distributing benefits through vouchers). Ryan suggested limiting benefits for the wealthiest Americans and increasing the amount of income that would be subject to the Social Security tax (ironically, similar proposals were made by Democratic hopeful Jesse Jackson in the 1980s, but they were dismissed as socialism). Some Republican hopefuls, most notably Governor Rick Perry of Texas, implied that they might be willing to make even more dramatic changes in the program. Perry became notorious for repeatedly calling Social Security a "Ponzi scheme" and suggesting that the program was a failed endeavor since its inception. Republican Mitt Romney acknowledged that the Social Security program had problems, but he expressed a commitment to saving it, although neither Romney nor Democratic incumbent Barack Obama explained in any detail their plans for "saving" the program. However, Obama did signal his willingness to raise the Medicare eligibility age and cut Social Security benefits as part of a deficit reduction strategy, angering many of his Democratic supporters.

Public Policy Polling conducted surveys of likely voters in New Hampshire and Iowa in May 2015 and found that overall, most voters were unwilling to vote for a candidate who suggested cuts to Social Security benefits. Republican voters were somewhat more likely than independent or Democratic voters to accept cuts to the program. Sizable majorities of voters across party lines in both states indicated that they would be more likely to vote for a candidate who was willing to protect Social Security benefits, and most were also supportive of increasing Social Security taxes paid by more affluent Americans as well as taxing investment income as a means of funding the program. In both instances, independents and Democrats again exhibited somewhat higher levels of support, although clear majorities of voters of every affiliation supported such propositions. Given the continued popularity of the program and the diversity in views about how to keep it solvent, political candidates will undoubtedly continue to bicker about how to best repair it for many years to come. Moreover, it appears unlikely that any candidate will find success in running against one of the few government programs that most voters have deemed valuable.

Additional Resources

Bacon, Perry, Jr. "The Candidates' Divide on How to Save Social Security." *Washington Post*, July 8, 2008.

Bosman, Julie. "The Ad Campaign: McCain and Social Security." *New York Times*, September 24, 2008.

Democrats.org. "Keeping Social Security Safe." http://www.democrats.org/news/blog/keeping_social_security_safe. Accessed September 18, 2015.

Klein, Ezra. "Why Liberals Should Thank Eric Cantor." *Washington Post* "Wonkbook" newsletter, July 12, 2011.

Krugman, Paul. "Social Security Finances." *New York Times*, August 13, 2010.

Pew Center for People and the Press. "Public Wants Changes in Entitlements, Not Changes in Benefits." July 7, 2011. http://people-press.org/2011/07/07/section-5-views-of-social-security/. Accessed September 18, 2015.

Ryan, Paul. "A Roadmap for America's Future: Social Security." http://www.gpo.gov/fdsys/pkg/BILLS-110hr6110ih/pdf/BILLS-110hr6110ih.pdf.

White, Ben. "Gore Reaches Out to Union, Candidate Attacks Bush on Texas Record, Social Security Plan." *Washington Post*, July 22, 2000, p. A5.

Sociotropic Voting

Sociotropic voting occurs when voters select a presidential candidate based on their perceptions of national economic conditions, as opposed to their own personal finances. Most political researchers believe that sociotropic voting is much more common than pocketbook voting. This means that voters gauge whether the state of the economy is improving or worsening, and they place a greater importance on the general state of affairs than they do on whether their personal financial situation has grown better or worse. There is also some evidence to suggest that women are more likely than men to evaluate general economic conditions, whereas men are somewhat more likely to make decisions based on their own pocketbooks.

See also Pocketbook Issue

Additional Resources

Feldman, Stanley. "Economic Self-Interest and Political Behavior." *American Journal of Political Science* 26, no. 3 (August 1982): 446–466.

Godbout, Jean-François, and Bélanger, Eric. "Economic Voting and Political Sophistication in the United States: A Reassessment." *Political Research Quarterly* 60, no. 3 (September 2007): 541–554.

Gomez, Brad T., and Wilson, Matthew J. "Political Sophistication and Economic Voting in the American Electorate: A Theory of Heterogeneous Attribution." *American Journal of Political Science* 45: 899–914.

Kinder, Donald R., and Kiewiet, Roderick D. "Sociotropic Politics: The American Case." *British Journal of Political Science* 11, no. 2 (April 1981): 129–161.

Soft News

Daytime and evening talk shows and late-night comedy shows have played an important role in recent electoral campaigns, as candidates have become more willing—in some cases, even eager—to talk about their campaigns with the hosts of entertainment shows in addition to being interviewed by more traditional news outlets. Soft news is news presented under the guise of entertainment; the emphasis is often on candidates and their personal lives rather than their policy positions, and the atmosphere tends to be more congenial than confrontational.

Presidential candidates appearing on late-night talk shows is a campaign custom reaching back to 1960, when Democratic nominee Sen. John F. Kennedy and Republican nominee Richard Nixon each appeared, at different times, on the old *Tonight Show* with host Jack Paar. Other candidates and prospective candidates would follow precedent. Robert Kennedy first appeared on the Jack Paar *Tonight Show* in 1964, and while he was not a candidate for the presidency at that point, it was well known that he was a name under consideration for future campaigns. He would later appear on *The Tonight Show* with new host Johnny Carson, and in 1967 and 1968, he appeared on the *Merv Griffin Show* and the *Joey Bishop Show*. During those appearances he was not an official candidate, but he would announce his candidacy in March 1968. During that 1968 campaign season, vice president and eventual Democratic nominee, Hubert Humphrey, appeared multiple times on the Dick Cavett and Joey Bishop shows, as well as appearing once on *It's Happening*, a short-lived rock/pop variety show, and his rival Sen. Eugene McCarthy also made appearances on the Cavett, Bishop, and Mike Douglas shows. Other examples could also be listed, but the most politically and culturally significant instance of a political candidate being interviewed in a non-news setting occurred in the **Campaign of 1992**, when Democratic nominee Bill Clinton famously appeared on the *Arsenio Hall Show* and played his saxophone with the house band. Clinton also appeared on the youth-oriented MTV cable channel, where he even answered a question regarding the type of underwear he wore (boxers or briefs). Despite receiving criticism from some quarters for these appearances, they helped Clinton connect with young voters. Later, candidates began to take their cues from Clinton's 1992 electoral success, becoming fixtures on *The Tonight Show with Jay Leno*, *The Tonight Show with Jimmy Fallon*, *The Late Show with David Letterman*, *The Late Show with Stephen Colbert*, *The Oprah Winfrey Show*, *Live with Regis and Kelly*, and *The View*. On occasion, appearances on such shows (or the lack thereof) can have serious political consequences for candidates. In the **Campaign of 2008**, John McCain notoriously canceled a September 24, 2008, planned appearance on Letterman's program to help shepherd the **TARP** legislation through Congress; when Letterman discovered that despite this last-minute cancellation, McCain stayed in town to do an interview with Katie Couric, he was outraged, and he lambasted McCain each evening on his show. Three weeks later, and declining in the polls, a chastened McCain returned to Letterman and offered an apology.

Matthew Baum argues that political candidates are increasingly seeking exposure on these entertainment-oriented shows because fewer voters are watching evening news broadcasts or tuning in to presidential debates. Moreover, he suggests, news-oriented shows have become more negative, or critical, in their campaign coverage over time. This has pushed candidates toward media environments that are less threatening and less partisan, where they can also gain valuable exposure with an audience that historically has been less likely to vote. Engaging in friendly banter with Oprah Winfrey or Regis Philbin may enhance a candidate's personal appeal among those potential voters who are most likely to cast their ballot on the basis of personal traits rather than policy issues. Indeed, Baum's research finds that candidate appearances on soft news programs improve their likeability among opposite-party voters, whereas appearances on traditional news programs only enhance their image among members of their own party.

Soft news can also set the agenda for other news organizations. For example, in the fall of 2010, Jon Stewart mocked Senate Republicans who had blocked a bill that would have provided medical benefits to September 11 first responders. The bill had gotten scant mention in the news media, which changed after Stewart took up the cause of the first responders. Like Stewart, the news media was critical of the senators who were blocking the bill; the bill was passed shortly thereafter. Similarly, Stewart's coverage of the Iowa straw poll in the early days of the **Campaign of 2012** pointed out a glaring omission in news coverage of the event—while Republican hopeful Ron Paul came in second in the poll, he received zero media coverage. Candidates who finished much farther behind were covered more, as were two individuals who were not even in the race at the time (Sarah Palin and Rick Perry). The Paul campaign successfully used Stewart's criticism to lobby news organizations for greater coverage.

Appearances on late-night television programming, particularly talk shows and comedy shows, remain a staple of presidential soft-news campaigning. Recently Stephen Colbert hosted Jeb Bush, Donald Trump, and Ted Cruz, for example, on his new version of *Late Night*. Hillary Clinton recently joined Jimmy Fallon to perform a comedy skit spoofing Donald Trump. No doubt many more candidates—most likely all of them—will eventually appear on these programs, especially as the campaign season moves into the actual upcoming primary and caucus schedule.

Additional Resources

Baum, Matthew A. "Talking the Vote: What Happens When Presidential Politics Hits the Talk Show Circuit?" *American Journal of Political Science* 49 (April 2005): 213–234.

Baum, Matthew A., and Angela Jamison. "The Oprah Effect: How Soft News Helps Inattentive Citizens Vote Consistently." *Journal of Politics* 68 (November 2006): 946–959.

Beam, Christopher. "No Joke: By Pushing for the 9/11 First Responders Health Bill, Jon Stewart Steps onto the Political Playing Field." Slate, December 20, 2010.

Hagey, Keach, and Dan Hirschhorn. "Paul Scores Success in Media Assault." Politico, August 25, 2011.

Parkin, Michael. *Talk Show Campaigns: Presidential Candidates on Daytime and Late Night Television.* Routledge Studies in Global Information, Politics and Society. New York: Routledge Press, 2014.

Sound Bite

The phrase "sound bite" refers to a pithy, preplanned phrase used by a political candidate to generate media coverage. The use of these canned, provocative phrases is a common practice of political candidates, campaign spokespersons, and other surrogates tasked with delivering a campaign message to the news media. Modern presidential campaigns recognize that they must make extensive use of free media or **earned media** to get their message out to prospective voters. To assure coverage of their candidate's speeches, campaigns carefully craft phrases designed to attract media coverage in news stories. During the **Campaign of 1980**, Republican nominee Ronald Reagan made effective use of the sound bite "There you go again" in a presidential debate with Democratic nominee Jimmy Carter, effectively making light of Carter's attacks against him. Similarly, in the **Campaign of 1984**, Reagan's question to voters, "Are you better off than you were four years ago?" became one of the most effective sound bites in modern presidential campaign history. In the **Campaign of 1988**, Republican nominee George H. W. Bush famously declared at his party's convention, "Read my lips, no new taxes." The sound bite came back to haunt Bush after he was forced to raise taxes to deal with the spiraling budget deficit.

Numbered among the more recent sound bites are "Drill, baby, drill" from the 2008 GOP campaign as well as "Yes we can" from the Democratic side, and more recently "You didn't build that" from the 2012 Democratic campaign. While the 2015–2016 presidential campaign season has certainly produced its share of provocative statements, a defining sound bite has yet to emerge.

The media's increasing reliance on sound bites has received a great deal of criticism from scholars, who argue that this tends to reduce media coverage of important issues to theatrics, depriving voters of the serious analysis they need to make an informed choice between the candidates. Instead, media analysts and pundits often evaluate the effectiveness of a campaign speech on whether the speech included a certain number of snappy sound bites.

Additional Resources

Hart, Roderick. *Seducing America: How Television Charms the Modern Voter.* New York: Oxford University Press, 1994.

Mickelson, Sig. *From Whistle Stop to Sound Bite: Four Decades of Politics and Television.* New York: Praeger, 1989.

Scheuer, Jeffrey. *The Sound Bite Society: Television and the American Mind.* New York: Four Walls Eight Windows, 1999.

Super PAC

In *Citizens United v. F.E.C.* (2010) the U.S. Supreme Court held that federal law could not prohibit corporations and labor unions from contributing private funds to political campaigns. On March 26, 2010, the Circuit Court of Appeals for the District of Columbia, in the case *Speechnow.org v. F.E.C.*, applied the *Citizens United* decision in holding that federal law could not limit either individual or corporate contributions to independent political advocacy groups. These two cases have provided the legal ground from which the super PAC phenomenon has grown and thrived, adding a controversial new method of working around older restrictions previously imposed against the influence of the corporate sector on presidential elections.

By the **Campaign of 2012**, these unlimited individual and corporate donations to independent advocacy groups assumed a different character. In 2010, such donations were centered primarily on broad-based conservative or liberal advocacy groups, such as the Chamber of Commerce. These groups promoted a range of candidates and policy issues at election time and were often formulated as **501(c) groups**, which were not required to disclose their donors. By 2012, these ostensibly independent groups were more likely to be organized as **527 groups,** and unlike earlier independent advocacy groups, they were increasingly dedicated to the election of a single political candidate, blurring the line between the candidate's own campaign organization and that of the outside group. Such groups were often staffed by individuals who had previously held paid jobs with the candidate and who retained personal relationships with a candidate's official campaign organization. While federal election law still prohibits coordination between a candidate's campaign and the activities of outside groups, candidates routinely ignore this distinction, making appearances at super PAC fund-raising events to promote their campaign and then ducking out the door minutes before the request for donations is made. Political analysts believe that the rise of the super PAC will effectively dismantle most federal campaign finance restrictions on political candidates as super PACs become a little-regulated back door through which affluent benefactors can skirt the few remaining limits on campaign donor activity.

In a notable moment of political satire, comedian Stephen Colbert formed his own super PAC in 2011 to raise and spend funds on activities related to the 2012 presidential election. While many observers dismissed Colbert's antics as a publicity stunt, he was in fact engaged in a serious critique of the role of money in contemporary campaigning. The Federal Election Commission eventually voted to approve Colbert's PAC, "Americans for a Better Tomorrow, Tomorrow," enabling Colbert to run ads in the Iowa Republican straw poll that implicitly mocked the process. Fellow comedian Jon Stewart took over stewardship of Colbert's super PAC for a time during the 2012 campaign so that Colbert could pursue a write-in campaign for president during the primary season; Colbert's candidacy was, of course, not serious, but his attempt to demonstrate the permissible level of coordination between his campaign and the super PAC was both serious and effective.

The limits of candidate coordination were further tested in the **Campaign of 2016**, most brazenly by GOP hopeful Jeb Bush. Federal election law prohibits candidates for office from coordinating with outside organizations, including super PACs. Bush sought to delay his "official" declaration of candidacy so that he could be actively involved in the organization of his Right to Rise super PAC (which shares a name with his leadership committee, as well as an election lawyer). Bush raised funds for his super PAC, hired staff, and mapped out a campaign strategy, all while claiming he was not actually running for president. Yet Bush was simultaneously making appearances at campaign events in his role as a presidential candidate and, indeed, telling the crowds gathered at such events that he was in fact running for president. Other Democratic and Republican hopefuls engaged in similar types of pretexts, albeit not on the same scale or for the same duration. Presidential candidates who already occupy a federal office (in the form of the presidency, vice presidency, House of Representatives, or Senate) may not engage in this charade; they are not permitted to associate with a super PAC prior to an official declaration of candidacy.

Democratic candidate Hillary Clinton also challenged the degree to which a candidate's campaign could coordinate with a super PAC in 2016. Her campaign created a super PAC called Correct the Record to disseminate opposition research and to form a rapid response team to handle negative attacks on her by other candidates. Correct the Record was used as a coordinated super PAC—because the group planned to have an online presence only, the campaign believed it had found a loophole in existing campaign finance law that it could exploit. However, the loophole the Clinton campaign sought to exploit was predicated on the assumption that staff members would be volunteers, probably not the case for Correct the Record. And it is questionable whether the online exemption was ever meant to give candidates the ability to accept potentially multimillion-dollar donations from a single donor for activities directly controlled by the candidate's campaign merely because those activities would be occurring online.

While candidates have generally viewed the rise of super PACs as an opportunity to collect large checks from affluent donors, it's not clear that relying on super PACs is always in a candidate's best interests. In 2012, Republican Mitt Romney collected far more donations from super PACs than did Democrat Barack Obama; however, Obama collected significantly more contributions from individual donors than did Romney. Because super PACs tend to be media-focused, much of Romney's funds went to purchase ads, rather than for activities such as voter mobilization. Ads aren't particularly effective at mobilizing the recalcitrant, and voters don't remember their content for long enough for them to have much long-term persuasive appeal. Moreover, super PACs pay a substantially higher rate for political ads purchased than do candidates' campaigns. Thus, relying too much on super PACs and too little on individual donors leads to wasteful, inefficient spending. The process of raising donations, particularly a sizable amount of small-dollar donations, is itself a grassroots mobilization tool for candidates. Getting voters to contribute even three dollars to a candidate causes them to have made an investment in that candidate, and to have a greater stake in the outcome of an election. When candidates don't have to ask voters for a donation, they also don't have to ask them for their vote.

In 2016, the earliest exits from the presidential context again demonstrated the pitfalls inherent in relying on super PACs at the expense of individual donations directly to the candidates' campaigns. Republicans Rick Perry and Scott Walker had pursued wealthy donors and raised sizable sums for their super PACs, but they had not spent much time or energy on their campaign organizations. As a consequence, they found themselves unable to pay staff, pay for travel, pay the bills that maintaining the campaign offices required, and pay for important things like filing fees—despite their super PACs having plenty of money in the bank.

See also Campaign Finance Reform; 527 Group; Independent Advocacy Groups; Negative Campaigning

Additional Resources

Carr, David. "Comic's PAC Is More Than a Gag." *New York Times*, August 21, 2011.
Confessore, Nicholas. "Lines Blur Between Candidates and PACs with Unlimited Cash." *New York Times*, August 27, 2011.
Gold, Matea. "Why Super PACs Have Moved From Sideshow to Center Stage for Presidential Hopefuls." *Washington Post*, March 12, 2015.

Super Tuesday

The term "Super Tuesday" originated during the **Campaign of 1988**. In that election, a number of states opted to hold their primaries (or caucuses) on March 8. In particular, most southern states opted to hold their contests on this day, hoping that if they banded together, they could generate media attention (and electoral influence) to rival that of New Hampshire and Iowa. In the **Campaign of 1992**, Democratic contender Bill Clinton secured his position as front-runner on Super Tuesday over rival Paul Tsongas (who had defeated him in the New Hampshire primary) by winning six southern states.

In more recent years, "Super Tuesday" has come to refer to the day in the primary season with the largest number of events (and, generally, the largest number of convention delegates up for grabs as well). So, for example, in the **Campaign of 2000**, the press referred to March 7 as Super Tuesday.

The largest ever Super Tuesday was held on February 5, in the **Campaign of 2008**. On that day, twenty states held some sort of campaign event; these events awarded half of the delegates to the parties' conventions. Critics have charged that having Super Tuesday dates early in the campaign season advantages establishment candidates at the expense of new faces; while this has been true for the most part, the Democratic primary season in 2008 defied these expectations (although this was more a function of competitive and evenly matched candidates, the existence of superdelegates, and a proportional allocation of electors than it was of the electoral schedule itself).

In the **Campaign of 2016**, Super Tuesday was reestablished as a primarily southern event, now popularly known as the SEC primary. On March 1, ten states (eight of them in the South) were slated to hold their primaries; also notable is that no other date in the primary schedule had as many state events being held at the same time (although other dates may have accounted for a similar number of delegates, as a function of the size of the states holding an event).

See also Frontloading

Additional Resources

Kettle, Martin. "Super Tuesday 2000 Accomplished Exactly What the Fixers Designed It to Do." *Guardian*, March 8, 2000.

Steele, Michael. "Southern GOP 'Super Tuesday' Could Be a 2016 Game Changer." MSNBC, May 22, 2015. www.msnbc/com/msnbc/southern-GOP-super-tuesday-could -be-2016-some -changes.

Superdelegate

Superdelegates are one of the types of delegates that vote to select the party's presidential nominee at the Democratic National Convention every four years. Their role came about as a consequence of the **McGovern-Fraser Reforms** of the early 1970s, when Democrats became concerned that the complete exclusion of party leaders from the selection process had led to the selection of risky, potentially unelectable candidates (such as McGovern himself). The role of superdelegate was officially created in 1984. Unlike the slates of delegates selected by Democratic Party voters in the primary or caucus process, a superdelegate is not pledged to vote for any particular candidate at the convention. Super delegates are appointed by party leaders (as an automatic consequence of their elected position), and are referred to in the party's delegate formula as "party leaders and elected officials," or PLEOs. Approximately 20 percent of the Democratic Party's nominating delegates are PLEOs, or super delegates.

Prior to the **Campaign of 2008**, super delegates played no discernible role in influencing Democratic nomination outcomes, although it could be argued that the support of superdelegates for former vice president Walter Mondale in his front-runner campaign for the 1984 Democratic nomination helped to deflect what at least for a time appeared to be a credible challenge by Colorado Senator Gary Hart. In that instance, Sen. Hart—who had actually won the New Hampshire primary—did trail the former vice president in the pledged delegate count as the primary season progressed, but Mr. Mondale's lead in that count was small and thus the nomination was not entirely secured. The former vice president's nomination may have hinged on his command of nearly all the superdelegates. However, in most presidential elections, the candidate who eventually receives the party's nomination has accrued more than enough delegates through primaries and caucuses that they easily earn a majority of the convention's votes. Nevertheless, in 2008, two strong Democratic candidates emerged in the primary process: Senator Hillary Clinton and Senator Barack Obama. Both candidates racked up impressive primary-season victories, and were running neck and neck as late as June, aided, in part, by the proportional allocation of delegates in Democratic primary contests (whereas Republican primaries at this time were still winner-take-all affairs).

It became clear by the end of June that neither Sen. Clinton nor Sen. Obama had won enough delegates to earn a majority at the convention. The decisions of the superdelegates became pivotal, and arguments erupted within the Democratic Party over how those delegates should vote. Some Democrats (including Obama) argued that superdelegates should be required to vote the way that their state as a whole voted. However, Obama was relying on the support of superdelegates such as Edward Kennedy, despite failing to win the Massachusetts primary. Clinton, on the other hand, argued that superdelegates should be able to vote independent of their state. The debate was never clearly resolved. Rather, the Clinton and Obama camps negotiated an agreement, and during the first vote counting at the convention, Clinton called to halt the vote and freed her delegates, effectively awarding their votes to Obama. Bill and Hillary Clinton campaigned for Obama throughout the fall, and after Obama won the election, he selected Hillary Clinton to serve as Secretary of State.

In the aftermath of the 2008 election, Obama's supporters formed the Democratic Change Commission, which lobbied the Rules and Bylaws Committee of the DNC for changes in the powers of the superdelegates, either by requiring them to vote the way their state's citizens voted (on the basis of the state's primary or caucus results), or by stripping them of their voting power altogether. While the Rules and Bylaws Committee agreed to expand the number of elected delegates at the convention, which would reduce the proportion of superdelegates to about 15 percent of the convention total, they were unwilling to place any other limits on the role of the super delegates.

Superdelegate clout, while potentially significant, in practice has remained mostly unremarkable. As Elaine C. Karmack of Harvard's Kennedy School of Government wrote after the 2008 presidential election, "Superdelegates have played a role in only two of the nine post-reform conventions, and in neither one did they act contrary to the will of the voters as expressed in the primaries." While many uncertainties cloud a reasonable forecast for 2016, the odds at least indicate that superdelegates should continue to behave as they have in the past.

See also Frontloading

Additional Resources

Curry, Tom. "What Role for Democratic 'Super-Delegates'?" MSNBC, April 26, 2007. http://www.msnbc.msn.com/id/18277678/ns/politics/t/what-role-democratic-super-delegates/. Accessed October 1, 2015.

Karmack, Elaine C. *Primary Politics: How Presidential Candidates Have Shaped the Modern Nominating System.* Washington, DC: The Brookings Institution, 2009.

Rudin, Ken. "Superdelegates Primer: What You Need to Know." NPR, April 14, 2008. www.npr.org/templates/story/story.php?storyId=89292254.

Woodard, Colin. "Democratic Party to Keep Controversial Superdelegates." *Newsweek*, August 2, 2010. http://www.newsweek.com/2010/08/02/democratic-party-to-keep-controversial-superdelegates.print.html. Accessed October 1, 2015.

Surge and Decline Theory

Surge and decline is a political science theory that attempts to explain why presidential candidates often begin their time in office with sizable majorities in the legislature, only to find these margins depleted at the midterm. According to the theory, a popular president enables lower-level officeholders to ride their coattails into office, often because voters base their decisions on their top-of-the-ticket selection. Once presidents begin their term in office, they take actions that invariably invite controversy, and the popular approval they once enjoyed dissipates as the honeymoon period comes to a close. Legislators of the president's party become an inviting target for dissatisfaction with the president's policies when the midterm rolls around.

Additionally, legislators at the midterm face a different electoral environment than is found in a presidential election year. Voter turnout in the midterm is lower, and the electorate is better educated, more affluent, older, and more white than it is in a presidential election year. Local issues play a larger role in midterm elections than in presidential elections as well. Some political researchers also suggest that negative voting is more common in the midterm, which means that voters who are more disgruntled with the status quo are more likely to turn out than are those who are satisfied with how things are going. And because newly elected legislators are more vulnerable to electoral defeat than are long-term incumbents, those legislators swept into office during a presidential election year are particularly susceptible to defeat at the next midterm.

Because presidents experience a surge in legislative support immediately after they're initially elected and can expect a decline in legislative support soon thereafter, there is immense pressure on presidents to pass the most important portions of their legislative agenda within the first year and a half of entering office.

Additional Resource

Campbell, James E. *The Presidential Pulse of Congressional Elections.* Lexington: University Press of Kentucky, 1997.

Swift Boating

This term refers to a series of political ads run in the **Campaign of 2004** by the Swift Boat Veterans for Truth, a **527 group**, against Democratic nominee John Kerry. In 1968, Kerry enlisted in the U.S. Navy and was sent to Vietnam to pilot a swift boat in the Mekong Delta. Kerry received three Purple Hearts, a Bronze Star, and a Silver Star for his heroic actions during the war and for the injuries he sustained. He later became an outspoken critic of the war when he returned from Vietnam. Republican nominee George W. Bush sat out Vietnam, serving instead in the Texas National Guard, a stateside role that virtually guaranteed that he would not be sent into combat overseas. The Swift Boat ads depict Kerry's military service in a less-than-favorable light, questioning whether Kerry fabricated events to earn the medals he was awarded and highlighting his later criticism of the war. The initial ad ran in three states for a week, but the ensuing controversy virtually guaranteed that most voters had some familiarity with the contents of the ad. Kerry, who had been touting his military service during the campaign, was slow to respond to this criticism of his record, and the group quickly followed up with even more provocative ads. The Swift Boat Veterans for Truth received most of their funding from a Texas supporter of George W. Bush, leading to suspicion that the Bush campaign was involved in the ad campaign. Former Bush opponent John McCain was an early and adamant critic of the Swift Boat ads, although he also defended Bush's military leadership during the campaign.

The term "swift boating" has come to be used as shorthand for a campaign ad that is both negative in tone and also takes a candidate's perceived strength and finds a way to portray it as a critical weakness. For example, in 2006, a former Marine and Iraq War critic, Representative John Murtha of Pennsylvania, faced a reelection campaign in which the legitimacy of his Purple Hearts, and ultimately his patriotism, was called into question. Like Kerry, the group criticizing Murtha was not associated with his political opponent's campaign but, rather, was an ideological organization operating independently of any campaign. In the **Campaign of 2012**, GOP nominee Mitt Romney's presumed strength, his private-sector experience running Bain Capital, was turned into a liability by the Obama campaign, which raised questions about the ethics of Bain when Romney was at its helm, accusing Bain of creating domestic unemployment and outsourcing jobs. This fed the Democrats' narrative that the Republicans were the party of the affluent elite and were ill prepared to deal with the growing gap between the haves and the have-nots. And it distracted voters from the Republican Party's argument that after four years in office, Obama had failed to produce the economic recovery that he'd promised.

Candidates appear to be vulnerable to swift boating by opponents who themselves have significant, visible liabilities that they expect to be exploited during the campaign. Opponents who are concerned about their own weaknesses may be more likely to cast the first stone, in the form of a swift-boat-style attack. Such a heavy-handed strategy may not be necessary when faced with a weak challenger who is unlikely to pose a serious threat. So an additional corollary may be that stronger candidates may, ironically, be more vulnerable to swift boating.

See also Negative Campaigning

Additional Resources

New York Times. Swift Boat Articles Archive. http://topics.nytimes.com/topics/reference/timestopics/organizations/s/swift_boat_veterans_for_truth/index.html. Accessed September 5, 2015.

Rainey, James, and Michael Finnegan. "More Bow Shots Fly in Swift Boat Controversy." *Los Angeles Times*, August 27, 2004.

Swift Vets and POWs for the Truth, Ad Archive. http://www.swiftvets.com/index.php?topic=Ads. Accessed September 5, 2015.

Washington Post. "Campaign 2004 Archive: The 'Swift Boat' Controversy." http://www.washingtonpost.com/wp-dyn/content/linkset/2007/11/19/LI2007111900952.html. Accessed September 5, 2015.

Symbolic Racism

In a nation with a history of slavery and its consequences, it is not surprising that there has been an element of racism in America's political rhetoric and its political policies. After the abolition of slavery, and particularly after the federal government's efforts to protect the civil rights of African Americans and others in the 1950s and 1960s, overt racism became less prevalent. Not only were racist policies (such as segregated public accommodations and schools, among other things) illegal, but also it was simply no longer socially acceptable to publicly denigrate or deprive someone on the basis of race, or to enact policies specifically designed to disadvantage or subjugate a racial group. As overt racism has declined, some political commentators have declared that America is now a post-racial society.

Political scientists, as well as other social scientists, are not so quick to agree. They note that merely because it is no longer acceptable to make racist statements does not mean that Americans do not still feel racial animosity toward others. Rather, they suggest, that animosity is now expressed in more subtle ways. These subtler expressions of racism constitute what is known as "symbolic racism." Symbolic racism involves the same kind of stereotyping that marks traditional racism—that is, to assume that a racial group is morally or intellectually inferior as a result of its biological traits or its racial subculture. But rather than complain about spending taxpayer money on education for African American children, for example, a symbolic racist attack would be to criticize education spending on inner-city schools. The intent is the same; in both instances, the target of such criticism is spending on economically disadvantaged African American youth. But the second criticism does not denigrate African Americans directly; rather, it relies on stereotypes about inner-city poverty, crime, and race.

Thus critics have maintained that Republican nominee Richard Nixon's law-and-order message in the **Campaign of 1968** was in reality thinly and cynically veiled symbolic racism. Nixon wanted to restore law and order to U.S. inner cities, which had been plagued by racial unrest and disrupted by rioting in recent years. By focusing on inner-city blight and crime, Nixon was able to imply that African Americans constituted a dangerous criminal element without actually saying so; voters intuitively understood what was being implied. Similarly, political scientists argue, if media images of poverty are dominated by African Americans, then attacks on "welfare queens" (most notably, by Republican nominee Ronald Reagan in the **Campaign of 1980**) may also appeal to underlying racial animosity among voters. In contemporary politics, most news stories about immigrants, both legal and illegal, focus on migrants from Mexico, or from Central or South America. Thus, the public debate over immigration reform is rooted, in a large part, in Americans' feelings about Latinos.

The conspiracy theorists who believe that President Barack Obama is secretly a Muslim (he is not) and the rising public concern about Muslims in the United States have similar roots. Most Americans believe that Muslims in the United States are primarily immigrants from the Middle East (in fact, approximately half are African Americans whose families have lived in the United States for many generations) and that, as Middle Eastern Muslims, they must be a threat to national security and the American way of life. Arab Americans are generally assumed to be Muslim (although many are, in fact, Christian, or even adherents of other religions such as the Baha'i faith or, in some cases, Zoroastrianism). And immigrants from the Middle East (depending on what area of the world one considers to be "Middle East" in the popular mind) are all assumed to be Arab (although many are Pakistani or Indian, or Persian—from countries that for geographers are not even technically Middle Eastern). What most Americans do know is that the September 11 terrorists were both Arab and Muslim, and this association has generated a great amount of fear about a religion and a culture of which most Americans know little. Public support for racial profiling of Arab Americans, opposition to the construction of mosques, and attempts to ban sharia law in various states all appear to emanate from a more general fear of the potential threat to American culture posed by individuals from the Middle East.

This fear became evident in the early Republican primary debates during the **Campaign of 2012**. When asked if they would be willing to appoint a Muslim to a position in the White House, Newt Gingrich compared Muslims in the United States with the threat posed by Nazis during World War II; Herman Cain said he would not permit a Muslim to serve in his cabinet; Rick Santorum expressed concerns about the spread of sharia law in the United States; only Mitt Romney dismissed the claim that Muslims were less loyal to the United States than members of other religious groups, expressing his belief that the country was founded on religious tolerance. Yet again, in the **Campaign of 2016**, GOP hopeful Ben Carson suggested that it might not be constitutional for a Muslim to be elected president of the United States. He argued that Muslims could not separate their religious beliefs from their public actions and were thus not fit to lead. Donald Trump has most recently caused considerable controversy through his proposal to impose a temporary ban on all Muslim immigrants to the United States, exploiting distrust of Muslims based on negative stereotypes held by segments of the general population. Mr. Trump's proposal has been met with strong condemnation in his own party. It is these issues of race, neatly cloaked by other, more policy-related concerns, that continue to divide American voters and thus continue to act as potential **wedge issues** at election time.

See also Birther; Race Relations Issue

Additional Resource

Valentino, Nicholas A., and David O. Sears. "Old Times Are Not Forgotten: Race and Partisan Realignment in the Contemporary South." *American Journal of Political Science* (July 2005): 672–688.

Talk Radio

Beginning in the 1980s, political talk radio became a major force in presidential politics. With increased competition for music programming from FM stations in the 1970s, many AM stations had converted to talk radio formats by the 1980s. One characteristic of the talk radio format is that it permitted listeners to call in and vent their frustrations with elected officials and with the political system at large. While this format had been common on local stations for decades, by the 1980s, nationally syndicated talk shows were beginning to use it as well. Conservative commentator Rush Limbaugh was an early pioneer of this format on the national scale, arraying an army of devoted listeners whom he affectionately referred to as "dittoheads." The popularity of Limbaugh's show attracted a slew of conservative competitors, including Glenn Beck, Sean Hannity, Laura Ingraham, Hugh Hewitt, Mark Levin, Michael Savage, and for a time, Bill O'Reilly, who is now exclusively a television and print personality. While liberal talk radio show hosts such as Jim Hightower, Stephanie Miller, Robert Kennedy, Jr., and Amy Goodman have also drawn listeners, political talk radio has predominately been the domain of conservatives.

It has become the custom of political candidates to do interviews with radio talk show hosts as part of their campaign strategy. For example, Republican incumbent George W. Bush and his running mate Dick Cheney were occasional guests on Limbaugh's show during the **Campaign of 2004** (and at other times as well). Because political talk radio is ideological in nature, listeners tend to be those individuals who are already committed to a particular political party. Democrats do not listen to Rush Limbaugh, and Republicans do not listen to Jim Hightower. Thus, while some of the most vicious attacks in presidential election campaigns can be heard on talk radio, there is little evidence that such attacks persuade voters. There were no real campaign consequences when Senators Obama and Clinton were besmirched by conservative talk radio personalities, for example, as the likely voters who would support either candidate were less likely to set their dial to a conservative broadcaster. This is programming that, as it were, "preaches to the choir." Nevertheless, some candidates, such as Mitt Romney in 2012, considered talk radio sufficiently important to devote at least some time to broadcast appearances. Romney, perceiving that former Republican nominee John McCain may have lost potential voters due to his lack of support among radio talk show person-alities, made an effort to preempt a similar situation in 2012 by reaching out to talk radio listeners. But again, the candidate's actions were an example of solidifying his position within the party rather than drumming up new supporters.

Political scientists have examined whether talk radio results in better-informed citizens or whether the format tends to promote disinformation and misperceptions about how government works. They have found that for people who already have a basic understanding of how the political system works, and a high level of interest in politics, exposure to talk radio can enhance voter knowledge at election time. For those who are less informed at the onset, and who are less interested in politics, the opposite occurs, and levels of misperception and inaccuracy increase among these individuals. Political talk radio's most enthusiastic audience is primarily composed of white males, potentially due to the structure of the format itself (e.g., alarming claims, angry callers, ranting hosts, dramatic catharsis), and the type of content that is usually involved (e.g., negative views about political institutions).

Additional Resources

Barker, David and Kathleen Knight. "Political Talk Radio and Public Opinion." *The Public Opinion Quarterly* 64, no. 2 (Summer 2000): 149–70.

Bolce, Louis, Gerald De Maio, and Douglas Muzzio. "Dial-In Democracy: Talk Radio and the 1994 Election." *Political Science Quarterly* III, no. 3 (Autumn 1996): 457–81.

Mintz, John. "Gore Team Assails Bush's Record in Texas." *Washington Post*, October 14, 2000, p. A10.

Troy, Gil. *See How They Ran: The Changing Role of the Presidential Candidate.* Cambridge, MA: Harvard University Press, 1996.

Talking Points

In an effort to better control the **twenty-four-hour news cycle**, political candidates, parties, and public officials have resorted to circulating their issue positions, arguments, and narratives to news organizations and political colleagues in an attempt to control how political events are framed. As a consequence, it is not uncommon to hear arguments, and even phrases, repeated by numerous political actors and news organizations throughout the course of a news day, giving the appearance that such remarks have been carefully orchestrated—which is in fact the case. Talking points are carefully constructed public relations devices designed to appeal to public opinion, to succinctly offer a persuasive comment regarding a larger issue, to symbolically represent a more involved position with regard to the issues, to avoid the appearance of blame when challenged on a position or question of character, to challenge another candidate through a shorthand phrase or single word, and to divert the media's focus in a way that benefits the candidate or political official.

For example, when Standard and Poor's rating organization downgraded the credit of the United States from a AAA to a AA+ rating in August 2011, many Democrats and liberal media outlets referred to the downgrade as "the Tea Party downgrade," whereas many Republicans and conservative media outlets referred to it as the "Obama downgrade." Whether the focus of the coverage was on Republicans in Congress or on President Obama influenced whom the public blamed for the downgrade. If prospective voters viewed Obama as primarily responsible for the downgrade, they would be more receptive to the economic proposals being made by his Republican rivals in the **Campaign of 2012**. If, on the other hand, most voters assigned blame to the Tea Party faction in the Republican Party in the House, then Obama would be better positioned to survive his reelection bid.

During the early days of the 2015–2016 presidential campaign season, the issue of immigration suddenly emerged as a prominent talking point, owing to the rhetoric of candidate Donald Trump. In response to Mr. Trump's provocative, even inflammatory statements, candidates across the GOP field weighed in on the immigration issue, and while the Democrats were less inclined to address immigration, Vermont's Sen. Bernie Sanders used this talking point opportunity to criticize the Trump campaign. Immigration continued to be a principal talking point even into the second GOP debate, but it was also clear that Mr. Trump himself—his qualifications and credentials—had become a prominent talking point.

See also Tea Party Movement

Additional Resource

Hopkinson, Jenny. "GOP Debate, Part 2: Immigration Dominates Again." Politico. http://www.politico.com/tipsheets/morning-agriculture/2015/09/gop-debate-part-2-immigration-dominates-again-210258. Accessed September 18, 2015.

TARP. *See* Troubled Asset Relief Program (TARP)

Tea Party Movement

The term "Tea Party" ("taxed enough already") is often attributed to CNBC commentator Rick Santelli, who made an impassioned on-air plea to citizens to rally in Chicago to oppose federal involvement in consumer mortgage relief shortly after President Obama took office in February 2009. Others claim that some conservatives were already organizing in small numbers even before Obama assumed office, united by growing discontent with the expansion of the federal government under George W. Bush.

The term "Tea Party" is a bit of a misnomer in that it does not describe an actual political party. Rather, it describes a loose coalition of state, local, and corporate-funded organizations who are united in a common set of core conservative beliefs, including negative views of the federal government, support for gun rights, opposition to taxes, opposition to Obama's health care reform policies ("Obamacare"), and opposition to the bailout of Wall Street (**Troubled Asset Relief Program [TARP]**). Because the Tea Party has a recognizable set of ideological principles but lacks an organizational structure, it is best characterized as a political movement.

Political scientists generally view the Tea Party movement as a faction of the Republican Party rather than an independent entity. This is due, in part, to the political behavior of its self-identifiers. Most self-identified Tea Party members have voted Republican in previous presidential elections and have higher approval ratings of George W. Bush than other portions of the electorate (including Republicans in general). Forty-three percent of Republicans and 57 percent of self-identified Tea Partyers believe the federal government is a major threat to their freedom, while only 18 percent of Democrats do.

While many of the public spokespersons for the Tea Party movement emphasize fiscal issues and carefully avoid controversial social issues, there appears to be a great deal of overlap among those who identify with the Tea Party movement and the Republican Party's contemporary evangelical Protestant base. In the months preceding the 2010 midterm elections, the Public Religion Research Institute (PRRI) conducted the American Values Survey and found that close to half of all self-identified Tea Party movement members also identified themselves with the Christian conservative movement. PRRI termed these individuals "teavangelical" voters. A recently completed panel study by Robert Putnam and David Campbell, both political scientists, found that individuals who were strong Republican Party identifiers in 2006 were those most likely to self-identify as Tea Partyers in 2011. Moreover, the strongest attitudinal correlate with Tea Party identification was a belief that religion should play a more prominent role in American politics; Tea Partyers did not exhibit a heightened level of concern about the economy relative to other Americans.

Moreover, the Tea Party's political efforts are aimed primarily at the Republican Party (as opposed to "swing voters" or Democrats). Republican Party elites such as former vice presidential nominee Sarah Palin, former Republican National Committee chair Michael Steele, South Carolina senator Jim DeMint, and Minnesota representative Michele Bachmann are among those who claim an affiliation with the Tea Party movement. In the summer of 2010, the House of Representatives recognized the Tea Party Caucus, organized by Bachmann. According to

Bachmann, the purpose of the group is to promote policy, rather than political goals. All fifty-three members of the caucus are Republicans.

Other organizations associated with the Tea Party movement include the Tea Party Express, **Americans for Prosperity** (AFP), the Tea Party Patriots, Glenn Beck's 9/12 Project, FreedomWorks, the Our Country Deserves Better PAC, the Club for Growth, Tea Party Nation, and numerous state and local entities. The training sessions and talking points that activists receive from groups like AFP have led critics to characterize the movement as being composed of **astroturfers**, rather than as a true grassroots movement.

The Tea Party movement is best noted for its Tax Day protest in April 2009 and its organized attacks on Democratic members of Congress at town hall meetings with constituents during the summer of 2009. Most of these attacks focused on the Democrats' proposed health care legislation, as opposed to the TARP legislation passed under the Bush administration or Obama's stimulus package. However, over time, Republican members of Congress who voted for TARP found themselves the target of Tea Party-sponsored challenges during the primaries.

During the **Campaign of 2012**, the Tea Party movement was expected to be a strong influence on the Republican nomination process, particularly in early contests such as the Iowa caucus and the South Carolina primary, where the conservative, evangelical party base is sizable. However, no clearly identifiable Tea Party coalition of voters, and no clearly preferred Tea Party candidate, emerged from these contests. Undoubtedly, those who self-identify with the Tea Party made up a sizable share of the voting public in the 2010 midterms. However, midterms tend to attract an electorate that is more affluent, better educated, more white, older, and more likely to be married than the population in general—demographics that are very highly correlated with the traits associated with the core elements of the Tea Party base. Presidential elections attract a far more diverse electorate. Voters in these elections are less white, younger, less affluent, and less educated, all of which are unfavorable for the Tea Party.

Not only are midterm electorates more conducive to Tea Party influence, but the overall political environment may be less favorable for the Tea Party more generally. Nate Silver has noted CNN polling data from March 2011 that confirmed a trend of growing unfavorable sentiment toward the Tea Party movement (while favorable sentiment is stable, or down slightly), suggesting that as the Tea Party has taken a more visible role in American politics, it has become more disliked by the public. Putnam and Campbell find that among the general public, the Tea Party is generally viewed unfavorably (even Muslims and atheists, two groups that are generally disliked, are more popular). Thus, Republican candidates with strong Tea Party support, particularly in presidential races, may alienate independent and swing voters, given the rising negative perceptions of this group.

As we move into the 2016 campaign season, three Republican candidates appear to have the closest affinity with Tea Party voters: Kentucky senator Rand

Paul, who delivered the Tea Party response to President Obama's 2013 State of the Union Address; Texas senator Ted Cruz, who has a reputation for embracing Tea Party positions; and Louisiana governor Bobby Jindal, currently losing traction in his campaign bid for the party nomination. Florida senator Marco Rubio has enjoyed Tea Party support in the past, but lately his stance on immigration reform has prompted a change in that relationship. Former Florida governor Jeb Bush, while not typically associated with the Tea Party brand, has recently stressed his conservatism, publically stating that he is the "most conservative" of the Bush family, assuring party supporters that he is noticeably more conservative than both his brother and his father. This is not to say that Gov. Bush is motivated by a desire to woo the Tea Party faction, but it is evident that he seeks ideological credibility from the Republican Party's right, which has been for the last seven years significantly influenced by the presence of the Tea Party. Perhaps even more interesting, a recent article for Politico by Michael Lind argues that a portion of the support for Donald Trump in the early stages of the 2015–2016 campaign season stems from Tea Party elements more populist than libertarian. Mr. Lind's argument stems from the incongruity between some of Mr. Trump's positions regarding health care and taxes and the ostensibly libertarian principles within the Tea Party faction. In effect, Trump's more flexible approach to these issues seems to be overlooked by his more conservative supporters, who, in the argument forwarded by Lind, are drawn to his populist rhetoric and the more nationalistic tenor of his campaign to this point. Again, as with the case of Gov. Bush, this is not to argue that Mr. Trump is the answer to the Tea Party's aspirations, but it does add new insight into the complexities behind the Tea Party movement.

Still remaining a faction rather than a formal political party, and not enjoying the clout that it appeared to have in the 2010 midterm elections, the Tea Party nevertheless remains a noteworthy and potentially influential element in presidential politics, particularly if an election promises to be close. In the age of the Internet and the twenty-four-hour news cycle, groups like the Tea Party are less likely to fizzle out the way they might have thirty years ago, and it would seem that the Tea Party will continue to play a role in the way Republican candidates address the issues as they compete for their party's nomination.

Additional Resources

Balz, Dan. "What the Tea Party Is—and Isn't." *Washington Post*, September 10, 2011.

Campbell, David E., and Robert D. Putnam. "Crashing the Tea Party." *New York Times*, August 16, 2011.

CNBC. "Rick Santelli's Shout Heard 'Round the World." February 22, 2009. http://www.cnbc.com/id/29283701/ Rick_Santelli_s_Shout_Heard_Round_the_World. Accessed October 6, 2015.

Fox News. "Tea Party Cautious Toward Congressional Caucus." July 22, 2010. http://www
.foxnews.com/politics/2010/07/22/grassroots-tea-party-cautious-caucus-capitol-hill.
Accessed October 6, 2015.

Gaynor, Tim. "Ron Paul, Herman Cain Win Tea Party Poll to Run against Obama."
Reuters, February 27, 2011. http://www.reuters.com/article/2011/02/27/us-teaparty
-idUSTRE71Q2SM20110227. Accessed October 6, 2015.

Herszenhorn, David. "Congress Now Has a 'Tea Party Caucus.'" *Washington Post*, "The
Caucus" section, July 20, 2010.

Jones, Robert B., and Daniel Cox. "Old Alignments, Emerging Fault Lines: Religion in the
2010 Election and Beyond: Findings from the 2010 Post-Election American Values Survey." Public Religion Research Institute, November 2010. http://publicreligion.org/site
/wp-content/uploads/2011/06/2010-Post-election-American-Values-Survey-Report.pdf.

Lind, Michael. "How Trump Exposed the Tea Party: The Proof Is In: the GOP Base Isn't
Small-Government Libertarian; It's Old-Fashioned Populist." Politico, September 3,
2015. http://www.politico.com/magazine/. Accessed October 6, 2015.

Pew Center for People and the Press. "Distrust, Discontent, Anger and Partisan Rancor:
The People and Their Government." April 18, 2010. http://people-press.org/2010/04/18
/distrust-discontent-anger-and-partisan-rancor/. Accessed October 6, 2015.

Silver, Nate. "Poll Shows More Americans Have Unfavorable Views of Tea Party." *New
York Times*, FiveThirtyEight blog, March 30, 2011.

Washington Post. "What Is the Tea Party? A Primer." September 15, 2010. http://voices
.washingtonpost.com/44/2010/09/what-is-the-tea-party-a-primer.html. Accessed October 6, 2015.

Tracking Poll

Also called "trend polls," tracking polls are conducted primarily by news organizations and specialized polling firms such as Reuters/Ipsos, Public Policy Polling
(PPP), Zogby, Rasmussen, and Gallup. They most commonly ask citizens whom
they plan to vote for on Election Day (or, alternately, whom the respondent would
vote for if they had to cast their ballot now). Such polls are designed to predict;
for this reason, they occur at fixed (and generally evenly spaced) intervals, such
as daily, once per week, or once every two weeks. At each interval, those sampled
for the poll are asked a question that is worded identically to the one of the week
before. News organizations, polling organizations, and candidates' campaigns use
tracking polls to determine which candidates are in the lead, which is integral to
horse-race campaign coverage. Significant surges in the polls are viewed as a
sign of a successful campaign strategy, whereas declines in support are viewed as
harbingers of a losing campaign.

Political scientists are critical of tracking polls because they are often misin-
terpreted by journalists and political pundits. Every poll has a margin of error, and

when the margins between candidates have overlap, journalists often portray one candidate as in the lead, treating apparent differences in support as statistically meaningful (when they are not). Moreover, while some movement in the polls may be due to campaign events, it is difficult to disentangle this from the short-term noise (measurement error) that is endemic to any poll. A more reliable estimate of candidate popularity can be found in a **poll of polls**, which is becoming a more common feature in political coverage of campaigns.

Another criticism of tracking polls is that they place excessive emphasis on the horse race itself, often at the expense of an in-depth analysis of the important issues of the day. Thomas Patterson argues that journalists treat elections as sporting events, in which every action by a candidate is geared toward winning the game. Polls are simply a means of keeping score in this type of coverage. Voters learn a great deal about which candidate is leading and which one is behind in the polls (that is, who is winning the game and who is losing), but they learn little else. Such coverage may mobilize voters who want to turn out to support their "team," but it isn't clear that horse-race coverage helps to mobilize voters who are not already strong partisans. When elections are viewed through the lens of a game, team loyalty becomes more important than other objectives such as good governance, and this may lead to partisan polarization, citizen distrust of government, and unwillingness by political leaders to discuss complex and controversial issues with voters.

Additional Resources

Green, Donald P., and Alan Gerber. "How to Interpret Tracking Polls." *Campaigns and Elections* 19 (August 1998): 23–27.

Patterson, Thomas E. *Out of Order.* New York: Knopf, 1993.

PBS Newshour. "Online Focus: Perplexing Polls." Transcript, October 31, 2000 http://www.pbs.org/newshour/bb/media/july-dec00/polls_10-31.html. Accessed September 5, 2015.

Trade Issue

After the slavery issue, no political dispute shaped nineteenth-century American politics (at least the first half of the century) more than the question regarding the rate of tariffs on imported goods. Under the Constitution, Congress has the exclusive authority to levy tariffs on all goods imported into the United States. In the aftermath of the War of 1812, the tariff issue gradually became enmeshed in a sectional conflict that seriously complicated the process of building national political coalitions. Throughout this period, the strongest opposition to protective goods came from the Deep South, where the agrarian economy benefited from low duties on raw materials exported to other nations (particularly cotton). In the industrial North, however, steep tariffs were viewed as a necessary protection from competition from cheap goods manufactured overseas.

In the candidate-saturated **Campaign of 1824**, four of the five presidential candidates had supported protective tariffs in some form. The **Campaign of 1828** was also marked by a debate over tariffs (as well as controversies surrounding the outcome of the previous election). Tariffs again emerged as a hot issue in the **Campaign of 1832**. South Carolina had, at one point, threatened to secede from the Union over the Tariff of Abominations, claiming that the state had a right of nullification for any federal legislation that it objected to.

Slavery dominated the political debate throughout the 1840s and 1850s, and although tariffs remained controversial, they were overshadowed by the lead-up to the Civil War. Throughout the nineteenth century and into the twentieth century, the Republican Party, with its base in the manufacturing centers of the Northeast and Midwest, remained a strong advocate of tariffs; while the Democratic Party, representing the more agrarian areas of the South, fought hard to limit tariffs to promote agricultural products. In response to the economic crises of the early 1890s, Republican nominee William McKinley ran on a platform of tariffs and sound money in the **Campaign of 1896**. His opponent, the populist-minded Democratic nominee William Jennings Bryan, opposed tariffs and wanted to make credit more available by the unlimited coining of silver currency.

After the election of Democratic nominee Woodrow Wilson in the **Campaign of 1912**, the tariffs rate on foreign imports plunged to a hundred-year low, only to rise again eight years later after Republicans regained control of Congress and the White House. Harding and the Republicans blamed the flagging economy in the aftermath of World War I on low tariffs, while Democrats argued that enacting new tariffs would hurt worldwide demand for U.S. goods. President Harding signed the Emergency Tariff Act in 1921 and the Fordney-McCumber Tariff in 1922. The purpose of the Emergency Tariff Act was to protect U.S. wheat farmers from low-priced Canadian wheat imports; Fordney-McCumber created a Tariff Commission and gave the president sweeping new powers to raise or lower tariff rates as he saw fit. All but a handful of Democratic legislators opposed the bill, and all but a handful of Republican legislators supported it. Nations around the world retaliated by hiking tariffs on U.S. goods, including products such as automobiles. Nevertheless, after the **Campaign of 1924**, Republican Herbert Hoover maintained the U.S. commitment to high tariffs, signing the Smoot-Hawley Tariff Act of 1930, which raised U.S. tariffs to record levels. Smoot-Hawley was opposed by large numbers of economists, the automobile industry, the banking industry, and other manufacturers who by now were seeking global markets for their goods. While imported goods sold in the United States declined, unemployment continued to surge.

In the **Campaign of 1932**, Democratic nominee Franklin Delano Roosevelt campaigned against Smoot-Hawley, and quickly sought to dismantle the tariffs after being elected (Smoot and Hawley had both been defeated in their reelection bids that same year), and to establish a series of bilateral and multilateral agreements with other countries as a means of resolving trade disputes. Roosevelt signed the Reciprocal Trade Agreements Act of 1934, giving him the authority to negotiate bilateral trade agreements with other nations. The General Agreement on Tariffs and Trade (GATT) was signed in 1947, and represented a commitment by many of the world's developed and developing nations to lower tariffs and other barriers to international trade. GATT was replaced in 1995 by the World Trade Organization (WTO).

While the United States has had a bipartisan commitment (among party leaders) to an international free trade regime, the country's long history of protectionism is still in evidence. In the early 1980s, the U.S. economy was in a tailspin, due in part to rising energy prices coupled with rising unemployment. The situation was particularly grim for American automakers, who found themselves losing market share to lower-priced, more fuel-efficient vehicles imported from Japan. Autoworkers were laid off in droves, and voters directed their anger at Japan. In the summer of 1982, two Detroit autoworkers beat twenty-seven-year-old Vincent Chin to death with a baseball bat outside of a McDonald's on the outskirts of the city. Chin was Chinese American, but his attackers had mistaken him for Japanese, taking out their economic frustrations on their hapless and confused victim. Chin's attackers were charged only with manslaughter and served no jail time, triggering outrage in the Asian American community. They were charged with federal civil rights violations two years later and were eventually cleared, although they were convicted in civil court.

In this perilous political climate, President Ronald Reagan sought to appease irate American autoworkers while still maintaining the appearance of a commitment to free trade. He called on Japanese auto producers to submit to voluntary import quotas, hinting that more drastic actions might be taken if Japanese auto exports to the United States continued to rise. Japan acquiesced, and Honda and Toyota soon began to build their own plants in the United States (called "transplants" at that time) to avoid potential import restrictions. With American workers being hired to assemble Japanese automobiles, they reasoned, they would not only be able to avoid any potential import quotas, but they could also argue that they were contributing to American economic growth. The strategy worked; as more Americans took jobs with foreign automakers, the line between American and foreign automobiles began to blur.

The next appearance of a trade issue in a presidential election was in the **Campaign of 1992**. The first major point of contention between the presidential candidates was over incumbent President George H. W. Bush's decision to renew the country's most-favored-nation (MFN) trading status with China. Democratic nominee Bill Clinton's running mate, Al Gore, argued that China's brutal crackdown on the peaceful demonstrators in Tiananmen Square in June 1989 should have been a factor in deciding whether to once again grant China the status of a privileged trading partner. Gore would also make this argument in the **Campaign of 2000**, when he was the Democratic nominee.

Also at issue in the Campaign of 1992 was the North American Free Trade Agreement (NAFTA), negotiated by the incumbent Bush administration, which was to create a free-trade zone between the United States, Canada, and Mexico. NAFTA had not yet been ratified by the Senate, and it was overwhelmingly unpopular in manufacturing states such as Michigan, Ohio, Wisconsin, Indiana, Illinois, and Pennsylvania. American workers had already begun to see job losses in the manufacturing sector as businesses relocated south of the border in an attempt to lower their labor costs, a trend that was poignantly captured by filmmaker Michael Moore in *Roger & Me*, a documentary about the demise of General Motors in his hometown of Flint. Independent candidate H. Ross Perot made NAFTA the centerpiece of his campaign, arguing that ratification of NAFTA would accelerate the flow of jobs to Mexico, such that Americans would hear "a giant sucking sound" as jobs and tax revenue disappeared across the border. Republican Pat Buchanan also joined the race, challenging Bush in the Republican primaries on the basis of both Bush's violation of his "no new taxes" pledge of four years earlier, and Bush's support of NAFTA.

Bush defended NAFTA, arguing that in the long run, it would help to create jobs in the United States. By this point, the Republican Party had become the standard-bearer for free trade, a complete about-face when compared to its electoral history. The Democrats, on the other hand, maintained a strong base of blue-collar workers and, as a consequence, sought to protect American jobs from outsourcing, overseas competition, and relocation of manufacturing industries to other locations. NAFTA was fast-tracked to passage during the last months of the elder Bush Administration, and supported, with modification, by his successor, President Bill Clinton, with the full approval of First Lady and future presidential candidate (2008 and 2016), Hillary Clinton. Ms. Clinton would eventually come to oppose NAFTA following her election to the United States Senate upon her departure from the White House, and she has devoted some energy throughout her political career since then to distancing herself from the principles behind NAFTA, conceding in her 2008 campaign that the pact had "had hurt a lot of American workers," an admission that was exploited by her 2008 rival, Senator Barack Obama, as an example of rhetorical flip-flopping.

The trade issue was again raised during the first few months of the 2015/2016 campaign as candidates considered a new and broader trade agreement, the

Trans-Pacific Partnership (TPP), negotiated by the Obama Administration. In early October 2015, Democratic candidate and former secretary of state Hillary Clinton went on the record against TPP even though she had supported it while serving as President Obama's secretary of state. In so doing, former Sec. Clinton publicly opposed President Obama's effort to obtain approval for the new multinational trade arrangement. Her Democratic rival, Sen. Bernie Sanders, has also criticized TPP. Republican candidates have been more divided on the issue, with Gov. Jeb Bush more consistently supportive of the arrangement. TPP has received its harshest criticism from the extreme ends of the political spectrum.

The parties continue to differ on this issue, although tariffs and trade are rarely an issue at election time. The Republican Party platform continues to advocate free trade without restrictions, whereas the Democrats support "fair trade," which makes trade relations subject to human rights considerations, working conditions and fair pay for labor, and environmental safeguards. Notably, while the political leadership of both parties has exhibited a strong preference for free trade in recent decades, the public in general is far more skeptical. The public has generally been considerably more willing than political leaders to make trade contingent on fair wages, job protection, and environmental quality standards.

Additional Resources

Irwin, Douglas A. "GATT Turns 60." *Wall Street Journal*, April 9, 2007. http://www.wsj .com/articles/SB117607482355263550. Accessed December 14, 2015.

Kaplan, Edward S. "The Fordney-McCumber Tariff of 1922." EH.net Encyclopedia, edited by Robert Whaples. March 16, 2008. https://eh.net/encyclopedia/the-fordney-mccumber-tariff-of-1922/. Accessed December 14, 2015.

Krugman, Paul. "A Tariff History of the United States." *New York Times*, November 7, 2009.

Merica, Dan, and Eric Bradner. "Hillary Clinton Comes Out against TPP Trade Deal." CNN Politics, October 7, 2015. http://www.cnn.com/2015/10/07/politics/hillary-clinton -opposes-tpp/index.html.

Perot, Ross, with Pat Choate. *Save Your Job, Save Our Country: Why NAFTA Must Be Stopped Now*. New York: Hyperion, 1993.

Taussig, F. W. "The Tariff History of the United States, Part II." 1892. http://teaching americanhistory.org/library/index.asp?document=1137. Accessed October 19, 2015.

Troubled Asset Relief Program (TARP)

The Troubled Asset Relief Program (TARP), often referred to as the "Wall Street bailout," was an effort to shore up major American banks and investment firms in the wake of a financial crisis caused in large part by risky bank investments in mortgage-backed securities. During the spring and summer months of the

Campaign of 2008, banks of all sizes, as well as major investment firms, began to fail as overleveraged homeowners were unable to pay their mortgages. Easy credit during the housing bubble earlier in the decade had led homeowners to borrow large sums that they were unable to manage once the economy became sluggish and many lost their jobs or were earning less. Investors who owned mortgage-backed securities quickly found themselves in financial peril. The FDIC shut down many financial institutions (at great cost to both taxpayers and investors), but some institutions were deemed "too big to fail."

When Lehman Brothers declared bankruptcy on September 15, 2008, the stock market took a nosedive, and economists feared that the bank crisis would quickly spread to other sectors of the economy as well. Advisers to President George W. Bush proposed a financial assistance program for these troubled institutions, wherein the Treasury Department would provide funds to assist eligible banks and investment firms in exchange for stock in the institution and quarterly dividend payments. However, getting Congress to approve the legislation proved problematic. Bush requested that Congress pass the bill over the course of a weekend to avoid further turmoil when the markets opened at the beginning of the week. Republican nominee John McCain famously put his campaign on hold to return to Washington to lobby his colleagues to support the bill. The Senate passed the bill on October 1, with support from both McCain and Democratic nominee Barack Obama. The House passed the bill two days later, on a mostly party-line vote (with most Democrats supporting President Bush and most Republicans in opposition).

Bush signed the Emergency Economic Stabilization Act on October 3, 2008, which provided $700 billion in federal funds to shore up failing firms. Later legislation related to TARP restricted the pay of top executives at institutions that still owed the federal government money under TARP, lowered the permissible government outlay from $700 billion to $475 billion, and required more transparency in how institutions used TARP funds. As of August 2011, the federal government disbursed a total of $579,766,309,727 to 928 entities. Major institutions (excluding subsidiaries) such as Citigroup, Bank of America, JP Morgan Chase, Wells Fargo, Goldman Sachs, and Morgan Stanley are among those that quickly repaid their loans. Additionally, the loans have thus far generated approximately $67 billion of revenue to the government in the form of dividends and interest payments.

The TARP program was controversial for a time, particularly among conservative voters. The **Tea Party movement** that developed during the early months of Barack Obama's presidency was a reaction, in part, to the bailout of financial firms that were viewed by many as precipitating an economic recession that continued to wreak havoc on the lives of working Americans. Tea Party critics of TARP noted that using government funds to ameliorate the consequences of risky investments seemed to advantage powerful Wall Street firms, while smaller American businesses continued to fail and average families continued to suffer. In the 2010 midterm elections, Tea Party candidates challenged Republican legislators who had voted for TARP, leading to some high-profile seat losses. TARP, the subsequent bailout of General Motors and Chrysler (government loans for which the companies were charged interest), and the bailout of Freddie Mac and Fannie Mae along with the stimulus bill served as rallying points for many conservative voters and Republican presidential candidates. In the **Campaign of 2012**, only one Republican presidential candidate served in Congress during the TARP vote—Michele Bachmann, who consistently lobbied against TARP and related legislation in 2008 and 2009. Other Republican candidates in the Campaign of 2012 were critical of TARP as well, although none were in a position to vote on the original legislation. Eventual 2012 Republican nominee and former Massachusetts governor Mitt Romney, however, appears to have "flip-flopped" on the issue of TARP, being critical of it on one hand, but then also accepting its role in helping to stabilize the economy on the other. As Gov. Romney wrote in *No Apology*, TARP "was intended to prevent a run on virtually every bank and financial institution in the country. It did in fact keep our economy from total meltdown."

While TARP was not particularly popular among liberal voters, President Obama and the Democrats focused their criticism on the lax regulations in the banking industry. Obama argued that without better financial oversight, risky investments would continue, and the financial sector could once again precipitate a major recession. At this point, TARP has not appeared as an issue in the 2016 presidential campaign.

Additional Resources

Cassidy, John. *How Markets Fail*. New York: Farrar, Straus and Giroux, 2009.

110th Congress. Public Law 110-343. http://www.gpo.gov/fdsys/pkg/PLAW-110publ343/html/PLAW-110publ343.htm. Accessed September 22, 2015.

Paulson, Henry M., Jr. *On the Brink: Inside the Race to Stop the Collapse of the Global Financial System*. New York: Business Plus, 2010.

ProPublica. "Bailout Recipients." http://projects.propublica.org/bailout/list/index. Accessed September 22, 2015.

ProPublica. "Companies That Have Refunded Bailout Money." http://projects.propublica.org/bailout/list/refunds. Accessed September 22, 2015.

Sorkin, Andrew Ross. *Too Big to Fail*. New York: Penguin, 2011.

Wessel, David. *In Fed We Trust*. New York: Crown Business, 2009.

Twenty-Four-Hour News Cycle

With the advent of CNN in 1980, Americans had access to media coverage of major political events twenty-four hours a day. Headline News followed in 1982, followed by the Fox News Network and MSNBC in 1996. In addition to twenty-four-hour cable news, the online distribution of previously printed news (i.e., online newspapers) meant that newspapers could inexpensively update their news content throughout the day in response to ongoing events. These two trends, combined with the rise of political blogs and social media, have served to diminish candidate control over news.

The twenty-four-hour news cycle poses a problem for presidential campaigns. Campaigns are expected to be on message and under scrutiny at all times. Any gaffe or misstep is instantly distributed to a national audience. It is not a coincidence that as news has become more available around the clock, candidates have increasingly sought to limit their interactions with reporters. Moreover, the twenty-four-hour news cycle has proven to be a boon for opposition research. Damaging information that candidates uncover about their opponents will always find an outlet in a world where cable, print media, online news, blogs, and tweets provide ample opportunities for the dissemination of information. Campaigns must maintain extreme vigilance in their efforts to engage in damage control, no matter how trivial the accusation. Critics of the twenty-four-hour news cycle argue that the new emphasis on the speedy distribution of information gives media organizations little time to vet stories for false or misleading information, and that it has harmed the professionalism and the credibility of the press as an institution.

Additional Resource

Rosenberg, Howard. *No Time to Think: The Menace of Media Speed and the 24-Hour News Cycle.* New York: Continuum, 2008.

Undecideds

The term "undecided" describes potential voters who express an intention to vote in a public opinion poll prior to Election Day but have not yet settled on a candidate choice. Journalists and political pundits often view such voters as up for grabs (or "swing voters"). Between 1972 and 1988, undecided voters constituted, on average, one in every five potential voters (with a range of 13% to 26%, depending on the specific election year). Political scientists have found few stable sociodemographic traits that characterize such voters; undecideds appear in all income and education levels. They are often more likely to be younger, however. Politically, these individuals tend to be less partisan than other voters, less interested in politics, and less likely to be concerned about the outcome of the election. This is especially true of chronic undecideds (also called "late deciders"), as opposed to occasional undecideds. In more recent years, political scientists have found the number of undecideds to be on the decline.

A more useful distinction may be between soft and firm voters. Soft voters, according to Kenski, Hardy, and Jamieson, are voters who are completely undecided, or who have made a tentative choice but are open to persuasion. Firm voters have a clear voting preference and express little willingness to change their mind prior to Election Day. In the **Campaign of 2008**, the National Annenberg Election Study found that 25.6 percent of voters were in the soft category in August, just prior to the Democratic National Convention. By mid-October, more than 85 percent of most of the sociodemographic groups in the electorate were in the firmly decided category (with slightly lower percentages for voters in the 18–29 age range and for individuals with a high school education or less). Sides and Vavreck's study of the **Campaign of 2012** found that many voters who claim to be undecided are partisans who, for some reason, are displeased with their party's candidate. Their unique analysis of the same voters at several points in time determined that almost half of the citizens who claimed to be undecided in December 2011 did not vote. Of the remainder, votes were divided fairly evenly among the candidates. To put it differently, they found that 88 percent of self-identified Republicans who voted ended up voting for Romney and 89 percent of self-identified Democrats who voted ended up voting for Obama. Fewer than 10 percent defected to vote for the opposite party, and some portion voted for someone other than a major party candidate. In short, disgruntled partisans end up either staying home or getting brought into the party fold. While the media often highlight the rule of undecided voters at election time, political scientists have long maintained that people who lack a candidate preference by the time that fall rolls around are less attentive to politics than other citizens, have lower levels of political information, and are substantially less likely to vote.

See also Microtargeting

Additional Resources

Faucheux, Ron. "Hitting the Bull's Eye: Winning Elections by Targeting Voters." *Campaigns and Elections* 20 (July 1999): 20–25.

Kelly, Tina. "Watching, Listening, Hoping for a President: Undecided Voters Weigh Options." *New York Times*, August 5, 2000, p. A1.

Kenski, Kate, Bruce W. Hardy, and Kathleen Hall Jamieson. *The Obama Victory: How Media, Money, and Message Shaped the 2008 Election.* New York: Oxford University Press, 2010.

New York Times. "The Power of the Undecideds." Editorial, November 5, 2000, Section 4, p. 14.

Sides, John, and Lynn Vavreck. *The Gamble: Choice and Chance in the 2012 Presidential Election.* Princeton, NJ: Princeton University Press, 2013.

Valence Issue

Originally coined by Butler and Stokes in their classic study of British politics, political scientists worldwide now use the term "valence issue" to describe political issues that either lack controversy or lack policy content, in contrast to a "position issue," which is both controversial and policy-specific. So, for example, leadership and experience are considered valence issues in a political campaign because they are personality references, as opposed to policy references. Moreover, they are lacking in controversy; while voters may disagree about which candidate possesses the best leadership qualities, no one argues against electing a president who will be a good leader. Similarly, few would suggest that inexperience is a desirable quality in a candidate. In the realm of policy issues, the term is used to describe a policy or a policy goal that has such widespread popular support that it is utterly lacking in controversy. Thus, "improving our nation's education system" is a valence issue because no one would support worsening our nation's education system; there are not two legitimate sides to this so-called issue. Additionally, the term "improving" is not specific; in practice, it is used as a placeholder for a variety of far more specific, technical policy solutions (such as No Child Left Behind, the use of Common Core standards, the establishment of a voucher system for private schools using public funds, or even the abolition of public schools in their entirety). The absence of a precise policy leaves much to the voters' imaginations and enables candidates to avoid alienating possible supporters by advocating a policy with which some may disagree.

In recent decades, particularly in the general election phase of a political campaign (as opposed to the primary phase), candidates have tended to emphasize valence issues over position issues in order to maximize possible votes. Valence issues offend no one, by their very nature, because they appeal to an existing social consensus. Position issues, however, tend to alienate some portion of the electorate and thus carry risk. **Median voter theory** suggests that a vote-maximizing strategy is one that appeals to the broadest possible segment of the electorate and blurs the candidate's position on controversial issues, thus enabling voters to imagine the smallest possible issue distance between themselves and the candidate. This strategy only becomes irrational, according to this model, if the electorate is extremely polarized across most issues and there is no real political center.

Additional Resources

Butler, D. E., and D. Stokes. *Political Change in Britain.* New York: Macmillan, 1969.
Downs, Anthony. *An Economic Theory of Democracy.* Indianapolis: Bobbs Merrill, 1957.

Values Voters

Values voters are those voters who support a candidate or political party based primarily upon the moral, religious, and philosophical principles that those actors embrace. While most voters are undoubtedly influenced in some part by their beliefs and principles, values voters are more inclined to base their political allegiances on one, two, or perhaps a handful of controversial issues that deeply reflect their moral beliefs. Throughout American electoral history, moral issues such as slavery, the rights of organized labor, civil rights, women's rights, nativism, and anti-communism influenced citizens' choices at the ballot box. Contemporary social issues such as abortion, prayer in school, gay rights (most recently, same-sex marriage or civil unions), gun control, the death penalty, global warming, and the theory of evolution all represent issues that speak to a voter's moral principles and beliefs.

Most frequently, what we technically call a "values voter" is meant to indicate those moral values and political dispositions held by social conservatives. The expression "values voters" came into vogue following the **Campaign of 2004**. The National Election Pool had an exit poll in that year in which voters were asked to indicate the "most important issue" influencing their vote choice. Voters were given a list of issues from which to choose, and among these was an item labeled "moral values." While the exit poll never asked voters to identify any moral value in particular, 22 percent of all voters selected this item as their most important issue. Of these, the vast majority also identified themselves as conservative Christians, and they overwhelmingly supported Republican nominee George W. Bush. On the basis of this poll, many political pundits heralded the rise of the new values voter in American politics.

Research in political science has challenged this interpretation of the 2004 election, finding, in many cases, that the number of values voters has not grown sharply over time (but, rather, has remained constant), and that even among such voters, other political issues may influence electoral choices. And there is disagreement among political scientists about the extent to which values voters uniquely contributed to Bush's reelection in 2004.

Nevertheless, it would be a mistake to underestimate the importance of political groups that represent the interests of socially conservative values voters. For example, the Family Research Council is a major influence in the study and promotion of the value vote, and beginning in 2006, the group has sponsored a Values Voter Summit to promote the agenda and policies of a social conservative ideology. Aspiring Republican political candidates have used this summit to court conservative voters (although Republican nominee John McCain and his running mate, Sarah Palin, notably did not make an appearance at the summit held during the **Campaign of 2008**). The 2009 Values Voter Summit featured Republican hopeful Tim Pawlenty, and the 2011 Values Voter Summit was attended by Republican hopeful Michele Bachmann, a leading voice among social conservatives and the **Tea Party movement**. In the Campaign of 2008, Democratic nominee Barack Obama and Republican nominee John McCain both made appearances at evangelical Christian preacher Rick Warren's Saddleback mega-church in Orange County, California.

In many ways, the Family Research Council and the Values Voter Summit are the products of the "culture wars" that emerged in the 1980s and 1990s (and as articulated at the GOP convention in 1992 by aspiring nominee Patrick Buchanan). The controversy over abortion has been, since the mid-1970s, probably the biggest hot-button issue in the values voter list of concerns, and more recently, the debate over the nature of marriage (and gay marriage in particular) has become a central concern for these voters as well. Given the current state of American politics, it is difficult to imagine a scenario in which the values voter would not be a factor in either setting the agenda for debate or influencing the outcome of an election. In particular, these voters are viewed as pivotal factors in determining the outcomes of Republican Party primaries, both as a function of their size and because they are more readily mobilized than other Republican primary voters. However, their influence on the general election is also unmistakable, as candidates of both parties increasingly address issues of personal faith on the campaign trail.

See also Culture War; Moral Majority

Additional Resources

Fiorina, Morris P., Samuel J. Abrams, and Jeremy C. Pope. *Culture War? The Myth of a Polarized America.* New York: Longman, 2005.

Langer, Gary, and Jon Cohen. "Voters and Values in the 2004 Election." *Public Opinion Quarterly* 69, no 5 (special issue, 2005): 744–759.

Muste, Christopher. "Hidden in Plain Sight: Polling Data Show Moral Values Aren't a New Factor." *Washington Post*, December 12, 2004, p. B4.

Silverleib, Alan. "Analysis: Candidates Can't Ignore Values-Based Voters." CNN, August 15, 2008.

Voting-Eligible Population (VEP) Turnout

Also known as "VEP turnout," this figure is calculated by dividing the total number of voters on Election Day by the total number of voting-eligible citizens. Calculating VEP turnout is complicated because the voting-age population turnout figures must be adjusted to account for residents of the United States who are not citizens (and thus are not eligible to vote), as well as citizens who are disenfranchised felons. Non-citizens may be in the United States legally or illegally, and the latter group is far more difficult to measure. Felon disenfranchisement laws vary greatly from one state to the next, further complicating matters.

Political scientist Michael McDonald has attempted to estimate VEP turnout for every presidential election, by state, from 1948 to 2012. The eight most recent presidential election comparisons are shown below:

	VEP Turnout	VAP Turnout
1980	54.2%	52.6%
1984	55.2%	53.3%
1988	52.8%	50.3%
1992	58.1%	54.7%
1996	51.7%	48.1%
2000	54.2%	50.0%
2004	60.1%	55.4%
2008	61.7%	56.9%
2012	58.6%	53.6%

Source: Michael McDonald, Voter Turnout, United States Election Project.

Additional Resource

McDonald, Michael. "Voter Turnout." United States Election Project. www.electproject .org/home/voter-turnout/voter-turnout-data. Accessed September 5, 2015.

Voting Reform Issue

The expansion of the franchise (the right to vote) has been a topic of controversy since the nation's inception. Over time, the public's role in the electoral process has been both expanded and limited by various political reforms. The first attempts to give the public a greater role in the electoral process focused on the Electoral College. The Constitution grants the Electoral College the right to select the president of the United States (except in cases of an Electoral College tie), but states were free to use any means they desired to select their electors. Most states permitted state legislatures to select their electors, rather than relying on a popular vote.

The problems that surfaced in the **Campaign of 1824** challenged these traditional practices. In this election, Andrew Jackson, running under the Democratic-Republican label, built a strong base of popular support. Jackson was running against John Quincy Adams, William Crawford, and Henry Clay, all of whom were using a variant of the Democratic-Republican label. At the time, eighteen states had begun using the popular vote to select their presidential electors, while six continued to let state legislatures assign their electors. One hundred and thirty-one electoral votes were necessary to win the election. Jackson had ninety-nine electoral votes (and 43.1% of the popular vote), Adams had eighty-four electoral votes (and 30.5% of the popular vote), Crawford had forty-one electoral votes (and 13.2% of the popular vote), and Clay had thirty-seven electoral votes (and 13.1% of the popular vote). As dictated by the Constitution, the House of Representatives was tasked with deciding the outcome of the election. Each state received a single vote, which they could cast for one of the top three vote earners. Clay, who came in fourth, threw his support behind Adams, who was ultimately selected by the House. In exchange, Adams appointed Clay to his cabinet. Jackson's supporters accused Adams and Clay of striking a "corrupt bargain," which fueled efforts by Jackson's supporters to expand the role of the public in the electoral process.

By the **Campaign of 1828**, the old King Caucus system, which relied on informal Congressional delegations gathered for the selection of presidential candidates, had ended. There were no informal nominating Congressional caucuses in the selection of the incumbent; rather, President Adams was nominated by the National Republicans through independent endorsements by state legislatures and party meetings. Jackson was again nominated by the Democratic-Republicans in a similar fashion (Jackson having been nominated to run again by the Tennessee state legislature as early as 1825, just a few months after President Adams's inauguration). Jackson handily won the election, dislodging the president by winning most regions outside of the Northeast. During the Jacksonian era, the proportion of states that required property ownership for voter eligibility and (by 1855) the majority of states that had required that voters be taxpayers had eliminated such restrictions. The elimination of property requirements in Virginia and North Carolina during this era increased the electorates of those states by more than 50 percent, and in New York, the electorate increased by an even greater percentage. Political historians estimate that this expansion of the franchise led to voting-eligible turnout rates of near 80 percent by the middle of the nineteenth century.

During this same era, many states that had not originally restricted voting to whites only began to do so, and states also began limiting voting to U.S. citizens (whereas previously, one needed only to be a resident of the state to vote). States also moved to restrict voting by Native Americans, and they were aided in this endeavor by Chief Justice Marshall, who claimed that Native American groups were "domestic, dependent nations." In short, Native Americans were not viewed as American citizens, and thus they had no right to participate in the American electoral process. While the Indian Citizenship Act of 1924 officially recognized Native Americans as U.S. citizens, many state constitutions continued to limit Native American political participation until 1948.

In the aftermath of the Civil War, the Thirteenth, Fourteenth, and Fifteenth amendments formally gave African Americans the right to vote, and the presence of federal troops in southern states during Reconstruction protected this right, for a time. When Reconstruction ended, states quickly moved to pass **Jim Crow laws**, which were designed to limit African American participation in elections (as well as other nonwhite groups). It was not until the Civil Rights Act of 1964 and the **Voting Rights Act of 1965** that the federal government offered real protections to African Americans seeking to register and vote in federal elections.

Asian Americans, who had historically come to the United States to construct the railroads, were also objects of suspicion in the political arena. Like African Americans, they were viewed as a source of cheap labor, but many Americans had no desire to extend political rights to Asian immigrants. A series of federal laws, beginning in 1882, severely limited the ability of Chinese and Japanese persons to immigrate to the United States and prevented them from applying for citizenship once they arrived. An assortment of alien land laws passed in the 1910s and 1920s barred Asians from owning land. It was not until the Magnuson Act of 1943 that persons of Chinese origin were eligible to become citizens. The Immigration Act of 1965 eliminated ethnic quotas for immigration to the United States and permitted Asian citizens to sponsor the immigration of family members to the United States.

While some territories and municipalities offered women the right to vote as early as the nineteenth century, women generally were not permitted to vote in federal elections. Numerous third parties (Greenbacks, Socialists, Bull Moose) backed women's suffrage, some as early as the 1800s; however, the Nineteenth Amendment, which granted women the right to vote, was not ratified until 1920. Similarly, some states permitted younger Americans to vote prior to the ratification of the Twenty-Sixth Amendment, although eighteen-to-twenty-year-olds across the nation gained federal voting rights in 1971. Still, other restrictions on the franchise remained. In *Dunn v. Blumstein* in 1972, the Supreme Court ruled that Tennessee's residency requirement was excessive. This effectively forced all states to limit the amount of time a voter must live in a state prior to being able to vote. It is now the norm for states to require a residency period of thirty days prior to voter registration (and registration deadlines are generally no earlier than thirty days prior to an election).

Overall, the history of voting for nonwhites in the United States has been one of exclusion; for centuries, laws regulating citizenship, access to property, poll taxes, arbitrary implementation of literacy and morals standards, and even threats and intimidation were used to keep these groups from voting, even when they appeared to have a legal right to do so. The numerous changes that occurred in the 1960s served to change the population of the United States in profound ways. The electorate became more diverse, both ethnically and socioeconomically. With the passage of the Twenty-Sixth Amendment, coinciding with the passage of the baby boom generation into adulthood, it also became younger (at least theoretically).

One of the remaining restrictions on access to the franchise is the laws that limit political participation by convicted felons. While the Constitution does not prohibit voting (or office holding) by felons, most states limit voting by individuals who have been convicted of a crime. Only two states (Vermont and Maine) do not limit the voting rights of felons. Thirteen other states and the District of Columbia restore voting rights automatically after a person is released from prison. Nineteen states require that felons complete their prison time, plus probation time on parole, before their voting rights are restored. Eleven states (primarily in the South and the West) permanently disenfranchise some portion of the felon population. Virginia and Kentucky have had the strictest rules, permanently disenfranchising all felons (although individuals may appeal to the governor to restore their rights), and they have been joined by Florida and Iowa. As Michelle Alexander points out, such rules are another way to limit political participation by persons of color. She finds that African Americans and Latinos are disproportionately targeted by law enforcement, particularly for drug-related crimes, and that they are far more likely than whites to be convicted and imprisoned for similar offenses. This disparity has both social and political consequences, and it tends to serve the same function as the **Jim Crow laws** of the twentieth century did—to permanently disenfranchise many people of color and relegate them to an economic and social underclass.

While there are few remaining restrictions on who is eligible to vote in the United States, political scientists have found that registration requirements and deadlines serve as one of the primary barriers in preventing many eligible Americans from casting a ballot. In an attempt to lower such barriers to voting, Congress passed the **National Voter Registration Act of 1993**. This law requires that states allow citizens to register to vote when they are obtaining a driver's license or state identification card, or when receiving a federal service, and provides several other options for registering that do not require that the voter show up in person. The Help America Vote Act of 2002 permits voters the option of casting a **provisional ballot** if the state has mishandled a voter's registration form. And several states have adopted Election Day registration to permit voters to register at the same time they cast a ballot. States also began to provide **early voting** opportunities, and more states offered no-excuse absentee ballots. Voter turnout surged in the **Campaign of 2004** and the **Campaign of 2008,** partly as a result of these reforms.

Some states have also attempted to lower the barriers to voting on their own, by offering Election Day registration (CO, CT, DC, ID, IL, IA, ME, MN, MT, NH, VY, WI, WY) or by eliminating the registration process altogether (ND), so that citizens need not plan in advance to vote. Vermont will have Election Day registration (EDR) in place by the **Campaign of 2016**, and California and Vermont will enact EDR in a subsequent election. Since 1998, Oregon has conducted all of its elections entirely by mail, sending each of its registered voters a ballot by mail several weeks before the election. This eliminates the need for voters to find their polling place and to allocate time to vote on Election Day. In March 2015, Oregon became the first state to implement automatic voter registration, whereby the state assumed responsibility for registering all eligible voters upon their eighteenth birthday. States with Election Day registration, as well as states such as Oregon that lower the barriers to voting in other ways, consistently demonstrate higher levels of voter turnout than do other states.

More recently, though, many states have been moving in the other direction, seeking to make both registration and voting more difficult. After the 2010 midterms, the Republican Party gained or solidified their control of many state legislative chambers. While the GOP had historically supported attempts to expand the franchise, the Tea Party faction of the GOP did not share this view. They feared that continued high turnout of young voters, minority voters, and poor voters would make it difficult for their party to regain the White House in 2012. At the urging of their Tea Party members, these GOP-dominated legislatures engaged in the first major effort in decades to limit the size of the eligible electorate, rather than to expand it. The rationale offered for these "reforms" was that they were necessary to prevent voter fraud.

By the **Campaign of 2012**, nine states created more stringent photo identification requirements for voter identification at the polls, and three states passed laws requiring proof of U.S. citizenship in order to register to vote. Five states dramatically reduced the time period allotted for early voting; as part of this process, both Florida and Ohio eliminated the Sunday prior to Election Day commonly used by African Americans and Latinos. Six states made it harder for citizens to register to vote, including restrictions on voter registration drives. Ironically, these restrictions on voter registration drives came back to haunt the GOP, particularly in Florida. Both parties had long relied on the League of Women Voters (LWV) and other groups that had traditionally conducted nonpartisan voter registration in the state (free of charge). In 2012, LWV refused to register voters in Florida, not wanting to navigate the onerous new state regulations or incur the draconian penalties. This disproportionately hampered the GOP, which had not devoted many resources to mobilization. Democrats, on the other hand, already had a successful in-house voter mobilization strategy in Florida that they had used in 2008 and had not yet dismantled.

In the aftermath of the 2012 election, the voting rights landscape changed dramatically. The Supreme Court ruled Section 4 of the Voting Rights Act invalid in *Shelby County v. Holder*, rejecting the formula used to subject states with a history of voter discrimination to preclearance by the Justice Department prior to making any changes in their electoral laws. While the Voting Rights Act remained intact, states that were previously subject to federal oversight were now free to pass whatever electoral or voting restrictions they liked, and citizens would have to petition the courts and demonstrate that they were being harmed by the new policy. Rather than the burden being on the state to show that its proposed policies would not be harmful, the burden was now on the citizen to show that they were. Texas, North Carolina, Mississippi, and Alabama proceeded with restrictive voter identification laws in the aftermath of *Shelby*. Other states have followed suit. The Maine legislature repealed its state's Election Day registration policy after the 2012 election, although voters reinstated it through a referendum in the fall of 2013.

In the summer of 2015, the Fifth Circuit Court of Appeals struck down Texas's voter identification law, ruling that it unfairly discriminated against African Americans and Latinos, in violation of the Voting Rights Act. Texas is appealing the decision. North Carolina and Wisconsin also have challenges to their voter identification laws that are winding their way through the federal courts.

While the rationale for voter identification laws is that they combat fraud, the evidence that they are effective in this endeavor is negligible, for a variety of reasons. First, rates of documented voter fraud in the United States are quite rare. News21, a Carnegie-Knight-funded investigative project, evaluated public records and claims of fraud in all fifty states since 2000. It documented 2,000 instances of improper ballots cast (out of 146 million votes cast), most of them absentee, or occurring as a result of error (by the clerk, or by voters confused about their eligibility). Moreover, in-person voter fraud is extremely uncommon—the News21 investigation documented ten cases total across twelve years and fifty states (less than one instance per year nationwide). When voter fraud does occur, it is most likely to occur with absentee ballots, or by tampering with ballots that have already been cast. Voter identification laws tend to address in-person voting only, and thus they provide no protection for fraudulent use of absentee ballots—the easiest type of fraud to commit. And they do not address more systemic instances of fraud, where ballots are tampered with by someone other than the voter (e.g., postal employees, election officials). Nor do such laws appear to protect the perceived integrity of the electoral process. Ansolabehere and Persily examined citizens' perceptions of ballot integrity in states with strict voter identification laws and contrasted them with views of citizens who lived in states without such laws. They found that views of fraud did not vary by electoral environment; citizens in states with strict laws did not view their electoral system as being fairer or safer from fraud. Rather, Ansolabehere and Persily found that the partisanship of the citizen and the party in power influenced perceptions of fairness. Citizens believe the electoral process is fair when their side wins an election, and they view the process as unfair when their side loses. Thus, fears of stolen elections are, essentially, rationalizations for electoral defeat.

Aside from their symbolic effects, though, voter identification laws can materially influence the cost of a citizen's participation, and thus, opponents have argued that they will drive down voter turnout of economically disadvantaged groups. The Government Accounting Office conducted a study on the effects of strict voter identification laws on voter turnout. They found that when they examined Kansas and Tennessee from 2008 to 2012, when both states had toughened up their identification laws substantially, compared to a group of control states that had not changed their laws during this period (Alabama, Arkansas, Delaware, and Maine) but otherwise had similar traits in terms of electoral competitiveness and other factors, the new laws did influence turnout. In Kansas, turnout dropped by 1.9 to 2.2 percentage points, and in Tennessee, it dropped by 2.2 to 3.2 percentage points. Moreover, the drop in turnout was not distributed evenly across the population; turnout was down far more among voters aged eighteen to twenty-three than it was among voters aged forty-four to fifty-three, turnout was down far more among voters who had been registered for a year or less than it was among voters who had been registered twenty years or more, and turnout was down among African Americans far more than it was among whites (with inconsistent patterns among other ethnic groups, who did not appear in large numbers in these states).

Voting reform promises to be a popular topic in the **Campaign of 2016,** in part because many of the Democratic candidates have made it a cornerstone of their agendas. Bernie Sanders is campaigning on a bill he introduced to make Election Day a national holiday, and he has proposed a constitutional amendment to preclude the kind of unlimited election spending by outside groups that the Supreme Court allowed in *Citizens United.* President Barack Obama has advocated a national system of automatic registration, which has been embraced by all of the Democratic Party hopefuls. Hillary Clinton has made voting rights a central theme of her campaign, advocating a mandatory minimum of twenty days of early voting in all states, automatic voter registration (with an opt-out feature), automatic updates to voter registration, online voter registration, more opportunities for felon re-enfranchisement, and strengthening the Voting Rights Act. Several of the GOP hopefuls are associated with efforts to enact more stringent voter identification requirements (Walker, Kasich, Perry) or have expressed support for such requirements (Rubio, Graham). Both Cruz and Paul have expressed opposition to the Voting Rights Act. Former Florida governor Jeb Bush, brother of Republican presidential nominee and eventual winner of the 2000 general election, George

W. Bush, presided over the notorious 2000 presidential election in which over ten thousand eligible voters, most of them African American and Latino, were purged from the electoral rolls for being suspected felons. It appears likely that there will be little partisan agreement on the topic of voter registration or voter identification.

There is one area, however, where the parties appear to be in agreement: online voter registration. The option was uncommon in 2008, with only two states providing voters the opportunity to complete the voter registration process online. By 2016, twenty-two states and the District of Columbia will permit voters to register online. The ideological makeup of the states that allow online registration is diverse, providing the only glimmer of bipartisanship on a topic that is growing increasingly partisan and polarized.

See also Civil Rights Issue; Get-Out-the-Vote (GOTV) Programs; Jim Crow Laws; Voting Eligible Population (VEP) Turnout; Voting Rights Act of 1965; Women's Rights Issue

Additional Resources

Alexander, Michelle. *The New Jim Crow.* Revised ed. New York: The New Press, 2011.

American Civil Liberties Union. "Timeline: Voting Rights Act." http://www.aclu.org/voting-rights/voting-rights-act-timeline. Accessed October 13, 2015.

Ansolabehere, Stephen, and Nathaniel Persily. "Vote Fraud in the Eye of the Beholder: The Role of Public Opinion in the Challenge to Voter Identification Requirements." Columbia Public Law Research Paper No. 08-170, February 21, 2008.

Berman, Ari. "The GOP War on Voting." *Rolling Stone*, August 30, 2011.

Berman, Ari. *Give Us the Ballot: The Modern Struggle for Voting Rights in America.* New York: Farrar, Straus and Giroux, 2015.

Brennan Center, New York University School of Law. "Voting Rights and Elections." http://www.brennancenter.org/content/section/category/voting_rights_elections/. Accessed October 13, 2015.

Government Accounting Office. "Elections: Issues Related to State Voter Identification Laws," GAO-14-634, September 2014 (revised February 27, 2015).

Keyssar, Alexander. "The Strange Career of Voter Suppression." *New York Times*, February 12, 2012.

Keyssar, Alexander. *The Right to Vote: The Contested History of Democracy in the United States.* New York: Basic Books, 2000.

News21. "Who Can Vote." http://votingrights.news21.com/. Accessed October 13, 2015.

Voting Rights Act of 1965

While the Civil War Amendments to the U.S. Constitution both guaranteed African Americans citizenship and protected their right to vote (as did the Civil Rights Acts of 1870 and 1871), the **Jim Crow laws** that followed Reconstruction placed serious limitations on African American political expression. Nonwhite Americans were not only subject to legal tactics such as literacy tests, poll taxes, "grandfather clauses" (i.e., restrictions on one's right to vote justified on the grounds that one's grandfather did not possess that right and the presumption that enfranchisement is somehow a function of ancestry or some other social requirement and not an objective, universal right), and the all-white primary; but they were also victims of a persistent climate of physical and emotional intimidation, and worse still, the deadly terror imposed on African Americans and other minorities through the brutality of lynching. Consequently, African American electoral participation plummeted in the latter nineteenth century and early decades of the twentieth century.

Confronted by considerable social and political resistance, organizations like the NAACP (National Association for the Advancement of Colored People) were founded near the turn of the century to promote and protect the constitutional rights of African Americans. At the presidential level, both President Theodore Roosevelt (in his 1906 State of the Union address) and President Warren Harding (in a speech delivered in Birmingham, Alabama, in October 1921) sternly condemned the lynching epidemic and began to publicly argue for the protection of African American political rights; and there was some movement by African Americans to press for their rights as guaranteed under the Constitution; but the crises, unprecedented in their scope and gravity, of the Great Depression and World War II delayed and eclipsed the struggle for minority rights. However, by the middle of the twentieth century, white voters outside of the South appeared ready to end the political and social discrimination faced by African Americans. The Republican Party platform in the **Campaign of 1944** called for the abolition of the poll tax, and the Democratic Party platform in the **Campaign of 1948** contained a civil rights platform that pledged "the right to full and equal political participation." The Supreme Court struck down the practice of all-white primaries in the 1940s, restrictive covenants in housing in the 1940s, and segregation in law schools and in public schools in the 1950s, and President Dwight Eisenhower used federal troops to enforce school desegregation orders in the South. Outside of the South, there was bipartisan support for the political enfranchisement of black voters. In the **Campaign of 1960**, both the Democratic and Republican parties supported a constitutional amendment to end poll taxes in federal elections; and the Twenty-Fourth Amendment was ratified in 1964. In *Harper v. Virginia Board of Elections* in 1966, the Supreme Court found the use of poll taxes in state elections to be unconstitutional as well.

The Voting Rights Act of 1965 (VRA) effectively ended the use of literacy tests in elections. Equally significant, the VRA provided for the appointment of federal registrars in southern states with a history of low rates of African American voter registration. Extensions of the VRA in 1970, 1975, 1982, and 2006 provided for the use of bilingual election materials in areas with sizable non-English-speaking populations, extended federal protections to disabled voters, required that states with a history of voting discrimination obtain federal preclearance for changes in their election laws, and provided for federal election monitors to ensure that voters were not intimidated at the polls on Election Day, a provision that has been used in more recent years to protect other vulnerable groups such as Chinese Americans, Latinos, and Arab Americans. The 1982 extensions of the VRA created majority-minority districts to improve the representation of ethnic minorities in the House of Representatives. The implementation of the VRA has paved the way for millions of African Americans, Latinos, and Asian Americans to register and vote throughout the nation, and it has also significantly increased the representation of nonwhites in the U.S. Congress. Writer Ari Berman counted upward of three thousand restrictive laws that were thwarted between 1965 and 2013 by the federal courts and the Justice Department under the VRA.

In June 2013, a divided Supreme Court overturned Section 4 of the VRA—the formula used to determine which states (and counties) were subject to the preclearance conditions of Section 5—in the landmark decision *Shelby County v. Holder*, arguing that the formula was dated and needed to be updated. While the remainder of the VRA was intact, states and counties that were previously required to clear any changes in their election laws (including the drawing of local, state, and federal electoral district lines) with the Department of Justice or the federal courts were now free to alter their laws at will. The effect was swiftly felt: Texas, North Dakota, and North Carolina enacted strict new voter identification laws; Arkansas, Tennessee, and Virginia enacted photo identification requirements; North Carolina and Ohio eliminated their same-day registration; North Carolina eliminated pre-registration for sixteen- and seventeen-year olds; Nebraska, Wisconsin, Ohio, and North Carolina reduced their early voting periods; Virginia placed stricter restrictions on third-party voter registration activities; Indiana permitted challengers to demand proof of identification from voters; Ohio made absentee ballot availability subject to funding; and Ohio prohibited individuals who lacked identification or a Social Security number from voting even with a provisional ballot. Changes were also felt at a local level, where most of the VRA's influence had resided; for example, Georgia moved some of its municipal elections (notably, in counties with significant African American populations) to dates that were not in November, and North Carolina downsized its voting districts, with many of the cuts taking place in districts that served low-income and minority communities. This forced the Department of Justice, joined by various groups committed to the protection of the franchise, to file suit against specific laws limiting access to the ballot. For example, in early August 2015, a federal appeals court struck down a voter identification law enacted by the Texas state legislature.

Congress proposed remedial legislation after the *Shelby* ruling; however, Republicans, who controlled both chambers after the 2014 midterm, expressed no interest in debating or voting on the proposed legislation (despite overwhelming bipartisan support for the renewal of the VRA as late as 2006, and the support of then-president George W. Bush for the legislation). The Voting Rights Advancement Act of 2015 is yet another attempt to revive the VRA, including a new formula for preclearance, federal approval of state voter identification laws, and prohibition of minority vote suppression. Senator Patrick Leahy (D-VT) is the Senate sponsor of the bill, and he has been joined by Senator Lisa Murkowski (R-AK). In the House, Rep. John Lewis (D-GA) is sponsoring the bill. A previous version of the bill had been authored by Rep. Jim Sensenbrenner (R-WI).

See also Civil Rights Issue; Race Relations Issue; Symbolic Racism; Voting Reform Issue

Additional Resources

American Civil Liberties Union. "Timeline: Voting Rights Act." http://www.aclu.org/voting-rights/voting-rights-act-timeline. Accessed September 15, 2015.

Berman, Ari. *Give Us the Ballot: The Modern Struggle for Voting Rights in America.* New York: Farrar, Straus and Giroux, 2015.

Davis, Ronald L. F. "Creating Jim Crow." The History of Jim Crow. http://www.jimcrow history.org/history/creating2.htm.

Flores, Henry. *Latinos and the Voting Rights Act: The Search for Racial Purpose.* New York: Lexington Books, 2015.

Office of the Clerk, U.S. House of Representatives. "Black Americans in Congress: Constitutional Amendments and Major Civil Rights Acts of Congress." http://baic.house.gov/historical-data/civil-rights-acts-and-amendments.html. Accessed September 15, 2015.

War and Peace Issue

The **Campaign of 1812** was the first presidential campaign conducted during wartime. The ongoing war between France, Britain, and other European powers had created sharp sectional divisions in the United States. A bloc of congressional war hawks, primarily from the South and the West, saw the European conflict as an opportunity to expand American power at the expense of British Canada and Spanish Florida, and they lobbied then-president James Madison for a declaration of war against Britain. Needing the support of the war hawks to obtain the Democratic-Republican nomination, Madison aligned himself with the hawks, and in June 1812, Madison asked Congress to declare war against Britain.

Rumors of war with Mexico over the annexation of Texas loomed over the **Campaign of 1844**. James K. Polk, the Democratic nominee, was a vocal advocate of the doctrine of manifest destiny. The Democratic platform endorsed the annexation of Texas and supported territorial claims to the whole of the Oregon Territory. The Whigs nominated Henry Clay, who opposed war with Mexico, fearing that it would undermine the nation's precarious sectional balance of power.

Polk turned the election into a referendum on the annexation of Texas. Democrats effectively used the slogans "Polk, Dallas, Texas, Oregon and the Tariff of '42," "Fifty-four Forty or Fight," and similar slogans to propel Polk to a stunning dark-horse upset over the statesmanlike Clay. Texas was annexed, and war soon followed. A treaty with Britain diplomatically settled the ongoing dispute over the Oregon Territory.

The future of the Union itself became the central issue of the **Campaign of 1860**. Demanding an end to the expansion of slavery, the fledgling Republican Party nominated Representative Abraham Lincoln of Illinois, long on record as critical of the "peculiar institution." Pro-slavery southern secessionists warned that the election of Lincoln would result in the dissolution of the Union. Supporters of Northern Democrat Stephen Douglas used the slogan "Douglas and Johnson: The Union Now and Forever" to frame the election as a referendum on preserving the Union rather than as a referendum on slavery. John Bell's Southern Constitutional Union Party borrowed a phrase from Daniel Webster in proclaiming the principle "Liberty and Union Now and Forever One and Inseparable. No North, No South, No East, No West, Nothing but the Union." Southern Democrat John C. Breckinridge represented the pro-slavery faction of his party. The result of this election forever transformed American society at all levels: politically, socially, economically, culturally, and morally. Lincoln and the Republicans won a plurality of the popular vote but a bare majority of the Electoral College vote, and by the spring of 1861, the nation's sectional divisions had descended into a civil war.

By the **Campaign of 1864**, Lincoln's reelection prospects were threatened by growing northern disenchantment over the painfully slow progress of the war. The Northern Democratic Party nominated Lincoln's former commander of the Army of the Potomac, General George B. McClellan, and its platform attacked Lincoln for allegedly using his war powers to abridge the constitutional rights of citizens. Burdened with the demands of executing a war and running for reelection, Republicans relied on slogans such as "Don't Change Horses in Mid-Stream" to persuade northern voters to stand with the president, and to imply the risks involved in selecting new political leadership during a national crisis. In the end, a string of Union victories beginning with Gettysburg turned the electoral tide in Lincoln's favor, and the Republicans won with ease in November.

While the Democratic and Republican parties were not divided in the run-up to the Spanish-American War, by the **Campaign of 1900**, many in the Democratic Party had turned against imperialism and opposed the Treaty of Paris that would bring the war to a close (Democratic nominee William Jennings Bryan, however, was not among them). Bryan later criticized McKinley during the campaign for not liberating the Philippines as he had liberated Cuba. By continuing its policies of territorial expansion, the United States came to exercise power over subjects far removed from its own borders, in locations as far-flung as Guam and the Philippine Islands. In addition to the moral dilemmas posed by imperialism (namely, the imposition of foreign rule by a government ostensibly committed to self-determination), the maintenance and security of these new territories required extensive defense commitments that not only were expensive but also taxed the nation's commitment to neutrality in foreign conflicts. In response to the 1914 outbreak of World War I in Europe, President Woodrow Wilson declared that the United States would adhere to a policy of strict neutrality in order to avoid being drawn into the Great War. On August 19, Wilson delivered an address to Congress, offering a Declaration of Neutrality: "The effect of the war upon the United States will depend upon what American citizens say and do. Every man who really loves America will act and speak in the true spirit of neutrality, which is the spirit of impartiality and fairness and friendliness to all concerned. The spirit of the nation in this critical matter will be determined largely by what individuals and society and those gathered in public meetings do and say, upon what newspapers and magazines contain, upon what ministers utter in their pulpits, and men proclaim as their opinions upon the street."

Early in 1916, Germany notified the world that it reserved the right to sink any ship approaching Britain. The United States announced, in turn, that it would not tolerate the sinking of any neutral vessel. Then, on May 7, 1916, a German U-boat sank the British steamship *Lusitania*, resulting in a loss of one hundred American lives. The U.S. reaction to the *Lusitania*'s sinking forced Germany to revoke its blockade. The Democratic Party and Woodrow Wilson turned the **Campaign of 1916** into a referendum on Wilson's neutrality policy. Peace slogans used by the Wilson campaign included "He Kept Us Out of War," "War in the East, Peace in the West, Thank God for Woodrow Wilson," and "War in Europe, Peace in America."

Controversy within the Republican Party over the neutrality issue complicated efforts by Charles Evans Hughes to convince voters that he had no intention of getting the United States involved in the conflict. Former Republican president Theodore Roosevelt publicly lobbied for the United States to enter the war on the side of the Triple Entente: Great Britain, France, and Russia. Strong isolationist sentiment in regions beyond the Northeast helped Wilson return for a second term. But by late 1917, the United States was nonetheless drawn into World War I.

The **Campaign of 1940** found the United States confronting the prospect of another world war. In Europe, Nazi Germany had swiftly and astonishingly defeated Poland and France, threatening an invasion of Great Britain. In the Pacific, Imperial Japan waged a war on China and seemed intent on extending its sphere of influence over all of East Asia and the Pacific Ocean. Given the exigency of the moment, popular president Franklin Delano Roosevelt wrestled with a decision to run for an unprecedented third term, defying the venerable two-term tradition established by George Washington.

Roosevelt also faced strong isolationist sentiment reminiscent of 1916. Roosevelt's decision to seek a third term, not his efforts to help Great Britain fight off Nazi Germany, turned out to be the main issue of the 1940 presidential campaign. Throughout the 1940 campaign, supporters of Wendell Willkie, the Republican nominee, chanted, "No Third Term." As a result, the Roosevelt campaign devoted most of its energy to rebutting Republican allegations that the election of Roosevelt would start the nation on the road toward dictatorship. Roosevelt also stressed that by providing Britain the tools to combat Nazi Germany, it was much less likely that the United States would become embroiled in another war. Roosevelt promoted the United States as the "Arsenal of Democracy," which boosted American industry, mitigating some of the economic distress of the lingering Great Depression. Americans backed Roosevelt once again for a third term.

The **Campaign of 1944** constituted the first wartime presidential election since the Campaign of 1864. Taking a page from Lincoln's 1864 campaign, Democrats advised Americans to "Never Swap Horses in Midstream," defusing the fourth-term issue. Thomas E. Dewey, the Republican candidate, failed to convince the American public that the election of Roosevelt to a fourth term would deliver the country to a homegrown dictator. Dewey also failed to convince voters that his administration would more quickly achieve victory in the ongoing war.

With the **Campaign of 1952**, the United States was locked in a military stalemate on the Korean Peninsula. An arms race with Stalin's Soviet Union intensified a dangerous world climate. Republican candidate General Dwight Eisenhower proved a credible candidate capable of dealing with crisis abroad. His opponent, Adlai Stevenson, a New Deal Democrat, was an able leader who emphasized the domestic legacy of his predecessors. The Stevenson campaign reminded voters that "You Never Had It So Good" under Roosevelt's New Deal, but the revered war hero overwhelmed Stevenson's otherwise solid credentials.

Between the 1952 election and the **Campaign of 1960**, persistent and intense Cold War competition with the Soviet Union and Communist China forced presidential campaigns to devote considerable time and energy to national security issues. Republican nominee Vice President Richard Nixon relied heavily on his experience to persuade voters that he was more qualified to be president than the Democratic presidential candidate, Massachusetts senator John F. Kennedy.

With slogans such as "Experience Counts" and "Keep America Strong," Nixon attempted to overshadow the young senator's inexperience. The Kennedy campaign countered with a new vision for the United States. At the same time, the Kennedy campaign attempted to close the experience gap by alleging the existence of a missile gap to the advantage of the Soviets. Kennedy's insistence that if elected president he would close the missile gap helped to reassure the public that Kennedy had the strength to deal with foreign threats. Kennedy won, but after the election, it became apparent that a missile gap never really existed.

Vice President Lyndon Johnson assumed the presidency in November 1963 upon the shocking assassination of President Kennedy. Johnson also was compelled to deal with war and peace, and in depicting Republican candidate Barry Goldwater as an unpredictable war hawk. LBJ won the November election in the biggest landslide since Franklin Roosevelt. Taking advantage of Goldwater's controversial positions on Vietnam and the feasibility of using nuclear weapons to achieve a tactical military victory, the Johnson campaign characterized Goldwater as an extremist. Johnson became the candidate for peace, an effective stance given the dangers of nuclear warfare. "The Stakes Are Too High for You to Stay Home" became a compelling slogan in Johnson's campaign.

From November 1964 through 1967, American involvement in the Vietnam War escalated. Against his 1964 campaign pledge, President Johnson deployed hundreds of thousands of troops to the conflict. The antiwar movement gathered strength in the lead-up to the 1968 election, providing momentum to the idealistic campaign of Minnesota senator Eugene McCarthy, who ultimately deflated Johnson's reelection hopes by nearly defeating the president in the critical New Hampshire primary. In late March, Johnson withdrew from the race, and shortly thereafter Vice President Hubert Humphrey and Senator Robert Kennedy joined the contest for the Democratic nomination. With his victory in the California primary, Robert Kennedy became the front-runner for the nomination, a fleeting moment of triumph violently obliterated by an assassin's bullet even while partisans celebrated the victory.

With the party in disarray, having lost the incumbent Johnson and the charismatic Kennedy, thousands of antiwar demonstrators descended upon the Democratic summer convention in Chicago. Rioting roiled the streets of Chicago while Humphrey received the nomination. Republicans turned to Richard Nixon, who claimed to hold a secret plan for ending U.S. involvement in the war. In a series of well-crafted ads, Nixon's campaign promised to lead the nation out of the turmoil of the 1960s and into the brighter decade ahead. "This Time Vote Like Your Whole World Depended on It" became one of the key slogans for the Nixon campaign. There is some evidence that candidate Nixon may have interfered with President Johnson's peace negotiations with the government in Hanoi to forestall any political momentum that could have been gained by Humphrey as a result.

Once elected, Nixon failed to end the conflict in Vietnam, instead expanding it into Cambodia. In his 1972 reelection campaign, Nixon stressed "peace with honor" in Vietnam, and emphasized his program of "Vietnamization" as means to reduce, but not eliminate, America's combat role in Southeast Asia. At the same time, Nixon entered into a series of arms control negotiations with the Soviet Union, producing the Anti-Ballistic Missile Treaty in the spring of 1972, which limited the two countries' ability to create missile defense systems, and the Strategic Arms Limitation Talks (SALT), which set ceilings on the maximum number of intercontinental ballistic missiles in each country's arsenal. The second phase of the SALT talks, which began during Nixon's administration, were concluded by Nixon's successor, Gerald Ford, and the SALT II treaty was sent to the U.S. Senate for ratification after Democrat Jimmy Carter had been elected in the **Campaign of 1976**. Relations with the Soviets had deteriorated during this time period, and Carter was forced to withdraw the treaty from the Senate, which had refused to ratify it. (The United States and the Soviet Union, however, adhered to the terms of the treaty regardless, until its expiration.) Also in the spring of 1972, Nixon made an official visit to China and normalized relations with the Communist country that had long been an adversary of the United States.

The **Campaign of 1980** was conducted in an environment of heightened Cold War tensions, a recent Soviet invasion of neighboring Afghanistan, and American hostages in Iran. Incumbent president Jimmy Carter, faced with public angst over what appeared to be an increasingly hostile world, advocated increased military spending and attempted (without success) a risky hostage rescue. He also boycotted the summer Olympics in Moscow (which the Soviets reciprocated by boycotting the Los Angeles Olympics in 1984). Republican nominee Ronald Reagan advocated an even larger increase in defense spending and suggested the need for a more aggressive posture in dealing with the Soviets as a means to regain American prestige abroad and protect the nation's security. While foreign policy concerns undoubtedly played a role in the outcome of the 1980 election, so too did the woeful state of the U.S. economy. While Carter had inherited a poor economy from his predecessor, he had not managed to find a workable solution to the nation's dual problems of joblessness and high prices. While foreign policy crises can create a rally-around-the-flag effect, generating an upswing in a president's domestic approval ratings, in Carter's case, it appeared that there was little that he was able to do right. His foreign policy problems compounded his domestic policy problems.

After being elected, President Reagan set about keeping his promise to increase defense spending. Beyond this, he invaded the tiny island nation of Grenada in October 1983, claiming that the Marxist government posed a threat to the hundreds of American tourists and medical students on the island. It later emerged that Reagan had failed to notify British Prime Minister Margaret Thatcher in advance of his actions; Grenada was a British protectorate. The Grenada action was controversial both at home and abroad. Supporters argued that defense of Americans abroad was important, and that this suggested that Reagan was willing to act militarily when American security was threatened. They viewed this as a warning to the nation's enemies that the United States would be willing to act if provoked. Critics suggested that Reagan was engaging in the politics of distraction, when there was no real, meaningful threat in Grenada. They pointed out that there were ample reasons why the president might want the public to focus its attention elsewhere—shortly before the Grenada invasion, also in October 1983, a suicide bomber drove a truck packed with explosives through the open gate of the Marine barracks in Beirut, killing 241 service members. Indeed, six months earlier, the U.S. embassy in Beirut had been targeted, and sixty-three people, seventeen of whom were Americans, died in the bombing; this gave the impression that the White House had not taken the previous events in Beirut seriously and thus risked the safety of the Marines unnecessarily. In the aftermath of these events, Congress conducted a bipartisan investigation, assessing the errors that led to the deaths and suggesting improved security measures. Yet, in March 1984, Beirut's CIA station chief, Bill Buckley, was kidnapped, tortured, and murdered, and in September 1984, an embassy annex in Beirut was bombed—apparently the security changes recommended by Congress were never implemented. In the end, Reagan withdrew U.S. forces from Lebanon.

In the **Campaign of 1984**, Reagan defended the military buildup, arguing that he only sought parity and not superiority, and in March 1983, he announced the Strategic Defense Initiative (SDI) program, which would have created a complicated ballistic missile defense system and would have led to the abrogation of the ABM Treaty. Journalists called this project the "Star Wars" system in a nod to the futuristic notion of ballistic missile defense, but the term was also sarcastic—the SDI system never managed to successfully target missiles in tests, where the timing and location of the missiles were known in advance, and most scientists of the day doubted that it was realistic to do so in the event of a real-world conflict (when foreign missiles needed to be targeted without mistake in the boost phase, which was over quite quickly). When asked about his previous use of the phrase "evil empire" to describe the USSR, Reagan backtracked slightly in 1984, suggesting that he would be willing to engage in arms control negotiations with the Soviets and that he did not seek the destruction of their political system. Democrat Walter Mondale, while also critical of the Soviets, suggested that the arms race was irresponsible, arguing that simply spending more on the military was not the same as spending money wisely. Mondale specifically criticized President Reagan for making no progress on arms control agreements during his time in office, further suggesting that the president was not interested in disarmament. Mondale also criticized the president for leaving Lebanon in humiliating circumstances, and he indicated that he would deploy the military to defend U.S. interests there. Mondale added that he would be willing to use U.S. military force in Central America as well to defend U.S. interests, but that he would not do so covertly and not without congressional approval, a criticism of Reagan's covert support for the contras and other actors in the region.

In October 1986, Reagan and Mikhail Gorbachev, the Soviet leader, met at a summit in Reykjavik. Gorbachev unexpectedly agreed to eliminate his country's nuclear weapons if the United States would do the same, but he was only willing to do so if the United States abandoned its plans for SDI. While the summit at Reykjavik produced no policy successes, it appeared to open the door to the possibility that the Soviets would be willing to reduce their nuclear stockpiles (previous agreements had had quotas but did not dismantle existing stockpiles). Gorbachev and Reagan eventually negotiated the Intermediate-Range Nuclear Forces (INF) Treaty in 1987, which was the first treaty to eliminate an entire class of nuclear weapons.

Reagan's vice president, George H. W. Bush, campaigned for president in the **Campaign of 1988** in a new world, one where the virulent conflict between the United States and the USSR appeared to be ending. He called for a "kinder, gentler nation," and while he suggested that the United States needed to be cautious in its dealings with its former adversary, he also noted that "our new relationship in part reflects the triumph of hope and strength over experience. But hope is good. And so is strength. And vigilance." Bush focused on specific defense programs, in particular the Midgetman missile system and the MX missile, suggesting that his opponent would do away with these programs, or would even support a unilateral nuclear freeze. Bush stated in a debate that he could not commit to cutting any portion of the defense budget, because if he were to mention a program that he did not believe was necessary, this could be giving away critical information to the Soviets that could be used against the United States. He cautioned against going back to the days when "we were the laughingstock of the world."

Bush's opponent, Massachusetts governor Mike Dukakis, criticized Bush and Reagan for enabling Panamanian dictator Manuel Noriega, arguing that U.S. complicity over Panama's involvement in drug trafficking was leading to problems of drug abuse and addiction on the home front. He also argued that Bush was actively involved in the decision to sell weapons to the Iranian government and use the funds for the contras, and that he was a supporter of Ferdinand Marcos before he was deposed, attempting to neutralize Bush's foreign policy experience by reminding voters of some of the more distasteful elements of that background. Dukakis was generally critical of the Reagan administration's efforts to destabilize regimes in Central America and Africa (i.e., Angola) and the lack of concern about economic inequality outside of the United States. In an unfortunate attempt to demonstrate his interest in foreign policy and the military, Dukakis paid a visit to the Chrysler tank factory outside of Detroit and was photographed taking a ride in a tank. Bush used the footage, which was visually unflattering, to mock him in a campaign ad. Ultimately, Bush was able to benefit from serving in a popular presidential administration and linking himself to the achievements of that administration. The arms control agreements at of Reagan's second term, and the demise of the Soviet Union, seemed to justify Reagan's earlier, more belligerent approach to the Soviet Union.

Once in office, Bush, with an experienced foreign policy team at his side, focused on negotiating additional agreements with the Soviets and dealing with the opening of eastern Europe. The Bush administration was not reluctant to engage in military conflict, despite Bush having been portrayed as soft by his detractors throughout the election campaign. In December 1989, less than a year after taking office, Bush sent tens of thousands of U.S. troops into Panama in order to arrest leader Manuel Noriega on charges of drug trafficking and extradite him to the United States (creating a regime change in the bargain). The conflict was over within weeks, and U.S. troops returned home. Twenty American soldiers were killed, and somewhere between three hundred and five hundred Panamanians died in the conflict. Bush sought neither UN nor OAS approval; the action was unilateral. A little more than a year later, in the winter of 1990, Iraq invaded Kuwait, and Bush once again supported an invasion. In this instance, he sought international support, but as was the case with Panama, the military objectives were limited: Iraq was to be driven out of Kuwait, the Kuwaiti government (in no way a democracy) was to be restored, and troops would then leave the region. The conflict in Kuwait was widely televised, akin to a sporting event, and Bush experienced a surge in public approval as people "rallied around the flag."

But the support did not last. While Bush had been concerned about foreign policy (the press had been counting how many days he had spent in the United States in recent years), economic conditions at home were grim. Once the conflict in Kuwait was over, Bush concentrated his efforts on getting reelected, moving Secretary of State James Baker out of the State Department to head up his reelection campaign. Bush touted the first Gulf War as a major foreign policy accomplishment and claimed primary responsibility for ending the Cold War as his major pitch to voters in the **Campaign of 1992**. However, the generally poor state of the domestic economy proved to be more important to voters, who were dismayed to note Bush's amazement at a cash register scanner at a campaign stop (clearly, the candidate had not shopped for groceries in quite some time), and Bush failed to win reelection. More than a decade later, in the **Campaign of 2004**, Bush's son George W. Bush ran for reelection after involving the United States in military interventions in both Afghanistan and Iraq in response to the September 11, 2001, terrorist attacks on the United States. While Bush had declared the end of hostilities in Iraq during his infamous "Mission Accomplished" speech in May 2003, the country was still at war in Iraq when Election Day rolled around. Bush urged voters to "stay the course" and suggested that with perseverance, the United States would be victorious in both conflicts. In a close election, Bush narrowly defeated Democratic nominee John Kerry. Kerry had initially supported U.S. involvement in both conflicts, but later he became critical of the war in Iraq. However, he was unwilling to state that with hindsight, he would have refused to enter the conflict. Kerry's inability to provide a clear alternative to the policies being pursued by the Bush administration undoubtedly hampered his candidacy.

The wars in both Iraq and Afghanistan were still going strong by the **Campaign of 2008**. Democratic nominee Barack Obama promised to quickly withdraw U.S. troops from Iraq and to reallocate them to Afghanistan, where he argued that U.S. efforts were seriously under-resourced. Republican nominee John McCain, on the other hand, campaigned to keep U.S. troops in Iraq indefinitely, and to consider an invasion of neighboring Iran if it appeared that the country was close to developing a nuclear capability. While political analysts originally viewed the two conflicts in the Middle East as the potential determinants of the 2008 election outcome, the quickly sinking economy appeared to eclipse most of voters' foreign policy concerns.

Once the **Campaign of 2012** was under way, initial similarities between the parties quickly ended. While Republican candidates appeared almost isolationist to some observers in the early days of the campaign, by the primary season, most were advocating increases in military spending and a more activist U.S. foreign policy (with Ron Paul as a notable exception). The Republican Party as a whole expressed a strong commitment to the ideals of **American exceptionalism**, accusing Obama and the Democrats of being willing to give up the country's role as a global hegemonic power in favor of a multipolar system. The Democrats argued that costs of continuing the war in Afghanistan should be weighed against the U.S. ability to pay for the conflict, given the challenges faced by Americans on the home front. Democrats supported a more limited U.S. role in conflicts overseas, with a greater emphasis on training and support for domestic security forces in Afghanistan and a near-term withdrawal of U.S. forces from the region. The Republican Party's response to the Arab Spring remained murky; while the party remained strongly pro-Israel, it was not clear how this should influence U.S. policy toward other states in the region (other than Iran). Obama, for his part, defended his use of force in Libya as part of the NATO mission to protect civilians (despite failing to consult Congress, as the War Powers Act said he must) and maintained his commitment to removing most U.S. troops from Iraq and setting a deadline for the removal of troops from Afghanistan. He touted the assassination of Osama bin Laden and the victory of U.S. and NATO forces in Libya as examples of his foreign policy successes. With the domestic economy still in a state of turmoil (but showing some signs of recovery), his foreign policy achievements, like those of presidents before him, were not the primary basis on which most voters judged him. As other elections have demonstrated, when the two are in competition, voters usually opt to vote on the basis of **bread-and-butter issues** rather than on the basis of foreign affairs.

U.S. policy in the Middle East remained a topic in the **Campaign of 2016**. By 2015, President Obama had negotiated a multilateral agreement with Iran and other western powers in which Iran agreed to limitations on its efforts to develop nuclear weapons in exchange for an internationally monitored foray into the use of nuclear power for the purpose of energy production and the lifting of international sanctions. Israel was a strong critic of the agreement, having long advocated for the use of military force in the short term against the regime in Iran. Democratic candidates for the White House generally supported President Obama and the agreement with Iran, whereas GOP candidates for the presidency were critical of both, affirming the GOP's commitment to Israel and to its ruling conservative Likud Party.

Partisan differences also emerged over whether to send ground troops to Syria to combat the presence of the Islamic State in the Levant (ISIL, often referred to by GOP supporters as ISIS) as well as the growing military presence of Russia. Democratic candidates supported groups opposed to ISIL and to Syrian president Asaad, but they tended to draw the line at ground troops, arguing that more resources and training should be directed at those groups in the region that already supported U.S. interests, such as the Kurds. Republican candidates tended to be more supportive of sending ground troops to Syria, and also of reintroducing American forces to Iraq, where ISIL had also been making inroads in the wake of the instability caused by the earlier American invasion. Not all GOP candidates agree on the use of ground troops in Syria. Donald Trump, still leading the polls in October 2015, has gone on record in support of allowing Russia to take the lead in managing the Syrian conflict, even to the point of yielding to Russian troops on Syrian soil. But Mr. Trump is not averse to using military force, claiming that he is "the most militaristic person" among the current candidates. While in the past (as late as 2013) he has called for withdrawal from Afghanistan, more recently he has "begrudgingly" conceded that the United States cannot realistically leave Afghanistan, and he has also stated (in August 2015) that he would not hesitate to use force in Iraq to impose American will and "take the oil."

By and large GOP candidates have blamed Obama for prematurely withdrawing troops from Iraq, leaving the door open to ISIL/ISIS; Democrats blamed George W. Bush and the Republicans for the crisis in Iraq, arguing that their support for the invasion and the inadequacy of the government backed by the Americans after the invasion created the basis for the current problems in the region. Republican candidates remain divided over the best approach to dealing with ISIL. Following the terrorist attacks in San Bernardino, California, in early December 2015, attacks linked to ISIL sympathizers, candidates from both parties have been compelled to address homeland security against these kinds of threats. Naturally, Donald Trump went so far as to propose a now widely condemned plan that would prohibit Muslim immigrants and travelers from entering the United States. More belligerently, and consistent with previous statements, Mr. Trump publicly recommended military force against ISIL, promising in an interview on *Fox and Friends* that he "would knock the hell out of ISIS," that he "would hit them so hard." Elaborating further, Mr. Trump darkly explained that, "When you get these terrorists, you have to take out their families. They care about their lives, don't kid yourself. When they say they don't care about their lives, you have to take out their families." Senator Cruz has seconded this sentiment, recommending that the United States should "carpet bomb" ISIL "into oblivion."

There has been somewhat less disagreement over the withdrawal of U.S. troops from Afghanistan, initially slated for the end of President Obama's first term in office. The failure of the Afghan military to maintain control over the region, and the continuing threat of Taliban resurgence (coupled with the new threat of the expansion of ISIL's influence in the region), led Obama to postpone troop withdrawal, and this effectively precluded political debate over the efficacy of ending that conflict in the near future.

See also Isolationism; Trade Issue

Additional Resources

Buchanan, Bruce. *The Policy Partnership: Presidential Elections and American Democracy.* New York: Routledge, 2004.

DeSilvio, David. *How Domestic Politics Influenced Foreign Policy in the 1940 Election.* Berlin: VDM Verlag Dr. Muller, 2008.

Hunt, Michael H. *Ideology and U.S. Foreign Policy.* New Haven, CT: Yale University Press, 1988.

Small, Melvin. *Democracy and Diplomacy: The Impact of Domestic Politics in U.S. Foreign Policy 1789–1994.* Baltimore: Johns Hopkins University Press, 1995.

Wedge Issue

Wedge issues are also referred to as "cross-cutting issues," because they tend to divide voters within political parties, rather than cutting across traditional party cleavages. Because American political parties are "big tents" that must incorporate a host of differing groups, invariably there will be some issues on which members of the same party hold differing beliefs. In the 1950s and early 1960s, civil rights was one of those cross-cutting issues. Northern Republicans had a long history of support for the rights of nonwhite Americans, making them far more liberal on this issue than other members of their party. At the same time, southern Democrats voiced strong opposition to federal efforts to promote civil rights, while the remainder of the Democratic Party was more supportive of such efforts.

Political parties use wedge issues as a means of splintering some voters away from their support for the opposition. In areas such as civil rights, where voters from both parties are divided, this tended to be a risky strategy because each party also has something to lose from taking up this issue. In other areas, supporters of only one of the parties may be divided, which provides the other party with a unique opportunity to exploit this division. One such example is Richard Nixon's "southern strategy," which he used to great effect in the **Campaign of 1968** (and again in the **Campaign of 1972**). Knowing that many southern Democrats were concerned about the expansion of civil rights, Nixon ran a law-and-order campaign promising to crack down on civil unrest. For many voters, "law and order" was a not-so-oblique reference to the race riots that had plagued numerous American cities in 1967 and 1968; concerns about the law-and-order issue were strongly linked with feelings about African Americans and Latinos, making the issue one of **symbolic racism** (as opposed to overt racism). Nixon did not have to come out and state that he was promising to keep African Americans in line; many voters received the message anyway. As a consequence, Nixon received very little of the African American vote but increased his popularity among white Southern voters, who were already trending Republican after the passage of several major civil rights laws a few years earlier.

In the **Campaign of 1980**, Republican nominee Ronald Reagan used his opposition to abortion to persuade some Catholic Democrats to support his bid for the White House. Prior to 1980, no presidential candidate had appealed to voters on the basis of abortion (in part, because there were still internal divisions in both parties on this issue). In the **Campaign of 2004**, Republican incumbent George W. Bush attempted to use support for the wars in Afghanistan and Iraq, patriotism, and support for antiterrorist policies to appeal to elements of the Democratic base (although there is little evidence that it was effective). In the **Campaign of 2008**, Democratic nominee Barack Obama used the economic recession as a wedge to attract fearful Republicans to his corner (although, again, there is little evidence of partisan defection in this election).

The **Campaign of 2012** was marked by the recurrence of the wedge issue. In this election, Democratic incumbent Barack Obama attempted to make the nation's growing economic inequality a campaign issue, suggesting that

Republican nominee Mitt Romney was seeking to continue the Bush-era tax cuts for the wealthiest Americans. While taxing the middle class tends to face strong public opposition, the public has historically had few objections to taxing the affluent. Moreover, Romney himself was affluent, enabling Obama to suggest that Romney's tax policies might be self-interested, while programs that the poor and middle class relied on would fall victim to the budget ax. In essence, Obama was attempting to divide Romney from a portion of his base. Romney was put in the difficult position of having to defend tax cuts for the well-to-do during a time when the economy was still struggling and many were out of work. His response was to rename the affluent "job creators" and suggest that if they were taxed at a higher rate, they would not spend the money needed to restart the economy and, ultimately, re-employ those who were currently out of work. While the GOP focused on "job creators" and their contributions to the economy in 2012, Obama may have struck a blow. In the **Campaign of 2016**, most of the GOP contenders for the party nomination are lamenting the level of economic inequality in American society and suggesting that it is a problem that needs to be resolved. This suggests that the GOP has real concerns that class is a viable, long-term wedge that the party may be susceptible to.

Also appearing in the Campaign of 2012 was the topic of women's access to contraception, as well as abortion, as part of the Affordable Care Act. Political scientists do not consider abortion access to be much of a wedge issue anymore, because, as a result of **partisan sorting**, most people with strong pro-life beliefs are now identified as Republicans and most people with strong pro-choice beliefs are now identified as Democrats. Moreover, abortion attitudes have been remarkably stable over time, suggesting that they are not amenable to persuasion. Contraception access, however, has not been seriously debated in over half a century (and the last time it was, evangelical Christians were far more supportive of it). By 2012, however, Republicans were arguing that the contraceptive coverage mandate in the ACA interfered with the religious rights of employers, particularly Catholic institutions, and they sought to pass a series of exemptions to permit employers the ability to deny coverage when they had moral objections. At the same time, several Republican-controlled state legislatures sought to pass sweeping new limits on abortion access, from invasive ultrasound requirements to personhood amendments that would potentially limit many forms of contraception as well (as well as in-vitro fertilization). For the first time, the parties appeared to be staking out opposite positions on contraceptive access, with the Democratic Party arguing that contraception should be both legal and free, and the Republican Party arguing that states, and even employers, should be able to limit a woman's access to contraception. This debate has continued into the Campaign of 2016, with the elimination of federal funding for Planned Parenthood (which only receives federal funds for non-abortion services such as contraceptives and cancer screening) a stated priority of almost every one of the GOP nominees. Some GOP candidates have suggested that they would support congressional legislation to make birth control pills available over the counter; however, this most likely would mean that women whose insurance coverage now pays for contraception would need to fund it on their own (although Congress cannot order the FDA to make sales over the counter, something that drug companies would likely resist). Contraception access is an issue that is unlikely to divide Democratic supporters, who are more likely to favor abortion access to begin with, who are less likely to be religious, and who tend to support the ACA. However, it is a topic that may be a wedge for Republican voters (male and female alike). It is unclear how voters will respond to a serious debate about contraceptive access.

LGBTQ rights promises to be another cross-cutting issue over the long term, as long as the two parties maintain separate positions on this topic. Historically, the Republican Party has used its opposition to gay rights to drive a wedge between more socially conservative Democrats and their party. However, in recent years, support for gay rights in general, and same-sex marriage in particular, has increased dramatically, and it is now the GOP that is divided on this issue (while the Democrats are united). Most opposition to same-sex marriage, and to gay people serving openly in the military, resides in the GOP and tends to increase with age (as it does among Democrats and independents). Thus, the issue has become a wedge for Democrats to exploit, emphasizing their support for LGBTQ rights as a means of garnering support from those Republicans who share their views and don't feel well represented by their party's platform or candidates. In the Campaign of 2012, Obama used this newfound support for same-sex marriage in this manner, and in the Campaign of 2016, the Democratic contenders are similarly expressing their support for federal civil rights protection for LGBTQ rights. The GOP candidates have been more reluctant to address this topic, suggesting its riskiness for their coalition and confirming its status as a wedge issue.

See also LGBTQ Issues; Women's Equality Issue

Additional Resources

Edsall, Thomas B. "Bush Abandons 'Southern Strategy'; Campaign Avoids Use of Polarizing Issues Employed by GOP Since Nixon's Time." *Washington Post*, August 6, 2000, p. A19.

Edsall, Thomas B. "GOP Honing Wedges for Next Campaign: Party Aims for Partisan Advantages by Making Corruption, Drugs and Crime Divisive Issues." *Washington Post*, February 26, 1989, p. A6.

Hillygus, Sunshine D., and Todd G. Shields. *The Persuadable Voter: Wedge Issues in Presidential Campaigns.* Princeton, NJ: Princeton University Press, 2008.

Women's Equality Issue

In Seneca Falls, New York, during the summer of 1848, abolitionists Lucretia Mott, Elizabeth Cady Stanton, and other progressive luminaries convened the first women's rights convention, endorsing (among other things) the right of women to vote. Historians view this meeting as the beginning of the women's suffrage movement in the United States.

Women had been a leading force in the abolition movement, and the ratification of the three Civil War amendments protecting the constitutional rights of freed slaves fueled women's demands for their own right to vote. In 1869, the new National Women's Suffrage Association selected Stanton as its president. That same year, the American Suffrage Association selected Henry Ward Beecher as its president, and the Wyoming Territory granted women the right to vote, followed by Colorado in 1893.

A turning point in the movement occurred in 1872, when Susan B. Anthony registered to vote in violation of New York state law and was jailed for refusing to pay the $100 fine. Anthony maintained that the Fourteenth Amendment permitted women the right to vote, although the Supreme Court disagreed, ruling that states had the authority to determine whether or not women could vote. In 1878, congressional supporters of women's suffrage responded by proposing a women's suffrage amendment to the U.S. Constitution.

Throughout the remainder of the nineteenth century, the women's suffrage movement continued to gain strength. In 1880, the Greenback Party endorsed women's right to vote. The growing electoral parity between the Democratic and Republican parties put pressure on both entities to support women's suffrage, as political campaigns looked for new sources of potential supporters. Equally important, the growing strength of third parties during this era contributed pressure as well. In 1892, the Prohibition Party included a plank in its platform stating, "No citizen should be denied the right to vote on account of sex." The 1908 platform of the Socialist Party called for "unrestricted and equal suffrage for men and women." And the 1912 Progressive Party platform pledged the party "to the task of securing equal suffrage to men and women alike." By the **Campaign of 1916**, both Republicans and Democrats supported the women's suffrage amendment.

In 1919, both chambers of Congress ratified a constitutional amendment granting women the right to vote and sent it to the states, and on August 26, 1920, a sufficient number ratified the Nineteenth Amendment, making it the law of the land. In the decades that followed, no single party benefited from women's enfranchisement. Rather, women tended to vote according to patterns of class, geography, race, and other traits, in much the same manner as men.

The publication of Simone de Beauvoir's *The Second Sex* (1949) and Betty Friedan's *The Feminine Mystique* (1963) heralded a new era in the women's rights movement. Women sought to define themselves as more than wives and mothers, and as part of that effort, they sought more political equality and more equality in the workplace as well. Many of the positions advocated by the new women's rights movement, however, did not sit well with conservative voters. These included legalizing access to contraception and abortion, equal pay in the workplace, legal protections against sexual harassment in the workplace, and more aggressive enforcement of Title VII of the Civil Rights Act of 1964, which prohibited workplace sex discrimination. The women's movement threw its full support behind a proposed Equal Rights Amendment (ERA) to the Constitution that would have made all governmental classifications based on gender subject to strict judicial scrutiny. The Senate and the House passed the Equal Rights Amendment in 1972. Within a short period of time, twenty-two of the required thirty-eight states had ratified the ERA. By the mid-1970s, an anti-ERA backlash significantly slowed the ratification by additional states. Critics argued that ratification of the ERA would strip states of the right to regulate abortions, would eliminate spousal support in cases of divorce, would require that the military allow women to serve in combat units, and would even eliminate same-sex public bathrooms and changing rooms. Nonetheless, in the **Campaign of 1976**, Republican presidential nominee Gerald Ford, egged on by his wife, Betty, voiced his support for the ERA, as did Democratic nominee Jimmy Carter. (Dismayed conservatives would support Ronald Reagan in the GOP primaries in this election, and again four years later.) Support for the ERA appeared in both parties' platforms, as it had in the **Campaign of 1972**.

Despite four decades of official Republican Party support for the ERA, it was removed from the GOP platform during the **Campaign of 1980**. In this same year, the Democratic Party, historically less enthusiastic about the ERA due to its perceived weakening of union workplace rules, not only endorsed the constitutional amendment, but also used it as a litmus test for funding political candidates. The parties also diverged sharply on abortion in 1980, with the Republican Party supporting a constitutional amendment to prohibit abortions (eliminating the commitment to public dialogue on the issue that had appeared in the 1976 platform) and the Democratic Party, for the first time, taking an explicitly pro-choice position. While both parties continued to support equal pay for women in 1980, such language disappeared entirely from the GOP platform by 1984, replaced by opposition to "quotas and preferential treatment." The Democrats continued to support the ERA in their party platform throughout the 1980s and into the 1990s, while the Republican Party platform remained silent on the topic.

By the late 1990s, the ERA had become a nonissue. Many women believed that the current legal protections against unequal pay and sexual harassment were similar to what the ERA would have provided—that is, until the Supreme Court ruled in a five-to-four decision in *Ledbetter v. Goodyear Tire and Rubber Company* (2007) that an employee who is subject to discriminatory pay cannot sue under Title VII of the Civil Rights Act or the Equal Pay Act if the actions had occurred more than 180 days previously. In the *Ledbetter* case, the employer had concealed the pay disparity for years, preventing the employee from taking action in a timely fashion, but the court maintained that this left Ledbetter with no grounds to sue. Democratic nominee Barack Obama campaigned on the issue in the **Campaign of 2008**, noting that his opponent, Republican nominee John McCain, opposed remedial legislation that would enable Ms. Ledbetter and other similarly situated employees to sue for equal pay. Obama signed the Lilly Ledbetter Fair Pay Act in 2009 as his first official action after taking office, which permitted women to sue within 180 days after discovering evidence of pay discrimination (with each paycheck constituting a separate event). More recently, the Supreme Court ruled in another five-to-four decision that a gender-pay discrimination case against Wal-Mart could not proceed as a class-action suit, which placed cumbersome new limits on women's ability to sue as a class.

In the **Campaign of 2012**, Democratic incumbent Barack Obama campaigned on equal pay and attempted to tie the contraception mandate in his Affordable Care Act to women's earnings. He argued that if women had to pay for contraception at market rate (because men rarely pay for contraception), this would further erode their wages, which were already lower than men's. He claimed that the ability to decide whether and when to have a child, and to not be overly burdened by the health care required to do this, was necessary for women to achieve economic parity with men. He highlighted GOP opposition to equal pay and suggested that his opponent did not support women's equality in the workplace. Republican nominee Mitt Romney, for his part, did not take a position on equal pay, but he suggested that as governor, he had promoted a record number of women in the workplace. Romney also backed off from his party's position on abortion, suggesting that he would be willing to permit access to abortion in cases of rape and incest, and that he was always in favor of contraception. He also propounded his opposition to Planned Parenthood—viewed by conservatives as a vehicle for abortion and viewed by liberals as a vehicle for contraception and wellness check-ups for economically disadvantaged women.

In the **Campaign of 2016**, the topic of women's equality and women's rights continues to be a focal point, particularly for Democrats, who view women voters as an important element of their party coalition. Moreover, the Democratic front-runner is a woman, whereas the crowded field of seventeen GOP hopefuls contains only one female candidate who is not viewed by any as a serious contender. But also, numerous events outside of the presidential campaign have drawn national attention to a debate about the role of public morality in influencing women's health care choices.

After GOP gains in the 2010 and 2014 midterms, state legislatures sought new restrictions on women's access to abortion, including bans on abortions after twenty weeks (on the grounds that the fetus, which would not yet be viable, might be able to feel pain); bans on abortion once a fetal heartbeat has been detected; requiring that abortion clinics be built and equipped as surgeries; requiring that abortion clinic doctors have admitting privileges at a local hospital; requiring that women submit to (and pay for) ultrasounds prior to receiving an abortion; requiring that women be compelled to look at an ultrasound prior to receiving an abortion; requiring that doctors deliver a state-authored script that states risks of an abortion (many of which the medical community disputes, such as suicide and mental illness) and that attempts to persuade a woman to forgo the procedure; requiring that non-surgical abortions use outdated (and dangerous) levels of prescribed drugs to induce abortions; bans on the use of insurance to pay for an abortion; bans on abortion for the purpose of sex or racial selection; bans on abortion if the fetus tests positive for Down syndrome; bans on abortion for reasons other than rape, incest, or to save the life of the mother; and bans on abortion for reasons other than to save the life of the mother.

The Democratic Party has the luxury of unity on the topic of abortion; all of its nominees generally support the pro-choice position and oppose additional state interference in access to abortion. The Democratic position is one of access, and the ability of the woman to make her own choices about her health care and when to raise a family. The party takes no position on the morality of abortions. The GOP field in 2016 is populated, in part, by governors (and former governors) who presided over numerous efforts to restrict abortion in their states. Some of these candidates, like Scott Walker, have been quite blunt—they would ban abortions even if the life of the mother was at stake, a measure that supporters of the pro-choice position and even some who identify as pro-life fear might in effect privilege the life of the fetus over that of the mother. Others, such as Ben Carson, would permit emergency contraception for rape victims (viewed as abortion by some) and potentially other measures as well. That there is internal conflict within the GOP, that the restrictions on access are more far-reaching than they have been in the past, and that there is some element of conflict for the GOP with its overall message of freedom, particularly from government regulation, are what will make this topic continue to be controversial. It seems also more likely to create disunity within the GOP, but not necessarily within the voting public. Public opinion on abortion has long been stable, and most voters who favor more access have sorted toward one party, while those who favor more regulation have sorted toward the other, in the years since the topic has come onto the political agenda.

Similarly, debates over access to contraception may appeal to these preexisting partisan divides. However, because the debate over contraception is newer, **partisan sorting** may be imperfect. Hillary Clinton is likely to borrow from Obama's framing of the contraception topic in 2012, where he argued that access to affordable contraception influenced women's ability to work, to earn, and to garner equal pay and provide their family with a decent standard of living. Research on issue evolution suggests that successfully reframing an issue (i.e., convincing people that an issue that they thought was moral is really one of economic inequality) may change the partisan divide in the long term.

Also at issue in the campaign is Title IX and the responsibility of colleges and universities to prevent the sexual assault (and sexual harassment) of students on their campuses. Sexual assault at U.S. military academies, and the greater problem of sexual assault throughout the armed forces in general, has been a topic of congressional hearings, and of proposed legislation, over the past several years. This is a problem most likely to be experienced by women (although men are also victimized), and candidates seeking their votes will undoubtedly find it useful to discuss potential reforms.

Other campaign topics, seemingly unrelated to women's equality, may still evoke such a controversy. Because women still earn less than men, and are often heads of households (particularly of households with children), they are disproportionately affected by changes to government programs for the disadvantaged. They are also affected by changes in the benefit structure of other programs, such as Social Security. According to the National Women's Law Center, women aged sixty-five and older are more likely to receive 90 percent or more of their total income from Social Security (even though they receive far less than men from the program, on average). Over a third of single women (unmarried, widowed, divorced) over sixty-five receive over 90 percent of their income from the program, while only 21 percent of married women do. Hispanic and African American women are more dependent on the program than are whites. And children of a deceased parent often rely on Social Security benefits to keep their families from sliding into poverty.

During the **Campaign of 2016**, Republican candidates directed their focus on controversies surrounding federal funding of Planned Parenthood, largely in reaction to provocative material circulated throughout social media alleging that a number of Planned Parenthood clinics were trading in body parts harvested from aborted fetuses, allegations that have been denied by the organization. In particular, GOP candidate Carly Fiorina, whose campaign at the time was on the upswing following her solid performances in the first two debates, drew attention for her pointed indictment of Planned Parenthood based on volatile images posted on the Internet; however, questions raised about the reliability of these video images soon blunted Ms. Fiorina's momentum, pushing the criticism of Planned Parenthood toward the margins of the campaign. Nevertheless, issues such as abortion and any attendant support supplied by the federal government, while often evaded by candidates, are likely to resurface at any given moment within a presidential campaign. Finally, questions regarding discrimination against Sec. Hillary Clinton were raised during the 2016 campaign. Republican front runner Donald Trump made juvenile, shamefully personal remarks about Sec. Clinton's physiology. Additionally, the secretary was also criticized for raising the volume of her voice during debates and other speaking events, describing her voice and delivery as "shrill." Meanwhile, Sen. Bernie Sanders as well as Mr. Trump, both noted for raising the decibel level at their own campaign events, received no such criticism. When Sen. Sanders raises his voice, as he frequently does, he is perceived in the media as a firebrand exuding righteous indignation. Mr. Trump's outbursts are but one more aspect of his hard-hitting personality, his bravado. That male candidates seem to raise their voices without raising an eyebrow while Sec. Clinton's raised volume is reported as "shrill" and "screaming" clearly indicates a media double-standard that can only be described as sexist.

See also Abortion Issue; Campaign of 1920; Gender Gap; Health Care Issue; Marriage Gap; Social Security Issue; Voting Reform Issue

Additional Resources

Hunter, Sara. *Woman Suffrage and the New Democracy.* New Haven, CT: Yale University Press, 1996.

Keyssar, Alexander. *The Right to Vote: The Contested History of Democracy in the United States.* New York: Basic Books, 2000.

National Women's Law Center. "Women and Social Security." February 23, 2015. http://www.nwlc.org/resource/women-and-social-security. Accessed September 6, 2015.

Wolbrecht, Christina. "Explaining Women's Rights Realignment: Convention Delegates, 1972–1992." *Political Behavior* (September 2002): 237–82.

Presidential Campaigns

Campaign of 1788–1789

The election of George Washington, who subsequently became the first president of the United States under the newly ratified Constitution, involved little suspense and held no surprises. Despite serious divisions resulting from the animated debate over ratification, almost all major political factions and interests considered Washington of Virginia the inevitable and only reasonable choice to serve as the nation's first true chief executive. By and large, Washington was, by personal choice, unaffiliated with any faction or party, but his ideas and attitudes about politics were in effect Federalist, at least for the most part. Even so, his sensibilities prevented him from regarding unqualified political allegiance with anything but cool indifference. He had his loyalties, but they were attached to persons more than they were to any specific political doctrine other than a keen and abiding commitment to republican government and the principled liberty that it secured. He enjoyed the ardent loyalties of many supporters, but his interest in drawing from those loyalties the support needed to obtain for himself the kind of political life that comes with republican governance was slight. After having scrupulously fulfilled his duty throughout the revolution as commander of the Continental army and later having served in the important role of presiding officer at the Constitutional Convention of 1789, Washington, at age fifty-seven, now preferred to embrace and enjoy the pleasures of private life warmly ensconced within his plantation at Mount Vernon, Virginia. The office of the presidency, Washington observed in a letter to the Marquis de Lafayette posted in April 1788, "has no enticing charms, and no fascinating allurements," and he said that the increasing "infirmities of nature and the growing love of retirement" did not permit any happy commitment to any occupation other than "living and dying an honest man on my own farm." And yet, recognizing the novelty of the Constitution and the sober care needed to successfully implement its various components combined with the serious circumstances under which it was ratified, Washington reluctantly, quietly agreed to serve as the first president if elected. Knowing this, supporters of Washington enthusiastically sang his praises throughout the summer and fall of 1788, unabashedly lauding him as the "New Cincinnatus," the "Great Washington," and the "Savior of America." Washington's old friend and comrade Alexander Hamilton in particular pressed hard for Washington's service in this capacity, writing to Washington in August and September 1788 to advise that his full participation in the new republic's "first operations" was no less than "indispensable," and that a "citizen of so much consequence" was "essential" to the "prosperity of [the] newly instituted government." Hamilton was not the only correspondent imploring Washington to accept the presidency. Mount Vernon was peppered with letters written by a broad variety of supporters encouraging Washington to respond again to the call of duty. While Washington remained demure, for the most part, he accepted this unwelcome conscription as one that he could neither too quickly embrace nor too deftly evade and still maintain his good name, so meticulously won for himself on the strength of his renowned virtues. His approach to the whole issue was marked by a nuanced admission of his duty to serve and a tempered insistence on remaining aloof to the prospect. A further complication added to the sensitivity of Washington's response; if his name was to be offered for the office, it needed to be so without dissent. It appears that Washington, while sincerely not desiring the office, simultaneously did not welcome the prospect of being challenged for the office or of having to engage in unseemly competition for political power, but rather to assume his duties without contest or self-promotion. Washington's lifelong care for reputation would not allow such a result. Hence, in a sense, the first presidential campaign was more about tactfully persuading the great statesman in a way that would defer to his sense of honor, which would not allow even the slightest hint of grasping for office. Owing to these sensibilities, Washington did not put forward a platform or publicly campaign for the presidency. He relied on that personal indispensability of which Hamilton spoke, all the while carefully sustaining a position that would neither invite accusations of unseemly ambition nor preclude his assumption of the post.

Washington succeeded in his efforts to avoid a campaign for the presidency, but the first presidential election was not without a contest—in this case, it involved the vice presidency, a position that at that time did not carry nearly the same degree of import that it does for us today. As Washington was from the South—and indeed, from the southern state that held the most electoral votes—deference to sectional interests drove the selection of a Northerner for the vice presidency, and it was to Massachusetts and New York that politicians turned. Governor George Clinton seemed a likely choice early, particularly from the old Anti-Federalists (those who had been critical of the new Constitution during the debates over its ratification), but his candidacy was thwarted by turmoil in the New York legislature over the method of selecting electors. Massachusetts was an incubator of notable statesmen, the most prominent being John Hancock, Samuel Adams, Henry Knox, Benjamin Lincoln (no relation to the future sixteenth president) and the erudite John Adams. Hancock drew some initial attention, but in the end it was John Adams, a seasoned, capable, and learned public servant, who commanded the most support. Hamilton, ever Washington's closest ally, was initially skeptical of Adams, suspecting him of being less than amenable to Washington and thus causing him to worry over the possibility that Adams might not exhibit the loyalty needed to strengthen a Federalist presidency. But in the end, Adams seemed to be nearly as inevitable as Washington, a fact that caused Hamilton to focus on ensuring that Adams did not receive the same kind of unanimity that was guaranteed to Washington, secretly working to ensure that only Washington would emerge unchallenged, a machination that, once Adams became aware of it in later years, drove an unhappy wedge between these two giants of the founding era.

It is important to note the context behind Hamilton's anxieties over Adams. Prior to the ratification of the Twelfth Amendment, the Constitution, as it was originally established, required that each elector cast two votes for president. The candidate with the highest number of votes became president. The candidate with the second-highest number of votes became vice president. Given the way in which Article II of the Constitution was originally designed, it was possible for a candidate who was intended for the vice presidency to actually win the most total votes and thus, by legal default, be elected president if a majority was obtained, even against the initial wishes of everyone involved. Although Washington constituted the consensus choice for president, rendering such a scenario unlikely, Adams, without additional challengers in the field, could possibly—at least in Hamilton's mind—inadvertently prevent Washington's unopposed election. For both Hamilton and Washington, the presidency should be assumed only with the kind of unanimity that Washington felt would preserve his reputation and establish the right kind of precedent for an office requiring dignity above public competition. That said, it was not simply the influence of Hamilton that prevented Adams from enjoying a similar acclamation, but also the presence of a number of candidates who managed to receive some degree of modest support. Adams was widely respected, but not universally as was Washington. Hence, Hamilton's concerns were largely ungrounded.

On the first Wednesday in January 1789, state legislatures selected the first members of the new Electoral College, in accordance with the requirements of the Constitution. (In the early years of the republic, the members of the Electoral College were selected by state legislatures in some states and the general voters in others, always under the advice and direction of prominent state and local figures. And while to this day, it is still the Electoral College and not the general public that technically elects the president, electors are currently chosen by the voters from a pool of candidates nominated by their respective parties and, for the most part, committed to vote accordingly.) Due to a delay in assembling a congressional quorum to count the ballots, the votes of the electors remained unopened until early April. North Carolina and Rhode Island did not select electors, because of their abiding hesitancy to ratify the Constitution. Because of the impasse between factions within its state legislature, New York also missed an opportunity to select electors for the 1789 presidential election. All the same, Washington's election was unanimous, winning all sixty-nine electoral votes that were cast, a unanimous total from among all participating electors. Owing to the impasse in New York and the ineligibility of North Carolina and Rhode Island, twenty-four electoral votes were not cast. Additionally, Maryland and Virginia were also shy two votes each. Hence, technically, Washington received around 85 percent of all *possible* Electoral College votes, and 100 percent of all votes cast by participating electors. His election was nonetheless unanimous, even with this qualification.

Adams, as anticipated, did win the vice presidency without any serious challenger, but enough alternative candidates received the votes needed to render a final count considerably smaller than Washington's, thus allaying Hamilton's concern. Most notable among these alternative candidates were Hancock and New York's John Jay, who received four and nine electoral votes, respectively (Jay's nine being third only to Washington's and Adams's); South Carolina's John Rutledge, who received six votes; Clinton, who received just three votes; and Lincoln, who received the support of one elector. Twelve electoral votes were distributed among figures less familiar to us today: Washington's close associate Robert H. Harrison of Maryland (6); governor of Connecticut and former president of the Continental Congress Samuel Huntington (2); and three favorite sons from Georgia, John Milton (2), James Armstrong (1), and Edward Telfair (1). In the end, Adams received thirty-four electoral votes for the vice presidency, just under half but still appreciably larger than even the closest challenger (Jay).

Thus the Campaign of 1789 ended in unanimity for Washington, but it masked deeper ideological and regional differences. The Federalists and Anti-Federalists held markedly different views regarding the structure of the new government and the respective powers of the federal and state governments. Southern states were sharply opposed to northern states on issues such as foreign policy and tariffs. The effort to fashion a North-South ticket provided a precedent that would become an important feature of the presidential contest. And while the support for Washington was from all quarters, his administration would not be immune from the strains of the factionalism against which he had famously warned. Washington, ever committed to his duty, rode to New York to become inaugurated as the first and one of the greatest presidents in American history, but he did so with an unshakable sense of reluctance mixed with apprehension. Musing on these feelings, he admitted, "I feel very much like a man who is condemned to death does when the time of his execution draws nigh."

Additional Resources

Allen, William B., ed. *George Washington: A Collection.* Indianapolis: Liberty Press, 1988.

Boller, Paul F., Jr. *Presidential Campaigns.* New York: Oxford University Press, 1984.

Cohen, Martin, David Karol, et al. *The Party Decides: Presidential Nominations before and after Reform.* Chicago: University of Chicago Press, 2008.

Cunliffe, Marcus. "Election of 1789." In Arthur M. Schlesinger, Fred Israel, and William P. Hansen, eds. *History of American Presidential Elections, 1789–1968.* Vol. 1. New York: Chelsea House, 1985.

Edwards, George C., III. *Why the Electoral College Is Bad for America.* New Haven, CT: Yale University Press, 2005.

Horsman, Reginald. "1788–89." In Arthur M. Schlesinger, Fred L. Israel, and David J. Frent, eds. *Running for President: The Candidates and Their Images.* New York: Simon & Schuster, 1994.

Leip, Dave. "Atlas of U.S. Presidential Elections." http://uselectionatlas.org/.

Miller Center for Public Affairs: American President On-Line Reference Resource. http://millercenter.org/academic/americanpresident.

The Papers of Alexander Hamilton. Vol. 5. New York: Columbia University Press, 1962.

Campaign of 1792

President George Washington, once again careful not to seem too eager for power and hoping with raised yearning to return to private life at Mount Vernon, agreed after considerable soul searching to serve a second term as president of the young republic, but not before nearly leaving office after just one term. Washington's physical health had deteriorated, but at the age of sixty, he remained keen enough of mind and resolved in his sense of duty to carry forward, however reluctantly, as the nation's leading executive. Had he done so, it would have been difficult for Washington to justify his resignation; the country faced serious internal divisions, particularly between the northern and southern sections, and a firm, moderating hand was needed to pilot the country through intersectional turbulence. Additionally, the young (and comparatively weak) country was in danger of being pulled into the entanglements that arise from conflict between great powers, in this case Britain and France. Again, it was unlikely to find anyone at this time who could apply the reasoned caution that was necessary in steering clear of the crossfire between these two ambitious, expansive, and exceedingly powerful European nations.

Washington's administration was more than capable in facing these prospects, as it included some of the finest minds of the day (or of any day, for that matter). Among their number were the brilliant Alexander Hamilton as secretary of the treasury, who had grown close to Washington and served as his closest adviser; his intellectual equal and ideological rival Thomas Jefferson as secretary of state; the capable Edmund Randolph as attorney general, who was often seen as the counterpoise balancing the disparate views of Hamilton and Jefferson; and the self-made, multitalented war hero and comrade of Washington, Henry Knox, as secretary of war. It does indeed seem from our perspective to have been a golden age of political leadership, but this extraordinarily talented administration was not immune from the divisiveness and factionalism that Washington had always considered inimical to the government of a unified republic.

Hamilton's extensive economic and financial policies—the more controversial measures involving federal assumption of state debts and the institution of a national bank—along with a rapidly widening schism within the administration between "Federalists" (led by Hamilton) and "Republicans" (led by Jefferson and not to be confused with our modern Republican Party), had drawn abundant criticism. Along with Hamilton, the Federalists numbered among their members such notable figures as John Adams (the incumbent vice president), John Jay and Gouverneur Morris of New York, John Marshall and Bushrod Washington of Virginia, James Wilson and Tench Coxe of Pennsylvania, and Paul Revere and Fisher Ames of Massachusetts. While the Anti-Federalists had earlier won the debate over the inclusion of the Bill of Rights—the first ten amendments having been quickly ratified during Washington's first term as president—their initial concerns about the potential for a large, centralized, and "consolidated" government under the new constitution were raised anew. The Republicans, following Jefferson and his friend and fellow Virginian James Madison, who was Hamilton's erstwhile ratification ally, along with other notable statesmen such as George Clinton of New York, Albert Gallatin of Pennsylvania (later to settle in New York), and Virginians James Monroe, John Taylor, and (at least for the moment) Roanoke's colorful John Randolph, for the most part embraced the Anti-Federalist mantle by advocating states' rights against the expansion of the power of the national government while also favoring the supremacy of the legislative branch. These Republicans (sometimes referred to as Jeffersonian Republicans or, referring specifically to the Southern wing, the "Old Republicans") focused their attacks on Hamilton and his policies, fervently opposing the national bank that had been approved by Congress in 1791. Not only did Jefferson set himself against Hamilton, but so did Randolph, who, even though he tried hard to remain neutral with regard to the Hamilton-Jefferson rivalry, considered the national bank an unconstitutional measure. Washington, while personally and philosophically close to Hamilton, deliberately did what he could to remain above the fray and maintain a cool distance from the more unseemly aspects of political infighting and doctrinal division. His ability to succeed in this effort further strengthened his reputation, fortifying his already solid and broad popularity and securing his legacy as a singularly unifying figure unlike any other in American history.

Perturbed by these divisions in his administration and longing to return again to his private life at Mount Vernon, Washington was seeking an honorable way out. As the election approached, he consulted with several eminent individuals—among them Hamilton, Jefferson, Edmund Randolph, Madison, and Knox (curiously, there is no evidence that he consulted his vice president, John Adams)—for advice on the best way to announce his decision not to stand for reelection to the presidency. But the advice offered from all quarters was to serve for a second term; even those who had fallen into bitter rivalry mutually agreed that, given the potential dangers ahead, Washington needed to remain at the head of the executive. Both Jefferson and Hamilton urged Washington to stay on; Randolph went as far as to warn Washington of the possibility of "civil war" as a result of the divisions that were beset upon them, and argued that Washington would be invaluable in the prevention of such an eventuality. It was clear to everyone that Washington was indeed indispensable after all.

While opposition to the activities of Washington's administration, or at least the Hamiltonian element within it, grew in both quantity and intensity, the president himself remained comparatively immune from public attack. This secured his universal support for reelection, and once again, by virtue of his character alone, Washington easily rode into a second term without a challenger to oppose him, receiving a unanimous 132 electoral votes from among those that were cast from 15 states, Vermont and Kentucky having been added since the last election. Additionally, this was also the first election in which the electoral votes were recorded from New York, Rhode Island, and North Carolina, given assorted reasons that had thwarted their participation in the previous election. Three electors did not cast their votes: two from Maryland and one from Vermont (thus Washington's unanimity was drawn from all votes cast, not from all electors available). State legislatures selected the electors in nine states, and the remaining states made use of the popular vote in district and statewide elections. As in the previous election, the real contest for the executive in 1792 shifted to the vice presidency.

Much like the first presidential campaign, the selection process in 1792 lacked any of the features commonly associated with modern presidential campaigns, but campaigning for other offices was vigorous. Throughout the campaign season, the battle lines were sharply drawn. To a large degree, Republicans and Federalists relied upon friendly newspapers to attack their opponents. Philadelphia's *National Gazette*, a pro-Jeffersonian (Republican) newspaper, launched broadside after broadside against the Federalists. The *Gazette of the United States* trumpeted the successes of the Washington administration and the Federalist philosophy. Insult freely flowed from both the Federalist and Republican press. The Federalist press accused the Jefferson faction of Jacobinism (a name for the radical and violent wing within the French Revolution), and the Republican press countered with allegations, based on his public writings and his alleged personal affinities, that Vice President Adams sought to establish a monarchy. The charge of monarchism against Adams was a serious one and would not easily be deflated, as he was admittedly a proponent of strong executive government and suspicious of the more volatile and demagogic aspects of democratic politics. But in this Adams was not alone, as many of the statesmen at the time, on both sides of the debate, harbored genuine reservations about pure democracy. Many who criticized Adams as a monarchist were forced to admit that they had not carefully read his extensive and erudite writings on his somewhat complex theories of politics and government, but rather only aped what they heard secondhand about these theories, or what they had read in excerpts cynically quoted in newspapers without context. Nonetheless, the charge of Adams as monarchist dogged his reputation and remained a sore point in his bid to remain Washington's vice president. These kinds of allegations were not confined to Adams. Republicans by and large accused Federalists of being elitists. As political scientists Marty Cohen, John Zaller, et al. report, James Madison, in a 1792 article titled "The Candid State of Parties," referred to the Federalists as the party of the "opulent class," in stark contrast to the Republicans, who "trusted the wisdom of the people." Further, Cohen, Karol, et al. related the decidedly exaggerated pose of the other side as well, citing statements from William Cobbett of the *Porcupine Gazette* (out of Philadelphia) wherein he described the Jeffersonians as the "refuse of nations," tools of "baboons," "vile old" wretches, and "frog-eating, man-eating, blood-drinking cannibals."

Mutual mudslinging aside, the facts indicate that these tactics were not needed by the Federalists, at least at this time, as support for Adams was for the most part strong. As expected, he was popular throughout New England, but he also commanded loyalty from key individuals throughout the Union. Jefferson—who was both a friend and a rival, sometimes more one than the other—simply assumed that Adams would remain in office, attesting to Adams's "personal worth" and admitting this to be more important than the "demerits of his political creed." Most leading Federalists backed Adams, and, significantly, Hamilton also continued his support of Adams, even though he continued to harbor reservations; Even so, those reservations would soon evaporate once it became clear whom the Republicans were preparing to support. Adams was not without controversy even within his own party, but in spite of his inability to foster an appealing popular image, he sustained the broad admiration needed to retain elected office.

That said, the Republican faction sought a challenger. Benjamin Rush and John Beckley in Pennsylvania, and Madison and Monroe in Virginia, emerged as important players in the Republican decision to challenge Adams. From the start, New York governor George Clinton, an old enemy of Hamilton, served as the logical choice to lead the Republican charge for the second spot. Strenuously opposed to Clinton, visible horror was stirred in Hamilton at the prospect of a challenge from his fateful nemesis, another New Yorker, the flamboyant junior senator Aaron Burr. Burr was highly regarded as a promising and fresh leader, one who provided an effective antidote to, as Rush phrased it, "the monarchical rubbish of our government," no doubt a direct slur against Adams (and quite possibly Hamilton). With the young Burr's name sent into currency along with Clinton's, a tristate axis involving politicians in New York, Pennsylvania, and Virginia briefly formed around the issue of displacing the incumbent vice president. But while Burr was a captivating prospect for some, the Virginians led by Madison and Monroe threw in their support behind the more mature Clinton; and independently, Pennsylvania Republicans would also decide for Clinton rather than Burr. Even though Burr's brief candidacy seemed to have fizzled out, Hamilton remained worried enough to continue his efforts against Burr. As much as Hamilton disliked Clinton, his antipathy to Burr was unrelenting: he considered him to be nothing less than a threat to the survival of the nation. Hamilton also suspected that the Clinton and Burr candidacies could be a diversion concealing Jefferson's own ambitions for the presidency, a suspicion that proved to be unfounded, and one that Hamilton was able to overcome once it became clear that support for Burr had dissipated. With Burr removed from the picture and his suspicions about Jefferson allayed, Hamilton directed his efforts against Clinton, this time working without thought to Washington's inevitable unanimity in order to ensure that Adams commanded a considerable number of votes, predicting that Adams would receive a "nearly unanimous vote" in New England and a high number throughout the Union, a public position in contrast to his more private attitude held in the previous election. Given his disdain for Clinton, Hamilton could not hide his newly found enthusiasm for Adams. "The success of the Vice President [in retaining office]," Hamilton wrote to Jay, "is as great a source of satisfaction as that of Mr. Clinton would have been of mortification & pain to me."

Even though Adams faced more opposition in a more divisive political climate than in 1789, the final tally of seventy-seven electoral votes was a larger percentage (just over 58%) of second-place votes than he had received in 1789. As Hamilton predicted, New England fell in behind Adams, delivering thirty-four votes (44% of his total count). Adams also finished strong in Pennsylvania (which delivered fourteen of its fifteen electoral votes), New Jersey, and in the border and southern states of Delaware, Maryland, Kentucky, and South Carolina. It was still far below Washington's unanimous 132 but nonetheless a strong showing that crossed regions, and more than sufficient to achieve reelection to the vice presidency, leaving him politically well positioned for 1796. Clinton received fifty votes, which represented a considerably more respectable third-place showing, in absolute numbers, compared to Jay's third-place tally (a meager nine votes) in the 1789 election. Jefferson received four votes from Rhode Island's electors (the state that spoiled Adams's unanimity in New England), and one elector from South Carolina cast his vote for Burr.

Significantly, Virginia, which with its twenty-one electoral votes was the giant of the Electoral College at the time, threw all of its support behind Clinton (thus accounting for just over 40% of Clinton's final tally). New York (Clinton's home state) and North Carolina, two other influential states with twelve electoral votes each, also fell in unanimously behind the Republican faction, to be joined by Georgia, which delivered a unanimous four votes for Clinton. New York's support of its native son was to be expected, but Clinton's strong showing in the South foreshadowed later developments in the establishment of the Jeffersonian base.

The real meaning of the election of 1792 is in what it portends. The factional divisions and growing rancor between the major figures that characterized the contest for vice president in 1792 serve as a foretaste of both 1796 and, even more importantly, 1800. Additionally, the sectional implications were becoming clearer, and they would become increasingly more evident through the divisive political controversies that would sharpen in the following decade, leading up to the War of 1812. The political battle lines were becoming clearer, and the trenches were rapidly deepening; the landscape of American presidential politics was being prepared for the full combat of two American titans.

Additional Resources

Boller, Paul F., Jr. *Presidential Campaigns*. New York: Oxford University Press, 1984.

Cohen, Martin, David Karol, Hans Noel, and John Zaller. *The Party Decides: Presidential Nominations before and after Reform*. Chicago: University of Chicago Press, 2008.

Cunliffe, Marcus. "Election of 1792." In Arthur M. Schlesinger, Fred Israel, and William P. Hansen, eds. *History of American Presidential Elections, 1789–1968*. Vol. 1. New York: Chelsea House, 1985.

Hoadley, John F. *Origins of American Political Parties, 1789–1803*. Lexington: University of Kentucky, 1986.

Horsman, Reginald. "1792." In Arthur M. Schlesinger, Fred L. Israel, and David J. Frent, eds. *Running for President: The Candidates and Their Images*. New York: Simon & Schuster, 1994.

Leip, Dave, "Atlas of U.S. Presidential Elections." http://uselectionatlas.org/.

Sharp, James Roger. *American Politics in the Early Republic: The New Nation in Crisis*. New Haven, CT: Yale University Press, 1995.

Campaign of 1796

Prior to 1796, there had not been a contest for the office of the presidency, George Washington unanimously twice winning the office without challenge or dispute. But the unanimity behind Washington's election and reelection could not conceal ongoing partisan aggravations, a condition that actually grew worse in Washington's second term, even to the point of eventually weakening the president's own popularity, hitherto undiluted. These divisions involved both domestic issues and foreign concerns and seemed to promote an unreflective politics that stifled dialogue between the various interests and perspectives. The ruling Federalist Party followed Alexander Hamilton in favoring active central government, which continued to include a national bank, government support for commerce and industry, a strong executive, and, despite his disappointments, public support for Jay's Treaty, which was designed to relieve an ongoing state of hostility between the United States and Britain. Perhaps most notably and definitely of lasting significance, the Hamiltonian mercantilist view toward commerce, finance, and industry led to strong Federalist support for the imposition of tariffs directed at protecting young industries from foreign competition. In pointed contrast, Jefferson's Republicans strongly criticized high protective tariffs, advocated local and state power, sought a comparatively weaker national government, opposed a national bank, were more disposed toward affiliations with the French republic than the old enemy Great Britain, and ultimately envisioned an economy rooted in the agrarian ideal. Thus, the Washington administration drew broad and sometimes bitter criticism from the Jeffersonian quarter in response to the economic policies designed and administered by Hamilton and bearing Washington's imprimatur. The same concerns over a powerful, centralized government that simmered throughout the previous election were heating to a slow boil. Hamilton's policies were developed and applied against the context of a small but evident rift in the economic terrain of the country, with the interests of commerce and industry—particularly strong in New England, the Atlantic Seaboard, and in the more urbanized areas—pitted against the agricultural economic base that dominated the South (particularly inland from the coast) as well as rural areas in the interior regions of the North and West; and in general the farmers—and in particular the Southern planter—who, to protect their perceived interests, supported low tariffs, opposed the national bank, and were suspicious of the more urbanized vision of the Hamiltonians.

These nettlesome domestic divisions, however, were overshadowed by disturbing developments abroad, particularly on the high seas, involving incidents that exposed American vulnerabilities and polarized its partisan factions, adding still more heat to the political pressure cooker. Much like the sharp division over domestic issues, interparty fissures quickly opened over foreign policy. The Federalists aligned themselves with the British largely because of the common heritage shared between the United States and Britain along with the obvious economic advantages of sustaining close ties with the industrial power of London and Manchester. In sharp contrast, Jeffersonian Republicans found spiritual kinship in the equalitarian principles of the French Revolution. As Britain and France were bitter enemies battling for international supremacy, any foreign policy directed at either nation would be a delicate matter. Although Washington sought to keep the United States clear of Great Power conflict by following a policy of careful neutrality toward Britain and France, many Federalists and Republicans rejected this approach in support of one of the belligerents. Washington, now no longer inoculated against partisanship, was subjected to increasingly more frequent and harsher criticism from Republicans over allegations that the president and his administration were passively sitting by while Britain's Royal Navy, seeking to add needed and experienced manpower to its ranks, brazenly and with utter impunity impressed American sailors into His Majesty's service. Ships were also seized by the Royal Navy while the U.S. government offered no resistance, and the British army remained fortressed on the northwestern frontier in violation of prior agreements. In spite of these insults, Washington held steady in his desire to maintain neutrality, but this position found him running against the grain of both pro-English Federalists who despised the excesses of the French Revolution and pro-French Republicans, the latter claiming to be especially aggrieved by Washington's refusal to stand with a sister republic against an old and common enemy.

As the humiliation caused by the impressment of men and the loss of ships continued to fester, President Washington, fully aware that the United States could not engage in another war against the might of Britain, sought ways to resolve tensions diplomatically. These developments along with Washington's state of mind led to the dispatching of then chief justice John Jay to London to negotiate the treaty that now bears his name. This action provoked severe antipathy from the Republicans, who perceived the treaty as not only inadequate in dealing with Britain's abuses—it most notably failed to solve the impressment issue—but also in effect drawing the United States into even closer relations with London. Moreover, while the British reduced their presence on at least a portion of the frontier, they remained in their fortifications in the Northwest, particularly in the Great Lakes region. Throughout the various states, angry Republican crowds burned Jay in effigy, and the French cockade in the tricolor of the Revolution was provocatively displayed on partisan clothing as a show of sympathy and allegiance. Angry partisans fought in the streets, and we have reports of violence erupting even in some church services. An impassioned mob burned a copy of the treaty on the doorstep of the British foreign ministry, for good measure shattering the windows of the ambassador's residence.

The hardening opposition to Hamilton's economic vision, combined with the violent reactions to Jay's Treaty and the overall disgust at the foreign situation behind it, led to discernible erosion in the president's popularity. Washington, who was once universally acclaimed as a leader above reproach, was now being scolded and attacked in the press with a personal bitterness with which he was entirely unfamiliar. For example, Benjamin Franklin Bache, editor of the Republican-affiliated *Aurora* (and who also happened to be the grandson of the eminent Benjamin Franklin), eviscerated Washington, impudently accusing him of harboring desires to become dictator and, with unabashed hyperbole, writing, "If ever a nation was debauched by a man, the American Nation has been debauched by Washington." Bache would later claim that Washington was nothing less than the "source of all the misfortunes of our country," and that, far from being the reputed paragon of virtue, the president's very name gave "currency to political iniquity and to legalized corruption."

Had Washington decided to stand for a third term, and even if he had managed another victory, which was not altogether unlikely as his inestimable prestige had not been entirely spent, the solid base of unanimity behind his presidency had certainly vanished. Thus, after eight years of service, a wearied Washington, now embattled where once he was embraced, offered his now famous, sobering observations about partisan politics, or what he referred to as the "Spirit of Party":

> This spirit, unfortunately, is inseparable from our nature, having its root in the strongest passions of the human Mind. It exists under different shapes in all Governments, more or less stifled, controuled or repressed; but in those of the popular form it is seen its greatest rankness and is truly their worst enemy.
>
> The alternate domination of one faction over another, sharpened by the spirit of revenge natural to party dissention, which in different ages and countries has perpetrated the most horrid enemies, is itself a frightful despotism. . . . It [the Spirit of Party] serves always to distract the Public Councils and enfeeble the Public administration. It agitates the Community with ill-founded jealousies and false alarms, kindles the animosity of one part against another, foments occasionally riot and insurrection. It opens the door to foreign influence and corruption, which find a facilitated access to the government itself through the channels of party passions. Thus the policy and will of one country, are subjected to the policy and will of another.

These reflections, looking back on the deepening partisan rifts within his own administration, testify to the sense of discouragement that descended upon Washington in the latter years of his administration, as well as to the prescience of his assessment. Indeed, they serve as an augury of an imminent change in the character of national politics—of two presidential elections that would expose two of the republic's more prominent and qualified statesmen, John Adams and Thomas Jefferson, to unleashed acrimony, thereby further driving the wedge between the nation's two leading, formative parties, the Federalists of Hamilton and the Republicans of Jefferson and James Madison.

While Vice President Adams never quite held the same kind of universal esteem that Washington had enjoyed—and would yet still enjoy once sufficiently removed from the current political turmoil—he was nonetheless respected as an accomplished, experienced public servant of the first order and a leading intellectual. But earlier doubts about his suspected "monarchist" proclivities lingered, even though he had proven his republican credentials through the important leadership role that he played during the American Revolution. Although he despised the social upheaval that had occurred during the French Revolution, Adams was, like his counterpart Jefferson—and for that matter, Washington—a revolutionary in his own right. But owing to his faith in moderate government and executive power, further boosted by his affinities for the British traditions of governance and magnified by his sustained distrust in popular democracy, Adams was perceived as possessing serious autocratic tendencies. This sustained misperception both clouded the sophisticated nature of Adams's republican principles and provided ammunition for his rivals in the Jeffersonian camp.

For his part, Adams was uncertain about the likelihood of succeeding Washington. As late as February 1796, Adams realized that the upcoming election would be a close match between him, Jefferson, and Jay, even considering the election of Jefferson as president and Jay as his vice president to be the probable result. The fact that Adams as vice president seemed to be the de facto successor was not by itself enough to assuage his doubts, particularly given the electoral trends that he had already observed in just the first two elections. In addition to his apparent uncertainties about his own electability, Adams attempted to follow Washington's example—at least initially—by maintaining a safe distance from the question and stating his intentions to not participate in an open political contest for the presidency. Like Washington, Adams disliked partisan politics, and he let it be known that he would rather quit public service than engage in such indignities.

Meanwhile, other names were floated: Jefferson and Jay, the most prominent in spite of the political baggage that they both carried (i.e., charges of Jacobinism in the case of the former and the ill-received Jay's Treaty in the case of the latter); James Madison and Patrick Henry of Virginia; and Hamilton himself, even though there were questions about his eligibility under the constitutional requirements for office (Hamilton having been born in the West Indies). Adams kept insisting that he would dutifully serve if selected by the Electoral College, but that he would not actively seek the office, preferring the office to come to him as it had to his noble predecessor. But as the prospects of his rivals increased, Adams's personal ambitions along with his distaste for the possibility of a Jeffersonian presidency overtook him—even though he remained well disposed to Jefferson as a person—and he discreetly sought ways to preserve the appearance of Washingtonian disinterest while quietly but clearly communicating his availability.

No hats were thrown in the ring in this election, as Jefferson took the same approach in following Washington's example and remaining publicly aloof to political office. In correspondence with Adams, he expressed his contempt for politics and reasserted his indifference to the presidency. This correspondence reveals Adams's worries over Jefferson's affection for the revolution in France, which appears to have been, more than any other difference between the two men, the anxiety that dominated Adams's doubts about his friend's potential candidacy. Even though Jefferson clearly stated that he did not seek the office, Adams, reading between the lines, was convinced that the Sage of Monticello was in the arena.

In spite of Adams's effort to keep his distance from any campaign for the presidency, he nonetheless privately considered himself the presumptive heir. He patiently waited, understandably as the vice president, for some sign from Washington that such was indeed the case, but no hint of endorsement was given. Washington endorsed no one and remained completely removed from the discussion. Nonetheless, Adams took every opportunity to emphasize his association with Washington's administration, and he freely praised Washington as a statesman. As Adams and Jefferson continued to cloak their ambitions, it was left to the press to promote their favorites. Bache put the *Aurora* to good use in Jefferson's behalf, writing in glowing terms that Jefferson was the only reasonable choice to succeed Washington. "Democratic clubs" began to appear in several locations, working for the Jeffersonian cause. Adams was praised for his virtue and intellect, and he was lauded by his supporters as "the first planet from our political sun." Unfortunately, less polite language was used in describing rivals. Jefferson's Republican supporters continued to trot out unfair accusations of monarchism against Adams. It was evident that Adams's republican credentials were sound, but the old scandalmongering would not abate. He was incessantly charged with being "an avowed friend of monarchy." Jefferson suffered as well, for Adams's Federalist supporters accused him of being an "atheist" with anarchistic tendencies. He was referred to as a demagogue and a coward, a "Franco-maniac" who led a following of ragged cutthroats, and quite willing to foment mobs for his own devious purposes. The level of hyperbole, as bad as it was, would be surpassed in subsequent elections, but it was enough to confirm at least in part some of Washington's misgivings about partisanship and electioneering.

In spite of their attempts to appear indifferent, and given the relentless hostility of their critics, Jefferson and Adams were nonetheless clearly the two best choices for the presidency available at that time (i.e., in light of Washington's unavailability for a third term). By contrast, the office of the vice presidency drew numerous candidates, but not all of them serious. Several names were offered: for the Federalists, Oliver Ellsworth of Connecticut, John Jay of New York, James Iredell and Samuel Johnston of North Carolina, and the brothers Charles Cotesworth Pinckney and Thomas Pinckney of South Carolina; from the Republicans, Samuel Adams of Massachusetts, George Henry of Maryland, and George Clinton and Aaron Burr of New York. Many Republicans turned to young Burr, who had made a brief appearance as a candidate for the vice presidency four years earlier and was in no sense averse to openly campaigning for office. Breaking form, Burr set out on the campaign trail, concentrating his efforts in New England, the incumbent vice president's home turf, and may have been responsible for arranging the selection of a political ally, Sam Adams, to serve as a Republican elector in Massachusetts. Burr and other Jeffersonian loyalists spoke directly to the people, not just to the electors (as was the favored approach of the Federalists), setting a tone that would be sounded with increasing frequency in all future elections.

Federalists, employing the same North-South strategy that was partially behind the selection of the Washington-Adams duo in the previous two elections, primarily supported Thomas Pinckney, the younger of the Pinckneys of South Carolina. Pinckney, unlike Jay, had recently succeeded in negotiating a popular treaty with Spain, a fact that was keenly understood by the Federalists as providing them with a smart antidote to the general hostility toward Jay's Treaty. Pinckney was an able candidate, and an appealing one to Hamilton, who was never fully behind an Adams presidency. Hamilton hatched a plot to steal the election for president from both Adams and Jefferson and deliver it to the younger Pinckney. Pinckney would unanimously carry South Carolina, and if Hamilton could convince New England Federalists to cast all their votes for both Adams and Thomas Pinckney while simultaneously managing to find enough electors outside of New England to support any candidates other than Adams and Jefferson, this would strengthen Pinckney's position while leeching away votes and preventing Adams from acquiring the needed majority. This scheme was thwarted when electors in New England caught wind of it and, on their own initiative, summarily removed Pinckney's name from their ballots. But as the election approached, anxieties over Pinckney's possible election did not dissipate until well into December, when the strength of Adams's position became clearer, and not only in comparison with Pinckney, but also against Jefferson. Hamilton's gambit to displace Adams did not succeed, but it did appear to have cut into support for Jefferson, an outcome that he doubtless found to be equally desirable, if not more so. Once Adams was in position to win the election, Republicans suddenly muted their criticism, thus allowing the election to proceed to a more amicable conclusion. The election was still strikingly close, with Adams receiving seventy-one electoral votes to Jefferson's sixty-eight. Predictably, Adams's strongest support was drawn from New England, which fell in unanimously behind the vice president (this time Rhode Island joining in the chorus of support), joined by New York and New Jersey—both delivering unanimous blocks. Twenty of Jefferson's sixty-eight votes came from his home state of Virginia, with solid support also drawn from Pennsylvania and the Carolinas. Thomas Pinckney managed a respectable fifty-nine, just twelve votes off the pace (and only nine out of second place), and drew twenty-one votes from New England in spite of the backlash against Hamilton's stratagem (it is to be remembered that, before the Twelfth Amendment, which would be passed in 1803 and then ratified in 1804, electors voted for two candidates for president; thus New Englanders and other electors could vote for both Adams and Pinckney if they chose to do so). Interestingly, Pinckney and Adams both carried New York, even though the Empire State had three favorite sons in the race. Burr gathered a total of thirty electoral votes (twenty-nine votes better than his showing in 1792), thirteen of which came from Pennsylvania; but, perhaps tellingly, none from his New York home. The remaining votes were tallied as follows: George Clinton and John Jay, who joined Burr in failing to win even a single vote in their home state of New York, took seven and five, respectively; Samuel Adams (15, all from Virginia); Oliver Ellsworth (11); Iredell (3); Samuel Johnson (2); John Henry (2); and Charles Pinckney (1). Two electors, one from North Carolina and one from Virginia, voted for Washington. When Adams was declared victorious, the press and popular opinion fell in behind him, with Jefferson, who was to now serve as vice president, making a point of visiting Adams in a show of unity. Goodwill was reestablished, and fears of irreparable fractures were for a time allayed.

The election of 1796 was the first in which party politics came to the foreground, even though formal parties still remained to be developed and political organization on a large scale did not as yet exist. Historian Page Smith noted that the election of 1796 was arguably the most important in American history, as its outcome proved that the selection of a president from among rival candidates and the transition of power from one president to the next could be peacefully achieved under the new constitution. In the end, once the participants dampened their hysteria, the result was indeed an amicable one. And at least for a time, the political waters were calmed and the ship of state steadied. But it would soon become evident that a far more tumultuous storm would yet appear over the horizon, made manifest as the **Campaign of 1800**.

Additional Resources

Boller, Paul F., Jr. *Presidential Campaigns.* New York: Oxford University Press, 1984.

Cohen, Martin, David Karol, Hans Noel, and John Zaller. *The Party Decides: Presidential Nominations before and after Reform.* Chicago: University of Chicago Press, 2008.

Freeman, Joanne. "The Presidential Election of 1796." In Richard Alan Ryerson, ed. *John Adams and the Founding of the Republic.* Charlottesville: University of Virginia Press, 2001.

Horsman, Reginald. "1796." In Arthur M. Schlesinger, Fred L. Israel, and David J. Frent, eds. *Running for President: The Candidates and Their Images.* New York: Simon & Schuster, 1994.

Sharp, James Roger. *American Politics in the Early Republic: The New Nation in Crisis.* New Haven, CT: Yale University Press, 1993.

Smith, Page. "Election of 1796." In Arthur M. Schlesinger, Fred Israel, and William P. Hansen, eds. *History of American Presidential Elections, 1789–1968.* Vol. 1. New York: Chelsea House, 1985.

Campaign of 1800

Students of politics and American history frequently point to the pivotal election of 1800 as the most significant in the story of American campaigns. The eventual winner of the election, Thomas Jefferson, once remarked that this election was "as real a revolution in the principles of our government as that of 1776 was in its form; not effected indeed by the sword, as that, but by the rational and peaceable instrument of reform, the suffrage of the people." This election was marked, even more than the previous one, by the kind of sharp theoretical disagreements that we would in our day call ideological, and the campaign that ensued reopened and then widened the deepening political and social rifts that had already been glimpsed in 1792 and still more noticeably in 1796. Once again, the election squared off John Adams, now the incumbent president, against Jefferson, his old friend and now the incumbent vice president. Few Americans were more important to the political leadership of the American Revolution than these old comrades and rivals. In 1776, they followed in essence the same ideals, agreed fully on their objectives, served as allies on the same revolutionary committees, took the same potentially deadly risks, and collaborated together on the Declaration of Independence (which, as it is well known, was largely written by Jefferson under the advice of Adams and Benjamin Franklin). But 1800 was not a year of political concord for these erstwhile allies. Even though the election of 1796 ended amicably, their philosophical differences had clearly sounded during the Washington administration, becoming further amplified during the campaign that followed Washington's retirement. This mutual support, freely given and enjoyed in the spirit of goodwill upon the outcome of the previous election, soon dissipated as events proceeded and philosophical differences further crystallized.

The disagreements of the 1790s were still there: reconciliation with England versus allegiance to France, centralized versus localized government along with federal versus state power, Hamilton's economic activism versus governmental minimalism, protectionist tariffs favored by commercial interests versus the disdain for tariffs felt by farming interests—especially, but not exclusively, in the South—and modernizing commerce, urbanization, and manufacturing industry versus a deep agrarian tradition, a division that also had North-South undercurrents even though the agrarian culture was also strong in the rural North and West. Soon, the rift was widened as the Jeffersonian Republicans excoriated President Adams for the Alien and Sedition Acts, a set of laws enacted by Congress with Adams's endorsement in an effort to quell anti-administration criticism and punish "Jacobin" newspapers. Naval hostilities, this time between the United States and France (in what has since been deemed the "Quasi War" pitting America against France), drew still further recriminations from Francophile Republicans, and the confusion surrounding the "XYZ Affair" raised nagging questions about the administration's diplomatic skills. Jefferson and the Republicans were infuriated by these events and sought a dramatic change in the upcoming election. Even some Federalists found the last four years under Adams distasteful and were reluctant to support a second term. The aggravated policy disagreements between Federalists and Jefferson's Republicans guaranteed a bruising campaign and, in some quarters, raised new doubts about the possibility of a peaceful transfer of power between the two factions. All conditions were ripe for a heated and, as it would turn out, momentous contest.

During Adams's administration, the naval war with France put the United States in a potentially perilous position. The French government was insulted by Jay's Treaty, signed between the United States and Britain, which had seemed to the French a clear indication that the United States was now leaning its allegiance toward Britain, which to the French was regarded askance given their substantial aid to the Americans against Britain in their war for independence. President Adams attempted to defuse the situation by sending three emissaries, Charles Cotesworth Pinckney, John Marshall, and Elbridge Gerry, to France to work toward a resolution. Represented by three French agents (later to be known anonymously as X, Y, and Z), the French demanded to be paid a large amount of money before they were to agree to any treaty that would resolve the growing hostilities between the two countries, a sum that included what was in effect a large (and embarrassing) bribe. Repulsed by such presumption, Pinckney's reaction came in his famous response: "No, no! Not a sixpence!" Later that summer, Rep. Robert Goodloe Harper of South Carolina is said to have echoed and further fortified this sentiment by declaiming a still more famous phrase, which was at one time well known to nearly all American elementary school students, "Millions for defense, not one cent for tribute!" It was now clear that any agreement between France and the United States was, at least momentarily, unattainable. The Quasi War between the former allies continued for two more years without a formal declaration of hostilities from either side. Politically, this hurt the Republican cause given their long and public sympathy for France, the effects of which were felt in the off-year elections of 1798. But any advantage held by the Federalists was soon negated by their actions.

In 1798, under this political climate and with Adams's support, the Federalist-dominated Congress passed four laws—soon to be together known as the Alien and Sedition Acts—designed to address domestic security in response to the growing threat of a belligerent France. Three laws addressing aliens and primarily directed at French and Irish (who were viewed as sympathetic to France) residents changed the requirements for naturalization, making it easier to deport and imprison aliens deemed to be a potential danger to domestic safety. Ominously, the Sedition Act broadened the definition of treason to include any publication of "false, scandalous and malicious writing." The execution of this act resulted in the arrests of twenty-five men, the majority of them being editors with Republican allegiances. This included Republican firebrand Benjamin Franklin Bache (a strident critic of both President Washington and President Adams), who was charged with seditious libel, an indictment that resulted in his being physically assaulted, his home and family threatened, and his office vandalized by a mob. (Bache died of yellow fever before his case went to trial.) Needless to say, the focus of the arrests led to the impression that the Sedition Act was aimed not so much at domestic security against potential French encroachments as it was at the discrediting and elimination of Republican opposition to Federalist policies. Response to the Alien and Sedition Acts also prompted Jefferson and his closest political ally, friend, and neighbor, James Madison, to anonymously write the Virginia and Kentucky Resolutions, documents used by Republicans in the campaign of 1800 but that would become more prominent as important theoretical arguments in the still more substantive debate over constitutional interpretation and the relationship between the several states and the federal government.

Such was the situation as the Campaign of 1800 drew close. Both parties prepared for a far more vigorous, polarized, and acrimonious contest than the Campaign of 1796. Because of this, the parties each began to exhibit more coherent organization than in the previous elections. While the true beginnings of the modern political party as we know it in America were still two or three decades away, party politics in some states began to show organizational characteristics that would later develop on a national scale. Formal party organization and structure emerged in those states in which allegiances were divided between the two factions. What can now, in retrospect, be identified as one of the earliest "party machines" was in operation in Virginia, the state with the most electoral votes at the time, as well as New York (which was becoming increasingly subject to the growing influence of the Tammany Society), with the Republicans being particularly diligent in incubating these formative versions of the political machine in the Empire State. New laws in the Old Dominion required voters to cast votes for all twenty-one electors instead of the previous practice of choosing one elector per voting district, a practice that encouraged statewide organization. The January before the election, Republican Party leaders—most (but not all) of them state legislators—met in Richmond in what was essentially a party caucus charged with establishing tighter organization throughout the commonwealth. The Federalists followed suit, although at least in Virginia, they operated on a smaller scale.

Organizing and electioneering in other states was far more effective than it had been in any previous campaign season. Party networks were becoming more sophisticated, especially in New York and Pennsylvania. As the party out of power, Republicans, by the virtues inspired by necessity, proved more adept at learning this new political game. One consequence of this was increased criticism of the congressional nominating caucus, which was the first formal presidential nominating instrument but was now, even at this early stage in the growth of the republic, being accused in some quarters of violating the constitutional rights of voting citizens. From all of this, it became apparent that the partisan politics so despised by Washington was in reality a political inevitability built into the structure of the political edifice. But caution must be added here to check exaggeration: The Electoral College was still selected by the various state legislatures in eleven of the now sixteen states, with only Kentucky, Maryland, North Carolina, Rhode Island, and Virginia choosing electors through popular vote (a popular vote not nearly as inclusive as that which we are accustomed to today); and given this control in the state legislatures, the type of political canvassing and stumping with which we are now familiar was still a distant development.

During the campaign, Republicans distributed their positions on policy in what could be called a forerunner to the party platform, with particular use of the friendly elements of the press in Virginia and Pennsylvania. In the *Examiner* of Richmond, several policy points formally adopted by state activists were published in the form of negative resolutions opposing current Federalist programs. Included among these resolutions were the Republican opposition to a standing military, reaffirmation of the need for neutrality in foreign affairs, criticism of the national debt, and denunciation of the Alien and Sedition Acts. In Philadelphia, the pro-Republican *Aurora*, now managed by Bache's widow Margaret, published a catalog of eleven antinomies punctuating the differences between "things as they have been" under the Federalists and "things as they will be" under the Republicans. Under this catalog, Republicans reaffirmed their dedication to the principles of the Revolution and further advocated peaceful neutrality abroad and domestic unity at home, fair and tolerant government separated from church hierarchy, elimination of public debt, reduction of taxes, a free press, and freedom of religion. By implication, the Federalists were depicted as opponents of these unassailable principles. In response, the Federalists stood their ground, choosing to claim their achievements rather than respond directly to Republican charges. They emphasized their proven experience in statesmanship earned through twelve years of predominantly Federalist government, the overall prosperity enjoyed under Federalist policies, and the need for continuity and stability in the face of incessant international tumult. One pro-Federalist address in Rhode Island pointedly asked why the nation should follow the lead of "aristocratic" Virginia, a state haughtily proud of its undemocratic class structure and institutionalized slavery. Through newspapers, pamphlets, posters, and handbills, both sides addressed the issues of the day with sincerity and offered their reasons as to why one party was superior to the other in the task of shaping the destiny of the young republic. But, inevitably and almost irresistibly, the question of character was also broached, lending to a particularly tense mood throughout the campaign.

Despite their genteel posture of civility, the Federalists were not above vituperation, describing Jefferson as cowardly, mean, the son of a "half-breed," a phony Southern rube who fed on coarse cornmeal and "fricasseed bullfrog," a robber of widows, and a profane threat to Christian civilization whose administration would foster fearsome crime and wretched malfeasance, in addition to the old charge of Jacobin heresy. In what nearly amounts to the coining and circulation of an early political slogan, Philadelphia's *Gazette of the United States* boldly and repeatedly framed the alternatives in the upcoming election as choosing between "God—and a religious president; or impiously declare for Jefferson—and no God!!!" Adams, of course, was in the eyes of the *Gazette* the "religious" president, in contrast to the "atheist" radical of Monticello.

Returning such verbal fire, personal insult was also heaped upon Adams by the Republicans. Tyrant, fool, and intemperate whirlwind of "malignant passions" were epithets hurled at Adams and now added to the old accusations of monarchism and aristocratic ambition. To further this tired canard charging Adams with blind devotion to the British monarchy, rumormongers disseminated a madcap fiction that the president was hatching a scandalous plan to reunite Britain and the United States through an arranged marriage between a scion of his household and a daughter of King George III. According to this fabrication, it was Washington himself who saved the country from the clutches of such cynical treason. With brandished sword, the story went, he was to have forced Adams to abandon his royalist ambitions. Preposterous as this all seems today, the story was for a while taken seriously by the Federalists' more gullible enemies.

Significantly, Alexander Hamilton's former ambivalence toward President Adams had degenerated into unequivocal dislike. Hamilton now regarded Adams as vain, self-promoting, and unpredictable. Indeed, Hamilton appeared to entertain some respect for his other rival, Jefferson, at least when compared to his assessment of the president, complaining, "If we must have an enemy at the head of the government, let it be one whom we can oppose, and for whom we are not responsible, who will not involve our party in the disgrace of his foolish bad measures." Hamilton, the true leader of the early Federalists and a stalwart of their principles, saw Adams as far too moderate in his attitudes toward the rabble-rousing Republicans and their dangerous French sympathies. Rejecting Adams outright, Hamilton supported Charles Pinckney, the elder Pinckney of South Carolina—famously and favorably associated with the XYZ Affair—whom he saw as decidedly truer to the party's principles and a person of stronger character. In a private letter addressed to South Carolina Federalists, Hamilton vilified Adams's record and character. A copy of this letter mysteriously fell into the hands of Republican Aaron Burr, and soon "Hamilton's Thunderbolt" decrying the meanness, incompetence, and petty egotism of Adams was widely circulated. Adams fueled this intraparty vitriol by sternly and publicly denouncing Hamilton as an unscrupulous "bastard" greatly schooled in cunning intrigue.

But in the end, in spite of the objections raised against President Adams by influential figures within his own party such as Hamilton, the popular candidates for the presidency were seen to be the incumbent president against his incumbent vice president, Jefferson. What was thus needed was to establish a pool of reasonable choices for vice president. This comparatively—by the standards of the times—tighter political organization provided for broader consensus in selecting candidates for the vice presidency. The Federalists, now generally committed to a second term for the president, threw in behind Hamilton's favorite, the elder Pinckney, for the vice presidency, while Burr was tapped by the Republicans. In doing so, both parties followed the North-South strategy (Massachusetts-South Carolina for the Federalists and Virginia-New York for the Republicans) that had been in practice since the first election (i.e., Washington of Virginia in the South and Adams of Massachusetts in the North). As the campaign unfolded, New York soon drew considerable attention from the Republicans, who believed they had a solid chance of securing a majority in the state legislature and thereby winning the twelve electoral votes that went to the Federalists in the previous election. Republicans also realized that victory in New York's elections for the state house would provide momentum that might influence other states as well. For Jefferson, New York was decisive, especially New York City, but victory would not come easy as

Hamilton, a New Yorker, led the Federalist charge there. But the Republicans were better organized and led by Burr, a rising star in state and national politics and now Hamilton's greatest nemesis. Burr proved energetic, determined, savvy, and perceptive, conducting the New York campaign for the state house with the expertise of a modern campaign manager. While Burr commonly has been associated with Tammany, in this election at least, he worked directly with state party committees and independently of the nascent machine's growing sway. Burr managed to deliver New York, a hard blow to the Federalists who had carried it for Adams in 1796. In a close election of this nature, a victory of this size proved the difference.

And the election was close—to this day the closest electoral vote in American history (the only tie in the history of the Electoral College). But in the end, the decision was not between Adams and Jefferson but between Jefferson and Burr, an outcome that some leading Republicans had actually anticipated but did little to prevent. To the contrary, their electoral strategy, particularly in Virginia and New York, seemed to guarantee it. President Adams won sixty-five Electoral College votes, sustaining his unanimous support in New England and New Jersey. (Pinckney received sixty-four, with one vote in Rhode Island going to New York's John Jay.) However, both Jefferson and Burr exceeded the president, each winning seventy-three electoral votes (taking the same electors in the same states, notably winning thirty-three of their seventy-three votes from Virginia and New York combined). The Federalists made inroads in Pennsylvania, which had favored Jefferson in 1796 by a margin of fourteen to one, in 1800 losing there by a margin of only eight to seven. Jefferson's position in North Carolina was also weakened by three votes, but Adams and Pinckney split Federalist loyalties, thus nullifying any gains. Significantly, Jefferson and Burr both managed to sweep Pinckney's home state of South Carolina, depriving the Federalists of any votes there. They also enjoyed unanimity in Georgia, Kentucky, and Tennessee. Maryland was an even split between the two parties.

While it was widely presumed that Jefferson was the party's candidate for president, under the Constitution, Burr's seventy-three votes were technically for president as well, not for vice president, the Constitution still at that time only stipulating that the candidate with the second-most votes was elected vice president (soon to be amended as a result of this election). Under the stipulations of the Constitution, any tie between presidential candidates in the Electoral College was to be resolved in the House of Representatives, who could decide for themselves—the intent of the electors, the preferences of the party, and the sway of public opinion notwithstanding—who should be elected president. Thus, entirely by accident, Burr was in a position to become the next president of the United States, even though from the outset, it was clear in everyone's mind that Jefferson was the intended Republican candidate for the presidency. It was therefore a matter now left to the members of the House, which at that time was still controlled by the Federalists, as the transition to the newly elected Republican majority had not yet transpired. In a twist of political fortune, the Federalists thus held the key to the immediate future of Republican leadership. As Jefferson dryly observed, the Republicans were "in the hands of the enemies."

Out of a sense of decorum, Burr publicly demurred to compete against Jefferson for the high office, stating that he did not desire to deprive the people of their first choice. And yet, it has been noted that he also failed to promise that he would refuse the presidency should the vote in the House go his way, and as such, he may have subtly encouraged a degree of uncertainty regarding his own ambitions. The Federalists in particular read it this way, and many interpreted Burr's lack of forthcoming clarity to be a sign that he did in fact seek the presidency for himself, and there were many Federalists who actually desired an outcome favoring Burr. For his part, Burr deflected offers of Federalist support in exchange for his allegiance to their policies. Hamilton was one Federalist who absolutely refused to make any such advances to Burr, for as much as Hamilton opposed Jefferson, he deeply dreaded a Burr presidency, referring to his fellow New Yorker as an unprincipled "American Catiline." Hamilton thus threw his considerable influence against Burr and, swallowing hard while holding his nose, worked for the election of the "contemptible hypocrite" Jefferson.

To complicate matters further, the voting in the House was by state, not by individual member; so the electoral vote tally could not supply any insight into what the House would in the end decide. A majority vote in the state delegation within the House carried the state. Ties did not count. On the first ballot, it was close; Jefferson received the votes of eight states, with six voting for Burr. Two states were deadlocked, delaying the needed majority and thus prompting further balloting. The balloting continued for six days, thirty-five ballots in all, before Jefferson finally emerged the winner, carrying ten states on the thirty-sixth and last ballot, cast on February 17, 1801. On that ballot, James A. Bayard, a Federalist and Delaware's sole representative to the House (Delaware at that time being allotted only one member in the House of Representatives), had prior to the voting announced his intention to abstain, and his example prompted other Federalists from Vermont, Maryland, and South Carolina to submit blank ballots. Although the actual facts are unclear, Hamilton appears to have played a key role in the outcome, convincing Bayard and at least some of the erstwhile pro-Burr Federalists to submit the blank ballots, thereby neutralizing the support that Burr needed from the Federalists in the House in order to win the presidency. Thus, by a vote of ten states to four in favor of Jefferson, Burr was to become vice president (Connecticut, Massachusetts, New Hampshire, and Rhode Island voted for Burr; Delaware and South Carolina cast no vote due to the submission of blank ballots). Thomas Jefferson, author of the Declaration of Independence and Virginia's statute for religious freedom as well as the founder of the University of Virginia, was now to become the third president of the United States. Personal animosities festered. Within four years, Alexander Hamilton, a true giant of the American founding, would be dead, mortally wounded by gunshot in a duel with Aaron Burr. Hamilton would openly oppose Burr's run for governor in New York in 1804, thus adding further fuel to their smoldering mutual enmity. Upon receiving news of a vigorous denunciation of Burr by Hamilton at a dinner party, Burr felt driven to resolve the issue once and for all by other, more final, and less forgiving means.

The election of 1800 and the subsequent peaceful transition of power from Federalists to Republicans represented a remarkable achievement, one that Jefferson, as stated above, considered an achievement as revolutionary as the American Revolution itself, an assessment that is not without support among historians today. As important as the election of 1796 was, the transition of power that occurred then was between members of the same faction or party. In 1800, power was exchanged between parties with which no love was lost, under conditions of deep, polarizing, and intensifying division within the republic. And yet the transition occurred, one party resigning power and another assuming it, without resorting to threat or violence. The election of 1800 also prompted the passage and ratification of the Twelfth Amendment, which solved the election confusion in Article II as it was originally written, by adding language explicitly separating the selection of the president from that of the vice president.

Finally, the election of 1800 foreshadowed in notable ways the emergence of modern political parties and even anticipated the influence of the political machine, which would dominate much of the political direction of the republic throughout the nineteenth century and even well into the twentieth. As an increasingly larger percentage of states were soon to move from legislative selection to the popular election of presidential electors, political parties became necessary to mobilize support for presidential tickets. While still lacking sophistication compared to the modern party apparatus that we today take for granted, political parties had, by 1800, become a durable feature in American society; and the politics of the boss-driven machine, while still in its earliest stages in the early 1800s, would grow up with the two-party system to expand and thrive for at least a century and a half. As the political world that beats within American democracy continued to reveal its competitive and antagonistic dimensions, James Madison's observation in *Federalist* 10 proved again vividly insightful; faction is indeed "sown in the nature of man."

Additional Resources

Boller, Paul F., Jr. *Presidential Campaigns.* New York: Oxford University Press, 1984.

Cunningham, Noble, "Election of 1800." In Arthur M. Schlesinger, Fred Israel, and William P. Hansen, eds. *History of American Presidential Elections, 1789–1968.* Vol. 1. New York: Chelsea House, 1985.

Cunningham, Noble E. "1800." In Arthur M. Schlesinger, Fred L. Israel, and David J. Frent, eds. *Running for President: The Candidates and Their Images.* New York: Simon & Schuster, 1994.

Peterson, Merrill D. *Thomas Jefferson and the New Nation.* Oxford: Oxford University Press, 1970.

Sharp, James Roger. *The Deadlocked Election of 1800: Jefferson, Burr and the Union in the Balance.* Lawrence: University Press of Kansas, 2010.

Smith, Page. *John Adams.* 2 vols. Garden City, NY: Doubleday, 1962.

Van der Linden, Frank. *The Turning Point: Jefferson's Battle for the Presidency.* Washington, DC: R. B. Luce, 1962.

Weisberger, Bernard A. *America Afire: Jefferson, Adams, and the Revolutionary Election of 1800.* New York: William Morrow, 2000.

Campaign of 1804

In his first inaugural address, President Thomas Jefferson urged a new spirit of unity in the wake of the most acrimonious campaign to date. "Every difference of opinion is not a difference of principle," the new president asserted, further declaiming, "We have called by different names brethren of the same principle. We are all Republicans. We are all Federalists. If there be any among us who would wish to dissolve this Union or to change its republican form, let them stand undisturbed as monuments of the safety with which error of opinion may be tolerated where reason is left free to combat it."

Unity and concord were uppermost in the president's mind at the inauguration, and he quickly set out to govern under the impulse of this aspiration. Two trends that developed between Jefferson's inauguration in 1801 and the campaign of 1804 helped to produce a calmer political climate: the growing popularity of Jefferson in response to notable achievements in his first term, and the continued growth of the Jeffersonian Republicans at the expense of the Federalists. It was becoming apparent that the party of Alexander Hamilton was waning in membership and influence. New England remained a Federalist stronghold, but the rest of the nation was gradually becoming dominated by the Republicans, increasing their influence in state legislatures as well as holding their gains in the federal Congress.

Jefferson's administration negotiated the Louisiana Purchase, oversaw the expiration of the despised Alien and Sedition Acts, successfully deployed the navy led by Stephen Decatur in a heroic campaign against the Barbary pirates, and benefited from the end of hostilities with France (it is important to note that it was Federalist and former president John Adams who actually negotiated the resolution of the crisis). Moreover, Jefferson had allayed the concerns of more moderate Federalists by incorporating friendly policies toward commerce and manufacturing as well as sustaining Hamilton's national bank, a branch being opened in

New Orleans shortly after its acquisition from the French. In effect, Jefferson, whose political principles are universally contrasted against Hamilton's, in practice adopted some Hamiltonian measures. Known for his record of criticizing the strong, activist, and ambitious executive recommended by Hamilton, President Jefferson would himself prove to be the strongest and most energetic chief executive to serve between Washington, the first president, and Andrew Jackson, the seventh. In sum, taxation was light, federal expenditures had been cut and the federal payroll reduced, the national debt cut by $6 million, and all the while the economy enjoyed a sustained period of growth.

By leaving untouched many of Hamilton's economic programs, most notably the national bank, the opposition was deprived of its own ammunition. Federalists found it exceptionally difficult to mount a viable campaign against the popular Jefferson. They attempted to criticize the Louisiana Purchase, but Jefferson's obvious coup in the peaceful acquisition of such an immense territory was difficult to challenge with any credibility, and certainly the American public was by and large not averse to the addition of an enormous tract of land that simultaneously cleared away an ambitious European power from the frontier. Their criticism of Jefferson's defense policy could only fall on deaf ears in light of the intrepid Decatur mission (which was, in Lord Nelson's view, "the most bold and daring act of the age") and the resolve that Jefferson exhibited in protecting American interests abroad. Denied any real political traction, in the end, the Federalists were reduced to falling back on worn incriminations of Jefferson's demagoguery and alleged atheism, scandalmongering about the president's relationship with Sally Hemings, a slave attached to the Jefferson plantation at Monticello, and deriding the president for the inland beaching of a gunboat in a Georgia cornfield in the aftermath of a hurricane—an act of God that had nothing to do with the president and everything to do with his critics clutching at straws. Jefferson's case for reelection in 1804 was as strong as any incumbent, then or now, could expect.

One of the more important features of the campaign and election of 1804 was the solidification of the caucus system, the first hint of which had informally appeared as early as 1796, and then again in 1800 under some noticeable criticism; but within four years of that controversial election, it would be taken for granted as routine. "King Caucus," as it would come to be called, especially as a pejorative by its critics, was effectively employed by congressional Jeffersonian Republicans in the summer of 1804 and was reinforced as the preferred method of nominating candidates for president on into the early to mid-1820s. Jefferson had no problem receiving the unanimous endorsement of the Republican caucus in February 1804 (considered to have been the first real congressional nominating caucus in history, although it is believed that informal caucuses met in the two previous campaigns). But Vice President Burr, his political fortunes rapidly deteriorating, was no longer considered a viable candidate for the second spot on the ticket. A replacement was therefore needed, and the caucus overwhelmingly supported the candidacy of New York's George Clinton, who received 67 out of 108 votes cast by the caucus, his nearest competitor, John Breckinridge of Kentucky, winning just 20—and the incumbent Burr winning none. (With the ratification of the Twelfth Amendment in September 1804, the issue of which candidate was nominated for what office was now clear.) Burr, who was never trusted by Jefferson and who was nothing more than a vice president by title, ran for governor of New York but was soundly defeated, due in large part to Alexander Hamilton's vehement—and highly personal—public opposition. The sudden collapse of Burr's once promising political career was accelerated later that year when he repaid Hamilton with fatal pistol fire. Burr, who in 1800 tied Jefferson for Electoral College votes for the presidency, coming as close to any man in American history to winning the presidency without becoming president, had quickly become a pariah.

By and large, the Federalists were a party in trouble. They lacked both vigorous organization and popular appeal outside of New England (where they still remained strong), although some stalwarts were active in Delaware, Maryland, and South Carolina. The new states recently admitted in the West were decidedly Republican. Unlike the Republicans, the Federalists did not adopt the caucus system, and throughout much of 1804, there was little discussion among Federalists about the nomination of a candidate for president. Without controversy, and largely through the support of Federalist-aligned newspapers, South Carolina's Charles Cotesworth Pinckney, one of the heroes of the XYZ Affair, and New York's Rufus King, a close ally of Hamilton, were tapped for the presidency and vice presidency, respectively. Once again, both parties carried forward the traditional North-South strategy. Republicans campaigned with enthusiasm throughout the various states and even promoted a set of doctrinal statements resembling a modern platform. But the Federalists were less inclined to participate in such popular politics. In some states, Federalist proponents were utterly invisible. However, several Federalists did seem to understand the need to make the party more accessible and appealing to the general voter. Before his death, a pragmatic Hamilton recommended that the party become more democratic in its procedures, admitting that the party needed to at least partially emulate the Republican style if it was to remain viable. While Republican political rallies and celebrations were more common, in some states the Federalists did make a show of it, but it was becoming clearer that the party was in danger of breaking apart. While some Federalists perceived the need for a more competitive presence in the campaign arena, other party leaders, particularly those in Congress, were simply not interested.

A group of Federalist diehards in New England, led by Fisher Ames, George Cabot, Stephen Higginson, Theophilus Parsons, and Timothy Pickering, confronted with what was to them the ignoble prospect of Republican domination in the rest of the Union, dramatically concluded that New England's only hope was to secede from the Union. Forming what would be called the "Essex Junto," as many of their members were from Essex County in Massachusetts, they appealed to Hamilton, whom they considered to be their philosophical inspiration, for support and leadership. Hamilton was unimpressed with their designs for secession and had abruptly spurned their overtures. Burr, Hamilton's nemesis, has been thinly connected to this group, but the evidence as to his support of or participation in a secessionist conspiracy involving the Essex Junto is still a matter of controversy and likely untrue.

Jefferson and Pinckney attempted to remain aloof from campaigning, as was the custom of the time (operating under the prevailing maxim, "The gentleman does not seek the office, but the office seeks the gentleman"), and they succeeded, for the most part, in exhibiting a quiet detachment. The campaign did at times deteriorate into scandalmongering and character assassination, but it was nothing compared to the viciousness of the campaign of 1800, in part due to the realization from nearly all quarters that Jefferson's reelection was guaranteed. Jefferson's association with Sally Hemings was again trotted out by his opponents, and he was continually accused of harboring irreligious doctrines and questionable morals. Regarding the more relevant policy matters, some of the president's critics attempted to take issue with the constitutionality of the Louisiana Purchase, but these efforts were too difficult to take seriously. For the most part, Jefferson demurred to engage in any potshots against the Federalists, but at one point, he referred to the opposing party as a "prigarchy," a swipe at the Federalists' alleged "priggish" attitudes and "aristocratic" pretensions.

Electors were chosen more democratically throughout the Union in comparison with previous elections. Seven states chose their electors via at-large popular voting, and in four other states, selection was determined, with some variation, by district. State legislatures chose electors in only six out of the seventeen states, a marked change from four years earlier when ten of sixteen state legislatures selected electors. This represented a prevailing turnaround in attitudes regarding the selection of electors, indicating that a democratization of the process of presidential selection was under way.

It was no surprise to anyone that Jefferson won in a landslide. His 162 electoral votes was, at that time, the highest total number earned by any candidate for president since the institution of the Electoral College; conversely, Pinckney's 14 votes was the worst showing of any candidate in a presidential election to that point. Owing to the Twelfth Amendment, the vote totals for the presidential and vice presidential candidates for the first time matched those of their running mates. Jefferson interpreted his triumph as a sign of renewed unity throughout the republic, and he wistfully reflected upon the late president Washington's vision of a unified republic beyond the reach of the divisive effects of faction. That vision was shortly to be thwarted, as partisanship would regain its influence in subsequent campaigns. The election of 1804 was a landslide that hastened the unraveling of the Federalist Party; but it would soon become evident that the election of 1808 would give them a second chance.

Additional Resources

Boller, Paul F., Jr. *Presidential Campaigns.* New York: Oxford University Press, 1984.

Cunningham, Noble E. "1804." In Arthur M. Schlesinger, Fred L. Israel, and David J. Frent, eds. *Running for President: The Candidates and Their Images.* New York: Simon & Schuster, 1994.

Dauer, Manning. "Election of 1804." In Arthur M. Schlesinger, Fred Israel, and William P. Hansen, eds. *History of American Presidential Elections, 1789–1968*, vol. 1. New York: Chelsea House, 1985.

McDonald, Forrest. *The Presidency of Thomas Jefferson.* Lawrence: University Press of Kansas, 1987.

Peterson, Merrill D. *Thomas Jefferson and the New Nation.* Oxford: Oxford University Press, 1970.

Campaign of 1808

The election of 1804 so weakened the Federalist Party that something akin to one-party government appeared, at least for a time, to be a very real possibility. After Thomas Jefferson's 1804 landslide, Federalist support regionally contracted to New England, with only a small number of stalwarts holding out in other parts of the Union, now thoroughly dominated by the Republicans. Yet a series of international disputes that occurred during Jefferson's second term seriously undermined his public support. Cracks began to appear in a hitherto tightly unified Republican structure, and the Federalist Party stumbled upon a real opportunity to reassert itself once again as a force in national politics.

The central controversy in Jefferson's second term revolved around the administration's unsatisfying response to renewed conflict abroad, this time with both Britain and France. Both the French and the British navies now brazenly seized American merchant ships, and the British resumed impressment of American sailors, a practice that they had first adopted during President Washington's administration. Additionally, in July 1807, the British ship-of-the-line HMS *Leopard* attacked an ill-prepared American frigate, the USS *Chesapeake*, on the pretense that it was harboring deserters from the Royal Navy. A badly damaged *Chesapeake*, with a wounded and demoralized crew, was forced to strike its colors and allow the British to board and capture four sailors. The resultant furor over this action fueled a growing contempt of the Royal Navy and an impassioned desire among American citizens for some kind of response against the arrogance of both navies. The president ordered British ships from American waters and issued a call for the mobilization of one hundred thousand militia troops, but he was fully aware of the weakness of the American position when compared to the formidable and expansive power of the British Royal Navy. Determined to prevent entanglement in the Napoleonic Wars under way in Europe, Jefferson rejected military options and, with the legislative support of Congress through the enactment of the Embargo Act that following December, resorted to punitive economic measures against both France and Britain. The Great Embargo of 1807, however, led to considerable economic discomfort at home and embarrassment for the young country's image abroad. Disenchanted New England merchants and grain farmers north and south suffered, and the domestic economy as a whole was strained.

Consequently, the fading, minority Federalists further solidified their New England base, and perturbed by the perception that aristocratic Virginians (Republican Virginians, no less) were the cause of their current entrepreneurial crisis, the engine of Federalist indignation was duly stoked. Jefferson's popularity plummeted, leaving the successor to his leadership of the Republican faction and the obvious favorite for the nomination in 1808, his close friend and secretary of state James Madison of Virginia, unhappily on the defensive and at a disadvantage. With Jefferson following Washington's worthy precedent and retiring after two terms, Madison was saddled with these festering problems left to him by President Jefferson. Moreover, it was Madison in his capacity as secretary of state who had formerly sponsored the vilified Embargo Act; hence it was as much his albatross as Jefferson's—even more so, as it threatened to pose more serious consequences for his political future.

Despite Madison's unsurpassed political insight and admirable record of political and administrative leadership, his anointing as Jefferson's heir was forcefully challenged within his own party. His campaign, which was directed by senators William Giles and Wilson Nicholas, both from Virginia, and who are now considered to be forerunners of the modern campaign manager, encountered serious intraparty resistance in three Electoral College powerhouses: his home state of Virginia (24 electoral votes), Pennsylvania (20 electoral votes), and New York (19 electoral votes). Even before Jefferson's reelection four years earlier, a small and (at the time) barely noticeable faction of Republican purists, who called themselves "Old Republicans," began to disassociate themselves from those aspects of Jefferson's policies that had followed Hamiltonian doctrine rather than that of their own party. As Jefferson's second administration slipped into controversy, the Old Republicans began to take the offensive.

Trouble erupted in Madison's home state of Virginia when the influential John Randolph of Roanoke, who had once been a Jeffersonian ally but who in recent years had moved away from the president, became more vocal in his distaste for the administration's drift toward Hamiltonian policy. Unable or unwilling to challenge the president directly, he targeted the man he knew the party would turn to in 1808, James Madison. In Randolph's estimation, Madison was as much a proponent of centralized government as any Federalist, and he was determined to redirect the party back to the "Principles of '98"—that is, those very decentralizing principles forthrightly advanced by a younger Jefferson and Madison in the Virginia and Kentucky Resolutions. Randolph contemptuously attacked Madison, pressing for an alternative in another of Virginia's favorite sons, James Monroe, who was currently the president's minister to Great Britain. Through correspondence, Randolph vigorously lobbied Monroe while relentlessly pitching heated diatribes against Madison.

Randolph's campaign against Madison deteriorated into invective, which after a time produced the boomerang effect of diminishing his credibility within the party leadership. However, through unkind and manipulative correspondence, Randolph succeeded in infecting Monroe with an unfair distrust of both Madison and Jefferson, leading to Monroe's decision to stand for the nomination. Interestingly, Jefferson attempted to blunt Randolph's appeals through correspondence of his own designed to forewarn Monroe of the misinformation about Madison that was likely to come his way. But the letter was lost and then, after several months, returned to Jefferson unopened. By the time Monroe returned from his duties in Britain in 1807, he had chilled to his old friends and was being drawn into Randolph's orbit. George H. May, father of George May, fiancé to Monroe's eldest daughter, Eliza, organized the Monroe faction, serving as the manager of the campaign. Randolph also worked through the press to further divide the state party between Madison and Monroe. Alert to this, the Cheetham Press in New York promptly homed in on the split in Madison's home state and seized the opportunity to promote its favorite son, the incumbent vice president George Clinton of New York.

New York being somewhat frustrated at Virginia's evident hold on the presidency (two of the first three presidents being Virginians, with the leading candidate to succeed Jefferson also a native of Virginia, as well as the challenger Monroe), the Republican critics of the administration within the Empire State looked toward both Vice President Clinton and his nephew, DeWitt, both native sons. Spurred forward by New York publisher James Cheetham, the "Clintonians" sought national office for either of the Clintons. The elder Clinton in particular was lauded by the New York press and packaged as a war hero (a reputation disputed by some) as well as the elder statesman of the republic, now assuming the mantle once unofficially held by the eminent American sage Benjamin Franklin. In May, as part of a long series of vehement attacks on Madison, Cheetham's paper endorsed George Clinton for president and Monroe for the vice presidency. Strange events unfolded in Pennsylvania, a state that for a time seemed to be in play. New Jersey's influential congressman James Sloan, an erstwhile Madison supporter, suddenly shifted his support to George Clinton and proposed to move the nation's capital back to Philadelphia, an obvious gambit directed at Pennsylvania voters and thus for a time raising the possibility of Madison losing vital Republican support in the populous Keystone State.

As the party splintered in critical swing states, a new term, "Quid" (shortened from *tertium quids* or a "third something"), usually used disparagingly, appeared in vogue. The term is commonly associated with Randolph and the "Monroeites" in Virginia, but there is some evidence that it might first have come into use four years earlier in Pennsylvania. Quids were treated by their critics as divisive factions accused of caring more for personal power than advancing the common political values and interests of their party. Thus, questions were raised as to what their principles actually were, and what, if anything, they really believed. Party Quids ultimately failed to secure the nomination for either Monroe or Clinton, as key Republican newspapers eventually supported Madison. The muddle in Pennsylvania was cleared by William Duane, who was now the editor for the *Aurora*, the reliable Republican paper published in Philadelphia. With some admitted reluctance, Duane endorsed Madison, arguing that in spite of recent problems, Jefferson's policies had been mainly correct. The Richmond *Enquirer* also went public for Madison, saving him the embarrassment of losing support in his home state to the younger Monroe. Madison's supporters in the press helped to reduce the influence of the Quid insurgency. The congressional caucus, attacked by the Monroe/Randolph and Clinton factions, also turned back to Madison. Randolph's influence waned, and Republicans were now able to submit a solidly supported candidate for election. To Cheetham's despair, the Clintonians lost their early momentum in New York, and by September, the state party, fearing a real challenge from the Federalists, announced its support for Madison. Having repelled a last-minute attempt by the Clintonians to capture the state committee, New York Republicans voted to approve the embargo, support the policies of the Jefferson administration, and recommend to the caucus James Madison for president and the reelection of George Clinton for vice president.

Dissenting Republicans were, needless to say, joined by the Federalists in blaming Madison for his visible role in the embargo—called the "Dambargo" by Federalist critics—and the resultant economic, military, and diplomatic problems. Added to this was the allegation of anti-English "Bonapartism," raised by spurious stories of Madison's fictional capitulation to Napoleon's ominous insistence that the United States was already at war with Britain and thus was expected to support France. Federalists also delighted in pointing out that the blood-soaked French revolutionary government had granted, *in absentia*, French citizenship to Madison in 1793, thus making him by association a fellow traveler with "bloody Robespi-erre" as well as the "Beast" Napoleon. Indeed, both Madison and Jefferson were accused of being French citizens and thus unqualified to hold any political office in the United States. Cheeky Republicans deflected this broadside by pointing out that Madison had received only *honorary* citizenship, a token of esteem granted by the French National Assembly that had also been bestowed upon both Citizen Washington and Citizen Hamilton, the Federalist Party's most venerated person-ages. Jefferson had not been so honored.

The Federalists were firm in their support of the familiar tandem of Charles Pinckney and Rufus King. There was a brief flirtation with the idea of combin-ing forces with the Republican Clintonites against Madison, but the idea failed to inspire interest outside of New York. The Federalist press continued to attack Madison as a toady of France and a slavish Bonapartist, but Madison's reputation, having finally been restored in the aftermath of intraparty grappling, remained ultimately unaffected by these tactics.

The Electoral College delivered the victory to Madison, who became the fourth president of the United States, continuing the Virginia dynasty. Madison managed 122 electoral votes, while the Federalist Pinckney received only 47, another deci-sive loss but a stronger showing when compared to the weaker effort in 1804. Six dissenting electors in New York threw their votes toward George Clinton for presi-dent. Clinton also won 113 votes for vice president, the remaining votes for that office being divided between Monroe, Madison (three New York electors indepen-dently sought to place Madison at the bottom of the ticket), and John Langdon of New Hampshire (who picked up 6 votes from Vermont and 3 from Ohio, but none from his native state). Madison's strength was drawn from his home state of Vir-ginia (now with 24 Electoral College votes and still the leader in electoral votes), Pennsylvania (winning all 20 votes), New York (taking 13 of 19 votes there), and the Carolinas (21 votes from these two southern states combined). Typically, the Federalists received most of their support from New England—Massachusetts's 19 votes being their biggest prize; but they did not do so unanimously, as Vermont went with Madison and the Republicans. While the Federalists did finish stronger in comparison to the previous election, Madison still won in what can only be deemed a landslide. Outside New England, the Federalists won only 8 votes and carried just one state, all three of Delaware's electors going to Pinckney. The other 5 non–New England votes for the Federalist ticket came from Maryland, where they won just 2 of 11, and North Carolina, where they took a mere 3 of 14. The out-come was far from what the Federalists had hoped for, given their initial encour-agement in light of Republican vulnerability as the campaign season opened.

The 1808 presidential election did not produce any enduring slogans, themes, or phrases. Yet the campaign demonstrated the growing importance of political parties and the influence of the press in the conduct and direction of presidential campaigns. The campaign also highlighted the continued weakness of the Federalist Party as a national political force, punctuated by its failure to sustain a credible challenge against the Republican administration's somewhat compromised position, at least when compared to the advantage enjoyed in 1804. Madison proved in the end to be a strong candidate, but he was initially vulnerable, and a focused, intelligent, and disciplined Federalist campaign could have led to a different result. Despite considerable popular anger over the impact of the embargo on the American economy, the Federalist Party proved unable to translate that anger into broader political support. But even though they were unable to regain the White House, they were not completely defeated, and another opportunity would arise four years later.

Additional Resources

Boller, Paul F., Jr. *Presidential Campaigns.* New York: Oxford University Press, 1984.

Bryant, Irving. "Election of 1808." In Arthur M. Schlesinger, Fred Israel, and William P. Hansen, eds. *History of American Presidential Elections, 1789–1968.* Vol. 1. New York: Chelsea House, 1985.

Cunningham, Noble E., Jr. "Who Were the Quids?" *Mississippi Valley Historical Review* 50, no. 2 (September 1963): 252–263.

McDonald, Forrest. *The Presidency of Thomas Jefferson.* Lawrence: University Press of Kansas, 1987.

Peterson, Merrill D. *Thomas Jefferson and the New Nation.* Oxford: Oxford University Press, 1970.

Rackove, Jack N. *James Madison and the Creation of the American Republic.* Glenview, IL: Scott, Foresman/Little Brown, 1990.

Roseboom, Eugene H. *A History of Presidential Elections.* New York: Macmillan 1964.

Rutland, Robert A. "1808." In Arthur M. Schlesinger, Fred L. Israel, and David J. Frent, eds. *Running for President: The Candidates and Their Images.* New York: Simon & Schuster, 1994.

Smith, Page. *John Adams.* Two vols. Garden City, NY: Doubleday, 1962.

Campaign of 1812

"Mr. Madison's War," "Virginia Dynasty," "No More Virginia," "Mr. Madison and War! Mr. Clinton and Peace," "Peace and Commerce," the "Peace Party," and "[Madison,] the Little Man in the Palace" were the quips, catchphrases, and slogans employed by the Federalists in their last credible challenge to regain the presidency, expressing attitudes that were also held by a minority of disillusioned Republicans. In addition to being the last real chance for the Federalist Party, the campaign and election of 1812 was the first in American history to occur during wartime. On June 18, 1812, just under five months before Election Day, Congress, at the recommendation of President Madison, declared war against the old nemesis, Great Britain, after a lengthy sequence of intolerable events. First, the British Royal Navy continued, with impunity and disregard for international protocol, its rogue practice of the impressment of American sailors, an ongoing insult to American sovereignty with a history running back to the Washington administration. Second, a long-standing dispute over the boundary between the United States and Canada remained unresolved, fueling border tension and fostering dangerous intrigues with Native American tribes that inhabited areas along or near the border. Third, a British embargo of French ports denied American ships access to lucrative French markets, a hindrance to the young nation's otherwise promising commercial prospects. Finally, Americans still seethed over the attack of their frigate the USS *Chesapeake* by the HMS *Leopard*, an incident that occurred five years earlier but that still evoked considerable anger throughout the United States.

War drums rolled within certain vocal and influential segments of the Republican Party. One of the nation's more promising young leaders, Congressman Henry Clay of Kentucky, who ascended to the position of Speaker of the House of Representatives in 1811, led a group of largely southern Republicans that soon came to be known as the "war hawks" (a term coined as a pejorative by antiwar congressman John Randolph of Virginia) for their bellicose attitude toward Great Britain. The war hawks were particularly troubled by Britain's role in fomenting violence within the Native American tribes on the frontier, violence directed at American forward settlements. This, along with the lingering and seemingly irresolvable impressment issue, was enough to stir the war hawks' ire; and intent on challenging Britain with armed force, they placed considerable and, in the end, effective pressure on the president to ask Congress for a declaration of war. Eventually the war hawks won the day, and with a majority in Congress and Madison's cooperation, war was declared, the first of five congressional declarations of war in American history.

Even though the war hawks won the debate, the nation as a whole was not as receptive to the sobering prospect of hostilities against what at that time was the world's greatest military power, and in particular against the unsurpassed reach and indomitable might of the Royal Navy. Madison's war message was delivered to Congress on June 1, but the vote in the House was far from an unqualified endorsement, seventy-nine voting for war and forty-nine against. A protracted debate prevented the Senate from voting for sixteen days after Madison's recommendation, and in the end the Senate's vote was nineteen for and thirteen against. Thus, while the president and his war hawk allies won their declaration, it was evident that the nation as a whole was not entirely committed, particularly when compared to later declarations of war in American history, and this lack of solid support for the war was an early sign of trouble to come. Once begun, the war would deeply divide the nation. Federalist merchants and export farmers, most of whom were located in the Northeast, with some interlaced as a minority faction in small pockets within the South, vocally opposed the war, primarily because it would impede access to British and other foreign markets. Those critical of the war would come to be known as "peace doves." War hawks and peace doves represented the polarized division throughout the country at the time, with the incumbent president Madison caught in the middle. In some regions where antiwar opinion was high, the Federalists clarified their position by explicitly referring to themselves as the "Peace Party," while not hesitating to label their Republican opponents as the "War Party." Thus, the main issue of the day drove the campaign for the White House.

In 1812, only New England retained a broad Federalist base and identity—but Republicans had made inroads into this region since the Jefferson administration, drawing support from the small farmers in the interior regions and among the newer merchants in the cities. The Federalists remained a force, but New England was no longer a guaranteed bloc for their party. New Jersey, New York, and Pennsylvania—the mid-Atlantic states—remained divided between the parties. Maryland was nearly dead even between the parties, the eastern shore of the Chesapeake Bay and the Potomac Valley largely Federalist at this time, the rest of the state Republican. Support for the Federalists in the northwestern state of Ohio, already slight, had attenuated still further. As mentioned above, the South was rapidly evolving into a Republican one-party region, with minority support active in scattered areas. The southern Federalists were strongest in the Potomac-Shenandoah watersheds of western Virginia, the eastern shore area of Virginia, Maryland, Delaware, and the Cape Fear Valley of North Carolina. The southernmost states were decidedly Republican and the most enthusiastic for the war, particularly in South Carolina. Yet the antiwar Federalists, in spite of their disadvantages when compared with the larger Republican base, retained influence and could be a strong and cohesive minority party given the right issue. At present, war against Britain was that issue; and in deciding for war, Madison's incumbent advantage had been compromised.

The issue over the war was not the only development that Madison needed to understand to successfully achieve reelection. Less dramatic but more enduring changes were rapidly occurring, at least in terms of long-term influence on the political culture. In addition to the continuing evolution of early parties, politically charged fraternal organizations such as the Tammany Society (or "Sons of Tammany," later to be known as "Tammany Hall") and the Washington Benevolent Societies were formed, particularly in New York where they had originated, as well as in parts of New England and Ohio. Claiming historical roots antecedent to the Revolution, the Tammany group was folded into the Republican faction due largely to the efforts of the notorious Aaron Burr, former vice president during

President Jefferson's first term and the adversary who slew Alexander Hamilton on the dueling field. In 1812, the Sons of Tammany held considerable power in New York City and were emulated by other local groups throughout the Northeast and into Ohio. In reluctant response, Federalists operating out of New York City established the Washington Benevolent Societies, first brought into existence in 1809 on the occasion of the observance of Washington's Birthday. These organizations acted as a bridge between political elites and the general public, developing a broader base of support through club activities, fund-raising events, public celebrations, political canvassing, and even secretive ritual. As mentioned in the entry on the **Campaign of 1804** above, these organizations would soon come to be called political "machines," or informal and tightly knit groups operating independently of public opinion or the discipline of formal parties and led by prominent individuals known as "bosses" who could effectually select candidates for elective office and control patronage appointments within nonelective administrative posts. A machine boss might or might not hold elective office himself, but in any event, the boss would become a dominant figure in the evolution of party politics in the nineteenth century and remain a force well into the twentieth.

Within the formal parties themselves, the Republican Party's congressional caucus unanimously supported Madison, nominating him on May 18, two weeks before the president's war message and a month before war was actually declared by Congress. Following the North-South precedent set by the Washington/Adams tandem in the first two presidential elections, the caucus nominated Elbridge Gerry of Massachusetts to replace the late vice president George Clinton, who had recently passed away. Clinton would become one of two vice presidents to have served under two distinct presidents: Thomas Jefferson in his second term and James Madison in his first (John C. Calhoun, serving under presidents John Quincy Adams and Andrew Jackson, would become the only other vice president to serve under two different presidents). Clinton's successor Gerry was a signer of the Declaration of Independence, one of the three diplomats in the famous XYZ trio, former governor of Massachusetts, and the namesake for the unfortunate political districting practice known as "gerrymandering." In turning to Gerry, Madison sustained the North-South strategy while drawing upon the well-established prominence of Virginia and Massachusetts, the only states to produce presidents to this point.

As both the parties and the machines increased in importance, the old congressional caucus institution no longer held the firm influence on the nominating process that it had previously asserted. Several state legislatures introduced nominating procedures of their own, independent of the congressional practice. For the most part, Madison's support was obtained throughout state legislatures—he received the formal endorsement of the legislatures within eight states shortly upon his nomination by the congressional caucus. But it was from a particularly nettle-some and familiar exception, the old "Clintonian" faction that had emerged in New York during the previous election, that Madison would be met with notable resistance. The New York legislature broke from the Republican majority in Congress and throughout other state legislatures and nominated native son DeWitt Clinton to replace Madison. DeWitt Clinton was currently the popular mayor of New York City and nephew of the late incumbent vice president. The younger Clinton sought to form a coalition between both pro-war and antiwar Republicans (the latter more common in the North than in the South) as well as those Federalists who were increasingly unhappy with Madison's economic policies and troubled by the long-term financial implications of war with Britain. Moreover, there were still many who shared concerns over what appeared to be the expectation of a fixed Virginia dynasty (three of the first four presidents were from Virginia, and the only non-Virginian, John Adams of Massachusetts, served just one term; thus the presidency had been occupied by Virginians in twenty of the past twenty-four years, and in the one term in which the presidency was held by someone from another state, the vice president had been from Virginia), and the Clintonians made an appeal to those who shared this concern. DeWitt Clinton's campaign, in contrast to Madison's more traditional detachment, was energetic. It was also chameleon. Here, he was against the war; there, he was all for it. For his running mate, he turned to Pennsylvania attorney general and signer of the Constitution Jared Ingersoll, whose father had been tarred and feathered by a mob of patriots during the Revolution. Ingersoll was a quiet, conservative Federalist who had participated in events of considerable importance but who, for the most part, kept a lower profile when compared to his colleagues. He was a stern critic of Jeffersonian policies, at one point warning against the election of the subversive Jefferson.

Throughout the campaign, the Federalists continued to exhibit inconsistency. When addressing pro-war Republicans, the Clinton faction declared its support for action against Britain; but when addressing peace doves, Clinton's advocates were known to vehemently criticize the president for the war. It was a Clintonian who, before a Federalist audience in New England, coined the phrase "Madison and War! Or Clinton and Peace!" and referred to Madison as that "base wretch" who sought to prosecute an unfair and "outrageous *war*." Resorting to this kind of unabashed vote-grubbing was much easier in the days before mass communication and the **twenty-four-hour news cycle** that we now take for granted. And in part because such inconsistency was harder to catch in 1812 than today, this tactic of playing to the crowd posed the president a serious challenge. New York was now the most populous state, carrying twenty-nine Electoral College votes as a result of the reapportionment that followed the 1810 census, and was thus an increasingly important electoral prize. Meanwhile, the Federalist Party was finding it difficult to forward a reasonable challenger on its own behalf. Chief Justice John Marshall was frequently mentioned as the only available person of stature equal to the task, but his role on the Supreme Court was considered indispensable and too dear to the Federalists to risk a potentially losing campaign for chief executive. With Marshall on the Supreme Court, the minority Federalist Party was assured the kind of influence that it was unable to muster in the other two branches. Drawn by Clinton's protean appearance as a dove/hawk and cognizant of his growing political base, the Federalists began to recruit the New York Republican to join their side. In September, the Federalists held a convention involving delegates from eleven states—a forerunner to the national nominating conventions of the late 1820s—but the results were inconclusive. Along with Marshall and John Jay, DeWitt Clinton was offered as a possible "fusion" candidate capable of mustering support against the war across party lines. Due to uncertainties about Clinton and hesitation regarding Marshall, a deadlocked convention was unable to produce a nominee, but Clinton emerged as the most visible choice and the only viable challenger.

Some Federalists took exception to the turncoat Republican. A Virginia state convention meeting (gathering shortly after the national meeting), held in the Shenandoah Valley town of Staunton, one of the few Federalist strongholds in the South, combated the Clintonian faction by endorsing its own candidate, Federalist stalwart Rufus King. But the Federalists in Virginia were a disaffected minority party within the incumbent president's home state. Furthermore, the electors pledged to King may have still voted for Clinton if conditions were favorable. By and large in most states, Clinton was able to successfully cross party lines and capture the Federalist nomination to run against Madison in the general election. However, in New York, the new colossus of the Electoral College and the center of Clinton's power, Republicans proved to be less organized and Federalists more resistant to crossing party lines in search of a fusion candidate. It was much easier for Clinton to secure support in Federalist-dominated New England but much harder to bring in his home state. In New York, the selection of presidential electors was still the province of the legislature, although the trend under way nationwide (including New England) was toward popular election of the members of the Electoral College. Republicans held a slight majority in the New York legislature, and the Clintonians were further compromised by the Federalists' reticence to join Republicans in support of Clinton, deciding instead to select electors loyal to the party. This was a commitment that might not have threatened Clinton had it not been for a minority faction for Madison among New York Republicans who were splitting the state party's loyalties and thus nearly destroying Clinton's chance at a majority of New York's electors.

To surmount these difficulties, Clinton allied himself with a youthful and politically savvy newcomer, Martin Van Buren, who, in spite of his age—twenty-nine at the time, but already well known for his acute political insight—deftly blunted the Madisonians and at the opportune moment secured the majority vote for Clinton. Interestingly, Van Buren was actually a supporter of Madison, but he was focused on party discipline and unity, and seeing that Clinton was the real choice of the New York Republicans, he applied his already considerable political skill against the candidate he preferred, for the sake of strengthening the party to which he was devoted. This and other examples of his political acumen earned him the nickname "the Little Magician," would make him a major force in New York state politics in the years ahead, and would eventually propel him into the uppermost reaches of the national arena.

Following the model of Washington, Madison preferred to remain aloof in the campaign, a posture that was now unofficially expected of candidates for the highest office (particularly incumbents), relying instead on the advocacy of friendly newspapers and local politicians. Aside from playing a role in the selection of Gerry as his running mate, Madison preferred to focus on steering the ship of state rather than on his bid for reelection. His primary concern was the war, and political campaigning—or pandering for votes—was viewed as unseemly for a Virginia gentleman otherwise occupied in attending to his civic duty. To this point, the war had not gone well for the United States, and the president was simply not available to worry over the upcoming election. Thus Madison depended on Republican newspapers to present his case to the voters, remaining for the most part quiet during the campaign, with a few modest exceptions, such as two letters stating his case for reelection, one to the New Jersey state convention and another to South Carolina's assembly. Madison's hope was that the party, and eventually the nation as a whole, would recognize that the country's honor was at stake and would come around to rally behind their president.

The election highlighted divisions within states and allowed the Federalists to reassert themselves in areas throughout the country that had traditionally supported them. The war and its unsteady prosecution was the main cause of Republican vulnerability. Ultimately, however, President Madison's prediction proved correct and thus vindicated his low profile during the campaign. In spite of a more energetic Federalist challenge compared to the election of 1808, the Republicans managed to hold the presidency. The Madison-Gerry ticket won 128 Electoral College votes, the highest total in history to this point but a smaller percentage compared with his 1808 victory (58.7% in 1812 versus 69.7% in 1808). By modern standards, both elections were Electoral College landslides; but the gains by the Federalist Party were evident. The eighty-nine electoral votes won by DeWitt Clinton represented an addition to the Federalist cause of thirty-six votes, or an increase of around 40 percent, a significant improvement. President Madison held firm and won reelection impressively, but it was clear that the Republicans, who in both 1804 and 1808 were on the verge of controlling a one-party government, at least at the federal level, could not be complacent in their continued predominance. The Federalists had acquired some momentum, but they needed to sustain and increase it if they were going to offer themselves as a viable alternative in the near future. The Republicans protected their majority in Congress and their hold on the White House (now having won four consecutive presidential elections) but failed to deliver the fatal blow to their Federalist rivals. Notably, it was also a sectionally polarized election. Madison received only six electoral votes in the North (Vermont's), while Clinton found support only in the nine Southern electoral votes cast by electors in the border states of Maryland and Delaware. The Deep South was even more solidly Republican than before, whereas New England and most of the Northeast and mid-Atlantic region (including New York) fell in behind the Federalists, but not as solidly as the South supported the Republicans. In terms of regional divisions, only the elections of 1860 (Abraham Lincoln) and 1964 (Lyndon Johnson) would surpass the election of 1812 in commanding such solid and sharply marked sectional loyalties.

Much was still in play after 1812. It would be left to the election of 1816 to produce the decisive moment in determining whether the Jeffersonian Republicans could gain a monopoly of power, or whether the Federalist Party could regain credible influence either as a strong minority party or possibly as a challenger to possibly regain the majority. The war, so divisive in 1812, would ultimately prove to be the critical issue in this decision.

Additional Resources

Boller, Paul F., Jr. *Presidential Campaigns*. New York: Oxford University Press, 1984.

Brown, Roger Hamilton. *The Republic in Peril: 1812*. New York: Columbia University Press, 1964.

Rackove, Jack N. *James Madison and the Creation of the American Republic*. Glenview, IL: Scott, Foresman/Little Brown, 1990.

Risjord, Norman K. "1812." In Arthur M. Schlesinger, Fred L. Israel, and David J. Frent, eds. *Running for President: The Candidates and Their Images*. New York: Simon & Schuster, 1994.

Risjord, Norman K. "Election of 1812." In Arthur M. Schlesinger, Fred Israel, and William P. Hansen, eds. *History of American Presidential Elections, 1789–1968*. Vol. 1. New York: Chelsea House, 1985.

Roseboom, Eugene H. *A History of Presidential Elections*. New York: Macmillan, 1964.

Rutland, Robert Allen. *The Presidency of James Madison*. Lawrence: University Press of Kansas, 1990.

Campaign of 1816

Between 1816 and 1824, the Jeffersonian Republican Party achieved the zenith of national preeminence and thus set the political tone for what would become known as the Era of Good Feelings, a period marked by what was virtually a one-party government and a political consensus unparalleled in American history (excepting the state of national unity achieved during World War II). But as late as 1814, this national unity was not a foregone conclusion. Two years into the war, many observers saw the American effort as ineffective. The war hawks' ambition to acquire Canada was thwarted by a combination of British strength and American ineptitude in the conduct of the war at the northern border. The city of Washington, DC, had been captured in the summer of 1814, the White House had been torched, and American troops in the field were desperate for reinforcements, in dire need of more and better supplies, and wanting able leadership. Adding insult to injury, the smuggling trade by American citizens with the enemy abroad could not be stopped or even blunted. The American forces in the field did not completely collapse; they fought valiantly, but they could not gain ground, and indeed, the failure to protect the capital only punctuated the deterioration of the war effort. With the exception of a surprisingly decent showing by the American navy against the British, who at that time deployed the world's greatest maritime fleet, the execution of the war was checkered with blunder, low morale, and stalemate.

The war's setbacks led to attenuated public support and thereby stimulated a brief but rapid resurgence of the political fortunes of the dissenting Federalists, who had gone on record as critics of "Mr. Madison's War." Owing to this state of affairs, the Federalists in 1814 were in their best position in twenty years to regain a broader support within the electorate, and even possibly political power; meanwhile, the Republicans were more divided and vulnerable than ever. Federalists had made gains in the off-year elections at both the state and federal levels, and the Republican war hawks in particular had suffered losses at the polls. Majorities were regained in states such as Maryland and Delaware, and minorities strengthened elsewhere; even in the southern Republican strongholds of Virginia and North Carolina, the renewed strength of the Federalist minority waxed significantly. Previous Republican advances into New England were reversed, and the Federalists seemed once more invincible in that part of the country. As a result of the war, the small Federalist gains that faintly glimmered in the election year of 1812 were now accelerating, fueled by disenchantment with a war that seemed to many a futile and costly adventure.

More zealous New England Federalists, political heirs of the Essex Junto, felt their complaint credible enough to strike hard against the current government. Delegates from five states (Massachusetts, Rhode Island, Vermont, New Hampshire—the delegates from the latter two states somewhat cautiously—and the host state, Connecticut) met in Hartford to discuss and propose constitutional amendments designed to protect the interests of the whole of New England against the encroaching power of the rest of the nation, and in particular, the South. The

Hartford Convention has been construed by many historians as an early effort toward secession, but no secession plan was actually adopted, at least not publicly. The Hartford Convention did publish proposals that were not unlike the Kentucky and Virginia resolutions of 1798 (in this instance written by Southern Republicans Thomas Jefferson and James Madison) aimed at strengthening state sovereignty against the growing power of the central government. Among its many proposals, the convention called for the prohibition of any trade embargo exceeding sixty days and for a two-thirds vote in Congress before any interdiction in foreign trade could be executed, as well as a two-thirds congressional vote to declare an "offensive war." The convention also insisted on removing the "three fifths of all other persons" electoral advantage that was held by the South, as many northerners felt that the ongoing southern dominance in past elections was the direct result of counting the larger portion of the (nonvoting) slave population in the assignment of Electoral College votes and the apportionment of congressional seats. Finally, the convention wanted to impose a one-year term limit on the presidency and, more importantly, stipulate that a candidate for president cannot be elected from the home state of the incumbent—two measures that were designed to break the "Virginia dynasty." Even though secession was not officially proposed at this time, many "Blue Light Federalists"—a term originally used to describe Connecticut Federalists who allegedly abetted the enemy through the use of "blue lights" to signal British warships in an effort to help them avoid the American naval blockade, but now applied in general to any Federalist presumed to be friendly to the British—and associates of the Essex Junto had desired this measure since at least 1804, so it was not unlikely that at least some of the delegates at Hartford were seriously thinking along these lines.

Unfolding events, however, quickly overtook the Federalists. Even as the Hartford Convention, buoyed by a rush of confidence in their cause, sent a delegation to Washington, DC, to assert their position, the nature and meaning of the war were thoroughly recast by two astonishing American victories. The U.S. Navy, under the command of Master Commandant Thomas Macdonough, soundly defeated the British Royal Navy on the waters of Lake Champlain and effectively secured the northern states against what had been a very real threat of British invasion from Canada. This was followed by the extraordinarily lopsided victory won outside of New Orleans by American forces under the command of General Andrew Jackson over a powerful contingent of the British army. As it would turn out, the latter land battle had absolutely no bearing on the outcome of the war—the Treaty of Ghent that formally ended the war had already been successfully negotiated and signed prior to the battle's first shot. But the combatants in Louisiana were oblivious to the peace that had just been settled by diplomats in Flanders, and thus in following their duty, the two armies joined battle in what would soon prove to be the decisive American land victory of the war. While the treaty rendered the battle technically needless, the battle's outcome made all the difference to the morale of the American public and, consequently, the political fortunes of the Republicans. The American triumph reconfigured overnight national attitudes regarding the war and, in the fascinating figure of the courageous and charismatic General Jackson, gave the country its biggest war hero since Washington himself.

In the short term, these two battles destroyed the Federalist Party. Their long-standing criticism of the war was now widely seen as wrongheaded and, in some quarters, regarded as blatantly unpatriotic, perhaps even treasonous. The actions of the Hartford Convention were henceforth sternly condemned. In matter of fact, the actual outcome of the war was inconclusive, but Macdonough and Jackson had delivered the end-game blows needed to alter the mood of an entire nation. The war, at one time controversial, was now almost universally deemed a "second war for independence," with the "new Washington," General Jackson, elevated as the exemplar of American resolve, resilience, and frontier virtue. After its fortuitous revival, enjoyed throughout the better part of 1814, the Federalist Party abruptly spun into a tailspin from which there was no escape, no pulling out. Before the victory on Lake Champlain in mid-September, the Federalists had enjoyed their strongest position within the public since before the death of Alexander Hamilton a decade prior. After Lake Champlain and then the triumph in New Orleans in early January 1815, the Federalists were utterly spent as a political force.

Additionally, President Madison's postwar programs actually implemented traditional Federalist principles such as the creation of a second national bank (anathema to the Republicans' Jeffersonian purists), the imposition of a protective tariff aimed at fortifying domestic industry and agriculture, and federally funded construction for turnpikes and canals to improve transportation infrastructure and thereby again boost the interests of commerce and industry. In effect, Hamilton's party had been absorbed into Jefferson's; there now appeared little reason to seek alternatives. In a way, it was now the remnants of the Federalist minority who became the advocates of decentralized power and limited government while the Jeffersonian Republicans were the party of centralization, nationalism, and active government, a reversal of polarity that would not be the last in the story of American political parties. The venerable John Adams, irretrievably retired from national politics but still an esteemed voice of political judgment, remarked in 1813, "Our two great parties have crossed over the valley and taken possession of each other's mountain." Adams himself had by this time thoroughly reconciled with his old friend and rival Thomas Jefferson, both recognizing a friendship larger than political differences, and a common experience formed in revolution far stronger than any divisions opened by those differences.

And so followed the campaign of 1816, one that Paul Boller has described as "dull as dishwater"—perhaps a slight exaggeration but, when contrasted to the previous four elections, perhaps a credible assessment. Even given the unprecedented strength of the Republicans, the political process still needed to play itself through. The emergence of a big-tent Republican Party did not mean a consensus existed on whom Republicans should nominate as president. James Monroe, an experienced public servant and a close friend of Thomas Jefferson, was the obvious heir. Monroe, who in spite of a former association with renegade senator John Randolph that prompted his Quidite challenge to Madison for the nomination in 1808, had been appointed by President Madison to serve as secretary of state in 1811, a position that had been particularly distinguished by its previous occupants, Jefferson (under President Washington) and Madison (under President Jefferson) themselves. (Other significant statesmen to hold that post within the first four administrations are John Jay, Edmund Randolph, and John Marshall.) To this point, two vice presidents— Adams and Jefferson—and two secretaries of state—Jefferson and Madison—had been elected to the presidency (Washington, as the first president, being the only one who was neither); hence both offices appeared to be effective staging areas for future presidents. Monroe had only one problem: He was from Virginia, and there was a growing discomfort from several quarters in response to the quasi-dynastic habit of relying too readily on the Old Dominion for presidential leadership. Popular New York governor Daniel Tompkins and the recently appointed secretary of war, William H. Crawford of Georgia, both challenged Monroe's candidacy. Tompkins's popularity did not cross state lines, and his hopes quickly faded, but for a brief moment, Crawford's candidacy mounted a viable challenge.

Monroe enjoyed a wider base of support throughout the party than Crawford, but his position was still vulnerable; hence his supporters vigorously lobbied Crawford to withdraw, implicitly suggesting the possible reward of future political support for high office. Crawford initially responded favorably to these overtures and graciously yielded to Monroe's claim. However, the anti-Virginia sentiment gained strength throughout several states, causing Crawford to reverse his position and work for the nomination. Growing opposition in New York (which now held twenty-nine Electoral College votes, the most of any state) to anyone from Virginia further tempted Crawford with the possibility of challenging Monroe at the Congressional Caucus. The ongoing criticism of the caucus system was increasing owing to a trend that with each election, more presidential electors were now being chosen by popular vote; but it still was a requisite factor in the nomination process, and New York delegates to the caucus sought to use this to their advantage. Monroe legitimately feared he might lose in the caucus, as there seemed to be considerable support for Secretary Crawford within Congress. But in reality, Monroe was more popular and better known among their constituents; and it would soon become clear to many that the move against him appeared to be coming primarily from "anti-Virginia" party organizers rather than from the electorate.

On February 24, anti-Virginia delegates met independently to consider their strategies. Both Tompkins and Crawford were supported as candidates, but both also met with enough opposition to cast some doubt on their ability to gain broader appeal. Now that Tompkins had also just been nominated for reelection as governor of New York, the New York delegates endorsed Crawford as their choice to challenge Monroe. Events began to displease Monroe and his supporters, who boycotted a March 12 caucus that they considered to be dominated by the anti-Virginia forces. The tactic worked, as only fifty-eight Republicans convened, well under the requisite number to nominate a candidate for president. As a result, the following March 16 caucus resulted in much greater participation, with 118 Republican congressmen (including several proxies) and the territorial delegate from Indiana also in attendance. Shortly thereafter, Republicans convened their official congressional nominating caucus. Monroe was favored to win, but Crawford was far from eliminated, as he still drew noticeable support. Interestingly and perhaps fatefully, Crawford's home state delegation, consisting of eleven delegates, had been instructed to attend the caucus and, at Crawford's request, formally defer to Monroe. But inexplicably, the eleven Georgia delegates simply decided not to attend. Once the final votes were counted, Crawford's real strength was revealed; somewhat to the surprise of the party leadership, Monroe won the nomination by only nine votes. Had the absent Georgia contingent attended, and had they rejected their nonbinding commission in light of circumstances and cast their votes for their own native son, William Crawford would have narrowly won the Republican nomination, and with the Federalist Party fast becoming an irrelevancy, Crawford assuredly would have become the nation's fifth president. So go the vicissitudes of history.

The weak and waning Federalist Party did not formally nominate a candidate. There was no consensus on a party champion among Federalist newspapers, and there seems to have been no effort on the part of congressional Federalists to forward an official nominee. Senator Rufus King of New York, the former Federalist candidate for vice president (1808) and an early opponent of slavery, somehow managed to receive a total of thirty-four electoral votes drawn from Massachusetts (22), Connecticut (9), and Delaware (3); but by some accounts, King might not have even been aware that he was a candidate for president until after the Electoral College had cast their votes. Four Federalists received votes for the vice presidency: John Howard of Maryland (22), James Ross of Pennsylvania (5), the venerable John Marshall of Virginia (4), and Robert Harper of Maryland (3). Resigned to defeat, the Federalist Party did not actively challenge Monroe's candidacy in Vermont, Ohio, New Jersey, or throughout the entire South. In Ohio, a Federalist editor candidly allowed that it was now "high time for the Federalists to give up an opposition which only serves to heighten the asperities of party spirit, and exhibit the thinness of their ranks." With no formal campaign to promote his candidacy, Rufus King would be the last person under the Federalist banner to receive any votes for president of the United States.

Monroe won 183 electoral votes in 1816—a new Electoral College record for total votes—carrying sixteen of nineteen states. Monroe's 84 percent of the Electoral College vote was exceeded only by Washington (1789 and 1792) and Jefferson (1804). For the sake of party unity, New York governor Tompkins stood as Monroe's running mate, once again duplicating the now seemingly obligatory North-South strategy that had marked every successful candidacy since Washington's first election. In James Monroe, the Virginia dynasty was to persist another eight years, marking a period of comparative political unity decidedly unusual within the more common American experience of competitive partisanship.

Additional Resources

Boller, Paul F., Jr. *Presidential Campaigns.* New York: Oxford University Press, 1984.

Brown, Roger Hamilton, and William G. Morgan. "The Congressional Nominating Caucus of 1816: The Struggle against the Virginia Dynasty." *Virginia Magazine of History and Biography* 80, no. 4 (October 1972): 461–475.

Cmiel, Kenneth. "1816." In Arthur M. Schlesinger, Fred L. Israel, and David J. Frent, eds. *Running for President: The Candidates and Their Images.* New York: Simon & Schuster, 1994.

Cunningham, Noble. *The Presidency of James Monroe.* Lawrence: University Press of Kansas, 1996.

Turner, Lynn W. "Election of 1816." In Arthur M. Schlesinger, Fred Israel, and William P. Hansen, eds. *History of American Presidential Elections, 1789–1968,* vol. 1. New York: Chelsea House, 1985.

Campaign of 1820

President James Monroe, running unopposed for a second term, fell just one vote short of a unanimous election—an accomplishment that, had it been achieved, would have placed him in the company of George Washington as one of two presidents elected without explicit opposition. By 1820, a pervasive attitude of general political consensus had settled in throughout the nation, and it appeared for a time that the young republic was in the midst of stability and a sense of like-mindedness that would endure for some time. The *Columbian Sentinel,* a Massachusetts newspaper long known for its uncompromising loyalty to the Federalists, is credited with first identifying Monroe's administration as the Era of Good Feelings. More skeptically, Roanoke's John Randolph described Monroe's acclamation in 1820 as the "unanimity of indifference, and not of approbation." Monroe governed in a time when significant party opposition appeared to have disappeared from the political sphere, a remarkable and welcome situation after two decades of heated interparty animosity (checkered by occasional intraparty rivalry). A one-party system appeared to have fallen into place.

In spite of these appearances, however, the Era of Good Feelings was not without problems. In 1819, the country faced its first major economic crisis, increased conflict with Native American tribes accompanied by rising international tension, and more visible evidence of potentially volatile antipathies over the issue of slavery. In 1819, the country faced a serious economic depression—what would become known as the Panic of 1819, and what would linger for nearly three years (lasting well into Monroe's second term) before it was all over. Numerous banks failed, due largely to the fact that they had indiscriminately made loans to land speculators who had predicted that land prices would continue to escalate and, as a result, were purchasing still more land in the blithe expectation of the continued trend toward rising land value. Simultaneously, high prices for farm goods led farmers to borrow more money so that they could deepen their investments in their own farms. But borrowers suddenly found themselves in too deep, and a large number of loans went into default, sending the national economy into a precipitous downturn. When the speculation bubble burst, a high number of banks closed, and subsequently the production of manufactured goods sharply dropped. Trade abroad, which had been steadily growing since the end of the War of 1812, suddenly froze. Unemployment in cities such as New York, Philadelphia, and Baltimore reached unprecedented levels. Factories closed throughout the country, and the price of crops such as cotton plummeted. Meanwhile, the government found itself slipping further into debt, thereby fueling the general sense of disquiet regarding the economic health of the country. Had there been an organized opposition to the Republicans, Monroe's reelection would have needed to surmount a serious challenge, requiring a second term to have been won against contenders rather than, as it was, merely assumed.

Regarding foreign policy, while trouble with Great Britain had subsided since the 1814 Treaty of Ghent that ended the War of 1812 six years earlier, a dispute with Spain over stalled negotiations in the matter of Florida, at that time still under Spanish sovereignty, threatened to pull the United States into yet another conflict with a European power. At the behest of President Monroe but without congressional permission, General Andrew Jackson, the hero of the Battle of New Orleans, audaciously led an occupation force into Spanish Florida in pursuit of a contingent of Seminole Indians who had conducted raids across the Georgia-Florida border after refusing to recognize federal claims to Indian lands that had, at least from the perspective of the U.S. government, been previously settled by the outcome of the

Creek War (or Red Stick War, in which General Jackson had also played a decisive role). While leading the military campaign in Florida, Gen. Jackson precipitated an international incident when he rashly ordered the unlawful execution of two British subjects on the charge that they were providing weapons to the Seminoles. Jackson's moves in Florida, which were more or less conducted under his own judgment, were at best only vaguely supported by the president, and certainly actions such as the summary execution of two foreigners was not within Monroe's design. The president's cabinet sternly criticized the general's actions, with the significant exception of Monroe's secretary of state (and former ambassador to Great Britain), John Quincy Adams, son of former president John Adams, who rebutted criticism of Jackson from both John C. Calhoun, Monroe's secretary of war, and Henry Clay, the Speaker of the House, and further argued that American intervention in Spain was legitimate given the inability of the Spanish governors to ensure peace in the Florida territory. A capable negotiator, Adams eventually persuaded Spain to sell outright the troublesome peninsula to the United States. Hence, what began as a potentially deadly crisis with yet another European Great Power ended in the first addition of land to the new country since Jefferson's Louisiana Purchase, a feather in the cap of the Monroe administration. Additionally, it was Adams who was the chief author of what would come to be known as the Monroe Doctrine, asserted in Monroe's 1823 annual message to Congress, and issuing a warning against European ambitions, particularly aimed at France and Spain in the Western Hemisphere. Well received by the general public, the Monroe Doctrine carried further weight owing to the tacit support of Great Britain, America's former enemy, now more than willing to cooperate with the young republic as a bulwark against Spanish and French ambitions in Latin America. Indeed, the force of the Monroe Doctrine, at least initially and thereafter through much of the nineteenth century, relied upon the quiet endorsement and steady forbearance of the British government.

In the West, the proposed admission of Missouri as the Union's newest state raised again the ugly issue of slavery, the immediate question being whether Missouri would be admitted as a slave or free state, with larger issues ominously brewing behind this question. In 1818 an amendment that had been attached to the Missouri statehouse admission bill prohibiting the future importation of slaves into the Missouri Territory had passed in the U.S. House of Representatives. The action ignited a firestorm of debate between slavery's supporters and opponents. Abolition sentiments, which had been simmering for decades, rapidly intensified, thereby alarming Southern supporters of the Peculiar Institution. Early in 1820, New York senator Rufus King, who had long opposed slavery (and who had also been the Federalist candidate for president in 1816), delivered a speech forthrightly calling for the exclusion of slavery as a condition for the admission of the new state of Missouri. King's speech helped fuel rumors of a possible new abolitionist party and further provoked slaveholding interests. In the months that followed, few could remain unaware that the struggle over the admission of Missouri, and the renewed debate over slavery that it had reignited, foreboded severe sectional antagonisms that would, among other things, reshape the landscape of presidential campaigns politics.

The Missouri Compromise was eventually settled in a manner that did not touch the political fortunes of President Monroe, but now that the issue of slavery was more visible to the public at large, it was becoming desperately clearer as to how the problem of slavery would stir future crises, and likely sooner rather than later. Famously, former president and revered elder statesman Thomas Jefferson, in retirement at Monticello, could hear in the Missouri Compromise what he likened to a "fire bell in the night," which had "awakened and filled" him with a palpable sense of "terror," and which had sounded what he feared would prove to be the "death knell of the Union." Jefferson's sense of doom notwithstanding, for the time being, President Monroe was not hampered by the pall of slavery, and he needed only to extinguish a few small and easily managed political fires to secure reelection. In Pennsylvania, for example, the influential and provocative Republican publisher William Duane, denouncing Monroe's administration as pro-slavery, sponsored a movement to draft New York's DeWitt Clinton for the upcoming presidential election and persuaded one-third of Pennsylvania's voters to choose electors pledged against Monroe. Despite this minor revolt, Monroe still controlled two-thirds of Pennsylvania's electors and subsequently received Pennsylvania's twenty-five electoral votes.

Monroe, in spite of significant crises foreign and domestic, economic, political, and moral, remained essentially unchallenged. In the end, Monroe carried every state (24 at the time) and received 231 out of 232 electoral votes cast—three electors having died before they could cast their ballot—which, excluding President Washington's two unanimous and atypical elections, remains down to this day the biggest Electoral College landslide in the history of American presidential elections, and one not likely to be matched. Unanimity was blocked by one lone elector, Republican (and former Essex Junto Federalist) William Plumer of New Hampshire, who voted for John Quincy Adams, Monroe's able secretary of state, and thereby prevented Monroe from duplicating Washington's still-unparalleled achievement. Folklore holds that Plumer voted against Monroe for no other reason than his belief that no comparison should be made between Monroe, or anyone for that matter, and the august Washington. However, historians have noted that there was no way Plumer could actually have known the exact final tally at the time he voted, and thus he would not have been aware that Monroe was in a position to receive a unanimous vote, although it is possible that he could have, through reasoned conjecture, anticipated Monroe's clean sweep. Some have claimed that Plumer's vote in reality may simply have been intended to draw attention to the younger Adams as a potential future candidate, or perhaps as the sole voice of opposition to the established policies of Monroe's administration. That aside, the actual reason behind Plumer's vote remains unknown. Incidentally, all nominal Federalists—there were thirteen in the Electoral College—voted for Monroe. Vice President Tompkins was also reelected, receiving 218 electoral votes; the remaining 14 votes were divided among four alternatives, none a serious challenge. New England electors had approached Adams, offering to support him to replace Tompkins as vice president, but Adams was not interested. Owing to his reelection as Monroe's vice president, Tompkins would come to be known as the last vice president to serve two consecutive terms under the same president until the early twentieth century. (Almost a century hence, Thomas R. Marshall, who would be elected as vice president along with President Woodrow Wilson and serve from 1913 to 1921, would become the first since Tompkins to serve two full terms under the same chief executive.)

While the Monroe administration was undeniably popular, and the president a capable leader and rightly esteemed public servant, it is to be remembered that an important reason behind this nearly unanimous landslide was the simple absence of any alternative. We do not know how Monroe would have fared against a credible challenger, and it is also to be remembered that Monroe's outstanding conduct in office was surely a factor in there being none. We do know one thing—the political consensus that made this landslide possible was soon to come to a swift and unseemly end.

Additional Resources

Boller, Paul F., Jr. *Presidential Campaigns*. New York: Oxford University Press, 1984.

Cmiel, Kenneth. "1820." In Arthur M. Schlesinger, Fred L. Israel, and David J. Frent, eds. *Running for President: The Candidates and Their Images*. New York: Simon & Schuster, 1994.

Cunningham, Noble. *The Presidency of James Monroe*. Lawrence: University Press of Kansas, 1996.

Turner, Lynn W. "Election of 1820." In Arthur M. Schlesinger, Fred Israel, and William P. Hansen, eds. *History of American Presidential Elections, 1789–1968*. Vol. 1. New York: Chelsea House, 1985.

Campaign of 1824

James Monroe, in following the now customary two-term limit set by President Washington's modest precedent, opted not to run for a third term in spite of his sustained popularity and influence. With Monroe removed from consideration, older political divisions that had been concealed during the Era of Good Feelings were reexposed and reanimated. The long, slow demise of the Federalist Party was now in fact precipitating a major struggle within the Republican Party (now referred to, with greater frequency, as the "Democratic-Republicans"), leaving the most open and competitive field of candidates to date in the history of American presidential campaigns. Not surprisingly, even as early as 1822, the names of over a dozen potential candidates were already in circulation.

By the election year of 1824, five prominent and respected names were still under serious consideration: John Quincy Adams of Massachusetts, the brilliant and talented son of former president John Adams, who was serving with considerable aplomb, skill, and influence as President Monroe's secretary of state; William H. Crawford, the elder statesman of Georgia and a Virginian by birth who was currently serving as Monroe's (and formerly President Madison's) secretary of the treasury (as well as having served for a short time as secretary of war under Madison), and who had come within a scant nine votes of the Republican nomination for president in 1816; Speaker of the House Henry Clay of Kentucky, an eloquent former war hawk and one of the foremost statesmen in Congress, experienced in both the House and the Senate; and Senator Andrew Jackson of Tennessee, the former general and magnetic hero of the Battle of New Orleans, renowned "Indian Fighter" (a reputation that meant something to those on the American frontier at that time), genuine self-made man, and universally popular figure prefiguring the type of politician that Americans increasingly would come to admire. Senator Jackson was held in such regard that his more ardent supporters considered him to be no less than a second Washington. Three other prominent candidates were also in play as late as the campaign year but were withdrawn from consideration for various reasons: DeWitt Clinton of New York, a former presidential candidate (losing to President Madison in the election of 1812) who had just recently served as the sixth governor of New York (and who was the principal political force behind the building of the Erie Canal); William Lowndes of South Carolina, who had in 1821 already obtained the official nomination of his home state, but who would suddenly pass away before his national campaign could get under way; and South Carolina's formidable John C. Calhoun, the promising young war hawk who, upon recognizing Crawford's strength in the South and Jackson's growing momentum in the West, temporarily withdrew from active campaigning. When it became clear that Jackson's popularity was eclipsing the field, Calhoun supported the Tennessean in the hope of obtaining the vice presidency.

Calhoun was correct about Crawford's strength, as the Georgian began the campaign season the early favorite; however, even as Calhoun was withdrawing, Crawford's fortunes had turned against him. All told, it was an impressive field of candidates, among the deepest in the history of American political campaigns.

And, in the end, absent the coherent two-party structure with which we are now all familiar, it became a four-way race that militated against the emergence of a decisive majority. When the votes were finally cast, Andrew Jackson would win pluralities in both the Electoral College (where the president is technically elected) and the popular vote (which in 1824 was only beginning to gain in importance within the contemporary political culture)—and yet still lose the election. It was John Quincy Adams who would emerge, once all the dust cleared, as the president-elect: the result of an exceedingly controversial outcome that was, with the possible exception of the election of 1800, the most divisive presidential election to date, and one of the more compelling stories in the history of American politics to this day.

While the result of the election to the frustrated twenty-first-century reader appears unreasoned and patently undemocratic (a conclusion that is not without merit), upon further reflection, the events leading to this outcome are brought somewhat into focus and, if not justified, at least better understood. Initially, outgoing president Monroe as well as former presidents Jefferson and Madison preferred Crawford, a trio of eminent endorsements that would doubtless be the envy of any presidential candidate in any age. Thus, as the election began to gain interest in the early stages, Crawford appeared to most as the likely successor to the august legacy of the previous six statesmen who had for the most part ably served as president for the young republic. Two events deflated Crawford's chances: rumors (the accuracy of which to this day remains unclear) of a debilitating stroke that he had suffered in September 1824, and, paradoxically, his nomination by the Democratic-Republican congressional caucus. Both were significant in casting a negative hue upon Crawford's candidacy: one for reasons of concern over the candidate's health and ability to govern soundly, and the other owing to an intensifying discontent with "King Caucus," by this time more broadly perceived as the by-product of a political system rigged by insiders, elites, and bigwigs. The general public sensed that this old nominating method was antiquated and thoroughly incompatible with the hard-won principles of republican government.

In October 1823, the Tennessee legislature in its official capacity jointly declared the caucus system undemocratic, called for the direct election of the president by the people, and passed a resolution requiring that the congressional delegation from Tennessee resist any nomination by caucus. Alabama and Maryland followed Tennessee's lead, while other states—including the ever-important electoral powerhouses New York and Virginia—were less willing to join the chorus now urging an end to the congressional caucus. As the issue drew more attention in Congress itself, Clay, the influential Speaker of the House, declared, "The Cause of a Caucus is on the decline, and I do not think there will be one, unless in a state of despair friends of Mr. Crawford determine to hold one of a minority of the Republicans." The situation developing against the caucus model in effect guaranteed multiple Democratic-Republican candidates competing for electoral votes. Crawford in fact did hold the support of those sixty-six members of Congress—the "minority of the Republicans" indicated by Clay—who chose to participate in the caucus, thus nominating him with near unanimity and naming Pennsylvania's able and experienced Albert Gallatin, former senator, representative, secretary of the treasury under both presidents Jefferson and Madison, and diplomat representing the United States in the signing of the Treaty of Ghent, as Crawford's running mate. While fourteen states did participate by sending delegates to the caucus, forty-eight of the sixty-six were drawn from just four states: New York, Virginia, North Carolina, and Georgia. That the numerous and influential delegates from New York and Virginia still supported the caucus and, by extension, boosted Crawford's chances was an important factor in the early part of the 1824 campaign. And thus Crawford enjoyed the full endorsement of the caucus; but its evident unpopularity in most states actually worked, in the end, to undermine the Crawford-Gallatin ticket. Rejecting the legitimacy of the caucus, the other candidates turned to their respective home states, where they were either nominated by their state legislatures or in separate state conventions. As campaign season moved into its latter stages, it became apparent that "King Caucus," the support of New York and Virginia notwithstanding, was in the process of being dethroned once and for all. As expected, Crawford received the endorsement of the Virginia state legislature, but he could not inspire other state assemblies to follow in kind.

Crawford's hopes were also diminished by the well-populated field of talented candidates. Even the savvy of the politically astute Martin Van Buren of New York, working behind the scenes on Crawford's behalf, proved insufficient in exploiting the Georgian's initial advantage against a broad and deep field of capable figures. While Crawford and Gallatin were both well regarded, and for good reason, Adams, Jackson, Clay, and Calhoun were all extraordinary men by any measure, and even the comparatively less promising candidates still in the field were appealing. While Adams, Jackson, and Clay were, along with Crawford, the leading candidates, the others were not so easily dismissed. Even though he withdrew from the early running, Calhoun continued to draw attention from potential supporters, and by 1823, he was again a serious presence in the field. As with Lowndes prior to his passing, DeWitt Clinton was nominated by a state convention, this one held in Steubenville, Ohio. With Crawford's candidacy hobbled by the stigma of the caucus, the high quality of the field overall, and the spreading news about his allegedly broken health, it was just a matter of time before Adams and Jackson soon established themselves as the new front-runners. Crawford's health had indeed been compromised, but the exact nature of his ailment was obscured by rumor and poor communication. His health apparently began to improve; at least enough for him to manage his personal affairs and to muster the will to persevere in his campaign, but complete recovery was by many accounts beyond reach. He suffered blindness and partial paralysis, maladies that he was able to cope with in the course of his daily activities but that also restricted his public engagements. To dispel the exaggerations about his condition, he needed visibility; but given his condition at the time, such visibility would actually do more to confirm doubts rather than allay them.

Clay, who was among the more energetic, affable, seasoned, and capable politicians of his time, might also have emerged as a major force, but he too was undercut by rumors that he had either withdrawn from the race or was facing unspecified health problems of his own. Other rumors held that Clay was really only angling for a cabinet post and thus was not serious about the main prize. These rumors were all groundless but nonetheless sufficient to weaken his position, particularly against Adams and Jackson.

At the time, all the candidates in the field identified themselves as Democratic-Republicans owing to de facto one-party dominance that was the consequence of the War of 1812, the demise of the Federalist Party, and the legacy of the Monroe's Era of Good Feelings. Given this, the Democratic-Republicans were not compelled to produce an official platform or develop a general party campaign strategy, as the absence of an opposition party did not produce a need. Consequently, no theme, set of issues, dramatic slogan, or persuasive phrase spun out of the campaign. Even though the major Democratic-Republican candidates avoided what we might today call hot-button issues, the press did not. Newspapers openly debated the three big polarizing issues—slavery, sectionalism, and tariffs. Despite sustained public interest in these problems, voters found it extremely difficult to distinguish the candidates on the basis of any real policy differences.

However, some policy differences did set the principal candidates apart. Clay's "American System" was a repackaging of Alexander Hamilton's federalism, favoring the national bank, federal funding of infrastructure development, and the imposition of protective tariffs. (By 1825, these policy positions would begin to serve as the distinctive doctrinal elements of a large faction that would be identified as the "National Republicans" and that would eventually become the precursors of the Whig Party. But for the moment, that delineation was not yet drawn.) For the most part, Adams and Calhoun, at least for the moment, joined Clay in these preferences. As with most Republicans by the time of the Monroe administration, Crawford had been a long-term supporter of the national bank and had on separate occasions both opposed and supported the notorious embargo of 1808, but he was also identified with the older doctrines of Jeffersonian Republicanism and was thus considered the candidate of the "Old Republicans" (now referred to as "Radicals" in some circles, but certainly not an apt description of Crawford as a politician). Unlike the other main candidates, Senator Jackson, who was prone to intense feelings, forcefully despised the national bank and was favorably disposed to limited, localized government and the encouragement of the free market. Jackson also openly criticized protective tariffs, although he was not always consistent in this regard, as he was also known to have supported them in the past on some occasions. As indicated above, among the major issues, the growing controversy over slavery festered as a latent source of severe, even violent conflict. There were also visible disagreements over economic issues in the wake of the severe and protracted depression of 1819 (which extended by most accounts into 1822), Clay's American System offering one solution, Jackson's less systematic but nonetheless ardently formed proclivities offering another. Even though the issues were compelling and, in at least the case of slavery, critical to the future of the republic, the campaign was ultimately overshadowed by the force of the powerful personalities involved. Candidate loyalties were based primarily on personal reputation, friendship, or regional allegiance.

As with the campaign of 1800, the discussion over the qualifications of the candidates grew increasingly personal. Scandalmongering and character assassination quickly and thoroughly replaced dialogue. Adams was unjustly accused of caving in to the British while he, along with Gallatin as well as Clay, had helped to negotiate the navigation agreements on the Mississippi River that had followed the Treaty of Ghent (with which he and Gallatin were also involved). It was sniffed with disapproval that he had an English wife, and he was also ridiculed by many who perceived him as slovenly and undignified. As to the other candidates, in addition to the pervasive anxieties over his health, Crawford was unfairly rumored to have mismanaged public funds. Clay was inaccurately rumored to be a gambler, a drunkard, and too ill to run for such a demanding office. Jackson's more exercised critics labeled him a murderer for, among other things, having summarily executed six mutinous deserters during the Creek War of 1813, a conflict that earned General Jackson a reputation for savagery, at least among some quarters. All the principal candidates were larger-than-life figures, inspiring fierce loyalties among some and drawing strident criticism among others.

Interestingly, these personal attacks initially did not directly come from the candidates. Adams, who was on record as having previously defended General Jackson's controversial actions in the First Seminole War in Florida, actually admired him, and when Adams's campaign enjoyed a surge that seemed to place him, for a time at least, as the front-runner, he seriously considered asking the general to join him on the same ticket as his vice presidential candidate. Among supporters of this suggestion, one of the campaign's few catch phrases was circulated: "John Quincy Adams who can write, Andrew Jackson who can fight." (The slogan would later be revised so as to give it an entirely different twist.) Adams was without any serious challenge in the Northeast, and if he could swing a few votes his way in other regions, he would enjoy a clear advantage. But Jackson's alpha-male personality was not geared for second best; his entire life was defined by his peerless ability to lead combined with his personal defiance against any submission to the authority of another. A Vice President Jackson was sheer fantasy, as plausible as Napoleon agreeing to submissively remain on Elba.

As the campaign deepened, Jackson emerged as the strongest figure in the field. Initially confined to the West, where Jackson enjoyed a firm base—particularly after he had gained ground against Clay in Indiana—the movement for the general soon gained momentum in the pivotal mid-Atlantic swing states. Pennsylvania propelled Jackson's effort in the East. Calhoun had anticipated winning the support of Pennsylvania, and he saw the Keystone State as the key state in his campaign; but Calhoun's campaign fizzled when a sudden grassroots movement supporting Jackson gained steam in the state's western portion. At this point, Calhoun saw the writing on the wall and lowered his ambitions, at least for the moment. Quickly spreading eastward to Philadelphia, the movement for the general gained credibility when a local group of Jackson supporters, simply calling themselves "democrats," voted to endorse Old Hickory, a nickname won in the military owing to his custom of resolutely sharing the same hardships experienced by the soldiers under his command, thus proving himself to be as tough as a hickory tree. This particular event in Pennsylvania is historically notable for two reasons: it could well be regarded as an early step, perhaps the first traceable step, toward the formation of what would become the Democratic Party; and, in the resolution itself, we find one of the earliest projections of the Jackson myth. The resolution endorsing Jackson described him as a virtuous patriot, a "consistent democrat," a "statesman and warrior," and a "friend to the rights of man and universal suffrage," all traits that would continue to define his image for voters in upcoming campaigns as well as for future Americans steeped in the stories of their own political heritage. For the moment, however, the pro-Jackson momentum that gathered energy in Pennsylvania carried into the state convention in Harrisburg, where Jackson received his first and perhaps most critical nomination outside his own state.

The "democratic" tenor of Jackson's campaign spread rapidly elsewhere. In New Jersey, which initially favored Adams, Jackson's supporters endorsed what they called the "People's Ticket" and successfully turned the state in their direction after a hotly contested campaign between all comers. Jackson, a slave owner and wealthy planter, a powerful member of the military elite, and currently a U.S. senator, had become the "man of the people"—a momentous development, as he was the first candidate of this kind in American history to emerge on the national stage, thus making Jackson the political archetype for all elections to come. Concurrently, the expansion of suffrage nourished Jackson's grassroots campaign. By the campaign of 1824, a growing number of states had declared all adult white males eligible to vote, irrespective of religious affiliation or property ownership—by 1820, nearly every state had already either abolished property qualifications attached to voting or imposed but a token poll tax. Only six states selected presidential electors in their state legislatures; the remaining eighteen states chose electors through the popular vote. The rapid expansion of the electorate and its increased influence on the Electoral College forced presidential candidates to make direct appeals to voting citizens instead of relying primarily on surrogates, political bosses, and friendly newspapers to argue their case. The seeds of the modern campaign were being planted, and their first fruits would soon be harvested.

The actual election was riddled with uncertainty and confusion and marked by fragmentation. Jackson did win a plurality of ninety-nine votes (37.9%) in the Electoral College, carrying eleven states, eight of them unanimously: Pennsylvania (which now delivered twenty-eight electoral votes, second only to New York), most of the South (but significantly not Virginia, now the third-largest electoral prize), and portions of the West. Adams placed well behind Jackson in the Electoral College with eighty-four votes (32.2%) cast from eleven states, predictably winning all of New England and easily taking New York (the Electoral College colossus, which delivered twenty-six of its thirty-six total votes to Adams, with just one for Jackson). Rebounding somewhat from rumors of illness and his unfortunate association with "King Caucus," Crawford managed to show forty-one votes from five states, including twenty-four from Virginia and nine from his home state of Georgia, as well as picking up five from New York. Clay held his home state of Kentucky as well as Ohio, Missouri, and four renegade votes from New York, for a total of thirty-one. Officially preserved on record for the first time, the national popular vote also leaned to Jackson, who managed, from among a field of four, a not inconsiderable plurality of just over 150,000 (or around 40%) votes recorded to Adams's tally of around 114,000 (just under 31%). Clay and Crawford each earned approximately 47,500 (just under 16%) and 41,000 (or about 14%) of recorded votes, respectively. Jackson's biggest victories were in his home state of Tennessee and in Pennsylvania; in the latter, he managed to win by around 30,000 over the second-place candidate, and in the former, his home state, he carried all but 528 votes. Adams showed similar success in New England, where Jackson did not receive a single vote, with a small minority turning to Crawford and thus allowing Adams to win his home region in a rout.

But neither the popular vote nor the Electoral College could produce the required majority that was mandatory for any candidate to win, hence Jackson's lead in both was not enough to send him to Washington. In marked contrast to the undecided presidential vote, Calhoun was elected to the vice presidency with ease; he was selected by both those electors who voted for Jackson and those who voted for Adams, giving him a total of 183 votes to 41 for North Carolina's Nathaniel

Macon, Crawford's running mate, and 37 for New York's Nathan Sanford, on the ticket with Clay. Unfortunately, the presidency was not so easily determined. Failing a majority in the Electoral College, the presidential election was decided in the House of Representatives as stipulated by the Constitution (originally under Article II, Section 1, and as amended in 1804 by the Twelfth Amendment). On February 9, 1825, John Quincy Adams won thirteen states in the House, the minimum required to capture a majority and thus electing him to become the sixth president of the United States. Jackson managed seven states, while four stood by Crawford. As only the top three candidates could receive votes in the House, Clay, who finished fourth in the Electoral College, was deemed ineligible.

For the second time in twenty-four years, the House of Representatives found itself in a position to determine the next president. Not bound to follow the electoral vote or the will of state legislatures, each House delegation held one vote; New York with thirty-two representatives had the same vote as Illinois with just one representative. Many at the time perceived Clay to be the key. Contrary to popular misconceptions, however, Clay could not direct anyone to support either of the two leading candidates, as those electors committed to him were not voters in the House of Representatives; thus, such a move would be pointless, as the election was now out of their hands. Nor could Clay, in spite of his authority as Speaker, command the voting in the House. His influence was indeed considerable, but it was not enough for him to single-handedly direct such an outcome. Furthermore, the voting was quite close in some cases, and it is less clear whether or not Clay could have (or indeed, would have) been able to exert his influence so extensively as to guarantee a decision for Adams. New York, for example, nearly went to Crawford. However, Adams's majority in New York was finally ensured when Representative Stephen Van Rensselaer, who had initially supported Crawford but, after having been buttonholed by both Clay and Daniel Webster on behalf of Adams, found himself paralyzed in such a state of indecision that he, by his own admission, left it in God's hands. So leaving it to divine intervention, he is said to have closed his eyes for a moment in prayer, thereby opening them by sheer chance, or perhaps in response to some inscrutable will, to the sight of a fateful Adams ballot that he had plucked from the House floor. Interpreting this as a true sign from above, his vote went to Adams. If this account, confirmed by Martin Van Buren, is accurate, then the election of Adams over Jackson was left as much to either divine will or blind luck as to any efforts, real or imagined, on the part of Clay and Webster.

Even so, Senator Jackson would not be consoled. Initially, Jackson appeared to cordially accept the outcome, but when he heard of the apparent cabinet-level benefit that Clay was about to receive after having supported Adams, his mood sharply changed. Stung by winning more votes than Adams in both the Electoral College and in the popular vote and yet still losing the election, Jackson brooded darkly, bristling when Clay received the plum position as Adams's secretary of state as a reward for, in Jackson's unsubstantiated perspective, marshaling his considerable influence in the House behind Adams. Clay did bear a dislike for Jackson and was known to have wondered aloud if killing 2,500 British soldiers qualified Jackson for the presidency, a statement that surely bore into Jackson's sense of honor. Incensed, Jackson famously described Clay's appointment as the fruit of a "corrupt bargain." As indicated above, while Clay, along with Webster, did attempt to influence the vote in Adams's favor, there is no evidence that an actual bargain behind the scenes, corrupt or otherwise, had been struck by anyone. While not particularly friendly to Adams as a person, Clay genuinely favored Adams's vast experience and proven qualifications over Jackson's. Moreover, the two men were already closely aligned in terms of policy, Clay's "American System" matching most of what Adams also envisioned for the future of the still-young republic. In a word, Adams and Clay were both Hamiltonians; Jackson was not. Ulterior motives are hard to prove, but we can say with confidence that Clay's general agreement with Adams on the issues, when combined with his dislike of Jackson, would naturally lead him to support Adams over Jackson at the decisive moment.

If a doubtful claim is made often and forcefully enough, it will eventually become widely adopted, consciously or subconsciously, even by the more well-informed students of history. We now tend to accept as true the old accusation by Jackson and his supporters of a "corrupt bargain" between Adams and Clay, even though there remains no evidence to prove or disprove it. Interestingly, in a 1998 article published in the *American Journal of Political Science*, professors Jeffrey Jenkins and Brian Sala, employing the methods of game theory, provide a basis for reexamining the "corrupt bargain," concluding that the House's election of Adams was actually consistent with "sincere voting models" that were not available to earlier critics of the outcome. In other words, according to Jenkins and Sala, there is no objective support for the popular, but misleading, "corrupt bargain" explanation. "Sincere voting models" aside, awarding a cabinet position to a political and doctrinal ally was not atypical; but Jackson, known to be somewhat thin-skinned and swift to judge, saw nothing but corruption and collusion in Clay's appointment to Adams's cabinet, an impression that would hound him over the next four years until he could be afforded an opportunity at revenge. In any event, for the moment, John Quincy Adams, with the lowest percentage of electoral votes as well as the lowest percentage of popular votes of any candidate in the history of American politics to win the presidency, followed the footsteps of his renowned father, John Adams, the second president of the United States, into the White House as the sixth president of the United States. The Virginia dynasty was now interrupted, as the second Adams was also the second president from the Commonwealth of Massachusetts.

There was no doubt, then or now, that Jackson was capable, confident, shrewd, intelligent, charismatic, dignified, and patriotic; but it must be admitted that at this point, Adams was far more qualified and experienced as a statesman. A prominent diplomat since the Washington administration, a former member of Congress, an accomplished secretary of state, coauthor of the highly regarded Monroe Doctrine, and a man of letters, Adams was at this point the ablest American statesman of his time. Jackson did have limited experience as a member of Congress (one year in the House, one year in the Senate) and as military governor of Florida, but it was his reputation as a warrior and his persona as self-made man that generated his popular appeal, not his record as a public servant. Jackson was lionized as Old Hickory, formidable war chief and archetypal man of the people. Adams, while respected among his peers, was perceived by the general public as an aloof aristocrat and vintage Federalist in Democratic-Republican clothing. And yet, unknown to most voters at the time, Adams was a sincere champion of republican values, while Jackson's personality was decidedly autocratic. More than most, this and the following campaign of 1828 revolved around a degree of inversion of image and fact, serving as examples of the power of appearances in democratic politics, even the politics of young democracies. These often confused elements of fact and image would soon play themselves out to their fullest in the following rematch of 1828.

Additional Resources

Boller, Paul F., Jr. *Presidential Campaigns*. New York: Oxford University Press, 1984.

Hargreaves, Mary W. M. *The Presidency of John Quincy Adams*. Lawrence: University Press of Kansas, 1986.

Hay, Melba Porter. "1824." In Arthur M. Schlesinger, Fred L. Israel, and David J. Frent, eds. *Running for President: The Candidates and Their Images*. New York: Simon & Schuster, 1994.

Hopkins, James F. "Election of 1824." In Arthur M. Schlesinger, Fred Israel, and William P. Hansen, eds. *History of American Presidential Elections, 1789–1968*. Vol. 1. New York, Chelsea House, 1985.

Jenkins, Jeffrey A., and Sala, Brian R. "The Spatial Theory of Voting and the Presidential Election of 1824." *American Journal of Political Science* 21, no. 4 (October 1998): 1157–1179.

Remini, Robert V. *Andrew Jackson and the Course of American Freedom, 1822–1832*. New York: Harper & Row, 1981.

Remini, Robert V. *The Election of Andrew Jackson*. Philadelphia: Lippincott, 1963.

Remini, Robert V. *Henry Clay: Statesman for the Union*. New York: W. W. Norton, 1991.

Campaign of 1828

"Expired at Washington on the 9th of February," a pro-Jackson editor groused, "of poison administered by the assassin John Quincy Adams, the usurper, and Henry Clay, the virtue, the liberty and independence of the United States." Losing the election of 1828 was one of the significant consequences of Adams's Pyrrhic victory in the election of 1824. Rightly or wrongly, Andrew Jackson, embittered by what he believed to be Adams's Machiavellian maneuver involving his ally Clay—the "corrupt bargain" of American political lore and perhaps a fiction adopted as truth—stormed back with a vengeance, this time to win clear margins in both the Electoral College and within the burgeoning popular vote. Given the vehemence behind Jackson's resolve to dislodge Adams combined with a growing acceptance of the charge that the Adams administration had not played fairly in 1824, the notable election of 1828 had likely already been decided four years earlier.

Acrimony between individuals and their supporters intensified before and during the Campaign of 1828. The Adams-Clay alliance had stirred enemies even before the inauguration. Clay found himself dueling with Virginia senator John Randolph over a particularly cutting insult publicly cast by the latter from the Senate floor against the integrity of the administration. Incumbent vice president John Calhoun, still harboring his own designs on the presidency, abandoned the Adams ship almost immediately for the Jacksonians, and thus served for four years as the vice president to a president he did not support. Truth notwithstanding, the phrase "corrupt bargain" dominated rhetorical currency for the four years between the Campaigns of 1824 and 1828. Against this backdrop, the first enduring and extant modern American political party was formed—the party of Jackson, eventually to be called Democrats, a label that had been first used by Jackson supporters four years earlier during his campaign in western Pennsylvania.

The Era of Good Feelings, largely killed by the controversy of the previous election, and "King Caucus" were now both relics of the past. Evolving in their stead was a distinctly bipartisan dynamic that was no longer attached to the congressional caucus. This was the incubator of modern political parties in the United States. Thoroughly polarized around both personal allegiance and political vision, the new factions carried further the policy debate ongoing since Alexander Hamilton and Thomas Jefferson fixed the initial parameters as early as the administration of President Washington, now four decades in the past. Adams was affiliated with Henry Clay's "American System," a vision of active governmental policy that included federally funded public works, protective tariffs, a strong central government, and an established national bank—in a word, the latest edition of the Hamiltonian vision. For his part, Jackson was not a committed ideologue; rather, he sought moderate, case-by-case positions on many of the pressing issues of the time, his zealous and abiding contempt for the national bank an important exception. While not a Jeffersonian purist, Jackson nonetheless gravitated toward the ideal of an agrarian republic, as well as embracing the strict constructionist and states' rights doctrines of the Old Republicans. The Old Republicans, or "Radicals," represented the remnant of the party's Jeffersonian origins—or at least

Jefferson's political attitudes prior to his election to the presidency, as his adoption of many of Hamilton's attitudes during his tenure in the White House caused the Old Republicans to break from their founder from Monticello. In 1824, their champion had been Crawford, curiously in spite of his support of a national bank and his vacillation on the embargo controversy. After losing the election to Adams, Crawford had retired to Georgia in 1825, leaving leadership of the Radicals to his erstwhile supporter Martin Van Buren of New York, known as the "Little Magician" and the "Red Fox of Kinderhook." As one of the keenest politicians of his age, Van Buren, an unlikely standard-bearer for the Radicals, assiduously avoided doctrinal zealotry—winning campaigns was his principal devotion.

Courting the popular Jackson thus became Van Buren's priority, and through Van Buren's efforts at adeptly exerting influence behind the scenes, Jackson's renewed challenge was given coherence and direction. Van Buren effortlessly guaranteed a majority of electors in his home state of New York and held enough influence among his allies in Virginia to deliver all twenty-four electoral votes of the Old Dominion to Jackson. Additionally, Van Buren, owing to his former allegiances, could muster support from among Crawford's base throughout a number of states. Van Buren was committed to the old North-South alliance, and in spite of his interest in votes above doctrine, he nonetheless adhered to a genuine desire to reanimate Jeffersonian principles against the Hamiltonian turn that had characterized public policy in recent years.

With the late Jefferson as their philosophical touchstone, Van Buren, Jackson, and Calhoun formed the leadership of what was now commonly known as the "Democratic-Republicans," frequently referred to as the "Jackson Party" in deference to its currently most dominant figure. By 1832, this party would generally come to accept the simplified alternative name mentioned above; that is, the Democrats. Adams and Clay, by contrast, were referred to as "National Republicans" (also, "Coalitionists"), the closest heirs to Hamilton and the direct forerunners of the Whigs, and through them, they are partially and indirectly connected to the modern Republican Party that would first form in the Northwest during the mid-1850s. Following Hamilton's political vision as reaffirmed through Clay's "American System," Adams and the National Republicans now clearly stood as a philosophical alternative to the Jackson/Calhoun/Van Buren faction. The National Republicans behind Adams also held strong sectional appeal, as they commanded the majority of their allegiance in New England and, to a lesser extent, New York, still the state with the most electoral votes. The South and West primarily leaned toward the Democratic-Republicans/Jacksonian Democrats. Additionally, two short-lived minor parties appeared at around this time. The Anti-Masonic Party suddenly materialized in response to an inflammatory wave of anti-Masonry that began with scandal and murder in New York. The Workingman's Party organized in 1828 as an advocate for the cause of labor, the only American political party of any renown exclusively standing as representative of the working class. But these minor parties would soon experience the fate of all "third" or minor parties in American history and fade out; the political landscape in the United States was being shaped largely by two primary visions of democracy, the direct legacy of the Hamiltonian-Jeffersonian debate.

Jackson's 1828 campaign ran throughout the duration of the Adams administration. As early as October 1825, only seven months after Adams's inauguration, the Tennessee state legislature nominated Jackson for president. Jackson supporters began working on his election soon after. Jackson partisans in Congress caucused regularly throughout Adams's term and worked as a coherent political faction. Jackson's cohort successfully accumulated an unprecedented campaign fund. Liberal use of the franking privilege for political purposes among Jackson's congressional supporters amplified the influence of the monies raised.

The role of money had expanded in proportion to the increase of eligible voters. With all states now having lifted property requirements attached to voting, and all but two states (Delaware and South Carolina) employing direct election of the Electoral College, democratization of American politics was accelerating. Creating partisans within such a large pool of new voters required money and organization, and the Jackson Party quickly mastered the necessary methods of obtaining funds and building a network of allied committees and clubs. "Hickory Clubs" sprouted throughout the various states—Jackson's nickname "Old Hickory," a reference to his straight and unbending character as well as to his practice as a military commander in resolutely sharing the burdens of his troops, providing the inspiration—working diligently at the local level to stage events, recruit supporters, and promote the cause. Hickory poles were raised in towns and cities nationwide as symbols of their man, and campaign workers distributed hickory paraphernalia in the form of hickory canes, sticks, and brooms, reminders of Jackson's heroic stature. Thus, Jackson became more firmly planted as the political *axis mundi* of grassroots democracy. Rallies and barbecues, accompanied by songs of Jackson's daring exploits, became commonplace events. The man who was increasingly called the "New Washington" had succeeded in stirring fervent support across the vast spaces of the new republic. Adams's more subdued followers were perplexed at the hoopla and mockingly inquired about any connection between hickory trees and republican principles.

The president's own efforts at reelection were quite another matter. The "American System" was continually emphasized—Adams and Clay choosing to focus on policy more than self-promotion. Adams, who lacked the personal warmth and social proclivities needed for the new style of campaigning, refused to engage in what he considered "vulgar politicking," leaving the task of working the public largely to Clay, Pennsylvania's Richard Rush, and other notables such as the young and eloquent Daniel Webster of Massachusetts, an important ally in the previous election. The National Republicans also held rallies and campaign events, but with less frequency and polish. The Nationals banked on Adams's reputation as a statesman as well as a strong self-confidence in their policies, counting on the Electoral College to again assert itself and perform its proper function as the best buffer between good government and popular passions. But after the off-year election of 1826, wherein the Jackson Party captured both chambers of Congress, the momentum for General Jackson was too strong to effectively resist.

More than ever, newspapers provided a visible and ubiquitous service to political partisans. The Jacksonians enjoyed the support of an impressive network of newspapers throughout the country. This network successfully defined the campaign as a decisive and historic contest pitting humble, egalitarian democracy against haughty and reactionary aristocracy. Unfortunately, this was accomplished through a combination of Jackson hagiography and *ad hominem* mudslinging aimed at Adams, who really did not deserve the accusations of autocratic pretensions that were persistently made against him. In the press, General Jackson was the self-made hero of the people, Adams the effete scion of New England aristocrats. Adams was depicted in the pro-Jackson press as undemocratic, misanthropic, anti-immigrant, and anti-Catholic—a "Unitarian," no less, an affiliation that more often than not was suspiciously perceived by the general public at that time as lacking piety and, even worse, as "atheistic." Jackson was depicted as a true American democrat, friend of the common man, and devout Presbyterian. Jackson himself tried to downplay his church affiliations for fear of turning religion into a political lever, even to the point of intentionally reducing his attendance at church while he remained active in politics. In the end, it is doubtful that the religious beliefs of either candidate influenced the outcome, but it nonetheless serves as another example of the willingness of political rivals, then as now, to play this particular card.

More than anything, the ongoing allegation of the "corrupt bargain" was Jackson's main weapon, as it was incessantly raised as proof of Adams's disdain for fair and unbiased electoral politics as well as his overall contempt of popular government. It would indeed prove to be the most effective weapon in the Jackson Party's arsenal, even though the truth of it remained unknown. Jackson's wartime heroics were touted as reminders of his steadfast courage and impeccable patriotism, and he was constantly referred to as the "People's Candidate," the "Hero of New Orleans," and the simple "Farmer from Tennessee." Causing scandal, the Jacksonian press without grounds accused Adams of vicious acts such as procuring a young American girl for the ignoble intentions of the czar of Russia, using the White House as a gaming den, and practicing loose habits regarding his relations with women. Above all, the theme of Adams's elitism was drummed throughout the campaign—the haughty "King John the Second" was no friend of the people and no choice for democracy, and the "corrupt bargain" was the one guiding note that sounded throughout the relentless attack on the president and his administration.

Not above responding in kind, partisan newspapers in support of Adams also joined in this untoward frenzy of mutual invective. Dragging the campaign further into the gutter, pro-Adams newspapers accused Jackson of murder, gambling, conspiracy with the disreputable Aaron Burr to commit treason, adultery, and bigamy—the latter charge being so vicious that it literally fractured the health of Jackson's wife, Rachel. The old indictment alleging Jackson's bloodthirsty murder of wrongly accused deserters in the 1813 Indian War was recycled. Philadelphia's *Democratic Press* published a morbid oblong flyer, known as the "Coffin Hand-bill," in an effort to expose the bloody incident. Nothing seemed beyond the pale; crossing yet another line separating decorum from opprobrium, even Jackson's mother was callously defamed.

More ominously for the future of American politics as such, Congress had recently imposed new tariff policies under the Tariff Bill of 1828, signed into law by President Adams in May of that year. The increased tariffs that the legislation required were enacted for the benefit of budding American industry and commerce, concentrated primarily in the Northeast; but, due to the increased prices on popular imported goods, they were perceived as unfair to consumers and, in particular, to Southern farmers who were now constrained to purchase manufactured materials as well as raw materials from New England producers at higher prices. Southerners felt singled out by the legislation, and in other parts of the country, the tariff was also criticized as not producing the desired effects of domestic economic growth. Tariffs had for some time been a matter of growing controversy between sections; the Southern planters and farmers desired low tariffs so that they could be free to purchase cheaper goods from abroad and thus reduce their costs, while Northern manufacturing enterprises supported higher tariffs to even their chances against stiff foreign competition, particularly from Great Britain, which was at that time the leading industrial power in the world. American industry was beginning to grow at a more rapid pace, and the Adams administration was invested in its continued expansion; thus, protective tariffs were well in line with both Adams's proclivities and Clay's "American System" as endorsed by the National Republicans. Southerners were unconvinced and, led by Vice President Calhoun, would soon come to call the new measures the "Tariff of Abominations." With the passage of this legislation, the debate over tariffs would begin to embitter the different sides against each other, and signs of an imminent constitutional crisis began to loom. When combined with the even more polarizing and acrimonious division over the slavery issue, the tariff issue would add still more volatility to sectional disputes. It was with the Tariff of Abominations that Calhoun, an old war hawk from his early days in Congress, would begin to abandon his erstwhile nationalism and assume the mantle as the most vigorous and preeminent defender of sectional interests and states' rights.

President Adams supported the legislation in the full knowledge that it could be to his political detriment. Jackson was not universally loved in the South, but he cut a more appealing figure to many Southerners, and the president knew that any misstep would lessen his chances at reelection. Furthermore, New Englanders were surprisingly divided on the issue of the new tariff, and it turned out to be more of a boon to Western interests than Northeastern interests, causing further trouble for Adams's efforts to retain the White House. Some argue that Jackson's supporters in Congress drove the tariff issue as a maneuver to weaken Adams, but if that is the case, these same supporters unwittingly banked more trouble for the future president than they, or Jackson, could have anticipated at the time.

Given the storm and stress of the campaign, the actual election was anticlimactic. Jackson won impressively in the popular vote: between 642,000 and 647,000 (around 55%–56%) going for Jackson, with somewhere between 500,000 and 508,000 (43%–44%) votes for the incumbent president. Jackson's margin of victory among the popular vote would stand as the highest in the nineteenth century. Reflecting the popular will, the Electoral College this time gave Jackson a decisive majority: 178 electoral votes to 83 (or 68% for Jackson to 32% for Adams). President Adams held all six New England states as anticipated and also won in New Jersey, Delaware, and Maryland, the Maryland vote being nearly split—six to five in favor of Adams. Even though Adams lost in New York, he managed to pluck sixteen of the Empire State's thirty-six electoral votes, Jackson still winning a majority of twenty. There was nothing left to question this time around; Andrew Jackson was decisively the president-elect. Three candidates received votes for vice president: the incumbent Calhoun, easily winning reelection with 171 votes and following the example of New York's George Clinton by becoming, along with Clinton, historically one of two vice presidents to serve two different presidents (Clinton having served under both Jefferson and Madison). Adams's secretary of the treasury, Richard Rush of Pennsylvania, received eighty-three vice presidential votes for the National Republicans, and William Smith of South Carolina won seven votes from the Georgia delegation as a protest against Calhoun's mistreatment of native son William Crawford when the two men worked together in the Monroe administration. It would not be the first time that Calhoun was the object of personal retribution.

The election of 1828 is often regarded by historians, political scientists, and students of electoral politics as the watershed event in the democratizing of presidential selection. To an extent this is accurate, as the election was characterized by what was at the time unprecedented citizen participation. But it is also misleading to an extent, as presidential elections had been gradually and noticeably moving in this direction for two decades. Whether or not historians can arrive at a clear enough understanding of this era to satisfy all the angles, the election of Andrew Jackson to the presidency definitely pointed the country toward the formal institutionalization of the modern two-party system and helped to establish the shape of things to come. Furthermore, Jackson's triumphs in 1828 and later in 1832 assembled and solidified a varied coalition within the Democratic Party that included the allegiance of aristocratic Southern planters (and thus slave owners), Western entrepreneurs, small farmers in the West as well as in the North, and diverse immigrants residing in larger numbers within the more heavily populated cities, particularly in the North. In a word, Jackson's ascent relied upon the first of many coalitions that would help to define the Democratic Party throughout much of its history. For these and other reasons, President Jackson would greatly contribute to the formation of the American political system that we know today. Indeed, the fact that these events opened what is now universally called "the Age of Jackson" speaks volumes with regard to his pivotal role in American history. And indeed, in many ways it was indeed Jackson's age, but it is only fair to remark that former president John Quincy Adams was not nearly finished with public life. President Adams may have left the executive branch under unfavorable conditions, but he would soon eagerly return to the public arena, serving with distinction in the House of Representatives—wherein his colleagues assigned him the nickname "Old Man Eloquent," due largely to his speeches condemning slavery—and thereby earning a name as one of the preeminent American statesmen in any era. And President Jackson's legend survived the mudslinging barrage of 1828 and continued to loom larger than life through the duration of his presidency and beyond.

Additional Resources

Boller, Paul F., Jr. *Presidential Campaigns*. New York: Oxford University Press, 1984.

Cohen, Martin, David Karol, Hans Noel, and John Zaller. *The Party Decides: Presidential Nominations before and after Reform*. Chicago: University of Chicago Press, 2008.

Cole, Donald B. *Vindicating Andrew Jackson: The 1828 Election and the Rise of the Two-Party System*. Lawrence: University Press of Kansas, 2009.

Parsons, Lynn Hudson. *The Birth of Modern Politics: Andrew Jackson, John Quincy Adams, and the Election of 1828*. New York: Oxford University Press, 2009.

Remini, Robert V. *Andrew Jackson and the Course of American Freedom, 1822–1832*. New York: Harper & Row, 1981.

Remini, Robert V. "1828." In Arthur M. Schlesinger, Fred L. Israel, and David J. Frent, eds. *Running for President: The Candidates and Their Images*. New York: Simon & Schuster, 1994.

Remini, Robert V. *The Election of Andrew Jackson*. Philadelphia: Lippincott, 1963.

Remini, Robert V. "Election of 1828." In Arthur M. Schlesinger, Fred Israel, and William P. Hansen, eds. *History of American Presidential Elections, 1789–1968.* Vol. 1. New York: Chelsea House, 1985.

Campaign of 1832

Lacking the passion and intensity of previous presidential campaigns such as those that occurred in 1800, 1824, and 1828, the Campaign of 1832 nonetheless played a crucial role in ensuring that organized, permanent political parties would become a fixture of American politics and an inseparable element of American political culture. And even though the Campaign of 1832 was not as provocative or as dramatic as those other elections mentioned above, it was not entirely without drama, for it is hard to conceive of any political contest involving personalities such as Andrew Jackson, John C. Calhoun, and Martin Van Buren, the "Little Magician," as just any ordinary affair. In this case, the drama that did arise was of a more personal nature, and one that serves as an important reminder about those facets of political life that are driven by emotion, sensitivity, empathy, antipathy, and loyalty.

By and large, President Andrew Jackson's first term has been described largely as one that solidified the position of what was by now commonly referred to as the Democratic Party (an outgrowth of the Jeffersonian Republicans, initially called simply "Republicans" and later referred to as "Democratic-Republicans," the direct progenitors of the Democrats, also known by some in the previous election as the "Jackson Party"). Jackson's administration was not without controversy and serious opposition, but for the most part, his first term as president had been successful, and thus his party's renomination was a *fait accompli.* And so, in late May 1832, the Democrats, holding their first national nominating convention in Baltimore, endorsed nominations that Jackson had previously secured in state conventions, the national nominating convention still an emergent force in presidential politics and thus still deferential to the state parties. Jackson's renomination was unopposed, but the vice presidency was now in play, a development that was incongruent with what had previously been anticipated shortly after Jackson's election in 1828. At that time, John Calhoun was moving into his second term as vice president, having already served under President John Quincy Adams, and at that time he was the popular choice to remain in office and thus serve under Jackson as well. Due to policy disagreements with then-president Adams, who was firmly committed to the comparatively activist government promoted by Henry Clay's "American System" (which was itself a revival of the policies of Alexander Hamilton), Calhoun's allegiances switched to the Jacksonians, who appeared at the time to be more inclined to support localized and limited governance. During his campaign for reelection to the vice presidency in 1828, Calhoun appeared to everyone as the obvious heir apparent, brimming with presidential potential and well situated to press for the office upon Jackson's departure. Indeed, Calhoun's name had been floated for a run for the presidency in the lead-up to the 1828 election, but in the end he withdrew from consideration. In 1829, it was not clear that the newly elected President Jackson would even be interested in running for a second term; thus, many were already considering Calhoun as the inevitable candidate in 1832. But very early in Jackson's administration, Calhoun found himself in a private conflict with the president, one that, when combined with real political differences that were becoming more apparent, would drive a rift between these two strong personalities and, in the end, not only diminish Calhoun's chances of becoming the next president, but actually ruin his tenure as vice president and guarantee that the nomination for the second spot on the ticket in 1832 would go to another rising star.

Much of what occurred was of an emotionally charged personal nature stemming from a nasty feud between Calhoun's wife, Floride, and Margaret "Peggy" Eaton, the wife of President Jackson's friend and secretary of war John Henry Eaton, former senator from Tennessee (for which, it turns out, he was constitutionally unqualified, at least initially, as he was first appointed to the Senate in 1818 while two years underage). When Jackson appointed Eaton to his cabinet, the Calhouns were caught off guard and set on the defensive. Eaton was, as it turned out, a stern critic and rival of Calhoun—even having opposed Calhoun's candidacy for the vice presidency; and his presence on the cabinet was an obvious impediment to the vice president's own ambitions, as he had hoped to use the vice presidency to become Jackson's most influential adviser and further secure his ascendency to the still higher office of the presidency in either 1832 or 1836. With Eaton on the cabinet, Calhoun suspected that his influence would be diluted, suspicions that were confirmed quite early in Jackson's administration, as Eaton proved to hold more sway with the president in promoting appointments for his friends while simultaneously impinging upon Calhoun's dwindling influence to do the same. Calhoun did manage to land cabinet positions for three of his friends (in a cabinet of six members, a not-so-inconsiderable number when Calhoun's voice was also added), but he nonetheless perceived the strength of his influence to have been sufficiently compromised by the unwelcome ascent of Eaton.

To make matters worse for Calhoun, another prominent figure, New York's Martin Van Buren, was tapped by Jackson for secretary of state, and Van Buren—the rising star alluded to above—was also widely regarded as promising presidential material and thus a still more formidable rival and potential impediment to Calhoun's expansive ambitions. With the darkening presence of both Eaton and Van Buren, Calhoun feared that what had once seemed to have been the brightest and surest of futures was now utterly in jeopardy. Thus the Calhouns, husband and wife, together went on the offensive, and for them it was undeniably personal.

Peggy Eaton was the soft target in the Calhouns' crosshairs. She was in her second marriage, her first husband, John Timberlake, having committed suicide as a consequence of what many alleged, proof or lack of proof notwithstanding, to have been illicit behavior between Peggy and John Eaton. After Timberlake's death, Eaton married the young widow with Jackson's full support and blessing. This caused considerable distress within Washington society owing to the rumors of marital impropriety, and in particular, among many members of the cabinet and their wives. Floride Calhoun in particular was offended by Peggy Eaton's past, or at least what was taken to be true about that past, and thus she led a faction of influential Washington wives in a successful collective snub of Mrs. Eaton. The president, whose own late wife, Rachel Donelson Jackson, had also been socially ostracized because of malicious rumors, was sensitive to this kind of treatment; he became intensely defensive of Mrs. Eaton and angry with those cabinet members, and especially with his vice president, for participating in such untoward pettiness. Even worse for both the president and the Eatons, Jackson's own niece, Emily Donelson, standing in for his late wife as a substitute First Lady, was allied with Floride Calhoun and had thus also refused to call upon Mrs. Eaton, confining her interactions with the Eatons only to her duties as White House hostess. Meanwhile, Calhoun's pettiness toward Jackson himself further angered the president against him. Van Buren, the Little Magician of political lore, took every opportunity to extend courtesy and sympathy to the Eatons, actions that did not go unnoticed by Jackson and his allies. While the meanness of this affair was not the only cause of the Jackson-Calhoun rift, it was an important factor in the deterioration of both their personal and professional relationships. The Eaton Affair, also known by some as the "Petticoat Affair," directly led to the formation of President Jackson's "Kitchen Cabinet," or his group of unseen, unofficial advisers that he now increasingly relied upon due to this estrangement from his appointed cabinet, or "Parlor Cabinet." Jackson's Kitchen Cabinet consisted of his most trustworthy political advisers and provided him with a body of friends with whom he could consult without having to suffer further irritation from the pettiness of his formal cabinet. Ultimately, the president fired a number of members of the official, appointed cabinet. Secretary of State Van Buren would also resign of his own volition from the cabinet but would remain an important participant in Jackson's Kitchen Cabinet, and would soon receive an appointment by the president to serve as ambassador to Great Britain at the Court of St. James.

The Eaton Affair was but one reason for the sudden decline of Calhoun's influence and prospects. Calhoun, who had once been a nationalist and war hawk prior to and during the War of 1812, had by his second term as vice president moved toward a position stridently advocating states' rights, one that was grounded in his "doctrine of nullification," which argued that states had the right to nullify federal laws within its own borders. A talented writer and proficient orator, Calhoun had fervently defended and helped to further develop the principle of nullification through his own writings and speeches—a doctrine that he combined with his theory of "concurrent majorities" to challenge the strength of the Northern section as well as the nationalism that he had once so successfully helped to promote. Nullification was advanced within the context of actual policy, the Tariff of 1828, a protectionist measure enacted by Congress, during the last full year of the Adams administration, aimed at supporting and strengthening domestic industry vis-à-vis foreign imports. With mixed results in the end, the legislation was meant to have benefited northern manufacturing economies, but it was perceived by Southerners as inimical to their own decidedly agrarian interests. Calhoun's home state of South Carolina, in particular, had been agitated by what was called, from their point of view, the "Tariff of Abominations," and with the argument of nullification now in play, a secessionist crisis was under way.

For his part, while Jackson certainly embraced states' rights in the spirit of Jeffersonian republicanism, he did so only to a point, finding the very notion of nullification to be treasonous. For Jackson, as for others such as his contemporary Senator Daniel Webster of Massachusetts, the Union was indissoluble, and to think and argue otherwise set a perilous course. Famously, the president exhibited his differences with the vice president at a Democratic commemoration of Thomas Jefferson's birthday, where, in a toast to Jefferson, he raised his glass and, targeting his imposing gaze directly at Calhoun, forcefully declaimed, "Our Federal Union. It must be preserved." Undaunted, Calhoun raised his glass in an equally famous reply, "The Union, next to our liberty, most dear. May we all remember that it can only be preserved by respecting the rights of the States and by distributing equally the benefits and burdens of the Union." Calhoun continued to even more aggressively espouse the nullification doctrine, and the government of his home state of South Carolina grew utterly recalcitrant; but with forceful determination, President Jackson made clear to South Carolina his willingness to even go so far as to send federal troops to enforce the tariff law. Given the president's reputation, this was a prospect not to be taken lightly; thus South Carolina would eventually back down, but not until after the doctrinal positions had been clarified and the sectional allegiances further crystallized and polarized. It was the first major secession crisis since the Hartford Convention during the War of 1812, and one that actually came closer to occurring and that signaled those unbridgeable divisions that remind us today that it would not be the last.

As if this were not enough, the final nail against Calhoun's incumbent vice presidency and his hope of inheriting the presidency from Jackson was delivered by the revelation that Calhoun had struck at Jackson much earlier in their respective careers. In opposing then-general Jackson's 1819 military expedition against the Seminoles in Florida during the Monroe administration, Calhoun, who was at that time serving President Monroe as secretary of war, had recommended that the president's cabinet collectively censure Jackson's conduct in Florida, with the further recommendation that punitive measures follow. Had it not been for the persuasive support of Jackson by another Monroe cabinet member and unforeseen political rival of Jackson, then-secretary of state John Quincy Adams, Calhoun likely would have won President Monroe over to his position. Jackson thus would have been censured and his political future dimmed by the young war hawk from South Carolina. It was Adams, whom Jackson so bitterly challenged in 1828, who actually protected him from Calhoun, the man who would become his own vice president and one of his most disdained rivals.

As it was, the censure never came, and Calhoun's push for it had remained unknown to Jackson until it came to light during this particularly tense moment between the two men; indeed, Jackson had always assumed, mistakenly, that Calhoun had defended his actions in Florida. The revelation as to the facts of the case came from William Crawford of Georgia, a candidate for the presidency in 1824 and who in 1830 exposed Calhoun's previous actions against Old Hickory. With this, the impasse led to a complete break, and an immediate confrontation between the president and vice president ensued. When Van Buren's appointment to the Court of St. James came before the Senate for confirmation, the vote was deadlocked, giving Vice President Calhoun, serving in his constitutional capacity as president of the Senate, the deciding vote. Calhoun promptly used that vote to break the tie and reject Van Buren, a move that Jackson found "base, hypocritical and unprincipled," and he referred to Calhoun as nothing less than a villain. His position in the administration now utterly destroyed, Calhoun resigned the vice presidency, an office that he had held since 1825, becoming the first of two vice presidents to resign from that office in American history (remember that he is also the first of two vice presidents to serve under two different presidents). Devoting his political energies to successfully obtaining a seat in the Senate, Calhoun would shake off this setback and continue on as one of the more important statesmen of his era, a member of what some historians call, owing to their exalted level of shared preeminence in Congress, the "Great Triumvirate": John C. Calhoun; Henry Clay, known as the Great Compromiser; and Daniel Webster. With Calhoun detached from Jackson, the party eagerly turned to Van Buren for the vice presidency in the upcoming campaign of 1832.

As important as this rift with Calhoun was for Jackson's administration and for the shape of the Democratic ticket in 1832 and the future leadership of the party for the next decade, an even more significant political issue commanded the attention of the electorate—that of the second national bank. Encouraged by Jackson's political opponents, most prominently Clay—who was at that time serving as the senator from Kentucky—Nicholas Biddle, an influential Pennsylvania financier, currently the president of the Second Bank of the United States, and thus by default President Jackson's sworn nemesis, petitioned Congress for an early renewal of the bank's charter, which reflexively incurred Jackson's ire. After a protracted congressional debate, both chambers of Congress approved the renewal of the national bank; this played into the hands of Clay and his allies, who were hoping to provoke Jackson into opposing the institution, a move that they knew would not require very much effort, given the president's abiding rancor toward the bank.

Owing to Jackson's personal experience as a young man involving financial losses incurred from unpaid promissory notes that were connected to land speculation in Tennessee, Jackson predictably reacted to the renewal of the bank charter as a personal affront. Previous loose lending practices practiced by Tennessee banks had helped to fuel a real estate bubble, and when the bubble burst, it ruined the lives of many Tennessee residents. Hence Jackson, who had himself directly suffered from the actions of the banks in Tennessee, harbored an intractable animosity toward banks in general and anything to do with the centralized banking systems. During his administration, he vigorously sought to dismantle once and for all the national bank that had been established, at the behest of Alexander Hamilton, during the Washington administration. On this issue, Jackson was more in line with the states' rights position, for he saw a national bank as unconstitutional and sought to reconfigure the banking system more in accord with the decentralized structures of the states themselves. Jackson also opposed easy credit and paper currency, and stated that "hard money," or "specie," was the only reputable medium of exchange in any context. Naturally, he distrusted speculators and viewed the Hamiltonian economic policies of Clay's "American System" askance. In Jackson's mind, banks and their "rag money," flimsy notes, and cheap credit were nothing less than despicable, and the more powerful the bank, the more it was to be a target for demolition, and the national bank was just such a bank.

Determined to eradicate the bank, the president eagerly vetoed the bill to renew the bank's charter in 1832. In a famous veto message, Jackson observed that the bank primarily served the interests of the wealthy, and he warned the nation against the designs of the rich who sought to convert their economic fortunes into expanded political influence throughout the country, to the detriment of republican ideals. Institutions such as the national bank served, according to Jackson, to "make the rich richer and the potent more powerful." In stifling the bank's charter, Jackson further clarified what were for him and his allies the now firm political boundaries of American democracy: the party of the people, the Democratic Party, was to slay the dragon bank once and for all; their opponents, on the other hand, were no less than plutocrats who kept their real interests obscured behind the bank's established reputation, seeking ways to secure and expand their position, all at the expense of the common man. Biddle was not impressed by any of this, and openly, unflinchingly scolded the president for what he perceived to be a cynical manipulation of the "Great Unwashed" for his own political gain.

It was left to the opposition party, still referred to as the National Republicans, to challenge this claim by the Democrats—viz., that Jackson and his party were the party of the common citizens, the people themselves. The National Republican Party held its nominating convention in December 1831. Made up primarily of businessmen, industrialists, small merchants, and some farmers, they looked to the venerable Clay to defeat Jackson and thereby secure the reestablishment of a new national bank, along with strengthening support for protective tariffs and increased federal expenditures on internal improvements. A former congressman and stalwart of Clay's "American System," John Sergeant of Pennsylvania, was selected to accompany Clay as his running mate. The strategy of the National Republicans and their candidate Clay hinged on persuading the electorate that Jackson, far from being a vaunted man of the people, had actually turned despotic, intent upon destroying the nation's democratic institutions and assuming absolute power. In effect, both sides insisted throughout the campaign that their opponents were antidemocratic autocrats, especially when the polemic turned to the bank issue. National Republicans blamed Jackson for introducing corrupt patronage practices, or what would become known as the "spoils system" (following the expression "To the victor belong the spoils") into American politics, a charge they felt was damning evidence of Jackson's true colors as an antidemocrat and a self-serving tyrant. The charge seemed to stick, as President Jackson's administration is to this day often associated, rightly or wrongly, with the practices and problems of the "spoils system," although it must be admitted that such practices were pervasive and even expected at the time, the president being no different from any other holder of high office in the 1830s, at least in this regard.

Far more serious than political patronage, representations of the specter of tyranny abounded throughout the election on both sides. Opponents of the national bank (primarily Jackson's Democrats) accused bank president Biddle of imperious conduct, calling him "Emperor Nicholas" or "Czar Nick," or even "Old Nick," an unsubtle (at the time) allusion to the Devil. Jackson's opponents followed suit, referring to the president as "King Andrew I" (an amusing reversal of insults by Jackson's supporters in the election of 1828, who had unkindly referred to then-president Adams as "King John II"), or simply the Tyrant or Usurper, a "King of Kings" (an allusion to the exalted emperors of ancient Persia, and not to another, very different figure also so named) who was bent on destroying the Constitution. In the wake of the bank veto, Daniel Webster accused Jackson of emulating King

Louis XIV, the Sun King of France, even to the point of identifying the famous claim of the Bourbon monarch, "I am the State" *("L'etat c'est Moi")* with Jackson's alleged lust for power. This message was driven by the desire to expose Jackson as a false man of the people who in reality sought office for the sake of power alone, "The King Upon the Throne, the People in the Dust!" as one anti-Jackson paper couched the charges of autocracy, charges that inspired several early political cartoonists to depict Jackson as a cheap, grasping despot. One cartoon depicts a fawning Van Buren crowning Jackson while a scepter is presented to the new King Andrew by none other than the Devil himself; another drew Jackson as a displaced Quixote, tilting against the marbled columns of the national bank only to shatter his lance in folly. In turn, supporters of Jackson made effective use of political cartoons to lampoon Henry Clay and to attack the national bank, and to their benefit, as the National Republicans miscalculated in their fixation on the president's bank veto. The National Republicans also misfired in their attempts to redefine Jackson as a despot. For example, political cartoons of the 1830s made frequent use of rats to symbolize corruption, quite frequently the corruption associated with the national bank, and it was not unusual to see cartoons depicting Jackson as a cat chasing down rats, cleaning out the vermin. Instead of politically hurting the president, his veto of the national bank bill ultimately reinforced his image as the protector of the common man and the enemy of the rich and powerful. President Jackson successfully seized the opportunity to frame his entire campaign around the national bank issue. Thus his decision to run on a populist platform hit a responsive chord with a rapidly expanding and engaged electorate.

The Democrats made good use of popular events—especially the barbecue and the parade. By some accounts, these parades were elaborate affairs, some reported to have extended a mile in length, involving torchlight, numerous and colorful banners, celebratory portraits of Jackson displayed alongside Washington and Jefferson, and the return of the familiar and effective hickory tree symbols that were ubiquitous in the previous election, honoring the president's nickname of "Old Hickory," won through his military discipline. National Republicans also held large rallies; one such rally in Philadelphia was reported to number around ten thousand Clay supporters, mostly naturalized citizens of Irish descent. But the Democrats appear to have been, by comparison, more effective in organizing rallies, while the National Republicans seem to have mastered the craft of the political cartoon. Jackson, Van Buren, and hickory poles were the more popular targets for lampooning cartoonists sympathetic to the National Republican cause.

Interestingly, a third party showed some support during the campaign of 1832, one that has often been referred to as actually having introduced the formal political party as a national institution wholly independent of governmental institutions and allegiances. In response to a bizarre series of events involving allegations against

Masons in the state of New York, the new Anti-Masonic Party formed in the late 1820s and formally entered the presidential campaign stage in 1832. Anti-Masonic sentiment traced its roots to the 1826 unsolved abduction of William Morgan of Batavia, New York. Morgan's unexplained disappearance raised suspicions owing to his plans to publish a book that he claimed would detail the allegedly sinister side of the Masonic organization. (Evidence connecting the disappearance of Morgan to anyone involved in Freemasonry was never found.) In the aftermath of Morgan's disappearance, anti-Masonic candidates began to run for office in New York and other states, leading to the formation of a formal Anti-Masonic Party, which held what some argue was the first truly and self-defined national political convention in American history, meeting in Baltimore in 1831, well before the first truly national conventions of both the Democrats and the National Republicans. The following year, the Anti-Masons nominated Maryland's William Wirt for president of the United States. Wirt, a former U.S. attorney general of notable renown as well as a prosecutor in the trial against Aaron Burr, was himself a former Mason. Amos Ellmaker of Pennsylvania was selected to run as Wirt's running mate. The party, as its name indicates, was primarily formed to oppose what they believed was the deleterious influence of Freemasonry in American society. But to gain political viability, it embraced policy positions not unlike those of the National Republicans, and for this reason, at least for a limited time, it eclipsed the National Republicans within the state of New York. By and large, while the Anti-Masonic Party serves as an interesting example an early challenge to the emerging two-party system, it was unable to muster the kind of broad appeal needed to sustain a national base.

Election Day vindicated President Jackson's first term, in spite of all the turmoil over protective tariffs (provoking a secessionist crisis), the banking system (stirring the populist pot), and the Peggy Eaton situation (shedding an unflattering light on the influence of scandalmongering, and those willing to engage in it, within the nation's capital). Accounts vary, but it appears that the president won between around 687,500 and 702,000 votes (at least 55% of those cast—what would be regarded as a landslide today), while his opponents (Clay and Wirt) together won around 474,000–530,000 votes. In some states, votes for Clay and Wirt were counted together on ballots simply marked "anti-Jackson," thus leading to our present confusion over just how many popular votes Clay was able to secure (although some records suggest that Wirt managed to collect close to 100,000 votes, which would have been a substantial reduction of Clay's total if accurate, and not a bad showing for a third-party candidate in the 1830s). But as we all know, the real votes are, then as now, in the Electoral College; and there, President Jackson won a truly significant victory, taking 219 votes to Clay's 49—a genuine landslide of 76 percent of the Electoral College for the president. Wirt won just seven electoral votes from Vermont, giving him the Green Mountain State. Eleven South Carolina Democrats, no doubt influenced by Calhoun, broke from the national party and cast their electoral votes for Virginia governor John Floyd, a proponent of Calhoun's doctrine of nullification and actually running under the banner of the Calhoun-inspired "Nullifier Party," based almost exclusively in South Carolina. Other than Vermont and South Carolina, which went to Wirt and Floyd, respectively, and the six states won by Clay—Massachusetts, Rhode Island, Connecticut, Delaware, Maryland, and the Great Compromiser's home state of Kentucky—Jackson took the rest of the Union, sixteen states in all. The president won over 60 percent of the popular vote in nine states, some of which reported an astonishing100 percent for Jackson. Clay's best showings were in Connecticut and, as expected, Kentucky, but in neither state did he win more than 55 percent. Predictably, the vice presidency went to Jackson's new running mate, Van Buren, who received 189 electoral votes, the remainder cast for Sergeant (matching Clay's total for president), 30 electoral votes from Pennsylvania for favorite son William Wilkins, 11 for Henry Lee from South Carolina (although unlike Floyd, Lee was not a nullifier), and 7 for Ellmaker to match Wirt's total.

All told, Jackson's victory solidified the Democratic Party as the dominant political voice in American politics, a strengthening voice that commanded diverse and wide-ranging appeal throughout the electorate, given its ability to more convincingly convey the image of being the real party of the people. It was apparent to the National Republicans that further victories were in the Democratic Party's future unless they could somehow provide a credible challenge to that image.

Additional Resources

The American Presidency Project. http://www.presidency.ucsb.edu.

Boller, Paul F., Jr. *Presidential Campaigns*. New York: Oxford University Press, 1984.

Cohen, Martin, David Karol, Hans Noel, and John Zaller. *The Party Decides: Presidential Nominations before and after Reform*. Chicago: University of Chicago Press, 2008.

Gammon, Samuel Rhea. *The Presidential Campaign of 1832*. Baltimore: Johns Hopkins Press, 1922.

Heidler, David S., and Jeanne T. Heidler. *Henry Clay: The Essential American*. New York: Random House, 2011.

Leip, Dave. Atlas of U.S. Presidential Elections. http://uselectionatlas.org/.

Meachem, John. *American Lion: Andrew Jackson in the White House*. New York: Random House, 2009.

Remini, Robert V. *Andrew Jackson and the Course of American Freedom*. New York, 1981.

Remini, Robert V. "1832." In Arthur M. Schlesinger, Fred L. Israel, and David J. Frent, eds. *Running for President: The Candidates and Their Images*. New York: Simon & Schuster, 1994.

Remini, Robert V. "Election of 1832." In Arthur M. Schlesinger, Fred Israel, and William P. Hansen, eds. *History of American Presidential Elections, 1789–1968.* Vol. 1. New York: Chelsea House, 1985.

Campaign of 1836

The 1832 defeat of Kentucky's Henry Clay and the National Republican Party by incumbent president Andrew Jackson and his Democratic Party proved to be the last act for the National Republicans, but it also opened the way for the establishment of the new, and more cohesive, Whig Party in 1834. The Whig Party, the latest heir to the ideas and policy positions of Alexander Hamilton, vividly carried forward by Clay and other notables such as Daniel Webster, the great orator from Massachusetts, became the political home for a number of anti-Jackson factions. The founders of the Whig Party took the name from the old English Whig Party that had opposed the Stuart monarchy in the seventeenth century—in particular the restored monarchy of James II—and who were largely responsible for the Glorious Revolution that shaped modern Britain's constitutional monarchy. But the term itself can be traced even farther back to those radical Scottish Presbyterians (also known as the Kirk Party) who were involved in the "Whiggamore Raid" against a rival faction in Edinburgh in 1648.

The choice of the name "Whig" thereby evokes defiance of autocratic power— in the case of the original British Whigs, it meant resistance to the Stuart Dynasty; for the American Whigs, it was "King Andrew" who drew their defiance. Since before the **Campaign of 1832**, opponents of President Jackson, and especially the now-defunct National Republicans, accused Jackson of conducting himself as more monarch than the man of the people that his supporters tirelessly maintained. This attempt at publicly reframing Jackson's image was resumed by the new Whig Party, now consisting mostly of former National Republicans as well as a smaller number of conservative Democrats disappointed with President Jackson's economic policies, and joined by erstwhile members of other anti-Jackson factions such as the Anti-Masonic Party (New York had already provided an example of an anti-Democrat alliance between Whigs and Anti-Masons, and indeed, some of the Whig Party's early leaders such as William H. Seward and Thurlow Weed were refugees from New York Anti-Masons, accompanied by another former member of the Anti-Masonic Party from Pennsylvania, Thaddeus Stevens) and finally a number of Southern nullifiers who were perhaps the most vehement opponents of "King Andrew." With the emergence of the Whigs, the American two-party system was still more firmly solidified within American political culture, with both parties, then as now, eager to demonstrate the democratic authenticity of their connection to the people as a whole. In a word, the Whigs had to find a way to claim for themselves what the Jacksonian Democrats had readily assumed since the election of 1828—that they were the real party of the common man, the champions of equality, the true bearers of American destiny.

This attitude was encouraged among Whigs, given the expectation that the incumbent vice president, Martin Van Buren of New York, was Jackson's unchallenged heir apparent, especially now that South Carolina's John C. Calhoun had long been removed from the picture. For the president's critics, the inevitable selection of Van Buren to succeed Jackson was more reminiscent of royal descent than of the kind of democratic pretensions the Jacksonian party incessantly made. But for the student of politics, it was difficult to imagine another successor to Jackson, at least from within the Democratic Party, quite as capable or prepared as the Little Magician. Looking back, Van Buren, a master of political nuance, seems to have been on a path to the presidency since his early days as the principal leader of the Bucktails (named for the deer tails—or "bucktails"—that they sported on their hats), a political faction that, among other things, had opposed the Federalist Party and, in particular, DeWitt Clinton. The Bucktails were cofounded by Van Buren and closely connected to the New York Tammany machine and a forerunner of the Van Buren-led Albany Regency, a powerful machine that managed to control much of New York state politics throughout the 1820s and 1830s, with Van Buren firmly in the midst of it. Van Buren's experience in government and his record as a competent public servant, combined with his many contributions to party politics and his deep connections within the state political machines, provided him with an expansive reservoir of practical political knowledge, a knack for the deal, and long-held alliances that made him the perfect candidate for high office in the mid-nineteenth century.

With the 1834 congressional midterm elections as well as various state elections held in 1834 and 1835, the Whig Party had shown substantial gains, proving its appeal to the broader electorate by winning majorities in state assemblies such as Virginia, and even in President Jackson's home state of Tennessee. The Whigs were a minority in Congress, but the gap was closing. The Democratic majority was not as pronounced as it had been in the wake of Jackson's 1832 landslide; and significantly, the Whigs had managed to make visible inroads into the South, which had been an important part of Jackson's base and a needed constituency to buttress Van Buren's credibility as a national candidate. Consequently, as the campaign of 1836 approached, the Whig Party had surfaced as not simply the best of the "other parties" on the national scene, but also as the most viable challenger to the dominance that the Democrats had enjoyed since 1828. Perhaps more importantly, the coalition that had been assembled and sustained within President Jackson's Democratic Party during the previous two elections was beginning to show signs, as coalitions inevitably do, of breaking apart.

By and large, the doctrinal principles and policy positions of the main parties remained unchanged; the Democrats reaffirmed the states' rights doctrine of Jefferson and Jackson, continued their recalcitrant opposition to the national bank, and sustained their general objection to Clay's "American System" and all that it entailed. The Whigs held fast to high tariffs, public works and internal improvements, ongoing support for the national bank, and the related spirit of governmental activism championed by Clay and inherited from Hamiltonian federalism. Where politically advantageous, some Whigs were willing to sing the tune of the other side; Illinois Whigs, for example, enthusiastically supported the candidacy of Tennessee senator Hugh Lawson White, who was known for consistently avowing the principles of Jefferson and Jackson usually associated with the Democrats, and choosing instead to personally attack Van Buren and the Democrats simply on the issue of their monopoly of power. For their part, the Democrats were more cohesive on party platform but just as likely to adjust their rhetoric to secure a regional advantage. Northern Democrats, aware of anti-Van Buren sentiment in the South, attacked abolition to mollify Southern voters, regardless of their own honest views on the issue of slavery. Generally the parties were sincere in their principles, but neither party was without division or blind to the necessity of political stratagem.

Even though both parties did advance coherent principles that marked their mutual differences, there were visible fissures within both the Democrats and the Whigs, and not the kind that are simply explained away by cynically playing to the local crowds. Not surprisingly, President Jackson had made enemies inside his own party; the Force Bill estranged South Carolina Democrats, led by his former vice president John C. Calhoun, along with other influential supporters throughout the South. All the same, President Jackson's personality, loyalties, and legend would likely have given him a third term had he chosen to pursue it; but it would have been at the cost of a weakened electoral mandate, a degree of cross-regional disaffection, a further fragmented party, and a diminished legacy. Additionally, it was remembered with some degree of pique that a younger Van Buren had, in 1820, opposed the admission of Missouri as a slave state, and though Van Buren was not an abolitionist (and would later, as president, oppose the abolition of slavery in the District of Columbia as an appeasement to the interests of Southern slaveholders), some—but certainly not all—Southerners were suspicious of his stand on the issue.

The Democrats were already experiencing internal dissent. In the Electoral College powerhouse of New York, the state Democratic Party had split into conservative and radical wings, the former being Tammany loyalists willing to modify their anti-bank position to permit banks chartered by party stalwarts, and the latter, the "Equal Rights" wing, adhering to a "purer" Jacksonian ideology and labeled the "Locofocos" by their estranged party brethren. Originally an insult, "Locofoco" soon became a moniker adopted nationally by the party populists, although "Equal Rights Party" was the preferred name during its formation and early days in New York City. (The nickname "Locofoco" actually comes from the use of what were called "locofoco matches," or matches that had been lit to save a particular meeting of the Equal Rights Party after the gas lamps had been extinguished by Tammany supporters in an unsuccessful attempt to throw the gathering into darkness and thereby thwart any further proceedings.) As one can surmise, the Locofocos were stern opponents of the growing influence of Tammany Hall, and they were also marked by the adoption of a laissez-faire approach to economic policies while simultaneously drawing allegiance from former members of the short-lived Workingmen's Party.

Even though the Whigs enjoyed the momentum that they had earned during the midterm elections of 1834, their lack of a national organization—or even the desire to really establish one—impaired their chances at winning the presidency. While the Democrats, at the urging of the outgoing president, held a national convention in Baltimore in May of the election year—a convention that easily nominated Van Buren as predicted—the Whigs followed a decentralized strategy, depending on legislative caucuses, state conventions, and other localized meetings. By 1836, the Democratic Party was nationally organized and, in spite of the factionalism that had diminished its once broader appeal, was able to muster a national effort in support of Van Buren. The Little Magician was indeed a master politician; but it was President Jackson, ever the man in charge, who choreographed the Democratic convention and ensured that his man was chosen.

The Whigs were, paradoxically, less inclined to follow the structured approach of the Democrats. They sought a government that effectively promoted a national set of policies and programs, a government that required a degree of centralization to institute the components of the "American System," and yet they almost stubbornly resisted the same kind of approach for the organization and operation of their own party. As a result, four different candidates were selected to stand for president under the endorsement of the Whig Party: White of Tennessee, Webster of Massachusetts, Willie P. Mangum from North Carolina, and war hero general William Henry Harrison of Ohio, who brought experience not only earned through his military achievements but also gained in the House of Representatives, Senate, diplomatic corps, and administrative leadership in the Northwest Territory. At the time, the nomination of four candidates was not necessarily that haphazard. Initially, many Whigs felt that the fielding of multiple candidates was a more plausible strategy against Van Buren, who, many admitted, was in fact much too formidable to challenge head-on with a single candidate. If the Whigs could divide the Electoral College and prevent Van Buren from gaining a majority, they might be able to throw the election into the House, where some Whigs felt they had a better chance of victory than if they ran a lone candidate against the Little Magician in a national election. Nicholas Biddle, for example, famed for his public rivalry with President Jackson over the national bank issue, simultaneously supported three Whig candidates—Webster in the North, Harrison in the West, and White in the South—arguing that the best way to resist the "disease" of Democratic policies was to treat it in force locally. If this was in fact the case—that is, if the Whigs really had generally and cohesively adopted a centrally organized decentralizing strategy, as it were—in the end it boomeranged, actually strengthening the Democrats and punctuating the perception among the electorate that the Whigs really were the party of disorganization.

William Henry Harrison's presence in the campaign was particularly of interest to the Democrats. Andrew Jackson's rise to power, it was well known, was directly the consequence of his military record, and Harrison was believed by many to have been cut from the same bolt. To counter this, the Democrats attempted to belittle Harrison's military record in an effort to demonstrate that, when compared to Jackson, Harrison was in reality exposed as a feeble leader. Furthermore, given that Van Buren himself did not bring a record of military success—or even military service—to the campaign, the Democrats, to supply this missing element, selected Kentucky's Colonel Richard M. Johnson, who was reported to have been responsible for actually striking down Tecumseh—or at the very least, one unknown chief in the Battle of the Thames—to run alongside the Little Magician.

But unlike Van Buren, who had enjoyed unanimous support from the convention, the selection of Johnson stirred some controversy. Johnson's record of fighting Native Americans on the frontier drew enough broad support in the West that many believed that his name, even more than Van Buren's, would be the decisive factor in securing Western allegiance. Having President Jackson behind Colonel Johnson was also of considerable importance for many throughout the party. However, Johnson's popularity did not extend into the South, where again the Jackson/Van Buren position was weakening. In this case, it was another example involving personal disdain and racial prejudice, as Southerners took offense at Johnson's past affections for a woman of mixed race. In objection to Johnson, President Jackson was on notice that his preferred candidate to run as second on the Van Buren ticket was "affirmatively odious" as a consequence of his "former domestic relations." Tennessee's James K. Polk, who as Speaker of the House of Representatives was gaining sustained attention on the national political stage, also warned the president against pushing for Johnson, claiming that the colonel's addition to the ticket would act as "dead weight" to the campaign. Against Johnson, Southerners floated the name of William Rives, the senator from Virginia. Even against this opposition, Johnson won the nomination on the first ballot, largely because of the force of President Jackson's charisma and the reach of his influence within the party, a deceptively easy victory given what this initial conflict would portend. But during the actual campaign, Johnson's presence as the hero of the Battle of the Thames gave the Democrats some effective ammunition against the image of Harrison as the Hero of Tippecanoe, for it was believed that in Johnson, the Democrats had found the real victor over Tecumseh. Who actually killed Tecumseh, whether Johnson or some other soldier shrouded within the fog of war, remains to this day unknown. But the fact remains that martial valor was still a powerful attractor for the electorate, and both sides maneuvered to exploit that fact.

During the campaign, both parties played hard to the people: the Democrats made much of the Whigs' alleged aristocratic pretensions, defined the Whigs as simply repackaged Federalist blue bloods, and continued to convey the image of both President Jackson and Vice President Van Buren as the true men of the people. The Democrats portrayed Van Buren as the "executor" of Jackson's political vision and attempted to focus on the principles of the party even more than the personality of its candidates, a difficult task in the wake of Jackson's inwardly contradictory presidency. By way of counterattack, Whigs delighted in promoting the image of King Andrew I accompanied by the diminutive caricature of a pipsqueak Van Buren presuming to be Jackson's autocratically aloof and imperious sycophant and successor. Grasping at straws, the Whigs reached a low point when, in an appeal to severe anti-Catholic prejudices that were common at the time, they attempted to represent Van Buren as a "papist" based upon his "shocking" record of correspondence with the Vatican during his service as secretary of state. One critic depicted this correspondence with the pope as "at once ridiculous and disgusting," and Van Buren was accused in the press of the "crime" of preferring Catholicism, which at that time, given strong and pervasive anti-Catholic feelings in the United States, was considered dangerous to the stability of the republic. Rumors of a "popish plot" to capture the election for some mysterious papal agenda circulated, reaching enough of a pitch to force Van Buren to stoop to a response. Not above these tactics, the Democrats countered in kind with charges that Whigs held a secret agenda to establish a national church in full violation of the Constitution and the spirit of the principle of the "wall of separation." It was claimed that Whigs were pushing for a religious test requisite to holding office, and some argued that prospective candidate Harrison supported adopting something akin to the old Alien and Sedition Acts of 1798 as a way to address an increase in the population of Irish Catholics.

But these more personal tactics aside, it is important to note that ideological differences did matter, and as such, the political culture in general was crystallizing around doctrinal positions. Whigs were adamant in their support of the national bank, and they sustained their belief in the need to fund internal improvements for industry and transportation. It must also be noted that the Democrats were now more eager to focus on party policies and ideas rather than simply relying on the power of personality. For all of Van Buren's considerable political skill and acuity, he was not Andrew Jackson, who was an undisputed war hero, a commanding chief executive, and a larger-than-life figure that had done nothing less than define an age. Van Buren, in spite of his many talents and impressive record, could not begin to match the inexhaustible force of Jackson's personality. In many ways, Jackson was indeed what he had been called for some time, viz., a "second Washington"; among all the presidents since the Great Man of Mount Vernon—all of whom had been among the most capable statesmen in American history—no one, not even the lionized Thomas Jefferson, could match the power of Jackson's charisma. Hence the party, absent the electricity that was so easily generated by Jackson, was now afforded the opportunity to reintroduce their ideas and values in support of Van Buren's cause, and to stand philosophically against the "Bankism," "nullification," and "anti-Jacksonianism" of the Whigs. "Principles are everything; men, nothing," as the Democrats affirmed, a maxim that certainly could not have been expressed so forthrightly with General Jackson leading the charge.

The year 1836 brought an election far closer than the Jackson landslides of 1828 and 1832. Van Buren easily took the Electoral College by winning 170 votes gathered from 15 states, or a not inconsiderable 58 percent; but the popular vote for Van Buren—which was slightly less than 51 percent—was noticeably smaller than both the corresponding electoral vote and Jackson's previous victories. But Van Buren's appeal had in fact proven to be national; he ran strongest in New Hampshire in the North (winning 75% of the popular vote in the Granite State) and Arkansas in the South (winning 64% there), as well as showing strength in Missouri (59%), Michigan (56%), and Virginia (56%), a truly cross-sectional achievement. In defeat, the Whigs had proven to be a viable political force in capturing nearly half of the popular vote; but the 124 Electoral College votes that they won were distributed across four candidates, the cost of their questionable strategy. All told, among the Whig candidates, 74 votes went for Ohio's Harrison, 26 for Tennessee's White, 14 for Massachusetts's Webster, and 11 for North Carolina's Magnum. Despite the outcome in the Electoral College, which delivered a clear election for Van Buren, the Whigs' electoral muscle had been duly and noticeably flexed in the popular vote. Harrison easily won the most popular votes among Whig candidates (around 550,000 votes or about 37 percent of the total popular vote), but he managed to take only seven states—Ohio, Indiana, Kentucky (the Democrats were not helped by Johnson there), Maryland, Delaware, New Jersey, and New Hampshire. Harrison was strongest in Vermont and Indiana, thus exhibiting indications of his own cross-regional appeal, and while he won his home state of Ohio, he did so with only 52 percent against Van Buren's 48 percent, a good showing but not what one would expect from a candidate on his own turf. White held his home state of Tennessee and picked up Georgia. Webster protected Massachusetts but could not gain elsewhere in spite of his growing influence and reputation as a preeminent statesman and acclaimed speaker. Magnum won the electors from South Carolina, which was at this time the only state in the Union wherein the electors were still selected by the state legislature. In all other states, the people voted for their electors to the Electoral College, who in turn officially elected the president typically in line with the expressed expectations of the voters themselves.

The controversy over Colonel Johnson, Van Buren's running mate and Jackson's preferred candidate for the vice presidency, resulted in his failure to win a majority in the Electoral College. Johnson took 147 electoral votes but was unable to gain the support of the electors of Virginia, who supported Van Buren but chose instead to cast their votes for South Carolina Democrat William Smith for vice president, thereby costing the colonel 23 electoral votes. Two Whig candidates for vice president, Francis Granger of New York and former senator John Tyler of Virginia, won 77 and 47 votes, respectively. Thus, unique to American history, the election of the vice president failed to produce an Electoral College majority (Johnson was one vote shy of the votes that he needed to secure the office), and in accordance with the protocols stipulated by the Constitution under the Twelfth Amendment, the election was put to the Senate, wherein Johnson managed to win his office by a vote of thirty-three to sixteen on the first ballot. Curiously, both senators from Virginia—the very state that had foiled his election in the Electoral College—voted for Johnson. New York representative Francis Granger received the other sixteen votes, including Webster's and Clay's. It is interesting to note that while much of the opposition to Johnson during the campaign was found in the South, most of the senatorial votes against Johnson and for Granger came from the North or West; Maryland, Delaware, and Kentucky (again, Johnson's home state) were the only states south of the Mason-Dixon Line with senators voting against him. Not one senator from a Deep South state opposed Johnson, even though it was there that Johnson was publicly repudiated.

The political mood of the country was beginning to change. In a real way, Van Buren symbolized that change as much as Jackson. Born into modest circumstances, he was the first president never to have been a subject of the British king, and he was the first president whose family heritage was not British, but rather Dutch. While he did not captivate the electorate as Jackson had, in important ways he embodied the spirit of party politics more thoroughly than Old Hickory; and in spite of his lack of familiarity to Americans today, he was just as important as Jackson in shaping modern American politics and ensuring the institutionalization, and for a time political dominance, of the Democratic Party. Given this, it must be noted that while the Democrats remained the majority party as a result of the election of 1836, they were somewhat more vulnerable to challenge than before, their victory less decisive in comparison to Jackson's earlier landslides.

The racial controversy over Johnson is hard to sort out given the actions of the Senate, but it is clear that race, particularly as it was associated with slavery, was steadily becoming a more imposing factor in in the realities of electoral politics. Democrats, self-described as the party of the people, increasingly displayed a self-serving eagerness to denounce and prohibit abolition to prevent any further erosion of their Southern base, a sign that politics in what would become known as the antebellum period was about to crystallize around this most volatile and ultimately destructive issue. At this point, the bank war, tariffs, and policy differences surrounding Clay's "American System" remained the dominant public issues; but with each election, the Peculiar Institution would further polarize Americans, stimulating a darkening climate of antipathy and vitriol.

Additional Resources

Boller, Paul F., Jr. *Presidential Campaigns.* New York: Oxford University Press, 1984.

Cohen, Martin, David Karol, Hans Noel, and John Zaller. *The Party Decides: Presidential Nominations before and after Reform.* Chicago: University of Chicago Press, 2008.

Feller, Daniel. "1836." In Arthur M. Schlesinger, Fred L. Israel, and David J. Frent, eds. *Running for President: The Candidates and Their Images.* New York: Simon & Schuster, 1994.

Miller Center for Public Affairs: American President On-Line Reference Resource. http://millercenter.org/academic/americanpresident.

Silbey, Joel H. "Election of 1836." In Arthur M. Schlesinger, Fred Israel, and William P. Hansen, eds. *History of American Presidential Elections, 1789–1968.* Vol. 1. New York: Chelsea House, 1985.

Silbey, Joel H. *Martin Van Buren and the Emergence of American Popular Politics.* Lanham, MD: Rowman & Littlefield, 2005.

Wilson, Major. *Presidency of Martin Van Buren.* Lawrence: University Press of Kansas, 1984.

Zuckert, Michael P. *The Natural Rights Republic.* Notre Dame, IN: University of Notre Dame Press, 1996.

Campaign of 1840

By any standard, the campaign of 1840 marks a watershed moment in the history of American politics that crystallized the many developments that had been unfolding throughout the previous three elections, particularly the campaign and election of 1828, establishing a firm base upon which the party structure and system would be framed and further developed over the years to come. The fairly rapid democratization of American political culture had already dramatically reshaped the electoral process by the early 1830s, and the "Age of Jackson" was marked by a far more expansive and comparatively inclusive political process than what had been experienced by the previous generation, developments and patterns that would prove the incubator of organized and directed bipartisan affiliations, managed national campaigns, hot-button issues tied into sustained and competing agendas, and a political rhetoric and emotive symbolism that appealed to the "common man" in the general sense, the "democratic man" in the abstract, and "the people" in the lowest common denominator. These developments were nothing more or less than a reasonable response to the expanded electorate, for by 1840, unqualified adult white male suffrage had become the norm, with all but three states (Rhode Island, Virginia, and Louisiana) successfully guaranteeing the right to vote for all white adult males without any stipulations as to the ownership of property (free African Americans were less fortunate, as only four New England states—Maine, New Hampshire, Vermont and Massachusetts—made a sustained effort to protect their right to vote).

Following hard upon these democratizing trends, the Campaign of 1840, as it is generally credited by political historians, is viewed as having fully ushered in a new era in presidential campaigns, in which the packaging of an attractive presidential candidate became as important as the more difficult labor of cobbling together a policy platform containing sufficient scope to draw in the widest possible support. Ideological attachments remained important, and in some cases they were drawn tighter still; but the focus of campaigns sharpened around the image of the candidate (a development already strikingly prefigured in the person of Andrew Jackson), the ability to communicate that image through the emotive shorthand of symbolism, and the ease with which a pool of voters beyond the diehard base could be marshaled behind a party's national nominee. Candidates with strong regional appeal and favorite sons were still in play, but their influence on the national party organizations and the overall tenor of presidential campaigns was receding from view. To win the White House, a candidate needed to represent something intuitively meaningful to the entire nation, as former president Andrew Jackson had, and as incumbent president Martin Van Buren, for all his considerable political acumen and abilities, never quite could. What thus transpired in 1840 was a campaign that came to symbolize the emergence of modern political parties as an irremovable fixture of the nation's political landscape.

Looking back, Jackson's Democratic Party had just managed to survive a scare from the new Whig Party during the Campaign of 1836. Had the Whigs directed a more cohesive and focused national organization, they might have won the White House. By 1838, Whig members of Congress came to recognize that if they had any chance of defeating the incumbent Democratic president Van Buren, they would have to avoid nominating multiple regional candidates as they had during the previous campaign. Thus, the only way to avoid repeating the failures of 1836 was for the Whig Party to abandon its regional approach and, emulating the Democrats and even other minor parties such as the Anti-Masonic Party, hold a national nominating convention to select a single, national standard-bearer.

Eager to capture the White House from the Democrats and confident in their chances, the Whigs deliberately sought a candidate that would appeal to an electorate that had previously and enthusiastically selected the inimitable Jackson for two terms and, subsequently, Jackson's heir apparent Van Buren, the famed "Little Magician" from New York. It was Andrew Jackson who had, through the possession of that rare personal magnetism that can through its own power command unflagging loyalty and adulation, provided the American prototype of the popular candidate—a charismatic leader, bona fide war hero, and resolute patriot who smoothly combined the nationalist sentiments favored by the Old Federalist/Hamiltonian element with the nagging distrust of national institutions and centralized power that marked the Jeffersonian-Madisonian Republicanism and that had for the most part dominated American political culture on the national level since 1800. All this was mixed in with a genuine populist disposition in spite of Jackson's own well-concealed aristocratic proclivities (which were developed without an actual aristocratic background, as Jackson was truly a self-made man, further adding to his mystique and popular appeal). Such an ostensible man of the people joined to his unsurpassed military legacy provided future campaigns with the best model to emulate, but also one that would be difficult to find among lesser mortals.

Fortunately for the Whigs, they already had someone in play—General William Henry Harrison of Ohio (originally from Virginia), the hero of the Battle of Tippecanoe and the Battle of the Thames, a familiar figure who previously had stood as one of the four Whig candidates in the loose campaign of 1836. *Prima facie*, Harrison fit the Jacksonian suit, a battle-hardened frontiersman who appeared to embody the American ideal of the man of action, at once a symbol of patriotic self-sacrifice and, as the story went, someone in touch with the sensibilities of a people increasingly committed to a broader political equality. And while Harrison may have been to a certain degree many of the things that were advertised about him, the image and the substance of the person behind it were not always consonant. He was indeed experienced in leading men in combat. Were his martial exploits in the same league as Jackson's? That seems to be less clear, at least to some historians, and it is a question that is more relevant for an account of military history than for our discussion of political campaigns.

Harrison's military record had served as a springboard into public service, serving the state of Ohio first as a member of the House of Representatives and then as senator, followed by a short assignment as President Jackson's minister to Colombia. After his diplomatic service, he quietly took up residence on a farm near North Bend, Ohio, working modestly as a county official. Such an unexpectedly unassuming lifestyle for a man favored by circumstances does, to a degree, draw some distance between Harrison and his upper-class roots, thus further clouding Harrison's frontiersman credentials. One thing is certain: He was far from representative of the "common man." Unlike both Jackson and Van Buren, Harrison came from a wealthy Virginia family, one of the richest in the young republic, which was influential politically and had already played a notable role in the direction of the nation; his father, Benjamin Harrison V, was both a signatory of the Declaration of Independence and a former governor of the Commonwealth of Virginia. He also had familial connections to the wealthy Carter family of Virginia, which also linked him to the family of Robert E. Lee. This is not to say that Harrison was insincere in his attempts to identify with the popular frontier spirit of the times, which may indeed have been genuinely pursued with good intentions. But such an admission must allow that such a "man of the people" was a decidedly well-connected one.

Another thing is certain: Harrison left his native Virginia and, through his own talents, earned a reputation as a leading figure in the development of the Northwest Territory, a fact of his biography that does support to some degree his frontier character and common connection to the people as such. Nonetheless, in many ways, Andrew Jackson, while he came to amass a significant fortune and harbored within his personality certain nondemocratic impulses, was, by way of contrast to Harrison, truly a man who through great effort and against much adversity achieved remarkable success from the humblest of beginnings, having been born to modest parents and orphaned at age fourteen—before Jackson was born, his father died as a result of injuries—and forced to fight to survive from a very young age. Even Van Buren, while not quite facing Jackson's hardships, was hardly a man of privilege, having come from a large, financially strapped family that could not afford college for young Martin (his father was a tavern owner and devoted follower of Thomas Jefferson). None of this was in Harrison's experience, but the imagery spun around "Old Buckeye," or "Old Tippecanoe" (or the abbreviated "Old Tip"), as he was to be called for obvious reasons, successfully evoked "Old Hickory" and all that he came to symbolize to the American people, and, quite unfairly, it emitted an image of Harrison as a man in touch with the people, in contrast to the alleged elitism of Van Buren. In this case, image and reality were by no means aligned.

Harrison's frontier-warrior/man of the people campaign image gave birth to one of the more famous political slogans in American history, "Tippecanoe and Tyler Too," Tyler being Virginia's John Tyler, Harrison's running mate on the Whig ticket. The phrase evoked his military record in a way that viscerally resonated with the American public, who wanted a new Jackson and expected their presidents to follow not only the model of Old Hickory, but even more importantly, the example of that first and greatest of American presidential archetypes, George Washington. Toward this end, the Whig Party unapologetically combined hagiographical promotion of its candidate, a festive atmosphere, exaggerated personal attack against the opposition, superficial treatment of the real issues, and an uninhibited appeal to the ever-multiplying, variegated voters to propel Harrison to victory. War hero Harrison was successfully depicted as the simple friend of the small farmer and all those who made their way through the hard world on their own initiative and by their own wits, a claim that was expertly encapsulated in a legend that circulated conveying an image of Harrison having been raised in a log cabin. Never mind that the closest the wealthy Harrison came to living in a log cabin was a brief residence with his bride as newlyweds in a five-room log house; the modest, rustic image stuck to him and again effectively set him apart from Van Buren, who, while not raised in a log cabin, actually was born into humbler circumstances than Old Tip.

The first Whig National Convention, attended by delegates from twenty-two of the twenty-six states, was held on December 4, 1839, in Harrisburg, Pennsylvania, an uncharacteristically early date for a presidential nominating convention. Along with Harrison, elder statesman Henry Clay of Kentucky and General Winfield Scott of Virginia all entered the convention with significant levels of support. The eloquent and capable Daniel Webster of Massachusetts was also a name in play early on, but as before in 1836, he lacked sufficient support outside of his New England base, and a Webster candidacy was openly opposed in a series of editorials by Richard Hildreth published in the *Boston Atlas*. This was a serious blow to Webster's credibility given that this print campaign against him originated from his home state. Webster's candidacy was thus stunted well before the convention was scheduled to be held.

It was the eminent Clay who actually enjoyed front-runner status prior to the convention. He drew extensive support in the South as well as enough support in the North and West, especially in Connecticut, Rhode Island, and Illinois, to demonstrate his continuing national appeal. Clay also seemed to benefit from support in New York, the critical northern state; but his position there was compromised when he encountered a mixed reception during an extended visit to the Empire State in the summer of 1839. For the most part, Whigs in New York City had expressed a general preference for Clay; but in Albany and the rest of upstate New York, there were enough doubts about running another Clay candidacy to darken his prospects. This may have been caused, at least in part, by Clay's Masonic affiliation, and it was here in New York that the Anti-Masonic movement originated and still enjoyed palpable influence. Clay was also connected to the national bank, still a point of contention even among some Whigs and thus a connection that might have further weakened his appeal in a general election. However, it must be noted that this issue may have just as easily been defused by 1840, especially given

Clay's own recent admission, for whatever reason, that he no longer considered the whole of his American System and all the policies associated with it as essential to any future candidacy. Rather, he began to cultivate a more moderate tone that placed his approach to national policy somewhere between his erstwhile Hamiltonianism and the more populist and prevailing Jacksonianism that had held sway for over a decade. Finally, the slaveholding Clay was on record as being in favor of preserving the peculiar institution; but this position would not necessarily hurt a campaign against Van Buren, who had, at least at this point of his political career, openly expressed reservations about abolitionism.

These three issues have been viewed as possible sources of doubt among Whig partisans, but it might also be the case that Clay's record as a national candidate worked against him. An otherwise highly successful politician and revered statesman, his inability to mount a successful presidential candidacy in earlier campaigns may have caused some hesitation within the leadership of the Whig Party, especially in the North (and particularly in New York, where the local politicos were well familiar with Van Buren's skills and just what would be needed to counter them). Clay was unsuccessful in the Campaigns of 1824 and 1832 (indeed, he had been thoroughly trounced by the incumbent president Andrew Jackson in 1832), and it is quite possible that a past marked by electoral failure at the national level was the one thing that kept the party leadership from rolling out a bandwagon for Kentucky's Great Compromiser. Broadly admired as a truly accomplished legislator (by many accounts the greatest of his era), his presidential ambitions were clouded behind the tarnish of past defeat. As with Webster, the bloom was off the rose with regard to Clay, his reputation as a statesman notwithstanding. This, more than any particular issue or political proclivity, seemed to weaken Clay's appeal as a presidential candidate. The young Abraham Lincoln of Illinois, for example, who would throughout his political life define himself as a Clay stalwart and protégé, would in the election year of 1840 turn to Harrison, whom he referred to as the "father of the Northwestern Territory" (not only had Harrison distinguished himself as a fighting general in combat against Native American warriors and the British army within the Northwest Territory during both the Northwest Indian War and the War of 1812, but he had also served as secretary of the Northwest Territory for a short time as well as governor of the Indiana Territory prior to statehood). Clay was a hero to Lincoln, but the Rail Splitter surmised that it was Harrison who could win the White House for the Whigs, and so he threw in behind Old Tip. Similar attitudes prevailed elsewhere. In Pennsylvania, for example, leadership in the Whig Party unreservedly praised Clay for his many achievements but turned to Harrison as offering the Whigs the best chance to unseat Van Buren. Thaddeus Stevens, who was in the process of making a name for himself in the Keystone State, was quick to commend Clay and, in the next breath, just as quick to recommend Harrison. Indebted as the party was to both Clay and Webster, other, fresher candidates were sought and found, not in the halls of Congress, but rather among those whose leadership had been tested on the field of battle, as with Old Hickory, who was now widely embraced and revered by the rank and file of both major parties as the prototype candidate for national office.

"Old Tip" was not the only candidate who fit that type. General Scott was another figure with growing appeal within the Whig ranks. His war experience included the Battle of Lundy's Lane near Niagara Falls during the War of 1812, an engagement in which Scott served admirably but that failed to produce a decisive outcome, and thus the memory of this battle failed to ring as emotionally as Harrison's exploits at Tippecanoe and the still more decisive Battle of the Thames. Scott was more recently lauded, especially in New York (and perhaps another reason why Clay's own appeal there declined), for his ability to successfully defuse border tensions with British Canada. This success gave Scott an advantage both over Clay (in that he could be promoted as a man of action with a record of success) and over Harrison (in that his latest accomplishments were more impressive, Harrison having kept a lower profile in recent years). Because of this, Harrison's nomination was not guaranteed, in spite of the inroads he was able to make in the losing effort of 1836.

Indeed, in spite of considerable hesitation about Clay, the Great Compromiser remained the front-runner as the convention opened. An informal straw poll signaled a likely plurality for Clay at the convention, Clay taking 103 noncommitted votes to 91 for Harrison and 57 for Scott. On closer examination, while it is true that Clay initially garnered more votes than the other two candidates, it was equally clear that a majority of delegates (148, the total votes for Harrison and Scott combined) sought a new champion to carry the party's banner against President Van Buren. Whether or not the convention would go to Harrison or Scott remained less clear, at least until Thaddeus Stevens somehow arranged to "accidentally" drop a letter among the Virginia delegation that had been privately penned by Scott to Pennsylvania delegate Francis Granger, the contents of which revealed Scott's antislavery position. Stevens's ploy, particularly cynical due to his own antislavery position, actually worked; Virginia delegates responded by throwing in behind Harrison, a turn of events that convinced the New York delegation, originally leaning toward Scott, to join in the endorsement of Harrison. On the fifth ballot, Harrison won the nomination, taking 148 votes, mostly from former Scott supporters, while Clay and Scott managed 90 and 16, respectively. The convention then nominated John Tyler of Virginia, a Clay delegate, as the Whig Party's vice presidential nominee, and thus was paired "Tip" and "Ty," and "Tippecanoe and Tyler Too!" was forever fixed in American political culture and history. In one of history's odd coincidences, Tyler's father, John Tyler Sr., ran for and won the Virginia governor's mansion in 1808 against Harrison's father, Benjamin, a shared history of political rivalry that again illustrates their high social standing within Virginia society.

As the Whig convention concluded, the *Baltimore Republican*, an anti-Whig newspaper, printed a comment attributed to a Clay supporter waggishly claiming that should one "give [Harrison] a barrel of hard cider and a pension of two thousand a year, my word for it, he will sit the remainder of his days in a log cabin, by the side of a 'sea-coal' fire and study moral philosophy." While this was meant to derogate Harrison's character, the Democrats inadvertently handed to the Whigs one-half of what would prove to be another of the more memorable, and more effective, slogans in presidential campaign history: "Log Cabin and Hard Cider." The image of Harrison living in a log cabin, a pint of cider in hand, became fixed in the minds of the electorate, and rather than impugning Harrison's habits as intended in the original remark, it actually worked to enhance the "common man" and pioneer persona that the Whigs had been trying to project. Here indeed was a frontiersman like Jackson and a man who lived in a modest dwelling and enjoyed his hard-earned cider just like the rest of us.

On May 6, 1840, the Democratic Party held its national convention in Baltimore, Maryland, and proceeded to renominate the president for a second term despite lukewarm support within Democratic ranks. Van Buren, the Little Magician or "Old Kinderhook," was at times called the less flattering "Slippery Elm" by some within party ranks, a feeble contrast to the party's real and beloved hero, Old Hickory. An economic downturn known as the Panic of 1837 had hurt Van Buren politically, tarnishing his appeal throughout the larger electorate and dampening his support even within the party. Conservative Democrats were defecting to the Whigs, and those Democrats who stood with Van Buren did so with muted commitment. The convention was even less enthusiastic about renominating Vice President Richard Johnson of Kentucky—reputed by some to have been the person actually responsible for slaying Tecumseh, and who had brought his own military credentials to the ticket in 1836. In spite of this military record, he was unable to supply the Democrats with the same dignified bearing and forceful persona as had Jackson, and he was regarded by some within the party as definitely expendable. But no other candidate for the vice presidency emerged at the convention; thus it was decided to allow the state parties to resolve the issue, and in time, it was therein resolved to Johnson's favor, but not before other names such as Senator Littleton Tazewell of Virginia and Governor James K. Polk of Tennessee were also considered in some quarters; Tazewell actually managed to win eleven electoral votes for the office, with Polk winning the attention of one Electoral College voter. With the convention adjourned, the Democrats found themselves in a vulnerable position as they opened their campaign to retain the White House.

Van Buren, whose credentials as a committed proponent of democracy were sound, was successfully (and quite unfairly) redefined by Whig campaigners as an Eastern aristocrat with no real connection to common Americans. It was brilliant deployment of creative imagery and unabashed sloganeering. The Democrats groused at having their populist thunder stolen by, in their minds, the phony Federalist-Whig usurpers. In response, Van Buren's supporters attempted to resuscitate the issues, particularly the battle over the bank, while dismissing the log-cabin story as the superficial trumpeting of mere celebrity mythmaking. In contrast, the Whigs intentionally steered from the issues. And the issues were still there, both parties hewing to their same positions advanced four years earlier, but now with the important addition that the issue of slavery was threatening to become a more visible and increasingly divisive concern. And yet the Whigs' campaign was, through all this, still marked by presentation and image management, popular entertainment and populist appeal.

Additionally, Whig strategists found themselves managing (or in modern parlance, "handling") their candidate. Harrison was not known for political acuity or philosophical clarity. His manner of speaking was often disjointed and confusing—incoherent to some and inspiring to none, he could appear both uninformed about and indifferent to the important questions of the day. Harrison's more influential supporters, particularly Nicholas Biddle (whose renown had been earned in political battle against President Jackson over the national bank), were understandably nervous whenever Harrison actively appeared on the campaign trail. A committee of campaign managers was hastily formed with the specific charge of monitoring and coaching Harrison's public statements. In a sense, Whig leaders devoted substantial energy to simply preventing their candidate from undermining himself. But for the most part, the polished Whig packaging—borrowing heavily from the Hickory Pole and public event tactics used to great effect by Jackson's campaigns in 1828 and 1832—stifled any real policy discussion through the slick organization of festivals, parades, and barbecues, all punctuated by a chorus of slogans, jingles, and catchphrases and lubricated by a glut of mock log cabins filled with both hard and soft cider free for the taking.

Merchandising was a signal mark of the Whig promotion. Baubles such as promotional handkerchiefs and campaign buttons were common. Boisterous Whig campaign songs were abundant and widely circulated through sheet music and songbooks. Familiar melodies such as "The Star Spangled Banner," "La Marseillaise," and "Yankee Doodle" now accompanied pro-Whig or anti-Van Buren lyrics. The Whig Party also made extremely effective use of campaign rallies, meetings, and bonfire events to build and fuel a grassroots following for Harrison. The slang term "booze" was invented due to the widespread consumption of whiskey sold in log-cabin-shaped packages and distributed by the E. G. Booz Distillery of Philadelphia to promote the Whig ticket. Even the phrase "keep the ball rolling" can be traced to the Whig campaign stunt of curiously rolling a large ball around Whig political rallies throughout 1840. The role of campaign songs was pronounced. The lyrics to one such Whig campaign song included the following doggerel:

> What has caused the great commotion, motion, motion
> Our country through?
> It is the ball a-rolling on,
> For Tippecanoe and Tyler too, Tippecanoe and Tyler too.
> And with them we'll beat the little Van, Van, Van;
> Van is a used-up man,
> And with them we'll beat little Van!

Political cartoons continued their comparatively new role as effective image-statements drawing quick and entertaining contrasts between the candidates. Harrison's Western frontiersman/ordinary fellow/log-cabin builder/hard cider drinker/no-nonsense ploughman/Indian fighting, Red Coat stomping war hero/ humble friend of the people imagery played out well in the cartoons and songs, and Van Buren's New York refinements and Eastern manners served as all-too-easy targets for exaggerated and unflattering comparisons. Van Buren, pinned with the pejorative "Sweet Sandy Whiskers" and denounced as "King Mat," was (quite falsely) accused by Whig politicians of indulging in opulent hedonism at the expense of the taxpayers, imbibing fine wines and clothed in delicate laces while General Harrison's simpler taste ran toward buckskins and the ubiquitous cider. In truth, Van Buren's White House was comparatively frugal and Harrison was not above extravagance, but the fiction was nonetheless swallowed by voters and thus politically devastating to the Democratic ticket.

The Democrats countered with attempts to humanize Van Buren, assigning to him the endearment of "Old Kinderhook" after his hometown, and pointing to his long record as a seasoned Jacksonian and heir to the ideals of Jefferson. President Jackson himself emerged from retirement to stump for his former vice president and political ally, but the presence of Jackson only served to remind voters of the clear differences between the two men, and it is likely to have caused Van Buren more harm than good in the comparison. Van Buren initially desired to avoid dem-agoguery and focus on issues, but the nature of the campaign eventually took hold, forcing the Democrats to play the image game as well. Typically, aspersions were exchanged in kind. Believing, rightly or wrongly, that Harrison's "war hero" legend was built on the thin foundations of a minor player in the War of 1812, the Demo-crats attacked the general's authenticity, competence, and manhood. "Granny Har-rison, the Petticoat General" was the nasty insult that Democrats hurled at the aging challenger. Working hard to demolish the general's war record, the Democrats accused Harrison of lacking political sensibility and moral spine, more the ignorant and effeminate poser than self-made rugged warrior. To the Democrats, Old Tippecanoe was in reality a dainty "General Mum." The Democrats delighted in referring to Harrison's speech coaches as a "Conscience-Keeping Committee," and they pointed out that the "doddering" general was really guided by the "leading strings" of his managers. Defamation and opprobrium were greedily pitched to and fro between the major parties. To the dismay of the Democrats and Van Buren, the attacks on Harrison did not stick. In the end, the Whigs amassed larger crowds, marshaled more effective support in the press, and sounded the populist chord more convincingly. President Van Buren, whose policies were well within the Jacksonian democratic vision, was simply unable to compete against the broad appeal of the log-cabin campaign.

On Election Day, the popular vote between Harrison and Van Buren was relatively close, or at least the closest tally in the popular vote since it was first recorded in 1824, with Harrison receiving just over 1,275,000 and Van Buren in the vicinity of 1,130,000 votes or approximately 53 percent to 47 percent (1840 marked the first election year in which any candidate for political office received over one million popular votes—four years earlier, Van Buren set a record with slightly over 760,000 popular votes, now substantially exceeded by both the winner and the loser of the 1840 campaign). A new third party, the abolitionist Liberty Party, managed to gain just approximately 7,000 votes for its candidates, James G. Birney, a Kentucky native residing in New York, and Pennsylvania's Thomas Earle. The Electoral College produced a more impressive decision, as Harrison enjoyed a landslide with 234 electoral votes against Van Buren's 60. Harrison carried twenty-one of the twenty-six states, including all the large states except Virginia, and significantly, the forty-two electoral votes won by the Whig ticket in Van Buren's home state of New York—a devastating blow to the president, who had well earned his reputation as a master politician by deftly navigating and, at least in the past, controlling the complexities of New York politics. Van Buren now became the third incumbent president to be denied a second term (John Adams and John Quincy Adams were the other two).

To everyone's dismay, thirty-two days after being sworn in as the nation's ninth president, William Henry Harrison died as a result of contracting a virulent strain of pneumonia, the onset of which was due, as many have believed and as legend still holds, to prolonged exposure to inclement weather during the inauguration, the result of an exceedingly protracted speech that Harrison delivered on that bitterly cold afternoon. Upon Harrison's death, Virginia's John Tyler became the first of eight vice presidents who would assume the office of the presidency upon the death of a president.

Additional Resources

Chambers, William Nisbet. "Election of 1840." In Arthur M. Schlesinger, Fred Israel, and William P. Hansen, eds. *History of American Presidential Elections, 1789–1968.* Vol. 1. New York: Chelsea House, 1985.

Cohen, Martin, David Karol, Hans Noel, and John Zaller. *The Party Decides: Presidential Nominations before and after Reform.* Chicago: University of Chicago Press, 2008.

Collins, Gail, Arthur M. Schlesinger, and Sean Wilentz. *William Henry Harrison: The American Presidents Series: The 9th President.* New York: Times Books, 2012.

Gunderson, Robert Gray. *The Log-Cabin Campaign.* Lexington: University of Kentucky Press, 1957.

Schlesinger, Arthur M., Fred Israel, and David J. Frent. *The Election of 1840 and the Harrison/Tyler Administrations.* Broomall, PA: Mason Crest Publishers, 2003.

Wilentz, Sean. "1840." In Arthur M. Schlesinger, Fred L. Israel, and David J. Frent, eds. *Running for President: The Candidates and Their Images.* New York: Simon & Schuster, 1994.

Campaign of 1844

Vice President John Tyler ascended to the presidency upon the death of President William Henry Harrison, just one month into Harrison's term. Tyler thus became the first vice president to assume the presidency as a result of the death of an incumbent president, an event that has occurred a total of eight times in American history as of this writing (in 1974, a ninth vice president, Gerald R. Ford, would assume the presidency upon the resignation of President Richard Nixon). The Whig Party had not only captured the White House with the Harrison-Tyler ticket, but they also dominated the 27th Congress (1841–1843), enjoying a thin majority in the Senate and a more comfortable majority in the House, and while they lost the House to the Democrats as a result of the midterm elections in 1842 that formed the 28th Congress, they retained their hold on the Senate. Hence for two full years, the Whigs held both the executive and legislative branches, and they continued to hold the advantage over the Democrats throughout Tyler's administration.

However, internal divisions in the party unexpectedly formed, quickly compromising its ability to govern as a cohesive majority party. The trouble began early, stemming in part from the discontent of that greatest of Whigs, Kentucky senator Henry Clay, who was nursing much bitterness for having been cast aside by the Whigs in their selection of General Harrison in the previous election, the bitterness no doubt amplified by the Whigs' victory that propelled Harrison, and not Clay, to the White House. In turning to Harrison in 1840, the Whig Party had, at least for the time being, turned aside the leadership of its most eminent statesman. Clay certainly must have felt that the presidency could have been his, had his own party invested more faith in him. As such, Clay desired to restore his leadership in the party and had planned to play a significant part in influencing the Harrison administration. He convinced President Harrison, in the brief time before he died, that Congress needed to be called into special session to aggressively press forward the Whig agenda, one that included elements of more traditional Whig policies—a national bank, high tariffs, etc.—thus signaling Clay's full return to Whig orthodoxy, to which he had seemed less devoted in the previous campaign. But Harrison's abrupt passing left the presidency to Tyler, whose own positions, it would soon become apparent, were not so fully aligned with those same Whig principles.

From the beginning of his presidency, Tyler's states' rights philosophy directly clashed with the Whig Party's support for a strong federal government. In particular, Tyler doubted the constitutionality of national banks (for some Whigs, still among their fundamental principles) and was thereby drawn into direct conflict with key Whig proponents of the bank. To the chagrin of Whig leadership, Tyler vetoed two consecutive bills aimed at chartering a new bank, this in an age when presidential vetoes were rare. Over the course of nearly four years, Tyler vetoed ten bills (four of them were pocket vetoes). Only Andrew Jackson, who vetoed twelve bills (seven pocket vetoes), exceeded that number, but those vetoes were employed by a two-term president over an eight-year period. The seven other presidents who had held office before Tyler vetoed among them a total of eleven bills; John Adams, Thomas Jefferson, and John Quincy Adams never used the veto at all, and Van Buren used the pocket veto one time. (The presidential veto would remain a rarely used procedure until the late 1860s and early 1870s, when President Andrew Johnson would nearly treble Tyler's number and, shortly after that, President Ulysses Grant would veto over ninety bills through two terms). Thus Tyler's comparatively liberal use of the veto (given the expectations of the times) seemed to his contemporaries an abuse of his executive office; and given that these vetoes were issued against congressional majorities mustered by his own party, they displayed the appearance of betrayal to the very party that had endorsed his vice presidency. From the very first veto, a groundswell began to gather against the president and for the leadership of Clay, and upon the second veto, Tyler was finished with the Whigs. Indeed, the Whig Congressional Caucus convened to officially declare the president *persona non grata*, rendering Tyler a man without a party. In effect, even though the Whigs won the White House with "Tippecanoe and Tyler Too" in 1840, before the end of 1841, they had lost it to an apparent political renegade. "His Accidency," as Tyler was called by his opponents (both within and without his own party), became increasingly isolated throughout his tenure in the White House.

It must be noted that Tyler's motivations may be more complex than his alleged attachment to non-Whig principles that made him appear to be a Democrat in Whig disguise. Edward P. Crapol has argued that Tyler's administration was more about the expansion of executive power and the extension of American territory than about states' rights and resistance to the national bank. However we understand it, it was clear that Tyler was abandoned by the party that gave him the vice presidency. With Tyler so quickly alienated from the leading members of his own party, Henry Clay naturally reassumed the mantle of the head of the Whig Party and thus reasserted himself as the Whigs' best choice for the presidency in the upcoming election. From the summer of 1841 onward, it was Senator Clay who was now clearly on track toward the Whig nomination for president in the 1844 election, the nomination that had eluded him in 1840 in favor of what appeared to have been a more "Jacksonian"—that is, a more charismatic and martial, and thus more boldly heroic—figure such as Harrison, or at least the somewhat incomplete perception of Harrison. General Winfield Scott, Senator Daniel Webster, and Supreme Court justice John McLean received some support for an 1844 nomination, particularly from antislavery elements in the party; but Clay's momentum was far too strong to deflect. By the summer of 1843, Clay had already received the official endorsement of thirteen state Whig nominating conventions, including major Electoral College powers New York, Pennsylvania, Virginia, and Massachusetts. By the spring of 1844, four more state Whig Party conventions threw in behind Clay.

Comfortable in the inevitability of his nomination and likely presidency, Clay, as early as 1842, retired from the Senate to his Kentucky estate to rest and wait. While there, he welcomed a visit from former president Martin Van Buren, who was at that time considered by most Democrats to be their clear front-runner for another run at the presidency. Van Buren, ever the practical politician, was seen in a far more favorable light now that at least some of the excitement stirred by the intense symbolism of 1840 had played out. He also retained the endorsement of his strongest political ally, the Great Man himself, Old Hickory, as well as other prominent figures such as Senator Thomas Hart Benton of Missouri and Van Buren's fellow New Yorker, Senator Silas Wright, one of his most loyal friends and a tireless campaign workhorse. Both Van Buren and Clay hoped to engage in a campaign that would steer clear of those volatile issues that were sure to ignite sectional antipathy, namely slavery and the closely related debate over the possible annexation of Texas, which was currently an autonomous republic having successfully won independence from Mexico in 1836. In a meeting of the minds, Clay and Van Buren were both determined to avoid those more divisive issues and agreed to emphasize traditional party differences, hewing close to less controversial issues and avoiding *ad hominem* tactics. But as fate (and other prominent politicians eager to advance their own careers) would have it, such cross-party choreography was not to be set in motion.

Even though Van Buren held the widest appeal within his party, he was not without challengers. Pennsylvania senator James Buchanan, a rising figure on the national stage, eagerly offered his services for the opposition, but his generosity was overshadowed by the reemergence of former vice president Richard M. Johnson of Kentucky, the other hero of the Battle of the Thames and a favorite of conservative Democrats. Having stolen Buchanan's thunder, Johnson saw his own re-ascendency quickly fade with the sudden appearance of Michigan's Lewis Cass, a former brigadier general (War of 1812) and secretary of war (succeeding John Eaton under President Jackson) and the current ambassador to France. Van Buren's front-runner position was not immediately threatened by these candidates, but the fact that they could arouse some interest early in the campaign season indicated that the Red Fox of Kinderhook was not invulnerable. And his most formidable intraparty rival had yet to enter the arena.

Meanwhile, Tyler's support in Congress continued to fade steadily, dwindling to a small minority by campaign season. The Senate and the Tyler White House were irreconcilably split, and Clay was now once again the undisputed leader of the Whigs. Even Tyler's cabinet deserted the ship, forcing the embattled president to reach beyond his nominal party to form a new cabinet. With the abandonment of Whig policy by the Tyler presidency, it became ever clearer to the Whigs that their true leader had been Clay all along. Animosity between Tyler and Whig members of Congress reached such a fevered pitch that a House committee drafted articles of impeachment against a president for the first time in American history. Nothing came of the threat, as Tyler was not impeached; but in drafting the articles against him, congressional leadership delivered a sharp rebuke and a final, irreconcilable break.

Initially, Tyler remained undaunted. Resigned to the recent ostracism from his erstwhile party, he sought new alliances, mainly with true believers in states' rights and more conservative figures from among the Democrats. But his new "friends" were hardly reliable, as they quickly took advantage of their new influence in the White House to promote their own self-serving gain. Tyler soon found himself without allies in either party. In an effort to restore his reputation and demonstrate his potential for bold statesmanship, Tyler began lobbying among Democratic Party leaders and insiders for the annexation of the Republic of Texas, a controversial and even risky proposition for a number of reasons, not the least of which was that the move surely meant war with Mexico. Tyler's motives were likely more than an attempt to merely recharge his political position and angle for reelection, as he was invested in the idea of westward expansion. By and large, the Democrats were divided on the issue. Some, like South Carolina's John C. Calhoun, were annexation enthusiasts, seeing in the addition of Texas the expansion and further fortification of slavery and the interests of the South in general. Others, such as former president Van Buren, quietly shared anti-annexation sentiments with a majority of Northern Democrats and Whigs. In truth, Van Buren was against immediate annexation, but he did not explicitly oppose the possibility of folding Texas into the Union in some distant future. As Van Buren still remained the favorite among Democrats, he continued to skirt the Texas question to avoid any intraparty cross-regional tension that might weaken his chances at a return to the White House. For Van Buren and his supporters, this meant an early nominating convention that would preempt the Texas question even before it could be raised. The "Texas faction," or "Texas men," as they were to be called, understanding this full well, pressed for a later convention, one that they hoped would be timed in such a way as to open the Texas question and force the nominee, whether it was Van Buren or any other candidate, to endorse annexation. Meanwhile, President Tyler's secretary of state, Abel P. Upshur of Virginia—whose loyalties were marked more by an association with Calhoun and his principles than any sense of fealty to Tyler—quietly crafted an annexation treaty that was to be signed by a special envoy from Austin upon the occasion of said envoy's arrival in Washington, DC. Tyler expected this move to propel him toward the Democratic nomination, but most of the "Texas men" were in fact lukewarm on the president in spite of his efforts on behalf of their cause; Calhoun actually was their man, and as such, the true threat to Van Buren's position had now finally come into full view.

An odd turn of events sealed President Tyler's fate. Secretary Upshur was killed in an explosion when a naval gun misfired during a firepower exhibition on the screw steam warship USS *Princeton*, a stunning accident that had also endangered Tyler's life and might have resulted in his death had he not chosen to remain below decks during the demonstration. When the explosion occurred, the president, most of his cabinet, and former First Lady Dolly Madison were among those aboard for a leisurely inspection tour down the Potomac. Among others, Colonel David Gardiner—the father, as chance would have it, of the president's future wife, Julia Gardiner Tyler—was also killed in the accident. In the wake of this tragedy, Calhoun was tapped to replace the late secretary, and from his new position he was able to strengthen his own political position and more evidently dominate the annexation movement, thereby sharpening his ambitions to move for the White House in the next election.

Meanwhile, Texas annexation as an issue was finding new allies within the Van Buren wing of the party, and Calhoun suspected that a public endorsement of a pro-slave state in Texas might soon come from his prospective opposition. Thus he delayed sending the treaty to the Senate for ratification, hoping to find a way to ensure the equation of annexation with the promotion of slavery. If he succeeded, he could chase northern support—and Van Buren—away from annexation and thus preserve the triumph for himself and his allies, a move that would work nicely against Van Buren while simultaneously strengthening southern influence at the convention. To do this, Calhoun let it be known that Great Britain, which had interests in an alliance with the Republic of Texas, had expressed support for the abolition of slavery in the Lone Star Republic, a development that, by extension, was viewed by Calhoun as a threat to slavery in the American South as a whole. Once annexation was conflated with the preservation of slavery, Northern politicians from both parties would withdraw all interest and support.

Thus Calhoun, while maintaining his commitment to the annexation of Texas, would nonetheless craftily use the issue to alienate antislavery/anti-annexation factions in the North and simultaneously strengthen his position among the powerful Southern bloc of the Democratic Party. Always a stalwart for the preservation of slavery, Calhoun was becoming an even more fervid apologist for the peculiar institution, a position that he was now attaching to an ardent portrayal of the South as the only dedicated bulwark preserving national integrity and political liberty against foreign interference. For Calhoun, Texas needed to be annexed both to strengthen the institution of slavery and to secure the integrity of the nation's standing in the world, particularly against a meddlesome Great Britain and the threat from Mexico; and all this had to be done without the participation of Northern politicians who could not be trusted to appreciate the need to preserve slavery. Calhoun's vigorous efforts led, in April 1844, to President Tyler's submission of a treaty to the Senate for ratification that would, if ratified, secure the annexation of Texas. Ratification was ultimately denied by the Senate, but the political effects of this "Texas Bombshell" reverberated throughout the following presidential campaign. Calhoun's tactics worked, and Van Buren abandoned the strategy that he had once privately agreed to with his rival Clay and no longer evaded the issues of annexation (and by implication, slavery). Now, as an act of conscience and against his proclivities for political electioneering and gamesmanship, he jeopardized his own chances for nomination by openly opposing annexation on principle. Clay also came out in opposition to annexation on behalf of the Whigs, although he would later vacillate upon realizing the political advantage gained in its support. It was now up to Calhoun and his pro-annexation faction to sell the addition of Texas to the American public in general. Meanwhile, President Tyler's role and influence continued to diminish even further as he was clearly overshadowed by his dynamic and powerful secretary of state.

By standing on principle, Van Buren, who still held his early advantage as the party's leading figure, had in effect denied himself another run at the White House. In correspondence with Congressman William Hammet of Mississippi, Van Buren wrote eloquently against annexation, "We have a character among the nations of the earth to maintain, and it has hitherto been our pride and our boast, that, whilst the lust of power, with fraud and violence in the train, has led other and differently constituted governments to aggression and conquest, our movements in these respects have always been regulated by reason and justice." The former president put the possibility of a second presidential term at risk in opposing the

Tyler-Calhoun treaty. Even though Van Buren did promise to support annexation if Congress enacted legislation for it, his public denunciation of annexation as a matter of principle was enough to lose support within the stronger elements of his party. Southern Democrats turned away from him in droves, and the strength of his Northern base was not enough to compensate for the loss. Virginia, which had provided support through the leadership of Van Buren's friend and political ally, the influential journalist Thomas Ritchie, a previous supporter of William Crawford and Andrew Jackson, and his "Richmond Junto," a political "machine" in the Old Dominion that had historically provided vital support for Van Buren and his "Albany Regency" (and thus sustaining, through loose alliance of two state political machines, the New York-Virginia axis that can be traced back to Thomas Jefferson, James Madison, and George Clinton), now suddenly and utterly abandoned Van Buren. Many Virginians were keen on immediate annexation, and thus their support for Van Buren evaporated overnight with the public dissemination of what appeared to be Van Buren's anti-annexation letter. Political leadership in Virginia now floated New York senator Silas Wright as a viable alternative to Van Buren at the top of the ticket in 1844. Wright, however, an old member of the Albany Regency, remained loyal to Van Buren and thus uninterested in taking his place as a candidate for the presidency. With Van Buren's fortunes rapidly declining and no one else appearing on the horizon, the way now appeared clear for Calhoun to step in and face Clay in the general election.

Had this then been the case, the election of 1844 would have pitted two of the century's more prominent American statesmen against each other, both of whom were former war hawks and allies during the Madison administration, and both of whom had already achieved legendary status in the annals of American statesmanship. But Calhoun's ambitions were in the end once again denied. Van Buren, despite his disappointment at the loss of his Southern supporters, especially the crucial support that he had once enjoyed in Virginia, was determined to fight on. He still held a thin majority among convention delegates, but he was short of the needed two-thirds majority under the convention rules currently in place, and his political influence was now irrevocably compromised by the sectional polarization that had set in. Nothing seemed guaranteed as the Democratic convention convened in Baltimore in May 1844, and yet Van Buren and his friends still dug in their heels, much to Calhoun's chagrin, and the secretary's earlier excitement over his prospects for the White House rapidly dissipated. He now realized that, owing to Van Buren's intransigence and the appearance of other more or less credible candidates diluting the field, his own nomination was becoming evidently unlikely. Uncharacteristically, the proud Calhoun, sensing that his moment was quickly evaporating, fell back on Tyler, more assertively supporting the very president that he had recently eclipsed.

President Tyler, bereft of support in either major party, convened a separate nominating convention to run as a third candidate under the "National Democratic" ticket, and thus he was no longer even on the margins of the Democratic Party. Colonel Johnson, by way of contrast, was determined to keep his name in play for either the presidency or the vice presidency, even though it was apparent that his nomination had now become a long shot. Even though Buchanan's candidacy had weakened, he held enough support to remain on convention ballots. Buchanan was cagey; he kept his name in the ring but avoided attacking Van Buren, and he even averred some degree of loyalty to the former president, an attitude that no doubt appeared too clever by half for many of the convention participants. Levi Woodbury, former governor of and senator from New Hampshire and secretary of the treasury under presidents Jackson and Van Buren, entered the pool as well, but it was Cass from Michigan who now seemed to pose the strongest challenge to Van Buren. Additionally, the anti-Van Buren faction managed to strong-arm the election of the convention's presiding officer, one of their own, Pennsylvania's Hendrick B. Wright, who was able to leverage his position against Van Buren as the convention proceeded. At one time having been clear on their front-runner, the Democrats, now in confusion with Calhoun's star fading and the rising tide flowing in against Van Buren, were ripe for the appearance of a dark horse.

Seven candidates were nominated for the first ballot: Van Buren, Calhoun, Cass, Buchanan, Johnson, Woodbury, and Charles Stewart, another Pennsylvanian and a naval war hero. Van Buren easily drew the most votes, carrying 146 of the 266 possible votes, or nearly 55 percent, with Cass landing a distant second place, receiving 86 votes. But the convention's two-thirds rule was a requirement that Van Buren, for all his political savvy, could not fill given the level of opposition. Former vice president Johnson finished third with 24. The extent of the sudden, dramatic slide for Calhoun was fully revealed through the mere 6 votes that he garnered on the first ballot. The second ballot offered the same 7 candidates, with Cass gaining 11 votes to bump to 94, Van Buren losing 19 to slip to 127. Buchanan and Johnson each took a total of 33 votes; Calhoun was down to one supporter from Georgia and joined Stewart at the bottom. With Stewart withdrawing on the third round, no candidate made any gains, with Van Buren continuing to slowly but steadily lose ground while no single rival really offered a credible challenge. Woodbury did not return for the fourth round, leaving five candidates in play, Cass finally closing the gap with Van Buren by gaining 105 votes to the Little Magician's 111. In round five, Cass managed to pass Van Buren by four votes, with Johnson and Buchanan receiving 29 and 26 respectively, Calhoun hanging on to his one supporter from Georgia. Cass managed to gain 9 more votes on the sixth ballot, but with 116 votes, he still fell far short of the 177 needed to win the nomination. The trend continued into the seventh ballot as Cass's total increased to 123 and Van Buren slipped to 99. The other candidates continued to remain distant also-rans. The mood of the convention was one of frustration, but a moment of levity was enjoyed when a delegate rose to propose a resolution to the stalled proceedings, calling for the unanimous nomination of General Andrew Jackson for the presidency, a jest that was met with a mixture of laughter and agitation as convention delegates grew anxious. The Ohio delegation was particularly vociferous and difficult to calm, forcing the convention into disarray and then adjournment for the evening in the wake of former president Jackson's perturbing "nomination."

By contrast, Clay had cruised easily to nomination at the Whig convention held a few weeks earlier. He received unanimous support on the first ballot, with the selection of his running mate going to New Jersey's former senator Theodore Frelinghuysen—well known for his strenuous opposition to the 1830 Indian Removal Act that was passed by Congress under the direction of President Jackson, who was at the time of his nomination for the vice presidency the president of New York University—after three ballots (winning over John Davis, Millard Fillmore, and John Sergeant). Given the news of the acclamation that Clay had received from the Whig Party, it was painfully obvious to the delegates present that a bold stroke was needed at the Democratic convention for fear that they could be decimated in the general election—thus a unifying candidate needed to be found and quickly, and none of the current names in the pool were able to deliver.

Keen on finding a solution, delegates Benjamin Butler of New York, Gideon J. Pillow of Tennessee, and George Bancroft, the renowned historian from Massachusetts, quietly laid plans to suggest Tennessee's James K. Polk, a former Speaker of the House of Representatives and governor of the Volunteer State and whose name had once already been mentioned for the vice presidency at the convention of 1840. Formerly a rising presence due in large part to his role in allying himself with President Jackson during his tenure in the House, in recent years Polk had been perceived as someone on his way out of politics; but he had recently managed an impressive political recovery following his failed gubernatorial reelection bid in the Volunteer State in 1841 and a subsequent frustrated comeback bid in 1843. Given his recent electoral defeats in his own home state, Polk seemed to most an unlikely solution; but Bancroft and an influential faction within the Massachusetts delegation were keen on the Tennessean and had actually been thinking of his name for the vice presidency even before the convention convened. Now he was viewed by Bancroft and Pillow, who also happened to be Polk's law partner, as a credible figure for the top of the ticket, and given the near crisis situation that the deadlocked convention was approaching, the timing seemed right. Bancroft lobbied delegates from New England, Ohio, and especially New York—Van Buren country—while Pillow drummed up support in the South and the Mississippi

Valley, helping to draw favorable attention to Polk and offer conventioneers renewed hope for a resolution. New complications arose when Silas Wright's name was once again floated, this time by Van Buren himself, who was considering withdrawing his own candidacy.

With Polk and Wright the new candidates under consideration, their respective supporters entertained the possibility of joining forces in an effort to advance either a Wright-Polk or Polk-Wright ticket. Yet there was some resistance to Wright, as his views on Texas were known to hew too closely to his friend Van Buren's, and it was the annexation issue, more than anything else, that was thwarting Van Buren's aspirations to return to the White House. On the eighth ballot, which was also the first to include his name, Polk won forty-four votes, and neither Van Buren nor Cass made any noticeable movement in either direction. Polk's candidacy was immediately seen as more viable than Johnson's or Buchanan's, and it had potential for support among the Van Buren faction, who appreciated Polk's past loyalties (namely his support of Van Buren in previous campaigns and his friendship with President Jackson), as well as the annexation men and other anti–Van Buren elements, who recognized in Polk a kindred spirit. With his appeal to both sides being apparent, Polk's star began to rise.

Going into the ninth ballot, Polk's supporters were optimistic, but as the voting began, considerable conflict remained. Things began to decisively shift in Polk's direction when Van Buren's camp conveyed its candidate's intent to withdraw, Old Kinderhook's supporters now finding Polk the most appealing alternative. Virginia, having earlier bolted from Van Buren, now came around to siding with his followers in support of Polk. New York, Van Buren's base, needed more persuading, but behind Butler's leadership, they became interested in Polk as well. Pennsylvania also came to Polk's support, and the tide was now carrying him toward victory. On the ninth ballot (the second since Polk's name was officially brought to the delegates), Polk took 243 votes to Cass's 29, with 2 Van Buren loyalists refusing to join the bandwagon. In light of this stunning dark-horse victory, the ninth ballot was "re-cast," this time all 275 delegates declared for Polk, giving him the same unanimity enjoyed by Clay, his Whig competitor. For vice president, the convention tapped Silas Wright on the first ballot, but he withdrew his candidacy as a show of allegiance to his old friend Van Buren, thus leading to a second ballot that produced a front-runner in Senator John Fairfield of Maine, who lacked the needed two-thirds support of the delegates (Colonel Johnson received 26 votes on this ballot); and so on a third ballot, the convention turned to George M. Dallas, among other things a former senator from Pennsylvania, who received 230 votes. The Polk-Dallas ticket moved forward to the general election to campaign against Clay and his running mate Frelinghuysen, two well-respected candidates who, by all indicators, promised to mount a strong effort.

President Tyler's desperate attempt to defend his incumbency through a third-party ticket came to no avail; his support quickly dissipated, and by late August, he withdrew his name from all consideration. Tyler's position was not without some leverage, as he held a degree of influence in the press and did hold the support of pro-business Democrats who were not without their own resources. But Tyler's main interest that summer was in his new marriage, and he was further persuaded to step down by former president Jackson, who worked to soften his determination at the behest of his friend Polk. The abolitionist Liberty Party repeated the nomination of its 1840 candidate, James G. Birney of New York (formerly of Kentucky and Michigan) and his running mate, Thomas Morris of Ohio. Little known to most Americans today, Joseph Smith Jr., the founder of the Church of Jesus Christ of Latter-day Saints (commonly known as the Mormon church), also declared for the presidency in an effort to promote what he called "theodemocracy," but his murder in June of the election year abruptly slammed shut that brief chapter of American political history.

Polk, or "Young Hickory," as he was known to many, adeptly provided the party with the unity that had recently eluded it, the party's more prominent members—Van Buren, Calhoun, Johnson, Cass, Buchanan, and Benton—all still harboring feelings that the White House remained in their respective futures. It was therefore evident to Polk that, even if he managed to win the White House in the contest against Clay, there remained a real possibility that he could face a powerful challenger from any one of these prominent names within his own party should he choose to run again during the election of 1848. Advised by associates to send a strong signal of deference to these influential figures among the party's elites, Polk declared almost immediately that he intended to serve only one term, promising that should he win the current campaign, he would not stand for reelection four years hence. From the outset, Polk was seen by his own party as a worthy albeit temporary compromise and one that might not win against Clay, but Polk's political mettle proved to be more than up to the task.

In the general campaign, Clay appeared to hold all the cards. A veteran politician and seasoned public servant, Polk was not without experience, but his name was not nearly as widely recognized as Clay's. The Democrats, still sporting scars from the strategically effective but substantively superficial "Log Cabin and Hard Cider" tactics employed by the Whigs against President Van Buren in 1840, openly called for a different approach and included among their convention statements of principle a resolution "That the American democracy place their trust not in factitious symbols, not in displays and appeals insulting to the judgments and subversive of the intellect of the people, but in a clear reliance upon the intelligence, the patriotism, and the discriminating justice of the American masses." No doubt it was a resolution sincerely made; but as the campaign unfolded, both sides, Whig and Democrat alike, fell back on the glamour of personality and sloganeering. Whigs scoffed at Polk's alleged obscurity with the prosaic slogan "Who is Polk?" (or, in some instances, "Who is James K. Polk?"), hardly a scintillating indictment but nonetheless evidence of the Whigs' dismissive tone in response to the Democrats' dark-horse candidate. Clay's campaign thus took every opportunity to depict Polk as inconsequential, a lightweight who happened to have the good fortune of knowing Andrew Jackson—a "blighted burr," complained Sergeant Prentiss of Mississippi, "that has fallen from the mane of the warhorse of the Hermitage" (i.e., Jackson). But like it or not, the Jackson-Polk connection worked in the Democrats' favor, the Old Hickory-to-Young Hickory lineage was proudly trotted out as frequently as possible by the Democrats, and any Whig efforts to belittle it only spoke to their own loyalists.

More seriously, the Democrats often ignored their own resolution and, taking the low road, went hard after Clay's character, accusing him of being "fiendish" and "vindictive," and worse still, an utter and "debauched" reprobate who had broken most of the Ten Commandments. Additionally, the old chestnut of associating any Whig candidate with aristocracy was recirculated. Clay was the favorite candidate, the Democrats claimed, of the European "crowned heads" eager to see American republican government undermined by despotic Whigs. Certainly not to be undone, Whigs responded by engaging in forgery, publishing an account (later to be known as the "Roerback Forgery") in an abolitionist newspaper published out of Ithaca alleging Polk's cruelty as a slave owner. Although the testimony against Polk's inhumanity was contrived and unproven, the best that the Democrats could offer in rejoinder was to claim that Polk was a "kind and humane master," not exactly a winning riposte from the vantage point of certain elements in the North who were more inclined to react to the phrase "humane master" with no small amount of derision. Democrats quietly circulated a pamphlet to Southern Whigs arguing that support for Clay would threaten slavery, but Whigs stumbled upon the document and circulated it in the North not only as evidence of the Democrats' cynicism, but also to further illustrate their alliance with the slaveholders of the South.

Additionally, another unseemly undercurrent became more visible as anti-immigrant and anti-Catholic attitudes began to infiltrate the election. Democrats were caught in a bind as they had, at least in the recent past, been more supportive of immigrant groups; but the anti-immigrant movement, which was closely tied to anti-Catholic prejudices (as many of the newer immigrants were Roman Catholic), was now drawing allegiance from both parties, threatening to add more toxins to the political culture already poisoned by slavery. Candidate Polk felt compelled to abandon the immigrants and fall silent on the issue if he was to retain support from the increasingly numerous and influential Nativists within his own party. Clay played both sides against the middle, as he supported the Nativists against the immigrants but at the same time formed a close alliance with Catholic archbishop John Hughes of New York, who himself had immigrated from Ireland as a young child and had gained a reputation for facing down Nativist intimidation. It was thus clear in the Campaign of 1844 that Nativism was dangerously on the rise.

Insults and prejudices aside, substantive policy distinctions were drawn. Not surprisingly, the sharp differences between the Whig Party and the Democratic Party over slavery and the annexation of Texas were the dominant (and interrelated) issues. Ironically, the Democrats, reputed defenders of states' rights and limited government, promoted the acquisition of new territories reaching to the Pacific; while their Whig counterparts, to add symmetry to the irony, adhered to their standard nationalist and governmental activist principles but cautiously eschewed continental and expansionist ambitions. The Whig Party and Clay saw the Texas annexation and slavery as inextricable and extremely divisive. Annexing Texas, it was clear to the Whigs, would certainly lead to a protracted and dangerous battle over the question of slavery in newly admitted states. And then there was the likely possibility that annexation would precipitate war with Mexico. Conversely, Southern leadership feared that any ban on new slave states would lead to the eventual abolition of slavery, which was to them a threat to the very social, economic, and cultural foundations of the South. In sharp contrast to the Whigs, Polk and many Democrats saw Texas annexation as a powerful **wedge issue** that could ensure their victory. Throughout his campaign, Polk espoused a position that would later come to be known as "manifest destiny" (a term actually coined by newsman and Irish American immigrant John L. O'Sullivan in 1845, the following year), in an effort to provide a moral justification for westward expansion (which of course included the annexation of Texas). To emphasize his point, Polk supporters made effective use of the laconic slogan "Polk and Texas, Clay and No Texas." Polk and the Democrats, to extend their expansionist vision, also demanded that the United States pursue its territorial claims in the Oregon Territory—a bold policy that could risk conflict with the world's greatest power at the time, Great Britain—but the fact that Oregon would, if successfully annexed, enter the Union as a counterbalancing free state was not enough to placate abolitionist opposition to the addition of Texas.

Whigs responded by contrasting the pro-slavery and expansionist attitudes of the Democrats to their own avowed dedication to liberty and union. Cassius M. Clay, the Whig candidate's cousin and an ardent Kentucky abolitionist, wrote that even though his cousin was not openly for "emancipation," he believed that his "feelings" were with the cause. He drew the contrast between "Polk, slavery, and Texas" on the one hand and "Clay, Union, and liberty" on the other. But candidate Clay did not embrace his abolitionist cousin's endorsement, and he was quick to disassociate himself from his cousin's position for fear of losing votes in the South.

This public repudiation of abolition boomeranged on Clay. Northern Whigs who were either abolitionists or at least sympathetic to emancipation protested. One Whig congressman, Seth Gates of New York, went so far as to describe Clay as being no less than "rotten as a stagnant fish pond" for his views on slavery, impugning as "diabolical" Clay's vaunted reputation as the Great Compromiser and predicting that Clay's "confounded" compromises would only lead to more slavery and ultimately to the future domination of "the lone star" in the Union's "galaxy" of states. Gates broke from the party and vociferously declared his support for Birney, the Liberty candidate. He was not alone among Northern Whigs in beating a path away from Clay's campaign. Uncharacteristically, Clay ineptly vacillated in addressing the question over Texas, and he was ridiculed for not taking a stand either way on the issue of slavery. Meanwhile, Polk retained his composure, maintaining a degree of consistency on the controversial issues (slavery, annexation, tariffs) that had escaped Clay. While Clay may have enjoyed the greater reputation as a statesman, in this instance Polk proved his superior in the way he conducted his campaign and in his unequivocal adherence to his principles.

Annexation and slavery, and to a lesser extent nativism, thus dominated the campaign, but the older issues, which Clay and Van Buren had previously hoped would shape the election, still lingered in the background, not far from view. The Whigs held to their pro-bank, soft currency position. The Whig platform advocated a protective tariff to bolster domestic industry and guard the interests of American labor from European (and especially British) competition, a tariff that Polk openly opposed in the forthright manner that seemed to be lacking in Clay's various positions. The Democrats, for the most part, maintained their traditional opposition to a national bank and stood firmly behind their hard money policy. Accordingly, the Democratic platform reaffirmed, in addition to resistance to abolitionism, their support for limited government, laissez-faire economic policies, governmental frugality, protection of presidential veto power, and further resistance to the chartering of national banks.

The election of 1844 turned out to be the closest since 1824. Polk and Dallas won 49.5 percent of the popular vote (just over 1,333,000) and carried 15 states with 170 electoral votes; their biggest victories came in New York (Van Buren's turf, delivering 36 electoral votes), Pennsylvania (26 electoral votes), and Virginia (17 electoral votes). Clay received a disappointing 48.1 percent of the popular vote (just under 1,300,000) and 105 electoral votes drawn from 11 states, Ohio's 23 electoral votes accounting for just over a fifth of his support. Significantly, Clay managed to win the slave states of Kentucky (his home state), Tennessee, and North Carolina. New York, with its huge bloc of votes, was decisive. A mere change of 2,554 votes in New York would have delivered New York's 36 Electoral College votes to Clay, thereby swinging the election, and at last the White House, to the Great Compromiser. In this instance, the presence of a third party proved the critical influence. Even though the Liberty Party only managed to receive 62,300 votes nationwide, in the state of New York, Birney, the Liberty Party's candidate, received 15,812, more than enough votes to influence the outcome between Clay and Polk in the Empire State and consequently in the general election as a whole. We cannot really know precisely where those votes would have gone if they had not been cast for Birney, but we can know that without the Liberty Party's third-party alternative in New York, Clay might have become president. If just 2,554 taken from the 15,812 Liberty Party votes (which amounted to only about 16% of the votes cast for the Liberty Party in the Empire State) had gone for Clay, New York would have gone to the Whig candidate. And if Clay had carried New York, his electoral vote total would have reached 141, while Polk's total would have fallen to 134. But New York went to Polk by a nose, thrusting him into the White House as the nation's eleventh chief executive, and dashing once and for all Clay's long-held presidential aspirations.

In the aftermath of the Campaign of 1844, President Polk would go forward to pursue the annexation of Texas, which as expected, meant war with Mexico. War fever with Great Britain also intensified. The slogan "Fifty-four Forty or Fight" (a slogan commonly but erroneously associated with Polk's 1844 election campaign) was coined in January 1846 and became the most frequent chant for Americans determined to secure the Oregon Territory from Britain. (The 54th parallel bordered what was then Russia's territory in North America and would have included much of British Columbia.) In the end, negotiations between Great Britain and the United States set the northern boundary of the United States at the 49th parallel. Before Polk left office in 1849, the United States had annexed Texas and had subsequently and consequently defeated Mexico in a brief war that stripped Mexico of all of its territory above the Rio Grande and guaranteed that the United States would stretch without interruption from the Atlantic to the Pacific.

Additional Resources

American Presidents Blog. http://www.american-presidents.org.

Bergeron, Paul H. *The Presidency of James K. Polk*. Lawrence: University Press of Kansas, 2008.

Cohen, Martin, David Karol, Hans Noel, and John Zaller. *The Party Decides: Presidential Nominations before and after Reform*. Chicago: University of Chicago Press, 2008.

Crapol, Edward P. *John Tyler: The Accidental President*. Chapel Hill: University of North Carolina Press, 2012.

Haynes, Sam W., and Oscar Handlin, eds. *James K. Polk and the Expansionist Impulse*. New York: Longman, 1997.

Holt, Michael F. *The Rise and Fall of the American Whig Party*. Oxford: Oxford University Press, 1999.

Our Campaigns. http://www.ourcampaigns.com.

Remini, Robert V. "1844." In Arthur M. Schlesinger, Fred L. Israel, and David J. Frent, eds. *Running for President: The Candidates and Their Images*. New York: Simon & Schuster, 1994.

Sellers, Charles. "Election of 1844." In Arthur M. Schlesinger, Fred Israel, and William P. Hansen, eds. *History of American Presidential Elections, 1789–1968*. Vol. 1. New York: Chelsea House, 1985.

Sheppard, Mike, "How Close Were U.S. Presidential Elections?" http://www.mit .edu/~mi22295/elections.

Campaign of 1848

Hunkers, Barnburners, Free Soilers, and "Old Rough and Ready" all entered the American political lexicon in the Campaign of 1848, a campaign that for the most part carried forward those practices and strategies that had been shaping electoral politics since the mid-1820s and that had taken firm root in the Whig's "Log Cabin and Hard Cider" campaign of 1840. By and large, the Campaign of 1848 does not exhibit any remarkable changes in the way campaigns were undertaken, but certain aspects of this campaign are noteworthy. Notably, the campaign season opened without the participation of the incumbent, President James K. Polk. Even before Polk won his party's nomination in the summer of 1844, he had formally declared his intent not to seek a second term. But even though he was a one-term president from the very beginning, he was hardly a lame duck. During his presidency, the United States annexed Texas, and it fought and won a sixteen-month war with Mexico. The victory led to the still further expansion of American territory. It include a vast territory, larger than Texas itself, that included what would eventually become California, Nevada, Utah, most of present-day Arizona, western New Mexico, the westernmost region of Colorado, and southwestern Wyoming. With the inclusion of Texas (which at that time contained not only present-day Texas but also a large region of territory in New Mexico as well as a significant section of Colorado and smaller portions of Wyoming, Oklahoma, and Kansas), the total territorial expansion under the Polk administration exceeds even the Louisiana Purchase acquired diplomatically by President Jefferson four decades earlier. Polk also managed to finally resolve the dispute with Great Britain over the Oregon Territory without going to war, this action further solidifying American expansion in the West and defusing a potentially disastrous situation in the Northwest.

Polk also, in working with Secretary of the Treasury Robert J. Walker (who happened to be his brother in-law), directed the passage of tariff legislation that at least temporarily reduced sectional tension over this ongoing domestic controversy (with the exception of slavery, the most volatile issue in the first half of the nation's history was the lingering argument over tariffs). Significantly, the immediate effects of Polk's tariff policy helped to improve relations with Great Britain, further alleviating the strain caused by the quarrel over Oregon. Additionally, the Independent Treasury Act, a legacy of the Van Buren administration, was resuscitated under Polk, offering a replacement to the national bank that President Jackson had assiduously worked to destroy. Under this legislation, the federal government could more effectively regulate certain elements in the economy (such as unbridled land speculation) without having to rely on the older Hamiltonian system that Democrats regarded as excessively centralizing and unduly beneficial to the interests of the wealthy. In a word, Polk's administration was widely viewed as a grand success, and yet the opportunity to retain Polk in the White House for another term was denied by a promise made four years earlier. No doubt Polk, who was actually a fallback choice for the Democrats in 1844, exceeded all contemporary expectations, and historians today rank him high, often among the ten best presidents in American history. To have such an accomplished president refuse to run for reelection after one term was unprecedented at the time and remains unique in the history of American presidential politics. (Later, incumbent president Theodore Roosevelt also did not stand for reelection in spite of his huge popularity and outstanding record, but owing to the assassination of President William McKinley, he had served out more than one term; as President McKinley died early in his second term, Roosevelt sat for nearly two terms, thus drawing a distinction from Polk in this regard.)

Polk's triumphs, however, were accompanied by grave problems, namely the further intensification of the most morally critical and dangerous issue in American politics: slavery. With the new territory that Polk secured for the growing nation, the issue over the future of slavery in these territories and in the republic as a whole was rekindled. Polk, himself a slave owner, opposed the Wilmot Proviso's prohibition against the expansion of slavery into what was called the "Mexican Cession." He desired to simply extend the Mason-Dixon Line dividing free states from slave states straight to the Pacific coast in the spirit of the Missouri Compromise, which meant the creation of an American Southwest that would likely resemble the Old South, fortifying slavery as a bicoastal, fully southern institution (what is now Arizona, New Mexico, Oklahoma, Southern California and the southern tip of Nevada would have joined Texas as those slave territories west of the Mississippi, and eventually states, under this arrangement). But impassioned elements in the North and South opposed such measures for predictable reasons. Polk's approach to the slavery issue did absolutely nothing to ease growing sectional animosities—a case can be made that the very success of his administration added fuel to the flames—and on this point, the Polk administration may have squandered an opportunity.

Furthermore, while the controversy over Oregon seemed from the perspective of many of Polk's contemporaries to have been reasonably solved, Northern Democrats felt that the added territory in the Pacific Northwest was not sufficient to counterbalance territorial expansion in the Southwest, with all the political, economic, and cultural implications therein. The Walker tariff, which was fairly popular (as the popularity of tariffs goes), did not fully appease industrialists in the Northeast. Hence Polk's administration, while commonly regarded as highly successful, even commendable in light of some of its significant accomplishments, was not without its limitations, mistakes, oversights, and critics. But for the most part, his contemporaries saw Polk as an accomplished president, a welcome surprise given his dark-horse status in 1844, thus further strengthening the Democratic Party's claims to an accomplished record of presidential governance, built on a legacy running from Old Hickory to Young Hickory through Old Kinderhook. That aside, history's conclusions about the management of the slavery crisis under Polk are difficult to ignore in the overall assessment of his administration's considerable achievements.

Without the incumbent Polk in the mix, the party turned to Senator Lewis Cass of Michigan, an experienced politician who had served in both the legislative and executive branches in a number of capacities as well as having distinguished himself as a war hero who had fought at the Battle of the Thames in the War of 1812 alongside William Henry Harrison (who had been elected the ninth president) and Richard M. Johnson (who had been elected the ninth vice president under President Van Buren). Lewis had been a candidate in the conflicted nominating convention of 1844 that produced candidate Polk, and thus he entered the convention in May 1848 as the principal contender. There was some competition against Cass during the convention from James Buchanan of Pennsylvania and New Hampshire's Levi Woodbury, two other holdovers from the 1844 contest; but unlike that convention, the eventual nominee, Cass, was more easily selected on the fourth ballot. Polk's vice president, George M. Dallas, was also available, but from the beginning, support for him was thin at best and, by the third ballot, had completely evaporated. Cass held a commanding lead from the first ballot, whereas in the convention of 1844, by contrast, the early front-runner, Van Buren, was unable to match his first-ballot support, and his standing declined with each ballot. Once the convention had decided for Cass, another veteran of the War of 1812 as well as the recent war against Mexico, Kentucky's William O. Butler was tapped for the bottom of the ticket, the delegates needing just two ballots in this instance.

Regarding the issue of slavery, Cass was an early proponent of what would come to be known as "popular sovereignty," or "squatter's sovereignty," the position holding that the states and territories were themselves responsible for deciding whether or not to allow or prohibit slavery. This position would later come to be more widely associated with Stephen Douglas of Illinois, but it was actually Cass's "Nicholson Letter," addressed to Tennessee's A. P. O. Nicholson and published in late 1847 in the *Washington Union*, that was likely the first formal affirmation of the doctrine, although Cass's friend Senator Daniel S. Dickerson of New York has also been credited as having originated the concept. In any event, this very letter may have led to his front-runner status as the convention approached in the spring of the following year. In the late 1840s, the Democratic Party was still divided over slavery, a division that mostly followed sectional lines. The Cass-Dickerson (and eventually Douglas) solution of "squatter's sovereignty," which would give all the authority (and responsibility) for the slavery issue to the states, seemed to many the most practical compromise at the time, although this position would later be utterly and forthrightly refuted by Douglas's great rival, Abraham Lincoln.

With the formal establishment of a new party, the Free Soil Party, the specter of slavery was brought into the foreground of presidential politics. Slavery had long divided both parties, and, as one would expect, generally but not necessarily along sectional lines. Outside the slaveholding states, the issue would divide the major parties in places like New York and New England. In the Democratic Party, an influential New York faction known as the Barnburners (who looked to former president and Bucktail Martin Van Buren for leadership) were open critics of slavery (and thus opponents of Cass's nomination), and they had been less than enthusiastic about President Polk. Meanwhile, conservative Democrats in the Empire State, known as the Hunkers, sympathized with the South and thus tended to evade or even repress the debate over slavery. Suffering the same intraparty divisions, the Whigs split into "Conscience Whigs" (eventually known as "Wooly Heads") who joined their Barnburner counterparts in criticizing slavery and "Cotton Whigs" who, as with the Hunkers, did their best to suppress interest in a slavery debate. These two Whig factions were primarily associated with New England. Charles Francis Adams (son and grandson of two presidents, John Quincy Adams and John Adams, respectively) and Charles Sumner numbered among the more prominent Conscience Whigs. Cotton Whigs, led by, among others, Edward Everett and Speaker of the House Robert C. Winthrop (both from Massachusetts), were sensitive to the reliance of the textile industry—which was located primarily in the Northeast—on the cotton plantations of the South. Thus, while Northern Cotton Whigs were not pro-slavery apologists of the variety found south of the Mason-Dixon Line, they were loath to make an issue of slavery and preferred to simply push it out of political discussion. Hence the antislavery Free Soilers attracted those supporters from both major parties who were disaffected from the mainstream over the inability or unwillingness to properly address slavery.

Along with the Liberty Party that had been established earlier, the Free Soil Party offered another alternative to those who sought either abolition—that is, those who gravitated to the Liberty Party—or at the very least the restriction of slavery to its current geographical range, which was explicitly the immediate goal of the Free Soilers. The Free Soil principle was encapsulated in the slogan "Free soil, free speech, free labor, free men," and while not demanding immediate or even gradual emancipation in the South, they insisted upon prohibiting the expansion of slavery, a policy that for many would eventually lead to slavery's gradual, peaceful extinction. The Free Soil Party was particularly important in Ohio, attracting Conscience Whigs who had been increasingly alienated by their party's lack of coherent principle regarding the issue of slavery. Ohio Whigs worked to overturn laws discriminating against free blacks in Ohio and managed to secure the election of Free Soiler Salmon Chase to the Senate. The Liberty Party was still active but had weakened considerably; hence the growing influence of the Free Soil Party gave antislavery voters some hope.

Among the complaints lodged by Ohio Free Soilers against the Whigs was their distaste over the Whig presidential candidate, General Zachary Taylor of Louisiana, during the campaign of 1848. As a result of his military exploits in the recent Mexican-American War, General Taylor enjoyed a level of popularity unseen since Andrew Jackson. Nicknamed "Old Rough and Ready" owing to his reputation for living under the same hard conditions that were experienced by his troops, Taylor first came to the public's attention for his meritorious record in the War of 1812 and then later as a renowned "Indian fighter," one who was known for not simply protecting settlers from hostile Native Americans but also for protecting the Native Americans from land-hungry settlers. But his real fame was created by his achievements on the battlefield during the Mexican-American War, particularly at the Battle of Buena Vista, where his contingent of approximately 4,800 Americans triumphed over General Santa Ana's much larger force of 22,000. Taylor's refusal to surrender to a superior force, combined with his own battlefield daring—exhibited in personally leading a charge on the enemy position that turned the battle in favor of the Americans—won for him the adulation of the American people. The triumph of Buena Vista was all the more remarkable in the wake of President Polk's wrath dealt against him in response to General Taylor negotiating, on his own authority, an eight-week armistice with Mexican forces at the resolution of the Battle of Monterey. As punishment, Polk reassigned all but five hundred of the professional soldiers under Taylor's command, leaving but a thin remnant to strengthen the now mostly volunteer force that he led into battle against Santa Ana at Buena Vista.

Buena Vista, Monterey, and another remarkable victory at Palo Alto fueled Taylor's legend; thus even as the war was under way, and much to Polk's growing disquiet back in Washington, Taylor's name was increasingly mentioned as a possible candidate for the White House. Hence this nonpolitical, lifelong soldier was suddenly in a position quite contrary to his habits, proclivities, and ambitions. Prior to the war against Mexico, he had never expressed any interest in politics, never affiliated himself with any party, and never held any political office of any kind at any level. Now he suddenly discovered that, based on his martial exploits alone, he was thrust onto the national political stage. He was a thoroughly apolitical figure; it is even said of him that at the time he ran for president, he had never voted in any election over the course of his life. He was intelligent but poorly educated, possessing enough charisma to lead men against long odds into deadly battle and yet incongruously cutting an unimposing, undistinguished figure under ordinary circumstances. In an age of eminent orators (e.g., Webster, Hayne, Clay, Everett, Calhoun, and Benton, among others), Taylor was an underwhelming public speaker. Yet he was a natural leader in spite of first impressions, and his military victories won for him the bona fide credentials of war hero. Many saw in Taylor the same qualities that were so appealing in Andrew Jackson and William Henry Harrison, a political type that seemed right for the moment animated by the enthusiasms of a war recently won.

Taylor fielded suggestions that he run for the White House with reticence. He was quick to admit that retirement was more appealing to him than presidential politics, and he mused that he would not refuse the office if the "good people were imprudent enough" to vote him into that position. Hardly an eager candidate, he waited for others to draft him into service rather than engage in typical campaigning. Whether this was a feature of his personality or coyly strategic is uncertain, but either way, it was clear that he had a loyal following. His lack of any real political allegiance proved to be an advantage; for two years prior to the campaign season of 1848, Whigs, Democrats, and Nativists at the local level forwarded to him their nominations for the presidency, which he willingly accepted without explicitly declaring his loyalty to any political party.

His ambiguous political principles aside, by the time of the opening of the Whig convention in Philadelphia, June 1948, Taylor was the party's front-runner, and he was well positioned for the nomination. Henry Clay, the Whig elder statesman from Kentucky and nominee in the previous election, was still very much a presence in the party and a main contender, even though his support had waned somewhat in the intervening years since the last campaign. As early as 1840, Clay was hampered by a record of defeat, at least at the presidential campaign level, losing in the famous four-way race against John Quincy Adams in 1824 and then being soundly trounced by Jackson in 1832. In spite of this, he won nomination from the Whigs in 1844, only to lose again to the dark horse Polk. Thus, even though Clay was the Whig Party's preeminent leader, he could not instill confidence among the delegates at Philadelphia. Another venerated Whig, Daniel Webster of Massachusetts, enjoyed some small allegiance in the party, particularly in the Northeast; but his opposition to the annexation of Texas and the war against Mexico diminished his chances. Another hero of the recent war, General Winfield Scott, who led the invasion force that eventually captured Mexico City, was also noticed as an alternative; but his public image—he was saddled with the unflattering nickname of "Old Fuss and Feathers"—was, to say the least, less compelling than "Old Rough and Ready" Taylor. As with the Democrats, four ballots were needed to settle the issue, and Taylor led from the outset.

Taylor's nomination, though fairly easy, was not without some controversy given that he owned over a hundred slaves. Northern Whigs in particular, who were naturally more inclined to support Clay or Webster, bristled at the sudden ascent of the slave-owning Taylor; but they conceded his national appeal given his war record and the association of his name with westward expansion. To allay this initial distaste for Taylor's slave-owning, the convention, embracing the commonly used North-South strategy, sought with even greater urgency to nominate a Northern candidate for the vice presidency. Abbott Lawrence, a longtime Clay supporter and former congressman from Massachusetts, and Millard Fillmore, state comptroller of New York, were the favorites, with Fillmore managing the nomination on the second ballot. Fillmore, long a Clay loyalist, was seen as an olive branch to the disappointed and long-frustrated Clay faction. On principle, Fillmore detested slavery and, through at least his early political career, was on record as favoring abolition. With the promise of higher office before him, however, he softened his tone and now even supported its continued existence in the South and possible expansion into the West. In an 1850 correspondence with Daniel Webster, two years after his nomination for vice president, Fillmore wrote, "God knows I detest slavery, but it is an existing evil, and we must endure it and give it such protection as is guaranteed by the Constitution, till we can get rid of it without destroying the last hope of free government in the world."

Between Fillmore and Taylor, the latter owning slaves in three states and who, quite typically, did not directly express any opinion regarding the expansion or containment of slavery as an issue, the Whig Party managed to strike a precarious balance between Northern and Southern Whigs. However, it should also be noted that Taylor did hint, somewhat unexpectedly, that he would not veto the Wilmot Proviso, an admission that raised some concern among Southern Whigs. If one looked closely enough, it could be observed that Taylor quietly favored the policy of limiting slavery to those states that presently allowed slavery. He saw no reason to institute slavery in areas where sugar and cotton were not major crops. Taylor's official views on slavery were thus somewhat obscured, but not entirely. Yet during the campaign, most Southerners believed that Taylor fully supported, as it would seem that any slave owner naturally would, the expansion of slavery into the new western territories. The Whig Party as a whole, on the other hand, evasively remained opaque on the controversy, deciding not to issue any official position on slavery.

In 1848, in the wake of the Mexican Cession, the conflict over slavery became larger and more intense than either major party could manage, and thus serious fissures opened in both parties along sectional lines. Consequently, more voters turned to Free Soil, which had become a haven for New York Barnburners, New England abolitionists, and disenchanted Conscience Whigs, and others who were dissatisfied with the fresh opportunities for expansion now enjoyed by the proponents of slavery owing to the addition of the new western territories. Significantly, and to the astonishment of some, the Free Soil Party that very August nominated former president and erstwhile Democrat Martin Van Buren as its candidate for president, with Charles Francis Adams, a leading Conscience Whig, tapped for the vice presidency. Van Buren and Adams were an unlikely pairing: Van Buren ran for the position of Andrew Jackson's vice president on the 1828 ticket that trounced the incumbent president, John Quincy Adams, Charles Francis Adams's father. Van Buren was a major mover and shaker in Democratic politics, at first for the state of New York during his years as a Bucktail and then as leader of the Albany Regency machine, and then later on the national stage. Adams was a lifelong abolitionist and occasional outsider who had previously been critical of Van Buren's reticence to address the Peculiar Institution. But Adams had also enjoyed some political success at the state level, and he brought with him to the ticket an impressive mind and one of the more distinguished American political lineages.

Like so many politicians at the time, Van Buren's views of slavery were complicated and prone to change. It was clear that, as with Fillmore, he considered slavery immoral. But when he was president, he did not challenge the institution, and like others, he preferred to leave the issue to be resolved by the states. Yet with the addition of expansive territories in the West, the issue was transformed, often pushing politicians more unequivocally to one side or the other. Van Buren seems to have been pushed toward a more forthright antislavery position after the events of the mid-1840s, and he joined the Barnburners in abandoning the Democrats for Free Soil. It should be noted that not a few historians question Van Buren's sincerity. Given his reputation for political maneuvering, assumptions are made, rightly or wrongly, about Van Buren's willingness to take positions that open opportunities. Others suspect Van Buren of even darker motives, such as a desire to exact revenge on the Democratic leadership that had rejected him in 1844 in favor of the lesser-known Polk, as well as retaliation against allies of Polk for undercutting the New York gubernatorial reelection of his friend Silas Wright. While it is difficult if not impossible to confidently plumb a person's interior motivations, these somewhat judgmental interpretations of Van Buren's political moves seem flawed. Given his political savvy, it is unlikely that he would risk his best chance at regaining the White House—that is, his leadership in the Democratic Party, which was in a position of strength due to Polk's success and wherein he still held some influence—without good reason, and a principled stand against slavery can be counted as one of them. The second interpretation of Van Buren's motives, revenge, while appealing to some, seems even less likely, as such a clumsy effort would have been incongruent with his shrewd command of political tactics. Only if his reputation as a magician in the public arena was undeserved would either of these explanations make sense, and it is unlikely that his contemporaries would be so wrong in their assessment of him. Ultimately, Van Buren's defection to the Free Soil Party is just as likely to be based on principle as it is to be evidence of cunning, and perhaps even more likely. At any rate, the election campaign was to assume a new shape with the entrance of a third-party candidate who brought considerable political loyalty, clout, experience, and expertise to the contest.

However, by today's standards the campaign was low-key, and even compared to the previous campaigns, it was somewhat mild. None of the candidates toured the country in the fashion of politicians at the national level today. The balance of the campaigning was handled by local surrogates, all loosely organized by the national party. Rallies for candidates were usually led by local and regional politicians of note. For the Whigs, William Seward of New York and Thomas Corwin were prominent campaigners on behalf of General Taylor in the North, with John J. Crittenden of Kentucky and Alexander H. Stephens as major figures working the South (Crittenden and Stephens were known in Whig circles as the "Young Indians"). For Cass, Democrats fielded the likes of Douglas of Illinois, William Allen of Ohio, and from the newly added state of Texas, Sam Houston. Van Buren's son John (nicknamed "Prince John" for the sole reason of having once danced with Queen Victoria) was active on the campaign trail, particularly in the North and Midwest. Ohio was particularly important, as it was decided by fewer than six thousand votes, with eight thousand going to the Liberty Party. Hence the campaign surrogates were commonly found stumping hard in the Buckeye State. With growing sympathy for Free Soil principles in Pennsylvania, the Keystone State, which had gone for Polk in 1844, was also seen as in play. But not only the slavery issue was on the minds of Pennsylvania voters; tariffs were also still a deep concern, and the industrial and mining strongholds of the Northeast, and especially Pennsylvania, were drawn to the Whigs in spite of doubts (real or imagined) about Taylor over slavery. In 1848, concerns over the effect of tariff policy over mining and manufacturing were strong enough to eclipse slavery in some corners such as Pittsburgh, and figures such as Thaddeus Stevens, who later would become an abolitionist firebrand, backed Taylor and the Whigs to protect their region's economic interests. New Orleans, for another example, was singular among southern cities in favoring protective tariffs and thus was given further cause to back Taylor.

In Illinois and Indiana, Whig projects directed at internal improvements, such as excavating canals, had resulted in unexpectedly high costs, thus throwing state finances into debt. In response, the Democrats grew in strength in these midwestern states out of economic dissatisfaction, while the Whigs struggled there for viability. Slavery was without doubt the elephant in the room, but numerous other large creatures also noticeably cluttered the policy arena.

Throughout the campaign, the numerous surrogates effectively spoke to the qualifications of the candidates they championed, the actual issues often being pushed to the background. In some cases, the success of the candidate relied heavily on the kind of connections he had in a particular part of any given state. It is not that the issues disappeared—slavery was certainly foremost in everyone's mind, whether they admitted it or not—but rather that, in the case of Taylor, whose positions were unformed or unclear, character was uppermost in the minds of the voters. Examples of this include, in the case of Cass, his record of public service (both military and political), and for Van Buren, his familiarity as a former president. Taylor in particular went about his affairs as if there were hardly a campaign under way at all, casually attending the occasional ceremony as a featured speaker but scarcely even mentioning the race for the presidency. In spite of Taylor's relaxed, almost nonchalant approach and the comparatively calmer atmosphere when compared to more heated battles such as those that had occurred in 1828 and 1840 (and even 1844), the campaign was not without its more dramatic moments. For example, Alexander Stephens, campaigning for Taylor in Georgia, was wounded by a knife-wielding Democrat. Allegations of financial misconduct were aimed at Taylor, who managed to brush them off with his dignity intact. The campaign was riddled with intraparty squabbles in various localities (usually dissatisfied with the candidate or disaffected because of positions, or lack thereof, regarding slavery), and anti-immigrant/anti-Catholic nativism, which had plagued the **Campaign of 1844**, surfaced in Pennsylvania.

When the votes were cast, Taylor won just under 1,400,000 popular votes or approximately 48.3 percent, which gave him 163 electoral votes, or 56 percent of the Electoral College total, thereby winning for him the presidency. Cass won just over 1,220,000 votes, taking 127 in the Electoral College. (South Carolina, alone among all the states, appointed its electors through the state legislature.) Van Buren's Free Soil effort managed slightly over 291,000 votes, a full 10 percent of the electorate (quite high for a third-party candidate), but it won him no votes from the Electoral College. In his home state of New York, Van Buren did out-poll Cass (surpassing him by over 6,000 votes) as well as in both Massachusetts (beating Cass by a margin of almost 3,000 votes) and Vermont. He polled over 35,000 votes in Ohio, a state that Cass won by 16,000 votes, thus inadvertently helping the Democrats avoid another close call there. Without modern tracking techniques, it is hard to draw firm conclusions, but a third party gaining a percentage of the popular vote reaching into double digits, however so slightly, is usually a significant factor in any presidential campaign.

Taylor won the election despite personally investing little effort. And yet it was clear to anyone that governing the nation burdened by the slavery crisis would take a monumental effort if any peaceful, just, and enduring resolution was to be found and applied. Taylor's administration was never fully tested in this regard, as the president passed away just sixteen months into his term. As it turned out, the only two Whigs ever to be elected to the presidency, Taylor and William Henry Harrison, died in office. With the death of Taylor, Millard Fillmore, born into a poor family at the turn of the century, was to become the thirteenth president, only to find himself fully immersed in those crises over the country's principles and purposes that would continue to deepen cross-sectional mistrust and domestic animosities. And it would only continue to get worse.

Additional Resources

Boller, Paul F., Jr. *Presidential Campaigns.* New York: Oxford University Press, 1984.

Cohen, Martin, David Karol, Hans Noel, and John Zaller. *The Party Decides: Presidential Nominations before and after Reform.* Chicago: University of Chicago Press, 2008.

Hamilton, Holman. "Election of 1848." In Arthur M. Schlesinger, Fred Israel, and William P. Hansen, eds. *History of American Presidential Elections, 1789–1968.* Vol. 1. New York: Chelsea House, 1985.

Holt, Michael F. *The Rise and Fall of the American Whig Party.* Oxford: Oxford University Press, 1999.

Miller Center of Public Affairs, University of Virginia. "Zachary Taylor (1784–1850." http://millercenter.org/president/taylor. Accessed December 18, 2015.

Potter, David M. *The Impending Crisis 1848–1861.* New York: Harper & Row, 1976.

Silbey, Joel. *Party over Section: The Rough and Ready Campaign of 1848.* Lawrence: University Press of Kansas, 2009.

Troy, Gil. "1848." In Arthur M. Schlesinger, Fred L. Israel, and David J. Frent, eds. *Running for President: The Candidates and Their Images.* New York: Simon & Schuster, 1994.

The White House. https://www.whitehouse.gov/1600/Presidents.

Campaign of 1852

During the late 1840s, the growing dispute over the future status of slavery in new states and territories continued to erode the strength of the Union. To prevent further decay, Congress, under the leadership of the Great Compromiser, Senator Henry Clay of Kentucky, and the Little Giant, Stephen Douglas of Illinois (who served an important role in assuming the reins of leadership toward the end of the process due to Clay's failing health), promulgated a sequence of five bills that constituted the Compromise of 1850. Clay, in response to antislavery legislation proposed before the House of Representatives by Congressman James Tallmadge Jr. of New York, had been an instrumental actor in forging the Missouri Compromise of 1820, under which slavery was prohibited in the territories of the Louisiana Purchase above the latitude demarcation of 36°30′ N and thereby left alone below the line, with the exception of the state of Missouri (with a southern border defined at 36°30′ N), admitted as a slave state in conjunction with the admission of Maine as a free state. At this compromise, the Union was balanced between twelve free states and twelve slave states, and the future admission of states followed this balancing rule. Arkansas (slave) and Michigan (free) were admitted in 1836 and 1837, respectively, followed in 1845 by two slave states, Florida and Texas (the annexation of Texas precipitating the war with Mexico and the consequent Mexican Cession), and two free states, Iowa and Wisconsin, in 1846 and 1848. Thus the Missouri Compromise successfully choreographed the equilibrium sought by Clay in 1820, restricting slavery to the South without weakening the influence of southern states compared to the North, a balance that was particularly important to the composition and actions of the U.S. Senate.

However, as the Campaigns of 1844 and 1848 illustrate, with the annexation of Texas and the subsequent Mexican Cession, debates over the expansion of slavery were renewed, intensified, and sectionally polarized. Both Southern and Northern politicians saw in the new territories ample opportunity to strengthen their respective positions, and abolitionists and pro-slavery apologists—including the radicalized Fire Eaters, a militant but vocal minority of Southern pro-slavery extremists who were already calling for secession as early as 1850—grew increasingly more active. Abolitionist activists demanding immediate and unconditional abolition, such as William Lloyd Garrison, were more than happy to let the slaveholding states go if it meant a Union rid of the curse of slavery. Thus by the late 1840s, division and cross-sectional distrust were intensifying.

Under the new compromise, Congress agreed, by a vote of 150 to 56, to admit California as a free state and end the slave trade, but not slavery itself, in the District of Columbia. In return, Congress enacted legislation requiring citizens of free states to return escaped slaves to their Southern masters. Additionally, Texas forfeited land claims in the far West (in territory that is now included in eastern New Mexico, central and southeastern Colorado, and portions of Wyoming, Oklahoma, and Kansas) and agreed to its current borders; in return, the state of Texas received monies to pay off the debt it had accrued during its brief period of political independence. Finally, and more controversially, the compromise left it up to the citizens of the new territories (i.e., the New Mexico Territory and the Utah Territory) to resolve for themselves the free state/slave state issue (under the principle of "popular sovereignty"). The compromise temporarily defused the situation, allowing more moderate voices to tame secessionist sentiments. But animosities lingered, and tensions, while somewhat mollified, nonetheless continued to stew just below the surface.

Political allegiances were shifting. In the South, supporters of the compromise crossed party lines to establish the "Union" coalition, while opponents from both parties converged around "States' Rights" candidates. In the North, the Free Soil Party remained an alternative home for opponents of slavery and, in particular, a refuge for disenchanted Whigs. By and large, the Free Soil Party displayed some influence in the North, most notably in Ohio, Pennsylvania, and New York; but for the most part, they were unable to build on the promise of the previous campaign, and thus their influence on the national stage remained marginal. Most Northerners seemed less willing to abandon their main party allegiances, and the efforts of the more fully committed abolitionists were undertaken well beyond the institutional parties. Nonetheless, the Whig Party was divided over slavery, with one faction, led by New York senator and former governor William Seward (the "Seward Whigs" or "free soil" Whigs—not to be confused with the independent Free Soil Party) and newspaperman Thurlow Weed, also of New York (a former anti-Mason who also had some political experience), becoming more influential in determining the course of the party's presidential ambitions. Seward and Weed were less interested in Clay's vision of the "American System," which had defined the Whig Party since its inception, and more interested in promoting a "free soil" agenda within the Whig organization. In this way, the Whig Party might accomplish more effectively what the smaller and more issue-confined Free Soil Party was unable to do given its status as a minor party.

It was within this potentially volatile context that the presidential campaign of 1852 commenced. The incumbent, President Millard Fillmore, who was elected as vice president in 1848 and had assumed office upon the death of President Zachary Taylor (now, after Virginia's John Tyler, the second vice president to ascend to the presidency), stood as the logical candidate for nomination for a second, full term; but his level of commitment to a second, full term was low and marked by the kind of indifference characteristic of candidate Taylor in 1848. There were supporters for a Fillmore candidacy in 1852—indeed, they had persuaded him not to withdraw his name upon hearing the news that his secretary of state, Daniel Webster, had announced his intention to run—but they were counterbalanced by the Seward Whigs, whose leader disliked Fillmore and tilted against the incumbent's nomination. This would have finished Fillmore had it not been for an endorsement from the party's eminent statesman, Clay. His health growing progressively worse, the venerable senator threw his full support behind the president. With the Great Compromiser leading one faction and the "free soil" Whigs coalescing around Seward's animosity toward Fillmore, the Whig Party began to splinter and drift apart.

As the Whig convention convened in Baltimore in June 1852, three serious candidates were under consideration: Fillmore, Webster, and General Winfield Scott. Seward and his allies backed Scott owing to his antislavery sentiments, and Southern "Union" Whigs preferred Fillmore, at least initially. Webster, in spite of his many talents, was the weakest of the three leading candidates. He was, however, still regarded as a viable alternative—the only viable alternative—candidate for the two leading factions behind Fillmore and Scott, and this fact kept his name in the pool. At one point during the convention balloting, Fillmore supporters offered to back Webster against Scott if Webster could bring at least 41 more votes to the table. Webster was unable to muster more than 32 on any given ballot, and thus the offered votes, and the nomination, remained out of reach. Fillmore managed 133 votes on the first ballot but was short of the 146 needed to gain the nomination. Scott was close with 131, Webster's total a meager 29 by comparison. Most of Fillmore's support in the initial balloting was from the South, with only 18 votes cast for him from Northern delegates. So began a seemingly endless sequence of ballots far exceeding even the deadlocked Democratic convention of 1844, with Fillmore and Scott, the two front-runners, unable to reach the needed majority through a tedious 52 ballots. Finally, Scott managed 159 votes on the 53rd ballot to 112 for President Fillmore and 21 for Webster. Fillmore's strength in the South was sustained, where he continued to dominate, winning all but 17 southern delegates; Scott, by contrast, won all but 11 delegates from states north of the Mason-Dixon Line. The secretary of the navy, William A. Graham of North Carolina (both a former governor and a former senator from the Tar Heel State), was unanimously nominated for vice president on the first ballot.

Rumors were floated about that Scott's victory was finally secured due to a secret "bargain" with Southern voters in which Scott—contradicting his antislavery attitudes—finally agreed to a party platform demanding strict enforcement of the Fugitive Slave Law; but while somewhat plausible given the frustrations of the convention, evidence for a prior bargain is thin. Scott did, however, publicly endorse the platform in its entirety once it was in place, a fact that alienated the antislavery wing of the Whig Party. Scott was in a bind: on the one hand, the antislavery faction that had initially been attracted to him now harbored second thoughts, given his recent embrace of a platform that compromised with pro-slavery elements; and on the other hand, the Southern wing of the party was suspicious that Scott was a vassal of Seward and the "free soil" Whigs. But in reality, many of the "free soil" Whigs were through with Scott after his unqualified endorsement of the platform, and they bolted to the Free Soil Party in support of its nominee, Senator John P. Hale of New Hampshire, and his running mate, Indiana congressman George

Washington Julian. For his part, President Fillmore, after having been rejected by his own party, nonetheless encouraged all Whigs to now rally behind their new nominee, General Scott. Webster, however, was less cooperative, suggesting to some of his close supporters that they might prefer to vote for the Democratic candidate. As events would have it, Webster himself would not live to see the outcome of the general campaign, as he would pass away just days before the general election, having suffered a mortal head injury, the result of a fall from his horse.

The Democratic Party faced similar divisions. Union Democrats and states' rights Democrats competed for allegiance in the South, with a "free soil" faction, consisting of New York Barnburners and antislavery elements in New England and Ohio, emerging among Democrats in the North. Notably, these "free soil" Democrats included former president Martin Van Buren of New York and Pennsylvania's David Wilmot, author of the controversial Wilmot Proviso. Hunker Democrats (prominent in New York) continued to avoid the slavery problem and focused instead on what had now become less controversial issues, namely banks and internal improvements; although some members of the Hunker faction, notably New York's William L. Marcy (former senator and governor as well as secretary of war under President Polk), did seek reconciliation with antislavery Barnburners. Thus the party needed a candidate that would appeal to an increasingly fragmented and divisive rank and file. Initially, the party's nominee from the previous election, General Lewis Cass, appeared to be the best solution. As one of Michigan's more prominent politicians, his true base was in the Midwest; but Hunkers and Southern Unionists also supported him, which provided him with a disciplined base but provoked resistance from Barnburners, Southern states' rights Democrats, and other, less conservatively minded factions. However, Cass was seventy years old and not as active in pursuit of the nomination as his followers were on his behalf; thus his early advantage as front-runner proved evanescent. Even in the West, his candidacy was vulnerable, for a younger and more dynamic person, the promising Stephen Douglas, was on the ascent in the Midwest and rapidly gaining a national reputation. Some Cass supporters looked elsewhere and found a promising alternative in Marcy, who had gained respect from within the Barnburners in spite of his Hunker associations.

More significantly, Pennsylvania's James Buchanan, who had previously been under consideration at the party's conventions in 1844 and 1848, was now in his best position yet to finally make a serious play for the nomination. A conservative Democrat like Cass, he was equally experienced in public life and perhaps, at least at this time in their respective careers, even better connected. His support of the Compromise of 1850 and his criticism of the Wilmot Proviso made him appealing in the South but won him enemies closer to his home base. His following was more numerous than his critics, but the latter were vocal and strident in their enmity toward him. Hence Buchanan, while credentialed and connected, was not at the time the obvious solution. Joining the contest was another veteran of previous attempts to win the Democratic nomination, New Hampshire's Levi Woodbury. Woodbury was neutral on the issue of slavery and thus would not arouse any distrust from the more polarized cohorts, and he seemed to many at the time a less divisive figure than either Cass or Buchanan. In 1851, a year out from the general election, Woodbury seemed to be in the best position; however, he passed away in September 1851, leaving the field to Cass, Buchanan, and Marcy, whose popularity began to eclipse Cass's as the New Year approached. A much younger and considerably more energetic Douglas began to draw more serious attention in the West, but his initial appeal was damaged by his aggressive personality, controversial ownership of a number of slaves who came to him through marriage (weakening his appeal in the North), and his youth. At age thirty-eight, he lacked the air of experience that was wanted in a president, particularly given the gravity of the issues at hand. As youthful as he was, Douglas was already a force in the party, but he was not yet ready for the national stage.

Additionally, Samuel Houston, formerly a president of the Republic of Texas and at that time senator from the state of Texas, began to draw interest as a potential national candidate in the mold of Jackson, Harrison, and Taylor. In the latter weeks of 1851, some Democratic leaders found him an appealing alternative to Cass (for whom he had campaigned in 1848), with Andrew Johnson of Tennessee even going so far as to confidently remark that Houston was the emerging frontrunner. Houston appeared to be an active candidate, as he had become a popular speaker at public events in the North and had even been inducted into the Tammany Society in New York. And yet, in spite of his high visibility as a popular and busy orator bearing an interesting personal biography, Houston did little to formally promote his candidacy, and interest from the party establishment soon declined. Moreover, like Douglas, he drew some animosity from certain quarters, in spite of his evident qualities. Even though Texas was considered a southern state, his support in the South was diluted by those who regarded him to be more of a nationalist than a sectionalist. It became clear by early 1852 that Houston would not draw the cross-sectional support he would need to carry forward Jackson's legacy. With Woodbury's untimely demise and no single candidate captivating the party on the national level, the Democrats were in flux.

Woodbury had been the favored son of New England, and many among the political leadership in that region, eager to see another New Englander in the White House (John Adams and John Quincy Adams having been at that point the only two from that part of the country), sought a replacement. They turned to Franklin Pierce, the forty-seven-year-old former senator from New Hampshire who had served as a colonel and brigadier general in the Mexican-American War, suffering a leg wound at the Battle of Contreras. Because of Pierce's comparative youth, he was initially considered as a candidate for the vice presidency; but as the weeks progressed and a strong front-runner for the top of the ticket failed to materialize, Pierce came into view as a possible contender for the presidency. Pierce himself declined consideration, but he quietly kept his name available to the delegates if the convention needed him as a last resort.

From its very commencement, the convention was divided and deadlocked, and the stage was arranged for a repeat of 1844—the emergence of a dark horse. Cass led on the first eight ballots, at one with as many as 119 votes, followed by Buchanan peaking at 95, Webster winning as much as 34, Marcy holding just over two dozen, and Houston and Joseph Lane of Oregon (former general and acting governor) each winning a handful of votes. On the tenth ballot, Cass began to noticeably decline while Webster rose to gain, at one point, as much as 80 votes. Buchanan was making the most progress, boosting his numbers to 104 by the twenty-second ballot, but it was still far below the 197 needed to win the two-thirds required majority. That was Buchanan's high mark; Douglas continued to charge forward as Buchanan now faded. At one point, Douglas won 92 votes; this provoked alarm among his enemies, who turned back to Cass, restoring him to the front-runner position with 123 votes, a turn of events that now raised the hackles of Cass's enemies. The convention began to experience wild swings in voting, some votes being cast in loyal support of a candidate, others simply to oppose a candidate they disliked. At one point, Marcy's support shot upward, and he found himself taking the lead with 97 votes on the forty-fifth ballot, increasing to 98 two ballots later and holding a slim lead for four ballots.

With no end in sight, Pierce's supporters began the drumbeat for their man. His name was first offered on the thirty-fifth ballot, immediately winning 15 votes, but he did not gather as much support as he had hoped, holding steady at 29 votes from the thirty-seventh ballot forward. But on the forty-sixth ballot, more delegates began to turn their interest toward him, so that by the forty-eighth ballot, he had gained solid support not only in his native New England, but also in Kentucky, Virginia, Maryland, and even Pennsylvania, cracking into Buchanan's home delegation. Marcy still led after the forty-eighth with 89 votes, Cass having slipped back to 72 and Pierce rising to 55. North Carolina and Georgia fell in behind Pierce on the forty-ninth ballot, thus demonstrating Pierce's appeal deeper into the South. North Carolina's delegate, James C. Dobbin, then stepped forward to deliver an impassioned and persuasive speech on Pierce's behalf, a moment that became a turning point for the Pierce effort. Delegations were thrown into confusion, previous allegiances were dissolved, and with New York's declaration for Pierce, the remainder of the state delegations mounted the bandwagon. All support for Marcy vanished, and delegates behind Buchanan abandoned their candidate. Announcing the results of the forty-ninth ballot, convention chair John Wesley Davis reported, "Cass 2, Douglas 2, [William O.] Butler 1, Houston 1, Franklin Pierce (God bless him) 282 votes." In just two ballots, the convention selected Alabama senator William Rufus King for the second spot on the ticket, following the long-established custom of providing the ticket sectional balance.

The more ideologically fixed wings of the Democratic Party, utterly dissatisfied, formally split from the Democratic Party, the states' rights wing forming the Southern Rights Party, which nominated Georgia's George M. Troup for president and John A. Quitman for vice president. The Union Democrats, unaware of the fate that awaited him, nominated Webster along with Charles Jenkins of Georgia. In the end, these factions had little effect on the election itself, but their withdrawal drew attention from disaffected party members seeking alternatives and served as a forewarning of further, still deeper divisions soon to come.

After two long and politically overheated conventions, the general campaign was less dramatic but not without its curious moments. Even though Pierce played a prominent role in the Mexican-American War, he was far less widely known than Scott, a disadvantage that the Pierce campaign tried hard to correct by engaging Nathaniel Hawthorne, a friend of Pierce from his college days, to write a campaign biography for the Democratic candidate. Scott's name was better known, and his campaign was less likely to seek out this avenue, perhaps to his detriment. The two campaigns also extensively utilized the press, and partisan papers devoted considerable ink to articles and editorials detailing their candidates' qualities and the platforms they were running on. The Democrats assembled local clubs, generally known as "Granite Clubs" (after "Granite State," the nickname for Pierce's home state of New Hampshire), to organize events and promote their candidate. The Hickory Pole, made famous by the legendary Andrew Jackson campaigns of the 1820s and 1830s in celebration of Old Hickory, were trotted out and posted in honor of "the Young Hickory of Granite Hills," General Pierce. "Young Hickory" was also a nickname previously associated with President Polk; thus the Hickory Pole symbolized the heroic lineage from Jackson through Polk and now to Pierce, implying that Pierce and Jackson were war heroes cut from the same bolt. To tighten the connection to Polk, the pugnacious slogan "We Polked 'em in '44, we'll Pierce 'em in '52" was circulated with considerable bravado. Mass meetings were held, notably in New York (one such meeting sponsored by Tammany Hall), Pennsylvania, and Hillsborough, New Hampshire, the birthplace of Pierce and the site of an enormous barbecue thrown to promote the cause of Pierce and the party. At the Tammany Hall event, both Douglas and Cass, the latter particularly impassioned, delivered speeches to promote Pierce and denounce "whiggism."

Both campaigns resorted to the obligatory slurs. Pierce was accused of cowardice for having fainted at one point during pitched combat in the war, and he was often mocked by Whigs as being the "Fainting General"; Democrats defended Pierce by informing the public that the wound that he had suffered at Contreras caused so much pain that he passed out during a subsequent battle. As a counter-attack, the Democrats dusted off the "Old Fuss and Feathers" sobriquet aimed at Scott during his unsuccessful 1844 campaign for the nomination, an insult that depicted Scott as a vainglorious, conceited, self-trumpeting, parading, and arrogant fop, and one that held some credibility among friends and foes alike. One editorial referred to Scott as the general with a "breastplate on his rear," an obvious slur against his virtues as a soldier. Whig supporters of Scott countered with a slogan, reminiscent of George Washington, honoring Scott as a candidate: "First in War, First in Peace." The Whigs further accused Pierce of being virtually inactive while in Congress, in the pocket of foreign interests, and anti-Catholic, the latter charge quite contrary to his record. Democrats returned the mud, accusing Scott of anti-Catholicism as well; they mocked his inadequacies as a speaker, labeled him an inept leader, and warned voters of his prickly personality. Buchanan, stumping in behalf of Pierce at a large Democratic rally in Greensburg, Pennsylvania, vigorously stressed Scott's disagreeable, conflictive personality. "General Scott," Buchanan reported, "has quarreled with General Wilkinson—he has quarreled with General Gaines—has quarreled with General Jackson—he has quarreled with DeWitt Clinton—he has quarreled with the administration of John Quincy Adams—he has quarreled with the people of Florida to such a degree that General Jackson was obliged to reluctantly recall him from the command of the army in the Seminole War—has quarreled with General Worth. . . he has quarreled with General Pillow—he has quarreled with the gallant and lamented Duncan—and unless reports speak falsely, he has quarreled with General Taylor." The operative word here is "quarrel," attempting to cause voters to doubt Scott's ability to effectively govern, let alone inspire, a nation that needed a leader capable of overcoming divisions, not adding to them.

Given the realities of Scott's unfortunate pomposity and argumentative demeanor, Whigs could not muster a credible defense, but they returned volley in another way, gladly taking advantage of old rumors about Pierce's heavy drinking, thus retorting that Pierce was indeed a hero after all, a "hero of many a well-fought bottle." It is a sad fact that such personal attacks are lobbed in most campaigns; in this one, they served not only as a dig against one's opponent, but also as an unsubtle way to evade the critical issues of the day, so urgent and volatile that one wrong suggestion from a candidate or campaign surrogate could wreck a candidate's chances overnight.

Additionally, both campaigns were sensitive to the growing importance of immigrant groups as a potentially decisive factor within the electorate, especially if the election would be close. Hence both Democrats and Whigs sought to win what today would be called the "immigrant vote." New citizens originally from Sweden, Ireland, and Germany, among others, were courted. Platforms and candidate biographies were written in Swedish and German, and immigrant populations were targeted for the stump. Not surprisingly, both parties took the low road in this regard, accusing the opposition of anti-immigrant prejudices, an accusation that actually hurt General Scott, as there was some evidence, at least through association, that he had at one time harbored nativist attitudes. This focus on immigrants helps to explain the mutual accusations of anti-Catholicism, for many new immigrants were Catholic, particularly in the Irish immigrant community, but also among some Germans (some of whom were Catholics, some Protestant).

In the nineteenth century, the actual candidates for president typically did not actively campaign. The usual practice was to leave the canvassing and oration to surrogates or local champions. In 1852, Pierce, although reputed to have been an effective speaker, followed this precedent, only making the customary rare appearance. Scott, on the other hand, broke from this practice, as it became evident to him that the Whig campaign might be in trouble, and he was thus needed to play a more active part. To address potential trouble among immigrant audiences, he sought them out and did his best to flatter them, hoping to allay their concerns about his nativist past. But Scott's style of speaking, irascibility, and public awkwardness militated against his efforts to remake his image. Meanwhile, coolly, Pierce bided his time and allowed his campaigners and biographers—Hawthorne among them—to burnish his image for him.

In November, the degree to which the Whigs had been weakened by intraparty fragmentation and defection and the clumsily arrogant efforts of their candidate became fully known. Pierce, who just months before was a comparative unknown, defeated Scott with ease. Pierce won just over 1,606,000 popular votes to Scott's total of approximately 1,387,000, with Hale, the Free Soil candidate, taking around 156,000, or just under 5 percent (less than half of the percentage of the popular vote won by former president Van Buren for the Free Soilers in 1844), with approximately 11,500 casting votes for splinter candidates (Webster, who had passed away two weeks before the election, still received around 5,000 votes from Georgia Whigs who were called "finality men" for their belief that the Compromise of 1850 was the final word on slavery, such was the enthusiasm in the fringes of the Whig Party for any candidate other than Scott). These figures gave Pierce a significant popular victory, just under 51 percent to Scott's 44 percent (rounded up), a seven-percentage-point gap between the two. Interestingly, Pierce would be the last Democrat to win over 50 percent of the popular vote and the White House until Franklin Roosevelt's election in 1932. (Samuel Tilden won a popular majority in 1876 but not the election.) As is usually the case, the real landslide was in the Electoral College, where Pierce, winning all but four states, won 254 to 42 (or 85%

to 15%). Scott took only Kentucky, Tennessee, Vermont, and Massachusetts (where Hale experienced his biggest showing, earning 22%). Pierce's victory reestablished Democratic supremacy throughout the government and exposed the weakness of the waning Whigs. And the Whig Party's demise was indeed imminent, as this would be the last election in which the Whigs would participate as a major party. Replacing the Whigs, a new party would form as the crisis over slavery magnified even further, sharply reconfiguring the political landscape and, as a result of the oncoming national strife, dramatically ascending to dominate presidential politics in the latter half of the nineteenth century.

Additional Resources

Boller, Paul F., Jr. *Presidential Campaigns.* New York: Oxford University Press, 1984.

Cohen, Martin, David Karol, Hans Noel, and John Zaller. *The Party Decides: Presidential Nominations before and after Reform.* Chicago: University of Chicago Press, 2008.

Gienapp, William E. *The Origins of the Republican Party: 1852–1856.* New York: Oxford University Press, 1988.

Greenberg, Amy S. "The Politics of Martial Manhood: Or Why Falling Off a Horse Was Worse than Falling Off the Wagon in 1852." *Common-Place* 9, no. 1. October 2008. http://common-place.org.

Holt, Michael F. *The Political Crisis of the 1850s.* New York: W. W. Norton, 1983.

Miller Center of Public Affairs, University of Virginia. http://millercenter.org/president /pierce.

Nichols, Roy, and Jeanette Nichols. "Election of 1852." In Arthur M. Schlesinger, Fred Israel, and William P. Hansen, eds. *History of American Presidential Elections, 1789– 1968.* Vol. 1. New York: Chelsea House, 1985.

Scary, Robert J. *Millard Fillmore.* Jefferson, NC: McFarland & Co., 2001.

Silbey, Joel H. "1852." In Arthur M. Schlesinger, Fred L. Israel, and David J. Frent, eds. *Running for President: The Candidates and Their Images.* New York: Simon & Schuster, 1994.

The White House. "The Presidents." https://www.whitehouse.gov/1600/Presidents. Accessed December 18, 2015.

Campaign of 1856

With the Compromise of 1850 and the subsequent election of Franklin Pierce, a Democrat from New Hampshire, as the republic's fourteenth president in 1852, the perpetual controversy over slavery slightly abated. There were still plenty of abolitionists and Fire Eaters actively affirming their positions and standing on their principles, and many politicians in both parties remained troubled by the issue, but upon Pierce's nomination a period of apparent calm settled in that it provided some respite for at least a brief time. With the exceptions mentioned above, the country as a whole seemed prepared to accept the "finality" of the Compromise of 1850 and make the best of an imperfect situation. But this reprieve from the explosive issue was illusory, and the extent to which it was in fact an illusion was soon revealed.

In 1854, Illinois senator Stephen Douglas, an unsuccessful candidate for the Democratic nomination for president in the previous campaign season and one of the more prominent rising stars on the national political stage, proposed and guided the passage of a bill that would bifurcate the Nebraska Territory, the lower half now to be called Kansas, and allow these territories to decide the issue of slavery for themselves. Employing the principle of "popular sovereignty" (or "squatter's sovereignty") that can be traced at least as far back as Lewis Cass's position in the late 1840s (and perhaps earlier), Douglas asserted that it was wholly within the authority of the territories themselves, in line with the will of their citizens, to decide with finality whether or not slavery would exist within their borders upon the eventual adoption of statehood. This was a dangerous turn of events, as the Missouri Compromise of 1820, recently reinforced by the Compromise of 1850, had prohibited slavery in the territories of the Louisiana Purchase (from which the Nebraska Territory had been carved) above the latitude 36°30′ N (with the exception of Missouri, which was at the heart of the compromise). With Pierce's somewhat half-hearted blessing—a presidential blessing that by some accounts was conceded as a consequence of having been politically strong-armed by Southern senators—Douglas drove the bill to enactment and, in so doing, utterly abolished all previous arrangements regarding where slavery was and was not legally permitted. This proved to be sheer folly, for with the passage of the Kansas-Nebraska Act in 1854, the country was set on a sure path to civil war.

Both slave-owning and "free soil" settlers began pouring into Kansas. Abolitionist firebrand John Brown, originally from Ohio and determined to strike a blow for the cause, moved into the territory in October of the following year. The shooting began in Kansas in November and was followed by pitched battles between increasingly violent pro-slavery and antislavery factions. On May 21, havoc cut loose in the core region of the Free State cause, Lawrence, Kansas, with many buildings burned, private homes ransacked, and families assaulted by a pro-slavery mob. The violence that roiled Kansas reached as far as the halls of Congress. Massachusetts senator and "free soil" Democrat Charles Sumner, who had at one time been affiliated with the Free Soil Party and, before that, one of the leaders of the Conscience Whigs, a faction of the Whig Party that would also become known as "Wooly Heads," publicly condemned the pro-slavery faction, and in the process, he rained insults on the character of Southern leadership. Sumner's caustic attack on the floor of the Senate infuriated South Carolina senator Preston Brooks, who, out of blind rage, brutally attacked and grievously injured his colleague from

Massachusetts. Sumner's injuries were so severe that he was incapable of returning to the Senate for three years. Brooks was vilified by the Northern press and lionized in the South. Meanwhile, the violence out west intensified. "Bleeding Kansas" proved to be a problem too big to manage for President Pierce, who had been distracted by personal tragedy (the loss of his only remaining child shortly before his inauguration, among other sad events in his life) since assuming office, thus quite literally ruining his presidency as well as imperiling the nation.

The Kansas-Nebraska Act was also the immediate cause of a political event of enduring significance for the nation's future: the birth of a new party. In January 1854, Ohio's Senator Salmon Chase, at the time a leader of the Free Soil Party, in collaboration with a fellow Ohioan, Congressman Joshua Giddings, penned the "Appeal of Independent Democrats of Congress to the People of the United States," a document excoriating Senator Douglas for conspiring to strengthen the "Slave Power" of the South, and in so doing, utterly demolish the work of the Founding Fathers who had, as Chase reasonably believed, intended for the eventual extinction of slavery and the full promotion of the principles of equality in the long course of time. The article succeeded in stirring the public, provoking public demonstrations in Northern cities throughout the early months of 1854. In March of that year, a meeting of antislavery groups (mostly disaffected Democrats and Whigs) occurred in Ripon, Wisconsin, under the leadership of local lawyer Alvan E. Bovay, refuting the Kansas-Nebraska Act and proposing the formation of a new party. That following June, approximately ten thousand antislavery activists participated in a meeting "Under the Oaks" in Jackson, Michigan; and a month later in Madison, Wisconsin, a convention was assembled with the intent of organizing a new political party publicly determined to challenge the "slave power" and that "in the defense of freedom will cooperate and be known as the Republican Party," a name that was first coined by New York's Horace Greeley to describe a movement "united to restore the Union to its true mission of champion and promulgator of Liberty rather than [disseminate the propaganda] of slavery." In response to the writings of Chase and Giddings followed by Greeley and the political events in Wisconsin and Michigan, numerous meetings were convened throughout the North under a variety of party names such as "Independent Democrats," "Fusion Party," "Reform Party," and "Anti-Nebraska Party." These all culminated in the organization of the Republican Party, which, assembling in Philadelphia, held its first official national nominating convention in June 1856.

Consisting mostly of antislavery Democrats and Northern Whigs, the party was initially identified as a "free soil," antislavery alternative to the Democrats, who now, both North and South, seemed to have embraced either pro-slavery policies or, at the very least, the position of "popular sovereignty" that had been forged and pushed by Cass and Douglas. Douglas was particularly prominent as one of the Democratic Party's Young Turks and a target of Republican antipathy. A good many of the new Republicans were in fact Old Whigs, some of whom brought with them the antislavery lineage of the "Wooly Head" Conscience Whigs and the "free soil" Whigs. Other Republicans were less concerned about slavery and more concerned with continuing the Hamiltonian vision that had been embodied in the "American System" of that most august of all Whigs, Henry Clay. Members of the fading Free Soil Party also found a natural home with the new Republican Party, which had also attracted fringe elements that injected a small but visible nativist element into the party. Thus the Republican Party was a hybrid at its birth; some of its members were drawn to it as a way to oppose slavery, others for reasons quite apart from the issue of slavery. But the fact remains that the main rallying principle for the Republicans in the mid-1850s was resolute opposition to the expansion of slavery, formed within a broader vision that aspired toward slavery's gradual eradication throughout the entirety of the Union.

The Democratic Party, in spite of the recent and strident criticism that it was receiving from some quarters in the North, still remained the dominant force in electoral politics and held the advantage that comes from established loyalties and institutional affiliations. Given the sustained strength of the Democrats taken as a whole, the Republicans needed a serious candidate who could at once be a credible champion and yet would not come from the party's leading ranks. To the party's leadership (i.e., men like Chase and William Seward of New York), winning the White House was an unlikely outcome for a newly organized party; thus the leading lights of the movement needed to be held back until the time was right to raise a more viable challenge. Allowing someone like Chase or Seward to be sacrificed now could thwart any promise of victory in the near future. Nonetheless, the party needed someone who would bring a degree of credentialed dignity to the fight, even if defeat was the foregone outcome in the face of the Democrats' hold on power.

Prior to the summer convention in Philadelphia, party leaders informally gathered in Silver Springs, Maryland, to discuss campaign strategy and select their standard-bearer. Chase and Seward, who were both participants in the Silver Springs meeting, were widely viewed as the best possible, as well as most deserving, candidates—but they were still inclined to wait for a more auspicious opportunity. Other names were floated, such as Ohio's Justice John McLean, a moderate candidate who held some appeal to both "free soil" elements in the party and those former Whigs who were dedicated to the sustained promotion of Clay's "American System." But McLean was elderly, already into his seventies, and the sentiment was toward a younger man for a young party. They found him in John C. Fremont, renowned explorer of the American West, a former army officer who, as lieutenant colonel, led the California Battalion in the Mexican-American War. Fremont also served as the military governor of California, followed by a short term as one of the first two senators representing the newly added Golden State.

Originally a Democrat, Fremont was a firm opponent of slavery and a serious enough individual to have received attention from the Democratic Party itself as a possible nominee to represent the party as a candidate for the White House. Fremont cut a commanding figure at the convention and won the nomination with comparative ease. With approximately one thousand total delegates in attendance, the convention drew many prominent figures. In addition to Seward, Chase, Giddings, Greeley, and McLean, such renowned leaders as Charles Francis Adams of Massachusetts, New York's Thurlow Weed, David Wilmot and Thaddeus Stevens of Pennsylvania, and Missouri Free Soiler Francis Blair Sr. were also in attendance. Some at the convention, at least initially, still favored nominating one of the leading figures (i.e., Chase or Seward) or perhaps patching together a McLean candidacy for president with the younger Fremont as his running mate; but as the balloting commenced, it was clear that Fremont was a stronger choice. An informal ballot prior to the official voting polled 369 for the Californian to 196 for McLean. By this time, Chase and Seward were clear in their decision not to stand for nomination, at least this time around; and on the first formal ballot, Fremont enjoyed the support of 530 delegates to McLean's meager 37. Thus it happened that John C. Fremont became the first candidate to run for the presidency under the banner of the Republican Party. (Readers will recall that the term "Republicans" had previously been used as a name for the Jeffersonian political faction that formed in the first two decades after the Constitution's ratification. Later to be called "Democratic-Republicans," the early party known as the Jeffersonian Republicans is not accurately linked to the modern Republican Party that was born in the mid-1850s.)

Selecting a nominee for vice president required sifting through a higher number of potential candidates. Fifteen names were in the running, but from the beginning, the clear front-runner was William L. Dayton, a former senator from New Jersey. Interestingly, the only candidate other than Dayton to receive any significant support for the vice presidential nomination was a young veteran of Illinois politics, Abraham Lincoln. In the informal poll before the official balloting, Dayton won 259 votes, a clear lead, but Lincoln received a noteworthy 110 votes. During the formal balloting, Dayton won with little effort, but the amount of interest in Lincoln can be interpreted as evidence that his political fortunes, which had been seriously diminished in the late 1840s, were about to turn in a different direction.

The Republicans were not the only alternative to the Democrats that were attracting supporters during the antebellum period. Since the 1830s, perhaps earlier, anti-immigrant (or nativist), anti-Catholic, and anti-Semitic sentiments were becoming more evident within the political arena, leading to the formation of the first nativist party in New York in 1843, from there spreading into other parts of the country. By 1845, nativist parties were not uncommon at the state level, and a national movement was clearly under way, with a national convention of what was then called the Native American Party convening in the summer of 1845 in Philadelphia, a violent hotbed of anti-Catholicism (riots in the City of Brotherly Love in 1844 resulted in over twenty deaths and the burning of two Catholic churches). Secret societies formed, remaining active enough to be known but anonymously underground. When members were asked about their nativist affiliations or activities, they would simply respond by saying, "I know nothing," a phrase that would evolve into the common name for a new nativist party, the Know-Nothings, officially called the American Party. Shedding their customary practice of secrecy, the American Party, or Know-Nothings, gathered again in Philadelphia in February 1856 to construct a formal party platform representative of the national nativist movement and to formally nominate a national candidate for the upcoming election.

But the slavery issue quickly and irreconcilably divided the Know-Nothings in the same way that it had divided the Democrats and the now moribund Whigs, with the result that the Northern antislavery delegates withdrew over their frustration with the influence of the pro-slavery element as well as over their objection to the inclusion of Louisiana delegates to the convention, a reaction to the fact that Louisiana was a state heavily populated by Roman Catholics.

With the Northerners abandoning ship, the Southern delegates controlled the course of the convention, nominating as their candidate for the top of the Know-Nothing ticket former Democratic president Millard Fillmore of New York, joined by Tennessee's Andrew Jackson Donelson, the nephew of President Andrew Jackson. Sam Houston, who at one time was viewed as a leader with national appeal in the Democratic Party, was among the eleven candidates who received votes from the Know-Nothings. But no one really challenged Fillmore. Some among the Know-Nothing supporters of the Fillmore/Donelson ticket hoped for the reconstitution of the Whig Party and were more interested in that long-term goal than they were in hewing to a strict nativist agenda. This served to strengthen Fillmore's broader appeal. These "Old Line" Whigs, supporters of Fillmore based mostly in the Northeast, who were also known as the "Silver Greys" or "Nationals," felt that their leader, given his prominence as the thirteenth president, was more than capable of accomplishing this goal through a return to the White House. The Northern faction, known as the "Northern Bolters" or "Republican Sympathizers," independently reconvened the following June in New York City and eventually supported the Republicans.

Remnants of the Whig Party assembled in Baltimore for what would become the last Whig convention, allying with the American Party in their joint nomination of the Fillmore/Donelson tandem. However, while some Whigs endorsed Fillmore as their own—and as fate would have it, final—candidate, and other Whigs joined in with the Republicans for different reasons (some to oppose the expansion of slavery, some to continue the legacy of Clay's "American System" under a new banner), a minority of Whigs, concerned that the new Republican Party could ruin the Union, preferred to throw what little influence they still retained behind the Democratic candidate. Most notably, Rufus Choate of Massachusetts, an old friend and political ally of the late Daniel Webster, regarded the Republicans as a divisive, "geographic" party that rested its principles on what he called the "glittering" generalities of the Declaration of Independence, scoffing at the revered documents underpinning the principle of natural rights. These divisions within the remnants of the Whig Party were a reflection of the broader divisions growing throughout the republic as a whole.

The Democratic convention met in Cincinnati, the first time a national presidential nominating convention convened in a city outside the original thirteen states. Even though the party had suffered fragmentation and defection over the issue of slavery, it remained the stronger, larger, and better-organized party in the now increasingly fragile Union. President Pierce, whose political strength had been depleted by the Kansas-Nebraska fiasco and subsequent disturbances, still sought a second term. Senator Douglas, who had also been stung by the consequences of his sponsorship of this now-infamous legislation, also held hopes for nomination. Both candidates appealed to the South, but in the North they were both slightly regarded as "Doughface" Democrats—that is, Northerners who cravenly held Southern sympathies, and thus their persona resembled the pliable doughface mask—a term of disparagement that would be hard to live down. Lewis Cass, the nominee in 1844 and prospective candidate in 1848, was still around and supported by a small minority.

But it was Pennsylvania's James Buchanan, a gradually rising star over the last dozen or so years, whose name had drawn some support during the previous two conventions. On experience alone, Buchanan was definitely qualified; one of the more experienced candidates in recent years, he had made a solid name for himself in both branches of government, having served as both congressman and senator from his home state, as well as diplomat abroad (Russia and the Court of St. James) and as a widely esteemed secretary of state under President Polk. His appeal was further enhanced by the fact that he had been serving abroad as a diplomat during much of the slavery controversy and thus had been fortunate to evade participation in the debate, leaving little record of his attitudes. Buchanan, a conservative Democrat (his roots reached back to the final years of the Federalist Party, his first political affiliation as a young man), also harbored affinities with Southern attitudes and positions, and in this sense, his name and reputation could also be added to the Doughface element of the party. But Buchanan's sympathy with the

South was at the time less noticeable when compared to the actions and policies of President Pierce and Senator Douglas.

Not supportive of Buchanan, front-runner President Pierce and Senator Douglas together agreed to collaborate against his nomination. For some time, Douglas and Buchanan had both been striving to ascend to the top of the party, and thus they viewed each other as natural rivals. By contrast, Douglas felt somewhat indebted to Pierce, given the latter's support (however reluctant in the beginning) of the Kansas-Nebraska Act, so the alliance between the two men naturally followed. But the violence in Kansas as well as on the floor of the Senate soured the current political mood, and anyone associated with the "crimes against Kansas," as Sumner referred to them, left a distasteful impression on the public's sensibilities. Buchanan's diplomatic service had, as stated above, mercifully removed him from the conversation, while Douglas and Pierce were under the glaring spotlight heated by the emotions that swelled in those particularly precipitous days. Thus when the convention was gaveled in session, Buchanan's loyalists were able to quickly gain the upper hand for their man.

On the first ballot, Buchanan held a clear lead, winning 135 votes but not the requisite majority. As expected, Buchanan, while failing a majority on the first ballot, did outpoll both the president (122 votes) and Douglas (33 votes), with Cass scarcely visible as a distant fourth (5 votes). This pattern would hold for 14 ballots. On the 15th ballot, the Pierce-Douglas alliance, frustrated by Buchanan's strength (peaking on the 6th ballot with 155 votes, and then dropping back to 143 on the 7th before gaining enough momentum to reach 152 votes after the 14th), shifted its direction to attempt a different tack. Pierce's supporters suddenly threw in behind Douglas in the desperate hope of braking Buchanan's momentum. The president was wiped out, losing all but 3 votes, leading him to withdraw before the 16th ballot. Douglas managed to win 122 votes on the 18th ballot, which was the same amount that Pierce had managed on the first ballot, but it was a total that he never surpassed. It was now evident that Buchanan's nomination could not be stopped, and thus on the 19th ballot, both Douglas and Cass (who never earned above 7 votes) also withdrew, allowing Buchanan to take all 296 delegates.

Even though the nomination went to nineteen ballots, it was not nearly as contested as those previous conventions that had led to the nomination of dark horses Polk (1844) and Pierce (1852). Buchanan led the entire way and, while temporarily frustrated, was never really in danger. Supporters of Douglas, believing that their moment was still to come, quickly conceded to Buchanan's nomination. The convention then proceeded to nominate in two ballots John C. Breckinridge of Kentucky, only thirty-five years old (and thus just eligible), from a field of eleven candidates, as the party's vice presidential nominee. (Upon the death in mid-April of Vice President William Rufus King scarcely six weeks into his term, the office of the vice presidency had been left vacant throughout most of President Pierce's term. King was the third vice president to have died in office, George Clinton, serving under presidents Jefferson and Madison, and Elbridge Gerry, serving under President Madison, being the other two to this date.)

Of particular importance in the Campaign of 1856, the Democratic convention passed a platform plank formally stating that the residents of territories and states should by themselves resolve the slavery issue, not Congress or any part of the federal government. This fact was kept fairly quiet by Buchanan during the campaign, as he was not at this time looking for a fight over popular sovereignty. Buchanan's ability to eschew sectional polarities seemed to many at the convention a reasonable antidote to the party's recent internal struggles, as well as a step in repairing the sectionally charged associations that the Democrats had earned for themselves since the debates over the annexation of Texas. His record of service in both branches of government was solid, and he appeared to be eminently qualified, if a bit less than charismatic. He lacked the oratorical flair of both President Pierce and Senator Douglas, but he appeared to many as a promising and much-needed stabilizing influence. In many ways he served as a clear alternative to the more passionate and adventurous Republican candidate, the soldier/explorer Fremont. Fillmore, the Know-Nothing/Whig candidate, in most ways resembled Buchanan. What was important to a good many voters was that none of the three major figures resembled Pierce, who had by 1856 become widely unpopular.

The campaign for the general election thus moved forward. In many ways the 1856 campaign resembled the famous log-cabin campaign of 1840. Mass events such as torchlight parades and barbecues were held in the North, as they had been in the 1840s, but things were oddly quiet in the South. This time, the difference could be seen in what was at stake, for unlike that earlier campaign that sang the praises of frontier living, hard-cider drinking, and Indian fighting, a truly substantively critical issue—slavery—shaped the nation's mood. Southerners could not bring themselves to support Fremont, and Fillmore was negatively associated with a previously failed administration. Once the nomination was secured, Buchanan's Doughface proclivities were exposed by his opponents, but such revelations served only to relieve Southern Democrats, who were encouraged by Buchanan's public statements repeatedly expressing concern over the threat to the Union of Republican antislavery activism, and his bold declaration that the "Black Republicans"—as the Republican Party was described by Democrats—"must be, as they can be with justice, boldly assailed as disunionists, and this charge must be reiterated again and again." In other words, to the Southern Democrats, encouraged by Buchanan's own words, it was the Republicans who were the sectional schismatics, and it was the Democratic Party that was committed to preserving the purity of the Constitution and the viability of the Union as it was originally designed. The Republicans, Buchanan would argue, were "abolitionists, free soilers and infidels against the Union." Only with a Democratic victory, in Buchanan's understanding, could the Union be preserved. This conclusion was not without merit, for many in the South were already drawing the division between the Democratic Party, the party of union, and the Republican Party, the party of disunion.

Southern Democrats dug in hard. Alabama's John Forsyth pointedly remarked that the election of Fremont would mean the end of the United States. Virginia's governor, Henry A. Wise, called up the state militia and belligerently declared that if "Fremont is elected, there will be a revolution." Throughout the South there were murmurs of secession, even among those who had only recently held more moderate positions. Fremont was viewed by many as a serious threat, and no small number were prepared to divide the Union permanently should the Republicans, through him, gain the White House. Such inflammatory posturing was not exclusive to the South. In the North, Joshua Giddings publicly wished for "a servile insurrection in the South," and Horace Greeley wrote that the two sections, slave and free, should resolve to divide and go their separate ways. The more radicalized Republicans petitioned Congress for the immediate abolition of slavery, and prominent Republicans such as Seward called for decisive action in the form of "an aggressive war on slavery." Speaking in Faneuil Hall in Boston, H. L. Raymond, in a particularly acerbic moment, crassly impugned the memory of the nation's most beloved Founder, George Washington. "Remembering that he was a slaveholder," Raymond declaimed, "I spit on George Washington." Comments such as these, coming from hard-liners both North and South, added fuel to an already combustible situation. And it was Fremont whose campaign suffered the most from this increasingly polarized, militant sectionalism.

To add still further to an already potentially explosive campaign season, the parties resorted to mean-spirited calumny and rumormongering. Democrats dismissed Fremont as a political lightweight, a coarse wilderness adventurer who lacked the qualities of statesmanship needed for the crisis at hand. Democrats also unabashedly played the anti-Catholic card, claiming that Fremont was a crypto-Catholic, a move that was cynically intended to thwart a possible Republican/Know-Nothing alliance. Fremont was in truth an Episcopalian, but to his credit, he remained silent regarding his faith and refused to respond to the claims that he was Catholic, forthrightly insisting that his campaign was not only about freedom from slavery, but also religious freedom, and Americans were free to be Catholics if they so desired. Additionally, Fremont was accused by his political enemies of being a heavy drinker, and doubts were cast about his background. He was also accused of having been at one time a slaveholder, and rumors were circulated that Fremont was actually of foreign birth. (Fremont was born in Savannah, Georgia; his father, who actually was a Catholic, was born in France but died when Fremont was a young child.) The Republicans were generally more inclined to avoid negative campaigning, focusing instead on the new vision they offered to the voters. But they were not above the occasional passing swipe, criticizing Fillmore for his age and ridiculing Buchanan, a lifelong bachelor, for his choice not to marry. The Democrats were accused of being corrupt and dated, and, given their support of the Kansas-Nebraska Act, immoral defenders of slavery, a charge that was not entirely without merit. In this campaign, the worst mudslinging came from the Democrats, who were given over to bigotry and slander.

Republicans were energized and enthusiastic. Clubs known as the "Wide-Awakes," "Rocky Mountain Clubs" (so named for Fremont's experience as an explorer), "Freedom Clubs," and "Bear Clubs" (an allusion to Fremont's role in liberating and governing California) formed to promote Fremont's campaign. They produced the old torchlight rallies that had been in use since the time of Andrew Jackson, and the more prominent Republican figures took to the campaign trail to give speeches on behalf of their candidate. These clubs consisted mostly of young unmarried men and assumed an air of quasi-military discipline, but, noticeably, some of these rallies involved the participation of a number of women, an atypical development for politics in the first half of the nineteenth century. Stumping for Fremont, a number of Republican surrogates, among them Chase, Greeley, Lincoln, and Sumner, were joined by luminaries such as Ralph Waldo Emerson and Wendell Phillips. Republicans saw themselves as the "hard-charging" party of change and reform, and they sought ways to stress Fremont's warrior spirit and the need for such a figure given the troubled times that the country now faced. Fremont supporters distributed thousands of copies of *The Republican Campaign Songster.* One such song included the following lyrics:

> BEHOLD! the furious storm is rolling
> Which Border Fields, confederate, raise.
> The Dogs of War, let loose, are howling,
> And lo! Our infant cities blaze.
> And shall we calmly view the ruin,
> While lawless force with giant stride
> Spreads desolation far and wide,
> In guiltless blood his hands imbruing?
> Arise, arise, ye braves,
> And let our war-cry be,
> Free Speech, Free Press, Free Soil, Free Men,
> FRE-MONT and Victory!

Such high-spirited effusions were common coming from the Republicans. The pervasively enthusiastic young party mounted a vigorous and compelling campaign, but in the end, it was one that would fall far short of victory. Strengthened by their experience, influence, and broader familiarity, the more established Democrats won the day.

Buchanan and Breckinridge won just over 1,800,000 popular votes (amounting to around 45%), with Fremont and Dayton taking slightly over 1,300,000 (33%). Fillmore-Donelson's anti-immigrant, anti-Catholic Know-Nothing (American Party)/Remnant Whig ticket impressively snared approximately 870,000 popular votes, which was then (as it remains now) a significant number for a third party, and at 21 percent, it would become the highest percentage of the popular vote won by a third party to that date; to this day, it remains the second-highest percentage received by a third party (to be exceeded only by the great Theodore Roosevelt's Bull Moose/Progressive campaign of 1912). Even though Buchanan could not muster a popular majority (falling a full 5% short), his election was far more impressive when considering the outcome of the Electoral College, where he won 174 votes (just under 59%) to Fremont's 114 (38.5%) and former president Fillmore's meager 8 (Maryland's electors, representing just under 3%). Portentously, Fremont did not win a single popular vote in the following states: Alabama, Arkansas, Florida, Georgia, Louisiana, Mississippi, Missouri, North Carolina, Tennessee, and Texas (electors were still appointed by the state legislature in South Carolina, which, predictably, committed its electoral votes to Buchanan); and in Kentucky, Virginia, and Maryland, the remaining Southern and border states, Fremont received separate totals of only 314 votes, 291 votes, and 281 votes, respectively.

Punctuating the sectional divide, Fremont swept in New England and won New York (still the largest Electoral College prize), and he also picked up the Midwestern states of Ohio, Michigan, Wisconsin, and Iowa, which were the stronghold of the Republican Party. As indicated above, the Democrats swept the South, and they picked up New Jersey and Buchanan's home state of Pennsylvania, as well as the four electors from Fremont's home state of California, where Buchanan won the popular vote by a two-to-one ratio. With the exceptions of Pennsylvania, New Jersey, and California, the sectional division was utterly crystallized, a reality magnified by the fact that Fremont won fewer than 1,000 votes throughout the entire South.

Looking back, the outcome of the Campaign of 1856 was a severe symptom of a country in crisis, one that was already so severely polarized that peaceful reconciliation was fast becoming no longer viable. There was no question that many in the South considered a result in Fremont's favor intolerable, and thus they were already firm in their belief that a Republican victory would serve as sufficient grounds for secession. The stage was clearly set, and the following election of 1860 would prove to be the fatal flashpoint.

Additional Resources

Boller, Paul F., Jr. *Presidential Campaigns*. New York: Oxford University Press, 1984.

Cohen, Martin, David Karol, Hans Noel, and John Zaller. *The Party Decides: Presidential Nominations before and after Reform*. Chicago: University of Chicago Press, 2008.

Gienapp, William E. *The Origins of the Republican Party: 1852–1856*. Oxford: Oxford University Press, 1987.

Holt, Michael. "1856." In Arthur M. Schlesinger, Fred L. Israel, and David J. Frent, eds. *Running for President: The Candidates and Their Images*. New York: Simon & Schuster, 1994.

Leip, Dave. Atlas of U.S. Presidential Elections. http://uselectionatlas.org/.

McPherson, James. *The Battle Cry of Freedom*. New York: Oxford University Press, 1988.

Miller Center of Public Affairs, University of Virginia. http://millercenter.org/president/pierce.

Nichols, Roy F., and Philip S. Klein. "Election of 1856." In Arthur M. Schlesinger, Fred Israel, and William P. Hansen, eds. *History of American Presidential Elections, 1789–1968*. Vol. 1. New York: Chelsea House, 1985.

Wisconsin Historical Society. http://www.wisconsinhistory.org/turningpoints.

Campaign of 1860

During the presidential election campaign of 1856, secessionist voices moved from the radicalized margins toward the political mainstream, and many within the nation's longest-running and most successful established party, the Democratic Party, had ominously warned that the election of a Republican president would provoke nothing less than "secession and revolution." The outcome of the election of 1860 pushed secession from threat to reality, and so began a deadly civil war that had been looming at least since the Missouri Compromise. The political landscape was fractured. There were still numerous policy issues to debate—tariffs, the old concerns involving the banking system, the administration of the western territories, allocation of resources for internal improvements, the location and building of railroad lines, etc.—and these issues did receive some attention. But only one issue overshadowed every other concern, and that was unequivocally the fate of the nation with regard to its long-standing Peculiar Institution, slavery. Differences over tariffs and banking could be peacefully resolved, and indeed they had been more or less resolved in the past, but slavery was the irresolvable problem and the single crisis that threatened the very Union itself.

The irresistible forces behind the nation's doom since the passage of the Kansas-Nebraska Act in 1854 gained momentum almost exponentially. Three events in particular rocketed the nation along the course toward civil war: the 1856 publication of Harriet Beecher Stowe's *Uncle Tom's Cabin*; Chief Justice Taney's untenable Supreme Court decision in the *Dred Scott* case (*Dred Scott v. Sandford*, 1857), which in effect stated that slavery could not be banned in the territories or in those new states derived from them; and militant abolitionist John Brown's violent raid on Harper's Ferry (then in Virginia) in the hope of sparking a slave rebellion that would result in the liberation of all slaves in the South and the establishment of a free republic in which they could live untouched by racial bigotry. These events cut a clear and seemingly irreconcilable schism between North and South. *Uncle Tom's Cabin* became widely popular and stirred throughout the North a groundswell of sympathy for the plight of the slave. The raid on Harper's Ferry filled Southerners with a palpable dread and gave all abolitionists a martyr for their cause. *Dred Scott* was roundly criticized by abolitionists and Republicans, and it even caused division within the Democratic Party itself. Northern Democrats disagreed with the decision because it destroyed the party doctrine of popular sovereignty. Southern Democrats regarded the decision as a vindication of the rights of individuals to own slaves anywhere within the boundaries of the entire United States. These three events, along with the crisis in Kansas that had occurred before the previous election, drove the nation hard toward the brink of secession and bloodshed. But it was still left to a fourth event to push the country into the maw of war. That decisive event was the election of Republican candidate Abraham Lincoln of Illinois to the presidency of the United States.

As stated above, the result of *Dred Scott* on the Democratic Party was to severely divide it along sectional lines. Up to this point, the party had remained fairly cohesive in spite of serious cross-sectional differences. It was the Whig Party that had been ripped apart over the issues of territorial expansion and slavery; the Democrats, by contrast, had weathered those forces and, at least for a time, enjoyed a position of political dominance because of it. The Republican Party, scarcely six years old and cobbled together from a diverse array of interests, was now the more unified party, but because it was inhabited by a sizeable number of party regulars who were critical of slavery, it was a party that was spurned throughout the South. Nonetheless, its cohesion in the North and the West gave the Republicans political and moral clarity, while the Democrats now suffered an internal fragmentation that thoroughly undercut their influence. They held the White House, but their incumbent, President Buchanan, who had already announced in his inaugural address that he would not seek a second term, had provoked controversy since the earliest days of his administration when he announced his public support of the *Dred Scott* decision and his open and insistent endorsement of "popular sovereignty."

From the first moments of his presidency, Buchanan made his position clear. "It is the imperative and indispensable duty of the government of the United States," Buchanan intoned in his inaugural address, "to secure to every resident inhabitant the free and independent expression of his opinion by his vote. This sacred right of each individual must be preserved. That being accomplished, nothing can be fairer than to leave the people of a territory free from all foreign interference to decide their own destiny for themselves, subject only to the Constitution of the United States." Buchanan also endorsed the pro-slavery Lecompton Constitution that would, if passed, place Kansas among the ranks of the slave states. The Lecompton Constitution was considered by many within Buchanan's own party to have been fraudulent, and even though Buchanan managed to persuade the House of Representatives to support it, the Senate, led by Illinois senator Stephen Douglas, blocked it. The contest pitted Douglas, who believed in popular sovereignty but opposed Lecompton because of the allegations of fraud, against Buchanan, an unwelcomed rivalry that the president could not withstand. The Lecompton instrument was rejected and returned, and in a second vote in 1861 (into the next administration), the people of Kansas eventually joined the Union as a free state. Both his public support of the *Dred Scott* decision and controversy over the fate of Kansas damaged Buchanan's administration; moreover, the country suffered an economic recession that further exacerbated the president's troubles.

In the midterm elections, the new Republican Party made huge strides, even stunning the Democrats by gaining the majority in the House, a Republican triumph that further eroded Buchanan's position as well as intensifying the sectional divisions in the government. Never before had a new party accomplished such remarkable gains in such a short time, and a young party that did not even exist scarcely more than four years ago was now in control of one-half of Congress. Meanwhile, among the Democrats, Senator Douglas gained in influence as Buchanan's fortunes turned increasingly sour. Prior to his election to the presidency, Buchanan distinguished himself as an able public servant. But his record was now tarnished by a sequence of questionable choices that both weakened his party and fueled the crisis that was threatening to break the Union. The Democrats needed leadership and unity—but the lack of the latter made it impossible to reach agreement on the former.

In April 1860, the Democratic Party convened in Charleston, South Carolina, to nominate its candidate for president and hammer out its platform. But the divisions between Northern and Southern Democrats were so deep that neither a single candidate nor a generally acceptable platform could be established. Senator Douglas had been, even as far back as the last convention, considered the party's frontrunner for the Campaign of 1860. In the past, his support of "popular sovereignty" had made him an appealing candidate in the South, but some Southerners regarded him to be a soft moderate on the issue of slavery. Douglas's open, albeit convoluted, criticism of the *Dred Scott* case (during one of his famed debates at Freeport, Illinois, against Abraham Lincoln, who also rejected the decision and reasoning in *Dred Scott* root and branch) in the 1858 Illinois senatorial campaign angered the

Fire Eaters, who now proposed an official endorsement of the *Dred Scott* decision as a platform plank and regarded Douglas as an unacceptable candidate. Douglas's Freeport Doctrine was, unlike Lincoln's stern rebuke against *Dred Scott*, a more qualified criticism. At Freeport, Douglas, fearing that the implications of the Supreme Court's decision might actually militate against popular sovereignty, asserted that citizens in the western territories could simply avoid passing legislation that would encourage the spread of slavery across their borders. Southern militants were highly agitated, but Northern Democrats managed to thwart the Fire Eaters' designs, thereby provoking fifty militant pro-slavery delegates to bolt the Charleston convention.

With the Fire Eaters holding their rump convention elsewhere, a Douglas victory seemed inevitable. But six other candidates emerged (notably including Tennessee's Andrew Johnson, who carried approximately a dozen supporters in the early ballots), and with the two-thirds majority required to gain the nomination, the large field forced a deadlock, even after the number was narrowed to four candidates after the thirty-eighth ballot. Douglas led by at least 80 votes on every ballot but continued to fall 50 or more votes short of the needed 202. No other candidate received more than the 66 votes won by Kentucky's James Guthrie on the thirty-eighth ballot, still trailing well behind Douglas's 151. Guthrie polled second on every ballot after the ninth but never came close to Douglas in absolute numbers. Virginia's Robert Hunter, who ran second on the first eight ballots, and Joseph Lane from the Union's newest state, Oregon, received as high as 42 and 21, respectively, and were the only other candidates to earn more than 20 votes at any point in the convention.

Given this irresolvable deadlock, a resigned convention adjourned, quitting Charleston and reconvening in Baltimore the following June. At Baltimore, a controversy immediately arose over the question of readmitting those delegates who had bolted from the previous Charleston convention. When the credentials committee, after some debate, decided to admit most of the bolters with the exception of the dissenting delegates from Alabama and Louisiana (preferring instead to recognize replacements from those two states), still more delegates were provoked into walking out, including almost the entire Southern bloc of delegates, along with a few sympathetic delegates from both the North and the West. With a good portion of the convention's delegates now absent, Douglas easily won the nomination on the second ballot with 181 votes to 7 for incumbent vice president John C. Breckinridge of Kentucky (who was not a candidate in the Charleston convention) and 5 votes for Guthrie. In an effort to patch sectional cracks, Alabama's Benjamin Fitzpatrick was nominated for the vice presidency, but he refused to accept; thus the convention turned to Herschel V. Johnson of Georgia to serve as Douglas's running mate. Those Democrats who bolted from this convention assembled in another rump session, nominating in one ballot Vice President Breckinridge, a competent, respected, experienced, yet youthful individual (he was thirty-nine years old at the time), to stand as their choice for the presidency, and Oregon's Lane as his running mate. Breckinridge, who received the blessing of President Buchanan as well as the endorsement of former presidents John Tyler and Franklin Pierce, embraced the pro-slavery platform, concluding that the nation's sectional fissures could never be closed. Douglas continued to hope for some kind of compromise between the divided sections, but his support in the South had utterly evaporated.

Much is revealed in looking at the platforms: (1) the Northern Democrats backing Douglas defended popular sovereignty and supported the Fugitive Slave Laws, the annexation of Cuba, and the westward expansion of the railroad; (2) the Southern Democrats behind Breckinridge included similar planks on less volatile issues such as Cuba and the railroads, but they added a more insistent demand for the protection of slavery, declaring that "all citizens of the United States have an equal right to settle with their property in [a] Territory, without their rights, either *of person* or property, being destroyed or impaired by Congressional or Territorial legislation" (emphasis added).

Meanwhile, another third party stepped into the picture. Known as the Constitutional Union Party, cobbled together from a combination of Old Line Whigs, Know-Nothings (i.e., the American Party), and a few Southern Unionist Democrats, the party attracted such prominent figures as Kentucky's John J. Crittenden (formerly associated with both the Whigs and the Know-Nothings), renowned orator and Massachusetts statesman Edward Everett, former senator and current governor Sam Houston of Texas, former associate justice John McLean of Ohio (who at one time had been considered as a candidate for president by the Whig Party and who also had received some support at the Republican convention), Georgia's Howell Cobb (a stern critic of Southern secessionism, at least until the outcome of the election of 1860, which apparently inspired him to change his mind), Henry Winter Davis of Maryland (another former Whig with Know-Nothing affiliations who would go on to become well known for the Wade-Davis Bill), and John Bell of Tennessee, who began his political career as a Jacksonian Democrat but, after having become disillusioned with Jackson over the bank controversy, joined the Whig Party in the mid-1830s. The convention nominated Bell for the presidency, to be joined by Everett as his running mate. Their concise platform was just a few sentences long; using uppercase letters for effect, they resolved "that it is both the part of patriotism and of duty to recognize no political principle other than THE CONSTITUTION OF THE COUNTRY, THE UNION OF THE STATES, AND THE ENFORCEMENT OF THE LAWS," and they pledged to "ourselves to maintain, protect, and defend, separately and unitedly, these great principles of public liberty and national safety, against all enemies, at home and abroad;

believing that thereby peace may once more be restored to the country; the rights of the People and of the States re-established, and the Government again placed in that condition of justice, fraternity and equality, which, under the example and Constitution of our fathers, has solemnly bound every citizen of the United States." Bell offered nothing on the issue of slavery, but he was on record as having earlier supported then-representative John Quincy Adams's fierce and sustained denunciation of the 1836 congressional gag order blocking petitions to Congress against slavery (Adams finally won the day in 1844 when Congress removed the ban). Bell's silence on slavery in the 1860 campaign caused critics to lampoon him as a "Do Nothing" candidate with no allegiance, "no North, no South, no East, no West—no anything." These attitudes were prevalent among the electorate; thus the Constitutional Union Party would, aside from the border states, receive only sporadic support throughout most of the Union.

Republicans fatefully met at Chicago in May to conduct their second national nominating convention. William Seward of New York and Ohio's Salmon Chase, "free soil" men from way back, were considered the front-runners at the commencement of the proceedings; also in the running were Charles Sumner of Massachusetts, Edward Bates of Missouri, Simon Cameron of Pennsylvania, William L. Dayton of New Jersey, John McLean (who, as mentioned above, also had supporters among the Constitutional Unionists), Jacob Collamer of Vermont, Ohio's Benjamin F. Wade, John M. Read of Pennsylvania, Cassius Clay of Kentucky (the abolitionist cousin of Henry Clay), and, rounding out the field, John C. Fremont (who had sportingly served in defeat as the party's standard-bearer in the election of 1856) and Abraham Lincoln, who had earned a reputation as a formidable debater, eloquent orator, keen intellect, and sober moderate. Lincoln had been considered, briefly, as a potential candidate to join as running mate on the Fremont ticket in 1856, and since then, he had increased his reputation as one of the party's more skilled debaters in the 1858 Illinois senatorial debates against Douglas, mentioned above. Chase, Sumner, Wade, and Fremont represented the wing of the party that embraced immediate abolition most ardently and who came to be known as the Radical Republicans.

Seward was the most confident coming into Chicago; he appeared to have the largest cohort of supporters and was, at that time, the party's biggest name. In the initial balloting, it was indeed Seward who led the field, gaining 173 votes on the first ballot with 233 needed for the nomination, a respectable first showing given the crowded field of over a dozen candidates. Lincoln, who was initially something of a dark horse, surprised the convention by pulling into second on the first ballot with 102 votes, followed by Cameron with 50, Chase with a surprisingly low 49, Bates with 48, and 42 votes scattered across the remaining candidates (Dayton's 14 votes being the largest share among the remainder). Through the vigorous efforts of Illinois delegate David Davis, a longtime friend and supporter of Lincoln who had stepped forward in Chicago to serve as something resembling Lincoln's campaign manager, Lincoln's position improved considerably on the second ballot, in which he won 181 delegates to Seward's 184. Chase with 42 and Bates with 35 were the only other candidates to win more than 10 votes, as the rest of the field faded quickly. Davis and Lincoln's other friends doubled their efforts, managing to win a stunning 231 votes on the third ballot, just 2 votes shy of the nomination, with Seward slipping to 180. After the initial tallies for the third ballot were announced, three members of the Ohio delegation, observing that Lincoln's victory was at hand, changed their votes to Lincoln, thus securing for him the nomination. This event prompted a wave of switched votes, and a "corrected" third ballot would result in Lincoln winning 349 delegates to Seward's 111, and the Republican nomination for the presidency.

Historians have noted that Lincoln's sudden ascent was in large part the result of Davis's Herculean labor on the convention floor in Chicago, for even though Lincoln had gained a much-deserved reputation as an intelligent voice for the new party, both Seward and Chase were considered the party's true leaders. Davis's achievement serves both as an example of the importance of energetic campaign canvassing and as a historical reminder of the importance that the national conventions once held in the selection of presidential candidates. Lincoln, now joining both Polk (1844) and Pierce (1852) as successful dark horses in the historical annals of convention politics, would now enter a cluttered field of four nominated candidates competing for the White House in 1860. From a field of nine candidates (including Cassius Clay and Sam Houston), former governor and current senator from Maine Hannibal Hamlin, a vocal opponent of slavery and ally of the Radical Republicans, was selected for the vice presidency, striking a balance between Midwest and Northeast. Hamlin won the nomination on the second ballot, with Cassius Clay placing a distant second.

Throughout his life, Lincoln found slavery reprehensible and a tyrannical stain that had soiled the young republic's founding principles of personal liberty, political equality, and rational self-government. Throughout his political career, Lincoln had openly criticized slavery on four counts: as blatantly immoral, patently illogical, directly contrary to the political creed of the nation as affirmed in the Declaration of Independence, and in unfair violation of the economic principles of free labor. He was also a true believer in constitutional government and the unadulterated rule of law, and as such, he realized that slavery needed to be addressed legally, formally, and gradually, soberly arguing for its immediate containment and, eventually, its natural and peaceful extinction. As a one-term congressman, Lincoln had opposed the Mexican War in the realization that the acquisition of vast new lands in the West would surely provide renewed opportunities for slavery to expand, something that Lincoln sorely dreaded, as he regarded such an eventuality to be the ruin of the Union and its republican principles. Abolitionists throughout the North criticized him for his comparatively moderate tone, arguing that Lincoln's more gradualist position was neither strong enough nor forthright enough in opposing slavery and working toward its swift elimination. And yet in the South, Lincoln was viewed with great apprehension, a sign that his was a position not entirely comforting to the slave owner and pro-slavery apologist.

As with Fremont in 1856, Southerners found Lincoln, solely based on his position toward slavery, to be completely intolerable and a real threat to their Peculiar Institution on the same order as John Brown and his militants. Lincoln abhorred such extremist measures as those employed by Brown, and while he continued to criticize slavery as a repugnant disgrace to the political creed of the American republic and the moral cultivation of the American character, he always insisted, out of his fealty to the Constitution, that the authority of the federal government was limited in what it could actually do to slavery where it already existed. His overall vision was that of a country neither half free nor half slave, but rather wholly free throughout all the states, but he stopped short of calling for immediate abolition. His strategy of containment and his moderate approach drew sharp criticism from all sides, North and South, and had the Democrats presented a united front behind one candidate as they did in 1856 behind Buchanan, Lincoln likely would have been defeated. As it was, the Democrats were split in two, with a third party also tossed into the mix; thus the Republicans were able to mount the serious campaign that eluded them four years earlier with Fremont then serving as their standard-bearer. Lincoln's views on other issues, such as the government's role in internal improvements, matched the Whig policies of his political hero, the Great Compromiser Henry Clay, and were typical of his proclivities as a political moderate.

But in the Campaign of 1860, as with the previous two campaigns of 1852 and 1856, no one paying attention really cared about any other issue but slavery, and Lincoln had always unabashedly held slavery to be a great evil; and on that one explosive question, Lincoln evoked nothing less than horror within the slaveholding South. In line with Lincoln's views, the Republican platform denounced the pro-slavery Lecompton Constitution of Kansas; scolded the Supreme Court for perversely, inhumanely, and criminally restoring the "slave trade, under cover of [the] national flag"; asserted that the "normal condition of all the territory of the United States is that of freedom"; and denied "the authority of Congress, or a territorial legislature, or of any individuals, to give legal existence to slavery in any territory of the United States." For many, Lincoln's victory on Election Day and the ascent of the Republicans would require nothing less than secession. It was the same reaction to Fremont, but this time, given the fragmentation of the political landscape and the unity enjoyed by Lincoln and the Republicans, advocating secession was now more than a simple threat.

The Republican Party conducted a vigorous campaign that made use of every available method to get out the vote for Lincoln. Republican slogans included "Free Homes for Free Men"; "Millions for Freedom, Not One Cent for Slavery" (riffing off the old phrase, "Millions for Defense, Not One Cent for Tribute"); "The Constitution and the Union, Now and Forever" (inspired no doubt by the late Daniel Webster's famous peroration exhorting both "liberty and union"); "Slavery Is a Moral, Social, and Political Wrong" (aptly summarizing Lincoln's views); "Vote Yourself a Farm" (seemingly incongruous given the way in which slavery overwhelmed all other issues); and, with a reference to a famous biblical line cited by Lincoln in his 1858 speech accepting his party's nomination to run for the U.S. Senate against Douglas, "A House Divided against Itself Cannot Stand." With the help of the organized and energetic Wide-Awake clubs, the Republican Party conducted numerous rallies and marches replete with songs celebrating Lincoln. To his supporters Lincoln was "Honest Abe," the "Rail Splitter," the "People's Nominee," slogans drawing upon his bona fide humble origins. That is to say, unlike William Henry Harrison, Lincoln was actually born on the frontier in a log cabin, was raised in rustic and modest circumstances, and was the best (but not sole) example since Andrew Jackson of a candidate who truly came from a humble background. Following previous custom, Lincoln cagily remained distant from the campaigning, leaving it to the Wide-Awakes and other political allies such Seward and Cassius Clay to mount the campaign stage. By contrast, Northern Democrat Stephen Douglas invested tremendous energy in the campaign. Unlike Lincoln, his old rival, the Little Giant traveled extensively, enthusiastically addressing large crowds throughout all sections. Throughout the campaign season, Douglas refused to abandon his support for the doctrine of popular sovereignty or to comment either way on the moral considerations of slavery. Shamefully, the Campaign of 1860 grew ugly. Hostile political prints presented cruel and racist images of a simian Lincoln fraternizing with monstrously drawn slaves and advocating interracial "free love." Such beastly behavior was the low point of the long tradition of the political cartoon.

In the election, Lincoln won the higher number of popular votes, a total of somewhere around 1,856,000 votes, which was actually a new record, in absolute numbers exceeding President Buchanan's 1856 total by over 25,000 votes; but in 1860, it was but a meager plurality of approximately 39.7 percent. Douglas polled second in the popular vote with approximately 1,380,000 votes (just under 30%), young Breckinridge taking around 850,000 (18%) and Bell somewhere in the neighborhood of 590,000 (slightly under 13%). The percentage of the 1860 popular vote for Lincoln is the second lowest for a winning candidate in the nation's history (John Quincy Adams won the election of 1824 after having polled only 31% of the popular vote and 32% of the electoral vote, that election having failed to produce a majority in the Electoral College and thus decided in the House of Representatives), and it was also the lowest in the era of modern parties that had quickly emerged after the election of Andrew Jackson in 1828. Lincoln was not even on the ballot in ten southern states, and in the only southern or border states where his name could be found on the ballot, the border states of Maryland and Kentucky (where he was born before moving to Indiana and from there to Illinois) and the southern state of Virginia, he won 2,294 votes, 1,929 votes, and 1,364 votes, respectively. In the popular vote, he ran strongest in Vermont, Pennsylvania, New York, Ohio, Massachusetts, Maine, Connecticut, Michigan, Wisconsin, Minnesota, and Iowa, all northern and midwestern states. All told, he won seventeen states for a total number of 180 electoral votes, or just over 59 percent, a substantial Electoral College victory in stark contrast to his thinner share of the popular vote (by comparison to recently held elections, even without any support in the southern states, Lincoln's Electoral College results were slightly stronger than Buchanan's in 1856 and Taylor's in 1848 and not nearly as strong as Pierce's 85% in 1852). Lincoln did win clear majorities in fifteen of the seventeen states that he carried in the Electoral College, the exceptions being California and Oregon, which he won with pluralities in the popular vote.

Although Douglas received the second-highest percentage of the popular vote, he managed to win only twelve electoral votes from the states of Missouri and New Jersey, starkly illustrating that the Democratic Party was dead in the North. Douglas nearly split the vote with Lincoln in Illinois, which was home to both candidates; but this time, unlike the senatorial campaign in the midterm election of 1858, the Rail Splitter edged out the Little Giant, taking his home state's eleven electoral votes. In the end, Lincoln won a clean sweep in the states that were carved from the old Northwest Territory, a region of the country in which Douglas might have run more successfully had it not been for the loss of votes to Bell and Breckinridge. In spite of the results of the popular vote, it was the much younger Breckinridge, not Douglas, who ran second in the Electoral College, taking seventy-two electoral votes, all from southern states. Even though he had the smallest percentage of the popular vote (and around 800,000 fewer votes than Douglas), Bell also exceeded Douglas's Electoral College total, winning thirty-nine electoral votes from Virginia, Kentucky, and Tennessee.

True to their word, Southern leaders, in response to Lincoln's electoral victory, began the movement to break from the Union. Buchanan's administration was utterly ineffective in forestalling secession. Prior to the final break, southern states managed to corner Congress into drafting a constitutional amendment protecting the institution of slavery where it had currently existed. Before the amendment was proposed for ratification, the war broke out, rendering such efforts irrelevant. South Carolina, historically at the center of Fire Eater agitation, moved first to secede from the Union. Other slave states soon joined South Carolina to form the rebellious Confederate States of America. Before Lincoln was inaugurated, seven states had left the Union, with the remainder seceding after Lincoln's military response to the assault on Fort Sumter in Charleston Harbor. After decades of debate, compromise, invective, posturing, agitation, repression, polarization, demonization, pleas, threats, and the occasional incidents of bloodshed from the slave uprisings in the South to the open plains of Kansas to the sullied floor of the Senate, the nation's original sin would finally be purged in the fires of war.

Additional Resources

The American Presidency Project. http://www.presidency.ucsb.edu.

Boller, Paul F., Jr. *Presidential Campaigns*. New York: Oxford University Press, 1984.

Cohen, Martin, David Karol, Hans Noel, and John Zaller. *The Party Decides: Presidential Nominations before and after Reform*. Chicago: University of Chicago Press, 2008.

Ecelbarger, Gary. *The Great Comeback: How Abraham Lincoln Beat the Odds to Win the 1860 Republican Nomination*. New York: Thomas Dunne Books, 2008.

Egerton, Douglas R. *Year of Meteors: Stephen Douglas, Abraham Lincoln and the Election that Brought on the Civil War*. New York: Bloomsbury Press, 2010.

Fite, David Emerson. *The Presidential Campaign of 1860*. Port Washington, NY: Kennikat Press, 1967.

Foner, Eric. *The Fiery Trial: Abraham Lincoln and American Slavery*. New York: W. W. Norton & Co., 2010.

Gienapp, William E. "1860." In Arthur M. Schlesinger, Fred L. Israel, and David J. Frent, eds. *Running for President: The Candidates and Their Images*. New York: Simon & Schuster, 1994.

Knoles, George Harmon. *The Crisis of the Union, 1860–1861*. Baton Rouge: Louisiana State University Press, 1965.

McPherson, James M. *Battle Cry of Freedom*. Oxford: Oxford University Press, 1988.

Morison, Elting. "Election of 1860." In Arthur M. Schlesinger, Fred Israel, and William P. Hansen, eds. *History of American Presidential Elections, 1789–1968*. Vol. 1. New York: Chelsea House, 1985.

Campaign of 1864

The presidential campaign of 1864 is remarkable for the very fact that it actually occurred, given the state of civil war in which the country was embroiled and the ease in which a postponement or suspension of a presidential election could have been justified given the circumstances at hand. President Abraham Lincoln, embattled as he was, understood that not only was an election feasible in spite of the tide of events, but it was both desirable and necessary, even critical for the future of the republic that now wrestled with its most fateful challenge since the Revolutionary War.

With eleven states in rebellion, the presidential election was confined to the Northeast, the Midwest, the West, and border states such as Kentucky, Maryland, Delaware, and Missouri, and the newly created state of West Virginia (those mountainous Unionist counties of western Virginia that refused to recognize the state of Virginia's Ordinance of Secession and subsequently were joined together and admitted to the Union as a free and separate state in 1863). Not only was the nation divided, but also the two main parties experienced serious divisions within their ranks. The party out of power, the Northern Democrats, broke into three factions, two of which shared the moniker "Peace Democrats": moderate Peace Democrats led by Horatio Seymour of New York, who were critical of the war and its conduct and who advocated negotiating an armistice with the Confederacy, but in a way that would leave the impression of at least a modicum of victory for the Union; and the more radical Peace Democrats, also known as "Copperheads" (pejoratively named by Republicans after the poisonous snake, a nickname that was soon embraced by the Peace Democrats, associating it with the image of Liberty portrayed on copper pennies), who, as the name implies, openly opposed the war, were sympathetic to the South (earning them another nickname, the "Butternuts," after a color worn on the Confederate uniform), and were prepared for peace at any price. Ohio's Clement Vallandigham, Connecticut's Thomas Seymour, and Daniel M. Voorhees of Indiana were the more influential leaders of the Copperhead cause. The third faction was the "War Democrats," or those Democrats who openly supported President Lincoln and the military effort to bring the South back into the Union while still distancing themselves from Lincoln's economic policies as well as some of his more controversial measures recently taken against political dissent. Among the more notable War Democrats were Andrew Johnson of Tennessee—who had become widely admired in the North for retaining his seat in the Senate and refusing to recognize his home state's act of secession—Edwin M. Stanton of Ohio (Lincoln's secretary of war), and Union generals such as U. S. Grant and George B. McClellan. Within the Democratic Party, the Copperheads held, at least during the first two years of the war, enough influence to prompt some War Democrats to drift away from their party and move toward an alliance with Republicans, eventually fully merging with the Republicans to form what would be called the Union Party, although some Democrats switched affiliation to the Republican Party outright. It was under the banner of the Union Party that President Lincoln sought reelection, a goal that seemed uncertain even as late as early 1864.

In 1832, Andrew Jackson was the last incumbent president to win reelection; since then, no sitting president had been returned to office (two—William

Henry Harrison and Zachary Taylor—died early in their first term; James K. Polk probably would have been reelected but, in keeping a promise, elected not to run; Buchanan also promised at the outset of his administration not to run for a second term, but had he changed his mind, he easily would have lost any reelection bid). Antebellum politics was hard on presidencies, setting a trend that President Lincoln would have to work diligently to break.

Moreover, Lincoln's particular position had been seriously weakened by the course of the war itself. The Union army did well in the West and along the Gulf of Mexico; but in the East, where it fought much closer to the nation's capital, its record was not nearly as encouraging. Indeed, in the first few months of the war, the Confederate army succeeded in throwing Union forces on their heels in Virginia and threatened major cities in the North, significantly including Washington, DC, itself. Meanwhile, Richmond, the Confederate capital, seemed invulnerable to the Union army, at least midway through 1863. The tide began to turn for the Union, first with stalemate at Antietam in September 1862 and then victory at Gettysburg in early July 1863, along with a simultaneous victory at Vicksburg along the Mississippi in the western theater. Much fighting, devastation, and bloodletting still remained in the nation's future, but the results of these three horrific battles signaled the beginning of the end for the Confederacy and restored confidence in the president. In the interval between these two battles, President Lincoln seized the opportunity and, having already decided to do so months earlier, famously issued the formal Emancipation Proclamation, an act that left no question—if any question genuinely remained—as to what the war was really about. The salvation of the Union was publicly, openly, unequivocally, and inextricably tied to the eradication of slavery, the precedent fact of which was now thoroughly congruent with what the public was willing to admit.

Politically, the president's fortunes began to improve and would steadily continue to strengthen, but even with the turning of the tide, fainter hearts within the Republican Party still harbored reservations. Secretary of the Treasury Salmon P. Chase, a leading figure in the party since its inception, drew the attention of a minority of supporters, but he withdrew his name from any consideration before the onset of spring. General Benjamin Butler, a recent defector from the War Democrats, was an appealing candidate to the party's more radical wing. The Radical Republicans, however, preferred John C. Fremont, the party's erstwhile nominee in 1856, and he was indeed actually nominated by bolting radicals who broke from the main party and held their own convention in Cleveland in late May. The main branch of the party, as indicated above, held firm and joined with War Democrats to form the coalition that was officially named the National Union Party, or simply Union Party, gathering in Baltimore in June to nominate Lincoln for reelection.

Prior to the convention, there were still murmurings of a challenge to Lincoln. As late as February 1864, Lyman Trumbull, a Republican senator from Lincoln's home state, for example, worried, "There is a distrust and fear that [Lincoln] is too undecided and inefficient to put down the rebellion," and Lincoln himself shared his doubts, writing in a memorandum as late as August 23 of that year, "It seems exceedingly probable that the Administration will not be reelected." But the president soldiered on and, in spite of his own doubts, managed to win the convention over to his cause, just as he had in 1860, but this time with surprising ease. And it eventually became apparent that all was not lost, for even though Lincoln had been roundly criticized in the first half of his term, he was nonetheless held in a high degree of esteem across the electorate. "Lincoln," William Cullen Bryant observed, "is popular with the plain people, who believe him honest, with the rich people, who believe him safe, with the soldiers, who believe him their friend, and with the religious people, who believe him to have been specially raised up for crisis." This reality led the leadership within the Union Party to fall in rank, and Lincoln cruised to renomination on the second ballot. Except for twenty-two first-ballot votes cast for General Grant, who was not seeking the nomination, the delegates unanimously backed Lincoln, a unanimity that became official on the second round.

As a part of his desire to form a coalition with the defecting War Democrats, the president worked to replace his current vice president, Radical Republican Hannibal Hamlin of Maine, with Tennessee's Andrew Johnson. Hamlin's desire was to remain in office, but Lincoln was insistent. By most accounts, it is not that Lincoln disliked Hamlin, but only that they never developed a close relationship; Hamlin remained somewhat aloof from the administration, which was not unusual for vice presidents in the nineteenth century, or even well into the twentieth century. Some have claimed that Hamlin's influence helped the president in his decision regarding emancipation; but on the whole, Hamlin's vice presidency was noted for its inactivity. More importantly in this case, Lincoln strongly felt the need to cement the Union Party coalition with a War Democrat as his running mate. Johnson had proven his loyalty to the Union, and as his reward, he had served successfully as military governor of Tennessee. At the time, he appeared to be a logical means to symbolize Lincoln's overall vision of restoration and reconciliation.

As a result of Lincoln's skill at behind-the-scene politics, Johnson was able to win 200 votes on the first ballot, to Hamlin's 150 and 108 for another War Democrat, Daniel Dickinson of New York. Sixty-one remaining votes were distributed across seven candidates, including generals Butler, Lovell Russell, Ambrose Burnside, and Indiana's Schuyler Colfax, who at the time was the Speaker of the House. The first ballot identified Johnson as Lincoln's new running mate, confirmed on the following ballot with 492 delegates in support of the change. Lincoln was also able to win over Radical Republicans, or at least those who did not join the bolters to nominate Fremont, through his inclusion of certain platform measures, including the demand for the unconditional surrender of rebel forces. The radical wing was also encouraged by emancipation and the real promise of a future amendment to the Constitution that would abolish slavery. After a protracted period of grave doubts about his prospects, victory on the battlefield and the moral victory of the Emancipation Proclamation, along with his own political savvy and firmness of character, propelled Lincoln toward electoral triumph in 1864.

The party platform was nailed together under the sway of the Radical Republicans, breaking from the gradualist/containment position regarding slavery affirmed in the platforms of 1856 and 1860 and now adopting a direct, immediate abolitionist position. The party officially admitted that the cause of the war was slavery and demanded its "utter and complete extirpation from the soil of the Republic." The Republican platform also demanded "unconditional surrender" of all rebel forces, rejecting all suggestions of compromise with Confederate rebels. Equally important, the platform endorsed Lincoln's Emancipation Proclamation by guaranteeing the "full protection of the laws" to freed slaves serving in the Union army. Rejecting the pre-Civil War nativism movement, the platform encouraged foreign immigration, particularly as a means of asylum for those fleeing from Old World oppression. Even though the party as a whole now supported immediate rather than gradual abolition, the Radical Republicans wanted still more extensive—some would say drastic—social reform at the end of the war, including punitive measures targeted at the old Southern slaveocracy. When Lincoln pocket-vetoed the Wade-Davis Manifesto outlining reconstruction measures more extreme than Lincoln's more moderate plan, Radical Republicans bristled, and at this point, a number of them bolted to endorse Fremont. This intraparty division was not lost on the general public, and particularly the Democrats, who detected vulnerable fracture lines dividing the radical wing that commanded the platform and the moderates who represented a solid base for the president. The Democrats needed a personality to match Lincoln's, an order that they would find exceedingly difficult to fill.

With the untimely death of Senator Stephen Douglas at the age of forty-eight, Lincoln's fellow Illinoisan and longtime rival, the Democrats lost their most influential and capable standard-bearer, and between the secession that cut the party in half and the many defections of a number of War Democrats to the Union Party, the Democrats experienced, for the first time in the party's history, a dearth of substantive leadership. Nonetheless, they were confident that they could unseat Lincoln, for they were convinced that the factionalism in the Republican Party was a clear indicator of the president's vulnerability.

Waiting until late August to hold their convention in Chicago in the hope that the war might by that time turn once again against Lincoln, the Democrats (also now known as the Northern Democrats or Grand National Democrats) proceeded with an apparent confidence that concealed their own inward doubts and divisions. The party turned to General George B. McClellan, still on active duty, a War Democrat who was zealously opposed to emancipation and who had served as President Lincoln's commander of the Army of the Potomac until he was relieved and reassigned after the Battle of Antietam. It was well known that McClellan and Lincoln were frequently at odds over war strategy, and it was natural for the Democrats to turn to such a notable figure to compete against the president. Even though he looked with disdain upon emancipation—while commanding the army, he refused to protect escaped slaves and chose to obey the old Fugitive Slave Law—and the recruitment of African Americans for military service, McClellan did support the war and the defeat of the Confederacy, a position that placed him in direct conflict with the Copperhead faction that was involved in building the party platform. The platform urged an end to the war and negotiation with the rebellious states, planks that McClellan could not support. Unlike Copperheads, McClellan believed fervently in preserving the Union. The platform of the Democratic Party reaffirmed its commitment to the Constitution and the Union and drew upon fidelity to both in demanding the "immediate cessation of hostilities [with the South]." Additionally, the Democratic platform accused Lincoln and his administration of violating the Constitution by suspending basic civil liberties in the conduct of the war. The platform remained silent on slavery, but Democrats in general supported its retention, at least those who had not defected to the coalition Union Party.

During the convention, General McClellan was not seriously challenged. Both Seymours—Thomas, the Copperhead from Connecticut, and Horatio, the moderate Peace Democrat from New York—drew limited and brief support early in the convention, but not enough to challenge McClellan, who was a figure nationally known and identified as someone who, through his history of conflict with Lincoln, might be the person capable of handling the president in a political campaign. Thus McClellan won nomination on the second ballot with little effort, the party then unanimously nominating George Pendleton of Ohio on the second ballot after he finished in second place to Kentucky's James Guthrie on the first. Pendleton, though only thirty-nine years old at the time of his nomination, was an old-school Jacksonian who, typically, was critical of centralized government; and yet, throughout his political career, he developed a pragmatist's disposition and would later become more famously known as an advocate for civil service reform, the famous Pendleton Act of 1883 (formally known as the Civil Service Reform Act) bearing his name.

Lincoln and his supporters made use of the same campaign tactics that had proven effective four years earlier. Wide-Awake clubs conducted torchlight parades through major northern cities. Lincoln supporters rallied around three prominent slogans: "Don't Change Horses in Mid-Stream," "The Constitution and the Union, Now and Forever," and "Slavery Is a Moral, Social, and Political Wrong," the latter two recycled from 1860. Lincoln partisans insulted McClellan's allegedly lackluster war record and made much of the tension between the two men during the early months of the war, which McClellan's critics in rebuttal claimed to have been to the detriment of the Union cause. Once the campaign was under way, all Republicans threw their full support behind the president. The Radicals backed away from their rump support of Fremont, and the party leadership stumped hard for the president, most notably—and energetically—Salmon Chase and William Seward. This time, the Democrats exhibited the unity that they lacked in 1860, closing ranks behind McClellan with a cohesion that had been elusive to them throughout the antebellum period, unseen really since the election of Martin Van Buren in 1836, in spite of their general dominance prior to the war. Along with the Wide-Awake clubs and the now-obligatory barbecues, fairs, and rallies, Republicans aggressively campaigned throughout the Union, publishing broadsides, pamphlets, and editorials and forming new associations such as the Union League and the Loyal Publication Society. Democrats responded with the Society for the Diffusion of Political Knowledge and similar groups.

Lincoln, as he had done in 1860, kept a quiet distance from the campaign, but McClellan waded in, an atypical (but not unheard-of) tactic at the time. The Democrats vigorously attacked Lincoln on the issue of civil liberties raised by some emergency measures adopted by the president against Confederate sympathizers that were openly questioned on constitutional grounds. In response, Republicans emphasized the choice between two possible futures: that of disunity, treason, and slavery offered by McClellan and the Democrats; or that of freedom, union, and the rule of law as embodied by President Lincoln and the Republicans. Taking the low road, McClellan's campaign resorted to attacks on Lincoln's character. Democrats accused Lincoln of corruption and tyranny, claimed him to be incompetent, insinuated that his racial background was ambiguous, and hurled a variety of insults at him, calling him a buffoon, a fanatic, a third-rate lawyer, a filthy storyteller, a ridiculous joke incarnate, a liar, an ignoramus, a butcher, and a baboon.

Lincoln's anxieties over reelection were soon allayed. With more Union military victories against Confederate forces and effective electioneering in the North, Lincoln enjoyed a pre-election boost that would carry him toward a genuine landslide, winning over 2,200,000 popular votes—setting a new record for total votes (Lincoln being the first candidate for president to win over 2 million votes)—which amounted to slightly more than 55 percent of the total vote, to McClellan's 1,800,000 votes, falling just under 46 percent. Lincoln's share of the popular vote, 55.03 percent, was second only to Andrew Jackson's share of 55.9 percent in 1828 (the popular vote first being recorded on a national scale in 1824), and only the second time since 1844 that a candidate for president won over 50 percent of the popular vote (Franklin Pierce winning just under 51% in 1852). The difference in the Electoral College was even greater. There, Lincoln won every state (not including the states in rebellion) except Kentucky, Delaware, and New Jersey, earning a total of 212 electoral votes to McClellan's 21, or 91 percent to 9 percent of the total electoral vote count, which was the biggest Electoral College landslide since President Monroe's nearly unanimous electoral reelection in 1820. In the popular vote, McClellan did come close in New York (losing by less than 1% in the Empire State) and Pennsylvania, but these two electoral giants in the end went for the president.

Thus Lincoln succeeded in becoming the first incumbent president to win reelection in thirty-two years, a remarkable achievement given the severe circumstances that he faced. Indeed, the situation was so dire that there was a general expectation that the election would be suspended or postponed until the cessation of hostilities; but to his credit, Lincoln insisted otherwise, a position that he summarized in an impromptu address delivered two days after his reelection, observing, "It has long been a grave question whether any government, not too strong for the liberties of its people, can be strong enough to maintain its own existence, in great emergencies." Lincoln continued, "We can not have free government without elections, and if the rebellion could force us to forego, or postpone a national election, it might fairly claim to have already conquered and ruined us. . . . [The recent election] has demonstrated that a people's government can sustain a national election, in the midst of a great civil war. Until now it has not been known to the world that this was a possibility."

Lincoln's peerless eloquence reached its zenith the following March, his second inaugural address being a triumph of sober reflection, honest assessment, unreserved confession, and compelling reaffirmation of principle, lucidity, and above all, compassionate reconciliation and transformation. These qualities, and the overall record of his conduct throughout the crisis, though certainly not without blemishes, have led historians and students of politics to regard Lincoln as one of the greatest presidents in American history, and perhaps the greatest. Only President George Washington before him and President Franklin Roosevelt after him are considered among his equals. Tragically, Lincoln would fall to an assassin's cruel bullet the following April, scarcely a month after his second inaugural address wherein he mercifully challenged the nation to hold "malice toward none" and to seek "charity of all." With Lincoln's death he would, as Edwin M. Stanton poignantly remarked, "belong to the ages" and become numbered among the fallen heroes of freedom. Vice President Andrew Johnson would thus ascend to the presidency, and the course of the nation would be irrevocably altered.

Additional Resources

Boller, Paul F., Jr. *Presidential Campaigns.* New York: Oxford University Press, 1984.

Flood, Charles Bracelen. *1864: Lincoln at the Gates of History.* New York: Simon & Schuster, 2012.

Hyman, Harold. "1864." In Arthur M. Schlesinger, Fred L. Israel, and David J. Frent, eds. *Running for President: The Candidates and Their Images.* New York: Simon & Schuster, 1994.

Hyman, Harold. "Election of 1864." In Arthur M. Schlesinger, Fred Israel, and William P. Hansen, eds. *History of American Presidential Elections, 1789–1968.* Vol. 1. New York: Chelsea House, 1985.

Lincoln, Abraham. *Speeches, Letters, Miscellaneous Writings, Presidential Messages and Proclamations, Vol. Two.* Edited by Don E. Fehrenbacher. New York: The Library of America, 1989.

Long, David E. *The Jewel of Liberty: Abraham Lincoln's Reelection and the End of Slavery.* Mechanicsburg, PA: Stackpole Books, 2008.

McPherson, James M. *Battle Cry of Freedom.* Oxford: Oxford University Press, 1988.

Waugh, John C. *Reelecting Lincoln: The Battle for the 1864 Presidency.* New York: Da Capo Press, 2001.

Campaign of 1868

The shattering and heartrending assassination of President Abraham Lincoln in April 1865 thrust Vice President Andrew Johnson of Tennessee into the White House, making Johnson the third vice president to assume the office of the presidency upon his predecessor's death. Lincoln placed Johnson on the 1864 ticket as part of an effort to cement the alliance between Republicans and Peace Democrats, resulting in the formation of the Union Party. Had Lincoln kept his first vice president, Maine's Hannibal Hamlin, on the ticket in 1864, a Radical Republican instead would have ascended to the presidency, an event that no doubt would have resulted in a dramatically different approach to Reconstruction. The Radical Republicans were already a driving force, and it was Lincoln who had supplied the voice of moderation, a voice that for some was too cautious, too compromising, too gradualist. Lincoln's vision involved a quick and thorough reconciliation with the defeated rebels and a full restoration of the former Confederate states to the Union, where they belonged. Lincoln remained committed to freedom for the emancipated slaves, but he was not interested in punitive measures against his old foes, for whom he had always felt responsible as their legitimate president. "With malice toward none," Lincoln instructed in his second inaugural address, "with charity for all, with firmness in the right as God gives us to see the right, let us strive on to finish the work we are in, to bind up the nation's wounds, to care for him who shall have borne the battle and for his widow and his orphan, to do all which may achieve and cherish a just and lasting peace among ourselves and with all nations."

President Lincoln's "new birth of freedom," as affirmed two years earlier in his Gettysburg Address, meant the abolition of slavery for good and all, but it did not mean vengeance upon the South. Both sides in the war, Lincoln noted in his second inaugural, shared mutual responsibility for all that had transpired, for in his view, it was the very will of God that gave "to both North and South this terrible war as the woe due to those by whom the offense came." Guilt for the sin of slavery was shared equally by the entire Union, all sections, and the only sure way to a restored republic was through dignified policies of charity, forgiveness, and mutual understanding. This understanding was also shared by Vice President Johnson, a Southerner and War Democrat who was invested in a lenient approach to the former rebels, and in this sense he carried forward Lincoln's desires. Johnson wished to follow Lincoln's plans for establishing amenable conditions hastening the South's full return to the Union. In sharp contrast, Radical Republicans, for various reasons, sought to impose numerous and more stringent requirements for readmission on the rebellious states.

However, Johnson, while more or less intending to follow the slain president's policy of swift reconciliation, was far less sympathetic than the Great Emancipator to the improvement of the position of the freedmen (i.e., recently emancipated slaves), thus putting him at odds with both the memory of Lincoln, who was now viewed as a martyred hero, and the Radical Republicans. President Johnson was unresponsive, watching with indifference as southern state governors whom he had recently appointed began to institute racist policies and practices, known as "black codes." To counter the black codes, congressional Republicans, both moderates and radicals, renewed and buttressed the Freedman's Bureau to assist all former slaves and, significantly, proposed civil rights legislation before Congress on behalf of the newly freed African Americans in an effort to protect their rights. President Johnson vetoed both the renewal of the Freedman's Bureau and the civil rights bill, reactionary moves that never would have occurred under President Lincoln. In rejecting the civil rights bill, Johnson's veto message asserted that such legislation was an undue encroachment on state power by the federal government, an early example of what would eventually become the all-too-common use of the states' rights argument against future civil rights legislation. For President Johnson, there was no discernible constitutional ground for such legislation, and it would only encourage a centralized federal government, to the detriment of the states. Additionally, the president wrote in his veto message, "In all our history . . . no such system as that contemplated by the details of this bill has ever before been proposed or adopted. [The bill establishes] for the security of the colored race safeguards which go beyond any that the General Government has ever provided for the white race."

More telling, in a letter to Missouri's governor, Thomas Fletcher, Johnson candidly wrote, "This is a country for white men, and as long as I am president, it shall be a government for white men." This attitude won him no friends in Congress, where a much different and more thoroughgoing approach to Reconstruction animated several of its more powerful members. Johnson's veto was promptly overridden, and Republicans of all stripes abandoned him; while Democrats, especially in the South, now embraced him. It is no stretch of the imagination to realize that these events are far from what the late President Lincoln had envisioned for the postwar reconciliation.

The conditions were in place for a grim confrontation between the executive and legislative branches. Congress was determined to act, and it moved to impeach Johnson in an immediate response to a controversy over the removal of Secretary of War Edwin Stanton, which was viewed as a defiant violation of the recently passed (again over Johnson's veto) Tenure of Office Act (1867). But this was in reality but a pretext; Congress had the Johnson administration in its crosshairs almost from the beginning. As a result of this controversy, the president was in fact impeached by the House (the first president to be so impeached; President Bill Clinton would also be impeached in 1998), but the Senate fell one vote short of conviction and removal from office. Johnson survived the impeachment move, but his presidency was in effect dead in the water, his prospects in the Union Party finished. With Johnson hobbled as a lame duck, the Republicans, now formally operating under the name of the National Union Republican Party, began a search for a candidate who would be more compliant with the agenda of the party's radical wing and the revolutionary party platform of 1864, a platform that had been endorsed by President Lincoln.

Ohio's Benjamin F. Wade, who, as president pro tempore of the Senate, was just one senatorial vote against Johnson from becoming the nation's president, was regarded by some as an early front-runner. But his age (sixty-seven at the time of the president's impeachment) was a significant disadvantage. Additionally, Chief Justice Salmon Chase, Speaker of the House Schuyler Colfax, and the eminent Charles Francis Adams, scion of the United States' most famous political family at the time and currently assigned as foreign minister to Great Britain, were other prominent names mentioned as possible candidates for the Campaign of 1868.

More significantly, the mood in the country tilted toward men of valor, and in the wake of the war, there was a surplus of war heroes and generals, the most prominent being General Ulysses S. Grant of Ohio. Other military leaders were mentioned, such as General William T. Sherman, Admiral David G. Farragut, and even General George McClellan, the man who had opposed Lincoln in 1864; but none of these other figures could match Grant in popularity. Grant had even been considered by a small minority of Republicans in the previous election as a possible replacement for Lincoln, but at the time Grant had exhibited no interest in political office, and Lincoln shook off doubts about his potential for reelection to secure that nomination with ease. Grant's political affiliations were vague—before the war, he had supported the Democrats and had voted for the Doughface James Buchanan in 1856—and because of his reputation as a wartime commander, he appealed to both parties. This reputation was solidified, especially for Republicans, when he refused to cooperate with President Johnson's attempt to have him appointed as Secretary Stanton's replacement during the controversy that directly led to the president's impeachment. Some Democrats, however, criticized Grant for refusing Johnson, a development that helped to prod him toward the Republicans. Grant had also been critical of slavery prior to the outbreak of war, and in American politics at that time, the Republican Party had become the political home of the antislavery factions. Grant had at every turn remained indifferent to ambitions for civil office, which only served to strengthen his appeal. More than any candidate, Grant drew the admiration of the broader electorate and thus was immediately identified as a formidable political force.

The National Union Republican Convention was held in Chicago in May 1868. The usual factions—moderates and Radical Republicans as well as former War Democrats—participated, and they were also joined by Southern Unionists who had remained loyal to the North throughout the war, as well as a few repentant former Confederates. Significantly, the convention included a dozen African Americans serving as delegates from the South, a visible sign of the changes brought to the South through Reconstruction policies. Grant was unanimously nominated without opposition on the first ballot. For the vice presidency, 11 different candidates received votes, including former vice president Hannibal Hamlin (vice president during President Lincoln's first term), who won as many as 30 votes on the second ballot. But in the end, his support was weak: the candidates that received the most votes were Benjamin Wade, the early favorite, winning a plurality of 147 votes on the first ballot, gaining votes on all subsequent ballots, peaking at 207 votes, and holding the lead on the first four ballots; Henry Wilson of Massachusetts, who peaked at 119 votes on the first ballot; Robert E. Fenton of New York, who won as many as 144 votes on the second and fourth ballots; and Speaker Colfax, who came in fourth place with 115 votes on the first ballot, but who steadily gained votes on every ballot until, finally on the fifth ballot, he won enough to secure the nomination, taking 226 delegates to 201 for Wade, 139 for Fenton, 56 for Wilson, and 20 for Hamlin. With Colfax's victory secured, a "second fifth ballot" was cast, this time with 541 delegates throwing their votes behind the winner. Colfax would become the first person to serve as both Speaker of the House and vice president, an achievement matched only by John Nance Garner, who would be vice president under President Franklin Roosevelt.

Both Grant, from Ohio, and Colfax, from Indiana, were Midwesterners, a sign that the party was, at least for this election, uninterested in sectional balance. Additionally, both Grant and Colfax were young by presidential standards, Grant being forty-six and Colfax forty-five, the youngest combined ticket to date. Younger men had been nominated for both offices, but no combination of candidates had been this youthful, at least by the standards of the times. Only the nomination of Bill Clinton and Al Gore in 1992 would promote a younger combination of candidates for a presidential ticket.

Framed by the slogan, "Let us have peace," taken from Grant's letter of acceptance, the Republican platform affirmed congressional control over Reconstruction, demanding equal political rights for all. Foreshadowing the emergence of the currency issue as one of the most contested policy areas during the post-Civil War period, the Republican Party adopted a hard-money currency position that opposed the printing of large numbers of greenbacks (paper money), a method that had been designed to permit debtors to pay back their debts with cheaper money, and one that ran against Republican instincts. The Republican platform also called for the restoration of citizenship rights to those former rebels who were fully cooperating with Republican Reconstruction efforts.

The Democrats came to the election of 1868 facing many difficult challenges. Southern Democrats were demoralized by the legacy of defeat, stained by accusations of treason, insulted by Reconstruction, burdened with a war-wrecked economy, wounded in their pride, and pained by the memories of slavery. Northern Democrats were, rightly or wrongly, associated with a lack of resolve during the Civil War and viewed by many as having been overly sympathetic to the Confederate cause, a charge that was in some instances justified, namely with regard to many of the former Copperheads. There were Democrats at the convention, such as the defiant Nathan Bedford Forrest of Tennessee, a founding member of the Ku Klux Klan, who vociferously resisted Reconstruction. The party needed to regroup, and in so doing, it attempted to move beyond the old attitudes behind the defense of slavery and the attempt at secession. The Democrats worked for the complete restoration of all former Confederate states as equal partners of the Union (four states at the time still remained under martial law—Virginia, Texas, Florida, and Mississippi—and thus would not able to participate in the election of 1868), general amnesty for all former Confederates, the return of suffrage regulations to the states themselves (prompted by racially charged concerns over the growing influence of freed African American voters within the South), and the abolition of the Freedmen's Bureau as well as more ordinary policy concerns such as elimination of the public debt, frugality in federal allocations, policies indicative of soft-money/pro-greenback positions, sympathy for and protection of the rights of labor, reduction of the military, and the correction of government corruption.

The Democratic Party was vocally critical of the "unparalleled oppression and tyranny" of the Radical Republicans, and the Democrats sought to offer themselves as a repudiation of what they saw as the more extreme elements driving the policies and practices behind Reconstruction. The platform attacked the Radicals, accusing them of subjecting "ten States, in time of profound peace, to military despotism and Negro supremacy." Included among anti-Reconstruction invective was an accusation by Democrats claiming that the Republicans were attempting to "Africanize" the South at the expense of white citizens and their heritage.

With their agenda in place, the Democrats needed a viable candidate to meet the challenge of the powerful Grant-Colfax ticket, a tall order for a party that had recently undergone a crisis of leadership. Curiously, Chief Justice Chase, a former ally of President Lincoln, prominent Republican, and former Free Soiler, was viewed by some as a potential Democratic candidate, and one who was evidently prepared to switch parties not out of any ideological sentiment, but rather as a means to fulfill a long-unsatisfied desire of achieving the White House. Chase seemed to be a strong candidate, as he agreed with a number of the Democrats' proposals; nonetheless, as a veteran of both the Free Soil and Republican parties, he was committed to universal suffrage, which was enough to cause alarm among most Southern Democrats, who were bent on retracting voting rights for the freed slaves. Thus a second candidate was sought and seemed to be available in George H. Pendleton of Ohio, a widely respected figure who had stood as the party's candidate for the vice presidency on the McClellan ticket four years earlier. Pendleton held strong support in the Midwest and the border states, but Eastern politicians distrusted him due to his former association with the Copperheads as well as his soft-money proclivities.

To complicate matters further, President Johnson, spurned by the Union Republicans, now sought to return to the Democratic fold, and he enjoyed some early support in gratitude for his lenient attitudes toward former Confederates as well as for his remarks on the status of freed blacks. But he was hampered by a lack of political connections and in the end drew only a few supporters; he had burned too many bridges and was now a politician adrift. Other candidates included Kentucky's Francis Preston Blair Jr., a more viable name than Johnson but not as strong as Pendleton; and General Winfield S. Hancock, as well as General McClellan, the Democrats' standard-bearer in 1864, were offered as military heroes to counter Grant, but McClellan was less than lukewarm at the prospect of another political campaign, and Hancock, while popular among Democrats, could not begin to match Grant's overall appeal throughout the North and the West.

With no decisive choice on the horizon, another candidate soon emerged—party chairman and former governor of New York Horatio Seymour, a former Peace Democrat and party stalwart considered by most to be a political moderate.

Seymour had been mentioned as a possible candidate in the previous election, but he demurred, a reaction that he repeated throughout the weeks leading up to the convention. In fact, he was insistent in his reluctance, but his popularity across the party soon translated into enough momentum on his behalf to make it difficult for him to refuse. Of all the candidates, he had the fewest enemies and the most consistent record as a tireless worker for the Democratic cause. Long before he resigned himself to the forces behind his nomination, party leaders canvassed delegates for Seymour, so that by the time the convention convened, Seymour's name was implicitly considered to be among the front-runners. Personally, Seymour preferred Chase, but his attempts to deflect attention away from himself and to Chase failed. Pendleton himself publicly held Seymour in high regard, a sentiment that did not go unnoticed. Still, Seymour genuinely did not want the nomination, and he did his best to prevent it.

Initially, nineteen names were in play (not counting Seymour, who refused to acknowledge his candidacy), and among the official front-runners were Pendleton, Hancock, Johnson, Senator Thomas Hendricks of Indiana, Sanford E. Church, a favorite son of New York, and Asa Parker of Pennsylvania, a railroad entrepreneur and founder of Lehigh College. Also among the wide field were Chase (who showed poorly on every ballot), former War Democrat Joel Parker of New Jersey, James English and Thomas Seymour of Connecticut, General McClellan, John Quincy Adams II (son of Charles Adams and grandson of John Quincy Adams), and former president Franklin Pierce. From among the field of 19 candidates, Pendleton managed to gather 105 delegates to support him on the first ballot, a number that made him the front-runner by a considerable amount and that steadily increased for eight ballots, peaking at 156 before dropping to 144 on the ninth, the beginning of a decline that indicated a deadlocked convention. By the sixteenth ballot, Pendleton lost his status as front-runner to Hancock, who outpolled him 113 to 107 and then peaked on the eighteenth ballot by winning 144 votes. Johnson never received more than 65 votes (enjoyed on the first and second ballots), and the only other candidate to receive more than 100 votes after 22 ballots was Hendricks, who won 107 on the nineteenth ballot to peak at 145 on the twenty-second, at which point he suddenly became the front-runner. But it was to no avail, as his newly found status at the top of the field was still far from the two-thirds majority needed to earn the nomination.

On the fourth ballot, the field was expanded to 20 as Seymour received 9 unwelcome votes from North Carolina, prompting him to temporarily leave the chair and deliver an impromptu speech reminding the delegates that he did not seek nomination. Convention delegates resisted casting any votes for Seymour through the next 17 ballots, but with the deadlock so evidently solidified, 22 delegates ignored Seymour's appeal and cast their votes in his direction. This time Seymour reluctantly accepted what had become a *fait accompli* and allowed his name to come forward. The twenty-second ballot was recast, and Seymour won all 317 votes. Wearied by the deadlocked presidential contest, the convention proceeded to unanimously nominate Blair for the vice presidency. Blair was a strident critic of Reconstruction and convinced that the white race was endangered by the enfranchisement of the freed slaves, whom he considered to be a "semi-barbarous race." Such attitudes were somewhat incongruous, given his family background (his father, Francis Sr., had supported both Free Soil and, later on, Republican causes before eventually returning to the Democratic fold; and his brother, Montgomery Blair, was an abolitionist and Lincoln loyalist), and decidedly impolitic, ultimately causing harm to the Democratic ticket.

Throughout the general campaign, Democrats persistently demanded the end of Reconstruction and the full restoration of rights to former rebels who had been stripped of their franchise and qualifications for office. Republicans remained steadfast in their support of the franchise for blacks. Incorporating the far-seeing resolutions of the Union League of America, an ardent pro-Union, pro-Lincoln organization that was formed in 1862, into their party platform, the Republicans declared that African Americans "had justified the reposing in their hands the highest boon of an American citizen, the ballot, and illustrated the truth that it is eminently wise and always safe to act with equity and justice to all men, without regard to race or color." In a famous speech, Robert G. Ingersoll of Maine asked, "Is not a negro who is an honor to the black race, better than a white man who is a disgrace to the white race?" Democrats countered these efforts by becoming even more vehemently opposed to the suffrage of African Americans. Southern journalists and politicians claimed that the African race was naturally inferior, lacking both the intelligence and character to participate in political life. Northern Democrats were not immune to such attitudes. The *New York Herald* criticized the Republicans' attachment to the cause of the franchise for blacks, even claiming a correlation between the improvement of conditions for African Americans and the growing oppression of whites, and doing so all the while by employing racist epithets. In a sense, the Civil War was still being fought, but now through the political process and within the opinion pages of the press over the fate of African Americans and their role in the future political direction of the republic. However, politics in the United States is seldom that simple; some Democrats recognized what Republicans had already realized: that the new "Negro vote" might be an untapped political resource. Democrats in Nashville made an appeal to the newly enfranchised by trying to convince them that the values represented by the Democratic Party were in fact closer to their interests as new citizens than those of the Republican Party.

Typically, the requisite mudslinging soon materialized. Democrats accused Grant of being a drunken, opportunistic, cold-hearted butcher. He was also accused of being an anti-Semite, an indictment that stemmed from Grant's actions as commander of the 13th Army Corps during the war. In December 1862, General Grant issued an order to expel Jewish citizens from the military district that he oversaw at the time, an area that included Tennessee, Mississippi, and Kentucky, based on a suspicion that Jewish merchants were supporting an underground market in the region. Responding to direct appeals from the Jewish community, President Lincoln revoked Grant's order, and historians are still unclear as to whether or not Grant was fully responsible for the incident. Nonetheless, Grant admitted responsibility, thus tainting with anti-Semitic overtones his record of tolerance. His running mate, Colfax, was also attacked, depicted as an office-grubbing and self-serving "politician by trade," and he was accused of having once been an anti-Catholic Know-Nothing, an indictment that appeared to hold a grain of truth, given that Colfax, a former Whig, was tempted to join the American Party upon the collapse of the Whig Party.

Seymour, while generally well liked within the party, was not immune to smear tactics. In the aftermath of the war, Republicans were prone to associating the Democratic Party as a whole with treason and rebellion, and they were not above questioning Seymour's loyalty, claiming that his wartime tenure as Democratic governor of New York was suspiciously cozy with elements among the Copperheads. Seymour became a target of the political cartoonist Thomas Nast, who drew for the popular *Harper's Weekly* and whose efforts would result in the introduction of cartooning as a major force in presidential politics and an important development in the evolution of presidential campaign politics. Nast portrayed Seymour as the instigator of the 1863 New York City draft riots, which led to numerous deaths and the destruction of large amounts of property. Nast and others alleged that Seymour had addressed the anti-draft rioters as "My Friends." Nast also used his cartoons to tie the Democratic Party to Forrest and the Ku Klux Klan. Seymour's running mate was another matter; he was far more vulnerable to smear tactics than Seymour. Blair was accused of being a drunk and a thief. Worse, untoward comments made by Blair recommending the nullification of Reconstruction and rashly calling for another war simply could not be answered. With the outlook dismal, Seymour felt compelled to go on the stump, touring several northern cities, a tactic that was seen as inconsonant with his good reputation. It also did not help that Seymour proved to be an awkward campaigner.

Given Blair's comments and Seymour's ineffective activity on the campaign trail, rumors about a movement to reconvene another convention to replace Seymour with Chase simmered but were eventually cooled. However, the damage to Seymour's candidacy had been done; Blair was a liability, and Seymour could not muster the skills needed to compensate. But the Democrats as a group were the more vulnerable target, and direct attacks against the candidates were not really necessary. "Scratch a Democrat and you will find a rebel" became a familiar accusatory refrain directed to Southern politicians. Massachusetts Radical Republican Benjamin Butler intensified the drama of the campaign by publicly exhibiting and waving the blood-stained garment of an unfortunate victim of the Ku Klux Klan. "Waving the Bloody Shirt" would henceforth become a visceral and recurring anti-Southern image in subsequent nineteenth-century campaigns.

To his credit, Grant remained above the fray throughout the campaign. Following the standard practice of nineteenth-century presidential candidates, Grant relied on surrogates to stump for him, choosing to spend most of his time receiving supporters in his home in Galena, Illinois, and committing himself to a few modest trips to his native Ohio, Missouri, Kentucky, and Denver in the Colorado Territory. On his way to Denver, he joined generals Sherman and Sheridan at Omaha, the three war heroes touring the West to popular acclaim.

Most importantly, the Campaign of 1868 was marked by the beginnings of antiblack violence in the South. Moderate Democrats were, as noted above, working to win the African American vote, but other elements sought to thwart efforts to enfranchise the emancipated slaves. Some Democratic candidates were warning African Americans away from the polls, and the Ku Klux Klan and similar terrorist groups employed violence against African Americans throughout the South; assaults became more frequent, often resulting in serious wounding and even death. These brutal tactics of intimidation, as bad as they were in 1868, would become even more pervasive and grave in the elections that followed. Lynching victimized both blacks and whites over the next few decades, grievously impairing the equal enforcement of the law and the progress of political democratization envisioned by the authors of the first civil rights legislation. Against the current of violent racism, the black vote, however whittled down by post-Reconstruction tactics effectively aimed at disenfranchisement, would subsequently remain Republican for six more decades. Against the currents of reaction, African Americans managed to participate in Republican politics in spite of the institutionalized discrimination against them, and they would continue the custom of sending delegates to Republican conventions.

Even though the campaign went badly for the Democrats, the demographics of electoral politics kept them in the race. The party held a monopoly among the white majority in the South, as no white Southerner would entertain even the thought of voting for the Party of Lincoln, and the minority African American vote, which was loyal to the Republicans, was not enough to counter the huge advantage held by the Democrats in the former Confederacy, with or without the criminal efforts to disenfranchise black voters. Democrats also managed to retain some loyalty within the urban North, a legacy of machine politics that began to take hold before the war and that gave Democrats some hope that they might crack the Republicans' Northern stronghold. By Election Day, the outcome was uncertain, even though Grant was clearly the more compelling candidate. But any uncertainties were soon dispelled as Grant easily won the popular vote, earning over 3,000,000 votes, more than any candidate in the history of presidential elections. Seymour did surprisingly well, winning just over 2,700,000 votes, or about 47 percent to Grant's 53 percent majority. The Electoral College was another matter, with Grant taking 214 electors, or 72 percent, to Seymour's 80. Seymour won just 8 states to Grant's 26, suffering a crushing defeat. However, the party held out some hope. Seymour did manage to win New York, which at the time had the highest number of electoral votes (33), as well as taking New Jersey's 7 and Oregon's 3. The Democrats also came close to winning in California, losing by a narrow margin and thus again showing surprising support in the Pacific West. The rest of Seymour's support came from the South and the border states, but the fact that he won New York and New Jersey, and barely lost in California, indicated that the Democratic Party, while clearly the minority party in the postwar era, was more resilient than expected and could possibly regain some cross-regional support. Republicans dismissed the Democrats' strong showing in New York, blaming their loss in the Empire State on allegations of voter fraud committed by New York City's famed political machine, Tammany Hall.

The Republican electoral victory instilled within the Republican Congress the confidence to pass the Fifteenth Amendment, which prohibited states from denying African American males the right to vote because of their race or color. By March 1870, the Fifteenth Amendment became law after a sufficient number of states ratified the amendment. Texas, Florida, Virginia, and Mississippi were readmitted into the Union as full partners following their respective ratification of the Fourteenth Amendment as well as amendments to their state constitutions guaranteeing universal male suffrage. Despite the ratification of the Fourteenth and Fifteenth Amendments, support for continued military occupation of the South and the implementation of Reconstruction policies would gradually decline within the Republican Party, thereby presenting a serious political challenge for Republicans in their Northern electoral base and new opportunities for the Democratic Party to continue to reassert and redefine itself outside the South. In the meantime, the Republicans would be prevented from making any inroads into the South for at least another century. The Republican Party would continue to dominate presidential politics throughout the remainder of the nineteenth century, but it could and would be challenged by a resurgent rival.

Additional Resources

Coleman, Charles H. *The Election of 1868: The Democratic Effort to Regain Control.* New York: Columbia University Press, 1933.

Franklin, John Hope. "Election of 1868." In Arthur M. Schlesinger, Fred Israel, and William P. Hansen, eds. *History of American Presidential Elections, 1789–1968*. Vol. 2. New York: Chelsea House, 1985.

Simpson, Brooks D. *Let Us Have Peace: Ulysses S. Grant and the Politics of War and Reconstruction 1861–1868*. Chapel Hill: University of North Carolina Press, 1991.

Trefousse, Hans L. "1868." In Arthur M. Schlesinger, Fred L. Israel, and David J. Frent, eds. *Running for President: The Candidates and Their Images*. New York: Simon & Schuster, 1994.

Campaign of 1872

Civilian leadership and military command are of different qualities. On the occasion of President Ulysses Grant's inauguration as the eighteenth president of the United States, a good portion of the nation responded with relief over the end of a failed Johnson administration and held high hopes in the prospect of the ascent of a widely acclaimed war hero and bold leader—at least so acclaimed throughout most sections of the country—to the White House. Many saw in Grant the qualities they admired in the legends of Washington and Jackson, and his ability to keep his dignity during the campaign lent support to that sentiment.

But President Grant's administration soon gave reason to disappoint. Corruption, incompetence, nepotism, and internal dissent against the continuation of Reconstruction shook the administration and severely fragmented the Republican Party. Grant himself was capable and essentially honest, but poor decisions regarding appointments, based more on loyalty and sentiment than professional considerations, damaged his reputation and undermined his personal integrity. Grant led what was far and away the most corrupt administration to date by filling offices with favorites and relatives, many of whom were either unfit for their appointments or devoid of any moral scruples. Scandal gripped the presidency. Vice President Schuyler Colfax had been implicated in the Crédit Mobilier scandal, an affair of bribery and graft that actually had occurred during the Johnson administration but came to light during Grant's term, one that entangled high officials who were now a part of his own administration. Because of the extensive corruption, a new term, "Grantism," was coined both to describe the condition of corruption that gripped the administration and to claim the location of its source directly in the president himself rather than the Republican Party. Many believed the president to be largely or wholly responsible and sought to begin governmental reform by directly targeting the White House. Others, however, observed that it was not so much the president as it was his closest advisers who exposed themselves as self-serving and venal flatterers who had poisoned the administration at the expense of Grant's good name and the administration's effectiveness. In either case, Republicans, in thinking about the upcoming election, were in a state of confusion and, in some quarters, either disenchantment or outright panic. The party that had proved so strong in the previous two elections was now vulnerable, and a president who had inspired so much confidence when inaugurated was now viewed by an ample number of voters as an inept failure.

As a result, as early as 1870, a number of leading Republicans saw themselves as a group in dissent against their president, and thus by the beginning of the 1872 campaign, a faction had emerged with the Republican Party that was clearly anti-Grant, demanding civil service reform as a way to control the unbridled corruption that was a consequence of the expansion and abuses of political patronage under the current president. This patronage system, often referred to as the "spoils system," had been the common way of assigning political appointments for decades, and it was taken for granted as the standard method of conducting the business of politics; but a movement was under way that sought a more meritocratic, professional civil service, and many Republicans, weary of "Grantism," were more than ready to pick up the cause. Members of this reform faction included some of the party's more talented and influential leaders, including famed journalist, reformer, and intellectual eccentric Horace Greeley, Republican elder statesman Charles Francis Adams (son and grandson of presidents), Justice Salmon P. Chase (who had also recently been courted by Democrats as a possible presidential candidate), Supreme Court justice and Abraham Lincoln's campaign manager David Davis, Senator Charles Sumner of Massachusetts, Illinois senator Lyman Trumbull (author of the Thirteenth Amendment and the Civil Rights Act of 1866), and Missouri senator Carl Schurz, who first made a political name for himself stumping within the German immigrant community in Illinois for Abraham Lincoln during his failed 1858 senatorial campaign. It was Schurz who, in a speech before the Senate in 1872, declaimed, "My country, right or wrong; if right, to be kept right; and if wrong, to be set right," a modification of the famous phrase that is also attributed to naval war hero Stephen Decatur. However, Grant, in spite of the myriad problems that weakened his administration, still held a strong base of supporters, enough to expose within the party a division so wide that it could not, at least at this time, be bridged.

Thus, largely through leadership of Schurz, this reform faction split from the main party, called themselves the Liberal Republicans of the United States, and convened in Cincinnati in May 1872 to independently nominate their own presidential candidate. Schurz, who was born in Germany and was thus ineligible to stand as a candidate, was nonetheless an important presence throughout the convention. His keynote speech was a critical moment, wherein he urged delegates to "rise above petty considerations" and "small bickerings" and instead seize the moment not only to defeat Grant, but also to infuse in the presidency, and in politics as such, a "loftier moral spirit." The campaign goal of "anybody but Grant" would not suffice to promote such lofty ends; a substantively credible challenger needed to be found. Chase, Sumner, and Adams were the more eminent figures, but Chase's flirtation with the Democrats in 1872 had eroded his once-considerable influence within the Republican Party. Sumner was slowed by poor health and hampered by a personality that many found difficult to manage. Greeley was also mentioned, but his support was almost exclusively concentrated in the Northeast, and particularly in New York; thus many viewed him as a potentially effective candidate for the vice presidency, one that could help bring New York's thirty-three electoral votes to the ticket. That said, Greeley had been promoting himself for the White House for at least a year, and it was clear to the delegates that Greeley might not settle for the second spot. Just how much of a force he would be at the convention was unclear, but his attempts to gain the nomination were known long before the delegates convened in Cincinnati. Three candidates were thus viewed as the more plausible contenders for the Liberal Republican campaign against Grant: Adams, Trumbull, and Davis, with a fourth, Greeley, looming ever larger on the horizon.

Adams was a brilliant and respected public servant, popular among Midwestern liberal Republicans and attractive to Democrats along the Eastern Seaboard. His moderate approach to the former Confederacy might have been an advantage in the South, even though as a Republican, Adams was already at a disadvantage there, for very few white Southerners were open to supporting a candidate from the Party of Lincoln. But he also brought some liabilities, beginning with his age (sixty-five), his disinterest in the competitive side of politics, and his close association with Schurz, who had over the years made a number of enemies. Trumbull, whose major triumphs were his leadership in the adoption of the Thirteenth Amendment and passage of the Civil Rights Act of 1866, came to the convention with a distinguished record and even more enemies than Schurz. He was a hardline Radical Republican whose vote on President Johnson's behalf during the Senate's removal proceedings saved the Johnson presidency, much to the chagrin of nearly everyone in his party. Trumbull was also aging, and like Adams, he found campaigning burdensome. Justice Davis was thus the front-runner as the convention opened. He had support in the Midwest and the South, but among the Liberal Republicans of the East, his record as a justice was not fittingly attuned to the spirit of liberal reform. His supporters offended delegates at the convention with their overconfidence and their indulgent behavior. Davis had been an important political asset to Lincoln back in the day, but his inability to conduct a disciplined campaign in his own behalf may suggest just who was in fact the bigger asset to whom in that particular relationship.

On the eve of the convention, four influential liberal editors targeted Davis, simultaneously lambasting him in their respective newspapers published in

Cincinnati, Louisville, Chicago, and Springfield, Illinois. It was now apparent that Davis had squandered his pre-convention political capital, and thus on the first ballot he finished a distant fifth, polling only 92 votes to 203 for Adams, 147 for Greeley, 110 for Trumbull, and 95 for Missouri's Benjamin Gatz Brown, numbered among Schurz's enemies. This initial result revealed the extent of Greeley's influence and served as a wave that he rode into the second ballot, where he gained 101 additional votes for a total of 245, moving just slightly ahead of Adams, who also gained votes to finish with 243. Trumbull gained as well, finishing third with 148, while Davis's fortunes slid dramatically, the preconvention front-runner polling only 75 votes. Andrew J. Curtin of Pennsylvania drew 62, with Chase pulling in just 2 votes. Brown, who now openly supported Greeley (his nemesis, Schurz, backed Adams), slid to just 2 votes, but his efforts provided Greeley with a significant bloc that helped propel him toward the top of the field.

On the fourth and fifth ballots, Adams once again pulled ahead of Greeley, as Greeley actually lost ground on the fourth ballot and scarcely made it up on the fifth. Adams, after five ballots, held a 309 to 258 vote lead, and the apparent momentum needed to propel him the nomination. But Adams's ascent suddenly stalled; enough delegates were on the floor who simply refused to vote for him under any circumstance, thus preventing him from achieving the needed 359 votes and victory. These delegates were more amenable to Greeley, particularly the Trumbull delegates, who now began to switch to the Greeley cause, helping to suddenly turn the tide away from Adams and toward the journalist/reformer from New York. Thus on the sixth ballot, Greeley pulled back into the lead, gaining 74 votes for a total of 332. Surprisingly, Adams also gained, increasing his delegate count to 324, but Greeley's more significant gain was a game changer. On the next round, the seventh, Greeley won 442 votes and thus the nomination. The convention then proceeded to reward Brown's alliance with Greeley by nominating him with ease on the second ballot. Trumbull also had some support for the second spot, but it was not enough to challenge Brown. The platform that was adopted by the Liberal Republican Party contained three central planks: civil service reform and the imposition of higher standards for public service, phasing out Reconstruction, and lowering tariffs.

Oddly enough, the Liberal Republicans were less interested in the situation facing African American voters and their increasingly frustrated attempts to exercise their rights now explicitly protected under the Constitution and supported by related federal laws. In 1871, intensified violence against African Americans forced President Grant to ask Congress to enact the Ku Klux Klan Act, which would thereby give federal officials the authority to arrest, prosecute, and punish individuals who engaged in the kind of intimidation and violence that had become a Klan specialty. Despite the frightening realities of terror and brutality directed against the freed slaves, Liberal Republicans sought to shift the focus from Reconstruction to government reform. While the Liberal platform sought to dismantle Reconstruction governments, it notwithstanding still endorsed the Reconstruction Amendments and the doctrine of equal rights under the law, a position that to their critics exposed inconsistencies. This platform also advocated a grant of universal amnesty to Southern citizens and withdrawal of federal troops from the South, a move that many felt would thoroughly undermine African American citizenship and the attempt to reform a former slave society. Advocating equal rights and yet proposing measures that put African Americans' vulnerable voting rights at risk was a contradiction that seems to have been lost on the delegates. But the mood of the country was changing, and the debate over what Reconstruction meant and what could be done on behalf of freedmen began to lose its energy. In addition to the Liberal wing, other Republicans had also grown tired of military occupation and became highly critical of arguably undemocratic and allegedly "carpetbag" Reconstruction governments in Southern states, thus sympathizing with some of the same complaints voiced by their counterparts among the Democrats, particularly those in the South.

Meanwhile, the Democratic Party convened in Baltimore the following July, and in a unique twist in American political history, the Democrats as a cohesive body joined a rival party to embrace its candidate, and thus they seconded Greeley's nomination for the presidency, hoping that the action would ultimately weaken the Republicans. Thus Greeley would run on the separate endorsements of both the Liberal Republicans and the Democrats. Greeley was far from being a hero to the Democrats; his political past was in part defined by his opposition to the Democratic Party and, in particular, what that party had meant to the South. Nonetheless, the Democrats concluded that they did not have a candidate anywhere near the stature needed to challenge Grant, whom they despised; and that for the long term, a strategy that would further divide the Republicans was their best opportunity for the upcoming election and beyond. The Democratic convention lasted but six hours, the shortest on record, Greeley having been nominated on the first ballot with 686 votes out of 724 delegates. Brown was also nominated for the second slot, winning 713 first-round votes. The Democrats adopted the Liberal Republican platform with a few minor changes and additions, mostly for show, as an attempt to appear to be a party apart. But in reality, the Democratic Party was, at least for the moment, almost at one with the Liberal Republicans, much in the same way that the War Democrats allied themselves closely with the Republicans in the Union Party coalition that had previously reelected Lincoln and subsequently elected Grant. The difference was that in this case, the Democrats were only lukewarm for Greeley.

Even though Greeley's nomination was virtually unopposed at the hastily concluded convention, there were a few dissenters. Democrats who were more conservatively disposed, forerunners of what would later be called the Bourbon Democrats, a faction that would soon become a powerful force in the party's future, were openly displeased. Alexander Stephens (former vice president of the Confederacy), for one, was appalled by the options left to the Democrats in the endorsement of Greeley, describing the choice between Grant and Greeley as akin to a choice between "hemlock and strychnine." A number of Bourbon Democrats bolted and nominated their own candidate, eminent lawyer Charles O'Conor of New York, under the banner of the "Straight-Out Democrats." The Straight-Out campaign was meager, winning in the end only slightly above 23,600 votes nationwide in the general election; but it is of interest as a historical first, for O'Conor, a Roman Catholic, became the first of his faith to be nominated by any party as a candidate for the presidency. It would not be until 1928 that another Catholic (Alfred E. Smith, another New Yorker) would receive a presidential nomination from either a major or a minor party. John Quincy Adams II, son of Charles Adams (recently defeated by Greeley for the Liberal nomination) and grandson of his presidential namesake, was nominated as his running mate. Adams, an erstwhile Republican, had switched to the Democratic Party as a result of his dissatisfaction with Republican Reconstruction policies. Neither O'Conor nor Adams sought their nominations, and both abstained from actively campaigning, although Adams in particular was publicly critical of the Greeley nomination.

A month after the Liberal Republicans met in Cincinnati, President Grant's diehard supporters, of whom there were many in spite of the stain of scandal, held their convention in Philadelphia, which was the official convention of the Republican Party (the hybrid Union Party moniker by now falling into disuse). As before, Grant was nominated without opposition, this time with considerable flourish resembling a coronation more than an election. The convention dropped controversial incumbent vice president Schuyler Colfax from the ticket and replaced him with Senator Henry Wilson of Massachusetts, an old opponent of slavery; but not without a fight, as Colfax still had numerous loyal supporters and an interest in high office. Grant, however, was annoyed at Colfax for making it publicly known that he would volunteer to run for president should Grant decide to step down, a statement that turned Grant's interest toward Wilson and to those delegates who chose to back him.

In an effort to defuse the crisis over the integrity of the Grant administration, as well as to counter the defection of the "Cincinnati Soreheads" that had nominated Greeley, convention delegates adopted a number of progressive planks. The platform reaffirmed statutory support for the Civil War amendments, begrudgingly endorsed civil service reform, and continued the traditional support for protective tariffs. Significantly, the party added a plank recognizing obligations to women, proposing their "admission to wider fields of usefulness," and suggesting the "respectful consideration" of "additional rights" for their sex. This constituted the first women's rights plank in American politics, and its inclusion won the endorsement of suffragette Susan B. Anthony, who had accused Greeley of publishing editorials unfriendly toward the cause of women. With the Civil War receding further into history, the political rights of women was now a cause regaining broader attention, and the Republican plank reflected a growing awareness, however gradually, of the justice of that cause. The convention was mostly a showcase for President Grant, but owing to these kinds of elements, it did promote a fairly farsighted platform. It was also the first convention to make full use of the instant communication now provided through the invention of the telegraph, as the electorate was now frequently alerted to the latest updates over the wire.

Events in the general election campaign broke well for President Grant. Liberal Republicans and their new allies, the Democrats, overestimated the effectiveness of the civil service reform and amnesty issues and underestimated Grant's personal popularity. Equally important, Greeley proved a weak candidate unable to deal with relentless Republican attacks. Greeley was certainly an idiosyncratic personality, even more so than Zachary Taylor, the blasé, albeit successful, Whig candidate in the campaign of 1848. Greeley's somewhat confused jumble of ideas and opinions revealed a restless and puzzling mind. He could appear farsighted and open-minded and then suddenly exhibit simple-minded intolerance. He was prone to dial into fads and fashionable causes, and he entertained cultish proclivities. His attraction to crackpot thinking weakened the credibility of his social vision. He was an abolitionist who excoriated hierarchy and privilege, and yet he was regarded in the women's movement as an enemy to that cause. He was once described by journalist Charles Dana as a "visionary without faith, a radical without root, an extremist without persistency, a strife-maker without courage." Grant, by comparison, was a safe and welcome alternative.

Some might regard the Greeley campaign as an unmitigated disaster, which may in part be true, but President Grant's success can also be attributed to his own personal resilience in deflecting criticism and marshaling his own loyal forces. Grant had, after all, vanquished far more formidable enemies in the past. Republican-aligned newspapers depicted Greeley as an eccentric troublemaker espousing weird ideas. For instance, political cartoonist Thomas Nast incessantly mocked Greeley with caricatures of a pumpkin-headed, mole-eyed know-it-all, easily corrupted, intellectually muddled, and foolishly arrogant. Nast's cartoons also strenuously impugned Greeley's loyalty and patriotism to great effect by portraying images of the Liberal candidate congratulating rebel soldiers, aiding and abetting murderous Klansmen, and scandalously joining hands with the notorious assassin John Wilkes Booth while wickedly gloating over Abraham Lincoln's grave. Once again, waving the bloody shirt and evoking President Lincoln's martyrdom worked to great effect against Republicans' opponents and helped further to seal Greeley's fate. At the end of the campaign, Greeley remarked, "I have been assailed so bitterly that I hardly know whether I was running for the presidency or the penitentiary." Memories of the Civil War and Grant's critical role in the Union victory were more powerful than any discontent over his administration's many problems. The Republican platform also helped Grant in his own efforts to address the problem of government corruption by supporting the establishment of a government commission charged with civil service reform.

Mudslinging was a tactic also employed by the Liberal Republican/Democratic coalition. Greeley supporters trotted out tired accusations of drunkenness and military butchery, and they attempted to tie Grant to scandals that had implicated his friends and associates. Matt Morgan, an editorial cartoonist stridently critical of Grant, drew the president as a cretinous, cigar-chomping crook, a crowned petty thief swilling huge quantities of liquor, raised palm opened for the bosses to grease. But in the end, Grant was again victorious, soundly defeating the politically naïve Greeley in spite of the serious scandals within his administration and the numerous biting insults launched against him.

Grant won in a landslide, carrying all but six states for a total of 286 electoral votes to Greeley's 66. Grant's electoral vote total was the highest ever in terms of raw numbers, exceeding the previous record of 254 won by Franklin Pierce in 1852 (President Lincoln impressively won 212 in the 1864 election, made more remarkable by the absence of 11 states). In the popular vote, Grant won close to 3,600,000 (55.6%), far exceeding his number in the previous election, while Greeley somehow managed to win approximately 2,800,000 (43.8%). Of note is the formation in 1869 of the Prohibition Party, which in 1872 nominated James Black of Pennsylvania, an advocate for temperance, for the presidency. Black scarcely won a total of 5,000 popular votes, but the temperance movement was under way, and when tied to the larger currents of progressivism, it would gain enough momentum to achieve its goals by the early twentieth century. Equally of interest is the candidacy of Victoria Woodhull for president, joined by the eminent Frederick Douglass for vice president on a ticket sponsored by what was called the Equal Rights Party. These two personages represent the first woman to officially run for president and the first African American to run for vice president, albeit on a minor party ticket. Whether or not the Equal Rights Party won any votes is unclear. Woodhull was a woman of some controversy, having been arrested on obscenity charges days before the general election.

Given Grant's vulnerability, the outcome more than anything exposed the weakness of the Democrats, who did not even select their own candidate. Interestingly, Grant won a majority of the former Confederate states, taking some of them decisively. An important factor was the African American vote, which was still exercised in spite of the many and increasing localized criminal efforts to blunt it. Sadly, this situation would soon change, as early as the following presidential election, and the black vote would not contribute significantly until well into the twentieth century.

Additional Resources

Gillette, William. "Election of 1872." In Arthur M. Schlesinger, Fred Israel, and William P. Hansen, eds., *History of American Presidential Elections, 1789–1968*. Vol. 2. New York: Chelsea House, 1985.

McFeely, William S. "1872." In Arthur M. Schlesinger, Fred L. Israel, and David J. Frent, eds. *Running for President: The Candidates and Their Images*. New York: Simon & Schuster, 1994.

Smith, Jean Edward. *Grant*. New York: Simon & Schuster, 2002.

Campaign of 1876

Coming a full century after the signing of the Declaration of Independence, the Campaign of 1876 demonstrates the ongoing tension between the egalitarian ideal of 1776 and its frustrated application throughout the social and political life of the republic. Reconstruction had been under way for over a decade, but the attempt to restructure politics and political culture in the United States along lines more congruent with the founding principles of liberty and equality continued to encounter sustained resistance. For most of the prior decade, Radical Republicans had pushed Southern Reconstruction as necessary to assure that these principles would take root and hold fast in the former slave states. But such measures required constant effort and resilience against those who would resist the dramatic changes needed to overcome the legacy of slavery that reached back to the colonial period and had itself pushed down its own strong roots, holding firm until the bloody constraint of an actual civil war forcefully dislodged it. Such prolonged and extensive effort often loses energy after a short time, and this was certainly the case for the cause of the Radical Republicans in the mid-1870s.

By 1876, intensified opposition to Reconstruction mounted from social and political forces, North and South, tired of the enthusiasms of reform and anxious to reestablish the traditional social order. From the perspective of the South, the Republican Party represented an oppressive occupation force, a conquering military regime depriving Southern civilization of the dignities of self-government. Even though Reconstruction was losing momentum, Southerners still bristled at the presence of federal troops in three states (South Carolina, Louisiana, and Florida), and the state governments—described in the pejorative as "carpetbag" regimes—that had been installed in the South after the war were deemed fraudulent, Jacobin, opportunistic, and utterly dependent on the presence of federal troops. Indeed, it was evident to many that the only thing that kept the despised Party of Lincoln viable anywhere in the old Confederacy was the federal military. In 1870 and 1871, Congress under the direction of the Radical Republicans passed the Enforcement Acts, promulgated to reinforce the radical governments that had been established in the separate southern states. But working against this, in 1872, the passage of the Amnesty Act granting amnesty to former Confederates enabled the return to politics of many Southern white leaders who could now openly muster their energies to officially oppose Reconstruction policies within their state governments, and to reenter government and influence policy at the federal level. The Civil War was long over, but sectionalism remained strong, and as the parties themselves were closely identified with the sections, residual postbellum enmities between North and South were the same enmities now converted to those held between Republicans and Democrats.

This deep sectional animosity, the immediate legacy of the Civil War, and what was regarded in the South as the bane of Reconstruction, reverberated throughout the Campaign of 1876 and infected any political debate or discussion at the national level. Republican politicians on the stump bluntly reminded the electorate that it was the Democratic Party that had supported slavery, betrayed the Union, and killed Northern sons—culminating in the assassination of the Great Emancipator himself. Campaigning in late September for the Republican candidate, firebrand Robert G. Ingersoll, one of the era's greatest orators, invoking the spirit of the waved bloody shirt, reiterated Democratic perfidy at a speech delivered before a veterans' association in Indianapolis:

"Every State that seceded from the Union was a Democratic State," he declaimed, "Every man that tried to destroy the nation was a Democrat. Every man that shot Union soldiers was a Democrat.. . .Every man that loved slavery better than liberty was a Democrat. The man that assassinated Abraham Lincoln was a Democrat.. . .Every man that wanted the privilege of whipping another man. . .was a Democrat. Every man that raised bloodhounds to pursue human beings was a Democrat.. . .Soldiers, every scar you have. . .was given you by a Democrat.. . .[E]very arm that is lacking, every limb that is gone, is a souvenir of a Democrat. I want you to recollect." (Ingersoll, Vol. 9)

The continuing dispute, often vituperative and always anguished, over Reconstruction was further darkened by the lingering shadow of "Grantism" (i.e., the public's reaction to years of maladministration under President Grant, an honest and sincere leader undercut by unscrupulous self-servers), a problem that Grant had already managed to dodge in 1872 but that was now again haunting the party as it moved into the general election season. Even though a series of investigations failed to tie the president directly to any of the scandals, the extent of the corruption did its damage to his party. Finally, the September 18, 1873, failure of Jay Cooke and Company, one of the most respected banking houses in the United States, touched off the Panic of 1873, the harbinger of a three-year depression during which more than ten thousand businesses failed. These three trends—discontent over Reconstruction, disenchantment over Republican corruption, and a troubled economy—created an almost perfect situation providing the Democratic Party with an opportunity to finally make a serious move to recapture the White House.

Within this context, the centennial election was nearly calamitous. The campaign prior to the election was pocked with bitter invective, prevarication, and scandalmongering. The election itself appeared to be an undemocratic fraud. It would seem to many that the only self-evident truth marking the centennial of the Declaration of Independence was that life, liberty, and the pursuit of happiness are ever mocked and occasionally trumped by callous partisan ambition. As the Republican Party held its convention in Cincinnati in June, James Gillespie Blaine of Maine, a former Speaker of the House who was about to move to the Senate and was an increasingly important personage within the Republican Party, and governor and war hero Rutherford B. Hayes of Ohio were the main contenders for the Republican nomination, despite the fact that President Grant had earlier indicated his willingness to break President Washington's hallowed precedent and accept a third term. Blaine appeared to have early momentum, and he received a famous and ringing endorsement from Ingersoll at the convention.

Many saw in Blaine, who projected a palpable magnetism (he was often referred to as "The Magnetic Man"), a figure of great promise. During the latter half of the Civil War, Blaine, who at that time was a junior member of the House of Representatives, had earned the trust of President Lincoln himself, and as a highly skilled speaker in his own right, Blaine became well known throughout the country for his inspirational oratory in support of Lincoln and on behalf of the Union cause. His rhetorical skills could be overwhelming; in a debate against his most bitter political rival, New York's Roscoe Conkling, his rebuttal was so withering that Conkling came away feeling publicly humiliated. Blaine was also involved in coauthoring the Fourteenth Amendment and had positioned himself as a moderate on the issue of Reconstruction, as well as a moderate on Republican positions in general. Indeed, Blaine had become one of the principal leaders— perhaps *the* principal leader—of the "Half Breeds," one of the two major factions in the Republican Party that had emerged during Reconstruction, the other being the "Stalwarts." The Half Breeds were so named because their moderate stance on most policies was described by their enemies as only "half Republican," or "half breed." The Half Breeds were not moderates when it came to their opposition to political patronage; they were the wing of the party most committed to civil service reform and the end of the "spoils system," whereas the Stalwarts were well entrenched behind the older practice of patronage. Blaine was without question a brilliant politician, and moving toward the convention, his appeal seemed to push him out in front of the field. And Ingersoll was perhaps his most fervent champion; in a now-famous nominating speech at the 1876 convention, a speech that is still regarded as one of the finest of its kind, the remarkable orator coined Blaine's most famous nickname, the Plumed Knight:

> Like an armed warrior, like a plumed knight, James G. Blaine marched down the halls of the American Congress and threw his shining lances full and fair against the brazen foreheads of every defamer of his country and maligner of its honor. For the Republican Party to desert a gallant man now is worse than if an army should desert their general upon the field of battle. James G. Blaine is now, and has been for years, the bearer of the sacred standard of the Republic. I call it sacred because no human being can stand beneath its folds without becoming, and without remaining, free. (Ingersoll, Vol. 9)

But to his political misfortune, Blaine's reputation had also suffered owing to a serious public scandal implicating him in unscrupulous railroad deals from which he had allegedly gained considerable personal profit. Indeed, Ingersoll's encomium celebrating Blaine on the convention floor was in part a defense of his candidate against these allegations. Apparently while serving Congress as the Speaker of the House of Representatives in 1869 (during the Andrew Johnson administration), Blaine had unduly used his weighty influence to pass legislation that would unfairly promote the business interests of the Little Rock & Fort Smith Railroad. In return for this favor, a contractor for the railroad, Warren Fisher Jr., made arrangements for Speaker Blaine to sell railroad securities, thereby allowing Blaine to line his own pockets with a generous commission in railroad bonds. The plan backfired as the value of the bonds plummeted, rendering them almost useless to Blaine. Another financier, Tom Scott, came to the aid of both Blaine and the railroad by purchasing Blaine's now nearly worthless bonds at a price that would garner a profit. In return for this favor, Speaker Blaine would ensure the passage of legislation that would benefit Scott's own railroad enterprise, the Texas & Pacific Railroad. A congressional investigation was established at the insistence of House Democrats, who alleged bribery and influence peddling, and the Speaker was now on trial before his colleagues. To the ever-alert cartoonist Thomas Nast, the Plumed Knight was sketched as a "Tattooed Man," displaying in ink the wages of shady deals, graft, and corruption. The cartoonist's pen was more perspicuous than Blaine, who seriously underestimated the impact of the scandal on the delegates at the 1876 convention.

The whole affair came to be known as the "Mulligan Letters" scandal after James Mulligan, a Boston bookkeeper (once employed by Blaine's brother in-law) who became a central figure in the controversy when he had claimed to keep in his possession personal letters of an incriminating nature that would expose the guilt of Blaine and his friends to the investigating committee. In late May, just as Blaine was about to clear his name before the committee (and in so doing, clear his way to the Republican nomination and, quite plausibly, the presidency), Mulligan revealed the existence of the letters and made it known that he was willing to share their contents. Immediately the committee went into recess, and in the interval, as Mulligan would claim, Blaine, in an allegedly desperate attempt to forestall the scandal, visited him at his home and, through a sustained battery of pleading, cajoling, and the promise of political office, tricked Mulligan into handing over the letters (said to number fourteen letters in all) to Blaine on the grounds that they were, after all, his own private and personal property. In Mulligan's account, Blaine was so distressed that he threatened suicide, although there is no evidence, other than Mulligan's own claim, that any of this happened. In fact, Blaine denied the entire story, asserting that he had never visited Mulligan's home; and on the House floor, after reading into the record what he claimed were the actual letters, he turned them over to the investigative committee. Mulligan claimed that the letters produced by Blaine did not account for the entire correspondence, and that other, more damaging letters were withheld by Blaine. Before it could go any further, the investigation stalled, and eventually the House lost its authority to investigate Blaine, as he received an appointment to the U.S. Senate, making him invulnerable to any further House action. Blaine's friends and political allies were satisfied that he had exonerated himself, but the odor of scandal would nonetheless dog him for the remainder of his political career, beginning with the nominating convention of 1876.

Erupting a few days before the beginning of the Republican convention, the Mulligan Letters scandal had altered the playing field. With the erstwhile Liberal Republicans now back in the party fold, and with suspicions about Blaine nagging at a number of party regulars, the cry for a reform candidate grew more forceful. Given Blaine's now weakened position, a number of candidates entered the fray; thus Blaine, Hayes, and Conkling were now joined by other viable contenders: Benjamin Bristow of Kentucky, Senator Oliver Morton of Indiana, and Governor John H. Hartranft of Pennsylvania, a former general and Medal of Honor winner who had served in the same army corps with Hayes during the war. Connecticut's Marshall Jewel, postmaster general, rounded out the field. As secretary of the treasury under President Grant, Bristow had broken yet another scandal, one known as the Whiskey Ring, a fairly elaborate conspiracy involving whiskey distillers and collateral businesses related to whiskey production and distribution, politicians, and government officials who were diverting tax revenues levied on their product to their own private profit. Grant was clear of the scandal and had no knowledge of it; but typically, one of his subordinates, his personal secretary, Orville Babcock, was enmeshed in the conspiracy and was thus indicted; the action infuriated Grant, prompting Bristow to resign as secretary of the treasury and to make his own run at the Republican presidential nomination. (Babcock was eventually acquitted, but it later became, by other means, apparent to Grant that he was in fact involved.) Because of bad blood between Grant and Bristow, his chances at the convention were compromised, given the influence that the president, who was not without a strong loyal following, still held in the party, corruption in his administration notwithstanding.

Even with this large field of challengers and the odor of the railroad scandal, the first ballot went to Blaine, who won 285 of the required 378 votes, with Morton a distant second at 124. Blaine, still a substantial political force, actually gained votes on the next three ballots and seemed to be close to the prize, dropped slightly on the fifth ballot, but then regained enough momentum to have won 308 sixth-ballot votes, just 70 shy of winning the nomination. Through the second through the fifth ballots, Bristow took and held second, peaking at 126 on the fourth, Conkling followed in third place through the fourth ballot, having peaked with 99 on the first, and Hayes and Hartranft exchanged fourth and fifth place throughout the first four ballots, with Hartranft peaking at 71 on the fourth. A deftly managed effort on behalf of Hayes steered the party toward the Ohio reformer, who suddenly leapt into third with 104 fifth-ballot votes, gaining nine more on the sixth to move into second. Between the sixth and seventh ballots, Hayes began to draw support away from other candidates, especially Bristow and Morton, narrowing it to a contest between Blaine and Hayes. On the seventh ballot, Hayes pulled in front, gaining 384 votes to 351 for Blaine. Even though it was Blaine's highest total, it was now not enough to hold off Hayes, who had what was needed to secure the nomination.

When the contest was over, nearly all the candidates who had received support at the convention, including Blaine (a dejected Conkling being the only exception), voiced a united front for Hayes and his vice presidential nominee, William A. Wheeler of New York, who needed just one ballot to win an easy nomination. Hayes, who was firmly in the Half Breed camp on the issue of civil service reform, vigorously attacked the spoils system, advocated "rigid responsibility" in civil service through extensive, effective reform, and recommended embracing a more conservative Republican platform that had now jettisoned its long commitment to Reconstruction. "Hurrah! For Hayes and Honest Ways" was the slogan leading the GOP onward, affirming distance from government scandal and abandoning the egalitarian commission of the party's radical wing. When it came time to stump for the nominee, Blaine et al. vigorously dove in, and they were joined by other skilled campaigners such as Blaine's champion, Ingersoll, who was now fully behind Hayes, and Carl Schurz, who had made a name for himself as a main force among the Liberal Republicans in the previous campaign, and whose influence among Midwestern German immigrants was highly regarded by Republican strategists. Hayes himself held to tradition, preferring to keep a low profile while his surrogate colleagues stumped and canvassed across the country.

Among the nineteen planks in the Republican platform, the party, as stated above, promised civil service reform, reaffirmed the need to guarantee civil rights equally for all citizens, endorsed the distribution of public lands to homesteaders rather than to "corporations and monopolies" and the adoption of protective tariffs, and charged Congress with the "duty" to "fully investigate the effects of the immigration and importation of Mongolians on the moral and material interests of the country." "Mongolian" in this sense was an unfortunate usage meant to describe anyone of Asian background; and the increase of Asian immigrants, especially from China, had, rightly or wrongly, raised concerns within the American electorate and was now a political issue strong enough to merit a platform plank.

The Democratic convention, held in St. Louis—the first national presidential nominating convention west of the Mississippi—was more easily settled. The front-runner, New York governor Samuel J. Tilden, an old Barnburner and Van Buren associate who temporarily broke from the party to support Old Kinderhook's 1848 campaign on the Free Soil ticket, enjoyed the full support of most of the party's leaders long before the opening of the convention. Like Hayes, Tilden was a reformer, and as such he had won a solid reputation for fighting corruption while serving as New York's governor. He provided the kind of strong and expert leadership that the party had lacked in the previous two elections, and he was eagerly embraced by both elites and the rank and file. Seven other candidates, most notably governors Thomas A. Hendricks of Indiana and Winfield Scott Hancock of Pennsylvania, also brought some support to the convention. But on the first ballot, Tilden gathered 401 votes to 140 for Hendricks and 75 for Scott (the remaining votes scattered among five additional candidates), and on the second ballot, Tilden easily reached 535 votes to meet the required two-thirds majority. Hendricks was then nominated to run for vice president with almost no competition on the first ballot, taking all but eight abstaining delegates. The platform, dominated by the issues of reform and Reconstruction, read as follows:

Reform is necessary to rebuild and establish in the hearts of the whole people the Union eleven years ago happily rescued from the danger of the secession

of States, but now to be saved from a corrupt centralism which, after inflict-
ing upon ten States the rapacity of carpet-bag tyrannies, has honeycombed
the offices of the Federal Government itself with incapacity, waste and fraud;
infected States and municipalities with the contagion of misrule, and locked
fast the prosperity of an industrious people in the paralysis of hard times.
Reform is necessary to establish a sound currency, restore the public credit
and maintain the national honor. (American Presidency Project, University
of California, Santa Barbara)

The platform joined the Republicans in criticizing the government's tolerance of
Chinese immigrants, and it also asserted the need to transfer public lands to homesteaders rather than the interests of big business.

Both platforms were similar, as were the candidates themselves, for in many
instances Tilden and Hayes were nearly identical in their approach to policy and
their proposals for reform. "Tilden and Reform" was the Democrats' primary slogan, a theme also stressed by the Hayes campaign. Tilden also favored rolling back
Reconstruction, an attitude now shared by an increasing number of Republicans;
along with Hayes, he favored advancing the policy of hard currency. With two
candidates nearly identical in attitude and policy, both parties relied upon worn
yet well-tested campaign techniques to mobilize their supporters. The Republican
Party made effective use of songs such as "The Voice of the Nation's Dead" and
"We Will Not Vote for Tilden." The emotive lyrics of "The Voice of the Nation's
Dead" left little to the imagination:

> From mountain hill, and valley
> A warning seems to come;
> It is the voice of silence
> From lips by death made dumb.
> *Refrain*: Oh hear the sad refrain
> From half a million slain,
> Ah do not now surrender
> What we have died to gain!
> Attend, ye living freemen,
> This call from out the grave;
> It comes from faithful soldiers
> Who died our land to save.

In the nineteenth century, sheet music was a popular medium for political boost-
erism. Republicans also used various songs to depict Hayes as a hero and leader.
Republicans took the still immensely popular Whig chant "Tippecanoe and Tyler,

Too!" from the legendary 1840 campaign and reworked it as "Hayes the True, Wheeler Too." The Republican Party released a Hayes-Wheeler songbook that was widely circulated. The Democrats countered in kind, composing their own songs and publishing songbooks celebrating the Tilden legend.

Given the candidates' similar positions, the parties yet again chose the low road, falling back on the familiar and reliable *ad hominem* rhetoric of the gutter to savage their opponents while promoting their respective champions. With the familiar rustling of the bloody shirt, Republicans impugned Tilden as a pro-slavery, pro-Confederate friend of the rich, accusing him of tax evasion and general swindling. Democrats charged Hayes with nothing less than murder—in an astonishing charge alleging the shooting of his own mother—as well as theft. The actual facts were not important to either side: Whoever was the opposition candidate was obviously a diabolical threat to the republic. In spite of the scandalmongering, more reasonable moments did occur. Mark Twain, the nation's greatest satirist, who had publicly tilted his pointed, incomparable wit toward an incompetent and corrupt system, endorsed Hayes; and the political songbooks mentioned above offered a more positive note, as it were. But the tone of the campaign, by and large, was decidedly mean-spirited.

In addition to the traditional parties, two new minor parties, the Greenback and Prohibitionist parties, offered alternative diversions, the former driven largely by agricultural concerns and promoting the expanded use of paper currency (i.e., greenbacks) and nominating New York industrialist Peter Cooper for president; and the latter, as the name indicates, calling for the prohibition of alcohol and nominating Green Clay Smith, former governor of the Montana Territory, for president. But for the most part, the campaign was burdened with scurrilous aspersions lobbed from both directions. Nastiness was the rule, wit and innovation the exception. The absurdity of the actual election was eclipsed by the malice of the campaign. Ballot boxes were stuffed, polling was woefully inaccurate, and African American voters suffered widespread intimidation and deprivation of their constitutionally protected voting rights. The brief period of limited, budding democratic participation briefly enjoyed by the former slaves and their descendants was coming to an abrupt end, and the Democratic Party in the South was reasserting the monopoly that it had previously achieved in the 1850s, a monopoly that would only serve to benefit the white voter.

The actual election was among the closest—and strangest—in the history of American politics. According to MIT's Mike Sheppard, had just a meager 445 votes in South Carolina shifted from Hayes to Tilden, the outcome would have been different, making the election of 1876, according to this measure, the second closest in history. Either way, it was certainly the most muddled to occur since the election of 1824, which was then marked by a four-way race; and as events unfolded, it was the first election since 1824 in which the winner of the popular vote was denied the presidency. But unlike 1824, when the winner of the popular vote, Andrew Jackson, polled a plurality of around 41 percent, Tilden won a clear popular majority by taking almost 51 percent to slightly under 48 percent for Hayes. When the polls did close, Tilden had apparently become the first Democrat in twenty years to win a presidential election, winning (if the numbers can be believed) 4.3 million popular votes, nearly a quarter of a million more than his opponent, and setting yet another record with the most popular votes gained by a candidate in American history to that point. But the dynamics of electoral politics conveyed a much different story. From within the Electoral College, Tilden managed only 184 electoral votes, just one shy of the needed majority, to Hayes's initial total of 165. But not all the votes were included in those totals; 20 electoral votes were in dispute in Louisiana (8 votes), South Carolina (7 votes), and Florida (4 votes)—the only three states that were still under federal military occupation—with one electoral vote from Oregon also thrown into the controversy over questions of legality. The two minor parties gathered over 90,000 votes between them—most of them going to the Greenbacks—but none of these votes affected the outcome, as the minor-party candidates were not on the ballots in the disputed states.

Tilden, the winner of the popular vote, needed just one more Electoral College vote to become president. From November 8 until March 2 of the following year, just two days before the scheduled presidential inauguration, the battle for the disputed votes lingered. Not unexpectedly, during the interval between Election Day and the final resolution, angry hotheads on both sides of the dispute went as far as to threaten actual violence. Militant Democrats warned of blood in the streets unless Tilden was sworn in as president. Headlines splashed on the front pages of Democratic newspapers menacingly promised "Tilden or War!" In the end, the threats proved more bluff and bluster than reality. Congress was severely divided and frustrated. The Constitution required that the president of the Senate, who also happens to be the vice president of the United States under the Constitution, certify the results. However, complication was in play, owing to the fact that Vice President Henry Wilson had died in 1875, leaving the vice presidency vacant (as was the practice before the Twenty-Fifth Amendment, ratified in 1967), and he was thus replaced as president of the Senate (but technically not as vice president) by Senator Thomas Ferry, a Republican from Michigan, through internal Senate appointment. Because he was clearly not the vice president, Senator Ferry refused to take responsibility for certifying the results from the disputed states. Still further complicating the situation, Democrats controlled the House of Representatives and Republicans controlled the Senate, adding to the impasse. Finally in December, with the results of the election still uncertain, the House and Senate agreed to the establishment of a fifteen-member independent Electoral Commission to resolve the disputes over the electoral votes within the states in question. The Electoral Commission included five members of the Supreme Court, five House members, and five senators. Eight Republicans and seven Democrats served on the panel, giving the Republicans a one-vote majority should the outcome be decided strictly according to partisan loyalties.

Of particular significance, Republicans also controlled the separate election returns boards in the three contested southern states. These returns boards had the responsibility for certifying election results within their states, which included the authority to disqualify disputed ballots. Not surprisingly, all three boards certified the Republican electors, even though there was some evidence supported by unofficial tallies that had indicated a win for Tilden in Louisiana by a margin of over 6,000 votes. Votes in South Carolina were discounted, with the returns boards citing fraud. In Oregon, a state that Hayes seemed to have carried, Tilden loyalists continued to question the legal eligibility of one of the electors. Florida was extremely close and thus was at the very center of the controversy. The initial count in Florida held that Hayes had won by the remarkably slim margin of 43 popular votes, and a recount showed Tilden winning by a thin margin of 93. In the course of its investigation, the Electoral Commission concluded, by a partisan vote of eight to seven, that a number of ballots had been corrupted in Florida and thus were to be disqualified and discarded. With the elimination of these corrupted ballots, Hayes was declared the winner of the popular vote in Florida by a margin of around 1,000. With the quagmire in Florida resolved, the special Electoral Commission thereby awarded Hayes all 20 disputed electoral votes in the four states (three of them Southern) at issue, giving him a total of 185 votes to Tilden's 184 and thus the presidency of the United States.

While the victory for Hayes boosted the spirits of the relieved Republicans after having lost the popular vote for the first time since 1856, it was, looking back, a portent of future problems for the party below the Mason-Dixon Line. Hayes won a majority of the states west of the Mississippi River—Texas, Missouri, and Arkansas being exceptions—all of New England except Connecticut, and the rest of the Northeast except for New York and New Jersey. Hayes also took the Midwest, losing only in Indiana. Tilden dominated the South and the border states, winning all but the three disputed states in that region, and showed the strength of the Democrats by retaking the Empire State (which had been lost to Grant in 1872 after it was won by Seymour in 1868). The election of 1876 would be the last time a Republican candidate for president would win any southern state until 1896, and it was the beginning of a Southern bloc that would not be cracked by Republicans until after World War II and that would prove impenetrable throughout the Deep South until the election of 1964 (not counting the Dixiecrat defection of 1948).

According to some accounts that have been largely accepted as true, a backroom compromise discreetly and secretly negotiated at Wormley's Hotel in Washington, DC, involving members of Congress representing both parties, allegedly prompted Tilden to withdraw any legal claims to the White House in exchange for the final removal of the remaining federal troops still stationed in the three southern states at the heart of the election controversy—i.e., Florida, Louisiana, and South Carolina—troops that were viewed there (at least by many among the white population) as an occupying force. This alleged deal was purported to have been further sweetened by an informal agreement to build a second transcontinental railroad through the South, along with the promise of new federal legislation to spur industrial improvements throughout the former Confederate states. While it is commonly held that these backroom deals, generally referred to as the "Compromise of 1877" (also called a "corrupt bargain," evocative of allegations in the aftermath of the election of 1824), ensured Hayes's presidency in exchange for the abandonment of federally directed political and social reforms in the South, some historians have noted that Hayes was in fact never really far from Tilden on the question of restoring home rule to all southern states, promising to allow every southern state the freedom to govern itself on the condition that it would guarantee equal rights for all citizens. Given this, there would have been little need for the Democrats to participate in such a needless arrangement as Tilden is said to have done in deferring to the election of Hayes. Furthermore, it is not clear to some historians that even if such a secret, informal agreement had actually been made, it would have done anything to alter the decision of the Electoral Commission. Thus, while the Compromise of 1877 has become widely assumed as fact, current historians are reconsidering its accuracy.

In any event, it is certain that, for various reasons that are difficult for us now to comprehend, Reconstruction was now over in the South, and this fact now seems to have less to do with the election of President Hayes than was previously held. It is unlikely that the termination of Reconstruction would have been prevented had Tilden become president rather than Hayes, and there is no evidence to lead us to that conclusion. Well before the election of Hayes, African American citizens were already threatened with reactionary white backlash and Klan terror throughout the South, even with the presence of federal troops in three states, and whether or not Tilden would have addressed that crisis any differently than Hayes cannot ever be known. Moreover, those troops were in reality only concentrated in a few areas within those three southern states; the rest of the South—including regions within the states in question—had already been free of any federal military presence for years. We also know that before finally removing the last federal occupation troops from the South, a newly inaugurated President Hayes had wrung a pledge from Southern leaders that they would support equal protection of the laws for whites and blacks throughout the South, a deal between Hayes and the southern states that, again, has no direct link to a "Hayes-Tilden Compromise." But in the end, the pledge was broken, the law of the land defied, and the position of African Americans reduced, in some parts of the South, to a condition slightly better than the slavery under which their ancestors had suffered for so long. In the end, only two things were certain: A candidate who had won more total popular votes than anyone in history would not be the president, the political rights of African Americans had been severely abridged and in some places utterly stolen, and the ramifications of these developments would plague the future of American democracy for nearly a century.

Additional Resources

The American Presidency Project. http://www.presidency.ucsb.edu.

Holt, Michael F. *By One Vote: The Disputed Presidential Election of 1876.* Lawrence: University Press of Kansas, 2011.

Ingersoll, Robert. "Speech at Indianapolis." In *The Works of Robert G. Ingersoll*, Dresden edition, vol. 9. New York: C. P. Farrell, 1900, pp. 157–187.

Morris, Roy. *Fraud of the Century: Rutherford B. Hayes, Samuel Tilden, and the Stolen Election of 1876.* New York: Simon & Schuster, 2003.

Polakoff, Keith Ian. *The Politics of Inertia: The Election of 1876 and the End of Reconstruction.* Baton Rouge: Louisiana State University Press, 1973.

Pomerantz, Sidney I. "Election of 1876." In Arthur M. Schlesinger, Fred Israel, and William P. Hansen, eds. *History of American Presidential Elections, 1789–1968.* Vol. 2. New York: Chelsea House, 1985.

Ritchie, Donald. "1876." In Arthur M. Schlesinger, Fred L. Israel, and David J. Frent, eds. *Running for President: The Candidates and Their Images.* New York: Simon & Schuster, 1994.

Roberts, Robert North. *Ethics in U.S. Government: An Encyclopedia of Investigations, Scandals, Reforms and Legislation.* Westport, CT: Greenwood Press, 2001.

Sheppard, Mike. "How Close Were U.S. Presidential Elections?" http://www.mit.edu/~mi22295/elections.html.

Campaign of 1880

After the protracted controversy revolving around the election of 1876, the campaign and general election of 1880 seem bland by comparison. Reconstruction was dead, and the candidates that the two major parties selected tended either to agree or to hold similar views on those important issues that remained: the tariff, immigration, and currency. This is not to say that politics on all levels had somehow been cured of conflict—there was certainly enough of it within the parties—but the similarities shared by the two major candidates for the presidency in 1880 reveal a level of consensus not seen since the Era of Good Feelings, or at least they successfully hid the most pressing social problems (i.e., deeper racial and economic questions) behind safer issues such as monetary policy and tariff levels. After the antebellum divisions of the late 1840s and throughout the 1850s, the bloodshed and destruction of the Civil War, and the struggles over Reconstruction in the aftermath, it seems almost as if the electorate, needing a reprieve, sought to return to a less dramatic, less urgent political mood.

Many historians view the Campaign of 1880 as the last campaign dominated by the legacy of the Civil War. Both the Republican and Democratic parties largely ignored the visible impact of the Industrial Revolution and the way it was reshaping the economic and social life of the country. Instead of looking forward, both parties looked backward in an effort to mobilize their respective party loyalists. But social and political problems certainly remained, becoming more aggravated the longer they were neglected; and the near accord of the two major candidates could not quite paper over that hard reality. Only the new Greenback-Labor Party (GLP), which nominated James B. Weaver of Iowa for president, sought to run on a spectrum of new economic and social issues including temperance, civil service reform, black suffrage, regulation of railroads, labor laws instituting an eight-hour workday and addressing child labor abuses, restrictions on immigration, the issuance of "greenbacks" as full payment of the public debt, universal suffrage, a personal income tax, extensive land reform, and sanitary codes for industry. Neither of the two main parties proposed such a far-reaching and (in most cases) forward-looking platform.

President Rutherford B. Hayes, keeping a promise that he had made upon entering the White House, chose not to seek reelection. Historians have been divided on the legacy of President Hayes. He has popularly been blamed for the end of Reconstruction, owing to the allegation of a corrupt bargain that ensured him the White House while denying that office to the winner of the popular vote in the election of 1876, Samuel Tilden. Hayes is also accused by some of being a strike buster (with no real evidence to support this) as well as engaging in damaging policies with regard to Native Americans, another long-standing accusation that is not without some degree of uncertainty as to its fairness; but then again, with regard to the plight of Native Americans in the nineteenth century, it is hard not to draw this kind of conclusion. Some have argued that Hayes was more effective than past commentators have allowed. His attempt at civil service reform was genuine and, to an extent, effective. He left the presidency having strengthened it in an era of congressional dominance, and even though this election was marred by implications of fraud from some quarters, he exhibited personal integrity, throughout his one term, that has long been underappreciated. Hayes's legacy will continue to be debated, but his decision to abide by his promise to serve only one term does provide us with one sure fact: The presidency was now thoroughly up for grabs in 1880. As is always the case when no incumbent is in play, the field was now wide open for both parties.

On the Republican side, former president Ulysses S. Grant sought renomination, with an almost rabidly loyal contingent eagerly falling in behind his cause. Grant had recently been out of the country on a world tour that lasted over two years, and while abroad he was consistently met with enthusiasm by crowds and with admiration by world leaders, a phenomenon that helped scour away the tarnish of his scandal-ridden presidency. As a former president and renowned Civil War general, Grant's popularity was never higher, and for a time, his name seemed to eclipse even Lincoln as the foremost hero of the Union. If his timing had been better, Grant might have gone unchallenged back to the White House, but he returned from abroad to his hero's welcome too early; by the time of the convention in the summer of 1880, six months after Grant's triumphant disembarking in San Francisco, party enthusiasm for the former president had waned in some quarters. Other candidates also brought delegates equally loyal to their own efforts, and a strong anti-Grant movement calling for "Anyone to Beat Grant" emerged along with them.

Thus two principal challengers against the Grant cause soon emerged: Maine's senator James Blaine, the magnetic "Plumed Knight" who came very close to winning the nomination in 1876; and Secretary of the Treasury John Sherman, an Ohioan and the younger brother of famed general William Tecumseh Sherman. Also joining the race was another Ohioan—former general James A. Garfield, a Civil War hero who, at the time the convention was gaveled to order, had recently been appointed by the Ohio legislature to serve as Ohio's senator-elect, to begin the following March. Elihu B. Washburne of Illinois, William Windom of Minnesota, and George Edmunds of Vermont were, along with Garfield, potential dark-horse candidates who rounded out the field. At various points in the convention, a handful of votes were cast for President Hayes (who was never a candidate); Philip Sheridan; John Hartranft, who had been a candidate in 1876; and former general Benjamin Harrison of Indiana, an official in the Hayes administration. Unlike Grant, Blaine had not quite shaken memories of scandal from the unseemly activities alleged in the Crédit Mobilier/Mulligan Letters scandal that had thwarted his nomination four years earlier; and Sherman was regarded as suspiciously sympathetic to Catholics, anti-Catholicism still being a prejudice harbored by elements in both parties. Even so, both candidates held enough support to serve as impediments to Grant's play for a third term. Garfield was initially not a candidate at all; but he enjoyed a following, and a quiet movement on his behalf began to work behind the scenes, waiting for the right moment to make its move. When Garfield drew the attention of the delegates by delivering a stirring speech on behalf of Sherman, that moment was upon them, and a Garfield candidacy became an increasingly attractive alternative.

In addition to the division over candidates, the party was now firmly split into the two main factions that had emerged in the previous election. The members of one faction, the Stalwarts, were generally more conservative in their adherence to party doctrine and, significantly, believed in the effectiveness and legitimacy of the old, machine-driven patronage (spoils) system; thus they were identified as opposing political and governmental reform, particularly civil service reform, and they also supported a third term for Grant. The other faction, the Half Breeds (derisively so labeled by the Stalwarts, who accused them of being only "half Republican"), were Republican moderates less inclined to ideological purity, were disenchanted with patronage and for the most part either supported or were sympathetic to civil service reform, and sought, at least initially, to nominate Blaine, believing him to have been innocent of all prior allegations and unfairly denied the nomination in the previous presidential election year. Blaine's old nemesis, New York senator Roscoe Conkling, who had also been a candidate for nomination in 1876, was the Stalwart boss and the leading Grant supporter, closely allied with another influential New York boss, Thomas C. Platt; naturally, Blaine himself led the Half Breeds. Together, Conkling and Blaine divided among themselves over 80 percent of the convention delegates.

Grant opened with a first-ballot lead, winning 304 votes to Blaine's 284 and Sherman's 75, and he was able to sustain a leading plurality of support through 33 ballots, reaching 309 and at one point dropping to 275. Even though he held the lead deep into the convention, he was unable to find the needed majority. On the thirty-fourth ballot, Garfield, who had received scattered support on a few ballots, was awarded all the votes from the Wisconsin delegation. In response to this turn of events, Garfield initially protested, but to no avail; on the next ballot his total jumped to 50, but Grant's also increased to 313, in what appeared to be encouraging movement in favor of the former president. Then suddenly, the anti-third-term forces, led by Conkling's old nemesis Blaine and Sherman, marshaled their support and swiftly fell in behind young Garfield, who suddenly took 399 votes, exceeding by 20 the required majority needed for the nomination, and leaving Grant's 306 far behind. Garfield—who would, as it turns out, never assume his Senate appointment—now joined the dark-horse legacy of previous successful candidates such as James K. Polk, Franklin Pierce, and Abraham Lincoln at his first convention.

Garfield's meteoric ascent surprised and humiliated the Stalwarts. It soon became clear to those who did a little investigating, and not without reason, that Garfield was in reality a faux dark horse, and that a degree of machination beginning some time before the convention had actually positioned Garfield into an unseen advantage, waiting for a well-timed moment. Garfield, in defeating Grant at the convention, was now the acknowledged de facto spokesman of the Half Breed faction, and realizing that a split party would be vulnerable in the general election, he successfully approached, in the spirit of reconciliation, the Stalwart Chester A. Arthur of New York to serve as his running mate. Arthur, a Conkling ally, had made a name for himself as President Grant's collector of the Port of New York, where he had managed to wield considerable power and, as his Half Breed critics were quick to point out, used his position to enhance his own private income. In 1878, President Hayes sought to remove Arthur and replace him with Theodore Roosevelt Sr., an influential New York philanthropist and father of a future president, but it was a battle that pitted the president directly against Conkling, and one that Conkling was able to win, blocking Roosevelt's ascent. Given the prospects of a joint Half Breed/Stalwart ticket, the delegates gladly nominated Arthur on the first ballot.

Democrats initially favored Samuel Tilden, the sentiment being that Tilden had been unjustly deprived of the presidency by what they felt to be the scandalous usurpation of "Rutherfraud" Hayes and was therefore entitled to another chance. But Tilden suffered declining health and the acrimony of Tammany Hall in his native New York, and thus he was unable to pursue the nomination. Several potential candidates were reviewed, but few leading personalities held wide appeal. Pennsylvania's Winfield Scott Hancock, supported in the North for his heroism at Gettysburg and in the South for the compassionate nature of his service as occupation governor in Texas and Louisiana, was now the front-runner. He was also challenged by Thomas F. Bayard of Delaware and Ohio's Henry Payne and Allen Thurman, along with numerous other candidates who came to the convention with scattered and thin support. On the first ballot, Hancock and Bayard left the rest of the field far behind, the former winning 171 votes, the latter 153. Given that numerous candidates shared the remaining 413 votes (with none of them exceeding 81), it looked as if the convention would grind toward deadlock. But on the second ballot, forces marshaled behind Hancock, and he won the nomination with 320 votes, with Bayard slipping to third and Speaker of the House Samuel J. Randall of Pennsylvania jumping into second with 128 votes. The second ballot was recast, with all but 33 delegates shifting to Hancock. William English of Indiana, known for his conservative management of state finances and his anti-greenback attitude, was plucked for the bottom half of the ticket without opposition.

With little difference between Garfield and Hancock, both parties once again resorted to the tedious tactics of the personal smear, albeit lacking the zeal of previous campaign nastiness. Republicans delighted in Hancock's allegedly thin record as a civilian leader and, ignoring his war heroism and his fair treatment of Texas and Louisiana, depicted him as a political lightweight. But Hancock's heroism for the Union army during the war prevented the Republicans from employing what had become, for them, a popular tactic of waving the bloody shirt against the Democrats as they had in the previous two elections, a worn and tacky display that was, by the 1880s, beginning to lose both its appeal and its effectiveness. The contrast between Hancock and Garfield, who could claim substantial experience and achievement in public life, was amplified. Democrats responded by finding dirt in Garfield's past, linking him to the Crédit Mobilier scandal of the late 1860s (the scandal that had been tied to James Blaine), thus evoking uncomfortable memories of the scandal-ridden Grant years, somewhat unfairly in this instance, as the Crédit Mobilier scandal occurred during the administration of President Andrew Johnson. Shamefully, Democrats circulated a phony Garfield letter supporting Chinese immigration, a cynical and racist move that probably cost the Republicans California. On the lighter side, the campaign songbook was again used as a means of promoting presidential candidates, a Garfield-Arthur songbook in particular making something of a splash.

In the end, the election, which proved to be a choice between two nearly identical candidates, was one of the closest in history. Garfield polled only 10,000 more popular votes than Hancock, winning just 48.3 percent of the popular vote to Hancock's 48.2 percent, with the remaining 3.5 percent going to candidates representing minor parties (mostly Weaver's Greenback ticket). However, in the Electoral College, Garfield succeeded in winning a substantial electoral vote majority of 214 to 155, ensuring that there would be no repeat of the bungled election of 1876. Now that the southern states were once again self-governing (and aggressively dominated by the white majority), the electoral result was strikingly sectional. Every former Confederate state voted as a solid bloc for Hancock along with the border states of Missouri, Kentucky, Maryland, and Delaware. New Jersey was the only northern state won by Hancock. The Chinese immigration issue helped Hancock to carry the states of California and Nevada, a blow that almost cost Garfield the presidency. Even though the election was again won by the Republicans, in just fifteen years after the end of the Civil War, the Democratic Party had reasserted itself, first by winning the popular vote (while losing the presidency) in the previous election of 1876, and now through a respectable showing in 1880. It was still largely a Southern political party, but it was one that was making inroads into the West and the more urban sections of the North, while the Republican Party remained solid with a largely Northern and Midwestern base.

From 1880 through the 1932 presidential election, the Democratic Party would continue to largely maintain control of southern states, mainly as a result of the widespread disenfranchisement of African American voters combined with sore memories among white voters of the Republican Party as the Party of Lincoln, the president responsible for defeating the Confederacy. The Republican Party would soon emerge, at least as general perceptions would have it, as the party of business and industry, but not before it would experience within its ranks the ascent of a strong, devoted, and for a time dominant reformist, progressive wing. With Garfield, the Grand Old Party (or GOP)—a nickname that was now associated with the Republicans—united its Half Breed and Stalwart factions and succeeded in preserving its dominance of the White House (a dominance that reached directly back to the Great Emancipator). However, Garfield's promising presidency was painfully brief; he was soon mortally wounded by a bullet from a gun ignobly fired by an assassin, one of history's small men who is almost universally described in the textbooks by some quirky default meme as a "disappointed office seeker," and who, upon the bloody completion of his murderous act, unabashedly confessed the cramped pettiness of his motivation: "I am a Stalwart, and now Arthur is president!"

Additional Resources

Dinnerstein, Leonard. "1880." In Arthur M. Schlesinger, Fred L. Israel, and David J. Frent, eds. *Running for President: The Candidates and Their Images.* New York: Simon & Schuster, 1994.

Dinnerstein, Leonard. "Election of 1880." In Arthur M. Schlesinger, Fred Israel, and William P. Hansen, eds. *History of American Presidential Elections, 1789–1968.* Vol. 2. New York: Chelsea House, 1985.

Herbert, John Clancy. *The Presidential Election of 1880.* Chicago: Loyola University Press, 1958.

Mach, Thomas S. *Reliving the "Hornet's Nest": James B. Weaver and the Election of 1880.* Lanham, MD: University Press of America, 2001.

Campaign of 1884

The Republican and Democratic parties entered the 1884 presidential campaign with the electorate now almost evenly split between them. With the end of Reconstruction, the Democratic Party had regained thorough dominance of the South; in effect, the southern bloc composed of the former Confederacy and border states was a one-party region, with only a small number of Southerners identifying with the Republican Party, many of those African Americans who still managed to remain politically active despite the efforts of southern states to disenfranchise them. On the other hand, the Republican Party had emerged as the party of free enterprise and industrialization; but within its ranks, a progressive, reformist faction was gaining in influence.

Given that the Republican Party was anathema throughout the South, it was clearly evident that in order to sustain its post-Civil War lock on the White House, the Grand Old Party needed an effective counterbalance, and it sought one by fortifying its base in the North and the Midwest. To finally retake the White House, the Democratic Party understood that it needed to pick off at least one populous northern state while holding its southern base. This was not out of the question, as both New York and New Jersey went with the Democratic candidate, Samuel Tilden, in 1876. The West was a slightly different story. In 1880, Colorado, Oregon, Kansas, and Nebraska went for James A. Garfield, the Republican candidate and eventual winner. Nevada and California supported Winfield Scott Hancock, the Democrat. California was particularly divided, as Hancock won by only a slender 144 popular votes in the Golden State. This was a new development, for in the previous elections involving states west of the Mississippi (with the exception of Texas, which in electoral politics is usually considered part of the southern bloc, or at least through the 1980s, depending upon one's perspective), Republicans dominated, losing only California to James Buchanan in 1856 and Oregon to Horace Seymour in 1868. Hence with the results of 1880, the western states now seemed to be in play, but their clout in the Electoral College at that time was not strong, California at that time was sparsely populated and thus in reality a "small" state in the Electoral College, far from the electoral colossus that it is today. Still, since the last two elections had been so close, the balance could be tipped anywhere.

The best chance for the Democrats outside the South was in the Northeast, and especially New York, where a tradition of Democratic strength had been established since the days of Martin Van Buren and the Albany Regency. New immigrants coming to New York and New England, as well as parts of the Midwest such as Chicago, also provided an opportunity for the Democrats to foster fresh loyalties unprejudiced by the ill feelings left by the Civil War and the stigma of the "bloody shirt." This actually gave the Democrats an advantage that the Republicans could not match in the South. But even though New York held out promise for the Democrats, they still needed to overcome the potent forces that could be mustered by Roscoe Conkling and Thomas C. Platt, two of New York's more powerful machine bosses. One thing was clear: Even though the Democrats had not sent a member of their party to the White House since 1856 (James Buchanan), the close (and for some, stolen) election of 1876 (it is to be remembered that the Democrats, with Tilden, actually won the popular vote in that election, and by no small margin) and the extremely close popular vote in 1880 proved that they were no longer simply a minority party in opposition to the more powerful GOP. The Republicans were still strong, but they were no longer invulnerable. The Democratic Party, with one or two lucky breaks, was on the verge of once again achieving the presidency.

The Republican National Convention met in Chicago, Illinois, on June 3–6. Even though incumbent president Chester A. Arthur, who had sadly assumed the presidency three years earlier after the assassination of President James A. Garfield, sought the nomination, he faced considerable opposition from within his own party. Arthur was a Stalwart (that faction of the party connected to the old machine system), but as president, he could not smooth over the discontent stewing within his own faction. He certainly was not the man for the Half Breeds (political moderates who opposed the machine patronage system and pushed for civil service reform); their man, Garfield, had been gunned down and replaced by a vice president that, fairly or unfairly, they could not bring themselves to trust. Even though Arthur had personally profited from his patronage position as collector of the Port of New York in the 1870s, he did possess a strong personal streak of honesty; but as a committed protégé of Roscoe Conkling, he was well accustomed to the spoils system, an attitude that had set him against President Garfield, who was committed to civil service reform. In short, Arthur perceived patronage to be more efficient and practical than the merit-based civil service system promoted by President Garfield and the Half Breeds. Nonetheless, once Arthur became president in the wake of Garfield's murder, he rose to the occasion, setting aside his Stalwart preconceptions and practices and thereby making a genuine effort to support civil service reform—a cause that had been given irresistible momentum in the wake of the assassination committed by a crazed and confessed Stalwart and murderous adherent to the spoils system. Arthur's surprising overnight transformation into a civil service reformer lost him a good deal of support among his old Stalwart associates. All this notwithstanding, Arthur soldiered on in spite of losing his friends among the Stalwarts and without having won over the Half Breeds. A further complication remained unknown to the party at the time: Arthur was terminally ill, suffering from a fatal kidney condition. Looking back, his quest for the nomination was likely less about any hopes over his political chances than about preserving his dignity and the legacy of his administration.

As expected, Republican Half Breeds threw their support behind their leader, former Speaker of the House and senator James G. Blaine of Maine. Eight years earlier, during the Campaign of 1876, Blaine lost the Republican nomination largely as the result of the Crédit Mobilier/Mulligan Letters scandal that had implicated Blaine in bribery, railroad influence peddling, and graft. He had also been a candidate for nomination in 1880, but he was overshadowed initially by former president Grant's bid for a third term and then by Garfield's spectacular rise to prominence. The Mulligan Letters scandal dogged him, but the "Plumed Knight" maintained his dignity and continued to exude a striking charisma; and by 1884, with the aid of a strong and numerous following, he was able to regain his reputation and was once again the front-runner at the opening of the convention. Senator Blaine cut the most impressive persona of any Republican since President Lincoln, and if he could shake off the scandals of the past and tap into his personal magnetism and many loyalties, he would indeed seem the inevitable choice for the White House.

President Arthur and Vermont senator George F. Edmunds were Blaine's main challengers. Interestingly, Edmunds, a reform candidate, enjoyed the ardent support of two of the Republican Party's more promising young activists: Henry Cabot Lodge of Massachusetts and his close friend, New York's Theodore Roosevelt, who even then, at the age of twenty-five, stormed the political stage as a highly charged, dominating force. While still lacking the sober judgment that comes from years of experience in the public arena, Roosevelt's intellect, dynamic personality, and sheer force of will made him an irresistible figure, one that, it was clear to those who made his acquaintance, might soon challenge the charisma of Blaine. General William Tecumseh Sherman was also a prospective candidate, leading Sherman, who genuinely held no interest in politics, to laconically spurn such advances with his famous quip, "I will not accept if nominated and will not serve if elected." Other candidates in the field were Sherman's younger brother, Senator John Sherman, a reformer who had been a candidate in play in the previous convention; John A. "Black Eagle" Logan of Illinois (sometimes referred to as "Black Jack" Logan); Senator Joseph R. Hawley of Connecticut; and Robert Todd Lincoln, President Lincoln's son, who had also made a name for himself in recent years as a political reformer.

As the Republican conventioneers gathered in Chicago, an interesting contest over who would serve as the convention chairman opened the proceedings. Blaine's supporters desired Powell Clayton as chair. Clayton, a former general and Reconstruction governor of Arkansas, was widely admired within the party; but a vocal faction, led by the youthful tandem of Lodge and Roosevelt, opposed Blaine's choice and sought to install John R. Lynch, an African American delegate and former congressman from Mississippi, as the convention chairman. Lobbying hard with Lodge, Roosevelt delivered an eloquent speech on Lynch's behalf, reflecting that it had now been "less than a quarter of a century since, in this city, the great Republican Party organized for victory and nominated Abraham Lincoln, of Illinois, who broke the fetters of the slaves and rent them asunder forever. It is a fitting thing for us to choose to preside over this convention one of that race whose right to sit within these walls is due to the blood and treasure so lavishly spent by the founders of the Republican Party" (Morgan, p. 50).

This, Roosevelt's debut on the national political stage after already having gained prominence in New York politics, was a stunning success. Against the resistance of the party's Old Guard, Lynch was elected by a vote of 424 to 384, the first African American to serve as the chairman of a national nominating committee, a feat done in 1884 during a period of particular strife for African American citizens. From this point and throughout the convention, Roosevelt, along with Lodge, would lead a faction of independents against both the Stalwart President Arthur and the Half Breed Blaine (owing to his connection to Conkling, who had deliberately thwarted the political career of his father, Theodore Sr., the younger Roosevelt was deeply opposed to Arthur, and he was also openly disdainful of Blaine); and for a time the Roosevelt-Lodge duo would impose their will on the convention. Eventually, they were overtaken by the party establishment, but not without first having memorably made a name for themselves, foreshadowing for both men still greater things to come.

On the eve of the convention, President Arthur and Senator Blaine had been evenly matched in terms of delegates, each relying on about 300 firm supporters. Vermont's Edmunds ran a distant third but, owing to the pre-convention efforts of Lodge and Roosevelt, held enough delegates to swing the balance of power. When the balloting finally began, Blaine opened with a lead of 334 to President Arthur's 278, the Edmunds faction led by Roosevelt and Lodge holding the pivotal 93 delegates, with the remainder of the candidates far behind (Logan led the also-rans with 63). Arthur's supporters began to angle for a coalition with the Edmunds faction, but Roosevelt and Lodge remained firm in their resistance; they sincerely meant to find a way for Edmunds to win, not simply to throw in with one of the front-runners when tactical considerations called for it. The second ballot did little to change the situation: Blaine's position improved slightly, with Arthur holding on to second, losing just two votes while the rest of the field faded slightly. President Arthur lost only two more votes on the next ballot, but Blaine's lead swelled to 375, only 36 shy of the nomination that had eluded him in 1876 and 1880. On the fourth ballot, Blaine's supporters, buoyed by the momentum, managed to convince large numbers of delegates to swing their way, in spite of the tireless efforts of Roosevelt and Lodge, thus managing to avoid another protracted deadlock. Blaine won with 541 votes. Robert Todd Lincoln, the son of President Abraham Lincoln who had served as secretary of war under presidents Garfield and Arthur, who never managed more than just a handful of votes, was considered by some as an appealing running mate for Blaine, but he refused to allow his name to be nominated for vice president. The delegates then turned to Black Jack Logan, nominating him with near unanimity on the first ballot. One of the heroes at the convention was a young William McKinley from the Ohio delegation, who, in the latter days of the convention, worked earnestly (and in the end, successfully) to counter Roosevelt's influence and help break the deadlock, ensuring Blaine's nomination.

The Democrats met in Chicago as well, with four candidates who had all been considered at some point in previous conventions—Samuel J. Randall of Pennsylvania, Allen G. Thurman of Ohio, Delaware's Thomas F. Bayard, and Thomas A. Hendricks, who ran for the vice presidency on the party's ticket with Samuel Tilden in 1876. A fifth candidate, Indiana's Joseph McDonald, enjoyed limited support as a favorite son. Even though there were four veterans of previous convention battles, including one who was nearly elected vice president eight years earlier, from the beginning the true front-runner was New York's Grover Cleveland (born Stephen Grover Cleveland), who emerged from near obscurity in just a few short years to rapidly become New York's leading statesman in spite of his open opposition to the powerful political machine of Tammany Hall. (In Albany, Governor Cleveland had formed a bipartisan reformist alliance with Roosevelt, who had, even at his young age, become one of the state assembly's most important leaders during his brief but productive tenure there.)

An imposing figure who in at least one instance had faced down the juggernaut Roosevelt, Cleveland was the leader of the Bourbon Democrats, a more conservative faction within the Democratic Party that supported unfettered business development and opposed high protective tariffs, fought against the old machine politics common in the nineteenth century and were thus committed to civil service reform, were wary of the growing sentiment for continued American expansionism (a political ambition that was now being referred to by some as "imperialism"), and opposed the free coinage of silver. The latter policy, commonly called "Free Silver" or "bimetallism" (the supporters of which were often referred to as "Silverites," and later "Silver Bugs," in contrast to the monometallist "Gold Bugs"), had its roots in the 1870s and was with each election becoming an increasingly divisive issue, to some as important or even more important than the old debate over tariffs. During Reconstruction in the United States, after a period of time during which the government relied on paper currency (or "greenbacks") to help defray Civil War debt, there arose a strong movement to establish gold alone as the official currency, thereby imposing a "monometal" policy that excluded the coinage of silver, which had previously been an option given the country's bimetal policies, but one that for the most part was decidedly less common than the more favored gold coinage. In 1873, under the Grant administration, Congress passed the U.S. Coinage Act, which effectively eliminated the silver dollar as a measure of value and thereby ensured the dominance of gold. The bimetallists referred to this act as the "Crime of '73" and argued that both gold and silver could be coined for circulation, whereas their opponents favored continuing with the monometal policy fixed on gold. During his tenure, President Hayes worked to continue the gold standard policy, thus further alarming the Silverites. This disagreement was not yet the key policy issue debated by politicians, but it would gain importance with each election, and it would develop into an issue that would cross party lines.

In many ways, Cleveland and the "Gold Bug" Bourbon Democrats resembled their more conservative counterparts in the Republican Party, which was mostly in favor of using gold as the standard currency (although the Republican Party would contain an activist Western faction known as the "Silver Republicans"), a fact that no doubt strengthened Cleveland's appeal in the North, especially among banking and financial interests. Cleveland had gained a reputation as a brave, disciplined, competent, and scrupulous public servant, and his ability to deflect the influence of Tammany proved to work to his advantage. As the convention opened, Cleveland took a commanding lead on the first ballot, winning 392 votes, with Bayard placing second at 170. Given Cleveland's strong early showing and the lack of real energy behind the other candidates, delegates quickly switched to Cleveland's cause. He won 683 votes on the next ballot, enough to deliver the nomination. Hendricks was then nominated, as he had been in 1876, for vice president on the first ballot, receiving all but four abstaining votes. Hendricks would become the first of three candidates to be nominated for vice president by a major party in two nonconsecutive years (the other two would be Adlai Stevenson and Charles Fairbanks).

Minor parties multiplied. Four in particular are worth mentioning: the Greenback Party and the Anti-Monopoly Party, which both nominated Benjamin F. Butler of Massachusetts and his running mate, Mississippi's A. M. West; the Prohibition (or Prohibition Reform) Party, which nominated John P. St. John of Kentucky; and the Equal Women's Rights Party, which nominated Belva C. Lockwood of the District of Columbia. These parties sprouted as part of a growing populist mood throughout the country, a mood that was particularly strong in the West and parts of the South. Both major parties responded by adopting some reform planks in their own platforms, such as regulation of the working day and the railroads. Both parties also contained factions that were divided over the more populist measures. This was particularly influential with regard to Republican unity, as elements within the party were not as keenly fixated on the pro-business, pro-industry attitudes of the party leadership. Among these elements in the party, a number of delegates were ripe for defection, particularly given their distaste for Blaine, Thomas Nast's "Tattooed Man" of the Mulligan Letters scandal. Those letters reappeared for a brief time to haunt Blaine, as they were actually published for public consumption in a number of major newspapers. One letter contained a postscript enjoining its recipient to "Burn this Letter," and as a result the phrase "Burn this Letter" became a wry campaign slogan for the Democratic cause.

This reformist and anti-Blaine element now gaining strength in the Republican Party was soon referred to, at first pejoratively, as the "Mugwumps." ("Mugwump" is a word that comes from the Native American Algonquin language, meaning "war leader" or "very important person," and initially it was used by the Republican Old Guard, or the party conservatives, to describe what they perceived to be the sanctimonious and presumptuous attitudes of the Republican reformists.) While they were a minority within the party, their influence would reach into the general election, as a number of Mugwumps would switch allegiance and support Cleveland—they admired Cleveland's defiance of Tammany Hall—rather than swallow their pride (and for some, deny their principles) and vote for Blaine. (Roosevelt and Lodge, in spite of their dislike of Blaine and intense opposition to him at the convention, refused to follow bolting Mugwumps to the other side, an act that, for a short time at least, cost them politically.) As before in the Campaign of 1880, the major candidates were not that distant on the issues, hence in switching to Cleveland rather than remaining loyal to their own party, the Mugwumps were indeed making a primarily (but not wholly) personal rejection of Blaine.

With partisan allegiance now evenly split within the electorate and the similarity of the two main parties on the major issues quite evident, the campaigns yet again resorted to the obligatory tactics of character assassination. Cleveland's personal character and public integrity while serving the state of New York had rightly earned him the nickname "Grover the Good," but Republican operatives working in support of Blaine went after his reputation nonetheless, and after enough digging, they uncovered an allegation that Cleveland had fathered a child out of wedlock. To the surprise of many observers, Cleveland willingly admitted paternity (even though it could not be proven) and hid nothing of his relationship with the mother and child, which included generously providing financial support and the placement of the child in a respectable home upon the collapse of the mother's health. Nonetheless, Blaine's supporters vilified Cleveland as a debauched libertine, cad, "gross and licentious man," and "moral leper," pounding Cleveland with the chant "Ma, Ma, Where's My Pa?" Cleveland's supporters retaliated, and given Blaine's own checkered past, it was not too difficult. Chanting, "Blaine, Blaine, James G. Blaine, the Continental Liar from the State of Maine," and referring to him as "Old Mulligan Letters," the "Tattooed Man," and "Slippery Jim," the Democrats delighted in dredging up Blaine's "mottled" record. As in 1876, Blaine continued to deny any wrongdoing in the railroad scandal, even despite the fact that newly found evidence raised yet again serious, unanswered questions about the veracity of Blaine's denials. The published "Burn this Letter" postscript no doubt worked effectively against him. Typically, all the personal attacks made against Blaine and Cleveland did little to shake their expected partisan allegiance, but it did fortify the Republican Mugwumps in their support of the Democrat Cleveland.

Following previous presidential campaigns, both major parties relied upon songbooks to boost their image and message. *The Blaine and Logan Song Book* contained numerous songs directed at reminding voters of the role of the Republican Party in defeating the rebellion, another installment in the "bloody shirt" strategy. In response, one of Cleveland's most effective campaign songs.contained the lyric, "Eight years ago we won the prize, but then were robbed by tricks and lies, of freedom's foes in friends' disguise, Democrats, good Democrats!"

Both parties realized that the electoral votes of New York, Cleveland's home state—and a state that Garfield and the Republicans had most recently carried in 1880 but that had been won by Democrats Tilden in 1876 and Horatio Seymour in 1868—could be the major factor in determining the outcome of the general election. Given recent developments, it was definitely a state in play and was thus a vital battleground. Pursuing New York votes nigh to the election, Blaine intensified his efforts in the Empire State, an effort that proved fateful owing to one peculiar incident. Attending a campaign event for pro-Republican Protestant ministers in New York City, Blaine made a mistake that could very well have cost him the presidency. During his introduction of the candidate Blaine, Reverend Samuel D. Burchard launched a stinging indictment of the Democratic Party and Grover Cleveland. Using an impolitic (and bigoted) phrase that was actually introduced eight years earlier, Burchard referred to the Democratic Party as the party of "Rum, Romanism, and Rebellion." It is unlikely that Blaine himself supported such views, as his own mother was Roman Catholic and one of his sisters was a nun (Blaine was himself a Congregationalist). But Blaine did nothing to publicly repudiate Burchard's remark. At one point he claimed to have heard Burchard say "Rum, Mormonism, and Rebellion" (an excuse that no doubt put him in swell with the Latter-day Saints, who also knew how to vote); other times he seemed to claim that he had not heard anything at all. But regardless of the status of Blaine's hearing, the comment was in fact made in his presence as he sat only a few feet away, and news of Burchard's gaffe and Blaine's lack of response to it spread rapidly. By the following day, a few anti-Catholic Republicans embraced the slogan, catching Blaine off guard when he saw the "three R's" prominently displayed in a Republican handbill endorsing the Blaine-Logan ticket. On November 1, with the election imminent, Blaine finally issued a weak and convoluted rejection of the "Romanism" sentiment. His apology, however, came too late; the damage was already done, as New York's Irish Catholic vote was now amassed against the Republicans. This, along with the Mugwump Republicans, wrecked Blaine in New York, a state that Cleveland barely carried by a margin of just over 1,100 votes.

New York was still the biggest electoral prize, and it proved to be the state the Democrats needed in order to crack the Republican stronghold and carry Cleveland into the White House, the first Democrat since James Buchanan to ascend to the presidency. But it is important to remember that he was the second Democratic candidate in that same period of time to win the popular vote in the general election, as Samuel Tilden had actually won a popular majority in 1876 but failed to carry the necessary majority in the Electoral College. Cleveland, with just over 4,914,000 votes, won election with a plurality of 48.5 percent of the popular vote, less than the clear majority won by Tilden in 1876. Blaine carried 48.3 percent (around 4,857,000), the Prohibition and Greenback parties taking approximately 151,000 and 134,000 votes, respectively. Cleveland won by just over 57,500 votes nationwide. The rum-and-Romanism crack no doubt damaged Blaine in New York, and given the narrow margin of the outcome there, it likely made the difference between victory and defeat. Cleveland finished with a narrow 1,100-vote lead in

New York, but according to statistician Mike Sheppard's MIT Web site, the margin was smaller still, at 575. If the latter is correct, had Blaine won just 575 more votes in New York, he would have then taken the Empire State's 36 electors, which would have been enough to give him an Electoral College victory and the presidency, even though Cleveland would have still won the most popular votes nationwide (which would have made this election a repeat of 1876). By this measure, the election of 1884, in terms of the popular vote, is the third closest in American history. But those 1,100 votes (or 575, depending on the angle from which you look) in New York amounted to the slim difference that gave Cleveland, not Blaine, the victory there and thus the White House, and it is hard to imagine that victory without an incensed and unified Irish Catholic population falling in behind Cleveland, their former governor. Thus James Blaine, the most influential Republican since the loss of President Lincoln with the exception of President Grant, became, as the result of one of the closest elections in history, only the second Republican to lose a presidential election, and the first since John C. Fremont in 1856.

Because Cleveland did manage to take New York with its 36 electors, his margin of victory in the Electoral College was not nearly so slight. The final count showed Cleveland winning 219 electoral votes (55%) to Blaine's 182 (45%). Blaine swept the six western states (not counting Texas, which Cleveland won, as it has historically been a part of the southern bloc), but there were not enough votes there to compensate for the inroads that the Democrats made in the North (Connecticut and New Jersey joining New York in going for Cleveland) as well as in the Midwest (Indiana going for the Democrats for the second time in twelve years). By carving these inroads and holding every southern and border state, Grover Cleveland became the twenty-second president of the United States, and he would also, as fate would have it, become the only Democrat to win the White House between Buchanan (1856) and Woodrow Wilson (1912). In the meantime, Democrats celebrated. With "Grover the Good" as the nation's new president, the Republican chant of "Ma, Ma, Where's My Pa?" could now be well answered by enthusiastic Democrats responding, "Gone to the White House, ha, ha, ha!" On a more sober note, Cleveland's vice president, Hendricks, whose health had been compromised by a stroke five years earlier, died suddenly eight months into the new administration. The office would remain empty throughout the remainder of President Cleveland's first term.

President Chester A. Arthur, known to some by the nickname "the Gentleman Boss," with his health failing, retired into private life, and he quietly passed away in November 1886. While Arthur had made enemies during his administration, enough to block his nomination in 1884, he came to be held in high esteem once out of office. Author, editor, and historian Alexander K. McClure wrote of Arthur, "No man ever entered the Presidency so profoundly and widely distrusted, and no one ever retired. . .more generally respected," a sentiment shared by the incomparable Mark Twain, who had once peevishly referred to Arthur as a "flathead," but who is reported by journalist Melville Stone to have later more thoughtfully remarked, "I am but one in 55,000,000; still, in the opinion of this one-fifty-five millionth of the country's population, it would be hard to better President Arthur's Administration. But don't decide until you hear from the rest."

Additional Resources

Gould, Lewis L. "1884." In Arthur M. Schlesinger, Fred L. Israel, and David J. Frent, eds. *Running for President: The Candidates and Their Images.* New York: Simon & Schuster, 1994.

Hirsch, Mark D. "Election of 1884." In Arthur M. Schlesinger, Fred Israel, and William P. Hansen, eds. *History of American Presidential Elections, 1789–1968.* Vol. 2. New York: Chelsea House, 1985.

Morgan, James. *Theodore Roosevelt: The Boy and the Man.* New York: Kessinger Publishing, 1907.

Morris, Edmund. *The Rise of Theodore Roosevelt.* New York: Random House, 1979.

Sheppard, Mike. "How Close Were U.S. Presidential Elections?" http://www.mit.edu/~mi22295/elections.html.

Summers, Mark Wahlgren. *Rum, Romanism and Rebellion: The Making of a President, 1884.* Chapel Hill: University of North Carolina Press, 2000.

The White House. http://www.whitehouse.gov.

Campaign of 1888

The Campaign of 1888 took place at the height of the Gilded Age. The Industrial Revolution was transforming at an increasing pace the economic and social structure of the United States. General prosperity accelerated throughout the nation, but the distribution of wealth and the political influence that followed it gravitated toward a small number of elites who ruled over American industry and transportation with a degree of power that evaded even the more prominent politicians of the day. The financial "combination," or "trust" (what we today call "monopoly"), was fast becoming the preferred way of amalgamating and directing the growing economy from within the private sector, and one that enabled just a few men—scarcely a handful, really—to gain nearly undisputed control of the nation's exponentially expanding wealth.

In response to growing anger expressed by Midwestern and Western farmers and small businessmen directed against monopolistic practices, particularly within the railroads, Congress passed the Interstate Commerce Act of 1877 under President Rutherford B. Hayes, creating and charging the new Interstate Commerce

Commission with the authority and means to investigate unfair rates set by the railroads, rates that favored corporate interests. Despite widespread popular concern over the intensifying concentration of economic power, the dominant factions within both the Republican and Democratic parties largely ignored populist issues and pressures during the Campaign of 1888. Conservatives in both parties (viz., Old Guard Republicans and Bourbon Democrats) tended to welcome the trust and the power it could deftly and, according to their point of view, intelligently wield, even to the point of considering the trust to be a more effective agent than the federal government's executive branch in guiding the country into a promising future of economic abundance. Thus instead of questioning the rise of the trust and all that it implied, the election was largely a battle over a familiar, and now (in the wake of the Civil War and the controversies over Reconstruction) comparatively safe, issue—protective tariffs, along with another issue that had been growing in importance, monetary policy.

Grover Cleveland's 1884 victory over James G. Blaine had surprised the dominant Republican Party. Even though Congress had passed the Civil Service Reform Act of 1883 that reduced (but did not eliminate) the influence of political patronage, the loss of the White House still meant that the Republican Party lost thousands of patronage appointments. Republicans believed that the reliable tariff debate would provide them with the best issue in their quest to regain the presidency without having to cater to the more populist elements within the party as well as the greater electorate. It was an argument that the Republicans managed to great effect. A high tariff, as the argument typically holds, would protect domestic industries from foreign competitors and encourage both expanding margins of profit and higher wages, and thus a general prosperity for all, capital and labor alike.

President Cleveland, as the incumbent Democrat, was affiliated with the conservative Bourbon faction of his party and thus held fast to laissez-faire economic policies, which at that time was in fact a traditional Democratic position going all the way back to President Jackson, and it could be traced even earlier to the Monroe Era. These policies included strong support for low tariffs. Because of their heavy reliance upon agricultural exports to generate income, southern states had historically opposed protective tariffs and thus were supportive of Bourbon candidates. Western states, which also relied heavily on agriculture, now joined, at least in part, the South in opposing protective tariffs. Although the anti-tariff position played well in southern states and parts of the West, the policy made it much more difficult for Democrats to attract votes in industrial midwestern and northeastern states; and it was in the Northeast, especially New York, where Cleveland's previous campaign had found the needed votes to break the GOP in the North, the tipping point that gave him the White House. At the same time, the rapidly strengthening temperance movement that was strongly aligned with various (but not all) Protestant churches could cause problems for both parties by potentially drawing away needed votes. Finally, the issue of bimetallism, or Free Silver, reappeared as a main point of division within both parties, but especially within the Democratic Party; Gold Bug Bourbon Democrats were pitted against the rest of the party that, for the most part, advocated Free Silver.

At the Democratic National Convention in St. Louis, a highly esteemed President Cleveland easily won renomination. Former senator and presidential contender Allen G. Thurman of Ohio, known as "the Nestor of the Democratic Party" owing to his reputation as a wise counselor, was nominated on the first ballot to fill the vacancy left by the death of Vice President Hendricks. Atypically for the time, Thurman was already identified prior to the convention by Cleveland and his advisers as the president's preferred running mate for the upcoming campaign, a practice that would not really take hold until well into the latter half of the twentieth century. An old Jacksonian, Thurman, also known as "the Old Roman," had gained a reputation as a venerable party sage, having devoted over five decades of distinguished service that began under the administration of President Polk. Both the party leadership and the rank and file embraced Thurman as a symbol of party unity and tradition, one that could bridge the growing divisions between the conservative and populist elements.

However, Thurman's health was deteriorating, and even though he accepted the responsibility that came with the nomination, the elder statesman had initially expressed dismay and no small degree of irritation at his selection. Many in the party would come to realize this soon after the convention. Moreover, Cleveland soon became aware that these growing divisions between the conservative and populist wings of the Democratic Party could not be repaired simply by nominating an esteemed, aging member for the second spot on the ticket. These divisions were not so easily closed, and they still threatened to split the coalition that Cleveland needed to win again in 1884. President Cleveland and the pro-business Bourbons of the Northeast, along with the Redeemers of the South (who were committed to states' rights), represented the conservative faction of the party. In contrast, the populist wing of the party placed bimetallism, or the free coinage of silver, at the center of its agenda. President Cleveland, leading the conservative Bourbons and Redeemers, supported the gold standard, a position that put him closer to the Republicans. To this end, Cleveland recommended the suspension of the circulation of silver coins, thereby alienating Democratic populists, especially in the West, where miners were invested in the currency of both gold and silver. Additionally, Cleveland's sincere efforts to expand civil service reform angered many partisans, who had concluded that once the Democrats were able to gain power in the election of 1884, the president should have made full use of his patronage powers to reward his partisan supporters and strengthen the influence of the party. Tammany Hall, never a friend to Cleveland, was particularly incensed over Cleveland's attempt to eliminate patronage, a situation that threatened Cleveland's ever-critical support in New York.

The Republican convention was held that June in Chicago. Even though their previous nominee, Senator James G. Blaine, had lost the presidential contest to Grover Cleveland in 1884, the popular vote had been very close (a change of 1,100 or so votes in New York would have swung the election in his favor); thus for a time, it seemed likely that Blaine would try one more time, forcing a rematch against the man whom he had nearly beaten in the prior election. However, Blaine realized that while he still had many loyal supporters, he also was opposed by a strident anti-Blaine faction, and that even if he managed to gain the votes to win the nomination, which was possible, the convention might take an ugly turn, dividing and weakening the party even more than it had been in the previous election due to the defection of the reformist Mugwumps. He was also uncomfortable about claiming the front-runner status after having already been defeated as the party's standard-bearer in that same election. Hence, shortly before the start of the convention, Blaine made it clear that he did not want the Republican nomination, an announcement that now produced a wide-open field. "A man," Blaine admitted, "who has once been the candidate of his party—and defeated—owes it to his party not to be a candidate again."

All told, eighteen candidates enjoyed some degree of support at the convention (including Blaine, whose loyalists remained hopeful for another run). Among this high number of candidates, a front-runner did emerge as the convention commenced—John Sherman of Ohio, the brother of General William Tecumseh Sherman and a notable figure in his own right, one who had already received some support for the presidency at the previous two conventions. Sherman—backed by industrialist Mark Hanna, an emerging player who was becoming a major force in the direction of Republican presidential campaigns—was well regarded for his intelligence and capable service in both the legislative and executive branches. It appeared to be Sherman's turn for the party's endorsement, particularly now that Blaine's star was clearly in the descendant. Thus, Sherman and his supporters worked hard to promote his candidacy in the weeks leading up to the convention. Most of the eighteen candidates were unable to win more than a handful of votes. In reality, only five candidates, in addition to Sherman, drew notable support: Russell Alger of Michigan; William Allison of Iowa; Chauncey Depew, a favorite of New York; and two from Indiana, William Q. Gresham and Benjamin Harrison, the grandson of President William Henry Harrison and great-grandson of Benjamin Harrison V, a signer of the Declaration of Independence. Harrison did not have the political record to match Sherman, but he had ably served as a general during the Civil War and he carried the renowned Harrison name. More importantly, he was supported by a cohort of savvy and influential political strategists, among them Wharton Barker and Stephen Elkins, a former Blaine lieutenant, who worked diligently behind the scenes to promote a Harrison candidacy. Harrison also enjoyed the support of Theodore Roosevelt and Henry Cabot Lodge, a tight political team who had fast gained national reputations as promising young leaders within the party. The rest of the field, which included notable personalities such as Frederick Douglass, Robert Todd Lincoln, and William McKinley (another Hanna protégé), never produced a serious challenger.

At the convention Sherman held his position as front-runner for six ballots but was not able to gain momentum, thus producing a degree of anxiety among his followers. His candidacy, it soon became apparent, depended too much upon support in the southern delegation, which was at that time the least reliable in the party and a poor forecast for Sherman's appeal in the general election. Additionally, Sherman's advisers built their strategy around the mistaken assumption that Blaine was still the major contender, and thus they were unprepared to stem competition from an alternate rival. During a recess between the third and fourth ballots, Depew, New York's favorite son, withdrew his name, leading the New York delegates, which included Roosevelt, to express their interest in General Harrison. Sherman's people were caught flatfooted and soon fell into despair, realizing that their efforts had been blunted and even entertaining the possibility of asking their candidate to withdraw with his dignity intact. But a determined Sherman was not prepared to quit just yet. However, a turn of events followed Depew's decision, propelling Harrison from a distant fourth to a close second on the fourth ballot, and by the seventh ballot, he had displaced Sherman in the lead. Building on this momentum, Harrison secured the nomination on the eighth ballot, winning 544 votes. The convention then nominated Levi P. Morton of New York, who had previously served both as governor and as a member of the House of Representatives, as well as in the diplomatic corps, for vice president on the first ballot.

There was sound electoral strategy behind this combination; Harrison was from Indiana, the only midwestern state lost to Cleveland in 1884 (and a state that also went for the Democrat Samuel Tilden in 1876), and Morton was from New York, the one state that had sealed Cleveland's victory, and the GOP's fate, in that very same election. With Harrison and Morton, it was believed that the Republicans could return Indiana and New York to their fold, which would virtually guarantee victory. Harrison also brought his distinguished military record to the ticket, strengthening his overall appeal; and Morton, a respected banker by profession, was attractive to the Republican base. Significantly, the roles filled by Hanna, Wharton, and Elkins behind the scenes indicated that the party was now being steered by a new leadership, one that was more interested in making presidents than actually being president. Such figures have always been present in the

American political landscape, but their efforts were now becoming more sophisticated and sustained, in effect creating the prototype for the modern campaign manager.

As stated above, the Republican Party platform again endorsed protective tariffs, which served to be a key issue in their cause; expressed support for the use of gold and silver as currency, stating that it "condemns the policy of the Democratic Administration in its efforts to demonetize silver"; opposed the practice of polygamy (a plank directed at the Mormon Church); supported the repeal of the federal tax on tobacco; opposed the use of Chinese contract labor; supported the regulation of railroad rates by the federal government and states; and endorsed free public education. Equally important, the Republican convention passed a prohibition resolution, asserting that "the first concern of all good government is the virtue and sobriety of the people and the purity of their homes. The Republican party cordially sympathizes with all wise and well-directed efforts for the promotion of temperance and morality."

The Republican temperance plank indicated just how important the issue had become in recent years. The Prohibition Party, gaining more adherents, held its convention in Indianapolis, nominating for the presidency New Jersey's Clinton B. Fisk, a principal supporter of Fisk College (which was named for him), and John A. Brooks of Missouri as vice president. Besides proposing a nationwide ban on the manufacture, importation, transportation, and sale of alcoholic beverages, the platform of the Prohibition Party included a number of principles that would be associated with progressivism: opposing protective tariffs, supporting the right of women to vote, endorsing the further expansion of civil service reforms, and calling for the abolition of polygamy. In addition to the Prohibition Party, a pro-labor party, the Union Labor Party, nominated Alson Streeter to head its ticket. Other minor parties, such as the Know-Nothing American Party, still offered candidates but drew little interest.

Both Harrison and Cleveland chose to conduct front-porch campaigns by remaining home and foregoing national tours. It was painfully remembered that the national tour was a tactic that had backfired on Blaine, for it was while he was on tour in New York that he ran into the problems caused by Reverend Samuel Burchard's anti-Catholic remarks. While Harrison benefited from the services of his surrogates on the campaign trail—numbering among them Theodore Roosevelt, whose rhetorical skills and captivating personality proved to be an invaluable asset to the Republican cause—he did not sit by passively. Remaining at home to conduct his own front-porch campaign, Harrison proved to be an elegant orator, meeting small gatherings almost daily and delivering a series of speeches that, when published for broader dissemination, were largely admired for their clean argument and intellectual force. President Cleveland, by contrast, was less involved, relying upon Thurman, his running mate, to wade into the fray while he remained "presidential" and aloof. But Thurman, because of his health, was no longer equal to the task, even though he made every effort to accept this responsibility. His speeches were usually cut short owing to his diminished energy, and they were often sprinkled with worrisome complaints about his deteriorating condition, a condition now visibly evident to a concerned public—he struggled on the platform, often wobbled, and on one occasion nearly fell into the audience. Making use of its greater financial resources, the Republican Party also put together a much more effective campaign organization, which included extensive canvassing by Republican Clubs, reminiscent of the Wide-Awakes who lobbied for Abraham Lincoln in the 1860s.

In comparison to the scandalmongering of previous campaigns, the Campaign of 1888 involved very little mudslinging, a refreshing and happy circumstance largely attributed to both Cleveland's and Harrison's personalities as well as their reputations for integrity. One unscrupulous dirty trick did damage Cleveland's chances to carry the ever-vital New York. Under the alias of Charles Murchison, George Osgoodby, a Republican fruit grower from California, wrote a phony letter to Britain's foreign minister currently assigned to Washington. In a politically motivated sting, Osgoodby pretended to be a newly nationalized American from Britain requesting advice on which candidate to support in the upcoming election. When the minister, duped by the ruse, responded favorably for Cleveland, Osgoodby shared the British endorsement with the press. The Murchison letter worked its intended result, angering New York's Irish Catholic (and decidedly anti-British) voters, a bloc within the Empire State's electorate that had proved decisive for Cleveland in the previous election, at that time favoring Cleveland in the wake of the "Rum, Romanism, and Rebellion" scandal that had detrimentally attached to Blaine's campaign. In a striking reversal of fortune, the Murchison letter did to Cleveland in New York exactly what Reverend Burchard's remarks did to Blaine in 1884, damaging the president's efforts and helping him to lose the biggest electoral cache in the nation. It must also be remembered that Cleveland's ongoing feud with New York City's Tammany Hall also cost him, for it is difficult to carry the state without the city—and, in the nineteenth century, to carry the city without Tammany. Historians have also concluded that the GOP position on the tariff, as well as other pro-business attitudes, was important in helping them to strengthen anew their base throughout the industrial North.

The actual election in November was a near carbon copy of 1884, with two key exceptions: New York and Indiana returned to the Republican fold, giving Harrison the Electoral College victory that had barely eluded Blaine. In the popular vote, President Cleveland actually won more votes than the challenger, a scenario reminiscent of the election of 1876. Cleveland's popular tally set a record of just around 5,540,000 votes (a 48.6% plurality) to the 5,450,000 (47.8%) for Harrison. But it was in the Electoral College where Harrison won the election, winning 233 to Cleveland's 168 (58% to 42%), thus dislodging the incumbent to become the twenty-third president, rendering irrelevant the fact that Cleveland outpolled Harrison in the popular vote by 90,000 votes, a wider margin of victory than the one he enjoyed over Blaine in the election of 1884 that sent him to the White House. Again, and as expected, New York made all the difference: Between the trouble with the Irish Catholic vote that was stirred up by the fake Murchison letter, Cleveland's ongoing conflict with Tammany Hall, and votes likely snatched away by the Prohibition Party (which won over 30,000 of its 250,000 total votes in New York, some of which, it must be noted, may have gone to the GOP), New York swung away from its native son and rallied behind Harrison, the gap between the two candidates in the Empire State being around 15,000 votes (compared to the 1,100-vote gap that leaned to Cleveland in 1884 in the wake of the rum-and-Romanism fiasco). Indiana was also lost to the Democrats, but it was losing New York that sealed Cleveland's fate.

For the third time in American history, a candidate who won the popular vote lost the election. All three cases were distinctive. In 1824, Andrew Jackson won a plurality in both the Electoral College and the popular vote, polling ahead of the three other candidates that election year, but lost the election when it was sent to the House of Representatives for resolution. In 1876, Samuel Tilden won a clear majority in the popular vote but lost by just one vote in the Electoral College after disputed votes had been granted to his rival, Rutherford B. Hayes, by an independent ad hoc Electoral Commission. In 1888, Cleveland, an incumbent president, won a plurality of the popular vote but lost decisively in the Electoral College, this time involving neither the House of Representatives nor a separate electoral board. While three elections in the nineteenth century were decided against the outcome of the popular vote, such a situation would become rare, occurring only one more time 112 years later in the controversial election of 2000. Thus Benjamin Harrison became the fifth Republican to be elected to the presidency since the party's inaugural campaign in 1856, and in so doing he restored, at least for the moment, Republican domination of the White House. But Grover Cleveland, who had been the sixth Democrat to be elected president since its first triumph under President Jackson in 1828, and the first Democrat to win since Abraham Lincoln began Republican primacy in 1860, was not quite finished. The following election would provide an opportunity for a rematch and a return.

Additional Resources

The American Presidency Project. http://www.presidency.ucsb.edu.

Calhoun, Charles W. *Minority Victory: Gilded Age Politics and the Front Porch Campaign of 1888*. Lawrence: University Press of Kansas, 2008.

Watts, J.F. "1888." In Arthur M. Schlesinger, Fred L. Israel, and David J. Frent, eds. *Running for President: The Candidates and Their Images*. New York: Simon & Schuster, 1994.

Wessen, Robert. "Election of 1888." In Arthur M. Schlesinger, Fred Israel, and William P. Hansen, eds. *History of American Presidential Elections, 1789–1968*. Vol. 2. New York: Chelsea House, 1985.

Campaign of 1892

Moving into the latter decade of the nineteenth century, American social and economic life was undergoing dramatic change. The Industrial Revolution, which had been under way for some time in North America, was now accelerating toward a high pitch. The United States was now a leading economic power, its industrial capacity surpassing even the Great Powers of Europe. As such, a massive restructuring of the nation's economy was under way, accompanied by any and all attendant changes within American society and culture. The United States was a prosperous and vibrant society like none before. These changes were also marked by the intense concentration of immense amounts of wealth and a reorganization of economic and political influence that to some observers gave far too much power to far too few people, and thus militated against the egalitarian principles upon which the republic was, at least in part, founded. This concentration of wealth led to corporate "combinations," also known as monopolies, or, in the parlance of the time, trusts; and trusts were widely declaimed as corrosive to a free and fair society.

To address this problem, Congress passed the Sherman Anti-Trust Act of 1890, named after the former candidate for the Republican presidential nomination, Senator John Sherman of Ohio, and designed to limit monopolies and provide regulative and investigative authority to prevent their future formation. The law was enacted with President Harrison's signature but scarcely enforced, much to the discontent of the American public. The two major parties were on record as supportive of the idea of busting trusts, but they were not always quick, at least initially, to execute those legal provisions that would actually allow government to solve the problem of monopolies. In other words, the law was in place, but a few years would still have to pass before the nation, under the leadership of a very different kind of president, would see it put into full and effective operation.

Equally important, neither the Republican Party nor the Democratic Party supported legislation to help improve the working conditions of millions of men, women, and children; or, if there was any sympathy, it was somewhat diluted by other interests, distractions, and allegiances. The reluctance of both parties to deal with these serious and fundamental issues opened the door for a third party that would challenge the status quo. It is true that American prosperity was moving off the charts, even when compared to the other affluent nations of the world; but it was equally true that a great many Americans were not able to enjoy the fruits of this wealth and, in many instances, suffered the dispiriting hardships of subsistence living. Finally, in addition to worry over combinations and trusts, the debate over monetary policy and the legitimate medium of currency, which can be traced to the early 1870s, began to intensify to the point of becoming the dominant issue in the campaigns of the 1890s.

President Harrison, who fought hard to win the election in 1888, soon discovered that being president was more onerous than he had anticipated. He regarded the White House as a confining fishbowl, exposing his family to constant scrutiny and restricting his own personal freedom. He would refer to it as "my jail," and thus he seemed to his friends quite prepared to follow the example of President Rutherford B. Hayes and make his administration a one-term presidency. Additionally, his wife suffered poor health, which had been a distraction for the president and a justification for his stepping back into private life. Nonetheless, as a former general, he felt an obliging sense of duty to soldier forth as his party's standard-bearer, personal feelings and needs notwithstanding, and that sense of duty checked his desires for retirement.

For the most part, the president had run an effective administration. He kept his campaign promise to impose, with the critical support of Congress, high tariffs (set under the McKinley Tariff Act of 1890, which was made possible largely by the efforts and skills of Representative William McKinley of Ohio, one of the Republican Party's more promising prospects), as well as signing into law the Sherman Anti-Trust Act. He worked to expand foreign markets and cooperated with Congress to address inflation. For the most part, the Harrison administration was considered a success; but the president had his critics, many within his own party, and he did absolutely nothing to reach out to them. Harrison was viewed by many as dispassionate and aloof, even cold, an independent thinker unbound by party discipline, unconcerned by the need to compromise with the various factions, and his Calvinist piety at times alienated even his close supporters.

Furthermore, many within the party rank and file still felt a strong allegiance to James G. Blaine, the venerable Plumed Knight, who was at that time President Harrison's secretary of state (and with whom Harrison had an amicable relationship). Blaine had again managed to slough off the old tarnish of corruption that had coated his political record since the mid-1870s and was still seen by many as the preferred candidate in the upcoming election. But Blaine suffered from ill health and depression, having recently lost two children within a time span of less than a month, and as a result of this heavy sadness was not in the proper state of mind to make another run at the White House. According to some accounts, while Blaine managed to keep up a cheerful appearance in public, once home and behind closed doors, he would collapse and take to his bed. Probably due to his ability to maintain an even keel in public, his followers worked hard prior to the convention to gather support for a Blaine candidacy that would displace the dispassionate President Harrison. Blaine was as popular as ever, and rumors of failed health and hardship could not dampen the spirits of his loyal diehards. The president, who had enjoyed a sound relationship with Blaine, now began to grow disenchanted with the Plumed Knight, and he worked to distance himself. Finally, Blaine issued a public statement clarifying his position: He would not be a candidate. Privately, Blaine remarked to a family member, "When the American people choose a President, they require him to remain awake four years. I have come to a time in my life [in] which I need my sleep." Blaine's more zealous supporters were nonetheless left with the impression that Blaine might still entertain the possibility of a draft, but the draft never happened.

By the time the convention opened in Minneapolis, Harrison was poised to lock up the nomination, which he managed to do on the first ballot in spite of the anti-Harrison/draft Blaine faction. The president gained 535 votes to Blaine's unsolicited 182. Interestingly, William McKinley, now Mark Hanna's favored protégé and who was currently serving as governor of Ohio after his successful tenure in Congress, matched Blaine to share second place, an important step toward future opportunities. Curiously, Robert Todd Lincoln, not a serious candidate and never expressing interest in the White House, still received one vote. Harrison thus reentered the campaign for the general election with solid Republican support, the party dissidents temporarily quieted. Whitelaw Reid of Ohio, Harrison's ambassador to France, was unanimously nominated on one ballot to replace incumbent vice president Levi Morton, who had disappointed the president by his failure, as president of the Senate, to quash a Senate filibuster against the passage of legislation, supported by Harrison, enforcing the voting rights of African Americans. The Republican platform reaffirmed its support for high protective tariffs, and in an effort to attract Western voters, the platform supported bimetallism. The platform also included a plank reaffirming the promise to protect the voting rights of African Americans in southern states, calling again for the passage of new voting rights laws designed to protect the franchise for all citizens. In an effort to appeal to urban Northeastern voters, the platform expressed support for the independence of Ireland from Britain. Among other items, the platform also endorsed the construction of a canal in Nicaragua that would create a channel joining the Atlantic and Pacific Oceans.

At the Democratic convention held in Chicago, former president Grover Cleveland became the first of only two people to win three consecutive nominations from a major party for president of the United States; Franklin Roosevelt is the only other candidate to match, and eventually surpass, Cleveland's political achievement (eventually winning four consecutive nominations in the 1930s and 1940s). William Jennings Bryan would earn three nominations as well, but only two consecutively. (It should also be noted that Eugene V. Debs would win five nominations as the candidate for the Socialist Party, which, while important, still remained a minor party.) Many in the party felt that Cleveland could regain the White House, for he did, after all, win the popular vote against Harrison in the previous election. Thus he came into the convention as the front-runner, but this time he faced opposition. Cleveland still had old enemies in Tammany Hall, which once again made him vulnerable in New York—the state that won him the presidency in 1884 and took it away in 1888. Furthermore, Cleveland's reputation as a Bourbon Democrat and his Gold Bug attitudes on the issue of currency won him strong critics from within his own party. Thus, ten other candidates were in play, the biggest challenges made by David B. Hill, a fellow New Yorker and Tammany man, whom many believed could deliver New York to the Democrats; and Horace Boies of Iowa, a bimetallist who might run strong in the West and the Midwest. Among the eight remaining candidates, none of whom became serious contenders, was Adlai E. Stevenson of Illinois, the grandfather of his famous namesake who would twice become the Democratic candidate in the 1950s. Stevenson was selected by the convention to run for the vice presidency, even though Cleveland initially favored Isaac Gray of Indiana. Stevenson, who supported Free Silver and greenbacks, was viewed as a counterweight to Cleveland's hard-currency, gold-standard principles and thus a concession to those elements at the convention who held reservations regarding Cleveland's return to the White House.

Cleveland's political triumph at gaining a third consecutive party nomination concealed the reality that he was not enthusiastically embraced, at least not this time around. His popularity was by default; the Democratic Party simply had not as yet produced a figure that could match his stature. As president, he was neither dynamic enough to capture the public imagination nor cunning enough to undercut his rivals, both good qualities stemming from his personal integrity but, unfortunately, not always the kind of qualities needed for the ego-driven world of high-powered politics. Hence, even though he was the obvious best choice available based upon his personal virtues and experience, he seemed vulnerable, and he might have been blocked had the rest of the field not been so disunited. But he managed a first-ballot win, not as convincing as Harrison's, as he earned just ten votes above the requirement, but convincing enough to rebuff the challenge from Tammany and the Silverites. Thus the former president was poised to challenge the incumbent president, the man who unseated him four years earlier.

In many ways, Cleveland resembled his once and present rival. Like Harrison, he had earned a reputation for obstinacy; he was an independent agent not willing to curry the favor of either the party elites or the general voters. Henry Adams, scholar, erudite social critic, and scion of the legendary Adams family, wrote, "The two candidates were singular persons of whom it was the common saying that one of them had no friends; the other only enemies." With the exception of the ever-important tariff issue that had defined the previous contest, his views on policy were not that different from Harrison's. Neither candidate was actively engaged in the campaign. Because of the ill health of the president's wife and his low spirits, the front-porch campaign tactics that he had used to great effect in 1888 were abandoned. He was virtually absent from the public arena during the campaign. Cleveland followed Harrison's example, thoughtfully forbearing from active campaigning out of respect for the First Lady.

Harrison and Cleveland were not the only notable candidates in 1892. In July, the People's Party, more commonly known as the Populist Party, held its first national nominating convention in Omaha, Nebraska. In the midterm elections of 1890, the emerging Populist Party had surprisingly won nine congressional seats. The Populists appealed to farmers, miners, ranchers, and rural Americans who blamed their economic problems on Eastern industrialists, bankers, financiers, speculators, and railroad magnates. Appealing to the "common man," Populists advocated extensive government action to more fully control the power of corporate trusts and monopolies. Bolstered by its midterm election victories, the Populist Party nominated former Greenback candidate James Weaver of Ohio for president and James Field of Virginia for vice president. Among other proposals, the Populist platform supported Free Silver and greenbacks, labor reform limiting the working day and providing protection against child-labor abuses, universal adult suffrage for both men and women, government control of the railroads, the use of the democratic procedures of the initiative and referendum, a graduated federal income tax, and amending the Constitution to provide for the popular election of senators as well as limiting presidential administrations to just one term. Interestingly, the Populist platform also included a plank calling for new laws prohibiting the importation of contract labor. In the preamble to their party platform, the Populists affirmed the following:

We have witnessed for more than a quarter of a century the struggles of the two great political parties for power and plunder, while grievous wrongs have been inflicted upon the suffering people. We charge that the controlling influences dominating both these parties have permitted the existing dreadful conditions to develop without serious effort to prevent or restrain them. Neither do they now promise us any substantial reform. They have agreed together to ignore, in the coming campaign, every issue but one. They propose to drown the outcries of a plundered people with the uproar of a sham battle over the tariff, so that capitalists, corporations, national banks, rings, trusts, watered stock, the demonetization of silver and the oppressions of the usurers may all be lost sight of. They propose to sacrifice our homes, lives, and children on the altar of mammon; to destroy the multitude to secure corruption funds from the millionaires. (American Presidency Project, University of California, Santa Barbara)

Effectively stirring recruits to the people's cause, Mary Lease of Kansas, a prominent suffragette, stumped with Weaver throughout the West and the South. Exhorting her audience to "raise less corn and more hell," Lease quickly became a leading figure in the campaign. Her attacks against the empires of finance epitomized the Populist attitude. "Wall Street owns the country," she declared, and, through parody of a mythic sentiment, she declaimed the American state as a "government of Wall Street, by Wall Street, and for Wall Street." Because both major parties found themselves vulnerable to charges of plutocracy and elitism, the Populists were able to attract their more disaffected elements.

While the People's (or Populist) Party attempted to build interest in its radical reform agenda, the Democratic and Republican parties focused on their traditional positions regarding tariffs and one's loyalty to the Union. Cleveland refused to compromise his steadfast low-tariff principles or to embrace the bimetallism supported by the Democratic Party's own populist wing. Labor unrest and Harrison's support for high tariffs created more serious problems for the Republicans than for the Democrats. Republican arguments holding that high tariffs strengthened American industry and produced jobs fell on deaf ears within labor. To many industrial workers, tariffs appeared to have the opposite impact. When leading industrialist Andrew Carnegie ordered a significant reduction in the wages of Pennsylvania steelworkers, the workers organized and went out on strike. The 1892 Homestead Strike led to intense violence between the strikers and Carnegie's private, armed Pinkerton security agents. Largely because of the growing alliance between the Republican Party, especially its conservative Old Guard, and powerful industrialists, many industrial workers blamed the Republicans for the antiunion tactics of Carnegie and other industrialists. Although the Democratic Party had its pro-business Bourbon wing, with which Cleveland was affiliated, the more populist, pro-labor elements in the party attracted labor votes, an advantage that would prove valuable in the upcoming election.

Some within the Republican Party again attempted to wave the "bloody shirt" by raising questions about the loyalty of Cleveland to the Union. Throughout the campaign, *Judge*, a popular illustrated newspaper, published cartoons reminding readers of the Democratic Party's historic association with the Confederacy. *Judge* and other Republican-leaning publications pointed out the fact that both Grover Cleveland and Adlai Stevenson had hired substitutes to fight for them after being drafted into the Union army. Comparisons were drawn to President Harrison and Reid, who had both served with distinction, Harrison achieving the rank of brigadier general and playing a crucial role under General Sherman, and Reid earning praise as a war correspondent who earned the military rank of captain. During the war, Cleveland was a War Democrat, and Stevenson, while remaining a civilian, helped to organize troops for the state of Illinois. But Stevenson had also been unfairly accused of being a Copperhead, and while the accusation was false, the stigma followed him throughout his political career.

In the final analysis, President Harrison's lifeless campaign and Cleveland's ability to attract the support of angry industrial workers in midwestern and northeastern states cost Harrison a second term. Cleveland received 46.1 percent of the popular vote against the 43 percent of the popular vote received by Harrison. In all three presidential elections in which he was involved, Cleveland won the popular vote but in each case fell short of an actual majority. In fact, he won a lower share of the popular vote in his successful 1892 bid than he had in either his winning 1884 campaign or his losing 1888 campaign. He was the first president twice elected without a popular majority, and one of only two, the other being President Bill Clinton a century later. More important, Cleveland received 277 electoral votes against the 145 electoral votes tallied for Harrison. To the dismay of the Republican Party leadership, Harrison failed to carry the Republican strongholds of Illinois, Indiana, Wisconsin, and the critical state of New York, a total loss of 87 electoral votes. Cleveland predictably swept the South, and he took California in the West, the first time since 1880 (when the state was won by Winfield Scott Hancock by a margin of less than 200 votes) that the Golden State went to the Democrats. The Populist Party won over a million votes, or 8.5 percent of the popular vote, the best showing of a third party since Millard Fillmore's Know-Nothings won 21 percent in 1856. However, the Know-Nothings won just one state in the Electoral College, while the Populists behind Weaver impressively won five states in 1892, all in the West—Colorado, Idaho, Kansas, Nevada, and North Dakota—for a total of 22 electoral votes, 5 percent of the total electoral count. While these states did not carry the electoral clout found in the East and the Midwest, they signaled a growing impatience with the established parties among a noticeable segment of the electorate, prompting sympathetic factions in both of the major parties to double their efforts. The effects of the populist influence were first felt in the Democratic Party as early as the next election, in the first campaign of Nebraska's William Jennings Bryan, and later in the Republican Party with the ascent of progressive figures such as Theodore Roosevelt. But for the moment, Bourbon Democrat Grover Cleveland was returned to the White House as the twenty-fourth president, to this day the only president in American history to serve two nonconsecutive terms. He would be the last Democratic president until the inauguration of Woodrow Wilson twenty years later.

Additional Resources

The American Presidency Project. http://www.presidency.ucsb.edu.

Boller, Paul F., Jr. *Presidential Campaigns.* Oxford: Oxford University Press, 2004.

Fratkin, Robert A. "1892." in Arthur M. Schlesinger, Fred L. Israel, and David J. Frent, eds. *Running for President: The Candidates and Their Images.* New York: Simon & Schuster, 1994.

Knoles, George Harmon. *The Presidential Campaign and Elections of 1892.* New York: AMS Press, 1971.

Morgan, H. Wayne. "Election of 1892." In Arthur M. Schlesinger, Fred Israel, and William P. Hansen, eds. *History of American Presidential Elections, 1789–1968.* Vol. 2. New York: Chelsea House, 1985.

Campaign of 1896

"You shall not press down upon the brow of labor this crown of thorns; you shall not crucify mankind upon a cross of gold!" Candidate William Jennings Bryan's famous declamation illustrates the overheated passion of the election of 1896, which reconfigured the parties primarily around the issue of bimetallism combined with a variety of policies inspired by an increasing populist sentiment within American political culture. Sectional allegiances remained solid in the South, accompanied by significant gains in the West for the Democrats, while the Northeast and the Midwest remained predominantly, but not exclusively, Republican. The decade of the 1890s was a turbulent one. An economic crisis that became known as the Panic of 1893, caused by a collapse of the railroad and banking industries, dragged the country into a depression, one that would be particularly harmful to farmers, who witnessed the value of their farms plummet and were subsequently driven into ever-burdensome debt. Additionally, disputes between business and a more active, organized labor movement led to increased tension and episodes of open conflict: Industrial labor experienced high unemployment and low wages, Pullman workers went on strike in 1894, violence erupted in the steel and mining industries, industrial workers marched on the nation's capital, and labor leaders grew increasingly frustrated by the intransigence of industrialists and the leaders of American commerce.

Amidst this storm and stress emerged two distinctly disparate candidates: the subdued yet self-assured conservative Republican William McKinley, governor of

Ohio, former leading member in the House of Representatives, committed protectionist who had helped set the nation's high-tariff policy, protégé of industrialist and kingmaker Mark Hanna, erstwhile pro-Blaine convention delegate, former Straddlebug now turned Gold Bug, and the last Civil War veteran to aspire toward the White House; and for the Democrats, the young, tempestuous, charismatic, and religiously devout populist Bryan of Nebraska—"the Great Commoner," "the Peerless One," the "Silver Knight of the West." The winner would become the last president to be inaugurated in the nineteenth century, a century that began with the inauguration of Thomas Jefferson and was drawing to a close still facing the many and difficult challenges of realizing a republic genuinely built upon the principle that "all men are created equal."

"Sixteen to One" was the proposed ratio between the two precious metals, sixteen ounces of silver holding the equivalent value of one ounce of gold. Thus the presidential campaign proceeded, framed by the state of the nation's monetary policy, an otherwise mundane concern that would quickly ignite into the most inflammatory political question since slavery, even to the point of eclipsing in importance the century-old debate over tariffs. Owing to economic depression and the intensifying activism among American workers, populist elements within the Democratic Party suddenly waxed in strength. Contrary to the conservative policies of the incumbent Democratic president, Grover Cleveland, who favored the gold standard and unrestricted markets, the party's more populist wing radicalized, committing partisan energies to a denunciation of the gold standard and steering their platform in a direction that aligned them more closely with the Populist Party than with the Bourbon Democrats of their own party. Attempting to shake, once and for all, the bloody shirt, rank-and-file Democrats now saw their future in returning to the powerful mythos of Jacksonian democracy. The common man wanted bimetallism and economic reform, and the newly aligned Democrats were intent upon delivering just that.

Supporters of Free Silver also numbered among the Republican ranks, but they were drawn primarily from the newly formed and sparsely populated western states and thus remained in the minority. At the 1896 convention in St. Louis, a small faction of Silverite Western Republicans objected to a plank in the party platform that, for the first time in the party's history, explicitly opposed the policy of Free Silver. Led by Colorado senator Henry Teller, the Silverites stalked out of the convention, established the National Silver Party, and eventually threw their support behind the Democrats. With the more populist-oriented Silverites abandoning the GOP, conservative elements in the party met little resistance in the nomination of McKinley, who (thanks to the tireless efforts of Hanna, who regarded McKinley as the greatest man he knew), came into the convention with a lock on the nomination and easily won on the first ballot with only token resistance. McKinley's friend and close adviser, Garret Hobart of New Jersey, was nominated for vice president on the first ballot. Since the end of Reconstruction in the late 1870s, the party of Abraham Lincoln, Frederick Douglass, and Thaddeus Stevens had been increasingly ignoring its progressive, reformist (in some cases radical) roots while drawing closer to the interests of the powerful industrial and commercial elite. With McKinley's nomination, the turn toward plutocracy seemed complete to critics both within the party and outside of it. The pro-business, protectionist, mono-metallist platform certainly seemed to confirm that impression, but other planks evinced a broader range of concerns, expressing support for Cuban independence from Spain and American control of a canal through Nicaragua, and denouncing the horrific practice of lynching. Interestingly, the Republican platform recommended greater opportunities for women in American society but did not explicitly endorse women's suffrage.

Unlike the Republican convention in St. Louis, the Democratic convention in Chicago was a real contest. Prior to the convention, a struggle developed between Gold Bug Democrats, who had embraced President Cleveland's sound money policies based on the gold standard, and the strengthening Silverites (or Silver Bugs). Given the economic stress that the country had recently faced, the policies of the Cleveland administration were under fire, and the Free Silver proponents made a strong move to gain more support throughout the party. There were Gold Bug holdouts within the party, but as the convention approached, the silver faction held the upper hand. All that was now required by the Silverites was a rallying voice. As the convention commenced, Missouri's Silverite champion, Richard Bland, who also shared with Bryan the "Great Commoner" moniker, appeared to be the strongest candidate (the party apparently being big enough for two "great commoners"). His Free Silver credentials reached back over two decades, and he was a coauthor of legislation—the Bland-Allison Act—that allowed for the limited circulation of some silver dollars as a compromise to the Coinage Act of 1873 that had struck the first blow against Free Silver. The Western miners and other Free Silver advocates thus saw in Bland a proven, credible ally. Bland, however, did not have many friends within the populist wing, and he was further hampered by his wife's Catholic faith, the old prejudices still skewing perceptions. Horace Boies of Iowa was both a populist and a bimetallist, and he appeared to be a more reasonable fit. Robert Pattison, governor of Pennsylvania (who achieved that office at the age of thirty-one), and Kentucky's Joseph C. S. Blackburn also brought loyal delegates, with Claude Matthews of Indiana and John R. McLean of Ohio joining the field of leading candidates. Numerous other candidates would receive some minor support.

Bland and Boies appeared to be the more credible candidates as the convention was gaveled into session, but Nebraska's Bryan, only thirty-six years old, soon emerged as an irresistible force. Prior to the convention, Bryan had already quietly worked to gather support for his name, but it was Bryan's oratory that propelled him well past all other candidates, with the exception of Bland. Bryan's rousing Cross of Gold speech convulsed the convention. During the speech, Bryan was interrupted several times by wild cheers, and his "crown of thorns, cross of gold" peroration sent the convention into a veritable frenzy. On the first ballot, Bland took the lead with 235 votes, but Bryan outpolled the rest, winning 137 delegates, with Pattison leading the "also-rans," falling well behind with 97. It was now a contest between the tested veteran of the Free Silver struggle and the youthful dynamo from Nebraska, a battle that Bland led through three ballots; but on the fourth, Bryan's momentum carried him into first, and on the fifth, he surged ahead with 652 delegates behind him and won the nomination—to this day the youngest man in American history to be nominated for president by a major party. Bland, Boies, and the other Silverites immediately closed ranks behind Bryan, much to the dismay of a disgruntled President Cleveland and the party's Bourbon/Gold Bug faction. Bland was considered for the vice presidency, and he led the balloting on the second and third rounds, populist Democrat Joseph C. Sibley having led on the first ballot. But in the end, after McLean took the lead on the fourth ballot, the convention tapped Maine's Arthur Sewall, an industrialist and shipbuilder, who was finally selected as an olive branch to the party conservatives.

While the Republicans—the Party of Lincoln, the humble Rail Splitter and Great Emancipator—were now widely perceived as the party of wealth, the Democrats—the party that had actually once guarded Southern aristocracy and defended slavery, even to the point of open war—were emerging as the new champion of the people: small farmer and industrial worker, immigrant and underprivileged alike. The Democrats nailed planks into their platform supporting populist reforms such as a graduated federal income tax, low tariffs, regulation of industries, and support for the cause of labor. And yet not all Democrats identified with their populist and bimetallist factions. After Bryan's oratorical triumph at the convention roiled the delegates into an agitated whirl, Gold Bug Democrats, unmoved by the inclusion of Sewall on the ticket, separated from the party to form the National Democratic Party, meeting in Indianapolis and nominating John M. Palmer of Illinois as their alternative to the populist Bryan, with Simon Bolivar Buckner Sr. tapped as his running mate. The National Democrats hewed more closely to the older values embodied by President Cleveland, who himself eagerly endorsed Palmer over Bryan. But their efforts were against the current; the Democratic Party was inexorably moving to incorporate the populist agenda, and as such, it offered an attractive platform and candidate to the swelling numbers of populist voters. Thus, when the actual Populist Party met in St. Louis, it joined the Democrats in endorsing Bryan. The Populists would not, however, second Sewall's nomination, preferring instead to nominate their own candidate for vice president from among their own ranks, Senator Thomas Watson of Georgia. Bryan happily acknowledged the Populist nomination, leaving the issue of his running mate—Sewall or Watson—ambiguous.

In perhaps the most ideologically charged campaign since 1860, the Great Commoner stumped with unprecedented abandon. McKinley tactically stayed home, playing it cool. Bryan's campaign events resembled charismatic tent revivals; McKinley effectively combined the proven front-porch strategy of Benjamin Harrison's first campaign with the seemingly inexhaustible fund-raising abilities of Hanna and the GOP elite. Bryan traveled thousands of miles to reach the people. The people traveled thousands of miles to reach McKinley. Bryan spoke for hours on end at innumerable venues at an impassioned and febrile pitch; McKinley's speeches were subdued and succinct—and all delivered from the same place; in a word, McKinley's campaign was "Harrisonian" in both strategy and demeanor. Learning from the success of the Democrats in 1892, Bryan concentrated much of his efforts in the key battleground states of the Midwest, primarily Michigan, Illinois, Ohio, Indiana, and Wisconsin.

But the campaign went beyond electoral politics, for both sides perceived the election as a battle between cosmic forces of good and evil: The bimetallist cause of silver was cast as a sacred battle against the iniquities of gold-standard plutocracy, the cause of gold monometallism explained as the only hope against the demonic forces of rabble-rousing anarchists and mob rule. Republicans openly charged the Democrats of moving so far to the left that they precipitated socialism, communism, and anarchy, in the style of European radicals. Democrats accused Republicans and Gold Bug/Bourbon Democrats of becoming duped pawns of the fat cats and robber barons. As did Harrison before him, McKinley, while remaining firmly planted in his home base, relied on surrogate campaigners who would travel the country canvassing on his behalf. Among these surrogates was the indomitable Theodore Roosevelt, now the party's most effective speaker and commanding personality. Hot on Bryan's trail, Roosevelt would soon prove to be more than a match for the Great Commoner. While Roosevelt's actual speeches were not, on paper, as powerful as Bryan's, his overwhelming persona simply electrified crowds, in many instances stealing Bryan's thunder. As such, it was becoming ever clearer to many party regulars that the GOP's future would to a great extent involve this incomparable personality.

The "Cross of Gold" remained the Democrats' central slogan. The Republicans defiantly maintained that the dollar itself was "good as gold." The most famous Republican slogan in that year punctuated the promise of economic stability and future prosperity with the less striking phrase "A Full Dinner Pail," emphasizing the traditional reliability of monometallism and conservative policies. The propaganda mill churned out disinformation from both sides: Workers collecting their wages would find their pay envelopes accompanied by enclosed Republican flyers admonishing them against the dangers of Democratic irresponsibility, alerting workers to the threat that a vote for Bryan would precede immediate unemployment. Democrats depicted McKinley as a mindless puppet of the kingmaker Hanna, a diminutive figure moved only by the commands of his party boss. Republicans returned the volley with shrill denunciations of Bryan as an ignorant, arrogant, irreligious madman seducing the uneducated masses with silken speeches wrought from the spirit of impiety. The "Cross of Gold" speech, widely acclaimed by Bryan's supporters in both the Democratic and Populist parties, was vehemently criticized by pro-Republican clergy as a thoroughly sacrilegious diatribe.

Following what had now become a customary method, the Republican Party widely circulated the Republican *Campaign Songster* to drum up the Republican message. One song titled "McKinley, 'Tis of Thee" sought to define McKinley as the savior of economic prosperity:

> McKinley, 'tis of thee,
> Proclaim from sea to sea
> Of thee we sing!
> We want prosperity;
> We want no anarchy,
> We want sweet liberty,
> Let Freedom ring.

Much like the McKinley campaign, the Bryan campaign relied upon campaign songs to disseminate its message. A song titled "Silver Lion Came Tearin' Out the Wilderness" sought to depict Free Silver as the solution to the nation's economic problems:

> The Silver Lion came tearing out the wilderness
> Tearing out the wilderness
> At sixteen to one
> William Bryan will be our next President,
> Be our next president, be our next president,
> William Bryan will be our next President,
> We'll get sixteen to one

On Election Day, McKinley held the Northeast-Midwest axis reflected in the ticket, collecting 271 Electoral College votes (an impressive 61%) and over 7 million popular votes (51%). Winning the entire South and most of the West was not enough for Bryan, who finished with just over 6,500,000 votes and an Electoral College total of 176 (39%). Bryan's sweep of the West was spoiled by McKinley holding Oregon and reclaiming California. But it was his ability to reclaim all the northern and midwestern states that had been lost to the Democrats in 1892 that sealed McKinley's victory. McKinley's showing in New York was utterly convincing, winning a statewide landslide of 57 percent of the vote in a state that had been a desperately close and decisive battleground in the previous four elections reaching back to 1880. Several minor parties were also on the ticket, led by the National Democrats, the Prohibition Party, and the recently formed Socialist Labor Party. Together, these three parties were unable to win 300,000 votes between them. With McKinley's victory along with the Populists' absorption into the Democratic Party, the establishment parties solidified their position among the voters. With impeccable timing, the Republicans regained the White House, for an economic recovery had begun toward the end of the campaign year, which, in the exchange of American politics, reliably translates into political capital of inestimable value, and it benefited the administration of the nation's twenty-fifth president at the close of the nineteenth century.

Additional Resources

Fite, Gilbert C. "Election of 1896." In Arthur M. Schlesinger, Fred Israel, and William P. Hansen, eds. *History of American Presidential Elections, 1789–1968.* Vol. 2. New York: Chelsea House, 1985.

Glad, Paul W. *McKinley, Bryan, and the People.* Philadelphia: Lippincott, 1964.

Jones, Stanley Llewellyn. *The Presidential Election of 1896.* Madison: University of Wisconsin Press, 1964.

Ritchie, Donald A. "1896." In Arthur M. Schlesinger, Fred L. Israel, and David J. Frent, eds. *Running for President: The Candidates and Their Images.* New York: Simon & Schuster, 1994.

Whicher, George Frisbe. *William Jennings Bryan and the Campaign of 1896.* Boston: Heath, 1953.

Williams, Hal. *Realigning America: McKinley, Bryan, and the Remarkable Election of 1896.* Lawrence: University Press of Kansas, 2010.

Campaign of 1900

The issues hovering over the Campaign of 1900 make the febrile debate over monetary policy that drove the **Campaign of 1896** seem almost comically overblown. A far more serious matter, the debate over the recently fought Spanish-American War and its implications for the country's future, dominated the Campaign of 1900. After a period of rising tension between the United States and Spain over increasingly dismal conditions in Cuba, the war had been touched off by the February 15, 1898, explosion of the American warship USS *Maine* in Havana Harbor. On April 25, following a long period of investigation into the incident by a board of naval inquiry, it was determined by the U.S. government that the *Maine* was deliberately attacked by the Spanish, using a "submarine mine." A Spanish inquiry drew a different conclusion, determining that the explosion was the result of an accident likely involving spontaneous combustion originating in the warship's coal supply. The United States was convinced otherwise, and thus Congress formally declared war against Spain on April 25. The subsequent and surprisingly quick and thorough defeat of Spain and its aftermath—the expansion of American territory into the Caribbean as well as the South Pacific, owing to a lopsided American naval victory in Manila Harbor in the Philippines—immediately transformed the United States into an imperial power over the slight time span of just a few short weeks. With this staggering success in war against a traditional European power, and with a growing economy that had by the turn of the century become the most productive in the world, eclipsing even the industrial might of Great Britain, a new, decidedly modernist twentieth-century America was laboring to be born.

But in spite of the remarkable success of the United States in the war, doubts about the causes—as well as the motivations—lingered, leading to a reexamination of the war from a number of critics. To these critics, the war was both unnecessary and without justification, offering disturbing evidence of a new and unbridled ambition for empire that was inconsonant with founding principles of the American republic—principles that, it was to be remembered, were affirmed through an act of defiance against a tyrannical colonial power. And now it seemed to the critics of the war that America itself was laboring to become such a power. Anti-imperialist leagues formed throughout the country to oppose continued American overseas expansion that was under way through the annexation of the Philippines (a war prize), as well as the Hawaiian Islands—a territory recently acquired under its own controversies—and any other territories far from the American mainland that had been acquired in the victory over Spain. Prior to the war, the popular doctrine of **manifest destiny** was indeed widely embraced; but it was a continental ambition based, rightly or wrongly, on a premise that the United States was fated by Providence to dominate the North American continent, and to establish a republic of, by, and for the people that was dedicated to the principles of liberty and equality stretching without interruption from the Atlantic to the Pacific. Throughout much of the nineteenth century, Americans almost universally embraced this concept, some more ardently than others. However, manifest destiny was not traditionally interpreted as including territory beyond the natural North American coastline; hence in some quarters—particularly within an exercised faction of the Democratic Party and those minor parties of a more populist/progressive hue—the move to establish a colonial presence overseas was regarded as imprudent at best and, at worst, evidence of imperial hubris that militated most stridently against the ideals of any free society.

Both William Jennings Bryan, the populist Democratic candidate for president in 1896, and the conservative former president Grover Cleveland, a Bourbon Democrat, vocally expressed concern over the fate of a republic that so eagerly sought empire abroad. Once he realized that Free Silver was yesterday's battle, Bryan would thus aim, after some hesitation, his rhetorical saber at the bloated and grasping: trusts that dominated the domestic economy, and imperialists who sought an undemocratic American empire. Some, however, favored and even promoted a stronger American presence within the world community, a presence that, in the age of European colonialism, would require the United States to extend itself in competition for territory abroad, out of a sense of duty to the greater good and improvement of civilized humanity. No one epitomized this belief more than Theodore Roosevelt, then the assistant secretary of the navy, who believed in America's destiny as a great force leading the entire world toward a higher stage of civilization, and Roosevelt was among those who led the United States along the war path against Spain, even though his president, the more reticent William McKinley, was less than enthusiastic. But events took over, and it was now incumbent upon President McKinley and the Republican Party to adopt Roosevelt's position, thereby standing firmly behind the prosecution of the Spanish-American War and its outcome against all critics and detractors. Thus Republicans embraced the war and the colonial expansion of the United States abroad as a boon to American interests and a boost to American destiny, and of equal importance, a blessing for the community of free nations.

And so a new controversy, imperialism (or "expansionism"), came to overshadow the other issues of the day, even drawing away attention from the continued debates over monetary policy that had been the central issue of the **Campaign of 1896**, as well as the unshakeable debate over tariffs, which had also been a major point of contention in the previous election and a perennially dominant concern in still earlier campaigns. Other serious domestic issues such as the economy or racial relations were pushed far into the background, almost out of sight. For the first time since the question of the annexation of Texas that, for good reason, generated heated debate in the 1840s, foreign policy became a principal issue in a presidential campaign. In spite of the partisan debate over the justification for the war and the future of the United States abroad, President McKinley felt confident in his bid for a second term. The favorable outcome of the war for the United States, combined with a general economic recovery after the depression that had occurred during the previous Democratic administration of President Cleveland, boosted Republican morale and gave the party considerable ammunition in the upcoming general election. The position enjoyed by President McKinley led to his nomination by acclaim at the party's national convention in Philadelphia the summer before the general election. Given his many successes, the president was simply too strong to dislodge, his nomination a *fait accompli.*

Vice President Hobart, who was for the times atypical in that he was an important participant in the president's administration (even referred to as "Assistant to the President," making him the most influential vice president since the ratification of the Twelfth Amendment altering the selection process), had sadly passed away the previous year; thus a new candidate was needed for the vacancy. Riding a wave of public adoration, convention delegates turned to the Rough Rider Theodore Roosevelt, who had earned a reputation for bravery by having previously resigned his post in the Department of the Navy to fight with the army in Cuba, and who had emerged from that enterprise a genuine war hero, an achievement that almost immediately rocketed him into the governor's mansion in Albany, New York. While governor, and before that throughout his already-storied political career, Roosevelt established a reputation as a reformer, thus incurring the wrath of the movers and shakers within the world of the New York political machine. But he greatly appealed to the reform wing within the party, and that, combined with his war record and his charismatic personality, made him the irresistible candidate for the moment at hand. In a rousing speech endorsing the renomination of President McKinley, Roosevelt had electrified an otherwise lethargic convention floor. Roosevelt's boundless energy, expansive intelligence, genuine courage, iron determination, and dominant personality were the stuff of legend. A fiery speaker who gave voters every reason to believe that he was more than capable of following his words with actions, he had been a rising force within the Republican Party since his days in the New York state legislature. As a reformer, he directly challenged the GOP's more conservative faction and gave the progressive wing a potent standard-bearer; but as war hero and worldly man of action, he was attractive to the conservatives as well. Thus Roosevelt was already viewed by a large number of delegates as the only real choice for the vice presidency.

Upon the death of Vice President Hobart, party members in the western states began to circulate Roosevelt's name as a replacement. Inadvertently, this caught the attention of one of Roosevelt's rivals, New York party boss Thomas Platt, who, eager to turn back the Rough Rider's political ascent as well as remove him from the governor's office in New York, realized that the vice presidency might actually be the best way to do it. Platt knew that the last vice president to gain the White House by means other than the death of a sitting president—that is, through the electoral process and not through blind fate—was Martin Van Buren in 1836, a full sixty-four years before. Because of this, the vice presidency was at that time regarded by many as a political dead end. Thus Platt cynically joined the chorus for

Roosevelt and, along with other enemies of the Rough Rider, voiced his approval. By contrast, Mark Hanna, who disliked "that damned cowboy" in a moment of despair, was openly against a Roosevelt vice presidency, asking his colleagues if any of them realized that there would be, if Roosevelt was indeed selected for the office, "only one life between this madman and the White House." Hanna, who revered McKinley, not only found Roosevelt to be an irresponsible choice on its own merits, but he was also concerned that this vibrant and imposing Rough Rider could quite easily overshadow the more subdued personality of the president.

Roosevelt himself was unsure and thus for a time demurred, suspecting that the vice presidency could in fact prove itself to be a political dead end, as many suspected; by the time of the convention, Roosevelt somewhat reluctantly began to warm to the idea, but Hanna did not. Behind the scenes, he worked hard to upset the Roosevelt bandwagon, lobbying prominent members of McKinley's cabinet along with Iowa's Senator Allison in an attempt to encourage them to mount an alternative campaign. It was to no avail. No candidate captured the delegates' imagination the way Roosevelt did, and all that was needed was Roosevelt's assent, which he finally gave after considerable resistance, and once done, he was nominated unanimously—with one abstention, Roosevelt himself—on a single ballot.

The Republican platform fell easily into place, lauding President McKinley and his leadership in the Spanish-American War, reaffirming its commitment to the gold standard while opposing the free coinage of silver, and renewing Republican adherence to a protective high tariff. Other planks advocated further restrictions on the importation of immigrant labor (a message aimed primarily at Chinese immigration), raising the minimum age for child labor, supporting the construction of a canal in Panama connecting the Atlantic with the Pacific, and criticizing southern states for enacting laws depriving African Americans of their full voting rights. The few black delegates from the South who were in attendance had hoped for more, their proposals suggesting, to no avail, a plank aimed at enacting anti-lynching laws as well as the repeal of state laws that had effectively disenfranchised African Americans throughout the South.

McKinley's opponent, William Jennings Bryan, also won renomination as his party's standard-bearer on the first ballot of an otherwise uninspired convention, forcing a rematch of the 1896 campaign. Prior to the convention, Admiral George Dewey, an eminent naval hero in the Civil War and more recently famous for leading the navy to the lopsided victory in the Battle of Manila Bay, attempted (on the somewhat questionable encouragement of friends) to muster a campaign for the Democratic ticket. But the admiral known for his famous command, "You may fire when ready, Gridley," proved to be an inept politician and withdrew from the race a month before the convention. Inept challenger or no, Bryan was clearly the party's favorite long before the convention, and at Kansas City he was nominated, like

McKinley, unanimously on the first ballot. Former vice president (under President Cleveland) Adlai E. Stevenson was nominated on the second ballot after rebuffing a temporary challenge from New York's David P. Hill, a Gold Bug conservative who would have been a poor fit for Bryan and an irritant to the Silverites. Stevenson became the second of three men to be nominated for the vice presidency on nonconsecutive tickets (Thomas Hendricks before him and Charles Fairbanks after him were the other two).

Looking backward to the previous campaign, a fixated Bryan began exactly where he ended four years earlier—relaunching jeremiads against the wickedness of gold and reaffirming his enthusiasm for the Free Silver movement, which he reiterated as "the paramount issue" in the upcoming battle. Bryan's recalcitrant reliance on the main issue of 1896 hardened before the convention, his dedication to silver more ardent than ever. However, with the dramatic revival and sustained expansion of the economy—boosted by a bountiful gold strike in the Klondike— bimetallism was an issue that could no longer spark the zealous and pseudo- religious devotions of the previous campaign. Furthermore, during the summer of that year, the Boxer Rebellion in China turned the attention of both parties away from domestic issues and toward questions regarding the growing U.S. presence and future role in the Far East. This, along with the heated discussion over imperi- alism, eclipsed bimetallism, a reality that eventually dawned on Bryan's campaign. Free Silver as political capital had been significantly devalued with the onset of prosperity, the new gold rush, recent military triumph, and the changing nature of American foreign interests and policies. As the campaign aged, Bryan's attack was retargeted, for the most part, on trusts and imperialism. This is not to say that the issue of Free Silver was entirely dead, but only to note that it was not nearly enough to fuel a substantial challenge against an incumbent who had presided over a significant economic recovery and who managed a quick and comparatively easy victory at war. Bryan was hard to convince about the traction of Free Silver, though, and at one point he threatened to end his campaign if silver were to be de- emphasized. He regarded silver to have been his only true base in 1896, and he felt that his campaign had to begin there. Only through a strenuous effort on his part to nail a Free Silver plank into the platform could a compromise be reached between Bryan and the northeastern Democrats.

During the convention, the Boxer Rebellion had gathered steam, and Presi- dent McKinley's response of deploying five thousand troops to China to help sup- press the rebellion drew considerable support. This development was the final proof needed to persuade Bryan that it was an election over American ambitions abroad. In his acceptance speech, actually given in Indianapolis, not Kansas City, Bryan was finally silent on Free Silver, choosing instead to state his opposition to McKinley's "imperialistic" presidency. This immediately won the allegiance of the anti-imperialists, but it was ultimately a miscalculation. Save for the South, which was already a firm Democratic bastion, the recent annexation of Pacific territories, along with American interaction with China, was a popular course of action. President McKinley knew this after touring extensively throughout the West and the Midwest, and thus he restated his commitment to the annexation of the Philippines. Bryan turned his oratory toward sympathy for "our brown brothers" in Mindanao, but with little effect. The popularity of the last war served the Republicans and placed the Democrats in the risky position of appearing unpatriotic. Bryan alienated his former allies outside the party, such as the minority Silver Bug and Mugwump Republicans, and was uncomfortably backed into the position of criticizing an administration that had overseen both unprecedented economic growth and astonishingly one-sided military victory. Events in China helped McKinley's cause, as his effective deployment of the U.S. Marines there deftly demonstrated the advantages of projected military power, especially naval power. With Roosevelt—fully equipped with martial bravado backed up by the credentials of his battlefield heroics—now on the ticket, and with the Boxers faced down, anti-imperialism soon withered in the breach. And, as always, economic prosperity helped. "Four More Years of the Full Dinner Pail" was the slogan that served the incumbent Republican message very well, and when tied to the image of the United States as a new power on the world stage, thanks to the leadership of President McKinley and Theodore Roosevelt, it was a formidable campaign to challenge. The Democrats were clearly on the defensive throughout: Gold, empire, and trusts were the plutocratic demons attacked by the Democrats, but the question was whether or not it would be enough to give the Republicans a real fight.

Once convinced of the limitations of the Free Silver issue, Bryan gladly turned to the trusts. The Great Commoner appealed to the working class against the excesses of the robber barons, and the Democratic Party disseminated literature denouncing the exorbitant wealth of American captains of industry and titans of finance. He set his sights on the "Full Dinner Pail," explaining that the use of such a metaphor was in truth demeaning to "the laboring man," who was implicitly and condescendingly portrayed by Republicans as "[being] all stomach [with] neither head nor heart." "The Republican Party," elaborated Bryan, "assumes that a laboring man is like the hog that squeals when it is hungry and sleeps when it is full." Bryan's appeal to labor resulted in the reanimation of his campaign and gained him needed support in the critical state of New York; and thus some momentum began to build in his favor until, in the latter weeks leading up to the election, his judgment began to cloud. In mid-October, Bryan inexplicably praised Tammany Hall and its associates, blindly ignoring the Tammany machine's own cozy and long-running ties to trusts and perennial allegations of corruption. Furthermore, Bryan, for example, ignored that Tammany Hall was deeply involved with the

Ice Trust, which effectively controlled the distribution of ice (an important commodity at the turn of the century) in New York City. Newspapers reported that the American Ice Company had given well-connected political figures hundreds of thousands of dollars in stock. Not surprisingly, the McKinley campaign made effective use of these allegations to undercut Bryan's credibility on the trust issue. In late October, Bryan realized his blunder and frantically altered course yet again, suddenly shelving his working-class appeal and returning to a reaffirmation of the failed 1896 platform—and by implication, dusting off Free Silver. He also began to revive the anti-imperialist rhetoric that he had previously concluded to be ineffective. By dropping labor issues and going back to imperialism and Free Silver, Bryan squandered his brief momentum.

McKinley's campaign also referred to the blueprint left from his 1896 campaign, but with one difference; unlike Bryan's blueprint from that election year, the Republicans' was proven successful and worth imitating. Senator Hanna was at the top of his game, raising millions of dollars to pay for the distribution of a large volume of campaign literature. McKinley surrogates campaigned hard and effectively while McKinley again stayed at home, greeting visitors in a reiteration of the front-porch strategy. Roosevelt in particular was outstanding. Charismatically more than a match for Bryan and at the height of his popularity, Roosevelt forged on as a self-described "bull moose," traveling across the country and captivating audiences with the force of his personality, giving 700 speeches and traveling some 21,000 miles. Even though Hanna continued to harbor deep doubts about the president's new running mate, his personal dislike for Roosevelt soon gave way to a new appreciation of the incalculable political capital that he brought to the Republican cause. McKinley's hard-money policy was also strengthened by the Klondike gold rush. As expected, Republican campaign songs touted the successes of the McKinley administration and sought to take advantage of Roosevelt's status as a war hero:

> In Cleveland's days we had to rest, no labor could be found;
> It did not matter where we'd go, above or under ground
> But when McKinley took his place he made the chimneys smoke
> And all the mills throughout the land, with one gigantic stroke,
> Then let us praise McKinley's name from Mexico to Maine
> And Teddy Roosevelt just the same for whipping treacherous Spain.

McKinley's victory was thorough, capturing nearly 900,000 more votes than Bryan and winning with 7,230,000 (or 52%) to 6,370,000 (46%) votes, accompanied by a substantial majority in the Electoral College, 292 to 165 (65% to 35%). Bryan held the automatic southern bloc, the Democrats' reliable stronghold, and took the Rocky Mountain states of Colorado, Montana, and Idaho as well as Nevada, all four states heavily involved in mining and supportive of bimetallism. California, the Golden State, did not follow suit and renewed its support for McKinley. The Northeast, Midwest, Great Plains, and Pacific Coast were swept by the president. A number of minor parties won votes, including 210,000 for John Woolley and the Prohibitionists, and 87,000 for the new Socialist Party under Eugene V. Debs. The Populist Party, which had been so successful in the 1890s, scarcely managed 50,000 votes for its candidate, Wharton Barker, with the Socialist Labor Party pulling in just over 40,000 behind Joseph Maloney. Building on the outcome of 1896, the election further solidified the strength of the two major parties, and especially, at least in presidential politics, the Republican Party.

Still regarding Roosevelt askance, Hanna famously admonished McKinley to remain alive through his full term as a guarantee against the Rough Rider's continued political ascent. Hanna never backed down from his description of Roosevelt as a "madman," and he hoped that Roosevelt's political future had been neatly controlled by his election to the vice presidency. But the Fates are capricious and even beyond the control of powerful politicians such as Mark Hanna. Within six months of McKinley's inauguration to his second term, an obscure anarchist gunned down McKinley at an exposition in Buffalo, making him the third American president to fall to an assassin. As McKinley fell back from his wounds, he maintained both his dignity and his sense of charity, asking his Secret Service guard not to harm his assailant. Eight days later, the president passed away, and the Rough Rider from New York was now the man behind the "bully pulpit," the very thing that Mark Hanna feared the most.

Additional Resources

Cooper, John Milton, Jr. "1900." In Arthur M. Schlesinger, Fred L. Israel, and David J. Frent, eds. *Running for President: The Candidates and Their Images.* Vol. 2. New York: Simon & Schuster, 1994.

Gould, Louis L. *The Presidency of William McKinley.* Lawrence: Regents Press of Kansas, 1980.

LaFeber, Walter. "Election of 1900." In Arthur M. Schlesinger, Fred Israel, and William P. Hansen, eds. *History of American Presidential Elections, 1789–1968.* Vol. 2. New York: Chelsea House, 1985.

Morris, Edmund. *The Rise of Theodore Roosevelt.* New York: Random House, 2010.

Campaign of 1904

Theodore Roosevelt, published historian and naturalist, conservationist, rancher, boxer, war hero, intellectual, outdoorsman extraordinaire, inhabitant of high society, Rough Rider, big-game hunter, experienced in both legislative and executive governance, and now propelled into the White House by an accident of history, quickly became the most popular president in recent memory—perhaps, as some have pointed out, the most popular president, at least while in the White House, since Andrew Jackson. (President Abraham Lincoln's popularity rose at the end of his presidency, and only at his death did he become a nearly universally admired and, for many, beloved political martyr; but during Lincoln's presidency, he never received the acclaim enjoyed by either Jackson before him or Roosevelt after him.) Owing to a truly rare charisma, indomitable will, intense focus, fearless character, overwhelming intellect, and genuine ebullience that can only be described as a true lust for living large, Roosevelt naturally drew a devoted following, and even before his ascent to the presidency, he was a widely acclaimed national hero. But he was not without his critics. Described by his detractors as a rough, wild "cowboy" and as "His Accidency," Roosevelt realized that he would need to work diligently to dispel doubts about him from both within and without the Republican Party. One would be hard pressed to deny that he in fact rapidly succeeded in earning at least the respect of his critics while commanding the admiration of the public at large. A vigorous and visionary leader unlike any other and, at the age of forty-two, the youngest man to ever fill the office, Roosevelt, to no one's surprise, began building a national reputation as a progressive.

During the **Campaigns of 1896 and 1900**, famed kingmaker Mark Hanna skillfully defined the Republican Party as the party of economic prosperity, sober fiscal policies, protection of American business, and, especially in 1900, American power and patriotism. His protégé, the slain President McKinley, had proven to be the perfect candidate to present this message to the American public. In both McKinley campaigns, Republicans successfully defined the Democratic Party and its populist standard-bearer, William Jennings Bryan, as too radical to be trusted with the presidency. Upon McKinley's death in 1901, Roosevelt entered the White House with an agenda that did not fit Hanna's blueprint for the McKinley administration or his vision of Republican principles. The new president initially affirmed his desire to continue McKinley's policies, but it was but a matter of time before Roosevelt's own outsized ambitions overtook him. Steeped in his own decidedly American vision of chivalry, Roosevelt recoiled at what he saw as the mob-manipulating radicalism stirred up by demagogic men like Bryan, regarding such ideas as utterly against the American vision of democracy and fairness on the one hand combined with the credo of self-reliance and personal achievement on the other.

Nonetheless, Roosevelt had always felt that democracy was stunted by the unchecked influence of wealth, and he sought means to prevent this. To control the excesses of corporate wealth, Roosevelt supported a more aggressive enforcement of the anti-trust laws that had been in place since the Harrison administration but that had not been effectively enforced or utilized. Through 1902 and 1903, Roosevelt pursued policies that unflinchingly challenged the status quo. The Roosevelt administration made use of the Sherman Antitrust Act to bring suit to break up J. P. Morgan's powerful Northern Securities Company railroad trust. This action and other anti-trust lawsuits brought by Roosevelt's Justice Department helped further his reputation as a trust-buster while angering many leaders of business and industry who had made generous donations to McKinley's campaigns. Additionally, to safeguard the natural resources of the country, Roosevelt, renowned as a naturalist, an outdoorsman, and one of the nation's first conservationists, pressured Congress to place millions of acres of forest under federal protection and sought to use these forests as wildlife preserves. He also tightened management of federally owned public land.

Reflecting the roots of the Republican Party, Roosevelt adopted a comparatively sympathetic attitude toward African Americans; upon reaching the White House, he immediately reached out to Booker T. Washington and other prominent black leaders. He punished a postal district in Mississippi for resisting the appointment of an African American postmistress by shutting down all postal services to that area. Roosevelt also continued to support, as he always had, black participation in Republican political conventions, and he publicly excoriated Americans for tolerating the lawless brutality of lynching. In steering the Republican Party—which, in many eyes both within and outside the party, had become the party of big business—back toward the Party of Lincoln and challenging the abuses of corporate wealth, Roosevelt estranged the new and well-connected generation of conservatives in the GOP. To the endless chagrin of monied interests, Roosevelt forced Hanna out as national party chair, replacing him with a less notable personality, his own secretary of commerce and labor, George B. Cortelyou, a person more amenable to Roosevelt's agenda and ambitions (and who had been present at the assassination of President McKinley). Although some Old Guard (or conservative) Republicans seriously circulated the name of Hanna as a potential challenger to Roosevelt for the 1904 nomination, support for such a move within the party quickly deflated in light of Roosevelt's overwhelming popularity. Moreover, Hanna, who had been a figure of great importance to the party since the 1880s, died unexpectedly in February 1904, a victim of typhoid fever; and thus even if Hanna had been in a position to challenge Roosevelt, his untimely death now left no one in the field even close to the president's stature. Given his many political gifts and extensive influence, Hanna might have been able to mount a credible challenge against Roosevelt if conditions had been more favorable to him. He had the resources of some of the party's wealthiest supporters at his disposal and a network of loyalists prepared to support him. But Roosevelt possessed his own resources, the most important of which was Roosevelt himself. Had Hanna lived, and had he managed to mount a charge in the weeks leading up the convention, the battle would have made for an interesting convention. As it was, there was hardly any real action at the 1904 convention at all.

Drawing upon his progressive philosophy (a progressivism tempered by his more conservative background and, in some cases, disposition), Roosevelt stated, "We must treat each man on his worth and merits as a man. We must see that each is given a square deal, because he is entitled to no more and should receive no less." For Roosevelt, when large trusts and monopolies fixed prices and established artificially low wage rates, government had a moral obligation to intervene to guarantee workers this "square deal." Roosevelt's promise of a square deal became the central principle of his campaign and one of the defining themes of his political career. All this was combined with an ambitious foreign policy designed to build on the legacy of President McKinley. With President Roosevelt, the United States would be a new force in the world, with the building of the Panama Canal and the assertion of the Roosevelt Corollary to the Monroe Doctrine representing his vision of the United States' new responsibilities abroad. Roosevelt also devoted attention to the suppression of guerillas in the Philippines and to the continued expansion of the U.S. Navy, showcased by the grand tour of the Great White Fleet. The president was determined to carve a new destiny for the American people that meant the exercise of power overseas in a way than no president before him had envisioned. "Walk softly and carry a big stick," a West African proverb that he used in a speech delivered in Minneapolis, encapsulated the president's approach to politics, both foreign and domestic. And it was always clear to all concerned that Roosevelt meant what he said and knew how to do what he claimed. Roosevelt's domestic progressivism, when combined with a vigorous nationalism and a muscular, rugged, energetic, no-nonsense persona, was a potent formula that the American public broadly embraced.

Roosevelt's progressivism and his anticorruption proclivities, marked by a genuine record of civil service reform, were incongruously accompanied by his accommodation for the old political patronage methods that had been so prevalent in the previous century and that he had fought throughout his political life. His dedication to civil service reform made him enemies, like New York's Thomas Platt, in the old machines. But his occasional reliance on the political bosses of the Northeast, again like Platt, was viewed by Roosevelt as simply a political reality. His long-held disdain for corruption was genuine, and when he did work with some bosses, it was simply seen as a deferral to those older practices still in use and comfortably embraced in certain parts of the country. Roosevelt was an idealist in many ways, but he held a politically realistic view of what was needed in politics to accomplish one's goals. Able to keep the bosses at bay while sustaining his immense popularity, Roosevelt won the GOP nomination at the convention in

Chicago on the first ballot without any challenge. Senator Charles W. Fairbanks of Indiana won the nomination for vice president, also without opposition.

Recognizing that he needed to unify all Republicans, Roosevelt embraced a platform that supported both conservative and progressive goals. The platform endorsed protective tariffs and the gold standard, and it praised Republican foreign policy, which had recently freed Cuba, constructed the Panama Canal, and enforced anti-trust laws. While sympathetic, Roosevelt shied away from supporting a proposed plank officially challenging the disenfranchisement of African Americans in the South and threatening punishment to states that violated voting rights by reducing the proportion of their votes in the Electoral College. Roosevelt's opposition was not from a sudden change of attitude toward the circumstances of African Americans, but rather from a concern that such a position could divide the party and thus weaken it as it moved toward the general election. Roosevelt also sought to bring Southern voters back to the party, and thus while his desire to bring more African American voters back into politics was sincere, this was offset by his olive branch to Southern whites. Roosevelt had been stung by the strident tone of Southern objections to his public overtures to Booker T. Washington and the African American leadership, and he worried over the electoral implications of losing the Southern bloc in 1904, hence his distancing himself from the proposed plank. Over Roosevelt's muted objections, the plank was adopted to read as follows: "We favor such Congressional action as shall determine whether by special discrimination the elective franchise in any State has been unconstitutionally limited, and, if such is the case, we demand that representation in Congress and in the Electoral College shall be proportionately reduced as directed by the Constitution of the United States."

The Democratic Party held its convention in St. Louis on July 6–9 somewhat subdued by the realization that actually defeating the immensely popular president was an almost impossible task. Since their harsh defeat in the previous election, party insiders reevaluated their position, and the conservative, Bourbon/Gold Bug wing saw an opportunity to challenge the Great Commoner, William Jennings Bryan, the nominee in the previous two failed elections, for party leadership. They sought a more conservative figure who was capable of assuming a more moderate tone within the party and thus possibly drawing more votes from outside the party, perhaps even luring conservative defectors from the GOP who were disenchanted with Roosevelt's trust-busting progressivism. Working to steer the party away from the Great Commoner long before the convention met, the anti-Bryan wing of the Democratic Party initially courted Maryland's Senator Arthur P. Gorman. However, Gorman opposed the widely popular Panama Canal project. After former president Grover Cleveland—perhaps the only American alive at the time who might be able to give Roosevelt a good fight—made it clear that he was not interested in a third term (it is of interest that the last five elections had seen either Cleveland or Bryan as the Democrats' standard-bearer), the Democratic Party nominated New York judge Alton B. Parker, a person widely respected for his abilities and integrity. The convention then selected eighty-year-old Henry Gassaway Davis of West Virginia as Parker's running mate. Born during the administration of President James Monroe (when West Virginia was still the westernmost quarter of Virginia), Davis was the oldest major party candidate to ever run for the vice presidency (or, for that matter, older than any candidate to stand for the presidency). In a victory for Gold Bug Democrats, Parker came out in favor of the gold standard, a direct reversal of the party's last two campaigns. Needless to say, Bryan was displeased; he openly criticized Parker's policies and stood by his own Free Silver and populist principles.

Prior to the convention, publisher William Randolph Hearst was also viewed by many as a potential challenger. Although Hearst's policies aligned with Bryan's on many domestic issues (e.g., progressive income tax and the eight-hour workday), his credentials as an ardent imperialist (to many, Hearst, more than anyone, was responsible for drumming the beat that urged the country to war against Spain) alienated Bryan and his followers, who thwarted Hearst's attempt to mount a viable campaign for the nomination. Bryan also attacked both Cleveland and Parker, thereby opening a rift within the party between his more ardent followers and those Democrats who were seeking a fresh approach. Bryan's influence was considerable and still broadly felt, and many of his policies had already been adopted by both major parties; but the invective he employed against any candidate who rejected his vision of the party's principles damaged his personal role as a respected former standard-bearer. And Bryan could not attack Roosevelt with any credibility, for much of the president's Republican administration had embodied the kind of progressivism that Bryan had so enthusiastically promoted over the past two decades. With a candidate in place and Bryan temporarily sidelined, the Democratic platform called for a reduction in government spending and continued its opposition to protective tariffs. In spite of the concerns of the party's anti-imperialist wing, the platform supported the construction of the Panama Canal but still criticized the imperialist policies of the McKinley-Roosevelt era. The platform also called for vigorous enforcement of the anti-trust laws and for expansion of the powers of the Interstate Commerce Commission, and it condemned the practice of polygamy (targeted at the Mormons). Interestingly, even though the Democratic platform remained silent on the gold standard, Parker publicly announced his support of it.

Parker never had a realistic chance against Roosevelt; however, the Democrats fought on, even resorting to smear tactics to tarnish the president's reputation, a ploy that was discordant with Parker's own sense of personal integrity. Democrats alleged that Republicans had obtained large campaign contributions from corporations and trusts in return for a "silent understanding" regarding the enforcement of anti-trust laws, allegations that implicated the party's new national chairman, George Cortelyou. Roosevelt refuted the charges, indignantly dismissing all allegations as "an atrocious falsehood," and defended Cortelyou's activities as party leader. When Parker failed to produce any hard evidence, the public quickly lost interest in the allegations.

Minor parties also offered candidates. The Socialist Party again nominated Eugene V. Debs, its candidate in 1900, tapping Benjamin Hanford for the second spot. Silas Comfort Swallow and George W. Carrol ran for the Prohibition Party, Thomas E. Watson and Thomas H. Tibbles carried the banner for the Populist Party, and the Socialist Labor Party put forward Charles H. Corregan and Wesley W. Cox.

President Theodore Roosevelt won a second term in a landslide, winning approximately 7,600,000 popular votes (56%) to Parker's total of just over 5,000,000 (38%). The victory in the Electoral College was even more impressive. The president won 336 electoral votes (the most total electoral votes, in raw numbers, won by any candidate to date), or 71 percent, to Parker's 140 votes, or 29 percent. It was the largest victory in the popular vote since Ulysses Grant's 56 percent in 1872 and the strongest showing in the Electoral College since Grant's 81 percent that same year. Roosevelt swept every state outside the solid Democratic South, illustrating once again the sectional polarization that channeled the nation's electoral allegiances. This is even more evident in looking at the state results; almost every state was won decisively, with Roosevelt winning big in every northern, midwestern, and western state, and Parker winning by huge margins in southern states (e.g., Parker beat Roosevelt in South Carolina, Mississippi, and Louisiana by winning 95%, 91%, and 89% respectively; while Roosevelt showed big margins in states such as Vermont, North Dakota—where he had once owned and worked a cattle ranch—and Minnesota, winning 78%, 75%, and 73% in those states, respectively). Only the border states of Maryland, Missouri, and Kentucky were close; Maryland was barely won by Roosevelt, Missouri was also close in going for Roosevelt, and Kentucky was taken by Parker in a tight race. Every other state was marked by a wide margin of victory. As for the minor parties, Debs and the Socialists did well, winning close to 403,000 votes, making them far and away the strongest minor party in the country. The Prohibition Party, while finishing a distant fourth, still gained about 50,000 votes. The landslide victory gave Roosevelt's policies wide approval and the president a strong and bully mandate as he moved with his usual alacrity into his second term.

Additional Resources

The American Presidency Project. http://www.presidency.ucsb.edu.

Arnold, Peri E. *Remaking the Presidency.* Lawrence: University Press of Kansas, 2009.

Boller, Paul F., Jr. *Presidential Campaigns*. New York: Oxford University Press, 1984.

Cooper, John Milton, Jr. "1904." In Arthur M. Schlesinger, Fred L. Israel, and David J. Frent, eds. *Running for President: The Candidates and Their Images*. Vol. 2. New York: Simon & Schuster, 1994.

Harbaugh, William H. "Election of 1904." In Arthur M. Schlesinger, Fred Israel, and William P. Hansen, eds. *History of American Presidential Elections, 1789–1968*. Vol. 2. New York: Chelsea House 1985.

Morris, Edmund. *Theodore Rex*. New York: Random House, 2010.

Mowry, George W. *The Era of Theodore Roosevelt and the Birth of Modern America*. New York: HarperCollins, 1968.

Campaign of 1908

Despite a level of popularity during his incumbency reminiscent of Andrew Jackson and even George Washington, Theodore Roosevelt, far and away the greatest president since Abraham Lincoln, decided to respect the informal two-term tradition by not seeking the 1908 Republican presidential nomination, even though it could have been easily his for the taking. From 1904 through 1908, Roosevelt had pursued an aggressive domestic and foreign affairs agenda. This was the age of muckrakers, or investigative journalists who scrutinized and exposed corruption and the abuse of power in politics and hardship and injustice in society as a whole, and Roosevelt was just the president suited to respond to this accordingly.

Additionally, the Roosevelt administration, in combination with a friendly Congress, addressed the serious problem of child labor, along with the debilitating working conditions for labor in general. The president and Congress responded to calls for reform in the insurance business and for closer supervision of the transportation industry (particularly the railroads) and interstate commerce; all told, the Republican president Roosevelt vigorously supported a major expansion of federal regulation extending deep into the private sector. The passage of the Pure Food and Drug Act provided for the establishment of the Food and Drug Administration. The Meat Inspection Act gave the Department of Agriculture responsibility for regulating the meatpacking industry. Roosevelt forthrightly spoke out and acted against the "dull, purblind folly of the very rich men; their greed and arrogance," against "the least attractive and most sordid of all aristocracies which regarded power as expressed only by its basest and most brutal forms, that of mere money," and "fortunes swollen beyond all healthy limits," and he envisioned an American prosperity and power that was not won at the expense of the laboring class. For this reason, he is rightly numbered among the more progressive thinkers and politicians of his time, and certainly among the more reform-minded presidents in American history. Indeed, with the exception of President Lincoln's Emancipation

Proclamation, no president had been as actively committed to extensive social reform as Theodore Roosevelt had up to this point. For these and a number of other reasons, too many to detail here, Roosevelt would be a tough act to follow for any candidate.

As the administration moved into its final months, the leading candidates for the Republican nomination were initially two Ohioans: Secretary of War William Howard Taft, a close friend of Roosevelt's who had vast experience in both the judicial (a former judge) and executive branches (serving in the administrations of presidents Harrison, McKinley, and Roosevelt); and Senator Joseph Foraker, who, as governor of Ohio in the 1880s, was appointed by Taft himself to his first post in public service, judge of the state superior court. Foraker and Taft were the only candidates who enjoyed any support at the national level. Taft was not a typical candidate. Not really a politician, Taft's heart's desire was to return to the bench and perhaps someday reach the Supreme Court (a dream eventually realized). By disposition more conservative than President Roosevelt, they had nonetheless struck up a strong friendship in the 1890s. In spite of Taft's own tendency to think for himself, he was often perceived as a mere imitation of the Great Man, a perception that was scarcely justified. Foraker, who by the election of 1908 had grown to dislike Taft in spite of their past connection, was also conservative, and he joined Taft; the powerful Speaker of the House, Joseph B. Cannon of Illinois; and Roosevelt's secretary of state, Elihu Root of New York (another close friend whom Roosevelt had initially considered his likely successor before eventually leaning toward Taft) as the candidates with the most initial support. Additionally, candidates such as Philander C. Knox of Pennsylvania, Charles Evans Hughes of New York, and Vice President Charles Fairbanks of Indiana drew the interests of party members who were seeking candidates who were viewed as either moderate or as leaning slightly toward the party's Old Guard wing. The progressive wing of the party, associated with the president's reformist vision, was represented most prominently by Robert M. La Follette Sr. of Wisconsin. Vice President Fairbanks also openly sought the nomination, but Taft was Roosevelt's choice and had been so privately since at least late 1905, a preference that the president formally announced to the public in March 1907. Fairbanks, without Roosevelt's support, was to be numbered among the also-rans.

For Taft, the president's blessing was an endorsement that was difficult for anyone in the party to ignore. Still preferring a return to the service on the courts rather than election as chief executive, Taft admitted as late as the summer of 1908 that he would rather see Root or Cannon nominated; but after enough cajoling from Roosevelt, not a person easily refused, as well as from other members of the president's cabinet and his wife, Helen Taft, he accepted the inevitable and assented to the Republican candidacy.

The Campaign of 1908 included the introduction of the presidential preference primary: a political event that some Republicans, such as Hughes, hoped would wean the nominating process away from the control of the influential political machines and their bosses. Although by some accounts the first official presidential primary occurred in Oregon in 1910, it is clear that the new approach to presidential selection was already under way at least two and perhaps even as much as six years prior. A forerunner of the primary had already been conducted by the Democratic Party in Florida during the **Campaign of 1904**, when voters within the general party participated in the selection of their delegates to the convention. In 1908, Republicans held primaries in four states: Pennsylvania, Wisconsin, California, and Ohio. Pennsylvania and Wisconsin chose delegates backing their favorite sons Knox and La Follette, respectively, while California indicated support for Taft. The significant primary occurred in Ohio, where two favorite sons, Taft and Foraker, were on the ballot, and where Taft won an impressive victory. This in effect abruptly eliminated Foraker as a serious candidate, and by the time of the convention, he was no longer under consideration. With Foraker now out of the way, Taft was without any serious challenge.

With the full blessing of President Roosevelt, the Republican Party decisively nominated Taft on the first ballot. Taft won 702 first-ballot votes to 262 for the rest of the field, Knox and Hughes leading the also-rans with 68 and 67 votes, respectively. The candidate from the progressive wing, La Follette, inspired only 25 votes. For the vice presidency, the convention chose, again on the first ballot, James S. Sherman, a member of the House of Representatives from New York. At the convention, a spontaneous, raucous celebration occurred in response to an affectionate tribute to Roosevelt, a display of emotion that was much more uplifting and protracted than the celebration that followed Taft's nomination, a fact that was not lost on either the delegates at the convention or Taft himself. Roosevelt was out of the running, but it was clear that he was, by consensus and acclaim, still the party's truest champion.

Once the encomiums for Roosevelt subsided, the Republicans turned to their platform, wherein they sought to abate major disagreements festering between the pro-business and progressive wings of the party. To keep the support of progressives, the platform endorsed shorter work hours for employees and a system to compensate employees for workplace injuries. The platform also endorsed legislation directed at providing greater workplace protection for women and children. To maintain the support of the business community, the platform reaffirmed the party's commitment to protective tariffs and embraced what was called "reasonable regulation" of business. Unlike Roosevelt, Taft lacked credentials in the progressive movement. However, Taft went out of the way during the Campaign of

1908 to underplay his corporate ties and to highlight his strong support for the progressive policies of the Roosevelt years.

William Jennings Bryan had been the Democrats' candidate in the Free Silver campaign of 1896 and again in the (quasi) anti-imperialism campaign of 1900, losing both times to McKinley and Roosevelt, respectively. Even more than President Roosevelt, Bryan's name evoked the aspirations and ideals of progressivism, and he continued to embrace that vision as passionately as before. All the progressive positions were long held by Bryan, such as labor reform, regulation of industry, tariff reform, the banning of child labor, term limits, popular election of the U.S. Senate, the initiative and referendum, a federal income tax, bimetallism (although as an issue, it had diminished in importance), and foreign policy positions stripped of the imperialist hue associated with McKinley-Roosevelt. It was only in Bryan's attitudes toward immigration (especially the controversial issue of Chinese immigrant labor, which he opposed and hoped to prevent) that he seemed to introduce an additive to his straight progressive line. More than Roosevelt, who was loath to engage in the rhetoric of class conflict, he excoriated the moneyed elite, openly regarding them to be a "menace to civilization." For Bryan, monopolies, protective tariffs, a financial system that favored the rich, and imperialism were destroying the Constitution and the American system in general.

Still known as the Great Commoner, Bryan opposed privilege at every turn, demanding thorough and immediate reform in contrast to what he considered to be a feeble gradualist approach followed by the president, and he vehemently stood against those conservatives in his own party who wanted to repeat their failed strategy of the previous election when they nominated the Bourbon Democrat Alton B. Parker. Even though the Roosevelt administration was progressive and had supported many of Bryan's proposed reforms, he continued to argue that the president's "conservatism" diluted any real reforms and thus called for a "bold new program" that would finally deliver the decisive reforms that were really needed. Nonetheless, some in the media spoke of a possible alliance between Roosevelt Republicans and Bryan Democrats, a progressive Roosevelt-Bryan alliance, as it were, to push reform; and Roosevelt himself, who had once called Bryan a dangerous demagogue, now softened, referring to his old rival as "kindly" and well-meaning, and seemed amenable to working with the Bryan Democrats. But Bryan was less receptive to the idea; he regarded himself as the true radical, and he was not taken in by Roosevelt's self-described label as a "progressive conservative." Still, Bryanite (i.e., progressive) Democrats and progressive Republicans were in accord in many issues, and were capable of recognizing their common ground. Bryan once informed Roosevelt that the president would have his support when he agreed with his own positions, and in some cases he had endorsed Roosevelt's actions. But when he found himself at odds with the president, he would speak with his customary intensity and boldness.

Additionally, Bryan's religious views became more pronounced and publicly interwoven into his overall critique of American society, politics, and culture, and he increasingly exhibited an evangelical tone in his speeches and pronouncements. He viewed himself as a voice for the social gospel, which understood egalitarian social reform as a moral and political imperative directing all sincere Christians in an effort to promote a more just society. These social gospel views embraced by Bryan were in direct opposition to the then-popular "gospel of wealth," a self-interest credo that justified the accumulation of riches, which had become a popular message for some during the Gilded Age especially but also into the early twentieth century. With President Roosevelt out of the running, Bryan was easily the most progressive major figure on the national scene. But Bryan would still have to overcome Roosevelt's legacy and charisma.

The Democratic convention, which was held in Denver, the first western city to host a national nominating convention, tapped Bryan without controversy. Even his old rival, former president Grover Cleveland, put aside his former animosity toward Bryan and quietly stated his support. Bryan joined Cleveland as the only other candidate from a major party to earn three party nominations for the presidency (Cleveland's were consecutive), an achievement that only Franklin Roosevelt would eventually surpass. Indiana's John W. Kern was unanimously nominated for the second spot on the ticket. The progressive wing of the party had, over the past four years, successfully regained control of the party, rendering the Great Commoner's nomination a rubber stamp. Still, the Bryanites realized the importance of party unity, particularly when going up against Taft, who might draw away some needed votes from the conservative wing of their own party. Therefore, much like the Republican platform, the Democratic platform sought to balance the concerns of conservative Democrats highly critical of increased government spending, and progressive Democrats who sought greater protections for workers and additional steps to reduce the concentration of economic wealth in corporate America. Consequently, the Democratic platform called for a significant reduction in government spending and opposed protective tariffs that produced revenue for the federal government to then, as the criticism held, simply waste. The platform also reaffirmed the exclusive authority of the states over matters of domestic concern. To satisfy the Bryanites, the platform called for much more vigorous enforcement of anti-trust laws, expansion of the power of the Interstate Commerce Commission to regulate the business practices of railroads, a constitutional amendment to permit the adoption of a personal income tax, the establishment of a department of labor to represent the interests of workers, and the establishment of a national bureau of health to safeguard the sanitary conditions of factories, mines, and tenements. Following Bryan's lead, the platform also sharply criticized the imperialistic policies of recent Republican administrations.

Both the Socialist and Prohibition parties nominated presidential candidates. The Socialist Party again nominated, also for a third time, Eugene V. Debs of Wisconsin for the presidency, with Benjamin Hanford of New York as his running mate (for the second time). The Prohibition Party nominated Eugene W. Chafing of Illinois, to be joined by Ohio's Aaron S. Watkins for the vice presidency.

Significantly, the Campaign of 1908 saw the first commercially recorded campaign speeches. At the request of the Thomas Edison National Phonograph Company, Bryan agreed to record a number of campaign speeches. Not wanting to be placed at a political disadvantage, Taft agreed to make recordings of a number of his campaign speeches. In the end, Bryan and Taft recorded some twenty-two campaign speeches. During the campaign, the recordings were frequently played at public meetings. Topics addressed by Bryan in his recordings included (1) imperialism, (2) popular election of senators, (3) the tariff question, (4) guaranty of bank deposits, (5) labor, (6) railroads, (7) trusts (monopolies), (8) the publication of campaign contributions, and (9) "swollen fortunes" and their effect on American democracy. In his recording on imperialism, for instance, Bryan called for the "independence of the Philippine Islands as soon as a stable government [could] be established." Bryan's speech on the guaranty of bank deposits proposed that all national banks should be required "to establish a guarantee fund for the prompt payment of the depositors of any insolvent national bank," a policy that would eventually be established under a future president. Recorded topics addressed by Taft included (1) encomiums for President Roosevelt, (2) the military, (3) postal savings banks, (4) comments regarding the progress of African Americans, (5) claims that the Democratic Party prevented national prosperity, (6) the rights of labor, (7) the Republican Party as the party of agriculture, (8) the possible effect of a proposal for jury trials in contempt cases, (9) foreign dependencies (Taft had once served as governor of the Philippines), (10) foreign missions, (11) trusts, (12) the anticipated functions of a Taft administration, and, for the sake of levity, (13) Irish humor.

Naturally, the Republican campaign sought to portray Taft as the true successor to Theodore Roosevelt. Throughout the campaign, Taft took moderate or even progressive positions on a wide range of issues. In sharp contrast to previous Republican campaigns, the party found it necessary to send Taft out on the campaign trail. Taft was a capable campaigner, but he lacked the oratorical skills of Bryan. He had help from others, such as Knox, La Follette, Albert J. Beveridge (a historian and progressive senator from Indiana), and most importantly, President Roosevelt himself, the only man alive who could rhetorically outduel Bryan.

Throughout the campaign, Bryan attempted to tie Taft and the Republican Party to big business and industry by attacking the Taft campaign for not making public the sources of its campaign contributions. As expected, Bryan depicted Taft and the Republican Party as the friend of high-finance fat cats and the enemy of workers and unions. Not surprisingly, Taft and the Republican campaign sought to define Taft as the best guardian of economic prosperity. An economic recovery in the summer of 1908, reversing setbacks experienced in the previous year, helped the Republicans in their arguments that they, not Bryan's Democrats, were the party of growth. More conservative than Roosevelt, La Follette, and Beveridge, Taft attempted to downplay his ties to big business and industry by expressing support for the right of workers to join unions and to strike.

Political songs again made their way into the campaign. One such song, "Get on the Raft with Taft," became the most popular Taft campaign song and slogan, and it included within the lyrics an interesting line: "Get on a raft with Taft. . . . He'll save the country sure, boys, from Bryan, Hearst, and graft. So all join in, we're sure to win. Get on a raft with Taft." The phrase "from Bryan, Hearst, and graft" sought to remind voters of Bryan's failure to effectively deal with the Standard Oil influence peddling scandal, which implicated high-level officials in both parties. During the middle of September 1908, powerful newspaper publisher William Randolph Hearst released a number of letters indicating that a number of Republican as well as Democratic leaders had accepted payments from the Standard Oil Company in return for blocking legislation that the powerful company opposed. The letters implicated Republican senator Foraker of Ohio and Democratic governor Charles Haskell of Oklahoma in the influence-peddling scandal. Of particular embarrassment to the Bryan campaign, Haskell also served as the treasurer for the Democratic National Committee. The scandal initially seemed to favor Bryan, who had railed against the close relationship between big business and the Republican Party—Foraker had, after all, once been mentioned by some Republicans as a possible successor to Roosevelt. But Bryan's inexplicable refusal to criticize Haskell permitted the Republican Party and President Roosevelt to expose the apparent hypocrisy and use the scandal to discredit Bryan's incessant attacks against big business. Taft was afforded the luxury of not having to address the controversy, for Roosevelt eagerly took the lead in storming Bryan and challenging him to distance himself from Haskell. Although Haskell resigned as treasurer, the damage to Bryan's campaign was already done.

As the election approached, Bryan lost confidence when facing Taft on policy and thus resorted to personal attacks. He criticized the religious beliefs of Taft, a Unitarian, arguing, apparently without consulting the Constitution, that rejection of the Trinity disqualified a man from holding the White House. Bryan also battled conservative elements within his own party who preferred the cautious policies of former president Cleveland. This led Bryan to soft-pedal some of his more progressive views and left him to fall back upon *ad hominem* tactics. Above all else, the potent combination of Taft's own substantial credentials as an accomplished and dedicated public servant and Roosevelt's prestige and energy made the GOP ticket formidable and, in the end, victorious.

The Bull Moose personally took the reins and charged forward, tirelessly campaigning on behalf of his friend and chosen heir. Bryan held a chance against Taft one-on-one; but he was thoroughly overshadowed by the progressive achievement and inexhaustible personal power of Taft's irrepressible ally, the heroic Rough Rider. Frustrated again, the Great Commoner led his party in defeat a third time. On reflection, Taft recognized the critical role that his friend President Roosevelt had played in his own election, and he also acknowledged the importance of support from a unified business community that viewed the Great Commoner as undesirable, as well as drawing some votes from labor in the aftermath of Hearst's unanswered attacks on Bryan. Taft was also helped by visible support from the Catholic and Jewish communities, two constituencies that represented solid and potentially pivotal voting blocs. Democratic crossover was also important, and Taft reminded reporters, "You must remember that I was elected by Democratic votes, probably polling almost as many as McKinley did in 1896."

In the end, Taft won almost 7,700,000 popular votes and 321 electoral votes, carrying every state outside of the Democrats' southern bloc except Colorado, Nevada, and Bryan's home state of Nebraska. While the South was held by the Democrats, the GOP swept the Northeast, the Midwest, and the Pacific coast, and it ruled the West with the exception of the three states mentioned above. Taft won decisively in New York and Pennsylvania, which at that time were the two powerhouse states in the Electoral College, holding 39 and 34 electoral votes, respectively. In Illinois, the state that held the third-highest number of electoral votes, Bryan could not quite manage 40 percent of the popular vote. Texas, with 18 electoral votes, was the biggest state won by Bryan, but he only managed a plurality there. Debs and the Socialists, along with Chafin and the Prohibition Party, won approximately 700,000 votes combined, with the Socialists taking the lion's share at just over 420,000, which was an increase of nearly 20,000 compared to 1904.

Thus William Howard Taft would enter the White House as the nation's twenty-seventh president, and the second president of the twentieth century that had been, to this point, largely defined by Roosevelt, McKinley, Hanna, and Bryan. Whether or not Taft himself was capable of emerging as a political force in his own right remained to be seen, but there was no question at the time that following Roosevelt promised to be Taft's most formidable challenge.

Additional Resources

Anderson, Donald F. *William Howard Taft: A Conservative's Conception of the Presidency*. Ithaca, NY: Cornell University Press, 1973.

Arnold, Peri E. *Remaking the Presidency*. Lawrence: University Press of Kansas, 2009.

Cohen, Martin, David Karol, Hans Noel, and John Zaller. *The Party Decides: Presidential Nominations before and after Reform*. Chicago: University of Chicago Press, 2008.

Coletta, Paolo E. "Election of 1908." In Arthur M. Schlesinger, Fred Israel, and William P. Hansen, eds. *History of American Presidential Elections, 1789–1968*. Vol. 2. New York: Chelsea House, 1985.

Coletta, Paolo E. "1908." In Arthur M. Schlesinger, Fred L. Israel, and David J. Frent, eds. *Running for President: The Candidates and Their Images*. Vol. 2. New York: Simon & Schuster, 1994.

"In Their Own Voices: Transcripts: The U.S. Presidential Election of 1908." http://www .marstonrecords.com/voices/transcripts.htm#1-4.

Morrisey, Will. *The Dilemma of Progressivism*. Lanham, MD: Rowman & Littlefield, 2009.

Campaign of 1912

The Campaign of 1912, one of the most theatric in American political history, generated a host of ear-snagging and mind-catching phrases, including "New Freedom," "New Nationalism," "Bull Moose Party," "Covenant with the People," "Bryanized," "My Hat Is in the Ring and I'm Stripped to the Buff!" "Have Another Cup of Coffee?" "I'll Do the Best I Can but There Is a Bullet in My Body," "What This Country Needs Is a Good Five-Cent Cigar," and finally, one that was more likely appealing to those who were the equivalent to our own present-day wonks, "Regulated Competition versus Regulated Monopoly." The campaign also involved a blistering contest between three candidates of considerable substance, and one that was electrified with a sudden and bitter rivalry between two formerly close friends, now fallen into harsh enmity. When the dust cleared, a respected academic named Woodrow Wilson would enter the national stage to signal a new direction for the development of the federal government in the United States.

The incumbent president William Howard Taft enjoyed considerable success during the first three years of his administration. In spite of his more conservative tendencies when compared to his predecessor, former president Theodore Roosevelt, he nonetheless continued the administration of the progressive agenda by dismantling trusts and supporting the enactment by Congress of progressive laws, achievements that were all built on the Roosevelt legacy. In trust busting alone, Taft proved his progressive credentials, as his administration actually dissolved more monopolies than Roosevelt, who had himself broken so many trusts that he picked up another nickname, the "Great Trustbuster." Indeed, as Taft set the enormous company U.S. Steel in his crosshairs, even the former president's concern was raised, worried that Taft's trust-busting was perhaps a little too indiscriminate. Unlike Roosevelt, Taft seemed less amenable to the notion that there were "bad trusts" and "good trusts." Taft also successfully helped to break the massive Standard Oil Trust as well as the American Tobacco Trust, and in so doing, he again surpassed the already significant achievements of the Great Trustbuster. Thus Taft's conservative disposition did not interfere with his commitment to continuing, and in many ways expanding, Roosevelt's reforms. The economy for the most part was sound, and general prosperity had been under way since the turn of the century; with the exception of a limited downturn in 1907 (occurring under Roosevelt), the nation's wealth and employment had been steadily improving. Taft's presidency had in many ways proven a successful heir to the McKinley and Roosevelt administrations.

Nonetheless, Taft encountered problems. His political troubles were already somewhat evident as early as 1910, even though his administration was accomplished in promoting continued reform. As his term moved into its latter months, Taft seemed to be devoting increasingly more time to socializing with his more conservative chums, in a way allowing himself to become distracted, less interested in the kind of progressive reforms that he adopted in the first part of his administration. Thus as the general election year of 1912 opened, Taft's incumbency was surprisingly vulnerable, and not since the defection of Liberal Republicans who were opposed to Grant in the election of 1872 was a Republican incumbent faced with this level of resistance from within his own party. Even the Plumed Knight, James Blaine, at his lowest moment still commanded considerable allegiance within the party; but President Taft was now facing large-scale abandonment. Those troubles stemmed from a split within the party that further divided the progressive wing from the conservative wing, and while Taft's policies had often followed the progressive agenda, he was readily identified as the leader of the conservatives. Former president Roosevelt was still regarded as the true great progressive, and he still commanded the unflagging loyalties of the party's reformist elements. In 1872, President Grant was able to quash the challenge from the Liberal Republicans and their eccentric candidate, Horace Greeley; but Taft now faced Roosevelt, the Great Man, which threw him into an impossibly difficult situation.

Owing to Taft's support of a number of reformist policies, the explanation for his troubles is more complex than the perception by some progressives—and in particular Roosevelt—that he had deserted them. The trouble began as early as the White House transition, as Taft did not retain key members of the Roosevelt cabinet, to the chagrin of the outgoing president, a man one did not want to vex. In particular, Taft replaced Roosevelt's trusted secretary of the interior,

James R. Garfield, the son of slain president James A. Garfield, with Richard Ballinger, who then returned to private use millions of acres of land that had been reserved for conservation under the leadership of Roosevelt and Garfield. Conservation was dear to the former president, and this act alone promised to drive a wedge between Roosevelt and Taft. To add fuel to the fire that was already intensifying, President Taft fired another member of Roosevelt's administration, Gifford Pinchot, originally an appointee of President McKinley, who had been running the U.S. Forest Service for Roosevelt since 1905. Pinchot, a close friend of Roosevelt's, was, among others, highly critical of Ballinger and convinced that Taft's new secretary of the interior would erase all progress made in the area of conservation. During the first two years of the Taft administration, the president, while continuing to support progressive legislation, nonetheless remained conservative in his inclinations and personal loyalties, which would eventually lead him to gradually abandon the trust-busting policies of the first part of his term, and in the end it would raise suspicions within his party's progressive wing.

From the left side of the party, Taft seemed too cozy with the oligarchs, a perception that completely ignored Taft's extensive public record as a reformer. By the midterm elections of 1910, the isolation of Taft was under way, and by 1911 it was evident that he had become associated with the conservative opponents of reform, a conclusion that, upon reflection, was unfairly drawn. But in campaign politics, the power of appearance is difficult to neutralize; and as Taft's administration moved closer toward the general election of 1912, some of his actions began to, at least in part, mirror the appearance while reshaping the reality. One such example is provided in Taft's reversal of his position on the tariff, now supporting protectionist legislation that, for his critics, signaled the negation of many of the earlier reforms that he had executed. For the progressives, high tariffs were closely allied to monopolies; thus, in switching from his former reformist policies to what now appeared to be a renewed protectionism, he raised another alarm.

As factions within the two parties began to quarrel, Roosevelt publicly refused to support either side, but privately he was displeased with the conservatives, and his old ally Taft had now seemed to join their number. The rift grew into a schism, and the schism tore a friendship apart. Four years out of office, an African safari and a European tour behind him, and again "feeling like a Bull Moose," Teddy Roosevelt charged back into the thicket of presidential politics like a force of nature determined to reclaim the Republican Party for the progressive cause. Friend and political benefactor to Taft just four years earlier, Roosevelt felt betrayed by both Taft and the conservative wing of the party, and he steeled himself to run for an unprecedented third term. Roosevelt hurled unkind epithets at his former friend, the "fathead" Taft, opening an irreconcilable breach. Taft defended himself, wildly claiming that Roosevelt had become too radical and warning voters that the election of the former president would initiate a "reign of terror" reminiscent of the darkest days of the French Revolution. Between an animated Roosevelt and the emerging Midwestern progressive star Robert La Follette of Wisconsin, who was also vying for the nomination, Taft's position in the party was undermined, and his very presidency now drifted in the doldrums at the launching of his own reelection campaign.

Roosevelt, back in the arena, loomed like a titan over the political landscape; but political parties traditionally favor incumbents, and this was no different in 1912, even with the popular Rough Rider again back in the fray. Taft still enjoyed the full support of party leaders—now largely conservative—and the institutional party's full endorsement. But Roosevelt remained universally beloved among the party regulars, and with the introduction of nonbinding presidential primary elections in the previous election year, now in practice in thirteen states, Taft's weakness was soon evident. The president was routinely beaten by Roosevelt in the primaries, in spite of the fact that he actively campaigned at the primary level, the first incumbent president to do so. Roosevelt took nine states in the primaries, La Follette surprisingly claimed two, and Taft managed to win only one. Even Taft's home state of Ohio went against him, an embarrassment for any presidential candidate under any set of circumstances, and exponentially worse for an incumbent president.

But in 1912, the primaries did not choose the nominee as they do today; the convention still did, and at the convention, it was Taft, not his former benefactor, who held the cards. It is also important to remember that even with Roosevelt's victories in the primaries, the majority of states still selected delegates in state conventions, and it was there that Taft still enjoyed influence and loyalty. Finally, the party itself made the final determination on the credentials of any delegate, primary politics notwithstanding. Roosevelt, as potent as ever in terms of his popularity among the electorate, still could not dislodge the party elite. At the Chicago convention, the Taft forces won the day. Vice President James S. Sherman was also chosen to continue as Taft's running mate on the first ballot, becoming the first incumbent vice president ever to be renominated for a second term at a national party convention (i.e., since the beginning of the national convention system in the late 1820s–early 1830s). By comparison, Vice President Richard Johnson, who served under President Van Buren and who did run with him twice, was not renominated but simply tacitly accepted in 1840 when the convention sought not to seek a replacement; and three previous two-term vice presidents, George Clinton (vice president under Thomas Jefferson and James Madison, one term each), David Tompkins (vice president during the two-term administration of James Monroe), and John C. Calhoun (vice president under John Quincy Adams and part of the first term of Andrew Jackson prior to his resignation), preceded the national nominating convention.

That said, Vice President Sherman unfortunately died on October 12, just a few weeks before the general election. Nicholas M. Butler, the president of Columbia University, was promptly selected to receive Sherman's electoral votes.

Undeterred by his failure to win over the party leadership and thus the convention, Roosevelt broke from the party (undertaking an action that he once found distasteful; he had once refused to bolt with the Mugwumps against the nominee, Blaine, in 1884), declared his candidacy as an independent, and promptly formed the Progressive Party, which naturally assumed the Bull Moose nickname, and which nominated the progressive governor of California, Hiram Johnson, as his running mate. This snapped the Republican Party in two: Taft, representing the conservative element friendlier to business—in spite of his proven record against trusts; and Roosevelt, the last eminent champion of progressive reform within the GOP. During the campaign, Roosevelt promoted what he referred to as his "New Nationalism," a conceptual vision for American politics that included the continuation of progressive reforms such as a proposed graduated income tax, close monitoring of corporations, lower tariffs, the expansion of the practice of direct presidential primaries, the initiative and referendum, and continued conservation efforts. As indicated above, Roosevelt had tempered some of his attitudes toward monopolies, arguing that in some cases they could be allowed (the "good trusts") and preferring tighter regulation to actual dissolution (a point in which Roosevelt appeared more conservative than Taft, who, it will be remembered, had attempted to disband U.S. Steel, another sore spot between the two men). For Roosevelt, if monopolies were accountable to government and the public it represented, they could, in some cases, be sustained under close scrutiny. In the final analysis, Lincoln's party was battling over its future and its soul, and in so doing, it opened the way to the first Democratic victory in a presidential campaign since Grover Cleveland's return to office in 1892.

Three-time Democratic nominee William Jennings Bryan, finally realizing his diminished appeal, concentrated his energies on helping to reshape the mentality of the Democrats. Even though he failed to gain the White House in three tries, Bryan nonetheless had made a lasting impact on American democracy. In large part due to Bryan's efforts, progressivism infused both parties, each battling its conservative wing, and Bryan had been a major figure at the center of the movement. Even Roosevelt acknowledged Bryan's qualified influence on his own proposals, admitting, "I have [taken ideas from Bryan]. That is quite true," but also adding the disclaimer, "I have taken every one of them except those suited for the inmates of lunatic asylums." More importantly, Bryan's failure to gain the presidency obscured his success at changing the ideological framework in his own party. The older states' rights, laissez-faire strain was still present in the Democratic Party, but it was fast becoming a minority voice representing the thinking of the past. Led forward by Bryan, the party was embracing the full scope of progressivism. The Democrats favored electoral and governmental reform that went beyond trust-busting and envisioned the remaking of American politics into a far more participatory form of democracy. Conservatives in both parties recoiled, but the tide was in favor of the reformers. The party was fully "Bryanized," but the Great Commoner would not lead it into victory; that task would fall upon a new Democratic hero, the erudite professor from Princeton.

As the Democratic convention opened in Baltimore, Speaker of the House Champ Clark of Missouri, who had recently replaced the legendary Joe Cannon in that position, was considered the front-runner based on his success in the nonbinding primaries that gave him the pre-convention lead in delegates. He was followed by the scholar/governor of New Jersey, Woodrow Wilson, along with Ohio's Governor Judson Harmon and House majority leader Oscar Underwood of Alabama. Clark, a progressive ally of Bryan, seemed the easy choice for the nomination. Wilson was harder to pin down ideologically. As a professor and university president, as well as in his early political career, Wilson adopted a more conservative tenor; but as governor of New Jersey, he became a reformist, supporting state legislation of a progressive nature. By 1912, Wilson was regarded as having become more liberal than Clark, who was now viewed as something of a moderate.

Clark had the lead as the convention proceeded in Baltimore, but he could not manage to gain the needed two-thirds majority to secure the nomination. According to some accounts, Clark lost his edge when Tammany Hall declared its support for him, a move that seemed to have locked up his nomination on the tenth ballot, but one that led Bryan and his loyalists to withdraw their support, a move that negated Tammany's influence. Bryan did not openly support Wilson, but rather he withdrew from Clark, leading some commentators to conclude that this was the turning point that drove the convention's delegates toward the professor. A speech by Bryan explaining the Nebraska delegation's sudden reversal against Clark is viewed by some observers as having been the decisive act leading to Wilson's nomination; in other words, it was Bryan who once again determined who would carry the party's standard, this time handing it to another candidate rather than embracing it himself. Other accounts tell a slightly different tale, that it was not so much the association of Clark with Tammany or the withdrawal of Bryan from Clark that ended his run, but rather skilled and subtle negotiations behind the scenes by William G. McAdoo and William F. McCombs on behalf of Wilson, who patiently held himself out of the spotlight while his allies discretely marshaled their forces. Even after the speech by Bryan, Wilson was not nominated until the forty-sixth ballot, perhaps lending some credence to this second account. Once the nomination was won by Wilson, Indiana's governor Thomas Marshall was quickly selected as his running mate without controversy.

The Democratic platform combined progressivism and the more agrarian strains of populism, and it was well received by both industrial labor and farmers. Even though former president Roosevelt had formed an independent Progressive Party that held nearly identical positions, it was clear to voters that among the two major parties, which still both had progressive wings, the Democratic Party was moving more in that direction than the GOP. Progressive Republicans were either following Roosevelt into his Bull Moose Party or considering the Democrats. With the renomination of Taft, the perception, whether fair or not, was that the Republican Party was abandoning its progressive agenda. Some progressive Republicans did, in the end, reconsider their initial enthusiasm for Roosevelt and, in so doing, returned to their own party. Progressivism was not entirely dead in the GOP, but there were signs that it was no longer the force that it had been just four years earlier.

Wilson possessed a different kind of charisma in contrast to Roosevelt's inexhaustible ebullience and bravado or Bryan's melodramatic yet emotively effective histrionics. Wilson lacked Roosevelt's colorful and domineering persona, but he possessed charms of his own that were more than capable of moving public audiences. Articulate, confident, astute, persuasive, professorial, quietly devout, indifferent to crowd pleasing, possessing a quick wit, and brimming with intelligence, Wilson knew how to communicate effectively. He neither spoke with the impassioned rhetoric of Bryan nor cut the commanding image of Roosevelt, but his audience immediately respected him, recognizing in him a sober, prudent approach combined with a larger vision of a greater purpose. He was the first Southerner (born and educated in Virginia, now a transplant to New Jersey) to win a major nomination since 1860, and the first (and to this day, the last) PhD to run for the White House. Recognizing the similarities shared by the progressive wings of both parties, Wilson redefined their respective positions on his own terms. Roosevelt's New Nationalism, which held much in common with the Democratic agenda, was reinterpreted by Wilson as a series of ideas and policies that actually worked to preserve monopoly power rather than eliminate it. Roosevelt, in Wilson's view, merely wanted to mildly regulate existing trusts but not banish the trust from the American economy. Wilson claimed to be the genuine trustbuster, and his own vision that he called the "New Freedom" was advanced as a way to restore real competition and opportunity to the American dream through the thoroughgoing abolition of a monopolist system. Wilson's message was strikingly effective in drawing out the contrasts within the progressive movement. In a sense, the "Bryanized" Wilson had succeeded in "Wilsonizing" Bryan, and in so doing, he regained the thunder for the Democrats that Bryan had accused Roosevelt of stealing away for the Republicans.

And so Taft, Roosevelt, and Wilson, three of the United States' most important historical figures, squared off in a single election. But they were not the only players drawing attention. The Socialist Party, showing optimism after slowly gaining votes in recent general elections as the leading third-party alternative, was now also enjoying considerable electoral success across the nation at various levels. But it too faced its own internal problems. The majority of the party in many ways resembled the progressive wings of the two major parties, and it advocated a gradualist approach toward the promotion and eventual development of a socialist society. However, a small but decidedly influential minority led by an outsized personality, Big Bill Haywood, and linked through close ties to the International Workers of the World (IWW, also known as the "Wobblies"), scolded the moderate majority for its doctrinal concessions, advocating a far more radical and revolutionary approach to the struggle. Eugene V. Debs himself, the party's standard-bearer for the past three elections, was closer to the radical position, at least in 1912, but he was seen by the moderates as the most appealing and reliable candidate, and thus he easily won renomination. In so doing, Debs became at this point in history the only person to be nominated four times to run for president (Bryan and Grover Cleveland had each been nominated three times to run on behalf of the Democratic Party). Eventually the radicals were expelled from the party; American socialism, at least to the Socialist Party, would employ the ballot and other peaceful methods, eschewing more extreme measures, to work toward the transformation of the political culture in the name of a more just and equitable society. Joining the Socialists against the mainstream, the small but inexplicably influential Prohibition Party tapped Eugene Chafin, its candidate in 1908, to again lead the charge in the general election of 1912.

During the campaign, Taft set aside his considerable record as a reformer and embraced the label of conservative. While he spoke against what he perceived to be the dangerous "schemes" of Roosevelt's Progressive Party, he nonetheless considered Wilson to be the bigger problem, the real challenge; thus most of his campaign statements were directed against the Democrats. As the nation had enjoyed prosperity during the Taft years, the president stressed that this was the result of the leadership of the Republican Party and argued that with the Democrats in power, their low-tariff, free-trade policies would blunt any further economic progress. But Taft saw the handwriting on the wall; he realized, from the moment that Roosevelt bolted the party and took the progressives with him, that his presidency was fated for one term.

Typically, Roosevelt traveled widely, stumping hard for his reformist principles. "I have been growing more radical instead of less radical," Roosevelt declared. "I'm even going further than the [Progressive Party] platform." He emphasized the conservatism of both the Republicans and even Wilson, describing the Democratic candidate as an "ultra-conservative" and claiming that the former professor's rise to political prominence was due to the support of his friends on Wall Street.

Roosevelt frequently referred to Wilson's more conservative positions held in the past, reminding voters that Wilson had only just recently adopted these more liberal views. Roosevelt was still a captivating speaker, but he addressed audiences less dramatically than he had in the past, projecting a more modest image even as his ideas were more provocative.

Some have referred to the policies proposed in Roosevelt's 1912 Bull Moose campaign as one of the more radical agendas in American history, at least by a candidate of such prominence, exceeding even the future 1936 campaign of his cousin Franklin Roosevelt and the 1948 campaign of Harry Truman in the extent of its reformist message. While the Great Man roamed far and wide, delivering his message from coast to coast and from the North into the Deep South, Wilson preferred economy of effort, going only as far west as Denver and ignoring the South altogether, which he knew to be loyal to the Democrats and not needing to be won over, save for stops in the border states of Missouri and Delaware, which had been close in recent years. He focused his rhetoric on distinguishing his New Freedom progressivism from Roosevelt's New Nationalism, and in so doing, at times he did reveal traces of a more conservative, non-Bryanist streak. For all his talk of reform, Wilson distrusted the power of government, and while he expressed sympathy with labor, he cautioned workers not to become too dependent on government to fight their battles, warning that if the government became too involved in the labor movement, the workers might become less independent and in the end actually resemble wards of the state. In this way, Wilson reminded reporters more of President Cleveland, the old Bourbon Democrat, than either William Jennings Bryan or President Roosevelt.

One of the more outrageous moments of the campaign involved a bizarre and dangerous attempt to assassinate Roosevelt. A delusional saloon keeper, still embittered by Roosevelt's enforcement of temperance ordinances during his tenure as a New York City police commissioner three decades earlier, ambushed the former president in Milwaukee, where he was due to give a speech, and shot him in the chest. The bullet was partially deflected by both Roosevelt's eyeglasses case and a multi-paged copy of his speech, and thus as the bullet lodged in his body, its momentum had been slowed considerably. But it was a life-threatening incident nonetheless. Ever fearless, Roosevelt calmly assessed his wound, concluded that it was not serious, and, to a stunned audience, nonchalantly proceeded to deliver his speech, which clocked in at around ninety minutes. In addressing the crowd, Roosevelt's initial remarks carried the following off-the-cuff disclaimer: "Friends, I shall ask you to be as quiet as possible. I don't know whether you fully understand that I have just been shot; but it takes more than that to kill a Bull Moose. But fortunately I had my manuscript, so you see I was going to make a long speech, and there is a bullet—there is where the bullet went through—and it probably saved me from it going into my heart. The bullet is in me now, so that I cannot make a very long speech, but I will try my best." Upon medical examination, doctors concluded that the candidate was right—the wound was not a particularly serious one. But it was still serious enough that the bullet's removal was determined to be potentially risky; thus Roosevelt carried the bullet in his chest for the remainder of his life. The entire incident epitomizes the incomparable character of the Rough Rider, further evidence that he was a man larger than his image, even larger than his age.

Even though the 1912 campaign was ideologically deeper than any campaign since 1860 and rhetorically more interesting than any campaign since 1896, the outcome of the election had more to do with the numbers game of electoral politics than with the high ideas under discussion or the provocative slogans that were spun out by the strategists. Due to the divisions between the Republican and Bull Moose progressives, Wilson won the election with slightly fewer than 6,300,000 popular votes (only 42%), which nonetheless converted to a stunning 435 votes (or 82%) in the Electoral College. Thus, even though Wilson's plurality in the popular vote was the third lowest for a winning candidate in history and second lowest in the era of the modern political party (only Lincoln's 39.7% in the four-candidate race of 1860 polled lower to win; and it should also be added that John Quincy Adams polled even lower at 30% in 1824, just before the beginnings of the modern political party), he paradoxically won more total electoral votes than any candidate before him in history, although this Electoral College landslide was not the biggest in terms of percentages. Since the 1804 election, wherein the Electoral College first began voting for the president and vice president separately, only Jefferson in 1804, Monroe in 1816 and 1824, Pierce in 1852, and Lincoln in 1864 (in an election that excluded eleven states) finished with a higher percentage in the electoral college than Wilson in 1912—this, of course, does not include Washington's unanimous support for the presidency for both of his two terms. Wilson won the presidency by holding, as expected, the entire South, still the Democrats' unyielding fortress, and making critical inroads into the North, which included winning in the ever-pivotal New York (which now carried 45 electoral votes), as well as the Midwest, where he won every state that Taft had managed to win in 1908 except Minnesota and Michigan (included in Wilson's tally was Taft's home of Ohio). Roosevelt succeeded in gaining more votes than any third-party candidate in history, winning over 4,100,000 popular votes and carrying six states in the Electoral College (California, Washington, South Dakota, and Pennsylvania in addition to Minnesota and Michigan) for a total of 88 electoral votes. Roosevelt became and would remain the only third-party candidate to outpace an incumbent president, and he did it in both the popular vote and the Electoral College vote.

Taft's loss was devastating—an incumbent president winning just under 3,500,000 votes and carrying only two states (New Hampshire and Utah) for a total of 8 electoral votes, showing third place against the challengers. This is all the more puzzling when looking at the overall record of the Taft administration, which on the whole was marked by a level of competence that exceeds that of a few chief executives who did manage to win a second term. But a divided Republican Party could not defeat the unified Democrats, particularly given the political muscle that Roosevelt quixotically took with him into his third party. The GOP lost in every region of the country, even in its northeastern/midwestern stronghold (e.g., for the first time in history, the Republican Party failed to carry Massachusetts, Maine, Michigan, and Minnesota). Had Roosevelt allied with Taft, they would have easily outpolled Wilson by 1.3 million votes, and the GOP could have maintained its long dominance of the White House. It has been noted, and it is important to do so, that Wilson in victory won fewer popular votes than Bryan in any of his three defeats; thus it is evident that the Democratic Party actually suffered a loss of popular support within the electorate in the 1912 election, even though it had enjoyed an Electoral College landslide on a scale seldom seen. The Democrats did experience a resurgence in Congress, taking majorities in both chambers for the first time since the 1850s, a boon that again was likely due to the split in the Republican Party. Meanwhile, Eugene Debs and the Socialist Party rode the progressive wave to their highest point to date, gathering more than 900,000 votes with increasing support in all states, and flexing considerable "third-party muscle" of their own. But the story of 1912 is more about division than unity. Even if all the minor-party votes went to the Democrats—and they would not have—the Republicans, if they had managed to prevent their split and combine their forces, still would have likely won the day, returned Taft to the White House, and held Congress as well. That said, the electorate was, at least for the moment, fragmented, and the two major parties were now facing new challenges. The vote total for the Socialists was nearly twice that of 1908; thus, in spite of its own internal divisions, the Debs campaign enjoyed a remarkable stride forward for the party, which would have been all the more impressive had it not been overshadowed by Roosevelt's Progressive campaign. The Prohibition Party won just over 208,000 votes, down from the nearly 255,000 votes that it won four years earlier. On Election Day at least, the Progressives and Socialists seemed to be pointing toward a new direction for the American electorate. As a nod to his role in supporting Wilson, and perhaps also for his role in helping to reshape both the mission of the Democratic Party and the language of American politics, William Jennings Bryan would serve as the incoming president Wilson's secretary of state.

But in the end, it was Wilson's victory, regardless of how it came about, and the Democrats were returned to the White House for the first time since President Cleveland left in 1897. Woodrow Wilson was only the second Democrat to win the White House since the Civil War, but it is significant to note that neither

Cleveland's two victories nor Wilson's recent victory was won with a popular majority. Cleveland won in 1884 with 48.5 percent of the popular vote and in 1892 with slightly over 46 percent to give him a nonconsecutive second term, while Wilson's 1912 victory was even lower at 42 percent. It was thus still apparent that the Democratic Party did not command the broad electoral base still enjoyed by the Republicans. But even though the Democrats had not convincingly broken through in terms of electoral allegiances, in the battle of ideas, the Republicans were in trouble. Thus, still more significantly, given the dominance of the Campaign of 1912 by the reform candidates—i.e., Wilson, Roosevelt, and Debs—it appeared that there was indeed a shift in attitudes among voters with regard to the responsibilities of governance in the direction of society. The American electorate was clearly focused on which vision would guide the country in the twentieth century. But the groundswell for new ideas would soon subside. Unlike in the **Campaigns of 1900** and **1904**, events abroad were scarcely considered during the election year of 1912; but before long, events abroad would soon signal to American voters that new priorities, and new anxieties, would again alter political necessities.

Additional Resources

Arnold, Peri E. *Remaking the Presidency.* Lawrence: University Press of Kansas, 2009.

Cohen, Martin, David Karol, Hans Noel, and John Zaller. *The Party Decides: Presidential Nominations before and after Reform.* Chicago: University of Chicago Press, 2008.

Gould, Lewis L., *Four Hats in the Ring.* Lawrence: University Press of Kansas, 2008.

Heckscher, August. "1912." In Arthur M. Schlesinger, Fred L. Israel, and David J. Frent, eds. *Running for President: The Candidates and Their Images.* Vol. 2. New York: Simon & Schuster, 1994.

Morrisey, Will. *The Dilemma of Progressivism.* Lanham, MD: Rowman & Littlefield, 2009.

Mowry, George E. "Election of 1912." In Arthur M. Schlesinger, Fred Israel, and William P. Hansen, eds. *History of American Presidential Elections, 1789–1968.* Vol.2. New York: Chelsea House, 1985.

Campaign of 1916

Between the election of 1912 and the Campaign of 1916, a terrible world war erupted in Europe, one that would soon devastate the European countryside and quite literally decimate the "flower of a generation." Throughout this horrific conflict, President Woodrow Wilson and his secretary of state, the veteran of the anti-imperialism movement, the Great Commoner William Jennings Bryan, worked diligently to establish a foreign policy rooted in moral principles and respect for the sovereignty of nations. Thus in 1916, the administration promised independence to the Philippine Islands, which had been acquired as the spoils of victory in the successful war against Spain under President McKinley. Other territories acquired as a consequence of the Spanish-American War, such as Puerto Rico, were given territorial status (Cuba having already been granted independence). The foreign policies of Wilson (who was the major force behind fashioning American policy abroad) and Bryan were quite apart from McKinley-Roosevelt and represented a visible change from American exertions at the turn of the century. (In 1915, Bryan would resign his post in disagreement over the president's response to the sinking of the *Lusitania*, having interpreted the president's protest against the U-boat strike as bellicose and precipitous of war.) Most important in this regard was the determination of Wilson to maintain American neutrality regarding the Great War that was bleeding Europe white. However, close American economic ties to Britain and France led to a de facto preference for those nations and a concomitant reaction away from Germany; this in turn led to a submarine blockade around the British Isles, aimed at American shipping in particular and resulting in a state of rising tension between the United States and the German government. Wilson's desire for neutrality was in many ways weakened by these developments. In addition to the growing difficulty in maintaining this neutrality, Wilson faced problems involving relations with Mexico, which was suffering internal violence that spilled over the border into the United States, provoking Wilson to send an American expeditionary force into Mexican territory in pursuit of the revolutionary Pancho Villa. Villa was never captured, and the troops were eventually withdrawn, but it proved a particularly unfortunate and embarrassing episode, marring Wilson's foreign policy record.

The slogan "He Kept Us Out of War," a reminder of Wilson's commitment to peace, was first uttered at the Democratic convention in St. Louis, and it quickly became the defining phrase of the election of 1916. Although the convention was intended to stress Wilson's achievement as an effective president in general—that is, both in terms of domestic as well as foreign policy ("Americanism" was chosen as the rallying theme of the convention, received somewhat blandly by the participants)—it was the issue of sustained peace for Americans that grabbed the delegates, a theme that was articulated from the beginning by the keynote speaker, New York governor Martin Glynn (the first Irish Catholic to reach the governor's office in any state), who extemporaneously thundered against the war and in praise of Wilson's policy of restraint. Poignantly, Glynn mentioned those mothers and wives who had been able to keep their sons and husbands near the hearth and out of "the moldering dissolution of the grave." In a call-and-response cadence, the delegates would answer Glynn's encomiums of Wilson with the chant, "We didn't go to war, we didn't go to war." By the second day of the convention, Wilson's persistent neutrality was *the* theme of the convention, and the slogan "He kept us out of the war" overshadowed all other achievements of the administration.

Within the party, Wilson was universally popular and easily won renomination, with his vice president, Thomas R. Marshall, picked once again for the bottom of the ticket. Wilson's domestic agenda, introduced as part of his New Freedom ideology, had been pursued vigorously and in close cooperation with Congress throughout his first term. Wilson pushed hard for tariff reform that would lower tariffs (a routine concern of the Democrats since long before the Civil War), currency reform, trust-busting (building on the legacy of his Republican predecessors, presidents Roosevelt and Taft), reforms supportive of labor and farming, and the establishment of the Federal Reserve System to better manage the banks as well as the economy in general. In most ways, Wilson's New Freedom was a continuation and slight variation of Roosevelt's New Nationalism, and it was the last major push for extensive social and political reforms until the 1930s. But even more than these policies, which were not inconsiderable, it was in foreign policy—and thus in successfully steering the United States away from the carnage now under way in Europe—that Wilson had made a visible difference when compared to his recent predecessors. (It is well known that had Roosevelt won election in 1912, he would have pushed hard to involve the United States in the war.) Going into his reelection effort, Wilson was convincing as the peace candidate, his record having proved his somewhat qualified success in maintaining neutrality.

One of the more poignant moments of the convention involved Bryan, who had fallen out of favor with the party due to his criticism of the president over the *Lusitania* protest and his attendant resignation from his position as secretary of state. This act led to his ostracism from the party; he was not even invited to serve in the Nebraska delegation, instead forced to attend the convention as a reporter. As the convention progressed, delegates experienced a change of heart, and the old Bryanites once again called for an appearance at the podium from the Great Commoner, the man who had carried the party's standard in three earlier elections. The rules suspended for this exception, Bryan, absent credentials, addressed the convention on Wilson's behalf. "I have differed with our President," Bryan admitted, "on some of the methods employed, but I join with the American people in thanking God that we have a President who does not want this nation plunged into war."

The Republican Party's principal goal was to restore unity, having been split in half in the election of 1912, a situation that directly led to the election of the Democrat Wilson. Having dominated presidential politics since 1860 (losing only three elections in 1884, 1892, and 1912 within that time period), the Republicans were unaccustomed to being the party out of power. As is often the case, the party did recover somewhat during the midterm elections of 1914, cutting the Democrats' congressional majority considerably, especially in the House of Representatives.

The party also appeared to have rebounded from the defection of its liberal wing to the Progressive Party. Many Republicans agreed with the Roosevelt/Progressive agenda but had refused to bolt permanently from the GOP. The leadership was still largely controlled by the conservative elements, but in the rank and file there was more diversity, including the reconciled Republican progressives. While the Republicans had reason to be optimistic after gains from the 1914 midterms, they were still vulnerable to division, as both the conservative and liberal wings of the party held their base. A candidate was needed who could somehow appeal to the progressive ranks as well as assure its conservative leadership.

Prior to the 1916 convention in Chicago, a number of potential candidates were suggested, including Elihu Root, the former senator from New York who had served in the cabinets of presidents McKinley and Roosevelt as both secretary of war and secretary of state; Ohio senator Theodore Burton; Lawrence Y. Sherman, the senator from Illinois; and Charles Evans Hughes from New York, associate justice of the Supreme Court. Neither former president Roosevelt nor former president Taft sought the nomination—nor realistically expected that they could win if they had—but both men still enjoyed enough of a following that their names were offered in spite of their own evident disinterest. All told, twenty-one candidates would receive at least one vote at the convention, just over a dozen of which would receive votes in double digits. Also among those mentioned prior to the convention or receiving support at the convention were former vice president (under Roosevelt) Charles Fairbanks of Indiana, Senator John Weeks of Massachusetts, the progressive senator Robert M. La Follette from Wisconsin, industrialist Henry Ford, Roosevelt's close friend Henry Cabot Lodge of Massachusetts, and Senator Philander Knox, who had been a candidate for the nomination in 1908 (losing to Taft, who at that time was Roosevelt's chosen heir). Not running themselves, Taft and Roosevelt, being former presidents (and Roosevelt being who he was), still held enough political clout to influence delegates. Roosevelt, however, was noncommittal. He admired Root's abilities, but he now held a grudge against his former cabinet member and friend due to Root's support of Taft in the bitter **Campaign of 1912**.

As the convention approached, Hughes seemed to move ahead as a front-runner, but he was by no means secure. Hughes was regarded as a safe choice; as an associate justice, he was not dogged by a potentially controversial political paper trail, and to many within the party, he seemed to be a moderate and thus the very kind of candidate that might unite both wings of the party. On the first convention ballot, Hughes won 253 delegates to 105 for Weeks and 103 for Root, with Fairbanks, progressive senator Albert Cummins of Iowa, and noncandidate Roosevelt trailing behind with 89, 85, and 81, respectively; the remainder of the votes were distributed among 15 additional candidates (including one vote for Senator Warren G. Harding of Ohio, a promising prospect gaining notice within the party).

Had those in the gallery been credentialed to vote, Roosevelt might have had a real chance, for when his name was nominated from the floor by Senator Albert Fall of New Mexico, a thunderous and protracted demonstration broke out in the gallery that lasted for over half an hour and was reported by witnesses as "deafening" in volume. Roosevelt sustained his fierce popularity among the party regulars, but the delegates on the floor were unmoved, and thus the Bull Moose, still keeping his hat from the ring, would not receive more than a sixth-best showing on the first ballot (with his support decreasing on subsequent ballots). Hughes gained more support on the second ballot, winning 326 to Weeks's 102, with all but two other candidates actually losing votes. The third ballot was all that Hughes needed, winning 950, with the second-best showing at 23 for La Follette (Weeks had withdrawn his name). Fairbanks was tapped to run once more for vice president—the third candidate, along with Thomas A. Hendricks (in 1876, running with Samuel Tilden, and in 1884, serving under President Cleveland) and Adlai Stevenson (in 1892, also serving under Cleveland, and in 1900, running with Bryan) to be nominated for vice president in nonconsecutive conventions.

Meanwhile, the Progressive Party that Roosevelt formed to oppose both Wilson and Taft in 1912 held its own convention across town. Without Roosevelt's participation, the Progressives lost their unity and their focus. In a letter to the convention, Roosevelt, whose main purpose was now to eject Wilson from the White House, recommended that the Progressives support the Republicans. At one point the Progressives, in a last signal of allegiance to Roosevelt and their reformist cause, nominated him nonetheless; but Roosevelt refused to accept, and in the end the party fell in behind the Republican ticket of Hughes-Fairbanks. Roosevelt could have again run as the Progressive nominee, but perhaps in a concession to the wisdom of the two-party system that had grown out of the American political tradition, he no longer felt it made sense to promote a third party, and thus he reconciled with his old affiliations. As for Hughes, Roosevelt had little regard for him, observing that only a good shave separated the bearded Hughes from the clean-shaven Wilson. But as lukewarm as he was regarding Hughes, he abjectly despised Wilson, whom he referred to as a hypocrite and a "Byzantine logothete." Thus Roosevelt again campaigned for the Republican cause, a cause that he understood as leading to American commitment to the war. Roosevelt notwithstanding, as a moderate it was clear that Hughes was acceptable to both wings of the party as well as those progressives who had bolted in 1912. With the nomination of Hughes, the Republican Party repeated for the third time the nomination of a jurist for the office of the presidency. Taft, nominated twice, had once served as a judge on the U.S. Sixth Court of Appeals; Hughes resigned his position as an associate justice of the Supreme Court to run for president, a body that Taft himself would eventually join as chief justice. Taft and Hughes were the only former judges to run for the presidency under the formal endorsement of a major party (although judges had been considered as potential candidates, but none had received an actual nomination other than Taft and Hughes).

Hughes was not a hawk on the war issue, but partisan attitudes led to equivocation. Roosevelt, who remained zealously hawkish and committed to immediate war against Germany, and who remained the Great Man of the party, still held pervasive influence within the GOP base; and because of this, many Republicans were less willing than the Democrats to insist on supporting Wilson's continued neutrality. Hughes was thus caught in the hotbox between a neutral "America First" position and the more pro-Anglo critique directed against Wilson for not protecting American maritime interests against German U-boat attacks in the North Atlantic. When speaking to audiences with a high Germanic mix, Hughes took a softer line than he would otherwise with a different audience. Such waffling on the war spurred the candidate's critics to assign him a new nickname—Charles *Evasive* Hughes.

With the Progressive Party moribund in the wake of Roosevelt's refusal to carry its banner, the Republicans now enjoyed the possibility of a united party against Wilson, a situation that would have guaranteed them victory four years earlier. But Wilson, enjoying the accomplishments that burnished his record, was now a formidable incumbent, much stronger than he had been in 1912. On the other side, though not as electrifying as Roosevelt or as canny as McKinley, Hughes was, as one would expect from a Supreme Court justice, quite capable, and he was personally commanding in his own right. However, Hughes carried three liabilities to the polls in November: the perception by many of a cold personality, Theodore Roosevelt's martial alarums, and California. To address the former, Hughes made a point of portraying himself as an ordinary chap: meeting crowds to shake hands and kiss babies, attending ball games and seeking out the players, and acting like a tourist at points of interest along the campaign trail. Hughes did enjoy some success in this, as he was gradually perceived as personally more appealing than his public speeches, which, owing no doubt to his considerable learning and juristic proclivities, could be long, dry, and dull in the context of a political campaign.

Eluding Roosevelt's shadow proved more difficult. Additionally, Roosevelt's militarism tagged the Republicans with the war party label, further muddying Hughes's real sentiments. The Democrats could plausibly claim, "The less is plain: if you want WAR, vote for Hughes! If you want Peace with Honor, VOTE for WILSON!" In spite of Hughes's waffling, there were moments when his actions inadvertently lent some credence to this claim. Hughes promised "unflinching maintenance of all American rights on land and sea," a gesture that could only mean a more aggressive posture to the Kaiser's U-boats, which in turn raised the real possibility of a shooting war with Germany. And yet his views were more complex; he excoriated the Wilson administration for its military adventures in Mexico, and as stated above, he at times assumed a more neutral tone, arguing for "America first" and the protection of its international standing, but then lowering his voice when addressing the prospects of armed conflict with Germany.

California is what, in the end, made the difference, and it was personal. An inadvertent snub by Hughes of California's progressive Republican governor Hiram Johnson (who stood as Roosevelt's Bull Moose running mate four years earlier) while visiting the Long Beach hotel where Johnson was also staying alienated the party faithful within the Golden State. Hughes would lose the state—which had in recent years been a frequently close battleground—by fewer than four thousand votes, allowing Wilson a clean sweep in the West and thus victory in what would become the closest election since 1888 (at that time former president Cleveland winning against incumbent president Harrison).

The early returns from the East (viz., New York, Pennsylvania, New Jersey, most of New England) favored Hughes in what was shaping up to be a possible landslide. Hughes took New York's popular vote by 7 percentage points and Pennsylvania's by a stunning 14 percentage points, thus allowing him to carry the Electoral College's two biggest prizes and converting his substantial popular majorities there into 83 electoral votes (45 from New York and 38 from Pennsylvania). As the election developed further, Hughes was further bolstered by winning in Illinois (with 29 electoral votes, now the third-largest prize). It was no surprise that Wilson held the solid South, but events seemed to be rolling against him. However, he managed to win in Ohio, his biggest state (with 24 electoral votes), and which, when combined with Texas (20 electoral votes)—where he enjoyed a staggering 76 percent of the popular vote—and both Virginia and North Carolina taken together (15 electoral college votes each, for a total of 30 votes), he was able to hold on and stave off an early defeat. But it still looked dire for the president. In the Northeast and the Midwest, where the balance of the electoral votes was distributed in 1916, Hughes won decisively, losing only to Wilson in Ohio and New Hampshire in those two regions. This meant that at midnight, Hughes had claimed 254 Electoral College votes, within easy reach of victory, and major newspapers prematurely announced in print the election of a new president.

By morning, however, Hughes had not shown any further gains, and returns from the West showed Wilson in much better shape. With the exception of Oregon and South Dakota, the president had taken every western state, and once California's returns were finally reported, Wilson was given victory by the slimmest of margins, taking California's popular vote by winning 46.7 percent to Hughes's 46.3 percent. This gave 13 electoral votes to Wilson, which proved to be the difference that propelled him to victory. Wilson won the popular vote by 600,000 votes, taking over 9,100,000 (or 49.2%) to Hughes's total of slightly below 8,500,000 (around 46%), and more importantly, he won in the Electoral College, 277 to 254. Repelling a stronger challenge than expected, President Wilson would return for a second term. The Socialist Party, this time running Allan Benson instead of its veteran standard-bearer, Eugene V. Debs (who had led their ticket in the previous four campaigns), won just over 590,000 votes, which was a considerable loss when compared to the party's encouraging 1912 total of over 900,000. The Prohibition Party, led by James Hanley, won just over 220,000 votes, which was a 12,000-vote improvement when compared to 1912.

California, which Hughes squandered all because of hurt feelings, was the clear difference in the election: the state that lost him the presidency. According to Mike Sheppard of MIT, a change of only 1,887 votes in California would have been enough to deliver the state, and the White House, to Hughes and send President Wilson home after one term. Interestingly, the election of 1916 demonstrated the power of the South and the West. Hughes dominated the Northeast and the Midwest, a veritable Electoral College bonanza, but won nothing in the South and only ten electoral votes in the West. With Wilson holding Ohio in the Midwest and the Democrats' one-party southern bloc, and decisively winning the West, he assured his second term. For the first time since 1892, when Cleveland won by splitting these regions with Harrison, and 1884, when Blaine edged out Cleveland in this part of the country, a presidential candidate won the Northeast and the Midwest but lost the general election. But Hughes's victory in these regions was decisive, winning more convincingly there than Blaine or Harrison in their defeats, a telling indicator of sustained Republican strength in spite of their failure to unseat Wilson. With the exceptions of the antebellum elections of Buchanan and Pierce in which California was the only true western state (Texas was then considered part of the southern bloc), never before had the South and the West combined to deliver the presidency as they had in 1916.

President Wilson was the second Democrat, along with Grover Cleveland, to win the presidency since the ascent of Republican dominance in 1860 behind President Lincoln, both Cleveland and Wilson also managing to win the White House twice. Surprisingly, even though the Democrats were the dominant party before the Civil War, Wilson became the only Democrat at that time to win the White House in consecutive elections (President Cleveland's victories being nonconsecutive) since President Andrew Jackson in 1828 and 1832. Like Cleveland, Wilson's two electoral victories were achieved without an absolute majority in the popular vote. The last Democratic candidate for president to win a genuine majority of the popular vote was Samuel Tilden in 1876, who won 50.9 percent of the popular vote but famously lost the election to Rutherford B. Hayes by just one vote in the Electoral College. In fact, only five Democrats to this point had managed to win a popular majority for the presidency: Andrew Jackson (twice in 1828 and 1832),

Martin Van Buren (in 1836), Franklin Pierce (in 1852), and Tilden (while losing in 1876), with neither Cleveland nor Wilson managing to join them. Even though Wilson kept the White House for another term, it was still evident that, at least in the politics of the presidency, the Democrats were far from dislodging GOP dominance.

History's many ironies mock great women and men. President Wilson, the candidate of peace throughout the summer and fall of 1916, would within a few months of his reelection commit Americans to join the blood-soaked, fire-scorched war in Europe. Thus Theodore Roosevelt's Big America joined the Great War, and Wilson's health would shatter in pursuit of the lasting peace that he had so strenuously guarded throughout his first term and that he so ardently desired in the war's aftermath. Collapsing during a speech in Pueblo, Colorado, in September 1919 while promoting the League of Nations and his broader policies of concerted, peaceful internationalism, Wilson would spend the last few months of his presidency infirm, with much of the daily conduct of his administration managed by his wife, Edith. He would pass away just slightly over three years after leaving office. Wilson's progressivism would recede with him, but the principles that he shared with his immediate Republican predecessors, Taft and Roosevelt, as well as his fellow Democrat, the Great Commoner Bryan, would eventually reemerge with still greater force a decade later, under far more desperate conditions, and under the direction of another and, as it would turn out, equally singular man named Roosevelt.

Additional Resources

Arnold, Peri E. *Remaking the Presidency*. Lawrence: University Press of Kansas, 2009.

Cohen, Martin, David Karol, Hans Noel, and John Zaller. *The Party Decides: Presidential Nominations before and after Reform*. Chicago: University of Chicago Press, 2008.

Heckscher, August. "1916." In Arthur M. Schlesinger, Fred L. Israel, and David J. Frent, eds. *Running for President: The Candidates and Their Images*. Vol. 2. New York: Simon & Schuster, 1994.

Link, Arthur S., and William M. Leary. "Election of 1916." In Arthur M. Schlesinger, Fred Israel, and William P. Hansen, eds. *History of American Presidential Elections, 1789–1968*. Vol. 2. New York: Chelsea House, 1985.

Lovell, S. D. *The Presidential Election of 1916*. Carbondale: Southern Illinois University Press, 1980.

Miller Center of Public Affairs, University of Virginia. http://millercenter.org/president /wilson.

Morrisey, Will. *The Dilemma of Progressivism*. Lanham, MD: Rowman & Littlefield, 2009.

Sheppard, Mike. "How Close Were U.S. Presidential Elections?" http://www.mit.edu /~mi22295/elections.html.

Campaign of 1920

The presidential election of 1920 might be the last in which neither major party, going into its national convention, had a clear image of who would emerge as its nominee, and thus it was the last of the truly wide-open seasons of presidential conventions. In all subsequent campaigns, even those in which there was no incumbent in the running, at least one of the major parties came to its nominating convention with an established front-runner; and with the final triumph of the primary system in the 1970s, no convention would again open with uncertainty about the inevitable nominee (the 1976 GOP convention being a possible exception). Thus 1920 was indeed the last convention of its kind.

By 1920, the euphoria that followed the end of World War I had been replaced with growing anxiety over the direction of the country and uncertainty as to how to conduct foreign affairs in an increasingly more dangerous world. The Great War (as World War I was then called) had amplified warfare to an entirely unprecedented level of mass slaughter, and many Americans, while on the whole having supported the war effort, were now even more reticent to become involved in foreign alliances. Even though Woodrow Wilson conducted a nationwide tour, giving some forty speeches promoting the League of Nations treaty during the late summer and throughout the fall of 1919, the Senate refused to ratify the treaty. Prior to the vote, Wilson suffered a stroke, which seriously weakened his health for the remainder of his second term. Meanwhile, labor unrest in the United States had sparked numerous strikes and concern over discontent among the working class. Recession had replaced the wartime boom. More than anything, the war had dramatically altered life in the United States. As historian Donald McCoy once wrote, "The First World War and its aftermath had struck the nation's political, social, and economic scene with earthquake force. Old ties and ways of life had been broken, the position of whole layers of society had been altered, and new fears and expectations had been unleashed, new leaders had arisen, and the role and status of the old ones had been changed."

American society was in the process of metamorphosis, and American political institutions were reacting. The energy of progressivism was, at least for the moment, spent. Isolationism, as evinced by the failure of Wilson's mission to commit the United States to the League of Nations, was emergent. Suspicion of foreign attitudes and ideologies was pervasive. Racism and religious animosity waxed with the reinvigoration of a once-moribund Ku Klux Klan. The American economy was becoming increasingly more industrial, commercial, and urban, and gradually less agricultural (although American agriculture still remained a major component of the economy), and the image of American life less rural.

Those large issues that had commanded attention during the last four campaigns—the policies of progressivism and, especially in 1916, the war—had exhausted both parties and the public mood in general. For the most part, progressivism had won the day, and it was only a matter of adjusting to the new shape the republic was now assuming. No candidate could effectively run against the legacy of both Theodore Roosevelt and Woodrow Wilson. The progressive movement had irrevocably transformed the American polity. The Great War had left the American public wary of what George Washington had referred to as "foreign entanglements," Wilson's grand vision for an international League of Nations now soundly rejected. Added to this was confusion and apprehension over events in Russia, where a communist revolution was under way, provoking a Red Scare throughout the United States against Bolshevism and, in effect, any type of "foreign-born" ideology. Internal divisions over the war and the Russian Revolution undermined the Socialist Party, which had become a thriving third party in the early decades of the century. Furthermore, a new amendment to the Constitution prohibited the sale and consumption of alcohol; thus while the Prohibition Party could never gain more than a quarter of a million votes in any given presidential election, its agenda had triumphed, and with the enactment of the Volstead Act to enforce this amendment, an entire nation was legally declared "dry." Additionally, in the midst of these many changes, many of them driven by disenchantment or uncertainty, the Nineteenth Amendment protecting the right of women to vote at the federal level was ratified, a positive stroke for democracy and electoral politics that was ratified in time for the 1920 election. Full women's suffrage had been gradually gaining strength since Wyoming (1869) and Utah (1870), as territories, guaranteed the franchise for women (a guarantee that was preempted at the federal level), with Wyoming becoming the first state to protect women's right to vote upon admission to the Union in 1890, Colorado following in 1893 as the second state to do so. Eastward, progress was also made on a smaller scale in Michigan and Minnesota in the 1870s and Kansas in the 1880s, through laws permitting women to vote at the local level in those states, and again on the West Coast in the Washington Territory in the mid-1880s (although this would not become established by the state of Washington until 1910). Before the turn of the century, the states of Wyoming and Colorado were soon joined by the states of Idaho and Utah in upholding the voting rights of women. What began in the Rocky Mountain West soon gained momentum in both directions, and within a generation, women had finally won the hard struggle to guarantee their voting rights at the federal level.

As a response to the turmoil of the past few years, "Back to Normalcy" was coined as the defining phrase of the Campaign of 1920; large men and even larger ideas were now a thing of the recent past. Wilson, Roosevelt, William Jennings Bryan, and Charles Evans Hughes were, for various reasons, no longer available as candidates to the American public. Hughes's prominence in GOP politics quickly faded in spite of his nearly defeating the incumbent Wilson four years earlier in a very tight, narrowly decided election. Bryan had been stigmatized by three embarrassing losses and had become, on a personal level, too eccentric for mainstream politics. Wilson was actually interested in a third term, but his broken health and recent inability to accomplish his foreign policy goals prevented him from mustering the energy and support. Finally, the age's defining figure, Theodore Roosevelt, who in running in 1912 had already through his actions established his position on the "no third term" tradition, had unexpectedly passed away in 1919. Had Roosevelt lived, he would probably have again been the Republican candidate, as there was simply no one else in either party who could exceed him; and had Wilson not suffered his stroke, he would have been in a good position to run for reelection as well—a lost scenario wherein the two great progressives would have met in battle again, this time without a third alternative (as in 1912 with President Taft), an alternate possibility that can only give students of politics and history pause. But with Roosevelt's death and the flagging of Wilson's health, along with the inexplicable political decline of Hughes and the dwindling of Bryan's base, the two parties were left without any major personality to drive their efforts forward. After two decades wherein the American electorate enjoyed a surplus of political giants, the Campaign of 1920 moved toward the acceptable, the safe, the ordinary.

As the campaign season approached, new leadership emerged in both parties. For the Republicans, the field was populated by any number of potential candidates, the more familiar names being Robert La Follette, Roosevelt's friend Hiram Johnson (governor of California and Roosevelt's Bull Moose running mate in 1912), and Nicholas Butler, who in 1912 had replaced Vice President James Sherman as President Taft's running mate upon Sherman's sudden passing. Among the many newer faces were Governor Frank Lowden of Illinois; Governor Calvin Coolidge of Massachusetts; Iowa's talented Herbert Hoover, who had risen to prominence due to his humanitarian efforts in Europe during and after the war; General Leonard Wood, a distinguished military figure, physician, and another close friend of Roosevelt's who had served as governor general of the Philippines as well as military governor of Cuba; Pennsylvania governor William C. Sproul; and Warren G. Harding, who had first received notice in the convention of 1916, and who was favorably regarded by Roosevelt.

As the convention opened, three candidates emerged as the principal competitors: Wood, who won 287 delegates on the first ballot; Lowden, who took 211 delegates on that round; and Johnson, who trailed in third with 133. Sproul led the rest of the field with 84 delegates, with Butler taking 69 and Harding a distant sixth place with 65 first-ballot delegates. The second ballot tightened the race at the top between Wood and Lowden, the former improving his position to 289, the latter following close with 259. Johnson gained 13 votes to remain a distant third, with every other candidate losing votes; thus it now appeared that a two-man race between General Wood and Governor Lowden was under way. Indeed, this trend persisted, with both candidates slowly gaining votes on each ballot while other challengers faded; Wood peaked with 314 on the fourth ballot, only to be surpassed by Lowden on the fifth, who led 303 to 299, Wood having lost 15 votes. But Lowden could not take advantage of this momentum; on the sixth ballot, the candidates each won 311 votes, and they exchanged leads on the following two ballots. Johnson remained a distant third through seven ballots, and on the fifth ballot, Harding suddenly moved into fourth place after having lost ground on the second through the fourth ballots, then jumping past Johnson to move into third on the seventh ballot and gaining further ground on the eighth. With no candidate able to make a significant move upward, it became evident that the convention was moving toward a deadlock.

With the convention in recess, the four leading candidates, Lowden, Wood, Harding, and Johnson, worked hard off the floor to win new delegates. Johnson, now in fourth, was approached as a possible vice presidential candidate, but he expressed no interest in again running for that position. Between the fifth and sixth ballots, the real work of nominating a candidate had quietly shifted behind the scenes. Gathering in a "smoke-filled room" that had been rented by the party chairman, Will Hays, the backroom bargaining began, with the influential senator from Massachusetts and devoted friend of Theodore Roosevelt, Henry Cabot Lodge, now supporting Harding as the only reasonable solution to the deadlock. While Lodge was a preeminent figure at the time, it was Harry M. Daugherty, Ohio political boss and Harding's campaign manager, who did the most to propel Harding's ascent. Coming from Ohio, Harding might help the Republicans retake the Buckeye State, the one state in the Midwest that had eluded them over the past two elections against Wilson, thereby having enabled the Democrats to crack into the Republicans' vital northern and midwestern bloc. Harding was also perceived as a "cleaner" candidate, in the sense that he was not as closely associated with big money. This gave Harding the boost he needed, so that by the ninth ballot, he jumped from a distant third to a significant first-place lead, winning 347 delegates to 249 for Wood, while Lowden faded to 121. On the tenth ballot, Harding pulled away, winning 644 delegates and the nomination.

The convention then selected Governor Coolidge, a refreshing new face in the party who never received more than thirty-two votes for the presidential nomination, on the first round to run as Harding's vice presidential candidate. Lodge was also approached by some delegates to run as second on the ticket, a proposal that he dismissed without hesitation. Coolidge's appeal actually stemmed from his lack of insider credentials. It was clear that he was not connected to the convention's principal kingmakers, and he seemed to be a refreshing antidote to the Old Guard who had dominated the backroom negotiations. In a sense, Harding was like Coolidge in this regard, and he fell into the nomination largely due to the fact that the initial front-runners, Wood, Lowden, and Johnson, could not bridge their differences and unify behind a single standard-bearer. Thus the Harding-Coolidge ticket represented a new kind of presidential candidacy—not as connected as the old leadership, and not as monumental as the candidates that had dominated the political landscape since the 1890s. The "Back to Normalcy" slogan was Harding's, and it typifies not only the desire of the times but also attitudes within both parties: The invigorating days of progressivism were coming to a close, and in the aftermath of a terrible war, the nation was prepared to stop and take a long break from those tumultuous times, to withdraw from ambitious domestic programs as well as the trending movement toward the expansion of America's role abroad. Reflecting these attitudes, the GOP platform was decidedly more conservative than it had been in years, another signal that the momentum of progressivism had played out.

Recognizing the key role California played in Woodrow Wilson's 1916 presidential election victory, the Democratic Party held its convention in San Francisco in the latter part of June and early July. Lacking a true front-runner, the Democrats were in the same situation as their Republican rivals. There was one possible front-runner for the Democrats—President Wilson's son in-law, William G. McAdoo of California, a former senator who had also served for five years as Wilson's secretary of the treasury. McAdoo, however, hesitated to formerly announce his candidacy, as there was still doubt about his father-in-law's campaign intentions. Wilson's attorney general, A. Mitchell Palmer, was in the early going an active candidate, but his fixation on the "Red Menace" of Bolshevism was the only issue that he seemed passionate about, and it did not take him very far in the party. Other candidates whose names received some mention were, along with Wilson himself, William Jennings Bryan (who still commanded a small but committed following); incumbent vice president Thomas R. Marshall, who enjoyed some initial support but withdrew his name from consideration early in the process; New York's impressive governor Alfred E. Smith; Speaker of the House Champ Clark of Missouri, who had actually at one point been the front-runner for the Democratic nomination in 1912 before the ascent of Wilson; John W. Davis, the current ambassador to the Court of St. James; New Jersey governor Edward I. Edwards; Senator Robert Latham Owen of Oklahoma; Senator Carter Glass of Virginia (who had succeeded McAdoo as Wilson's treasury secretary, leaving that office for the Senate in early 1920); and a popular two-term former governor from Ohio, James M. Cox. When counting the numerous also-rans and favorite sons, all told, twenty-three candidates would receive some delegate votes at the Democratic convention.

After one ballot, McAdoo won the support of 266 delegates, making him the slim front-runner, followed by Palmer with 256 votes, Cox with 134, and Smith holding 109 delegates. After just one ballot, President Wilson made it known through back channels that he would be available to step forward and break what already appeared to be a deadlocked convention; but not every delegate was convinced, many thinking that the nomination would eventually go to McAdoo or one of the other leaders—possibly Cox, who was showing more appeal among the delegates than initially expected. Wilson's name remained officially out of the running, but unofficially, the delegates were fully aware of the possibility of a last-minute draft for the president. As the balloting continued, the candidates pulled away from the pack: McAdoo, who held and increased his lead through six ballots; Palmer; and Cox, who remained a distant third to McAdoo but remained viable. McAdoo led through eleven ballots, but on the twelfth, Cox managed to pull ahead, winning the support of 404 delegates to McAdoo's 375, with Palmer receding far behind. There was little movement until the thirty-eighth ballot, when Palmer, realizing that his position was no longer tenable, withdrew from the contest; and with his delegates now in play, both Cox and McAdoo drew into a tighter race. By the forty-first ballot, Cox held 497 delegates, McAdoo 440, leading the latter's supporters to propose a recess to negotiate off the convention floor. But Cox's supporters, realizing the stratagem and aware of the power of the "smoke-filled room" and the advantage it would give to McAdoo, refused to accede to adjournment and, slugging out for two more ballots, managed to gain the majority needed to nominate their candidate. Having done so, McAdoo withdrew his name, and his delegates were released to Cox as a sign of party unity. Thus the campaign for the White House would entail a battle between two Ohioans, the third time that major party candidates from the same state would square off for the White House—the first being Lincoln against Douglas, both from Illinois, in 1860; and the second being Theodore Roosevelt against Alton Parker, both of New York, in 1904.

Notably, for the vice presidency, the delegates nominated Cox's preferred choice, a young, luminous, and rapidly emerging star within the party, President Wilson's assistant secretary of the navy, Franklin Delano Roosevelt of New York, who was also a cousin of the late Republican former president Theodore Roosevelt (Theodore Roosevelt had also served as assistant secretary of the navy under President McKinley). Franklin Roosevelt—who, in spite of disparate party affiliations, deliberately emulated his famous cousin, whom he once referred to as the greatest man he ever met—was supported by, among others, both Cox and Al Smith, the latter having become something of a mentor for young Franklin. Young Roosevelt had already made his own mark, for he was well known and highly regarded within the Wilson administration and among most of the delegates at the convention.

The Socialist Party was still the strongest minor party in spite of the anxieties of the times, nominating for a fifth run its most prominent figure, Eugene V. Debs, even though he had been imprisoned for violating the Espionage Act. With Debs in prison and unable to campaign, the job of stumping for the Socialist cause fell to his lawyer, Seymour Stedman. Other minor parties nominating candidates include the newly formed Farmer-Labor Party, which nominated Parley P. Christensen of Utah, and the Prohibition Party, still active and nominating Aaron S. Watkins from Ohio.

Among the issues under discussion during the campaign were the enforcement of Prohibition under the Volstead Act, continuation of progressive reforms on behalf of labor, government regulation of industry and transportation, the rising cost of living, conservation and reclamation of natural resources, the state of American farming, immigration, campaign funding, and the League of Nations. The debate over joining the League of Nations stood out as the principal single issue of 1920. Led by Cox and Franklin Roosevelt and motivated to fulfill the promise of Wilson's foreign policy efforts, the Democrats regarded the League as the paramount issue and placed it as the central plank of their platform. For the most part, Democrats were united behind the League, but Republicans remained divided. Harding felt pressure from both supporters and opponents of the League, and awkwardly he tried to steer a middle course. Cox attempted to make it his defining principle, and he attacked Harding for equivocating on the issue. Pro-League Republicans backed Harding in spite of his confused stance, but the party reiterated within the platform its position against the controversial Treaty of Versailles, praising the Senate for its opposition. Harding made clear his support for some type of international organization, but the League itself was implicitly rejected in the Republican platform.

The Harding campaign defined "Back to Normalcy" in terms that proposed significantly reducing government regulation of business. Throughout the campaign, Harding made use of the slogan "Less Government in business and more business in Government" to describe how his administration would reduce government regulation of the private sector and improve the efficiency of the federal government by adopting successful business practices. Significantly, Harding largely conducted a front-porch campaign, along with making several phonograph recordings of his speeches for distribution to a much wider audience than otherwise possible. In one speech, Harding expressed a refrain that would typify the Republican's new approach, one that in all its elements poses a direct contrast to the legacy of Theodore Roosevelt: "America's present need is not heroics, but healing; not nostrums, but normalcy; not revolution, but restoration; not agitation, but adjustment; not surgery, but serenity; not the dramatic, but the dispassionate; not experiment, but equipoise; not submergence in internationality, but sustainment in triumphant nationality."

Even though the majority of Americans supported the progressive reforms of Theodore Roosevelt and Wilson, the Harding campaign made effective use of the growing distrust of government and the great reluctance of the American public to become involved in new "foreign entanglements." Equally important, the Republican Party attempted to blame the Red Scare on the failed foreign policies of the Wilson administration.

Significantly, the Harding campaign raised approximately $8 million, the largest amount in the history of presidential campaigns up to that point in time. To help Daugherty manage his campaign, Harding hired ad man Albert Lasker, who made use of modern advertising techniques to create a new image of Harding as a down-to-earth, ordinary American. Lasker distributed thousands of pictures of Harding and his wife to newspapers from coast to coast, and he hired Al Jolson, who was at that time the best-known entertainer in the United States, to compose a song, "Harding You're the Man for Us," to further publicize his candidate's image. Like Harding, Cox made a number of phonograph recordings as well, arguing on record, as it were, that Wilson's successful prosecution of World War I had in the end saved "civilization." In sharp contrast to the Republican campaign strategy, Cox and Roosevelt both campaigned extensively across the United States. On behalf of the Democrats' cause, Franklin Roosevelt delivered over a thousand speeches in thirty-two states, a feat reminiscent of his famous cousin.

In spite of their strenuous efforts on the stump, it was difficult for Cox and Roosevelt to counteract the kind of money that was backing Harding-Coolidge. In the successful tradition of Benjamin Harrison in 1888 and William McKinley in 1896 and 1900, Harding was also an effective campaigner from the front porch (leaving his home on only a few occasions to deliver a handful of speeches in major cities); through his speeches, he was able to persuade voters that the promise of normalcy was real, and that stability would be the consequence of a Republican victory. "Let's be done with wiggle and wobble," Harding wrote, indicating that with a GOP victory, the country would be stabilized in the coming administration. The press liked him, and he cut a dignified figure, attracting large numbers to his front-porch events. In addressing the issues, Harding preferred restraint, letting the enthusiastic Democrats assert large and unrealistic claims while he and Coolidge exhibited sober forbearance. Coolidge, who would become famous for his laconic demeanor, was particularly effective in this regard, and he criticized the Democrats Cox and Roosevelt for conducting a campaign that became "coarser and coarser" and "wilder and wilder." The alternative that the Republicans offered was one of calm and fixity, and they succeeded in depicting the Democrats as offering more turmoil and instability. Roosevelt was, by contrast, a vigorous campaigner, proudly pointing out during his extensive travels that Cox was not prone to hiding behind the comforts of the front porch, away from the people and the political debates. For his part, Cox reaffirmed the principles of progressivism and claimed that the Republicans were promising not stability or normalcy, but instead reactionary retreat from the positive reforms that the Democrats had delivered to all Americans.

But as the election approached, it became clear to many observers that the Republican team, in spite of the many talents of the Democrats, was better positioned, more abundantly funded, and tactically sharper. The situation for the Democrats was not helped by the breaking of a scandal involving allegations about Franklin Roosevelt. By and large, Roosevelt's record as assistant secretary of the navy was solid, winning him widespread respect; however, to weaken the Democratic ticket, members of the Republican National Committee released a letter from a Providence, Rhode Island, publisher, John Rathon, alleging that Roosevelt had lied before a congressional investigating committee when he denied removing the files of a man convicted of a morals charge during his service in the navy. The dispute involved what was then called the Newport Scandal, a sting conducted by the navy that was aimed at identifying homosexual sailors. Roosevelt vigorously denied the allegations and quickly filed libel suits against Rathon and his *Providence Journal* along with officials in the Republican National Committee. However, the controversy embarrassed the campaign and, at the time, was seen as a potential impediment to Roosevelt's continued political fortunes. In the end, this imbroglio proved to be of almost no significance to young Roosevelt, given the grave crisis that he, quite unknowingly at the time, was about to face in his personal life shortly after the end of the campaign.

On Election Day, the Harding-Coolidge campaign enjoyed what was then the biggest popular-vote landslide in American history, winning over 16,000,000 votes (an astonishing 60.3%, at that time far and away the highest percentage ever accumulated by a presidential ticket), 5,000,000 more than the total that President Wilson had gained for victory in the previous election. Cox-Roosevelt managed slightly over 9,100,000 votes (about 34%), which was actually slightly higher than Wilson's popular total won in 1916. Looking at the popular vote alone, Harding's margin of victory amounted to a stunning 26 percent, which still remains the highest margin of victory in the history of presidential elections. On the whole, in spite of the inclusion of women voters nationwide within the electorate, the Democrats made, in effect, absolutely no gains from their close but successful election four years earlier, while the Republicans had nearly doubled their support. From his prison cell, Debs won 913,000 votes, the best showing yet for the Socialists, a remarkable feat given Debs's situation and the onset of the Red Scare. The Farmer-Labor Party managed just over 260,000 votes. For the first time in six consecutive elections, the Prohibition Party dipped below 200,000 votes, winning just under 190,000, its worst showing since 1896. But party members could take some solace in the passage of the Eighteenth Amendment.

In the Electoral College, Harding-Coolidge won 404 electoral votes to 127 for Cox-Roosevelt, sweeping the Northeast, the Midwest, and the West, and even cracking into the Democrats' southern bloc by taking Tennessee for the first time since 1868, during the early years of Reconstruction. Harding clobbered Cox in their common home state of Ohio and demolished the Democrats in Roosevelt's home state of New York. Aside from Tennessee, the Democrats held their southern bloc (including Texas here); but it was a decisive retreat from Wilson's electoral victory four years earlier, made possible by a solid southern-western combination.

Thus Warren G. Harding decisively became the twenty-ninth president of the United States. But in two years, Harding would die suddenly, and his vice president, the taciturn Calvin Coolidge, would be inaugurated as the thirtieth president, only to find that in the pursuit of "normalcy," he would lead the nation through an era of rapid economic and cultural change in American history that would come to be known as the Roaring Twenties.

Additional Resources

Bagby, Wesley. *The Road to Normalcy: The Presidential Campaign and Election of 1920*. Baltimore: Johns Hopkins Press, 1962.

Cebula, James E. *James M. Cox: Journalist and Politician*. New York: Garland, 1985.

McCoy, Donald. "1920." In Arthur M. Schlesinger, Fred L. Israel, and David J. Frent, eds. *Running for President: The Candidates and Their Images*. Vol. 2. New York: Simon & Schuster, 1994.

McCoy, Donald R. "Election of 1920." In Arthur M. Schlesinger, Fred Israel, and William P. Hansen, eds. *History of American Presidential Elections, 1789–1968*. Vol. 2. New York: Chelsea House, 1985.

Morello, John A. *Selling the President, 1920: Albert D. Lasker, Advertising, and the Election of Warren G. Harding*. Westport, CT: Praeger, 2001.

Campaign of 1924

The election of 1920 threw the Democratic Party back on its heels. After eight years under the largely successful leadership of the progressive administration of President Woodrow Wilson, the party's fortunes took a sudden turn back toward the minority status that it had come to know, for the most part, in presidential politics since the Civil War. After the Harding landslide, the Democrats were again reminded that the White House had become Republican turf, for only two Democrats—Wilson and Grover Cleveland—had taken up occupancy there since 1861; or in other words, in the sixty years between the inauguration of Abraham Lincoln and the election of Harding, the Democrats held the presidency for only sixteen of those years, and they did so without winning a majority of the popular vote. In the election of 1920, those sixteen years now appeared more than ever to be an aberration from the trend.

Nonetheless, in the midterm elections of 1922, the Democrats, as is ordinarily the case during midterms, recovered, regaining eighty seats in Congress. This was in part due to a reaction to an economic downturn, and partly a predictable reoccurrence of a patterned tendency in midterm elections for a party to regain lost ground. But it was also in part due to continued divisions between progressives and conservatives within the Republican Party itself, and these divisions were again weakening party unity and frustrating coherent leadership. Recapturing eighty seats exceeds the expected midterm gains; thus the Democrats had reason to be optimistic going into the campaign season of 1924. The midterm elections also signaled important trends regarding regional loyalties. Democrats showed strength in traditional Republican areas, particularly the Northeast, where increased votes for Democrats were observed in the larger cities. Additionally, the infamous Teapot Dome bribery scandal (which involved illegalities surrounding the improper use of the federal oil reserves at Teapot Dome, Wyoming, and Elk Hills, California) associated with the Harding administration came to light, threatening to compromise Republican efforts at holding the White House. At the time, Teapot Dome was regarded as the most damaging scandal in the history of presidential administrations, and while President Harding himself seemed to be uninvolved, the public felt outraged and were unlikely to disassociate the president from the corruption within his administration. The scandal, as investigations revealed, was not confined to Republicans alone, as some prominent Democrats were also implicated. But a far sadder event intervened, for in August 1923, President Harding passed away after only two years and five months in office, leaving his vice president, Calvin Coolidge, as his heir to the office of the presidency, an unexpected and sobering development that deflated the effect of the scandal in the upcoming election year. Furthermore, as the economy recovered from the downturn that had been experienced in the early part of the decade, the reputation of the administration's policies and overall leadership rebounded.

In mid-June of the election year 1924, Republicans convened in Cleveland, and as expected, President Coolidge was easily nominated to run for a full term. Coolidge, known for his laconic manner and respected for his honesty and work ethic, had gained a reputation as a liberal while serving as governor of Massachusetts before his election to the vice presidency in 1920. However, other liberal/progressive Republicans were not persuaded by his credentials. In fact, Coolidge was a firm advocate of limited government and free markets, a preference that in today's political culture would place him in the fiscal conservative camp. For a short time, the progressive Republican Hiram Johnson, former running mate of Theodore Roosevelt on the 1912 Progressive (Bull Moose) ticket and current senator from California, appeared once again as a challenger; and the party's other famous progressive, Senator Robert La Follette of Wisconsin, was preparing to bolt and run under the Progressive banner. Both Hiram and La Follette sharply criticized the pro-business policies of the Harding administration and, by extension, the Coolidge administration. Coolidge and his supporters thus worked to win more liberal Republicans to his side. To the surprise of many political observers, Coolidge defeated Johnson in numerous primaries leading up to the convention, leaving little doubt as to the incumbent president's political strength. To the more conservative leadership, Coolidge also seemed to raise questions; but after the president's primary showing, it was evident that no candidate from either wing of the party held the promise of winning in November other than Coolidge.

But Coolidge, to solidify his position, still needed to underplay the more liberal aspects of his thinking so as to appease the Old Guard conservatives without chasing too many progressives away from the party. The memories of 1912 were still strong; hence Coolidge sought to reach out to both wings, and apparently with a high degree of success—he managed to deflect Johnson's primary season challenge, a prelude to his convincing nomination on the convention's first ballot, winning 1,065 votes to LaFollette's 34 and Johnson's 10. This can be explained in part as a consequence of the advantage of incumbency, and also in part to Coolidge's own skill in assuming the presidency without difficulty and acquitting himself as a capable leader—in the eyes of many, more capable than the late President Harding. It may also be viewed as evidence that the Republican Party, by unequivocally rejecting both Johnson and La Follette, was shifting still further away from the progressive legacy that had been built by Theodore Roosevelt.

The Republican platform of that year, reflecting a less progressive tone, applauded the decision of the Republican Congress to significantly decrease taxes and federal expenditures, reaffirmed Republican support of high protective tariffs to protect American business and industry from foreign competition, and, significantly, opposed federal crop subsidies. However, it included more moderate-to-liberal positions as well, endorsing the eight-hour workday, advocating restrictions on child labor, and proposing a federal anti-lynching law. Above all, the platform described Coolidge as a "practical idealist," a phrase that reveals much about the new attitude of the party that once held the allegiance of some of the more important figures in the progressive movement.

The convention selected Charles Dawes of Illinois, the dramatic and provocative orator and former budget director—stylistically, the "anti-Coolidge"—to balance the ticket. For a time, a number of candidates were suggested, including Herbert Hoover, the party's most exciting prospect, who was at that time viewed by some as too invaluable to Coolidge's cabinet as secretary of commerce to be shifted to the vice presidency, and viewed by others as potentially capable of overshadowing his own president, and thus better kept, at least for the moment, from the limelight of a presidential campaign. Frank Lowden, the former governor of Illinois who was a serious candidate (he held brief leads in the balloting for president in 1920, winning the most delegates on two of the ten ballots before the nomination of Harding) for the GOP nomination four years earlier, was also in the running and actually led the field after one ballot. Congressman Theodore Burton of Ohio and Senator William S. Kenyon of Iowa were also considered and received some support, but on the third ballot, Dawes was nominated by winning 682 delegates, with Hoover in second, commanding 234 delegates.

Coolidge-Dawes, the former from Massachusetts and the latter from Illinois, reflected Republican regional strongholds of the Northeast and the Midwest. The delegates also saw Dawes as a partisan lance wielder, on the attack while the ever-reticent Coolidge would coolly remain aloof and above it all. This tactic was a forerunner of a similar approach in later campaigns: choosing a hard-nosed hatchet man, such as Dawes, Richard Nixon (1952 and 1956), or Bob Dole (1976) for the bottom of the ticket to deflect political heat away from the more mellow top half—Coolidge, Dwight Eisenhower, and Gerald Ford, respectively. Indeed, "Keep Cool with Coolidge" was the Republicans' defining slogan, "Silent Cal" himself their central and defining image.

Democrats, while hopeful of recapturing the White House, experienced the widest field of candidates in the history of American presidential campaigns to that point. The Democrats entered their convention divided along numerous lines: conservative versus progressive, pro-Prohibition (known as the "drys") versus anti-Prohibition (the "wets"), urban versus rural, Protestant versus Catholic (two candidates at the convention were Roman Catholics), and pro-Catholic/anti-Ku Klux Klan versus anti-Catholic/ pro-Klan. Significantly, the Klan, after nearly dying out, experienced a resurgence in the postwar period that was marked by the Red Scare, xenophobia, anti-Semitism, anti-Catholicism in some parts of the country, and, as one would expect, increased racism throughout the country. Some have blamed the Klan's comeback, at least in part, on the release of D. W. Griffith's racist 1915 film, *Birth of a Nation*, an event that would prove to be a culturally significant moment, and not for the better. For whatever reasons, the Klan now enjoyed more political influence than it had at any point since the post-Reconstruction period, and it even held sway over large segments within the political mainstream, particularly among Southern Democrats, but certainly not exclusively, as the Klan was also increasingly popular in parts of the Midwest and the West. Indeed, the Klan had become so influential that it would play a principal part in the direction of the convention, a most unwelcome part for many delegates representing the more liberal and ethnically diverse Northeast, but one that was encouraged among Southern delegates. Owing to the Klan's visible role at the convention's proceedings—and more particularly, to a large and well-publicized Klan rally that occurred within the vicinity of the convention hall and in which several convention delegates participated—the 1924 Democratic Convention has come to be known as the "Klanbake" convention. Additionally, the issue of Prohibition—which was largely divided along sectional lines, with the Northeastern Democrats (the wets) favoring repeal of Prohibition, and Southern and Western Democrats tending to be dry—divided the party and compromised unity. Similarly, Northeastern Democrats tended to be liberal, either pro-Catholic or tolerant of Catholics, and anti-Klan, while the Klan held strong support in the South and parts of the Midwest. These divisions fueled considerable tension throughout the convention, thus weakening any chance the Democrats might have had in challenging the Coolidge-Dawes ticket.

In the months prior to the convention, the front-runners in this highly populated field were former secretary of the treasury William G. McAdoo of California; Governor Al Smith of New York; and John Davis of West Virginia, a former diplomat and member of the House of Representatives. McAdoo, a serious candidate at the 1920 convention who was also former president Wilson's son-in-law, was a "dry" who appealed to Southern delegates and especially to the Klan faction, largely due to his opposition to a proposed anti-Klan platform plank (although McAdoo himself was not a Klan member). The plank, which was proposed by Forney Johnston, an anti-Klan delegate from Alabama, called for the party to rebuke the Klan for its practice of engaging in intimidation and violence. It was this proposal that sparked the Klanbake rally in proximity to the convention venue, one that was marked by burning crosses, inflammatory speeches against African Americans and Catholics, and effigies of Al Smith put to the torch. Governor Smith, a Roman Catholic who had received some minor support for the nomination in 1920 and who was particularly popular with the liberal wing of the party, was well known as an enemy of the Klan, a "wet" critic of Prohibition, and a candidate that would, it was hoped, help to raise interest among African American voters (Smith was also know for his mentoring friendship with Franklin Roosevelt, the party's 1920 candidate for the vice presidency). Davis was a former ambassador to Britain; a severe, frequent, and explicit critic of the Klan; and, like McAdoo and Smith, a candidate who had been in play for nomination in the previous convention. Joining these front-runners, among many others, were notably Alabama's Senator Oscar Underwood, Indiana's Governor Samuel Ralston, and Senator Thomas Walsh of Montana. James M. Cox, who received the party's nomination in 1920, was also in the running; but he was not considered to be among the convention favorites. In all, fifty-eight individuals received at least one vote at the convention, a cohort that included in its numbers a large portion who, such as the popular satirist Will Rogers, were not really considered as serious choices but were nonetheless mentioned as symbolic gestures.

Nonetheless, the list included numerous substantive candidates—even Franklin Roosevelt, who now quite sadly suffered debilitating paralysis as a result of having contracted polio, received two votes at the convention. Roosevelt had been Cox's running mate in 1920, and had it not been for his tragic illness, he might have been a strong contender for the top of the ticket in 1924, perhaps the front-runner himself. Roosevelt's hour had not yet come, but he nonetheless was a visible and important presence at the 1924 convention in spite of his many struggles. But following the example of his famous cousin, Franklin Roosevelt was thoroughly irrepressible, and he exerted his influence at the convention, the state of his health notwithstanding. It was Roosevelt who nominated his friend Smith, whom he generously referred to as the "Happy Warrior" in an enthusiastic and rousingly memorable speech. The Happy Warrior, which could describe Roosevelt himself just as easily as it would define Smith, was a reference to the beloved poem by William Wordsworth, which opens with the following lines:

> Who is the happy Warrior? Who is he
> That every man in arms should wish to be?
> It is the generous Spirit, who, when brought
> Among the tasks of real life, hath wrought
> Upon the plan that pleased his boyish thought:
> Whose high endeavors are an inward light
> That makes the path before him always bright

Wordsworth's verse was meant to encapsulate those qualities most admired of Smith, and because of his recitation of this verse in Smith's honor, Roosevelt is usually given credit for assigning this nickname to his friend and mentor; but it has also been traced to Judge Joseph M. K. Proskauer, who had earlier managed Smith's gubernatorial campaign in 1920, and who, as the story goes, incorporated the Wordsworth phrase into one of Smith's own speeches. Regardless of its original source, Roosevelt turned the phrase into one of the convention's more inspiring moments. From this point, the nickname took hold, and throughout his political career, Smith was associated with the image of the Happy Warrior, an image that, as stated above, could be applied to Roosevelt with equal accuracy, and that would also later be inherited by another great optimist of the political arena, Hubert Humphrey.

From the beginning, it seemed that the convention, based on the early balloting, would select McAdoo. He held a substantial lead on the first ballot, winning 431 delegates, with Smith a distant second, supported by 241. Cox, Davis, and Underwood all finished far back, and no other candidate received more than 59 first-ballot votes (Cox). As the convention progressed, McAdoo and Smith emerged as the main rivals. Smith was a rallying point for the Catholic bloc, while the Protestant McAdoo, as one would expect, held the Protestant delegates. Smith supporters were mainly urban and Northeastern and consisted of numerous ethnic groups, while McAdoo enjoyed influence over rural and small-town delegates, primarily in the South. McAdoo was favored by the Klan delegates, and as one would expect, the Catholic Smith was vilified by them. McAdoo's early success seemed to indicate a clear preference from the floor, but front-runner status can be weakened in such a large field, and as the balloting droned on without any end in sight, McAdoo was unable to muster enough delegates for the needed majority.

McAdoo kept the lead through most of the convention, peaking at 528 votes on the unprecedented seventieth ballot, an extraordinary number; but at this peak, he was still unable to gain the two-thirds majority, or 729 votes, needed to win the nomination. Smith did not fare any better, as his best showing was no higher than 368 votes, still far below McAdoo's best, although Smith did come within one vote of McAdoo on the ninety-ninth ballot. As the convention moved toward its staggering one-hundredth ballot, both wearied candidates reluctantly agreed to withdraw; but diehards, refusing to abandon their allegiances, boosted the Happy Warrior into first with 351 votes to McAdoo's 190 on a ballot that now placed Davis in second, winning 203 delegates, his highest number to that point. The most dead-locked, protracted convention in history appeared to be at an irresolvable impasse. Compromise candidates were floated, among them Governor Ralston, who, like McAdoo, was supported by the Klan, and who had begun to draw more interest in the latter ballots. But for personal reasons, Ralston withdrew his name as the convention wore on. The balloting had lurched along for such a long time with no end to it in sight that some delegates, due to depleted funds, had to quit the convention and return home.

However, things finally began to move. After the hundred-and-first ballot, Davis, the former ambassador, suddenly jumped into the lead, carrying 316 votes to 229 for Underwood, with Smith now fading to 121 delegates. The following ballot strengthened Davis's position at 415, Underwood moving up as well to win 307, and Senator Walsh (who, like Smith, was also a Roman Catholic and thus anathema to the Klan element at the convention) suddenly moving into third with 123. Finally, on the hundred-and-third ballot, the frazzled convention rejected McAdoo and Smith and selected Davis, nominating him by acclamation at the end of the longest nominating process in the history of national political conventions. Davis was clearly not the convention's preferred choice, but given no solution to the McAdoo-Smith deadlock, he emerged as the most reasonable compromise. Throughout the convention, Davis ran mostly in third place, slipping to fourth on a few ballots and only leading on the last two, and his nomination by acclamation seems to have been an act of acquiescence more than affirmation. But in the end, it was John W. Davis of West Virginia who now bore the standard for the Democratic Party.

For the vice presidency, the convention selected Charles W. Bryan, the brother of William Jennings Bryan, the Great Commoner still holding some influence within the party and the abiding devotion of its more progressive wing. Thus the ticket consisted of a career public servant with diverse experience (having served not only as ambassador to the Court of St. James but also as solicitor general as well as a member of the House of Representatives), a Wall Street lawyer who was viewed by many as a moderate-to-conservative candidate; and Bryan, who, like his more famous brother, was regarded by most within the party as a radical, thus causing some displeasure within the leadership. But the top of the ticket is what matters; and in Davis, the Democrats chose a candidate who to some appeared more conservative than his Republican counterpart, Vice President Coolidge. It should be noted that even though the Democratic convention was infected with racism and religious bigotry, it is also noteworthy for being the first time in American history that a major party considered a woman for the vice presidency (the first woman to receive a vice presidential nomination from any party was Marietta Stow in 1884, for what was called the National Equal Rights Party). Lena Springs, originally from Tennessee and a delegate from South Carolina, a scholar at North Carolina's Queens College, an activist for women's rights, and a well-known delegate at the convention, was nominated to run with Davis. Springs received some support from the floor, but not enough to make anything more than a symbolic run at the office.

The Democratic platform sharply criticized widespread corruption within the Harding administration. The platform also opposed protective tariffs imposed by the Republican Congress and the lowering of income tax rates on the wealthy. As to the controversy surrounding the Klan's influence at the convention, the delegates, as stated above, following McAdoo's leadership on the issue, rejected the platform plank proposed by liberal Democrats that would have formally, explicitly censured the Klan. William Jennings Bryan, still in many ways the titular leader of the party, opposed the Klan in principle but argued against directly censuring the Klan by name, fearing that such an action might drive a further wedge between the liberal and conservative wings of the Democratic Party. In the end, the party settled on compromise language that affirmed that Democrats "insist at all times upon obedience to the orderly processes of the law and deplore and condemn any effort to arouse religious or racial dissension."

Meanwhile, Robert La Follette broke from the Republican Party, becoming the latest nominee of the Progressive Party that had been founded by former president Theodore Roosevelt twelve years earlier. La Follette drew support from the Socialist Party as well, along with disenchanted progressives from both the Republican and Democratic parties, various farming and labor associations, and a variety of progressive and radical groups. For the vice presidency, the Progressive Party nominated a renegade Democrat, Montana's Senator Burton L. Wheeler. The Prohibition Party returned with another candidate, Herman P. Farris of Missouri, and it was joined by two other minor parties—the American Party; and, for the first time in a presidential campaign, an officially nominated candidate from the Communist Party, William Z. Foster. But the Progressive Party commanded the most attention among the minor parties. La Follette, who was a severe critic of the two establishment parties and viewed them as equally tied to monied interests, was an appealing candidate to a number of disenchanted and disaffected citizens. As such, his candidacy could cause the same kind of problems for either party as Theodore Roosevelt's schismatic campaign had for the Republicans in 1912. As one would expect, the Progressive platform called for stricter enforcement of anti-trust laws, public ownership of railroads and water resources, higher estate taxes, government crop price supports, a constitutional amendment to prohibit child labor, and a number of other progressive proposals.

Technology was becoming increasingly evident in political campaigning, and the presidential contest of 1924 was certainly influenced by innovation. The use of radio as a tool for campaign coverage, as well as reporting election results, became widespread during this campaign season. The coverage constituted the first time the American people had the opportunity to listen in on the national political conventions. During the campaign, Coolidge and Davis made frequent radio appearances. And in further use of the latest technology, a group of Coolidge supporters conducted a cross-country automobile tour to promote their man, caravanning from Vermont (Coolidge's home state) to California from early September into the first week of November, ending just before the election. Traveling to around three hundred cities and towns, the bicoastal tour would stop for boisterous rallies highlighted by speeches from local dignitaries on behalf of the GOP ticket; and aging Civil War veterans who had actually voted for Abraham Lincoln were called upon to sign a movable guest roster, thus drawing the direct connection between Silent Cal and the Great Emancipator.

Not surprisingly, the Republican Party and Coolidge ran a careful campaign that highlighted the strong national economy and Coolidge's experience as president as well as a former governor. Coolidge's laconic style proved to be an asset in the end, as "Silent Cal" measured his comments well. As was his custom, Coolidge was careful not to engage in any mudslinging, kept his remarks to the issues, and upheld his reputation for concise speech. Davis was a dignified candidate and, like Coolidge, well regarded as a man of integrity, but he was not viewed as inspired or inspiring; even within his own party, his campaign appeared bland. Perhaps the most notable aspect of his campaign was his eagerness, now that the campaign was clear of the convention, to openly face down the Klan, but it was not enough when running against a president who was at that moment regarded as largely successful. That perception was reinforced by an economic boom that was currently under way, a factor that typically makes incumbents virtually invulnerable to even the most compelling challenger.

Without a unifying theme or defining slogan, the Democrats were unable to sustain a credible challenge against the solid Coolidge. La Follette only added to their troubles, drawing more votes away from them than from the Republicans (a reversal of 1912) and even showing better than the Democrats in twelve states on Election Day, all in the West or the Midwest.

On Election Day, the president won the popular vote by a firm majority, taking over 15,700,000 votes (54%), which converted to 382 votes in the Electoral College. Davis won just under 8,400,000 (around 29%), a margin of victory for Coolidge of 25 percent, just shy of the record set by Harding four years earlier. Coolidge swept the northeastern and western states (not counting Texas, which in 1924 was still more properly considered as within the Southern bloc; and Oklahoma, which can be characterized, as Texas is now, as both southern and western) and won every state in the Midwest except Wisconsin, which rejected both major parties and went with native son La Follette, giving him 13 votes in the Electoral College. Davis won the Southern bloc, where he enjoyed huge majorities (e.g., an astonishing 96% in South Carolina, a state that in recent years put up numbers ranging between 93% and 96% for Democrats Alton Parker, William Jennings Bryan, Woodrow Wilson, and James Cox, and where only 1,100 voters cast their ballots for Coolidge in 1924; 89% in Mississippi; 76% in Louisiana; and 74% in Texas and Georgia) but could not gain a single electoral vote beyond the South (other than Oklahoma, where he did manage to win with a plurality), finishing with a national tally just under 8,400,000 (just slightly below 29%, the worst showing for a Democratic candidate in history and historically the second worst for a candidate from one of the two major parties, behind only Republican incumbent President William Howard Taft, with 23%, in 1912) among the popular votes for a total of 136 electoral votes. Davis's feeble showing in the West negated his strength in the South: in North Dakota, for example, only 7 percent of the electorate supported him; while California, which had been so evenly divided between the two major parties in the recent past, barely gave Davis 8 percent, the state of Washington scarcely over 10 percent, South Dakota 13 percent, and Idaho, Montana, and Wyoming around 16–19 percent. Davis's best showing in the West was in New Mexico, where he managed to win the easternmost counties (nearer to Texas) and finished with 43 percent of the popular vote statewide, but he still well short of Coolidge by 5 percentage points. Davis also suffered huge losses in the Midwest, gaining only 6 percent in Minnesota (his worst showing in any state—and if you combine Minnesota and North Dakota, two bordering states in which he won less than 7% of the vote, Davis's popular vote total in those two states was around 70,000), 8 percent in Wisconsin (where La Follette beat Coolidge as well), 13 percent in Michigan, and 16 percent in Iowa. Following the pattern set in Harding's victory in 1920, in most western states, Davis failed to win even one county. La Follette's 13 electoral votes were accompanied by nearly 5,000,000 popular votes, or 16 percent, which in terms of percentage is an impressive figure for a third-party candidate (exceeded only by former presidents who had returned to challenge the field, viz., Theodore Roosevelt's 27% in the 1912 Bull Moose campaign and Millard Fillmore's 21% in 1856, and not counting the splintered four-way **Campaigns of 1824 and 1860**).

The landslide, although not as impressive as Harding's in 1920, was just as complete. Coolidge ran an effortless campaign, steadily keeping his cool while Democrats undermined their campaign with internal division, the odor of burned crosses, and, eventually, disinterest. Upon his election to a second term, Silent Cal would continue on as the leading American political figure of the Roaring Twenties.

Additional Resources

Burner, David. "Election of 1924." In Arthur M. Schlesinger, Fred Israel, and William P. Hansen, eds. *History of American Presidential Elections, 1789–1968.* Vol. 2. New York: Chelsea House, 1985.

Burner, David. "1924." In Arthur M. Schlesinger, Fred L. Israel, and David J. Frent, eds. *Running for President: The Candidates and Their Images.* Vol. 2. New York: Simon & Schuster, 1994.

Ferrell, Robert H. *The Presidency of Calvin Coolidge.* Lawrence: University Press of Kansas, 1998.

Krug, Larry L. *The 1924 Coolidge-Dawes Lincoln Tour.* New York: Schiffer Publishing, 2007.

Noggle, Burl. *Teapot Dome: Oil and Politics in the 1920s.* Baton Rouge: Louisiana State University Press, 1962.

Ranson, Edward. *The American Presidential Election of 1924: A Study of Calvin Coolidge.* Lewiston, NY: Edwin Mellen Press, 2008.

Campaign of 1928

In 1928, Democratic governor Al Smith of New York became the first Roman Catholic in American history nominated by a major political party to run for president of the United States. Smith was a progressive Democrat, advocating reformist social policies, economic programs favorable to labor, federal control of the power industry, and the repeal of Prohibition. Smith's progressive bent was both alike and dissimilar to the legacy of William Jennings Bryan, the Great Commoner. Smith, who lacked a college education and who spoke with the accent of a New York workingman, was representative of common folk, much like Bryan, the archetypal prairie politician. But in an important contrast to Bryan, Smith's reforms spoke to the immigrant and Catholic citizens of the industrial and urban Northeast, whereas Bryan's populism was spun from the more traditional, agrarian, Protestant attitudes of the South and the more rural areas of the Midwest and the West. But Bryan's influence had been fading, and Smith, like other New York governors before and since, had emerged as the principal leader in the party in the aftermath of the disastrous **Campaign of 1924**.

Smith would face Republican candidate Herbert Hoover, an engineer, humanitarian, and expert administrator for both Democrats (under Wilson) and Republicans (under Harding and Coolidge) alike, and one of the most capable men of his time. Hoover, in some ways, was a marked contrast to Smith: a Quaker from rural Iowa, educated as an engineer at Stanford, a supporter of Prohibition, and a firm adherent to the principles of government frugality; but in other ways, he was like Smith in that he was a thoroughly self-made man who had combined real talent with discipline and integrity to rise to the top of his calling, public service. Hoover and Smith held other things in common as well: Both men were genuinely dedicated to principles of honest service, and both had earned their reputations as solid and trustworthy statesmen. Furthermore, the two men also held in common the angularity, compared to predominant social norms, of their religious beliefs. Although they were important elements in helping to shape, along with so many other groups, an exceedingly heterogeneous American society and culture, both Quakers and Catholics were nonetheless still very rare breeds of cat at the highest level of national politics. Catholics might pull considerable weight in state and local politics in places like New York and Massachusetts, and particularly in the urbanized areas of the Northeast and the Midwest; but presidential politics at the national level was still a game largely enjoyed by Protestants and one that, as the previous campaign in 1924 once again proved, did not welcome Catholics. The same could also be said of Quakers, who were never until now players in the presidential hunt. (Curiously, the only other time a Roman Catholic Democrat would run for president as a major party's nominee, in that case John F. Kennedy, would be coincidentally against another Republican from a Quaker background, Richard M. Nixon—thirty-two years after the Hoover-Smith contest.) It might well be said that together, these two presidential candidates (and Kennedy and Nixon after them) embodied the meaning of the First Amendment's protection of religious liberty.

The Republican National Convention in Kansas City was uneventful. With President Coolidge refusing to seek a second term in spite of his popularity and efforts by some of his supporters to initiate a "draft Coolidge" movement, Hoover easily emerged as the clear front-runner long before the convention convened. Hoover had drawn national attention since the convention of 1920 and had already been considered the future of the party. Thus Hoover effortlessly polled 837 delegates on the first ballot to 247 for the rest of the field of eight—Frank Lowden, the former governor of Illinois who had been considered as a candidate in 1920, and Charles Curtis, Senate majority leader from Kansas, leading the also-rans with 74 and 64 votes, respectively. For the vice presidency, the party tapped Curtis with virtually no contest.

The Republicans carried into the campaign a gleaming record of four years of unprecedented prosperity under Coolidge. That said, there were signs of trouble in some sectors of the economy, especially in agriculture, where farmers were experiencing significant economic stress. Looking back, the problems of American farms prefigured things to come; but in 1928, most Americans were swept up in the tide of economic growth and vitality, and this greatly fueled Hoover's campaign. "Who but Hoover?" was the rallying slogan, and indeed, given the Republicans' history of dominating the White House since the Civil War and the general mood of the country, it would be hard to imagine Hoover falling short. His campaign was nearly flawless. As Coolidge had before him, Hoover managed to minimize controversial issues, and he projected a statesmanlike image of competence and nonpartisan expertise that made him appear irreproachable. His record of public service, easy for all to see, was far more impressive than either of his two most recent Republican predecessors—or for that matter, any of the candidates nominated by either party in the past two elections, all of whom seemed to pale in comparison to Hoover. Even Wilson, whose image had been somewhat tarnished by disappointment over the war and its aftermath, seemed to some critics at that time to be less capable than Hoover.

In Houston, the Democrats mirrored the Republicans, nominating Governor Smith on the first ballot; and for the third time (running back to the convention of 1916), Smith was nominated by his close friend and protégé Franklin Roosevelt, who, as he had in 1924, again delighted in referring to his candidate as the Wordsworthian "Happy Warrior." In marked contrast to the seemingly interminable balloting at the deadlocked 1924 convention, at this convention, Smith won 849 delegates to 379 scattered among a field of 13 also-rans (Tennessee's Cordell Hull leading this group with a meager 71 votes). Joseph T. Robinson of Arkansas was selected on the first ballot to run for the vice presidency without any significant challenge. Smith was a colorful, able, and engaging candidate, but he faced a nearly insurmountable task: decades of Republican dominance in presidential politics; a strong economy that, at least on appearances, seemed to be primed for an even more prosperous future; a skilled and respected opponent in Hoover; and social prejudice against his religious affiliation.

Anti-Catholicism was again on the rise in American society and politics. The United States had already experienced waves of Know-Nothing anti-Catholic sentiment in the nineteenth century, and a new wave was swelling through American political culture in the 1920s. Set into motion by disenchantment with "foreign" influences owing to the rise of immigration and the social aftershocks of the Great War, and fueled by the reemergence of the Ku Klux Klan and other militant nativist groups, anti-Catholic prejudice climaxed as Smith accepted his party's standard for president. The new edition of anti-Catholicism that strengthened in the early 1920s was mixed with attitudes of racism that had been tinged by social Darwinism, making for an even more virulent strain. The Anglo-Nordic race was viewed as somehow inherently superior, a naturally more successful race that had, as it so happened, embraced Protestantism while "less desirable" ethnic groups clung to Catholicism and Judaism. To counter these attitudes, Robinson, a Southern Protestant and a "dry," was selected as Smith's running mate, in part to serve as a counterpoise in the hopes of easing the concerns harbored by the Protestant majority within the national electorate; but as it is a maxim of electoral politics that no one really votes for the vice presidency, Smith's Catholicism remained a central issue throughout, Robinson's faith being of no interest. Extremist groups like the Klan warned that a "vote for Al Smith [was] a vote for the Pope," and, given Smith's support of the repeal of Prohibition, the old chestnut, dating back to the 1880s, of "Rum, Romanism, and Rebellion" (one that actually had then backfired against its purveyors) was this time intentionally repackaged as "Rum, Romanism, and Ruin." Adding further insult, critics, connecting Smith's Catholicism to his "wet" attitudes but twisting them to indict the candidate's personal habits, asked, "Shall America Elect a Cocktail President?" "Al-coholic" Smith, according to his less restrained (and pun-induced) enemies, secretly planned to move the pope to Washington and annul Protestant marriages once in office. Such was the hysteria of the times in the minds of those who combined religious prejudice with xenophobia and racialism.

The South in particular harbored anti-Catholicism (although not every Southerner shared these views), and a great deal of propaganda was circulated claiming that the pope's designs on dominating American society were so strong that they would turn any Catholic politician (viz., Democratic candidate for president Al Smith) into a puppet of the Vatican. Anti-Semitism also increased. Embarrassingly, public figures such as Henry Ford advocated purging the country of unwelcome foreign influence, a prescription that included a dark suggestion to "put down the Jews." Predictably, the Klan combined its hatred of African Americans with bigotry against both Jews and Catholics, and the lynching of individuals from all three groups—African Americans, Jews, and Catholics—was not uncommon. Any adherents of non-Protestant religions and any members of ethnic groups other than Americans descended from northern Europeans were vulnerable to the attacks of extremist groups. Many of those who exhibited these bigoted attitudes were indeed on the social fringe, but enough individuals in both the mainstream of society and the political leadership of both parties held similar prejudices, enough to severely impair Smith's efforts. In the *Atlantic Monthly*, for instance, an invited open letter questioned the compatibility of Catholic theology and the Canon Law of the Catholic Church with the principles of the U.S. Constitution, and Smith's alleged subservience to papal leadership was a common refrain. In the *Christian Century*, a Protestant (nondenominational) journal, Smith's religion was described as "an alien culture, a Medieval Latin mentality, of an undemocratic hierarchy."

Smith was at a loss as to how to respond to all of this. At one point, upon being asked how he would apply papal decrees to public policy, a perplexed Smith admitted that he had never even read a papal encyclical or bull, even though he was an observant Catholic. Initially, Smith deliberately ignored the issue of his religious affiliation, but eventually he found himself forced to circulate a response in an effort to mollify the concerns of the public at large. "I recognize," Smith averred, "no power in the institutions of my Church to interfere with the operations of the Constitution of the United States or the enforcement of the law of the land." While the statement, which also stressed the inviolability of freedom of conscience, separation of church and state, and secular public education, was well received in the mainstream press and among most leaders in the Protestant clergy, the anti-Catholic propaganda engine continued its relentless attack on Smith's faith. Smith tried again, this time broadcasting his position to a national audience from a radio station in Oklahoma City, wherein he shared the campaign endorsements of prominent Protestant supporters of goodwill, emphasizing the close connection between religious bigotry and groups like the Ku Klux Klan and reminding listeners that religious intolerance was anathema to the principles of the American founding, especially as epitomized in the writings of Thomas Jefferson. Even with many of the country's more notable Protestant leaders defending Smith, prejudices against him nonetheless continued.

Making matters still worse, these prejudices were further amplified by Smith's erstwhile association with Tammany Hall, an affiliation that no longer held his allegiance but nonetheless a past connection that he could not shake. Typical of New York political culture, Smith owed his initial political success to the support of Tammany, and now the chickens were coming home to roost. The corrupt image of the urban political machine was, understandably, an easy target for critics of big-city politics, and many voters saw Smith as the product of the political boss and the iniquitous culture of graft. These machine connections hurt Smith's case, perhaps as much as his religion. By contrast, Hoover was genuinely independent of the machine system; having made his mark through skillful performance and enduring achievement, he owed absolutely nothing to any power brokers or patrons. Hoover thus projected a safer, cleaner, more reassuring image of political autonomy and administrative competence that appealed to the heartland; Smith seemed at once far too atypical in his beliefs and far too typical in his associations. Piling on more negative imagery, Smith and his wife were unkindly represented as too unsophisticated for the White House, often depicted by their more strident critics as coarse, even vulgar, and a potential embarrassment to the American public, especially when dealing with sophisticated foreign dignitaries who would be more accustomed to and comfortable with the refinements of diplomacy. Finally, among the many scare tactics employed by the Republicans were claims that the election of a social progressive such as Smith would result in other minority groups—especially African Americans (who as voters were still loyal to the GOP)—gaining unfairly at the expense of the white majority. Thus both the religion card and the race card were cynically dealt and, combined with unkind rumors about Smith's character and manners, effectively damaged the Democrats' strongest candidate, at least in terms of proven ability, since Wilson.

For his part, Hoover avoided mudslinging and openly expressed his feelings that Smith's religious views were irrelevant, running a no-nonsense campaign stressing his own outstanding record, the sane policies that he favored, the achievements of his predecessor President Coolidge, and the prosperity historically secured by Republican administrations. Hoover not only did not need to resort to vulgar tactics and *ad hominem* attacks, but it really was not his practice. Hoover's professionalism and sense of personal dignity prevented him from stooping to the nastiness displayed by a good many of his supporters. The advantages for Hoover of a strong economy, at least on the surface of things, cannot be overstated. While Smith was distracted by the controversies regarding his religion, past connections to Tammany Hall, the implications that his election might have for racial and ethnic issues, his personal habits and alleged weaknesses, his upbringing, and his stand on Prohibition, Hoover was able to emulate Coolidge by keeping cool, hovering above the fray, staying close to Washington, and quietly relying on the proven Republican record. "A Chicken in Every Pot" became the defining Republican slogan, as the voters would be asked, "Is your bread buttered?" and then prompted to "remember hard times when we had a Democratic president. You can't eat promises. Play safe! Vote a straight Republican ticket!" Smith could not dismantle the claims of his opponents, and Hoover benefited from the good times, high spirits, and general optimism of the Roaring Twenties, especially in the urban centers where the real electoral clout was to be found.

Thus on Election Day, the Republicans enjoyed yet another electoral triumph in a sequence of recent landslide victories. How much of this was attributed to religious bigotry is unclear. The GOP did hold a strong suit of cards going into the campaign, and the odds are that Smith would have lost even if he had not been Catholic. Would he have fought a closer race? Again, that is a question that eludes any readily available answer. In any event, the results of the race were evident—the Republicans held their dominance with ease. While losing in a landslide, Smith's numbers were not as meager as either those of Davis in 1924 or Cox in 1920. Hoover impressively won over 21,400,000 votes, or 58 percent of the popular total, far exceeding even Coolidge's considerable victory over Davis in 1924. Smith fared better than Davis in the total popular vote, winning just over 15,000,000, which almost doubled Davis's total and actually was close to what Coolidge needed to win in the previous general election. But it amounted to only 40 percent of the popular vote—a larger share than what Davis or Cox had drawn, it is true, but still 18 percentage points behind Hoover. Socialist candidate Norman Thomas won just over 267,000 votes for the balance of the remainder, evidence that the heyday of this minor party was behind it.

In the Electoral College, Hoover carried a record 40 states to Smith's 8 for a total of 444 electoral votes to Smith's 87. Not only did Hoover hold the traditional GOP strongholds for the time, but he also cracked into the South, winning Virginia, Florida, Tennessee, Texas, North Carolina, and the border state of Kentucky. It was the first time since the controversial election of 1876 that Florida went to a Republican, the first time since 1872 that Virginia and North Carolina voted for a Republican, and the first time ever that a Republican took Texas. Even though Hoover had decimated the Democrats, there was one small glimmer of hope, for the Democrats won Massachusetts and Rhode Island, traditional Republican bastions, for the first time since the Republican Party fielded a national candidate in 1856. The last time the Democrats took Rhode Island was 1852, when it went with Franklin Pierce; and the only time prior to 1928 that the Democrats won Massachusetts was in 1836: the Van Buren election. Smith also showed well in his home state of New York, where he lost by only two percentage points (Davis and Cox had been utterly humiliated there in the previous two elections). Smith's defeat was indeed thorough, but the fact that he managed to snag two hitherto impenetrable Republican bastions and vastly improve the party's position in New York, even in the face of what was otherwise a complete landslide, served as a vague portent of things to come.

Hoover became the thirty-first president, and the country appeared to be moving optimistically forward into ever-expanding affluence at home and assured peace abroad. With another electoral landslide behind them, the Republicans as a party were at the height of their power, prepared to meet the promise of the oncoming decade and confident that the voters had made the intelligent choice in answer to a question posed by one of their more ironic campaign boilerplates: "Prosperity didn't just happen. Hoover and happiness or Smith and soup houses? Which shall it be?" But just under the surface, menacing forces were already stirring, both at home and abroad, that would soon show a dramatically different future for the American people—one that would bear unprecedented suffering for the human race, and one that would produce the preeminent politician of the twentieth century.

Additional Resources

Finan, Christopher M. *Alfred E. Smith: The Happy Warrior.* New York: Hill & Wang, 2002.

Fuchs, Lawrence. "Election of 1928." In Arthur M. Schlesinger and Fred L. Israel, eds. *History of American Presidential Politics, 1789–1968.* Vol. 3. New York: McGraw-Hill, 1971.

Graff, Henry. "1928," In Arthur M. Schlesinger, Fred L. Israel, and David J. Frent, eds. *Running for President: The Candidates and Their Images.* Vol. 2. New York: Simon & Schuster, 1994.

Leuchtenburg, William E. *Herbert Hoover.* New York: Times Books, 2009.

Lichtman, Allan. *Prejudice and Old Politics: The Presidential Election of 1928.* Chapel Hill: University of North Carolina Press, 1970.

Campaign of 1932

The year 1932 is remarkable in the history of American presidential elections for four principal reasons. First, the outcome of the election of 1932 would signal the end of the presidential dynasty that Republicans had enjoyed since 1860 with only three interruptions—the two nonconsecutive terms of Grover Cleveland and the two-term presidency of Woodrow Wilson, which effectively arose as the result of internal schisms within the Republican Party that more than halved its electoral clout. With the end of the Republicans' near monopoly at the federal level (and especially in the White House, which they held for fifty-six of the last seventy-two years), the election of 1932 would initiate a new era of Democratic dominance of a kind unknown since before the Civil War, Democrats achieving and then holding a political predominance that would remain, with some important exceptions, the shape of American politics until the late 1970s–early 1980s.

Second, with 1932, and beginning with trends that became visible four years earlier during the contest between Herbert Hoover and Al Smith, African Americans slowly began to move away from the Republicans. This process did not occur all at once, as some accounts have led us to believe; it happened gradually and steadily, beginning in the latter half of the 1920s, accelerating in the 1930s, and solidifying in the 1950s and early 1960s. In 1928, Smith enjoyed modestly better support from African Americans than had previous Democratic candidates, but on the whole, blacks still voted in high numbers for the Republican Hoover in both the elections of 1928 and 1932. But some evidence of a trend away from the GOP can be seen, such that by the mid-1930s, the African American vote began the slow shift en masse from the Republicans to the Democrats. Thus, the Party of Lincoln, the Great Emancipator, was in danger of losing its formerly loyal African American support to the party that, more than any other, was formerly associated with the Confederacy. As a result, throughout the better portion of the twentieth century, the majority of African Americans would support the Democrats after having held allegiance to the Republicans since Emancipation, and into the 1930s.

Third, the Democratic Party, building on trends already under way, would establish a new, unprecedented coalition of widely disparate groups, ethnicities, and interests, and thus would evolve as the more heterogeneous of the two parties throughout the remainder of the century. The most liberal Northern Democrats would become allies of the most traditional Southern conservatives; blue-collar industrial workers and tweedy intellectuals would find common cause in the party's platform; farmers and urbanites would be drawn to the activist policies of the Democrats; Roman Catholics and Jews as well as Southern Baptists would each represent an important voting bloc for the Democrats; and a variety of racial and ethnic groups—Irish Americans, Italian Americans, Polish Americans, African Americans, and Hispanics, among others—would give the Democratic Party a pluralistic flavor seldom seen in democratic politics of any kind.

Finally, and perhaps most importantly for American politics as it would unfold over the following five decades, the campaign and election of 1932 reflected a deep shift within American political culture on ideological grounds. Beginning with the populist and progressive movements of the late nineteenth and early twentieth centuries, American political consciousness, for good or ill, had been drawing a new vision of the relationship between government and social responsibility. Throughout the first two decades of the twentieth century, both of the two major parties—Republicans and Democrats alike—included among their diverse ranks influential progressive elements that insisted upon various degrees of governmental activism in the social and economic life of Americans, and both parties also included equally among their membership influential conservative wings. Republican presidents Theodore Roosevelt and William Howard Taft—the latter reputed, not always accurately, to be more conservative—instituted progressive reforms that preceded the liberal policies of Democratic president Woodrow Wilson. But in the early 1920s, following the death of the Republican Roosevelt, one of the century's truly great reformers, the progressive wing of the GOP waned significantly;

and by 1928, the contrast between Republican president Hoover's self-reliant "rugged individualism" and Democrat Al Smith's understanding of a more expansive role for government had further clarified the growing distinctions between the two major parties. In 1932, with the Great Depression smothering all vestiges of the prosperity that helped elect Harding, Coolidge, and Hoover in the landslides of the previous decade, these differences were sharply polarized as never before. While some pundits and wits complained of little real difference between the two parties and their candidates, even casual attention to their speeches, statements, and attitudes regarding the crisis at hand reveal the bold outlines of the ideological shift. By the mid-1920s, the Republicans had abandoned the progressive legacy of Theodore Roosevelt and fallen back on the mythos of self-reliance and restrained government. The Democrats were no longer the laissez-faire party of Andrew Jackson and Martin Van Buren, nor for that matter the party of Bourbon Democrat Grover Cleveland; instead, they were now developing along lines that would lead them to champion the imminent emergence of what would come to be called the "welfare state," which for some was a high compliment, for others opprobrium; they were becoming the party of Al Smith and Franklin Roosevelt.

Franklin Delano Roosevelt, cousin of Theodore Roosevelt, had been one of the Democrats' rising stars since his campaign for the vice presidency twelve years earlier. A crippling battle against polio interrupted his ambitions; but blessed with a measure of resolve beyond the reach of most human beings, Roosevelt willed himself back into the political arena, even though the paralysis that resulted from the disease left him without the use of his legs. By 1924, three years after contracting the disease, Roosevelt was fully back in the political game and, having become one of the party's more influential forces, appeared on crutches at the national convention that year to personally nominate his friend Al Smith, delivering a speech that energized the convention and helped to seal Smith's reputation as the "Happy Warrior." Roosevelt furthered his comeback in 1928, successfully campaigning for the governorship of New York and winning election in a landslide. Given that Republican gains were extensive in 1928, Roosevelt's successful campaign as a Democrat was seen as all the more remarkable; as the decade was drawing toward a close, it was clear that FDR had indeed recovered the political momentum that he had lost due to the terrible affliction that he suffered near the decade's opening.

As Roosevelt ascended, President Herbert Hoover, confronted with the demoralizing effects of the Great Depression, dug in. Hoover, who had been elected in a landslide four years earlier, was an intelligent, honest, and capable leader; but the crisis was so extensive that his efforts, rooted in his commitment to the principles of "rugged individualism" and limited government, seemed too little and ultimately too late. Hoover firmly believed that the dynamics of private markets would inevitably pull the country up and out of the Depression, holding fast to the belief that the federal government needed to be cautious in the extent of its activity. It is not fair to Hoover's reputation to depict him as indifferent to the sufferings of Americans during the Great Depression, or as merely the tool of monied interests looking out only for themselves. Hoover did have close ties to business, but he also had a long record of humanitarian service reaching back to his efforts to help Europeans recover in the aftermath of the Great War. But by the time of the election, the shantytowns of the homeless and unemployed that pockmarked the American urban landscape were known as "Hoovervilles," and the candidate that once rode to a stunning political victory on the wave of prosperity was now buffeted hard by circumstances that he considered beyond his legitimate control. By 1932, the mood at the White House was somber and withdrawn, further adding to the perception that Hoover had become a distant, indifferent figure.

Nonetheless, when the Republican Party held its convention in Chicago during that summer, Hoover was nominated without any real opposition, winning over 98 percent of the delegates on the first round. Vice President Charles Curtis was also renominated, with just over 55 percent of the delegates on the first ballot. With the exception of a small number of delegates, the party rallied behind Hoover, praising his sober forbearance in responding to the economic crisis and reaffirming the principles of frugality in government and balanced budgets. The American people, the language of the platform averred, will emerge from the economic calamity even stronger, and Hoover's leadership was noted as the principal assurance of this outcome. "This will be due in large measure," the platform stated, "to the quality of the leadership that this country has had during this crisis. We have had in the White House a leader—wise, courageous, patient, understanding, resourceful, ever present at his post of duty, tireless in his efforts and unswervingly faithful to American principles and ideals." The platform also reminded Americans that "true to American traditions and principles of government, the administration has regarded the relief problem as one of State and local responsibility. The work of local agencies, public and private has been coordinated and enlarged on a nation-wide scale under the leadership of the President."

As the Democratic convention, also held in Chicago late that July, opened, Governor Roosevelt held the advantage of the front-runner. Two other candidates emerged: Al Smith, Roosevelt's friend and predecessor as governor of New York as well as the Democratic nominee for president in 1928; and John Nance Garner from Texas, the current Speaker of the House of Representatives. Nine other names were mentioned as well, but none drew any serious support. What was once a close friendship between Roosevelt and Smith had sadly become strained since the previous convention. Smith felt that his former protégé had deliberately cut him out of the inner circle of New York politics, and by the time of the convention, both men had cooled toward each other. Smith, who had been associated with the party's liberal/progressive wing four years earlier—and thus the heir apparent to the legacies of William Jennings Bryan and President Woodrow Wilson—had since gravitated more toward the conservative side of the party. It was now Roosevelt who most resembled Wilson, and who best drew the contrast between the Democrats' progressive vision and the conservatism of President Hoover.

Thus at the convention, Roosevelt's lead was commanding from the beginning, winning 666 delegates on the first ballot, Smith following in second with 201 delegates and Garner showing a distant third with 90. While it was an impressive lead, a two-thirds majority was required to win nomination; thus the balloting continued, with Roosevelt making small gains on each ballot, Smith falling further back, and Garner gaining only 11 more votes by the third ballot. Even though Roosevelt gained a few votes on both the second and third ballots, there was no evident momentum, and a strange deadlock seemed to be forming in spite of Roosevelt's overwhelming popularity at the convention. After the third ballot, the convention recessed, and in the interim, Garner, realizing that a deadlock could sour the upcoming effort against the Republicans, was persuaded to throw in behind Roosevelt. On the fourth ballot, the California delegation, led by William McAdoo (the son-in-law of President Wilson who had almost won the nomination in 1920 and again in 1924), swung its support from Garner to Roosevelt, spurring other Garner delegates on the convention floor to follow suit. With Garner's delegates released to Roosevelt along with several supporters of scattered also-rans, FDR was nominated with 945 votes, Smith retaining 190. The convention then selected Garner to run for the vice presidency. The long friendship between Roosevelt and Smith was now even more troubled, and while Smith joined the chorus of prominent Democrats in support of FDR, his campaign efforts were less than enthusiastic for the Democratic nominee. Editors at the *Denver Post* mused, for example, that one of Smith's speeches on behalf of the Roosevelt-Garner ticket was in effect the "best speech yet for Hoover."

With his convention victory in hand, Roosevelt went on the stump, campaigning so energetically that the frail state of his health was completely overlooked. Assisted by James Farley and Louis Howe, his closest advisers, as well as what would become known as his "brains trust" (later referred to in the singular as "brain trust")—an informal circle of campaign managers and academics led, at least in its original form, by men such as Professor Raymond Moley of Columbia University, Adolf Berle, James Warburg, and Rexford Tugwell—Roosevelt mapped a campaign strategy and executed it with aplomb, surprising even those critics who had, as recently as the convention, underestimated him, mistaking him for something of a political lightweight. His numerous friends, supporters, and advisers provided considerable counsel and support, but Roosevelt ran the show in a way that had scarcely been seen in the politics of presidential elections. Thus with FDR, a new era of campaign politics seemed to have been ushered in. Roosevelt's vigor, confidence, high-spiritedness, and optimism were infectious, particularly when compared to Hoover, whom some had perceived as dour and resigned to defeat. "Happy Days Are Here Again," Roosevelt's campaign theme song, typified the campaign's mood more effectively than any speech or slogan, with the possible exception of one phrase, assuredly coined by Roosevelt in the following promise: "I pledge you, I pledge myself, to a New Deal for the American people." By the next day, the New Deal was the most important slogan promoting the Roosevelt campaign and would become the defining vision of his presidency. Indeed, the Roosevelt New Deal would henceforth come to mean much more, defining the Democratic Party as well as encapsulating a new approach to the role of the public sector in American democratic thought and practice.

Naturally, the campaign focused primarily on the Great Depression and how to address it. In other areas, such as foreign policy, there was no significant difference between the two candidates; and even on some domestic issues, Roosevelt and Hoover were not as divided as our limited understanding of history has led us to believe. Roosevelt, while genuinely feared in some quarters as dangerously progressive, for the most part embraced the laissez-faire principles of free-market capitalism and, along with Hoover, believed in a balanced budget and responsible federal spending. Nonetheless, Roosevelt did draw important distinctions between himself and the president. In his Commonwealth Club address delivered in San Francisco, Roosevelt set aside his free-market proclivities and sketched ideas and policies that would constitute the basics of the New Deal, proposals that called for greater government responsibility in the economic direction of the country. "As I see it," Roosevelt explained,

> The task of government in relation to business is to assist the development of an economic declaration of rights, an economic constitutional order. This is the common task of statesman and business man. It is the minimum requirement of a more permanently safe order of things. Every man has a right to life; and this means that he has also a right to make a comfortable living. He may by sloth or crime decline to exercise that right; but it may not be denied him. We have no actual famine or death; our industrial and agricultural mechanism can produce enough and to spare. Our government formal and informal, political and economic, owes to every one an avenue to possess himself of a portion of that plenty sufficient for his needs, through his own work. (Quoted in Hammond, Hardwick, and Lubert 2007, p. 407)

President Hoover seemed defeated from the outset; in contrast to the endlessly active and enthusiastic Roosevelt, he did little to campaign throughout the summer, and it was only in October, extremely late in the campaign, that he really entered the fray, and then primarily as a defense against his critics. Hoover attempted to inform the public of those measures that he actually had taken to address the crisis, insisting that had it not been for his administration, the Depression would have been "infinitely worse." He pointedly contrasted his rugged individualism with Roosevelt's "alien" ideas, insinuating that with FDR and the Democrats, the very ideals that underpin American society would be replaced by "sinister" foreign doctrines similar to Bolshevism. Hoover warned that if the electorate turned to the "radicalism" of Roosevelt, "the same philosophy of government which has poisoned all Europe" would infect the values of American society as well. Roosevelt blithely dismissed Hoover, describing the latter's administration, in apocalyptic and alliterative terms, as being spurred by "the Horsemen Destruction, Delay, Deceit, Despair."

Roosevelt was elected president in a landslide, although it was not as quite as large as Hoover's victory over Smith four years earlier, FDR winning 57 percent of the popular vote to Hoover's 39 percent. The actual margin of victory was approximately the same, both elections coming in at around a winning margin of 17–18 percent. Socialist candidate Norman Thomas managed what seemed an impressive 885,000 votes (approximately), but it was only just over 2 percent of the voting electorate, a poor showing given the economically distressed times and the intensity of the discontent that had been raised over the past three years. The margin of victory for Roosevelt in the Electoral College was even more impressive: He won all but six states for a total of 472 electoral votes to Hoover's 59, or 89 percent to 11 percent, the highest percentage of electoral votes won by a candidate since Abraham Lincoln's 91 percent (in an election in which the southern states did not participate) in his 1864 reelection. Interestingly, even though Democrats Grover Cleveland and Woodrow Wilson had both been twice elected to the White House (1884, 1892, 1912, 1916), Franklin Roosevelt was the first Democratic candidate to receive at least 50 percent of the popular vote since Samuel Tilden in 1876 (an election that Tilden actually lost by one vote in the Electoral College) and the first Democrat to receive a true popular majority and win election to the presidency since Franklin Pierce in 1852—in other words, eighty years had passed since a Democrat had last won the White House by carrying both the Electoral College and a total exceeding a simple majority of the popular vote. After Election Day 1932, the only Democrats to whom that applied—that is, who were elected to the presidency with simple majorities (50.1% or above) in the popular vote as well as the requisite majority in the Electoral College—were Roosevelt (1932), Pierce (1852), Martin Van Buren (1836), and Andrew Jackson (1828 and 1832). One could also add Tilden to this company as the six Democrats between the party's founding in the late 1820s/early 1830s through 1932 to have gained a majority of the popular vote in a presidential election. Roosevelt swept the South, the West, and the Midwest, and while Hoover won five of his six states in the Northeast (Maine, New Hampshire, Vermont, Connecticut, and Pennsylvania—his only other state being the border state of Delaware)—Roosevelt carried his home state of New York with its 47 electoral votes (10% of the total votes in the Electoral College) and again took what was now becoming a *former* Republican stronghold, Massachusetts, for the Democrats, thus repeating and reinforcing the trend that had been initiated by candidate Smith in the previous election.

In the wake of such a devastating victory, Roosevelt and the Democrats now ruled the political landscape; the Republican Party, which had dominated the federal government since Lincoln, and which had as recently as the last three elections produced a string of landslides that made the party appear invulnerable, at least in presidential elections, was now in the minority. The middle decades of the twentieth century—those decades that were marked by the worst global crises in the history of humankind, the Great Depression, World War II, and the earliest years of the Cold War—in American politics were to be dominated by the Democrats.

Additional Resources

The American Presidency Project. http://www.presidency.ucsb.edu and http://www.presidency .ucsb.edu/ws/index.php?pid=29638#ixzz1IP4Mu8Pv.

Brands, H. W. *Traitor to His Class: The Privileged Life and Radical Presidency of Franklin Roosevelt.* New York: Doubleday, 2008.

Freidel, Frank. "Election of 1932." In Arthur M. Schlesinger and Fred L. Israel, eds. *History of American Presidential Politics, 1789–1968.* Vol. 3. New York: McGraw-Hill, 1971.

Freidel, Frank. "1932." In Arthur M. Schlesinger, Fred L. Israel, and David J. Frent, eds. *Running for President: The Candidates and Their Images.* Vol. 2. New York: Simon & Schuster, 1994.

Hammond, Scott J., Kevin R. Hardwick, and Howard L. Lubert. *Classics of American Political and Constitutional Thought.* Vol. 2. Indianapolis, IN: Hackett Publishing Co., 2007.

Lichtman, Allan. *Prejudice and Old Politics: The Presidential Election of 1928.* Chapel Hill: University of North Carolina Press, 1970.

Ritchie, Donald. *Electing FDR: The New Deal Campaign of 1932.* Lawrence: University Press of Kansas, 2010.

Smith, Jean Edward. *FDR.* New York: Random House, 2008.

Topping, Simon. *Lincoln's Lost Legacy: The Republican Party and the African American Vote, 1928–1952.* Gainesville: University Press of Florida, 2008.

Campaign of 1936

During his inaugural address delivered on March 4, 1933, Franklin Delano Roosevelt, in his inimitable style, confidently and forthrightly affirmed his own genuine "firm belief that the only thing we have to fear is fear itself—nameless, unreasoning, unjustified terror which paralyzes needed efforts to convert retreat into advance. In every dark hour of our national life, a leadership of frankness and of vigor has met with that understanding and support of the people themselves which is essential to victory. And I am convinced that you will again give that support to leadership in these critical days."

In this spirit, the new president, with the full cooperation of a Democratic-controlled Congress, initiated numerous and sweeping programs designed for one purpose: the complete recovery of the American economy and the end of the Great Depression that had burdened American citizens for the better part of four years. Banks were closed for four days under the Emergency Banking Act signed into law by the new president shortly after his inauguration that imposed a "bank holiday," and when reopened they were certified under federal authority, and their deposits were guaranteed by the treasury of the federal government; farmers' crops were also insured by the federal government; Social Security was established; the federal government refinanced homes; and a variety of government programs were instituted to employ workers, execute internal improvements, provide electricity to more remote areas of the country (electricity still being a novelty within large regions of the country), address poverty in both rural and urban areas, and generate money in the economy. These included federal programs such as the Works Progress Administration, the Public Works Administration, the Civilian Conservation Corps, the Tennessee Valley Authority (TVA), the National Industrial Recovery Act, the Rural Electrification Act, and the National Labor Relations Act, to name only a few of the dozens of government programs initiated during Roosevelt's first term, a staggering panoply of government-funded and government-administered programs that have been referred to by supporters and critics alike as the "alphabet soup" of the New Deal. Where they could, state and local governments followed suit with programs of their own. Franklin Roosevelt's presidency was in effect restructuring a wide array of American institutions in an unprecedented manner, surpassing even the aspirations of the progressive movement of the late nineteenth and early twentieth centuries (a movement that included his famous cousin, the equally expansive Theodore Roosevelt).

By 1936, Roosevelt's New Deal had indeed succeeded in improving conditions for most Americans in a variety of ways, but it had nonetheless failed to fully restore overall prosperity. It should be noted that to this day, economists, political scientists, and historians still disagree on the correlation between FDR's

programs and the economic recovery that would eventually come—some arguing that Roosevelt saved the country from collapse, others arguing that his efforts
actually impeded the recovery and that other events, namely the war, were the
real force that reversed the situation. At any rate, as the election year approached,
President Roosevelt still faced many challenges. The Depression still gripped the
American and global economies, and in spite of some successes here and there,
the future remained uncertain. While the success of the president's programs to
abate the effects of the Great Depression remains a topic of debate among scholars, it is still accurate to say that by the Campaign of 1936, Americans understood
the nature and reach of the federal government—and by extension, the office of
the presidency—in a new way. Even when the federal government fell short, Roosevelt's willingness to experiment and try again reassured many Americans that
something was being done to address the crisis, a marked contrast to perceptions,
fair or unfair, that former president Hoover did little to nothing to help. (To be
fair, it is important to note that some of President Roosevelt's programs, such as
the Reconstruction Finance Corporation, actually began with President Hoover;
but the New Deal in general far exceeded the efforts of Roosevelt's more cautious predecessor.) Most Americans accepted and even welcomed some programs
that would have been foreign to them just five or six years earlier, such as Social
Security and federal guarantees for bank deposits, and it is clear that programs
such as the TVA and rural electrification supplied needed economic relief and the
general improvement of life to large sections of the country. The public responded
favorably in the 1934 midterm elections, and the Democrats were generally in a
fairly strong position going into the season of 1936. Nonetheless, discontent was
still widespread throughout the country, and the president's reelection efforts were
sobered by recent polls indicating a close contest ahead. Roosevelt was demon-
ized by his harshest critics, even to the point of portraying him as a "puppet of
Moscow" (viz., a communist stooge in liberal clothing); but the American public in general embraced Roosevelt, many with uncommon enthusiasm. No president could inspire such a mix of devoted adoration and intemperate condemnation
as Franklin Roosevelt. His image became anathema among the powerful in the
United States—tycoon households were known to have forbidden the use of his
name. To some, Roosevelt was a shining savior, to others—especially among the
high social strata—he was scornfully and curtly referred to as "that man." Polls
of the day, although often inaccurate, indicated that the general population loved
the person of Roosevelt more than the policies of the New Deal. One poll from
the *Literary Digest*, which at the time was regarded as a reliable predictor but has
since been discredited owing to its skewed, biased sampling, measured an overwhelming disagreement with the policies of the New Deal, thus causing some concern within the Democratic Party. Even the Democrats' own consultants were not

encouraging; the polls were showing a tight election and warning of the president's vulnerability. But as mentioned above, polling in the 1930s was far from accurate, as the final results would soon indicate.

At their national nominating convention in Philadelphia in the summer of 1936, the Democrats unanimously nominated Roosevelt and his vice president, John Nance Garner, on the first ballot. In the primaries, a few Democratic challengers tested the waters, notably Henry S. Breckenridge, the president's assistant secretary of war and a critic of the New Deal; popular novelist and muckraker Upton Sinclair; Father Charles Coughlin, a radio demagogue, notorious anti-Semite, and rogue priest whose political rhetoric and ambitions were officially disowned by the Vatican, but who had received, in defiance of Rome, the support of his direct superior, the archbishop of Detroit; and former governor Al Smith, the Democratic nominee in 1928, who had once been a beloved friend and mentor to the president but who had now sadly become an embittered rival. All of these primary challengers soon discovered that, in spite of the polls, the president's position within the party was invulnerable, and the platform adopted at the convention reaffirmed Roosevelt's New Deal. Closely paraphrasing the Declaration of Independence for dramatic effect, the platform intoned,

> We hold these truths to be self-evident, that the test of a representative government is its ability to promote the safety and happiness of the people. We hold this truth to be self-evident—that 12 years of Republican leadership left our Nation sorely stricken in body, mind, and spirit; and that three years of Democratic leadership have put it back on the road to restored health and prosperity. We hold this truth to be self-evident—that 12 years of Republican surrender to the dictatorship of a privileged few have been supplanted by a Democratic leadership which has returned the people themselves to the places of authority, and has revived in them new faith and restored the hope which they had almost lost. We hold this truth to be self-evident—that this three-year recovery in all the basic values of life and the reestablishment of the American way of living has been brought about by humanizing the policies of the Federal Government as they affect the personal, financial, industrial, and agricultural well-being of the American people. We hold this truth to be self-evident—that government in a modern civilization has certain inescapable obligations to its citizens, [and among these are]: (1) Protection of the family and the home. (2) Establishment of a democracy of opportunity for all the people. (3) Aid to those overtaken by disaster. These obligations, neglected through 12 years of the old leadership, have once more been recognized by American Government. Under the new leadership they will never be neglected. (American Presidency Project, University of California, Santa Barbara)

The Republican Party felt chastened by its landslide defeat in 1932 as well as the equally discouraging outcome of the 1934 midterms. It was clear that the GOP, for the first time in memory, was now the minority party at the federal level. Hoover and the Republicans were blamed for the Depression, and the party was fully aware that its only chance was to find a new approach and a fresher face. It was apparent that the Republican Party needed to concede, at least to some limited extent, that the liberal reforms that had been instituted under FDR were not easily challenged and were now unlikely to be undone. It was equally apparent that the Old Guard conservative leadership needed to cast a broader net for a candidate that was distinct enough from Roosevelt to salvage the party's integrity while, rightly or wrongly, remaining as far from Hoover as possible. Some turned to Senator William E. Borah, the "Lion of Idaho"; others turned to Stephen Day of Ohio and Rough Rider Frank Knox from Illinois (who had served with the president's cousin, Theodore Roosevelt, in Cuba during the Spanish-American War). Diehard Hoover loyalists still held out hope that their man might muster a comeback. Borah, Knox, and Day all had support among the rank and file, but the party leadership showed its preference for Kansas governor Alfred "Alf" Landon. Other names were also floated as possible candidates (including famous personalities such as aviator and popular hero Charles Lindbergh and industrialist Henry Ford, as well as rising stars such as Robert Taft and Earl Warren), but by the opening of the GOP convention in Cleveland, Landon's nomination was inevitable.

Landon's political roots reached back to the Republican progressivism of Theodore Roosevelt, and his cautious approach to fiscal policy leaned conservatively; thus it follows that he was viewed within the party as a moderate. Strategically, Landon was an intelligent choice to challenge Roosevelt. He was a proven ally of business and an advocate of free enterprise, and yet his old Bull Moose credentials and link to Theodore Roosevelt appealed to the progressive mood of the times. As governor of Kansas, he had openly supported many of the president's New Deal reforms, and yet he forthrightly championed fiscal frugality, the gold standard, and the implementation of policies favorable to business and industry. In Kansas, he expanded state government for the sake of regulation while at the same time reducing taxes. And as a governor, he was inclined to political tolerance and avoided the kind of "red-baiting" that was not uncommon within the party's Old Guard wing. Like his Democratic counterpart, he won his party's nomination on the first ballot; only Borah's nineteen delegates committed from Wisconsin prevented a Landon sweep. Knox, whose even closer affiliation with Theodore Roosevelt drew upon those now increasingly important progressive Republican legacies, was selected as Landon's running mate.

The GOP platform sounded a direct challenge to the Democratic Party and the New Deal that the Democrats had, from the perspective of Republicans, foisted upon the American public. Opening with the words "America is in peril," the platform continued as follows:

> The welfare of American men and women and the future of our youth are at stake. We dedicate ourselves to the preservation of their political liberty, their individual opportunity and their character as free citizens, which today for the first time are threatened by Government itself. For three long years the New Deal Administration has dishonored American traditions and flagrantly betrayed the pledges upon which the Democratic Party sought and received public support. The powers of Congress have been usurped by the President. The integrity and authority of the Supreme Court have been flouted. The rights and liberties of American citizens have been violated. Regulated monopoly has displaced free enterprise. The New Deal Administration constantly seeks to usurp the rights reserved to the States and to the people. It has insisted on the passage of laws contrary to the Constitution. It has intimidated witnesses and interfered with the right of petition. It has dishonored our country by repudiating its most sacred obligations. It has been guilty of frightful waste and extravagance, using public funds for partisan political purposes. It has promoted investigations to harass and intimidate American citizens, at the same time denying investigations into its own improper expenditures. It has created a vast multitude of new offices, filled them with its favorites, set up a centralized bureaucracy, and sent out swarms of inspectors to harass our people. It has bred fear and hesitation in commerce and industry, thus discouraging new enterprises, preventing employment and prolonging the depression. It secretly has made tariff agreements with our foreign competitors, flooding our markets with foreign commodities. It has coerced and intimidated voters by withholding relief to those opposing its tyrannical policies. It has destroyed the morale of our people and made them dependent upon government. Appeals to passion and class prejudice have replaced reason and tolerance. To a free people, these actions are insufferable. This campaign cannot be waged on the traditional differences between the Republican and Democratic parties. The responsibility of this election transcends all previous political divisions. We invite all Americans, irrespective of party, to join us in defense of American institutions. (American Presidency Project, University of California, Santa Barbara)

In comparing the two platforms, it was obvious to all that the lines were clearly drawn, and yet the Republicans moved ahead with caution in challenging some of the New Deal's more popular achievements. Landon, in many ways, was the best candidate in this regard; but as a personality on the stump, he fell short of

Roosevelt's incomparable natural skill as a campaigner. The public recognized Landon as a man of integrity but was not stirred by him as it was by Roosevelt. Biting social critic and irrepressible wag H. L. Mencken observed that Landon lacked the "power to inflame the boobs" and, while admiring Landon for his personal virtues, saw in him a bland candidate not equal to the task of meeting FDR in an even contest. Landon had the support of several powerful newspaper publishers such as William Randolph Hearst, who was particularly aggressive in deploying reporters to convey Landon's common-man attributes to his readers. Reporters working for Hearst described Landon as the "Lincoln of Kansas," a "liberal Coolidge," and the "Horse and Buggy Governor," an unpretentious man of simple tastes, self-reliance, and prairie common sense.

Landon was an able governor and an adept politician, but Franklin Roosevelt, by contrast, was nothing less than an authentic political genius. Charismatic, vigorous, forthright, visionary, courageous, graceful, articulate, quick-witted, warm, and genuinely friendly in crowds, Roosevelt was the one and only political colossus of his time. Given to opening his remarks with the simple and reassuring phrase, "My friends," Roosevelt exuded trust, resolve, and ability. His amiability was genuine, he was able to win over a crowded room or a single person that he met on the street, and he always left an impression of openness and attentiveness. He was a master of the uses of radio, and in personal appearances, he emitted the raw presence of naturally gifted leadership. Rhetorically, he was without peer in his day. In accepting his renomination at the convention in Philadelphia, Roosevelt delivered a dazzling speech, wherein he coined, with the help of his brain trust, a new phrase that would aptly encapsulate his entire presidency, proclaiming that his generation of Americans had a "rendezvous with destiny." Not knowing what world events awaited the United States over the next ten years, Roosevelt had spoken with uncanny prescience. The phrase would itself become as iconic as the president who first coined it, and it would be quoted to great effect by future politicians from both parties, including future presidents John F. Kennedy and Ronald Reagan. Such was the power and enduring appeal of the Roosevelt legacy.

As the election drew near, the Republicans, nervous about their chances, increased the volume of attacks on the New Deal, even to the point of challenging Social Security, a move that was wisely avoided earlier in the campaign, given the program's popularity. Still, polls such as those issued by the *Literary Digest* (as mentioned above) encouraged Republicans. In a particularly curious and embarrassing act of self-deception, the media—highlighting for its readers a favorable straw poll that predicted Landon's imminent victory—participated in spinning the illusion that Roosevelt's reelection was in peril. In the recent past, the periodical's straw poll had predicted with some accuracy (compared to the expectations of the times) the outcome of the four previous elections, but the sample was hampered by a self-selecting bias, as it was confined to the comparatively more affluent sub-scribers of the *Digest* who were inclined to respond, and thus it was not a reliable reflection of the mood of the voters in general. Roosevelt and his brain trust were not intimidated by the *Digest*'s previous record; they went into November with full confidence in spite of the appearance of uncertainty that had been generated by the media on the eve of the election.

Their confidence, events proved, was utterly justified. When the election came, the results were no less than stunning. Roosevelt shattered every electoral record, winning 28.7 million total popular votes, amounting to 60.8 percent of the entire popular vote cast (breaking the old record set by Warren Harding in 1920 and eventually exceeded in only one other election—Lyndon B. Johnson in 1964), and taking 523 electoral votes, or 98.5 percent (a percentage of the Electoral College exceeded only by George Washington and James Monroe before the rise of the modern two-party system and the broadening of the franchise), leaving Landon with just 8 electoral votes from 2 states, Vermont and Maine. Roosevelt's margin of victory of 24 percent was the third highest in history (exceeded only by Harding in 1920 and Calvin Coolidge in 1924). Impressively, Roosevelt won at least 60 per-cent of the vote in 30 states. Landon's approximately 16,700,000 votes represented around 38 percent of the electorate, the remaining votes going to the populist Union Party (their candidate, William Lemke of North Dakota, winning just over 930,000 votes), the Socialist Party (campaign veteran Norman Thomas, in his third election, winning just under 188,000 votes, a poor showing for the Socialists, who at one time enjoyed a promising position as a growing third party), and the Communist Party (scarcely managing 79,000 votes for their obscure candidate, Earl Browder).

The diverse Roosevelt Coalition, which was forged in the election of 1932 and somewhat foreshadowed in the Smith campaign of 1928, had not only held its base, but also expanded its reach. For the first time in history, for example, the majority (in this case, 71%) of voting African Americans cast their votes for a Democrat. More importantly, the New Deal programs that Roosevelt and the Democratic Congress established were earnestly embraced by a substantial majority of the American electorate, signaling that a dramatic change had indeed occurred and taken root, a change in the way in which the role of the federal government was understood by the majority of American citizens. The 1930s would continue to be marked by hardship at home and ever more menacing dangers abroad; but for the moment, Franklin Roosevelt was the most successful politician of his time, and the Democrats enjoyed unprecedented power throughout the federal government.

Additional Resources

The American Presidency Project. http://www.presidency.ucsb.edu/ws/index.php?pid= 29596#ixzz1IfGCKPvm).

Brands, H. W. *Traitor to His Class: The Privileged Life and Radical Presidency of Franklin Roosevelt.* New York: Doubleday, 2008.

Brinkley, Alan. "1936." In Arthur M. Schlesinger, Fred L. Israel, and David J. Frent, eds. *Running for President: The Candidates and Their Images.* Vol. 2. New York: Simon & Schuster, 1994.

Leuchtenburg, William. "Election of 1936." In Arthur M. Schlesinger and Fred L. Israel, eds. *History of America Presidential Politics, 1789–1968.* Vol. 3. New York: McGraw-Hill, 1971.

Lichtman, Allan. *Prejudice and Old Politics: The Presidential Election of 1928.* Chapel Hill: University of North Carolina Press, 1970.

Smith, Jean Edward. *FDR.* New York: Random House, 2008.

Webber, Michael J. *New Deal Fat Cats: Business, Labor, and Campaign Finance in the 1936 Presidential Election.* New York: Fordham University Press, 2000.

Campaign of 1940

When Americans turned their attention to the presidential campaign of 1940, a world war had once again ravaged the community of nations. Wars and rumors of war had been brewing throughout the 1930s, first with the invasion of Manchuria by the forces of the Japanese Imperial Army, and then in Europe through the aggression of Nazi Germany led by Adolf Hitler and Fascist Italy under Benito Mussolini, as well as the invasion of Finland by Stalinist Russia. On September 1, 1939, Hitler's forces poured across the frontier between Poland and Germany, and what would come to be known as the Second World War followed. Great Britain and France declared war on Germany, and in the spring of 1940, France fell after only a few short weeks of resisting the Nazi juggernaut. Britain stood courageously, resolutely alone against what was then the most powerful military force in history, with the United States under the direction of President Franklin Roosevelt providing material aid and, for a time, nonmilitary support.

Thus the crisis of the Great Depression, which had burdened Americans and the world in general for a full decade, gave way to the howling cataclysm of war—not just any war, but a war that would soon surpass even the Great War fought a generation earlier in its total destruction and brutal extermination of human lives, and the burning issue in the American heartland revolved around the nature of the United States' ultimate response. Hawks and doves, interventionists and isolationists again flocked to their respective corners of the political arena, and the country confronted the choice between internationalism and commitment to war on the one hand, and peace, neutrality, and self-imposed isolation on the other. Roosevelt unequivocally supported the Allies against the totalitarian menace, but he was unable to offer more than material support, owing to the strength of isolationism within the country at that time. Eventually, the president would provide the active protection of the U.S. Navy in convoy escorts across the northern Atlantic well before Pearl Harbor, a deployment that would lead to shooting between the American and German navies months before the Japanese attack in the Pacific; but during the Campaign of 1940, Roosevelt was compelled to reassert, against his own instincts and desires, American neutrality. The crisis was such that for the first time in American political history, an incumbent president broke the tradition of the venerable *Pater Patriae*, George Washington, and stood for a third consecutive term. (Presidents Grant and Theodore Roosevelt each sought a third term four years after their presidencies had ended, without success.)

As late as 1939, Roosevelt had indicated ambivalence regarding a third term, and he even encouraged other party members to seek the nomination. But with war exploding in Europe and expanding through the first half of 1940, the president, realizing the unprecedented gravity of the situation abroad, decided there was good reason to break tradition. Officially, Roosevelt demurred; but unofficially, he expected to be drafted by the convention, an expectation that was realized on the first ballot. Initially, there was some minority grousing in both parties about Roosevelt's alleged dictatorial ambitions (and even some supportive of Roosevelt who wanted him to be more like a dictator, at least in the ancient Roman understanding of that role), but the broken tradition, while previously cherished, now seemed insignificant given the magnitude of the decisions at stake. By and large, the critics of Roosevelt's third run were Roosevelt bashers to begin with.

It is the case that Roosevelt's second term was not without serious problems. The president committed a costly political miscalculation in his efforts to expand the Supreme Court, a measure that he attempted as a response to a judiciary that was not amenable to some of his New Deal programs, and which therefore blocked some of his efforts on constitutional grounds. Additionally, while it was apparent that many New Deal programs had helped the economy to a certain extent, another economic downturn in 1937—which would be embarrassingly called the "Roosevelt Recession"—was so severe that it threatened to roll back any and all gains made since Roosevelt took office in early 1933. The recession resulted in part from the president's own efforts to balance the budget, which drained away funds needed to "prime the pump" of the economy. Additionally, some of the New Deal relief programs were reduced, while other programs were simply cut. By 1939, the economic situation was still serious, and it was not until the election year of 1940 that signs of recovery were evident. The Republicans, still in the minority in Congress, became more effective in either blocking or forcing revisions of Roosevelt's programs, a development that revived their confidence. And Roosevelt himself pulled back from some of his earlier progressivism, concerned that federal spending was becoming too high. Nonetheless, at least within the Democratic

Party, the Roosevelt administration was highly lauded, his popularity within the party remained high, and his attempt at a third term, while unconventional, clearly seemed to the Democrats the best course for both party and country.

One significant voice of dissent came from the president's close confidant James Farley, the postmaster general under Roosevelt, who had been at one time one of his more trusted advisers since his early days in New York politics. Farley had objected to Roosevelt's attempted court-packing and also was unhappy with his decision to run a third time. Having his own presidential ambitions, Farley made it known that he was available as an alternative to FDR. This resulted in a personal break between the two old friends and political allies, and while Farley remained close to First Lady Eleanor Roosevelt, he would never fully reconcile with the president. Vice President John Nance Garner, a more conservative Democrat who had in his second term come to reject the New Deal, also broke from FDR and stood for the nomination. But aside from these minor challenges, Roosevelt's renomination went smoothly. Roosevelt remained the party's standard-bearer, and the Democratic platform again stressed its commitment to the social and economic reforms associated with the New Deal. Roosevelt had also cultivated strong affiliations with a number of influential Republicans, as several members of his administration were drawn from Republican ranks. Thus the president, in spite of the recession and controversies such as the court-packing maneuver, maintained the kind of political strength seldom sustained by a national figure under any circumstances.

The only real controversy at the 1940 Democratic convention involved the choice of a new running mate to replace Garner. Roosevelt wanted zealous New Dealer Henry A. Wallace (formerly a progressive Republican), who was serving as his secretary of agriculture. Delegates wanted to open the nomination for vice president to other candidates, there being a large groundswell from conservative Democrats against Wallace and his more radical approach to the New Deal. Roosevelt bristled upon hearing of resistance to Wallace, threatening to withdraw his name from consideration. This was prevented by the efforts of Harry Hopkins, the First Lady, and others from the brain trust who worked arduously at the convention to successfully generate support for Wallace. Thanks to these efforts, Wallace won nomination on the first ballot, supported by 629 delegates, with conservative Democrat William B. Bankhead receiving 329, former Indiana governor Paul V. McNutt taking 68, and a field of 11 additional candidates (which included Farley and Senate majority leader Alben Barkley) sharing the remaining 32 votes. Aside from this slight difficulty, the path was clear for Roosevelt's precedent-breaking renomination.

The Roosevelt Coalition, which was forged in the 1930s (and traced back, in some of its elements, to Al Smith's 1928 campaign), was a strong, diverse, and formidable political force. While it had been gathering and coalescing throughout the 1930s and even the late 1920s, by the election of 1940, it was fully solidified. The Democratic Party was now the home of a mosaic of social and political interests: organized labor, the Catholic voting bloc, the Jewish voting bloc, Southern conservatives who remained loyal to the Democrats in spite of their progressive social policies, nearly every new immigrant group that had gained larger shares of the overall population after the Civil War, the more liberal/progressive farm organizations, urbanites, intellectuals, and notably African Americans, who had begun their mass defection from the Party of Lincoln, their political home since Reconstruction, as early as the election of 1936 (a majority of African Americans still supported incumbent republican President Herbert Hoover in the 1932 election), and had by the election of 1940 generally, but not entirely, moved into the Democratic camp. As many African Americans were de facto disenfranchised throughout much of the country, the African American vote did not carry the national clout that it would in later elections; but in response to FDR and the New Deal policies and programs that he and the Democrats had established, the allegiance had been shifted, and where African Americans could be politically engaged, they were now mostly for Roosevelt and the Democrats.

The Republican convention was more dramatic; the party was sharply divided between isolationists and internationalists, but among the party leadership, isolationism was gaining strength. The leading candidates at the beginning of the convention were Thomas Dewey, a moderate from New York who had gradually drifted toward isolationism; the Old Guard conservative Robert Taft, son of former president and chief justice of the Supreme Court William Howard Taft, of Ohio, and who was a prominent opponent of the New Deal as well as an isolationist; and Michigan senator Arthur H. Vandenberg, another firm opponent of Roosevelt (whom he scornfully referred to as a dictator) and most of the New Deal measures, and who had also moved toward isolationism after having been, for a time and with some qualification, an internationalist. Early polls indicated that Dewey held the strongest support in the party, and he won most of the presidential preference primaries that were held that election season, with Vandenberg and Taft a distant second and third, respectively, and a number of also-rans trailing still farther behind. All three of the front-runners, however, showed their vulnerability in their inability to respond with confidence in the face of developments in Europe. By the time the convention convened in late June, France, Denmark, Norway, and the Netherlands had all fallen to Hitler's armies, and none of the Republican front-runners seemed to know how to address the crisis.

On the first ballot of the convention, Dewey won the most delegates with 360. Taft came in second at 189, but Vandenberg, who had shown stronger than Taft in the primaries and earlier polls, managed just 76 delegates and trailed far behind in fourth. A number of also-rans (including former president Herbert Hoover, who won 17 delegates on the first round and would peak at 32 delegates on the third) shared 270 first-round votes. Significantly, in third place, with 105 delegates, was a newly emergent candidate, Wendell Willkie, a liberal Republican, former Democrat (having only recently switched parties), and Wall Street lawyer. Willkie, who had little political experience but who had recently earned a national reputation for his skilled leadership as president of the privately owned power company Commonwealth and Southern, had suddenly appeared as a serious candidate in the wake of the Nazi push in Europe. A recent radio debate between Willkie and Roosevelt's solicitor general, Robert H. Jackson, on the merits of free enterprise, had also drawn considerable attention to the Republicans, as many listeners were impressed by Willkie's presence and command of the issues. Willkie was also a more appealing choice to the internationalist wing of the party, having identified with the internationalism of President Woodrow Wilson in the 1920s, and he now supported increased measures to assist Great Britain against Nazi Germany.

With the front-runners wavering, Willkie pressed forward, stumping the country prior to the convention to gain momentum; the move paid off, as he outvoted Vandenberg on the first round. On the second ballot, Dewey still held the lead, but he lost ground, winning 338 delegates as both Taft and Willkie gained strength, winning 203 and 171 delegates, respectively. In part, Dewey's age—at thirty-seven, he was one of the youngest candidates to have ever sought the nomination from a major party (only William Jennings Bryan, at thirty-six in 1896, was younger), prompting Democrats to joke that he had "thrown his diaper in the ring"—worked against him, now that the crisis in Europe was spiraling quickly downward and tensions in the Pacific were increasing; and both Taft and Willkie were regarded as more seasoned and ready to confront what was sure to lie ahead. On the next ballot, Dewey slipped to 315 delegates, with Willkie leaping over Taft to win 259 delegates to Taft's 212.

By the fourth ballot, Willkie took the lead with 306, with Dewey slipping to third behind Taft, setting up a fifth ballot in which Willkie showed 429 delegates to Taft's 377, with Dewey fading fast to 57 delegates and now in fourth place behind Pennsylvania's governor, Arthur H. James, who took third with 59 delegates. Even though Taft's position had improved, and though he won more delegates on the fifth ballot than Dewey had held at any point in the balloting, it was clear that the momentum was Willkie's. On the next ballot, moved by spirited chants of "We Want Willkie" loudly cascading from the gallery, the delegates cast 655 votes for Willkie, giving him the nomination. Taft finished with 318 delegates, while Dewey dropped to just 11, just one vote ahead of Hoover. Willkie's victory hinged on New York, Pennsylvania, and Michigan, all of which switched to Willkie as a bloc on the sixth ballot. "Win with Willkie" was now the Republican battle cry as the campaign moved toward the general election. Anticlimactically, Oregon's Senator Charles McNary (the Senate minority leader) was selected to run for the vice presidency.

The Republican platform, as one would expect, criticized Roosevelt's New Deal, even though by 1940, most of the New Deal programs were supported, at various levels, by the majority of members in both parties. Significantly, the party stated its opposition to any involvement of American troops in a "foreign war," expressing the GOP's affinity with the isolationist elements that FDR was fighting against in his efforts to aid the Allied cause. The Republicans did call for renewed defense spending to prepare in the event of conflict, and they also added support for the provision of aid to "all peoples fighting for liberty," so long as that aid did not violate international law and treaties or compromise the United States' own self-defense. Interestingly, the Republican Party added a forward-looking clause promoting "equal rights for men and women," the first such clause to appear in the platform of either of the two major parties; the Democrats would follow suit four years later. Among the other planks, Republicans issued a sharp warning to those engaged in un-American activities, associated such activity with the New Deal (and by implication, the president), and promised to thwart all attempts by those fifth-column "borers from within" who threatened the American way of life.

Against Roosevelt, Willkie deployed a two-pronged attack. The first prong depicted the Republicans as the best party to ensure that the United States remained at peace; but Willkie's approach was not isolationist, as he agreed that the current administration's defense program was, for the most part, reasonable. He did openly question the president's foreign policy, musing aloud that Roosevelt seemed to be "deliberately inciting us to war," a refrain that did appeal to the isolationists. But he also made it known that he sympathized with those countries that had recently lost their freedom, and on the whole, he appeared more of an internationalist than an isolationist. His main charge was against Roosevelt's apparent eagerness to fight a foreign war. The second prong of Willkie's challenge attempted to associate the New Deal with European totalitarianism. "[If] you return this Administration to office," he declaimed in California, "you will be serving under an American totalitarian government before the long third term is up." However, it must be noted that while Willkie criticized the "defeatism" of the New Deal and spoke vaguely about its threat to freedom, he had in fact supported many of Roosevelt's programs, and he continued to do so as he accepted the Republican standard. His vision for the future was framed in terms of "unlimited productivity," which he contrasted to the "distributed scarcity" of the New Deal. Willkie consistently made claims that Roosevelt was an enemy of liberty, and he punctuated claims of his opponent's authoritarian ambition by referring to Roosevelt as "the third term candidate." Understandably, "No Third Term" became one of the key Republican slogans.

Most voters were not persuaded by this line of reasoning, but Willkie's first prong, the promise of peace, did draw some attention and, subsequently, support to his campaign. Lend-Lease, Roosevelt's plan to supply Great Britain with fifty destroyers in exchange for the use of British naval bases, helped to provoke the issue. Initially, FDR had requested Willkie's public endorsement of the plan. Willkie declined the invitation and initially issued a lukewarm rebuke of the president for not allowing enough time for public debate over the issue of military aid to Britain. However, Willkie soon changed his tone when political allies urged him to assume a more severe criticism. "The most arbitrary and dictatorial action ever taken by a President in the history of the United States" was Willkie's second, modified response to Lend-Lease; and from this point, Willkie increased the volume of his antiwar rhetoric and showed some drift toward a de facto isolationism.

Willkie, who began the campaign from a position supportive of Britain, thus transformed himself into an isolationist; in the process, he became increasingly shrill, alarming his audience with memories of the Great War (now called World War I) and the specter of "wooden crosses for sons and brothers and sweethearts" if Roosevelt returned for a third term. The Republican's rhetoric intensified even to the point of acrimony directed against Roosevelt, with whom he had actually enjoyed an amicable relationship. Typically, Roosevelt remained above the fray, choosing to ignore Willkie's newly found isolationist rhetoric. But when polls indicated that Willkie had gained support, Roosevelt reassured the American public that he did not intend to lead the United States into another foreign war. Toward the end of the campaign, Roosevelt placated nervous handlers with a bold reminder: "I have said this before, but I shall say it again and again and again: Your boys are not going to be sent into any foreign war." Roosevelt quietly instructed his more nervous advisers and handlers that a direct attack on the United States was not a "foreign" war, and he was careful to remark, "Of course we'll fight if attacked."

Willkie was an energetic campaigner, stumping hard across the country, but not always with good results. This was particularly true in the early days of his campaign; then, his speeches, while earnest, were amateurish compared to those of the president, and when he committed himself to outlandish charges about Roosevelt "selling Czechoslovakia down the river at Munich"—making a false claim, as neither Roosevelt nor any of his emissaries were present at Munich or even remotely involved in the appeasement that occurred there—Willkie's press secretary had to withdraw the claim to save face. On domestic policy, Willkie continued to criticize the New Deal in the abstract but tended to concede some of its successes. As the campaign moved into its latter weeks, Willkie's charge that Roosevelt's domestic policy was a step toward totalitarianism, along with his claims that the president was tilting toward war, began to gain some traction. The polls began to show gains, and there was a sense of momentum in the Republican camp.

Roosevelt responded with restraint. When he spoke, he spoke as the president, even when it was clear that his pronouncements were thinly veiled to address issues in the campaign. And he sustained his typical grace and eloquence, an effective contrast to Willkie's unskilled, almost awkward oratory. After a period of reserve, and beginning in late October as the election approached, the president finally made his move and, with impeccable timing, delivered a series of five extraordinary speeches that were more openly political than his previous, low-keyed responses to Willkie, and that forthrightly and expertly defended his administration. This set of speeches, which have been regarded as among his best, succeeded in deflating much of Willkie's rhetoric. In the fifth speech, given in Cleveland in early November just days before Election Day, Roosevelt gave what many regard to be one of his greatest speeches, observing that

There are certain forces within our national community, composed of men who call themselves American but who would destroy America. They are the forces of dictatorship in our land—on one hand, the Communists, and on the other, the Girdlers. It is their constant purpose in this as in other lands to weaken democracy, to destroy the free man's faith in his own cause. In this election all the representatives of those forces, without exception, are voting against the New Deal. You and I are proud of that opposition. It is positive proof that what we have built and strengthened in the past seven years is democracy! This generation of Americans is living in a tremendous moment of history. The surge of events abroad has made some few doubters among us ask: Is this the end of a story that has been told? Is the book of democracy now to be closed and placed away upon the dusty shelves of time? My answer is this: All we have known of the glories of democracy—its freedom, its efficiency as a mode of living, its ability to meet the aspirations of the common man—all these are merely an introduction to the greater story of a more glorious future. We Americans of today—all of us—we are characters in this living book of democracy. But we are also its author. It falls upon us now to say whether the chapters that are to come will tell a story of retreat or a story of continued advance. I believe that the American people will say: "Forward!" (American Presidency Project)

It was a brilliant speech delivered in FDR's incomparable style, striking a noble chord throughout. Bringing the speech to its conclusion, the president confidently affirmed that

In that building of [the future] we shall prove that our faith is strong enough to survive the most fearsome storms that have ever swept over the earth. In the days and months and years to come, we shall be making history—hewing out a new shape for the future. And we shall make very sure that that future of ours bears the likeness of liberty. Always the heart and the soul of our country will be the heart and the soul of the common man—the men and the women who never have ceased to believe in democracy, who never have ceased to love their families, their homes and their country. The spirit of the common man is the spirit of peace and good will. It is the spirit of God. And in His faith is the strength of all America. (American Presidency Project)

If there had been any doubt that the president could deflect Willkie's challenge, it was now allayed. Willkie did not have an effective counter-response to the president's latest volley, and on Election Day, Franklin Delano Roosevelt became the first, and only, president to be elected to a third term.

Roosevelt won in another landslide, but it was not nearly as staggering as the previous two victories. FDR won over 27,300,000 popular votes (or just under 55%), which was about 400,000 less than in 1936, and which converted to 449 votes in the Electoral College drawn from 38 states (winning 85% to 15% in the Electoral College). Willkie won over 22,300,000 popular votes (just over 45%) and 10 states for a total of 82 electoral votes. He took Michigan, Iowa (the home state of Henry Wallace, FDR's running mate), and Indiana from Roosevelt in the Midwest, and Maine and New Hampshire in New England; he was particularly strong in the Great Plains states, where he took North Dakota, South Dakota, Nebraska, and Kansas; and finally, in the Intermountain West, he won in Colorado, which had twice gone for Roosevelt in 1932 and 1936. By any standard except his own past triumphs, Roosevelt's victory was impressive.

Willkie, while soundly defeated, still offered signs of hope for the Republicans. Against a very popular president, he won six million more votes than Landon had in 1936, and seven million more than Hoover in 1932. In fact, Willkie's total popular vote amounted to the highest number of votes for a Republican candidate in history, exceeding Hoover's previous record, set in 1928, by over 900,000 votes—a figure that demonstrated that the GOP, while now out of the White House for the longest streak in the party's history, still a minority in both houses of Congress (although gains were made in the Senate, with some ground lost in the House), and still burdened by the blame for the Great Depression, was nonetheless still a viable political force. Willkie also won 1,147 counties in 1940 compared to Landon's meager 459 in 1936. Interestingly, while Roosevelt took what was, at that time, the six largest Electoral College states (in order, New York, Pennsylvania, Illinois, Ohio, Texas, and California), his margin of victory in New York, his home state, was much slimmer than in the previous two elections; significantly, Willkie actually outpolled FDR among New York Democrats (48% to 45%), even to the point of beating Roosevelt in all but three New York counties. Only with the addition to Roosevelt's cause of just over 400,000 votes from the minor American Labor Party was the president able to carry New York. Willkie also beat Roosevelt in a majority of the counties in Pennsylvania, Illinois, and Ohio—the second-, third-, and fourth-largest Electoral College states—but FDR won in the bigger cities in those states, notably Philadelphia, Pittsburgh, Chicago, Cleveland, and Youngstown (Cincinnati, by leaning toward Willkie, being the only exception), and thus by holding his urban base managed to retain the big states for the Democratic ticket. While Roosevelt won in every major city (except Cincinnati) throughout the country, Willkie took the Great Plains and Midwestern farm vote away from FDR, winning significant swaths of rural country. In Nebraska and Kansas, for example, Willkie almost shut FDR out, winning in all but four counties in Kansas and all but eight counties in Nebraska, with similar results in the Dakotas.

Unfortunately, the Campaign of 1940 grew acrimonious toward the end; but shortly after the election, Roosevelt and Willkie reconciled. Willkie's finest moment came in his defeat when he delivered a gracious concession, calling for the end of antagonistic politics. Willkie became a political ally of Roosevelt's, working closely with the president throughout his next term and winning the president's deepening friendship. This was a most fitting turn, for such amity and mutual loyalty among American leaders became vital during the terrible challenges and hardships that awaited the country in the months and years ahead.

Additional Resources

The American Presidency Project. http://www.presidency.ucsb.edu/ws/index.php?pid= 15893#ixzz1IrXVzcXp.

Burke, Robert E. "Election of 1940." In Arthur M. Schlesinger and Fred L. Israel, eds. *History of American Presidential Politics, 1789–1968*. Vol. 3. New York: McGraw-Hill, 1971.

Doenecke, Justus. "1940." In Arthur M. Schlesinger, Fred L. Israel, and David J. Frent, eds. *Running for President: The Candidates and Their Images*. Vol. 2. New York: Simon & Schuster, 1994.

Moscow, Warren. *Roosevelt and Willkie*. Englewood Cliffs, NJ: Prentice-Hall, 1968.

Peters, Charles. *Five Days in Philadelphia: 1940, Wendell Willkie, FDR, and the Political Convention that Freed FDR to Win World War II*. New York: Public Affairs, 2006.

Smith, Jean Edward. *FDR*. New York: Random House, 2008.

Campaign of 1944

"The Republican Party accepts the purposes of the National Labor Relations Act, the Wage and Hour Act, the Social Security Act and all other Federal statutes designed to promote and protect the welfare of American working men and women, and we promise a fair and just administration of these laws." Inserting this plank into its 1944 campaign platform, the GOP pledged to sustain these as well as many other programs that were generated by the Democrats under President Franklin Roosevelt's New Deal. Even though the Republican platform abstractly vilified the New Deal on principle, when it came to specifics, much of Roosevelt's social and economic vision for the country had now been accepted across party lines. Roosevelt grew bolder: In his 1944 State of the Union address, FDR sketched what he deemed a "second Bill of Rights," or "economic rights" that he conceived as encapsulating his vision of a postwar United States, rights that reaffirmed his general progressive vision and that resonated with the majority of American voters. Roosevelt was so dominant in the political landscape that there was no question of his standing for renomination by his party for a fourth term. Few leaders were trusted to cope with the apocalyptic crises that had roiled across the globe over the past five years, and the Democrats knew better than anyone that FDR had to continue on. Conservatives within the party were far from enamored with the president, but they were in the minority, and they were savvy enough to know that the Roosevelt name was enough by itself to guarantee the nomination.

The only concern at the convention involved the vice presidency. The incumbent vice president, Henry Wallace, was viewed by moderates and conservatives in the party as far too radical, and by most in the party from both sides of the aisle as too eccentric, to be trusted with the responsibilities that might arise in light of the president's current health. Rumors circulated that Roosevelt's health had turned for the worse; thus it did not take much imagination to fear the worst-case scenario. Delegates at the convention were determined to prepare for that dreaded possibility in the event that the president was lost, and they were convinced that in the event of such a tragedy, should it come, a President Wallace in command of the enormous military might of the United States was not a prospect to be entertained. Thus the convention sought to replace Wallace, even though Roosevelt himself enjoyed a good relationship with his vice president and would not openly support a movement to dislodge him. Nor would he oppose it, and a brief contest ensued between liberals (who favored renominating Wallace) and moderates (who sought to replace him with Missouri senator Harry S. Truman, a widely respected, capable, plain-spoken, no-nonsense son of the Show Me State). With Roosevelt and Truman on the ticket, the Democrats yet again entered the campaign from a position of strength.

Nonetheless, the Republican Party, while still in the minority and facing an enormously popular incumbent president, had already started to close the gap and had begun to show strength of its own, gaining considerable ground in the 1942 midterm elections, which infused the party with a new sense of confidence.

Roosevelt had been pressed by congressional Republicans on tax policy and found himself in the unusual condition of being at a disadvantage. When Roosevelt did not get the tax bill that he wanted, but rather a compromise hammered out between the majority Democrats and minority Republicans, Roosevelt acerbically attacked Congress in general. This provoked Senate majority leader Alben Barkley, a fellow Democrat, to issue a strong rebuttal to the president and, in an act of defiance, resign his position as majority leader (he was immediately reelected by his fellow senators in a show of solidarity, in itself an unexpected swipe at the president). Stung by the actions of his fellow Democrats in the Senate, Roosevelt backed down and sent out olive branches to the Senate leadership.

But the domestic conflicts between the executive and legislative branches were rendered trivial when compared to the events abroad. Between the Japanese attack on Pearl Harbor in December 1941 and the opening of the presidential campaign of 1944, the United States had entered the most destructive and horrific war in history, the devastation of which, in terms of both human life and property, was of a scale hitherto unimaginable, even by the terrible measures set by World War I. The full force and might of American resources were brought to bear in that dreadful cataclysm, resulting in the creation of astonishing military and economic power, the likes of which had not been seen before, even when compared to the greatest empires of the past. Franklin Roosevelt was at the helm of this Herculean effort, and while some grumbled about his disorganized style of management and his odd proclivity for stimulating conflict among his subordinates, he was widely lionized at home and, even more significantly, beloved abroad, acclaimed as a statesman of world caliber.

After the United States struggled in the first months of the war, partially accounting for Republican gains in the midterms of 1942, the tide had been turned well before the presidential campaign of 1944. Even though a year of warfare remained ahead as the national conventions commenced (less than a year in Europe, just over a year in the Pacific), there was a strong, confident sense that the Allied powers would in the end be victorious. By the 1944 election season, the U.S. Navy ruled the oceans, and the successful invasion of Normandy was just under way. Roosevelt was an able commander in chief, and the recent successes of the Allies boosted his image at home. Even though Republicans were tempted to publicize scandalous rumors (which have subsequently been proven to be unfounded) that Roosevelt might have known beforehand about the imminent Pearl Harbor attack in time to intercept it but failed to do so, in the end they suppressed the temptation, partly for national security reasons and partly because of Roosevelt's formidable stature. Even Roosevelt's strongest critics would not touch him on his statesmanship as a leader of the Allied war effort. The fact that he was admired by both the British leader Sir Winston Churchill and the Soviet leader Josef Stalin lent further credence to his reputation as a statesman. His political enemies might object to his principles and even his personality, but they openly saluted his wartime leadership. Republicans would not, and could not, base their campaign strategy against President Roosevelt on either the New Deal or his leadership at war. Another tack was needed.

Three strategic options remained for the Republicans. First, they could amplify allegations about Roosevelt's administrative inefficiency and claim that the administration had become enervated, and even slightly corrupt, with age; the argument being that it is natural for the rot to set in if an organization, such as a president's administration, is around long enough. Second, they could draw attention to what they perceived to be dangerous connections to communism and communist sympathizers, in the same spirit that would later produce the McCarthy hearings of the next decade. And third, they could dwell at length on the health of the president, who at only sixty-two years of age was showing visible signs of fatigue and physical decline. All three approaches would eventually be floated once the Republicans found their candidate.

As the campaign season opened, seven candidates were in the mix: Wendell Willkie, a friendly rival of the president, who had been the Republican candidate in the previous election; Senator Robert Taft, who had come to be known as "Mr. Republican" and who had also been, for a brief time, a possible candidate for the nomination four years earlier; General Douglas MacArthur, the flamboyant current Allied commander in the Pacific theater and a favorite of GOP conservatives; Minnesota's former governor, Harold Stassen, another naval officer deployed abroad under Admiral Halsey and a supporter of Willkie in 1940; Governor John W. Bricker of Ohio, who received the support of Taft after he himself announced he would not pursue the nomination; Illinois representative Everett Dirksen; and the eventual front-runner, Thomas Dewey of New York, who, like Taft, had also been in the running for the nomination in 1940.

Early in the campaign season, Willkie was the name that entered the minds of most Republicans as the likely nominee. Owing to his restless energy and ongoing achievements, Willkie remained in the public eye and continued to be a popular figure. Even though he and Roosevelt remained friendly toward each other, in public Willkie did not hesitate to criticize the president, and he had continued to draw attention as a leading spokesman for the GOP. By November 1943, a Gallup poll indicated that just under 34 percent of registered Republicans desired that Willkie run again, putting him ahead of the field, with Dewey finishing a distant second at slightly below 18 percent. Hence Willkie once again seemed to be the man for the GOP, and as the campaign season opened, Willkie won the New Hampshire primary and was thus in the position of front-runner. But when Dewey won the Wisconsin primary, crushing the opposition in spite of Willkie's hard campaigning, a resigned Willkie withdrew from the campaign (not one delegate had committed to his cause), leaving Dewey in a contest with a fairly weak pool. The celebrated MacArthur, who was running war operations in the Far East, could not campaign owing to his command responsibilities in the Pacific, and the other candidates lacked Dewey's national reputation. In 1940, Dewey was regarded within the party leadership as too young to handle Roosevelt; but now he had more experience and influence in the party, and as a moderate, he easily bridged the gap between Old Guard Republicans and the party's liberal wing, and he also promised wider appeal in a contest against a widely beloved incumbent. Dewey was easily nominated on the first ballot at the national convention in Chicago; Bricker was selected to run with Dewey in the second spot.

Dewey was youthful, energetic, serious, and buttoned-down. In sharp contrast to the relationship between Roosevelt and Willkie, a tangible animosity existed between Roosevelt and Dewey, both New Yorkers. Dewey had an abrasive, humorless, and somewhat aloof personality that had alienated most of the members of the press working the campaign trail. He deliberately presented himself as the epitome of efficiency, formality, planning, and organization; but for the most part, it left those around him cold. That aside, Dewey was fixated on his desire to portray an image of administrative competence, a key element of the Republicans' strategy for the general election. However, the claim that Roosevelt was an incompetent and manipulative administrator—one of the three strategic options that the Republicans saw as available to them—was unconvincing. After twelve years of dealing with social, economic, and foreign crises of previously unknown magnitude and gravity, the public was unmoved by such arguments. But Dewey and his supporters continued to strike at what they considered one of Roosevelt's few weaknesses, and in so doing, they managed to gain some verification for their claims from within the Roosevelt administration. FDR's secretary of war, Henry Stimson, admitted his disappointment with Roosevelt as an administrator, and there were rumors of discontent at the State Department as well. Roosevelt and the State Department often worked either at cross-purposes or in the dark as to each other's intentions, causing a climate of confusion among the leadership at State. The Republicans exploited the divisions between Roosevelt and his underlings in the State Department, employing personal attacks and mudslinging to depict the entire department as corrupt and incompetent.

The Republicans' second strategic approach, alleging communist sympathies in the administration, failed to gain much traction. The red-baiting they employed played well in some parts of the country—but again, only in those parts that were already anti-Roosevelt and thus looking for more reasons to hate "that man." The old canard that Roosevelt was, in effect, a dictator was no longer available to his enemies, as the American public—indeed, the entire world—had become all too familiar with the real meaning of dictatorship during the course of the war.

The GOP's last approach, the president's health concerns, seemed to offer a more promising weapon. However, the president's critics could only suggest, imply, or insinuate; no one wanted to publicly embarrass Roosevelt over the issue of his physical condition, particularly given the heroic manner in which he overcame his disability, combined with the custom in those days of overlooking and not publicizing the health problems of public figures, and especially personages of Roosevelt's stature and importance. Everyone knew that such a ploy would also play all too well in Berlin or Tokyo; thus the health issue, which was in fact the best that they had in their arsenal, could only be hinted at obliquely.

Because Republicans had made substantial gains during the congressional and state elections of 1942, Dewey's candidacy was able to feed off that momentum. Dewey worked hard to make the most of it, and even though Roosevelt's strengths were formidable, he campaigned aggressively. Dewey assaulted the administration, describing it as an inefficient, backbiting, quasi-socialistic, geriatric empire in decay. Dewey boasted that his administration would be "fresh and vigorous," bringing needed professionalism and effective leadership to a decaying presidency that was marked by exhaustion and internal bickering. Roosevelt had, in Dewey's estimation, led the country down the "road to total control of our daily lives" and had left the federal government in a condition of corruption and "disrepute." Upon closer observation, though, Dewey's criticisms of the New Deal were not entirely aligned with his views regarding specific New Deal programs; for by and large, he reflected the level to which the Republican Party had indeed, by the mid-1940s, accepted many of the innovations that came out of the Roosevelt years. One wag at the *New York Times* observed that Dewey had "just about completed the process of running for the Presidency on the domestic platform of the New Deal," an observation that was shared by the more conservative elements in the GOP, who felt Dewey was too moderate, maybe even liberal.

Dewey tried to compensate in his rhetoric, becoming more acerbic when referring to FDR's leadership and the moral questions behind the New Deal in the abstract. Roosevelt, Dewey insisted, had governed above the law, and the restoration of the rule of law under a Republican administration was now necessary. Much of what Dewey claimed was not far from Willkie's criticisms in 1940, or even some of the criticisms that Willkie had offered in the interval; but when the assault came from Dewey, his fellow New Yorker whom Roosevelt disliked, the president took it more personally and, in retrospect, referred to Dewey's challenge as "the meanest campaign of my life." Many in the press, whether they supported Dewey or not, found him far less agreeable than Roosevelt. Even with his health in decline, the president remained at ease in conversation and inviting in his demeanor, and he was far more approachable than the officious Dewey.

Roosevelt maintained his preferred tactic of remaining above the fray, not mentioning his opponent by name, running on his own record, and reminding the voters of the troubles brought to the country by the former dominance of the Grand Old Party. His lieutenants, however, would target Dewey personally. Harold Ickes had already mocked Dewey's youth. When the Republican unsuccessfully ran for his party's nomination in 1940, Ickes commented that Dewey had "thrown his diaper in the ring." Now in 1944, when the candidate Dewey adopted positions consonant with New Deal accomplishments, Ickes, riffing on the earlier diaper quip, remarked that the Republican nominee had "thrown a sponge into the ring." For the most part, Roosevelt spent the campaign season dealing with the war, which in itself was the most effective campaigning strategy.

It was not until the final eight weeks of the campaign that the president turned his attention to the Republican challenge. On September 23, with Election Day six weeks away, the president spoke before a meeting of the International Brotherhood of Teamsters in an address that was broadcast live to the American public. Roosevelt appeared as vigorous and spirited as ever, dispelling, at least to the audience present and those following the event over radio, the rumors of his poor health. Tapping into the Roosevelt magic, which was palpable even to those tuning in on the broadcast, the speech was immediately recognized as yet another masterpiece, reminiscent of the set of five speeches that he gave late in the **Campaign of 1940** that successfully obliterated, once and for all, any serious challenge.

In Lincolnesque fashion, Roosevelt humorously demonstrated his famed mastery of rhetorical wit and timing, a dramatic contrast to the comparatively dry and dour speeches by the ever-serious Dewey. Roosevelt blithely dissected the Republican platform. Like a surgeon, he effortlessly deflated the GOP charge that the country had still been in a depression as it entered the war in 1941. Instructing his audience, Roosevelt quipped, "Now there is an old and somewhat lugubrious adage which says: 'Never speak of a rope in the house of a man who's been hanged.' In the same way, if I were a Republican leader speaking to a mixed audience, the last word in the whole dictionary that I would be using is that word depression." The highlight of the speech came toward the end, when the president, in a brilliant stroke that epitomized everything about him as a politician, answered Republican allegations that Roosevelt had cavalierly squandered naval resources during wartime to retrieve his lost dog Fala, a Scottish terrier who, as the story goes, had been inadvertently abandoned in the Aleutians during a recent visit to that region by the president. In good humor, Roosevelt chided the Republicans and deflected Republican charges of inefficiency and wasteful self-indulgence in the prosecution of the war:

These Republican leaders have not been content with attacks on me, or on my wife, or on my sons. No, not content with that, they now include my little dog Fala. Well, of course, I don't resent attacks, and my family doesn't resent attacks, but Fala does resent them. You know, you know, Fala's Scotch, and being a Scottie, as soon as he learned that the Republicans' fiction writers in Congress had concocted a story that I had left him behind on an Aleutian island and had sent a destroyer back to find him—at a cost to the taxpayers of two or three or eight or twenty million dollars—his Scotch soul was furious. He has not been the same dog since. I am accustomed to hearing malicious falsehoods about myself—such as that old, worm-eaten chestnut that I have represented myself to be indispensable. But I think I have a right to resent, to object to libelous statements about my dog.

Those who were in the audience responded with waves of laughter, and with what would become known as the "Fala speech," Roosevelt had, with just a few expertly timed, humorous sentences, deftly and comically demolished the Dewey campaign. Pining for some excitement after weeks of suffering Dewey's arid and fussy campaign, the press was yet again completely won over by FDR's inexhaustible good nature. Reporting on the Fala speech, *Time* magazine declared that "[Roosevelt] was like a veteran virtuoso playing a piece he has loved for years, who fingers his way through it with a delicate fire, a perfection of tuning and tone, and an assurance that no young player, no matter how gifted, can equal. The President was playing what he loves to play—politics." Samuel Rosenman, one of the members of Roosevelt's famous brain trust, remarked that it was Roosevelt's finest campaign speech, exceeding even his highly lauded efforts toward the end of the 1940 campaign. To this day, it remains a model of political mastery, and it is the sort of rhetorical performance that places Franklin Roosevelt in the same rarified company as Abraham Lincoln.

No doubt the Fala speech was not the only reason why President Roosevelt was elected to a fourth term, but it reveals, perhaps more than any other moment in the campaign, the difference between Franklin Roosevelt and just about every other politician then or now. On Election Day, Roosevelt won slightly more than 25,600,000 votes to approximately 22,000,000 for Dewey (or approximately 53% to 46%, with the remaining 1% going to minor candidates), which converted to an Electoral College victory of 432 to 99 (or 81% to 19%). It was another Roosevelt landslide, at least in terms of electoral votes; but compared to his previous three victories, it was the least impressive. Dewey won the ten states that Willkie won in 1940, with the exception of Michigan, which went to FDR, and also added three more—Wyoming, Wisconsin, and Ohio—for a net gain of two states in what was overall the strongest Electoral College finish by a Republican since Hoover in

1928, which was at that time the last GOP victory. It should be noted, however, that Dewey received about 220,000 fewer popular votes than Willkie had in 1940. In defeat, Willkie's total popular vote in 1940 was still the highest ever received by a Republican candidate to that date, Dewey unable to surpass that figure in spite of his gains in the Electoral College. Interestingly, Dewey failed to win New York, which many felt was in play after Willkie nearly took it from Roosevelt four years earlier (and would have taken if it had not been for the support for Roosevelt from the American Labor Party, which made the difference for FDR in New York on Election Day), and Roosevelt actually showed strength in the home state of the two rivals, beating Dewey there by taking 52 percent of the vote, 2 percentage points better than his finish against Willkie.

To the sorrow of a nation, President Franklin Delano Roosevelt's fourth term came to an abrupt end nearly three months after his fourth inauguration. As some anticipated might happen, the indomitable Harry Truman became the thirty-third president of the United States on April 12, 1945, shortly after President Roosevelt passed away. Even though it was apparent to many that the president's health had declined, and obvious to insiders that he was indeed failing, his death was still a traumatic shock. Roosevelt was the kind of politician that one would either fervently love or despise, but in the end, the entire nation mourned his loss. Roosevelt's combination of courageous leadership, illimitable optimism, high-spirited wit, stirring vision, fearless commitment, and genuine goodwill were difficult to resist, even to his enemies. A young congressman from Texas, Lyndon Johnson, on hearing of the president's death, tearfully professed an affection nearly universally shared: "He was like a daddy to me always, he always talked to me just that way. He was the one person I ever knew—anywhere—who was never afraid. Whatever you talked to him about, whatever you asked him for, like projects for your district, there was just one way to figure it with him. I know some of them called it demagoguery; they can call it anything they want but you could be damn sure that the only test he had was this: Was it good for the folks?"

Regardless of one's final assessment of the wisdom of his political principles and the ultimate success or failure of their application, or of the nature of his ambitions and the motivations behind his ascent, Franklin Roosevelt was and remains the defining political figure of what many have called the "American Century," and he was a towering international statesman during what was, by any and all criteria, far and away the worst war in human history. His importance in that capacity cannot be overstated. Perhaps, as recounted by biographer Jean Smith, the testimony of Sir Winston Churchill, the eminent British prime minister who worked with FDR as closely as anyone possibly could, provides the final word on both the personal character and lasting importance of Franklin Roosevelt. As Roosevelt and Churchill parted company at the conclusion of one of their many wartime meetings, Churchill, nervously watching as the president's plane taxied toward departure, candidly and perhaps in a rare moment of unguarded humility, confessed to an aide his innermost feelings about Roosevelt: "He is the truest friend; he has the furthest vision; he is the greatest man I have ever known."

Additional Resources

Divine, Robert. *Foreign Policy and the U.S. Presidential Elections, 1940–1948.* New York: New Viewpoints, 1974.

Evans, Hugh. *The Hidden Campaign: FDR's Health and the 1944 Election.* Armonk, NY: M. E. Sharpe, 2002.

Fraser, Steven. "1944." In Arthur M. Schlesinger, Fred L. Israel, and David J. Frent, eds. *Running for President: The Candidates and Their Images.* Vol. 2. New York: Simon & Schuster, 1994.

Friedman, Leon. "Election of 1944." In Arthur M. Schlesinger, Fred Israel, and William P. Hansen, eds. *History of American Presidential Elections, 1789–1968.* Vol. 2. New York: Chelsea House, 1985.

Smith, Jean Edward. *FDR.* New York: Random House, 2007.

Campaign of 1948

In the summer of 1944, Missouri senator Harry S. Truman was nominated by the Democratic Party for the vice presidency, joining the ticket that sought to reelect for a fourth term the incumbent president Franklin Roosevelt. At the nominating convention held in Chicago that summer, Senator Truman issued a brief statement accepting the nomination. Well over a month later, Truman gave a second, longer acceptance speech at an event in his birthplace of Lamar, Missouri, in which, while stressing the need to reelect FDR owing to the president's experience, leadership, and intimate knowledge of the war, he observed, "The end of hostilities may come suddenly. Decisions that will determine our future for years, and even generations to come, will have to be made quickly. If they are made quickly and wisely by those who have had years of experience and the fullest opportunities to become well informed with respect to our national and international problems, we can have confidence that the next generation will not have to spill its blood to rectify our mistakes and failures."

In sharing these thoughts, Truman was emphasizing the need for experience in the Oval Office, the experience that was guaranteed in the reelection of the incumbent president, the implication being that his opposition, Republican candidate Thomas Dewey, could not bring that same guarantee to the presidency, given the nature of the times and what was at stake. Truman further remarked, "It takes time for anyone to familiarize himself with a new job. This is particularly true of the presidency of the United States, the most difficult and complex job in the world.... There will be no time to learn, and mistakes once made cannot be unmade."

Truman's observations were widely shared. Even though some were uncomfortable with the prospect of a four-term president, and others were concerned over the health of a visibly aging, physically weakened Roosevelt, the argument that the president's unmatched experience was vital, given the dangers of the times and the demands of the war, was a persuasive one. One could not fight Hitler and the Japanese Empire, or meet with Churchill and Stalin, without the confidence, probity, and fortitude that come from the experience of having braved terrible ordeals and the maturity that follows the necessities of hard decision. Questions of health and ideological differences could not outweigh that one fact. Few people seriously believed that Dewey could bring to the war what Roosevelt had and still could. Within eight months, Harry Truman, elected as the thirty-fourth vice president of the United States, came into intimate knowledge of the meaning behind the rhetoric; just eighty-two days after his inauguration as the vice president, President Roosevelt passed away, and Truman became the thirty-third president of the United States.

The war, while drawing to a close in Europe, was still raging in the Pacific, and while the military might of the United States had nearly destroyed the Japanese Imperial Navy, Japanese forces bravely fought with a resolution and ferocity that indicated they were far from defeat. Thus into the fray, the newly inaugurated President Truman, a capable senator and skilled politician, came to his responsibilities every bit as inexperienced as the Republican challenger of whom he spoke in that acceptance speech at Lamar. He was now faced with continuing the leadership of the American forces as they concluded the most destructive war in history, and the responsibility of diplomatically dealing with the strong leadership of the United States' allies, and in particular Josef Stalin. As the fighting in the Pacific seemed to intensify even as the Nazis fell in Europe, Truman found himself facing one of the more momentous decisions that had ever been expected of any world leader, let alone an American president. The decision, the use of newly invented atomic weapons against the Japanese homeland, finally ended the horrors of World War II, ushering in the "atomic age," and within just four months of his inauguration, thrusting upon President Truman the kind of responsibility that no man, regardless of experience, temperament, and character, should have to bear. But bear it Truman did; the plain-spoken, unassuming son of Missouri farmers, former army captain (having served with distinction during World War I), former businessman and product of Missouri's Pendergast political machine, became the first (and, it can only be hoped, the only) world leader ever to order the deployment of nuclear weapons, a dread decision that was spared his beloved predecessor. With the war over, President Truman now turned to managing a new peace won through an unimaginable sacrifice drawn from the peoples of many nations, confronting a resurgent Republican Party, and absorbing the petty discontents that were brewing throughout the political landscape.

With the war won and the Great Depression over, the Republicans finally recaptured a majority in Congress for the first time since 1930. The GOP had been making gradual gains over the past few election cycles, and it finally broke the Democratic majority during the 1946 midterms. While the Democrats still held the White House, Congressional Republicans outnumbered the Democrats 246 to 188 in the House of Representatives, and 51 to 45 in the Senate. The transition from wartime to a peacetime economy created a multitude of problems for the young Truman administration. With the end to wartime wage and price controls, inflation soared as the demand of American consumers, tired of wartime rationing and frugality, drove increased prices for scarce consumer goods. Seeking to protect wages, labor unions called a record number of strikes. In response to labor unrest, a Republican-led Congress passed the Taft-Hartley Act of 1947, which prohibited labor unions from making campaign contributions to candidates for federal office and authorized states to pass right-to-work laws. With the labor unions agitated, disunity was now more evident within the Democratic Party; the liberal wing was displeased with Truman over his antagonistic stance toward labor, an important bloc within the Roosevelt Coalition. Liberals feared that as former Roosevelt appointees within the executive branch were replaced by more moderate and conservative Truman appointees, the New Deal was being abandoned by the new administration.

Equally important, by the beginning of the 1948 campaign, the euphoria associated with the end of World War II and the establishment of the United Nations gave way to a cold war between the United States and its former ally, the Soviet Union. Concern increased over the activities of communist subversives inside the United States. While the Republican Party for the most part strongly supported new domestic security measures, liberal Democrats expressed reservations about the potential impact of such measures on the civil liberties of American citizens. Additionally, Southern Democrats were aggravated by Truman's open sympathies with the African American community and his support of recommendations offered by his Committee on Civil Rights, which conservative Democrats perceived as too radical and a sign of ingratitude, given their support of Truman for the vice presidency over then-incumbent Henry Wallace at the convention of 1944. Southern conservatives interpreted Truman's actions as a cynical attempt to curry the African American vote in the North, and for the first time since the end of Reconstruction, it appeared that the southern bloc, the Democratic Party's most reliable reservoir of electoral power, might now be in play, jeopardizing the party's plans to retain the White House.

Worst of all, Truman's popularity had greatly suffered. In April 1948, during the early weeks of the campaign season, polls indicated that the president's approval rating had dipped to just 36 percent, nineteen percentage points below more favorable numbers that he had enjoyed as recently as the previous October. In another poll asking respondents to indicate who they thought would serve as the most effective president, only 11 percent selected Truman, with 24 percent naming General Dwight D. Eisenhower, even though he was openly disinterested. Since the conclusion of the war, Eisenhower had been courted by both parties, and many in the Democratic Party saw in the general a stronger, more capable leader than the president. Eisenhower, who kept his party affinities to himself, eventually announced that he was a Republican, but in late 1947–early 1948, an effort to dump Truman for Eisenhower was set in motion, and even after Eisenhower refused to accept any nomination from either party, some still worked for that result well into spring.

Thus Truman was vulnerable on many fronts; nonetheless, when the Democratic convention opened in Philadelphia, he was the clear candidate to bear the Democratic standard. This was to a considerable extent the result of efforts by energetic and intelligent supporters on Truman's behalf, led by prominent members of the president's inner circle of advisers such as Clark Clifford and Charles S. Murphy, supportive members of Congress such as Rhode Island senator J. Howard McGrath (who also served as both the party's national chairman and the president's campaign manager), and key individuals in the party leadership such as the former party chair Robert Hannegan. With Eisenhower no longer an option, the only challenger to Truman was conservative senator Richard Russell of Georgia, but as events unfolded at the convention, Russell's challenge was quickly blunted. Truman won the nomination on the first ballot, with Kentucky senator and veteran New Dealer Alben W. Barkley selected as the vice presidential nominee.

But Russell was the least of Truman's worries. Even though Truman easily won the nomination on the first ballot, a remarkable recovery from the feeble approval ratings exhibited by the polls leading up to the convention, a battle ensued over the platform that caused a full breach within the party. Now that the war was over, liberal Democrats (particularly in the Northeast and the Midwest) intensified their focus on the issue of civil rights, particularly for African Americans; and at the convention, the liberal wing of the party proposed and succeeded in securing the adoption of a progressive civil rights plank that exceeded the plank added in 1944:

> The Democratic Party is responsible for the great civil rights gains made in recent years in eliminating unfair and illegal discrimination based on race, creed or color. The Democratic Party commits itself to continuing its efforts to eradicate all racial, religious and economic discrimination. We again state

our belief that racial and religious minorities must have the right to live, the right to work, the right to vote, the full and equal protection of the laws, on a basis of equality with all citizens as guaranteed by the Constitution. We highly commend President Harry S. Truman for his courageous stand on the issue of civil rights. We call upon the Congress to support our President in guaranteeing these basic and fundamental American Principles: (1) the right of full and equal political participation; (2) the right to equal opportunity of employment; (3) the right of security of person; (4) and the right of equal treatment in the service and defense of our nation. (American Presidency Project, University of California, Santa Barbara)

The latter clause referring to military service was a direct endorsement of President Truman's Executive Order 9981, which had formerly desegregated the U.S. military, although the process of desegregation had already incrementally begun during World War II under the leadership of both the late President Roosevelt (counseled by First Lady Eleanor Roosevelt) and General Eisenhower. Truman, who was satisfied with the party's 1944 platform on issues of this nature, was regarded by most within the party as a moderate on civil rights, but his decision to officially desegregate the entire military is regarded by many historians as the first of many significant postwar steps in the civil rights movement. Southern conservatives were frustrated with Truman, causing them to turn to leaders such as Senator Russell, who unabashedly sought to preserve racial segregation. Thus a simmering discontent between the liberal wing and the conservative, Southern wing percolated into the national convention, intensified by the proposed civil rights plank, and brought to a boil by the eloquence of the progressive mayor of Minneapolis, Hubert H. Humphrey, an ebullient rising star within the party. Humphrey's stirring speech galvanized pro-civil rights delegates, and that, in prompting the passage of their plank, also prompted a number of Southern conservatives to walk out of the convention, leaving those who remained steeled in their opposition against both the platform and the president. Led by South Carolina's Governor J. Strom Thurmond, these bolting Southern conservative Democrats, known as "Dixiecrats" (or formally, the States' Rights Democratic Party), would convene their own convention in Birmingham and nominate Thurmond as their candidate for president, tapping Governor Fielding L. Wright of Mississippi as his running mate. Strongly defending the practice of segregation, the Dixiecrat platform warned that increased federal power put the nation on course toward a totalitarian police state. Not mincing words, the Dixiecrats averred, "We oppose and condemn the action of the Democratic Convention in sponsoring a civil rights program calling for the elimination of segregation, social equality by Federal fiat, regulations of private employment practices, voting, and local law enforcement." With the defection of the Dixiecrats, an important affiliate of the Roosevelt Coalition had now become alienated, and the Democrats' traditional and virtually unbreakable hold on the South (which reached back to the end of Reconstruction) was slipping away.

To make matters even worse for the president and the Democratic Party in general, a movement to revive the Progressive Party (which had not run a presidential candidate since Senator La Follette's campaign in 1924) drew more votes away from the liberal side of the Democratic Party, nominating former vice president Henry Wallace to carry its standard in the general election. Thus elements of both the left and right wings of the party were shaved off, leaving a divided and weakened party to confront the more unified Republican challenge, which, given the evidence of the polls, promised to come in full strength.

There was less drama at the Republican convention held in Philadelphia, the first national convention to be broadcast over television, but it was not without its own divisions. New York governor Thomas R. Dewey, the GOP's nominee against President Roosevelt in 1944, came into the convention riding a wave of momentum that was the result of his winning an important radio debate against his competitors during the Oregon primary. But a number of influential party leaders—among them Harold Stassen, the former governor of Minnesota; "Mr. Republican," Senator Robert Taft of Ohio; and Michigan's venerated senator Arthur Vandenberg— were still able to attract attention and together worked to block a Dewey movement. During the primaries, Dewey's support was tepid, showing a distant fourth, winning only 11.5 percent among those voting in the candidate preference polls, just ahead of entrepreneur and prizefighter Riley Bender of Illinois, who polled 11.3 percent, and well behind the leader, Governor Earl Warren of California (27%), who was followed by Stassen (22%) and Taft (16%). But the Oregon campaign and radio debate boosted Dewey back into the spotlight, and when the convention was gaveled to order, he was perceived as holding the best position.

The Stassen-Taft-Vandenberg alliance against Dewey failed to produce an alternative candidate, causing each of them to guardedly retain his delegates and independently engage against Dewey's rising tide. (Vandenberg managed less than 1% of the preference vote in the primaries but was nonetheless an esteemed figure and was thus able to pull some influence on the convention floor.) Dewey, a veteran of two campaigns for the GOP nomination, winning in 1944, had the better campaign organization and was well prepared to counter the alliance against him. On the first ballot, Dewey won 434 votes to Taft's 224, Stassen's 157, and Vandenberg's 62. Warren, who showed strongest in the primaries, came in fifth with 59. The remainder of the field consisted of seven candidates, none of them winning more than 56 votes. On the second ballot, Dewey gained strength, winning 515 delegates, at which point Senator Taft withdrew, thereby guaranteeing Dewey's nomination, which was unanimously affirmed on the third ballot. Governor Warren, the leader in the primaries whose growing popularity had drawn attention from party leaders, was then selected to join Dewey as his running mate. With no one bolting from the GOP convention, and the party in the end exhibiting a unity that the Democrats clearly seemed to have lost, the Republicans were optimistic as they moved into the general election, a confidence that was verified in the media, where Dewey's impending victory seemed no less than a *fait accompli.*

From the close of the conventions to the eve of Election Day, all the indicators predicted a Dewey landslide. Truman responded by campaigning tirelessly, engaging in a whistle-stop campaign that has become legendary in the annals of American politics. Beginning in September and covering more than 30,000 miles by rail, making as many as eight speeches a day at a total of 201 stops as he moved from town to town, Truman's cross-country tour effectively brought the message and, more importantly, the fighting character of the undaunted president to the people. Senator Barkley also stumped aggressively; as the president took to the rails, Barkley took to the air, becoming one of the earliest candidates to make frequent use of air travel during a presidential campaign. As he journeyed throughout the lower forty-eight, Truman's plain-speaking, hard-hitting, candid, and occasionally colorful delivery worked well in his favor, and his attacks on the "do-nothing Republican Congress" made for good press. The president did not hesitate to target his opponent, ridiculing Dewey's campaign for its failure to deliver nothing more than "soothing syrup" to the voters. Much in the style of William Jennings Bryan, Truman positioned himself as the friend of working men and women. At every stop, Truman supporters would yell, "Give 'em Hell, Harry!" To counter Dewey's financial advantage, the Truman campaign depended upon organized labor to get out the Democratic vote. Overcoming past resentment, Truman managed to finally win over labor, calling for the repeal of the Taft-Hartley Act that had been passed over his veto the previous year. Throughout the campaign, Truman returned to his roots as the true heir to President Roosevelt, arguing that a Republican victory would threaten the very survival of the important New Deal programs that had been established by Democrats and since accepted by moderate and liberal Republicans. He pledged to continue the New Deal system of farm price supports and, steeled against the Dixiecrat bolters, urged the passage of new civil rights laws.

With a large war chest, the Dewey campaign had almost unlimited funds to convey its message to the voters. As in the past, however, Dewey proved to be his own worst enemy. To many voters, Dewey still came across as cold and calculating. At each campaign stop, Dewey repeated the same rote stump speech with little emotion. He frequently repeated bland lines such as "Your future lies ahead of you" (as if one's future could possibly be behind one), and he claimed that when he got to Washington, he "would do the greatest pruning and weeding operation in American history" by cutting the size of government. To his credit, he stumped hard and earnestly; but as he had in 1944, Dewey annoyed his audiences by ending sentences with the word "period," and he continued to come off as priggish and self-important. "The only man who could strut sitting down," one wag cracked; "A man you had to really get to know to dislike," commented another. Equally important, Dewey made a series of campaign gaffes that permitted Truman to punctuate the image of Dewey as unapproachable and uncaring. The most famous of the Dewey gaffes took place in early October 1948, when Dewey was speaking from the back of his own campaign train. The train suddenly lurched backward toward the crowd. Surprised, Dewey responded by telling the crowd, "That's the first lunatic I've had for an engineer. He probably ought to be shot at sunrise but I guess we can let him off because no one was hurt." Meant to be a joke, the awkward comment was widely reported, and Truman and his supporters gleefully used the incident to portray Dewey as no friend of the working man. Responding to Dewey's comment, Truman wryly observed that his rival "objects to having engineers back up. He doesn't mention that under that great engineer, Hoover, we backed up into the worst depression in history."

Dewey, wanting to remain above the fray in the model of his former rival, the incomparable President Roosevelt, made every effort to ignore Truman's jibes. But eventually he lost his forbearance and was goaded to react, accusing the president of slinging mud and resorting to allegations of communists and fellow travelers in the Truman administration. Even so, on the eve of the election, the polls continued to forecast a Dewey victory and the press spoke quite confidently of a "Dewey Presidency." Pundits and analysts wrote columns speculating on the configuration of Dewey's cabinet, and journalists were already referring to Dewey as "our next president." Even Truman himself was braced for defeat, quietly slipping away to his hometown of Independence, Missouri, to await the election returns, while Dewey camped out in New York's Roosevelt Hotel, primed to celebrate his impending victory. But that victory never came; "President-Elect Dewey" did not materialize.

As the first returns came in just after the polls closed, President Truman surprisingly showed a slight lead. Nonetheless, pollsters and journalists were so persuaded that Dewey's election was inevitable that these early indicators were universally dismissed. Newspapers casually went to press declaring that Dewey had been elected as the next president. But as the following day dawned and all the returns were in, the final count in both the popular vote and the Electoral College revealed the contrary—President Truman had been, against all prior signs and indicators, convincingly elected to another term. In a famous photograph snapped the day after the election, a grinning and triumphant President Truman held up the front page of the *Chicago Daily Tribune*, its headline boldly declaring, "Dewey Defeats Truman." But to the embarrassment of the *Tribune*'s editors, such was not the case: Truman won just over 24,180,000 popular votes (49.5%) to Dewey's total of slightly under 22,000,000 (45%), which in comparison to his 1944 campaign against FDR was actually a slight reduction. Strom Thurmond's Dixiecrat ticket managed just under 1,200,000 votes, while Wallace's Progressive ticket took approximately 160,000 votes, and the Socialist Party's eternal candidate Norman Thomas won around 140,000 votes.

The Dixiecrat effort had hurt the Democrats, as Dixiecrats took away four traditionally Democratic states: Louisiana, Mississippi, Alabama, and Thurmond's home state of South Carolina. After Theodore Roosevelt's Bull Moose campaign (which won six states in 1912), it was to that date the second-best showing in the Electoral College enjoyed by any third party (not counting the four-way elections of 1828 and 1860). The final Electoral College tally was 303 for Truman, 189 for Dewey, and 39 for Thurmond. Dewey did take Pennsylvania and his home state of New York, winning also all of New England except Massachusetts (which had, since its support of Al Smith in 1928, converted from a Republican bastion to a Democratic one, which it remains to this day), and swapping Ohio (won in 1944, lost in 1948) for Michigan (lost in 1944, won in 1948). Republicans gained Oregon but lost to the Democrats Wisconsin, Iowa, and the Intermountain states of Colorado and Wyoming.

As one pundit remarked, Dewey, who by all signs should have defeated the incumbent, "extracted defeat from the jaws of victory." Truman became the first candidate since Woodrow Wilson to be elected president without a popular majority but rather with a popular plurality, mustering 49.5 percent of the electorate (Wilson's plurality was slightly below 42% in the multiparty race of 1912). And with Truman, the Democratic Party returned to the pattern of winning the White House without gaining a simple majority (i.e., at least 50.1%), a trend going back to 1852 that Franklin Roosevelt had broken (four times) but that now seemed to have resurfaced. In any event, instead of finding himself moving toward retirement as he had anticipated, the president now prepared for a second term, one in which he would build on Roosevelt's New Deal with his own "Fair Deal," and one in which he would, like Roosevelt, face the hard challenges of open war.

Additional Resources

The American Presidency Project. http://www.presidency.ucsb.edu.

Boller, Paul F., Jr. *Presidential Campaigns*. Oxford: Oxford University Press, 2004.

Donaldson, Gary. *Truman Defeats Dewey*. Lexington: University Press of Kentucky, 1999.

Karabell, Zackery. *The Last Campaign: How Harry Truman Won the 1948 Election*. New York: Knopf, 2000.

Kirkendall, Richard S. "Election of 1948." In Arthur M. Schlesinger, Fred Israel, and William P. Hansen, eds. *History of American Presidential Elections, 1789–1968*. Vol. 2. New York: Chelsea House, 1985.

McCullough, David. *Truman*. New York: Simon & Schuster, 1992.

Pietrusza, David. *1948: Harry Truman's Improbable Victory and the Year That Transformed America*. New York: Union Square Press, 2011.

Ross, Irwin. *The Loneliest Campaign: The Truman Victory of 1948*. New York: New American Library, 1968.

Ross, Irwin. "1948." In Arthur M. Schlesinger, Fred L. Israel, and David J. Frent, eds. *Running for President: The Candidates and Their Images*. Vol. 2. New York: Simon & Schuster, 1994.

Truman Presidential Museum and Library. "Project Whistlestop." http://www.trumanlibrary.org/whistlestop.

Campaign of 1952

In March 1952, President Harry Truman announced his intention to retire from the presidency and not to seek another term. The recently ratified Twenty-Second Amendment limiting a presidency to two terms did not apply to the current incumbent, and throughout much of his second term, it was assumed by many that he would stand for reelection. But the president's political fortunes, which held so much promise after his stunning upset of Thomas Dewey in the election of 1948, dramatically turned. By early 1952, Truman's popularity had rapidly spiraled downward to a new low; a poll conducted in February indicated an approval rating of 22 percent, which has remained the lowest rating of any president since the late 1930s when pollster George Gallup invented the practice of polling as an ongoing measure of presidential approval within the general public. By contrast, in June 1945 during the final months of World War II and the first few months of the new president's administration, Truman enjoyed an approval rating of 87 percent, which exceeded by 3 percent even the highest measured rating reached by his predecessor, the late president Franklin Roosevelt, and which has remained the third highest in the history of the poll. Prior to his election in 1948, he had also suffered approval ratings in the low thirties, but he managed to recover, in large part due to an energetic and aggressive campaign made famous by his whistle-stop strategy.

But after Truman's election, events overtook the administration. China, an ally of the United States during World War II, fell to the forces of Mao Zedong's (or Mao tse-Tung's) communist revolution, an event that caught the United States by surprise, and for which the president was held partly to blame by many critics within both parties, especially from both sides of the aisle in Congress. Republican senator Robert Taft of Ohio, a conservative elder statesman who at that time was considered by many as the GOP's most likely presidential candidate in 1952, made the bold assertion that President Truman's attitude toward China and East Asia in general was "guided by a left-wing group who obviously have wanted to get rid of [Chinese Nationalist leader and general Chiang Kai-shek], and were willing at least to turn China over to the communists for that purpose." In the House of Representatives, a young Democrat from Massachusetts, John F. Kennedy, scolded the administration for blunders committed with regard to Chiang's—and China's—fall, sharply observing that "what our young men had saved, our diplomats and our president frittered away." Congressman Kennedy urged resolute support of Chiang's government now exiled in Taiwan, arguing that Americans must "prepare ourselves vigorously to hold the line in the rest of Asia." Another young congressman, Republican Richard Nixon of California—who had previously praised the president's postwar policies in Europe—now accused Truman and his "blundering" State Department of "losing China to the communists." And so the administration's reputation in the handling of situations abroad was perhaps irreparably damaged, courtesy of Chairman Mao, and yet another dangerous player, and dimension, had been added to the Cold War.

The international situation worsened with the outbreak of the Korean War in the summer of 1950. Involving the forces of the United Nations, and primarily the military power of the United States in the protection of South Korea from Soviet-sponsored North Korean aggression, the war eventually led to what many had feared since the fall of China to Mao's revolution the previous year: American troops joined in battle against Chinese forces. By the campaign season of 1952, the war had lingered for more than two years and had cost the lives of thousands of American soldiers, sailors, airmen, and marines and their allies, and had devastated the Korean Peninsula. Even though Truman's bold response to the invasion of South Korea from the north was praised by some, and the announcement of the Truman Doctrine designed to contain the spread of communism was well received in both parties and thus led to the partial restoration of his credibility as an international leader, Truman's direction of the war had been questioned by some. Among Truman's more controversial moves was his decision to fire General Douglas MacArthur, a celebrated figure from the Pacific combat theater in World War II.

Given the West's confrontation with communism abroad, there was growing concern about the presence of radicalism at home, and a new Red Scare descended upon American public life, darkening the nation's discontent as the campaign season approached. Senator Joseph McCarthy, a Republican from Wisconsin, made himself into a national celebrity by "exposing" alleged subversives within the American government, further adding to the general anxiety over the deepening Cold War. Senator McCarthy's notoriety was crystallized by a series of hearings conducted by the House Un-American Activities Committee (HUAC), which was charged with ferreting out communists and fellow travelers and addressing what was claimed to be the dangers of domestic radicalism. While McCarthy's efforts were embraced by many conservatives, moderates and liberals in both parties were made uncomfortable by the tenor and extent of HUAC's activities, worried that McCarthy was trading in fearmongering and injecting paranoia into the political process. Many of McCarthy's allegations were later revealed to have been exaggerated or patently false, but for a time, his charges were taken seriously and his zealotry was in many quarters applauded. From the beginning, President Truman disliked McCarthy and distrusted his ambitions; but at that time, the senator held so much influence that a direct attack on his activities was politically risky. Those criticisms that were directed at McCarthy, mostly by liberal and moderate Democrats, were muted.

In addition to fears of communism at home and abroad, the president was mired in troubling domestic controversies. Continuing labor unrest led to numerous strikes, including strikes in the steel industry that had caused Truman to seize manufacturing facilities and place them under the direction of the federal government so that production of steel, a vital wartime commodity, would not be impeded. In a famous case, *Youngstown Sheet and Tube Co. v. Sawyer* (Charles Sawyer was the president's secretary of commerce), the U.S. Supreme Court ruled that Truman had overstepped his authority, and it ruled against the steel seizure. Finally, a series of influence-peddling scandals involving members of the Truman administration, and especially Harry Vaughn, a close associate of the president, damaged Truman's formerly clean reputation and seriously degraded the public's perception of his personal integrity.

All of these factors, when added to the alienation within the party of the conservative Southern bloc that began in the previous election season of 1948, removed any possibility of a second Truman election campaign. Early polls showed some support within the party; just over one-third of Democrats polled preferred that Truman run again over the rest of the field (Tennessee senator Estes Kefauver demonstrated the second-highest support with 18%), but his approval rating among independent voters plunged to 18 percent (in a reversal of the figures, Senator Kefauver drew 36% among independents). Truman did enter the New Hampshire primary, but he was defeated by Kefauver, losing by over three thousand votes, allowing Kefauver to claim all of the state's Democratic delegates. Thus on March 29, 1952, the president, resigned to events, formally announced that he would not be a candidate for reelection. With the president's withdrawal, the election was now wide open; for the first time since 1920, an incumbent president did not stand for reelection, nor was there an incumbent vice president waiting in the wings, as the office had been vacant since Truman's ascent to the presidency (prior to the adoption of the Twenty-Fifth Amendment, any vacancy in the office of the vice presidency, for whatever reason, would not be filled until the beginning of a new presidential term). Given the low approval ratings of the

Democratic incumbent, the Republican Party had good reason to be optimistic; the White House seemed once again within its grasp. But it had also seemed that way four years earlier when the Republicans nominated New York's Thomas Dewey, a clear favorite in the polls to win the White House, and yet President Truman still managed to win on Election Day. Thus the GOP was particularly focused on finding the right candidate to avoid a repeat of 1948 and to guarantee a victory in November.

As the campaign season opened, the Republicans focused primarily on two candidates: Senator Taft, who had received support in previous nominating conventions and was the preferred candidate of the party's conservative wing as well as the early front-runner; and General Dwight David Eisenhower, supreme commander of the Allied forces in Europe during World War II and a universally admired figure. In 1948, Eisenhower had been courted by both parties until he eventually disclosed, in January 1952, that he was a Republican. Owing to his high profile, Eisenhower represented the strongest challenge to Taft, who admitted that the 1952 campaign was likely his last chance at winning the White House. Three other candidates—former Minnesota governor Harold Stassen; California governor Earl Warren, who ran for the vice presidency in 1948 with Dewey; and General MacArthur—were also in the field of play. Dewey still held some support among the party moderates, but he chose not to run in 1952, instead endorsing General Eisenhower.

In spite of Eisenhower's strong appeal, Taft was well liked within the party and was considered to be in line for the nomination. Taft promised to dismantle much of the New Deal/Fair Deal institutions that had been firmly established by the Democrats, under the leadership of presidents Franklin Roosevelt and Truman, over the past two decades, and also to return to a more isolationist foreign policy. For Taft and his conservative supporters, the New Deal was nothing less than a milder version of socialism and, as such, was in the process of depriving Americans of their sacred liberties. (In spite of Senator Taft's rhetoric, as a member of the Senate, he often supported government spending to assist the poor.) Eisenhower, by contrast, was a moderate on domestic issues and an internationalist on foreign policy. Because he announced his party affiliation only in January of the election year, his campaign started later than Taft's, but he quickly made up ground. In the New Hampshire primary, Eisenhower outpolled Taft by 50 percent to 39 percent, with Stassen taking most of the remainder.

With the win in New Hampshire, Eisenhower proved his viability, and as with Kefauver's victory over Truman, the Granite State suddenly appeared to be a critical political arena. New Hampshire had held preference primaries since the **Campaign of 1916**, but with the Campaign of 1952, the importance of the state in the process of selecting presidential candidates was first realized. Beginning in the early 1970s, subsequent campaigns would look to New Hampshire as well as the Iowa caucus as bellwether indicators of a candidate's strength and base. As expected, Stassen won the following primary in his home state of Minnesota, but Eisenhower again showed strength, polling second to Taft's distant third. Taft recovered by winning in the Nebraska primary and then following with five more victories (including his home state of Ohio), to four more for Eisenhower, with one victory for Warren in his home state of California. All told, going into the convention, Taft had won six states to Eisenhower's five (Stassen and Warren taking their home states for one each), while polling 35 percent of the popular vote to Eisenhower's 26 percent—the rest of the field left behind.

As the GOP convention opened, Taft was in the front-runner position, but most delegates considered Eisenhower to have tightened the race; hence even though Taft appeared to be at an advantage, Eisenhower loomed large. The general's cause was greatly aided by the efforts of Dewey, Massachusetts senator Henry Cabot Lodge Jr. (it was Lodge who, more than anyone, lobbied the general to run for the presidency), and Governor Sherman Adams of New Hampshire, all of whom campaigned vigorously for Eisenhower before and during the convention, attacking the Taft campaign by accusing Taft's managers of having violated convention rules to block the seating of Eisenhower delegates. The strategy worked: On the first ballot, Eisenhower won 595 delegates, putting him in first as Taft placed with 500, the rest of the field far behind (Warren showed 81 votes, leading the also-rans). Given Eisenhower's strong support, and the sentiment among many conservatives that the general actually had the best chance of defeating the Democrats owing to his popularity, delegates began to shift. On the second round, Eisenhower won 845 delegates and the nomination. California's Richard Milhous Nixon, now a young senator who had gained considerable fame as a resolute anti-communist, was tapped to serve as the general's running mate.

The Republican platform consisted of a laundry list of attacks against the Roosevelt and Truman administrations, which amounted to twenty years of Democratic control of the presidency, the longest run enjoyed by the Democrats at any point in American history. (The Republicans' longest run at keeping the White House— and the longest streak for any party—is still twenty-four years, from March 1861, the inauguration of Abraham Lincoln, through the Garfield/Arthur administration, followed by the Democratic administration of Grover Cleveland beginning in March 1885. That time span would likely have been exceeded between 1897 and 1933 had not former Republican president Theodore Roosevelt split from the party to run for president, thus depriving the incumbent, President William Howard Taft, a second term and providing an inroad for the Democrats to win and keep the White House for eight years during what was otherwise an era of Republican domination in the executive branch.)

As one would expect, the Republican Party platform blamed the spread of communism on the Democrats, accusing the Truman administration of "appeasement of Communism at home and abroad" (the word "appeasement" evoking images of Chamberlain and Daladier at Munich in 1938) and permitting "communists and their fellow travelers to serve in many key agencies and to infiltrate our American life." Aside from the hysteria churned by the era of Senator McCarthy, the platform did include substantive policy proposals, promising to create a new environment for business by significantly lowering taxes and reducing government regulations. The platform blamed the Truman administration for the stalemate in Korea and for "corruption in high places" that had shamed the "moral standards of the American people."

With the decision by President Truman to withdraw his name from the field, and with no incumbent vice president, the Democrats were also facing a wide-open race. Senator Kefauver, who dislodged the president in the New Hampshire primary, used that victory to sustain momentum throughout the primary season, winning primaries in every state except Florida, Minnesota, and West Virginia; all told, Kefauver entered fifteen primaries and won twelve, taking almost 65 percent of the primary votes. But in the 1950s, while the primaries were important as evidence of a candidate's national appeal, they were not as yet the requisite path to nomination that they are today. A candidate could win every primary, and the party leadership could still prevent nomination. Senator Kefauver was viewed by some in the party as a renegade. His investigation of organized crime implicated machine politics in the East, causing considerable discomfort within the party leadership, many of whom were still products of the old machine/patronage system. Southern Democrats found Kefauver to be too sympathetic to the problems of African Americans, and given their recent decision to bolt from the party rather than concede on the issue of civil rights, Southern Democrats were at that time a nearly indivisible faction of the party that caused considerable worry. President Truman in particular opposed a Kefauver nomination, and even though Truman had lost the clout needed to run for reelection, he still remained an important figure in Democratic politics. Other candidates were considered by the party leaders, such as Senator Richard Russell of Georgia, who was appealing to the segregationist Dixiecrats and who had won the Florida primary); Truman's secretary of commerce, Averell Harriman, who won the West Virginia primary; incumbent vice president Alben Barkley; California's attorney general Edmund Gerald "Pat" Brown (who actually won the second-most primary votes, just under 10%, behind Kefauver, but who failed to take any states); and the young senator Hubert H. Humphrey (who won the primary in his home state of Minnesota), one of the party's more promising personalities. Each of these candidates, while capable individuals, was somehow incomplete: Russell could deliver the Southern bloc that had fragmented in 1948, but as an enemy of the New Deal and a committed segregationist, he held little appeal beyond the Deep South; Harriman was a noncommittal candidate; Barkley was capable but, at age seventy-four, was considered too old; Humphrey, at age forty-one, was too young.

Eventually, the party leadership turned to Adlai Stevenson II, the popular governor of Illinois and grandson of Vice President Adlai Stevenson, who had served in that capacity under President Grover Cleveland during his second term. Stevenson was a moderate and could smooth divisions between Northern and Midwestern liberals on the one hand and Southern conservatives on the other, and he spoke with eloquence and clear intelligence. It was clear that in many ways Stevenson was also an idealist, but his approach to politics was far more pragmatic than Kefauver's; and even though he supported civil rights reform, he was not viewed as a hard-liner, which made him more palatable than Kefauver. President Truman worked hard to persuade a reluctant Stevenson to enter the race, but even as late as the opening of the convention, Stevenson demurred. Nonetheless, after his opening address at the Chicago convention, the delegates were awakened to his talents and appeal, and subsequently the movement to draft Stevenson intensified. Thus, without having won—or, for that matter, entered—a single primary, Stevenson managed to place second on the first convention ballot. Kefauver won that initial ballot with 340 votes to Stevenson's 270, and even though he held first, it was a poor showing for a candidate that had seemed unstoppable in the primaries. Russell showed 263 votes, with Harriman in fourth at 123. On the second ballot, Kefauver gained 22 votes, but Stevenson's support increased considerably, jumping to 324, with Russell also gaining to show at 291.

Even though Kefauver still held the lead, the momentum was Stevenson's. On the third ballot, Stevenson took the nomination. Kefauver was still under consideration as a potential vice presidential candidate, along with incumbent vice president Barkley and Senator Russell. Under the offstage direction of President Truman and others working behind the scenes, the convention tapped Senator John Sparkman of Alabama, who was liberal on economic policy but was also a segregationist, to serve as Stevenson's running mate in an effort to heal the divisions of 1948 that led to the Dixiecrat defection. But Sparkman's nomination did provoke a reaction at the convention, this time from African American delegates, many of whom bolted the convention in protest.

The Democratic platform again reaffirmed support for the New Deal/Fair Deal programs of the Roosevelt and Truman administrations. Equally important, the platform called for the repeal of the Taft-Hartley Act that permitted states to enact anti-union right-to-work laws. "An objective appraisal of the past record clearly demonstrates," the language of the platform intoned, "that the Democratic Party has been the chosen American instrument to achieve prosperity, build a stronger democracy, erect the structure of world peace, and continue on the path of progress." The platform also vigorously defended the leadership of President Truman during the Korean crisis.

By the early 1950s, the newly emerging medium of television had become a more prominent feature of American life and a more frequent presence in the habits of American citizens. By the beginning of the 1952 presidential campaign, a television set was a new and exciting feature in millions of homes in the United States, and while radio was still popular, it was clear to many that television was the next wave in mass media. The major networks had already televised the Republican and Democratic conventions in 1948. The two parties used broadcast media extensively, and the first television advertisements promoting presidential candidates were received in American living rooms. Having made use of radio for decades, political campaigns initially broadcast thirty-minute discussions or policy addresses similar to traditional speeches that had been previously broadcast over radio, or even in some cases, recorded for dissemination. Candidates in the earliest days of television did not as yet understand the effectiveness of the thirty-second TV ad or the sound bite, but that was about to change. Madison Avenue advertising executive Rosser Reeves, for example, convinced the Eisenhower campaign that it should broadcast short advertisements that would be inserted during television programming in what was called "prime time"—that is, that interval of time during evenings in which American audiences were likely to be largest— to more effectively connect Eisenhower to a mass audience of potential voters. Eisenhower's advisers recognized the importance of this, given that the general had never before faced the task of running for elective office; and even though he enjoyed the kind of fame that reaches global proportions, he was a neophyte to the rituals and methods of the political contest. The effective use of television was seen as a quick and effective way to humanize the iconic Eisenhower and to foster a more intimate familiarity between the general and the voting public.

In a series of thirty-second spots titled "Eisenhower Answers America," the Republican candidate fielded questions from ordinary citizens, discussing inflation, the war in Korea, and political inefficiency in Washington. The Eisenhower campaign spent millions of dollars broadcasting television ads in key battleground states. Focusing on the theme of change, the Republicans promised a new direction for the country after twenty years of now-stagnant Democratic administrations. In addition to the change motif, one of the catchiest slogans in American politics, "I like Ike," was a fixture of television ads, campaign buttons, and posters throughout the country.

The Democratic Party and the Stevenson campaign found themselves on the defensive throughout most of the 1952 presidential campaign. For the first time since 1936, Republicans were not attacking an incumbent, now turning their sights more abstractly toward the recent record of Democratic governance; and so Stevenson and his fellow Democrats found themselves forced to refute allegations that they were "soft on communism" as well as to deflect the scandals that had hurt President Truman's integrity, and thus the party as a whole, in the final months of his administration. It was a difficult task, particularly given that the Republican candidate was a beloved war hero, an international leader, and—absent a political record—immune from charges of excessive ambition, inconsistency, incompetence, or corruption. Equally important in the weakening of the Democrats' position, Stevenson disliked the idea of using television, which he considered superficial and demeaning. He preferred the traditional approach established in radio, one that allowed candidates extended discussions of complex issues. Stevenson's reputation as an intellectual was earned in part through his ability to speak at length with clarity and purpose, something that the candidate found to be utterly frustrated in the new medium of television. As such, the Stevenson campaign used radio to broadcast eighteen half-hour speeches focusing on issues in detail and providing his audience with a sense of the Democratic candidate's vision for the future. Many consider Stevenson's stubborn refusal to fully utilize television to be a factor that significantly reduced the effectiveness of his other campaign efforts.

Because of his proclivities and personality, Stevenson also faced the problem of frequently coming across as much more of an academic rather than a man of the people; and he experienced difficulty in providing simple answers to complex problems. Hence Stevenson and his inner circle were described in the press (as well as by Richard Nixon) as "eggheads," a mild insult that Stevenson embraced in his cheeky response, "Eggheads of the world unite; you have nothing to lose but your yolks!" And in responding to a remark connecting the egghead label to his own bald head, Stevenson drew upon his Latin, declaiming, "Via ovicipitum dura est," or "The way of the egghead is hard." Other, more ordinary, slogans such as "All the Way with Adlai" and "Madly for Adlai" proved of little help against the much more polished Eisenhower campaign. However, the Stevenson campaign definitely had its moments. Much was made of a candid photograph of Stevenson sporting a hole worn in one of his shoes, an image that actually benefited the campaign, as it helped to connect the otherwise "aristocratic" Stevenson with taxpaying voters. Stevenson played along, quipping that it is better to "have a hole in one's shoe than a hole in one's head." However, these entertaining episodes aside, in terms of long-range campaign strategies, tactics, and the way in which they were conceived and deployed, the general's team was not only ahead of the cerebral Stevenson effort, but also more anticipatory of the shape of things to come, in the way it was able to utilize the media at all levels.

But the Eisenhower campaign was not without its own problems, nor was the candidate above committing mistakes that he would later regret. He was not accustomed to the necessity of projecting a certain image to the public, but rather he maintained his steady, commanding persona that, while effective in simultaneously dealing with men like the British field marshal Montgomery and the American general Patton, was not necessarily gripping his audiences at home. Eisenhower did have political experience of a kind, as he had to deal with some of history's greatest statesmen and generals during the war, but that was for the most part out of sight and behind the scenes. Running for office was another matter, and on the campaign trail, he often appeared dry, monotonous, ambiguous, and at times even ill-informed, a decided weakness compared to the scholarly Stevenson, who also spoke more fluidly by comparison. Additionally, Eisenhower, who for the most part was a political moderate, perhaps went too far to allay the concerns of the party's conservative elements, a tendency that made him look less the redoubtable war commander and more the pliable vote grubber, a perception made all the more disappointing to his supporters given the certainty that the Taft wing of the party realistically could not support any candidate other than Ike.

Perhaps Eisenhower's most egregious error was one of omission, revolving around the controversies that were stirred by Senator McCarthy in his role as chairman of HUAC. For the most part, Eisenhower, who disdained McCarthy, kept the senator at arm's length, but an opportunity arose in which the general could have rebuked McCarthy over accusations that the senator had made against General George Marshall, Eisenhower's friend and former superior and the director of the Marshall Plan. McCarthy had scandalously called Marshall a traitor, and during a campaign swing through the senator's home state of Wisconsin, Eisenhower had planned to defend Marshall in McCarthy's presence during a stop in Milwaukee. But at the last minute, Eisenhower uncharacteristically lost his nerve and omitted a passage from his speech that would have honored Marshall while dismissing McCarthy's charges. Even prior to that, a similar incident involving Indiana senator William Jenner, an ardent ally of McCarthy who had added his voice to accusations against Marshall, occurred at an event attended by both Eisenhower and Jenner. Rather than confront Jenner then and there, Eisenhower played it safe and held his tongue. These missed opportunities to speak up against McCarthyism disappointed many of Ike's supporters, casting, at least for a time, a palpable shadow over his campaign. Stevenson did not hesitate to describe Eisenhower's behavior as spineless, and a chorus of Democrats, and even a few Republicans, chimed in to criticize the general's strange unwillingness to take on McCarthy.

An angry President Truman, who in the past had always admired and liked Eisenhower, and who had, since his withdrawal, remained quietly cloaked behind the scenes, now openly campaigned against Eisenhower and for Stevenson. Truman publicly scolded Ike, stating that he "had never thought the man who is now the Republican candidate would stoop so low," and he took to the campaign trail confessing that at one time he thought Eisenhower would serve the country well as president, but that he had been mistaken and was now determined to oppose his candidacy. Before Election Day, Eisenhower finally referred to Marshall as a great patriot; but by then, few were impressed by his late display of loyalty in defense of his friend and former commander. Sadly, this episode in the Eisenhower campaign ended what had been a genuine friendship between Truman and Eisenhower. Embittered over Eisenhower's lack of response to McCarthy when it was needed, Truman, roused from his silence, now referred to Ike as a Wall Street stooge and a willing tool of "reactionary" forces (viz., McCarthyism) in the GOP. Fueling the president's wrath, Eisenhower, toward the end of the campaign, boldly promised the voters that if elected, he would "go to Korea," a remark that further angered Truman, who shot back that such a promise was "cheap" and deceptive.

As embarrassing as Eisenhower's capitulation to McCarthy was, the biggest challenge to the GOP ticket involved Nixon. Prior to his nomination for the vice presidency, Nixon had made many enemies in both parties due to a reputation for having allegedly employed unscrupulous campaign tactics in the past, particularly during his 1948 campaign for a seat in the House of Representatives, won against Jerry Voorhis in what some argue was a particularly nasty fashion, and an even more allegedly brutal campaign for the Senate against Congresswoman Helen Gahagan Douglas in 1950. His campaign's success in painting Congresswoman Douglas "red"—that is to say, a potentially disloyal left-winger—led to the circulation of a new nickname for Nixon, "Tricky Dick." And now as the campaign for the presidency turned hotter, the California senator was accused of receiving an illegal campaign slush fund of around $16,000–$18,000 from a private donor, a charge that, if proved true, would render hypocritical Eisenhower's criticism of corruption in the Truman administration and his own pledge to honesty in government. A movement to force Nixon off the ticket began in the press, even among newspapers that supported Eisenhower's candidacy, and gained traction among Eisenhower volunteers at the state and local levels. For a brief moment, some among the party leadership considered catching the rising swell against Nixon, and to save face, they began to consider the possibility of dropping Nixon from the ticket. But Eisenhower was convinced that the campaign would suffer irreversible damage by making such a move, and at one point, he privately admitted to Sherman Adams that the election was lost without Nixon on the ticket. In a public statement addressing the indictment, Eisenhower confidently asserted, "Knowing Nixon as I do, I believe that when the facts are known to all of us, they will show Dick Nixon would not compromise with what is right. Both he and I believe in a single standard of morality in public life." Nixon did not hesitate to defend himself, countercharging that the smear tactic was somehow traceable back to "communists and crooks" inside the government.

Eisenhower coolly stepped back to measure Nixon's response, and under the advice of Thomas Dewey, the vice presidential candidate made his stand before a nationally broadcast television audience. During the address, which at that time was the highest-rated broadcast in the short history of television to that point, Nixon explained his side of the story, discussing the funds in question (identified as being $18,000)—where they came from, indicating that there was never any secret as to how the funds were raised, and accounting for "every penny" having been spent for the campaign while assuring the public that none had gone to his personal use or remuneration. Additionally, Nixon avowed his objectivity as a public servant, noting that "no contributor to this fund, no contributor to any of my campaigns, has ever received any consideration that he would not have received as an ordinary constituent." Continuing further, Nixon appealed to the public's sympathies, supplying his life story: his rise from "modest circumstances" and the history of his family's finances, including income raised and debts accrued, punctuating the fact that he did not come from the privileges of wealth. With a particularly effective show of familial loyalty and strength, Nixon defended his wife and family against Democratic claims that the Nixons were living in luxury on revenues illegally peddled. "Pat does not have a mink coat," Nixon parried, "but she does have a respectable Republican cloth coat, and I always tell her she'd look good in anything." Even more dramatically, just over halfway through the speech, the Republican candidate for vice president delivered one of the more famous moments in the history of campaign politics. In speaking of a dog that was given to his family as a personal gift from a supporter, Nixon disclosed the following:

> One other thing I probably should tell you because if we don't they'll probably be saying this about me too, we did get something—a gift—after the election. A man down in Texas heard Pat on the radio mention the fact that our two youngsters would like to have a dog. And believe it or not, the day before we left on this campaign trip we got a message from Union Station in Baltimore, saying they had a package for us. We went down to get it. You know what it was? It was a little cocker spaniel dog in a crate that he'd sent all the way from Texas, black and white, spotted. And our little girl Tricia, the six year old, named it "Checkers." And you know, the kids, like all kids, love the dog, and I just want to say this, right now, that regardless of what they say about it, we're gonna keep it.

In his peroration, Nixon promised that he would not quit, that he would continue to battle against "crooks and communists and those who defend them" in government, and that he believed that the best thing for the United States was to vote for Eisenhower, whom he described as "a great man." After the speech, Nixon's critics accused him of cynical, maudlin manipulation, turning the political campaign into a soap opera. However, others argued that it was nothing less than a campaign masterpiece; and what would soon become known as the "Checkers speech" was in some quarters compared to FDR's brilliant "Fala speech," another example of a presidential candidate in one deft stroke defending both his integrity and his dog. Democrats, however, were not convinced of any fair comparison between Roosevelt's good humor and what they saw as Nixon's cynicism. What really mattered, however, was General Eisenhower's reaction.

That same night, Eisenhower was scheduled to give a speech at a Cleveland auditorium. Prior to the general's address, the Nixon speech was broadcast live to the audience present. The audience was moved, women wept, and as Eisenhower mounted the stage, he discarded his prepared remarks and announced, "Tonight I saw an example of courage." As telegrams in support of Nixon's retention on the ticket inundated the party's national headquarters, Eisenhower met Nixon at the airport in their first encounter since the broadcast, embraced him, and enthusiastically avowed, "You're my boy." The Checkers speech signals the first effective use of the new medium of television by a candidate involved in a presidential campaign, and it provided the first precedent for the power of the medium that would help propel and sustain those political aspirants who would come after Nixon. Years later, as Nixon's political career matured, he would often be described as awkward on television, out of touch, and incapable of using the medium effectively; but in the annals of presidential politics, it was Richard Nixon who first demonstrated with great skill the power of television to move public emotions and sway opinions, signaling the way in which candidates would be promoted in the near future. While Adlai Stevenson continued to adhere to radio for valid reasons of his own, Richard Nixon helped to usher in the era in which television would become, for good or ill, the primary medium for political rhetoric in national campaigns.

Although the Eisenhower campaign in 1952 encountered its problems, the country in the end seemed prepared for change, and the results of Election Day proved it. Eisenhower won slightly over 34,000,000 votes, at that time the highest number of popular votes won by a presidential candidate in history, and representing 55 percent of the voting electorate. Stevenson polled 27,375,000 votes, just over 44 percent, with around 300,000 votes cast for minor parties. Stevenson actually won three million more votes than President Truman had won in his victory over Dewey four years earlier, but the high turnout of the "stay-at-home voters" that the GOP campaigned to win over for its candidate helped boost Eisenhower to victory. The landslide was, as is usually the case, more impressive in the Electoral College, where Eisenhower won 442 electoral votes to Stevenson's 89, sweeping the Northeast, the Midwest, and the West, and by winning Virginia, Tennessee, Texas, and Florida, cracking into the Democrats' Southern base and winning a higher percentage of popular votes in once-solid southern states than any Republican candidate in history, a stunning blow to the Democrats. While the Democrats had lost considerable Southern support to the Dixiecrat defectors in 1948, they had not lost any state in the Old South to the Republicans since Hoover took six southern states (including Texas) in 1928. Additionally, the Republican Party rode Ike's coattails to reclaim both the House and the Senate.

It was the most successful year politically for the GOP since 1928, but it would not, as some had anticipated, initiate the reversal of the legacy of the New Deal. The 1950s would, however, be marked by other concerns: pressing social movements urging cultural changes at home, and new dangers lurking just over the horizon abroad.

Additional Resources

The American Experience. "The Presidents." PBS. http://www.pbs.org/wgbh/amex/presidents.

Bernstein, Barton J. "Election of 1952." In Arthur M. Schlesinger, Fred Israel, and William P. Hansen, eds. *History of American Presidential Elections, 1789–1968.* Vol. 2. New York: Chelsea House, 1985.

Boller, Paul F., Jr. *Presidential Campaigns.* Oxford: Oxford University Press, 2004.

Cohen, Martin, David Karol, Hans Noel, and John Zaller. *The Party Decides: Presidential Nominations before and after Reform.* Chicago: University of Chicago Press, 2008.

Eulau, Heinz. *Class and Party in the Eisenhower Years.* New York: Free Press of Glencoe, 1962.

Greene, John Robert. *The Crusade: The Presidential Election of 1952.* Lanham, MD: University Press of America, 1985.

Miller Center of the Presidency. http://millercenter.org/president/Eisenhower.

Thompson, Charles. *The 1956 Presidential Campaign.* Washington, DC: Brookings Institution, 1960.

West, Darell. *Air Wars: Television Advertising in Election Campaigns, 1952–1992.* Washington, DC: Congressional Quarterly, 1993.

White, Theodore. *America in Search of Itself: The Making of the President, 1956–1980.* New York: Harper & Row, 1982.

Campaign of 1956

The many changes that marked the first term of President Dwight Eisenhower consisted of, among other things, increased pressure for long-overdue reforms toward the protection of the constitutional rights of African Americans and, eventually, of women and other minorities as well. To say that the civil rights movement began in the 1950s, or even reached a greater level of activism and attention during that decade, would be to speak inaccurately. Since the abolition of slavery, American citizens of all races, religious traditions, and persuasions, and in both major parties, have worked either for or against the protection of civil rights for African Americans, and the movement for greater civil rights protected under the law and enforced by it reaches back to the end of the Civil War. If one also counts the struggle for abolition that predates the Civil War, the first stirrings of a movement that promoted the rights of all citizens can be observed even before the American Revolution.

But in the 1950s, a confluence of events and variables finally merged to make the movement more visible, sustained, and pervasive, and its victory inevitable. And it was under the administration of President Eisenhower, for the most part, that the civil rights movement began to finally break through and command the attention of the broader citizenry. This is not to say that civil rights were ignored in previous decades; but only to say that during Eisenhower's presidency, the stage was being set for the struggles and triumphs that would unfold during his administration and in the following decade of the 1960s. While a common image of Eisenhower portrays him as indifferent to civil rights, a closer examination reveals another side to him. Eisenhower saw himself as a man of the people, and as such he was firmly committed to equality under the law. This attitude made him amenable to reforms against racial discrimination. As the Allied commander in Europe, he directed, on a limited scale, the racial integration of the military forces under him, long before President Truman would formally desegregate the military three years after the war's end, and it was indeed a cooperative General Eisenhower who worked diligently to implement Truman's executive order. In fact, most of the desegregation of the armed forces was actually accomplished under President Eisenhower after President Truman left office. Truman issued the order; Eisenhower carried it through.

When in 1954, the U.S. Supreme Court overturned the principle of "separate but equal" in the public education case of *Brown v. Board of Education*, Eisenhower announced that as president, he was bound to enforce the law as henceforth defined. In his Supreme Court appointments, he avoided segregationists and Southerners altogether, a fact that Chief Justice Earl Warren, in reflecting back on these appointments, observed as critical to the success of the civil rights movement as supported by the courts. (Although, to be fair, it must also be pointed out that President Eisenhower would later regret the liberal tenor of some of the justices that he appointed—especially Justice William Brennan.) In 1957, President Eisenhower introduced civil rights legislation to Congress that, with the help of Senate majority leader Lyndon Baines Johnson of Texas, became law and a necessary forerunner of the still more extensive legislation that would be passed seven years later. While certainly not perfect owing to the diluting efforts, especially in the Senate, of the powerful Southern bloc, it was in fact the first legislation of its kind since Reconstruction, and it was, significantly, bipartisan—due in large part to the collaboration of President Eisenhower and the liberal and moderate Democratic and Republican leadership in Congress. This legislation was an outgrowth of Eisenhower's public commitment to ending segregation, a commitment that he made early in his administration. Any shortcomings in the legislation cannot be blamed on the president, who was openly in favor of a more integrated society. Finally, President Eisenhower, acting on his authority as commander in chief, deployed the U.S. Army to enforce desegregation in the South, as firm a commitment as a president can make within the limits set by the Constitution.

Change was in the making in some areas of American public life during the 1950s, but not in others. Even though President Eisenhower had extended a campaign olive branch to the conservative wing of the Republican Party (still loyal to Ohio's senator Robert Taft and determined to dismantle the New Deal), during his presidency he moved back to the center; and on many issues, he found more allies among the Democrats than from within his own party. For Eisenhower, Roosevelt's legacy was complete and unalterable. In a letter to his brother in November 1954, Eisenhower remarked, "Should any political party attempt to abolish social security, unemployment insurance, and eliminate labor laws and farm programs, you would not hear of that party again in our political history." In other words, should any party seek to roll back the achievements of Franklin Roosevelt, it would risk self-destruction. It was no longer at issue for Eisenhower; the programs of the New Deal were entrenched and invulnerable to any reasonable attack. In Eisenhower's view of the political universe, both parties were now New Deal parties. This was less a statement of belief than acknowledgment of political realities, less an affirmation of any principle than a realization of the practical. Conservative Republicans could not look to Ike for an ally, or even for a sympathetic friend. To Eisenhower, that brand of conservatism—that is, the anti-New Deal conservatism that still appealed to strong elements within his own party—was growing increasingly "negligible and stupid." And liberal Democrats gladly recognized in President Eisenhower the voice of moderation, a Republican who was almost a New Dealer by default. Indeed, the Republican president enjoyed a close and genuinely affectionate relationship with the two most powerful Democrats in Congress: Johnson and another Texan, Speaker of the House Sam Rayburn. This relationship forged a uniquely bipartisan mood in Washington, and the old animosities between the parties seemed to have abated. This is not to say that there were no disagreements, but any criticism of the president from the Democratic leadership was offered absent invective, and any support for him by that same leadership was given without qualification. Eisenhower was liked and appreciated in a Congress that was controlled by the Democrats. Finally, Eisenhower oversaw the ending of the war in Korea, and his reputation as a proven international leader lent confidence to the voting public—and again would prove hard for any opposing candidate to rebuke. Thus it would be difficult, for these and other reasons, to mount a credible challenge to this popular president in 1956. But a challenge was mounted, as it had to be, and once again it was through the candidacy of the erudite Adlai Stevenson.

As the campaign season approached, many Democrats hoped Stevenson would run again, even though Stevenson himself again met such a prospect with reluctance. However, Stevenson was not unchallenged. Estes Kefauver entered the New Hampshire primary unopposed, taking New Hampshire's delegates and showing early strength (although Stevenson, who was not on the ballot there, managed a high number of write-in votes, enough to reach about 15%). More impressively, Kefauver won the Minnesota primary outright, this time with Stevenson on the ballot, thus prompting Stevenson to begin a serious effort. In so doing, Stevenson assented to a televised debate with Kefauver, the first televised presidential debate in history. The debate itself was uninspiring, as both candidates were fairly close on nearly all the issues; and in subsequent events, it was largely ignored by the candidates themselves. But it sparked in Stevenson a renewed interest in running, and from this point forward, his campaign was more focused. Following the debate (but evidently not a consequence of it), Stevenson won in Florida and California, and from there, the way to his renomination at the convention was eased. Kefauver continued to win primaries, but Stevenson's support grew.

By the end of the primaries, Stevenson had won just over 50 percent of the popular vote, with slightly less than 38 percent going for Kefauver, who subsequently withdrew from the race prior to the convention. Stevenson, now the clear front-runner going into the Chicago convention, won the nomination on the first ballot, although a last-minute challenge from Averell Harriman forced a contest, largely due to the efforts of former president Truman, who felt Harriman could beat Eisenhower. Despite the entrance of a last-minute contender, the nomination was easily won by Stevenson, taking 905 delegates to Harriman's 210, the rest of the delegates scattered among seven also-rans led by Senator Johnson's 80 delegates. For the vice presidency, Stevenson unexpectedly asked the convention to decide, thus initiating a spontaneous contest between a number of unprepared candidates led by Kefauver, who was challenged by Senator Hubert Humphrey of Minnesota, Senator Albert Gore Sr. of Tennessee, Mayor Robert F. Wagner Jr. of New York City, and a youthful first-term senator and former congressman from Massachusetts, John F. Kennedy.

From the start, Kennedy was the more visible candidate, and it appeared that his chances at becoming Stevenson's running mate in 1956 were strong. He was an appealing figure; his particular combination of rhetorical eloquence, quick wit, confident disposition, and personal grace were of a kind not seen in either party since the passing of Franklin Roosevelt, and his record as a war hero—having won the Purple Heart in the Pacific theater while displaying extreme courage, strength, and resourcefulness in saving many lives after a PT boat under his command was sliced in half by an enemy destroyer—only added to his appeal. The Campaign of 1956 occurred just eleven years after the end of World War II; thus personal stories of combat bravery were better than gold during a political campaign, and young Jack Kennedy's story was certainly stirring. Additionally, Stevenson quietly preferred Kennedy, but he kept to his pledge to allow the convention to make the decision and thus remained silent in the contest. Kennedy was also Roman Catholic, a fact that might have lacked purchase for the nomination, particularly given memories of Al Smith's frustrated campaign for the presidency in 1928, the last and only time a Catholic received a presidential nomination from a major party. Aware of this, the Kennedy faction went to great lengths to demonstrate that their man's Catholicism would actually give the Democrats an advantage in the larger northern cities that were so vital to winning the bigger prizes in the Electoral College; but this effort backfired, provoking some to respond that Kennedy's religion should not be a factor for or against him.

On the first ballot, Kefauver took the lead in delegates, winning 466 to Kennedy's 294, with 178 going to Gore, 162 to Wagner, 134 to Humphrey, and the rest of the votes scattered among a variety of favorite sons and also-rans. On the second ballot, Kennedy actually pulled ahead, gaining a significant lead with 618 delegates to Kefauver's 515, but these results were not announced quickly enough to stem a sudden shifting of delegates initially supporting favorite sons but now moving toward Kefauver, resulting in Kefauver regaining the lead before it was clear that it had even been lost. Senator Kennedy came very close to winning the nomination to run on the ticket with Stevenson, but in the end, Kefauver won the official vote, 755 to Kennedy's 589. As the convention was nationally televised, Kennedy, in losing the nomination, gained greatly by winning national recognition, his gracious concession speech in particular receiving broad acclaim; hence his narrow loss for the vice presidential nomination in 1956 has been viewed as a first important step toward other goals of a still larger scale that were yet to be achieved. But for the moment, Stevenson-Kefauver was the ticket promoted by the Democrats, two candidates that not only resembled each other on the issues, but in many ways were not that far from their Republican counterpart, President Eisenhower.

With the economy strong and expanding, the Korean War long over, relations with the Soviet Union comparatively less tense, and his reputation solid, renomination to run for a second term seemed an inevitability for the incumbent president. However, the pre-campaign picture suddenly became muddied by questions over the condition of the president's health. In September 1955, while on a visit to Denver, the president suffered what was later discovered to have been a fairly serious heart attack, causing him to be hospitalized for several days and, even after his release, raising lingering doubts about his long-term health and his viability as a two-term president. Under this climate of uncertainty, other possibilities for the upcoming election year were floated, and for a short time, a field of potential replacement candidates emerged, including the incumbent vice president Richard Nixon; two-time GOP presidential nominee (1944 and 1948) Thomas Dewey; Henry Cabot Lodge Jr., a longtime Eisenhower supporter currently sitting as ambassador to the United Nations; Eisenhower's chief of staff, Sherman Adams; Senate minority leader William Knowland, a prominent member of the party's conservative wing; Minnesota's former governor Harold Stassen; Massachusetts governor Christian Herter; and even the president's brother, Milton Eisenhower. In time, Eisenhower's health did improve; but the president, considering his options, privately entertained the possibility of stepping down after one term. Eisenhower slowly began to change his mind after January, but it was not until March 1956 that he officially announced that he would stand for a second term. But then in June, the president suffered another setback to his health, this time involving an occurrence of ileitis that required surgery, prompting a renewal of rumors regarding his possible withdrawal from the race and, once again, the consideration of possible alternatives. Again his health recovered, and the discussion of his replacement silenced.

Throughout these changes and uncertainties, Vice President Nixon's name provoked intraparty controversy: he was, on the one hand, floated as a strong alternative to succeed President Eisenhower; and on the other hand, as a liability who needed to be dropped from the ticket altogether. Stassen in particular wanted Nixon out, claiming that with the president's health no longer a certainty, a more mature man was needed in the event of the worst-case scenario. Nixon was still fairly young; when he was inaugurated as vice president four years earlier, he was only thirty-nine years old, making him the second-youngest vice president in history, behind only John Breckinridge (who served under President Buchanan and was himself a candidate for president in 1860), who was thirty-six at his inauguration and to this day remains the youngest. By and large, Nixon was seen as a capable vice president, and he had taken an active role in running cabinet meetings during the president's convalescence. Thus by the time of the convention, Stassen's attempt to dislodge Nixon fizzled out.

The Republicans moved on from the convention with confidence. "In four years we have achieved the highest economic level with the most widely shared benefits that the world has ever seen," stressed the GOP platform. "We of the Republican Party have fostered this prosperity and are dedicated to its expansion and to the preservation of the climate in which it has thrived," the platform continued. With respect to the Eisenhower administration's foreign policy, the platform stressed that under "the leadership of President Eisenhower, the United States has advanced foreign policies which enable our people to enjoy the blessings of liberty and peace."

The post-convention campaign seemed anticlimactic. Stevenson, a moderately liberal (or perhaps liberally moderate) New Dealer, ran in defense of the social programs established by Roosevelt and Truman, but as the president himself had openly endorsed many of those programs and policies, it seemed to make little difference. Additionally, with the economy at its healthiest, the Democrats were deprived of an important set of issues to bring forward in debate. Equally important, Stevenson, a foreign policy expert, supported efforts to slow the arms race between the United States and the Soviet Union, including a ban on atmospheric testing of nuclear weapons, especially the city-busting hydrogen bomb. Throughout the campaign, Stevenson attempted to lead a national debate over the direction of the nation's foreign policy, a somewhat risky strategy given the president's own solid reputation in this area. Stevenson argued that Eisenhower's foreign policy was bringing the United States closer to war than to peace, claiming that efforts to contain communism needed to involve more than just building and testing increasingly powerful nuclear weapons. The United States needed to understand what made communism attractive to many within the developing countries around the world. These were reasonable arguments and for the most part well received; but even so, it remained difficult to credibly challenge a figure such as President Eisenhower, whose experience in the international arena could not be matched, and who had already gone to great lengths to develop a better rapport with the Soviet Union. Toward the end of the campaign, a series of international crises erupted, again driving home the desire among Americans for foreign policy experience in the White House, and none was more qualified than the man who commanded all Allied forces in Europe just one decade ago, and that same man was in the Oval Office.

In the domestic arena, many Democratic loyalists wanted Stevenson to attack the close ties between big business and the Eisenhower administration in an effort to mobilize working-class men and women to support the Stevenson candidacy. However, because of his privileged upbringing and academic demeanor, Stevenson did not make a credible populist, even though his credentials as a New Deal liberal were real. The slogans "Get the Country Moving Again" and "Give 'em Hell, Adlai" failed to ignite the passion that led to President Truman's last-minute, come-from-behind victory in 1948. Stevenson's distaste for modern campaigning once again worked against him. His commendable desire to raise the level of debate also prevented him from considering the kinds of tactics that were becoming more compulsory in the age of visual media. "The idea that you can merchandise candidates for high office like breakfast cereal," Stevenson lamented, "is the ultimate indignity to the democratic process." As before, the GOP won the battle of the slogans and sound bites, and it helped that the country's overall outlook was bright in spite of dangers abroad. Much like the **Campaigns of 1896, 1924, and 1928**, good economic times permitted Eisenhower to run on the slogans of "Peace, Progress, Prosperity" and "Keep America Strong with Ike."

Following the model set during the contest in 1952, Eisenhower's 1956 campaign focused on assuring voters that their president was in touch with the lives of ordinary Americans. For example, the Eisenhower ad campaign relied heavily on testimonies of average voters, making a point to include support from people such as a "Taxi Driver and His Dog." Perhaps even more importantly, the Eisenhower campaign effectively portrayed Stevenson's experience in foreign policy as too thin compared to that of the president, and it treated his support of a nuclear test ban as naïve. Besides raising questions regarding the effectiveness of Eisenhower's foreign policy to preserve peace, the Stevenson campaign faced the problem of changing the lingering image of Stevenson as an "egghead." To accomplish this, the campaign ran a series of ads entitled "The Man from Libertyville," portraying Stevenson as a somewhat folksy man of the people. Taking everything into consideration, Stevenson had little hope of defeating the president. Americans simply trusted Eisenhower to sustain prosperity and keep the peace.

On Election Day, President Eisenhower was returned to office in a landslide, winning over 35,000,000 popular votes, or 57 percent, to Stevenson's approximately 26,000,000 votes, which amounted to just under 42 percent, a crushing victory that converted to a still more impressive win in the Electoral College, where the president won 457 electoral votes (86%) to Stevenson's 73 (14%). Eisenhower again swept the Northeast, the Midwest, and the West, holding every state that he had won in 1952 except the border state of Missouri, and in exchange he gained three states: Louisiana, Kentucky, and West Virginia. To this point, only four candidates had won a larger percentage of the popular vote: Franklin Roosevelt in 1936 and 1932 (Eisenhower's victory was .04 percentage points behind FDR's 1932 landslide), Warren Harding in 1920, and Herbert Hoover in 1928. Perhaps even more telling, Eisenhower's separate percentages of the popular vote in 1952 and 1956 were both higher than President Roosevelt's in the elections of 1940 and 1944; and as stated above, his 1956 share was virtually the same as Roosevelt's 1932 share, evidence that the Republican Party had completely rebounded from the doldrums of the 1930s and the lingering effects in the early 1940s. Eisenhower was also the first Republican to win a second term since Theodore Roosevelt (and the first Republican to be elected twice—Roosevelt's first term being the result of ascension upon the death of a president—since President McKinley in 1900). Eisenhower's immense popularity did not come with very long coattails, for the Democrats retained control of both houses of Congress.

President Eisenhower would leave office in 1960 as the last president to have been born in the nineteenth century, and as the country moved into the decade of the 1960s, youth and the fresh outlooks that come with it would set the tone for the politics and culture of the next generation. Nonetheless, the Eisenhower administration was an important factor in prompting those myriad changes that would be later associated with the youth movement of the future, and it stood at a critical moment in the history of the republic. And at the center of it was the steady presence of President Eisenhower himself, whose calm influence may have been the right element for the times. Today Eisenhower's legacy is viewed positively; most presidential scholars and historians rank him among the nation's ten best chief executives and regard him as a "near-great" president. Rankings aside, his presidency fares well when considering the things at stake during his administration and his steady demeanor throughout his two terms. In the words of journalist Andy Rooney, "Eisenhower was the quintessential American to me. He meant to do the right thing. He was honest. I think he is the great American hero of our time."

Additional Resources

The American Experience. "The Presidents." PBS. http://www.pbs.org/wgbh/amex/presidents.

Boller, Paul F., Jr. *Presidential Campaigns.* Oxford: Oxford University Press, 2004.

Cohen, Marty, David Karol, Hans Noel, and John Zaller. *The Party Decides: Presidential Nominations before and after Reform.* Chicago: University of Chicago Press, 2008.

Eulau, Heinz. *Class and Party in the Eisenhower Years.* New York: Free Press of Glencoe, 1962.

Greene, John Robert. *The Crusade: The Presidential Election of 1952.* Lanham, MD: University Press of America, 1985.

Hamby, Alonzo L. "1956." In Arthur M. Schlesinger, Fred L. Israel, and David J. Frent, eds. *Running for President: The Candidates and Their Images.* Vol. 2. New York: Simon & Schuster, 1994.

Miller Center of the Presidency. http://millercenter.org/president/Eisenhower.

Moos, Malcolm. "Election of 1956." In Arthur M. Schlesinger, Fred Israel, and William P. Hansen, eds. *History of American Presidential Elections, 1789–1968.* Vol. 2. New York: Chelsea House, 1985.

Thompson, Charles. *The 1956 Presidential Campaign.* Washington, DC: Brookings Institution, 1960.

West, Darell. *Air Wars: Television Advertising in Election Campaigns, 1952–1992.* Washington, DC: Congressional Quarterly, 1993.

White, Theodore. *America in Search of Itself: The Making of the President, 1956–1980.* New York: Harper & Row, 1982.

Campaign of 1960

With the campaign and election of 1960, the political culture of the United States experienced the beginnings of a series of dramatic changes that would reshape the political and social landscape for decades to come. One can surely identify more critical elections in American history (e.g., Jefferson in 1800, Jackson in 1828, Polk in 1844, Lincoln in 1860, and Franklin Roosevelt in 1932 and then again in 1940) that produced still greater consequences in driving the republic's destiny. But the election of 1960, at least in terms of campaign methods, shifting structures of party organization and challenges to traditional party leadership, rapid innovation in media, generational identity, emerging demographic configurations, shifting social perceptions, and cultural aspirations, is a pivotal moment in its own right and, with the possible exception of 1980, may be the most important election in the latter half of the twentieth century. As Theodore Sorenson once wrote, "The 1960 presidential election was a watershed in American history. The oldest man ever to serve in the Presidency was succeeded by the youngest man ever elected to it. It was the first time the nation had elected a Catholic President; the first time that a major party had nominated two incumbent senators for President and Vice President; and the first time that the Democrats had sent a sitting senator to the White House. He [Kennedy] was in addition the first Democratic presidential nominee from New England in over a hundred years."

One might also add that it was the first election in which an incumbent president was deemed under the Constitution ineligible to run for reelection, this being the first time that the provisions under the Twenty-Second Amendment, ratified and added to the Constitution in 1951, were applicable. Even though President Eisenhower's second term faced more difficulties than his first—the country was experiencing a mild recession, civil rights issues were intensifying, relations with the Soviet Union had chilled (and would become tense owing to the embarrassing U-2 incident in 1960), the Soviets' successful launching of the Sputnik satellite had provoked national concern over the state of American science and technological progress, a scandal involved the president's chief of staff, Sherman Adams—he still remained a popular president, and had he been eligible and so inclined, he could have mounted a strong reelection campaign. But under the Constitution, Ike was out of the picture, and the field was again wide open for the second time since the end of the war and the fourth time this century (the other wide-open elections in the twentieth century—that is, elections without an incumbent president seeking reelection—were 1920, 1928, and 1952).

For the Republicans, the party holding the White House for the past eight years, the choice was obvious. Over his eight years as vice president, Richard Nixon had worked to credential himself as a foreign policy expert capable of standing up to the dual threats of the Soviet Union and Communist China. He had also received favorable notice for the calm manner in which he had conducted himself during the crises over President Eisenhower's health in the autumn of 1955. Nixon's record was not without some blemishes—a particularly embarrassing trip to Latin America did not serve the administration well, and many Democrats as well as a few Republicans had long considered him to be a dirty campaigner—"Tricky Dick," as he was often called by his enemies—but all told, he was considered by most insiders as the clear heir to Eisenhower's legacy. At one point early in 1959, a prospective challenger seemed to be emerging in the figure of Nelson Rockefeller, a liberal Republican and popular governor of New York. But Rockefeller withdrew his name from consideration, clearing the way for Nixon to run for the nomination without a serious challenger to face.

At the convention, Nixon won easily on the first ballot, sweeping all but ten conservative delegates, who cast their votes for Arizona's Senator Barry Goldwater. Ideologically, Nixon was viewed as a moderate, gravitating somewhere between the conservative wing of the party led by Goldwater and the liberal wing represented best by Rockefeller. But given his Cold Warrior credentials, Nixon appealed to conservatives as well as moderates, with the liberal wing resigned to his inevitable ascent and preferring him to Goldwater. He promised to be a strong candidate, his only weakness stemming from a personality and style less comforting and avuncular than Eisenhower's, and the fact that within the party as well as outside it, Nixon had made more political enemies than the retiring president, and these enemies were almost zealous in their disdain for "Tricky Dick." Nonetheless, Nixon was a disciplined, resolute campaigner, intelligent, well prepared, and far more experienced in government than most of his contemporaries, a fact that was punctuated by his comparative youth (elected to the vice presidency at thirty-nine, he stood for the presidency at the age of forty-seven). Nixon's approach was to stress foreign policy as the campaign season unfolded, and to emphasize this he selected UN ambassador Henry Cabot Lodge Jr. to serve as his running mate. Nixon-Lodge provided a formidable combination that in many ways embodied the moderate views of the Eisenhower presidency and brought breadth of experience to the contest.

Ever since his acclaimed performance during the 1956 Democratic nominating convention, in which he came close to winning the party's nomination for the vice presidency, Massachusetts senator John F. Kennedy, a Roman Catholic of Irish descent, was regarded by many within the party as a leading contender for the presidency in the upcoming election season. Kennedy was even younger than Nixon and, like Nixon, had earned a reputation as a Cold Warrior throughout his political career. Nixon and Kennedy shared their ascent together, first as members of the House of Representatives, and then as U.S. senators. Often forgotten in the annals of popular history, Nixon and Kennedy had formed a friendship in the late 1940s, one that was based on mutual respect and a shared vision for America's role as a world leader, and on a friendship that endured through the 1950s. Kennedy, at least for a number of years, felt that Nixon's enemies misjudged him, and he found in his rival many admirable qualities. Eventually, politics would lead to strained relations, but throughout most of their working lives in government, they included each other among their broader circle of political friends.

Even though Nixon had the visibility of the vice presidency to his advantage, Kennedy had become as widely known, and his personal magnetism easily made him the most charismatic national politician since FDR. But unlike Nixon, he faced a battle for the nomination. Senate majority leader Lyndon Baines Johnson of Texas, one of the more powerful senators in American history, posed a serious challenge. Kennedy, Johnson, and Minnesota senator Hubert Humphrey (another young senator who had been considered a rising star in the party since his stirring speech for civil rights at the 1948 convention) were the heavyweights in the contest; but other candidates were also in the field, namely Stuart Symington, the first secretary of the Air Force and the favorite of former president Harry Truman; Governor Edmund "Pat" Brown Sr. of California, who had some limited visibility in the 1952 presidential primaries; and, in addition to a handful of favorite sons, Governor Adlai Stevenson, former First Lady Eleanor Roosevelt's choice, who had won the party's nomination in the two previous campaigns and was thus given the unenviable job of twice opposing Eisenhower. As before, Stevenson had announced that he was not actively seeking the nomination but that he would accept if drafted by the convention, thus indirectly keeping his name in the running.

During the primary season, Kennedy had impressively won ten states, including an early victory over Humphrey in Wisconsin that showed his appeal in the Midwest, where Humphrey, being from Minnesota, had been expected to dominate. But Kennedy's victory was boosted by a strong showing from Wisconsin's large Roman Catholic population. In looking closely at the discrete precincts, Kennedy won handily in areas that were majority Catholic, Humphrey won in Protestant precincts, and where there was an even split between Catholics and Protestants, Kennedy barely edged out his rival from Minnesota. Even though Kennedy continued to dominate the primaries, the strong divisions in Wisconsin along religious lines indicated that Kennedy's religion would be at issue throughout the primaries, and perhaps a liability in states with Protestant majorities, and especially in those parts of the country that still harbored anti-Catholic sentiments. This would be tested in West Virginia, a predominantly Protestant state that was of further concern owing to a tradition of anti-Catholic bigotry there. However, through the efforts of an energetic, polished, and well-funded campaign involving the Kennedy family against Senator Humphrey's shoestring budget and barely visible organization, Senator Kennedy scored a dramatic victory in West Virginia, settling the religion question, at least for the moment. Senator Kennedy's performance in a televised debate against Humphrey, in which polls indicated Kennedy the winner, no doubt further helped his cause. The extent of the victory in West Virginia was enough to prompt Senator Humphrey to withdraw, leaving only Lyndon Johnson to deal with at the convention.

Johnson did not enter the primaries, relying on his solid support among the party leadership and his renowned ability to deal behind the scenes. As Senate majority leader, Johnson was formidable; and even without a single primary under his belt, he raised serious problems for the Kennedy campaign. It must be remembered that in 1952, Estes Kefauver dominated the Democratic primaries but was never nominated to the presidency; and with a politician of Johnson's depth, the Kennedys were well aware that history could be repeated. Adlai Stevenson himself was still in the mix, and the possibility that the convention could turn back to the party's old standard-bearer, perhaps out of a sense of obligation to a faithful champion, was certainly plausible. Just prior to the convention, Johnson challenged Kennedy to another televised debate, wherein again Kennedy outperformed the more experienced politician and confirmed for many delegates that he was a solid match for Nixon, the prospective Republican nominee. On the only ballot cast, Kennedy won the nomination with 806 delegates to Johnson's 409, the remaining votes scattered among a field of 10 additional candidates, Symington and Stevenson leading the also-rans with only 86 and 79 votes, respectively.

Surprisingly, Kennedy offered the second spot on the ticket to Johnson, who just as surprisingly agreed, and the Democratic candidates for the 1960 election were set. According to some accounts, the Kennedys offered the second spot to Johnson as a courtesy, expecting him to turn it down. Other accounts indicate that it was primarily about electoral politics, employing the North-South strategy (in this variation, Massachusetts-Texas) as well as blending Kennedy's charisma and grace with Johnson's grit and experience. Other accounts have JFK's younger brother and closest adviser, Robert Kennedy, privately visiting Johnson after the Texas senator had accepted the invitation to join the ticket, in an effort to goad him into withdrawing his name, an episode that is said to have embittered both men to each other. In any event, Kennedy-Johnson carried the Democratic standard into the general campaign against the experienced tandem of Nixon-Lodge.

Both candidates were moderates on the issues; hence the Campaign of 1960 quickly evolved into a debate over leadership abilities. Republicans argued that Kennedy lacked the foreign policy experience to deal with the threat of global communism. To counter the charges, Democrats pointed to Kennedy's wartime record and the personal character to which it testified. While serving as a PT boat commander in the U.S. Navy during World War II, a Japanese destroyer rammed and cut Lieutenant Kennedy's boat in half; but under Kennedy's command leadership and heroic actions, only two members of his crew were lost, and Kennedy himself shook off his own wounds to personally save the life of at least one crew member. The evident leadership of the young lieutenant boosted his reputation as a man of action and courage. Equally effective, the Kennedy campaign raised doubts about the Eisenhower-Nixon team by claiming the existence of a "missile gap" that favored the ever-menacing Red Army, the result of the current administration's lack of foresight and resolve in dealing with the Soviets. The Eisenhower administration denied the gap, and the facts were actually on its side; but in the wake of the *Sputnik* shock, the tactic was persuasive and harmed Nixon's claim to toughness with the Soviet Union.

Although the Nixon-Lodge campaign never raised the issue of religion, other critics of the Democratic standard-bearer argued that a Kennedy victory would give the pope far too much influence over an American president, the same argument that was aimed at Al Smith in his 1928 campaign against Herbert Hoover that preceded Hoover's landslide victory. (As in the **Campaign of 1928**, a Catholic Democrat—Smith and Kennedy—competed against a Republican with a Quaker background—Hoover and Nixon. Throughout the history of American presidential politics, only two Quakers and two Catholics have received nominations from a major political party to run for president, and, coincidentally, on both occasions candidates from these faith traditions faced each other.) Kennedy repeatedly responded by clearly stating that there was absolutely no conflict between being a Roman Catholic and serving as president of the United States, assuring the public that the pope would not dictate White House policy on any issue at any time. Throughout the campaign, Kennedy approached controversies raised by his religion with his characteristic grace. At times he managed to turn the tables and, with good humor, expose anxieties over religious differences as needless and unfounded. Journalist Chris Matthews recounts one particularly amusing opportunity seized by Kennedy in an effort to deflate concerns surrounding his religion, one that was inadvertently opened by none other than the straight-shooting, irrepressible former president Truman. While stumping for Kennedy, Truman displayed, as was his way, great and unrestrained distaste for supporters of Vice President Nixon, at one campaign event directly telling them that they could quite simply "go to hell." The vice president was not amused, and he publicly scolded the former president for his somewhat less than perspicuous choice of words. Kennedy, not passing over this opportunity for levity, dashed off a telegram to Truman, wherein he quipped, "I have noted with interest your suggestion as to where those who vote for my opponent should go. While I understand and sympathize with your deep motivation, I think it is important that our side try to refrain from raising the religion issue."

But levity aside, the issue was important and impossible to ignore, and so Kennedy, who would rather have remained aloof to it, began to feel a growing need to address it directly and soberly once and for all. Finally, Senator Kennedy, speaking before a conference of Baptist ministers in Houston, Texas, shared his definitive statement and final word on the issue:

> I believe in an America where the separation of church and state is absolute; where no Catholic Prelate would tell the President—should he be a Catholic—how to act, and no Protestant minister would tell his parishioners for whom to vote . . . and where no man is denied public office merely because his religion differs from the President who might appoint him, or the people who might elect him. I believe in an America that is officially neither Catholic, Protestant nor Jewish; . . . where no religious body seeks to impose its will directly or indirectly upon the general populace or the public acts of its officials, and where religious liberty is so indivisible that an act against one church is treated as an act against all.

On a cautionary note, the candidate continued, "For while this year it may be a Catholic against whom the finger of suspicion is pointed, in other years it has been—and may someday be again—a Jew, or a Quaker, or a Unitarian, or a Baptist. It was Virginia's harassment of Baptist preachers, for example, that led to Jefferson's statute of religious freedom. Today, I may be the victim, but tomorrow it may be you—until the whole fabric of our harmonious society is ripped apart at a time of great national peril." And in a spirit of optimism, Kennedy added, "Finally, I believe in an America where religious intolerance will someday end, where all men and all churches are treated as equals, where every man has the same right to attend or not to attend the church of his choice, where there is no Catholic vote, no anti-Catholic vote, no bloc voting of any kind, and where Catholics, Protestants, and Jews, at both the lay and the pastoral levels, will refrain from those attitudes of disdain and division which have so often marred their works in the past, and promote instead the American ideal of brotherhood." It may have been the candidate's finest moment yet, and the speech remains one of the clearest statements of religious tolerance in American politics.

In terms of ideas and principles, Kennedy's Houston address might be the substantively most important moment of the 1960 campaign; it certainly remains today one of the finest statements from anyone on the issue. But in terms of immediate impact on the election and overall influence on the future direction of presidential campaign strategies, the definitive moment of the campaign was reached in a series of four televised debates between Nixon and Kennedy, the first time that two candidates nominated by the major parties met in public debate during a presidential campaign, and, as it happens, the first such debates broadcast over both television and radio. (In the most famous debating event in American history, Abraham Lincoln met Stephen Douglas in a series of debates during their Illinois contest for the U.S. Senate, two years before they would run against each other in a four-way race for president; but there was no debate in that latter contest or in any other presidential campaign involving the nominees of the two major parties before Kennedy-Nixon. It is to be noted that the first televised debate involving presidential candidates occurred in 1956, between Adlai Stevenson and Estes Kefauver, both running for the Democratic nomination. Kennedy-Nixon is the first of its kind in that it set the two nominees against each other.) Not only was this the first time such a debate was held, but it was also televised, making it another innovation and setting a precedent that would be followed in every subsequent presidential campaign, with the exceptions of 1964, 1968, and 1972.

During the debates, Kennedy appeared before the huge television audience of seventy million viewers in good form (by 1960, nearly 90% of all American households now owned a television, compared to only 11% just ten years earlier), exhibiting the famous Kennedy "vigor" and cutting an image of polish and command. As the first debate opened, Vice President Nixon, who had just finished a stressful marathon tour of all fifty states and was suffering the effects of a knee injury for which he had been temporarily hospitalized, appeared exhausted, ashen, and drawn. He had lost twenty pounds, and while he was clean-shaven, his five o'clock shadow was unflatteringly highlighted by the harsh contrasts of black-and-white television, giving him a slightly disheveled look and, for some, making him appear slightly ill (his own mother is said to have telephoned him after the debates out of worry over his health). Kennedy, by contrast, looked fit, relaxed, youthful, self-contained, and robust, an image that actually concealed even more serious health problems of his own, of which the voting audience remained completely unaware. Kennedy's image of robust health concealed severe illnesses that he had suffered since childhood; and on at least two occasions, he was considered to have been close to death, even having last rites administered to him. Hence, even though Nixon had the appearance of illness on that night, it was Kennedy who was saddled with debilitating and at times grave illness.

Kennedy's opening remarks that evening exhibited a confidence and resolve that exposed television viewers to a different side of his personality. Drawing from the abundant rhetorical well of Franklin Roosevelt, Senator Kennedy observed that the current generation of Americans was appointed to a "rendezvous with destiny," defined in terms of the responsibilities of the United States to bravely confront the enemies of freedom and democracy throughout the world. Vice President Nixon touched on many of the same themes and even at times conceded that he and his opponent were in principle not all that different, the only main difference being his rejection of Kennedy's claim that the Eisenhower administration had "stood still" while the power and purpose of the Soviet Union had pushed them forward.

As presidential debates go, it proved to be a valuable forum for the exchange of ideas. Both candidates actually performed well in responding to questions, delivering their positions, and addressing the issues; both were equally well prepared, intelligent, articulate, dignified, professional, sincere, and sure in their responses. When one views old film footage of the Kennedy-Nixon debates, one cannot help but feel struck by the quality of both personal bearing and informed answers from the two candidates, particularly when compared to the tenor and mood of more recent debates. Both candidates delivered thoughtful answers, but on black-and-white television, Nixon's bedraggled appearance was to many viewers a constant distraction. Polls indicated that those who viewed the debate on television overwhelmingly considered Kennedy the winner, while those who listened on radio leaned slightly to Nixon. This proved to be a turning point for the Kennedy campaign, as the post-debate polls indicated that his candidacy was now slightly in the lead in a very tight race. Nixon recovered for the following three debates, and by some accounts he actually matched Kennedy and perhaps even slightly bested him in the second and third debates; but these later debates drew twenty million fewer viewers, and the powerful images of the first debate, which had reached a higher number of viewers, were difficult to erase. It was an impression that Nixon never forgot. In subsequent campaigns for the presidency, Nixon refused to participate in televised debates. There is some irony in all this, as it was actually Nixon in 1952, then a candidate for vice president, who quite deftly broke new ground in the effective use of television through the famous "Checkers speech" that saved his candidacy and boosted his popularity as a national figure. But in just eight years, the rapidly changing medium of television seemed to have passed him, and from the debates with Kennedy forward, Nixon would never trust the medium again.

The vice president did enjoy a surge as Election Day approached, and in part due to his ability to finally respond more forcefully to Senator Kennedy's criticism of the Eisenhower administration's foreign policy. Nixon was able to gain traction against his opponent over the issue of two islands off the coast of China, Quemoy and Matsu, both of which had been a point of conflict between the communist mainland government, the People's Republic of China, and the Republic of China (the Nationalists) now in exile on Taiwan and currently supported by the United States and thus protected by the might of the U.S. Pacific Fleet. The islands had recently been shelled by the communists and had thus become a potential hot spot in the Cold War. President Eisenhower drew the line at these two remote islands, and Vice President Nixon reasserted that position, making a particular point of mentioning it in the second televised debate, a debate in which he presented himself with more strength. But Senator Kennedy, who had hit the administration hard on the "missile gap," was put back on his own heels over these two islands, for he had exhibited a considerable degree of waffling on the issue. Senator Kennedy personally harbored serious doubts about committing the United States to another war against China over what he regarded as two small, obscure islands. Defending the Nationalist government on Taiwan, which he certainly endorsed, was one thing; spilling American blood for Quemoy and Matsu was quite another. But Nixon came back at Kennedy hard, implying that the unwillingness to take a stand to hold these islands amounted to an appeasement. This was a particularly sensitive accusation to the senator, who was painfully aware of the appearance of appeasement on the part of his own father, Joseph Kennedy Sr., who, when serving as the U.S. ambassador to the Court of St. James, agreed with the appeasement policies of the British prime minister Neville Chamberlain's government, a source of embarrassment for the younger Kennedy, who identified far more with Sir Winston Churchill than with Chamberlain. Nixon delivered a well-placed blow against Kennedy, forcefully explaining that

The question is not these two little pieces of real estate—they are unimportant. It isn't the few people who live on them—they are not too important. It's the principle involved. These two islands are in the area of freedom. We should not force our Nationalist allies to get off them and give them to the Communists. If we do that, we start a chain reaction. In my opinion, this is the same kind of wooly thinking that led to disaster for America in Korea. I am against it. I would not tolerate it as president of the United States, and I will hope that Senator Kennedy will change his mind if he should be elected. (Matthews, p. 302)

Owing to this parry, Nixon, who had suffered a setback in the first debate and had also been dogged by Kennedy's "missile gap" charge, had managed to recover his balance and push back against the Democrats. Thus the race heated up again, with both candidates having enjoyed gains and suffered losses.

Throughout the campaign season of 1960, both candidates campaigned hard and aggressively. The fifty-state tour that had compromised Nixon's health was but one example of his determination. Kennedy played a different strategy, focusing intensely on the swing states and maintaining a visible presence in those areas that were known to be tight. Both candidates consistently performed well in their campaign engagements, and in many ways and in spite of their visible differences in style, they both represented the new kind of politician that was needed in the age of mass communication and ever-increasingly rapid transportation.

Election Night brought one of the closest elections in history, certainly the closest of the twentieth century. The early returns initially indicated a large lead for Senator Kennedy; but as the night wore on, the vote for Nixon came out, and he closed the gap. As expected, Kennedy showed his greatest strength in urban areas, particularly in the Northeast, most of the Atlantic coast (sharing the Pacific coast with Nixon), and the larger midwestern cities. He won all the major cities at the time except Los Angeles, taking New York, Chicago, Philadelphia, Detroit, Boston, and Pittsburgh in the early going, thus exaggerating his lead. Nixon won heavily in suburbia and rural America, and as returns came in from the West, he found himself in a dead heat with Kennedy. Kennedy carried the old Roosevelt Coalition blocs, as expected; but the support he received from African Americans was even higher than usual, owing to his public sympathy for Reverend Martin Luther King Jr. during King's incarceration in Georgia, an event that was ignored by the Nixon camp in a display of apparent disinterest that did not go unnoticed among black voters. On the morning after Election Day, no winner had been declared, although earlier that morning, Nixon expressed his opinion that the election was going Kennedy's way. Still, it was not until that afternoon that the vice president finally conceded defeat. Unknown to the voting public at the time, there were suspicions of voter fraud in both Illinois and Texas that had allegedly worked in Kennedy's favor; but Nixon, apprised of the allegations, refused to pursue the issue and congratulated Kennedy for his victory. It should be noted that recent political science research has, in reexamining the data, now cast some doubt upon the old claims that Nixon in reality won Illinois but then lost it due to corruption. That there was fraud in Illinois is not disputed, but it is not clear whether the fraud that did occur was extensive enough to have made a difference. And the issue, for the moment, remains controversial and inconclusive.

But we know one thing: The election was close. In five states won by Kennedy (Hawaii, Illinois, Missouri, New Jersey, and New Mexico), Kennedy's margin of victory was less than 1 percent, and in the case of Hawaii and Illinois (the latter state being where the allegations of voter fraud were circulating), the margin of victory was a staggeringly slender 0.06 percent and 0.19 percent, respectively. The closest race in a state won by Nixon, his home state of California, was decided by 0.55 percent of the vote. In all, twenty states were decided by margins of victory of less than 5 percent, nine states by less than 2 percent. Kennedy won a total of 34,222,984 popular votes to Nixon's 34,108,157, or 49.72 percent to 49.55 percent in favor of Kennedy, with the remainder of the vote going to minor candidates. Kennedy's popular vote plurality was razor-thin, but it converted to a clearer victory in the Electoral College, wherein Kennedy won 303 (56%) of the electors to Nixon's 219 (41%), with 15 electors remaining unpledged (14 in Mississippi who refused to vote for Kennedy and instead announced for conservative, segregationist Democrat Harry Byrd of Virginia; and one elector in Alabama who voted for Senator Goldwater).

Kennedy's victory regained the White House for the Democrats, reasserting the party dominance that they had won in the election of 1932 and held for two solid decades before being unseated by Dwight Eisenhower. President Kennedy's vision of a New Frontier energized the nation in a way that resembled Franklin Roosevelt, and his perception of the torch of liberty being passed to a new generation inspired many within that same generation to public service. The Kennedy administration suffered setbacks in its first few months, especially in foreign policy, but once it settled in, it began to show promise of great things to come. President Kennedy's conduct during the Cuban Missile Crisis in October 1962, his emboldened vow to win the space race, his resolute support of West Germany and in particular West Berlin against the Soviet threat, and his growing commitment to civil rights, particularly as his administration matured, illustrated the depth and scope of his leadership.

All this came to a cruel end. On November 22, 1963, as President Kennedy was beginning to accelerate his campaign for reelection to a second term, he was brutally assassinated by a delusional sociopath in Dallas, Texas, a cruel and murderous blow that wounded the entire country and, for many, signaled the "end of American innocence." The youngest man to be elected president was now also the youngest to die in office, and the bright promise of a decade was instantly snatched away without warning and without any sense. The collective grief that suddenly struck the American people would linger heavily within American political culture throughout the remainder of the century; and while the raw and painful emotions surrounding those times have for the most part dissipated and Americans no longer mourn their fallen president as they once had, the influence of his life, the example of his commitment, and the effects of his death remain a vivid element in the story of American democracy.

Additional Resources

Donalson, Gary. *The First Modern Campaign: Kennedy, Nixon and the Election of 1960*. Lanham, MD: Rowman & Littlefield, 2007.

Pietrusza, David. *1960: LBJ v. Kennedy v. Nixon: The Epic Campaign that Forged Three Presidencies*. New York: Union Square Press, 2008.

Rorabaugh, W. J. *The Real Making of the President*. Lawrence: University Press of Kansas, 2009.

Sorenson, Theodore. "Election of 1960." In Arthur M. Schlesinger, Fred Israel, and William P. Hansen, eds. *History of American Presidential Elections, 1789–1968*. Vol. 2. New York: Chelsea House, 1985.

Troy, Gil. "1960." In Arthur M. Schlesinger, Fred L. Israel, and David J. Frent, eds. *Running for President: The Candidates and Their Images*. Vol. 2. New York: Simon & Schuster, 1994.

White, Theodore. *The Making of the President: 1960*. New York: Harper Perennial Reissue Edition, 2009.

Campaign of 1964

With an informal beginning in 1963, looking ahead, the Campaign of 1964 was shaping up as a likely contest between the charismatic, young incumbent president, John F. Kennedy, whose presidency seemed to be just hitting its stride after a series of setbacks in the early months of his term; and an ascending leader within the resurgent conservative wing of the Republican Party, the redoubtable and inimitable Senator Barry Goldwater from Arizona. Goldwater had emerged as a captivating alternative, riding a wave of conservative discontent within the GOP over what they viewed as the betrayal of their core principles by moderate and liberal Republicans who had either accepted or even embraced the tenets of the New Deal, tenets that they viewed as contrary to the American way of life.

Supporting states' rights, low taxes, a much smaller federal government, and restrictions on the power of the Supreme Court as well as opposing a nuclear test ban treaty, and stridently anticommunist while advocating direct confrontation with the Soviet bloc and China rather than negotiation, which was likened to appeasement, the new brand of Republican conservatism was energized and emboldened, and the party was thus more sharply divided than it had been since the **Campaign of 1912**. The old GOP that had, in the eyes of the Goldwater conservatives, capitulated to New Deal statism had to be rehabilitated from the pernicious influence of the New Deal. So strong was this belief among the party's right that even a figure as respected as former president Eisenhower, who was among the more popular Republican presidents in history, was viewed as allowing his moderate attitudes and policies to drift toward what they deemed leftward ideology. For Senator Goldwater, Eisenhower's presidency had been simply "New Deal light" and thus a radical break from the purer Republican principles of small, localized government and individual self-reliance. This movement had already been in evidence during President Eisenhower's two terms, as he often felt more closely aligned to the moderate Democrats on key domestic issues, thus in a way validating the conservative complaint about interparty cross-pollination. Goldwater thus represented a voice in the GOP that had been, in their estimation, pushed aside by the wake of FDR's New Deal, a wake that had reshaped both parties (or perhaps upset, in the case of the GOP, at least from the viewpoint of the conservatives), and the Goldwater Republicans wanted to set their party aright.

President Kennedy, by and large a moderate Democrat, whose defining vision, the New Frontier, was tempered by a consistent political pragmatism that in many ways was closer to the bipartisanship of his Republican predecessor, nonetheless was viewed as a stark contrast to Goldwater, particularly in the realm of civil rights. Kennedy was hardly soft on communism—he cut his political teeth as a Cold Warrior and had proven his mettle against the Soviets during the precipitous Cuban Missile Crisis in October 1962, and in this sense he was not far from many Republicans—in spite of the protestations of the Goldwater faction. But his views on civil rights were liberal, particularly for the times, even though they had been somewhat soft-peddled earlier in his administration out of concern over alienating the South, a Democratic stronghold that at that time was considered a critical asset that needed to be held to mount any successful Democratic bid for the White House.

While many of President Kennedy's critics, then and now, feel that he moved too slowly in addressing the political and social disadvantages of African Americans, the record shows that he did exhibit ongoing concern for civil rights during his 1960 campaign, and, more to the point, his administration had recently proposed the most far-reaching civil rights legislation since Reconstruction. Now that the recent and menacing international crisis was behind him, Kennedy had begun, at political risk, to accelerate his efforts in the promotion of his civil rights agenda, describing in a nationally broadcast civil rights address his administration's renewed push for a more equitable society for all races as a moral imperative. "We are confronted primarily with a moral issue," Kennedy explained in his civil rights address. "It is as old as the Scriptures and is as clear as the American Constitution." It was, along with his inaugural address and his campaign speech to the Baptist ministers in Houston, one of his greatest speeches, applauded by none other than the Rev. Martin Luther King Jr. as the "most sweeping and forthright ever presented by an American president."

These increased efforts by the Kennedy administration in addressing civil rights for minorities, and the speech that defined those efforts, threatened to split the party along the same lines that divided it in 1948. Indeed, Kennedy's fateful trip to Texas was an attempt to mend broken relations within his important Southern base, which was the consequence of the president's now more candidly shared progressive attitudes toward equality between the races. Many in the South were angered over Kennedy's speech, the recently proposed civil rights bill, and the future policies that it implied, and the trip to Dallas and other Texas cities was largely an effort by Kennedy to win back Texas Democrats, who were a crucial cohort in the upcoming election against what was likely to be a conservative Republican, and who were in danger of being lost over the issue.

In this regard and in comparison to Kennedy, and even in comparison to the liberal wing and moderate center of his own party, Goldwater's conservatism leaned toward a libertarian position that preferred nonpolitical solutions to social problems, denying that racial prejudice was the federal government's responsibility to correct. Goldwater himself was not personally invested in maintaining segregation; rather, he was deeply committed to preventing the continued growth of federal power and its expanding intervention in policy areas that he considered the province of the states and their localities. Given his perception of a serious divide between his principles and those of the current administration, Goldwater looked forward to debating Kennedy in 1964; the two candidates even planned a national tour in which they would together travel cross-country to various locations where they would stop to debate the issues and problems of the times. Both men respected each other and enjoyed a friendly relationship in spite of their disparate political visions, agreeing to a civil campaign based on issues and values. But what promised to be an engaging contest of ideas and styles was obliterated in a split second by the death of the president at the hand of a delusional assassin, a most loathsome act against the ideals that are so palpably expressed through the democratic process of free and open elections. A shocked and saddened Senator Goldwater joined all Americans in grieving for the slain president, and he dreaded the thought of facing the new president and now the new Democratic candidate for the upcoming campaign of 1964, Lyndon Baines Johnson.

If charisma, urbanity, and sophistication aptly describe President Kennedy, President Johnson can, with equal aptness, be referred to as larger than life, even overpowering. More domineering than charismatic, and unimpressed by the graceful charm of the Kennedys, LBJ was a genuine master at shaping political brokering and insider negotiations. His forceful, dogged personality could overwhelm most of his colleagues, and his ability to buttonhole and persuade his way to legislative victory as Senate majority leader is legendary. He has often been described as an "arm twister" and a master manipulator, but those are more epithet than accurate characterization. Johnson's strength stemmed from a lifetime study of the political craft; an ability to know the intimate details of any issue and, more importantly, the principal actors involved; and to track this knowledge, compile it, thoroughly understand it, and use it to his advantage. He could intimidate, but mostly when he worked on a person, it was more a combination of an intuitive knowledge of human nature, insight into character, and sheer persistence that made Johnson one of the very best in influencing the course of events. Beneath what appeared to some to be a rough, even uncultured exterior, a keen intelligence surveyed the political landscape and, with intuition sharpened by years of careful observation, knew just exactly how to traverse the often obscured and entangled pathways of political negotiation.

In contrast to President Kennedy, who never enjoyed the gamesmanship of politics and preferred a more personable style—which, as many believed, made him at times less effective in dealing with Congress (although to be completely fair, JFK could, in those times when necessity pressed in, play very hardball politics)—Johnson relished the art of honing the political deal and bringing pressure to bear on friend and foe alike. Kennedy exuded charm; even his political opponents admitted that it was difficult not to like him. Johnson was more a force of nature; even his worst enemies discovered that it was difficult to resist him. He was one of the more effective politicians in the history of the Senate, in many ways surpassing Kennedy, who was no slouch, in the mechanics of politicking. This is not to say that Kennedy lacked political skill; he certainly possessed a different set of qualities that made him an effective president. But whereas Kennedy drew upon his inexhaustible personal magnetism to assure his friends and to win his opponents to his side, Johnson applied the sheer force of his outsized personality to impose his will. Where Kennedy was charmingly persuasive, Johnson was formidable, and few if any could match his sheer determination and capacity to achieve his goals. On a personal level, Goldwater disliked Johnson; there would be no debate between these two men should they both receive, as was expected, their respective party nominations in the following summer.

With the loss of President Kennedy, the liberal wing of the Democratic Party feared that Johnson might reject Kennedy's progressive reform agenda. Instead, Johnson seized the moment, embraced Kennedy's vision, and even expanded it. Without a moment's hesitation, he took the lead in pushing through Congress, as only Lyndon Johnson could, the Civil Rights Act of 1964, an act that began with President Kennedy and, through President Johnson's leadership, became the most extensive civil rights legislation in a century—which, among other things, prohibited discrimination on the basis of race, religion, sex, and national origin on many levels throughout society: in the workplace, in public accommodations, in education, in the political arena. Johnson further reinforced his support with the liberal wing of the Democratic Party by announcing his plans for a series of new "Great Society" social programs and a "war on poverty" aimed at nothing less than the elimination of poverty in the United States. Johnson's vision was now seen as exceeding Kennedy's and more progressive than even FDR's; it captivated the imagination of moderate and liberal Democrats as well as liberal Republicans, and it was received favorably by large segments of the American electorate.

Hence, just as Senator Goldwater was steering his party to the right, LBJ was driving his party further left, setting the stage for the most ideologically charged election since 1932, and perhaps more so. By comparison, the candidates in the previous general election, Kennedy and then vice president Richard Nixon, were centrists, in reality fairly close on the issues, and well accustomed to the bipartisanship that had defined the Eisenhower years. Differences in policy and vision have always been important in American political history, and 1960 is no exception. But in the 1964 candidacies of Johnson and Goldwater, the election was clearly polarized: Lyndon Johnson's activist state and the promise of a Great Society beyond poverty and prejudice, directly challenged by Barry Goldwater's clarion call for a restoration of the principles of self-reliance, small government, and individual initiative that he and his supporters considered under threat by

New Deal/Fair Deal/Great Society ambitions and the seemingly limitless growth of federal power.

But before the fated Johnson-Goldwater campaign could begin, both candidates still needed to win their respective party nominations. Even though Goldwater had emerged as the GOP front-runner in the latter half of 1963, to the point of drawing the principal focus from the Kennedy campaign camp, it was New York governor Nelson Rockefeller, from the party's liberal wing, who was the front-runner as late as the spring of 1963. But the idea of a Rockefeller candidacy was intolerable to the conservative wing, and his sudden marriage to a recently divorced woman fifteen years his younger, a choice that raised eyebrows in the mid-1960s, had caused many in the party to question his personal judgment. As a result, his numbers in the poll dropped precipitously, helping to propel Goldwater into the front-runner position. Surprisingly, Henry Cabot Lodge Jr., Nixon's running mate in 1960, beat both Goldwater and Rockefeller in the increasingly important New Hampshire primary; but it was Lodge's only promising moment in the campaign.

With Richard Nixon, the party standard-bearer four years earlier, temporarily out of politics and embittered by his treatment in the press after his failed 1962 gubernatorial campaign in California, and with Rockefeller compromised, Goldwater did not face a serious challenge after June 1963, and he was already preparing for a run at Kennedy in 1964. During the primaries Rockefeller managed some support, but Goldwater led in the popular voting, 38 percent to 22 percent, with a handful of also-rans claiming the rest, and he took eight states to Rockefeller's two. By the time of the convention, Goldwater's nomination seemed inevitable, the senator winning easily on the first ballot, with Rockefeller actually showing third behind Pennsylvania governor William Scranton, who placed a distant second to the nominee. Of historical interest, Maine senator Margaret Chase Smith became the first woman to receive support for the presidency at a major party's nominating convention, after having won 227 votes in the primaries. (Victoria Woodhull, nominated in 1872 by the Equal Rights Party, is technically the first woman to receive an official endorsement for president from any political party; but Smith, at the 1964 GOP convention, was the first woman to have been mentioned as a potential presidential candidate from a major party, and she was the first woman to receive votes of any kind for the White House, having received the support of those 227 delegates mentioned above.) Following Goldwater's nomination for the top of the ticket, Representative William E. Miller of New York, a former prosecutor at the Nuremburg Trials, was tapped to serve as Goldwater's running mate, the first Roman Catholic to be nominated for the vice presidency (by a major party), and to this date the only Roman Catholic to be nominated by the Republican Party for either the presidency or the vice presidency.

With control of the majority of delegates, Goldwater pushed through the convention an exceptionally conservative platform. Much of the platform focused on the alleged failures of the Kennedy and Johnson administrations in their approach to the threat of communist expansion. To counter this threat abroad, the platform demanded that the United States acquire military superiority over possible enemies and refuse to settle for mere parity. "We will maintain a superior, not merely equal, military capability as long as the Communist drive for world domination continues. It will be a capability of balanced force, superior in all its arms, maintaining flexibility for effective performance in the rapidly changing science of war," stressed a key platform plank. Of equal importance, the platform called for a significantly smaller federal government and a return of power to the several states. "Within our Republic the Federal Government should act only in areas where it has Constitutional authority to act, and then only in respect to proven needs where individuals and local or state governments will not or cannot adequately perform. Great power, whether governmental or private, political or economic, must be so checked, balanced and restrained and, where necessary, so dispersed as to prevent it from becoming a threat to freedom any place in the land," the platform announced. To the dismay of those civil rights advocates in the liberal and moderate factions of the party, the GOP platform also included a plank that implied less commitment to the enforcement of civil rights laws. "We recognize that the elimination of any such discrimination is a matter of heart, conscience, and education, as well as of equal rights under law," stated the platform. Goldwater and his supporters saw the future of the Republican Party as drawing its strength from the more fiscally and socially conservative West and South and not in the liberal Northeast, which was the center of the Republican Party's civil rights support.

The convention was acrimonious; Governor Rockefeller was booed by conservatives, and tension was high between the various factions in the party. Two speeches were delivered at the convention that are of particular importance: a deftly delivered nominating speech by Ronald Reagan, a Hollywood actor and former Democrat, who, after Goldwater, was rapidly becoming the favorite of the conservative wing; and Goldwater's own acceptance speech. Reagan's speech, now commonly referred to as "A Time for Choosing," became an instant classic in American political rhetoric and a touchstone of the postwar conservative movement, as well as a launching point toward his own eventual election as governor of California. Reagan encapsulated the conservative ethos and conviction that the United States was the "last stand" in the world for the principles of individual liberty, affirming as an article of faith that the Founders opposed the "full power of centralized government." Refusing to accept the treatment of the American people as the "masses" to whom government must supply comfort at the expense of independence, Reagan skillfully presented the renewed conservative creed. Linking the rejection of the welfare state to the ideological struggle between the superpowers abroad, Reagan intoned,

> Those who would trade our freedom for the soup kitchen of the welfare state have told us they have a utopian solution of peace without victory. They call their policy "accommodation." And they say if we'll only avoid any direct confrontation with the enemy, he'll forget his evil ways and learn to love us. All who oppose them are indicted as warmongers. They say we offer simple answers to complex problems. Well, perhaps there is a simple answer—not an easy answer—but simple: If you and I have the courage to tell our elected officials that we want our national policy based on what we know in our hearts is morally right.
>
> We cannot buy our security, our freedom from the threat of the bomb by committing an immorality so great as saying to a billion human beings now enslaved behind the Iron Curtain, "Give up your dreams of freedom because to save our own skins, we're willing to make a deal with your slave masters." Alexander Hamilton said, "A nation which can prefer disgrace to danger is prepared for a master, and deserves one." Now let's set the record straight. There's no argument over the choice between peace and war, but there's only one guaranteed way you can have peace—and you can have it in the next second—surrender. . . . You and I know and do not believe that life is so dear and peace so sweet as to be purchased at the price of chains and slavery. If nothing in life is worth dying for, when did this begin—just in the face of this enemy? Or should Moses have told the children of Israel to live in slavery under the pharaohs? Should Christ have refused the cross? Should the patriots at Concord Bridge have thrown down their guns and refused to fire the shot heard 'round the world? The martyrs of history were not fools, and our honored dead who gave their lives to stop the advance of the Nazis didn't die in vain. Where, then, is the road to peace?

In his peroration, Reagan effectively quoted President Franklin Roosevelt, whom he had always admired in spite of their ideological differences (differences that developed only later in Reagan's life), by proclaiming that this generation also faced its own "rendezvous with destiny." Roosevelt's familiar phrase was also famously quoted by John Kennedy during his first debate against Richard Nixon in the 1960 campaign just four years earlier; but in a sense, Reagan's reiteration of FDR's famous line has become more familiar within our political culture, almost to the point of the phrase being commonly identified as much with Reagan as with Roosevelt. Goldwater's acceptance speech was equally provocative, if not as memorable, save for one phrase inspired by a similar line from the Roman philosopher-statesman

Cicero at the suggestion of scholar Harry Jaffa. "I would remind you that extremism in the defense of liberty is no vice." Goldwater declaimed. "And let me remind you also that moderation in the pursuit of justice is no virtue." (Cicero actually said, "I must remind you, Lords, Senators, that extreme patriotism in the defense of freedom is no crime, and let me respectfully remind you that pusillanimity in the pursuit of justice is no virtue in a Roman.") After Goldwater delivered this now-famous line, many were led to conclude, rightly or wrongly, that the candidate was endorsing extremism as the default policy. Hence for Goldwater's followers, it served as an inspiring maxim that embodied the brave-hearted virtues of more rugged conservatives; but to many voters, it came off as at best a cavalier defense of provocation abroad, and at worst, a dangerous, even deadly impulse simmering just below the surface of the Goldwater campaign. It did fuel the efforts on the part of Democrats to depict Goldwater as a hothead who could not be trusted, an extremist who could precipitate total war.

President Johnson was clearly the only choice for the Democrats in 1964; thus, long before the convention, he was considered a lock. In the presidential preference primaries, Johnson actually finished well behind California governor Edmund "Pat" Brown; but in 1964, these primaries were nonbinding, expressing preference rather than commitment, and the power to nominate was still firmly in the party leadership, where Johnson held sway. There were two problems that LBJ had to face: renewed discontent in the Southern wing that could possibly lead to a Dixiecrat defection similar to what had happened in 1948; and Johnson's prickly relationship with his attorney general, Robert F. Kennedy, brother and close adviser of the slain president. LBJ and RFK harbored mutual animosity that stemmed from Bobby Kennedy's attempts to block Johnson's inclusion on the bottom of the Kennedy ticket at the 1960 convention. Since that time, the two men's disdain for each other festered: Bobby regarded Johnson as coarse, domineering, and insincere (RFK seethed at what he viewed to be LBJ's sudden conversion on civil rights and his self-serving appropriation of what should have been his brother's finest legacy); Johnson, although he personally liked Bobby's brother, President Kennedy, was uncomfortable with what he regarded as the elitist Kennedy clan, and he found Bobby in particular to be an arrogant and pretentious child of privilege. Both men had more in common than they would likely admit—they were equally confident, resolute, committed, impossible to intimidate, fearless, and blunt, and whether fairly or unfairly, they shared a reputation for ruthlessness. Many believed that Bobby should be offered the vice presidential nomination, but LBJ bristled at the suggestion, tapping instead another liberal Democrat, Senator Hubert Humphrey of Minnesota. So intent was Johnson on blocking any possible movement to draft Bobby for the vice presidency that he had Bobby's appearance before the convention scheduled for the final day of the convention, long after the vice presidential nomination would have been settled. As it turned out, Bobby Kennedy's appearance proved to be the most powerful moment in the entire convention, a tribute to his fallen brother and a visual reminder that the Kennedy legacy remained a strong force within the party.

Not surprisingly, the Democratic platform sought to define the Democratic Party as the party of peace. The Johnson campaign knew full well that it could easily depict Barry Goldwater as temperamentally and ideologically too reckless to serve as president. "At the start of the third decade of the nuclear age, the preservation of peace requires the strength to wage war and the wisdom to avoid it. The search for peace requires the utmost intelligence, the clearest vision, and a strong sense of reality," the platform proclaimed. With respect to an expanded domestic agenda, the platform called for further expansion of the Social Security program to provide "medical care benefits for the aged" and new "federal programs to aid urban communities to clear their slums, dispose of their sewage, educate their children, transport suburban commuters to and from their jobs, and combat juvenile delinquency," all promoted as part of Johnson's Great Society initiative.

In spite of Johnson's evident strength in the polls, his campaign took the Goldwater challenge seriously. Instead of trying to sell the American people on the need for new Great Society programs and a "war on poverty," the campaign opted for a strategy of convincing the American people that the election of Barry Goldwater was so risky that it could even lead to a nuclear war. Goldwater's own tendencies to issue controversial pronouncements proved to be the Democrats' best weapon. On domestic policy, for example, Goldwater openly mused that Social Security, which had become politically inviolate to both parties, would be better were it voluntary. More critically, in the arena of foreign policy, Goldwater could not help but issue provocative, even frightening statements; at one point, he even openly speculated that nuclear weapons might help to end the Vietnam War. The Democrats' slogan "Vote for President Johnson on November 3: The Stakes Are Too High to Stay Home" was meant to convey without equivocation the alarming message that Goldwater was dangerous. To further this effort, the Johnson campaign hired the Madison Avenue ad agency Doyle Dane Bernbach to produce its television ad campaign. The ads developed by the agency ushered in a new era of political campaign "attack ads." Goldwater was effectively depicted as bellicose, trigger-happy, and politically immature, a crackpot loose cannon who had no business controlling the nation's nuclear arsenal.

Although only broadcast one time, the now famous "Daisy Girl" campaign ad depicting a carefree young girl happily playing in a bed of flowers is the best example of Johnson's negative strategy. In the ad, the little girl, in her idyllic reverie, innocently pulls the petals from a freshly plucked daisy. As her sweet voice playfully counts the petals away, another voice, this one mechanically ominous, begins a countdown of its own; suddenly the girl's attention is drawn to something in the sky, and the picture immediately dissolves to be terrifyingly replaced by the fiery mushroom cloud of a massive nuclear explosion—all childhood, all hope, all that is living forever obliterated in a single moment. This astonishing image was followed by President Johnson's somber voice-over punctuating the gravity and high stakes of the upcoming election. "These are the stakes," Johnson warns. "To make a world in which all of God's children can live, or to go into the dark. We must either love each other, or we must die." The advertisement was met with immediate criticism, accused of being an exercise in blatant fearmongering; but its lone broadcast on September 7, 1964, even though it was quickly withdrawn, produced the intended effect. The message to the voters was clear: The election of 1964 was a matter of life and death, and the wrong choice (viz., Senator Goldwater) could lead to the end of everything.

In addition to the nuclear war issue, Johnson campaign ads pounded Goldwater for his controversial approach to domestic programs. One ad made no bones about Goldwater's appeal to the Ku Klux Klan, even quoting, against the backdrop of burning crosses and hooded degenerates, one of the Klan's poobahs who, after denouncing African Americans, Catholics, and Jews, encourages his followers to vote for Goldwater, saying, "He needs our help." To Senator Goldwater and the Republicans, it was an embarrassing example of the old saying, "With friends like that, who needs enemies?" Other, less hysterical ads attacked Goldwater for voting against a measure before Congress that would expand the Social Security program to include health care coverage for the elderly. In the same ads, Johnson pledged to push the Medicare program through Congress. The president himself remained in the White House, quietly keeping his distance from the brutal ad campaign mounted by his managers.

While the Johnson campaign was aggressive, Goldwater did not help his own cause. He was inclined to speak his mind without reserve and with little concern for the consequences of his statements. Even loyal supporters would wince, knowing that reporters were recording verbatim some of his more controversial comments, usually made off the cuff. Hence, instead of enjoying the freedom to craft an effective campaign that delivered its candidate's vision and personality to the voters, the Goldwater campaign found itself forced to squander scarce media dollars to explain, clarify, and defend Goldwater's pronouncements. Goldwater was forced to clarify a statement indicating that he believed NATO commanders should have the option of using nuclear weapons to counter a Soviet threat without first receiving approval from the president. Goldwater also did not rule out the use of low-yield nuclear weapons in Vietnam to remove forests that provided the enemy cover. Goldwater's ham-handed attempt at humor suggesting that it might be a good idea to lob a nuclear weapon into the men's room at the Kremlin fell flat and did little to help Goldwater shake the image of recklessness.

The Goldwater campaign believed that its primary slogans, "In Your Heart You Know He's Right" and "Extremism in the Defense of Liberty Is No Vice," aptly defined its candidate as a courageous leader of strong principle who unflinchingly and unapologetically stood by his beliefs. Johnson supporters cleverly reworked these slogans to humorously but effectively raise doubts about Goldwater's mental fitness to serve as president. Slogans such as "In Your Heart You Know He's Nuts," "In Your Heart You Know He Might," and "In Your Guts You Know He's Nuts" parodied Goldwater's real slogan as an indictment of the Republican candidate's risky proclivities and ideas. Joining the mudslinging, the Goldwater campaign tried hard to tie Johnson to influence-peddling scandals, but voters were either not convinced or not interested. Perhaps most significantly, strong economic growth and relatively low inflation made it difficult for Goldwater, as it does for any candidate who challenges an incumbent in times of prosperity, to convince voters that the country needed lower taxes and less government spending.

Come Election Day, President Lyndon Johnson enjoyed one of the largest landslides in American history, winning just over 43,000,000 votes (a shade over 61%) to Goldwater's total of around 27,000,000 (approximately 38%). Johnson's 61.1 percent of the total popular vote nationwide still stands as the highest percentage of the popular vote ever received by a candidate for the American presidency (slightly exceeding even Franklin Roosevelt's 60.8% in 1936). Significantly, and as a further sign of future trouble for the Democrats, LBJ did lose the formerly reliable Democratic bastion, the Southern bloc, largely due to his positions and achievements regarding civil rights; Mississippi, Alabama, Louisiana, Georgia, and South Carolina—that is, the Deep South—all went with Goldwater. Other southern states such as Virginia, Florida, and North Carolina did stick with the Democrats, but it was clear that the effects of the Dixiecrat revolt of 1948 had come back to bite the party hard, and it was equally clear now that in two of the last five elections, the Deep South had rejected the Democratic candidate. Thus the election of 1964 (prefigured by 1948) marked a shift in the South away from its former role as a Democratic bastion and the beginning of its movement toward the GOP. The only other state that Goldwater was able to win was his home state of Arizona (and there he barely won by just a 1% margin). As a historical note, due to the ratification of the Twenty-Third Amendment, the District of Columbia was for the first time allotted electors, all of whom voted for Johnson. All told, Johnson's popular-vote landslide converted to an Electoral College victory of 486 (90%) to Goldwater's 52 (10%), an electoral-vote figure that, not counting the elections of Washington and Monroe that had occurred well before the maturity of the modern party system, is exceeded only by FDR in 1936 (98.5%) and by Abraham Lincoln in 1864 (91%), the latter in an election that did not involve the entire Union. (Washington and Monroe, of course, enjoyed a still higher percentage of electoral votes under different circumstances, the former unanimously selected and the latter falling one electoral vote shy of unanimity within a different political landscape.) Eventually both Richard Nixon (1972) and Ronald Reagan (1984) would surpass LBJ's Electoral College figure.

Johnson's landslide victory provided him with the mandate to push through his Great Society programs. Yet, within a relatively short period of time, the war in Vietnam began to transform the Johnson presidency, a transformation that had been neither anticipated nor desired, and that painfully reflected one of the more turbulent eras in American history. Lyndon Johnson would, for a time, be regarded as one of the United States' more successful presidents, owing to his accomplishments in civil rights and the promotion of social programs aimed at addressing poverty and other forms of social and political disadvantage. But before his departure from the White House, he would experience a rapid and merciless fall from grace that would make a mockery of his astonishing election victory in 1964 and drive him fully out of the presidency; and like Shakespeare's Cardinal Wolsey in *Henry VIII*, having once put forth "the tender leaves of hopes" as tomorrow's promises, like a field of bright daisies, blossomed before him, he would soon feel the "killing frost" that nips the root of ripening greatness, to which he would be left to bid a long farewell.

Additional Resources

Dallek, Robert. "1964." In Arthur M. Schlesinger, Fred L. Israel, and David J. Frent, eds. *Running for President: The Candidates and Their Images.* Vol. 2. New York: Simon & Schuster, 1994.

Faber, Harold, et al. *The Road to the White House: The Story of the Election of 1964.* New York: McGraw-Hill, 1965.

Martin, John Barlow. "Election of 1964." In Arthur M. Schlesinger, Fred Israel, and William P. Hansen, eds. *History of American Presidential Elections, 1789–1968.* Vol. 2. New York: Chelsea House, 1985.

White, Theodore. *The Making of the President, 1964.* New York: Atheneum Publishers, 1965.

Campaign of 1968

There has never been a campaign like the one that preceded the presidential election of 1968. As dramatic changes convulsed American society on a number of levels, an embattled incumbent president surprised the nation by withdrawing from the race, a former vice president that many believed was out of politics made a stunning comeback, a youthful presidential candidate who inspired multitudes was assassinated, rioting broke out at a national nominating convention, a potent segregationist third party formed to drain electoral votes away from the main parties, and the general mood of the country was rocked by tragedy, anger, disaffection, disappointment, fragmentation, and grief. The Vietnam War, which had now involved Americans for three administrations, was widely protested. The civil rights movement, in spite of the significant legislative victories of 1964 and 1965, was beleaguered by a sense of frustration that in some instances turned toward bitterness, and the peaceful methods that defined the movement in the 1950s and early 1960s were now undercut by an increase in blind violence. In April of that year, the most prominent leader of the movement, the Reverend Martin Luther King Jr., was gunned down by an assassin, fueling the despair and confusion that seemed to mark those times. The 1960s were both hopeful and disorienting, promising an uplifting cultural transformation while often delivering social disillusionment. Against this backdrop, the presidential campaign of 1968 remains a singular moment in American political history.

Incumbent president Johnson had enjoyed a staggering electoral victory in 1964, and the early months of his first full term as president (he had earlier succeeded to the presidency on the death of President John F. Kennedy, who was struck down by an assassin's bullet, a far too frequent event in the 1960s) were characterized by a series of legislative triumphs. But to his eventual downfall, the ambitious president did the very thing that he promised he would not do during the **Campaign of 1964**. Critical of his campaign opponent of that year, Senator Barry Goldwater of Arizona, for his bellicose attitudes regarding foreign policy, and especially with regard to Vietnam, President Johnson had pledged that he would not send "American boys" to fight a war that should be fought by "Asian boys." But early in his term, LBJ, in an effort to seize control of the situation, escalated the American presence in Indochina, and the Vietnam War turned far more controversial, a controversy that severely divided the country and stained what had otherwise been, at least by many accounts, a successful presidency.

In February 1964, just three months after the death of President Kennedy, Johnson's approval rating peaked at 79 percent, but by the spring of 1965, it dipped below 50 percent, dropping to below 40 percent before the end of 1966 and swinging widely back and forth throughout 1967. Even so, LBJ was considered the party's clear front-runner going into the 1968 campaign. His lowest approval rating had not dropped as low as President Truman's had prior to the campaign season of 1948 (Truman had also ascended to the White House upon the death of a president), and Truman somehow managed reelection against what were then seen as long odds. In the initial days of the 1968 campaign, no one would directly challenge Johnson, even though the war had severely compromised his popularity and had caused visible divisions within his own party. Incumbent presidents are seldom denied their party's renomination; the last time this occurred was in 1884, when the Republicans chose not to nominate the incumbent president Arthur (yet another vice president to have ascended to the presidency upon the death of a president, and in this case, an assassination as well). Within the party, if there were to be a challenge, the obvious choice was New York senator Robert F. Kennedy, the younger brother and most trusted adviser of the late President Kennedy, as well as former attorney general in both the Kennedy and Johnson administrations. Kennedy, no friend of Johnson's, had become over the past few months increasingly disenchanted with the war and, by the latter part of 1967, more vocal in his criticism. Friends and close associates were prodding Kennedy to oppose Johnson, but Kennedy held back, fully aware of the divisiveness that would ensue in the wake of such an intraparty challenge. But as he became more critical of the war, it was difficult for Kennedy to remain out of the race; by February 1968, he had privately decided to enter the race, but he was advised to withhold announcing the decision until later.

However, another challenger had announced—Senator Eugene McCarthy of Minnesota, part poet, part scholar, and fully resolute in his strong and vocal opposition to the war. McCarthy held considerable appeal for young Americans, who were referred to as the "McCarthy Million" and who made a point of abandoning the countercultural fashions of the day that encouraged long hair and unconventional dress to go "Clean for Gene" while canvassing neighborhoods throughout the nation for votes. The McCarthy Million—a number of whom were actually Kennedy loyalists looking for a surrogate—were a devoted, enthusiastic, disciplined, and focused cohort, determined to bring McCarthy's antiwar message to the American public. McCarthy understood the quixotic nature of challenging an incumbent president within one's own party, and particularly one as politically savvy as Lyndon Johnson, but his primary goal was, at least initially, to challenge the war itself more than to unseat LBJ. The first round occured in the New Hampshire primary in March, where McCarthy's strong performance against the president stunned the media and sent shockwaves through the party. In the primary, LBJ tallied the most votes, taking 49 percent; but McCarthy won 42 percent, an unheard-of figure against a sitting president; and more importantly, twenty of the twenty-four New Hampshire delegates pledged for Senator McCarthy, boosting the senator's confidence and prompting him to publicly predict that he would beat Johnson and win the nomination. It was now no longer a campaign to force the party in power to reconsider its policies in Vietnam; it was now a real contest to dislodge President Johnson from within his own party.

Shortly after, Senator Kennedy announced he was joining the race. Even though most insiders testify that prior to New Hampshire, Kennedy had already decided to announce, McCarthy and his followers took offense at the timing of RFK's announcement coming so close to McCarthy's triumph. McCarthy harbored feelings of resentment against Bobby Kennedy, whom he saw as having waited behind the lines for him to do the dirty work in weakening the president, and was now suiting up to ride in for the kill. Kennedy announced that his campaign was "not in opposition to McCarthy's candidacy, but in harmony" with it. But a breach had been opened between Kennedy and McCarthy; throughout the campaign, the latter took umbrage at the appearance of opportunism on the part of the former. Whether or not that assessment is fair remains beyond anyone's perception, but it is clear that not only was there a fissure between the president and the liberal wing of the party over Vietnam, but now there was also a serious division between the McCarthy and Kennedy factions of that wing. The Democratic Party was fragmenting.

With McCarthy and Kennedy marshaled against him, and in the wake of the Tet Offensive—a comparatively extensive and coordinated assault throughout South Vietnam committed by the forces of North Vietnam in combination with the Viet Cong rebels, an assault that was in reality soundly defeated by U.S. military forces but that had nonetheless illustrated the full resolve of the enemy and, in the judgment of the media, the strategic mistakes of the administration—President Johnson stunned the nation when he announced on national television that he "would not seek [or] accept the nomination of my party for another term as your President." The president explained that he was withdrawing from the election in order to devote all his efforts to bringing the war to a swift resolution. With the exception of those closest to the president, the announcement came as a complete surprise, one that threw the campaign wide open and initiated one of the most chaotic episodes in American political history.

With President Johnson now out, it initially came down to McCarthy and Kennedy; but they were quickly joined by Vice President Hubert Humphrey, another liberal Democrat but with a much longer public record of progressivism, reaching back to the Truman administration. Owing to Humphrey's stature as vice president, he was immediately regarded the front-runner and likely heir apparent by the party leadership. But both McCarthy and Kennedy enjoyed enthusiastic groundswells of popular support, and as the campaign moved into the spring, it was apparent that Humphrey's advantage was vulnerable. Kennedy toured the country at a frenzied pace, energizing crowds and, in turn, being energized by them. Kennedy spoke brilliantly and courageously, and while McCarthy was more than capable of matching Kennedy on the level of intellect and in the promotion of ideas, Kennedy's passion and the power of his message, which called for a just, compassionate, and ennobled America, in many ways eclipsed McCarthy's more cerebral style. McCarthy, while sincere in his beliefs, seemed personally detached, and observers would often note that he gave the impression that he really did not want the presidency that much. By contrast, Kennedy was driven; he carried the much-touted mystique of his family's name and the legacy and promise of his brother's lost presidency, as well as his own emerging voice, which had become a powerful clarion call on behalf of the poor and marginalized:

> We must recognize peace in the world means little to us unless we can preserve it at home. We cannot continue to deny and postpone the demands of our people while spending billions in the name of freedom for others. No country can lead the fight for social justice of its own capital. No government can sustain international law and order unless it can do so at home. No country can lead the fight for social justice unless its commitment to its own people is credible and determined—unless it seeks jobs and not the dole for its men, unless it feels anguish as long as any of its children are hungry, unless it believes in opportunity for all its citizens. Our future may lie beyond our vision, but it is not beyond our control. Alfred Lord Tennyson once wrote: "The lights begin to twinkle from the rocks/The long day wanes/the low moon climbs/the deep moans round with many voices/Come, my friends, 'Tis not too late to seek a newer world."

Kennedy was particularly beloved within minority communities. In California, he joined activist Cesar Chavez in meeting migrant farm workers; he made a point of introducing himself to leaders of local African American communities wherever he went; and he campaigned hard in predominantly black neighborhoods, where he was embraced with genuine and reciprocated affection. African American voters, as a general population, still felt disaffected in spite of recent attempts to address the painful history of their disfranchisement; but in Kennedy, many African Americans found a kindred spirit. On the night of the murder of Reverend King, Bobby Kennedy appeared at a previously scheduled rally in downtown Indianapolis, a rally that was intended to be a simple campaign event; but the senator turned his attention to the tragedy, announcing the terrible news to the crowd that had gathered to hear him and then lingering to share his reflections and grief, an act that is widely recognized as the only explanation as to why rioting did not erupt in Indianapolis as it had in nearly every other American city over the next few days. Kennedy's compassion for African Americans on that night, as well as his courage in calming what easily could have become an angry, destructive crowd, were well noted and long appreciated.

After Reverend King's funeral, Kennedy continued to cross the country at a nearly frenzied pace, sharing his message of a gentle and just society for all, a theme that quickly eclipsed his criticism of the war. His concern for the poor was commended, but his own campaign staffers were upset by some of his campaign trail decisions. On one occasion, rather than attend a larger rally for more visible media exposure, Bobby devoted the better part of an entire day to visiting, away from the media spotlight, a Native American reservation and forming a friendship with a young child who resided there. This attention endeared him to the tribe, but his handlers were frustrated by the lack of press exposure and the remoteness of the location. Kennedy seemed to be indifferent to those frustrations; always empathetic toward the many injustices suffered by Native American tribes, RFK felt more comfortable spending time on a reservation rather than attending staged campaign events that would draw the big crowds. But when Kennedy did appear before those larger crowds, the response was always a spontaneous outpouring of a kind of fervor unseen even in American politics, the kind of crowd reaction usually accorded a rock star, not a politician. McCarthy, even though he possessed an intelligence and charisma of his own, was still no match for this; but his campaign carried forward, and he managed to win one primary against the steaming RFK juggernaut, the first time any Kennedy had lost an election of any kind. But for the most part, RFK's momentum seemed unstoppable as the campaign moved toward what many regarded to be the decisive primary—California.

Meanwhile, with LBJ no longer a problem, the Republicans marshaled their forces. The Republican field consisted of Michigan governor George Romney, the former president of American Motors and the most prominent Mormon politician in the country; New York governor Nelson Rockefeller, the leader of the liberal wing of the Republican Party, who for a brief time had been considered a potential candidate in 1964; California governor Ronald Reagan, the new favorite of the conservatives and a rapidly rising force in the party; and former vice president and the party's nominee in 1960, Richard M. Nixon. In 1962, after a campaign for governor of California, Nixon, resentful of his treatment in the press, curtly announced his retirement from politics, punctuated at his purported "last press conference" by his famous declaration, "You won't have Nixon to kick around anymore." But by 1964, Nixon was back in. While he was not at that time positioned to challenge Barry Goldwater for the GOP nomination, he appeared at the convention to speak on Goldwater's behalf, and he stumped for Goldwater after the convention.

Even as Goldwater's 1964 campaign was circling the drain, Nixon was thinking of ways to run in 1968, but he played it coy. Throughout 1967, he kept a low profile, taking time away from politics to write and travel, allowing Romney— who for a time was the more visible candidate and appeared to be shaping up as the front-runner—and the others plenty of room to advertise their names. Romney made himself known in the media, and his activities were clearly marked by the tenor of a presidential campaign. He did indeed begin to emerge as the GOP front-runner, with Nixon virtually out of sight. Like Bobby Kennedy, Nixon held back and allowed the rest in the field to make their respective plays. Many of Romney's ideas were compelling and even later adopted by politicians in both parties, but he lacked the focus and discipline needed to speak clearly and consistently, and to avoid costly gaffes. The worst gaffe was when Romney stated that he had been "brainwashed" by the government and the military to accept the Vietnam War, a self-destructive, hyperbolic statement that he could not live down and that, more than anything else, killed his prospects. By the time of the New Hampshire primary, Romney's campaign was out of steam, and sensing a lack of support, he withdrew. Nixon, who had deftly sustained low visibility on the campaign trail but, through his writings and well-selected appearances, was looking ever more presidential, easily won the New Hampshire primary, taking 78 percent of the votes, a victory that was followed by equally impressive wins in Wisconsin and Ohio. He was outpolled by Governor Rockefeller in a much more competitive field in the Massachusetts primary, but not by much, as Rockefeller and favorite son John Volpe took 30 percent each to Nixon's 26 percent; but in the following two midwestern primaries in Indiana and Ohio, he made his statement, polling 100 percent of the vote. He won all but one of the remaining contested primaries, losing only to Governor Reagan in California, Reagan's home turf. In total votes throughout all the primaries, Reagan actually won slightly more than Nixon, but that was accounted for by Reagan's victory in California, where Nixon did not bother to campaign. In terms of delegates, it was Nixon who had the leverage.

Moving toward the convention, Nixon was clearly the indisputable GOP front-runner and likely nominee. For a brief moment, the conservative Reagan and the liberal Rockefeller seemed prepared to unite their efforts against Nixon, but they were unable to give each other their unqualified support. Thus Nixon took a commanding 692 delegates on the first ballot to 277 for Rockefeller and 182 for Reagan, with the remaining votes dispersed across a field of eight minor candidates. On the second round, over 1,200 delegates announced for Nixon, and for the second time in three election years, he was nominated as the standard-bearer for the Republican Party. For vice president, Nixon inexplicably picked Maryland governor Spiro Agnew, a virtual unknown outside his home state, in a move that disappointed many at the convention who were actually hoping to see Romney join the Nixon ticket. Agnew, who was really a Rockefeller man and was himself disappointed at Rockefeller's withdrawal, found himself surprised at the opportunity. But now Agnew was suddenly Nixon's man in spite of his lack of high visibility in the public arena. Even though Nixon had many rivals and even some enemies in his own party, he was able to accomplish what Goldwater could not four years earlier—to pull all factions of the party together.

Nixon's acceptance speech was among his better rhetorical moments. He spoke lucidly and candidly of "forgotten Americans" who were frustrated by inflation, war, and violence on American streets:

Let us look at America, let us listen to America to find the answer to that question. As we look at America, we see cities enveloped in smoke and flame. We hear sirens in the night. We see Americans dying on distant battlefields abroad. We see Americans hating each other; fighting each other; killing each other at home. And as we see and hear these things, millions of Americans cry out in anguish. Did we come all this way for this? Did American boys die in Normandy, and Korea, and in Valley Forge for this? Listen to the answer to those questions. It is another voice. It is the quiet voice in the tumult and the shouting. It is the voice of the great majority of Americans, the forgotten Americans—the non-shouters; the non-demonstrators. They are not racists or sick; they are not guilty of the crime that plagues the land. They are black and they are white—they're native born and foreign born— they're young and they're old. They work in America's factories. They run America's businesses. They serve in government. They provide most of the soldiers who died to keep us free. They give drive to the spirit of America. They give lift to the American Dream. They give steel to the backbone of America. They are good people, they are decent people; they work, and they save, and they pay their taxes, and they care. Like Theodore Roosevelt, they know that this country will not be a good place for any of us to live in unless it is a good place for all of us to live in. This I say to you tonight is the real voice of America. In this year 1968, this is the message it will broadcast to America and to the world. Let's never forget that despite her faults, America is a great nation. And America is great because her people are great.

In the end, the Republican convention produced a cohesive, focused ticket and entered the final push for the White House as a unified and confident force. The Democrats, on the other hand, met nothing but division, chaos, disaffection, despair, violence, and heartbreaking tragedy.

The United States in the 1960s was a violent, destructive place. Perhaps this can be said, with requisite qualifications, of any given era in American history; but in the 1960s, a decade often viewed as a touchstone of liberation and renewal, the prevalence of social turmoil and the frequency of violence seems, in retrospect, particularly incongruous. The war in Vietnam and persistent frustration in the civil rights movement fueled a roiling undercurrent of discontent that could not remain static; it had to discharge, and when it did, something was destroyed. Whether this destruction came in the shape of the many urban riots that marred the American landscape, or the assault on civil rights protesters, or the seizure of public buildings on campuses and, in some cases, acts of arson on those very campuses, it was jarringly dissonant with the potent countercultural aspirations for a more harmonious, peaceful, and loving human community. Peace and love were popular sentiments, but they were not popularly practiced. And few acts reminded the public of this more viscerally than the assassinations of their moral and political leadership.

President Kennedy was but the first to fall to such murderous acts. Others followed, and on June 5, 1968, the very night of his impressive and pivotal victory in the California primary, the late president's younger brother Robert Francis Kennedy was mortally wounded by the bullet of a demented assassin; he would die the following day. It was a particularly senseless and demoralizing moment, one that ended the life of a beloved public figure and, simultaneously, killed what might have been the most morally compelling political campaign in modern American politics. Yet again, just two months after the murder of Reverend King, and not quite five years after the murder of a president, the nation was again thrown into mourning. The loss of Bobby Kennedy was every bit as bitter as the loss of his brother, a loss felt beyond the constraints of partisan politics. But if we are to look at the partisan effects that followed, the Democratic Party was utterly wrecked, and it would not be until the next decade that it could begin to recover. With two Kennedy brothers slain and the fall from grace of the once-indefatigable Lyndon Johnson, the Democrats were thrown into chaos, and this chaos erupted yet again into violence, at the national nominating convention in Chicago later that summer.

When Bobby Kennedy was slain, the contest for the nomination was reduced to two contenders: Humphrey and McCarthy. Other names were entertained, most notably South Dakota senator George McGovern, a close ally of RFK; and for a brief moment, the youngest and surviving Kennedy brother, Senator Edward Moore "Ted" Kennedy, even was proposed as a write-in candidate, one who might have been able to rely on McCarthy's delegates had he entered the race. By convention time, McCarthy had lost interest and focus, his campaign inconsistent since California. Ted Kennedy might have had a chance if McCarthy's delegates threw in, but it was clear that Vice President Humphrey was the likely nominee. (An offer for the vice presidency was floated to Ted Kennedy from Humphrey, but the senator declined.) As the convention approached, rumors also circulated that President Johnson was preparing another surprise move, hinting that he was about to change his mind and enter the convention as a candidate for reelection, a prospect that to some now seemed, after the turbulent summer, a tolerable and maybe even safe fallback. But Johnson stood by his decision to retire; thus, in the end, it was either Humphrey, the favorite, or McCarthy, who was now the dark horse; the former had the support of the party leadership, while the latter still appealed to the antiwar element—one was seen as the candidate of "the Establishment," the other as the wave of the future.

While the convention proceeded, antiwar protests erupted outside. At one point, Chicago police, in response to what was seen as an insult to the American flag, responded with force. The protesters reacted in kind, further provoking the police and escalating levels of violence leading to sheer mayhem. Young people were bludgeoned and brutalized, tear gas was deployed in such quantities that the fumes wafted into the hotel room where Senator Humphrey was lodged awaiting his nomination, and, equally important, the shameful debacle was broadcast on television, viewed by millions of utterly bewildered viewers. What was later called a "police riot" quickly divided the delegates on the convention floor; many supported the actions of the police against what was perceived to be nothing more than a savage, unpatriotic mob, but many others found the level of force used against the protesters excessive and reprehensible. A pugnacious, aggressive Mayor Richard Daley, the convention host, defended the Chicago police and the forces of the Illinois National Guard who were called in for support, and he was unapologetic for having ordered the crackdown.

Inside the convention, acrimony reigned and political debate gave way to angry outbursts as tempers rose and flared. Television journalists Mike Wallace and Dan Rather were physically manhandled by police on the convention floor, and a rancorous Daley loudly cursed anti-Semitic epithets at Connecticut senator Abraham Ribicoff when the latter accused the mayor's police force of resembling the Nazi Gestapo. But in the end, and in spite of the emotional and even physical turmoil on the convention floor, Vice President Humphrey was nominated through the chaos on the first ballot, gaining 1,760 votes to McCarthy's 601 and McGovern's 146, with the District of Columbia nominating its favorite son, the Reverend Channing Philips, the first African American to receive nominating votes at a Democratic convention. Vice President Humphrey then tapped the able and respected Maine senator Edmund Muskie for the second spot on the ticket. Senator Muskie would become the second Roman Catholic to be nominated for the vice presidency by a major party, after William E. Miller, the GOP nominee for the vice presidency four years earlier (on the Goldwater ticket), and along with Al Smith and John Kennedy, who were both nominated for president, only the fourth Roman Catholic to be nominated to national elective office (which, in effect, is a set of two: the presidency and the vice presidency). As capable as Muskie was, his selection to join the ticket was almost lost in the turbulence around the candidates. In the front rooms of the United States, dismayed television viewers were treated to the specter of parallel images of political celebrations staged inside the convention as rioting raged outside the convention. The party was immediately divided, with many Democrats who had supported either Kennedy or McCarthy, and in the latter days McGovern, expressing their feelings with a new chant: "Dump the Hump!" It was an unmitigated disaster, and it was perhaps the inevitable final chapter of a campaign initiated by antiwar dissent and shattered by assassination.

However, Humphrey's campaign was not a complete disappointment. In late October, President Johnson suspended bombing operations over North Vietnam, a move well received by the American public and which gave Humphrey's campaign renewed support. At one point, he actually passed Nixon in the polls, leading him by around 3 percent just a few days away from Election Day, a surprising development given the recent fiasco at Chicago. Nixon responded by addressing the nation during a campaign telethon in which he claimed that the North Vietnamese were now able to move massive amounts of supplies and troops southbound along the Ho Chi Minh Trail without any resistance. Nixon personally felt that Johnson's move in Vietnam was a cynical ploy to give Humphrey a late surge on the eve of Election Day, but he promised not to publicly question the president's interior motivations. Vice President Humphrey, appearing before the nation during his own telethon, rejected Nixon's claims regarding North Vietnam's troop and supply movements. Recent evidence seems to support charges that Nixon may have privately interfered with President Johnson's peace negotiations with North Vietnam, an alleged ploy that an infuriated Johnson kept quiet rather than cause further turmoil in an already tumultuous campaign season.

The smooth nomination of Nixon and the turmoil surrounding the nomination of Humphrey was not the whole story in 1968. In 1967, a conservative alternative party, the American Independent Party, was formed, and in the summer of 1968, the party nominated its own candidate for the presidency, the controversial governor from Alabama, George Wallace, a conservative Southern Democrat known for his zealous opposition to the civil rights movement, confrontational attitude toward the federal government during attempts to enforce segregation, and blunt statements such as one in which he expressed admiration for the Chicago police for their "restraint" in indiscriminately assaulting the protesters during the convention. Assuming the mantle of the "common man's" candidate, he inveighed against the intellectuals, bureaucrats, dewy-eyed do-gooders, and "pointy-heads" who were, in Wallace's estimation, social-engineering the United States into something entirely un-American. Wallace tapped as his running mate the vociferous Cold Warrior general Curtis LeMay, who in fact was uninterested in Wallace's views on segregation and race, but rather was more concerned by what he deemed to be Nixon's apparent softened views toward the Soviet Union, and thus he wanted to campaign to sustain and strengthen the United States' nuclear first-strike advantage.

Wallace's campaign drew interest and appealed to those white voters who were disenchanted, in some cases angry, with what they perceived to be dangerous social and cultural upheaval. Not unlike minority voters who had found a voice in Robert Kennedy, a minority of conservative white voters felt equally disaffected owing to the manner in which, at least in their eyes, the countercultural trends of the mid-to-late 1960s seemed to be on the verge of taking hold of the political process and forever altering society, and in their opinion, for worse. These fears were exaggerated, as the 1960s really were not what we remember them to be, thanks to pop culture's tendency to glamorize the decade—even though there were significant cultural and social changes under way, most Americans were not grooving on a new wave of transcendent consciousness as it is often now depicted. But for this small group of traditionally oriented voters—mostly white and Southern—the cherished values of American culture were imperiled by subversive countercultural forces, and supporting Wallace seemed to be the first step in responding to this threat. At the extremes of this attitude, one can find a certain degree of palpable "white backlash" in response to irrational fears drawn, rightly or wrongly, about the meaning of the social changes under way. Cynically, certain (but not all) Republican strategists sharply tuned into this sentiment, and they began to develop a different approach to tapping into what they considered to be growing discontent among the white middle class, particularly in the South.

Developing what would later be called the "southern strategy," the Nixon campaign began for the first time to stress states' rights, a position that to this point had, at least historically, been assumed by Southern Democrats and either ignored or scarcely discussed by GOP candidates in the past. For example, this kind of thinking was largely foreign to Eisenhower's campaigning in the 1950s; Barry Goldwater's emphasis on state government in 1964 stemmed more from an attitude of small-scale government and the defense of individual liberties against the expanded powers of the modern state, rather than from the more shadowed impulses behind Nixon's "southern strategy." Now the Nixon camp was subtly appealing to those white voters who were most concerned about the overall social consequences of the civil rights movement. Recently, more visible and active militant elements within minority communities had fueled the backlash, and Nixon's campaign strategists seized the opportunity to tap into the fears and suspicions of nervous white Southern voters as well as less political elements in the white middle class in general. Social unrest, urban riots, militant radicalism, and increased urban crime would be addressed, according to the Nixon campaign, by the restoration of "law and order," another catchphrase that some consider to be a racially charged "code word" directed at minority discontent. While Nixon's more reasoned appeal to the "forgotten Americans" resonated with many within the electorate who were anxious over the state of the nation, the unseen "southern strategy" stealthily established a potentially dangerous precedent for racial division within the course of mainstream politics. In a word, certain elements within the GOP seemed to have been willing to finally surrender the African American vote—which had been, prior to 1936, fiercely loyal to the Party of Lincoln—to the Democrats in return for a larger and more solid political base in the South.

In the end, the Nixon campaign proved to be far more organized, savvy, and capable of riding through the swells and storms of the rough political seas that churned the late 1960s. While the ebullient Hubert Humphrey—who attempted to tap into the cultural movements of the time by speaking of a "politics of joy," and who had inherited from Al Smith the moniker of the "Happy Warrior"—ran a frustratingly ill-managed campaign, Nixon, as well as Wallace, charged forward with a sense of focus and resolve that the Democrats seemed to have left behind after their heady triumph in 1964. Humphrey's efforts were partly hampered by his incumbency. As vice president, he could hardly denounce his president, the man who had supported him throughout his political career, and whose policies he had endorsed down the line. But as the candidate in a party fractured over the war, he could not further alienate the antiwar factions—the supporters of McCarthy, McGovern, and the late Bobby Kennedy. Humphrey had earned a reputation for decency and honesty, as well as for possessing some political skill of his own; but on this campaign, he seemed unable to inspire.

The only advantage the Democrats seemed to have going for them was the presence of Muskie, who, in contrast to Agnew, seemed cool, composed, and strikingly competent. On the campaign trail in 1968, Muskie could not be rattled, even when raucously heckled, as was often the case during these times, while stumping for votes. One incident played well on the nightly news when Muskie, heckled mercilessly at one campaign event, invited one of the leaders of the dissenters to come to the microphone, and stepping aside, the candidate allowed a forum for the venting of the oppositional opinion. It was not the sort of thing that Agnew, or Nixon or Wallace, or even Humphrey, could have pulled off, and it was one of the few high points in the Democratic campaign. Still, the polls indicated a tight race, and a victory for Vice President Humphrey was certainly possible, a position all the more striking given the complete disarray within the Democratic Party since the death of Robert Kennedy and the tumultuous convention that followed.

On Election Night, the returns revealed just how close the race was, well reminding voters, at least initially, of another tight election that had previously involved Nixon, the election of President Kennedy eight years earlier; and as with that election, Americans retired for the night not knowing who had won, and they still did not know until noon the following day, when the Illinois returns had finally come in for Nixon. Nixon took a popular total of slightly over 31,780,000 (43.4%), Humphrey trailing with just under 31,280,000 (42.7%), and Wallace showing just over 9,900,000 votes—the highest absolute total of votes ever won by a third-party candidate and, at 13.5 percent, the fourth-highest percentage of popular votes won by a third-party candidate (following Theodore Roosevelt's 27% in 1912, Millard Fillmore's 21% in 1856, and Robert La Follette's 16.7% in 1924); by contrast, Strom Thurmond's pro-segregation Dixiecrat candidacy in 1948 garnered only 2.4 percent of the popular vote. President-elect Nixon's 43 percent was the lowest percentage of the popular vote for the winning candidate since Woodrow Wilson's 41.8 percent in 1912, and only two other presidents were elected with a lower percentage of popular votes—Abraham Lincoln in 1860 with just over 39 percent, and John Quincy Adams in 1824 with slightly under 31 percent. It was also the sixth-lowest total of the popular vote for any Republican candidate in the history of American political campaigns (only Taft in 1912, John C. Fremont—the Republicans' first candidate—in 1856, Alfred Landon in 1936 and Herbert Hoover in 1932—both defeated by Franklin Roosevelt—and Lincoln, who won, in 1860, were lower) and, with the exception of Lincoln's first election—which involved a four-way race—the lowest percentage of the popular vote ever enjoyed by a winning GOP candidate. However, Nixon's win in the Electoral College was more convincing, taking 301 electoral votes to 191 for Humphrey, with Wallace taking five states carrying 46 electoral votes, all from the Deep South (Alabama, Mississippi, Louisiana, Georgia, and Arkansas). Nixon took 32 states to Humphrey's 14; Humphrey did manage to win in New York, Pennsylvania, Texas, and Michigan, four states that claimed a high number of Electoral College votes, but Nixon countered with wins in California, Ohio, Illinois, and New Jersey, strengthened by a near sweep west of the Mississippi. The Wallace campaign made a difference; in taking a large segment of what was once the solid South for Democrats along with conservative Democrats in other parts of the country, Wallace was a factor in Nixon's election. The Republicans drew most support from business, the various professions and white-collar workers, small farmers, and Protestants; Humphrey ran strongest among African Americans, Catholic and Jewish voters, and labor. In a word, the Democrats managed to keep most elements of the old New Deal coalition forged by Franklin Roosevelt in the 1930s; but they again lost the southern bloc, as they had in 1948 and the previous election of 1964, and it became apparent that the Roosevelt Coalition was unraveling. Nevertheless, the new president faced many difficulties from the first moments of his presidency. Even his inaugural procession was met with a barrage of rocks and other objects courtesy of angry antiwar protesters.

After what was the most traumatic election since 1860, Richard M. Nixon, out of politics just six years earlier, had ascended through sheer tenacity to the pinnacle of American political life; only the second Republican to be elected to the White House since the beginning of the Depression, he was now to become the thirty-seventh president of the United States.

Additional Resources

Ambrose, Stephen. "1968." In Arthur M. Schlesinger, Fred L. Israel, and David J. Frent, eds. *Running for President: The Candidates and Their Images*. Vol. 2. New York: Simon & Schuster, 1994.

The American Presidency Project. http://www.presidency.ucsb.edu/ws/index.php?pid=25968#ixzz1KNKabhcI.

Broder, David S. "Election of 1968." In Arthur M. Schlesinger and Fred L. Israel. *History of American Presidential Elections: 1789–1968*. Vol. 4. New York: McGraw-Hill Book Co., 1971.

Chester, Lewis, Godfrey Hodgson, and Bruce Page. *American Melodrama: The Presidential Campaign of 1968*. New York: Viking Press, 1969.

Clarke, Thurston. *The Last Campaign: Robert F. Kennedy and 82 Days that Inspired America*. New York: Henry Holt and Company, 2008.

Cohen, Martin, David Karol, Hans Noel, and John Zaller. *The Party Decides: Presidential Nominations before and after Reform*. Chicago: University of Chicago Press, 2008.

Gould, Lewis. *1968: The Election that Changed America*. New York: Ivan R. Dee, 1993.

McGinniss, Joe. *The Selling of the President*. New York: Penguin, 1988.

White, Theodore. *The Making of the President: 1968*. New York: Harper Perennial, 2005.

Campaign of 1972

While the election of 1968 occurred as the culmination of perhaps the most singularly aberrant campaign season since 1860, in hindsight, the outcome seems to follow logically from the events that preceded it. The election of Richard Nixon, given the violence and social confusion driving the political currents of the time, in retrospect holds the weight of inevitability. By contrast, the outcome of the Campaign of 1972—one of the biggest landslide victories on record and an unequivocal reaffirmation of an incumbent's successful administration—seems incongruous with the events that, again in retrospect, define that election. As President Nixon basked in his greatest electoral moment, unknown to the majority of Americans, a simmering scandal was about to break open in such a way that would, within a matter of months, bring the Nixon presidency to an abrupt and unexpected halt. Given the ease of Nixon's reelection, the Watergate scandal that destroyed his political career is difficult to comprehend.

The first two years of the Nixon administration were buffeted by economic uncertainty and renewed protests over the war in Vietnam, a war that had been expanded across the border into Cambodia, spreading into Laos. The president's promise to restore a mood of "law and order" throughout the country, and his appeal to the "great silent majority," had been met with frustration. (The phrase "silent majority" was a variation of Nixon's "forgotten majority," so identified in his 1968 campaign; "silent majority" also can be attributed to Spiro Agnew, Nixon's running mate, during that same campaign—interestingly, the phrase is also used by then senator John F. Kennedy in his *Profiles in Courage*, a copy of which he presented to Nixon as a gift in 1956; whether or not this influenced Nixon's use of the phrase is unknown.) The antiwar protests became yet again violent, with the campus shootings of students by national guardsmen at Kent State in Ohio and Jackson State in Mississippi. Nixon had promised voters that he had a "secret plan" to end the war in Vietnam, but by 1970, well into Nixon's presidency, the American public saw no evident end in sight. The economy suffered both unemployment and inflation, or "stagflation," and the administration seemed wanting for answers. As 1970 rolled into 1971, and as 1971 moved from winter into spring, Nixon's approval rating dipped below 50 percent for the first time.

After floundering, Nixon finally found his bearings and instituted a set of economic policies that were well received and that coincided (whether or not there is a causal connection is a matter of debate among economists and other scholars) with an economic recovery as the 1972 campaign approached. Additionally, the president's foreign policy was regarded as the most far-sighted since President Franklin Roosevelt. He had gone to great lengths to relieve tension between the United States and the Soviet Union through the implementation of the policy of détente; and, perhaps still more impressively, he initiated a stunning reconciliation with the People's Republic of China, a major foreign policy triumph for the old Cold Warrior who had once lambasted President Harry Truman for having "lost China." His foreign policy was also critical to managing tension in the Middle East, and under the Nixon White House, the prestige of the United States abroad was reasserted in spite of the onus of Vietnam. As the 1972 campaign season unfolded, the president enjoyed approval ratings ranging from around 50 percent in January of that year and climbing to just over 60 percent by mid-spring. Nixon seemed unbeatable, particularly when contrasted with the continuing divisions in the Democratic Party, the shockwaves of the disastrous 1968 campaign.

Why the Nixon administration then chose the "dirty tricks" strategy that led to the Watergate break-in and subsequent cover-up seems all the more puzzling. Some have argued that Nixon had himself been stung by rough treatment in previous campaigns, and, as the argument goes, the source of much of this came from the Kennedy camp in 1960. From that election forward, some have argued, Richard Nixon was resolved to fight dirty. Still others claim that Nixon was this kind of politician all along, and that his moniker "Tricky Dick," which had been first used against him in 1948, was well deserved and had nothing to do with any reaction to similar dirty tricks by the Kennedys. One thing is for certain: Nixon, who had once been friendly with John Kennedy, had never forgotten his slender loss to JFK in the tough campaign of 1960.

In any event, wishing to maintain total control over his reelection effort, Nixon, even as president, let his own insecurities get the best of him, and so he established the Committee to Re-Elect the President (CREEP) to more closely manage the upcoming campaign. Despite having a huge lead over all potential candidates in all polls, Nixon worried incessantly about the competition and sincerely believed that the Democratic Party was no longer a moderate party, having been captured by the leftists since the 1968 election, perhaps even earlier. To fund the campaign, CREEP raised millions of dollars of illegal campaign contributions from corporations and individuals, and it used some of that money to fund dirty tricks and illegal activities such as the Watergate break-in. In reality, Nixon was so strong that he never needed such cloak-and-dagger methods to defeat his political opponents; more to the point, the Democrats at this time were so divisive they were doing the job of defeating themselves, while Nixon, using the power and prominence of his office, was seen everywhere, from Beijing to Middle America, "looking presidential" and carving a name for himself as the statesman of his generation, his reelection an inevitability.

Thus Nixon won renomination virtually unchallenged. Two candidates from within the GOP—a conservative representative from Ohio, John Ashbrook, who challenged Nixon's policy of détente; and Representative Pete McCloskey from California, a liberal Republican (by 1972, a dying breed) who ran primarily against the war—opposed Nixon in the primaries, but the president won over 5,300,000 primary votes to fewer than 500,000 for McCloskey and Ashcroft combined. At the convention in Miami, the president and Vice President Agnew were renominated without serious opposition.

The Republican platform praised the accomplishments of the Nixon administration on the domestic and foreign fronts. "Now, four years later," the platform proclaimed, "a new leadership with new policies and new programs has restored reason and order and hope. No longer buffeted by internal violence and division, we are on course in calmer seas with a sure, steady hand at the helm. A new spirit, buoyant and confident, is on the rise in our land, nourished by the changes we have made." At the time, it was a credible message. With respect to Vietnam and other foreign policy issues, the platform stressed that the United States had "moved far toward peace: withdrawal of our fighting men from Vietnam, constructive new relationships with the Soviet Union and the People's Republic of China, the nuclear arms race checked, the Mid-East crisis dampened, our alliances revitalized." The platform declared that the new Nixon Doctrine would hopefully lead "the peace-loving nations to undertake an exhaustive, coordinated analysis of the root causes of war and the most promising paths of peace, so that those causes may in time be removed and the prospects for enduring peace strengthened year by year." The Republican platform also continued to endorse the ratification of the Equal Rights Amendment as it had been doing since 1940, but the political mood was such that intensified efforts in this area was expected of any serious political party or position. On the whole, Nixon looked impossible to beat. He had established himself as a moderate on domestic issues and a visionary in foreign policy. Even before the conventions, he enjoyed support from some Democrats and was well positioned for a major victory—all the more reason to wonder about the events that led to the Watergate scandal.

Once again, the Democrats struggled. The calamitous 1968 Democratic convention and the subsequent defeat of their candidate, the incumbent vice president Hubert Humphrey, had left deep divisions within the Democratic Party. Between 1969 and the beginning of the 1972 presidential campaign, changes in the rules governing the manner in which party delegates were selected shifted the focus to the primaries and significantly increased their importance, signaling the beginning of the end of the convention as a meaningful forum for the actual nomination of presidential candidates (this is not to say that the conventions are without merit; only to say that candidates are now selected prior to the conventions). These rules changes also significantly increased the number of women, African Americans, and other minority voters, raised the number of young people involved in the process, and significantly diminished the role of the old-style "party bosses" that had been central to past nominations. However, this is not to say that, as some have argued, political parties lost their effectiveness. Recently, political scientists Marty Cohen, John Zaller, et al., for example, have closely reexamined what has been called the "end-of-parties" argument in the wake of the strengthened primaries, and in their study, they found that political parties still played the critical role in nominating and directing candidates at all levels, and in particular, at the level of the presidency. The rules had changed, but with those changes, the parties continued to provide a framework and sustain continuity.

Between the end of Election Day 1968 and June 1969, the favorite candidate among the Democrats to challenge Nixon in 1972 was Senator Edward "Ted" Kennedy, the heir to the legacies of his slain brothers, President John Kennedy and Senator Robert Kennedy, the latter having recently run an inspired campaign in the spring and early summer of 1968 before losing his life to an assassin's bullet. Ted Kennedy was widely regarded as the best hope for the Democrats in the next election, but all this ended when the senator was involved in an automobile accident that caused the drowning death of a young woman, Mary Jo Kopechne, a Kennedy loyalist and former worker for Bobby Kennedy's 1968 campaign. Ted Kennedy's behavior both before and especially after the accident was called into question by the press, and rumors were circulated about Kennedy's overall character in the days and weeks that followed. As a result, the senator quietly maintained his distance from any discussion of the presidency, leaving the field once again wide open, at least among Democrats, for a number of competing candidates.

Early in the primary season, Maine senator Edmund Muskie, Humphrey's running mate in 1968, appeared to be the front-runner for the Democratic presidential nomination. Muskie managed to win the Iowa caucus, with Senator George McGovern, a late candidate for the presidential nomination in 1968, showing a strong second; but in the now ever-critical New Hampshire primary, events turned against Muskie. First, a strange document insulting to Canadians and purportedly written by Muskie, which soon came to be known as the "Canuck Letter," raised concerns upon its publication in the *Manchester Union-Leader*. In truth, the letter was a forgery, and it was later revealed that Donald Segretti, a dirty trickster working for the Nixon campaign, was behind it. At the time, however, the letter was attributed to Muskie and caused considerable trouble for his efforts in

New Hampshire. Second, and perhaps even more damaging, was Muskie's public response to allegations that his wife was an alcoholic and given to spout vulgarities. While defending the honor of his wife against the press at a small gathering outdoors during a mild snowfall, Muskie suddenly appeared tearful to those present, his voice cracking, his eyes watering, and his face showing signs of emotional stress. Muskie later claimed that what had appeared to be tears in his eyes was actually caused by the melting snowfall and the cold air, but the impression held firm: Muskie had "cried," even though by some accounts the evidence was thin at best, and his campaign was now in jeopardy.

That Muskie was a target of CREEP follows from President Nixon's own fears of the Maine senator, who, after Ted Kennedy (who was now out of the picture, to Nixon's relief), was the one candidate that the president did not want to face in 1972. CREEP's dirty tricksters also went after Humphrey and Washington senator Henry "Scoop" Jackson, but the damage to Muskie was the most significant. In 1972, if anyone could have challenged Nixon, it was Muskie; but his campaign had been literally sabotaged by the underhanded methods of dirty tricksters on the president's behalf. Muskie's collapse in the wake of the scandals caused by the sabotage was a stark and unexpected contrast to Muskie's calm response to the heated campaign that he experienced as the vice presidential candidate four years earlier; in 1968, he seemed unflappable, but now he appeared to many as fragile. Even though Muskie did actually win the New Hampshire primary with 46 percent of the vote in spite of the "crying" incident, McGovern, who was emerging as his main challenger, did sufficiently well at 37 percent to infuse his campaign with the energy needed to stoke momentum. Humphrey; Alabama governor George Wallace, now back in the Democrats' fold after running as the American Independent Party candidate in 1968; Minnesota senator Eugene McCarthy, the man who brought down President Lyndon Johnson in 1968; Senator Jackson, known for his past support of the Vietnam War; and Democratic representative Shirley Chisholm of New York, the first African American woman to run for president from within a major party, all participated as candidates within the Democratic primaries, along with a handful of additional candidates.

One week after the New Hampshire primary, Wallace scored an important victory by winning in Florida, taking 42 percent of the vote, far ahead of the rest of the field (Muskie, the erstwhile front-runner, slipped from his New Hampshire victory to a dismal 9 percent—and third place—in Florida). McCarthy scored high in Illinois, with Jackson a distant second; McGovern then won in Wisconsin with a plurality and, more impressively, in Massachusetts with a majority, thus tightening the race. Representative Walter Fauntroy, who ran only in the District of Columbia, winning there with 72 percent of the delegates, became the first African American in American campaign history to win a presidential primary. (Four years earlier,

Delegate Channing E. Phillips was given the recently slain Senator Robert Kennedy's delegates at the Chicago convention, making him the first African American to win nominating votes at a Democratic presidential convention.) Humphrey made it even more interesting, first by taking Pennsylvania with 35 percent of the primary vote (Wallace with 21% and Humphrey and Muskie both around 20%), and then winning two consecutive primaries in Indiana and Ohio, while McGovern maintained a close second (only 1 percent separated Humphrey and McGovern in Ohio). Wallace soundly won the next two primaries in Tennessee and North Carolina, McGovern won convincingly in Nebraska, and Humphrey took West Virginia, the state he lost to John Kennedy in the 1960 primary. With Muskie no longer a factor, the primaries had developed into a three-way race between Humphrey, McGovern, and Wallace (McCarthy's big win in Illinois proved to be anomalous; he never finished with more than 2% of the vote in any given primary after his 63% in Illinois).

However, as in 1968, the campaign was abruptly changed by another act of violence, this time against Wallace, who was brutally shot five times in an attempted assassination in a Laurel, Maryland, shopping center. Wallace survived the shooting but was sadly left paralyzed, prompting him to eventually withdraw from the race. Nonetheless, he still won the Maryland primary and received another big primary win in Michigan on the same day; but because of the severe wounding from which he never fully recovered (he would remain bound to a wheelchair for the remainder of his life), Wallace's campaign was over. Wallace's campaign theme, "Send Them a Message," appeared to have some traction with angry white voters, especially in the South, who were unlikely to turn to the liberal Humphrey or McGovern and more inclined to support the Republican president before anyone from the Democratic left. After the shooting of Wallace, Senator McGovern managed to win five of the remaining six primaries, beating Humphrey convincingly. Of historical note, New York's Chisholm won primaries in New Jersey, Louisiana, and Mississippi, making her the first woman and the second African American (after Fauntroy) to have won a presidential primary. Arkansas congressman Wilbur Mills took the Arkansas primary as a favorite son. Eight years earlier, Republican Margaret Chase Smith won a handful of primary votes and was the first woman to receive support for nomination at a major party convention. Chisholm, a woman of high principles who enjoyed a reputation for being "unbought and unbossed," was actually criticized by the intolerant for having the decency to pay a visit to Wallace, her ideological opposite, while he was in the hospital recovering from his wounds.

Even though Humphrey actually ended the primary season with the largest popular primary vote among all Democrats, with 4,121,375 total votes (or 25.8%) to McGovern's 4,053,451 (or 25.3%), with Wallace showing at 3,755,424, McGovern succeeded in winning the largest number of primaries (winning 8 contests to 5 for Wallace, 4 for Humphrey, 3 for Chisholm, 2 for Muskie, along with the Iowa caucus, and 1 for Mills) and thereby enjoyed a significant lead in delegates going into the Democratic convention. Humphrey withdrew from the race after the first day of the convention (Muskie withdrew as well, but he had not actively campaigned since that awkward moment in New Hampshire), allowing George McGovern to enjoy a first-ballot victory, taking 1,864 delegates to 525 for Scoop Jackson, 381 for Wallace, and 151 for Chisholm, with the remaining votes distributed across 12 additional individuals. Besides calling for an immediate unconditional withdrawal of all U.S. forces from Vietnam, the Democratic platform included a long list of proposals directed at ending inequality in American society. The platform called for significantly increasing the income tax rate on high-income earners, the ratification of the Equal Rights Amendment, the end to discrimination against individuals with physical or mental disabilities, a system of universal national health insurance, handgun legislation to end the sale of "Saturday night specials," the abolition of the draft, universal voter registration by mail, a constitutional amendment to end the Electoral College with the requirement of a runoff election if no candidate received more than 40 percent of the vote, and comprehensive campaign finance reform.

The outcome of the convention was largely the result of a new system, for which McGovern himself was partially responsible, instituting reforms shifting the selection process away from the actual convention to the primaries. Even though primaries had become increasingly important over the decades as a sign of political viability and general appeal, from the beginning of the national nominating conventions in the late 1820s through the recent **Campaign of 1968**, presidential nominations were mostly controlled by the party leadership at the convention, as well as by the powerful machine bosses, such as Tammany Hall in New York. With the Campaign of 1972, all of that changed, and the McGovern nomination became the first fruit of the new procedure. But many influential delegates who had benefited from the old system felt estranged, overlooked, and in some cases angry, refusing to actively support McGovern in the post-convention phase of the campaign, and some joining the "Democrats for Nixon" movement that drew considerable support from conservative and moderate Democrats. With the convention once again showing divisions within the party, a large field of over seventy names received votes for vice president (including one impish vote for Mao Zedong); but in the end, McGovern's own preferred choice, liberal Missouri senator Thomas Eagleton, was selected to run on the bottom of the ticket.

But disaster soon befell the McGovern-Eagleton campaign, as it was leaked to the press that Senator Eagleton at one time had received electroshock therapy as a treatment for depression, prompting Eagleton to back out in reaction to concerns about his emotional stability. It was the first time in history that a candidate for either the vice presidency or the presidency was forced to withdraw from the race after having received a party's official nomination. Perhaps more damaging to the campaign than Eagleton's medical record was McGovern's waffling in reaction to the crisis. When the news broke, over 77 percent of Americans polled indicated that Eagleton's medical record would have no bearing on their vote; and McGovern himself declaimed, with no small degree of hyperbole, that he was behind Eagleton "1,000 percent." But in a matter of days, McGovern had changed his mind, mostly due to a fixation in the press with Eagleton's "shock therapy," a new obsession that the media could not let go and that became increasingly distracting. Realizing the damage to the campaign, Eagleton fell on his sword and took himself out of the picture.

McGovern then tried to convince, in sequence, several prominent Democrats to join his ticket, to no avail. An old Kennedy loyalist, he finally turned once again to what for him was safer and more familiar territory, the Kennedy family, tapping Sergeant Shriver (who was married to Eunice Kennedy Shriver and thus the brother-in-law of Jack, Bobby, and Ted Kennedy) to run for the vice presidency. Shriver had actually at one time been considered as a possible running mate for President Johnson in 1964, but he had demurred so as not to draw away any future political attention that might otherwise be devoted to Bobby Kennedy. Shriver was a well-respected figure throughout the public arena, but the damage done to the campaign by the resignation of Eagleton was difficult to repair. As Nixon grew even stronger, the Democrats continued to lose confidence. The McGovern campaign seems to have unraveled even before it could tightly spool its forces together.

As he had in 1968, Nixon, still shy from the aftereffects of his first debate in the 1960 presidential campaign against JFK, refused to debate McGovern, which also served as part of a larger strategy to deny McGovern a national platform. Nixon's ad campaign placed a heavy emphasis on his genuine diplomatic achievements, including withdrawing an increasing number of American troops from Vietnam as well as the improved relations with China and the Soviet Union for which he and his secretary of state, Henry Kissinger, were largely responsible. Nixon argued with conviction that his approach in the war had forced North Vietnam to the bargaining table in Paris. Slogans including "Peace with Honor" and "President Nixon, Now More Than Ever" sought to emphasize the importance of leaving Nixon and his foreign policy team in office. Equally important, the Nixon media campaign used attack ads to sharply criticize McGovern for proposing large reductions in the defense budget.

On Election Day, Nixon received just under 47,200,000 votes, or 60.7 percent of the popular vote, to McGovern's total of slightly over 29,000,000, or 37.5 percent. The American Independent Party, which ran George Wallace in 1968, received over 1,000,000 votes with its new candidate, California representative John Schmitz, on the ticket; but this time, in terms of percentages, it barely registered. Nixon's popular-vote landslide—which was and remains the third-highest percentage of the popular vote to date (behind only LBJ in 1964 and FDR in 1936, and slightly ahead of Harding in 1920) and was marked by a difference of 23.2 percent, still the fourth-largest gap between candidates in a presidential election—represented the zenith of his career and an enormous reassertion of the GOP's newly recovered prominence in the White House. The numbers in the Electoral College were equally staggering: Nixon won 520 electoral votes to a mere 17 for McGovern, and more impressively, he won every state in the country with the lone exception of Massachusetts. It was an Electoral College victory exceeding every prior election except those of Washington and Monroe, and it was easily the most impressive win in the Electoral College since the institution of the modern party system in the late 1820s–early 1830s. This Electoral College landslide would only be surpassed by one other election twelve years later.

However, even before President Nixon had enjoyed this crowning achievement, his Shakespearian downfall had been set in motion by the mysterious June 23 arrest of five burglars at the Watergate Hotel. After the election, the *Washington Post*, the *New York Times*, congressional investigations, and the investigation of two Watergate special prosecutors soon uncovered direct White House involvement in the break-in and its cover-up, as well as other illegal campaign operations (which included the unseemly activities of Segretti). These investigations led to the criminal prosecution of a number of high-level officials within the Nixon administration, precipitating a serious constitutional crisis that was without historical precedent. After a long struggle, an embattled, embittered President Nixon was backed into an untenable legal and political corner, and he was forced to submit his resignation on August 9, 1974, thus becoming the first American president to ever resign from office, the final consequence of actions that, when analyzed through the lens of his landslide reelection, seem utterly inexplicable and, for the American people, painfully tragic.

Additional Resources

Bernstein, Carl, and Bob Woodward. *All the President's Men*. Reprint ed. New York: Simon & Schuster, 1996.

Cohen, Martin, David Karol, Hans Noel, and John Zaller. *The Party Decides: Presidential Nominations before and after Reform*. Chicago: University of Chicago Press, 2008.

Crouse, Timothy. *The Boys on the Bus*. New York: Random House, 2003.

Parmet, Herbert S. "1972." In Arthur M. Schlesinger, Fred L. Israel, and David J. Frent, eds. *Running for President: The Candidates and Their Images*. Vol. 2. New York: Simon & Schuster, 1994.

Roberts, Robert North. *Ethics in U.S. Government: An Encyclopedia of Investigations, Scandals, Reforms and Legislation.* Westport, CT: Greenwood Press, 2001.

Thompson, Hunter S. *Fear and Loathing: On the Campaign Trail '72.* New York: Grand Central Publishing, 2006.

Wade, Richard. "Election of 1972." In Arthur M. Schlesinger, Fred Israel, and William P. Hansen, eds. *History of American Presidential Elections, 1789–1984.* Vol. 9. New York: Chelsea House, 1986.

Weil, Gordon. *The Long Shot: George McGovern Runs for President.* New York: Norton, 1973.

White, Theodore. *The Making of the President, 1972.* New York: Atheneum Publishers, 1973.

Witcover, Jules. *Marathon: The Pursuit of the Presidency, 1972–1976.* New York: Viking Press, 1977.

Campaign of 1976

Throughout his political life, Michigan congressman Gerald R. Ford's principal ambition and heart's desire was to ascend to the office of the Speaker of the House of Representatives, and as House minority leader from 1965 through most of 1973, he was well positioned to achieve that goal should his party—the minority Republican Party—enjoy a favorable change in political fortune. But with the resignation of Vice President Spiro Agnew, who was under indictment for tax evasion and money laundering, President Richard Nixon, on advice of congressional leadership, selected Ford to fill the vacancy under the provisions of the recently adopted Twenty-Fifth Amendment. Prior to this amendment, once the vice presidency was left vacant, it would have remained an open office until the next presidential election. Seven vice presidents died in office and were not replaced; eight ascended to the presidency owing to the death or resignation of their president (and again, were not replaced), four of whom did so as the result of an assassination. Prior to Agnew, only one vice president had resigned, John C. Calhoun (under President Andrew Jackson), who was not replaced; hence Agnew would become the second vice president to resign and the first to be replaced under the stipulations of the Twenty-Fifth Amendment.

Under the new amendment, this vacancy problem was solved, and Vice President Ford was sworn in as the nation's fortieth vice president on December 6, 1973. Nine months later, he was sworn in again as the thirty-eighth president of the United States upon the resignation of President Nixon, the consequence of new and damaging revelations in the infamous Watergate scandal. "Our long national nightmare is over," the new president assured the American public, and he began a process of healing the wounds of the protracted Watergate scandal in an attempt to quickly restore confidence in government and unity within the public sphere. In pursuit of this goal, President Ford preemptively pardoned former president Nixon, a move that stirred considerable controversy and even false rumors of a corrupt backroom deal between Ford and Nixon, the latter allegedly promising the former the White House in exchange for a full pardon. Politically, it was a risky move for the new president that was at the time harshly criticized. It was only years later that many came around to the view of the pardon as a needed, dignified act of compassion.

With the resignation of President Nixon, who in 1972 appeared invulnerable and on track to earn a reputation as a great president, and with huge losses in the midterm elections as a result of the Watergate scandal, the Republican Party faced its biggest crisis since the Depression, or perhaps since the assassination of President Lincoln and the controversies that grew out of the administration of his successor, President Andrew Johnson. Many predicted that the GOP would not recover from the blow of a disgraced presidency, and some even anticipated that the Republican Party could fade out, as had the Whig Party in the 1850s. What was in the wings as a possible replacement for the GOP was unclear, but in late 1974 and the early months of 1975, the Republican Party was viewed by many as being in critical condition.

Thus, as the campaign season began, leading up to an election that would coincide with the nation's bicentennial celebration, those within the Republican Party began looking for a solution to the GOP's weakened state. Some remained loyal to President Ford, in part because they valued the office of the presidency in and of itself, and in part because Ford was admired within the party as a person representing needed integrity in public service. Others felt that Ford was uninspiring, or maybe too close to the disgraced Nixon White House (even though Ford had nothing to do with Watergate), or politically too moderate to lead the Republican cause in stemming the tide of what they perceived to be a new and dangerous statism promoted by an increasingly liberal and high-spending Democratic Party. For them, the crisis of the failed Nixon presidency was an opportunity, and the nomination and election of former California governor Ronald Reagan, the champion of the conservative wing of the party since the failed Goldwater campaign of 1964, was the best solution. It was at the 1964 Republican convention that Reagan experienced his breakthrough as a national political figure, and from that point, he was regarded by conservatives as the true rallying figure in their cause. Thus, as the campaign season moved ahead, the Republican nomination became a two-way race between the moderate incumbent president Gerald Ford—who by accident had become the first person to fill the presidency without being elected to either the presidency or the vice presidency—and the challenger, Reagan—popular, personable, disarmingly charismatic, and resolved.

Given the vulnerability of the Republican Party, the Democrats were handed the rare, perfect conditions for a major political triumph, perhaps on the order of Franklin Roosevelt's landslide defeat of President Hoover forty-four years earlier, accompanied by considerable gains in Congress. But there was no one around like FDR (nor has anyone like him materialized since), and the Democrats continued to remain divided, the residues of the fragmented, polarizing **Campaigns of 1968 and 1972** still lingering; and thus the party that should have rode easily to victory nearly lost. The field of candidates was among the largest in history, and while it included numerous personalities who were not serious contenders, it was populated by a large number of figures who were indeed quite serious contenders, and who had a chance in the opened field.

In 1975, one of the early front-runners, Washington senator Henry "Scoop" Jackson drew considerable attention owing to his outspoken views on foreign policy (especially his unwavering support of Israel), but he earned the wrath of the liberal wing for his support of the Vietnam War. Former vice president and 1968 party nominee Hubert Humphrey of Minnesota was also regarded as an early contender, along with his former running mate and the early 1972 front-runner, Senator Edmund Muskie of Maine; but Humphrey faced health problems and declined to run, while Muskie seemed to have lost his taste for national campaigns after the debacle of 1972. Other familiar names were floated, such as Senator Edward Kennedy of Massachusetts and former senator Eugene McCarthy of Minnesota; but for different reasons, they could not find traction within the party. (McCarthy would eventually run as an independent, drawing little attention and less support.) Former governor George Wallace, an independent candidate in 1968 who had been paralyzed by a would-be assassin in the 1972 campaign, an incident that caused his withdrawal at the very moment he began to gain momentum, was also once again in the ring. Also joining the field were the 1972 nominee for vice president, Sargent Shriver; Arizona senator Mo Udall; West Virginia senator Robert Byrd; Indiana senator Birch Bayh; former North Carolina governor and former president of Duke University Terry Sanford; Texas senator Lloyd Bentsen; Idaho senator Frank Church; and two new faces on the national stage, Georgia governor James Earl "Jimmy" Carter, to be joined later in the campaign by another governor, California's free-thinking, free-speaking governor, Edmund G. "Jerry" Brown Jr., the son of another California governor, Edmund "Pat" Brown Sr. (who had himself been a candidate for the Democratic nomination in 1956, at that time running a distant second in the primaries to Estes Kefauver before the party nominated Adlai Stevenson at the convention later that summer). Thus while the Republican race was shaping up to be a close duel between two major public figures, the Democrats were busily sifting through a truly mixed bag of candidates in search of a bona fide front-runner. At the Iowa caucus, things began to clarify.

While the choice of "uncommitted" received more votes than any candidate at the Iowa caucus, Governor Carter sent shockwaves through the party and the press by tallying 28 percent of the delegates in play, 15 percent more than his nearest competitor, Senator Bayh. Carter's campaign followed with a critical, jolting win in the bellwether New Hampshire primary, where Carter again snagged 28 percent of the vote, followed by Senator Udall with 23 percent, Bayh showing third with 15 percent, and Senator Jackson, an early front-runner who did not participate in Iowa, receiving a meager 2 percent (he won 1% in the Iowa caucus). Jackson's decision not to compete in Iowa was, looking back, a serious mistake, but it was one that he seemed to correct after winning the Massachusetts primary, taking 22 percent of the vote, with Carter finishing fourth behind Jackson, Wallace, and Udall. But on that same day, Carter won a crushing victory in Vermont, taking 42 percent of the delegates, with Shriver a distant second, winning 28 percent; and from the Vermont poll forward, Carter seemed unstoppable, winning the next nine primaries, soaking up delegates like a sponge, and leaving the rest of the field far behind. On May 11, he finished in a first-place tie with Frank Church in Nebraska, did not compete against Senator Byrd in the West Virginia primary, and was finally defeated by Governor Brown in the Maryland primary. Brown was a compelling candidate, and he might have given Carter a contest, but he entered the campaign season too late, winning two more primaries in the West (Nevada and his home state of California) while watching Carter take eight more primaries, scarcely contested. It was an astonishing development, as prior to the Iowa caucus, Carter was a virtual unknown outside of his home state of Georgia. It was also in 1972 that the importance of Iowa became fully realized, and subsequent campaigns would, at least until very recently, look to the combination of the Iowa caucus and the following New Hampshire primary to set the tone, serving as early indicators of a candidate's promise.

After Carter campaigned brilliantly in the primaries, the Democratic Convention was left with the simple task of making it official, nominating him on the first ballot to bear the standard of the party in the bicentennial election. To complement the Democrats' moderate Southern presidential nominee, Minnesota senator Walter Mondale, a liberal Northerner schooled in the Midwestern populism of his fellow Minnesotan Hubert Humphrey, was chosen by Carter to run in the second spot. Carter initiated an unprecedented process of interviewing vice presidential candidates. Prior to the convention, many political observers anticipated that Carter would invite Senator Church to run with him; but Carter harbored second thoughts about Church, conducted interviews of three candidates in his home—Mondale, Muskie, and Ohio senator and former Mercury astronaut John Glenn—and two at the convention—Jackson and Adlai Stevenson III. In the end, Carter chose Mondale on grounds of personal compatibility more than for any concern over North-South strategy (which was, coincidentally, the result) or ideological balance. Mondale proved to be an energetic, knowledgeable, and competent choice as the campaign developed.

Throughout American political history, the presence of an incumbent president usually makes for a *fait accompli* in the renomination of the incumbent to run for reelection. There are exceptions, the most recent being President Johnson twelve years earlier; but for the most part, an incumbent in the mix makes for no contest within the incumbent's party. With Reagan's presence, however, President Ford faced a genuine battle, and one that, it soon became evident, could have gone either way. Ford did show early strength, winning the first six primaries, but he barely beat Reagan in New Hampshire; and as President Johnson discovered in 1968, scarcely winning in New Hampshire is, for incumbents, tantamount to a loss. Once the dust had settled on the primary season, Ford had won eighteen primaries to Reagan's eleven, and again, had Ford not been the incumbent, there might have been less of an issue with regard to Reagan's performance; but Reagan had shown strength against the president and at one point won four consecutive primaries, exposing vulnerabilities in the president's bid. More importantly, where Reagan actively campaigned, things were close, and even though Ford held a narrow lead in delegates going into the convention, there was much hope within the Reagan campaign that the convention might play out differently. Ford's slight lead over Reagan in delegates did not give him the needed majority, so there was reason in the Reagan campaign to draw that conclusion.

It was the tightest convention since the 1924 Democratic convention, and as the candidates maneuvered for position, Reagan, a conservative who felt that he needed to woo delegates away from the more moderate Ford, announced that if nominated, he would select moderate/liberal Republican Richard Schweiker as his running mate. The move boomeranged, as enough conservatives were offended at what they perceived to be a betrayal of principle to stalk away and switch to Ford, and few if any moderates were drawn to Reagan because of Schweiker. Thus Ford snatched enough delegates to win the nomination, ending one of the more compelling conventions since the ascent of the primaries as the key impetus toward nomination. Ford came very close to asking Reagan to serve as his running mate, but in the end he selected Kansas senator Robert Dole, known for his acerbic wit and who, by some accounts, was chosen for his ability to aggressively attack the Democratic nominee, allowing Ford to remain true to his more affable persona. In a show of unity, Ford invited Reagan to speak at the end of the convention, an invitation accepted by the former governor, who again performed well, and in the opinion of many, he outshone the nominee as he had upstaged Goldwater at the 1964 convention, the event that launched him into the national spotlight. The 1976 Republican convention is the last one in which the party's nomination was actually in play as the convention began, and at that time, this was an anomaly, given that the primary system had overtaken the process over the course of the past few elections.

Thus the outcome of the primary season was, in retrospect, counterintuitive. The incumbent president, who would under typical circumstances have glided to his nomination, limped out of the convention having barely staved off a significant challenge from an appealing competitor. Governor Carter, comparatively new to the national stage and in most respects an unknown quantity who under typical circumstances would have found himself quickly winnowed out by more seasoned, familiar, and influential candidates, in actuality proved an adept campaigner, winning his party's nomination with comparative ease and delivering to the Democrats the most unifying candidacy in twelve years. In part this was due to a general desire within the electorate for someone fresh. After Vietnam and Watergate, many Americans were looking for new directions, and the unassuming outsider from Georgia seemed to point the way. Carter's confidence and ease of victory was not lost on the voters, and Ford's narrow escape from the Reagan challenge hovered over him throughout the remainder of the campaign season. Thus at the end of the Republican convention in mid-August, national presidential preference polls showed Carter enjoying a double-digit lead over Ford; in some polls Carter led by as much as thirty-four points.

On the issues, the two candidates were both generally moderate, easily the most moderate rivals since the 1960 election pitted Senator John Kennedy against Vice President Nixon. Carter had keenly positioned himself as a moderate on budget and crime issues and a liberal on social issues such as abortion and affirmative action. Instead of calling for higher taxes to pay for the expansion of federal programs, Carter pledged spending discipline and frugality, touting "zero-based budgeting" as a method to control government spending and promising to set firm budgetary priorities. Furthermore, Carter promised to restore honesty in government in the aftermath of the Watergate scandal. The Carter campaign made the return of integrity in government its top priority, and so the phrase "Return Integrity to the White House" became the keynote slogan of the Carter campaign.

Fighting back from a huge deficit in the polls, the Ford campaign adopted a strategy that was aimed at convincing the American people that the country was now finally on a promising course, thanks to the president's leadership, and it emphasized the strong Midwestern values that shaped his upbringing, a countermove to the stress that Governor Carter's campaign had placed on the values of public service that he developed throughout his life as an observant Southern Baptist. Carter's religious devotion, never really an issue for the voters, nonetheless defined his persona in a way not seen since the campaign of John Kennedy, a Roman Catholic. However, Kennedy preferred to steer clear of the issue, and he only addressed it to allay concerns from some quarters that he was politically beholden to the pope, and address it he did, in a powerful speech before a gathering of Baptist ministers in Houston during the 1960 campaign. But Carter's faith visibly shaped his public image, and while not influencing voters either way, it became, along with the perception that he was a "Washington outsider," a prevalent theme in describing the governor's background, character, and vision. Ford, an Episcopalian and also devoutly religious, chose not to mention that aspect of his life and instead drew on his long record as a public official with experience in both Congress and the presidency.

Ford's approach worked; with each poll he incrementally closed the gap, and soon the momentum was clearly his. A slowing rate of inflation and falling unemployment made it easier for the Ford campaign to make the case that his presidency was accomplished, and that given a firm mandate from the people (the only thing he lacked), he could then go on to achieve still greater things. While Carter spoke of personal intimacies, Ford was effectively looking presidential, strengthening his campaign at the right moment. The slogans "The Man Who Made Us Proud Again" and "Peace, Prosperity and the Public Trust" sought to stress these points. Many voters were still disappointed over the pardoning of former President Nixon, and thus Ford avoided raising the issue; but his campaign also emphasized, as did Carter's, the integrity of Ford and the role he had already played in helping to restore trust in government, a claim that held some merit. Additionally, the Ford campaign sought to raise doubts about Carter's preparation for the Oval Office, and it challenged the Democrat's claim that he was ready to take on the responsibilities of the presidency after having only served as governor of Georgia for a relatively short period of time.

For only the second time in history, the two presidential candidates nominated by the major political parties agreed to meet in televised debate. Additionally, for the first time in campaign history, the two vice presidential nominees, Bob Dole and Walter Mondale, also met in a televised debate. In the first presidential debate, both Ford and Carter did well, but many analysts concluded that the president came away holding a slight edge. Ford seemed confident and calm, while Carter appeared at some points unsure and even a little prickly. The polls indicated that the first debate helped Ford: Before the debate, the president had trailed by 18 points, but after the debate, he had gained 10 points on Carter and was now only 8 points behind, significantly narrowing the gap. The momentum was clearly still his.

But in the second debate, the president committed an egregious gaffe that blunted his momentum and, to many observers and analysts, cost him the election. One element of the campaign that had previously worked in Ford's favor was his experience in foreign policy. After having served in the Oval Office since

December 1974, Ford had gained considerable expertise in dealing with foreign leaders and international issues, something that Governor Carter could not easily dismiss. But during the second debate, President Ford, in speaking of the status of Soviet Bloc nations, inexplicably refused to admit that the Soviet Union dominated Eastern European nations, a statement that to everyone seemed to be either patently naïve or, worse, lacking basic understanding of geopolitical dynamics. The president made the comment in defense of the Helsinki Accords that he had negotiated with the Soviet leadership, agreements that to some critics amounted to a concession to Russian hegemony in Eastern Europe, with serious implications for Western Europe and evoking anxiety over the future. In explaining the Helsinki Accords, the president stated, "There is no Soviet domination of Eastern Europe and there never will be under a Ford administration." When pressed further to explain himself, the president curiously insisted on digging himself into a deep hole. "I don't believe," the president claimed, "that the Yugoslavians consider themselves dominated by the Soviet Union. I don't believe that the Rumanians consider themselves dominated by the Soviet Union. I don't believe that the Poles consider themselves dominated by the Soviet Union." For a candidate who was relying heavily on his foreign policy reputation, it was an epic blunder. Still worse, the following day when the president again attempted to explain still further, he stubbornly refused to admit that he had misspoken. Surprisingly, the polls told a slightly different story, indicating a loss of only one or two points after the second debate; hence it may not have been as deleterious as some analysts, then and now, have concluded. Nonetheless, the mistake effactually broke Ford's momentum and restrengthened Carter's position.

As it turned out, Carter did not help his own cause, as he also committed a weird gaffe that directly hurt his numbers. In an injudicious interview with *Playboy* magazine, some untoward impulse possessed Carter to confess to having "lusted in his heart," an admission that was viewed by many as far too personal, undignified, and somewhat troubling for a presidential candidate. The very decision to interview with *Playboy*, in its essence a pin-up centerfold magazine with pretentions to urbane discussion and social relevance, was in itself unusual, but the content of Carter's remarks in the course of the interview was simply too much to resist. The "lust in my heart" incident drew jokes and jibes from all corners, from popular late-night talk shows (such as *The Tonight Show Starring Johnny Carson)* to numerous political cartoons, and Carter faced his first serious setback since entering the very beginning of his campaign in Iowa. The news media and late-night comedians alike gleefully pounced on Carter, but they also continued to mock Ford. Even though he was probably the most athletic president since Theodore Roosevelt, Ford was portrayed as clumsy and somewhat doltish. On more than one occasion, the president had been caught stumbling on camera, images that fed into the misperception that he was physically inept and, by implication, somehow slow of mind. *Saturday Night Live* comedian Chevy Chase routinely satirized the president as an awkward and incompetent dunce. Ford took it all in stride, even sportingly making a brief appearance to introduce the popular show. Whether or not either of these major gaffes—Ford's baffling Eastern Europe comment or Carter's embarrassing frankness about his salacious urges—in the end made any difference in the race's outcome is not clear, but neither incident helped them, and both men retrospectively regretted their mistakes.

On Election Night, the early returns indicated a favorable outcome for Governor Carter, as projections for New York, Pennsylvania, Ohio, Florida, and Massachusetts went his way. But as the night developed, Ford came back, taking Illinois, Michigan, Indiana, and Virginia, and thereby providing his supporters with a degree of hope. But when Texas was announced for Carter, it appeared that the governor would be the next president, even though Ford swept every western state in the lower forty-eight, including California, the biggest electoral prize; the only state Ford lost west of Texas was Hawaii, which was significant given the closeness of the election. The popular tally was tight, Carter winning just over 40,800,000 votes (or 50.1%) with Ford taking just under 39,150,000 votes (a whisker over 48%), the remainder of the votes (less than 2%) going to independent candidate Eugene McCarthy and a variety of obscure minor-party candidates. Governor Carter's popular victory converted to 297 Electoral College votes (55%) to President Ford's 240 (45%); it was the closest margin of victory in the Electoral College since 1916 (President Wilson's 277 votes, or 52%, to 254, or 48%, for Charles Evans Hughes). President Ford was the first incumbent president to lose a general election since President Hoover in 1932. (All told, Ford was now the eighth incumbent to lose an election, joining Hoover, John Adams, John Quincy Adams, Martin Van Buren, Grover Cleveland, Benjamin Harrison, and William Howard Taft.) Even though on the surface the defeat of an incumbent president was a severe blow to the Republican Party, which was still suffering the aftershocks of the Watergate scandal that brought down a once-popular Republican president, the close election revealed another story. As stated above, in 1974, many considered the GOP on its way to extinction based on the assessment that Watergate had so stained the reputation of Republicans that a complete recovery would be nearly impossible. But even in defeat, and in spite of serious campaign errors, the Ford candidacy proved that his party remained resilient.

Just two years after the resignation of President Nixon, the Republicans were thus showing evidence of rebounding. They only required the right kind of candidate and a favorable turn of circumstances to complete their recovery. With the Ford presidency over, that candidate would have to come from somewhere else. As it turned out, the candidate the GOP was looking for had already proven himself a formidable force in the primaries of 1976, and he would again enter the arena four years hence.

Additional Resources

Anderson, Patrick. *Electing Jimmy Carter: The Campaign of 1976*. Baton Rouge: Louisiana State University Press, 1994.

Cohen, Martin, David Karol, Hans Noel, and John Zaller. *The Party Decides: Presidential Nominations before and after Reform*. Chicago: University of Chicago Press, 2008.

Glad, Betty. "Election of 1976." In Arthur M. Schlesinger, Fred Israel, and William P. Hansen, eds. *History of American Presidential Elections, 1789–1984*. Vol. 9. New York: Chelsea House, 1986.

Green, Robert. *The Presidency of Gerald R. Ford*. Lawrence: University Press of Kansas, 1995.

Kraus, Sidney. *The Great Debates: Carter v. Ford, 1976*. Bloomington: Indiana University Press, 1979.

Ribuffo, Leo P. "1976." In Arthur M. Schlesinger, Fred L. Israel, and David J. Frent, eds. *Running for President: The Candidates and Their Images*. Vol. 2. New York: Simon & Schuster, 1994.

Witcover, Jules. *Marathon: The Pursuit of the Presidency, 1972–1976*. New York: Viking Press, 1977.

Campaign of 1980

President Jimmy Carter's administration opened with a palpable sense of promise. He was elected to the presidency during the nation's bicentennial observance, and in the wake of Watergate and the residual aftereffects of Vietnam, he appeared on the scene as a refreshing antidote to a political system that, for many Americans, had betrayed their ideals and disappointed their aspirations. The newly inaugurated president made every effort to portray himself as a man of the people, and the promise of personal integrity and pragmatic, nonideological leadership was embraced by the American public. In March 1979, three months into his presidency, Carter enjoyed an approval rating of 75 percent, the highest since Lyndon Johnson in February 1964 (only three months after the death of President Kennedy). President Carter's ratings remained above 50 percent throughout 1977. But moving into 1978, economic problems (high unemployment combined with double-digit inflation—a phenomenon called "stagflation") weighed on the Carter presidency along with growing concerns over the cost of energy, particularly oil; and from this point, his ratings would fluctuate for the remainder of his administration.

The president had established himself as an important international figure through his role in brokering peace between Israel and Egypt, but these domestic problems dogged his presidency. Liberal Democrats were angry with the president for not cooperating with their efforts to establish a national health program, or at least for not supporting the kind of program that the liberals in Congress desired, as President Carter did in fact support national health care as a policy. Conservatives in both parties felt that Carter was soft on defense and were incensed that he had canceled production of the new-generation B-1 long-range bomber. As the Cold War was still under way, the canceling of such a big-budget item would guarantee controversy.

Carter did not help matters when he spoke of a "crisis of confidence" that had insinuated itself throughout American political culture. It was a well-meaning effort at avuncular frankness toward the American people, but the message was as distasteful as bad medicine and of questionable effect. "The threat is nearly invisible in ordinary ways," the president declaimed in a nationally televised speech in the summer of 1979. "It is a crisis of confidence. It is a crisis that strikes at the very heart and soul and spirit of our national will. We can see this crisis in the growing doubt about the meaning of our own lives and in the loss of a unity of purpose for our nation." While the president was merely responding to what pollsters had already observed in the wake of the Watergate scandal, the fate of Vietnam, fears of a stagnating economy without respite, and painful memories of the assassinations of President John Kennedy, his brother Senator Robert Kennedy, and civil rights leader Martin Luther King Jr., the speech appeared too somber, even morose—and it came to be called the "malaise speech" in the press, even though the word "malaise" was nowhere to be found in the actual text of his address. President Carter had promised honesty and candor, and he delivered it; but its ultimate effect was to tint the White House with a shade of resignation, a presidency in the doldrums. While perhaps an overreaction to President Carter's overall purpose, there was something to the criticism. Past presidents had encountered far worse problems and still managed to deliver stirring, hopeful speeches—examples in recent times included Franklin Roosevelt and John Kennedy; but in his "crisis of confidence" or "malaise" speech, President Carter inadvertently announced a self-fulfilling prophecy, not about the mood of the country, but more directly about the timbre of his own presidency. Even in the president's own party, there was enough disgruntlement to throw into doubt Carter's renomination.

For a brief moment, this changed. When an agitated mob of Iranian revolutionaries, in violation of all standards of international protocol, violently stormed the American embassy in Tehran and held a number of Americans hostage, the president enjoyed a favorable bump in his approval ratings, as is often the case when the nation faces a new crisis abroad. But as the hostage crisis worsened and then reached what appeared to be an impasse, the president was seen by many within the American public as ineffective, lacking the fortitude needed to manage such a crisis. A disastrous rescue effort only punctuated the "crisis in confidence" in President Carter's judgment, competence, and resolve. Additionally, President Carter's decision to boycott the Summer Olympic Games, to be held in Moscow, in protest over the Soviet invasion of Afghanistan further damaged his popularity in the polls, as it was seen by some as grandstanding, and by others as a futile gesture that would not be taken seriously, something to be dismissed by the emboldened Soviets, who gladly exhibited their indifference to the opinions of the Americans.

Furthermore, discontent brewed within the Democratic Party itself. Liberal Democrats in Congress found it difficult to work with the president, in part due to ideological disagreements but also as a result of irreconcilable personality differences. Thus President Carter lost considerable support throughout the party in the second half of his administration. Rumors circulated that elements in the party wanted to dump Carter in 1980 and replace him with a more visionary, charismatic leader. Many turned back to the Kennedys—in this case, Senator Edward Kennedy, the youngest of the Kennedy brothers, who had, over the course of the past decade, managed to shake personal scandal to become an esteemed leader in the U.S. Senate. Kennedy's presidential ambitions had been virtually demolished by the horrible Chappaquiddick incident in 1969, but over the years his position had recovered, and to many within the party, he was the only figure capable of dislodging an incumbent president. However, one poll indicated that Senator Edmund Muskie, the Democratic candidate for vice president in 1968, would be a more preferable candidate for the general election. Governor Jerry Brown of California was also a possible candidate to run against Carter for the nomination, but his campaign never received enough traction to be considered a serious threat. It was Kennedy who led Carter 58 percent to 29 percent in an August 1979 poll, and even after a bungled television interview with Roger Mudd of *CBS News* in which Kennedy awkwardly failed to coherently explain why he felt he should be president, he still held a 49-to-39 lead when pitted against Carter.

The Iran hostage crisis, which would eventually become a principal factor in Carter's downfall, in its earliest days gave Carter the advantage over Kennedy as the two candidates squared off in the early primaries. Kennedy campaigned hard in Iowa, but Carter won a stunning victory there, to be followed by another convincing win in New Hampshire. Kennedy did manage to win the Massachusetts primary, his home state, but Carter continued to win in subsequent primaries. As the campaign season moved into the summer and the American public grew anxious over the unresolved hostage crisis, Kennedy finally began to win a series of primaries, including a significant victory in New York, always a key state, even though it was no longer the biggest electoral prize (that now being California, thanks to the 1970 census). In the face of Kennedy's assault, Carter suddenly withdrew from campaigning and adopted the "Rose Garden approach" of remaining in the White House and away from the campaign trail, a decision he explained as stemming from the need to manage the hostage crisis. Carter's tactic may actually have allowed Kennedy to make late gains, but it was not enough. Going into the convention, Carter's lead in delegates was too large, and in spite of one final effort to persuade the convention to release all delegates from their prior commitments, the Kennedy campaign was defeated.

President Carter won his party's renomination (Vice President Walter Mondale also was renominated), but the fight with Kennedy had exposed divisions and discontent within the party that illustrated a gravely vulnerable incumbent. At the convention, Kennedy, in defeat, delivered an eloquent and inspiring speech, considered by many to have been Ted Kennedy's finest hour, while the president's acceptance speech fell flat. Carter awkwardly appeared before the delegates, cutting a pale image when compared to Kennedy, and at times his enthusiasm for the upcoming campaign against the Republicans appeared somewhat forced, and it even contained an egregious error in referring to the late Senator Hubert Humphrey, whose memory was honored at the convention, as "Hubert Horatio Hornblower—Humphrey." As an incumbent, President Carter was in a poor position moving into the general election, and he was to face a formidable opponent.

Ronald Wilson Reagan broke through as a major figure on the national political stage in 1964, owing to a stirring speech delivered at the national convention that eclipsed the party's nominee, then senator Barry Goldwater. Since that time, Reagan had remained the most visible and popular voice of American conservatism. He nearly dislodged incumbent president Ford in a tight battle for the 1976 GOP nomination, and since that convention, he had remained a visible spokesperson for conservative values and policies. Given his reputation, and in light of his near victory against an incumbent for the nomination four years earlier, Reagan was considered to be far and away the only serious Republican front-runner for 1980, particularly given that Ford himself had decided not to compete for the nomination. This led Reagan's campaign managers to adopt a policy that set their candidate above the fray, keeping him away from campaign events that they deemed to be of little relevance. However, this approach nearly backfired, as a number of talented candidates then stepped into the field, including several prominent Republicans, among them Senator Robert Dole, the GOP's vice presidential candidate in 1976; Senator Howard Baker; former governor (and former Democrat) John Connolly of Texas, who had been wounded by a bullet during the assassination of President Kennedy; perennial candidate Harold Stassen of Minnesota; rising moderate congressman John Anderson of Illinois; and former CIA director and diplomat (who had also served two terms in the House of Representatives) George Herbert Walker Bush of Texas.

Bush, who like Anderson was a moderate, soon proved to be the most effective challenger, participating in as many campaign events as possible, leading to
payoffs in the polls; he began to actually show better than Reagan in informal and
straw polls conducted after events in which Bush had participated. Bush won a
straw poll in Iowa, dispelling any illusions that Reagan's nomination was inevitable. Reagan finally took notice and actively joined the campaign, beginning in
New Hampshire, which included a candidates' forum that was partially funded
by Reagan's own campaign and that was meant to bring together all the current
candidates for an open debate. The Bush camp, confident with the momentum (the
"Big Mo," as Bush was wont to call it) it had gained in Iowa, welcomed the debate
with Reagan but was caught off guard when the rest of the field, none of whom by
this time were serious challengers, also appeared. Wanting to debate Reagan alone
and not interested in providing the also-rans with a public stage, Bush's campaign
manager, Howard Baker, promptly advised Bush not to participate, leaving the two
front-runners silently stewing on stage while four of the other candidates waited
on stage behind them. With the audience confused and fidgeting, Reagan took the
microphone to begin to explain his reasons for including all the candidates out
of a sense of fairness. At that moment, the debate moderator ordered Reagan's
microphone to be silenced, to which a clearly vexed and roused Reagan forcefully replied, to the vigorous applause of all those present, "I am paying for this
microphone!"

Reagan's refusal to be silenced and the strength he reflexively revealed in the
heat of the moment was pivotal; from that point, Reagan commanded all the attention, and the Bush campaign, which had been up to that point successful and well
managed, began to look bland by comparison. Reagan won the New Hampshire
primary with 50 percent of the vote, with just 23 percent going to Bush. New
Hampshire was followed by Massachusetts, which gave Bush and Anderson a tie
for first and a narrow two-percentage-point victory over Reagan; but after that,
Reagan won six primaries in a row and nearly all of the primaries afterward.
Bush ran second in most of these primaries (usually a distant second), and where
he did not take second, he either won (just three more primaries after Massachusetts) or finished third to Anderson. At the end of the primary season, Reagan had
won nearly 60 percent of the popular vote to Bush's 24 percent and Anderson's
12 percent.

Prior to the convention, Anderson's campaign bolted and established an independent candidacy in an attempt to offer a moderate alternative to Republicans
uneasy with Reagan's conservatism and to Democrats disappointed by Carter's
alleged lack of leadership. Reagan cruised to nomination at the GOP convention,
with George Bush invited to join Reagan as his running mate. The Republican platform proposed a significant reduction in federal income tax rates. It also proposed

to reduce welfare allocations by "removing ineligibles from the welfare rolls, tightening food stamp eligibility requirements, and ending aid to illegal aliens and the voluntarily unemployed." The platform refused to either endorse or oppose the ratification of the Equal Rights Amendment, the ratification of which had recently been stifled. Additionally, the platform supported a constitutional amendment "to restore protection of the right to life for unborn children," supported legislative action to "to restore the right of individuals to participate in voluntary, non-denominational prayer in schools and other public facilities," and demanded a halt to forced busing of public school students. The platform also opposed any new national health insurance program and supported the transfer of all welfare program functions to the states. One platform plank opposed any federal registration of firearms and supported mandatory sentencing for the commission of armed felonies.

Thus the stage was set for the general election. The Reagan campaign employed a two-prong strategy to convince Americans to deny Jimmy Carter a second term. First, the campaign sought to make the American people comfortable with Reagan as a person and a proven leader. By focusing on the actions of Reagan as governor of California for eight years as well as his leadership in the party, the campaign angled a defense that would prevent the Carter campaign from characterizing Reagan as simply a former actor who knew little about running a government. The slogan "It's Time for Strong Leadership" reflected this strategy. The second prong forthrightly blamed the Carter administration for not dealing with the serious domestic and foreign policy problems facing the country. Slogans such as "Are You Better Off Than You Were Four Years Ago?" "Make American Great Again," and "Together—A New Beginning" sought to persuade American voters that Reagan offered the nation a way out of its domestic and foreign problems. Reagan ads blasted Carter for high inflation, rising energy costs, and foreign policy disasters. Even though Reagan gave few detailed suggestions as to how he would address these problems, his spirited optimism was a marked contrast to the cloud of malaise that had settled over the Carter presidency, and the strategies employed to illustrate this were effective.

The Carter campaign relied upon a three-prong strategy. First, the Carter campaign sought to emphasize his foreign policy achievements—viz., the Camp David accord between Egypt and Israel that he helped broker, and his careful and deliberate responses to dangerous international situations, which helped to prevent the United States from becoming involved in another war. Second, the Carter campaign sought to depict Carter as a hard-working chief executive devoting countless hours to find solutions to the nation's problems. Third, the Carter campaign sought to depict Reagan as potentially dangerous, a move reminiscent of President Johnson's campaign against Senator Goldwater in the 1964 presidential contest. Carter campaign ads argued that Reagan, if elected, would shoot from the hip and thus might involve the United States in another unwanted war. Slogans such as "Stand by the President," "Leadership and Strength," and "A Solid Man in a Sensitive Job" were designed to convince voters that Carter, after four years managing crises in the White House, was far better prepared to serve as president under strained circumstances than his GOP counterpart.

Following his Rose Garden strategy (reminiscent of the "front-porch campaigns" of the late nineteenth century), President Carter remained in the White House through much of the post-primary phase of the campaign, under the belief that this approach permitted Carter to look presidential and convince voters that it was too dangerous to change presidents in the middle of so many domestic and international problems. But Carter was eventually forced to leave the Rose Garden and face his challenger head-on. Following the precedent set by the campaigns of 1960 (Kennedy-Nixon) and 1976 (Ford-Carter), the candidates agreed to a series of televised presidential debates. As the polls showed the candidates in a tight race, many observers believed that the debates might determine the outcome of the election. Through much of the fall, the Carter campaign had refused to debate Reagan, owing to Reagan's insistence that third-party candidate John Anderson also be included. Anderson's numbers in the polls had increased to around 20 percent, a significant amount for a third-party candidate, and Reagan desired to engage him in a national debate. The first debate went as scheduled, but President Carter still withheld, refusing to debate Anderson. While some had anticipated that Anderson, who was a skilled debater and a cool presence under media fire, could get the best of Reagan, quite the opposite resulted; after the first debate, Anderson's percentage in the polls was halved. The Reagan camp continued to insist on three-way debates, and President Carter continued to refuse. Finally, President Carter managed to persuade Reagan to drop his insistence on including Anderson, and a second debate involving only Reagan and the president was held just one week before Election Day.

Carter was well prepared to deliver complex facts and demonstrate the expertise that he had acquired over the past four years as the nation's chief executive, but Reagan's personal charm and sense of vision shined brighter, at least on that one evening. Carter, who often seemed irritated or put-upon, could not match Reagan's disarming manner and telegenic image. In addition to Reagan's more comfortable, poised performance, Carter seemed out of his league, a marked contrast to his evident successes on the campaign trail in 1976. Reagan managed to ably deflect any effort by Carter to depict him as "hawkish" or extreme, and when the president focused on Reagan's domestic policies, the challenger would shrug it off. "There you go again," Reagan casually responded to Carter's criticism of Reagan's past record on entitlement programs, dismissively sweeping away the president's attempt to depict Reagan as too conservative to trust with "third rail" spending programs and policies. Carter appeared risible when, in debating nuclear weapons policy with Reagan, he shared with the television viewers his "consultation" over the future of nuclear weaponry with his eleven-year-old daughter Amy, a debate moment that fueled many jokes and one-liners on late-night television and helped to generate more than one satirical opinion column. But Reagan's best moment came at the end of the debate, when in his concluding reflection and with the uncanny timing that he had learned from his years as an actor, he turned toward the viewing audience and asked,

> Are you better off now than you were four years ago? Is it easier for you to go and buy things in the stores than it was four years ago? Is there more or less unemployment in the country than there was four years ago? Is America as respected throughout the world as it was? Do you feel that our security is as safe, that we're as strong as we were four years ago? And if you answer all of those questions yes, why then, I think your choice is very obvious as to whom you will vote for. If you don't agree, if you don't think that this course that we've been on for the last four years is what you would like to see us follow for the next four, then I could suggest another choice that you have.

If there had ever been a single, defining turning point in any presidential campaign, this was it. Immediately before the debate, the polls indicated the candidates were locked in a dead heat, with some polls showing a slim lead for the president. The following day, after Reagan's masterstroke, public opinion polls conducted by Carter's own advisers showed Reagan steadily moving ahead.

Still, the polls leading up to the evening of Election Day predicted a close election, but the pollsters were caught by surprise. Reagan won in a landslide. Even though he managed just 50.7 percent of the popular vote, it was still nearly ten points higher than President Carter, who took only 40.9 percent of the popular vote, with John Anderson winning 6 percent, an impressive amount for a third-party candidate, and the remainder of the popular votes (just over 1%) scattered among a handful of minor-party candidates. More impressively, Reagan won 489 electoral votes (91%) to President Carter's meager 49 (9%), with Anderson taking none. Carter took only six states and the District of Columbia, Reagan all the rest, winning big in every region of the country including the South (the only southern state that went for Carter was his home state of Georgia). With the GOP's clean sweep of the South in 1972 and near sweep in 1980, as well as strong showings there in both 1964 and 1968, it was now more than evident that the Democrats' dominance in that region was finished once and for all. The Reagan election signaled the end of the old Roosevelt Coalition; the Democrats could no longer take the South for granted, lost ground among the labor vote, appeared to be losing ground among Catholics, and found no one region of the country that could get behind the Democratic president. Moreover, it was the worst showing for an incumbent since William Howard Taft lost his bid for reelection in the wild three-way race of 1912 (President Taft actually finished third in a three-way race), and the worst showing in the Electoral College by an incumbent president in any two-way race for reelection (incumbent president Hoover lost by a bigger margin in the popular vote during the 1932 election but finished slightly better than President Carter in the Electoral College).

Given the scope of the loss, some analysts at the time concluded that the country was undergoing, at the very least, what was described as a political "de-alignment," and possibly what some preferred to call realignment. Most political scientists today reject this assessment, arguing that the election of Ronald Reagan was the inevitable outcome of events already set into motion in the early 1960s. Either way, President-elect Reagan seemed to have pulled the country toward the right, working a kind of reconfiguration of the institutional political arrangements; but once in office, President Reagan would surprise many as a far more moderate figure than most observers could have anticipated.

Additional Resources

Busch, Andrew E. *Reagan's Victory: The Presidential Election of 1980 and the Rise of the Right*. Lawrence: University Press of Kansas, 2005.

Cohen, Martin, David Karol, Hans Noel, and John Zaller. *The Party Decides: Presidential Nominations before and after Reform*. Chicago: University of Chicago Press, 2008.

Drew, Elizabeth. *Portrait of an Election*. New York: Simon & Schuster, 1981.

Stanley, Timothy. *Kennedy v. Carter: The 1980 Battle for the Democratic Party's Soul*. Lawrence: University of Kansas Press, 2010.

Troy, Gil. *The Reagan Revolution: A Very Short Introduction*. Oxford: Oxford University Press, 2009.

Witcover, Jules. "The Election of 1980." In Arthur M. Schlesinger, Fred Israel, and William P. Hansen, eds. *History of American Presidential Elections, 1789–1984*. Vol. 9. New York: Chelsea House, 1986.

Witcover, Jules. "1980." In Arthur M. Schlesinger, Fred L. Israel, and David J. Frent, eds. *Running for President: The Candidates and Their Images*. Vol. 2. New York: Simon & Schuster, 1994.

Campaign of 1984

Ronald Reagan was sworn in as the fortieth president of the United States on January 20, 1981. Just barely two months later, on March 30, he was struck by the bullet of a would-be assassin, fired by a dispirited loner. The president was critically wounded, and it was later revealed that the assault nearly cost him his life; but in the end, he survived to see his popularity soar in the polls and his legislative proposals adopted by Congress. As promised, President Reagan proposed and managed to secure from Congress cuts in both taxation and spending, but these were not as extensive as his conservative supporters had hoped (nor as his liberal opponents had feared).

Reagan's willingness to modify his proposals in the direction of compromise indicated his more pragmatic side. Often viewed by his critics and supporters alike as an ideological "true believer," Reagan was more than amenable to supporting more moderate solutions. He would at times assume a harder line, as in the case of his battle against the Professional Air Traffic Controllers union, in which the president actually fired air controllers in retaliation for their attempt to initiate a strike; but in many instances, he could work toward compromise. He was and remains the central figure in American conservatism; but as a matter of course, as president, he could and did work with those on the other side. This ability and willingness was one of the reasons behind his early success in seeing his legislative agenda through Congress, providing the foundation for a surprisingly bipartisan spirit shared between the conservative president and the Democratic leadership in Congress. This is not to say that there was a return to the "Era of Good Feelings," or even a restoration of the kind of bipartisanship experienced under presidents Eisenhower and Kennedy; but rather to note that the many fears over Reagan's ideological purity were somewhat allayed by his inclination to principled compromise.

The early success of the Reagan administration gave way to an economic recession that, by some accounts, was (at that time) the worst economic downturn since the Great Depression. The tax and spending cuts that the president and Congress had together developed were chewed away by falling revenues on one side and Reagan's determination to continue increasing the defense budget on the other. Reagan, who pledged in his campaign to balance the budget in three years, now oversaw deficit spending of unprecedented proportions. However, within a few months, the economy improved and continued to show improvement throughout much of Reagan's presidency. During this economic upswing, President Reagan supported slight increases in the tax rate, another example of his decision to break from his earlier supply-side policies and pursue more pragmatic, or perhaps more accurately, less ideological approaches. Reagan had also shown strength as a leader in the international arena, and his firm stance with the Soviet Union—even, to some controversy, referring to the Soviet Union as an "evil empire"—along with his determination to increase the size of the American military were seen by many as a restoration of American resolve, although a growing anti-nuclear weapons movement visibly challenged the president's policies.

Thus, going into the election campaign of 1984, the Reagan incumbency did not appear to face the same problems that brought down the previous two incumbents, President Ford (who lost the White House to Jimmy Carter) and President Carter (who then lost the White House to Ronald Reagan). And, unlike Presidents Ford and Carter, who faced challenges from within their own parties (Reagan challenging Ford in 1976 and nearly winning, and Senator Edward Kennedy challenging Carter in 1980), Reagan and Vice President Bush were unopposed (although technically, perennial presidential candidate Harold Stassen ran against Reagan for good measure, but his opposition was neither serious nor noticeable). On the first ballot at the GOP national convention, the Reagan-Bush ticket was renominated, with both candidates named at the same time for the first time during the roll-call vote.

The Republican platform praised the Reagan administration for successfully leading the economic recovery and avoiding a more severe recession, and for restoring the respect for the United States around the world. The platform called for still further tax cuts, endorsed a constitutional amendment requiring a balanced federal budget, supported a constitutional amendment to ban abortions, and expressed opposition to hiring quotas in the workplace to increase the number of women and minorities. The platform also praised the president for his resolve in dealing with the Soviet Union.

After the defeat of Democratic incumbent president Jimmy Carter in 1980, many in the party regarded the logical front-runner for the 1984 campaign to be Senator Kennedy, who had himself challenged Carter in the 1980 campaign season. Throughout much of 1982, Kennedy considered it, and he was even working on plans for a run against Reagan. But by the end of that year, after much consultation with his family, he renounced any further presidential ambitions. With Senator Kennedy no longer a possibility, the field was opened, and a new front-runner, former vice president Walter Mondale of Minnesota, quickly emerged. Mondale was joined by Colorado senator Gary Hart, civil rights activist Jesse Jackson (the second African American, after Shirley Chisholm, to campaign on the national level), former Mercury astronaut and Ohio senator John Glenn, California senator Alan Cranston, Senator Ernest Hollings of South Carolina, former Florida governor Reuben Askew, and former senator and the party's 1972 nominee for president, George McGovern of South Dakota. It was a populated field, but from the beginning, the principal candidates were Mondale, Hart, and Jackson. Mondale easily won the Iowa caucus, but he was surprised in the New Hampshire primary, which Hart won by taking 37 percent of the vote to Mondale's 28 percent, with Glenn showing third at 12 percent. Hart followed with two more substantial victories in Vermont and Wyoming, and he appeared to have all the momentum.

But the Mondale organization was polished and well funded, and it fought back hard. Hart had promoted himself as a new kind of Democrat, and by implication, he promised a departure from the allegedly stale policies of the old New Deal mentality that had defined the party since President Franklin Roosevelt. Mondale, who was a protégé of his fellow Minnesotan, the late senator Hubert Humphrey, cut his teeth on the legacy of FDR's New Deal as well as on the Great Society of President Lyndon Johnson, and he was thus steeped in the more conventional attitudes of the party as it had been defined by Roosevelt, Truman, Kennedy, and Johnson as well as his mentor Humphrey. Mondale criticized Hart's "new ideas," complaining that they lacked real substance, and famously quipping during a televised debate that, in considering Hart's claim to innovation, he was reminded of a fast-food hamburger advertisement that employed the catchphrase "Where's the beef?" It was an effective line that was immediately latched onto by Mondale's supporters, becoming the signal statement of the Mondale response to any challenge from the younger Hart. While Mondale successfully depicted Hart as superficial, Jackson's efforts were damaged by an anti-Semitic remark that he made during a visit to New York City. Jackson apologized, but he was unable to shake off the effects of the remark, which was particularly appalling to those who had always considered Jackson to be a champion of the rights and dignity of minorities.

As the primary season developed, Hart managed to continue doing well in the primaries, actually winning seventeen primaries to Mondale's eleven; but Mondale was able to win more delegates due to his larger margins of victory in the more densely populated states such as New York, Illinois, Pennsylvania, and New Jersey (Hart won the California primary, the biggest electoral state, but by a smaller margin, as well as the Ohio primary by, again, a slim margin; and many of Hart's other primary victories did not promise a high number of delegates), and in a proportional system as employed in the Democratic primaries, the margin of victory makes all the difference. Furthermore, when the superdelegates (i.e., those delegates who are not determined or committed by primary or caucus votes) were added, Mondale had more than enough to win the nomination. The decision to create superdelegates was made in an attempt to prevent a repeat of the 1980 battle between incumbent president Carter and Ted Kennedy, which many felt had internally damaged the party and weakened their nominee's case against the Republican challenger, who did eventually win that election. Determined to avoid repeating that mistake, the Democrats relied on superdelegates to help gain the nomination for Mondale, the party leadership' preferred candidate. Now with the 1984 nomination in hand, Mondale followed the example of Jimmy Carter, interviewing numerous candidates for the vice presidential spot, which resulted in the selection of New York representative Geraldine Ferraro, the first woman to receive the nomination from a major party for the vice presidency, and the third Roman Catholic to be so nominated (following William Miller in 1964 and Edmund Muskie in 1968). To many, Ferraro, a personable, appealing, and enthusiastic figure, provided a possible counterforce to President Reagan's popularity and personal magnetism, and she proved to be an effective campaigner, often drawing more enthusiastic crowds on the campaign trail than Mondale himself.

The Democratic platform attacked the performance of the Reagan administration on a number of fronts. The platform blamed the growing deficit on the large Reagan tax cuts and massive increases in defense spending. To deal with the growing deficit, the platform proposed moderate reductions in defense spending and reform of the tax system to place a heavier burden on the wealthy and reduce the burden on the poor and middle class. The platform also called for the ratification of the Equal Rights Amendment, opposition to the balanced budget amendment proposed by the Republicans, and significant new investments in serving children, education, infrastructure, cities, housing, and transportation. The platform also included a plank that reaffirmed the right of women to undergo an abortion, as established by the U.S. Supreme Court under *Roe v. Wade* in 1973. In his acceptance speech, Mondale, in an attempt at honesty in campaigning, promised the delegates present and the television viewing audience that he would raise taxes, claiming that Reagan would also raise taxes (which, in fact, he did); but Mondale emphasized that, in his honesty as the Democratic standard-bearer, he was willing to openly admit it. Whether or not this statement had any effect on the outcome of the election is unclear, but most analysts consider Mondale's admission, although well intentioned, to have been a serious mistake, particularly in a campaign against a popular incumbent.

The Reagan campaign adopted a three-part strategy against Mondale. The first part of the strategy involved highlighting the successes of the Reagan administration, particularly the nation's evident economic recovery. The second part of the strategy involved raising public doubts about the ability of Walter Mondale to deal with threats around the world, an approach that emphasized President Reagan's record of firmness with the Soviet Union. The third part of the strategy involved attacking Mondale for his proposals to raise taxes and expand liberal social programs. Mondale's affiliation with the Carter presidency also worked to Reagan's advantage, as many still considered the Carter years to have been a failed effort. By contrast, the Reagan campaign drew attention to the achievements of the Reagan administration and the way in which those achievements had provided a needed corrective to the Carter-Mondale administration. Republicans stressed that the cloud of "malaise" that shrouded the Carter years had been cleared away by the fresh optimism of the Reagan White House.

To this end, the Reagan campaign produced one of the more effective advertising campaigns in history, with a spot ad running on the theme of a new "Morning in America." Using images of Americans enjoying their affluence in the calm that comes with security, the commercials stressed that with President Reagan, the country had moved far beyond the "crisis of confidence" that had become associated with former President Carter, and by association, his vice president, Walter Mondale. Shifting from domestic tranquility and prosperity to national security, the Reagan ad campaign focused on doubts about Mondale's ability to deal with the ongoing Soviet menace, producing a lurking "bear in the woods" commercial designed to remind viewers of the dangers of ignoring, or taking too lightly, the power and ambition of Russia. In the ad, a lone bear—a Russian bear—lumbers aimlessly through a wilderness landscape as a voice-over raises questions about the bear's concealed intentions and suggests a preemptive course of preparedness: "Isn't it smart," the narrator asks, "to be as strong as the bear—if there is a bear?" President Reagan had proven his mettle against the Russian bear; by contrast, the Carter-Mondale years were marked by indecision, lack of resolve, naïveté, and the diminution of American power. The GOP message was clear: For both international prestige and domestic prosperity, the nation could not afford to turn back to the weaknesses and failures of the previous administration. Republicans pointedly described those years as the "Carter-Mondale" administration, a frequent reminder of the difference between the president and his current challenger.

If there was one weapon that the Mondale campaign could use, it was the president's age. At seventy-three, Reagan was now the oldest person to have ever served in the White House. Following the precedent that was now becoming an obligatory component of presidential campaigns, the two candidates agreed to meet in a series of debates, and Reagan's uncharacteristically lackluster performance in the first debate seemed to feed into the sense that he might be growing too old for the extreme stress of the White House. Mondale looked sharp and prepared, Reagan at times out of sorts, and at one point Reagan made a reference to being in Washington, when the debate was actually occurring live in Louisville. Reagan's political reputation had been earned throughout his career largely due to his ability to shine under the spotlight at just the right moment, to think on his feet and jovially disarm his opponents; but in this first debate against Mondale, he projected a less competent and far less magnetic image.

The age issue would not go away until Reagan himself decided that it would, and thus, in the second debate, in a moment worthy of FDR or JFK, a revived Reagan deftly turned the tables on Mondale, promising that he would "not make age an issue of this campaign. I am not going to exploit," Reagan amiably explained, "for political purposes, my opponent's youth and inexperience." Those in the audience were instantly delighted; Mondale himself was seen laughing at his podium. It was another Reagan masterstroke coming at just the right time, reminiscent of, and perhaps surpassing, his "There you go again" remark in the debate against then president Carter four years earlier. After the election, Mondale explained that this moment was, in his mind, the end of his campaign. In describing what had appeared on camera to be Mondale's amusement over President Reagan's quip, Mondale commented, "If [television] can tell the truth. . .you'll see that I was smiling. But I think if you come in close, you'll see some tears coming down because I knew he had gotten me there. That was really the end of my campaign that night, I think." Between Mondale's pledge to raise taxes and President Reagan's sterling recovery in the second debate, it was difficult for Mondale to mount a serious charge. Soldiering on, Ferraro continued to add excitement to the campaign, but in the end, the American public voted for the president, not the vice president; and on Election Day, they voted in a landslide to return Ronald Reagan to the White House.

Measured by the popular vote, President Reagan's reelection was the fifth-biggest landslide in history: Reagan won just under 54,500,000 votes to Mondale's total of just slightly under 37,600,000 votes, or in terms of percentages, 58.8 percent for Reagan, 40.6 percent for Mondale. In terms of percentage of the popular vote, only Lyndon Johnson in 1964, Franklin Roosevelt in 1936, Richard Nixon in 1972, and Warren Harding in 1920 managed a higher number. Measured by the number of votes in the Electoral College, however, the Reagan landslide was even bigger. Setting a new record for total electoral votes, Reagan won every state except Mondale's home state of Minnesota and the District of Columbia, for a total of 525 electoral votes, two more than the 523 electoral votes won by FDR in 1936, the previous record. However, FDR's percentage of the electoral vote is still slightly higher—98.5 percent to Reagan's 97.6 percent—given that Roosevelt's landslide occurred before the admission of Alaska and Hawaii and the inclusion of electoral votes from the District of Columbia; thus there were seven fewer total electoral votes in 1936 than in 1984. By any measurement, the only landslide elections in terms of the Electoral College that are comparable to Reagan's are FDR's in 1936 and Nixon's in 1972 (not counting the unanimity enjoyed by George Washington and the near unanimity given to James Monroe before the emergence of the modern party system). It was a thorough triumph and reaffirmation of the Reagan presidency.

President Reagan's second term would not be without serious difficulties. The scandal over the Iran-Contra affair, and the investigation into it, at one point seemed enough to actually bring down the Reagan presidency. But President Reagan had a gift for landing on his feet, as he had in the 1984 campaign, when through his own personal qualities, he managed to correct what might have been a serious problem after the first debate. Among Reagan's critics, he was labeled the "Teflon President," a phrase coined by Colorado congresswoman Patricia Schroeder, describing a president mysteriously evading the stigma of scandal that would have adhered to other, less personally gifted politicians. But his followers held fast to the notion that President Reagan was the most important American statesman of their time. In the end, the Reagan presidency became a defining aspect of the decade of the 1980s, much like the Eisenhower administration in the 1950s and the Roosevelt administration in the 1930s and 1940s. President Reagan, as it turned out, was also the first president since Eisenhower to serve two full terms, further illustrating his resilience as a politician, the kindness of fortune, and his enduring appeal as a symbol to the American public.

Additional Resources

Bunch, William. *Tear Down This Myth: The Right-Wing Distortion of the Reagan Legacy.* New York: Free Press, 2010.

Germond, Jack, and Jules Witcover. *Wake Us When It's Over: Presidential Politics of 1984.* New York: Macmillan, 1985.

Gillon, Stephen M. "1984." In Arthur M. Schlesinger, Fred L. Israel, and David J. Frent, eds. *Running for President: The Candidates and Their Images.* Vol. 2. New York: Simon & Schuster, 1994.

Hayward, Steven. *The Age of Reagan: The Conservative Counterrevolution, 1980–1989.* New York: Three Rivers Press, 2009.

Leuchtenburg, William. *The 1984 Election in Historical Perspective.* Waco, TX: Baylor University Press, 1986.

Noonan, Peggy. *What I Saw at the Revolution.* New York: Random House, 2003.

Pomper, Gerald. *The Election of 1984.* New York: Chatham House Publishing, 1985.

Shannon, William V. "Election of 1984." In Arthur M. Schlesinger, Fred Israel, and William P. Hansen, eds. *History of American Presidential Elections, 1789–1984.* Vol. 9. New York: Chelsea House, 1986.

Campaign of 1988

In 1984, President Ronald Reagan was reelected by a convincing landslide, but beginning in 1985 and running through 1987, a series of episodes significantly reduced public trust in the Reagan administration in particular and the Republican Party in general. High-level Reagan administration officials were implicated in what was called by the press the "Iran-Contra scandal," a convoluted scheme to sell American military parts to Iran, which only a few years earlier had, in violation of international law and the standards of common decency, held American diplomats hostage during the latter months of the Carter administration and that had referred to the United States as "the Great Satan." The military parts were exchanged for Iranian help in releasing a different set of American hostages that were at that time being held in Lebanon. The proceeds from the sale of the spare parts and weapons were then illegally diverted to a covert program underwriting the Nicaraguan contras in their insurgent campaigns against the Marxist Sandinista government. For a time, the scandal appeared on the verge of toppling the Reagan presidency—more than one member of Congress was prepared to submit articles of impeachment—and the president himself seemed to be either evading the responsibility or clueless about the events behind the scandal, the latter a possibility that for some was equally worrisome. Additionally, on October 19, 1987, the stock market lost 22.6 percent of its value, raising new fears about the viability of the nation's recent economic recovery, which had, to this point, been largely attributed to the administration's policies.

By the election of 1984, the economy had recovered and was undergoing a period of expansion; but with the stock market downturn in the autumn of 1987, all the confidence over domestic policy that had been won by the administration evaporated. An increasing number of economists argued that the exploding federal deficit threatened the nation's economic future. In addition to these developments, on October 23, 1987, the Senate refused to confirm Reagan Supreme Court appointee Robert Bork. The confirmation battle cast a harsh spotlight on the growing tensions between Republicans and Democrats over social issues such as abortion and affirmative action. During the first term of the Reagan presidency, a spirit of bipartisanship had developed between the conservative president and congressional Democrats, particularly the more moderate elements of the party. President Reagan's conservatism in many ways had not proven as ideologically fixed as his critics feared and his supporters had hoped. But with the Iran-Contra scandal and intensified disagreements over social issues, the spirit of bipartisanship fostered by Reagan and congressional leaders such as Democratic Speaker of the House Tip O'Neil had been compromised. The Bork hearings demonstrated how much that spirit had waned.

The problems of the Reagan administration buoyed Democratic hopes for the upcoming election of 1988, and in the opinion of many analysts, there existed a real opportunity for the Democrats to win back the White House. Not surprisingly, a large field of Democrats entered the race for the nomination. Shortly after the 1984 defeat of Walter Mondale, two figures were mentioned as likely front-runners for 1988: New York governor Mario Cuomo, who had enjoyed rising popularity in response to an eloquent keynote speech in the 1984 convention; and, once again, Senator Edward Kennedy, who was quick to publicly remove his name from any consideration. Cuomo also refused to run; thus, with both Cuomo and Kennedy out, the number of prospective candidates swelled. The list included former Colorado senator Gary Hart, a main contender in the 1984 campaign and considered the front-runner at the opening of the 1988 campaign season; civil rights leader Jesse Jackson, who had also drawn attention in 1984; Tennessee senator Albert Gore Jr.; Missouri representative Dick Gephardt; Illinois senator Paul Simon; former Arizona senator Bruce Babbitt; Delaware senator Joe Biden; and popular governor Michael Dukakis of Massachusetts. The press deemed this cohort "Gary Hart and the Seven Dwarfs," waggishly stressing Senator Hart's early advantage.

Hart was both a moderate and a candidate who symbolized a new direction for the Democratic Party, and his experience in the 1984 campaign, where he proved to be a serious challenge to the eventual nominee Mondale, gave him a clear edge against the rest of the field. However, allegations circulated that Hart was prone to marital infidelity, raising speculation about Hart's character. These allegations were vigorously denied by the former senator, and he even challenged the press to follow him around to see for themselves how mundane his personal life really was. Some in the media accepted the challenge and began to dog his trail; and early in May 1987, a story broke that confirmed suspicions about Hart's indiscretions, implicating him, with photographic support, in an extramarital relationship. Given that Hart had openly dared the press to find anything untoward in his private life, the revelation was too damaging for him to deflect. In a Nixonian moment in which Hart blasted the press for its behavior, he petulantly withdrew from the race. Even though Hart would eventually reenter the race later that year, he was never able to regain his earlier front-runner status. Senator Biden also suffered from allegations that one of his defining campaign stump speeches was in reality plagiarized from British Labor leader Neil Kinnock. The allegations were unfair, as Biden in most cases properly attributed Kinnock as his source; but on at least one occasion, he neglected to do so, and it was on that occasion that the media indicted him for mimicking Kinnock without proper attribution. Eventually Biden's name was cleared, but by then it was too late; his chances in 1988 had been derailed.

With Hart out of the picture, the Democratic field was more open than it had been since 1976, the year that produced the nomination and eventual election of Jimmy Carter. Gephardt took the Iowa caucus to launch the campaign season, with both Simon and Dukakis showing early strength. In New Hampshire, it was Dukakis who finished first, with Gephardt placing second; thus the two candidates emerged as early front-runners, even though the race remained competitive. To blunt Gephardt's momentum, both the Dukakis and Gore campaigns ran a series of attack ads impugning his record on labor, which had actually been among Gephardt's more important voting blocs. The attack campaign worked; labor withdrew support for Gephardt, thus depriving him of a critical element for a credible run. The Super Tuesday primaries, a new event that combined a high number of primaries in a single day, proved revealing, allowing Dukakis, who won six, and Gore and Jackson, who each won five, to pull away from the rest of the field (Gephardt managed to win just one primary on Super Tuesday).

For a time, the battle was between Dukakis, Gore, and Jackson; and at one point, after having scored an impressive victory in the Michigan primary, Jackson appeared to pull ahead as the front-runner, a historic moment, as no African American had ever been a strong candidate for president this late in the process. But Dukakis responded with a solid win in Wisconsin and then pulled ahead of Jackson by taking the critical primaries of New York and Pennsylvania. Hence, moving toward the convention, Dukakis had won 42.5 percent of the primary vote to Jackson's 29 percent, with Gore showing around 13 percent for third. Dukakis had managed to surge ahead at the right moment, and thus he carried the party's nomination with ease. In an effort to duplicate the successful North-South strategy of previous campaigns, Texas senator Lloyd Bentsen, who himself had been a brief candidate for the presidential nomination four years earlier, was selected as Dukakis's running mate, the Massachusetts-Texas combination reminiscent of the 1960 ticket consisting of John Kennedy and Lyndon Johnson. But as the campaign developed, it was clear that, at least in the case of Dukakis, the ticket was far removed from that potent combination.

The Democratic platform pledged to support national health insurance regardless of income or employment status. The platform also supported a ban on "cop killer" bullets, renewed the call for the ratification of the Equal Rights Amendment, and reasserted "that the fundamental right of reproductive choice should be guaranteed regardless of ability to pay." Additionally, the platform promised vigorous enforcement of environmental laws. In response to public outcry, the platform called for the classification of South Africa as a terrorist state for its refusal to dismantle apartheid.

Having served as Ronald Reagan's vice president for eight years, George H. W. Bush was the clear favorite to win the Republican nomination. However, a significant number of conservative Republicans continued to have doubts about Bush's ideological commitment. Throughout his political career, Bush had earned a reputation as a moderate, and during the campaign season of 1980, he ran against President Reagan as the centrist alternative. Hence, even though he was the incumbent vice president, Bush was not without competitors for the nomination. Seeking to capitalize on the growing influence of evangelical conservatives within the Republican Party, prominent televangelist Pat Robertson sought to challenge Bush for the Republican nomination. Also joining the contest was Senate minority leader Bob Dole, who had run for the vice presidency on the 1976 ticket with then president Ford, and who hoped to draw from both conservatives who could not accept Bush and moderates who were concerned over Robertson. The field was rounded out by New York representative Jack Kemp and Delaware governor Pierre "Pete" DuPont.

To the surprise of many political experts, Dole convincingly won the February 8 Iowa caucus, with Robinson placing a strong second, while the vice president lagged behind, a distant third. The strength of Dole and Robertson prompted a more aggressive approach from the Bush campaign, which turned to a series of attack ads to halt Dole's momentum. The strategy worked, and coming from behind in the polls, Bush regained his front-runner status by winning soundly in New Hampshire, carrying 38 percent of the vote to Dole's 29 percent, Robertson fading to just 9 percent and fifth place. In the next seven primaries, Bush won four, with Dole taking three, the rest of the field no longer contending. On the March 8 Super Tuesday primaries, Bush locked up the nomination—stunning the Dole campaign—by winning all sixteen state contests, losing only in the District of Columbia, in a near sweep of unprecedented proportions. In every primary that followed, Bush was virtually uncontested, winning most primaries by taking over 70 percent of the vote, in many cases much higher. The nomination was well in hand when he addressed the GOP convention in an acceptance speech that expressed a desire for a "kinder, gentler nation," celebrated a "thousand points of light" illuminating the hope of America, and delivering a stern message to Congress about tax policy in which he coined the famous phrase, "Read my lips: no new taxes." In an effort to appeal to the new generation of Republicans, the Bush campaign selected Indiana senator Dan Quayle—a surprise move, given his youth and lack of national exposure.

As expected, the Republican Party platform praised the foreign policy and domestic achievements of the Reagan administration and sought to remind voters of the situation the country had found itself in during the Carter-Mondale administration. The text of the platform observed, "We are in the midst of the longest peacetime expansion in our country's history. Where once we measured new businesses in the thousands, we now count millions. These small businesses have helped create more than seventeen million well-paying, high-quality new jobs, more than twice the number of jobs that were created during that time in Japan, Canada, and Western Europe combined! Small business has accounted for 80 percent of the jobs created during the recovery." Additionally, the platform restated Vice President Bush's pledge to oppose increased federal taxes: "The Republican Party restates the unequivocal promise we made in 1984: We oppose any attempts to increase taxes. Tax increases harm the economic expansion and reverse the trend restoring control of the economy to individual Americans." Following precedent, the platform reaffirmed the Republican position on the issue of federally funded abortion, stating that "the unborn child has a fundamental individual right to life which cannot be infringed." The platform then reaffirmed continued Republican support "for a human life amendment to the Constitution," stating further, "We endorse legislation to make clear that the Fourteenth Amendment's protections apply to unborn children." The platform also supported the reestablishment of the federal death penalty and expressed strong opposition to "furloughs for those criminals convicted of first-degree murder and others who are serving a life sentence without possibility of parole," a plank that deliberately stressed their opposition to programs such as those previously supported by Governor Dukakis.

After the Democratic convention, presidential preference polls showed Dukakis with a double-digit lead over Vice President Bush. The Dukakis-Benson ticket seemed well positioned to return a Democrat to the White House, and many pundits believed the American people were ready for a change, even though President Reagan remained surprisingly popular in spite of the Iran-Contra affair, an episode that for the most part did not affect Vice President Bush, as by his own public admission, he could honestly claim that he was well "out of the loop." But the Democrats enjoyed the early lead in the polls, so a Dukakis presidency seemed at this point a strong possibility. To reverse this situation, the Bush campaign hired long-time Republican media consultant Roger Ailes to craft a hard-hitting, "take no prisoners" negative campaign designed to define Dukakis as a "tax-and-spend liberal" who was also soft on crime, a weak candidate with no experience in foreign affairs or any appreciation for the responsibilities of commanding the world's most powerful military, and, to make matters worse, a former governor tainted by a poor record regarding environmental protection.

The result of this decision was one of the dirtiest campaign efforts in recent memory. Most campaigns at some point resort to a degree of mudslinging, character assassination, and embarrassing innuendo; but for the most part, the presidential campaigns in the twentieth century were quite tame when compared to those conducted in the nineteenth century. There are exceptions, of course—1928 Democratic candidate Al Smith was smeared by the Hoover campaign (not only was he criticized for his religious views, but he was depicted as a lush), but not by Hoover himself; Lyndon Johnson's campaign against Barry Goldwater employed tactics that were unabashedly designed to depict Goldwater as an unstable warmonger supported by racists; "dirty tricks" were employed without compunction by the Nixon campaign; and Ronald Reagan was often unfairly drawn by his critics as shallow, even unintelligent. But the level of mudslinging reached by the 1988 Bush campaign matched or exceeded nearly every twentieth-century precedent. In a particularly aggressive manner somewhat reminiscent of Johnson's 1964 attack-ad blitz against Goldwater, the Bush campaign tore into the Dukakis record as Massachusetts governor.

Three attack ads in particular are of note: the "Revolving Door" ad that was used to depict Governor Dukakis as soft on crime; the "Boston Harbor" ad that impugned the governor's environmental record, which was supposedly a strength of the Democratic candidate; and the "Tank and Rider" ad that used embarrassing visual imagery to caricature Dukakis in a particularly foolish manner. In its "Revolving Door" ad, the Bush campaign implied that the rape of a Maryland woman was in fact the consequence of a Massachusetts prison-furlough program approved by Dukakis during his term as governor, as the rapist also happened to be a furloughed prisoner enjoying the benefits of the Massachusetts program. It was a particularly nasty charge, made all the worse by a similar ad, sponsored independently of the Bush campaign, that was broadcast just prior to the airing of the "Revolving Door" ad. This independent ad used the same scare tactics as in the "Revolving Door" spot, this time identifying by name a Massachusetts prisoner, Willie Horton, who committed an act of rape while on furlough. The Willie Horton ad displayed a typically menacing mug shot of Horton, an African American convict, as a prelude to a report of the incident that boldly indicted the Dukakis administration as largely to blame for Horton's crime. Given the way the images were used in the ad, many critics charged the Bush campaign with open racism. Bush loyalists focused not on the racial elements of the ad, but rather on the wrong-headed policy, associated with Governor Dukakis, of coddling criminals to the point that they were even capable of committing crimes while still technically prisoners of the commonwealth. Either way, the Willie Horton image raised tension over racial questions on a level not seen since the 1960s.

In the "Harbor" attack ad, the producers employed visual imagery to effectively indict Governor Dukakis for allegedly having done absolutely nothing to clean up the heavily polluted Boston Harbor. As the ad bitingly concludes, a narrator observes that "Michael Dukakis promises to do for America what he's done for Massachusetts." Finally, the Bush campaign's "Tank" ad mocked an incident, caught on film, in which Dukakis, at a campaign event designed to showcase him as tough on defense, rode atop an army tank sporting a tank commander's helmet that appeared, at least on film, as so oversized that he resembled more the child "playing army" than a serious presidential candidate. The visual image was merciless, and the message was clear—Dukakis was but a poser and not the man to lead the world's most powerful military. In yet another example of aggressive negative ads employed by the Bush campaign, Governor Dukakis was pounded for vetoing a bill requiring all Massachusetts public school students to recite the Pledge of Allegiance. Finally, Bush campaign operative Lee Atwater allegedly engaged in "dirty tricks" tactics that floated embarrassing rumors about both Governor Dukakis and his wife, Kitty; the latter was rumored to have at one time burned an American flag at an antiwar protest, while scandalmongering about the former involved rumors that the governor had at one time been treated for mental illness.

The Dukakis campaign was unprepared for the public response to the Bush attack ads. Assuming that the American people would not be swayed merely by the ads, the Dukakis camp waited, in the assessment of some analysts, far too long to respond and did not do what was necessary to discredit the charges coming from the Bush handlers. The issues and themes that the Dukakis campaign had hoped would work simply did not. The American people turned out not to be particularly concerned with the Iran-Contra scandal. And the American people did not blame the Republican Party or the Reagan-Bush administration for the increasing federal deficit. Equally important, the Dukakis campaign devoted considerable resources to attempting to make Republican vice presidential nominee Dan Quayle a major campaign issue. Even though public opinion polls indicated that the American people had doubts about the ability of Quayle to assume the duties of the presidency, few voters indicated that having Quayle on the ticket would cause them to change their vote, further verifying the maxim that Americans do not vote according to who is running for vice president. Finally, slogans from the Dukakis campaign such as "The Best America Is Yet to Come," "Good Jobs at Good Pay in the Old USA," and "the Next Frontier" (an attempt to connect Dukakis with the "New Frontier" of another famous politician from Massachusetts, President Kennedy) simply did not have any impact on key swing voters.

Dukakis did not help his own case. In the now-obligatory presidential debates, Dukakis seemed wooden, blasé, disconnected, and mechanical. Vice President Bush was by no means a great debater—his fractured, idiosyncratic way of speaking was gleefully parodied by comedians, and to great effect by *Saturday Night Live*'s Dana Carvey—hence neither candidate appeared able to execute a signature debating moment as Ronald Reagan had in both the 1980 and 1984 campaigns. If Dukakis came off disinterested or perhaps even a little smug to some observers, Bush appeared superficial, dropping maddeningly shallow phrases such as "vision thing" and going through the motions as if he were merely entitled to be the president, an impression that does not fairly reflect George Bush's sincerity and lifelong dedication to public service (reaching back to his heroism in the Pacific theater in World War II) any more than did similarly unfair impressions formed of Dukakis reflect his genuine commitment to the public trust. But in the small-screen age of television, image has become crucial, and to some, Machiavelli's principle that in politics one must be concerned more about appearance than the reality behind it has won the day in the practical nuts-and-bolts of media-driven elections. Both candidates brought a long record of public service, but both had to overcome serious image problems, whether unfair or not.

These image problems were distorted and amplified in the glare of live television during the debates. In the first debate, both candidates performed satisfactorily, which to the press meant the avoidance of any noticeable slips or gaffes, with Dukakis enjoying perhaps a slight advantage in the analysis. But in the second debate, Dukakis's inner robot emerged and left viewers and pundits alike cold by his exasperatingly detached response to an emotionally, and quite frankly unconscionably, charged question. When loutishly asked by a panelist whether or not he would reconsider his position against the death penalty if his wife had been raped, an unaffected Dukakis responded by impassively emitting statistics as the best evidence against the death penalty. To many voters, it was a revealing and unsettling moment, and it was enough to cause most to come away with the impression that the vice president won the debate, due not to any persuasion on behalf of his policies or to his own conduct during the event, but entirely because of Dukakis's perceived limitations. Had he rightly taken umbrage to the question or at the very least responded with more passion, the viewers likely would have identified with him (by way of contrast, a roused Ronald Reagan was a key moment in his 1980 run for the nomination), but his bland and emotionless demeanor in response to the very thought fell flat.

During the vice presidential debates, also now an obligatory feature since 1976 (Mondale versus Dole), the Democratic candidate Lloyd Bentsen scored the biggest television coup in the entire campaign. At one point in the debate, Senator Quayle, who had been attacked by the Dukakis camp as too green to stand but a heartbeat away from the presidency, noted that his experience in Congress was comparable to then senator John Kennedy's during his successful run for president twenty-eight earlier. Senator Bentsen, a respected senior member of Congress's upper chamber, did not hesitate to pounce: "Senator," Bentsen retorted, "I served with Jack Kennedy. I knew Jack Kennedy. Jack Kennedy was a friend of mine. Senator, you're no Jack Kennedy." Senator Quayle was caught flat-footed and out of position; trying to muster a response, he replied that what Senator Bentsen had said was "really uncalled for," at which Bentsen, now more aroused and forceful than ever, moved in for the killing blow: "You are the one that was making the comparison, Senator," Bentsen lectured, "and I'm one who knew him well. And frankly I think you are so far apart in the objectives you choose for your country that I did not think the comparison was well-taken."

Had this exchange occurred between the presidential candidates, it would easily have been the defining moment of the campaign, no doubt a pivotal one to the benefit of one candidate and the detriment of the other; but this was the debate between vice presidential candidates, and while it did receive a high volume of attention in the media and in late-night comedy monologues, it barely had any effect in the polls. Again, no one really chooses a ticket based on the running mate; Americans always get behind the top man. And the top man, Vice President Bush, was scarcely moved by the errors and stumbles of his running mate. To be fair, Senator Quayle was not as seasoned at campaigning as the other candidates, and the press certainly did not hesitate to stress this fact. But in the end, it was really a contest between Bush and Dukakis: it was Dukakis's persona, not Quayle's, that the voters found lacking; and it was Bush's experience, not Bentsen's own fine record, that the voters relied on.

When Election Day came, George Herbert Walker Bush became only the fourth sitting vice president to be elected directly to the presidency, the last being Martin Van Buren, who, as the incumbent vice president under President Jackson, was elected in 1836. John Adams and Thomas Jefferson were the other two; in the pre-Twelfth Amendment era, Jefferson ran for election and won against the president under whom he served. (Former vice presidents who eventually became presidents—Theodore Roosevelt, Calvin Coolidge, Harry Truman, Lyndon Johnson, and Richard Nixon—were indeed all eventually elected to the presidency for another term, but not while they were incumbent vice presidents—all other vice presidents who ascended directly to the presidency owing to the death or resignation of their president were not returned to office.)

George Bush's election, though not a landslide when compared to some, was nonetheless substantial, with Bush winning just under 48,900,000 votes to Dukakis's approximately 41,800,000, or 53 percent to 46 percent, with Libertarian candidate Ron Paul winning slightly over 400,000 votes, which was less than half a percent. Bush's 53 percent of the vote, while far below the figure of nearly 59 percent enjoyed by the Reagan-Bush ticket of 1984, was still impressive, and it exceeds every other winning candidate between 1988 and the present. As usual, the margin of victory in the popular vote was even more impressive in the electoral vote: Bush carried 40 states for 426 votes (79%) in the Electoral College, with Dukakis winning 10 states and the District of Columbia for a total of 111 electoral votes (21%). Bush swept the South, further solidifying the GOP's strength in that region, and took every western state except Oregon and Washington. In addition to the Northwest, Dukakis won in New York; the upper midwestern states of Minnesota, Wisconsin, and Iowa; Hawaii; West Virginia; Rhode Island; his home state of Massachusetts (recaptured from the GOP after the Democrats atypically lost it to Reagan in 1984); and the District of Columbia. With the exception of New York's 36 electoral votes and Massachusetts's 13, both claimed by Dukakis, Bush took 9 of the 11 biggest Electoral College prizes: California (47), Texas (29), Pennsylvania (25), Illinois (24), Ohio (23), Florida (21), Michigan (20), New Jersey (16), and North Carolina (13).

Given Vice President Bush's perceived vulnerability as the campaign season began, it was a crushing disappointment for the Democrats and a significant triumph for the Republicans, who were intent on building on the legacy of Ronald Reagan. With the sequential elections of Reagan (twice) and now Bush, it was the first time since Roosevelt-Truman (1932–1948) that either party had won more than two consecutive general elections, a pattern not uncommon in the history of presidential elections, having occurred five times before Reagan-Bush; but that had, since President Truman's 1948 election, become difficult to repeat, given recent events and developments. The Republicans, who had dominated the presidency from Abraham Lincoln through William Howard Taft (with only one Democrat serving in the White House during that time span), appeared to have restored their advantage, at least in the executive branch of the government, leaving the Democrats searching for a new champion to challenge the GOP in the next round. On the day after Election Day, 1988, not many prospects came to mind as President-elect Bush enjoyed the zenith of his long career in public service. But before the next Election Day, all of that would soon change for the Democrats.

Additional Resources

Blumenthal, Sidney. *Pledging Allegiance: The Last Campaign of the Cold War.* New York: HarperCollins, 1994.

Boller, Paul F., Jr. *Presidential Campaigns: From George Washington to George W. Bush.* Oxford: Oxford University Press, 2004.

Cohen, Marty, David Karol, Hans Noel, and John Zaller . *The Party Decides.* Chicago: University of Chicago Press, 2008.

Germond, Jack. *Whose Broad Stripes and Bright Stars? The Trivial Pursuit of the Presidency, 1988.* New York: Warner Books, 1989.

Runkel, David R. *Campaign for President: The Managers Look at '88.* Westport, CT: Auburn House, 1989.

Squier, Robert. "1988." In Arthur M. Schlesinger, Fred L. Israel, and David J. Frent, eds. *Running for President: The Candidates and Their Images.* Vol. 2. New York: Simon & Schuster, 1994.

Campaign of 1992

In late February 1991, in the wake of the successful completion of the First Persian Gulf War, in which the United States, leading a coalition of allies, liberated the country of Kuwait by repelling the invading forces of Iraq, then under the control of dictator Saddam Hussein, President George Bush's approval ratings as measured in the polls soared to a fraction under 90 percent, the highest that had ever been observed since pollsters began measuring approval ratings during the second term of Franklin Roosevelt's administration (the previous record, 87%, was enjoyed by President Truman after his swearing in as president upon the death of FDR and during the final months of World War II; FDR's highest measured approval rating was 84%, which at that time had only been exceeded, briefly, by Truman). Bush's ratings remained above 70 percent through the remainder of the spring and into summer, and even as late as July and August of that year, the president enjoyed approval ratings oscillating between 70 and 75 percent, and they remained above 60 percent well into October.

With the 1992 campaign season around the corner, no Democrat considered a run against the president to be anything other than a quixotic enterprise. Under this measurement, Bush seemed invulnerable, and in comparison to other popular presidents who enjoyed similar numbers measured within the same time frame (i.e., the October before election year), his approval ratings matched Eisenhower's and Reagan's, slightly exceeded Kennedy's, and had only been surpassed by Lyndon Johnson, who went on to win in a landslide. All other presidents measured at this time fell far below these figures; thus Bush was in good company and in a solid position. His prosecution of the First Persian Gulf War was widely praised at home and abroad, and a second Bush term seemed guaranteed. But the opinion and approval of the American voters is decidedly fickle, particularly in the age of mass media and the endless news cycle; and within just two months, in mid-December as the year was drawing to a close, his ratings rapidly fell to 50 percent, a full twelve-point drop from October and almost forty points when compared to his highest level ten months earlier; and by the opening of the following year—election year—his numbers dipped below 50 percent, never to recover, reaching a low of 29 percent that August in what can only be described as a genuine reversal of fortune. Bush, who seemed invincible throughout 1991, now appeared doomed.

"It's the economy, stupid," Arkansas governor and 1992 Democratic nominee for president William Jefferson Clinton quipped while instructing the media on what matters most in presidential campaigns, a pithy and insightful comment on the causes of the electorate's historical pattern of fickleness and impatience. Bush's record abroad, while initially inspiring to most, could not deflect damage that had occurred to his presidency owing to a soured economic situation. With the fall of the Soviet Union and the Eastern bloc, Bush's strength—foreign policy—seemed less vital when compared to the economic downturn. Clinton's Reaganesque line defined the decline and fall of the Bush presidency as well as encapsulating, in one moment, the native brilliance of this new star within the Democratic Party. Given Bush's strong position in 1991, many of the party's heavy-hitters, such as New York governor Mario Cuomo, displayed no interest in running. None of the party's more prominent leaders were looking to lead a futile campaign against such a strong incumbent, at least a strength that the polls were indicating in the year prior to election season. Clinton, who had been the youngest person to serve as governor in the state of Arkansas, had been noticed for some time now as a potential national figure and possible future candidate for president, but he almost squandered his growing reputation with a garrulous, meandering nominating speech at the Democratic National Convention in 1988.

Nonetheless, Clinton, known to some as the "Comeback Kid" for his reputation of resilience (a nickname that some associate with his uncanny ability to shake off personal indiscretions and land catlike on his nimble political feet), joined a crowded field that included former California governor Jerry Brown, who had briefly made noise in 1976; former Massachusetts senator Paul Tsongas;

Iowa senator Tom Harkin, Nebraska senator Bob Kerrey, Virginia governor Doug Wilder, Pennsylvania governor Robert Casey, Colorado representative Patricia Schroeder (briefly and never officially), and former Minnesota senator Eugene McCarthy, who had famously challenged President Lyndon Johnson in 1968 and was credited as having been a crucial player in ending LBJ's presidency.

Clinton's early campaign received the kind of blow that causes less resilient candidates to fold. After the Iowa caucus, which Harkin easily won, as it was his home state, a scandal surrounding Clinton's marriage surfaced involving allegations of infidelity reminiscent of those circulated against Colorado senator Gary Hart in 1988. In Hart's case, his campaign was mortally wounded by the allegations and the manner in which Hart had responded to them. Clinton and his wife, Hillary Rodham Clinton, who was herself a savvy campaigner, closed ranks and charged full ahead into the allegation, appearing on a broadcast of the television news show *60 Minutes* to candidly share their personal life and, in the process, completely defuse the situation. It was an intelligent decision masterfully executed. In the following New Hampshire primary, Clinton, who before the broadcast appeared to have been in trouble, finished second to Tsongas, who was the favorite going into the primary, given his familiarity to the voters there (Tsongas being from a neighboring state). Clinton's second-place finish, while nine points behind Tsongas, was double that of the third-place candidate, Kerrey; thus it was evident that his campaign had shaken off the scandal and was back on track.

On Super Tuesday, Clinton made huge gains, sweeping the southern states and winning heavy support elsewhere; Tsongas's campaign was seriously weakened, never to recover. For a time, Governor Brown surged forward, as he had against Governor Carter in 1976, to challenge Clinton with wins in Colorado, Connecticut, and Vermont, briefly gaining the momentum; but again the Clinton campaign recovered (even winning in Brown's home state of California); thus as the convention commenced in New York City, Clinton held all the cards, eclipsing what by then was Brown's meager support. Clinton locked up the nomination, and his choice for the vice presidency, Tennessee senator Albert Gore Jr., was accepted by acclamation. At one point, Gore was considered by many to be, along with Cuomo, one of the likely nominees against Bush; but an accident involving his son caused him to take a hiatus from politics as the campaign season opened. Clinton, identifying himself as a "New Democrat" (in language reminiscent of Hart) and promising a "third way" between the left and the right, moved energetically toward the confrontation with the president.

In an effort to appeal to a larger cross-section of the American people, the Democratic platform followed Clinton's lead and took moderate positions on a number of issues, careful not to propose expensive new government programs. Significantly, the platform identified reducing the national debt as a leading priority. To accomplish this, the platform proposed to put "everything on the table; eliminate nonproductive programs; achieve defense savings; reform entitlement programs to control soaring health care costs; cut federal administrative costs by 3 percent annually for four years; limit increases in the 'present budget' to the rate of growth in the average American's paycheck; apply a strict 'pay as you go' rule to new non-investment spending; and make the rich pay their fair share in taxes." Additionally, the platform proposed to make health care available to all Americans regardless of "pre-existing conditions" by putting "tough controls on health costs." The platform also reaffirmed the Democratic Party's position on the right to choose an abortion, and it supported background checks for those wishing to purchase firearms and a prohibition on the sale of assault weapons.

Following the convention, the Clinton-Gore team would stump hard, touring the country as a duo in a campaign bus and advertising their youthful enthusiasm and their innovative, pragmatic approach to governing. They were intent on abandoning the politics of the past and the old, failed methods of government that had become entrenched in Washington, and they promised a presidency that would build a "bridge to the twenty-first century." In contrast to most presidential candidates in the latter half of the twentieth century, Clinton was the first Democratic presidential candidate since Franklin Roosevelt who had not served in the military. Gore served in Vietnam, but Clinton, who had been criticized by his opponents for his refusal to join the military during the Vietnam War, had no military record, and thus he was the first presidential candidate from a major party since Thomas Dewey, President Truman's 1948 Republican challenger, not to have served in the armed forces (Dewey was sixteen at the end of World War I). With Fleetwood Mac's "Don't Stop Thinking about Tomorrow" adopted as the campaign theme, the Clinton-Gore collaboration was clearly emblematic of a new generation. Clinton saw a connection between himself and President Kennedy, whom he at one point met as a young man, and even Clinton's mannerisms at times seemed to emulate JFK. Clinton, while not as charismatic and sophisticated as Kennedy or that other magnetic personality of the post-World War II era, Ronald Reagan, was nonetheless at ease with people, quite capable of speaking to any kind of audience in a welcoming manner, exuding the kind of personal warmth and affability that gave both Kennedy and Reagan, as well as FDR before them, such broad appeal. In a word, Clinton was a natural politician—genial, quick on his feet, confident, good-natured, comfortable in his skin, and at his best before crowds. These qualities, combined with a quick intellect and hidden toughness, made Clinton the dominant politician of his times, and along with Reagan the most accomplished campaigner since Kennedy.

As Clinton's image deflected scandal and innuendo over infidelity and allegations of draft evasion to ascend in the polls, President Bush's popularity continued to decline rapidly. In addition to an economic downturn, which Bush was slow to take seriously, he had incurred the wrath of the Republican right, beginning with what the conservatives took to be an act of betrayal: the decision to support tax increases against his own 1988 pledge to fight against "new taxes," pronounced with pugnacity through the famous "Read my lips" line coined in his acceptance speech. Conservatives by and large had never really adopted Bush; he was seen as too moderate, even liberal to some, and with the reneging of his promise not to impose new taxes, the conservatives bolted, provoking controversial pundit and former aide to the Nixon White House Pat Buchanan, a leading conservative figure since the 1970s, to declare his candidacy as a challenge to the president. In the New Hampshire primary, the president won 53 percent, but Buchanan took just under 38 percent, a high number against an incumbent, and to some, reminiscent of the damage done to Lyndon Johnson by Eugene McCarthy in 1968 (although the margin of victory was not nearly as narrow as it had been in 1968). The Buchanan campaign was stoked to move forward, stirred by images of storming the castle in a spasm of "pitchfork" populism that exposed Bush's vulnerability. The president eventually went on to defeat Buchanan (as well as Ku Klux Klansman David Duke, whose provocative but idiosyncratic challenge to both Bush and Buchanan received much press but scarcely any votes) in the primaries, and to take the nomination. But the damage was inflicted and the soft spots revealed, and Bush found himself having to walk on eggshells when dealing with the conservative wing.

At the convention, Buchanan stole the show with his clarion call announcing a "culture war," with Clinton and the Democrats on the wrong side of the line. Moderates in the party were put off by Buchanan's jeremiad, but the party's far right wing was once again energized. Even though their candidate could not dislodge Bush, the conservatives felt the strength needed to influence the party's platform and agenda. Specifically, the conservative wing managed to win the inclusion of a number of socially conservative planks that could potentially alienate moderate Republicans as well as many centrist independents. Following Buchanan's lead, the platform scolded the Democrats and the "liberal left." "Our opponents," the platform read, had "declared that the dogmas of the Left were the final and victorious faith. From kremlins and ivory towers, their planners proclaimed the bureaucratic millennium. But in a tragic century of illusion, Five Year Plans and Great Leaps Forward failed to summon a Brave New World. One hundred and fifty years of slogans and manifestos came crashing down in an ironic cascade of unintended consequences. All that is left are the ruins of a failed scoundrel ideology."

The platform further accused the Democratic Party of waging war against traditional cultural values. "Elements within the media, the entertainment industry, academia, and the Democrat Party are waging a guerrilla war against American values," the platform maintained; "they deny personal responsibility, disparage traditional morality, denigrate religion, and promote hostility toward the family's way of life." The platform also opposed "any legislation or law which legally recognizes same-sex marriages and allows such couples to adopt children or provide foster care." Among many other things associated with conservative policy, the platform reaffirmed Republican support for a constitutional amendment to protect human life and "legislation to make clear that the Fourteenth Amendment's protections apply to unborn children."

Another wrinkle was added to the campaign with the addition of a particularly strong third-party challenge. During the late spring of 1992, Texas billionaire H. Ross Perot announced his intention to conduct an independent bid for the presidency. Perot argued that neither the Republican Party nor the Democratic Party had any intention of dealing seriously and maturely with the growing debt and deficit spending. Perot also argued that both the major parties supported free-trade agreements that led to millions of well-paying American jobs shifting permanently abroad, specifically to Mexico and Asia. Even though Perot had little confidence that Bill Clinton would deal with the growing federal deficit or oppose free-trade agreements, Perot reserved his strongest criticism for President Bush. Perot's blunt, plain-spoken, businessman's style and persona appealed to a number of centrist, non-ideological Americans disaffected by the more conservative tone of the GOP and disappointed in Bush's leadership in failing to steer the party away from the right, as well as to those Americans who either did not trust Clinton's character (in the wake of the infidelity and draft evasion scandals) or were not persuaded by the ostensibly new Democratic Party that they represented. Perot, armed with graphs, charts, and the data behind them, promised to "open the hood, look inside, and fix the problem" of an ailing economy and uncontained national debt. The appeal of Perot excited many: In June, the polls surprisingly showed Perot in the lead, polling 39 percent of participants to Bush's 31 percent and Clinton's 25 percent.

However, the Perot campaign was troubled by internal dissent, sparked primarily by Perot's disagreement with his leading advisers. Perot also expressed concern that a three-way race might cause the election to be thrown into the House of Representatives (as it had in 1800 and 1824), a possibility that he considered damaging to the democratic process. His numbers did begin to show signs of slipping downward, plunging to 25 percent only a few short weeks after his peak. Thus, to the disappointment of his followers, Perot announced on television his withdrawal from the race. Perot would also later claim that his withdrawal was out of fear over dirty tricks that were being used by the Bush campaign to invade his family's privacy with the intent of sullying his family's reputation. But in early October, Perot reentered the campaign, just in time to participate in the presidential debates against Bush and Clinton. Perot's campaign, which had gathered significant support just a few months earlier, had been irreparably damaged by his withdrawal; nonetheless, with his hat back in the ring, the election once again had a new shape.

For the first time, the now-standard presidential debates included a third candidate, in this case Perot. Four debates were held and, again for the first time, different formats were used—e.g., one debate was held as a town hall event rather than in the standard lectern-centered format. In the first debate, Perot's humor and blunt manner seemed a refreshing contrast to both of the major-party candidates. Clinton, who was capable of charming audiences, was unexpectedly reserved and low-key throughout much of the debate, but he was roused to defend himself when the president criticized him for his youthful participation in antiwar protests. Exhibiting strong disapproval of Clinton's choices, the president asked how he could have protested against his own county and in a foreign land (Clinton was a Rhodes Scholar at Oxford at the time of his antiwar activism) "when young men were held prisoner in Hanoi or kids out of the ghetto were drafted." Bush, needing to score a winning blow to help bolster his sagging poll numbers, angled for the killing blow: "It's not a question of patriotism," the president instructed the viewers, "it's a question of character and judgment."

Clinton, who had been fairly unemotional the entire evening, became agitated and turned toward President Bush to respond with strength. "When Joe McCarthy went around this country attacking people's patriotism, he was wrong," Clinton noted, effectively going on to further explain that, against McCarthy's tactics, "a Senator from Connecticut stood up to him, named Prescott Bush. Your father was right to stand up to Joe McCarthy. You were wrong to attack my patriotism. I was opposed to the war but I love my country." Even though post-debate polls showed that the highest number of viewers—47 percent—felt Perot had won the day, Clinton's swift and emotionally charged rebuttal of the president, made all the more effective owing to the well-targeted reference to the president's own father, was the key moment; 30 percent of those polled felt that Clinton had won the debate, while Bush managed only 16 percent. To many observers, the debate proved that Clinton would not defer to the president, who was a war hero, on issues of character and patriotism, and thus it was a pivotal moment in his campaign.

Things got worse for the president. In the second debate, held in the style of a town hall forum, Bush seemed disinterested, distracted, even bored. At one point, he was caught on camera checking his watch; at another point, he appeared not to be paying close attention to the questions. While neither Clinton nor Perot was necessarily impressive that night, Bush's apparent disinterest was hard to miss and incessantly commented upon in the post-debate chatter. This helped Clinton more than Perot: Post-debate polls indicated that well over half of the viewers saw Clinton as the winner, just 16 percent believed Perot to have won, and only 15 percent felt that Bush had performed the better of the three. Bush fared better after the third debate, with viewers concluding the two major-party candidates to be about even, but Perot was again elevated by a 38 percent plurality as the winner (the rest of the viewers split between Bush and Clinton).

Throughout the campaign, Clinton ran as a centrist, critical of both the right and the left. His promotion of his ideas as representing a new kind of Democrat was compelling to a large population of voters weary of the old political language framed by tired dichotomies of the "left" and the "right." Furthermore, the Clinton campaign was far more effective in deflecting attacks on his character and competency than the Dukakis campaign four years earlier. Then, the Bush campaign successfully depicted Dukakis as "too liberal," too "soft on crime," and lacking the fortitude needed for the Oval Office. Bush's campaign operatives were even more aggressive against Clinton, for given Clinton's personal past, they had far more ammunition than they had against Dukakis. But the difference this time around was found in the Clinton "war room" strategy, on guard twenty-four hours a day for immediate counterattack. Bush's other main strength, his foreign policy experience and achievements, was underplayed in the press to Clinton's advantage, and the theme "It's the Economy, Stupid," as well as a combination of Kennedyesque youth and vigor and Reaganesque affability, provided the Clinton-Gore challenge with substantial force.

On Election Day, Governor Clinton won a plurality of the popular vote, winning just under 45,000,000 votes, or 43 percent of the voting electorate, with President Bush taking just over 39,100,000 popular votes (about 37%), and Perot showing just over 19,700,000 (or slightly under 19%). Historically, Perot's 19 percent of the popular vote is the third-highest percentage of the total vote to go to a third-party candidate, exceeded only by Theodore Roosevelt (27% in 1912) and Millard Fillmore (22% in 1856), who were both former presidents at the time they ran on a third ticket, and surpassing Senator La Follette's 16 percent in 1924. However, unlike Teddy Roosevelt, Millard Fillmore, LaFollette, or, for that matter, George Wallace (1968), Strom Thurmond (1948), and James Weaver (1892), Perot's impressive third-party run did not produce any votes in the Electoral College, as Perot, while finishing strong in some states, did not manage to win even one. There, in the Electoral College, Clinton's plurality was converted to a solid majority, winning 370 electoral votes (or 69%) to the president's 168 (31%). In the popular vote, President Bush's percentage was the second worst received by an incumbent; President Taft (who also lost in a three-way race) finished lower with 23 percent. If we count John Quincy Adams's election in which he won the White House in 1824 with just 31 percent of the popular votes cast, President-elect Clinton's popular vote was the fourth lowest in history for a winning candidate; along with the younger Adams, only Abraham Lincoln's 39 percent in 1860 and Woodrow Wilson's 41 percent were lower (Richard Nixon's 1968 plurality of 43.4% was a fraction higher than Clinton's in 1992).

But Clinton's victory in the Electoral College was certainly more convincing. Dominating the Northeast and the Midwest, he also showed strength in every other region of the country, including the Deep South—where Bush still carried more states, but Clinton managed to cut into what had since the 1960s become an important region for the GOP—and the Intermountain West, where the GOP had also recently been dominant. Clinton won the two biggest states—California, now, with an enormous 54 electoral votes, the Electoral College colossus; and New York (33)—as well as taking other leaders in the electoral vote: Pennsylvania (23), Illinois (22), Ohio (21), New Jersey (15), and Georgia (13). The biggest states won by Bush were Texas (now, thanks to the 1990 census, the third-largest prize with 32, just one vote behind New York), Florida (25), North Carolina (14), and Virginia (13). Clinton became the first Democrat in history to win the White House without winning Texas since its annexation in 1845 (Democrats Andrew Jackson, Martin Van Buren, and Franklin Pierce were elected prior to Texas joining the Union), and only the second Democrat (Kennedy being the first) to win election without Florida. In looking more closely at the results by county, Clinton drew strength throughout every region of the country with the exception of the Great Basin, the Great Plains, and a large swath of the rural Midwest (which was countered by Clinton's strength in the more densely populated midwestern urban areas).

Even though Clinton fell seven percentage points shy of a popular majority, his election signaled a significant change in the mood of the country. After rwelve years of Republican control of the executive branch, a new kind of Democrat was back in the White House—not unlike 1976, when eight years of Republican control produced another "new" kind of Democrat in Jimmy Carter. Thus the Reagan-Bush years were bookended by the ascent of two Southerners who ran as outsiders and promised a new, pragmatic approach to governing. Whether or not the Clinton presidency would follow President Carter's fate would remain to be seen. But for the moment, it was clear that the political pendulum had shifted back toward the Democrats, and a new youth movement was under way.

Additional Resources

American Presidency Project. http://www.presidency.ucsb.edu and http://www.presidency .ucsb.edu/ws/index.php?pid=25847#ixzz1meEUz4EE.

Boller, Paul F., Jr. *Presidential Campaigns: From George Washington to George W. Bush.* Oxford: Oxford University Press, 2004.

Chancellor, John. "1992." In Arthur M. Schlesinger, Fred L. Israel, and David J. Frent, eds. *Running for President: The Candidates and Their Images.* Vol. 2. New York: Simon & Schuster, 1994.

Germond, Jack, and Jules Witcover. *Mad as Hell: Revolt at the Ballot Box, 1992*. New York: Warner Books, 1993.

Goldman, Peter, Thomas M. DeFrank, et al. *Quest for the Presidency: 1992*. New York: Newsweek, Inc., 1994.

Pomper, Gerald M., et al. *The Election of 1992: Reports and Interpretations*. New York: Chatham House, 1993.

Campaign of 1996

Two years before the election of 1996, many political pundits boldly predicted that President Bill Clinton had little chance of winning reelection, some going so far as to declare the Clinton presidency effectively dead. The administration's efforts, under the active leadership of First Lady Hillary Clinton, to reform the nation's health care system, a major pledge of candidate Bill Clinton's 1992 campaign, had utterly failed. Democrats were divided over the president's support of the North American Free Trade Agreement, many in the party fearing the loss of millions of jobs to companies overseas. Additionally, the Clintons continued to absorb a barrage of personal attacks, impugning their personal character and qualifications for public service. Among these, the most politically damaging revolved around what was called the "Whitewater Scandal," alleging that the Clintons had illegally profited from a soured real estate scheme. Sinister innuendo followed the suicide of top Clinton aide Vince Foster, and the culture warriors on the radio made a cottage industry out of routinely and incessantly blasting Clinton and the Democrats, to an expanding and receptive audience.

In the November 1994 midterm congressional elections, the Republican Party took control of the House of Representatives for the first time since 1952, a dramatic turnaround from the party's embarrassing loss of the White House to the Clinton-Gore ticket only two years earlier. With both the House and the Senate now under Republican control, a hostile Congress blocked President Clinton's agenda and instead passed key provisions endorsed by Speaker of the House Newt Gingrich's "Contract with America," provoking a veto strategy from the president and causing an impasse between the legislative and executive branches. Although excoriated by the Republicans in Congress, the stalemate permitted President Clinton the opportunity to reintroduce himself to the American people as a strong leader. Clinton adapted better than had been anticipated and adjusted his legislative agenda to help reestablish himself as a fiscally responsible and socially moderate president. Despite strong opposition from liberal Democrats, Clinton agreed to support major welfare reform legislation, pushed by the Republican Congress, that abolished the Aid to Families with Dependent Children program, in place since

Franklin Roosevelt's New Deal, and replaced it with a block grant program under the Personal Responsibility and Work Opportunity Act, limiting the length of time that assistance recipients could receive benefits.

By 1996, Clinton's "dead' presidency had been resuscitated. After having bottomed out at 37 percent approval in June 1993, his numbers slowly climbed, and in late September of that year, he enjoyed a ten-point jump that put him again over 50 percent. Over the next few months, his numbers fluctuated, but on average he managed, with a few exceptions dipping back into the forties, to sustain numbers at or just over 50 percent. But again, beginning in June 1994, the year of the GOP's big midterm wins, and running through April 1995, his ratings dropped into the forties to stay, reaching again as low as 39 percent. He would begin to turn things around eventually, but for the moment, Republicans smelled blood in the water, and they went after it.

A number of Republican candidates set up exploratory committees to compete for the Republican presidential nomination. These included Kansas senator and former vice presidential candidate (1976) Bob Dole, conservative commentator and culture warrior Pat Buchanan, newspaper and magazine editor Steve Forbes, former Tennessee governor Lamar Alexander, Indiana senator Richard Lugar, Texas senator Phil Graham, and Alan Keyes of Maryland. Bob Dole began the 1996 primary contests by narrowly winning the Iowa caucus to establish himself as the front-runner; but to the surprise of political observers, Buchanan narrowly defeated Dole in the important New Hampshire primary, muddying the waters considerably. They were further muddied when Forbes then narrowly defeated Dole in the Delaware and Arizona primaries, raising growing doubts about the viability of a Dole candidacy. However, Dole won a critical victory in the South Carolina primary on March 2, and three days later, Dole won in Colorado, Connecticut, Georgia, Maine, Maryland, Massachusetts, Rhode Island, and Vermont. From that point forward, Dole did not lose another primary on his way to the GOP nomination at the national convention in San Diego.

With Dole the easy winner, New York congressman Jack Kemp, a former professional football player who had earned a reputation as a leading moderate Republican, was tapped to serve as Dole's running mate. The platform called for new revenue structures designed to allow Americans to keep more of their earnings, pledging extensive tax reform, avowing that the party was committed to "a tax code for the 21st century that will raise revenue sufficient for a smaller, more effective and less wasteful government without increasing the national debt. That new tax system must be flatter, fairer, and simpler, with a minimum of exclusions from its coverage, and one set of rules applying to all. It must be simple enough to be understood by all and enforced by few, with a low cost of compliance which replaces the current stack of endless forms with a calculation which can be performed on the back of a postcard." Specifically, the platform proposed "an across-the-board, 15-percent tax cut to marginal tax rates." Another platform plank endorsed a renewed effort to adopt a balanced budget amendment to the Constitution. As part of a plan to reduce the size of the federal government, the platform proposed the "elimination of the Departments of Commerce, Housing and Urban Development, Education, and Energy." Additionally, the platform again reaffirmed support for "a human life amendment to the Constitution," endorsing "legislation to make clear that the Fourteenth Amendment's protections apply to unborn children."

As the Republican field first formed, President Clinton appeared vulnerable, even likely to lose if the Republicans could sustain the offensive and find the right candidate. But in a battle with President Clinton over the federal budget, the GOP-dominated Congress allowed the national government to shut down, a gambit that from the perspective of many voters, and especially those in the center, exposed stiff-necked stubbornness on their part, contrasted against the appearance of a more moderate, responsible, and less ideologically fixated president. Meanwhile, the economy, which had experienced a minor downturn, was improving once again. Thus beginning in the spring of 1995, the polls turned around for President Clinton; and moving toward election year, it appeared that he had gathered strength; and peaking at the right moment, the president reached approval ratings as high as he had seen. The Comeback Kid again proved his resilience, reaffirming his status as the most significant political figure in the post-Reagan era.

Freed from the task of competing in a long series of primaries, Clinton and his campaign team focused upon building a case for reelection. To accomplish this task, the Clinton camp made efficient use of the "soft money" campaign finance loophole. Since the late 1970s, the Federal Election Commission (FEC) had interpreted federal campaign finance laws as permitting political parties to raise unlimited amounts of money for party-building activities such as voter registration and nonspecific **get-out-the-vote** operations. The Clinton campaign broadly construed the "soft money" exception to permit the use of these kinds of contributions to pay for televised issue ads. These ads would highlight the accomplishments of the Clinton administration without directly advocating the reelection of Bill Clinton. Through the late winter and spring of 1996, the Clinton campaign invested large quantities of money in issue ads praising the accomplishments of the Clinton administration. It was an effective strategy that helped to further fortify the president as he prepared to meet the Republican challenge. With a healthy economy and renewed confidence in light of once-again-favorable polls, Clinton coasted to renomination and emerged the favorite against Dole throughout the remainder of the campaign season.

The platform of the Democratic Party praised the achievements of the Clinton administration in bringing down the federal deficit, as well as other accomplishments that were tied to peace and prosperity. "Today, America is moving forward with the strong Presidential leadership it deserves," the platform assured. "The economy is stronger, the deficit is lower, and government is smaller. Education is better, our environment is cleaner, families are healthier, and our streets are safer. There is more opportunity in America, more responsibility in our homes, and more peace in the world." Of particular significance, the platform stressed that during Clinton's first term, the economy had created ten million new jobs and that the rate of inflation and interest rates were the lowest in decades. Stealing the GOP's thunder, the platform praised the Clinton administration for providing funds to put one hundred thousand new police officers on the streets and for having provided states with $8 billion to build new prisons to hold violent offenders. The platform reaffirmed Democratic support for the right to choose an abortion. Additionally, the platform praised the Clinton administration for its foreign policy, celebrating four years of the United States' prominent role in keeping peace around the world.

The Clinton campaign adopted a two-part strategy to help win reelection. The first part of the strategy involved attacking Speaker Gingrich and the GOP majority in Congress for shutting down the federal government during the federal budget impasse, and also for seeking major changes in the popular Medicare and Social Security programs (the "third rail" of American politics). By the summer of 1996, public opinion had shifted against the Republican-controlled Congress. The second part of the strategy involved stressing the achievements of the Clinton administration, particularly the fact that the country was experiencing an exceptionally strong period of economic growth fed by the "dot-com revolution." Equally important, Clinton ads stressed that the president wanted new legislation designed to protect children by supporting a number of measures such as the adoption of school uniforms, tougher penalties for drug pushers, revoking the licenses of teenagers who drive drunk, and tougher penalties for the distribution of child pornography. By supporting these actions, Clinton ads rebutted conservative culture warriors by demonstrating that the president was in fact fiercely "protecting the values" of the American people. Indeed, Democrats portrayed Bill and Hillary Clinton as the candidates who believed in the American family, appealing to a generation of "soccer moms" who epitomized a child-centric culture. The effectiveness and positive attitude of the Clinton ad campaign evoked memories of Reagan's upbeat 1984 reelection campaign, drawing yet another comparison between the respective styles of the Comeback Kid and the Great Communicator.

Dole's campaign tried hard to depict its candidate as a moderate, disassociating him as much as possible from the party's powerful conservative wing. Personal integrity was a strength of the Dole record, stirringly matched with his service in World War II, wherein he performed with valor in combat while being seriously wounded, providing the senator with the strongest dimension of his campaign against the incumbent president. But rather than focus on Dole's personal character and admirable achievements, the campaign turned down the low road. Much like the effort of President Bush's campaign in 1992, the Dole campaign unleashed a steady stream of attack ads critical of President Clinton's character, making use of slogans such as "A Better Man for a Better America" to suggest that Clinton was not morally fit to serve in such a high office. Specifically, the Dole campaign alleged that Clinton, sometimes unflatteringly referred to as "Slick Willie," had a history of lying to the American people and playing fast and loose with his personal life, to the embarrassment of his family and to the disgrace of the nation's highest office. The alleged prevarication included promising not to raise taxes when he ran for president in 1992 but, once elected, reneging on his pledge and supporting a major tax increase. Late in the campaign, the Dole camp adopted the slogan "Wake up America" to attack Clinton and the media, the latter being accused, in general, as not doing enough to criticize the president. Specifically, the Dole campaign alleged that the media, dominated by a liberal narrative and agenda, applied an unfair double standard when comparing the two parties, one that worked to the benefit of the Democrats and the disadvantage of the Republicans. Conservative pundits delighted in referring to the "liberal" or "leftist" media, waggishly referring to CNN (Cable News Network) as the "Clinton News Network." Efforts by conservatives to raise anew President Clinton's lack of military service and to reopen draft-dodging allegations were stepped up, and the personal lawsuit brought by former Arkansas state employee Paula Jones alleging that Clinton had sexually harassed her while he served as Arkansas governor fueled conservative rage against the White House, but it failed to move the public opinion polls, which continued to give Clinton a comfortable lead as Election Day approached.

In the end, Dole seemed out of touch with a more youthful America as it moved toward a new century. At one point, taking a page from Spiro Agnew and Pat Buchanan, the senator sternly criticized Hollywood for its amoral values and unpatriotic attitudes; but instead of giving him a boost, the pitch came across to many as crabbed, the discontent of a curmudgeon fed up with the whippersnappers who were running the show and ruining the country. Dole, at age seventy-three, would turn out to be the last candidate to run for president who had served in World War II, and for many younger Americans, the war seemed too distant to inform them about the quality of those who had sacrificed so much during that horrific period in history. Dole's grit certainly won him the respect of his colleagues, and rightly so, but his persona came off as far too rooted in the worn attitudes of the past. By contrast, Clinton was a man that appealed to an age of rapid change, and his ability to shrug off what to other politicians would have been career-ending disasters gave much to recommend to a generation that had become accustomed to personalities and celebrities able to recover from their checkered pasts to remake themselves. Dole, who had earned a reputation in the Senate for his quick and caustic wit, did not play well on the national stage, especially against the unflappable Clinton, who seemed to be at his best when cornered.

President Clinton thus joined Grover Cleveland as the only two-term presidents to win the White House without ever having received a majority in the popular vote, and Clinton is the only president to have done it in consecutive terms (President Cleveland's terms being nonconsecutive). On Election Day, he won just over 47,400,000 votes; at 49.2 percent of the popular vote, this failed to reach that simple majority for the second consecutive election. But his showing was decidedly better than in 1992, a difference of seven points compared to his first election; whereas Dole, who won just over 39,000,000 votes, finished with slightly more than 40 percent of the voting electorate, fewer than 100,000 votes and around one percentage point higher than incumbent president George Bush's failed bid for reelection four years earlier. Clinton's 49 percent was the best showing for a Democratic candidate since Carter's 50.1 percent in 1976. In the Electoral College, Clinton won 379 electoral votes to Dole's 159, which was only slightly better than his electoral victory in 1992. The remaining 9–10 percent of the popular vote was divided among a handful of minor-party candidates, the balance of which went again to Ross Perot, who had returned as the standard-bearer of the newly created Reform Party, a third-party alternative that carried forward the Perotian pragmatism of his impressive minor-party run four years earlier, but to less effect. Consumer advocate Ralph Nader mounted a campaign as the standard-bearer of the Green Party and managed to win over 685,000 votes. The Libertarians also fielded a candidate, Harry Brown, who managed around 485,000 votes; other minor candidates shared just over 420,000 votes.

East of the Mississippi, Clinton won, for the most part, the same states that he carried in 1992, with the exception of losing Georgia to Dole but this time winning Florida, a net gain in the Electoral College. In the West, Clinton lost Colorado and Montana to Dole while gaining Arizona. A solid block of eleven western states supported Dole, running from the southern border of Texas (included here as a western state) to the northern border of Montana and dividing the country in half, with the Pacific coast going to Clinton; and a second solid block of states in the South, running from Virginia to Louisiana (or Texas, if it is to be included in the South as well, as it has been historically), going to Dole, with Clinton taking only Florida, Vice President Gore's home state of Tennessee, and the border states of Kentucky and Maryland. But the old Deep South was again a solid Republican bloc. Outside these two regions (i.e., the South and the Great Plains/Intermountain states), which voted solidly Republican, the only states that voted for Dole were Alaska and Indiana. County by county, the Democrats again showed more strongly east of the Mississippi, where population density is higher, with the GOP taking more counties west of the Mississippi. However, the Democrats still scored the more highly populated areas in the West, specifically the urban counties on the Pacific coast and interior metropolitan areas such as Phoenix, Denver, Las Vegas, San Antonio, Dallas, and Houston. In examining the political trends, it was becoming evident that a coastal-interior and urban-rural divide had formed and crystalized, one that would become further exaggerated in subsequent elections, with Democrats drawing strength from both coasts and the larger urban areas, and Republicans drawing their strength from the nation's interior and more rural regions; this divide would even influence the political mood of the country during President Clinton's second term.

In sum, while the Democrats enjoyed a noticeably better showing in 1996, the Republicans gained little to no ground, in spite of the vulnerabilities exhibited by President Clinton at the midterm in 1994. Clinton proved that he could compensate for those vulnerabilities, smoothing them over through the strength of his personality combined with a knack for stressing the more positive features of his record and somehow managing to let rumor and scandal slide off his back. In so doing, he became the first incumbent Democrat to win reelection since Franklin Roosevelt (who was elected four times and reelected thrice) in 1944, and only the fifth Democrat in history to be elected two or more times (joining Andrew Jackson, Grover Cleveland, Woodrow Wilson, and Franklin Roosevelt; two other Democrats served more than one term—viz., Harry Truman and Lyndon Johnson—but were only elected once). Clinton would also become one of only five presidents (along with Wilson, Franklin Roosevelt, Dwight Eisenhower, and Ronald Reagan) in the twentieth century to serve two complete terms (or, again, in the case of FDR, more than two).

The president enjoyed another electoral triumph, but in spite of being the most politically successful Democrat since FDR, Clinton did not ride the wave of a unified political culture. Divisions continued to grow, widen, intensify, and, for a brief moment, threaten the Clinton presidency. The Comeback Kid would again nimbly deflect his attackers and complete his term, but the political costs for the Democrats would prove to be very high.

Additional Resources

American Presidency Project. http://www.presidency.ucsb.edu.

Boller, Paul F., Jr. *Presidential Campaigns: From George Washington to George W. Bush.* Oxford: Oxford University Press, 2004.

Burnham, Walter Dean, et al. *The Election of 1996: Reports and Interpretations.* New York: Chatham House, 1997.

Burns, James MacGregor, and Georgia J. Sorenson. *Dead Center.* New York: Scribner, 1999.

Hanes, Walter, Jr. *Reelection.* New York: Columbia University Press, 2000.

Hohenberg, John. *Re-Electing Bill Clinton: Why Americans Chose a "New Democrat."* Syracuse, NY: Syracuse University Press, 1997.

Campaign of 2000

The campaign and election of 2000, depending on whom you agree with, was either the first or last American presidential election of the century and millennium. But regardless of how one counts it, it was without question one of the strangest political events in memory. By all accounts, it produced more frustration, anger, and bewilderment than any presidential election since 1968. The actual campaign season itself was strangely unremarkable, even bland; rather, it was the outcome of the election that agitated an entire country.

In the 2000 election, the incumbent vice president and Democratic standard-bearer for president, Albert Gore Jr., won more total popular votes than any American in history to that point, and yet he still lost the election. The forces that led to his defeat were likely set in motion two years earlier in a failed attempt by the Republican-dominated Congress to discredit President Bill Clinton and remove him from office. President Clinton, the epitome of political survival, weathered the storm, but the toll was exacted, the unity of the party shaken, the resolve of the Republicans steeled. Even though the Clinton administration had been successful on many fronts—a healthy, expanding economy, the first balanced budget in decades—the Republicans were in a good position to mount a serious challenge to return one of their own the White House. The odor of personal scandal associated with the Clinton White House clung to the Democrats, and in particular to the vice president, who had nothing to do with Clinton's humiliating indiscretions but was now paying a high political price for them. Going into the 2000 campaign, Gore was clearly the Democratic front-runner, but he found himself behind the GOP contender in the polls. The electorate seemed primed for a change, and the prospect of a Gore presidency was, to many, not change enough.

Vice President Gore's only opposition in the 2000 primaries was former senator Bill Bradley from New Jersey. From the beginning, Gore clearly held the advantage, winning decisively in the Iowa caucus, somewhat narrowly in the New Hampshire primary (where Bradley enjoyed his best showing, losing by just four points), and then dominating every primary after that. Hence, instead of having to worry about a costly primary fight for the nomination, the Gore campaign focused on developing a strategy for the fall campaign against the likely GOP nominee, Texas governor George W. Bush, the son of the forty-first president, George H. W. Bush, whose presidency had been limited to one term owing to a successful challenge from Bill Clinton and, of course, his running mate, Al Gore.

The central issue at hand involved the question of how closely Gore should be tied to Clinton. As stated above, the Clinton presidency could boast significant achievements, but the Clinton White House was tarnished by shameful personal misconduct. The Gore campaign needed to distance itself from Clinton's character issues while at the same time sharing credit for the healthy economy and balanced budget that had been achieved during the Clinton years. Gore prided himself on being, by many accounts (especially his own), the most involved vice president in history, assuming leadership in a number of ways that few previous vice presidents could claim. The Gore vice presidency was the culmination of a more active role for the vice president that many consider to have begun during the presidency of John Kennedy, during which Kennedy, more than any previous president, included Vice President Lyndon Johnson among his closest advisers and quietly deployed the vice president on his behalf on diplomatic missions; prior to that, Vice President Nixon also stepped forward to carry much responsibility during President Eisenhower's health crises. (Under President McKinley, Vice President Garret Hobart, a close confident of McKinley's, provides a late nineteenth-century precedent, anomalous for the era and abruptly shortened by the vice president's death in November 1899. Most vice presidents before Nixon and LBJ were not deeply involved in their administrations. And it is only fair to note that some accounts regarding LBJ claim that his role has been exaggerated.) This new approach to the vice presidency was further developed by President Carter in the late 1970s, involving then vice president Mondale in ways that stretched the office of the vice presidency; and under President Reagan, then vice president Bush was also more engaged, following the model established by the Kennedy-Johnson and Carter-Mondale tandems. During the Clinton administration, these precedents were expanded still further, and Vice President Gore emerged as an integral actor in the formation and direction of the administration's policies. Hence Gore's position between the horns of a dilemma: either stress his close involvement with President Clinton's administration, taking credit for what was earned and risking blame for the many embarrassments for which he had no responsibility; or detach himself completely from President Clinton and thereby suppress his record of service over the past eight years.

For the most part, Clinton and Gore had indeed enjoyed a close working relationship; but in the latter months of President Clinton's second term, the relationship was strained owing to the damage that was done in the wake of the president's poor personal choices. But Gore was dialed into the administration of his president more thoroughly than any previous vice president, a fact that worked both for and against him. This was not unlike Vice President Hubert Humphrey, who was forced to strike a delicate balance between supporting his president, who had been politically wounded by the Vietnam War, and not endorsing or owning every act that his president made. However, it must be noted that the Clinton-Gore relationship was more complex. The Vietnam War forced Johnson to withdraw from a reelection bid after having attracted considerable wrath from within his own party. President Clinton, in many ways and in spite of himself, continued to remain popular and even admired in many quarters, although his private behavior drew

sharp criticism. If Gore was to associate himself with Clinton, he had to negotiate the complex psychological terrain of an electorate that appreciated Clinton for
his many talents and at the same time found his actions and impaired judgment
embarrassing, if not disgraceful. It was a difficult situation for Gore, and it provided the GOP strategists with considerable ammunition. It was the kind of situation that Clinton would always find a way to control, but the question remained
whether or not Gore could prove himself as politically adept.

Gore's nomination to run for the presidency in 2000 was rubber-stamped at
the convention in San Diego that August. After vetting a number of candidates for
the second spot on the ticket, Gore selected Connecticut senator Joseph Lieberman, a political moderate and the first Jewish candidate to run on a presidential
ticket from a major party. Concerned about alienating the center, the Democratic
platform sought to convey the moderate nature of its ticket by stressing the commitment of the Democratic Party to fiscal discipline. Focusing on the positive
aspects of the Clinton-Gore years, the platform observed, "Today, America has
gone from the biggest deficits in history to the biggest surpluses in history. Fiscal
discipline keeps interest rates low and investment rates high—and it has helped
fuel America's remarkable prosperity." The platform pledged to protect the Social
Security system and opposed the Republican plan to privatize Social Security by
permitting Americans to invest part of their Social Security contributions. The
platform vaguely reaffirmed Democratic support for some type of universal health
coverage. The platform also supported the expansion of the Medicare program to
include prescription drug coverage.

At the beginning of the primary season, Governor George W. Bush was the
clear favorite to win the Republican presidential nomination. Bush, however, faced
a number of Republican challengers. The list included newspaper and magazine publisher Steve Forbes; Arizona senator John McCain, a Vietnam war hero;
Utah senator Orrin Hatch; conservative activist and former diplomat Alan Keyes;
and Gary Bauer, formerly of the Reagan administration, president of the Family
Research Council, and also a senior vice president for Focus on the Family, a conservative evangelical Christian organization concerned with social issues. Bush
had the funding, the organization, the name, and the support of the party leadership. It was apparent that he could run a winning campaign without any serious
problems all the way to the convention, and he significantly outpolled everyone in
the Iowa caucus (in the Alaska caucus, Bush and Forbes tied with 36% each); but
in the New Hampshire primary, an unexpected situation emerged. There, Senator
McCain scored a major victory, outpolling Bush by eighteen points and dislodging him from the position of front-runner that he had enjoyed for over a year prior
to the primary season. Bush recovered by winning the Delaware primary, but the
race hinged on South Carolina. It was there that the campaign turned ugly. Reports

emerged of mudslinging and dirty tricks, mostly instigated by the Bush campaign, including some tactics that were racially charged and involved McCain's family. Whether or not these tactics made a difference is not clear, but it can be said that the campaigning in the South Carolina primary was among the most bitter in recent years, particularly within a party.

Whether or not the nasty mudslinging helped, Bush scored an important victory in South Carolina, winning 53 percent to 42 percent, with 5 percent going to Keyes. McCain followed with a victory in his home state of Arizona and an important victory in Michigan that offered a glimmer of encouragement, with Bush taking four primaries and caucuses after that. The decisive moment was the March 7 Super Tuesday set of primaries in which Bush won ten primaries to McCain's four, including a convincing victory in California, where he beat McCain by over 25 points. After Super Tuesday, Bush swept with ease the remainder of the primary season, and he had the nomination sealed well before the convention. The Bush campaign then turned to its choice for vice president, engaging in a long vetting process, personally managed by seasoned political insider Dick Cheney, who had been a visible presence in every GOP administration reaching back to the administration of President Richard Nixon, and who most notably served as the chief of staff for President Gerald Ford. Several prominent Republicans were considered for the second spot on the ticket, but Bush remained unsatisfied, eventually turning to Cheney himself as his choice for running mate.

Saddled with the memory of two consecutive presidential election losses to the Clinton-Gore team, the Bush campaign sought to soften the tone of the Republican Party platform, aiming for a more moderate tenor in an attempt to move the party back to the center and to abandon the "culture wars" attitude that pervaded elements of the party throughout the 1990s. As the platform explained, "We seek to be faithful to the best traditions of our party. We are the party that ended slavery, granted homesteads, built land grant colleges, and moved control of government out of Washington, back into the hands of the people. We believe in service to the common good—and that good is not common until it is shared." The platform made education reform a top priority: "For dramatic and swift improvement, we endorse Governor Bush's principles of local control [in education], with accountability, parental choice, and meaningful student achievement as essential to education reform." Additionally, the platform reaffirmed ongoing Republican support for a "human life amendment to the Constitution," and with equal significance, the platform included a plank supporting a ban on all partial-birth abortions. The platform also included a separate plank protecting the Second Amendment rights of Americans to "safely use and store firearms."

In addition to the nominations of Gore and Bush by the major parties, celebrated consumer advocate Ralph Nader ran again under the banner of the Green

Party, this time drawing considerably more attention, and support, than with his previous effort four years earlier. Even though Al Gore had established himself as a strong environmentalist and a leader in the cause, Democrats feared that Nader might draw off those voters who had concerns about the commitment of the Democratic Party to environmental problems and the policies that were required to address them. The Reform Party, the attenuated remnant of Ross Perot's 1992 and 1996 alternative campaigns, had curiously gravitated toward the right, nominating for president conservative firebrand Pat Buchanan, while Libertarians again turned to Harry Brown to carry their standard.

Throughout the general election campaign, presidential preference polls fluctuated. Without any major domestic or foreign policy issues to sway voters, both parties focused their energies on mobilizing key voting blocs. Even though Bush held a substantial lead in the polls after the Republican convention, Gore, making a comeback of his own, would pull even with him after the Democratic convention. Both parties were well funded, having already raised tens of millions of dollars in soft money contributions to supplement the public funds they would receive to conduct their fall presidential campaigns. Early in the campaign, both the media analysts and the candidates identified a relatively small number of battleground states that would probably determine the outcome of the race. These included the states of Arkansas, Florida, Iowa, Kentucky, Michigan, Missouri, New Hampshire, New Mexico, Ohio, Oregon, Pennsylvania, Tennessee, Washington, West Virginia, and Wisconsin; thus it was in these states that a high volume of campaigning would be concentrated.

The Gore campaign adopted a strategy of focusing on traditional Democratic messages to hold together the diverse coalition that proved crucial in both of Bill Clinton's 1992 and 1996 presidential election victories. The coalition included young, college-educated women invested in the issue of reproductive rights, older Americans fearing cuts to Social Security and Medicare, and African American voters who had strongly supported Clinton due to his enforcement of civil rights and an ongoing, healthy relationship between Clinton and the African American community. Gore's media campaign sought to remind voters of the success of the Clinton-Gore administration in bringing economic prosperity to the nation. But again, Gore could not weave the Clinton connection too tightly. Throughout the campaign, Gore chose to run as much as possible on his own qualities, not relying on his president to support him on the stump. For some, the selection of Senator Liebermann, a stern critic of the president's misconduct, was a blunt message to the voters that the vice president was a different sort of man from the president.

By and large, the Gore campaign attempted to restrict the amount of negative campaigning, a decision at which both camps arrived, given the growing discontent in the electorate over too many attack ads and too little discussion of the issues. Some negative campaigning was employed: Gore's campaign questioned the qualifications and experience of Bush, and the Bush campaign reminded voters of the undignified manner in which the Clinton White House had conducted itself (an indirect indictment of Gore and all Democrats); but by and large, the tone of the campaign was less vitriolic. However, things changed in early October, as Governor Bush committed a gaffe that provided the Gore campaign with an irresistible opportunity to unleash the most negative attack ads of the campaign. In a speech, Bush puzzlingly asserted that Social Security was not a federal program. Bush made the statement as part of his defense of allowing young workers to contribute part of their Social Security contributions to private investment accounts. "They want the federal government controlling the Social Security like it's some sort of federal program," Bush publicly announced, leaving himself open to the impression that he was unaware of the structure, funding, and history of the program. The gaffe did not really affect Bush's campaign, but it did allow the Gore camp to mount an aggressive charge, renewing their assertion that Bush lacked the experience and depth necessary to manage the vast network of agencies that constituted the federal executive.

The Bush campaign worked hard to disabuse the political center of its assumptions about the nature of Republican conservatism. To appeal to the independents that had defected to Clinton in 1992 and 1996, Bush attempted to define himself as a "compassionate conservative" committed to education reform and to strengthening key entitlement programs such as Social Security and Medicare. Using ideas reminiscent of Ronald Reagan's 1980 campaign, Bush proposed a large, across-the-board tax cut on the grounds that it was better to return part of the government surplus to taxpayers rather than enabling further government spending. Even though the Bush campaign also avoided making use of heavily negative ads, it did attempt to persuade voters that Gore had a history of embellishing his role in key events—for example, Bush operatives made effective use of an earlier, risible statement by Gore claiming that he had "invented the Internet," in addition to noting the loss of dignity in the White House as a consequence of the Clinton-Gore presidency.

Probably more significant, the Bush campaign devoted considerable resources and energies to those states where certain Democratic issues might cause voters to shift from the Democratic to the Republican column. In West Virginia, for example, the Bush campaign, concluding that many West Virginians feared that an environmentalist Gore administration might crack down on the use of coal as an energy source, a move that could put West Virginia coal miners out of work, did its best to depict Gore as a "tree hugger" unconcerned with the problems of "average Americans" and the real needs of their families. The Bush campaign also understood that many West Virginia voters relied on hunting to help feed their families, and feared that a Gore administration might support further restrictions on gun ownership. Interestingly, while Republicans at all levels in the 2000 campaign did not hesitate to share their grievances against President Clinton's personal improprieties and to impugn his overall character, Governor Bush was not interested in smearing Gore with Clinton's reputation. While Bush firmly stated that the shenanigans of the Clinton administration were an embarrassment to the dignified office of the presidency, promising that his presidency would work hard to restore that dignity, when pressed by reporters on whether or not Vice President Gore was also capable of repairing the White House's reputation, Bush replied without hesitation, "I think he can," further assuring the media, "I don't think Clinton is an issue as we move forward."

In the obligatory presidential debates, many predicted that Gore would perform better than Bush, anticipating a boost to his campaign just in time for the general election. But in the first debate, neither candidate showed the upper hand, and the post-debate polling indicated that Bush, who was eight points behind Gore on the evening of the debates, had now pulled even, dispelling all assumptions about the candidates' respective debating skills. However, before the second debate, Gore bounced back in the polls, regaining most of the ground that he had lost; but after the second debate, Bush again surged back, with polls showing Bush enjoying a slight lead. Those questioned about the debates seemed to agree that while Gore was clearer in expressing his positions, Bush was generally considered to be more personally likable. Throughout his political career, Gore had unwittingly gained a reputation as a stilted, wooden, and wonkish campaigner—although as his convention acceptance speech illustrated, he possessed a dry humor often lost on audiences. Bush, while given to fractured grammar, disjointed logic, and slips of the tongue, was received by most as a warmer, more identifiable person, not quite as magnetic as Reagan or Clinton, but possessing a folksy manner that belied his inner ambitions and abilities.

During the debates, Gore could speak intelligently, even impressively at times, to the issues; but his inflection and mannerisms often grated. One incident that involved Gore leaving his podium to approach Bush during the debate seemed to irritate viewers (although Gore apologists were quick to point out that this was only to be expected from an alpha male like their candidate); thus, even though Gore managed to speak informatively, he lost on the important intangibles owing to his presentation and what was seen as an untoward slip to poor form in leaving his lectern to move toward Bush. As the poll numbers oscillated back and forth, it was clear that the race was tightening. After the third debate, those polled regarding the performance of the candidates in the actual debate slightly favored Gore, but not by much; and in the post-debate polling, Bush again surged ahead, now enjoying a four-point lead. But Gore closed the gap again, and thus on the eve of the election, the race was considered a toss-up.

Throughout Election Day and into the night, television viewers following the results witnessed an extremely tight, tense election. Early results showed Gore running strong in the Northeast, where he would eventually win a solid bloc with the exception of New Hampshire—a block that delivered the big prizes of New York (33 electoral votes), Pennsylvania (23), and New Jersey (15). As more results were reported, it was clear that Gore's early lead was tenuous. Bush won solidly in the South, and the early returns in the Midwest also provided his camp with some good news in Ohio and Indiana; but Gore took the lead in Illinois, Michigan, and Minnesota, which altogether would amount to a substantial bloc of electors. Nonetheless, races in the midwestern states of Wisconsin and Iowa were extremely close, and deep into the night they remained uncertain. From that point, state after state went to Bush, nearly sweeping the West, and significantly, Bush snatched Gore's home state of Tennessee, which delivered 11 electoral votes; however, the Pacific coast states went for Gore, which included the Electoral College grand prize of California, which, at 54 votes, represented by itself a full 20 percent of the electoral votes needed to win the election.

Hence as the evening wore on, most of the states were clearly committed, but four states remained far too close to call: Wisconsin, Oregon, New Mexico, and Florida. At one point, the exit polls in Florida seemed to predict with confidence a Gore victory there; the state had gone for Clinton in 1996; many expected the same result for the Democrats in 2000; and some broadcasters, upon seeing the early numbers from the Atlantic side of Florida, projected Gore as the winner. But the counties of western and northern Florida, particularly the panhandle, leaned to Bush, throwing the announced projection in doubt. The northern and western segments of Florida have historically been part of the southern bloc, at least politically, and thus the voting patterns there are more aligned to those of the Deep South states on the northern border (Alabama and Georgia), whereas the more urbanized Atlantic side and southern tip of Florida resemble voting patterns farther north; thus the disparity in the polling projections as the night grew long. Similarly, New Mexico was showing a margin that separated the candidates by only a few hundred votes throughout the entire state. Later that evening, media projections, sensing a change in the direction of the voting, were now calling the election in Florida for Bush, a response to his success in the western counties that had earlier delayed reporting their results. With Florida, Bush would win the election, prompting Gore to telephone Bush to concede, but as the vote tallying moved into the wee hours of the following day, new reports about the Florida results placed the outcome once again in doubt, causing Gore to withdraw his concession.

On Wednesday morning after Election Day, the election still had yet to be called. At that point, it was evident that Vice President Gore had clearly won the popular vote, winning approximately (pending further sorting) over 51,000,000 votes, which was a record number in absolute terms, and which amounted to just over 48.3 percent counted, with Governor Bush taking around 50,460,000 votes, or slightly over 47.8 percent. With three states—Oregon, New Mexico, and Florida— so close that recounts were required, the electoral vote leaned to Gore, 255 to 246, with 88 of Gore's votes coming from two states, California (54) and New York (33), amounting to 37.5 percent of Gore's electoral total. Bush won far more states, but Gore's numbers were still higher given his ability to win the larger states; that is, measured as the more highly populated states. The election thus could not be called until the votes had been recounted in the three states in question, and it was mathematically obvious to all concerned that it was in Florida that the election would be determined. The process remained unresolved long after Election Day had passed. Within two or three days, Oregon and New Mexico had determined their totals, Gore taking Oregon by just under seven thousand votes, thanks largely to his higher numbers in the Portland metropolitan area and the more urbanized counties in the state's northwestern quadrant. New Mexico was ridiculously close; a margin of 366 votes gave Gore the state. Together Oregon and New Mexico, now declared for Gore, delivered 16 electoral votes, raising Gore's Electoral College lead to 266, a full 20 votes ahead of Bush, setting him on the verge of the presidency.

To win the election, a candidate must have 270 electoral votes, and Gore remained four votes shy of the White House even though it was clear that he had won a plurality of the popular vote nationwide, polling over a half-million more votes than Bush. But under the Constitution, the states, through their electors in the Electoral College, who are now all selected by the voters within the various states, cast the deciding votes for the president, and the fate of the candidates in the election of 2000 hinged, in an eerie repetition of the election of 1876, on Florida. In 1876, Democratic candidate Samuel Tilden won the popular vote (by actually taking a slight majority of the popular vote, not simply a plurality), but after the vote in Florida was too close to call, and after months of investigation into the true outcome of the Florida vote, the state was, hard upon the eve of the scheduled inauguration, declared for Republican Rutherford B. Hayes. The 1876 election was the third in which a candidate had won the most popular votes but was denied the presidency under the requirements of the Constitution, and now history appeared to be in the process of repeating itself in 2000, with Florida again at the center of the controversy.

For days on end, votes were recounted in Florida, and revelations of voting improprieties, technical problems, and general incompetence threw the legitimacy of thousands of votes into doubt. At one point, Bush's whisper-thin lead seemed to be at just around three hundred votes in the entire state. The inclusion of military ballots would increase Bush's lead to a slim nine hundred. But Gore demanded further recounting, particularly in four counties where he was convinced that his totals should have been higher. Under threat of approaching deadlines that would automatically shut down any recount, Gore used the courts, successfully, to extend the time allotted for recounting, and the process continued. It became apparent that in many counties, the "butterfly ballots" that had been used there were unreliable, and because of idiosyncratic problems such as "hanging chads," some ballots were decidedly unclear, the intent of individual voters thus concealed. Meanwhile, as the **twenty-four-hour news cycle** spooled into overdrive, the press enjoyed a bonanza of airtime devoted to explaining the myriad problems in the Florida recount and routinely broadcasting the "latest developments." All the while, teams of attorneys representing the two candidates met in court to argue for extended deadlines. On November 26, the Florida Election Commission finally declared Governor Bush the winner in the Sunshine State by a scant 537 votes, but the announcement was immediately challenged by the Gore camp, receiving a favorable ruling by the Florida Supreme Court to recount seventy thousand ballots that had been rejected by machine counters. Bush's attorneys challenged the decision, and the case made its way to the U.S. Supreme Court, where, in the case of *Bush v. Gore*, the Supreme Court ruled in a five-to-four vote that the Florida court's support for a statewide recount was unconstitutional, and further ruled that any additional recounts could not be completed before a final December 12 deadline and thus should be promptly discontinued. Whether or not any revealing recounts would have been conducted had Gore won his case in court, the precise result remains uncertain. What is certain is that the election of 2000, one of the closest in American history, was settled in the judicial branch.

Thus, the election was called for Bush in Florida by the slimmest of margins, thereby delivering the coveted prize of 25 electoral votes, pushing Bush's total to 271, one vote above the minimum required majority in the Electoral College, and propelling Governor Bush to the presidency. It was the fourth time in American history that the presidency was won by a candidate who lost in the popular vote. (John Quincy Adams lost both the popular vote and the electoral vote in 1824, with the election decided in the House of Representatives owing to Andrew Jackson's failure to win a clear Electoral College majority; Thomas Jefferson's election was also decided by the House after having tied Aaron Burr's vote in the Electoral College, no popular vote then being recorded; Hayes in 1876 and Benjamin Harrison in 1888 both won the electoral vote while losing the popular tally, now joined by the younger Bush in that company.) It was also the third consecutive presidential election wherein no candidate managed to win a majority in the popular vote. Green Party candidate Ralph Nader managed close to 2,900,000 votes, or just over 2.7 percent, including 97,000 votes in Florida, which was clearly enough to have made a difference in the outcome there. It is more than likely that Gore would have carried well over half of those votes that went to Nader; thus it is easy and quite plausible to conclude that the actions of the Green Party in Florida, more than any other single factor, led to Gore's defeat. Had Vice President Gore won just 538 more votes in Florida, he would have been the forty-third president of the United States; thus in terms of the minimum number of votes required to change an election, it was the closest in American history.

Significantly, Gore's failure to win in his home state could also be considered a deciding factor. Had Gore won Tennessee, he would have managed to field 277 votes; thus, even with Florida, Bush would have fallen short with 260. West Virginia, with five electoral votes, may also have been a factor. Since 1932 and the formation of the Roosevelt Coalition, West Virginia stood as a consistently Democratic state, voting for Democratic presidential candidates in most elections beginning with Franklin Roosevelt's first victory, with the notable exceptions of 1956 (Eisenhower), 1972 (Nixon), and 1984 (Reagan). Had Gore carried West Virginia, he would have won enough votes to push his total over the needed majority by one. However, in 2000, the Mountain State went strong for the GOP, and it continued to back Republicans for president in the subsequent two elections. But it is in Florida where the real difference was made, where the election was ultimately decided.

And so goes the tale of one of the most unusual presidential contests in American history. Between Election Day and the final certification of the electors in George Bush's favor, the country experienced frustration, bewilderment, acrimony, and sideshow hyperbole from all corners. And even after the issue was settled, a great many Americans were left disenchanted by a democratic process that was resolved, at least on appearances, so undemocratically. Given this, the incoming administration was in a precarious situation. Thus the Bush White House, aware of the close election and committed to a more moderate tone, opened its administration with designs to reconfigure the culture of Washington, with the intention of steering it toward a more bipartisan environment, something that Governor Bush had prided himself on while he served as the chief executive of the state of Texas. With the economy sound and the budget manageable, the Bush administration anticipated a first term committed to an agenda that promised to unite the country in the spirit of cross-partisan comity and political pragmatism. Seeking to work fairly with both parties in Congress, and with a spirit of interparty cooperation stirring on Capitol Hill, calm seas were forecast for the Bush administration. But a new reality hit like a thunderbolt, reminding all that even the sunniest day can suddenly succumb to the darkest storms.

Additional Resources

Boller, Paul F., Jr. *Presidential Campaigns: From George Washington to George W. Bush.* Oxford: Oxford University Press, 2004.

Cohen, Martin, David Karol, Hans Noel, and John Zaller. *The Party Decides: Presidential Nominations before and after Reform.* Chicago: University of Chicago Press, 2008.

Dershowitz, Alan M. *Supreme Injustice: How the High Court Hijacked the Election of 2000.* New York: Oxford University Press, 2001.

Dworkin, Ronald, ed. *A Badly Flawed Election.* New York: New Press, 2002.

Federal Election Commission. http://www.fec.gov.

Sabato, Larry. *Overtime: The Election of 2000 Thriller.* New York: Longman, 2001.

Shaw, Daron R. *The Race to 270: The Electoral College and Campaign Strategies of 2000 and 2004.* Chicago: University of Chicago Press, 2006.

Simon, Roger. *Divided We Stand: How Al Gore Beat George Bush and Lost the Presidency.* New York: Crown, 2001.

Tobin, Jeffrey. *Too Close to Call: The Thirty-Six-Day Battle to Decide the 2000 Election.* New York: Random House, 2002.

Campaign of 2004

The September 11, 2001, terrorist attacks on New York City's World Trade Center towers and the Pentagon in Washington, DC, instantaneously and irrevocably changed the Bush presidency. It would also, consequently, shape the Campaign of 2004. Pushing aside his domestic agenda with its ambitions to promote "compassionate conservatism" and a new bipartisan mood of governmental pragmatism, President George W. Bush announced a worldwide war on terrorism that led directly to the deployment of the power of the U.S. military overseas, destroying the Taliban regime in Afghanistan and moving into Iraq to dislodge the tyrannical regime of Saddam Hussein on the premise that the dictator was harboring "weapons of mass destruction" that had destabilized the region and that now posed a threat to the interests of the United States and her allies. Thus the Bush administration, fully expecting a presidency marked by peace, prosperity, and pragmatism, was suddenly transformed into a wartime presidency, buoyed by bipartisan unity in response to the attacks and initially riding a wave of popular support upon which President Bush enjoyed the highest presidential approval rating ever recorded (Bush's rating was 90% ten days after the terrorist attacks, slightly higher than the record set by his father, George H. W. Bush, in 1991 during another wartime crisis) and sustained favorable ratings through 2002 and even into the spring of 2003.

But controversies emerged that began to alienate many voters; thus by early 2004, President Bush's approval ratings were oscillating back and forth across the 50 percent threshold, and by that summer, his ratings reached their lowest point. Nonetheless, the polls continued to rise and drop, and it was clear that while he no longer enjoyed the **"rally around the flag"** effects that invariably follow international crises, many Americans were behind his efforts to fight terrorism. A growing number, though, had turned against Bush, either criticizing the nature of the effort itself or criticizing Bush for what they perceived was an incompetent response to international terrorism. Moving toward campaign season, Bush firmly held the loyalties of the GOP, as no challengers emerged. Hence the 2004 version of the Bush-Cheney campaign would be directed at moderate independents, outside the party, knowing that it could fully count on its Republican base and that it could not win over the liberal Democrats, nor would it be likely for the campaign to persuade even most moderate Democrats. Regardless of ideological persuasion, all knew that the 2004 campaign would become a referendum on the Bush administration's prosecution of the war on terrorism.

As President Bush was unopposed in his own party, the 2004 primary contest was entirely within the Democratic Party, where a large field of candidates lobbied for support. The front-runner, beginning in the summer of 2003, was former Vermont governor Howard Dean, who had amassed an impressive campaign war chest owing in large part to his ability to use new media (particularly the Internet) for fund-raising and dissemination of his campaign materials. Other candidates in the field were North Carolina senator John Edwards; retired general Wesley Clark; Connecticut senator Joe Lieberman, who had run for the vice presidency on the Gore ticket in 2000; former Illinois senator Carol Moseley Braun; former Missouri representative Dick Gephardt; Reverend Al Sharpton; Senator Bob Graham of Florida; Ohio representative Dennis Kucinich; and Massachusetts senator John Kerry.

While the nomination appeared to be up for grabs, Dean held a commanding lead in all the polls leading up to the Iowa caucus. In Iowa, most analysts predicted a battle between the well-funded, Internet-driven Dean campaign and Gephardt, who was well known and supported in the Midwest; but pre-primary polls hinted at a different story, revealing Kerry and Edwards to be in better shape than expected. These signs were confirmed the following day as the caucus votes were tallied, revealing a stunning win for Kerry at 38 percent, with Edwards placing second at 32 percent. Dean, who had been considered by many as just one or two steps away from coronation, showed a dismal 18 percent, his purportedly strongest rival Gephardt taking but 11 percent. The Dean camp was sent reeling, and the candidate made matters worse by a frantic post-caucus performance marked by a now-infamous high-pitched scream—ostensibly intended to whip up enthusiasm for his now-wounded campaign, but in effect providing grist for the eager comedian and the hostile pundit—that effectually in one stroke blunted any possibility of a comeback. It was referred to in the press as a meltdown for Dean; but looking back at the images, it seems less disintegrative than desperate. But at the time, Dean's seemingly manic scream conveyed the wrong image to the voters, one that did not evoke presidential timbre; and it was but a matter of time before Dean was winnowed out.

In New Hampshire, Kerry again gathered the highest total, winning there with 36 percent to Dean's second-place tally of 26 percent, a better showing than Iowa for Dean but still ten points below the new front-runner. Edwards finished in a tie for third place with Clark at 12 percent, Lieberman taking around 9 percent. Following New Hampshire, Kerry won five more primaries before Edwards won convincingly in South Carolina, bordering his home state of North Carolina. Edwards also managed a first-place tie with Clark in Oklahoma, and it was thus evident that Kerry was now the sole leader, with Edwards a rising challenger. Meanwhile, Dean did poorly, his campaign obviously spent and going through the motions. It was Kerry's nomination to be had from this point on, sweeping every primary on Super Tuesday with the exception of Vermont, which gave its native son Dean his second and last victory (the other being in the District of Columbia) of the 2004 primary season. Dean had in effect withdrawn, but a small number of diehard supporters still voted for him right to the bitter end. With Kerry's sweep on Super Tuesday, Edwards withdrew, clearing the way for Kerry's nomination by acclamation.

At the national convention, Kerry was formally nominated, tapping Edwards to run with him on the ticket's second spot. The convention highlighted Kerry's record of public service, including his heroism in the Vietnam War, which was followed by a period of personal disillusionment that led to his open opposition to the war. Two speeches drew the attention of the viewing audience: former president Clinton's nomination speech on behalf of Kerry, and an opening address by a young candidate for the U.S. Senate from Illinois, Barack Obama. Obama's keynote speech was a scene-stealer, reminiscent of past seminal speeches delivered by figures other than the party nominees in past conventions, such as Ronald Reagan's 1964 nominating speech for Barry Goldwater at the Republican convention, Democratic representative Barbara Jordan's speech in 1972, Senator Edward Kennedy's speech in 1980, and Governor Mario Cuomo's speech in 1984. Speaking of the "audacity of hope," Obama exhorted Americans to embrace a more optimistic vision of the American future and, with a "righteous wind" propelling them forward, to meet all challenges ahead. Like Reagan's eloquent speech in 1964, it was a breakthrough moment for an important, rapidly ascending figure in American political life.

In the post-convention campaign, the Democratic Party was confronted with issues revolving around the ongoing wars in Iraq and Afghanistan, and thus it faced the difficult task of supporting, on the one hand, the many sacrifices of the various members of the U.S. armed forces while, on the other hand, as forthrightly and as patriotically as possible, criticizing the foreign and military policies of President Bush's wartime administration. The platform attempted to state the terms: "Today, the Bush Administration is waging a war against a global terrorist movement committed to our destruction with insufficient understanding of our enemy or effort to address the underlying factors that can give rise to new recruits. This war isn't just a manhunt." The platform sharply criticized the Bush war effort for allegedly failing to build an international coalition in support of its military and foreign policy goals. To counter charges that the Democratic Party was weak on defense, the platform called for the expansion of the armed forces to reduce the strain on the National Guard and Reserves. "We will add 40,000 new soldiers—not to increase the number of soldiers in Iraq, but to sustain our overseas deployments and prevent and prepare for other possible conflicts. This will help relieve the strain on our troops and bring back more of our soldiers, guardsmen and reservists. We are dedicated to keeping our military operating on a volunteer basis. We are committed to management reform both to ensure that our defense funding is spent effectively and to help pay for these new forces," the platform explained. With respect to the domestic agenda, the Democratic platform promised affordable health care for all Americans and the adoption of advanced technology to improve the environment while creating new jobs. The platform also continued to oppose perennial Republican proposals to pass constitutional amendments that would ban abortions and that would legally define marriage as solely between a man and a woman.

The Republican platform, in addition to maintaining its positions on abortion and same-sex marriage, praised President Bush for his prosecution of the War on Terror in the aftermath of the 9/11 terrorist attacks. The platform recounted, "When America was struck by terrorists on September 11, 2001, President Bush immediately realized that it was an act of war, not just a crime. Working with Congress, the President drew up plans to take the fight to the enemy, vowing to bring the terrorists to justice, or bring justice to the terrorists." The platform promised to continue to fight terrorism on every front. With respect to domestic issues, the platform reaffirmed Republican support for allowing younger workers to divert part of their Social Security contributions to personal investment accounts. Additionally, the platform reaffirmed Republican support for the objectives of the No Child Left Behind education reform law enacted by Congress in a bipartisan effort during the first year of the Bush administration, in the pre-9/11 world of interparty comity.

The Bush campaign employed a dual strategy, the first element depicting the president as an effective wartime leader. The second element involved using attack ads aimed at defining Kerry as a stereotypical "tax-and-spend" liberal Democrat who was too weak on defense and thus unprepared to face enemies abroad. The Bush campaign used the slogan "Safer, Stronger" to convey the message that the president had both restored the nation's security and military power in the wake of 9/11 and revived the nation's economy after the bubble burst during the dot-com bust of the late 1990s during the Clinton administration. To raise doubts with respect to Kerry's ability to serve as commander in chief, the Bush ad campaign accused Kerry of having supported massive cuts in major weapons systems and even blocked the use of body armor for the troops.

The most effective of the attack ads, now known as the "Any Questions?" ad, was produced by an independent group working out of Texas. In a move reminiscent of the attempt in the 1852 campaign to discredit the military valor of Franklin Pierce, who fought in the Mexican-American War, the ad was aimed at impugning Kerry's otherwise vaunted military record during the war in Vietnam, and it involved interviews with former military personnel who served under Kerry as their commander on a U.S. Navy Fast Patrol Craft, or "swift boat"—small and quick naval patrol boats that would steam upriver in an attempt to interdict the flow of enemy supplies downriver, and to engage the enemy when the opportunity arose. Those interviewed alleged that Kerry had lied with respect to the events that led to his being awarded the Purple Heart and the Bronze Star. Besides claiming that Kerry prevaricated regarding his Vietnam heroics, those interviewed attacked Kerry for his April 22, 1972, testimony before the Senate Armed Services Committee. In his testimony, young Kerry entered the political spotlight for the first time in his condemnation of American involvement in the Vietnam War, an act that many of his former comrades-in-arms considered to be at the very least insubordinate. As one would expect, Kerry denied the claims of his former swift boat crew regarding his combat record, and he defended as an act of patriotism his decision to speak out against the conduct of the war in Vietnam. But the Bush attack had been particularly effective, casting considerable doubt on Kerry's willingness to engage a dangerous enemy such as al-Qaeda and similar terrorists, thugs, and bullies.

Kerry's counterpunch was also basically two-pronged. The first part of the Democrats' strategy involved familiarizing voters with Kerry's biography to convince them that his personal attributes were equal to the task of the presidency. The second sequence in the counterpunch was to hit back at Bush, drawing attention to what was perceived among the Democrats as the many serious failures of the administration, and most critically, the decision to invade Iraq in force based on vague and unproven allegations that the Hussein regime was actively developing and storing weapons of mass destruction (WMDs) without sufficient hard evidence to justify the military action.

By and large, while many voters were indeed confused or angry over the manner in which the war in Iraq was justified, Kerry faced a difficult campaign. Polls indicated that many states were solidly behind President Bush, with Kerry realistically holding almost no chance of gaining any ground in those areas of the country that were solidly with the president; hence the Kerry campaign selected a strategy to canvas and stump hard in key battleground states that he might be able to win over to their side should events cut their way. Much like the **Campaign of 2000**, these battleground states were, for the most part, Florida (which had been infamously tight, and confused, in 2000), Missouri, Arkansas, West Virginia, New Hampshire, Maine, Michigan, Minnesota, Wisconsin, New Mexico, Nevada, Pennsylvania, Washington, Oregon, Colorado (not as close in 2000 as other swing states, but shaping up, according to the polls, as very tight), and Ohio. Again, much like the 2000 election, the outcome of the election hinged upon turning out the respective core groups of each party. To win, the Bush campaign needed the support of white, middle-class male voters and social conservatives as well as to break even with women. The Kerry campaign needed to turn out union members and African Americans and to win over more women voters.

Catholic voters were also in play. While historically the clear majority of Catholics had supported Democratic candidates (with a minority backing Republicans), since the mid-to-late 1970s, the trend had been in a different direction, with Catholics more divided in their party allegiance, mostly owing to discomfort with the Democratic Party's public positions on certain moral issues, primarily abortion, that were incompatible with Church doctrine. Democrats had appealed to Catholics in the past, given their commitment to a more progressive social agenda with regard to problems such as poverty; but since the 1970s, the allegiance between the majority of Catholics and the Democrats had been seriously weakened. Hence the Democrats would have to win back Catholic voters if they were to boost their chances in purple states (i.e., states that were neither "red," or Republican, nor "blue," or Democratic—viz., the battleground or swing states) and possibly pull an upset. Kerry was himself an observant Roman Catholic, only the third Roman Catholic to be nominated by a major party for the presidency (the other two, Al Smith in 1928 and John Kennedy in 1960, were also liberal/moderate Democrats from the Northeast; Kennedy, like Kerry, was from Massachusetts), but his position on abortion was not entirely in line with the teachings of the Church; hence Kerry was not as appealing to the more conservative elements among the Catholic voters, who were more likely to support the Protestant Bush based on his more traditional views regarding certain social issues, and who were growing in numbers and influence. Liberal and moderate Catholics would still support Kerry, but the Catholic vote as a whole was not the solid bloc that had helped Democrats, with some exceptions, since the nineteenth century.

When the dust settled, President Bush was reelected by winning just over 62,000,000 votes, or 50.7 percent, to Senator Kerry's approximately 59,000,000 (about 48.3%), with Ralph Nader returning, this time as an independent, to win just over 460,000 votes. The Libertarian candidate Michael Badnarik managed to win around 397,000. The states won by Bush and Kerry in 2004 were almost identical to those states that were won by Bush and Gore in 2000, the only differences being New Mexico, which was won by Gore in 2000 but by Bush in 2004; and New Hampshire, which was the only northeastern state to vote for Bush in 2000 but which now, in voting for Kerry, gave the Democrats their first solid northeastern bloc since 1992. This time around, Bush won decisively in Florida, allaying fears by some analysts that another deadlock in Florida might possibly be repeated.

In looking at the finer grain at the county level, the trend set in motion in the 1990s and more clearly observed in 2000 was becoming even more evident; the Republican Bush won heavily in suburban and rural counties throughout the country, and especially in the interior, while the Democrat Kerry dominated the larger metropolitan areas and their urban cores scattered across the country, as well as counties along both the California and northeastern coasts. This trend appears to be the dominant pattern within electoral politics, at least for the moment. It has been noted that had Kerry won in Ohio, a reversal of the election of 2000 would have occurred, with Kerry winning the White House via the Electoral College (the electoral votes of Ohio, not Florida, this time making the difference) over Bush's win in the popular vote, with the only difference being that Bush would have lost with a majority given this alternative scenario. But according to data on statistician Mike Sheppard's MIT Web site detailing the easiest way to reverse any given election, the 59,000 votes that separated Bush from Kerry would have been slightly more difficult for Kerry to win than a switch of votes across Colorado, New Mexico, and Iowa that would have more likely given Kerry an Electoral College victory than the switching of sides in Ohio alone. Had Kerry won just 2,995 more votes in Iowa, another 5,030 votes in New Mexico, and then another 49,762 votes in Colorado, he would have managed a total switch of 57,787 votes, almost 2,000 fewer than a scenario in which he would gain over 59,000 votes in Ohio, and thus he could have won the election via those states. In other words, according to this source, the Bush-Kerry election was not nearly as close as some have believed; whereas the previous election, Bush over Gore, was indeed one of the closest elections in history, thanks primarily to Florida (Gore enjoying a much more significant margin in the national tally), and one in which the Electoral College made all the difference. Indeed, had just 29,525 votes changed in Nevada (which Bush won by only 21,500 votes) along with Iowa and New Mexico (and still giving Colorado to Bush), the Electoral College would have resulted in a tie at 269 to 269, even though Bush would have easily held a majority in the popular vote in that scenario.

Whether the Bush-Kerry contest was close or not, it is clear that the Bush presidency—in spite of the many controversies associated with it owing to the questions involving the war in Iraq as well as the manner in which the White House was first won in 2000, and in spite of the embattled nature of the last two years of the Bush administration—would nonetheless define the first decade of the twenty-first century. However, as crucial as the Bush White House had been in shaping

American politics at the start of the millennia, it would not be the last word in that first decade; and in 2004, no one could anticipate the manner in which politics in the United States would dramatically change in the campaign and election of 2008.

Additional Resources

Boller, Paul F., Jr. *Presidential Campaigns: From George Washington to George W. Bush.* Oxford: Oxford University Press, 2004.

Ceaser, James W. *Red over Blue: The 2004 Elections and American Politics.* Lanham, MD: Rowman & Littlefield, 2005.

Federal Election Commission. http://www.fec.gov.

Institute of Politics, Harvard University. *Campaign for President: The Managers Look at 2004.* Lanham, MD: Rowman & Littlefield, 2006.

Sabato, Larry. *Divided States of America: The Slash and Burn Politics of the 2004 Presidential Election.* New York: Longman, 2005.

Shaw, Daron R. *The Race to 270: The Electoral College and Campaign Strategies of 2000 and 2004.* Chicago: University of Chicago Press, 2006.

Sheppard, Mike. "How Close Were U.S. Presidential Elections?" http://www.mit.edu /~mi22295/elections.html.

Campaign of 2008

It is difficult to overstate the importance of the campaign and election of 2008 as a touchstone in the development of American political culture. For the first time in American political history, a woman candidate enjoyed front-runner status for several months moving into the campaign season, and she was viewed by many as not only the likely nominee from a major party, but also the odds-on favorite to become the next president. However, that eventuality never materialized, as a surprising new challenge suddenly emerged to thwart what many regarded to have been a *fait accompli*, a challenge that blocked the nomination and election of the first woman president but that nonetheless led to an electoral achievement equally remarkable and no less significant.

Prior to the election season of 2008, the 2006 midterm elections led to the Democratic Party's reemergence as it regained control of the House of Representatives. Growing anger over the lack of progress in Iraq contributed directly to the outcome of the congressional elections. But as dissatisfied as many American voters were with regard to the course of the war, troubling signs in the economy also weighed heavily on the voters and exposed the vulnerability of the Republican Party. The first quarter of 2007 saw the housing bubble burst with the decline of the subprime mortgage industry. First in California and then in the rest of the country, home prices collapsed as mortgage money began to disappear. By 2008, the bursting of the housing bubble would contribute to a severe recession that would become the most serious economic downturn since the Great Depression (although still not nearly as grave as the crisis in the 1930s). As a result, the Bush presidency lost a great deal of support, President Bush's approval ratings having dipped to the low thirties through the latter half of 2007 and clearly moving down (they would reach, according to some polls, as low as 19% before the president left office, the lowest ever measured since the approval ratings polls were instituted in the late 1930s, the second term of President Franklin Roosevelt). The country as a whole seemed not just anxious for change but insistent upon it, and the field of candidates exploring their options seemed to grow with each month as the 2008 season approached. President Bush, who remained resolute in his commitment to his policies, was increasingly isolated. His vice president, Richard Cheney, who had served an important role in the Bush administration, was almost universally unpopular and blamed for many of the policies that were now either rejected by large segments of the population or under close scrutiny and reevaluation. It was clear that the president would not pass along the legacy of his administration to a chosen heir; Vice President Cheney expressed no desire to run for nomination, and no other major GOP figure sought President Bush's imprimatur.

And so, for the first time since 1960, the 2008 campaign season opened without either an incumbent president seeking reelection or an incumbent vice president hoping to inherit the party's nomination (as in 1960 with then vice president Richard Nixon), and for the first time since 1952 (Dwight D. Eisenhower versus Adlai Stevenson), no incumbent president, incumbent vice president, or former vice president stood as a candidate for nomination. It was the most wide-open field since at least the 1968 election, an election thrown into turmoil with the withdrawal of the incumbent president (Lyndon Johnson) and the assassination of a leading candidate (Robert Kennedy); and to some, given that in 1968 the GOP was dominated on one side by a former vice president (Nixon, who would go on to win that year) and the 1952 campaign included the towering figure of General Dwight D. Eisenhower (who would win both his party's nomination and the presidency), it was in reality the most wide-open field since 1920 (the campaign season that produced, out of a pool of numerous candidates of all stripes and levels of ability, the Harding-Cox contest). Even if Vice President Cheney had chosen to run for president, he likely would not have garnered much support, given his controversial tenure. Thus the Republican nomination was up for grabs.

The Democratic Party, as mentioned above, did have a front-runner: New York senator and former First Lady Hillary Rodham Clinton, whose campaign for the presidency was already a cultural milestone. In past elections, one woman, Representative Geraldine Ferraro, had been nominated by a major party for the vice presidency (running alongside Senator Walter Mondale in 1984), and other women had been mentioned as presidential candidates in the past, most of them, beginning with suffragette Victoria Woodhull in 1872, representing minor parties, with a few, most notably Shirley Chisholm—the first woman candidate to win a major party primary in 1972—running under the banner of a major party (as a Democrat). But Senator Clinton was the first woman candidate ever to be considered the top contender. She was joined by a broad field of Democrats, including former North Carolina senator John Edwards, the vice presidential candidate in 2004 and considered by most to be Senator Clinton's main challenger; Senator Joe Biden of Delaware, who had briefly been a candidate in the 1988 campaign; New Mexico governor Bill Richardson, a prominent member of President Bill Clinton's administration and one of the more notable Hispanic politicians in the country; Senator Evan Bayh of Indiana; Senator Christopher Dodd of Connecticut; Ohio representative Dennis Kucinich, a candidate in 2004; former senator Mike Gravel of Alaska; former Iowa governor Tom Vilsack; and Senator Barack Obama of Illinois, an ascending figure in the party who had launched his national career via a breakthrough moment delivering a captivating keynote address at the 2004 convention.

While many analysts anticipated, over the long term, a battle between Clinton and Edwards, early polls indicated surprising strength for Obama. Interestingly, former vice president Al Gore was viewed by many as a potential contender, and in the early polls he ran second to Clinton, with some polls indicating that a significant number of voters might shift their support from Clinton to Gore should he formally announce. But Gore remained detached from the electoral process, having met with bitter disappointment in 2000 when, in winning the popular vote by nearly half a million ballots, he lost the election in the Electoral College. By the campaign season for the 2008 election, Gore was not a serious consideration, although a number of Democrats were prepared to fall in behind him. Other candidates that drew early attention but who ultimately decided not to run were Massachusetts senator John Kerry, the party standard-bearer in 2004; Howard Dean of Vermont, famous for his Iowa caucus "meltdown scream" in 2004; activist Al Sharpton; and Virginia senator Mark Warner. Each of these candidates drew a loyal core of followers but, for various reasons, decided not to mount a campaign.

Of all the candidates, Clinton, Obama, Edwards, Biden, and Dodd drew the most attention early, but it became clear that once Gore and Kerry were eliminated from the mix, it was shaping up as a contest between Clinton and Obama. Senator Clinton drew from a well-funded campaign war chest; enjoyed the support of the party leadership; built, along with her famous husband and former president Bill Clinton, a well-constructed and well-managed campaign organization; and seemed to be the only sure bet to take the nomination. Senator Obama, while popular and appealing, was considered by many within the party to be moving prematurely toward the White House, and when compared to the skilled Clinton campaign, he appeared to be out of his depth. Nonetheless, Obama possessed personal qualities that exuded confidence and competence, and as a fresh face in the eyes of the American electorate, he posed an attractive alternative. Obama ably ran a sharp campaign, borrowing lessons from Howard Dean's 2004 use of new media to generate attention, support, and donations, while avoiding the pitfalls that damaged Dean by also undertaking more traditional tactics and running, in some ways, a more conventional campaign by comparison. Senator Obama was clearly the underdog to Senator Clinton, who was looking more and more like a juggernaut prior to the commencement of the primary season; but he was nonetheless carving inroads toward electoral support. The Iowa caucus revealed that the 2008 contest would promise to be a battle.

In Iowa, Obama stunned the Clinton campaign. Obama won a substantial 38 percent in the caucus to 30 percent for Edwards; falling to third, Clinton showed a respectable but disappointing 29 percent. It was an unforeseen and heavy early blow to the Clinton campaign, and her front-runner status immediately evaporated; Obama enjoyed a ten-point lead in the polls just prior to the New Hampshire primary, while Edwards, sensing Clinton's weakness, began targeting her campaign in what appeared to be a joint effort with Obama to deliver the *coup de grâce* to Clinton's hopes, some pundits and wags declaring her candidacy moribund if not already dead.

However, Edwards's tactic of attempting to ally with Obama to gang up on Clinton backfired. In a particularly powerful moment during a debate at New Hampshire's St. Anselm College, Senator Clinton responded to Edwards's claim that her campaign could not promise real change, and that a Clinton presidency could not deliver genuine change. Playing to both his supporters and Obama's, Edwards claimed that they (i.e., he and Obama) could effect change, while Clinton was simply another version of the status quo. Roused, Clinton shot back, "Making change is not about what you believe; it's not about a speech you make. It's about working hard. I'm not just running on a promise for change. I'm running on thirty-five years of change. What we need is somebody who can deliver change. We don't need to be raising false hopes." It was seen by many as a pivotal moment for the Clinton campaign. Clinton, who had been the epitome of restrained and disciplined professionalism in the early stages of her campaign, was now opening up to the voters, revealing a more emotional and impassioned candidate. The voters responded favorably and rallied behind her, pushing her toward a three-point victory—39 percent to 36 percent—over Obama after having at one point trailed by as much as 13 percent, amounting to at least a 16 percent turnaround. Edwards's decision to pile on Clinton backfired; he won slightly under 17 percent of the vote, a distant third, with Richardson a still more distant fourth at around 4.5 percent, causing him to withdraw from the campaign. It was now shaping up to be a protracted battle between Senator Clinton and Senator Obama.

Senator Clinton's comeback was worthy of her husband, the "Comeback Kid," tightening and complicating the primary race and promising the most interesting primary season since 1976 (which pitted President Ford against former governor Ronald Reagan). It was clear that Clinton and Obama, who had actually split the delegates in New Hampshire, were the only real candidates for the party's nomination, and it was equally clear that neither one could confidently claim sole frontrunner status. It was also evident that winning the popular vote in a given primary was not enough; the delegate count was not determined by the straight overall percentages. In New Hampshire, Clinton had won the popular vote, but the delegates were split between her and Obama. In the following Nevada primary, Clinton won the popular vote but took a close second to Obama in the delegate count, winning twelve delegates to Obama's thirteen; by the Nevada primary, Edwards was no longer a factor.

With the primary season now in a dead heat, former president Clinton stepped in to assume a more active role, but it nearly backfired. In South Carolina, where Senator Obama was projected to win, Bill Clinton, in an uncharacteristically foolish campaigning moment, dismissively attributed Obama's likely victory in the Palmetto State as being akin to Jesse Jackson's win there twenty years earlier during the 1988 campaign, a win that was largely due to heavy support among African Americans there. Perceived as an unnecessary and pointless observation that, for the first time in the campaign, made an issue of Obama's race, many Democrats were understandably put off by Clinton's awkward remarks, which were atypical of the former president, owing both to his experience on the stump and to his solid reputation within the African American community. Obama did win South Carolina, as expected; but the campaign now turned more negative moving into Super Tuesday, and the party was dividing along Clinton and Obama loyalties. Significantly, after South Carolina, both Senator Edward Kennedy and his niece, Caroline Kennedy, daughter of President John F. Kennedy, openly supported the Obama campaign, significant endorsements tapping into an important Democratic legacy that boosted Senator Obama's confidence.

Prior to Super Tuesday, Clinton won in both Michigan and Florida, her campaign once again moving forward. Super Tuesday was a heated battle. In the end, Senator Obama could claim victories in twelve primaries, Senator Clinton ten primaries, with Missouri deadlocked. While Obama won slightly more states, Clinton's victories occurred in heavily populated states, including by far the largest electoral prize, California, as well as another big state, New York, and adding Massachusetts, a key Democratic stronghold and indicator of a candidate's strength among the party rank and file. For the first time since 1988, the Super

Tuesday cluster of primaries failed to solve the issue, and a prospective nominee still had not emerged.

Most pundits considered the race up in the air. However, when Clinton admitted that her campaign was experiencing funding problems (announcing that she had to pony up $5 million of her own money to stay afloat), while Obama's campaign enjoyed ample and growing funding, the mood began to shift toward Obama. Looking ahead at the demographics in the upcoming round of primaries, pundits and forecasters began to predict a momentum change for Obama. In a series of primaries and caucuses beginning on February 9 and running intermittently for ten days, Senator Obama swept all eleven contests in a spectacular breakthrough move. Even before it was over, on February 13, *NBC News* was referring to Obama as the front-runner, the Clinton campaign now viewed as on the descent.

But Clinton was far from defeated. Thanks in part to incendiary comments by Senator Obama's pastor, a particularly controversial cleric who impudently "damned" the United States while delivering a self-indulgent and inflammatory sermon denouncing its domestic and foreign policies, Obama's momentum was temporarily mired in a thicket of criticism impugning both the young senator's religious values and the sincerity of his patriotism. Obama responded admirably, delivering his most important speech since the 2004 keynote address at the Democratic Convention, and certainly the most important speech of the 2008 campaign, in which he spoke candidly and reasonably on the complexities of race and disaffection within the context of American history and social development. Simultaneously expressing an understanding of the reasons behind such comments and rejecting their substance as being "profoundly distorted," Obama managed to define his campaign in terms of the ongoing quest for "a more perfect union."

Obama's deft response notwithstanding, Clinton rebounded to win three more primaries, including convincing wins in Ohio and Rhode Island and a close victory in the Texas primary, with Obama winning in the parallel Texas caucus. In an effort to build on its new momentum, the Clinton campaign focused on the importance of record and achievement, claiming that Obama lacked the experience and political maturity that is needed to competently manage international crises. A dramatic television ad asked voters to consider which candidate would be better prepared to answer the inevitable "3:00 AM phone call" alerting the president to news of an unfolding international crisis requiring swift action and intelligent, courageous leadership. The "red phone" television ad was visually and viscerally effective, but it was not enough to dampen Obama's attempts to restoke his campaign. Parrying Clinton's thrust, he managed to win primaries and caucuses in Wisconsin, Vermont, and Mississippi, thus marshaling his forces for an important charge at the late primaries running from late April into June and hard upon the threshold of the upcoming convention in Denver. As predicted in the polls, Clinton opened this last phase of the primary season with a solid win in Pennsylvania, and she also managed to win more primaries and caucuses between April 22 and June 3 than Obama. But in spite of Clinton's successes in the latter primaries, Obama kept winning more pledged delegates, and significantly, he began receiving more pledges from the important and influential cohort of superdelegates than his adversary.

Thus, on the eve of the Denver convention, Obama held a slight lead in delegates even though Clinton had actually won more primaries; but as close as it was, it proved to be just enough of a lead to win the nomination in just one ballot. Shortly before the Denver convention, the media began to refer to Obama as the "presumptive nominee" after recent wins in the Montana and South Dakota primaries, which were accompanied by the commitment of sixty additional superdelegates pledging for Obama. On June 7, a crestfallen Clinton, who just narrowly fell short after the most competitive primary season campaign in thirty-two years (Ford and Reagan), conceded the nomination. At the Denver convention, Senator Obama officially became the first African American to be nominated for the presidency by a major political party. Obama selected Delaware senator Biden as his running mate, even though Biden had at one point early in the campaign put his foot in his mouth with what was perceived as a well-intentioned but poorly worded, racially suggestive comment about Obama's "clean" image. But all of that was put well behind the two men as they now moved forward to carry forth the Democratic standard in 2008; they were among the most diverse tandem in memory— Obama an African American with biracial roots, and Biden a Roman Catholic (only three other Roman Catholics had been nominated by a major party to run for vice president—Republican William Miller in 1964 and Democrats Edmund Muskie in 1968 and Geraldine Ferraro in 1984).

In his acceptance speech, candidate Obama declared, "Our government should work for us, not against us. It should ensure opportunity, not for just those with the most money and influence, but for every American who is willing to work. That's the promise of America, the idea that we are responsible for ourselves, but that we also rise and fall as one nation, the fundamental belief that I am my brother's keeper, I am my sister's keeper. That's the promise we need to keep, that's the change we need right now."

The contest for the Republican nomination was in some ways the reverse of the Democratic campaign. While former New York mayor Rudy Giuliani was widely considered the front-runner in the early phase of the process, as the campaign year approached, it became evident that Giuliani's political capital was not as strong as initially anticipated. In other words, while both Clinton and Giuliani were widely regarded as the front-runners in 2006 and 2007, as the actual campaign season approached, Giuliani's position was revealed as quite weak, leaving the impression that the GOP field was even more open than the Democrats'. Along with Mayor Giuliani, the major Republican candidates consisted of former governor of Massachusetts Mitt Romney, son of George Romney, who ran for the GOP nomination against Richard Nixon in 1968; former Arkansas governor Mike Huckabee; and Arizona senator John McCain, who ran for the nomination against George W. Bush in 2000. Other candidates of note included former Tennessee senator Fred Thompson (currently a television actor), Representative Ron Paul from Texas, and California representative Duncan Hunter.

The exact nature of Giuliani's vulnerability was exposed in Iowa, where Governor Huckabee surprised the field by taking 34 percent of the popular vote, with Romney placing a respectable second at 25 percent. McCain and Thompson landed in a tie for third with 13 percent, and the previously assumed front-runner Giuliani fell far behind the field, winning a meager 4 percent. New Hampshire thus became critical for Giuliani, but his showing there was again discouraging, taking just slightly below 9 percent and less than half a percentage point ahead of fifth-place Ron Paul. The big surprise in New Hampshire came from Senator McCain, whom many pundits and analysts had proclaimed finished the previous year. Both McCain and Romney campaigned vigorously in the Granite State, with the payoff of just under 38 percent of the vote for the former and 32 percent for the latter. Huckabee finished a distant third with approximately 11 percent, Thompson barely registered in sixth with slightly above 1 percent.

After Iowa and New Hampshire, it was clear that the once broad field was narrowed to three major figures: McCain, the New Hampshire winner; Huckabee, the Iowa winner; and Romney, who finished a respectable second in both events. Romney won the next primary in Wyoming, but the big test for his campaign was in Michigan, where his father had served as governor in the 1960s. Pollsters detected a dead heat between McCain, who carried the momentum of New Hampshire, and Romney, who was well known in Michigan owing to his upbringing, with Huckabee also showing the likelihood of a close third, and possibly higher. In the actual primary voting, Romney surged ahead with 39 percent to McCain's 30 percent, injecting energy into his campaign and tightening the race still further. Huckabee fell farther behind than anticipated, taking just over 16 percent. The following primary in Nevada proved an even bigger victory for Romney, as he took over 51 percent of the vote. Saving their resources and energies for South Carolina, neither McCain nor Huckabee campaigned in Nevada, thus allowing Ron Paul to place behind Romney in the Silver State. Romney's victory in Nevada pushed him ahead in the delegate count and thus gave him, at least for some, front-runner status.

South Carolina was the site of McCain's pivotal loss to George W. Bush in 2000, and, given Romney's recent successes, it was a state critical to both the McCain and Huckabee campaigns. South Carolina was also Fred Thompson's last stand. Thompson entered the race late, in response to what was perceived to be a grassroots groundswell for the conservative former senator. Thus Thompson devoted considerable energy to South Carolina, particularly focusing his efforts on challenging Huckabee's conservative credentials and claiming that he, Thompson, offered the real choice for conservatives. But it was McCain's moment; in a reversal of his 2000 fortunes, McCain won in South Carolina with just over 33 percent, Huckabee placing with slightly below 30 percent, with Thompson lagging far behind, showing a dismal 15.6 percent, scarcely above the 15 percent taken by Romney, who did not mount a campaign there.

Meanwhile, Mayor Giuliani, after being chastened in Iowa and New Hampshire, opted to ignore every state except Florida, gambling that a big win there would reignite his campaign. Florida was a genuine battleground state, as the last two elections had proved; thus if Giuliani could impress in Florida, he would be in a good position to turn his campaign around. Giuliani devoted all of his energy, resources, and focus to the Sunshine State, and for a time pollsters agreed that the strategy might work. But after South Carolina, the other candidates and their supporters began to canvass Florida hard. The result of the Florida primary obliterated Giuliani's campaign and propelled McCain into the status of the clear frontrunner: McCain won 36 percent of the popular vote and took all of Florida's 57 delegates; Romney placed at 31 percent, with Giuliani limping into third at only just under 15 percent, Huckabee lagging farther behind with only 13 percent. After Florida, McCain began receiving the endorsements of the party's more prominent leadership, setting him up for more success on Super Tuesday, when twenty-one states would be in play for GOP candidates: nine states would be won by McCain, seven would go to Romney, and five would see wins for Huckabee. Significantly, following the endorsement of California's "Governator," Arnold Schwarzenegger, McCain won the Golden State. With California's weight behind him, McCain's campaign now could claim around three-fifths of the delegates needed to win the nomination, and he clearly held momentum going into to the later primaries. Huckabee followed Super Tuesday with wins in Kansas and Louisiana, but the McCain camp remained confident, and on February 12, in what is called the "Potomac Primaries" (consisting of Virginia, Maryland, and the District of Columbia), McCain swept up all the delegates in play and was deemed by the media as the "presumptive nominee." And so it was—on March 4, McCain swept four more primaries (Texas, Ohio, Vermont, and Rhode Island) and clinched the nomination. Moving toward the convention in St. Paul, Minnesota, all that was left was to find a running mate.

It was a reasonable assumption to expect a possible McCain-Romney or McCain-Huckabee ticket, but the McCain camp, anticipating a tough contest with the Democrats, who were guaranteed to nominate a historic candidacy (either the first-ever African American or the first woman nominee from a major party), sought a running mate that would similarly excite the voters. Upon the advice of his inner circle, McCain tapped Alaska governor Sarah Palin, scarcely known outside her home state, as his vice presidential running mate. Palin, who was to most voters an unknown quantity, was a bold, dramatic, and risky choice; but her debut performance at the national convention introducing her to the general public proved outstanding, injecting the McCain campaign with renewed energy and drawing considerable interest to the GOP ticket. Thus the 2008 election, regardless of the result, was guaranteed the result of a watershed moment: either the first African American president or the first woman vice president would be elected come November.

The campaign for the general election thus drew more excitement within the voting public, as well as within the media, than any campaign in recent memory. The Obama campaign stressed the renewing themes of hope and change; the McCain campaign emphasized experience, heroism, and patriotic commitment. Both candidates and their running mates stumped hard throughout the country, with the polls indicating a tightening race in the post-convention stretch. The McCain campaign worked hard to connect to the average working American, making a pop culture hero out of an otherwise anonymous citizen who would come to be known as "Joe the Plumber," an Ohio plumbing contractor who had vocally challenged candidate Obama during a stump event in his home state. To the McCain-Palin campaign, "Joe the Plumber" represented the industrious, self-reliant, middle-class working man who would be hampered by the typical "tax and regulate" policies that were once again offered by a liberal, activist Democrat, and hence he became a symbol of the values of small government and personal initiative that were central to the Republican Party's core principles. Republicans followed the lead of the Clinton strategy and attacked Obama's lack of experience, McCain drawing upon decades of public service and his status as a seasoned and accomplished elder in the Senate, Obama depicted as too young and too green, a veritable backbencher not having even completed his first term in the Senate. Stumping Republicans, egged on by Rudy Giuliani's St. Paul convention speech, mocked Obama's record as a "community organizer" in Chicago, and it was frequently implied that an Obama presidency would move the country too far to the left, setting national policies upon a slippery slope that would precipitate an insidiously more "socialist" United States.

Rhetorically, the Obama campaign focused on associating McCain with the Bush presidency, something that the McCain people had labored hard to prevent (not unlike Gore's efforts to distance himself from Bill Clinton in 2000, and to a lesser extent Hubert Humphrey's similar efforts to detach himself from President Johnson in 1968). The Democrats indicted the Bush administration and the GOP leadership, which included Senator McCain, for mistakes and deceptions leading to and nearly ruining U.S. efforts in Iraq. Senator Obama, while critical of the war in Iraq, was clearly in support of increased efforts in Afghanistan forcefully directed against al-Qaeda. Thus, while Obama was embraced by many who were against the war, it was clear that Obama's main criticism was only against the conduct of the war in Iraq. The Obama campaign also targeted Governor Palin. After her dramatic and surprisingly effective debut, the Alaska governor seemed slightly out of her depth on the campaign trail, unable to perform as well on the stump as she had at the convention. With Palin's every slight miscue or gaffe, the Democrats pounced, gleefully depicting her as shallow and clueless. Thus, while both campaigns did send positive messages to the voters, there was plenty of mud slung across both camps.

In the presidential debates, Senator Obama played well to the viewing audience. Evincing a cool and collected demeanor, and well equipped to recall facts and form arguments in a style that was no doubt cultivated during his days as a law school professor, Obama seemed increasingly more qualified than his critics would allow. Senator McCain's performance was uneven. At times he seemed strong and seasoned, but at other times, he appeared clumsy and out of touch. Tellingly, both candidates were parodied by television comedians, but the manner in which McCain was spoofed was decidedly unflattering compared to comic interpretations and parodies of Obama. After the first debate, polls indicated that 40 percent of viewers thought Obama the victor and another 30 percent called it a draw, while only 22 percent felt that McCain had won the day. Polling also revealed that Obama was viewed more favorably on economic issues, while McCain was seen as more adept in foreign policy.

A second debate was scheduled shortly after, but in the wake of the recession crisis that interrupted the campaign season, Senator McCain announced that he was suspending his campaign (and thus postponing the next debate) so that he could direct all of his energies to the current crisis. Both candidates flew to Washington, DC, and participated in a roundtable meeting about the crisis with President Bush and several key advisers, but insiders soon leaked that McCain's presence was scarcely relevant, while Obama, at least according to the accounts of those present, was at least more engaged. McCain's effort to demonstrate the need for nonpartisan responsibility during the crisis was viewed in the media, rightly or wrongly, as cynical grandstanding. On September 26, after the short emergency hiatus from the campaign trail, McCain agreed to a second debate.

The second debate went poorly for Senator McCain. Senator Obama again appeared fluid and in command; McCain spoke haltingly and committed a number of slight but nagging mistakes, such as calling Senator Obama "that one" and seemingly wandering around stage while Obama spoke. These goofball moves were easily exaggerated in the press and were all too ripe for the late-night wags and the armchair critics. Afterward, polls universally indicated that voters saw Obama as the winner; in some polls, Obama's favorable ratings were as high as 55 percent, with McCain scarcely making 30 percent in his best showing. Sarah Palin's debate against Joe Biden did not play as well as the Republicans had hoped. Her convention triumph was now a distant memory, as both she and Senator McCain were, fairly or unfairly, viewed as unable to manage their counterparts in public debate. Governor Palin did develop an ardent and energized following, but her campaign performance on the whole was not sufficient to win over many voters beyond the loyal corps of true believers. The third debate showed even better for Obama. Thus, after the round of debating was over, what began as a dead heat in the polls between the two candidates had evolved into a significant lead for Senator Obama. All polls indicated that the senator from Illinois would prevail and thus become the first African American to be elected president of the United States.

And so it was. On Election Day, Barack Obama was elected to serve as the forty-fourth president of the United States by winning a record number of total votes, coming in at just a fraction under 69,500,000 (or 52.9%), with Senator McCain winning just over 59,850,000 (45.6%) and no minor-party candidate managing above 0.5 percent. Significantly, Obama's percentage of the popular vote, at just under 53 percent, was the highest for a Democratic candidate since 1964 (Lyndon Johnson's 61% landslide), and he was the first Democratic candidate to win over 50 percent since Jimmy Carter's 50.08 percent in 1976. In fact, only three Democratic candidates in history have won a larger percentage of the popular vote than Barack Obama: Franklin Roosevelt (whose percentage of the vote exceeds Obama's on four occasions, winning 57.4%, 60.8%, 54.7%, and 53.4%), Lyndon Johnson (61.1%), and Andrew Jackson (on two occasions, 55.9% and 54.7%). Furthermore, Obama won the highest percentage of the popular vote by any candidate since the elder Bush's 53.4 percent in 1988, although it should be noted that President Clinton's margin of victory of 8.5 percent in 1996 was noticeably higher than Obama's margin of 7.3 percent, even though Clinton never won more than 49 percent of the vote. In the Electoral College, Obama's popular-vote victory converted to 365 electoral votes (68%) to 173 for McCain (32%), with Obama carrying every state won by John Kerry in 2004 but significantly adding the battleground states of Florida, Ohio, Indiana, Iowa, Colorado (going to the Democrats for the first time since 1992 and only the second time since 1964), Nevada, North Carolina, and Virginia, the latter won by the Democrats for the first time since the Johnson landslide in 1964 (a state that even bucked the trend in 1976 and went for the Republican candidate, President Ford, preventing Carter from sweeping the South that year).

If not a landslide, it was nonetheless clearly a decisive victory for Obama; more importantly, it was one of the most important electoral events in American political history and a cultural marker of monumental proportions. A nation that once permitted the brutish enslavement of millions of Africans and people of African descent had just elected, through a decent democratic process, a man of biracial birth to the highest office in the land, an act that for many reflects the nobler principles of that more perfect union toward which the Founders aspired and to which thoughtful Americans to this day remain ardently committed. President Barack Obama has proven to all Americans, and indeed, to the world at large, that the democratic process, when duly framed by the principles of equal rights and liberties and protected by the rule of law, can draw from all of us the sense of fairness and the commitment to dignity that all human beings should ever expect and that every human being always deserves.

Additional Resources

Abrahamson, Paul R., John H. Aldrich, and David W. Rohde. *Change and Continuity in the 2008 and 2010 Elections.* Washington, DC: CQ Press, 2011.

Ceaser, James W., et al. *Epic Journey: The 2008 Elections and American Politics.* Lanham, MD: Rowman & Littlefield, 2011.

Cohen, Martin, David Karol, Hans Noel, and John Zaller. *The Party Decides: Presidential Nominations before and after Reform.* Chicago: University of Chicago Press, 2008.

Johnson, Haynes, and Dan Balz. *The Battle for America 2008: The Story of an Extraordinary Election.* New York: Viking, 2009.

Norrander, Barbara. *The Imperfect Primary: Oddities, Biases and Strengths of U.S. Presidential Nomination Politics.* New York: Routledge, 2010.

Sabato, Larry. *The Year of Obama: How Barack Obama Won the White House.* New York: Longman, 2009.

Telser, Michael, and David O. Sears. *Obama's Race: The 2008 Election and the Dream of Post-Racial America.* Chicago: University of Chicago Press, 2010.

Todd, Chuck, and Sheldon Gawiser. *How Barack Obama Won.* New York: Vintage Books, 2009.

Campaign of 2012

There are a small number of political campaigns in which the surface conceals the substance, campaigns in which the dissonance between appearance and reality is pronounced. Consequently, these campaigns are remembered for having been in some way surprising, shaped by unexpected developments or an unforeseen outcome, an outcome that upon reflection might not have been so unexpected if the perception of events had been more aligned with the reality of essential conditions. The general election of 1948 might serve as the most prominent example of this—President Truman's defeat seemingly so inevitable that one of the country's foremost newspapers, the *Chicago Tribune*, ran the now famous headline declaring it so, an inky blooper that famously delighted the victorious incumbent. While the presidential campaign of 2012 was in no way marked by such a dramatic disjunction between expectations formed by misperception and the realities of the case at hand, it was nonetheless a campaign season in which opinions about the candidates and their prospects did not always jibe with the actual circumstances. The actual substance behind the political drama as spotlighted through the media was obscured by disconnected suppositions and skewed perceptions.

The disjunction begins with a curious misreading of the position of the incumbent, President Barack Obama, combined with equally puzzling assumptions fashioned around the challenging Republican Party's commitment to its front-runner, former Massachusetts governor Mitt Romney. Had the perceptions regarding the former been, in fact, an accurate reflection of the reality of things, then the president might have been limited by the voters to a single term; and conversely, had the assumptions regarding the Republican Party's presumably lukewarm interest in its nominee been accurate, then the incumbent president would have enjoyed a still more impressive victory on Election Day. Neither was the case: The president was never in threat of being dislodged as some had anticipated, nor was the challenger politically incompetent and undercut by diluted support. The Campaign of 2012 did not produce a surprising outcome comparable to 1948, at least as the story goes, but upon reflection the 2012 outcome was quite apart from the expectations held by divergent segments of the electorate.

Notably, political scientists John Sides and Lynn Vavreck examined this dissonance between appearance and reality in their important study of the 2012 presidential campaign, *The Gamble*. Avoiding anecdotal distractions and methodically inquiring into the manner in which the "fundamental factors" (e.g., the ever-important state of the economy) influence elections, Sides and Vavreck's study has prompted a number of questions. Just how vulnerable was the incumbent? How thin was the GOP's support for its front-runner? Did the Republicans in reality delay their commitment to Governor Romney in the hope that a stronger standard-bearer would eventually emerge? Was President Obama's reelection more likely, and therefore less surprising, than commentators had allowed during the campaign? Appearances aside, was the "conventional wisdom" about both candidates aligned with real factors fundamental to the outcome?

Unchallenged in his own party, President Obama held the advantage of incumbency running up to the election year. Historically, incumbent presidents typically win reelection, losing only nine times since the pivotal election of 1800, the first instance of an incumbent president (John Adams) failing to retain office, and throughout the sweep of American political history, the blind odds have favored incumbents. Nevertheless, upon closer observation, more recent elections seem to have followed a newer, different trend. Among the last six presidents to hold office prior to 2008, only three managed to win reelection: Reagan, Clinton, and the younger Bush in 1984, 1996, and 2004, respectively. The remaining three incumbents within this time frame—Ford (1976), Carter (1980), and the elder Bush (1992)—were voted out. If we include President Lyndon Johnson—who withdrew from the race influenced by what he deemed the constraints of insurmountable exigencies—then we observe that *four of the last eight* sitting presidents were unable to secure their reelection. This is an observable trend that may warrant a reduced confidence in the presumed advantage of incumbency. All four of those sitting presidents who were unable to win a second term were at some point challenged within their own party: President Johnson by Senator Gene McCarthy, President Ford by former governor Reagan, President Carter by Senator Edward Kennedy, and the elder President Bush by political firebrand and former adviser to President Nixon, Pat Buchanan. The incumbent presidents among the last eight who managed reelection went unchallenged within their party (save for a quixotic, mostly symbolic, and largely ignored antiwar campaign advanced by Republican California representative Pete McCloskey in 1972 during the Nixon incumbency), as was the case for President Obama. Nevertheless, as the campaign for 2012 began to stir into motion, there hovered a palpable assumption that the president was somehow vulnerable; that given a credible challenge, his reelection could be thwarted.

A variety of factors may have encouraged these assumptions, beginning with the state of the economy, which, while improving, was nevertheless generally perceived to be sufficiently stressed to sustain general anxiety. True, the nation was gradually emerging from the severe recession that hampered the last year of the Bush administration and plagued the first three years of the Obama administration, but progress was slow and not widely perceived. Additionally, the expected Republican gains in the midterm congressional elections were extensive; the scale of the seat changes in the House of Representatives was particularly astonishing. Republicans gained sixty-three new seats while recapturing the majority, the biggest shift in that chamber in sixty-two years. Senate Democrats, while protecting an ever-receding majority in their chamber, were weakened by the loss of six seats. Republicans also enjoyed gains throughout the Union at the state level. Media pundits read these signs as a plebiscitary rebuke of the policies and performance of the Obama administration. Humbled by the Republican triumph, the president candidly referred to the numbers on the midterm scorecard as a "shellacking."

Some of these Republican gains were influenced by the activism of the Tea Party faction, boosting the confidence of the ideological right through its ostensibly newly won leverage. Tea Party influence was unexpectedly persistent, but given that slightly less than a third of the Republicans elected in Congress were directly associated with the faction, its image as a ubiquitous and irresistible force may be exaggerated. Clearly the Tea Party had markedly influenced GOP politics, especially through activity in the primaries and success in local elections, but its focus had been scattered by crackpot distractions such as the "birther" allegations and oddly pointed criticisms of President Obama's religious affiliation, somehow oblivious to the Constitution's prohibition against religious tests. While not every Tea Party adherent had adopted these bizarre opinions, the more exercised and vigorous elements of the movement viewed them seriously. Fringe extremists aside, the Tea Party seemed formidable.

Furthering this perception of vulnerability, raised voices of discontent from within the president's own party, primarily from the liberal wing, reacted in frustration to what they deemed an ideologically moderate and politically conciliatory administration. In spite of caricatures of the president's ideological positions from the right, President Obama, a pragmatist, gravitated toward the middle, perhaps a left-leaning centrist but a centrist nonetheless, to the chagrin of the left. Historically, such criticisms from within a president's own party are expected; one cannot be president without drawing criticism from all directions. In the case of President Obama, the liberal criticism seemed to expose fading confidence in the administration growing into disillusionment. In 2008, candidate Obama raised hopes for those who sought a genuine answer to the "failed system in Washington," an answer that had eluded the leadership in both parties. This virtue of hope and the promise of change were central elements of Senator Obama's rhetoric, winning over the left with the promise of institutional reform and progressive initiative. By 2010 President Obama was stridently criticized from the party's left for failing to make good on his promises to transform government and in the process transform American political culture. In office, President Obama appeared to have abandoned the idealism of his campaign for the realism of the pragmatist, prompting complaints of betrayal from the left. While some would argue that the president's efforts in reforming public support for health care, regulating the financial system, stimulating the economy, addressing environmental degradation, improving fair-pay legislation, and seeking solutions to the burden of student debt were significant efforts toward fulfilling those promises, others—especially in the liberal wing of the party—received his policies as gradualist half-measures and cynical compromises with the right, more politics as usual from the man who had won the election under the clarion of hope and change. Finally, voters left and right were stridently critical of the president's foreign policy, especially the conduct of military action abroad. To the disappointment of those Obama supporters who had anticipated a reduction of military operations abroad, the fighting continued, and the unfinished business regarding the prison at Guantanamo Bay Naval Base drew sharp criticism against the administration. For some Democrats, the president had become part of the establishment.

The president, however, was not entirely disengaged from the left. As the Occupy Wall Street protest commenced in September 2011, the president took notice, sympathetic to grievances against income inequality and the influence of Wall Street, symbolized by the contrast between the wealthiest "one percent" and the rest of us, the "ninety-nine percent." Shedding the caution recommended from within his inner circle, the president resolved to acknowledge the concerns of the Occupy protestors, reaffirming his own commitment to social justice. In Osawatomie, Kansas (already an important place in American history owing to the connection to militant abolitionist John Brown in the mid-1850s and former president Theodore Roosevelt's speech introducing his "New Nationalism" in August 1910), the president joined his own bully pulpit in rebuking the "one percent," inveighing against the greed of Wall Street, along with the insurance and mortgage industries, and, fairly or unfairly, implicating the Republican Party for its alleged role in promoting a heartless "you're-on-your-own economics." Occupy Wall Street protesters, the president intoned, were justified in speaking to the "broad-based frustration about how our financial system works." Forceful as it was, the speech only made a modest splash. It received media coverage, but more as a routine event than a major address in the mold of Teddy Roosevelt's Osawatomie touchstone. Interestingly, and with some insight, the president even-handedly observed similarities shared between both the Occupy and Tea Party movements. "Both on the left and the right," the president explained, ". . . people feel separated from government. They feel that their institutions aren't looking out for them."

Not everyone associated with Occupy Wall Street embraced this. Within a month of Osawatomie, Occupy protestors heckled the president at a New Hampshire event, shouts of "Mic check!" cueing a cascade of chants that temporarily halted the president's remarks. These "mic check" tactics, dubbed "the People's Microphone," were a by-product of the Occupy movement, now aimed at a president friendly to their cause. Nevertheless, the 2011 Osawatomie speech and subsequent comments signaled, at least rhetorically, the president's recommitment to social transformation, supplying the scaffolding for the upcoming campaign for reelection.

Naturally, ongoing anxieties, however realistic, over economic progress loomed over the president, the principal feature casting the shadow of vulnerability. The Great Recession of 2008–2009 did not further deteriorate into a second Great Depression as many feared; however, the effects of the recession lingered, prolonging the recovery and constraining the administration's ambitions. Polls indicated sustained misgivings within the general public, even though the economy was evincing slow growth. Significantly, unemployment remained above 8 percent through most of the president's term, and while this is hardly close to the calamitous 30 percent and more experienced during the darkest days of the Great

Depression, the perception among the general public was influenced by nervous pessimism and diminished confidence in the president's policies. For this reason alone, President Obama was from various quarters compared to President Carter, who was also constrained and dogged by a stressed economy, in the late seventies. As with President Carter, congressional Democrats had become disconnected from the administration, especially those Democrats that leaned left. President Carter had also become isolated from the left wing of his party, thus prompting the intraparty challenge from Senator Kennedy. The deep recession that buffeted President Obama's first years in office exceeded the problems that plagued the Carter administration and the first year of President Reagan's subsequent presidency. President Reagan enjoyed the benefits of an economic recovery during his first term, but a comparable recovery did not occur under President Obama, and public opinion circled in a holding pattern of disquiet and diffidence. Plans for an unprecedented and exhaustive economic stimulus were blunted by partisan opposition; nevertheless, the bipartisan package that was approved in Congress exponentially exceeded a previous extensive stimulus attempt by the federal government under President Clinton during the downturn of 1993. Public support was lukewarm at best. In April 2010, seven months prior to the dramatic midterm elections, a Pew Center poll indicated growing disillusionment, over 60 percent of participants expressing mounting pessimism. To compound the president's problems, the general public also remained unenthusiastic about—and in certain segments of the electorate (viz., the conservative right), vehemently opposed to—the Patient Protection and Affordable Care Act (ACA). Critics pejoratively labeled the president's health care reform "Obamacare," but the tag evolved into the vernacular for the ACA. With the ideological right lobbing broadsides against the administration, the ideological left standing aloof, and the public in general anxious, the president's prospects appeared compromised. Finally, no one could anticipate how President Obama's race would figure into the equation; would he encounter a racially charged backlash in 2012? While it is a fact of political history that the American public did elect an African American for the nation's highest office, it is also evident to honest observers that the electoral triumph of 2008 had not inaugurated, as it was hoped, a racially more tolerant climate. All these factors considered together seemed to cloud the president's outlook for 2012, consequently energizing Republican opposition.

Nevertheless, these fundamental conditions were dissonant with one important fact: the president was popular. This is not to dismiss those factions within the general public who were critical of the president, some severely so (even to the point of hatred, at times stirred by racist undercurrents, simmering at the crackpot fringe), but rather to indicate that in spite of the many difficulties encountered in his first administration, many Americans still embraced President Obama as a person, even as his policies still invited broad criticism. Sides and Vavreck's original study of polling data reveals that the president was "unexpectedly popular"; they noticed that the president's approval ratings were persistently stable, even comparing the president's actual approval ratings with "expected approval" ratings based on a protracted study of presidential approval ratings dating from the Truman administration. In studying the relationship between fundamental conditions (e.g., the economy, always a central factor) and how these conditions correlate to public reactions to a president's policies, an "expected approval" rating can be determined and then compared to the actual numbers drawn from a poll. According this study, President Obama's actual approval ratings were consistently higher than what should have been expected based on external conditions, and furthermore, with the exception of President Kennedy, the difference between President Obama's actual and expected approval was higher than any administration in the database, which extends back through President Truman. Moreover, in measuring party loyalty and comparing presidents Obama and Carter, Sides and Vavrick observed that Obama was "more popular with Democratic voters than every president since Truman except Kennedy." Thus, even though disenchantment among Democrats in Congress was real, the data nonetheless reveals more party loyalty than that which had been inspired by fellow Democratic presidents Truman, Johnson, Carter, and Clinton.

Additionally, Sides and Vavreck address the issue of the president's image. Obama is often depicted as aloof, intellectually distant, and dispassionate—compared by some media wags to the stoic fictional character Mr. Spock (an analogy that seems strangely oblivious to the fact that Mr. Spock is an admired, beloved character to even the most casual *Star Trek* viewer). Polling data reveals a different impression of Obama's persona, with most Americans polled—as high as 71 percent, according to Pew—regarding him as "warm and friendly," a "good communicator" sympathetic to their troubles. Furthermore, while it would appear that the president's response to the recession was often a focus of criticism, and that the public was at best lukewarm toward his reforms in health care and other domestic programs, the president as a person was still viewed favorably by the majority. For many Americans, it didn't hurt the president's image as commander in chief when U.S. Navy Seals killed the murderous al-Qaeda ringleader Osama bin Laden in May 2011. Shrill critics right and left remained adamantine in their intense dislike of the president, but the majority of the public, at least according to the polling data, while tentative in response to his achievements, were nonetheless well disposed toward the man.

While the GOP appeared perched on the catbird seat in November 2010, by the summer of 2011 its advantage, though still evident, began to weaken. Tea Party influence, while still present, was thinning, or at least according to recent polling, the clout that it held in 2010 slightly weakened. Nevertheless, while the GOP seemed to have lost some ground since the midterms, the party remained confident and generated a number of prospective candidates. At the outset former governor Romney, Senator John McCain's principal challenger for the 2008 nomination, was the obvious front-runner. This populated field of challengers helped shape the impression that Romney's status as front-runner was temporary, that the gathering of competitors was motivated by distaste for Romney. Thus the whispered petition "Anyone but Romney" appeared to reveal the party's mood, especially within the noisy conservative wing of the party. This ostensible aversion to Romney encouraged all comers, boosted by the perception that Romney lacked presidential stature. From the influential right, Romney was irredeemably moderate, suspiciously liberal on some issues—the despised "Obamacare" was, after all, akin to the health care policies adopted by Romney himself when he served as governor of Massachusetts. Romney campaigned to rescind President Obama's health care program, but his fellow Republican rivals were unmoved by Romney's protestations, given the resemblance shared between Obamacare and the health care program that he helped to establish while governor in Massachusetts. Basking from their influential role in the 2010 midterms, the Tea Party faction insisted on being courted, and Romney was not the kind of suitor for which they pined.

Moreover, Romney's wealth and the perception of his patrician demeanor worked against him. There may indeed be something to the electorate's wariness of wealth; beginning with President Truman, only three presidents—Kennedy, the elder Bush, and the younger Bush—were raised in wealth. Even before President Truman, the only other twentieth-century president that came from substantial wealth was Franklin Roosevelt. (Theodore Roosevelt enjoyed great wealth, but as a younger man, he could not be described as having come from wealth.) All told, American voters historically elect candidates from more modest backgrounds, infrequently supporting the wealthiest. Romney's wealth might not be an endearing quality.

On a personal level, trouble was expected over Romney's Mormon faith, but ultimately it had no effect. However, his personal image was underappreciated; he was sometimes unfairly described as "boring," "bland," blasé, socially awkward, even "weird" or "robotic." Clearly these were exaggerations to be taken with a grain of salt; nonetheless, his image within the voting public had been distorted by this caricature. *Prima facie*, Romney just didn't seem to have the juice to lead a credible campaign against an incumbent, even one that was purportedly vulnerable.

Among the earliest names that were floated as alternatives to Romney were former Alaska governor and 2008 GOP nominee for vice president Sarah Palin, and the popular New Jersey governor Chris Christie. Palin in particular seemed to suit the Tea Party faction, and a Palin candidacy was anticipated, she having already periodically hinted her interest even prior to the 2010 midterm results. However, her showing in various party straw polls conducted throughout the country from January 2011 forward were less than heartening. Still, during the summer of 2011, rumors of a Palin candidacy remained in circulation. Meanwhile, Christie's name also remained prominent, even though his public intentions were vague. The ambiguity around Christie and the speculation about Palin were dispelled when both prospective candidates announced in October 2011 that they would not run. With Christie and Palin removed from the pool, and with interest in Romney still apparently lackluster, other presidential ambitions were encouraged.

Throwing in early were Representative Michelle Bachman of Minnesota; former Speaker of the House Newt Gingrich; Texas governor Rick Perry; former Washington lobbyist, entrepreneur, and pizza magnate Herman Cain; Texas representative Ron Paul; Jon Huntsman, ambassador to China; former Pennsylvania senator Rick Santorum; former Minnesota governor Tim Pawlenty; former New Mexico governor Gary Johnson; and former Louisiana governor Buddy Roemer, along with numerous other, less familiar faces. Names such as Wisconsin representative Paul Ryan, Indiana governor Mitch Daniels, Louisiana governor Bobby Jindal, South Dakota senator John Thune, and real estate mogul and reality television entertainer Donald Trump, among several others, were also mentioned as possible candidates, all of whom publicly demurred. As the media coverage of the early primary season began to increase, Gingrich, Perry, and Cain quickly attracted the most attention, each experiencing a surge in the polls and further reinforcing the appearance of doubt regarding the party's interest in Romney.

Governor Perry surged early, his record and background appealing to conservatives, his fund-raising temporarily surpassing Romney's, and he polled strong numbers from mid-August into early September. However, these figures spiked and soon began to decline in the aftermath of a damaging sequence of missteps and gaffes, beginning with Perry's pugnacious and unguarded comments about the Federal Reserve Board and its chairman, Ben Bernanke—whom he accused of treasonous conduct—combined with additional prior claims now leaking into the press of his comparing Social Security to a Ponzi scam, and deteriorating from there. By the time a Florida Republican Party straw poll was conducted in late September, it was clear that the governor's support was diminishing, his numbers cut in half, enough to finish second but well behind the winner of the straw poll, Herman Cain, who was supported by 37 percent of those polled. This turnaround represented both the ascent of Mr. Cain and the rapid descent of Governor Perry, whose campaign was then doomed by more embarrassing episodes: comments sympathetic to the weird "birther" conspiracy, his association with a hunting ranch saddled with a racially offensive name, and a pointless passing swipe at the upbringing of the Bush family at which the revered family matriarch, Barbara Bush, took umbrage. Worse still was his inane reaction upon losing his train of thought during a November 9 debate while detailing which three cabinet-level departments he would, if elected, eliminate from the executive branch. After identifying both Commerce and Education, forgetting the third department, and then becoming flustered when the EPA was raised by the debate moderator and then withdrawn by the candidate, an exchange causing laughter among the audience, Perry halted, still unable to name the third department, and said, "Oops!" in an attempt to brush off the evident bungle as an insignificant lapse. Perhaps it was insignificant, but Perry's shrugging reaction came off as shallow. What has since come to be called the "oops moment" was Perry's *coup de grâce*, the governor now appearing either unfocused under pressure or incapable of sustaining a serious conversation about policy. Harry Enten, at the Web site FiveThirtyEight, marked Perry's precipitous decline, losing twenty-seven points in the polls, the steepest on record. Meanwhile, Mr. Cain's fortunes rose in the wake of his winning the Florida straw poll, framed by persistent promotion of his trademark "9-9-9" plan to replace the current federal tax structure with a three-pronged approach that was a species of flat tax: viz., 9 percent levied on personal income tax, 9 percent drawn from businesses, and imposition of a 9 percent federal sales tax. Cain briefly pulled ahead of the field after the October straw poll, but as with Perry, the surge would break and his support would soon collapse.

Cain's decline began with criticisms of the 9-9-9 plan, many analysts describing it as a regressive tax that would burden most Americans, although his supporters were unfazed. In one interview he compared himself to Moses, but that raised only mild reaction. A more damaging incident occurred during an October television interview. Having previously boasted that he stood prepared to deflect "gotcha questions," he garrulously explained that were he to be asked to identify "the president of Ubeki-beki-beki-beki-stan-stan," he would say, "You know, I don't know. Do you know?" Hoping to demonstrate a common bond with the average American, Mr. Cain obviously meant to inject a modicum of self-effacing humor into this frank admission, mining Uzbekistan for material; but it was a misfire, inviting mocking criticisms portraying him as pridefully ignorant about global politics. Finally Cain's *coup de grâce* came on Halloween 2011, when charges of sexual harassment and infidelity were aimed at Mr. Cain, allegations he firmly denied but that he was unable to deflect, effectively deflating his prospects; the fleeting Cain surge dissipated, the candidate underscoring his retreat with a sentimental reference to a lyric from a *Pokémon* movie soundtrack during a December address conceding the end. Romney remained the front-runner.

One might expect the Romney candidacy to quickly gain momentum in the aftermath, but for the moment at least, a third challenger, former Speaker of the House and standard-bearer of the 1994 "Contract with America," Newt Gingrich, now stepped forward to lure the media's gaze. Having announced his candidacy months earlier, Gingrich's campaign languished, as the former Speaker appeared to lack commitment, but also owing to reservations about Gingrich among party insiders. Even so, during an ongoing series of intraparty debates, Mr. Gingrich began to stand out, stimulating renewed public interest in his prospects in spite of his problems inside the party leadership. Drawing upon his background, the former Speaker began to look like a credible challenger, perhaps even displacing Romney as the new front-runner, polling around 37 percent in early December. The former Speaker, however, carried substantial baggage stemming from his personal history as well as his prickly personality. While Gingrich had made a name for himself as a conservative firebrand in the early 1990s, his ideas could be idiosyncratic and unappealing to the purist. Additionally, even party insiders were wary of what they interpreted as Gingrich's tendency toward self-promotion. Ambivalence surrounded Gingrich: On one hand he could appear as a forthright, intelligent, and informed critic of corruption and a champion of character in political leadership, but then on the other hand, his own foibles would peek through the chinks in his personal armor—bad blood with the House Ethics Committee, marital infidelities from the very man who had attacked President Clinton's indiscretions, etc. Any Gingrich surge might be dampened by a counter-undercurrent of resistance flowing from the public's sense of unease about this past. Added to this was a tendency to fluctuate across the ideological terrain while discussing policy, an open-mined quality that was not in itself problematic, but that nonetheless scrambled any potential commitment from the more ardently ideological. From the more conservative perspective, Gingrich enjoyed some support, but he was also capable of tendering bemusing suggestions that would reintroduce old doubts about his real principles. His curious lack of diplomacy and nuance, his oddball musings, and his checkered past neutralized his strengths. By January, the Gingrich surge seemed spent, but a last gasp remained.

As the campaign season developed, a number of other candidates moved in and out of media focus. Among conservatives, there were no candidates more appealing, at least on ideological grounds, than Congresswoman Bachmann and Senator Santorum. Bachmann had announced her candidacy as early as June 2011; she polled encouraging numbers the following July and won an Iowa straw poll (the Ames Straw Poll) in August, receiving over 28 percent among the field (her closest competitor in this poll was Congressman Ron Paul, who came within a percentage point). For this reason Bachman's candidacy initially looked solid, but as with Perry and Cain, gaffes and errors quickly smothered her momentum. Her gaffes ranged from kooky and inaccurate accusations about Governor Perry and state-sponsored vaccinations in Texas to risible declamations about American history. By the time of the Iowa caucus in early January, her campaign had fizzled out with only 5 percent support.

Gaffes, muffs, and blown opportunities were embarrassing for these challengers; however, front-runner Mitt Romney, who could have been crowned the King of Gaffes, having committed more than his fair share of injudicious comments, managed to soldier on somehow. To emphasize a point at one debate event, he challenged Governor Perry to bet ten thousand dollars. He sprinkled his public comments with blue-blooded flourishes—nonchalant asides about his wife's two Cadillacs, disclosures about the illegal immigrants who tended his garden, and indecorous confessions that he liked "being able to fire people" on grounds of personal dissatisfaction; and while exhibiting his support for the middle class during one interview, casually remarking that he was "not concerned about the very poor." Imprudent comments abounded from nearly all the candidates, especially from Romney, and while his numerous, gob-stopping gaffes were duly disseminated through the media—and there was ample derision aimed at everyone's mistakes, Romney's included—he nevertheless mysteriously avoided the self-destruction visited hard upon his challengers resulting from similar indiscretions. A curious situation unfolded, one that may be better explained by the factual solidity of Romney's support concealed behind the appearance of hesitation and doubt. His challengers were not as poorly credentialed as they have since been depicted, and their blunders were by and large no worse, and no more frequent, than those of the front-runner. Even though each of the surging candidates had promptly crashed while Romney held steady, there was still an "anyone but Romney" tinge coloring the campaign. There remained a demand for a credible challenger among segments of the GOP, at least based on appearances, and one more figure would step forward to fill that role.

Beginning with the Iowa caucus, it became evident that former senator Santorum was that challenger; his campaign had already shown signs of increased energy in late December, and on the eve of the Iowa caucus, now held in the first week in January, Santorum's uptick in the polls could not have been better timed. Fervent and unbowed, Santorum was unabashedly conservative down the line, and he began to draw crowds. Having referred to himself in the past as "the Popeye candidate," explaining "I am what I am," Santorum was a marked contrast to the comparatively more moderate and reserved Romney, and at least for the moment, he seemed like the impassioned antidote to the governor's purported patrician detachment. One episode in particular fueled this momentum: a plaintive, tearful, powerful moment in Boone's Pizza Ranch Restaurant wherein Santorum and his wife, Karen, in an emotionally charged defense against callous criticisms lambasting their very personal reaction to a heartbreaking family tragedy, drew sympathy, touched nerves, and won support. It had little to do with the issues and much to do about what Iowa conservatives seemed to be seeking and not finding in Governor Romney. On the evening of the Iowa caucus, the numbers rolling in could not have been tighter, with both Romney and Santorum in front and running at 25 percent, Ron Paul polling around 21 percent, Gingrich drawing around 13–14 percent, Perry at 10 percent, and the rest of the pack followed in single digits or less. The day after the caucus, Romney appeared to be the winner but only by the slimmest of margins—a mere eight votes. Such a result was viewed by many as a draw; in a public e-mail message, Romney himself called it a "virtual tie," and with a feeling of relief, he was quick to move forward full tilt into New Hampshire. Iowa was important to Romney, but he was anxious to move on, as he had never felt comfortable in the Hawkeye State, having lost there by six percentage points to Mike Huckabee in the 2008 caucus, thereafter referring to Iowa as the "La Brea Tar Pits of politics." A split decision in Iowa was, for Romney, as good as a victory. Spirits were high in Santorum's camp, buoyed further by a recount in Iowa indicating a new result in which Santorum actually polled higher than Romney by thirty-four votes; however, the final tally remained unofficial, as the results in eight precincts had been lost. By the time news of Santorum's unofficial slender victory in Iowa broke, Romney had already easily won the New Hampshire primary, with Santorum finishing in fifth place and Iowa's significance receding.

In New Hampshire, Gingrich and Huntsman went into a full-court press against Romney in an attempt to, as the former Speaker explained, "make Romney radioactive"; but it was to no avail, as Romney, with deep ties in New England, won just over 39 percent in the Granite State and was well ahead of the rest of the pack. Mr. Gingrich's campaign seemed to undergo a modest revival in the public, polling respectable numbers in selected primaries and caucuses, but his numbers would soon fluctuate and fade. Congressman Paul also managed to remain in the arena, as he showed respectable numbers placing second but far behind Romney. Jon Huntsman showed third, a result that encouraged him to stay in for a short while longer, but he too was soon gone. In spite of a weak run in New Hampshire, Santorum's prospects were recharged by February victories in Colorado, Minnesota, and Missouri, while also nationally outpolling the president by a percentage point in a hypothetical Santorum-Obama contest conducted by Rasmussen Reports. Significantly, Santorum's gains were more sustained than those of candidates who had previously surged and then fizzled. For the moment, Santorum appeared to be stiff competition for Romney.

Relying on the South for his pivot move, Gingrich scored a convincing victory in South Carolina, polling 40 percent to Romney's distant second (just under 28%). This second surge seemed to renew the former Speaker's strength, but Romney remained undaunted, having anticipated that he was likely to lose Southern support to more conservative candidates. South Carolina proved to be Gingrich's zenith; a few days later, Romney won an impressive victory in the Florida primary, bolstered by his own performance in debates against Gingrich as well as

Gingrich's tendency to suffocate his own chances with an all-too-frequent controversial or, in this case, oddball remark about establishing space stations on the Moon by 2020—a laudable goal, to be sure, but a remark misplaced and divergent to common sense. Romney assayed the Gingrich Moon Plan, weighing in that as an executive, he would naturally fire any employee who would submit such an unlikely scheme. Conservatives derided Gingrich, who was castigated by both the *National Review* and *American Spectator*, and columnist Ann Coulter quipped, "Reelect Obama/Vote Newt." Gingrich would win Georgia, his home state, on Super Tuesday, but his campaign was unable to convert the South Carolina surge into the energy needed for a prolonged fight with Romney and Santorum.

Santorum continued to push Romney, winning the popular vote among primary and caucus participants in eleven states—twelve, if one counts the confused result in New Hampshire—and he pressed the governor hard in Michigan, the state where Romney was raised, his father, George Romney, having been Michigan's Republican governor through the better part of the 1960s, and prior to that, president and chairman of American Motors. George Romney had himself campaigned for the Republican nomination in 1968 as a liberal alternative to Richard Nixon. Moreover, Mitt Romney had a record of success in Michigan, winning the primary there in 2008, besting the eventual party nominee, Senator John McCain, by nine percentage points. Nevertheless, he was hardly a native son in Michigan; it had been decades since Romney had resided there—he was governor in Massachusetts, not Michigan—and a controversial *New York Times* editorial that Romney wrote in November 2008, critical of a federally funded rescue of the struggling American automobile industry, did not endear him to Michigan residents. Worse still, the editors at the *New York Times* elected to misleadingly title Romney's op-ed, "Let Detroit Go Bankrupt," a phrase that has since been attributed to Romney himself, even though he neither explicitly nor even implicitly suggested such a course of action. But like Marie Antoinette, Romney couldn't shake the misattributed phrase. Meanwhile, Santorum's steely conservatism continued to animate crowds, and when compared to what was perceived as Romney's more pliable ideological inclinations combined with a reputation for, however fairly or unfairly ascribed, patrician disdain, the governor's advantages seemed tenuous. In the days leading toward the Michigan primary, Santorum, who initially polled more than ten percentage points behind, was now drawing almost even with Romney, his campaign appearing increasingly vibrant. Imagined scenarios suggesting a brokered convention were now percolating within the party; Chris Christie's name was again being whispered as a possible "white knight" to charge forward at the denouement. Governor Daniels of Indiana and Congressman Ryan of Wisconsin were additional names popping up in the buzz among worried insiders. Grumblings about Romney's alleged ineptitude murmuring throughout the party leadership and persisting through the media dismayed the front-runner and appeared to weaken his support. However, while Santorum had mounted the most effective, consistent, and prolonged challenge to the governor, Romney still managed to take the Michigan prize by three percentage points. Again the clear front-runner, Romney moved toward the primary in Pennsylvania, Santorum's home turf, in April with the nomination finally in sight.

Soon gaffes and injudicious declamations began to cost the senator—in particular, a scathing criticism of fellow Catholic John F. Kennedy's famous position, delivered during his 1960 presidential campaign for the assurance of Baptists in Houston and Protestants more generally, defending the doctrine of the separation of church and state. It was actually the second time he raked over President Kennedy's Houston address, but this time it made news, and it was mixed in with the claim that his fellow communicants who adopted Kennedy's position were "not real Catholics." After receiving flak from nearly every candidate in the field, including another Catholic, Newt Gingrich, as well as Governor Romney, Santorum soon publicly admitted to television personality Laura Ingraham that he regretted the remark, but the damage had been done. However, when Santorum focused on policy, he proved more effective. As Super Tuesday approached, he continued to impugn Romney's credentials as a conservative, stressing a lack of ideological consistency, especially on issues such as health care. "Romneycare" was the label Santorum deployed in his attempt to expose his opponent as a liberal in conservative clothing, hitting the governor hard on issues more effectively than other challengers.

Super Tuesday on March 6 was decisive for Romney, as he won 38 percent of the popular vote spread across eleven separate primaries, converting to 238 delegates secured to 85 for Santorum, 79 for Gingrich, and 21 for Paul. Santorum did manage to win three states (with Gingrich winning in Georgia), but it was essentially a triumph for Romney. Ohio was the tightest contest, Romney there edging out Santorum by only one percentage point. Santorum campaigned hard in Ohio, but in the end he fell short, and his campaign seemed to now be on the wane. Clearly Santorum's exit was a matter of time after Super Tuesday, and perhaps even after Michigan, but it was a family crisis that forced his withdrawal; his youngest daughter had just been diagnosed with a serious medical disorder, prompting the senator's judicious decision to withdraw from the campaign two weeks shy of the Pennsylvania primary, even though he would remain on the ballot. The way to the party nomination was now graded smooth for Governor Romney.

Having emerged the presumptive nominee by outdueling more conservative challengers, one might conclude that Romney's accomplishment had come at a cost. Like Senator John McCain in 2008, Romney, a natural moderate, seemed to have allowed himself to be pulled to the right, causing confusion and doubt among supporters. Research findings offered by Sides and Vavreck supply a fuller account. According to their data, the GOP's conservative extreme, while influential, "do not comprise the majority of Republican voters"; consequently, Romney's campaign relied on nearly a third of the party rank and file who were already closer to his comparatively more moderate positions than those held by the Tea Party. In spite of the clear influence of the party's right, Sides and Vavreck remind students of politics that "moderates and pragmatists in the Republican Party have tended to prevail in presidential primaries." This is not to dismiss the real influence of the "archconservative" faction, but rather to question "stereotypes like the Molotov Party" that many consider to be the dominant feature of the current GOP. In other words, Romney, whose political history indicates a more moderate approach, could not have defeated a strong challenger such as Santorum if the party were in fact truly dominated by the Tea Party faction and other diehard conservatives. Compared to the Republican Party of the 1950s or even the 1970s, there is no question that the party is currently more homogeneous and that it leans toward the conservative pole; and yet the whole picture is distorted if we focus on just one visible and vocal element. Governor Romney was required to allay the concerns of conservatives, but then President Obama faced a similar situation with his party's left wing. Both candidates share a pragmatism that is easily lost in ideologically refracted rhetoric and *ad hominem* punditry.

By the actual primary season, informed voters, those who were likely voters, knew full well the political principles represented by the two candidates. Democrats began to raise questions about Romney's background in the private sector. Lauded as the savior of the Salt Lake Olympic Games and admired for his success as a businessman, his association with Bain Capital was often scrutinized by opponents looking for the unseemly, cold-hearted side of Romney. Largely initiated by the Gingrich camp, the light shed on Bain was meant to depict Romney as, in the words of Governor Perry, a "vulture capitalist," the type of "Wall Street wolf" casually wrecking lives by pursuing larger profits while thoughtlessly eliminating jobs. True enough, Romney's numbers did decline shortly after the Bain allegations against him arose, but it is difficult to prove a correlation. Nevertheless, issues surrounding Romney's tenure at Bain would reappear in the contest against the president.

President Obama, even though unchallenged in his party, was still a presence during the campaign season, especially since the Osawatomie event in December 2011. On April 4 he delivered a speech criticizing the proposed federal budget, a tight, frugal plan now emerging from House Republicans steered under the leadership of Paul Ryan, a plan that the president condemned as a "Trojan horse" concealing within it the political principles of "social Darwinism," and observing that it reflected an ideological agenda so extreme that, by comparison, the conservative 1994 "Contract with America" looked "like the New Deal." Claiming that Romney's own policies were tightly aligned with the Ryan plan, the president warned that the Republican presumptive nominee was tacking toward the extreme right. Employing a contradictory strategy that simultaneously criticized Romney for playing to the conservatives but also renewing older charges that Romney was a flip-flopper, analogous to an Etch A Sketch (an image actually culled from a gaffe committed by one of Romney's own campaign advisers, Eric Fehrnstrom, who, in speaking to the mutability of political campaigns and Romney's willingness to adapt to the concerns of the voters, inadvertently formed the impression that he thought of Romney as a candidate lacking permanent positions, a comment that had also been exploited by Senator Santorum), his positions easily wiped away, leaving no real ground, commitment, or enduring principles: moderate Romney is shaken and wiped away; a conservative Romney is sketched in and then erased again; a politician who "has no core," but who has, in order to become president, allowed the far right to rewrite his script, filling in a new sketch. With the tapping of Representative Ryan as Romney's running mate, whom analyst Nate Silver deemed "the most conservative Republican member of Congress to be picked for the vice-presidential slot since at least 1900," the president's campaign was supplied with more evidence in support of the charge that the erstwhile moderate Romney was pandering to the right. The president's campaign would also continue to hammer the governor with his background at Bain—perhaps pandering to its party's left. In both campaigns, the presumptive nominees were both speaking to the true believers; whether or not this approach made a difference is unclear.

In July Governor Romney, traveling abroad, insulted his London hosts by observing that the city was not prepared to manage the upcoming Olympic Games. This may or may not have had any consequences, but his polling numbers coincidentally began to recede; from July 27 to August 12, the president's lead widened from a negligible one percent to just under five percent. As Romney's numbers dipped, Republicans hoped to reverse their fortunes, beginning with the national convention opening in Tampa in late August. The first night of the convention was postponed due to a hurricane warning; on the second night, keynote speaker Governor Chris Christie seemed to have the reverse effect of cyclonic winds, sucking all the oxygen out of the convention hall. As though he had drifted into the doldrums, Christie offered a languid endorsement of Romney through a speech that scarcely mentioned the candidate's name. While most of the speakers in the lineup performed well, especially former Secretary of State Condoleezza Rice, Christi's prime time keynote address folded the sails. Things continued to deteriorate when the presumptive nominee for vice president, Paul Ryan, delivered a speech riddled with errors, providing more grist for the media mill. More seriously, on Wednesday, mystified viewers watched as movie legend Clint Eastwood performed a stunningly embarrassing improvisation involving an empty chair as a prop and an imaginary President Obama as a punchline. Between Christie's tepid keynote and Eastwood's extemporized wreck, the convention fell into a tailspin; there were but two speakers remaining to prevent a catastrophe: Florida senator Marco Rubio and the candidate himself. Although he confused one of his lines—inadvertently calling for more government over more freedom (but everyone knew what he meant)— Senator Rubio's speech was competent and sincere, halting the dive. It was Romney's own speech that salvaged the night. Critics who had previously described Romney as patrician, robotic, or awkward were silenced as he spoke with passion, resolve, and poise, recounting an America that "has been a story of the many becoming one, uniting to preserve liberty, uniting to build the greatest economy in the world, uniting to save the world from unspeakable darkness." It was through this address that Romney, whose campaigning had been decidedly inconsistent and often sidetracked by gaffes and self-inflicted wounds, began to manifest his strength. It was a crucial moment and a clutch save, perhaps rescuing his campaign altogether. A fiasco averted, Wilson Mitt Romney, the first Mormon to be nominated by a major party for president of the United States, at last looked equal to the task. More mistakes would be made by the governor in the weeks ahead, but they were reparable. The blunders at the convention nearly wrecked everything, and it was the candidate himself, with little support from the other principal players, that saved the campaign. Even though the poor performances by Christie and Eastwood were morsels for the media and inspiration for satirists, the polls did not indicate any damage. In fact, within a week, polling numbers showed that the two candidates had drawn even.

From the beginning Romney's punch and counterpunch combination relentlessly and predominantly targeted the president on the economy while also stressing Republican opposition to Obama's health care reforms, the president's economic stimulus package, climate change, international trade, and immigration, while also publicizing the governor's own record as a successful executive in both the public and private sectors. Increasing his efforts to appear less the patrician and more plebian, Romney's rhetoric was aimed at the middle class. From late February through early March, the polling numbers for the president ran around 48–49 percent favorable; for the governor, between 43 and 44 percent. In early May the gap closed, the governor moving within approximately a percentage point, but then the gap again widened in the president's favor, fluctuating throughout the summer, and by mid-August, on average the president enjoyed a four-to-five-percentahe-point lead. Again this gap suddenly closed; by the first week of September, as the Democrats' national convention opened in Charlotte, North Carolina, polls showed Romney within less than a percentage point, virtually dead even. The convention as a whole was smooth and unremarkable, minor protests from an Occupy Wall

Street spin-off excepted. In prime time the oratory did not disappoint the party faithful: First Lady Michelle Obama, Massachusetts senator Elizabeth Warren, Vice President Joe Biden, and San Antonio mayor Julian Castro delivered effective speeches—the First Lady's being particularly vibrant, and Mayor Castro writing history as the first Hispanic American to serve as keynote speaker at a Democratic national convention. As expected, the president's own acceptance speech exhibited his rhetorical proficiency, and while not as stirring as speeches from his past, such as his own 2004 convention keynote address or the historic 2008 acceptance speech, it was nonetheless a polished performance. Foremost among the speakers, former president Bill Clinton reached the convention's high notes. Back in center stage, the former president exhibited a command of the issues conveyed through a lighthearted optimism. He was reassuring, playfully incisive, intellectually agile, and fearlessly spontaneous, cautioning that Romney would "double down on trickle-down" and raising "the most important question . . . what kind of country do you want to live in? If you want a you're-on-your-own, winner-take-all society, you should support the Republican ticket. If you want a country of shared prosperity and shared responsibility—a we're-all-in-this-together society—you should vote for Barack Obama and Joe Biden." While President Obama's own well-crafted speech was a success, he appeared reserved and measured in comparison to his captivating predecessor—Bill Clinton, one of the more adept politicians in the history of presidential campaigning, simply could not be upstaged. He injected new energy into the president's campaign, generating enough dynamism to distract Romney's advisers with a new anxiety over the "Clinton problem." With two months remaining in the seemingly interminable campaign season, the incumbent was well positioned for reelection, and with former president Clinton now charging ahead full bore in his behalf, the Democrats' prospects brightened. Nonetheless, the Romney campaign was on the verge of staging a late rally, one that would reveal the reality of Romney's strength that had been concealed behind the appearances.

On September 11, the anniversary of the 2001 terrorist attacks, a United States diplomatic outpost was attacked and destroyed in Benghazi, Libya, resulting in the death of the American ambassador at the hands of malevolent and criminal fanatics. Prior to the Benghazi assault, the American embassy in Egypt had issued a general apology regretting the posting by an American citizen of a juvenile and tasteless YouTube video insulting the Islamic prophet and provoking the anger of religious fundamentalists, purportedly initiating the events in Benghazi. Candidate Romney issued a statement stridently critical of the president for ordering the Cairo embassy to apologize, for sympathizing with the militants, and for failing to properly condemn the attack in Libya. The following day, the president announced that the Cairo apology was not issued from or approved by the White House, denouncing Governor Romney's reproach as irresponsible and self-serving.

In reality, the outrage in Benghazi was a blow to the president, to Secretary of State Hillary Clinton, and to Obama's record on foreign policy in the Middle East; but the Romney campaign fumbled badly in its apparent eagerness to gain advantage from the misfortune.

Then, to worsen matters for the Republicans, on September 17, just a little more than two weeks before the opening of the presidential debates and approximately seven weeks before the general election, Governor Romney's campaign was distracted by the sudden appearance of a furtively recorded video in which the candidate, removed from context, conveyed plutocratic insensitivity. During an appearance before a private fund-raiser the previous May, Romney, speaking frankly, dropped a passing dismissal of the "forty-seven percent of the people who . . . are dependent upon government, who believe they are victims . . . who pay no income tax." He explained that these "forty-seven percent" would dutifully, blindly vote for President Obama, and consequently, Romney would not worry about "those people. I'll never convince them that they should take personal responsibility and care for their lives." Compared to previous gaffes, this one appeared to exceed them all. As the recording was leaked, the media and the president's campaign pounced, the term "forty-seven percent" now representing for the Obama campaign the gulf between the party that genuinely cared for the people, the Democrats, and the Scrooge McDucks in the GOP. Initially the Romney campaign was dazed by the unexpected exposure of these remarks, but the candidate himself, while concerned, seemed loath to be drawn into the controversy. Refusing a public display of contrition, the governor chose to wait until the first debate for an opportunity to explain his meaning. Even before the debate, the effects of the gaffe began to weaken. Polls averaged a dip of just 1 percent a week after the remark was publicized, while the president's own numbers actually dropped slightly, less than 1 percent. Indubitably, the comments did not reflect well on Romney's attitude toward certain segments of the American public, but the data does seem to indicate that in spite of his perturbed advisers, Romney managed to avoid significant damage, offering further evidence that, in spite of himself, the governor's campaign was stronger than his critics assumed, his candidacy more credible than appearances allowed.

Governor Romney gained momentum from the first debate held in Denver, in which he visibly outperformed a seemingly unprepared president. Romney prevailed throughout, the president hesitant and unconvincing. Forthrightly the governor hammered the president for imposing "trickle-down government . . . bigger government, spending more, taxing more, regulating more" and consequently "crushing" a "buried middle class." It was a decisive victory for the Republicans; the following week Romney for the first time enjoyed a slight lead in several polls, although on average the numbers were again showing a dead heat. With the general election close, the governor was invigorated, and it seemed that Romney had finally begun to show both substance and style at just the right moment. Now it was the Obama campaign that appeared to be sliding backward as Romney charged forward. At the second debate, held at Hofstra University on Long Island, the president righted himself, resembling more the vibrant candidate of 2008 than the halting incumbent during the fiasco in Denver. By contrast, Romney lived up to his exaggerated awkwardness. While discussing the issue of pay equity for women, Romney boasted that he could have hired "binders full of women" while governor of Massachusetts. Worse still, Romney bungled an attempt to challenge the president on the attack in Benghazi. Improving his performance in the third debate, the governor managed to put the missteps over Benghazi and other gaffes behind him, but most analysts, while acknowledging Romney's stronger performance, considered the third debate a victory for the president. At one point, responding to Romney's criticism that the U.S. Navy had fewer ships than in 1916, the president retorted that the military also had more "horses and bayonets" in 1916. As the general election approached, the polls continued to indicate a tight outcome. Governor Romney and the Republican leadership were anticipating victory, and friendlier analysts in the media shared the same optimism.

On the eve of the election, Mitt Romney believed he would be the next president. Many Republican activists and commentators shared this confidence. Twenty-four hours later, it was clear that the external appearance of imminent victory concealed a harsher reality. Similar to the manner in which Romney's own nomination illuminated the difference between the appearance of his vulnerability and the reality of his strength, the results of the 2012 general election revealed the abiding popularity of the president. The Romney challenge did exceed John McCain's efforts four years earlier; Mitt Romney actually became the second person, after Barack Obama in both 2008 and 2012, in American political history to win over sixty million popular votes, which was no small achievement. Whereas McCain lost by a margin of ten million votes in 2008, Romney fell five million short. In comparison to 2008, the Romney campaign performed better, but that gap of five million stunned the Romney family and its supporters. As the returns rolled in from the pivotal battleground state, Ohio, Karl Rove, appearing on the Fox television network, stubbornly resisted the meaning underneath the data. Even as experts were calling Ohio for the president, Rove insisted otherwise, convinced that the numbers weren't adding up and recommending caution in calling the state for the president. Impatiently, anchorwoman Megyn Kelly famously asked, "Is this just math that you do as a Republican to make yourself feel better or is this real?" Ms. Kelly's question encapsulates much of what this campaign season reveals about the disparity between perceptions drawn from preferences and hard data that reflect what is real. While some pundits had anticipated a tight outcome allowing the possibility of a Romney upset, most polls did not support this expectation: the best among them (e.g., Public Policy Polling and Nate Silver's analysis while still at the *New York Times*) accurately sounded the data and had forecasted with precision a convincing reelection for the president.

In the Electoral College, Obama won 332 to 206 (61% to 39%), retaining all but two of the states won in 2008 (surrendering only Indiana and North Carolina). Even though Obama's 51 percent of the popular vote to Romney's 47 percent was not as impressive as his election four years earlier, he deemed it personally more satisfying. Barack Obama became the third consecutive incumbent president to win reelection (following two-term presidents Clinton and the younger Bush), a sequence that has only happened one other time in American history (Jefferson, Madison, and Monroe). To punctuate his success with the American electorate, President Obama stands now as one of only seven presidents to have won *two* elections by polling more than 50 percent of the popular vote, joining presidents Andrew Jackson (1828, 1832), Ulysses S. Grant (1868, 1872), William McKinley (1896, 1900), the inimitable Franklin Roosevelt (1932, 1936, 1940, 1944), Dwight D. Eisenhower (1952, 1956), and Ronald Reagan (1980, 1984). Still more notably, he is only the third Democrat to accomplish this electoral feat, along with Jackson and FDR, and just one of two Democrats over the course of the past century—the other being no less than Franklin Roosevelt. By contrast, Bill Clinton, the singular politician of his generation, fell below 50 percent of the popular vote in both of his election victories. Interestingly, only seven Democrats have won over 50 percent of the popular vote in presidential elections: Jackson (twice), Martin Van Buren, Franklin Pierce, Samuel Tilden (who lost the election in the Electoral College), Roosevelt (four times), Jimmy Carter, and Barack Obama (twice). Ultimately the reality of the case shed the opaque veil of insubstantial appearance; in spite of the many difficulties that the president faced, and what proved in the end to be a respectable effort from his Republican opponent, Barack Obama's tally of the popular vote was hardly the consequence of a weakened, vulnerable incumbent, affirming instead his position as one of the more accomplished politicians and noteworthy presidents in American history.

Additional Resources

Balz, Dan. *Collision 2012: Obama vs. Romney and the Future of Elections in America.* New York: Viking, 2013.

Denton, Robert E., Jr., ed. *The 2012 Presidential Campaign: A Communication Perspective.* Lanham, MD: Rowman & Littlefield, 2014.

Halperin, Mark, and John Heilemann. *Double Down: Game Change 2012.* New York: Penguin Books, 2014.

Sides, John, and Lynn Vavreck. *The Gamble: Choice and Chance in the 2012 Presidential Election.* Princeton, NJ: Princeton University Press, 2013.

Campaign of 2016: A Provisional Review and Tentative Preview

Presidential campaigns are markedly regular; from election to election, patterns emerge, tendencies are charted, and affinities are asserted. Variation is certainly expected, as nothing in politics is exactly the same as it was before; and yet there are structures and propensities that both frame and steer the development of any given presidential contest. Among those structures that frame an election, the condition of the economy stands as preeminent. Few, if any, factors are more important than the economy in determining the outcome of an election. This is especially the case when an incumbent is standing for reelection, but even when there is no incumbency to be defended, the party that holds the White House is typically boosted when likely voters are confident and hopeful about the economy. A strong or stable economy always helps the party of the incumbent, whether or not the incumbent is eligible for or working toward reelection. Moreover, unease about the economy is, in almost every case, the principal cause of an incumbent's failure to gain reelection. Reelection efforts by presidents Herbert Hoover, Jimmy Carter, and George H. W. Bush were thwarted by the economic situation during the year prior to the general election. Events abroad can also influence a campaign, particularly international crises that are perceived as a threat to national security or that have stirred controversy at home. Two instances spring readily to mind: the outbreak of World War II, which led to President Franklin Roosevelt breaking from the unwritten two-term tradition to successfully run for and win a third term; and perceptions formed in the media and within public opinion regarding the conduct and purpose of the war in Vietnam, prompting incumbent president Lyndon Johnson to withdraw from the 1968 campaign. Less dramatically, but no less significantly, diplomatic success can also boost the efforts of an incumbent, a notable example being the stunning diplomatic achievements of the Nixon administration in opening China and improving relations with the Soviet Union; another example is the Middle East shuttle diplomacy conducted by Henry Kissinger on behalf of President Nixon. Realistically, the economy is ultimately beyond the control of any single political actor, and while an incumbent president, through the application of policy decisions in tandem with other actors within Congress and the executive branch (notably the Federal Reserve Board), can indeed influence the economy in both positive and negative ways, in the end no president can singlehandedly steer or subdue economic forces. Every president learns quickly the ancient tension between free will and fate. Foreign events are different from domestic economic affairs only in that the response of the president is more directly and visibly influential, but again, they are dependent on numerous other actors (e.g., foreign heads of state) beyond the president's control. That said, while many actors and variables make it difficult for a president to influence the decisions of foreign governments and the actions of all other foreign actors, the manner in which a president responds is more evidently critical to the way in which crises abroad are managed when compared to domestic problems and situations, particularly economic ones. In any event, these two factors—the state of the economy and the presence or absence of international crises—are likely to be the most important elements in shaping the outcome of a presidential election. These factors are also related to presidential approval ratings among likely voters in cases involving the prospect of reelecting an incumbent. Even more than apparent standing in polls that measure support from among a pool of candidates, a favorable rating in job approval is a more reliable indicator of an incumbent's strength moving toward and throughout the campaign season from its opening to the eve of the general election. Approval ratings are doubtless directly influenced by perceptions formed around the condition of the economy as well as a president's success in managing crises and other important issues involving situations abroad. And they do matter. While it is often claimed that incumbency adds additional electoral armor to a president, such a claim is not in accord with the reality of elections over the past few decades. Beginning with 1972, eight incumbents have run for reelection, and over one-third (three of eight) were not returned to the White House: Nixon, Reagan, Clinton, the younger Bush, and Obama were reelected; however, Ford, Carter, and the elder Bush were turned out of office. This reality strengthens the case for the predominance of the state of the economy as well as the situation abroad, for the three incumbents who failed to return to the White House all were confronted with a distressed economy; and in the case of President Carter, economic problems were accompanied by lingering frustrations with a crisis abroad—the Iranian hostage crisis that defined the last fourteen months of his presidency.

Another factor in predicting the outcome of a presidential campaign may simply be the length of time in which a party has held the White House. In cases where the two candidates appear to be viewed equally favorably, voters may choose the candidate from the party that has recently been out of power, a result of voters collectively seeking a change of direction for its own sake. However, this is less certain as an influence when compared to other factors such as a slowed or stressed economy, a crisis situation abroad, and an incumbent's approval rating. From 1969 to January 1977, the Republican Party held the White House, and even though the Democratic nominee, former Georgia governor Jimmy Carter, managed to unseat the incumbent Republican president, Gerald Ford, in a close election in 1976, the voters quickly turned back to the GOP in the next election. The Republicans then managed to protect occupancy of the White House for three more terms through 1992, thus losing only one presidential election—one that occurred in the wake of the tumultuous Watergate scandal—between 1968 and 1988, a period of twenty years covering six elections, five of which were won by the GOP. The Democrats managed to control the White House from 1933 to January 1953, another twenty-year period, but it must be allowed that four terms were won by Franklin Roosevelt, a singular statesman who served during extraordinary and dangerous times (the Great Depression and World War II). In any event, while there may be something to the desire for change among voters—change for its own sake—it is decidedly less reliable as a predictor than the health of the economy or threats from abroad. Party unity, particularly unified support among party insiders, also contributes to the success or (when that support is attenuated) failure of a candidate's campaign. President Carter, already hampered by economic uncertainty and burdened by the Iran hostage crisis, lost the confidence of his party's leadership, and even though he managed to deflect a serious challenge for the 1980 nomination from Massachusetts senator Edward Kennedy, his position had been significantly weakened moving into the general campaign against a charismatic Republican challenger, former California governor Ronald Reagan, who had managed to build solid support both within the party leadership and among the rank and file. But even if the GOP had nominated a weaker candidate, or had the Democratic Party thrown its full support behind their incumbent, President Carter may have still encountered difficulties in securing reelection, given discontent at home with regard to the economy and growing public impatience over the protracted Iran hostage crisis, which had initially stimulated public support of the president, though that support deteriorated as the crisis lingered. Additionally, the manner in which the media treats the candidates before and during a campaign can contribute to the outcome. No doubt Senator John Kennedy's 1960 campaign benefited from the favorable way in which the press treated not only him but also his family, especially his youthful and sophisticated wife, Jacqueline Kennedy. This is not to say that the press won the election for Kennedy or that Kennedy glamor was sufficient in gaining the White House; there were certainly other, more substantive factors involved; but the press had been fascinated by the Kennedy family both prior to and during the campaign, and a certain mythology was already being woven around the Kennedy charisma, the photogenic and telegenic images of "Jack and Jackie" captivating the media and embraced by a significant segment of the American public. If we were to imagine that Senator Lyndon Johnson had managed to win the Democratic nomination in 1960 instead of Senator Kennedy, we would naturally wonder how press coverage might have been different. How would the media have treated Johnson? How would Vice President Richard Nixon, the GOP nominee that year, have been treated by the press in a campaign involving Johnson as his rival rather than the more magnetic Kennedy? Any answer would rest, of course, on pure speculation, but the question might prompt us to consider the role that media coverage plays in the promotion, however inadvertent, of a specific candidate. Charismatic candidates, such as either of the Roosevelts, Kennedy, Reagan, or Bill Clinton, unsurprisingly attract media attention, and a comparatively controversial candidate such as Barry Goldwater or George McGovern will also draw pointed coverage, but with a different, more negative slant.

Finally, the outcome of a presidential campaign is to a large extent shaped by ongoing voter allegiance to one of the major parties. Protestations aside, nearly all likely voters are to some degree partisan, even when they are not explicitly affiliated with or active in a particular party. The voter that genuinely remains undecided on the eve of the election is rare; most already are committed to the candidate of one party or another, regardless of who manages to win the nomination. Campaigning is important in helping to spur voters to the polls, and in a tight election, the conduct of a campaign is important in winning over the small number of voters who are genuinely independent; but in the end, most voters are not moved to abandon their previous voting patterns. There is considerable inertia in the dynamic, and a successful campaign knows how to ride that inertia.

These factors—the state of the economy, the magnitude of events abroad (and, significantly, whether or not an incumbent president effectively responds to those events), the level of unity and support within the nominee's party, and the manner in which campaigns and candidates are covered throughout the media—serve as the principal preconditions affecting the success or failure of a presidential campaign. Doubtless other interesting factors and apparent correlations can be identified and examined, but these conditions are constant, providing presidential forecasters with the necessary regularity needed to encourage confidence in predicting the outcome of an upcoming election.

Regularity is a fact of life in the cycle of presidential campaigning; still, it is fair to say that no two presidential elections are identical. There are constants in the cycle of elections, but owing to the unpredictability of human behavior, there are enough variations to ensure that each campaign will possess characteristics of its own. The campaign season leading into the 2016 election, even in its earliest stages as they have unfolded through the summer, fall, and winter of 2015/early 2016, has already earned a distinction of its own. Were one to glance back to late spring 2015, one would observe a field of candidates led by apparent front-runners in both major parties: the clear Democratic front-runner being former First Lady, former New York senator, and former Secretary of State Hillary Rodham Clinton; and the provisional Republican front-runner being former Florida governor Jeb Bush—thus another Bush-Clinton contest was already anticipated by numerous commentators, analysts and party insiders. Both the Bush and the Clinton families have stamped a deep impression on American political culture in the latter half of the twentieth and early twenty-first centuries beginning with Senator Prescott Bush, who won national office in 1952, and on the Clinton side, the ascent of former Arkansas governor Bill Clinton to the presidency forty years later. With the exception of the campaign and election of 2012, a member of either the Bush family or the Clinton family has prominently participated at some point in every presidential campaign since 1980: George H. W. Bush was elected to the vice presidency in 1980 and 1984, elected to the presidency in 1988, and lost reelection in 1992 to Bill Clinton, who was subsequently reelected in 1996. In 2000 and 2004, Texas governor George W. Bush, son of President George H. W. Bush, was himself elected to the presidency; and in 2008 former First Lady (as the spouse of President Clinton) and New York senator Hillary Clinton ran for, and nearly won, the Democratic nomination for president. Had it not been for the astonishingly rapid ascent of Senator Barack Obama, Sen. Clinton would have secured the nomination and would likely have been elected president that year. Now, in 2016, Hillary Clinton and Jeb Bush once again represented their respective families in the pool of presidential candidates. Including the 2016 campaign season that is now under way, this brings to a total of nine the number of presidential campaigns in which a Bush or a Clinton—in two instances both—has or have been involved in a substantial way, either in a general election as a candidate for the presidency (1988, 1992, 1996, 2000, 2004) or vice presidency (1980, 1984) or as a frontrunner or leading candidate during a campaign for a party nomination (2008, 2016). The campaign of 2012 is the only one since 1976 in which neither a Bush nor a Clinton was a candidate for their respective party's nomination. Nonetheless, name recognition and family pedigree aside, neither Secretary Clinton nor (especially) Governor Bush campaigned unchallenged. Indeed, campaign events throughout the summer and early fall of 2015 exposed vulnerabilities in both candidates that had not been anticipated prior to their respective announcements. Jeb Bush, the favorite among party insiders, failed to answer the unexpected and rapid ascent of Donald Trump, his campaign unable to gain traction once it became clear that Mr. Trump's idiosyncratic approach held an enduring appeal for a significant segment of GOP voters. In February 2016, Bush withdrew from the race following a disappointing showing in the South Carolina primary.

On the Democratic side, Vermont senator Bernie Sanders, known for deeply engrained and unorthodox ideological propensities atypical of a serious presidential candidate, quickly emerged as a compelling alternative to what many had initially assumed would be, in effect, a coronation for Secretary Clinton as party standard-bearer. By mid-summer, three other Democratic candidates announced their intentions: former Maryland governor Martin O'Malley, former Virginia senator Jim Webb, and former Rhode Island governor, senator, and erstwhile Republican Lincoln Chafee (as a Republican, Governor Chafee supported Democratic candidate Senator Barack Obama in 2008, and he later officially joined the Democratic Party in 2013). By October 2016, both Chafee and Webb had withdrawn their candidacies, leaving only Clinton, Sanders, and O'Malley. Since announcing in April 2015, Sanders commanded an abundance of media attention through his posture as a crusader against what he and his followers perceive to be a political system manipulated by a corrupt plutocracy that has supplanted the democratic ideals toward which the American polity has historically aspired. For disciples of the Sanders message, Clinton is too closely associated with Wall Street financial interests who are perceived as existentially tainted with the sin of greed, big banks deemed inimical to the public good, and what they believe to be the unresponsive and corrupt Washington Beltway establishment disconnected from the needs and ideals of the majority of Americans. Even though her past and even her current tendencies exhibit a history of progressive attitudes and sympathies, Clinton has over the years become so deeply entrenched in the establishment, at least in the judgment of the Sanders camp, that the amount of separation between her policies and those of some of her Republican rivals is thereby deemed inconsequential. In the forum of ideas and the arena of attitudes, those who adopt positions advanced by the Vermont senator generally regard Clinton, and Democrats of her kind, askance, and in some cases even with contempt. Whether or not this is a fair assessment of Sec. Clinton's record—and one could make a case for her record as a consistent liberal—it is the case that Sanders has stood out as the alternative candidate—the candidate claiming for himself genuine progressive credentials and the truer, more consistent vision for an authentically fair society. Through his clarion call against the system, Senator Sanders seems to have resonated with a new generation of voters. Nonetheless, Clinton, a major political figure since the 1992 presidential campaign that led to the election of her husband, cannot be so easily dismissed. This was not the case, through November 2015, with the early Republican front-runner, Governor Jeb Bush, who, at least on appearances, seemed eminently dismissible. Moving into 2016, the Bush campaign failed to make headway.

The Republican field in 2015 was one of the more heavily populated in presidential campaign history. As stated above, in the late spring of 2015, the apparent (but by no means overwhelming) front-runner was Jeb Bush, whose candidacy was grounded primarily in name recognition and broad support from establishment party insiders. However, even the earliest polls indicated that his support within the base was thin. In the first few months of 2015, other candidates managed to draw sufficient interest, most notably former Arkansas governor Mike Huckabee, Kentucky senator Rand Paul, and former Massachusetts governor and 2012 Republican nominee Mitt Romney. In early January 2015, Romney briefly considered joining the race for a third consecutive run at the presidency, but in the end he demurred, likely owing, as speculation might have it, to lack of support within the "invisible primary," that unseen or at best only partially observed aspect of a presidential campaign wherein a prospective candidate not only tests the possible level of financial support but also, equally importantly, seeks the provisional approval of the party establishment (i.e., public and semi-public endorsements from party insiders, recognized activists, credentialed partisans, and prominent officeholders). With Romney no longer available, the principal challenger to Bush's front-runner status seemed in the early stages to be Wisconsin governor Scott Walker, who at least through late spring 2015 showed well in polls conducted in Iowa, leading with as much as 21 percent in the Quinnipiac poll of May 6. Other candidates in the field by late May included Senator Marco Rubio of Florida, Senator Ted Cruz of Texas, New Jersey governor Chris Christie, neurosurgeon and conservative commentator Dr. Ben Carson, business executive Carly Fiorina, South Carolina senator Lindsey Graham, former Pennsylvania senator Rick Santorum, former New York governor George Pataki, and former Virginia governor Jim Gilmore. Among this group, Bush remained the establishment front-runner; but in some early polls, Walker, Huckabee, and Paul drew better numbers. Nevertheless, even though Bush was not the obvious front-runner according to the polling numbers, his status as the principal candidate in the race seemed plain to most students of campaign politics, and if any single candidate seemed to be his strongest challenger, it would have been, at least on appearances during the early period of the campaign season, Governor Walker. Walker's early numbers in the polls aside, another Bush-Clinton contest in the general election seemed to be a strong possibility.

This situation suddenly changed with the garish entrance of billionaire real estate magnate and television celebrity Donald Trump, who officially announced his candidacy on June 1. Mr. Trump was soon joined by former Texas governor Rick Perry, current Louisiana governor Bobby Jindal, and current Ohio governor John Kasich. The Trump campaign immediately proved to be a formidable force. Mr. Trump's larger-than-life personality quickly grabbed media attention, and his unfiltered, shoot-from-the-hip, astringent rhetorical style and take-it-or-leave-it attitude appealed to a percentage of the Republican rank and file who, in a way similar to supporters of Senator Sanders among disenchanted Democrats, had grown weary of politics as usual, wary of establishment elites, and wanting a personality who would speak candidly to their frustrations. Exuding a confidence that nearly everyone—supporters and detractors alike—recognized as brazen and that some would perceive as arrogant and even outlandish, and emitting what was for many the alluring magnetism of the wildcat outsider, Trump launched a meteoric ascent to the top of the polls. By mid-July, the polls revealed a dead heat between Mr. Trump and Governor Bush, and within another two weeks, Trump was pulling well ahead of Bush, Walker, and the rest of the field. In one poll conducted by the *Washington Post* and *ABC News*, Trump polled at 24 percent, with Walker placed well behind in second at 13 percent. By August, it was clear that Trump's early support was more than a temporary surge or anomaly and that his campaign was on the move, enjoying a substantial lead in every nationwide poll. Meanwhile, after having peaked in mid-July at around 17 percent, Bush's numbers suffered a steady decline. As Trump moved rapidly upward, Bush steadily declined toward the lower tier. Thus, by the first week of August, Trump was polling 23–24 percent across a number of polls nationwide, while Bush and Walker were holding at around 12–13 percent. When Trump broke 25 percent (mind you, in a crowded field of sixteen candidates), Bush and Walker both dipped into single digits, with Walker's descent being particularly rapid, a situation that no one had anticipated two months earlier. Bush was at that point a distant third behind Mr. Trump and Dr. Carson, who had also begun to show more promising polling numbers beginning around mid-July. In mid-September, Trump peaked at 30 percent and Carson, surprisingly, reached 20 percent, while the rest of the field, including Bush and Walker, clustered below 8 percent. Walker's campaign would not recover, and he would be among the first candidates to withdraw from the race.

Even though it remained reasonable to argue that in spite of his chronically poor showing in the polls, Bush was in fact still the front-runner through autumn 2015 because of his connection to establishment insiders—the leader in the "invisible primary," as it were—credulity was stretched by Trump's substantial and sustained lead. According to Nate Silver at FiveThirtyEight, by assigning points to party endorsements—ten points for an endorsement from a sitting governor, five from a senator, and one from a member of the House of Representatives—a candidate's position in the invisible primary, or what Mr. Silver refers to as the "endorsement primary," can be more tangibly tracked. Over the six months prior to November 2015, Bush's endorsement points hovered between thirty and forty, by early January 2016 reaching 46 points by this metric. Meanwhile Trump, even as late as early January, did not, according to Silver's criteria, possess a single point or a solitary endorsement (by February 2016 Trump would finally receive four endorsements—including Gov. Chris Christie's—for 22 points). Even so, the perception shared across the media up to early January holds Trump as the true front-runner. On January 6, according to an average of national polls calculated by RealClearPolitics, Mr. Trump still drew around 35 percent nationwide among Republican participants, with Sen. Cruz making significant inroads and placing at 20 percent. Sen. Rubio—who at that point enjoyed second in the invisible primary as measured in the first week of January—showed slightly over 11 percent, and Dr. Carson, who for a short time appeared to be Mr. Trump's principal challenger, slipping back into single digits. Bush's popular appeal ebbed irreversibly, his money and political capital squandered regardless of his strong position in the invisible primary. Not only was Gov. Bush ineffective in meeting the challenge from Mr. Trump, who overtook him in all polls, he was also surpassed by, at various times, Dr. Carson, Sen. Cruz, and Sen. Rubio, unable to even assume the position as the top contender to Trump's front-runner status, his poll numbers consistently showing single digits.

Whether or not Trump (the leader in the polls) or Bush (consistently stronger in the invisible primary through insider endorsements) could be identified as a true front-runner, a curious phenomenon emerged in the presidential campaign of 2015/2016. Quite unexpectedly, Trump's lead in the polls inexplicably survived a series of controversial statements, discourteous and even vulgar language, and impolitic claims tendered with apparent disregard for self-restraint, observations and assertions that would have caused irreparable damage had they been uttered by more typical politicians. In his remarks about immigration and undocumented aliens, Trump not only insulted many voters of Hispanic descent, but he also committed himself to indicting the government of Mexico with the charge of collusion. It was the kind of gaffe that prompts ordinary candidates to plaintively abase themselves with immediate and earnest apologies, or, more likely, ending a campaign entirely; however, Trump, rather than apologizing or even attempting an excusatory explanation, forcefully reasserted his claims, "doubling down" in the argot of punditry. Through tweets complaining of the debate moderation of Fox anchorwoman Megyn Kelly, Trump posted comments disrespectful of Ms. Kelly in particular and women in general. Again, Trump did not apologize for the gaffe but instead dismissively explained it away. Significantly, these comments did not damage Mr. Trump in the polls, at least in the long term. Rather, his numbers continued to rise even after the inflammatory remarks about undocumented immigrants, and while his numbers dipped two percentage points shortly after the episode involving Ms. Kelly, within two weeks that trend had reversed toward his polling peak in mid-September. Trump's rise to the top was also unhindered by a brief controversy over comments, perceived as unseemly, regarding the war record of Arizona senator John McCain, the GOP nominee in 2008. To be fair to Trump, the full context of the remarks reveals an intent apart from what was reported in the media and perceived throughout the public, but it nonetheless was broadly perceived that Trump was impeaching McCain's reputation as a war hero. Yet, in the midst of this, whether the perception aligned with the reality of his intent or not, Trump did not lose any momentum at the polls. Trump has lambasted Syrian refugees and proposed unconstitutional and uncivil prohibitions against all Muslims, used crass language while referring to Hillary Clinton's failed 2008 campaign, and in general continues to speak without filters and without consequences, at one point committing embarrassing and adolescent comments about Sec. Clinton, another time egging on, and then repeating on mic, a Trump follower's crudely inappropriate insult against Sen. Cruz at a campaign event. These and other statements, either uttered during the multi-candidate "debate" showcases that began in July, or at press conferences, during speaking engagements, or posted on Twitter, have not impeded his popularity. To the contrary, each unsavory or controversial comment was followed by improved numbers in the polls. By sheer force of personality, Trump achieved an unprecedented position wherein he could speak without reservation or forethought about any subject and remain unscathed in the backlash, every time seemingly gaining strength in inverse proportion to the level of criticism against him. Certainly there have been other major party candidates in the past who were able to speak with a frankness eschewed by typical candidates: President Theodore Roosevelt relished the bully pulpit and was successful at speaking his mind, President Harry Truman was well known for his straight-shooting candor, Arizona senator Barry Goldwater made no apologies for the intensity of his convictions, Minnesota senator Eugene McCarthy could display an intellectual's high-minded disregard for standard campaign protocols, and New York senator Robert Kennedy exhibited an atypical fearlessness in challenging his audiences with a flinty indifference to the risk of provoking a hostile reaction. But Mr. Trump's knack for casually trumpeting confrontational comments or personal insults while deflecting the consequent outcry has been unique. In a way, Trump entered the scene as a new political species: the major party candidate of no consequences; and it is this that made him *sui generis.*

During the first of the GOP debates, Trump was indeed a domineering presence. By contrast, a nonplussed Bush, described as tepid in his campaign appearances and ineffective on stage during the debate events, seemed either unwilling or unable to deflect the Trump charge. Owing to the unusually crowded field, the first two debates were divided into upper and lower tiers, with candidates qualifying for the "top card" of the debates based on their success in the polls. In the second card, Carly Fiorina, who polled quite low initially, drew the most attention and the most acclaim, adding strength to her position in the polls and consequently qualifying her for a slot in the second debate's first card, where she appeared to be the candidate on the move with, at least for the moment, the best chance at challenging the dominance of Trump. In that same debate, Senator Rubio also began to show promise, and Dr. Carson, managing to avoid mistakes, sustained his steady drive upward toward the second spot behind Trump. Fiorina managed to peak at around 11 percent, third behind only Trump and Carson, but owing to her controversial claims regarding allegations targeting abortion practices within Planned Parenthood, her support quickly eroded. By the third debate, she was polling just over 5 percent, having lost, at least based on the polling data, over half of her temporary support. By mid-autumn, Carson's numbers pressed Trump, whose lead across the national polls was now around five percentage points. In some polls, Dr. Carson actually gained a slight lead; but it must be noted that the several polls varied considerably. By Halloween, Carson's best showing was a four-percentage-point lead in a CBS/*New York Times* poll; however, in most polls, Trump still led the pack by just under 5 percent, his biggest lead being ten percentage points in both the Monmouth poll and the ABC/*Washington Post* poll. After steady performances in all three GOP debate showcases, including a particularly strong effort in the third debate, Rubio replaced Fiorina as the candidate with momentum, showing third across the polls nationwide as well as in most of the specific polls conducted. Rubio's best number was 13 percent, reached in the *NBC News/Wall Street Journal* poll. Rubio had been gradually gaining more attention in the preceding weeks, but it was in the third debate on October 28 that he managed to energize his campaign though his firm and cool-headed reaction to a badly misfired criticism aimed in his direction by Bush, who thereby appeared to be an increasingly desperate candidate. With aikido-like agility, Rubio deflected Bush's awkward schoolyard gibe, which had in effect accused the senator of shirking his sworn responsibilities to his constituents, with a deftly executed move that reversed the weight of the clumsily delivered (and obviously scripted) charge, directing it back upon his accuser. Bush's condescending jab, met by Rubio's decisive block, put the governor on the ropes where he remained throughout the rest of the debate while Rubio and Sen. Cruz seemed to score the most points. Additionally, at one moment during the debate, Bush, in an attempt to interject a modicum of levity, generously offered to plant "a warm kiss" on any Democrat who was "for cutting taxes," an unappetizing jest so self-consciously and uncomfortably delivered that it was less likely to raise a knowing chuckle and more likely to give a serious person the willies. In the aftermath of the debate, even observers amenable to Governor Bush came away with the impression that his campaign was perilously close to collapsing. Loyal Bush supporters openly expressed disappointment and frustration, and Bush himself was forced to admit that he was not a good debater. Following the debate, it seemed that Bush's only remaining hope rested on the fundamental fact that the Bush campaign held in reserve a dragon's hoard of money—and, one would expect, the ongoing support of the largest number of established party insiders. The money and the endorsements did not give Bush enough juice to make a credible run, his campaign continued to spiral down and land foul, and ultimately he withdrew following a weak result in the South Carolina primary. Bush's failure again demonstrates that it takes a lot more than money and establishment credentials to be elected president.

The third Republican debate as a whole was poorly conducted. The candidates vocally criticized the behavior of the moderators both during and after the debate—for example, Senator Cruz gained approval and real momentum for his impatient criticism of the media during the event—and proposals to cancel the next scheduled event were openly submitted. In previous campaigns, a decision to postpone or cancel a debate showcasing prospective nominees several months before the Iowa caucus would have received, at best, passing notice in the media, and likely on the national level; but given the recent emphasis assigned by candidates and media alike to these early debate events, the prospect of such a postponement or cancellation bears a new degree of import. (The proposed postponement was not implemented.) Indeed, these early debate-style showcases have exhibited more significance in the process than they could have had in past campaigns, even the debate-saturated **Campaign of 2012**. In that campaign, eventual nominee Mitt Romney was the established Republican front-runner throughout, regardless of gaffe-riddled incidents within each debate and the cycle of other candidates surging from the middle of the pack to the ostensible lead. Such incidents only meant that the reality of Romney's front-runner status was not always congruent with appearances derived solely from the polls. In the 2015 lead-in to the 2016 season, Governor Bush's steady decline seems to have been accelerated owing to his bland performance in the debates and at other speaking engagements, and not just because of the Trump juggernaut. Unlike previous presidential campaigns, these early intraparty debates have drawn large national audiences, in unprecedented numbers to the detriment of the one candidate who should have been in the best position to strengthen his credentials months before the first caucus in Iowa. As it happens, in part owing to the debates, and in part to other speaking appearances and events, political outsiders Donald Trump and Ben Carson, and to a lesser degree Carly Fiorina (although her fortunes eventually turned in the other direction), drew far more interest and (at least in the polls) support than the purported choice of the party insiders. Throughout the months of November, December, and January, Cruz and Rubio continued to enjoy far more success in the polls than Bush, even though the quality of the debates deteriorated noticeably, the polls showing that no one seemed to care that the intraparty debates, especially on the Republican side, were embarrassingly unprofessional, the behavior of the candidates increasingly immature. After months of shouting each other down, the candidates faced off in the Iowa caucus, where Sen. Cruz scored the first victory of the official primary/caucus cycle. By contrast, Jeb Bush's negatives were the highest among the field according to polls conducted in December and January, and his performance in Iowa and subsequent primaries was dismal, although he attempted enthusiasm after a weak fourth-place finish in New Hampshire. Significantly, Sen. Rubio gained considerable momentum in the endorsements that mark the invisible primary, garnering as of January 2016 more endorsements from prominent insiders than any candidate other than Jeb Bush, and then surpassing Bush in early February following the Iowa caucus and New Hampshire primary. Bush's aimless drifting in the doldrums compromised his credibility before the voting public and within the media. Careful students of presidential campaign politics are prompted to ask just exactly to what degree can a lead among endorsements and a bountiful campaign war chest compensate for a candidate's strategic errors, tactical miscues, and casual overconfidence. Will Bush's enervated campaign signal a new trend in presidential campaign politics with regard to the invisible primary that is shaped by the endorsements of prominent insiders? Having scored 150 endorsement points (Sen. Cruz well behind with only 34 endorsement points), Rubio's lead in endorsements may still provide some friction against the growing Trump bandwagon, but it remains too early to tell as of this writing. As of late February, Mr. Trump had finally managed to win some endorsements but still had a weak endorsement score of 22, behind both Rubio and Cruz as well as Gov. Kasich. As political science professor Marty Cohen has observed, these "early endorsements in the invisible primary are the most important cause of candidate success in the state primaries and caucuses." Should Mr. Trump manage an end run around the party establishment by relying strictly on the polls, it will represent an anomalous case in the study of the nominating process. It will remain to be seen what this anomaly may mean in the long term.

On the Democratic side, Secretary Clinton, also the early and clear front-runner for the nomination in the spring of 2015, had appeared vulnerable to an energetic and captivating challenge from Senator Sanders, a candidate moving against her from the left. Throughout the summer, Clinton's campaign seemed dormant as Sanders, touring the country and drawing large, animated crowds, received substantial attention from the media. Indeed, Clinton's campaign for a time seemed to resemble the troubled, lackluster Bush campaign, exacerbated by ongoing allegations of wrongdoing and incompetence in responding to the trag-edy in Benghazi, Libya, while she was secretary of state under President Obama. Clinton seemed unconcerned about the lassitude that had slowed her campaign, and she also appeared unable to shake off criticisms over the Benghazi incident. Consequently, for a few weeks during the summer of 2015, there were serious conversations revolving around the possibility that Vice President Joe Biden might announce his intention to run for the nomination. In the end, Vice President Biden, still mourning the sad loss of his son on May 30, 2015, withdrew his name from consideration on October 24. This announcement came within the same week as Clinton's strong performance in the first Democratic debate and her successful appearance before a congressional committee investigating the Benghazi incident. (Vice President Biden has recently expressed regret over his decision.) The revival of Clinton's fortunes animated by her debate performance may have been the deci-sive factor in the grieving vice president's decision to step back from the campaign and yield to Clinton. Perhaps more importantly, in the invisible primary, Clinton currently (as of late February 2016) enjoys a score of 474 "endorsement points," according to the metric used at FiveThirtyEight (i.e., ten points for a governor's endorsement, five for a senator's, and one for a member of the House). Sanders has just two endorsements for a score of two points, a clear indication that only one candidate—Sec. Clinton—holds any genuine support among the party establish-ment. Nevertheless, the fact that she is such a potent establishment force is one of the reasons more disillusioned Democrats identify with Sanders.

The Iowa caucus was narrowly won by Sec. Clinton, and the New Hampshire primary provided a more substantial victory for Sen. Sanders, which was followed by another close but significant win for Clinton in Nevada.

Sanders, in spite of his status as underdog and antiestablishment outsider, remains a compelling figure. For the first time in decades a presidential candidate with authentic left-wing proclivities and a progressive voting record in the Senate has been taken seriously by the press as well as by a visible number of likely voters, drawing large, enthusiastic crowds in sharp contrast to Sec. Clinton's more subdued campaign. That Sanders unabashedly defines himself as a democratic socialist while still managing to hold sustained media attention and enjoy unexpectedly strong numbers in the polls lends further credence to the unusual properties of the 2015/2016 campaign season to date. A candidate with Sanders's ideological proclivities is typically more likely to poll well below 5 percent nationally in a presidential campaign; thus if a candidate as far to the left as Senator Sanders, even though he is behind Clinton in nearly every measure, still manages to poll in double digits, it must indicate something different when compared to other presidential campaigns. Socialists candidates like Eugene Debs and Progressive candidates such as Robert LaFollette have appeared in the past, and even drawn considerable support, but they were not seeking the nomination of one of the two major parties nor did they receive the sustained media attention now witnessed by the Sanders campaign. In the long term, the Sanders campaign may prove to be anomalous, but at present it reveals developments within the Democratic Party that cannot be ignored. In a close general election, Clinton, if she is the nominee, will need votes from Sanders supporters; thus her campaign must rhetorically adjust to at least some of the concerns and frustrations of the progressive left.

In the 2015 Democratic intraparty debates, both Clinton and Sanders, as well as O'Malley, performed well. Clinton put to rest growing anxiety over her abilities as a presidential candidate, and Sanders demonstrated before a national audience that his efforts are those of a serious and thoughtful politician. The contest between the candidates was initially congenial even though hackles were temporarily raised over an incident involving a computer security breach committed by Sanders operatives against the Clinton organization. Sen. Sanders has apologized for any possible improprieties, an apology accepted by Sec. Clinton. In later debates, the interaction between the candidates was more tense, although when compared to the GOP debates, more civil by and large if nonetheless more strained than the earlier events. In the most recent debate, the candidates continued to address a variety of substantive issues, from the recent shootings involving law enforcement and African Americans that have spurred movements such as Black Lives Matter, to issues such as ISIL/ISIS and the contemptuous criticism of the campaign rhetoric of Republican candidate Donald Trump. Following the debates, while Sen. Sanders appears to be sustaining his momentum, a more thorough examination of the polling data reinforces what many analysts have been claiming since she lost her attempt at the nomination to Sen. Obama in 2008; to wit, Hillary Clinton remains the likely Democratic nominee for the 2016 general election.

Predicting the outcome of a presidential campaign is an inexact and mildly risky commitment, even though there are reliable predictive measures available to us, such as (most notably) the condition of the economy, as well as numerous other factors, such as those mentioned above. Based upon events as they unfolded from April through October 2015, it would appear that the more likely GOP nominee is still difficult to discern. At this point, Trump, winner in New Hampshire, Nevada, and South Carolina, and Cruz, who won in the Iowa caucus, lead the pack in the polls, but Rubio is not far behind the latter. The events of the summer and fall, 2015, and the first two months of 2016, have seriously fogged the prognosticator's crystal ball. It is unlikely that either Trump or Cruz will lose ground in the polls any time soon. Trump's gaffe-proof, reverse-English, tough-talkin' persona has proven to be a persistent strength on the campaign trail (but holds no persuasive power within the party establishment). In the weeks ahead Cruz should continue to draw enough support to push the leader, especially given his success as the winner of the Iowa caucus. There are clear signs that Rubio, who polled nearly even with Cruz in Nevada, may be able to fuel his current momentum if he continues to perform with confidence and resolve in future campaign events, whether at the national level or within the various primary and caucus contests that will open in early February. With the disappearance of Jeb Bush, there is a better chance for Kasich to move up in the polls, as he now appears to be the more appealing alternative to those seeking a comparatively moderate nominee. It is unlikely that Kasich will overtake Trump or displace Rubio as the leading alternative, but he may show strength in primaries outside the South. Should Cruz or Rubio and Clinton both win their respective party nominations, for the first time in the history of U.S. presidential elections, both a woman and an Hispanic would serve as major-party standard-bearers, thereby making 2016 a significant cultural moment on the same level as 2008. Should Clinton manage to deflect Sanders's progressivist charge—and it seems likely that she will—and should Bush reanimate his campaign and regain the confidence of the voters as well as the endorsements of the party leadership, then we would witness a second presidential contest between a Bush and a Clinton. Prima facie, the possibility that both of the antiestablishment candidates, Trump and Sanders, could win the nominations of their respective parties remains, but the months ahead should reveal a different outcome. Having won in Iowa, Nevada, and most notably a landslide victory in the South Carolina primary, Hillary Clinton seems to have finally energized her campaign. While the Sanders camp remains hopeful, it is unlikely that their candidate can now regain sufficient momentum to match Clinton.

Be that as it may, it must be acknowledged that any prediction made so early in the campaign season lacks reliability—a lot can happen in the months remaining prior to the party conventions and the general election of 2016. And yet, based on long-term trends in presidential campaigning, it is safe to say that should likely voters perceive the economy to be stable and growing, however gradually, a Democrat—more likely Hillary Clinton—should hold the White House for his or her party in 2016. A brief glance at the constants and variations within the electoral map over the past few elections might serve as a baseline indicator for 2016. In doing so, one of the first questions to be raised is whether or not the eventual Republican nominee can persuade enough voters in the handful of battleground states to support a party change in the White House. Since Bill Clinton defeated the incumbent president George H. W. Bush in 1992, Democrats have won over 300 votes in the Electoral College four times (370 in 1992, 379 in 1996, 365 in 2008, and 332 in 2012). Republican candidate George W. Bush won in 2000 and 2004 with 271 electoral votes (a tenuous single vote above the required minimum) and 286 votes, respectively—the latter being the second-lowest percentage of electoral votes, 53.2 percent, won by a winning incumbent (President Woodrow Wilson was reelected with 52.3% of the votes in the Electoral College in 1916). Beginning with the 1992 election, a majority in the popular vote has been won only three times—50.7 percent for the incumbent president George W. Bush in 2004, 52.9 percent for Senator Barack Obama in 2008, and then just over 51 percent for incumbent president Obama in 2012. While the GOP dominated both the electoral vote and the popular vote in the 1980s (the Reagan-Bush years), since 1992 the Democrats have enjoyed more success both among the electorate and within the Electoral College. Part of this can be attributed to voting patterns in California, which at fifty-five electoral votes is the colossus of the electoral map, and since the first election of Clinton in 1992, it has become a reliably Democratic prize. California has not been, by any stretch of the term, a battleground state since (at best) the 1988 campaign when the difference in California was less than 5 percent. Indeed, since 1992, the difference between Democrats, who consistently win California, and Republicans has shown double digits in all six elections, the GOP's best showing since 1992 in California being 10 percent *behind* the Democratic candidate in 2004, when incumbent president Bush won reelection. In itself, this is a decisive factor, as no candidate has won California and lost the election since President Ford in 1976; thus it is evident that if the Republican Party is to strengthen its overall performance in the Electoral College, significant changes must occur in the Golden State. Republicans have commanded Texas, the state with the second most Electoral College votes, over the same time period, but the gap between the two states is seventeen votes in California's favor. New York and Florida, with twenty-nine each, are the states with the next highest electoral votes, and Republican candidates have not won in New York since President Reagan's landslide reelection in 1984. Florida has famously been the most important battleground state since 2000, a purple state that can swing either way. That said, Barack Obama's victories in Florida have been convincing, outpolling his Republican rivals, Sen. John McCain (2008) and Gov. Mitt Romney (2012), by 9.5 million against the former and around 5 million against the latter, figures that might serve as a prelude to a trend shifting Florida from purple to blue. The election of 2016 will prove a still more important indicator.

In other words, barring a sudden and improbably wide-ranging shift in electoral patterns, Democratic candidates are guaranteed 84 electoral votes in California and New York alone, and they have an even chance or better at winning Florida's 29, which, if that were to be the result, would deliver to their ticket 113 votes from just these three states. Republicans can rely on the 38 electoral votes in Texas, and at best can add Florida's 29, should the election swing in that direction, for a possible, best-case scenario total of 67 electoral votes among those two states, which, compared to the 84–113 that the Democrats are likely to win in 2016, is decidedly insufficient. Additionally, the two states with the fourth highest amount of electoral votes, Illinois and Pennsylvania, have been won by Democrats in every election since 1992, the election of the elder Bush in 1988 being the last time a Republican candidate won in either of those two states. Moreover, while Pennsylvania has at times been described as a battleground state, the popular vote there has in fact only been close on two occasions since 1992—around a 3.5 percent margin for Vice President Gore in 2000, and just over 5 percent for incumbent President Bush in 2004. Illinois has not been close since the Republicans won there by 2 percent in 1988 (the elder Bush versus Michael Dukakis after running a weak campaign); since then, Democrats have won Illinois by no less than 8 percent (in 1992) and at least 10 percent in every other election during that time period. Of the big-ticket states, only Florida (29 electoral votes) and Ohio (now claiming 18 Electoral College votes) have been won by Republicans since the Reagan-Bush years (when both states were won by the GOP in three consecutive elections—1980, 1984, and 1988). The elder Bush won Florida in a losing effort in 1992, and the younger Bush won both Ohio and Florida in 2000 (including the improbably narrow and controversial Florida count resolved by the Supreme Court) and 2004. Additionally, Michigan, which still delivers 16 electoral votes, has also been won consistently by Democrats since 1992, the elder Bush in 1988 being the last Republican to win there. Even Mitt Romney, who has a public family history in the Wolverine State, was unable to mount a credible challenge there, losing Michigan by over four million votes. All told, these electorally dominant states have, by and large, been the province of the Democrats since the Clinton election in 1992, with the few exceptions noted above. In other words, this hard fact alone illustrates the current favorable position enjoyed by any given Democratic nominee in the current political environment.

Nevertheless, any economic downturn between now and November 2016, along with intensified crises abroad as well as the possibility of lowered approval ratings for the current incumbent Democrat (President Obama), may cause the White House to again be occupied by a Republican. Nevertheless, unless the long-term economic outlook does turn in another direction, the odds for a Democratic victory are stronger. At the opening of 2016 and just weeks from the beginning of the caucus and primary season, Hillary Clinton appears to hold the advantage moving toward the 2016 general election. Barring a serious reversal of economic fortune, she is at present the likeliest person to succeed President Obama.

Additional Resources

Bycoffe, Aaron. "The Endorsement Primary." FiveThirtyEight. http://projects.fivethirtyeight .com/2016-endorsement-primary/. November 6, 2015.

Cohen, Marty, David Karol, Hans Noel, and John Zaller. *The Party Decides: Presidential Nominations Before and After Reform.* Chicago: The University of Chicago Press, 2008.

Issenberg, Sasha. *The Victory Lab: The Secret Science of Winning Campaigns.* New York: Crown Publishers, 2012.

Politico.com. Accessed November 6, 2015.

Reston, Laura. "When Endorsements Matter: Marco Rubio and the Race to Win the Invisible Primary." *New Republic,* November 3, 2015. http://www.newrepublic.com/article /123332/. Accessed November 6, 2015.

Selected Bibliography

Abrahamson, James L. *The Men of Secession and Civil War, 1859–1961.* Wilmington, DE: SR Books, 2000.

Abrahamson, Paul R., John H. Aldrich, Brad. T. Gomez, and David W. Rohde. *Change and Continuity in the 2012 and 2014 Elections.* Washington, DC: CQ Press, 2016.

Abrahamson, Paul R., John H. Aldrich, and David W. Rohde. *Change and Continuity in the 2008 and 2010 Elections.* Washington, DC: CQ Press, 2011.

Alter, Jonathon. *The Center Holds: Obama and His Enemies.* New York: Simon & Schuster, 2013.

Alvarez, R. Michael, and John Brehm. *Hard Choices, Easy Answers: Values, Information, and American Public Opinion.* Princeton, NJ: Princeton University Press, 2002.

American Presidency Project. University of California, Santa Barbara. http://www.presidency.ucsb.edu.

Ammon, Harry. *James Monroe: The Quest for National Identity.* New York: McGraw-Hill, 1971.

Anbinder, Tyler. *Nativism and Slavery: The Northern Know Nothings and the Politics of the 1850s.* New York: Oxford University Press, 1992.

Anderson, Donald F. *William Howard Taft: A Conservative's Conception of the Presidency.* Ithaca, NY: Cornell University Press, 1973.

Anderson, Keith. *The Creation of a Democratic Majority, 1928–1936.* Chicago: University of Chicago Press, 1979.

Anderson, Patrick. *Electing Jimmy Carter: The Campaign of 1976.* Baton Rouge: Louisiana State University Press, 1994.

Ansolabehere, Stephen, and Shanto Iyenger. *Going Negative: How Attack Ads Shrink and Polarize the Electorate.* New York: Free Press, 1995.

Arnold, Peri E. *Remaking the Presidency.* Lawrence: University Press of Kansas, 2009.

Bagby, Wesley Marvin. *The Road to Normalcy: The Presidential Campaign and Election of 1920.* Baltimore: Johns Hopkins Press, 1962.

Bailey, Thomas. *Presidential Saints and Sinners.* New York: Free Press, 1981.

Balz, Dan. *Collision 2012: Obama vs. Romney and the Future of Elections in America.* New York: Viking, 2013.

Balz, Dan. "What the Tea Party Is—and Isn't." *Washington Post*, September 10, 2011.

Barrett, Grant, ed. *The Oxford Dictionary of American Political Slang.* Oxford: Oxford University Press, 2004.

Bartels, Larry. *Presidential Primaries and the Dynamics of Public Choice.* Princeton, NJ: Princeton University Press, 1988.

Baum, Matthew A. "Talking the Vote: What Happens When Presidential Politics Hits the Talk Show Circuit?" *American Journal of Political Science* 49 (April 2005): 213–234.

Baum, Matthew A., and Angela Jamison. "The Oprah Effect: How Soft News Helps Inattentive Citizens Vote Consistently." *Journal of Politics* 68 (November 2006): 946–959.

Beck, Paul Allen. *Party Politics in America.* 8th ed. New York: Longman, 1997.

Beer, Thomas. *Hanna.* New York: A. A. Knopf, 1929.

Bell, Rudolph. *Party and Faction in American Politics.* Westport, CT: Greenwood Press, 1973.

Berman, Ari. "The GOP War on Voting," *Rolling Stone,* August 30, 2011.

Bishop, Bill. *The Big Sort: Why Clustering of Like-Minded Americans Is Tearing Us Apart.* New York: Houghton Mifflin Harcourt, 2008.

Bisnow, Mark. *Diary of a Dark Horse: The 1980 Anderson Presidential Campaign.* Carbondale: Southern Illinois University Press, 1983.

Bloom, Allen. *The Closing of the American Mind.* New York: Simon & Schuster, 1988.

Blue, Frederick. *The Free Soilers: Third Party Politics 1848–54.* Urbana: University of Illinois Press, 1973.

Blumenthal, Sidney. *Pledging Allegiance: The Last Campaign of the Cold War.* New York: HarperCollins, 1994.

Boller, Paul F. *Presidential Campaigns.* Oxford: Oxford University Press, 2004.

Brady, John. *Bad Boy: The Life and Politics of Lee Atwater.* Reading, MA: Addison Wesley, 1991.

Brewer, Mark D., and Jeffrey M. Stonecash. *Dynamics of American Political Parties.* Cambridge: Cambridge University Press, 2009.

Broadwater, Jeff. *Adlai Stevenson and American Politics: The Odyssey of a Cold War Liberal.* New York: Twayne, 1994.

Broder, David S. *The Party's Over: The Failure of Politics in America.* New York: Harper & Row, 1972.

Broder, David S., and Richard Harwood. *The Pursuit of the Presidency 1980.* New York: Berkley Books, 1980.

Broderick, Francis L. *Progressivism at Risk: Electing a President in 1912.* Westport, CT: Greenwood Press, 1989.

Brody, Richard A. *Assessing the President.* Palo Alto, CA: Stanford University Press, 1991.

Brown, Roger Hamilton. *The Republic in Peril: 1812.* New York: Columbia University Press, 1964.

Buell, Emmett H., and Lee Sigelman. *Attack Politics: Negativity in Presidential Campaigns since 1960.* Lawrence: University Press of Kansas, 2008.

Buell, Emmet H., Jr., and Lee Sigelman, eds. *Nominating the President.* Knoxville, TN: University of Tennessee Press, 1991.

Bunch, William. *Tear Down This Myth: The Right Wing Distortion of the Reagan Legacy.* New York: Free Press, 2010.

Burnham, Walter Dean, et al. *The Election of 1996: Reports and Interpretations.* New York: Chatham House, 1997.

Busch, Andrew E. *The Front-Loading Problem in Presidential Nominations.* Washington, DC: Brookings Institution Press, 2003.

Busch, Andrew E., *Reagan's Victory: The Presidential Election of 1980 and the Rise of the Right.* Lawrence: University Press of Kansas, 2005.

Busch, Andrew E., *Truman's Triumphs: The 1948 Election and the Making of Postwar America* (American Presidential Elections). Lawrence: University Press of Kansas, 2012.

Calhoun, Charles W. *Minority Victory: Gilded Age Politics and the Front Porch Campaign of 1888.* Lawrence: University Press of Kansas, 2008.

Campbell, David E., and Robert D. Putnam. "Crashing the Tea Party." *New York Times,* August 16, 2011.

Carmines, Edward G., and James A. Stimson. *Issue Evolution: Race and the Transformation of American Politics.* Princeton, NJ: Princeton University Press, 1989.

Carroll, Susan J., and Richard Logan Fox. *Gender and Elections: Shaping the Future of American Politics.* New York: Cambridge University Press, 2010.

Carty, Thomas J. *A Catholic in the White House? Religion, Politics, and John F. Kennedy's Presidential Campaign.* New York: Palgrave MacMillan, 2004.

Ceaser, James W. *Presidential Selection: Theory and Development.* Princeton, NJ: Princeton University Press, 1979.

Ceaser, James W. *Red over Blue: The 2004 Elections and American Politics.* Lanham, MD: Rowman & Littlefield, 2005.

Ceaser, James W., and Andrew Busch. *The Perfect Tie: The True Story of the 2000 Presidential Election.* Lanham, MD: Rowman & Littlefield, 2001.

Ceaser, James W., and Andrew Busch. *Upside Down and Inside Out: The 1992 Elections and American Politics.* Lanham, MD: Rowman & Littlefield, 1993.

Ceaser, James W., et al. *Epic Journey: The 2008 Elections and American Politics.* Lanham, MD: Rowman & Littlefield, 2011.

Cebula, James E. *James M. Cox: Journalist and Politician.* New York: Garland, 1985.

Chase, James. *1912: Wilson, Roosevelt, Taft and Debs—The Election that Changed the Country.* New York: Simon & Schuster, 2005.

Chester, Lewis, Godfrey Hodgson, and Bruce Page. *American Melodrama: The Presidential Campaign of 1968.* New York: Viking Press, 1969.

Chinni, Dante, and James Gimpel. *Our Patchwork Nation.* New York: Gotham, 2010.

Clancy, Herbert John. *The Presidential Election of 1880.* Chicago: Loyola University Press, 1958.

Clarke, Thurston. *The Last Campaign: Robert F. Kennedy and 82 Days That Inspired America.* New York: Henry Holt and Company, 2008.

Clayton, Dewey M. *The Presidential Campaign of Barack Obama: A Critical Analysis of a Racially Transcendent Strategy.* Lanham, MD: Routledge Press, 2010.

Coffey, Thomas. *The Long Thirst: Prohibition in America, 1920–1933.* New York: Norton, 1975.

Cohen, Marty, David Karol, Hans Noel, and John Zaller. *The Party Decides: Presidential Nominations before and after Reform.* Chicago: University of Chicago Press, 2008.

Cole, Donald B. *Vindicating Andrew Jackson: The 1828 Election and the Rise of the Two-Party System.* Lawrence: University Press of Kansas, 2009.

Coleman, Charles H. *The Election of 1868: The Democratic Effort to Regain Control.* New York: Columbia University Press, 1933.

CQ Press, eds. *Presidential Elections: 1789–2008.* Washington DC: CQ Press, 2009.

Cramer, Richard. *What It Takes: The Way to the White House.* New York: Random House, 1992.

Crotty, William. *The Party Game.* New York: W. H. Freeman, 1985.

Crotty, William, and John S. Jackson. *The Politics of Presidential Selection.* New York: Longman, 2001.

Crouse, Timothy. *The Boys on the Bus.* New York: Ballantine Books, 1974.

Cunningham, Noble E. *The Presidency of James Monroe.* Lawrence: University Press of Kansas, 1996.

David, Mark. *Going Dirty: The Art of Negative Campaigning.* Lanham, MD: Rowman & Littlefield, 2009.

Davis, Burke. *Old Hickory: A Life of Andrew Jackson.* New York: Dial Press, 1977.

Davis, Michael A. *Politics as Usual: Thomas Dewey, Franklin Roosevelt, and the Wartime Presidential Campaign of 1944.* DeKalb: Northern Illinois University Press, 2014.

Deaver, Michael. *Behind the Scenes.* New York: Morrow, 1987.

Denton, Robert E., Jr., ed. *The 2004 Presidential Campaign: A Communication Perspective.* Lanham, MD: Rowman & Littlefield, 2005.

Denton, Robert E., Jr., ed. *The 2008 Presidential Campaign: A Communication Perspective.* Lanham, MD: Rowman & Littlefield, 2009.

Denton, Robert E., Jr., ed. *The 2012 Presidential Campaign: A Communication Perspective.* Lanham, MD: Rowman & Littlefield, 2014.

Denton, Robert E., Jr. *Studies of Communication in the 2012 Presidential Campaign.* Lanham, MD: Lexington Books, 2014.

Denton, Robert E., Jr. *Studies of Identity in the 2008 Presidential Campaign.* Lanham, MD: Lexington Books, 2010.

Dershowitz, Alan M. *Supreme Injustice: How the High Court Hijacked the Election of 2000.* New York: Oxford University Press, 2001.

Dewey, Donald. *The Antitrust Experiment in America.* New York: Columbia University Press, 1990.

Divine, Robert E. *Foreign Policy and the U.S. Presidential Elections, 1940–1948.* New York: New Viewpoints, 1974.

Donaldson, Gary. *The First Modern Campaign: Kennedy, Nixon, and the Election of 1960.* Lanham, MD: Rowman & Littlefield, 2007.

Donaldson, Gary. *Truman Defeats Dewey.* Lexington: University Press of Kentucky, 1999.

Drew, Elizabeth. *Campaign Journal: The Political Events of 1983–1984.* New York: Macmillan, 1985.

Drew, Elizabeth. *Portrait of an Election: The 1980 Presidential Campaign.* New York: Simon & Schuster, 1981.

Drew, Elizabeth. *Whatever It Takes: The Real Struggle for Political Power in America.* New York: Viking Press, 1997.

Du Bois, W. E. B. *Black Reconstruction in America, 1860–1880.* n.p.: S.A. Russell Co., 1956.

Dulce, Benton, and Edward J. Richter. *Religion and the Presidency: A Recurring American Problem.* New York: Macmillan, 1962.

Dunn, Susan. *1940: FDR, Willkie, Lindbergh, Hitler—The Election amid the Storm.* New Haven, CT: Yale University Press, 2013.

Dworkin, Ronald, ed. *A Badly Flawed Election.* New York: New Press, 2002.

Ecelbarger, Gary. *The Great Comeback: How Abraham Lincoln Beat the Odds to Win the 1860 Republican Nomination.* New York: Thomas Dunne Books, 2008.

Edwards, George C. *Why the Electoral College Is Bad for America.* 2nd ed. New Haven, CT: Yale University Press, 2011.

Egerton, Douglas R. *Year of Meteors: Stephen Douglas, Abraham Lincoln and the Election That Brought on the Civil War.* New York: Bloomsbury Press, 2010.

Eisenhower, John S. D. *Agent of Destiny: The Life and Times of General Winfield Scott.* New York: Free Press, 1997.

Erikson, Robert S., Michael B. Mackuen, and James A. Stimson. *The Macro Polity.* New York: Cambridge University Press, 2002.

Erikson, Robert S., and Christopher Wlezien. *The Timeline of Presidential Elections: How Campaigns Do (and Do Not) Matter* (Chicago Studies in American Politics). Chicago: University of Chicago Press, 2012.

Eulau, Heinz. *Class and Party in the Eisenhower Years.* New York: Free Press of Glencoe, 1962.

Eulau, Heinz, and Michael Lewis-Beck, eds. *Economic Conditions and Electoral Outcomes: The United States and Western Europe.* New York: Algora Publishing, 1985.

Evans, Hugh. *The Hidden Campaign: FDR's Health and the 1944 Election.* Armonk, NY: M. E. Sharpe, 2002.

Faber, Harold. *The Road to the White House: The Story of the Election of 1964.* New York: McGraw-Hill, 1965.

Farley, James Aloysisus. *Jim Farley's Story: The Roosevelt Tears.* Westport, CT: Greenwood Press, 1984.

Federal Election Commission. http://www.fec.gov.

Felknor, Bruce L. *Political Mischief, Smear, Sabotage, and Reform in U.S. Elections.* New York: Praeger, 1992.

Ferling, John. *Adams vs. Jefferson: The Tumultuous Election of 1800.* Oxford: Oxford University Press, 2005.

Ferling, John. The Ascent of George Washington: The Hidden Political Genius of an American Icon. New York: Bloomsbury Press, 2009.

Fiorina, Morris P., Samuel J. Abrams, and Jeremy C. Pope. *Culture War? The Myth of a Polarized America*. New York: Longman, 2005.

Fisher, Roger A. *Them Damned Pictures: Explorations in American Political Cartoon Art*. North Haven, CT: Archon, 1996.

Fisher, Roger A. *Tippecanoe and Trinkets Too: The Material Culture of American Presidential Campaigns, 1828–1984*. Urbana: University of Illinois Press, 1988.

Fite, David Emerson. *The Presidential Campaign of 1860*. Port Washington, NY: Kennikat Press, 1967.

FiveThirtyEightPolitics. www.fivethirtyeight.com.

Flanigan, William H., and Nancy H. Zingale. *Political Behavior of the American Electorate*. Washington, DC: CQ Press, 2010.

Flood, Charles Bracelen, *1864: Lincoln at the Gates of History*. New York: Simon & Schuster, 2012.

Foner, Eric. *The Fiery Trial: Abraham Lincoln and American Slavery*. New York: W. W. Norton, 2010.

Foner, Eric. *Free Soil, Free Labor, Free Men: The Ideology of the Republican Party before the Civil War*. New York: Oxford University Press, 1970.

Freehling, William. *The Road to Disunion*. New York: Oxford University Press, 1990.

Friedenberg, Robert V. *Communication Consultants in Political Campaigns: Ballot Box Warriors*. Westport, CT: Praeger, 1997.

Friedenberg, Robert V. *Notable Speeches in Contemporary Presidential Campaigns*. Annotated ed. Westport, CT.: Greenwood Press, 2002.

Friedman, Milton, and Anna Jacobson. *A Monetary History of the United States, 1867–1960*. Princeton, NJ: Princeton University Press, 1963.

Frymer, Paul. *Uneasy Alliances: Race and Party Competition in America*. Princeton, NJ: Princeton University Press, 1999.

Gammon, Samuel Rhea. *The Presidential Campaign of 1832*. Baltimore: Johns Hopkins Press, 1922.

Geer, John G. *In Defense of Negativity: Attack Ads in Presidential Campaigns*. Chicago: University of Chicago Press, 2006.

Gelman, Andrew. *Red State, Blue State, Rich State, Poor State*. Expanded ed. Princeton, NJ: Princeton University Press, 2009.

Germond, Jack. *Whose Broad Stripes and Bright Stars? The Trivial Pursuit of the Presidency, 1988*. New York: Warner Books, 1989.

Germond, Jack, and Jules Witcover. *Blue Smoke and Mirrors: How Reagan Won and Why Carter Lost the Election of 1980*. New York: Viking, 1981.

Germond, Jack, and Jules Witcover. *Mad as Hell: Revolt at the Ballot Box, 1992*. New York: Warner Books, 1993.

Germond, Jack, and Jules Witcover. *Wake Us When It's Over: Presidential Politics of 1984*. New York: Macmillan, 1985.

Gienapp, William E. *The Origins of the Republican Party 1852–1856*. New York: Oxford University Press, 1987.

Gilens, Martin. *Why Americans Hate Welfare: Race, Media, and the Politics of Anti-Poverty Policy*. Chicago: University of Chicago Press, 2000.

Glad, Paul W. *McKinley, Bryan, and the People*. Philadelphia: Lippincott, 1964.

Glasser, Joshua M. *The Eighteen-Day Running Mate: McGovern, Eagleton, and a Campaign in Crisis*. New Haven, CT: Yale University Press, 2012.

Goldberg, Ava C. *Men Who Lost the Presidency: Profiles of the 29 Men Who Lost Elections to Be President of the United States*. Brentwood, TN: J.M. Press, 1992.

Goldman, Peter, Tony Fuller, and Thomas DeFrank. *The Quest for the Presidency 1984*. New York: Bantam Books, 1985.

Goldman, Peter, Tom Mathews, and the Newsweek Special Election Team. *The Quest for the Presidency, 1988*. New York: Simon & Schuster, 1989.

Goldzwig, Stephen R. *Truman's Whistle-Stop Campaign* (Library of Presidential Rhetoric). College Station: Texas A&M University Press, 2008.

Gould, Louis L. *Four Hats in the Ring: The 1912 Election and the Birth of Modern American Politics* (American Presidential Elections). Lawrence: University Press of Kansas, 2008.

Gould, Louis L. *The Presidency of William McKinley*. Lawrence: Regents Press of Kansas, 1980.

Gould, Lewis L. The Republicans: A History of the Grand Old Party. Oxford: Oxford University Press, 2014.

Green, Donald J. *Third Party Matters: Politics, Presidents and Third Parties in American Politics*. Santa Barbara, CA: ABC-CLIO, 2010.

Green, Donald P., and Alan S. Gerber. *Get Out the Vote: How to Increase Voter Turnout*. 2nd ed. Washington, DC: Brookings Institution Press, 2008.

Green, Donald P., Bradley Palmquist, and Eric Schickler. *Partisan Hearts and Minds*. New Haven, CT: Yale University Press, 2002.

Green, John C., and Daniel J. Coffey. *The State of Parties: The Changing Role of Contemporary American Parties*. Lanham, MD: Rowman & Littlefield, 2011.

Green, Michael S. *Lincoln and the Election of 1860* (Concise Lincoln Library). Carbondale: Southern Illinois University Press, 2011.

Greene, John Robert. *The Crusade: The Presidential Election of 1952*. Lanham, MD: University Press of America, 1985.

Gumbel, Andrew. *Steal This Vote: Dirty Elections and the Rotten History of Democracy in America*. New York: Nation Books, 2005.

Gunderson, Robert Gray. *The Log-Cabin Campaign*. Lexington: University of Kentucky Press, 1957.

Gutgold, Nicola D. *Paving the Way for Madam President* (Lexington Studies in Political Communication). Lanham, MD: Lexington Books, 2006.

Halperin, Mark, and John Heilemann. *Double Down: Game Change 2012*. New York: Penguin Books, 2014.

Hammond, Scott John. *Political Theory: An Encyclopedia of Contemporary and Classic Terms*. Westport, CT: Greenwood Press, 2009.

Hammond, Scott J., Kevin R. Hardwick, and Howard L. Lubert. *Classics of American Political and Constitutional Thought.* Vols. 1 and 2. Indianapolis, IN: Hackett Publishing, 2007.

Hanes, Walter, Jr. *Reelection.* New York: Columbia University Press, 2000.

Hansen, Bruce E. "Recounts from Undervotes: Evidence from the 2000 Presidential Election." *Journal of the American Statistical Association* 98, no. 462 (June 2003): 292–298.

Harpine, William D. *From the Front Porch to the Front Page: McKinley and Bryan in the 1896 Presidential Campaign* (Presidential Rhetoric and Political Communication). College Station: Texas A&M University Press, 2005.

Haynes, Sam W., and Oscar Handlin, eds. *James K. Polk and the Expansionist Impulse.* New York: Longman, 1997.

Hayward, Steven. *The Age of Reagan: The Conservative Counterrevolution, 1980–1989.* New York: Three Rivers Press, 2009.

Heilemann, John, and Mark Halperin. *Game Change: Obama and the Clintons, McCain and Palin, and the Race of a Lifetime.* New York: Random House, 2010.

Hendricks, John Allen, and Dan Schill. *Presidential Campaigning and Social Media: An Analysis of the 2012 Campaign.* Oxford: Oxford University Press, 2015.

Hernson, Paul S. ed. *CQ's Guide to Political Campaigns.* Thousand Oaks, CA: CQ Press, 2006.

Hersh, Eitan D. *Hacking the Electorate: How Campaigns Perceive Voters.* New York: Cambridge University Press, 2015

Hershey, Marjorie. *Party Politics in America.* White Plains, NY: Longman Publishers, 2010.

Hess, Steven, and Sandy Northrop. *Drawn and Quartered: The History of American Political Cartoons.* Washington, DC: Elliott & Clark, 1996.

Hillygus, D. Sunshine, and Todd G. Shields. *The Persuadable Voter: Wedge Issues in Presidential Campaigns.* Princeton, NJ: Princeton University Press, 2008.

Hirshon, Stanley. *Farewell to the Bloody Shirt.* Bloomington: Indiana University Press, 1962.

Hoadley, John F. *Origins of American Political Parties, 1789–1803.* Lexington: University Press of Kentucky, 1986.

Hofstader, Richard. *The Idea of a Party System.* Berkeley: University of California Press, 1970.

Hohenberg, John. *Re-Electing Bill Clinton: Why Americans Chose a "New Democrat."* Syracuse, NY: Syracuse University Press, 1997.

Holbrook. Thomas M. *Do Campaigns Matter?* Thousand Oaks, CA: Sage Publications, 1996.

Holt, Michael F. *The Rise and Fall of the American Whig Party.* Oxford: Oxford University Press, 1999.

Howard, Philip M. *New Media Campaigns and the Managed Citizen.* New York: Cambridge University Press, 2006.

Howe, Daniel Walker. *What Hath God Wrought: The Transformation of America, 1815–1848.* Oxford: Oxford University Press, 2009.

Hunter, James Davison. *Culture Wars: The Struggle to Define America.* New York: Basic Books, 1992.

Hunter, Sara. *Woman Suffrage and the New Democracy.* New Haven, CT: Yale University Press, 1996.

Israel, Fred. *History of American Presidential Elections, 1789–1884.* New York: Chelsea House, 1986.

Issenburg, Sasha. *The Victory Lab: The Secret Science of Winning Campaigns.* New York: Crown Publishers, 2012.

Iyengar, Shanto. *Is Anyone Responsible? How Television Frames Political Issues.* Chicago: University of Chicago Press, 1991.

Jacobson, Gary C. *A Divider, Not a Uniter: George W. Bush and the American People.* New York: Longman, 2010.

Jaffa, Harry. *A New Birth of Freedom: Abraham Lincoln and the Coming Civil War.* Lanham, MD: Rowman & Littlefield, 2000.

Jamieson, Kathleen Hall. *Electing the President, 2012: The Insiders' View.* Philadelphia: University of Pennsylvania Press, 2013.

Jamieson, Kathleen Hall. *Packaging the Presidency: A History and Criticism of Presidential Campaign Advertising.* New York: Oxford University Press, 1996.

Jamieson, Kathleen Hall, and David S. Birdsell. *Presidential Debates: The Challenge of Creating an Informed Electorate.* New York: Oxford University Press, 1990.

Jelen, Ted. *Ross for Boss: The Perot Phenomena and Beyond* (SUNY Series in the Presidency). Albany, NY: State University of New York Press, 2001.

Johannsen, Robert Walter, Sam W. Haynes, and Christopher Morris. *Manifest Destiny and Empire: American Antebellum Expansion.* College Station: Texas A&M University Press, 1997.

Johnson, David. *All the Way with LBJ: The 1964 Presidential Election.* Cambridge: University of Cambridge Press, 2009.

Johnson, Dennis W. *No Place for Amateurs: How Political Consultants Are Reshaping American Democracy.* New York: Routledge, 2001.

Johnson, Haynes, and Dan Balz. *The Battle for America 2008: The Story of an Extraordinary Election.* New York: Viking, 2009.

Jones, Stanley Llewellyn. *The Presidential Election of 1896.* Madison: University of Wisconsin Press, 1964.

Just, Marion R., ed. *Crosstalk: Citizens, Candidates, and the Media in a Presidential Campaign.* Chicago: University of Chicago Press, 1996.

Kallina, Edmund F., Jr. *Kennedy v. Nixon: The Presidential Election of 1960.* Gainesville: University of Florida Press, 2011.

Kaplan, Richard L. *Politics and the American Press: The Rise of Objectivity, 1865–1920.* Cambridge: Cambridge University Press, 2002.

Karabell, Zackery. *The Last Campaign: How Harry Truman Won the 1948 Election.* New York: Knopf, 2000.

Karmack, Elaine C. *Primary Politics: How Presidential Candidates Have Shaped the Modern Nominating System.* Washington, DC: Brookings Institution Press, 2009.

Kazin, Michael. *The Populist Persuasion: An American History*. Ithaca, NY: Cornell University Press, 1998.

Keith, Bruce E., David B. Magleby, Candice J. Nelson, Elizabeth Orr, and Mark C. Westlye. *The Myth of the Independent Voter*. Berkeley: University of California Press, 1992.

Kelly, Frank K. *The Fight for the White House: The Story of 1912*. New York: Crowell, 1961.

Kensky, Kate, Bruce W. Hardy, and Kathleen Hall Jamieson. *The Obama Victory: How Media, Money, and Message Shaped the 2008 Election*. New York: Oxford University Press, 2010.

Keyssar, Alexander. *The Right to Vote: The Contested History of Democracy in the United States*. New York: Basic Books, 2000.

Kiewet, D. Roderick. *Microeconomics and Micropolitics: Electoral Effects of Economic Issues*. Chicago: University of Chicago Press, 1983.

Knoles, George Harmon. *The Crisis of the Union, 1860–1861*. Baton Rouge: Louisiana State University Press, 1965.

Kraus, Sidney. *The Great Debates: Carter v. Ford, 1976*. Bloomington: Indiana University Press, 1979.

Kraus, Sidney. *The Great Debates: Kennedy vs. Nixon, 1960*. Bloomington: Indiana University Press, 2001.

Krug, Larry L. *The 1924 Coolidge-Dawes Lincoln Tour*. New York: Schiffer Publishing, 2007.

Langer, Gary, and Jon Cohen. "Voters and Values in the 2004 Election." *Public Opinion Quarterly* 69, no. 5 (Special Issue), 2005.

Leech, Margaret. *In the Days of McKinley*. New York: Harper, 1959.

LeMay, Michael, and Elliot Robert Barkan. *U.S. Immigration and Naturalization Laws and Issues*. Westport, CT: Greenwood Press, 1999.

Levendusky, Matthew. *The Partisan Sort*. Chicago: University of Chicago Press, 2009.

Levine, Lawrence W. *The Opening of the American Mind*. Boston: Beacon Press, 1997.

Levy, Peter B. *Encyclopedia of the Reagan-Bush Years*. Westport, CT: Praeger, 2001.

Lichtman, Alan. *Prejudice and the Old Politics: The Presidential Election of 1928*. Chapel Hill: University of North Carolina Press, 1979.

Link, Arthur Stanley. *Wilson: The New Freedom*. Princeton, NJ: Princeton University Press, 1956.

Lipset, Seymour Martin. *American Exceptionalism: A Double-Edged Sword*. New York: W. W. Norton, 1997.

Long, David E. *The Jewel of Liberty: Abraham Lincoln's Reelection and the End of Slavery*. Mechanicsburg, PA: Stackpole Books, 2008.

Lovell, S. D. *The Presidential Election of 1916*. Carbondale: Southern Illinois University Press, 1980.

Mach, Thomas S. *Reliving the "Hornet's Nest": James B. Weaver and the Election of 1880*. Lanham, MD: University Press of America, 2001.

Maisel, Sandy L., and Mark D. Brewer. *Parties and Elections in America: The Electoral Process*. Lanham, MD: Rowman & Littlefield, 2008.

Malbin, Michael J. *The Election after Reform: Money, Politics, and the Bipartisan Campaign Reform Act*. Lanham, MD: Rowman & Littlefield, 2006.

Mann, Robert. *Daisy Petals and Mushroom Clouds: LBJ, Barry Goldwater, and the Ad That Changed American Politics*. Baton Rouge: Louisiana State University Press, 2011.

Matalin, Mary, and James Carville. *All's Fair: Love, War, and Running for President*. New York: Random House, Simon & Schuster, 1994.

Matthews, Christopher. *Jack Kennedy: Elusive Hero*. New York: Simon & Schuster, 2011.

Matthews, Christopher. *Kennedy and Nixon: The Rivalry That Shaped Postwar America*. New York: Simon & Schuster, 1996.

Mayer, Jeremy D. *Running on Race: Racial Politics in Presidential Campaigns, 1960–2000*. New York: Random House, 2002.

Mayer, William G., ed. *The Swing Voter in American Politics*. Washington, DC: Brookings Institution Press, 2007.

Mayer, William G., and Jonathan Bernstein, eds. *The Making of Presidential Candidates, 2012*. New York: Rowman & Littlefield, 2011.

Mayer, William G., et al. *The Making of Presidential Candidates, 2008*. New York: Rowman & Littlefield, 2007.

Mayfield, John. *Rehearsal for Republicanism: Free Soil and the Politics of Antislavery*. Port Washington, NY: Kennikat Press, 1980.

McClosky, Herbert, and John Zaller. *The American Ethos: Public Attitudes toward Capitalism and Democracy*. Cambridge, MA: Harvard University Press, 1987.

McCubbins, Matthew D. *Under the Watchful Eye: Managing Presidential Campaigns in the Television Era*. Washington, DC: CQ Press, 1992.

McDougall, Malcolm D. *We Almost Made It*. New York: Crown Publishers, 1977.

McNair, Brian. *An Introduction to Political Communication*, 5th ed. Lanham, MD: Routledge Press, 2011.

McPherson, James. *The Battle Cry of Freedom*. New York: Oxford University Press, 1988.

Mebane, Walter R., Jr. "The Wrong Man Is President! Overvotes in the 2000 Election in Florida." *Perspectives on Politics* 2, no. 3 (September 2004): 525–535.

Melder, Keith. *Hail to the Candidate: Presidential Campaigns from Banners to Broadcasts*. Washington, DC: Smithsonian Institution Press, 1992.

Minow, Newton N., and Craig L. LaMay. *Inside the Presidential Debates: Their Improbable Past and Promising Future*. Chicago: University of Chicago Press, 2008.

Mitchell, Jack. *How to Get Elected: An Anecdotal History of Mudslinging, Redbaiting, Vote Stealing and Dirty Tricks in American Politics*. New York: St. Martin's Press, 1992.

Moe, Richard. *Roosevelt's Second Act: The Election of 1940 and the Politics of War* (Pivotal Moments in American History). Oxford: Oxford University Press, 2013.

Monkey Cage. http://www.themonkeycage.org.

Moore, Jonathan, ed. *Campaign for President: The Campaign Managers Look at '84*. Dover, MA: Auburn House Publishing, 1986.

Morello, John A. *Selling the President, 1920: Albert D. Lasker, Advertising, and the Election of Warren G. Harding*. Westport, CT: Praeger, 2001.

Morgan, James. *Theodore Roosevelt: The Boy and the Man*. New York: Kessinger Publishing, 1907.

Morris, Dick. *Behind the Oval Office: Winning the Presidency in the Nineties*. New York: Random House, 1997.

Morris, Edmund. *The Rise of Theodore Roosevelt*. New York: Random House, 1979.

Morris, Edmund. *Theodore Rex*. New York: Random House, 2001.

Morris, Roy. *Fraud of the Century: Rutherford B. Hayes, Samuel Tilden, and the Stolen Election of 1876*. New York: Simon & Schuster, 2003.

Moscow, Warren. *Roosevelt and Willkie*. Englewood Cliffs, NJ: Prentice-Hall, 1968.

Mosher, Frederick C. *Democracy and the Public Service*. New York: Oxford University Press, 1982.

Mowry, George W. *The Era of Theodore Roosevelt and the Birth of Modern America*. New York: HarperCollins, 1968.

Mucciaroni, Gary, *Same Sex, Different Politics: Success and Failure in the Struggles Over Gay Rights* Chicago: University of Chicago Press, 2008.

Mueller, James E. *Tag Teaming the Press: How Bill and Hillary Clinton Work Together to Handle the Media* (Communication, Media, and Politics). Lanham, MD: Rowman & Littlefield, 2008.

Neal, Steve. *Dark Horse: A Biography of Wendell Willkie*. Garden City, NY: Doubleday, 1984.

Nelson, Michael. *Resilient America: Electing Nixon in 1968, Channeling Dissent, and Dividing Government* (American Presidential Elections). Lawrence: University Press of Kansas, 2014.

Noggle, Burl. *Teapot Dome: Oil and Politics in the 1920s*. Baton Rouge: Louisiana State University Press, 1962.

Noonan, Peggy. *What I Saw at the Revolution*. New York: Random House, 2003.

Norpath, Helmut, Jean-Dominique Lafay, and Michael S. Lewis-Beck, eds. *Economics and Politics: The Calculus of Support*. Ann Arbor: University of Michigan Press, 1991.

Norrander, Barbara. *The Imperfect Primary: Oddities, Biases and Strengths of U.S. Presidential Nomination Politics*. New York: Routledge, 2010.

Oates, Stephen. *The Approaching Fury: Voices of the Storm, 1820–1861*. New York: HarperCollins, 1997.

Owen, Diana. *Media Messages in American Presidential Elections*. Westport, CN: Greenwood Press, 1991.

Panagopoulos, Costas. "Campaign Dynamics in Battleground and Nonbattleground States." *Public Opinion Quarterly* 73, no. 1 (Spring 2009): 119–129.

Parker, Christoper S., and Matt A. Barreto. *Change They Can't Believe In: The Tea Party and Reactionary Politics in America*. Princeton, NJ: Princeton University Press, 2013.

Parmet, Herbert S., and Marie B. Hecht. *Never Again: A President Runs for a Third Term*. New York: Macmillan, 1968.

Parsons, Lynn Hudson. *The Birth of Modern Politics: Andrew Jackson, John Quincy Adams, and the Election of 1828*. New York: Oxford University Press, 2009.

Pasley, Jeffrey L. *The First Presidential Contest: 1796 and the Founding of American Democracy* (American Presidential Elections). Lawrence: University Press of Kansas, 2013.

Patterson, Thomas E. *Out of Order.* New York: Knopf, 1993.

Pegram, Thomas R. *Battling Demon Rum: The Struggle for a Dry America, 1800–1933.* Chicago: Ivan R. Dee, 1998.

Perlstein, Rick. *Before the Storm: Barry Goldwater and the Unmaking of the American Consensus.* New York: Hill and Wang, 2001.

Perry, Luke. *Mitt Romney, Mormonism, and the 2012 Election* (Palgrave Studies in Religion, Politics, and Policy). New York: Palgrave MacMillan, 2014.

Peters, Charles. *Five Days in Philadelphia: 1940, Wendell Willkie, FDR, and the Political Convention That Freed FDR to Win World War II.* New York: Public Affairs, 2006.

Picket, William B. *Eisenhower Decides to Run: Presidential Politics and Cold War Strategy.* Chicago: Ivan R. Dee, 2000.

Pietrusza, David. *1948: Harry Truman's Improbable Victory and the Year That Transformed America.* New York: Union Square Press, 2011.

Pietrusza, David. *1960: LBJ v. Kennedy v. Nixon: The Epic Campaign That Forged Three Presidencies.* New York: Union Square Press, 2008.

Piven, Frances Fox, and Richard A. Cloward. *Poor People's Movements: Why They Succeed, How They Fail.* New York: Vintage, 1978.

Pleasants, Julian M. *Hanging Chads: The Inside Story of the 2000 Presidential Recount in Florida.* New York: Palgrave MacMillan, 2004.

Plissner, Martin. *The Control Room: How Television Calls the Shots in Presidential Elections.* New York: Free Press, 1999.

Polakoff, Keith Ian. *The Politics of Inertia: The Election of 1876 and the End of Reconstruction.* Baton Rouge: Louisiana State University Press, 1973.

Politico. http://www.politico.com.

Polsby, Nelson W. *Consequences of Party Reform.* Oxford: Oxford University Press, 1983.

Polsby, Nelson W., Aaron Wildavsky, Steven E. Schier, and David A. Nelson. *Presidential Elections: Strategies and Structures of American Politics.* 13th ed. New York: Rowman & Littlefield, 2012.

Posner, Richard A. *Breaking the Deadlock: The 2000 Election, the Constitution, and the Courts.* Princeton, NJ: Princeton University Press, 2001.

Public Policy Polling. www.publicpolicypolling.com

Putnam, Robert, and David E. Campbell. *American Grace: How Religion Divides and Unities Us.* New York: Simon & Schuster, 2010.

Ranson, Edward. *The American Presidential Election of 1924: A Study of Calvin Coolidge.* Lewiston, NY: Edwin Mellen Press, 2008.

Rapaport, Ronald B., and Walter J. Stone. *Three's a Crowd: The Dynamic of Third Parties, Ross Perot, and Republican Resurgence.* Ann Arbor: University of Michigan Press, 2007.

Ratcliffe, Donald. *The One-Party Presidential Contest: Adams, Jackson, and 1824's Five-Horse Race* (American Presidential Elections). Lawrence: University Press of Kansas, 2015.

Rawley, James A. *Race and Politics: "Bleeding Kansas" and the Coming of the Civil War.* Philadelphia: Lippincott, 1969.

Real Clear Politics. http://www.realclearpolitics.com.

Reiter, Howard. *Selecting the President: The Nominating Process in Transition*. Philadelphia: University of Pennsylvania Press, 1985.

Remini, Robert V. *Andrew Jackson and the Bank War: A Study in the Growth of Presidential Power*. New York: Norton, 1967.

Remini, Robert V. *Andrew Jackson and the Course of American Freedom, 1822–1832*. New York: Harper & Row, 1981.

Remini, Robert V. *The Election of Andrew Jackson*. Philadelphia: Lippincott, 1963.

Rimmerman, Craig A., Kenneth D. Wald, and Clyde Wilcox, eds. *The Politics of Gay Rights*. Chicago: University of Chicago Press, 2000.

Ritter, Gretchen. *Goldbugs and Greenbacks: The Antimonopoly Tradition and the Politics of Finance in America*. Cambridge: Cambridge University Press, 1997.

Roberts, Robert North. *Ethics in U.S. Government: An Encyclopedia of Investigations, Scandals, Reforms, and Legislation*. Westport, CT: Greenwood Press, 2001.

Rorabaugh, W. J. *The Real Making of the President: Kennedy, Nixon, and the 1960 Election* (American Presidential Elections). Lawrence: University Press of Kansas, 2009.

Roseboom, Eugene H. *A History of Presidential Elections*. New York: Macmillan, 1964.

Roseboom, Eugene H. *Presidential Campaigns*. New York: Oxford University Press, 1984.

Rosen, Elliot. *Hoover, Roosevelt, and the Brains Trust: From Depression to the New Deal*. New York: Columbia University Press, 1977.

Rosenstone, Steven J., and John Mark Hansen. *Mobilization, Participation, and Democracy in America*. New York: Longman, 2002.

Ross, Irwin. *The Loneliest Campaign: The Truman Victory of 1948*. New York: New American Library, 1968.

Ross, Shelly. *Fall from Grace: Sex, Scandal, and Corruption in American Politics from 1702 to the Present*. New York: Ballantine Books, 1988.

Ross, Tara. *Enlightened Democracy: The Case for the Electoral College*. Dallas, TX: Colonial Press, 2004.

Rossiter, Clinton. *The American Presidency*. New York: Harcourt-Brace, 1960.

Rudin, Ken. "Superdelegates Primer: What You Need to Know." NPR, April 14, 2008.

Runkel, David R. *Campaign for President: The Managers Look at '88*. Westport, CT: Auburn House, 1989.

Russell, Francis. *The President Makers: From Mark Hanna to Joseph P. Kennedy*. Boston: Little, Brown, 1976.

Sabato, Larry. *Divided States of America: Slash and Burn Politics*. New York: Longman, 2005.

Sabato, Larry. *Feeding Frenzy: How Attack Journalism Transformed American Politics*. New York: Free Press, 1991.

Sabato, Larry, *Overtime: The Election of 2008 Thriller*. New York: Longman, 2001.

Sabato, Larry. *The Rise of Political Consultants: New Ways of Winning Elections*. New York: Basic Books, 1981.

Sabato, Larry, *The Year of Obama: How Barack Obama Won the White House*. New York: Longman, 2009.

Schill, Dan. *Stagecraft and Statecraft: Advance and Media Events in Political Communication* (Lexington Studies in Political Communication). Lanham, MD: Lexington Books, 2009.

Schlesinger, Arthur M., Fred Israel, and William P. Hansen, eds. *History of American Presidential Elections, 1789–1968*. Vol. 1. New York: Chelsea House, 1971.

Schlesinger, Arthur M., Fred L. Israel, and David J. Frent. *Running for President: The Candidates and Their Images*. New York: Simon & Schuster, 1994.

Schall, Marianne. *What Will It Take to Make A Woman President? Conversations About Women, Leadership and Power*. Berkeley, CA: Seal Press, 2013.

Schram, Martin. *The Great American Video Game: Presidential Politics in the Television Age*. New York: Morrow, 1987.

Schram, Martin. *Running for President, 1976: The Carter Campaign*. New York: Stein and Day, 1977.

Schroder, Alan, *Presidential Debates: Fifty Years of High-Risk TV*. New York: Columbia University Press, 2008.

Schultz, Jeffrey D. *Presidential Scandals*. Washington, DC: CQ Press, 2000.

Sellers, Charles Grier. *Andrew Jackson, Nullification and the State-Rights Tradition*. Chicago: Rand McNally, 1963.

Sharp, James Roger. *American Politics in the Early Republic: The New Nation in Crisis*. New Haven, CT: Yale University Press, 1993.

Sharp, James Roger. *The Deadlocked Election of 1800: Jefferson, Burr and the Union in the Balance*. Lawrence: University Press of Kansas, 2010.

Shaw, Daron R. *The Race to 270: The Electoral College and the Campaign Strategies of 2000 and 2004*. Chicago: University of Chicago Press, 2006.

Sheppard, Mike. "How Close Were U.S. Presidential Elections?" http://www.mit.edu /~mi22295/elections.html.

Sides, John, and Daniel Hopkins, eds. *Political Polarization in American Politics*. New York: Bloomsbury Academic, 2015.

Sides, John, Daron Shaw, Matt Grossman, and Keena Lipsitz. *Campaigns and Elections: Rules, Reality, Strategy, Choice*. New York: W. W. Norton and Co., 2011.

Sides, John, and Lynn Vavreck. *The Gamble: Choice and Chance in the 2012 Presidential Election*. Princeton, NJ: Princeton University Press, 2013.

Sievers, Rodney M. *The Last Puritan? Adlai Stevenson in American Politics*. Port Washington, NY: Associated Faculty Press, 1983.

Silber, Irwin. *Songs America Voted By: With the Words and Music That Won and Lost Elections and Influenced the Democratic Process*. Harrisburg, PA: Stackpole Books, 1971.

Silbey, Joel H. *Party over Section: The Rough and Ready Presidential Election of 1848* (American Presidential Elections). Lawrence: University Press of Kansas, 2009.

Silva, Ruth. *Rum, Religion, and Votes: 1928 Re-Examined*. University Park: Pennsylvania State University Press, 1962.

Simon, Roger. *Divided We Stand: How Al Gore Beat George Bush and Lost the Presidency*. New York: Crown, 2001.

Simon, Roger. *Show Time: The American Political Circus and the Race for the White House*. New York: Times Books, 1998.

Simpson, Brooks D. *Let Us Have Peace: Ulysses S. Grant and the Politics of War and Reconstruction, 1861–1868*. Chapel Hill: University of North Carolina Press, 1991.

Skewes, Elizabeth A. *Message Control: How News Is Made on the Presidential Campaign Trail* (Communication, Media, and Politics). Lanham, MD: Rowman & Littlefield, 2007.

Skocpol, Theda. *Boomerang: Health Care Reform and the Turn against Government*. New York: W. W. Norton, 1997.

Skocpol, Theda, and Vanessa Williamson. *The Tea Party and the Remaking of Republican Conservatism*. Oxford: Oxford University Press, 2013.

Slayton, Robert. *Empire Statesman: The Rise and Redemption of Al Smith*. New York: Free Press, 2001.

Smith, Elbert B. *The Presidency of James Buchanan*. Lawrence: University Press of Kansas, 1975.

Smith, Jean. *FDR*. New York: Random House Publishing, 2007.

Socolofsky, Edward Homer. *The Presidency of Benjamin Harrison*. Lawrence: University Press of Kansas, 1987.

Sperber, Hans, and Travis Trittschuh. *American Political Terms*. Detroit: Wayne State University Press, 1962.

Stanley, Timothy. *Kennedy v. Carter: The 1980 Battle for the Democratic Party's Soul*. Lawrence: University Press of Kansas, 2010.

Stephanson, Anders. *Manifest Destiny: American Expansionism and the Empire of Right*. New York: Hill and Wang, 1995.

Stonecash, Jeffrey M. *Political Polling: Strategic Information in Campaigns*. Lanham, MD: Rowman & Littlefield, 2008.

Summers, Mark Wahlgren. *The Press Gang: Newspapers and Politics, 1865–1878*. Chapel Hill: University of North Carolina Press, 1994.

Summers, Mark Wahlgren. *Rum, Romanism and Rebellion: The Making of a President, 1884*. Chapel Hill: University of North Carolina Press, 2000.

Sundquist, James L. *Dynamics of the Party System: Alignment and Realignment of Political Parties in the United States*. Washington, DC: Brookings Institution Press, 1983.

Telser, Michael, and David O. Sears. *Obama's Race: The 2008 Election and the Dream of Post-Racial America*. Chicago: University of Chicago Press, 2010.

Tetrault, Lisa. *The Myth of Seneca Falls: Memory and the Women's Suffrage Movement, 1848-1898*. Chapel Hill: University of North Carolina Press, 2014.

Thompson, Hunter S. *Fear and Loathing: On the Campaign Trail '72*. New York: Grand Central Publishing, 2006.

Thompson, Kenneth W., ed. *Lessons from Defeated Presidential Candidates*. Lanham, MD: University Press of America, 1994.

Thomson, Charles. *The 1956 Presidential Campaign*. Washington, DC: Brookings Institution Press, 1960.

Thurber, James A., and Candice J. Nelson. *Campaign Warriors: The Role of Political Consultants in Elections*. Washington, DC: Brookings Institution Press, 2000.

Thurber, James A., Candice J. Nelson, and David A. Dulio, eds. *Crowded Airwaves: Campaign Advertising in Elections.* Washington, DC: Brookings Institution Press, 2000.

Tobin, Jeffrey. *Too Close to Call: The Thirty-Six-Day Battle to Decide the 2000 Election.* New York: Random House, 2002.

Todd, Chuck, and Sheldon Gawiser. *How Barack Obama Won.* New York: Vintage Books, 2009.

Topping, Simon. *Lincoln's Lost Legacy: The Republican Party and the African American Vote, 1928–1952.* Gainesville: University Press of Florida, 2008.

Tocqueville, Alexis de. *Democracy in America.* Translated and edited by Harvey C. Mansfield and Delba Winthrop. Chicago: University of Chicago Press, 2000.

Trent, Judith, Robert V. Friedenberg, and Robert E. Denton Jr. *Political Campaign Communication: Principles and Practices* (Communication, Media, and Politics). Lanham, MD: Rowman & Littlefield, 2011.

Tufte, Edward R., Political *Control of the Economy.* Princeton, NJ: Princeton University Press, 1980.

Tugwell, Rexford. *The Brains Trust.* New York: Viking Press, 1968.

Valentino, Nicholas A., and David O. Sears. "Old Times There Are Not Forgotten: Race and Partisan Realignment in the Contemporary South." *American Journal of Political Science* 49, no. 3 (July 2005): 672–688.

Van der Linden, Frank. *The Turning Point: Jefferson's Battle for the Presidency.* Washington, DC: R. B. Luce, 1962.

Van Zoonen, Liesbet. *Entertaining the Citizen: When Politics and Popular Culture Converge.* Lanham, MD: Rowman & Littlefield, 2004.

Vavreck, Lynn. *The Message Matters: The Economy and Presidential Campaigns.* Princeton, NJ: Princeton University Press, 2009.

Wald, Kenneth D. *Religion and Politics in the United States.* Washington, DC: Congressional Quarterly Press, 1997.

Walker, Clarence E., and Gregory D. Smithers. *The Preacher and the Politician: Jeremiah Wright, Barack Obama, and Race in America.* Charlottesville: University of Virginia Press, 2009.

Wattenberg, Martin P. *The Rise of Candidate-Centered Politics: The Politics of Presidential Elections.* Boston: Bedford/St. Martin's Press, 1991.

Waugh, John C. *Reelecting Lincoln: The Battle for the 1864 Presidency.* New York: Da Capo Press, 2001.

Webber, Michael J. *New Deal Fat Cats: Business, Labor, and Campaign Finance in the 1936 Presidential Election.* New York: Fordham University Press, 2000.

Weed, Clyde P. *The Nemesis of Reform: The Republican Party during the New Deal.* New York: Columbia University Press, 1994.

Weil, Gordon. *The Long Shot: George McGovern Runs for President.* New York: Norton, 1973.

Weintraub, Stanley. *Final Victory: FDR's Extraordinary World War II Presidential Campaign.* Boston: De Capo Press, 2012.

Weisberger, Bernard A. *America Afire: Jefferson, Adams, and the Revolutionary Election of 1800.* New York: William Morrow, 2000.

West, Darrell. *Air Wars: Television Advertising in Election Campaigns, 1952–1992.* Washington, DC: Congressional Quarterly, 1993.

Whicher, George Frisbe. *William Jennings Bryan and the Campaign of 1896.* Boston: Heath, 1953.

White, Theodore. *America in Search of Itself: The Making of the President, 1956–1980.* New York: Harper & Row, 1982.

White, Theodore. *The Making of the President, 1960.* New York: Atheneum Publishers, 1961.

White, Theodore. *The Making of the President, 1964.* New York: Atheneum Publishers, 1965.

White, Theodore. *The Making of the President, 1968.* New York: Atheneum Publishers, 1969.

White, Theodore. *The Making of the President, 1972.* New York: Atheneum Publishers, 1973.

Wilcox, Clyde, and Carin Robinson. *Onward Christian Soldiers? The Religious Right in American Politics.* Boulder, CO: Westview Press, 2000.

Wilensky, Norman M. *Conservatives in the Progressive Era: The Taft Republicans of 1912.* Gainesville: University Press of Florida, 1965.

Williams, Hal. *Realigning America: McKinley, Bryan and the Remarkable Election of 1896.* Lawrence: University Press of Kansas, 2010.

Williams, Andrew Paul, and John C. Tedesco, eds. *The Internet Election: Perspectives on the Web in Campaign 2004* (Communication, Media, and Politics). Lanham, MD: Rowman & Littlefield, 2006.

Witcover, Jules. *Marathon: The Pursuit of the Presidency, 1972–1976.* New York: Viking Press, 1977.

Witcover, Jules. *Party of the People: A History of the Democrats.* New York: Random House, 2003.

Wlezian, Christopher, and Robert S. Erikson. "The Timeline of Presidential Election Campaigns." *The Journal of Politics* 64, no. 4 (November 2002): 969–993.

Wolak, Jennifer "The Consequences of Presidential Battleground Strategies for Citizen Engagement." *Political Research Quarterly* 59 (September 2006): 353–361.

Wolbrecht, Christina. "Explaining Women's Rights Realignment: Convention Delegates, 1972–1992." *Political Behavior* (September 2002): 237–282.

Wolter, Kirk, Diana Jergovic, Whitney Moore, Joe Murphy, and Colm O'Muircheartaigh. "Reliability of the Uncertified Ballots in the 2000 Presidential Election in Florida." *American Statistician* 57, no. 1 (February 2003): 1–14.

Woodward, C. Vann. *Origins of the New South, 1877–1913.* Baton Rouge: Louisiana State University Press, 1971.

Woodward, C. Vann. *The Strange Career of Jim Crow.* Rev. ed. New York: Oxford University Press, 1971.

Young, Min. "Intertwining of Campaign News and Advertising: The Content and Electoral Effects of Newspaper Ad Watches." *Journalism and Mass Communication Quarterly* 79, no. 4 (Winter 2002): 927–944.

Zuckert, Michael P. *The Natural Rights Republic.* Notre Dame, IN: University of Notre Dame Press, 1996.

Index

abolitionist movement, 344, 472, 473, 485, 486, 498, 504, 511. *See also names of specific abolitionists*

Abood v. Detroit Bd. of Educ., 271

abortion issue/controversy, 1–3, 54, 144, 267, 341, 788, 789, 814, 825; culture wars and, 73, 75; Democratic Party stance, 347; internal GOP conflict, 347; partial birth abortion, 814; Republican Party stance, 347; wedge issue, 341, 342. *See also names of specific candidates*; Campaigns of 1972, 1976, 1980, 1992, 1996, 2000, 2004, 2012, 2016; *Griswold v. Connecticut*; *Roe v. Wade*

activist community, rugged individualism versus, 257

Adams, Charles Francis, 468, 472, 489, 517, 521, 527, 528, 529, 531

Adams, John, 356, 358, 377, 390, 449, 794; attacks against, 372–373; campaign of 1792, 359; campaign of 1796, 366–367; campaign of 1800, 364, 368, 842; criticism of, 369, 370; first vice presidential election, 354; Hamilton rejection of, 373; nomination, 40. *See also* Alien and Sedition Acts; Quasi War; XYZ Affair

Adams, John Quincy: campaign and election of 1824, 404, 406, 407, 408–409, 411, 412–413, 414, 415, 506, 750, 802; campaign of 1820, 401, 402, 403; campaign of 1828, 413–414, 415, 416–417; congressman, 420; "corrupt bargain" with Clay, 412, 414, 417, 418; House of Representatives election role, 820; rumors, 42; tariffs, 418

Adams, John Quincy II, 521, 531

Adams, Samuel, 353; campaign of 1796, 366, 367

Adams, Sherman, 698, 704, 716

advertisements, campaign, 33–35; billboards, 35; campaign speech broadcasts, 33; "Daisy Girl" campaign ad, 33–34, 76–77, 229–230, 735–736; "Eisenhower Answers America," 33; first televised, 229, 701; focus groups and, 112; issue ads, 33, 38; Internet, 35; KKK ad, 34; negative, 33–35; print media, 33, 35; radio, 33, 35; Swift Boat ads, 30–31, 157; television, 33, 35; testimonials, 33; "Willie Horton" ad, 30, 54, 112, 157, 244, 262; YouTube videos, 35. *See also specific presidential campaigns and candidates*; advertisements, political

advertisements, political, 229–231; biographical, 229; campaign speeches, 229; emotions associated with, 231; first television, 229; issue, 229; manner of dissemination, 229, 231; negative, 229–230; spot, 229; testimonial, 229;

About the Authors

Scott John Hammond is Professor of Political Science at James Madison University, specializing primarily in political theory while having taught courses in American government and politics as well as other areas within political science.

Robert North Roberts is Professor of Political Science at James Madison University, specializing in public administration, state and local politics, and American politics.

Valerie A. Sulfaro is Professor of Political Science at James Madison University, specializing in American government and politics, campaigns and elections, and political behavior.